W9-BYA-345

# GO!

## with Microsoft® Office

# Word 2003
## Comprehensive

## John Preston, Sally Preston, and Robert L. Ferrett

## Shelley Gaskin, Series Editor

**PEARSON**

Prentice
Hall

*Upper Saddle River, New Jersey*

**Library of Congress Cataloging-in-Publication Data**

The Library of Congress has catalogued Volume 1 as follows:

Preston, John.
  Go! with Microsoft Office Word 2003. Volume 1 / John Preston, Sally Preston,
Robert L. Ferrett.
        p. cm.— (Go! with Microsoft Office 2003)
Includes index.
    ISBN 0-13-145102-2 (perfect bound : alk. paper)—ISBN 0-13-143431-4 (spiral : alk.
paper)
    1. Microsoft Word. 2. Word processing. I. Title: Word 2003. II. Preston, Sally.
III. Ferrett, Robert. IV. Title. V. Series.
Z52.5.M52P738 2004
005.52—dc22

                                                                    2003026105


ISBN 0-13-143422-5 (Comprehensive)

**Vice President and Publisher:** Natalie E. Anderson
**Executive Acquisitions Editor:** Jodi McPherson
**Senior Marketing Manager:** Emily Williams Knight
**Marketing Assistant:** Nicole Beaudry
**Senior Project Manager, Editorial:** Mike Ruel
**Project Manager, Editorial:** Jodi Bolognese
**Senior Media Project Manager:** Cathi Profitko
**Editorial Assistant:** Alana Meyers
**Senior Managing Editor, Production:** Gail Steier de Acevedo
**Senior Project Manager, Production:** Tim Tate
**Manufacturing Buyer:** Tim Tate
**Design Manager:** Maria Lange
**Art Director:** Pat Smythe
**Cover Designer:** Brian Salisbury
**Cover Photo:** Steve Bloom/Getty Images, Inc.
**Interior Designer:** Quorum Creative Services
**Full Service Composition:** Black Dot Group
**Printer/Binder:** Von Hoffmann Corporation
**Cover Printer:** Phoenix Color Corporation

Credits and acknowledgments borrowed from other sources and reproduced,
with permission, in this textbook are as follows or on the appropriate page
within the text.

Microsoft, Windows, PowerPoint, Outlook, FrontPage, Visual Basic, MSN, The
Microsoft Network, and/or other Microsoft products referenced herein are
either trademarks or registered trademarks of Microsoft Corporation in the
U.S.A. and other countries. Screen shots and icons reprinted with permission
from the Microsoft Corporation. This book is not sponsored or endorsed by or
affiliated with Microsoft Corporation.

Microsoft and the Microsoft Office Specialist logo are trademarks or registered
trademarks of Microsoft Corporation in the United States and/or other countries. Pearson Education is independent from Microsoft Corporation and not
affiliated with Microsoft in any manner. This text may be used in assisting
students to prepare for a Microsoft Office Specialist Exam. Neither Microsoft,
its designated review company, nor Pearson Education warrants that use of
this text will ensure passing the relevant exam.

**Copyright © 2004 by Pearson Education, Inc., Upper Saddle River, New Jersey, 07458.** All rights reserved. Printed in
the United States of America. This publication is protected by Copyright and permission should be obtained from the
publisher prior to any prohibited reproduction, storage in a retrieval system, or transmission in any form or by any means,
electronic, mechanical, photocopying, recording, or likewise. For information regarding permission(s), write to the Rights
and Permissions Department.

10 9 8 7 6 5 4 3 2
ISBN 0-13-143422-5

### What does this logo mean?

It means this courseware has been approved by the Microsoft® Office Specialist Program to be among the finest available for learning **Microsoft® Office Word 2003, Microsoft® Office Excel 2003, Microsoft® Office PowerPoint® 2003, and Microsoft® Office Access 2003**. It also means that upon completion of this courseware, you may be prepared to take an exam for Microsoft Office Specialist qualification.

### What is a Microsoft Office Specialist?

A Microsoft Office Specialist is an individual who has passed exams for certifying his or her skills in one or more of the Microsoft Office desktop applications such as Microsoft Word, Microsoft Excel, Microsoft PowerPoint, Microsoft Outlook, Microsoft Access, or Microsoft Project. The Microsoft Office Specialist Program typically offers certification exams at the "Specialist" and "Expert" skill levels.* The Microsoft Office Specialist Program is the only program approved by Microsoft for testing proficiency in Microsoft Office desktop applications and Microsoft Project. This testing program can be a valuable asset in any job search or career advancement.

### More Information:

To learn more about becoming a Microsoft Office Specialist, visit **www.microsoft.com/officespecialist**

To learn about other Microsoft Office Specialist approved courseware from Pearson Education, visit **www.prenhall.com/phit**

*The availability of Microsoft Office Specialist certification exams varies by application, application version, and language. Visit www.microsoft.com/officespecialist for exam availability.

Microsoft, the Microsoft Office Logo, PowerPoint, and Outlook are trademarks or registered trademarks of Microsoft Corporation in the United States and/or other countries, and the Microsoft Office Specialist Logo is used under license from owner.

# GO!

## Series for Microsoft® Office System 2003

### Series Editor: **Shelley Gaskin**

**Office**
**Getting Started**
**Brief**
**Intermediate**
**Advanced**

**Word**
**Brief**
**Volume 1**
**Volume 2**
**Comprehensive**

**Excel**
**Brief**
**Volume 1**
**Volume 2**
**Comprehensive**

**PowerPoint**
**Brief**
**Volume 1**
**Volume 2**
**Comprehensive**

**Access**
**Brief**
**Volume 1**
**Volume 2**
**Comprehensive**

# GO! Series Reviewers

We would like to thank the following "Super Reviewers" for both their subject matter expertise and attention to detail from the instructors' perspective. Your time, effort, hard work, and diligence has helped us create the best books in the world. Prentice Hall and your author partners thank you:

| | |
|---|---|
| **Rocky Belcher** | Sinclair CC |
| **Judy Cameron** | Spokane CC |
| **Gail Cope** | Sinclair CC |
| **Larry Farrer** | Guilford Tech CC |
| **Janet Enck** | Columbus State CC |
| **Susan Fry** | Boise State |
| **Lewis Hall** | Riverside CC |
| **Jeff Howard** | Finger Lakes CC |
| **Jason Hu** | Pasadena City College |
| **Michele Hulett** | Southwest Missouri State U. |
| **Donna Madsen** | Kirkwood CC |
| **Cheryl Reindl-Johnson** | Sinclair CC |
| **Jan Spaar** | Spokane CC |
| **Mary Ann Zlotow** | College of DuPage |

We would also like to thank our valuable student reviewers who bring us vital input from those who will someday study from our books:

| | |
|---|---|
| **Nicholas J. Bene** | Southwest Missouri State U. |
| **Anup Jonathan** | Southwest Missouri State U. |
| **Kimber Miller** | Pasadena City College |
| **Kelly Moline** | Southwest Missouri State U. |
| **Adam Morris** | Southwest Missouri State U. |
| **Robert Murphy** | Southwest Missouri State U. |
| **Drucilla Owenby** | Southwest Missouri State U. |
| **Vince Withee** | Southwest Missouri State U. |

Finally, we have been lucky to have so many of you respond to review our chapter manuscripts. You have given us tremendous feedback and helped make a fantastic series. We could not have done it without you.

| | | | |
|---|---|---|---|
| Abraham, Reni | Houston CC | Challa, Chandrashekar | Virginia State University |
| Agatston, Ann | Agatston Consulting | Chamlou, Afsaneh | NOVA Alexandria |
| Alejandro, Manuel | Southwest Texas Junior College | Chapman, Pam | Wabaunsee CC |
| Ali, Farha | Lander University | Christensen, Dan | Iowa Western CC |
| Anik, Mazhar | Tiffin University | Conroy-Link, Janet | Holy Family College |
| Armstrong, Gary | Shippensburg University | Cosgrove, Janet | Northwestern CT Community |
| Bagui, Sikha | Univ. West Florida | | Technical College |
| Belton, Linda | Springfield Tech. Com College | Cox, Rollie | Madison Area Technical College |
| Bennett, Judith | Sam Houston State University | Crawford, Hiram | Olive Harvey College |
| Bishop, Frances | DeVry Institute- Alpharetta (ATL) | Danno, John | DeVry University/ |
| Branigan, Dave | DeVry University | | Keller Graduate School |
| Bray, Patricia | Allegany College of Maryland | Davis, Phillip Md. | Del Mar College |
| Buehler, Lesley | Ohlone College | Doroshow, Mike | Eastfield College |
| Buell, C | Central Oregon CC | Douglas, Gretchen | SUNY Cortland |
| Byars, Pat | Brookhaven College | Driskel, Loretta | Niagara CC |
| Cacace, Rich | Pensacola Jr. College | Duckwiler, Carol | Wabaunsee CC |
| Cadenhead, Charles | Brookhaven College | Duncan, Mimi | University of Missouri-St. Louis |
| Calhoun, Ric | Gordon College | Duvall, Annette | Albuquerque Technical |
| Carriker, Sandra | North Shore CC | | Vocational Institute |

*Reviewers continues*

Ecklund, Paula — Duke University
Edmondson, Jeremy — Mount Pisgah School
Erickson, John — University of South Dakota
Falkenstein, Todd — Indiana University East
Fite, Beverly — Amarillo College
Foltz, Brian — East Carolina University
Friedrichsen, Lisa — Johnson County CC
Fustos, Janos — Metro State
Gallup, Jeanette — Blinn College
Gentry, Barb — Parkland College
Gerace, Karin — St. Angela Merici School
Gerace, Tom — Tulane University
Ghajar, Homa — Oklahoma State University
Gifford, Steve — Northwest Iowa CC
Gregoryk, Kerry — Virginia Commonwealth State University
Griggs, Debra — Bellevue CC
Grimm, Carol — Palm Beach CC
Helms, Liz — Columbus State CC
Hernandez, Leticia — TCI College of Technology
Hogan, Pat — Cape Fear CC
Horvath, Carrie — Albertus Magnus College
Howard, Chris — DeVry University
Huckabay, Jamie — Austin CC
Hunt, Laura — Tulsa CC
Jacob, Sherry — Jefferson CC
Jacobs, Duane — Salt Lake CC
Johnson, Kathy — Wright College
Jones, Stacey — Benedict College
Kasai, Susumu — Salt Lake CC
Keen, Debby — Univ. of Kentucky
Kirk, Colleen — Mercy College
Kliston, Linda — Broward CC
Kramer, Ed — Northern Virginia CC
Laird, Jeff — Northeast State CC
Lange, David — Grand Valley State
LaPointe, Deb — Albuquerque TVI
Lenhart, Sheryl — Terra CC
Letavec, Chris — University of Cincinnati
Lightner, Renee — Broward CC
Lindberg, Martha — Minnesota State University
Linge, Richard — Arizona Western College
Loizeaux, Barbara — Westchester CC
Lopez, Don — Clovis- State Center CC District
Low, Willy Hui — Joliet Junior College
Lowe, Rita — Harold Washington College
Lucas, Vickie — Broward CC
Lynam, Linda — Central Missouri State University
Machuca, Wayne — College of the Sequoias
Madison, Dana — Clarion University
Maguire, Trish — Eastern New Mexico University
Malkan, Rajiv — Montgomery College
Manning, David — Northern Kentucky University
Marghitu, Daniela — Auburn University
Marks, Suzanne — Bellevue CC
Marquez, Juanita — El Centro College
Marucco, Toni — Lincoln Land CC
Mason, Lynn — Lubbock Christian University
Matutis, Audrone — Houston CC
McCannon, Melinda (Mindy) — Gordon College
McClure, Darlean — College of Sequoias
McCue, Stacy — Harrisburg Area CC
McEntire-Orbach, Teresa — Middlesex County College
McManus, Illyana — Grossmont College

Menking, Rick — Hardin-Simmons University
Meredith, Mary — U. of Louisiana at Lafayette
Mermelstein, Lisa — Baruch College
Metos, Linda — Salt Lake CC
Meurer, Daniel — University of Cincinnati
Monk, Ellen — University of Delaware
Morris, Nancy — Hudson Valley CC
Nadas, Erika — Wright College
Nadelman, Cindi — New England College
Ncube, Cathy — University of West Florida
Nicholls, Doreen — Mohawk Valley CC
Orr, Claudia — New Mexico State University
Otieno, Derek — DeVry University
Otton, Diana Hill — Chesapeake College
Oxendale, Lucia — West Virginia Institute of Technology
Paiano, Frank — Southwestern College
Proietti, Kathleen — Northern Essex CC
Pusins, Delores — HCCC
Reeves, Karen — High Point University
Rhue, Shelly — DeVry University
Richards, Karen — Maplewoods CC
Ross, Dianne — Univ. of Louisiana in Lafayette
Rousseau, Mary — Broward CC
Sams, Todd — University of Cincinnati
Sandoval, Everett — Reedley College
Sardone, Nancy — Seton Hall University
Scafide, Jean — Mississippi Gulf Coast CC
Scheeren, Judy — Westmoreland County CC
Schneider, Sol — Sam Houston State University
Scroggins, Michael — Southwest Missouri State University
Sever, Suzanne — Northwest Arkansas CC
Sheridan, Rick — California State University-Chico
Sinha, Atin — Albany State University
Smith, T. Michael — Austin CC
Smith, Tammy — Tompkins Cortland CC
Stefanelli, Greg — Carroll CC
Steiner, Ester — New Mexico State University
Sterling, Janet — Houston CC
Stroup, Tracey — Pasadena City College
Sullivan, Angela — Joliet Junior College
Szurek, Joseph — University of Pittsburgh at Greensburg
Taylor, Michael — Seattle Central CC
Thangiah, Sam — Slippery Rock University
Thompson-Sellers, Ingrid — Georgia Perimeter College
Tomasi, Erik — Baruch College
Toreson, Karen — Shoreline CC
Turgeon, Cheryl — Asnuntuck CC
Turpen, Linda — Albuquerque TVI
Upshaw, Susan — Del Mar College
Vargas, Tony — El Paso CC
Vicars, Mitzi — Hampton University
Vitrano, Mary Ellen — Palm Beach CC
Wahila, Lori — Tompkins Cortland CC
Wavle, Sharon — Tompkins Cortland CC
White, Bruce — Quinnipiac University
Willer, Ann — Solano CC
Williams, Mark — Lane CC
Wimberly, Leanne — International Academy of Design and Technology
Worthington, Paula — NOVA Woodbridge
Yauney, Annette — Herkimer CCC
Zavala, Ben — Webster Tech

# Dedications

*We dedicate this book to our granddaughters, who bring us
great joy and happiness: Clara and Siena & Alexis and Grace.*

—John Preston, Sally Preston, and Robert L. Ferrett

*This book is dedicated to my students,
who inspire me every day, and to my husband, Fred Gaskin.*

—Shelley Gaskin

# About the Authors/Acknowledgments

## About John Preston, Sally Preston, and Robert L. Ferrett

**John Preston** is an Associate Professor at Eastern Michigan University in the College of Technology, where he teaches microcomputer application courses at the undergraduate and graduate levels. He has been teaching, writing, and designing computer training courses since the advent of PCs and has authored and co-authored over 60 books on Microsoft Word, Excel, Access, and PowerPoint. He is a series editor for the *Learn 97*, *Learn 2000*, and *Learn XP* books. Two books on Microsoft Access that he co-authored with Robert Ferrett have been translated into Greek and Chinese. He has received grants from the Detroit Edison Institute and the Department of Energy to develop Web sites for energy education and alternative fuels. He has also developed one of the first Internet-based microcomputer applications courses at an accredited university. He has a BS from the University of Michigan in Physics, Mathematics, and Education and an MS from Eastern Michigan University in Physics Education. His doctoral studies were in Instructional Technology at Wayne State University.

**Sally Preston** is president of Preston & Associates, which provides software consulting and training. She teaches computing in a variety of settings, which provides her with ample opportunity to observe how people learn, what works best, and what challenges are present when learning a new software program. This diverse experience provides a complementary set of skills and knowledge that blends into her writing. Prior to writing for the *GO! Series*, Sally was a co-author on the *Learn* series since its inception and has authored books for the *Essentials* and *Microsoft Office User Specialist (MOUS) Essentials* series. Sally has an MBA from Eastern Michigan University. When away from her computer, she is often found planting flowers in her garden.

**Robert L. Ferrett** recently retired as the director of the Center for Instructional Computing at Eastern Michigan University, where he provided computer training and support to faculty. He has authored or co-authored more than 60 books on Access, PowerPoint, Excel, Publisher, WordPerfect, and Word and was the editor of the *1994 ACM SIGUCCS Conference Proceedings*. He has been designing, developing, and delivering computer workshops for nearly two decades. Before writing for the *GO! Series*, Bob was a series editor for the *Learn 97*, *Learn 2000*, and *Learn XP* books. He has a BA in Psychology, an MS in Geography, and an MS in Interdisciplinary Technology from Eastern Michigan University. His doctoral studies were in Instructional Technology at Wayne State University. For fun, Bob teaches a four-week Computers and Genealogy class and has written genealogy and local history books.

### Acknowledgments from John Preston, Sally Preston, and Robert L. Ferrett

We would like to acknowledge the efforts of a fine team of editing professionals, with whom we have had the pleasure of working. Jodi McPherson, Jodi Bolognese, Mike Ruel, and Shelley Gaskin did a great job managing and coordinating this effort. We would also like to acknowledge the contributions of Tim Tate, Production Project Manager, and Emily Knight, Marketing Manager, as well as the many reviewers who gave invaluable criticism and suggestions.

## About Shelley Gaskin

**Shelley Gaskin**, Series Editor, is a professor of business and computer technology at Pasadena City College in Pasadena, California. She holds a master's degree in business education from Northern Illinois University and a doctorate in adult and community education from Ball State University. Dr. Gaskin has 15 years of experience in the computer industry with several Fortune 500 companies and has developed and written training materials for custom systems applications in both the public and private sector. She is also the author of books on Microsoft Outlook and word processing.

### Acknowledgments from Shelley Gaskin

Many talented individuals worked to produce this book, and I thank them for their continuous support. My Executive Acquisitions Editor, Jodi McPherson, gave me much latitude to experiment with new things. Editorial Project Manager Mike Ruel worked with me through each stage of writing and production. Emily Knight and the Prentice Hall Marketing team worked with me throughout this process to make sure both instructors and students are informed about the benefits of using this series. Also, very big thanks and appreciation goes to Prentice Halls' top-notch Production and Design team: Associate Director Product Development Melonie Salvati, Manager of Production Gail Steier de Acevedo, Senior Production Project Manager and Manufacturing Buyer Tim Tate, Design Manager Maria Lange, Art Director Pat Smythe, Interior Designer Quorum Creative Services, and Cover Designer Brian Salisbury.

Thanks to all!
Shelley Gaskin, Series Editor

# Why I Wrote This Series

Dear Professor,

If you are like me, you are frantically busy trying to implement new course delivery methods (e.g., online) while also maintaining your regular campus schedule of classes and academic responsibilities. I developed this series for colleagues like you, who are long on commitment and expertise but short on time and assistance.

The primary goal of the **GO! Series**, aside from the obvious one of teaching **Microsoft® Office 2003** concepts and skills, is ease of implementation using any delivery method—traditional, self-paced, or online.

There are no lengthy passages of text; instead, bits of expository text are woven into the steps at the teachable moment. This is the point at which the student has a context within which he or she can understand the concept. A scenario-like approach is used in a manner that makes sense, but it does not attempt to have the student "pretend" to be someone else.

A key feature of this series is the use of Microsoft procedural syntax. That is, steps begin with where the action is to take place, followed by the action itself. This prevents the student from doing the right thing in the wrong place!

The *GO! Series* is written with all of your everyday classroom realities in mind. For example, in each project, the student is instructed to insert his or her name in a footer and to save the document with his or her name. Thus, unidentified printouts do not show up at the printer nor do unidentified documents get stored on the hard drives.

Finally, an overriding consideration is that the student is not always working in a classroom with a teacher. Students frequently work at home or in a lab staffed only with instructional aides. Thus, the instruction must be error-free, clearly written, and logically arranged.

My students enjoy learning the Microsoft Office software. The goal of the instruction in the *GO! Series* is to provide students with the skills to solve business problems using the computer as a tool, for both themselves and the organizations for which they might be employed.

Thank you for using the **GO! Series for Microsoft® Office System 2003** for your students.

Regards,

*Shelley Gaskin*

Shelley Gaskin, Series Editor

# Preface

## Philosophy

Our overall philosophy is ease of implementation for the instructor, whether instruction is via lecture, lab, online, or partially self-paced. Right from the start, the *GO! Series* was created with constant input from professors just like you. You've told us what works, how you teach, and what we can do to make your classroom time problem free, creative, and smooth running—to allow you to concentrate on not what you are teaching from but who you are teaching to—your students. We feel that we have succeeded with the *GO! Series*. Our aim is to make this instruction high quality in both content and presentation, and the classroom management aids complete—an instructor could begin teaching the course with only 15 minutes advance notice. An instructor could leave the classroom or computer lab; students would know exactly how to proceed in the text, know exactly what to produce to demonstrate mastery of the objectives, and feel that they had achieved success in their learning. Indeed, this philosophy is essential for real-world use in today's diverse educational environment.

## How did we do it?

- All steps utilize **Microsoft Procedural Syntax**. The *GO! Series* puts students where they need to be, before instructing them what to do. For example, instead of instructing students to "Save the file," we go a few steps further and phrase the instruction as "On the **Menu** bar, click **File**, and then select **Save As**."

- A unique teaching system (packaged together in one easy to use **Instructor's Edition** binder set) that enables you to teach anywhere you have to—online, lab, lecture, self-paced, and so forth. The supplements are designed to save you time:

  - *Expert Demonstration Document*—A new project that mirrors the learning objectives of the in-chapter project, with a full demonstration script for you to give a lecture overview quickly and clearly.

  - *Chapter Assignment Sheets*—A sheet listing all the assignments for the chapter. An instructor can quickly insert his or her name, course information, due dates, and points.

  - *Custom Assignment Tags*—These cutout tags include a brief list of common errors that students could make on each project, with check boxes so instructors don't have to keep writing the same error description over and over! These tags serve a dual purpose: The student can do a final check to make sure all the listed items are correct, and the instructor can check off the items that need to be corrected.

- **Highlighted Overlays**—These are printed and transparent overlays that the instructor lays over the student's assignment paper to see at a glance if the student changed what he or she needed to. Coupled with the Custom Assignment Tags, this creates a "grading and scoring system" that is easy for the instructor to implement.

- **Point Counted Chapter Production Test**—Working hand-in-hand with the Expert Demonstration Document, this is a final test for the student to demonstrate mastery of the objectives.

## Goals of the GO! Series

The goals of the *GO! Series* are as follows:

- Make it *easy for the instructor to implement* in any instructional setting through high-quality content and instructional aids and provide the student with a valuable, interesting, important, satisfying, and clearly defined learning experience.

- Enable true diverse delivery for today's diverse audience. The *GO! Series* employs various instructional techniques that address the needs of all types of students in all types of delivery modes.

- Provide *turn-key implementation* in the following instructional settings:

    - Traditional computer classroom—Students experience a mix of lecture and lab.

    - Online instruction—Students complete instruction at a remote location and submit assignments to the instructor electronically—questions answered by instructor through electronic queries.

    - Partially self-paced, individualized instruction—Students meet with an instructor for part of the class, and complete part of the class in a lab setting.

    - Completely self-paced, individualized instruction—Students complete all instruction in an instructor-staffed lab setting.

    - Independent self-paced, individualized instruction—Students complete all instruction in a campus lab staffed with instructional aides.

- Teach—*to maximize the moment*. The *GO! Series* is based on the Teachable Moment Theory. There are no long passages of text; instead, concepts are woven into the steps at the teachable moment. Students always know what they need to do and where to do it.

## Pedagogical Approach

The *GO! Series* uses an instructional system approach that incorporates three elements:

- *Steps are written in **Microsoft Procedural Syntax**, which prevents the student from doing the right thing but in the wrong place. This makes it easy for the instructor to teach instead of untangle. It tells the student where to go first, then what to do. For example—"On the File Menu, click Properties."

- *Instructional strategies* including five new, unique ancillary pieces to support the instructor experience. The foundation of the instructional strategies is performance based instruction that is constructed in a manner that makes it *easy for the instructor* to demonstrate the content with the GO Series Expert Demonstration Document, guide the practice by using our many end-of-chapter projects with varying guidance levels, and assess the level of mastery with tools such as our Point Counted Production Test and Custom Assignment Tags.

- *A physical design* that makes it *easy for the instructor* to answer the question, "What do they have to do?" and makes it easy for the student to answer the question, "What do I have to do?" Most importantly, you told us what was needed in the design. We held several focus groups throughout the country where we showed **you** our design drafts and let you tell us what you thought of them. We revised our design based on your input to be functional and support the classroom experience. For example, you told us that a common problem is students not realizing where a project ends. So, we added an "END. You have completed the Project" at the close of every project.

## Microsoft Procedural Syntax

Do you ever do something right but in the wrong place?

That's why we've written the *GO! Series* step text using Microsoft procedural syntax. That is, the student is informed where the action should take place before describing the action to take. For example, "On the menu bar, click File," versus "Click File on the menu bar." This prevents the student from doing the right thing in the wrong place. This means that step text usually begins with a preposition—a locator—rather than a verb. Other texts often misunderstand the theory of performance-based instruction and frequently attempt to begin steps with a verb. In fact, the objectives should begin with a verb, not the steps.

The use of Microsoft procedural syntax is one of the key reasons that the *GO! Series* eases the burden for the instructor. The instructor spends less time untangling students' unnecessary actions and more time assisting students with real questions. No longer will students become frustrated and say "But I did what it said!" only to discover that, indeed, they *did* do "what it said" but in the wrong place!

## Chapter Organization—Color-Coded Projects

All of the chapters in every *GO! Series* book are organized around interesting projects. Within each chapter, all of the instructional activities will cluster around these projects without any long passages of text for the student to read. Thus, every instructional activity contributes to the completion of the project to which it is associated. Students learn skills to solve real business problems; they don't waste time learning every feature the software has. The end-of-chapter material consists of additional projects with varying levels of difficulty.

The chapters are based on the following basic hierarchy:

**Project Name**

> **Objective Name** (begins with a verb)
>
> > **Activity Name** (begins with a gerund)
> >
> > > **Numbered Steps** (begins with a preposition or a verb using Microsoft Procedural Syntax.)

Project Name → **Project 1A Exploring Outlook 2003**

Objective Name → **Objective 1**
**Start Outlook and Identify Outlook Window Elements**

Activity Name → **Activity 1.1** Starting Outlook

Numbered Steps → **1** On the Windows taskbar, click the Start button, determine from your instructor or lab coordinator where the Microsoft Office Outlook 2003 program is located on your system, and then click Microsoft Office Outlook 2003.

A project will have a number of objectives associated with it, and the objectives, in turn, will have one or more activities associated with them. Each activity will have a series of numbered steps. To further enhance understanding, each project, and its objectives and numbered steps, is color coded for fast, easy recognition.

# Instructor and Student Resources

## Instructor's Resource Center and Instructor's Edition

The *GO! Series* was designed for you—instructors who are long on commitment and short on time. *We asked you how you use our books and supplements and how we can make it easier for you and save you valuable time.* We listened to what you told us and created this Instructor's Resource Center for you—different from anything you have ever had access to from other texts and publishers.

What is the Instructor's Edition?

# 1) Instructor's Edition

New from Prentice Hall, exclusively for the *GO! Series*, the Instructor's Edition contains the entire book, wrapped with vital margin notes—things like objectives, a list of the files needed for the chapter, teaching tips, Microsoft Office Specialist objectives covered, and MORE! Below is a sample of the many helpful elements in the Instructor's Edition.

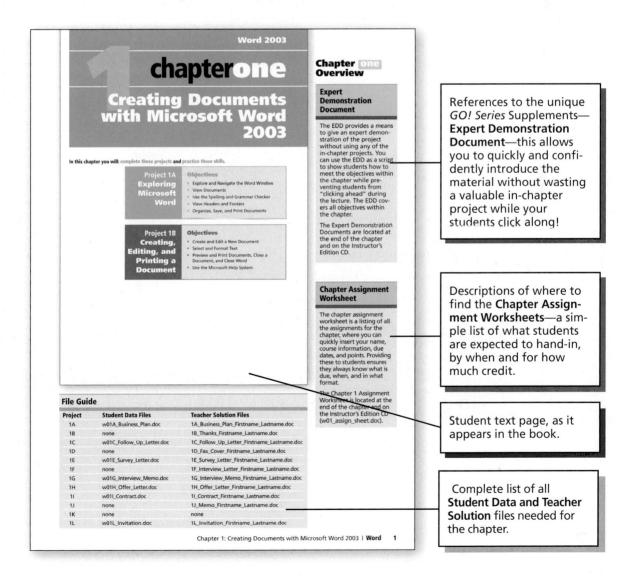

References to the unique *GO! Series* Supplements—**Expert Demonstration Document**—this allows you to quickly and confidently introduce the material without wasting a valuable in-chapter project while your students click along!

Descriptions of where to find the **Chapter Assignment Worksheets**—a simple list of what students are expected to hand-in, by when and for how much credit.

Student text page, as it appears in the book.

Complete list of all **Student Data and Teacher Solution** files needed for the chapter.

Reference to Prentice Hall's Companion Website for the *GO! Series*: **www.prenhall.com/go**

Each chapter also tells you where to find another unique *GO! Series* Supplement—the **Custom Assignment Tags**—use these in combination with the highlighted overlays to save you time! Simply check off what the students missed or if they completed all the tasks correctly.

**CW**

Companion Website

www.prenhall.com/go

*The Companion Website is an online training tool that includes personalization features for registered instructors. Data files are available here for download as well as access to additional quizzing exercises.*

**Custom Assignment Tags**

Custom Assignment Tags, which are meant to be cut out and attached to assignments, serve a dual purpose: the student can do a final check to make sure all the listed items are correct, and the instructor can quickly check off the items that need to be corrected and simply return the assignment.

The Chapter 1 Custom Assignment Tags are located at the end of the chapter and on the Instructor's Edition CD (w01_assign_tags.doc).

### The Perfect Party

The Perfect Party store, owned by two partners, provides a wide variety of party accessories including invitations, favors, banners and flags, balloons, piñatas, etc. Party-planning services include both custom parties with pre-filled custom "goodie bags" and "parties in a box" that include everything needed to throw a theme party. Big sellers in this category are the Football and Luau themes. The owners are planning to open a second store and expand their party-planning services to include catering.

© Getty Images, Inc.

## Getting Started with Microsoft Office Word 2003

Word processing is the most common program found on personal computers and one that almost everyone has a reason to use. When you learn word processing you are also learning skills and techniques that you need to work efficiently on a personal computer. Use Microsoft Word to do basic word processing tasks such as writing a memo, a report, or a letter. You can also use Word to do complex word processing tasks, including sophisticated tables, embedded graphics, and links to other documents and the Internet. Word is a program that you can learn gradually, adding more advanced skills one at a time.

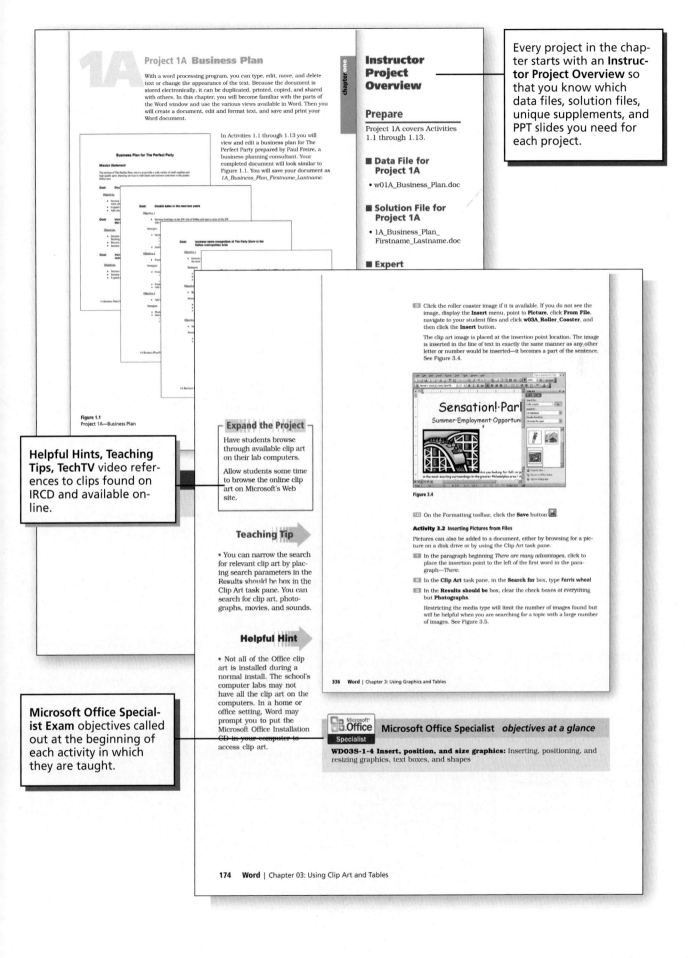

**Every project in the chapter starts with an Instructor Project Overview** so that you know which data files, solution files, unique supplements, and PPT slides you need for each project.

**Helpful Hints, Teaching Tips, TechTV** video references to clips found on IRCD and available online.

**Microsoft Office Specialist Exam** objectives called out at the beginning of each activity in which they are taught.

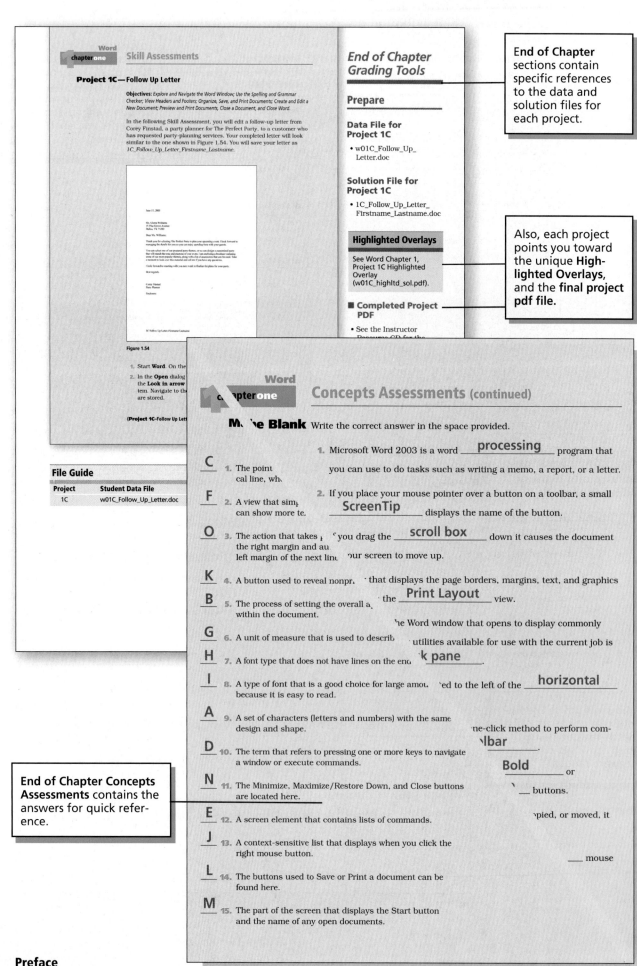

**End of Chapter** sections contain specific references to the data and solution files for each project.

Also, each project points you toward the unique **Highlighted Overlays**, and the **final project pdf file**.

**End of Chapter Concepts Assessments** contains the answers for quick reference.

**Chapter summary pages** contain links to Glossary and Key Terms, as well as information about Online Courses and Prentice Hall's Train and Assess Generation IT—online training and assessment.

Another supplement exclusive to the *GO! Series* is the **Point Counted Production Test.** Reminders are put on each chapter summary page, the printed documents are provided in the back of each chapter, and we also provide electronic versions in Word format on the IE CD-ROM for easy customization.

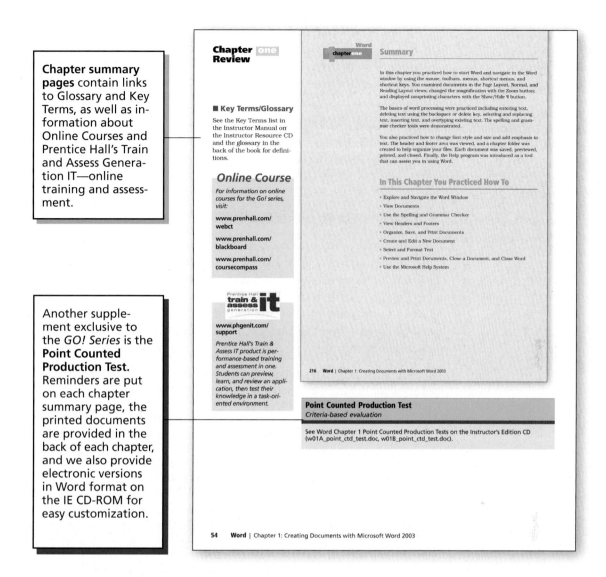

The Instructor's Edition also contains printed copies of these supplement materials *unique* to the *GO! Series*:

- ***Expert Demonstration Document (EDD)*—A mirror image of each in-chapter project, accompanied by a brief script. The instructor can use it to give an expert demonstration of each objective that will be covered in the chapter, without having to use one of the chapter's projects. This EDD also prevents students from "working ahead during the presentation," as they do not have access to this document/project.

- ***Chapter Assignment Sheets*—With a sheet listing all the assignments for the chapter, the instructor can quickly insert his or her name, course information, due dates, and points.

- ***Custom Assignment Tags*—These cutout tags include a brief list of common errors that students could make on each project, with check boxes so instructors don't have to keep writing the same error description over and over! These tags serve a dual purpose: The student can do a final check to make sure all the listed items are correct, and the instructor can check off the items that need to be corrected.

- **Highlighted Overlays**—These are printed and transparent overlays that the instructor lays over the student's assignment paper to see at a glance if the student changed what he or she needed to. Coupled with the Custom Assignment Tags, this creates a "grading and scoring system" that is easy for the instructor to implement.

- **Point Counted Chapter Production Test**—Working hand-in-hand with the EDD, this is a final test for the student to demonstrate mastery of the objectives.

## 2) Enhanced Instructor's Resource CD-ROM

The Instructor's Resource CD-ROM is an interactive library of assets and links. The Instructor's Resource CD-ROM writes custom "index" pages that can be used as the foundation of a class presentation or online lecture. By navigating through the CD-ROM, you can collect the materials that are most relevant to your interests, edit them to create powerful class lectures, copy them to your own computer's hard drive, and/or upload them to an online course management system.

The new and improved Prentice Hall Instructor's Resource CD-ROM includes tools you expect from a Prentice Hall text:

- The Instructor's Manual in Word and PDF formats—includes solutions to all questions and exercises from the book and Companion Website

- Multiple, customizable PowerPoint slide presentations for each chapter

- Data and Solution Files

- Complete Test Bank

- Image library of all figures from the text

- TestGen Software with QuizMaster

  - TestGen is a test generator that lets you view and easily edit test bank questions, transfer them to tests, and print in a variety of formats suitable to your teaching situation. The program also offers many options for organizing and displaying test banks and tests. A built-in random number and text generator makes it ideal for creating multiple versions of tests that involve calculations and provides more possible test items than test bank questions. Powerful search and sort functions let you easily locate questions and arrange them in the order you prefer.

  - QuizMaster allows students to take tests created with TestGen on a local area network. The QuizMaster utility built into TestGen lets instructors view student records and print a variety of reports. Building tests is easy with TestGen, and exams can be easily uploaded into WebCT, Blackboard, and CourseCompass.

### 3) Instructor's Edition CD-ROM

The Instructor's Edition CD-ROM contains PDF versions of the Instructor's Edition as well as Word versions of the *GO! Series* unique supplements for easy instructor customization.

### Training and Assessment— www2.phgenit.com/support

Prentice Hall offers performance-based training and assessment in one product— Train&Assess IT. The training component offers computer-based training that a student can use to preview, learn, and review Microsoft Office application skills. Web or CD-ROM delivered, Train IT offers interactive, multimedia, computer-based training to augment classroom learning. Built-in prescriptive testing suggests a study path based not only on student test results but also on the specific textbook chosen for the course.

The assessment component offers computer-based testing that shares the same user interface as Train IT and is used to evaluate a student's knowledge about specific topics in Word, Excel, Access, PowerPoint, Outlook, the Internet, and Computing Concepts. It does this in a task-oriented environment to demonstrate proficiency as well as comprehension of the topics by the students. More extensive than the testing in Train IT, Assess IT offers more administrative features for the instructor and additional questions for the student.

Assess IT also allows professors to test students out of a course, place students in appropriate courses, and evaluate skill sets.

### OneKey— www.prenhall.com/onekey

OneKey lets you in to the best teaching and learning resources all in one place. OneKey for the *GO! Series* is all your students need for anywhere-anytime access to your course materials conveniently organized by textbook chapter to reinforce and apply what they've learned in class. OneKey is all you need to plan and administer your course. All your instructor resources are in one place to maximize your effectiveness and minimize your time and effort. OneKey for convenience, simplicity, and success... for you and your students.

### Companion Website @ www.prenhall.com/go

This text is accompanied by a Companion Website at www.prenhall.com/go. Features of this new site include an interactive study guide, downloadable supplements, online end-of-chapter materials, additional practice projects, Web resource links, and technology updates and bonus chapters on the latest trends and hottest topics in information technology. All links to Web exercises will be constantly updated to ensure accuracy for students.

## CourseCompass—www.coursecompass.com

 CourseCompass is a dynamic, interactive online course-management tool powered exclusively for Pearson Education by Blackboard. This exciting product allows you to teach market-leading Pearson Education content in an easy-to-use, customizable format.

## Blackboard—www.prenhall.com/blackboard

Prentice Hall's abundant online content, combined with Blackboard's popular tools and interface, result in robust Web-based courses that are easy to implement, manage, and use—taking your courses to new heights in student interaction and learning.

## WebCT—www.prenhall.com/webct

WebCT Course-management tools within WebCT include page tracking, progress tracking, class and student management, gradebook, communication, calendar, reporting tools, and more. Gold Level Customer Support, available exclusively to adopters of Prentice Hall courses, is provided free-of-charge on adoption and provides you with priority assistance, training discounts, and dedicated technical support.

## TechTV—www.techtv.com

 TechTV is the San Francisco-based cable network that showcases the smart, edgy, and unexpected side of technology. By telling stories through the prism of technology, TechTV provides programming that celebrates its viewers' passion, creativity, and lifestyle.

TechTV's programming falls into three categories:

1. **Help and Information**, with shows like *The Screen Savers*, TechTV's daily live variety show featuring everything from guest interviews and celebrities to product advice and demos; *Tech Live*, featuring the latest news on the industry's most important people, companies, products, and issues; and *Call for Help*, a live help and how-to show providing computing tips and live viewer questions.

2. **Cool Docs**, with shows like *The Tech Of...*, a series that goes behind the scenes of modern life and shows you the technology that makes things tick; *Performance*, an investigation into how technology and science are molding the perfect athlete; and *Future Fighting Machines*, a fascinating look at the technology and tactics of warfare.

3. **Outrageous Fun**, with shows like *X-Play*, exploring the latest and greatest in videogaming; and *Unscrewed* with Martin Sargent, a new late-night series showcasing the darker, funnier world of technology.

For more information, log onto www.techtv.com or contact your local cable or satellite provider to get TechTV in your area.

# Visual Walk-Through

## Project-based Instruction

Students do not practice features of the application; they create real projects that they will need in the real world. Projects are color coded for easy reference.

Projects are named to reflect skills the student will be practicing, not vague project names.

Each chapter opens with a story that sets the stage for the projects the student will create, not force them to pretend to be someone or make up a scenario themselves.

---

**Word 2003**

## chapterone

## Creating Documents with Microsoft Word 2003

In this chapter you will: complete these projects and practice these skills.

| Project 1A **Exploring Microsoft Word** | **Objectives** |
| --- | --- |
| | • Explore and Navigate the Word Window |
| | • View Documents |
| | • Use the Spelling and Grammar Checker |
| | • View Headers and Footers |
| | • Organize, Save, and Print Documents |

| Project 1B **Creating, Editing, and Printing a Document** | **Objectives** |
| --- | --- |
| | • Create and Edit a New Document |
| | • Select and Format Text |
| | • Preview and Print Documents, Close a Document, and Close Word |
| | • Use the Microsoft Help System |

## Learning Objectives

Objectives are clustered around projects. They help students to learn how to solve problems, not just learn software features.

---

### The Greater Atlanta Job Fair

The Greater Atlanta Job Fair is a nonprofit organization that holds targeted job fairs in and around the greater Atlanta area several times each year. The fairs are widely marketed to companies nationwide and locally. The organization also presents an annual Atlanta Job Fair that draws over 2,000 employers in more than 70 industries and generally registers more than 5,000 candidates.

©Getty Images, Inc.

### Getting Started with Outlook 2003

Do you sometimes find it a challenge to manage and complete all the tasks related to your job, family, and class work? Microsoft Office Outlook 2003 can help. Outlook 2003 is a personal information management program (also known as a PIM) that does two things: (1) it helps you get organized, and (2) it helps you communicate with others efficiently. Successful people know that good organizational and communication skills are important. Outlook 2003 electronically stores and organizes appointments and due dates; names, addresses, and phone numbers; to do lists; and notes. Another major use of Outlook 2003 is its e-mail and fax capabilities, along with features with which you can manage group work such as the tasks assigned to a group of coworkers. In this introduction to Microsoft Office Outlook 2003, you will explore the modules available in Outlook and enter data into each module.

Each chapter has an introductory paragraph that briefs students on what is important.

## Visual Summary

Shows students up front what their projects will look like when they are done.

## Project Summary

Stated clearly and quickly in one paragraph with the Visual Summary formatted as a caption so your students won't skip it.

## Objective

The skills they will learn are clearly stated at the beginning of each project and color coded to match projects listed on the chapter opener page.

## Teachable Moment

Expository text is woven into the steps—at the moment students need to know it—not chunked together in a block of text that will go unread.

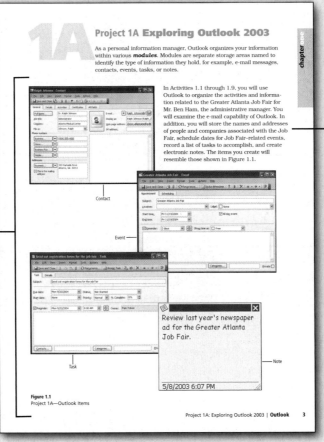

### Project 1A Exploring Outlook 2003

As a personal information manager, Outlook organizes your information within various **modules**. Modules are separate storage areas named to identify the type of information they hold, for example, e-mail messages, contacts, events, tasks, or notes.

In Activities 1.1 through 1.9, you will use Outlook to organize the activities and information related to the Greater Atlanta Job Fair for Mr. Ben Ham, the administrative manager. You will examine the e-mail capability of Outlook. In addition, you will store the names and addresses of people and companies associated with the Job Fair, schedule dates for Job Fair–related events, record a list of tasks to accomplish, and create electronic notes. The items you create will resemble those shown in Figure 1.1.

Review last year's newspaper ad for the Greater Atlanta Job Fair.

5/8/2003 6:07 PM

**Figure 1.1**
Project 1A—Outlook Items

Project 1A: Exploring Outlook 2003 | **Outlook**   3

### Objective 1
**Start Outlook and Identify Outlook Window Elements**

**Activity 1.1** Starting Outlook

1. Find out from your instructor or lab coordinator where the microsoft office 2003 program is located on your system. On the Windows taskbar, click the **Start** button, then click **Microsoft Office Outlook 2003**.

   Organizations and individuals store computer programs in a variety of ways. In organizations where Outlook is used as the standard e-mail program, it may display at the top of the Start menu along with Internet Explorer. Or it may display on the All Programs list, either by itself or on a submenu associated with the Microsoft Office suite. Refer to Figure 1.2 for an example.

**Figure 1.2**

**Alert!**   **Server Connection Dialog Box**

If a message displays indicating that a connection to the server could not be established, click OK. Even without a mail server connection, you can still use the personal information management features of Outlook.

2. If the Outlook window is not already maximized, on the Microsoft Office Outlook 2003 title bar, click the **Maximize** button.

   The default and most common Outlook setup is for the Mail module to open when you start Outlook 2003. The Mail module organizes your e-mail messages into various folders.

## Steps

Color coded to the current project, easy to read, and not too many to confuse the student or too few to be meaningless.

## Sequential Page Numbering

No more confusing letters and abbreviations.

## End of Project Icon

All projects in the *GO! Series* have clearly identifiable end points, useful in self-paced or on-line environments.

### Objective 5
### Organize, Save, and Print Documents

In the same way that you use file folders to organize your paper documents, Windows uses a hierarchy of electronic folders to keep your electronic files organized. Check with your instructor or lab coordinator to see where you will be storing your documents (for example, on your own disk or on a network drive) and whether there is any suggested file folder arrangement. Throughout this textbook, you will be instructed to save your files using the file name followed by your first and last name. Check with your instructor to see if there is some other file naming arrangement for your course.

#### Activity 1.12 Creating Folders for Document Storage and Saving a Document

When you save a document file, the Windows operating system stores your document permanently on a storage medium—either a disk that you have inserted into the computer, the hard drive of your computer, or a network drive connected to your computer system. Changes that you make to existing documents, such as changing text or typing in new text, are not permanently saved until you perform a Save operation.

🔲 On the menu bar, click **File**, and then click **Save As**.

The Save As dialog box displays.

🔲 In the **Save As** dialog box, at the right edge of the **Save in** box, click the **Save in arrow** to view a list of the drives available to you as shown in Figure 1.30. The list of drives and folders will differ from the one shown.

**Figure 1.30**

## Microsoft Procedural Syntax

All steps are written in Microsoft Procedural Syntax in order to put the student in the right place at the right time.

#### Activity 1.13 Printing a Document From the Toolbar

In Activity 1.13, you will print your document from the toolbar.

🔲 On the Standard toolbar, click the **Print** button.

One copy of your document prints on the default printer. A total of four pages will print, and your name and file name will print in the footer area of each page.

🔲 On your printed copy, notice that the formatting marks designating spaces, paragraphs, and tabs, do not print.

🔲 From the **File** menu, click **Exit**, saving any changes if prompted to do so.

Both the document and the Word program close.

**Another Way**

**Printing a Document**

*There are two ways to print a document:*

- On the Standard or Print Preview toolbar, click the Print button, which will print a single copy of the entire document on the default printer.
- From the File menu, click Print to display the Print dialog box, from which you can select a variety of different options, such as printing multiple copies, printing on a different printer, and printing some but not all pages.

**End**  You have completed Project 1A

chapter one

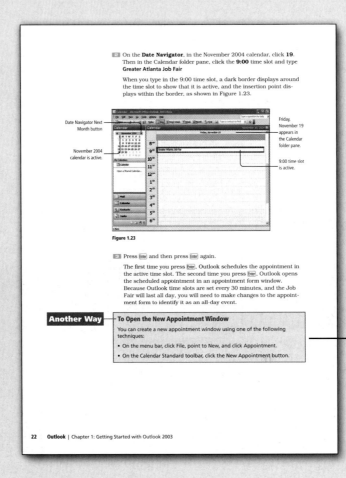

**Alert box**
Draws students' attention to make sure they aren't getting too far off course.

**Another Way box**
Shows students other ways of doing tasks.

**More Knowledge box**
Expands on a topic by going deeper into the material.

**Note box**
Points out important items to remember.

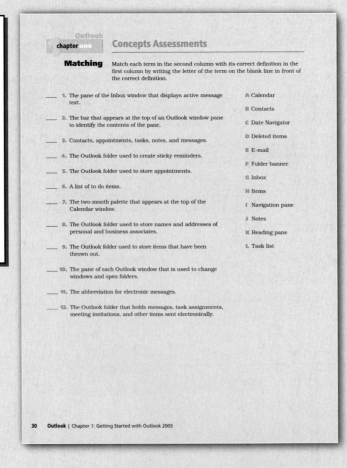

**End-of-Chapter Material**
Take your pick… Skills Assessment, Performance Assessment, or Mastery Assessment. Real-world projects with high, medium, or low guidance levels.

## Objectives List

Each project in the GO! Series end-of-chapter section starts with a list of the objectives covered, in order to easily find the exercises you need to hone your skills.

**Project 1D —** Creating Folders for College Fairs

**Objectives:** *Start Outlook and Create Outlook Folders.*

The fairs for Mercer College and Georgia Tech have been set for April 2005. As a result, you need to create folders to hold vendor information for the fairs. When you have created the contact folders for these two fairs, your Contacts list will appear as in Figure 1.35.

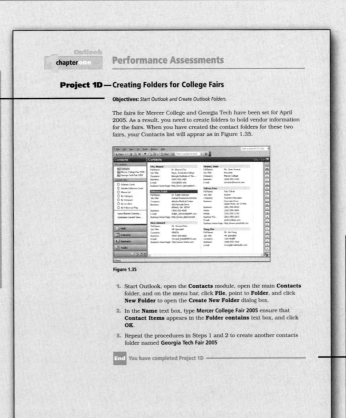

**Figure 1.35**

1. Start Outlook, open the **Contacts** module, open the main **Contacts** folder, and on the menu bar, click **File**, point to **Folder**, and click **New Folder** to open the **Create New Folder** dialog box.

2. In the **Name** text box, type Mercer College Fair 2005 ensure that **Contact Items** appears in the **Folder contains** text box, and click **OK**.

3. Repeat the procedures in Steps 1 and 2 to create another contacts folder named **Georgia Tech Fair 2005**

**End** You have completed Project 1D

## End of Each Project Clearly Marked

Groups of steps that the student performs; the guided practice in order to master the learning objective.

## On the Internet

In this section, students are directed to go out to the Internet for independent study.

**Locating Friends on the Web**

The World Wide Web not only stores information about companies, Web sites for bidding on items, and so forth, but it also contains telephone book information as well as e-mail addresses for many people—especially those who are students at universities! Search the Web for the colleges that three of your friends attend. After you locate the sites, search each university's e-mail directory for one of your friends. Then record these friends and their university e-mail addresses in your contacts list. Print a copy of each contact form as you create it.

**GO! with Help**

**Training on Outlook**

Microsoft Online has set up a series of training lessons at its online Web site. You can access Microsoft.com and review these training sessions directly from the Help menu in Outlook. In this project, you will work your way through the links on the Microsoft Web site to see what training topics they currently offer for Outlook. Log onto the required networks, connect to the Internet, and then follow these steps to complete the exercise.

1. If necessary, start Outlook. On the menu bar, click **Help** and then click **Office on Microsoft.com**.

   The Microsoft Office Online Web page opens in the default browser window.

2. On the left side of the Microsoft Office Online Web page, click the **Training** link.

   The Training Home Web page opens.

3. On the Training Home page, under Browse Training Courses, click **Outlook**.

   The Outlook Courses Web page opens.

4. On the Outlook Courses Web page list, click **Address your e-mail: Get it on the To line fast.**

   The Overview Web page displays information about the training session, identifies the goals of the session, and displays links for continuing the session. Navigation buttons appear in a grey bar toward the top of the Overview page for playing, pausing, and stopping the session. Yellow arrows appear above the navigation bar to advance to the next session page.

5. In the upper right side of the Overview page, on the gray navigation bar, click **Play**.

## GO! with Help

A special section where students practice using the HELP feature of the Office application.

# Contents in Brief

# Table of Contents

# chapterone

# Creating Documents with Microsoft Word 2003

**In this chapter you will:** complete these projects **and** practice these skills.

## Project 1A
### Exploring Microsoft Word

**Objectives**

- Explore and Navigate the Word Window
- View Documents
- Use the Spelling and Grammar Checker
- View Headers and Footers
- Organize, Save, and Print Documents

## Project 1B
### Creating, Editing, and Printing a Document

**Objectives**

- Create and Edit a New Document
- Select and Format Text
- Preview and Print Documents, Close a Document, and Close Word
- Use the Microsoft Help System

# The Perfect Party

The Perfect Party store, owned by two partners, provides a wide variety of party accessories including invitations, favors, banners and flags, balloons, piñatas, etc. Party-planning services include both custom parties with pre-filled custom "goodie bags" and "parties in a box" that include everything needed to throw a theme party. Big sellers in this category are the Football and Luau themes. The owners are planning to open a second store and expand their party-planning services to include catering.

© Getty Images, Inc.

# Getting Started with Microsoft Office Word 2003

Word processing is the most common program found on personal computers and one that almost everyone has a reason to use. When you learn word processing you are also learning skills and techniques that you need to work efficiently on a personal computer. Use Microsoft Word to do basic word processing tasks such as writing a memo, a report, or a letter. You can also use Word to do complex word processing tasks, including sophisticated tables, embedded graphics, and links to other documents and the Internet. Word is a program that you can learn gradually, adding more advanced skills one at a time.

# Project 1A **Business Plan**

With a word processing program, you can type, edit, move, and delete text or change the appearance of the text. Because the document is stored electronically, it can be duplicated, printed, copied, and shared with others. In this chapter, you will become familiar with the parts of the Word window and use the various views available in Word. Then you will create a document, edit and format text, and save and print your Word document.

In Activities 1.1 through 1.13 you will view and edit a business plan for The Perfect Party prepared by Paul Freire, a business planning consultant. Your completed document will look similar to Figure 1.1. You will save your document as *1A_Business_Plan_Firstname_Lastname.*

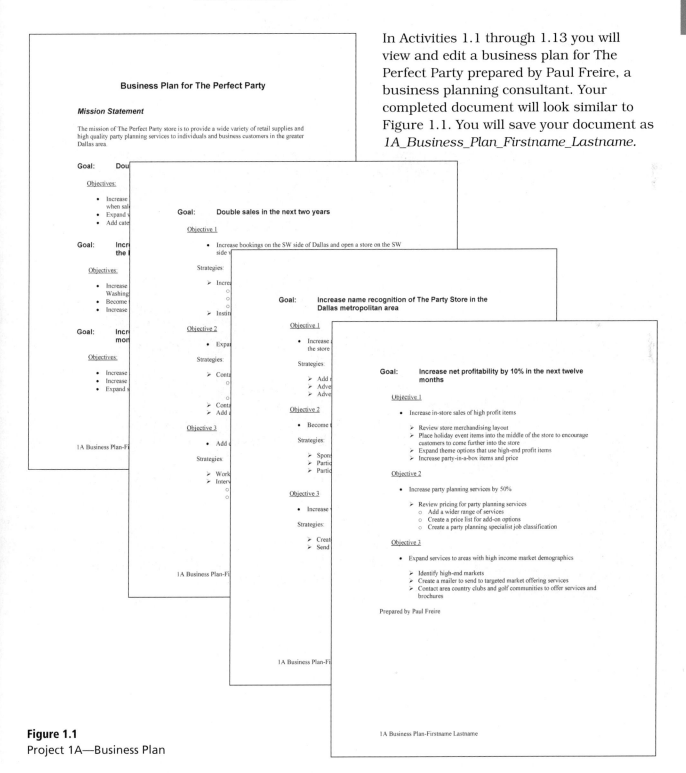

**Figure 1.1**
Project 1A—Business Plan

## Objective 1
## Explore and Navigate the Word Window

**Activity 1.1** Starting Word and Identifying Parts of the Word Window

**1** On the left side of the Windows taskbar, point to and then click the **Start** button ![start](start button) .

The Start menu displays.

**2** On the computer you are using, locate the Word program and then click **Microsoft Office Word 2003**.

Organizations and individuals store computer programs in a variety of ways. The Word program might be located under All Programs or Microsoft Office or at the top of the main Start menu. Refer to Figure 1.2 as an example.

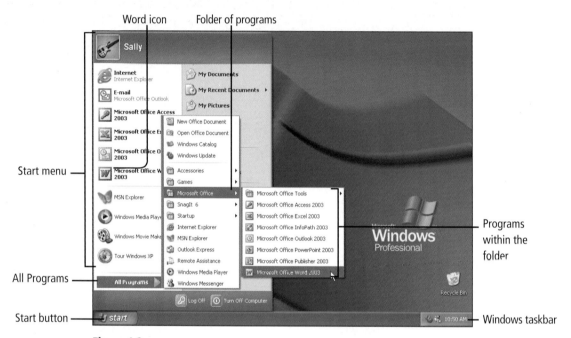

**Figure 1.2**

**3** Look at the opening Word screen, and then take a moment to study the main parts of the screen as shown in Figure 1.3 and described in the table in Figure 1.4.

**Alert!**

### Does your screen differ?

There are several ways to look at a document in the Word window. The appearance of the screen depends on various settings that your system administrator established when the program was installed and how the program has been modified since installation. In many cases, whether a screen element displays depends on how the program was last used.

**4** On the Formatting toolbar, click the **Toolbar Options** button ▊. If the Standard and Formatting toolbars are on two separate rows as shown in Figure 1.3, move the pointer into the Word document window and click to close the list without making any changes. If the toolbars are sharing a single row, click **Show Buttons on Two Rows**.

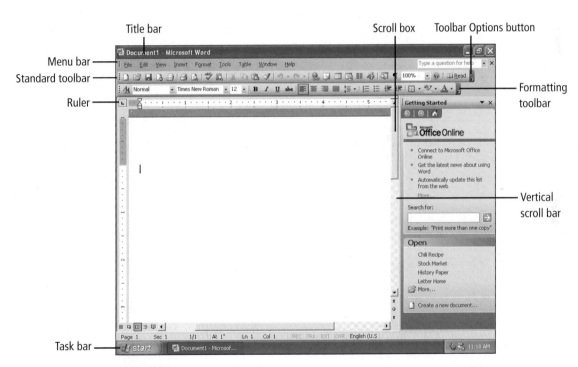

Figure 1.3a

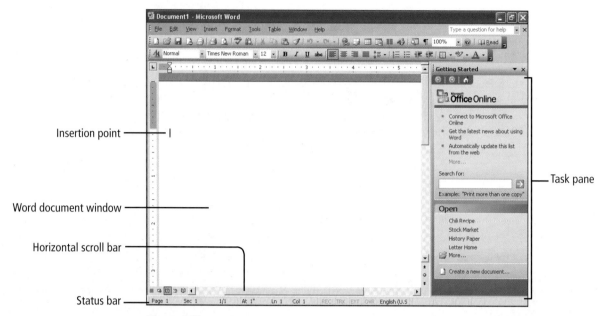

Insertion point ———— |

Word document window ————

Horizontal scroll bar ————

Status bar ————

**Figure 1.3b**

Task pane ————

It is easier to use the toolbars if all of the most commonly used buttons are displayed. Most Word users keep the Standard and Formatting toolbars displayed on separate rows.

## More Knowledge — Turning on Toolbars

If a toolbar is missing entirely, point to an existing toolbar or to the menu bar and click the right mouse button (also known as right-clicking). On the shortcut menu that displays, point to the name of the toolbar you want to display and click the left mouse button. A shortcut menu is a context-sensitive menu of commands relevant to the particular item. Alternatively, display the View menu, click Toolbars, and then click the name of the toolbar you want to display. If a toolbar is open, a check mark displays to the left of the toolbar name.

## Microsoft Word Screen Elements

| Screen Element | Description |
|---|---|
| Title bar | Displays the program icon, the name of the document, and the name of the program. The Minimize, Maximize/Restore Down, and Close buttons are grouped on the right side of the title bar. |
| Menu bar | Contains a list of commands. To display a menu, click on the menu name. |
| Standard toolbar | Contains buttons for some of the most common commands in Word. It may occupy an entire row or share a row with the Formatting toolbar. |
| Formatting toolbar | Contains buttons for some of the most common formatting options in Word. It may occupy an entire row or share a row with the Standard toolbar. |
| Ruler | Displays the location of margins, indents, columns, and tab stops. |
| Vertical scroll bar | Enables you to move up and down in a document to display text that is not visible. |
| Horizontal scroll bar | Enables you to move left and right in a document to display text that is not visible. |
| Scroll box | Provides a visual indication of your location in a document. It can also be used with the mouse to drag a document up and down. |
| Toolbar Options button | Displays a list of all of the buttons associated with a toolbar. It also enables you to place the Standard and Formatting toolbars on separate rows or on the same row. |
| Word document window | Displays the active document. |
| Insertion point | Indicates, with a blinking vertical line, where text or graphics will be inserted. |
| Task pane | Displays commonly used commands related to the current task. |
| Taskbar | Displays the Start button and the name of any open documents. The taskbar may also display shortcut buttons for other programs. |
| Status bar | Displays the page and section number and other Word settings. |

**Figure 1.4**

### Activity 1.2 Opening an Existing Document

**1** On the Standard toolbar, click the **Open** button 📄.

The Open dialog box displays.

**2** In the **Open** dialog box, click the **Look in arrow** at the right edge of the **Look in** box to view a list of the drives available on your system. See Figure 1.5 as an example—the drives and folders displayed on your screen will differ.

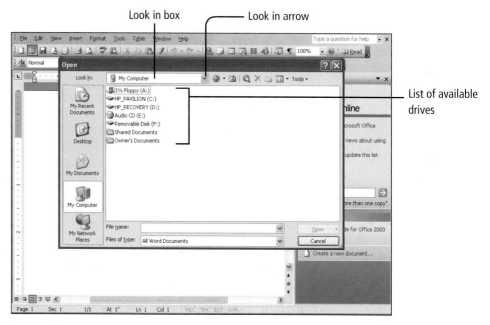

**Figure 1.5**

**3** Navigate to the location where the student files for this textbook are stored.

**4** Locate **w01A_Business_Plan** and click once to select it. Then, in the lower right corner of the **Open** dialog box, click the **Open** button. Alternatively, **double-click** the file name to open it—click the left mouse button twice in rapid succession.

The document displays in the Word window. See Figure 1.6.

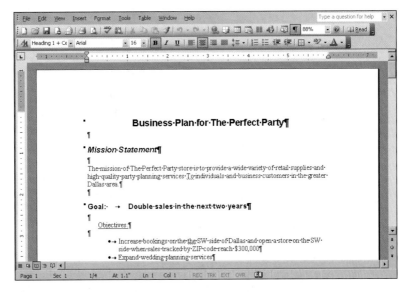

**Figure 1.6**

**Note** — Turning Off the Office Assistant

One of Word's Help features is an animated object called the Office Assistant. Many people like to turn this feature off. To hide the Office Assistant, click the right mouse button on the Office Assistant. In the menu that displays, click Hide with the left mouse button. The instruction in this textbook assumes that the Office Assistant is turned off.

**Activity 1.3** Accessing Menu Commands and Displaying the Task Pane

Word commands are organized in *menus*—lists of commands within a category. The *menu bar* at the top of the screen provides access to the Word commands. The buttons on the toolbars provide one-click shortcuts to menu commands.

**1** On the menu bar, click **View**.

The View menu displays in either the short format as shown in Figure 1.7, or in the full format, which displays all of the menu commands. If the full menu does not display, you can do one of three things:

- Wait a moment and the full menu will display if your system is set to do so.

- At the bottom of the menu, click the double arrows to expand the menu to display all commands.

- Before opening a menu, point to the menu name in the menu bar, and then double-click. This ensures that the full menu displays.

Short menu format

Menu bar

Double arrows for
expanding menu

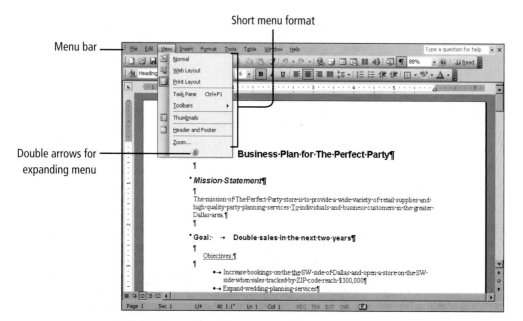

**Figure 1.7**

## Note — Turning On Full Menus

The instruction in this textbook assumes that the full menus display when you click a menu command. To turn on full menus, go to the menu bar, click Tools, and then click Customize. In the Customize dialog box, click the Options tab, and then click the *Always show full menus* check box. Click the Close button to close the dialog box.

**2** Be sure that the full menu is displayed as shown in Figure 1.8, and notice to the right of some commands there is a ***keyboard shortcut***; for example, *Ctrl+F1* for the task pane.

A keyboard shortcut enables you to perform commands using a combination of keys from your keyboard. For example, if you press and hold down Ctrl and then press F1, the result is the same as clicking View on the menu bar and then clicking Task Pane. Many commands in Word can be accomplished in more than one way.

Keyboard shortcut

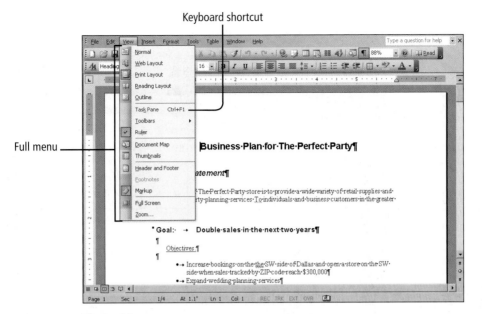

Full menu

**Figure 1.8**

**3** On the displayed **View** menu, to the left of some command names, notice the image of the button that represents this command on a toolbar.

This is a reminder that you can initiate the command with one click from a toolbar, rather than initiating the command with multiple clicks from the menu.

**4** On the displayed **View** menu, pause the mouse pointer over **Toolbars** but do not click.

An arrow to the right of a command name indicates that a submenu is available. When you point to this type of menu command, a submenu displays. See Figure 1.9.

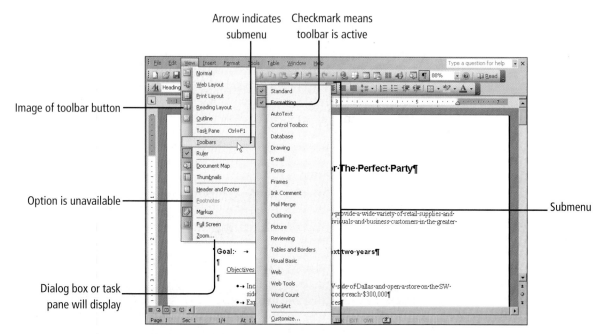

Arrow indicates submenu    Checkmark means toolbar is active

Image of toolbar button

Option is unavailable

Dialog box or task pane will display

Submenu

**Figure 1.9**

**5** Look at the full **View** menu on your screen, and notice the various symbols and characters. These are standard across all Microsoft products. Take a moment to study the table in Figure 1.10 for a description of these elements.

## Word Menu Characteristics

| Characteristic | Description | Example |
|---|---|---|
| … (ellipsis) | Indicates that either a dialog box requesting more information or a task pane will display. | Zoom… |
| ▶ (right arrow) | Indicates that a submenu—another menu of choices—will display. | Toolbars ▶ |
| No symbol | Indicates that the command will perform immediately. | Web Layout |
| ✔ (check mark) | Indicates that a command is turned on or active. | ✔ Ruler |
| Gray option name | Indicates that the command is currently unavailable. | Footnotes |

**Figure 1.10**

**6** With the **View** menu still displayed, click **Task Pane**.

The Getting Started task pane displays as shown in Figure 1.11. If the task pane was already displayed, it will close. If the task pane was not visible, it will display on the right side of the screen. As you progress in your study of Word, you will see various task panes to assist you in accomplishing Word tasks.

Task Pane

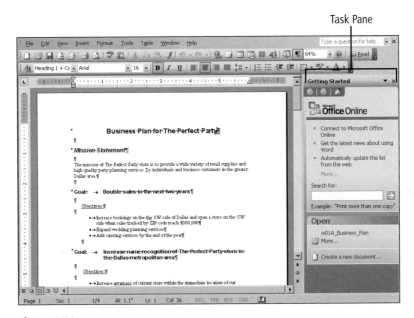

**Figure 1.11**

**7** On the menu bar, click **View**, and then click **Task Pane** again to close the task pane.

For the remainder of this book the task pane should be closed, except when otherwise instructed.

**Activity 1.4** Navigating a Document Using the Vertical Scroll Bar

Most Word documents are larger than the Word window. Therefore, there are several ways to **navigate** (move) in a document.

**1** At the right of your screen, in the vertical scroll bar, locate the down arrow at the bottom of the bar as shown in Figure 1.12. Then, click the **down scroll arrow** five times.

Notice that the document scrolls up a line at a time. In this document, Word has flagged some spelling and grammar errors (red and green wavy lines), which you will correct in Activity 1.9.

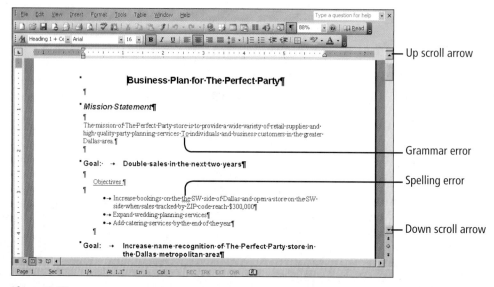

Up scroll arrow

Grammar error

Spelling error

Down scroll arrow

**Figure 1.12**

**2** Point to the **down scroll arrow** again, and then click and hold down the mouse button for several seconds.

The document text scrolls up continuously, a line at a time.

**3** At the top of the vertical scroll bar, point to the **up scroll arrow**, and then click and hold down the mouse button until you have scrolled back to the top of the document. As you do so, notice that the scroll box moves up in the scroll bar.

**4** At the top of the vertical scroll bar point to the scroll box, and then press and hold down the left mouse button.

A **ScreenTip**—a small box that displays information about, or the name of, a screen element—displays. In this instance, the ScreenTip indicates the page number and the first line of text at the top of the page. See Figure 1.13.

ScreenTip

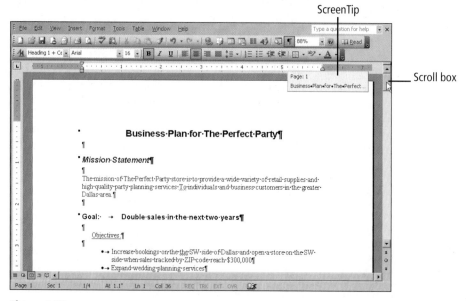

Scroll box

**Figure 1.13**

**5** *Drag* (hold down the left mouse button while moving your mouse) the scroll box down to the bottom of the scroll bar. As you do so, watch the ScreenTip.

The ScreenTip changes as each new page reaches the top of the screen. See Figure 1.14.

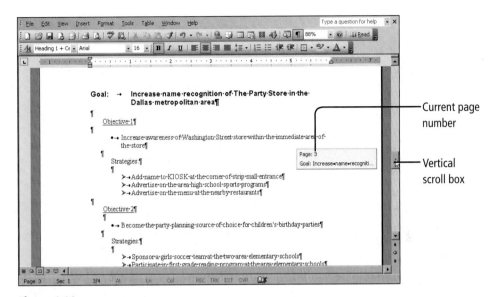

Current page number

Vertical scroll box

**Figure 1.14**

**6** Release the mouse button, and then click in the gray area above the scroll box.

The document scrolls up one screen.

**7** Practice clicking in the area above and below the scroll box.

This is a quick way to scan a document.

---

**Another Way** — **Using the Wheel Button on the Mouse**

If your mouse has a small wheel button between the left and right mouse buttons, you can scroll up and down in the document by rotating the wheel.

---

**Activity 1.5** Navigating a Document Using the Keyboard

***Keyboard shortcuts*** are another way to navigate your document quickly. Keyboard shortcuts provide additional navigation techniques that you cannot accomplish with the vertical scroll bar. For example, using keyboard shortcuts, you can move the insertion point to the beginning or end of a word or line.

**1** On your keyboard, hold down Ctrl and press Home.

The top of the document displays, and the insertion point moves to the left of the first word in the document.

**2** Hold down Ctrl and press End.

The text at the bottom of the last page in the document displays, and the insertion point moves to the right of the last word in the document.

**3** Press Page Up.

The document scrolls up one screen.

**4** Press End.

The insertion point moves to the end of the current line of text. Take a moment to study the table shown in Figure 1.15, which lists the most commonly used keyboard shortcuts.

## Navigating a Document Using Keyboard Shortcuts

| To Move | Press |
|---|---|
| To the beginning of a document | Ctrl + Home |
| To the end of a document | Ctrl + End |
| To the beginning of a line | Home |
| To the end of a line | End |
| To the beginning of the previous word | Ctrl + ← |
| To the beginning of the next word | Ctrl + → |
| To the beginning of the current word (if insertion point is in the middle of a word) | Ctrl + ← |
| To the beginning of the previous paragraph | Ctrl + ↑ |
| To the end of the next paragraph | Ctrl + ↓ |
| To the beginning of the current paragraph (if insertion point is in the middle of a paragraph) | Ctrl + ↑ |
| Up one screen | Page Up |
| Down one screen | PageDown |

**Figure 1.15**

**5** Hold down Ctrl and press Home to position the insertion point at the beginning of the document.

# Objective 2
## View Documents

In addition to different document views, there is a method to view characters on your screen that do not print on paper. Examples of these characters include paragraph marks, tabs, and spaces.

### Activity 1.6 Displaying Formatting Marks

When you press Enter, Spacebar, or Tab on your keyboard, characters are placed in your document to represent these keystrokes. These characters do not print, and are referred to as ***formatting marks*** or ***nonprinting characters***. Because formatting marks guide your eye in a document like a map and road signs guide you along a highway, these marks will be displayed throughout this instruction.

**1** In the displayed document, look at the document title *Business Plan for The Perfect Party* and determine if a paragraph symbol (¶) displays at the end of the title as shown in Figure 1.16. If you do *not* see the paragraph symbol, on the Standard toolbar, click the **Show/Hide ¶** button ¶ to display the formatting marks.

Paragraph marks display at the end of every paragraph. Every time you press Enter, a new paragraph is created, and a paragraph mark is inserted. Paragraph marks are especially helpful in showing the number of blank lines inserted in a document. Spaces are indicated by dots, and tabs are indicated by arrows as shown in Figure 1.16.

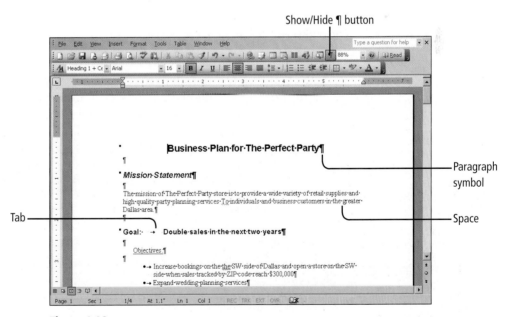

Show/Hide ¶ button

Paragraph symbol

Tab

Space

**Figure 1.16**

**2** Click the **Show/Hide ¶** button ¶. This turns off the display of nonprinting characters. Then, click the **Show/Hide ¶** button ¶ once more to turn it on again.

**Another Way** **Viewing Documents**

*There are five ways to view your document on the screen. Each view is useful in different situations.*

- The Print Layout view displays the page borders, margins, text, and graphics as they will look when you print the document. Most Word users prefer this view for most tasks, and it is the default view.

- The Normal view simplifies the page layout for quick typing, and shows a little more text on the screen than the Print Layout view. Graphics, headers, and footers do not display.

- The Web Layout view shows how the document will look when saved as a Web page and viewed in a Web browser.

- The Reading Layout view creates easy-to-read pages that fit on the screen to increase legibility. This view does not represent the pages as they would print. Each screen page is labeled with a screen number, rather than a page number.

- The Outline view shows the organizational structure of your document by headings and subheadings and can be collapsed and expanded to look at individual sections of a document.

### Activity 1.7 Changing Views

**1** To the left of the horizontal scroll bar, locate the **View buttons**.

These buttons are used to switch to different document views. Alternatively, you can switch views using the commands on the View menu.

**2** Click the **Normal View** button ≡.

The work area covers the entire width of the screen. See Figure 1.17. Page margins are not displayed, and any inserted graphics, *headers*, or *footers* do not display. A header is information at the top of every page, and a footer is information at the bottom of every printed page.

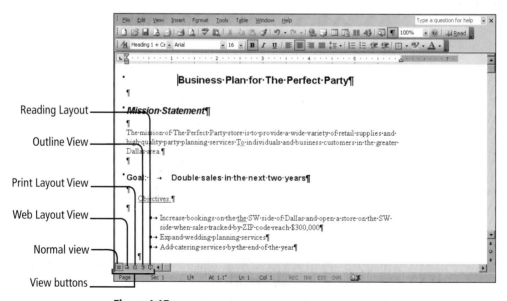

Reading Layout
Outline View
Print Layout View
Web Layout View
Normal view
View buttons

**Figure 1.17**

**3** Click the **Reading Layout** button 📖.

An entire page is displayed, and the text reaches nearly to the bottom. However, this is only about half of the text that is actually on the page as it is formatted and if it were printed. This view has its own toolbars and is optimized for easy reading. You can display side-by-side pages in longer documents, and you can *edit*—make changes to—the document in this view.

> ## Note — Opening the Reading Layout view
>
> The Reading Layout view is also accessible by clicking the Read button 📖 Read on the Standard toolbar.

**4** At the top of the screen, in the Reading Layout toolbar, click **Close** button 📖 Close.

Closing the Reading Layout view returns you to the previous view, which was Normal view.

**5** At the left of the horizontal scroll bar, click the **Print Layout View** button 🗒.

In this view you can see all of the elements that will display on paper when you print the document. The instruction in this textbook will use the Print Layout View for most documents.

### Activity 1.8 Using the Zoom Button

To *zoom* means to increase or to decrease the viewing area of the screen. You can zoom in to look closely at a particular section of a document, and then zoom out to see a whole page on the screen. It is also possible to view multiple pages on the screen.

**1** On the Standard toolbar, click the **Zoom button arrow** 100% ▾.

The Zoom list displays as shown in Figure 1.18.

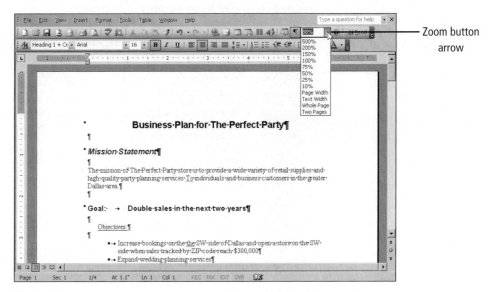

Figure 1.18

**2** On the displayed list, click **150%**.

The view of the text is magnified. See Figure 1.19.

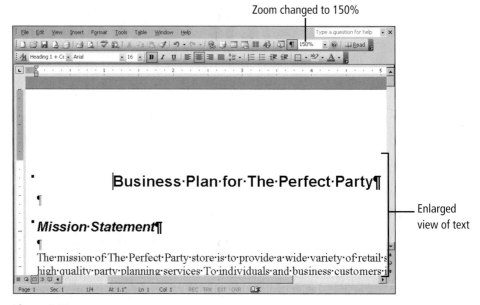

Zoom changed to 150%

Enlarged view of text

**Figure 1.19**

**3** On the Standard toolbar, click the **Zoom button arrow** 100% ▼ again and then click **Two Pages**.

Two full pages display on the screen. This magnification enables you to see how the text is laid out on the page and to check the location of other document elements, such as graphics.

**4** On the vertical scroll bar, click the down scroll arrow five times.

Notice that you can now see parts of four pages, and you can see how the text flows from one page to another. See Figure 1.20.

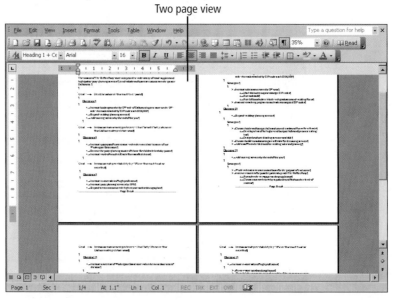

Two page view

**Figure 1.20**

**5** On the Standard toolbar, click the **Zoom button arrow** `100% ▾` and from the displayed list click **Page Width**.

This is a flexible magnification, displaying the maximum page width, regardless of the size of your screen. The size shown in the Zoom box will vary depending on screen size and resolution.

**6** On the Standard toolbar, click on the number in the Zoom box to highlight the number currently displayed. Type **100** and then press `Enter`.

Typing a number directly into the Zoom box is another method of changing the zoom level.

## Objective 3
## Use the Spelling and Grammar Checker

As you type, Word compares your words to those in the Word dictionary and compares your phrases and punctuation to a list of grammar rules. Words that are not in the Word dictionary are marked with a wavy red underline. Phrases and punctuation that differ from the grammar rules are marked with a wavy green underline. Because a list of grammar rules applied by a computer program can never be exact, and because a computer dictionary cannot contain all known words and proper names, you will need to check any words flagged by Word as misspellings or grammar errors.

Finally, Word does not check for usage. For example, Word will not flag the word *sign* as misspelled, even though you intended to type *sing a song* rather than *sign a song,* because both are legitimate words contained within Word's dictionary.

### Activity 1.9 Checking Individual Spelling and Grammar Errors

One way to check spelling and grammar errors flagged by Word is to right-click the flagged word or phrase and, from the displayed shortcut menu, select a suitable correction or instruction.

**1** Hold down `Ctrl` and press `Home` to move the insertion point to the top of the document. Scan the text on the screen to locate green and red wavy underlines.

### Note — Activating Spelling and Grammar Checking

If you do not see any wavy red or green lines under words, the automatic spelling and/or grammar checking has been turned off on your system. To activate the spelling and grammar checking, display the Tools menu, click Options, and then click the Spelling & Grammar tab. Under Spelling, click the *Check spelling as you type* check box. Under Grammar, click the *Check grammar as you type* check box. There are also check boxes for hiding spelling and grammar errors. These should not be checked. Close the dialog box.

**2** In the second line of the *Mission Statement*, locate the word *To* with the wavy green underline. Position your mouse pointer over the word and right-click.

A shortcut menu displays as shown in Figure 1.21. A suggested replacement is shown in the top section of the shortcut menu. In this instance, Word has identified an incorrectly capitalized word in the middle of a sentence.

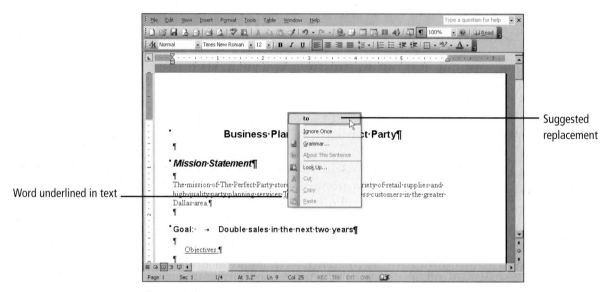

**Figure 1.21**

**3** On the shortcut menu, click **to**.

The incorrect word is replaced.

**4** In the first bullet point, find the word *the* with a wavy red underline. Position the mouse pointer over the word and right-click.

Word identified a duplicate word, and provides two suggestions—*Delete Repeated Word* or *Ignore*. See Figure 1.22. The second option is included because sometimes the same word will be used twice in succession.

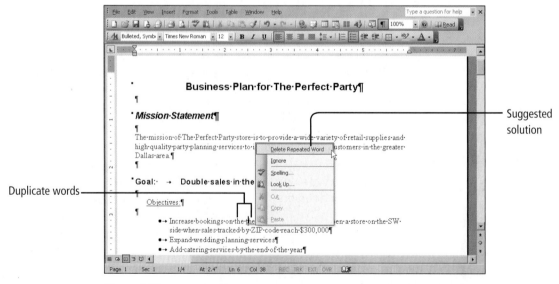

**Figure 1.22**

**5** On the displayed shortcut menu, click **Delete Repeated Word**.

The repeated word is deleted.

**Activity 1.10** Checking Spelling and Grammar in an Entire Document

Initiating the spelling and grammar checking feature from the menu or toolbar displays the Spelling and Grammar dialog box, which provides more options than the shortcut menus.

**1** On the Standard toolbar, click the **Spelling and Grammar** button

 to begin a check of the document. If necessary, move your mouse pointer to the title bar of the dialog box, and drag the dialog box out of the way so you can see the misspelled word *awarness*.

The Spelling and Grammar dialog box displays. Under Not in Dictionary, a misspelled word is highlighted, and under Suggestions, two suggestions are presented. See Figure 1.23.

**2** Take moment to study the spelling and grammar options available in the **Spelling and Grammar** dialog box as shown in the table in Figure 1.24.

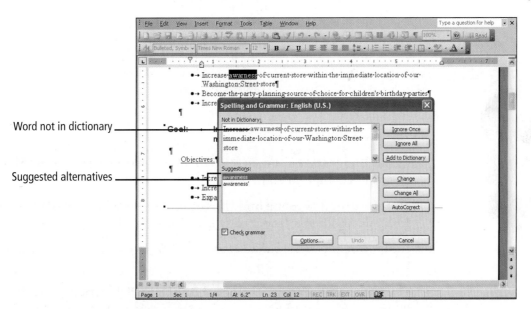

Word not in dictionary

Suggested alternatives

**Figure 1.23**

## Spelling and Grammar Dialog Box Buttons

| Button | Action |
| --- | --- |
| Ignore Once | Ignores the identified word one time, but flags it in other locations in the document. |
| Ignore All | Discontinues flagging any instance of the word anywhere in the document. |
| Add to Dictionary | Adds the word to a custom dictionary, which can be edited. This option does not change the built-in Microsoft Office dictionary. |
| Change | Changes the identified word to the word highlighted under Suggestions. |
| Change All | Changes every instance of the word in the document to the word highlighted under Suggestions. |
| AutoCorrect | Adds the flagged word to the AutoCorrect list, which will subsequently correct the word automatically if misspelled in any documents typed in the future. |
| Ignore Rule (Grammar) | Ignores the specific rule used to determine a grammar error and removes the green wavy line. |
| Next Sentence (Grammar) | Moves to the next identified error. |
| Explain (Grammar) | Displays the rule used to identify a grammar error. |
| Options | Displays the Spelling and Grammar tab of the Options dialog box. |

**Figure 1.24**

**3** Under **Suggestions**, make sure *awareness* is selected, and then click the **Change** button.

The correction is made and the next identified error is highlighted, which is another misspelled word, *merchandixing*.

**4** Under **Suggestions**, make sure *merchandising* is selected, and then click the **Change** button.

The misspelled word is corrected, the next identified error is highlighted, and a number of suggestions are provided. This time the word is a proper noun, and it is spelled correctly. You could add this word to your dictionary, or choose to ignore it. See Figure 1.25.

Proper noun

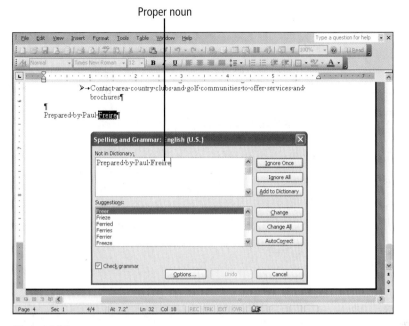

**Figure 1.25**

5 Click the **Ignore Once** button.

A dialog box displays indicating that the spelling and grammar check is complete. See Figure 1.26.

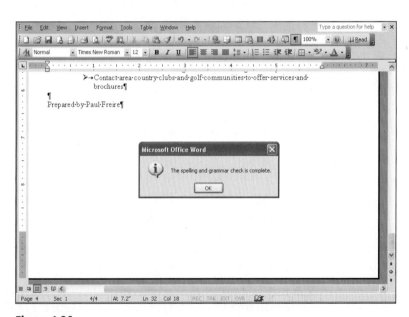

**Figure 1.26**

6 Click **OK** to close the dialog box.

## Objective 4
## View Headers and Footers

Headers and footers are areas reserved for text and graphics that repeat at the top (header) or bottom (footer) of each page in a document.

### Activity 1.11 Accessing Headers and Footers

**1** Display the **View** menu, and then click **Header and Footer**.

The first page of the document displays with the Header area outlined with a dotted line. By default, headers and footers are placed 0.5 inch from the top and bottom of the page, respectively. The Header and Footer toolbar displays, floating on your screen as shown in Figure 1.27.

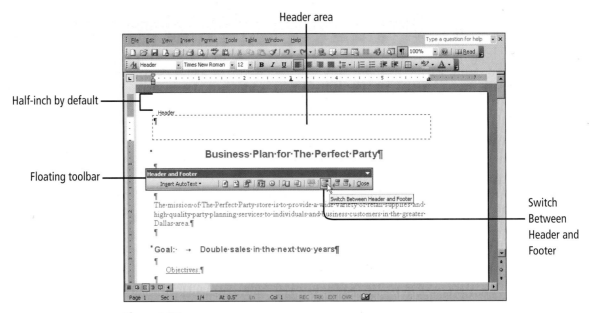

**Figure 1.27**

**2** On the Header and Footer toolbar, click the **Switch Between Header and Footer** button 🖳.

The footer area displays with the insertion point blinking at the left edge of the footer area.

**3** In the footer area, using your own name, type **1A Business Plan-Firstname Lastname** as shown in Figure 1.28.

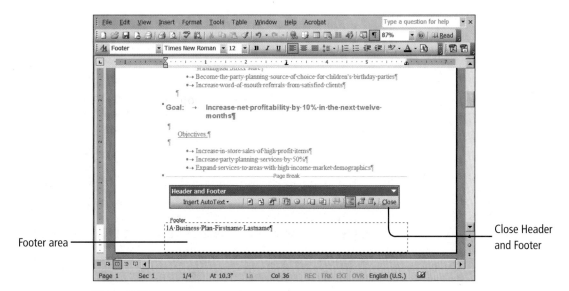

Footer area ——

—— Close Header
and Footer

**Figure 1.28**

4 On the Header and Footer toolbar, click the **Close** button Close.
Alternatively, double-click anywhere in the text area of the document
to close the Header and Footer toolbar.

5 Scroll down until you can see the footer on the first page.

The footer displays in light gray as shown in Figure 1.29. Because
it is a proper name, your name in the footer may display with wavy
red lines.

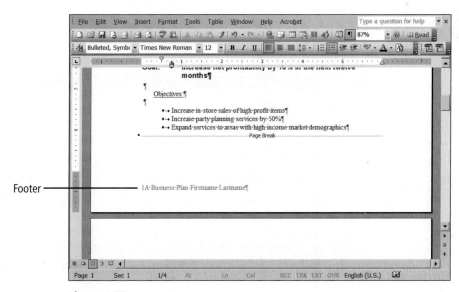

Footer ——

**Figure 1.29**

## More Knowledge — Moving to the Header or Footer

A quick way to edit an existing header or footer is to double-click in the
header or footer area. This will display the Header and Footer toolbar, and
also place the insertion point at the beginning of the header or footer.

# Objective 5
## Organize, Save, and Print Documents

In the same way that you use file folders to organize your paper documents, Windows uses a hierarchy of electronic folders to keep your electronic files organized. Check with your instructor or lab coordinator to see where you will be storing your documents (for example, on your own disk or on a network drive) and whether there is any suggested file folder arrangement. Throughout this textbook, you will be instructed to save your files using the file name followed by your first and last name. Check with your instructor to see if there is some other file naming arrangement for your course.

### Activity 1.12 Creating Folders for Document Storage and Saving a Document

When you save a document file, the Windows operating system stores your document permanently on a storage medium—either a disk that you have inserted into the computer, the hard drive of your computer, or a network drive connected to your computer system. Changes that you make to existing documents, such as changing text or typing in new text, are not permanently saved until you perform a Save operation.

**1** On the menu bar, click **File**, and then click **Save As**.

The Save As dialog box displays.

**2** In the **Save As** dialog box, at the right edge of the **Save in** box, click the **Save in arrow** to view a list of the drives available to you as shown in Figure 1.30. Your list of drives and folders will differ from the one shown.

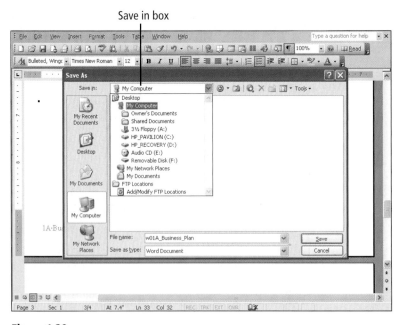

Figure 1.30

**3** Navigate to the drive on which you will be storing your folders and projects for this chapter—for example, 3½ Floppy (A:) or the drive designated by your instructor or lab coordinator.

**4** In the **Save As** dialog box toolbar, click the **Create New Folder** button ▣.

The New Folder dialog box displays.

**5** In the **Name** box, type **Chapter 1** as shown in Figure 1.31, and then click **OK**.

The new folder name displays in the Save in box, indicating that the folder is open and ready to store your document.

Create New Folder button

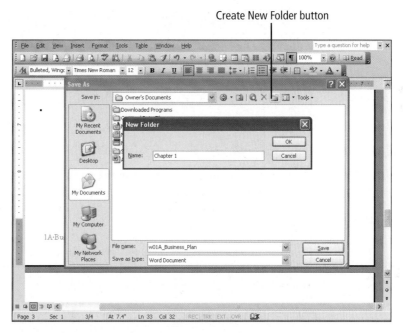

**Figure 1.31**

**6** In the lower portion of the **Save As** dialog box, locate the **File name** box.

The file name *w01A_Business_Plan* may be highlighted in blue, in which case your new typing will delete the existing text.

## More Knowledge — Renaming a Folder

You can rename folders as well as files. To rename a folder, right-click the folder in the Save As dialog box, click Rename from the shortcut menu, and then type a new folder name. This procedure also works in My Computer or Windows Explorer.

**7** If necessary, select or delete the existing text, and then in the **File name** box, using your own first and last name, type **1A_Business_Plan_Firstname_Lastname** as shown in Figure 1.32.

The Microsoft Windows operating system recognizes file names with spaces. However, some Internet file transfer programs do not. To facilitate sending your files over the Internet using a course management system such as Blackboard, eCollege, or WebCT, in this textbook you will be instructed to save files using an underscore instead of a space. The underscore key is the shift of the ⎯ key, located two keys to the left of ⎣←Bksp⎦.

Underscore characters in file name

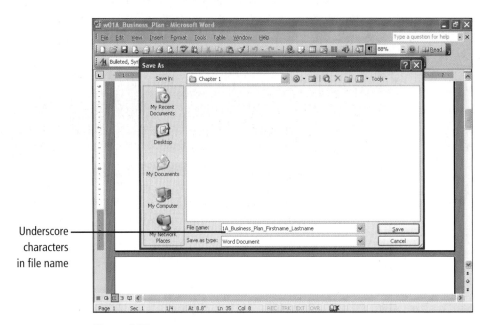

**Figure 1.32**

**8** In the lower portion of the **Save As** dialog box, click the **Save** button, or press ⎣Enter⎦.

Your file is saved in the new folder with the new file name.

## More Knowledge — Saving Your Document Often

Save your documents frequently to avoid losing the information you have created in a new document or the changes you have made to an existing document. In rare instances, problems arise with your computer system or your electrical power source. After a document is saved, hardware or electrical problems will not harm your document. However, you could lose any new editing that you performed on the document after the last save operation.

### Activity 1.13 Printing a Document from the Toolbar

In Activity 1.13, you will print your document from the toolbar.

**1** On the Standard toolbar, click the **Print** button.

One copy of your document prints on the default printer. A total of four pages will print, and your name will print in the footer area of each page.

**2** On your printed copy, notice that the formatting marks designating spaces, paragraphs, and tabs do not print.

**3** From the **File** menu, click **Exit**, saving any changes if prompted to do so.

Both the document and the Word program close.

**Another Way** ─── **Printing a Document**

***There are two ways to print a document:***

- On the Standard or Print Preview toolbar, click the Print button, which will print a single copy of the entire document on the default printer.

- From the File menu, click Print to display the Print dialog box, from which you can select a variety of different options, such as printing multiple copies, printing on a different printer, and printing some but not all pages.

**End** You have completed Project 1A ───────────────

# Project 1B **Thank You Letter**

In Project 1A you opened and edited an existing document. In Project 1B you will create and edit a new document.

In Activities 1.14 through 1.22 you will create a letter from Gabriela Quinones, a co-owner of The Perfect Party, to Paul Freire, a business consultant who was involved in preparing the business plan. Your completed document will look similar to Figure 1.33. You will save your document as *1B_ Thanks_Firstname_Lastname.*

September 12, 2005


Mr. Paul Freire
Business Consulting Services
123 Jackson Street, Suite 100
Dallas, TX 75202

Dear Paul:

*Subject: Your participation in the planning retreat*

Thank you for participating in the planning retreat for **The Perfect Party**. We are very excited about the next two years. One of the reasons our future looks so bright is because of the contributions you have made!

I would also like to thank you personally for taking notes and summarizing the ideas expressed at the retreat.

Yours truly,


Gabriela Quinones




1B Thanks-Firstname Lastname

**Figure 1.33**
Project 1B—Thank you letter

# Objective 6
## Create and Edit a New Document

In Activities 1.14 through 1.17, you will practice the basic skills needed to create a new document, insert and delete text, and edit text.

### Activity 1.14 Creating a New Document

**1** Start Word. If necessary, close the Getting Started task pane by clicking the small Close button ⊠ in the upper right corner of the task pane.

When Word is started, a new blank document displays.

**2** In the blue title bar, notice that *Document1* displays.

Word displays the file name of a document in both the blue title bar at the top of the screen and on a button in the taskbar at the lower edge of the screen—including new unsaved documents. The new unsaved document displays *Document1* or *Document2* depending on how many times you have started a new document during your current Word session. See Figure 1.34.

Default document name ——

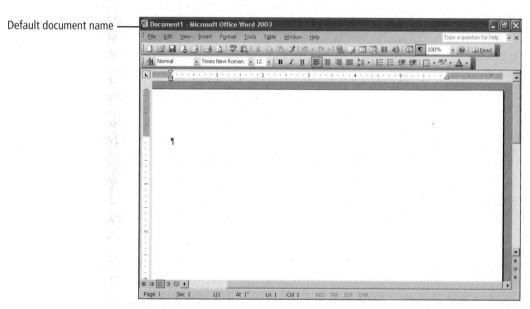

**Figure 1.34**

chapter one

**Another Way**

### Opening a New Document

*There are five ways to begin a new document in Word:*

- Start the Word program; a new blank document displays.

- On the Standard toolbar, click the New Blank Document button.

- From the menu bar, click File, and then click New.

- From the Getting Started task pane, under Open, click *Create a new document.*

- From the New Document task pane, under New, click *Blank document.*

**Activity 1.15** Entering Text and Inserting Blank Lines

**1** Verify that formatting marks are displayed. If necessary, click the Show/Hide ¶ button ¶ to display them. With the insertion point blinking in the upper left corner of the document to the left of the default first paragraph mark, type **Sept**

A ScreenTip displays *September (Press ENTER to Insert)* as shown in Figure 1.35. This feature, called ***AutoComplete***, assists in your typing by suggesting commonly used words and phrases after you type the first few characters.

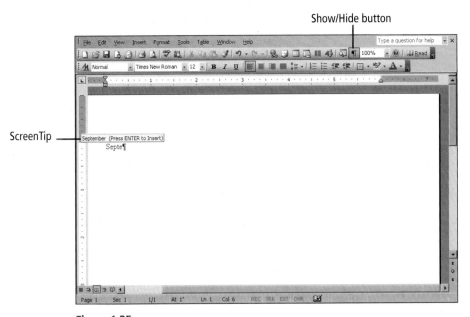

Figure 1.35

**2** To finish the word *September*, press [Enter]. Press [Spacebar] once and then type **12, 2005** and press [Enter]. (If you are completing this activity during the month of September, AutoComplete may offer to fill in the current date. To ignore the suggestion, type as indicated.)

The first paragraph is complete and the insertion point is positioned at the beginning of the next line. A paragraph is created when you press [Enter]. Thus, a paragraph can be a single line like the date line, or a blank line.

A purple dotted underscore beneath the date indicates that Word has flagged this as a ***recognizer***. A recognizer indicates that Word recognizes this as a date. As you progress in your study of Microsoft Office, you will discover how dates such as this one can be added to other Office programs like Microsoft Outlook.

**3** Press [Enter] three more times.

Three empty paragraphs, which function as blank lines, display below the typed date.

**4** Type **Mr. Paul Freire** and then press [Enter].

**5** On three lines, type the following address:

**Business Consulting Services**

**123 Jackson Street, Suite 100**

**Dallas, TX 75202**

**6** Press [Enter] twice. Type **Dear Paul:** and then press [Enter] twice.

**7** Type **Subject: Your participation in the planning retreat** and press [Enter] twice.

Compare your screen to Figure 1.36. The purple dotted line under the street address is another recognizer, indicating that you could add the address to your Microsoft Outlook address book or perform other useful tasks with the address. Additionally, the proper name *Freire* is flagged as misspelled because it is a proper name not contained in the Word dictionary.

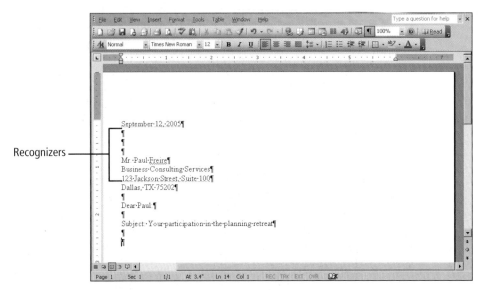

Recognizers

**Figure 1.36**

**8** As you type the following text, press the Spacebar only once at the end of a sentence: **Thank you for participating in the retreat for The Perfect Party. We are really very excited about the next two years. One of the reasons our future looks so bright is because of the contributions you have made!** Press Enter twice.

As you type, the insertion point moves to the right, and when it reaches the right margin, Word determines whether or not the next word in the line will fit within the established right margin. If the word does not fit, Word will move the whole word down to the next line. This feature is **_wordwrap_**.

## Note — Spacing at the End of Sentences

Although you may have learned to press Spacebar twice at the end of a sentence, it is common practice now to space only once at the end of a sentence.

**9** Type **I would also like to thank you personally for taking notes and also for summarizing the ideas expressed at the retreat.**

**10** Press [Enter] two times. Type **Your** and when the ScreenTip *Yours truly,* *(Press ENTER to Insert)* displays, press [Enter] to have AutoComplete complete the closing of the letter.

**11** Press [Enter] four times, and then type **Angie Nguyen**

Compare your screen to Figure 1.37.

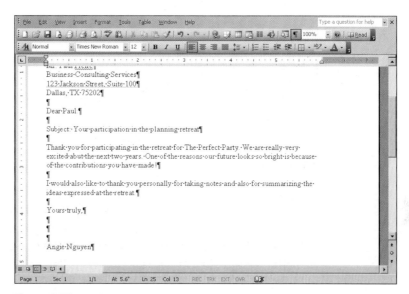

**Figure 1.37**

**12** On the Standard toolbar, click the **Print Preview** button . If necessary, change the Zoom setting on the Print Preview toolbar to Whole Page to see the entire page as it will print.

Your document displays as it will print on paper. Notice that there is a large amount of blank space at the bottom of this short letter.

**13** On the Print Preview toolbar, click **Close**. Display the **File** menu, and then click **Page Setup**.

**14** On the displayed **Page Setup** dialog box, click the **Layout tab**. Under **Page**, click the **Vertical alignment arrow**. From the displayed list, click **Center** as shown in Figure 1.38.

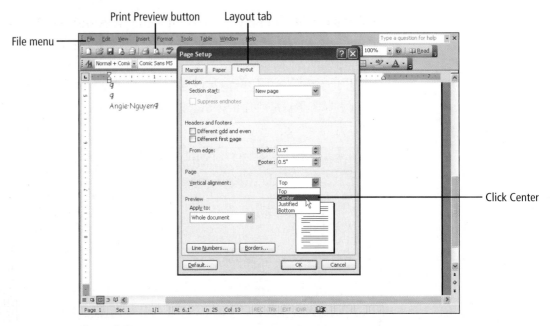

**Figure 1.38**

**15** In the lower right corner of the **Page Setup** dialog box, click **OK**. On the Standard toolbar, click the **Print Preview** button ![Print Preview icon].

Your document displays as it will print on paper. The text is centered on the page between the top and bottom margin. You can see that vertically centering one-page letters results in a more attractive and professional looking document.

**16** On the Print Preview toolbar, click the **Close** button ![Close button]. On the Standard toolbar, click the **Save** button ![Save button].

Because this document has never been saved, the Save As dialog box displays.

**17** Use the **Save in arrow** to navigate to the **Chapter 1 folder** that you created in your storage location. In the lower portion of the **Save As** dialog box, in the **File name** box, delete any existing text and then type **1B_Thanks_Firstname_Lastname**

Make sure you type your own first name and last name as the last two parts of the new file name.

**18** In the lower right portion of the **Save As** dialog box, click the **Save** button or press Enter.

Your file is saved in your Chapter 1 folder with the new file name.

**Activity 1.16** Editing Text with the Delete and Backspace Keys

**1** Scroll as necessary to view the upper portion of your document. In the paragraph beginning *Thank you,* at the end of the first line, click to position your insertion point to the left of the word *very.*

The insertion point is blinking to the left of the word *very.*

**2** Press ⟨←Bksp⟩ once.

The space between the words *really* and *very* is removed. See Figure 1.39.

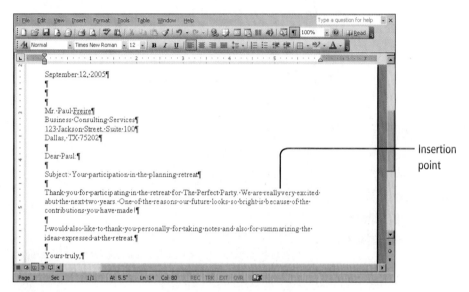

Insertion point

**Figure 1.39**

**3** With the insertion point between the two words, press ⟨←Bksp⟩ six times.

The word *really* is removed. Make sure there is only one dot (dots are the formatting marks that indicate spaces) between *are* and *very.* You can see that when editing text, it is useful to display formatting marks.

**4** In the paragraph beginning *I would,* in the first line, locate the phrase *for summarizing* and then click to position the insertion point to the left of the word *for.*

**5** Press ⟨←Bksp⟩ five times.

The word *also* and the space between the words is removed.

**6** Press ⟨Delete⟩ four times.

The word *for* to the right of the insertion point is removed, along with the space following the word. Make sure there is only one dot (space) between *and* and *summarizing.* See Figure 1.40.

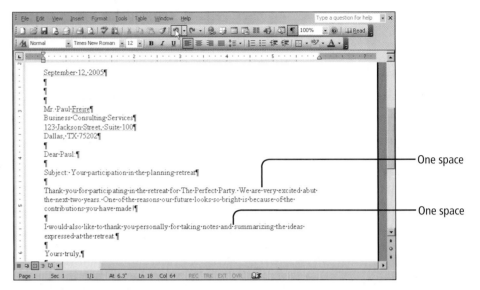

One space

One space

**Figure 1.40**

**7** On the Standard toolbar, click the **Save** button to save the changes you have made to your document since your last save operation.

**Another Way**

**Removing Characters**

*There are two ways to remove individual characters in a document:*

- Press [Delete] to remove characters to the right of the insertion point.
- Press [←Bksp] to remove characters to the left of the insertion point.

**Activity 1.17** Inserting New Text and Overtyping Existing Text

When you place the insertion point in the middle of a word or sentence and start typing, the existing text moves to the right to make space for your new keystrokes. This is called **insert mode** and is the default setting in Word. If you press the [Insert] key once, **overtype mode** is turned on. In overtype mode, existing text is replaced as you type. When overtype mode is active, the letters *OVR* display in black in the status bar. When insert mode is active, the letters *OVR* are light gray.

**1** In the paragraph beginning *Thank you*, in the first line, click to place the insertion point to the left of the word *retreat*.

The space should be to the left of the insertion point.

**2** Type **planning** and then press Spacebar.

As you type, the existing text moves to the right to make space for your new keystrokes, and the overtype indicator (OVR) in the status bar is gray. See Figure 1.41.

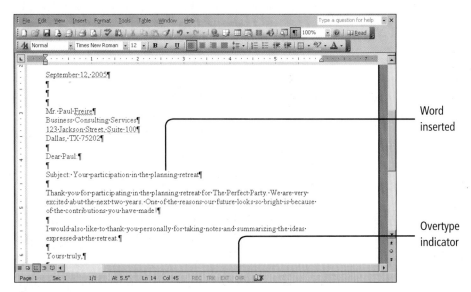

Word inserted

Overtype indicator

**Figure 1.41**

**3** In the last line of the document, click to place the insertion point to the left of *Angie Nguyen*.

**4** Press Insert, and notice that in the status bar, the OVR indicator is black, indicating that overtype mode is active.

When you begin to type, the new text will replace the old text, rather than move it to the right.

**5** Type **Gabriela Quinones**

Notice that as you type, the characters replace the existing text.

**6** Press Insert to turn off overtype mode. Alternatively, double-click the overtype indicator in the status bar.

**7** On the Standard toolbar, click the **Save** button 🖫 to save the changes you have made to your document.

# Objective 7
## Select and Format Text

***Selecting text*** refers to highlighting, by dragging with your mouse, areas of text so that the text can be edited, formatted, copied, or moved. Word recognizes a selected area of text as one unit, to which you can make changes. ***Formatting text*** is the process of setting the overall appearance of the text within the document by changing the color, shading, or emphasis of text.

### Activity 1.18 Selecting Text

To perform an action on text—for example, to move, delete, or emphasize text—you must first select it. You can select text using either the mouse or the keyboard.

**1** In the paragraph beginning *Thank you,* position the I-beam pointer $\boxed{I}$ to the left of *Thank,* hold down the left mouse button, and then drag to the right to select the first sentence including the ending period and its following space as shown in Figure 1.42. Release the mouse button.

The first sentence of the paragraph is selected. Dragging is the technique of holding down the left mouse button and moving over an area of text. Selected text is indicated when the background and color of the characters are reversed—the characters are white and the background is black as shown in Figure 1.42. Selecting takes a steady hand. If you are not satisfied with your result, click anywhere in a blank area of the document and begin again.

Period and space included in the selection

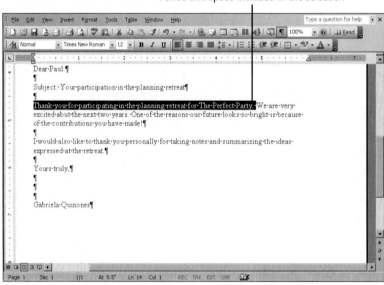

**Figure 1.42**

**2** Click anywhere in the document to deselect the sentence. Then, in the same sentence, move the pointer over the word *Perfect* and double-click the mouse button.

The entire word is selected. Double-clicking takes a steady hand. The speed of the two clicks is not difficult (although you only have about a second between clicks), but you must hold the mouse perfectly still between the two clicks. If you are not satisfied with your result, try again.

**3** Click anywhere to deselect the word *Perfect*. Then, move the pointer over the word *Perfect* and triple-click the mouse button.

The entire paragraph is selected. Recall that keeping the mouse perfectly still between the clicks is critical.

**4** Hold down ⌨Ctrl and press ⌨A.

The entire document is selected. See Figure 1.43. There are many shortcuts for selecting text. Take a moment to study the shortcuts shown in the table in Figure 1.44.

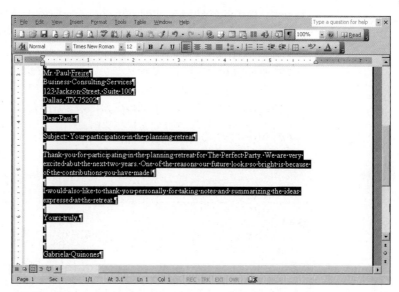

**Figure 1.43**

## Selecting Text in a Document

| To Select | Do This |
|---|---|
| A portion of text | Click to position the insertion point at the beginning of the text you want to select, hold down Shift, and then click at the end of the text you want to select. Alternatively, hold down the left mouse button and drag from the beginning to the end of the text you want to select. |
| A word | Double-click the word. |
| A sentence | Hold down Ctrl and click anywhere in the sentence. |
| A paragraph | Triple-click anywhere in the paragraph; or, move the pointer to the left of the line, into the margin area. When the pointer changes to a right-pointing white arrow, double-click. |
| A line | Move the pointer to the left of the line. When the pointer turns to a right-pointing white arrow, click once. |
| One character at a time | Position the insertion point at the left of the first character, hold down Shift and press → or ← as many times as desired. |
| A string of words | Position the insertion point to the left of the first word, hold down Shift and Ctrl, and then press → or ←. |
| Consecutive lines | Hold down Shift and press ↑ or ↓. |
| Consecutive paragraphs | Hold down Shift and Ctrl and press ↑ or ↓. |
| The entire document | Hold down Ctrl and press A or move the pointer to the left of the line. When it turns to a right-pointing white arrow, triple-click. |

**Figure 1.44**

**5** Click anywhere in the document to cancel the text selection.

### Activity 1.19 Changing Font and Font Size

A *font* is a set of characters with the same design and shape. There are two basic types of fonts—serif and sans serif. *Serif fonts* contain extensions or lines on the ends of the characters and are good choices for large amounts of text because they are easy to read. Examples of serif fonts include Times New Roman, Garamond, and Century Schoolbook. *Sans serif fonts* do not have lines on the ends of characters. Sans serif fonts are good choices for headings and titles. Examples of sans serif fonts include Arial, Verdana, and Comic Sans MS. The table in Figure 1.45 shows examples of Serif and Sans Serif fonts.

| Examples of Serif and Sans Serif Fonts | |
|---|---|
| **Serif Fonts** | **Sans Serif Fonts** |
| Times New Roman | Arial |
| Garamond | Verdana |
| Century Schoolbook | Comic Sans MS |

**Figure 1.45**

**1** Move the mouse pointer anywhere over the subject line in the letter and triple-click.

The entire paragraph is selected. Recall that a paragraph is defined as one paragraph mark and anything in front of it, which could be one or more lines of text or no text at all in the case of a blank line.

**2** On the Formatting toolbar, locate the **Font Size button arrow** [12 ▼] and click the arrow. On the displayed list, click **14** as shown in Figure 1.46.

Font size

Selected text

**Figure 1.46**

Fonts are measured in ***points***, with one point equal to 1/72 of an inch. A higher point size indicates a larger font size. For large amounts of text, font sizes between 10 point and 12 point are good choices. Headings and titles are often formatted using a larger font size. The word *point* is abbreviated as ***pt.***

**3** On the Formatting toolbar, locate the **Font button arrow** [Times New Roman ▾] and click the arrow.

On the displayed list, the fonts are displayed in alphabetical order. Word assists in your font selection by placing fonts recently used on this computer at the top of the list.

**4** Scroll the displayed list as necessary and then click **Arial**. Click anywhere in the document to cancel the selection.

**5** Hold down ⌈Ctrl⌉ and press ⌈A⌉ to select the document.

**6** With the document selected, click the **Font button arrow** [Times New Roman ▾]. On the displayed list, scroll as necessary and then click **Comic Sans MS**.

The selected text changes to the Comic Sans MS font. In a letter, it is good practice to use only one font for the entire letter. This font is less formal than the default font of Times New Roman.

**7** With the entire document selected, click the **Font Size button arrow** [12 ▾] and change the font size to **11**. Alternatively, you can type **11** in the Font Size box. Click anywhere in the document to cancel the text selection.

**8** Compare your screen to Figure 1.47.

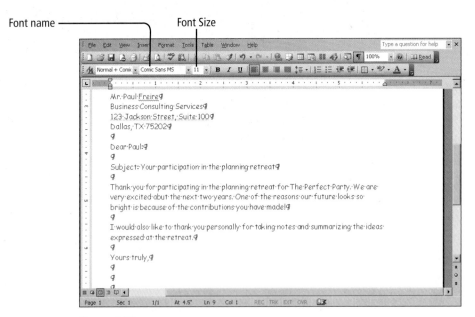

Font name ——————  Font Size

**Figure 1.47**

**9** On the Standard toolbar, click the **Save** button ⊞ to save the changes you have made to your document. Leave the document open for Activity 1.20.

### Activity 1.20  Adding Emphasis to Text

*Font styles* emphasize text and are a visual cue to draw the reader's eye to important text. Font styles include bold, italic, and underline, although underline is not commonly used for emphasis. You can add emphasis to existing text, or you can turn the emphasis on before you start typing the word or phrase and then turn it off.

**1** Move the pointer over the subject line and triple-click to select the paragraph.

**2** On the Formatting toolbar, click the **Italic** button ⟦*I*⟧.

Italic is applied to the paragraph that forms the Subject line.

**3** In the paragraph beginning *Thank you*, use any method to select the text *The Perfect Party*.

---

**Another Way** ──┤ **Applying Font Styles**

*There are three methods to apply font styles:*

- On the Standard toolbar, click the Bold, Italic, or Underline button.

- From the menu bar, click Format, click Font, and apply styles from the Font dialog box.

- From the keyboard, use the keyboard shortcuts of ⟦Ctrl⟧ + ⟦B⟧ for bold, ⟦Ctrl⟧ + ⟦I⟧ for italic, or ⟦Ctrl⟧ + ⟦U⟧ for underline.

---

**4** On the Formatting toolbar, click the **Bold** button ⟦**B**⟧. Click anywhere in the document to cancel the selection.

**5** On the Standard toolbar, click the **Print Preview** button ⟦🔍⟧ and compare your screen to Figure 1.48.

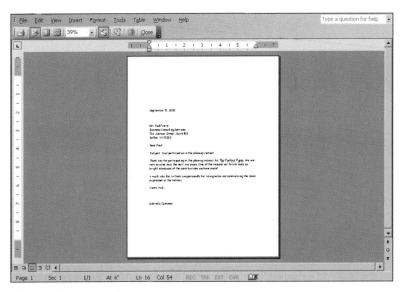

**Figure 1.48**

6. On the Print Preview toolbar, click **Close**.

7. In the inside address, right-click *Freire* and then click **Ignore All**. Correct any other spelling or grammar errors in your document.

8. On the Standard toolbar, click the **Save** button ⊞ to save your changes.

---

### More Knowledge — Using Toggle Buttons

The bold, italic, and underline buttons are toggle buttons; that is, you can click the button once to turn it on and again to turn it off.

---

## Objective 8
## Preview and Print Documents, Close a Document, and Close Word

While creating your document, it is helpful to check the print preview to make sure you are getting the result you want. Before printing, make a final check with print preview to make sure the document layout is exactly what you want.

### Activity 1.21 Previewing and Printing a Document and Closing Word

1. From the **View** menu, click **Header and Footer**. (The large header area at the top is a result of vertically centering the document on the page.) On the displayed Header and Footer toolbar, click the **Switch Between Header and Footer** button 🗐.

The footer area displays. The insertion point is at the left edge of the footer area.

**2** In the footer area, using your own name, type **1B Thanks-Firstname Lastname** as shown in Figure 1.49.

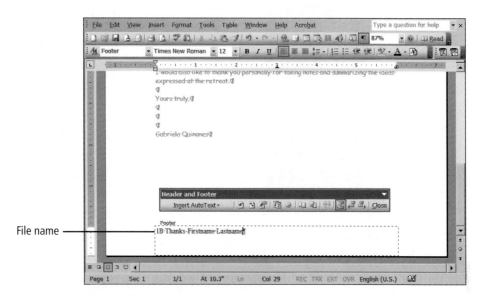

File name

**Figure 1.49**

**3** Double-click anywhere in the text area of the document to close the Header and Footer toolbar. Alternatively, on the Header and Footer toolbar, click the Close button Close .

**4** On the Standard toolbar, click the **Print Preview** button.

Your document displays exactly as it will print. The formatting marks, which do not print, are not displayed.

**5** In the **Print Preview** window, move the mouse pointer anywhere over the document.

The pointer becomes a magnifying glass with a plus in it, indicating that you can magnify the view. See Figure 1.50.

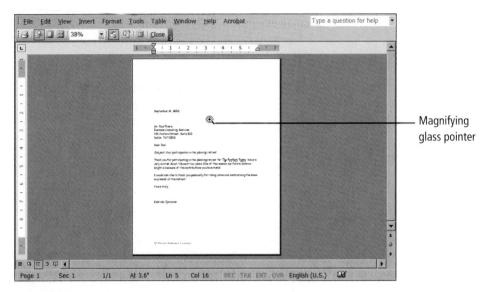

Magnifying glass pointer

**Figure 1.50**

**6** Move the pointer over the upper portion of the document and click once.

The top portion of the document is magnified, and is easier to read. The pointer changes to a magnifying glass with a minus sign.

**7** Click anywhere on the document.

The full page displays again.

**8** On the Print Preview toolbar, click **Close**. On the Standard toolbar, click the **Save** button 🖫 to save your changes.

**9** Display the **File** menu, and then click **Print**.

The Print dialog box displays. See Figure 1.51. Here you can specify which pages to print and how many copies you want. Additional command buttons for Options and Properties provide additional printing choices. The printer that displays will be the printer that is selected for your computer.

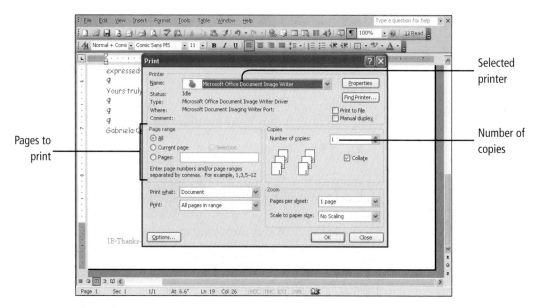

**Figure 1.51**

Selected printer

Number of copies

Pages to print

**10** In the displayed **Print** dialog box, under **Copies**, change the number of copies to 2 by either typing **2** in the text box or clicking the **up arrow** in the spin box. See Figure 1.51. At the bottom of the **Print** dialog box, click **OK**.

Two copies will print.

**11** From the **File** menu, click **Close**, saving any changes if prompted to do so. At the far right edge of the blue title bar, click the **Close** button ☒.

The Word program is closed.

## Objective 9
## Use the Microsoft Help System

As you work with Word, you can get assistance by using the Help feature. You can ask questions and Help will provide you with information and step-by-step instructions for performing tasks.

### Activity 1.22 Typing a Question for Help

The easiest way to use Help is to type a question in the *Type a question for help* box, located at the right side of the menu bar.

**1** If necessary, start Word. Move your pointer to the right side of the menu bar and click in the **Type a question for help** box. With the insertion point blinking in the box, type **How do I open a file?** and then press Enter.

The Search Results task pane displays a list of topics related to opening a file. Your list may be quite different than the one shown in Figure 1.52.

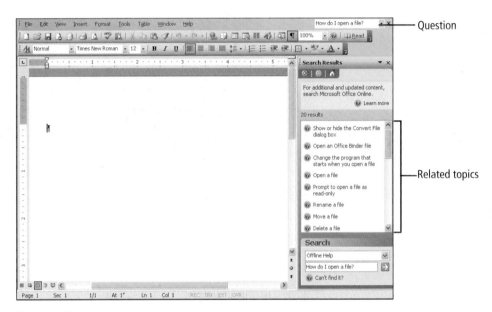

**Figure 1.52**

**2** On the displayed list in the task pane, point to and then click **Open a file**.

The Microsoft Word Help window opens at listing instructions for opening a file. Text in blue at the bottom of the Help window indicates links to related instructions or related information.

**3** At the bottom of the **Microsoft Office Word Help** window, click **Tips** to display additional information about opening files.

**4** In the second bulleted item, point to and then click the blue highlighted words **task pane** to display a green definition of a task pane as shown in Figure 1.53.

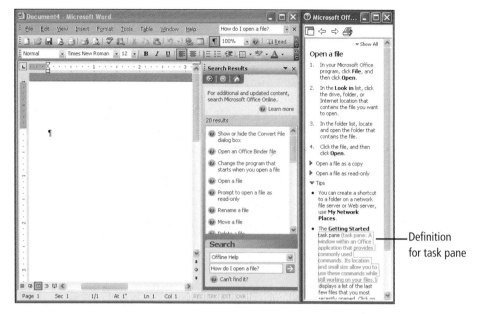

Definition for task pane

**Figure 1.53**

5 Click **task pane** again to close the definition.

6 In the **Microsoft Office Word Help** window, click the **Close** button ☒.

On the **Search Results** task pane, click the **Close** button ☒.

7 From the **File** menu, click **Exit** to close the Word program.

**Another Way** ── **Getting Help Using the Task Pane and the Office Assistant**

You can access Help by clicking the Microsoft Word Help button on the Standard toolbar. This action opens the Help task pane. In the Search box, type a topic that you want to learn more about and then press ⏎. Results are displayed in the Search Results task pane. The Office Assistant, an animated character that provides tips as you work, can be displayed from the Help menu by clicking Show the Office Assistant.

**End** You have completed Project 1B ─────────────────

# Summary

In this chapter you practiced how to start Word and navigate in the Word window by using the mouse, toolbars, menus, shortcut menus, and shortcut keys. You examined documents in the Page Layout, Normal, and Reading Layout views; changed the magnification with the Zoom button; and displayed nonprinting characters with the Show/Hide ¶ button.

The basics of word processing were practiced including entering text, deleting text using the backspace or delete key, selecting and replacing text, inserting text, and overtyping existing text. The spelling and grammar checker tools were demonstrated.

You also practiced how to change font style and size and add emphasis to text. The header and footer area was viewed, and a chapter folder was created to help organize your files. Each document was saved, previewed, printed, and closed. Finally, the Help program was introduced as a tool that can assist you in using Word.

## In This Chapter You Practiced How To

- Explore and Navigate the Word Window
- View Documents
- Use the Spelling and Grammar Checker
- View Headers and Footers
- Organize, Save, and Print Documents
- Create and Edit a New Document
- Select and Format Text
- Preview and Print Documents, Close a Document, and Close Word
- Use the Microsoft Help System

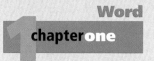
# Concepts Assessments

**Matching** Match each term in the second column with its correct definition in the first column by writing the letter of the term on the blank line in front of the correct definition.

_____ 1. The point in the Word window, indicated by a blinking vertical line, where text will be inserted when you start to type.

_____ 2. A view that simplifies the page layout for quick typing and can show more text on a smaller screen.

_____ 3. The action that takes place when the insertion point reaches the right margin and automatically moves down and to the left margin of the next line.

_____ 4. A button used to reveal nonprinting characters.

_____ 5. The process of setting the overall appearance of the text within the document.

_____ 6. A unit of measure that is used to describe the size of a font.

_____ 7. A font type that does not have lines on the ends of characters.

_____ 8. A type of font that is a good choice for large amounts of text because it is easy to read.

_____ 9. A set of characters (letters and numbers) with the same design and shape.

_____ 10. The term that refers to pressing one or more keys to navigate a window or execute commands.

_____ 11. The Minimize, Maximize/Restore Down, and Close buttons are located here.

_____ 12. A screen element that contains lists of commands.

_____ 13. A context-sensitive list that displays when you click the right mouse button.

_____ 14. The buttons used to Save or Print a document can be found here.

_____ 15. The part of the screen that displays the Start button and the name of any open documents.

**A** Font

**B** Formatting

**C** Insertion point

**D** Keyboard shortcuts

**E** Menu bar

**F** Normal

**G** Point

**H** Sans serif

**I** Serif

**J** Shortcut menu

**K** Show/Hide ¶

**L** Standard toolbar

**M** Taskbar

**N** Title bar

**O** Wordwrap

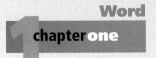

**Fill in the Blank** Write the correct answer in the space provided.

1. Microsoft Word 2003 is a word _____ program that you can use to do tasks such as writing a memo, a report, or a letter.

2. If you place your mouse pointer over a button on a toolbar, a small _____ displays the name of the button.

3. If you drag the _____ down it causes the document on your screen to move up.

4. The view that displays the page borders, margins, text, and graphics is known as the _____ view.

5. The portion of the Word window that opens to display commonly used commands or utilities available for use with the current job is known as the _____.

6. The View buttons are located to the left of the _____ scroll bar.

7. A row of buttons that provides a one-click method to perform common commands is called a _____.

8. To add emphasis to text, use the _____ or _____ or _____ buttons.

9. Before text can be edited, changed, formatted, copied, or moved, it must first be _____.

10. To display a shortcut menu, click the _____ mouse button.

# Project 1C—Follow Up Letter

**Objectives:** *Explore and Navigate the Word Window; Use the Spelling and Grammar Checker; View Headers and Footers; Organize, Save, and Print Documents; Create and Edit a New Document; Preview and Print Documents, Close a Document, and Close Word.*

In the following Skill Assessment, you will edit a follow-up letter from Corey Finstad, a party planner for The Perfect Party, to a customer who has requested party-planning services. Your completed letter will look similar to the one shown in Figure 1.54. You will save your letter as *1C_Follow_Up_Letter_Firstname_Lastname.*

June 15, 2003

Ms. Gloria Williams
35 Pine Grove Avenue
Dallas, TX 75202

Dear Ms. Williams:

Thank you for selecting The Perfect Party to plan your upcoming event. I look forward to managing the details for you so you can enjoy spending time with your guests.

You can select one of our prepared party themes, or we can design a customized party that will match the tone and purpose of your event. I am enclosing a brochure outlining some of our more popular themes, along with a list of accessories that can be used. Take a moment to look over this material and call me if you have any questions.

I look forward to meeting with you next week to finalize the plans for your party.

Best regards,

Corey Finstad
Party Planner

Enclosure

1C Follow Up Letter-Firstname Lastname

**Figure 1.54**

1. Start **Word**. On the Standard toolbar, click the **Open** button.

2. In the **Open** dialog box, at the right edge of the **Look in** box, click the **Look in arrow** to view a list of the drives available on your system. Navigate to the location where the student files for this textbook are stored.

**(Project 1C–Follow Up Letter continues on the next page)**

**(Project 1C–Follow Up Letter continued)**

3. Locate and click the file **w01C_Follow_Up_Letter**. In the lower portion of the **Open** dialog box, click the **Open** button.

4. If necessary, on the Standard toolbar click the **Show/Hide ¶** button to display formatting marks.

5. On the menu bar, click **File**, and then click **Save As**. In the **Save As** dialog box, click the **Save in arrow**, and then navigate to the location where you are saving your projects for this chapter. Recall that you created a Chapter 1 folder for this purpose.

6. In the **File name** box, using your own first and last name, type
   **1C_Follow_Up_Letter_Firstname_Lastname**

7. In the lower portion of the **Save As** dialog box click the **Save** button.

8. Be sure the insertion point is positioned to the left of the blank line at the top of the document. If necessary, hold down Ctrl and press Home to move the insertion point to the top of the document.

9. Begin typing today's date and let AutoComplete assist in your typing by pressing Enter when the ScreenTip displays. Press Enter four times. Notice the purple dotted line under the date, which is the recognizer that could add this date to your Outlook calendar. Type the following on three lines:

   **Ms. Gloria Williams**

   **35 Pine Grove Avenue**

   **Dallas, TX 75202**

10. Press Enter twice, type **Dear Ms. Williams:** and then press Enter once.

11. Hold down Ctrl and press End to move the insertion point to the end of the document. Press Enter twice, type **Best regards,** and then press Enter four times.

12. Finish the letter by typing the following on two lines:

    **Corey Finstad**

    **Party Planner**

13. Press Enter twice and type **Enclosure**

14. On the Standard toolbar, click the **Spelling and Grammar** button. The first error—a duplicated word—is highlighted, unless you made a typing error earlier in the document.

15. In the **Spelling and Grammar** dialog box, click the **Delete** button to delete the second occurrence of *the*. The next error is highlighted.

**(Project 1C–Follow Up Letter continues on the next page)**

**(Project 1C–Follow Up Letter continued)**

16. Under **Suggestions**, the first suggestion is correct. Click the **Change** button to change the misspelled word to the highlighted suggestion of *brochure*. The next error is highlighted.

17. Be sure *themes* is highlighted under **Suggestions**, and then click the **Change** button. Correct the next two errors, and then click **Ignore Once** to ignore the name *Finstad*. Click **OK** to close the box indicating the check is complete.

18. Drag the vertical scroll box to the top of the scroll bar to display the top of the document. In the paragraph beginning *Thank you*, double-click the word *handle* to select it and type **plan**

   Notice that your typing replaces the selected word.

19. In the paragraph beginning *You can select*, locate the first occurrence of the word *party*, click to the left of the word, type **prepared** and then press Spacebar once.

20. On the menu bar, click **View**, and then click **Header and Footer**. Click the **Switch Between Header and Footer** button. In the footer area, using your own name, type **1C Follow Up Letter-Firstname Lastname**

21. On the Header and Footer toolbar, click the **Close** button.

22. Display the **File** menu, click **Page Setup**, and then in the displayed **Page Setup** dialog box, click the **Layout tab**. Under **Page**, click the **Vertical alignment arrow**, and from the displayed list, click **Center**. Recall that vertically centering one-page letters results in a more attractive letter. In the lower right corner of the dialog box, click **OK**.

23. On the Standard toolbar, click the **Save** button to save the changes you have made to your document.

24. On the Standard toolbar, click the **Print Preview** button to make a final check of your letter before printing. On the Print Preview toolbar, click the **Print** button, and then on the same toolbar, click the **Close** button.

25. From the **File** menu, click **Close** to close the document, saving any changes if prompted to do so. Display the **File** menu again and click **Exit** to close Word. Alternatively, you can close Word by clicking the **Close** button at the extreme right end of the blue title bar.

**End** You have completed Project 1C

## Project 1D — Fax Cover

**Objectives:** *Explore and Navigate the Word Window; Create and Edit a New Document; View Documents; View Headers and Footers; Select and Format Text; Preview and Print Documents, Close a Document, and Close Word.*

In the following Skill Assessment, you will create a cover sheet for a facsimile (fax) transmission. When sending a fax, it is common practice to include a cover sheet with a note describing the pages that will follow. Your completed document will look similar to Figure 1.55. You will save your document as *1D_Fax_Cover_Firstname_Lastname.*

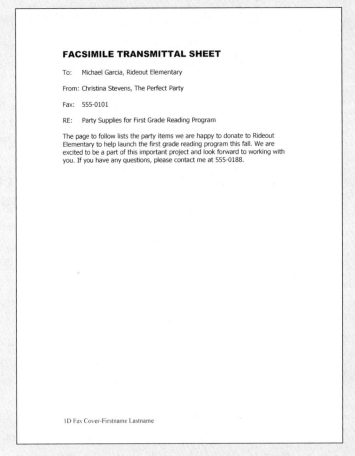

**FACSIMILE TRANSMITTAL SHEET**

To:     Michael Garcia, Rideout Elementary

From: Christina Stevens, The Perfect Party

Fax:    555-0101

RE:     Party Supplies for First Grade Reading Program

The page to follow lists the party items we are happy to donate to Rideout Elementary to help launch the first grade reading program this fall. We are excited to be a part of this important project and look forward to working with you. If you have any questions, please contact me at 555-0188.

1D Fax Cover-Firstname Lastname

**Figure 1.55**

1. Start **Word** and make sure the **Show/Hide ¶** button is active so you can view formatting marks. If necessary, close the task pane.

2. On your keyboard, press CapsLock. With the insertion point at the top of the document, type **FACSIMILE TRANSMITTAL SHEET** and then press Enter twice. Press CapsLock again to turn the feature off.

**(Project 1D–Fax Cover continues on the next page)**

**(Project 1D–Fax Cover continued)**

3.  On the Standard toolbar click the **Save** button. Because this new document has never been saved, the **Save As** dialog box displays. Click the **Save in arrow**, and then navigate to the location where you are saving your projects for this chapter. In the **File name** box type **1D_Fax_Cover_Firstname_Lastname** and in the lower portion of the **Save As** dialog box, click the **Save** button.

4.  Type **To:** press ⌷Tab⌷, type **Michael Garcia, Rideout Elementary** and then press ⌷Enter⌷ twice. Type the remainder of the fax headings as follows, pressing ⌷Tab⌷ after each colon (:) and pressing ⌷Enter⌷ twice at the end of each line. Refer to Figure 1.55.

    **From:  Christina Stevens, The Perfect Party**

    **Fax:     555-0101**

    **RE:      Party Supplies for First Grade Reading Program**

5.  Type the following, and as you do so, remember to let wordwrap end the lines for you and to press the ⌷Spacebar⌷ only once at the end of a sentence:

    **The page to follow lists the party items we are happy to donate to Rideout Elementary to help launch the first grade reading program this fall. We are excited to be a part of this important project and look forward to working with you. If you have any questions, please contact me at 555-0188.**

6.  On the Standard toolbar click the **Save** button to save your work.

7.  Press ⌷Ctrl⌷ + ⌷A⌷ to select the entire document. On the Formatting toolbar, click the **Font arrow**, scroll as necessary, and then click **Tahoma**. Click anywhere in the document to cancel the selection.

8.  Move the mouse pointer into the margin area to the left of *FACSIMILE TRANSMITTAL SHEET* until the pointer displays as a white arrow. Click to select the title line only. On the Formatting toolbar, click the **Font arrow**, scroll as necessary, and then click **Arial Black**. You can also type the first letter of the font to move quickly in the Font box. With the text still selected, click the **Font Size arrow**, and then click **16**. Click anywhere to cancel the text selection.

**(Project 1D–Fax Cover continues on the next page)**

**(Project 1D–Fax Cover continued)**

9. On the menu bar, click **View**, and then click **Header and Footer**. On the Header and Footer toolbar, click the **Switch Between Header and Footer** button. In the footer area, type **1D Fax Cover-Firstname Lastname** using your own name. On the Header and Footer toolbar, click the **Close** button.

10. On your screen, notice that the word *Rideout*, which appears twice, is flagged as misspelled, and *The* is flagged as a grammar error. On the Standard toolbar, click the **Spelling and Grammar** button.

11. At the first occurrence of *Rideout*, click **Ignore All**. This action will remove the red flag from the second occurrence of the word. For the grammar error *The*, click **Ignore Once**. Because the word *The* is part of the proper name of the company, it is correct as written. If the Spelling and Grammar checker stops on your name, click **Ignore Once**. Click **OK** when the check is complete or, if necessary, click the **Close** button on the title bar of the **Spelling and Grammar** dialog box.

12. On the Standard toolbar, click the **Save** button to save your changes.

13. On the Standard toolbar, click the **Print Preview** button. On the Print Preview toolbar, click the **Print** button, and then click the **Close** button. From the **File** menu, click **Close**.

14. At right end of the title bar, click the **Close** button to close Word.

**End** You have completed Project 1D

# Project 1E — Survey Letter

**Objectives:** *Explore and Navigate the Word Window; View Documents; Create and Edit a New Document; Use the Spelling and Grammar Checker; Select and Format Text; View Headers and Footers; Organize, Save, and Print Documents; Preview and Print Documents, Close a Document, and Close Word.*

In the following Skill Assessment, you will edit a cover letter that will be sent with a survey to clients. Your completed document will look similar to Figure 1.56. You will save your document as *1E_Survey_Letter_Firstname_Lastname.*

November 23, 2005

Dear Customer:

**Subject: We want to hear your opinion!**

Thank you for using The Perfect Party services for your recent event. We hope that the party exceeded your expectations and that you will recommend us to your friends and associates.

As a new business, we are always looking for ways to expand our services. We know that our customers are our best advertising, and often they provide excellent suggestions that can help us develop our services. Please take a few moments to complete the short survey that is enclosed. Your candid comments and feedback are welcomed.

We look forward to working with you again when you want to throw another *Perfect Party.*

Best regards,

Angie Nguyen
Owner

Enclosure

1E Survey Letter-Firstname Lastname

**Figure 1.56**

1. Start **Word**. On the Standard toolbar, click the **Open** button.

2. In the **Open** dialog box, at the right edge of the **Look in** box, click the **Look in arrow** to view a list of the drives available on your system. Navigate to the location where the student files for this textbook are stored.

**(Project 1E–Survey Letter continues on the next page)**

**(Project 1E–Survey Letter continued)**

3.  Locate and click the file **w01E_Survey_Letter**. In the lower portion of the **Open** dialog box, click the **Open** button.

4.  If necessary, on the Standard toolbar, click the **Show/Hide ¶** button to display formatting marks.

5.  On the menu bar, click **File**, and then click **Save As**. In the **Save As** dialog box, click the **Save in arrow**, and then navigate to the location where you are saving your projects for this chapter.

6.  In the **File name** box, using your own first and last name, type **1E_Survey_Letter_Firstname_Lastname** and then click the **Save** button.

7.  Move the pointer into the left margin to the left of the subject line until the pointer takes the shape of a white arrow. Click once to select the subject line. On the Formatting toolbar, click the **Font arrow**, and then click **Arial Black**.

8.  In the sentence beginning *We once again*, drag to select the phrase *We once again want to* and then press Delete to remove this phrase. Press Delete to delete the *t* in *thank*, and then type **T**

9.  In the same paragraph, select the phrase *hopes and dreams* and then type **expectations** and adjust spacing if necessary.

10. In the same paragraph, click to place your insertion point to the left of the word *recommend* and type **will** and then press Spacebar.

11. In the paragraph beginning *As a new*, right-click *adverticing*, which is flagged as a spelling error. On the displayed shortcut menu, click *advertising*. In the same sentence double-click *ideas* to select it, and then type **suggestions** to replace it. In the same sentence replace the word *expand* with **develop**

12. In the same paragraph, right-click *moment*, which is flagged as a grammar error. From the displayed shortcut menu, click *moments*.

13. In the paragraph beginning *We look*, click to position the insertion point to the left of *Perfect Party*. Hold down Shift and Ctrl and then press → twice to select *Perfect* and then *Party*. Recall that this is a keyboard shortcut for selecting a string of words. On the Formatting toolbar, click the **Italic** button to apply the Italic font style to this phrase.

**(Project 1E–Survey Letter continues on the next page)**

**(Project 1E–Survey Letter continued)**

14. In the closing of the letter, click to position the insertion point to the left of *Sincerely* and then press [Insert] on your keyboard to activate Overtype mode. The OVR indicator on the status bar displays in black. Type **Best regards,** and then press [Delete] three times to delete the remaining unnecessary characters. Press [Insert] again to turn off Overtype mode and dim the OVR indicator.

15. Hold down [Ctrl] and press [End] to position the insertion point at the end of the document. Press [Enter] twice and then type **Enclosure**

16. On the menu bar, click **View**, and then click **Header and Footer**. On the Header and Footer toolbar, click the **Switch Between Header and Footer** button. In the footer area, type **1E Survey Letter-Firstname Lastname** and then on the Header and Footer toolbar, click the **Close** button.

17. From the **File** menu, click **Page Setup**, and then on the displayed **Page Setup** dialog box, click the **Layout tab**. Under **Page**, click the **Vertical alignment arrow**, and then click **Center**. In the lower right corner of the dialog box, click **OK**. Recall that one-page letters are commonly centered vertically on the page to give a more professional appearance.

18. On the Standard toolbar, click the **Save** button to save the changes you have made to your document. On the Standard toolbar, click the **Print Preview** button to view your document as it will print. On the Print Preview toolbar, click the **Print** button to print the letter, and then on the same toolbar, click the **Close** button.

19. From the **File** menu, click **Close** to close the document. At the right edge of the blue title bar, click the **Close** button to close Word.

 **End** **You have completed Project 1E**

## Project 1F — Interview Letter

**Objectives:** *View Headers and Footers; Create and Edit a New Document; Organize, Save, and Print Documents; and Preview and Print Documents, Close a Document, and Close Word.*

In the following Performance Assessment, you will create a letter to schedule an interview for Gabriela Quinones with a catering service. Your completed document will look similar to Figure 1.57. You will save your document as *1F_Interview_Letter_Firstname_Lastname*.

The Perfect Party
700 Washington Street
Dallas, TX 75202


September 22, 2005

Louise's Catering
2302 Boardwalk
Dallas, TX 75202

RE: Catering Services

Dear Ms. Gomez:

We have received a tremendous response to our ad for catering services. Your resume and sample menus are outstanding and seem to fit with the vision for our business. We would like to interview you and give you a chance to ask us questions. We will be conducting interviews the week of October 10. My assistant, Ms. Finstad, will call to schedule a time that will be convenient for you.

For the interview, we would invite you to bring a sample of your favorite dishes so we can have an opportunity to taste your creations. There will be only two people conducting the interview so a small sample would be appropriate.

We are looking forward to meeting with you.

Cordially,


Gabriela Quinones
Owner



1F Interview Letter-Firstname Lastname

**Figure 1.57**

**(Project 1F–Interview Letter continues on the next page)**

**(Project 1F–Interview Letter continued)**

1. Start **Word** and, if necessary, close the task pane. Beginning at the top of the page type the address on three lines as shown:

   **The Perfect Party
   700 Washington Street
   Dallas, TX 75202**

2. Press Enter four times. Type **September 22, 2005** and press Enter twice. Type the following on three lines:

   **Louise's Catering
   2302 Boardwalk
   Dallas, TX 75202**

3. Press Enter two times and then type **RE: Catering Services**
   Press Enter two times and type the salutation **Dear Ms. Gomez:**

4. Press Enter twice and type the body of the letter as follows, pressing Enter two times at the end of each paragraph:

   **We have received a tremendous response to our ad for catering services. Your resume and sample menus are outstanding and seem to fit with the vision for our business. We would like to interview you and give you a chance to ask us questions. We will be conducting interviews the week of October 10. My assistant, Ms. Finstad, will call to schedule a time that will be convenient for you.**

   **For the interview, we would invite you to bring a sample of your favorite dishes so we can have an opportunity to taste your creations. There will be only two people conducting the interview so a small sample would be appropriate.**

   **We are looking forward to meeting with you.**

5. Press Enter twice and type **Cordially,** create three blank lines (press Enter four times), and then type the following on two lines:

   **Gabriela Quinones
   Owner**

**(Project 1F–**Interview Letter continues on the next page**)**

**(Project 1F–Interview Letter continued)**

6.  On the Standard toolbar, click the **Save** button. In the **Save As** dialog box, navigate to the location where you are saving your projects for this chapter. In the **File name** box, using your own name, type **1F_Interview_Letter_Firstname_Lastname** and then click the **Save** button.

7.  Display the **View** menu, and then click **Header and Footer**. Click the **Switch Between Header and Footer** button. In the footer area, using your own information, type **1F Interview Letter-Firstname Lastname**

8.  Double-click in the body of the document to close the Header and Footer toolbar and return to the document.

9.  Display the **File** menu, click **Page Setup**, and then click the **Layout tab**. Under **Page**, click the **Vertical alignment arrow**, and then click **Center**. Click **OK** to center the letter on the page.

10. Proofread the letter to make sure it does not contain any typographical or spelling errors. Use the Spelling and Grammar checker to correct any errors.

11. On the Standard toolbar, click the **Print Preview** button to see how the letter will print on paper. On the Print Preview toolbar, click the **Print** button to print the letter. Close Print Preview and then click the **Save** button to save your changes. Close the document and close Word.

 **End** You have completed Project 1F

# Project 1G — Interview Memo

**Objectives:** *Create and Edit a New Document; Select and Format Text; View Headers and Footers; and Organize, Save, and Print Documents.*

In the following Performance Assessment, you will edit a memo for Corey Finstad to Gabriela Quinones listing interviews that The Perfect Party has scheduled with catering firms. Your completed document will look similar to Figure 1.58. You will save your document as *1G_Interview_Memo_Firstname_Lastname.*

---

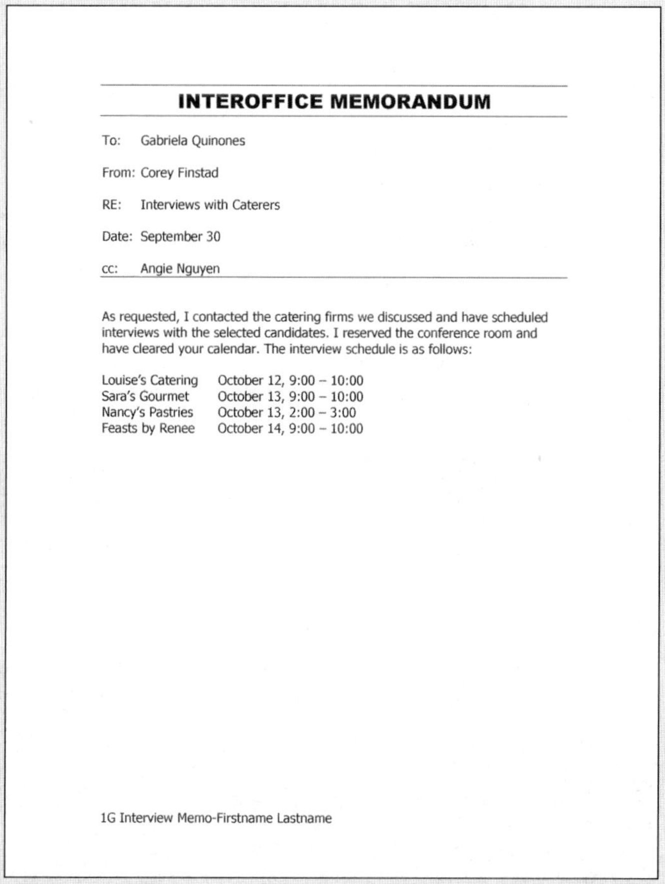

**INTEROFFICE MEMORANDUM**

To:     Gabriela Quinones

From:  Corey Finstad

RE:     Interviews with Caterers

Date:  September 30

cc:      Angie Nguyen

---

As requested, I contacted the catering firms we discussed and have scheduled interviews with the selected candidates. I reserved the conference room and have cleared your calendar. The interview schedule is as follows:

| | |
|---|---|
| Louise's Catering | October 12, 9:00 – 10:00 |
| Sara's Gourmet | October 13, 9:00 – 10:00 |
| Nancy's Pastries | October 13, 2:00 – 3:00 |
| Feasts by Renee | October 14, 9:00 – 10:00 |

1G Interview Memo-Firstname Lastname

**Figure 1.58**

**(Project 1G–Interview Memo continues on the next page)**

**(Project 1G–Interview Memo continued)**

1. Start **Word**. On the Standard toolbar, click the **Open** button. Navigate to the location where the student files for this textbook are stored. Locate and open the file *w01G_Interview_Memo*.

2. From the **File** menu, click **Save As**. In the **Save As** dialog box, navigate to the location where you are saving your projects for this chapter. In the **File name** box, type **1G_Interview_Memo_Firstname_Lastname** and then click the **Save** button.

3. Click after the colon in the word *To:* then press Tab and type **Gabriela Quinones**

   Press ↓ twice to move to right of *From:* then press Tab and type **Corey Finstad**

4. Use the same keystroke technique to complete the heading portion of the memo as shown:

   **RE:      Interviews with Caterers**

   **Date:   September 30**

   **CC:      Angie Nguyen**

5. Click to position the insertion point at the beginning of the third empty line in the body of the memo, and then type the following:

   **As requested, I contacted the catering firms we discussed and have scheduled interviews with the selected candidates. I reserved the conference room and have cleared your calendar. The interview schedule is as follows:**

6. Press Enter twice. Type **Louise's Catering** Press Tab and type **October 12, 9:00 –10:00** and then press Enter. Repeat this pattern to enter the remainder of the interview dates.

   | | |
   |---|---|
   | **Sara's Gourmet** | **October 12, 9:00–10:00** |
   | **Chef Michelangelo** | **October 13, 9:00–10:00** |
   | **Nancy's Pastries** | **October 13, 2:00–3:00** |
   | **Feasts by Renee** | **October 14, 9:00–10:00** |

**(Project 1G–Interview Memo continues on the next page)**

**(Project 1G–Interview Memo continued)**

7. On the Standard toolbar, click the **Spelling and Grammar** button. Click **Ignore Once** to ignore the any proper names that are flagged and correct any other errors that may be identified.

8. Beginning with the paragraph *As requested*, select all of the text of the memo and change the font to **Tahoma**, which is the same font used in the top portion of the memo.

9. Navigate to the top of the document and select the text *INTEROFFICE MEMORANDUM*. Change the font to **Arial Black** and the font size to **18** point.

10. Display the **View** menu and click **Header and Footer**. Click the **Switch Between Header and Footer** button. In the footer area, using your own information, type **1G Interview Memo-Firstname Lastname**

    Select the text you just typed in the footer and change the font to **Tahoma**, **12** point. Double-click the body of the document to close the Header and Footer toolbar and return to the document.

11. On the Standard toolbar, click the **Save** button to save your changes. On the Standard toolbar, click the **Print Preview** button to preview the document before it is printed. Print the document. Close the file and close Word.

**End** You have completed Project 1G

## Project 1H—Offer Letter

**Objectives:** *Explore and Navigate the Word Window; View Documents; Use the Spelling and Grammar Checker; View Headers and Footers; Create and Edit a New Document; Select and Format Text; and Preview and Print Documents, Close a Document, and Close Word.*

In the following Performance Assessment, you will edit a letter for Gabriela Quinones to Sara's Gourmet requesting a follow-up meeting to discuss a possible business partnership. Your completed document will look similar to Figure 1.59. You will save your letter as *1H_Offer_Letter_Firstname_Lastname.*

The Perfect Party
700 Washington Street
Dallas, TX 75202

October 20, 2005

Sara's Gourmet
3200 Penny Lane
Dallas, TX 75202

Dear Sara:

We enjoyed meeting with you last week and were absolutely delighted with the appetizers you brought to the interview. You presented some unique ideas for party food, and demonstrated skill in the art of food presentation.

We would like to meet with you again before the end of the month to explore some possible business arrangements that would be mutually satisfying. As we stated in the interview, we are interested in working with someone on a contract basis initially, with a view to a longer term relationship that could include becoming a partner in **The Perfect Party**. We would like to discuss how your plans to grow your business might intersect with our need to add a catering component to our party planning business.

Please call my office at (214)-555-0188 to set up a time when you could meet with us. My partner, Angie Nguyen, is looking forward to meeting you.

Yours truly,

Gabriela Quinones
Owner

1H Offer Letter-Firstname Lastname

**Figure 1.59**

1. Start **Word**. On the Standard toolbar, click the **Open** button. Navigate to the location where the student files for this textbook are stored. Locate and open the file *w01H_Offer_Letter.*

2. Display the **File** menu, click **Save As**, and then use the **Save in arrow** to navigate to the location where you are storing your projects for this chapter. In the **File name** box, using your own information, type **1H_Offer_Letter_Firstname_Lastname**

**(Project 1H–Offer Letter continues on the next page)**

**(Project 1H–Offer Letter continued)**

3. In the paragraph that begins *We enjoyed meeting*, select *liked* and type **were absolutely delighted with** and then adjust the spacing if necessary.

4. In the same paragraph, select *interesting* and replace it with **unique** In the same sentence delete the word *alternatives*. In the same sentence, select the phrase *are very skillful* and replace it with **demonstrated skill**

5. In the paragraph that begins *We would like*, delete the word *once*. In the same sentence, replace the word *consider* with **explore** In the same sentence, place the insertion point at the end of the word *mutual* and type **ly**

6. There are some grammar and spelling errors that need to be corrected. Right-click on the duplicate or misspelled words and correct as necessary.

7. In the paragraph that begins with *We would like*, use the technique of Ctrl + Shift + → to select the three words *The Perfect Party* and then change the font to **Lucida Calligraphy**. If you do not have that font, choose a similar font from the list. Change the font size to **11** point. With the name still selected, click the **Bold** button.

8. Click in the blank line following *Yours truly* and add two more blank lines by pressing Enter two times. Three blank lines is the standard space allotted for a signature in a letter. Display the Page Setup dialog box and center the letter vertically on the page.

9. Display the **View** menu and then click **Header and Footer**. Click the **Switch Between Header and Footer** button. In the footer area, using your own information, type **1H Offer Letter-Firstname Lastname** Double-click in the body of the document to close the Header and Footer toolbar and return to the document.

10. Use Ctrl + Home to navigate to the top of the letter. On the Standard toolbar, click the **Read** button to display the document in Reading Layout view. Proofread the letter to make sure it is correct. In this format, two pages display to make the reading easier, but recall that this is not the page preview. When printed, the document will print on one page.

11. On the Reading Layout toolbar, click the **Close** button to return to the Page Layout view. Click the **Save** button to save your changes. Preview the letter in Print Preview and then print the document. Close the file and then close Word.

**End** You have completed Project 1H

## Project 1I — Contract

**Objectives:** *Explore and Navigate the Word Window; View Documents; View Headers and Footers; Create and Edit a New Document; Use the Spelling and Grammar Checker; Select and Format Text; Organize, Save, and Print Documents; and Preview and Print Documents, Close a Document, and Close Word.*

In the following Mastery Assessment, you will complete a contract that is given to clients of The Perfect Party. Your completed document will look similar to Figure 1.60. You will save your document as *1I_Contract_Firstname_Lastname.*

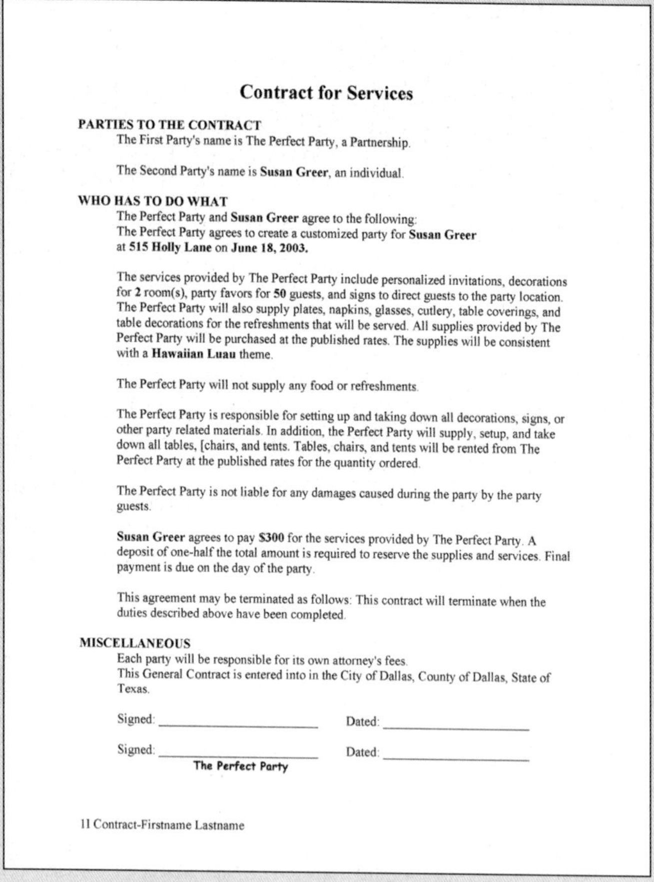

**Contract for Services**

**PARTIES TO THE CONTRACT**
The First Party's name is The Perfect Party, a Partnership.

The Second Party's name is **Susan Greer**, an individual.

**WHO HAS TO DO WHAT**
The Perfect Party and **Susan Greer** agree to the following:
The Perfect Party agrees to create a customized party for **Susan Greer** at **515 Holly Lane on June 18, 2003.**

The services provided by The Perfect Party include personalized invitations, decorations for **2** room(s), party favors for **50** guests, and signs to direct guests to the party location. The Perfect Party will also supply plates, napkins, glasses, cutlery, table coverings, and table decorations for the refreshments that will be served. All supplies provided by The Perfect Party will be purchased at the published rates. The supplies will be consistent with a **Hawaiian Luau** theme.

The Perfect Party will not supply any food or refreshments.

The Perfect Party is responsible for setting up and taking down all decorations, signs, or other party related materials. In addition, the Perfect Party will supply, setup, and take down all tables, [chairs, and tents. Tables, chairs, and tents will be rented from The Perfect Party at the published rates for the quantity ordered.

The Perfect Party is not liable for any damages caused during the party by the party guests.

**Susan Greer** agrees to pay **$300** for the services provided by The Perfect Party. A deposit of one-half the total amount is required to reserve the supplies and services. Final payment is due on the day of the party.

This agreement may be terminated as follows: This contract will terminate when the duties described above have been completed.

**MISCELLANEOUS**
Each party will be responsible for its own attorney's fees.
This General Contract is entered into in the City of Dallas, County of Dallas, State of Texas.

Signed: _____     Dated: _____

Signed: _____     Dated: _____
       **The Perfect Party**

1I Contract-Firstname Lastname

**Figure 1.60**

1. Display the **Open** dialog box. Navigate to the student files, and then locate and open the file *w01I_Contract*. Display the **File** menu, click **Save As**, and then use the **Save in arrow** to navigate to the location where you are storing your projects for this chapter. In the **File name** box, type **1I_Contract_Firstname_Lastname**

2. Click the **Read** button to view this document and read through the contents of the contract. In the reading view, text size is increased to ease your reading of the document on the screen. Notice that there are three headings that are shown in all uppercase letters.

**(Project 1I–Contract continues on the next page)**

**(Project 1I–Contract continued)**

3. On the Reading View toolbar, click the **Close** button to return to the Print Layout view. Use the **Spelling and Grammar** checker to correct the errors in the document. The last error flagged shows *State*, and suggests that this needs to be changed to *and State*. Click **Ignore Once** to ignore this occurrence.

4. Locate the three headings in uppercase letters. Select each one and add bold emphasis.

5. Locate the black lines in the document that represent blanks to be filled in. Press [Insert] on your keyboard to turn on the overtype feature. Alternatively, double-click the **OVR** button displayed in the Status bar at the bottom of the Word Window.

6. In the line beginning *The Second Party's name*, click to position your insertion point after the space following *is*. Type **Susan Greer** and notice that as you type, your typing will be displayed in bold. Make sure you do not type over any of the words in the contract. Then, use [Delete] or [←Bksp] to remove the unused portion of the black line. On the next two black lines, type **Susan Greer** again and delete the rest of both black lines. On the fourth black line, following the word *at*, type **515 Holly Lane** and delete the rest of the black line. At the beginning of the next black line, type the current date followed by a period and delete the rest of the black line. Delete unused portions of the black lines using [Delete] or [←Bksp] as needed in the remaining steps.

7. In the paragraph that begins with *The services provided*, type **2** for the number of rooms to be decorated, and type **50** for the number of guests. On the last black line in this paragraph, type **Hawaiian Luau** as the theme for the party.

8. Locate the next black line, and type **Susan Greer** and in the next black line type **300** following the dollar sign.

9. At the end of the contract, under *Signed*, select *The Perfect Party* and change the font size to **10**, change the font to **Comic Sans MS**, and add bold emphasis.

10. Display the footer area, and then, using your own information, type **1I Contract-Firstname Lastname**

11. Save the changes. Preview the document and then print it. Close the file. On the Status bar, double-click the **OVR** button to turn off the overtype feature. Close Word.

**End** You have completed Project 1I

## Project 1J — Memo

**Objectives:** *Create and Edit a New Document; View Documents; View Headers and Footers; Organize, Save, and Print Documents; Select and Format Text; Preview and Print Documents, Close a Document, and Close Word.*

In the following Mastery Assessment, you will create a memo for Christina Stevens requesting a copy of a contract from another Perfect Party employee and asking him to work at an upcoming event. Your completed memo will look similar to Figure 1.61. You will save your document as *1J_Memo_Firstname_Lastname.*

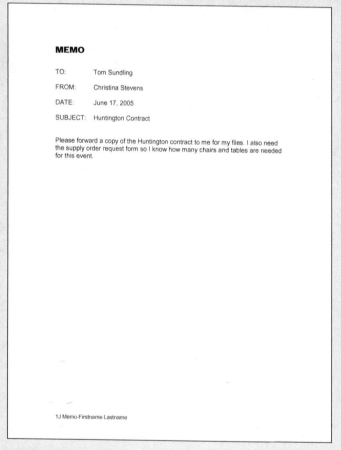

**MEMO**

TO:        Tom Sundling

FROM:    Christina Stevens

DATE:    June 17, 2005

SUBJECT:  Huntington Contract

Please forward a copy of the Huntington contract to me for my files. I also need the supply order request form so I know how many chairs and tables are needed for this event.

1J Memo-Firstname Lastname

**Figure 1.61**

1. Open **Word** and begin with a new document. Change the font to **Arial Black**, and the font size to **16**. Press CapsLock, type **MEMO** and press Enter twice.  Change the font to **12-point Arial**.

2. Save the project in your storage location as **1J_Memo_Firstname_Lastname**

**(Project 1J–Memo continues on the next page)**

**(Project 1J–Memo continued)**

3. Change the font to **12-point Arial**. Type **TO:** and press Tab twice. Type **Tom Sundling** and press Enter twice. Follow the same pattern to enter the remainder of the heading, pressing Enter twice to create a blank line between each heading line. You will need to press Tab twice after *DATE* and then type the current date for the date line. Use the appropriate number of tabs to line up the text. Press CapsLock to turn it off.

   **FROM:**    Christina Stevens

   **DATE:**

   **SUBJECT:**  Huntington Contract Party

4. Make sure the information entered in the memo heading aligns as shown in Figure 1.61. Save your document.

5. At the end of the Subject line, press Enter three times and type the body of the memo as follows:

   **Please forward a copy of the Huntington contract to me for my files. I also need the supply order request form so I know how many chairs and tables are needed for this event.**

6. Save your document. Create a footer and type **1J Memo-Firstname Lastname** and then format the text in the footer to **10-point Arial** font.

7. Proofread the document and use the Spelling and Grammar checker to correct any errors if necessary.

8. Print the memo, save your changes, and close the file.

**End** **You have completed Project 1J**

## Project 1K — Party

**Objectives:** *Create and Edit a New Document; View Headers and Footers; Organize, Save, and Print Documents; Select and Format Text; Preview and Print Documents, Close a Document, and Close Word.*

Using the information provided, draft a letter for the owners of The Perfect Party describing the services available to potential customers. Save your document as *1K_Party_Firstname_Lastname.*

1.  Open **Word**. Type the current date and press Enter four times to create two blank lines. Type **Dear** and then create a blank line.

2.  Compose a letter that explains the services offered by The Perfect Party. The tone of the letter should be positive and sales oriented. The letter should answer the question "why do I need this service?" As you write the letter, use your own imagination along with the information in the beginning of the chapter that describes the company. The letter should contain three paragraphs—an introductory paragraph, a second paragraph describing the services offered, and a closing paragraph.

3.  Add an appropriate closing, such as **Sincerely**
    Create three blank lines and then type:

    **Angie Nguyen**

    **Owner**

4.  Proofread the letter and correct any spelling or grammar errors.

5.  Change the font of the letter to a font and font size of your choosing.

6.  Create a footer and, using your own information, type **1K Party-Firstname Lastname**

7.  Preview the letter. Use the **Page Setup** dialog box to center the letter vertically on the page.

8.  Save the letter in your storage location as **1K_Party_Firstname_Lastname** Print the letter. Close the file and close Word.

**End** **You have completed Project 1K** ————————————————

## Project 1L—Invitation

**Objectives:** *Create and Edit a New Document; View Headers and Footers; Organize, Save, and Print Documents; Select and Format Text; Preview and Print Documents, Close a Document, and Close Word.*

Create a sample invitation for The Perfect Party that could be used for birthday parties. Save your invitation as *1L_Invitation_Firstname_Lastname.*

1. From your student files, open the file *w01L_Invitation* and save it in your storage location as **1L_Invitation_Firstname_Lastname**. This document contains only a title. On separate lines add labels for information that is typically found on an invitation, such as who the party is for; when, where, and why it is being held; any party theme; refreshments provided; and an R.S.V.P line. Place a blank line between each line of information.

2. Change the font of the title to **Batang** and increase the font size so the title is large and easy to read. Add bold emphasis to the title. If Batang is not available on your computer, choose another font.

3. Format the labels to **12-point Batang**. Add bold emphasis to the labels.

4. Next to each label, add a statement in brackets that describes the information to enter in each empty space; for example, **[Enter address of party]**

5. Change the font of the instructions on each line to a font of your choice in an appropriate font size.

6. View the footer area and, using your own information, type **1L Invitation-Firstname Lastname**

7. Save your changes and print the invitation. Close the file and close Word.

**End** You have completed Project 1L

## Microsoft Word Specialist Certification

As you progress through this textbook, you will practice skills necessary to complete the Microsoft certification test for Word 2003. Access your Internet connection and go to the Microsoft certification Web site at **www.microsoft.com/traincert/mcp/officespecialist/requirements.asp**. Navigate to the Microsoft Word objectives for the certification exam. Print the Core (Specialist) objectives for the Microsoft Word user certification and any other information about taking the test.

# GO! with Help

## Getting Help While You Work

The Word Help system is extensive and can help you as you work. In this exercise, you will view information about getting help as you work in Word.

1. Start **Word**. On the Standard toolbar, click the **Microsoft Office Word Help** button. In the **Search for** box, on the **Microsoft Word Help** task pane type **help.** Click the green **Start searching** button to the right of the *Search for* box.

2. In the displayed **Search Results** task pane, click *About getting help while you work*. Maximize the displayed window, and at the top of the window, click the **Show All** link. Scroll through and read all the various ways you can get help while working in Word.

3. If you want, print a copy of the information by clicking the printer button at the top of Microsoft Office Word Help task pane.

4. Close the Help window, and then close Word.

# 2 chaptertwo

# Formatting and Organizing Text

**In this chapter, you will:** complete these projects **and** practice these skills.

| Project 2A **Changing the Appearance of a Document** | **Objectives** |
|---|---|
| | • Change Document and Paragraph Layout |
| | • Change and Reorganize Text |

| Project 2B **Working with Lists and References** | **Objectives** |
|---|---|
| | • Create and Modify Lists |
| | • Work with Headers and Footers |
| | • Insert Frequently Used Text |
| | • Insert References |

# Lake Michigan City College

Lake Michigan City College is located along the lakefront of Chicago—one of the nation's most exciting cities. The college serves its large and diverse student body and makes positive contributions to the community through relevant curricula, partnerships with businesses and nonprofit organizations, and learning experiences that allow students to be full participants in the global community. The college offers three associate degrees in 20 academic areas, adult education programs, and continuing education offerings on campus, at satellite locations, and online.

© Getty Images, Inc.

# Formatting and Organizing Text

Typing text is just the beginning of the process of creating an effective, professional-looking document. Microsoft Word also provides many tools for formatting paragraphs and documents; tools to create shortcuts for entering commonly used text; and quick ways to copy, cut, and move text.

Word also provides tools to create specialized formats, such as endnotes, bulleted and numbered lists, and indented paragraphs.

In this chapter you will edit a report about a groupware database and how it is being used.

# Project 2A Campus Software

You have practiced opening existing documents and creating and editing new documents. In this chapter you will go further and learn how to change paragraph layouts, work with lists, headers and footers, and references.

In Activities 2.1 through 2.12 you will edit a document that describes the groupware software used by Lake Michigan City College. Your completed document will look similar to Figure 2.1. You will save your document as *2A_Campus_Software_Firstname_Lastname.*

---

**TSF Database 4**
**Background and Usage Within the Academic Counseling Department**
**Lake Michigan City College**

**Presented to the Database Development Committee**
**of the Intensive English Department**

TSF Database 4 is the platform used to make information of the Academic Counseling Department at the College available internally to staff, faculty, and students at the main campus and satellite campuses. The College previously conducted much of the administration of this department at the main campus, but recent budget redistributions and staff changes have shifted much of the responsibility for the administration to the satellite campuses.

TSF Database 4 is a program that captures unstructured information created by diverse entities and allows it to be viewed and manipulated by users within the system. It is considered a form of groupware—programs that help some work together collectively while located remotely from each other. Groupware services can include:

shared calendars

shared information

collaborative writing

e-mail

electronic meetings with shared information

TSF Database 4 is a database, workflow engine, document store, client/server environment, electronic mail service, and data distribution system.

TSF 4 collects information with the goal of collecting knowledge. "Information taking data and putting it into a meaningful pattern. Knowledge is the ability to use that information." Since much information is stored in various places, TSF Database 4 attempt collect the information in an accessible manner available to the entire organization.

**How is information collected?**

TSF Database 4 is a collection of databases, but the databases consist of docume just data that must be manipulated in some way to make sense. This concept is called d oriented data modeling. "Data modeling is the analysis of data objects that are used in a or other context and the identification of the relationships among these data objects." Ea document contains keyword fields that allow it to be sorted and retrieved. Documents al contain fields called rich text fields that can contain formatted text, sounds, pictures, an other programs. Such fields are designed to contain loosely structured information.

2A_Campus_Software_Firstname_Lastname

---

**How is information shared?**

TSF Database 4 clients connect to a database server and to each other. Each client and server has a unique ID file that establishes their identity and is also used for security purposes. Replication manages changes to documents and keeps their contents synchronized on various servers and clients. (Database replication is the copying and maintenance of data on multiple servers.) During replication, only information that has changed is moved across the network. This allows users working online to see the latest information almost instantly, and users working offline can update, or replicate, their work to the network very quickly.

Mail enabling is another important feature of TSF Database 4. It allows servers to route documents as messages and allows users to send information to a database.

**How does the ACD use TSF Database 4?**

The five main types of applications, discussion, broadcasting, reference, tracking, and workflow/approval, are all used by the Academic Counseling Department. Broadcasting refers to using the system to deliver non-critical college-wide information. Reference refers to using the system to replace printed reference materials, such as policy manuals, class information, and so forth. For tracking applications, the replication and security features make the system a useful tool for applications such as personnel and student tracking. Workflow/approval refers to applications where it is necessary to route knowledge according to defined protocols.

TSF Database 4 is not suited for applications requiring heavy analysis of numbers, real time analysis, or relational linking or record locking. It is, however, useful for collecting the results of such analysis and manipulation and presenting it in a format easily accessed by users throughout the College, including students. It is well suited, therefore, for use by the department.

**Training Schedule:**

Training will begin in May, and should be finished by the end of the month. The tentative training schedule follows.

2A_Campus_Software_Firstname_Lastname

---

**Figure 2.1**
Project 2A—Campus Software Document

## Objective 1
## Change Document and Paragraph Layout

Document layout includes *margins*—the space between the text and the top, bottom, left, and right edges of the page. Paragraph layout includes line spacing, indents, tabs, and so forth. Information about paragraph formats is stored in the paragraph mark at the end of a paragraph. When you press the Enter key, the new paragraph mark contains the formatting of the previous paragraph.

### Activity 2.1 Setting Margins

You can change each of the four page margins independently. You can also change the margins for the whole document at once or change the margins for only a portion of the document.

**1** Start Word. On the Standard toolbar, click the **Open** button . Navigate to the location where the student files for this textbook are stored. Locate **w02A_Campus_Software** and click once to select it. Then, in the lower right corner of the **Open** dialog box, click **Open**.

The *w02A_Campus_Software* file opens. See Figure 2.2.

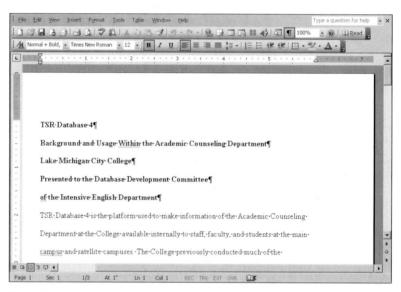

**Figure 2.2**

**2** If your formatting marks are not displayed as shown in Figure 2.2, on the Standard toolbar, click the **Show/Hide ¶** button to display the formatting marks on your screen.

**3** On the **File** menu, click **Save As**.

The Save As dialog box displays.

**4** Use the **Save in arrow** to navigate to the location where you are saving your files. In the **File name** box, delete the existing text, and using your own name, type **2A_Campus_Software_Firstname_Lastname**

**5** Click **Save**.

The document is saved with a new name.

**6** On the Standard toolbar, click the **Zoom button arrow** [100% ▼] and click **Page Width**.

**7** On the **File** menu, click **Page Setup**.

The Page Setup dialog box displays.

**8** In the **Page Setup** dialog box, if necessary, click the **Margins tab**. Under **Margins**, with *1″* highlighted in the **Top** box, type **1.5**

This will change the top margin to 1.5 inches on all pages of the document. (Note: You do not need to type the inch (″) mark.)

**9** Press Tab two times to highlight the measurement in the **Left** box, type **1** and then press Tab again. With the measurement in the **Right** box highlighted, type **1**

The new margins will be applied to the entire document. Compare your Page Setup dialog box to Figure 2.3.

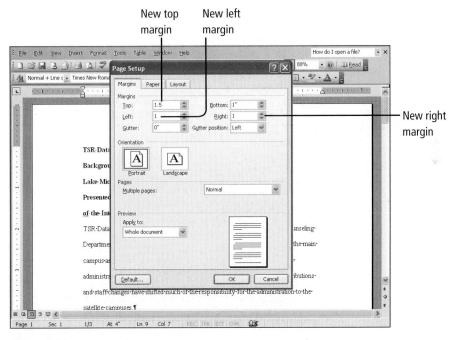

New top margin    New left margin                                                            New right margin

**Figure 2.3**

**10** In the lower right corner of the dialog box, click **OK**.

The dialog box closes, and the new margins are applied to your document. The width of the document is displayed on the ruler. If the ruler is not displayed, from the View menu, click Ruler. With 1″ left and right margins, the document width will be 6.5″.

### Activity 2.2  Aligning Text

*Alignment* is the placement of paragraph text relative to the left and right margins. Most paragraph text is *aligned left*—aligned at the left margin, leaving the right margin uneven. Three other types of paragraph alignment are available: *center alignment*, which is centered between the left and right margin, *right alignment*, which is aligned on the right margin, and *justified alignment*, which is text aligned on both the left and right margins. Examples are shown in the table in Figure 2.4.

| Paragraph Alignment Options | | |
| --- | --- | --- |
| **Alignment** | **Button** | **Description and Example** |
| Align Left | ▤ | Align Left is the default paragraph alignment in Word. Text in the paragraph aligns at the left margin and the right margin is ragged. |
| Center | ▤ | The Center alignment option aligns text in the paragraph so that it is centered between the left and right margins. |
| Align Right | ▤ | Align Right is used to align text at the right margin. Using Align Right, the left margin, which is normally even, is ragged. |
| Justify | ▤ | The Justify alignment option adds additional space between words so that both the left and right margins are even. Justify is often used when formatting newspaper-style columns. |

**Figure 2.4**

**1** Place the insertion point anywhere in the first line of text in the document.

To format a paragraph, you only need to have the insertion point somewhere in the paragraph—you do not need to select all of the text in the paragraph.

**2** On the Formatting toolbar, click the **Center** button ▤.

The first paragraph, which is a title, is centered.

**3** Move the pointer into the left margin area, just to the left of the second line of text. When the pointer changes to a white arrow, drag down to select the second, third, fourth, and fifth lines of text as shown in Figure 2.5.

Recall that a paragraph consists of a paragraph mark and all the text in front of it. To format multiple paragraphs, they need to be selected.

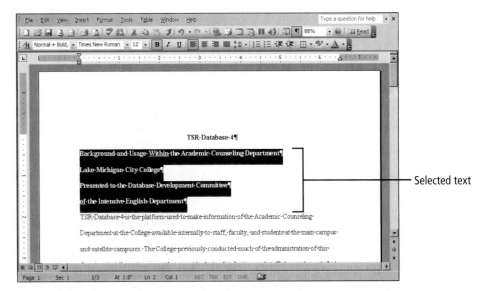

Selected text

**Figure 2.5**

4 On the Formatting toolbar, click the **Center** button [image].

All five of the title lines of bold text are centered. The last four lines are still selected. See Figure 2.6.

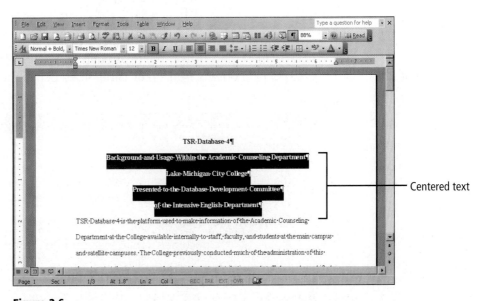

Centered text

**Figure 2.6**

5 Click the down arrow at the bottom of the vertical scrollbar until you can see all of the paragraph that begins *TSR Database 4 is the platform* and click anywhere in this paragraph. Make sure that you can see the first two or three lines of the following paragraph also.

6 On the Formatting toolbar, click the **Justify** button [image].

Both the left and right edges of the paragraph are even. The other paragraphs are not affected. See Figure 2.7.

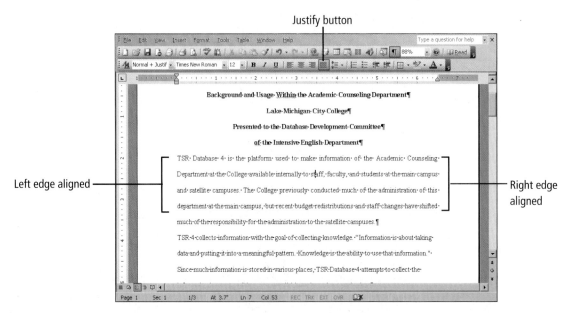

Justify button

Left edge aligned

Right edge aligned

**Figure 2.7**

**7** On the Formatting toolbar, click the **Align Left** button ▣.

The paragraph is returned to the left aligned format.

### Activity 2.3 Changing Line Spacing

**Line spacing** is the distance between lines of text in a paragraph. A single-spaced paragraph of 12-point text has six lines per vertical inch. If you double-space the same text, each line will be 24 points high (12 points of text, 12 points of space), or three lines per inch. See Figure 2.8.

| Line Spacing Options | |
|---|---|
| **Spacing** | **Example** |
| Single (1.0) | Most business documents are single spaced. This means that the spacing between lines is just enough to separate the text. |
| Double (2.0) | Many college research papers and reports, and many draft documents that need room for notes are double spaced; there is room for a full line of text between each document line. |

**Figure 2.8**

**1** Move the pointer to the left margin just to the left of the first title line. When the pointer changes to a white arrow, drag downward to highlight the first and second lines of the title.

**2** On the Formatting toolbar, click the arrow on the right of the **Line Spacing** button ▤▾.

A list displays. A check mark next to 2.0 indicates that the selected paragraphs are double spaced. See Figure 2.9.

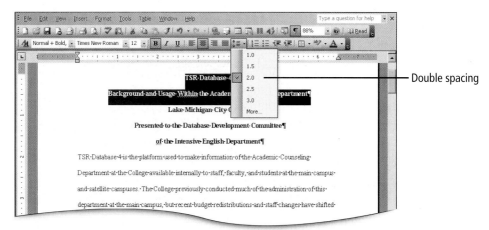

Figure 2.9

**3** On the displayed **Line Spacing** list, click **1.0**.

The selected paragraphs are single spaced. The third title line is part of the first group of titles, so its spacing was left as double spaced to separate it from the following title lines. See Figure 2.10.

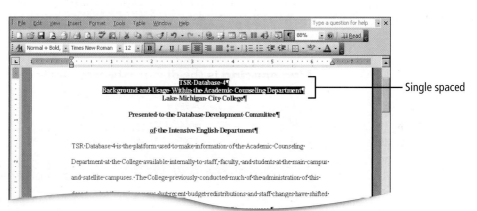

Figure 2.10

**4** Click to place the insertion point anywhere in the fourth line of the title. On the **Formatting** toolbar, move the pointer over the **Line Spacing** button.

A ScreenTip displays, indicating *Line Spacing (1)*. This means that the last operation performed using this button is now the default when you click the button.

**5** On the Formatting toolbar, click the **Line Spacing** button. Make sure you click the button and not the arrow on the right side of the button.

The line is single spaced.

**6** In the paragraph that begins *TSR Database 4 is the platform*, click to place the insertion point to the left of the first word in the paragraph.

**7** Use the vertical scrollbar to scroll to the bottom of the document, position the I-beam pointer $\boxed{I}$ to the right of the last word in the text, hold down [Shift] and click.

All text between the insertion point and the point at which you clicked is selected. This [Shift] + click technique is convenient to select a block of text between two points that span several pages.

**8** On the Formatting toolbar, click the **Line Spacing** button [icon].

The selected text is formatted with single spacing.

**9** Scroll to the top of the document and click anywhere to cancel the text selection.

Compare your screen to Figure 2.11.

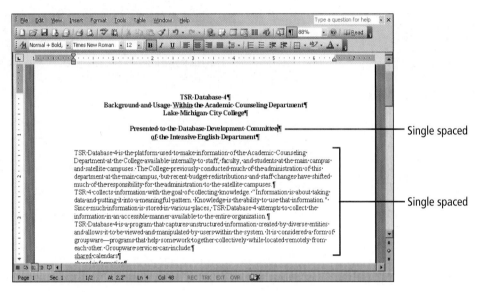

**Figure 2.11**

**10** On the Standard toolbar, click the **Save** button [icon].

**Activity 2.4** Adding Space After Paragraphs

Adjusting paragraph spacing from the Paragraph dialog box gives you the most control, because you can control the space before or after paragraphs using points as the unit of measure. Remember, there are 72 points per inch.

**1** Click anywhere in the paragraph that begins *TSR Database 4 is the platform.*

**2** On the **Format** menu, click **Paragraph**.

The Paragraph dialog box displays. You can also open this dialog box by clicking the arrow on the Line Spacing button [icon] and clicking More from the displayed list.

**3** If necessary, click the Indents and Spacing tab. Under **Spacing**, in the **After** box, click the up arrow twice.

The value in the box changes from 0 pt. to 12 pt. The up and down arrows, called *spin box arrows*, increment the point size by six points at a time. Alternatively, type a number of your choice directly into the text box. See Figure 2.12.

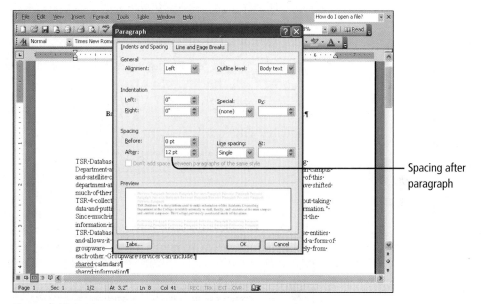

Spacing after paragraph

**Figure 2.12**

**4** Click **OK**.

A 12-point space is added to the end of the paragraph. See Figure 2.13.

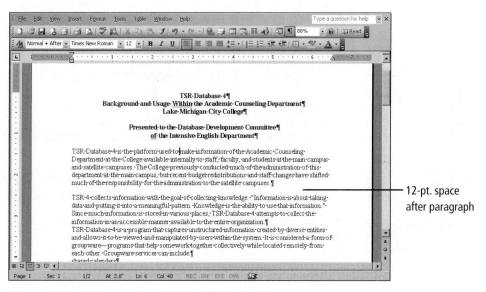

12-pt. space after paragraph

**Figure 2.13**

**5** In the paragraph that begins *TSR 4 collects information*, click to the left of first word in the paragraph. Use the vertical scrollbar to scroll to the end of the document, position the I-beam pointer 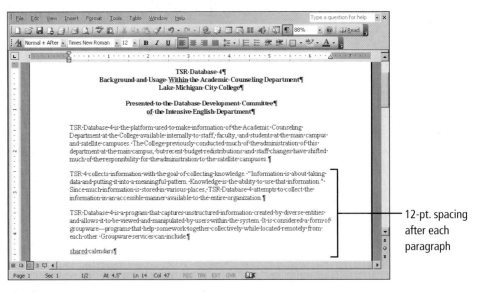 to the right of the last word in the document, hold down Shift and click.

The text between the insertion point and the end of the document is selected.

**6** With the text selected, display the **Format** menu, and then click **Paragraph**. Alternatively, you can right-click in the selected text and then click Paragraph from the shortcut menu.

**7** In the displayed **Paragraph** dialog box, under **Spacing**, in the **After** box, click the **up spin arrow** twice.

The value in the box changes from 0 pt. to 12 pt.

**8** Click **OK**. Click anywhere in the document to cancel the selection. Scroll through the document to examine the result of adding extra space between the paragraphs.

Recall that paragraph formatting instructions are stored in the paragraph marks at the end of each paragraph. When you select more than one paragraph, these instructions are placed in the paragraph mark for each selected paragraph but not for any other paragraphs in the document. Compare your screen to Figure 2.14.

12-pt. spacing after each paragraph

**Figure 2.14**

**9** On the Standard toolbar, click the **Save** button.

**Another Way**

**Adding Space**

*You can add space to the end of a paragraph in the following ways:*

- Press Enter to add a blank line.

- Change the line spacing to double.

- From the Paragraph dialog box, adjust the spacing after the paragraph.

### Activity 2.5 Indenting Paragraphs

In addition to adding space at the end of paragraphs, indenting the first lines of paragraphs provides visual cues to the reader to help break the document up and make it easier to read.

**1** Hold down Ctrl and press Home to move to the top of page 1. Then, click anywhere in the paragraph that begins *TSR Database 4 is the platform*.

**2** On the **Format** menu, click **Paragraph**.

The Paragraph dialog box displays.

**3** Be sure that the **Indents and Spacing tab** is displayed. Under **Indentation**, click the **Special arrow**, and from the displayed list, click **First line**.

**4** Under **Indentation**, in the **By** box, make sure *0.5"* is displayed. See Figure 2.15.

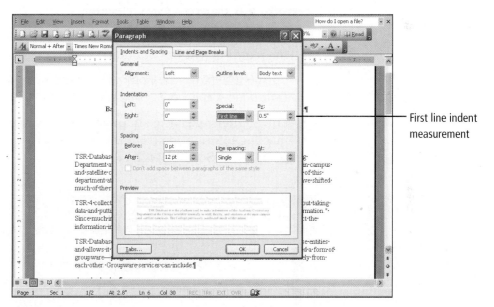

First line indent measurement

**Figure 2.15**

**5** In the lower right corner of the dialog box, click **OK**.

The first line of the paragraph is indented by 0.5 inch, and the First Line Indent marker on the ruler moves to the 0.5 inch mark. See Figure 2.16.

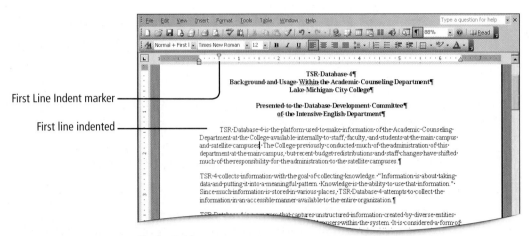

First Line Indent marker

First line indented

**Figure 2.16**

**6** On the Standard toolbar, click the **Save** button 🖫.

### Activity 2.6  Using the Format Painter

**1** Click anywhere in the paragraph that begins *TSR Database 4 is the platform.* On the Standard toolbar, click the **Format Painter** button 🖌. Move the pointer over the next paragraph, beginning *TSR Database 4 collects information.*

The pointer takes the shape of a paintbrush, and contains the formatting information from the paragraph where the insertion point is positioned. See Figure 2.17.

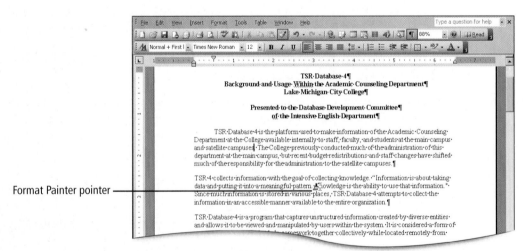

Format Painter pointer

**Figure 2.17**

**2** Click once.

The paragraph is formatted with the same formatting as the previous paragraph.

The pointer returns to its normal I-beam 🔲 shape.

**3** On the Standard toolbar, *double-click* the **Format Painter** button [icon]. Move the pointer over the paragraph that begins *TSR Database 4 is a program that captures.*

**4** Click once.

The paragraph is indented, but this time the Format Painter paintbrush remains active.

**5** Scroll down using the down scroll arrow and move the pointer over the paragraph that begins *TSR Database 4 is a database.* Click once.

**6** Scroll down and click once in each of the remaining paragraphs that are not bold subheadings.

This is much faster than clicking on each paragraph and then opening the Paragraph dialog box to set the indentation parameters.

**7** On the Standard toolbar, click the **Format Painter** button [icon].

The Format Painter feature is turned off. You can also turn it off by pressing Esc.

**8** On the Standard toolbar, click the **Save** button [icon].

## Objective 2
## Change and Reorganize Text

Changing and reorganizing text is accomplished using Word tools such as the **Office Clipboard**, a temporary storage area that holds text. Text can be moved to the Office Clipboard by **copying** existing text, which leaves the original text in place, or by **cutting** text, which removes it from its original location. You can then **paste** the contents of the clipboard in a new location. There are keyboard shortcuts for many of these tools, as shown in Figure 2.18.

### Activity 2.7 Finding and Replacing Text

Finding and then replacing text is a quick way to make a change in a document that occurs more than one time. For example, if you misspelled someone's last name, Word can search for all instances of the name and replace it with the correct spelling.

## Keyboard Shortcuts for Editing Text

| Keyboard Shortcut | Action |
| --- | --- |
| Ctrl + X | Cut text or graphic and place it on the Office Clipboard |
| Ctrl + C | Copy text or graphic and place it on the Office Clipboard |
| Ctrl + V | Paste the contents of the Office Clipboard |
| Ctrl + Z | Undo an action |
| Ctrl + Y | Redo an action |
| Ctrl + F | Find text |
| Ctrl + H | Find and replace text |

**Figure 2.18**

**1** Press `Ctrl` + `Home` to position the insertion point at the beginning of the document.

When you initiate a find-and-replace operation, it begins from the location of the insertion point and proceeds to the end of the document. If you begin a search in the middle of a document, Word will prompt you to return to the beginning of the document and continue the search.

**2** On the **Edit** menu, click **Replace**.

**3** In the displayed **Find and Replace** dialog box, in the **Find what** box, type **TSR**

**4** In the **Find and Replace** dialog box, in the **Replace with** box, type **TSF**

**5** Click **Find Next**.

The first instance of *TSR* is highlighted, and the Find and Replace dialog box remains open. See Figure 2.19.

First instance of found text ——

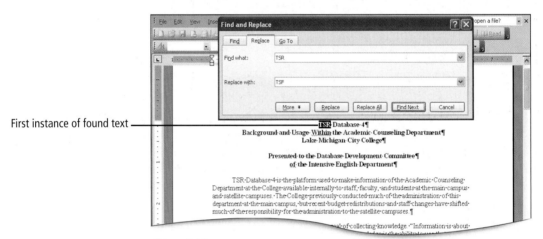

**Figure 2.19**

**6** Click the **Replace** button.

The first instance of TSR is replaced by TSF, and the next instance of TSR is highlighted. See Figure 2.20.

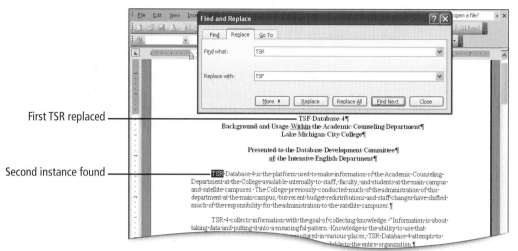

First TSR replaced

Second instance found

**Figure 2.20**

---

**7** Click the **Replace All** button.

Every occurrence of TSR is replaced with TSF, and a dialog box indicates the number of replacements made. See Figure 2.21.

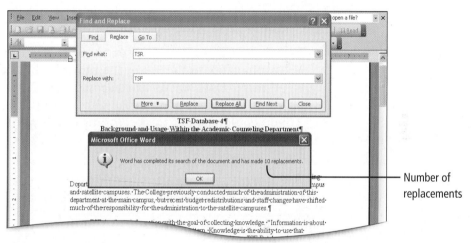

Number of replacements

**Figure 2.21**

---

**8** Click **OK** to close the dialog box. In the **Find and Replace** dialog box click **Close**.

The Find and Replace dialog box closes.

### Activity 2.8 Selecting and Deleting Text

You have practiced removing text one letter at a time using the Backspace key and the Delete key. For removing larger blocks of text, it is more efficient to select the block of text and then delete it.

**1** Scroll down until you can see the lower portion of page 1 and locate the paragraph that begins *TSF Database 4 is a collection of databases.*

**2** At the end of the fifth line in the paragraph, locate the word *can*, and then double-click to select the word. See Figure 2.22.

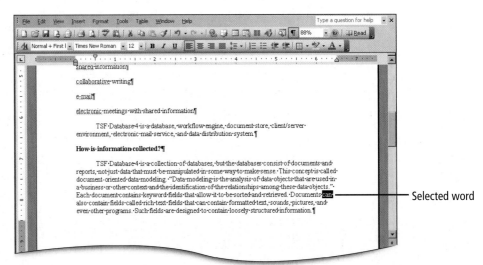

Selected word

**Figure 2.22**

**3** Press ⌊Delete⌋.

The word is removed from the paragraph.

**4** Locate the phrase *and reports* in the first sentence of the same paragraph. Click to the left of the phrase, hold down ⌊Ctrl⌋ + ⌊Shift⌋, and press ➜ twice. Both words are selected. See Figure 2.23. Alternatively, you could click to the left of the phrase and drag to select both words, or you could click at the beginning of the phrase and ⌊Shift⌋ + click at the end of the phrase.

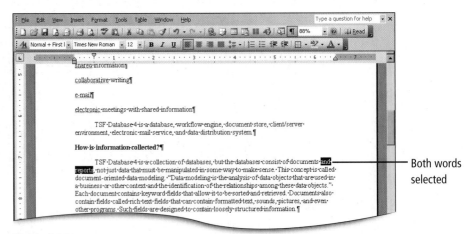

Both words selected

**Figure 2.23**

**5** Press ⌊Delete⌋.

Both words are deleted.

**6** On the Standard toolbar, click the **Save** button 🖫.

### Activity 2.9  Cutting and Pasting Text

You can move text from one location in a document to a different location in the same document with the commands cut and paste. The *cut* command moves text out of the document and onto the Office Clipboard—the temporary storage location for text or graphics. Then, use the *paste* command to paste the contents of the Office Clipboard into the new location.

**1** Scroll down to view the upper portion of page 2, and locate the paragraph that begins *TSF Database 4 clients connect.*

**2** Locate the second sentence, that begins with *Replication manages changes.* Hold down [Ctrl] and click anywhere in the sentence.

The entire sentence is selected. See Figure 2.24.

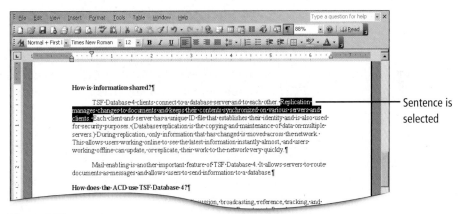

Figure 2.24

**3** On the Standard toolbar, click the **Cut** button .

The sentence is removed from the document and moved to the Office Clipboard.

---

**Note** — **The Difference Between Using Delete, Backspace, and Cut**

When you use the Cut command to remove text, it is stored on the Office Clipboard and can be pasted into the same (or another) document. When you use Delete or Backspace to remove text, the text is not stored on the Office Clipboard. The only way you can retrieve text removed with Delete or Backspace is by using the Undo feature.

---

**4** In the third line of the paragraph, click to position the insertion point to the left of the sentence that begins *(Database replication.* See Figure 2.25.

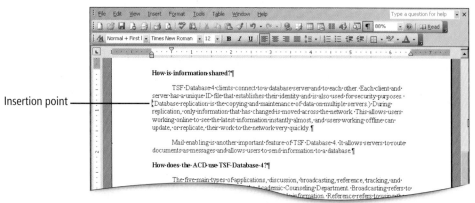

Insertion point

**Figure 2.25**

**5** On the Standard toolbar, click the **Paste** button. Adjust the spacing before and after the sentence if needed.

The sentence is moved from the Office Clipboard and pasted into the document at the insertion point. A **smart tag** with a clipboard image also displays below the pasted sentence. A smart tag is a button that lets you control the result of certain actions, for example, a cut and paste operation.

**6** Point to the smart tag until its ScreenTip *Paste Options* displays, and then click its small arrow.

A short menu provides commands related specifically to pasting, as shown in Figure 2.26. You can determine whether you want to format the pasted text the same as the surrounding text or retain its original formatting. Performing another screen action will cancel the display of the smart tag; alternatively press Esc to cancel its display.

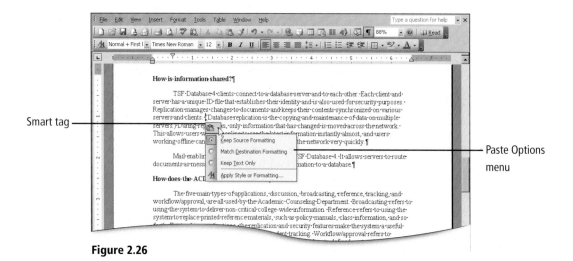

Smart tag

Paste Options menu

**Figure 2.26**

**7** Click anywhere in the document to close the **Paste Options** menu.

**8** Scroll up to position the insertion point at the top of page 1 on your screen, locate the paragraph that begins *TSF 4 collects information*, and then triple-click in the paragraph.

The entire paragraph is selected. Recall that double- and triple-clicking takes a steady hand. The speed of the clicks is important, but the mouse must also remain steady. If you did not select the entire paragraph, begin again. See Figure 2.27.

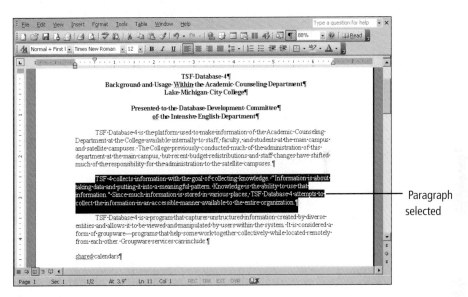

Paragraph selected

**Figure 2.27**

**9** On the Standard toolbar, click the **Cut** button.

The paragraph is moved from the document onto the Office Clipboard.

| **Alert!** | **If the Clipboard Task Pane Opens** |
|---|---|
| | The Clipboard task pane may display on your screen depending on the options that have been set for the clipboard on your computer. If the Clipboard task pane opens, click the close button on the task pane title bar. |

**10** Scroll down as necessary and click to position the insertion point to the left of the word *How* in the subheading, *How is information collected?*

**11** On the Standard toolbar, click the **Paste** button.

The paragraph is pasted from the Office Clipboard into the document at the insertion point, and the Paste Options smart tag displays. See Figure 2.28.

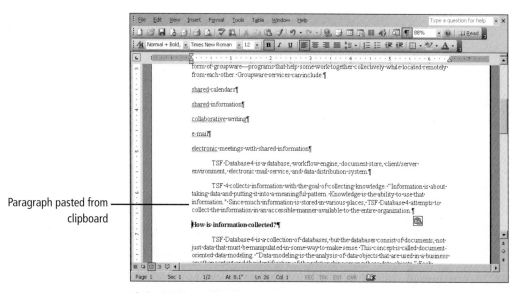

**Paragraph pasted from clipboard**

**Figure 2.28**

### Activity 2.10 Copying and Pasting Text

The copy command places a copy of selected text on the Office Clipboard, which you can then paste to another location. Unlike the cut command, the copy command does not remove the selected text from its original location.

**1** Be sure that the lower portion of page 1 is in view and then triple-click on the subheading *How is information collected?*

The subheading is selected. See Figure 2.29.

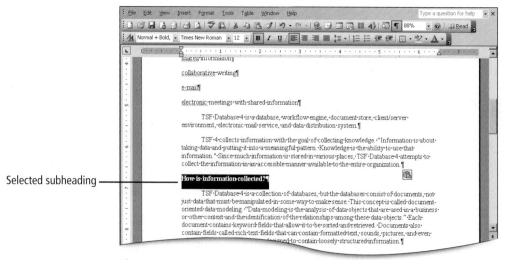

**Selected subheading**

**Figure 2.29**

**2** On the Standard toolbar, click the **Copy** button [icon]. Alternatively, you can right-click on the selected text and click Copy from the shortcut menu, or press [Ctrl] + [C].

The heading remains in its original location, but a copy has been moved onto the Office Clipboard.

**3** Hold down Ctrl and press End to move to the end of the document.

**4** In the last paragraph, click to position the insertion point to the left of the word *Training*. On the Standard toolbar, click the **Paste** button 📋.

The text is copied from the Office Clipboard to the insertion point location. The spacing following the heading is also included because the information about the spacing following the paragraph is stored in its paragraph mark. See Figure 2.30.

Subheading pasted from clipboard —

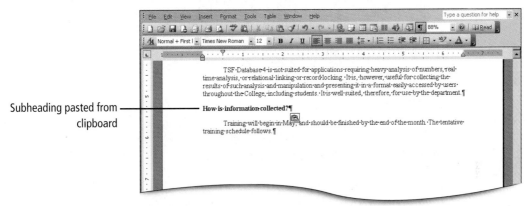

**Figure 2.30**

**5** Triple-click on the new subheading to select it. Type **Training Schedule:** to replace the selected text.

The original text is replaced, but the formatting is retained. See Figure 2.31.

Replacement text —

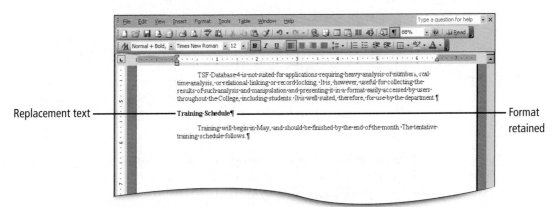

— Format retained

**Figure 2.31**

## More Knowledge — Using the Office Clipboard Task Pane

If you use the copy command twice without pasting, a Clipboard task pane may open. This enables you to copy up to 24 pieces of text, graphics, and other objects into the Office Clipboard, and then paste them by selecting the desired item from the task pane. Clipboard task pane options are accessed by clicking the Options button at the bottom of the task pane. The Clipboard task pane can also be opened by clicking Edit on the menu bar, and then clicking Office Clipboard.

### Activity 2.11 Dragging Text to a New Location

Another method of moving text is ***drag-and-drop***. This technique uses the mouse to drag selected text from one location to another. This method is useful if the text to be moved is on the same screen as the destination location.

**1** Scroll as necessary to position the upper portion of page 2 at the top of your screen.

**2** In the paragraph that begins *TSF Database 4 clients*, in the next to the last line, locate and select the word *almost*.

**3** Move the pointer over the selected word.

The pointer becomes a white arrow that points up and to the left. This is the drag and drop pointer. See Figure 2.32.

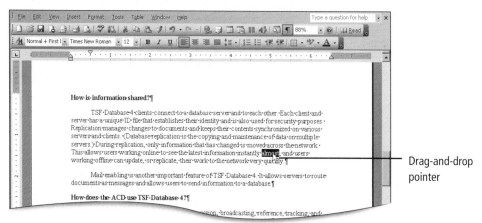

Drag-and-drop pointer

**Figure 2.32**

---

## Note — Turning on the Drag-and-Drop Option

If you do not see the drag-and-drop pointer, you will need to turn this feature on. On the Tools menu, click Options, and then click the Edit tab. Under Editing options, select the *Drag-and-drop text editing* text box.

---

**4** Hold down the left mouse button and drag to the left until the dotted vertical line that floats next to the pointer is positioned to the left of the word *instantly* and then release the left mouse button.

The word is moved to the insertion point location. The vertical line of the pointer assists you in dropping the moved text in the place where you want it. The small box attached to the pointer indicates that there is text attached to the pointer. See Figure 2.33.

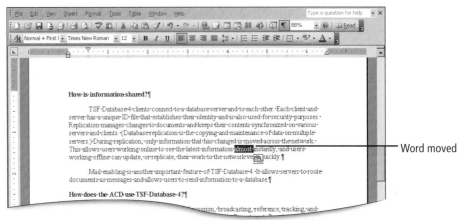

**Figure 2.33**

Word moved

---

**5** Press [Ctrl] + [End] to move to the end of the document. Then scroll as necessary so that you can view the last four paragraphs on your screen as shown in Figure 2.34.

**6** Hold down [Ctrl] and click anywhere in the sentence *It is well suited, therefore, for use by the department* at the end of the second-to-last paragraph.

The sentence is selected.

**7** Move the pointer over the selected sentence to display the drag-and-drop pointer, and then drag up to the paragraph above and position the vertical line to the right of the period at the end of *defined protocols.* as shown in Figure 2.34.

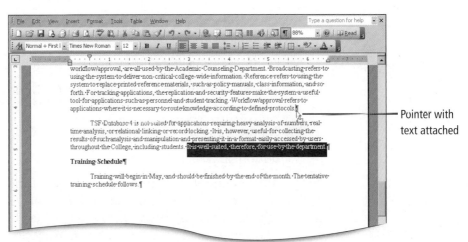

Pointer with text attached

**Figure 2.34**

**8** Release the mouse button. The sentence you moved becomes the last sentence in the paragraph. Notice that a space was automatically added before the sentence.

### Activity 2.12 Undoing and Redoing Changes

You can Undo one or more actions that you made to a document since the last time you saved it. An Undo action can be reversed with the Redo command.

**1** On the Standard toolbar, click the **Undo** button.

The sentence you dragged and dropped returns to its original location as shown in Figure 2.35.

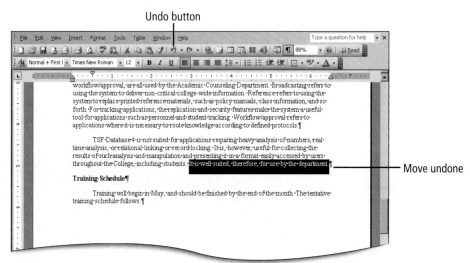

**Figure 2.35**

**2** On the Standard toolbar, click the **Undo** button again.

The word you moved prior to moving the sentence returns to its original location.

**3** On the Standard toolbar, click the **Redo** button.

The word is moved back. Clicking the Undo and Redo buttons changes one action at a time.

**4** On the Standard toolbar, click the arrow on the right of the **Undo** button.

A list of changes displays showing all of the changes made since your last save operation. From the displayed list, you can click any of the actions and undo it, but all of the changes above the one you select will also be undone. See Figure 2.36.

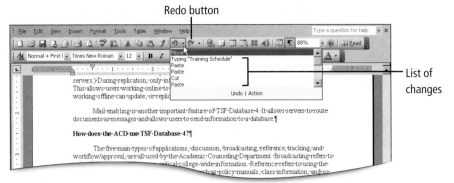

**Figure 2.36**

**5** Click anywhere in the document to close the Undo menu without selecting any actions.

**6** From the **View** menu, click **Header and Footer**.

**7** From the Header and Footer toolbar, click the **Switch Between Header and Footer** button ⊞. Using your own name, type **2A Campus Software_Firstname_Lastname** in the footer.

**8** On the Header and Footer toolbar, click the **Close** button Close.

**9** On the Standard toolbar, click the **Save** button 🖫 and then click the **Print Preview** button 🔍 to preview the document. Close the Print Preview window. Use the PgUp and PgDn keys as necessary to view both pages in Print Preview. Make any necessary changes, and then click the **Print** button 🖨. Close the document saving any changes.

**End** You have completed Project 2A ———————————————

# Project 2B **Software**

Word has numerous features to help you create a report. In this project, you will use report features such as lists, headers and footers, and footnote references.

In Activities 2.13 through 2.27 you will make further changes to a document that describes the groupware software being used by Lake Michigan City College. This document is similar to the one you worked on in Project 2A. Your completed document will look similar to Figure 2.37. You will save your document as *2B_Software_Firstname_Lastname*.

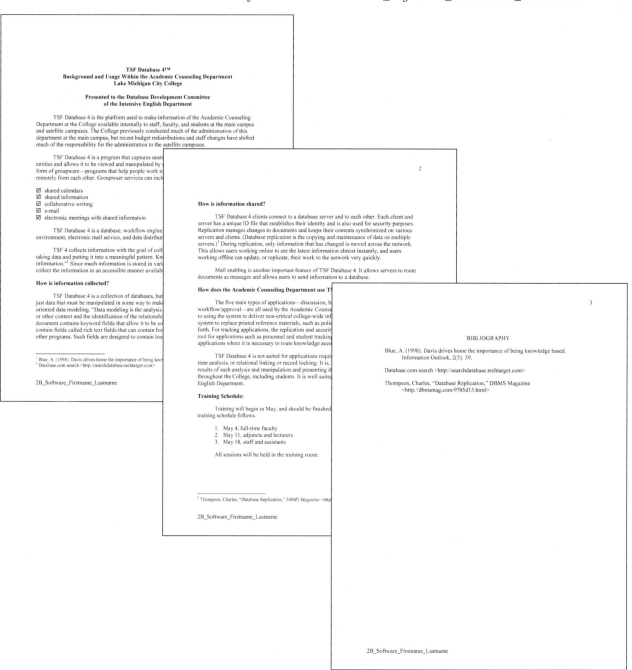

**Figure 2.37**
Project 2B—Software

# Objective 3
## Create and Modify Lists

Lists of information can be displayed two ways. A bulleted list uses bullets, which are text symbols such as small circles or check marks, to introduce each piece of information. Numbered lists use consecutive numbers to introduce each item in a list. Bulleted lists are used when the items in the list can be displayed in any order; numbered lists are used for items that have definite steps, a sequence of actions, or are in chronological order.

### Activity 2.13 Creating a Bulleted List

**1** Start Word. On the Standard toolbar, click the **Open** button. Navigate to the location where the student files for this textbook are stored. Locate **w02B_Software** and click once to select it. Then, in the lower right corner of the **Open** dialog box, click the **Open** button.

The *w02B_ Software* file opens.

**2** If the formatting marks are not already displayed on your screen, on the Standard toolbar, click the Show/Hide ¶ button.

**3** On the **File** menu, click **Save As**.

The Save As dialog box displays.

**4** Use the **Save in arrow** to navigate to the location where you are saving your files. In the **File name** box, delete the existing text and, using your own name, type **2B_Software_Firstname_Lastname**

**5** Near the bottom of the **Save As** dialog box, click **Save**.

The document is saved with a new name.

**6** On the Standard toolbar, click the **Zoom button arrow** and click **Page Width**.

**7** Scroll as necessary to display the middle of page 1 on your screen, and locate the five short paragraphs that begin with *shared calendars*.

**8** Move the pointer into the left margin to the left of *shared calendars*, and when the pointer changes to a white arrow, drag down to select the five short paragraphs as shown in Figure 2.38.

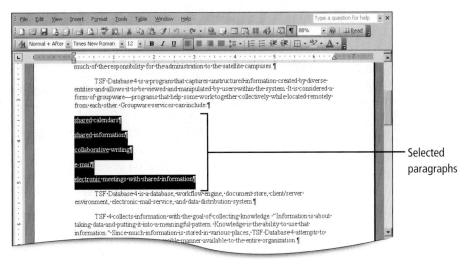

Selected paragraphs

**Figure 2.38**

To create a list from existing text, the paragraphs need to be selected.

**9** On the Formatting toolbar, click the **Bullets** button ⊞.

A symbol is placed to the left of each of the five paragraphs, and the text is moved to the right. The bullet symbol displayed on your screen depends on previous bullet usage of the computer at which you are seated. The default bullet is a large, round, black dot centered vertically on the line of text.

**10** Click anywhere in the document to deselect the text. Click the **Show/Hide ¶** button ¶.

This enables you to see the bulleted list without the formatting marks. Notice that the line spacing remains the same as it was before you created the list. See Figure 2.39.

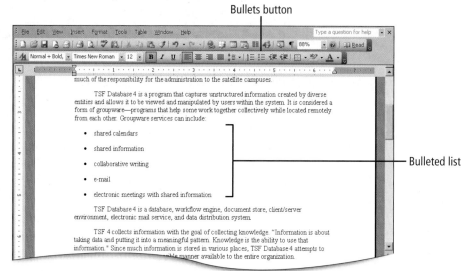

Figure 2.39

**11** Click the **Show/Hide ¶** button ¶ again to turn on formatting marks.

**12** On the Standard toolbar, click the **Save** button 💾.

### Activity 2.14 Creating a Numbered List

In the previous activity you created a list using existing text. You can also turn on the list feature and create a new list.

**1** Press Ctrl + End to move to the end of the document and then press Enter once.

Notice that the insertion point is indented. This paragraph retains the formatting of the previous paragraph, which is stored in the paragraph mark you just created when you pressed Enter.

**2** On the Formatting toolbar, click the **Numbering** button ⊞.

The number *1* is inserted to begin a numbered list as shown in Figure 2.40.

Numbering button

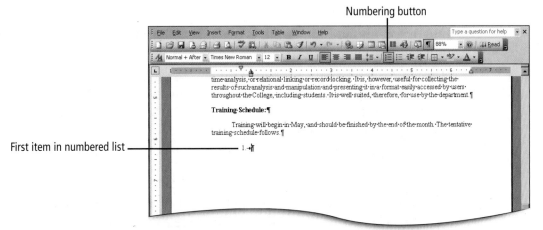

First item in numbered list

**Figure 2.40**

**3** Type **May 4, full-time faculty** and press Enter.

The text is entered, and a second number is added.

**4** Type **May 11, adjuncts and lecturers** and press Enter.

**5** Type **May 18, staff and assistants** and press Enter.

Although this list will contain only the three lines you typed, the paragraph marker for the new paragraph retains the formatting of the previous paragraph, which is a numbered list. See Figure 2.41.

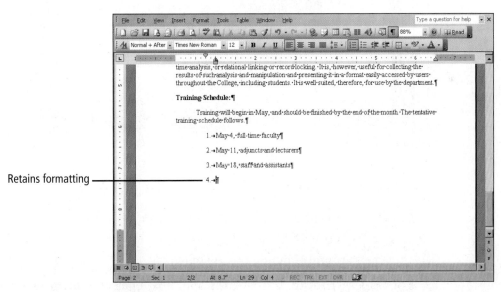

Retains formatting

**Figure 2.41**

**6** On the Formatting toolbar, click the **Numbering** button again.

The numbering format is turned off. Both list buttons, Numbering and Bullets, act as a *toggle switch*; that is, clicking the button once turns the feature on, and clicking the button again turns the feature off.

**7** Type **All sessions will be held in the training room.**

**8** On the Standard toolbar, click the **Save** button.

## Activity 2.15 Formatting Lists

Lists are columns of paragraphs and can be formatted in the same way other paragraphs are formatted.

**1** Move the pointer into the left margin to the left of *1.* and when the pointer changes to a white arrow, drag down to select the three numbered items.

The three items are selected, even though the list numbers are outside the highlighted area.

**2** On the Formatting toolbar, click the **Decrease Indent** button 📑.

All of the items in the list move to the left, and the decreased indent is reflected in the ruler. See Figure 2.42.

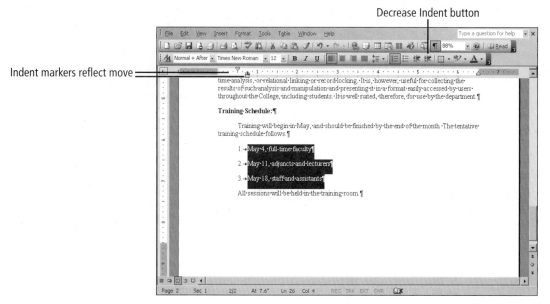

Figure 2.42

**3** Select only the first two numbered items in the list.

**4** On the **Format** menu, click **Paragraph**. If necessary, click the Indents and Spacing tab.

The Paragraph dialog box displays.

**5** Under **Spacing**, in the **After** spin box, click the **down arrow** twice.

The value in the box changes from 12 pt. to 0 pt. as shown in Figure 2.43.

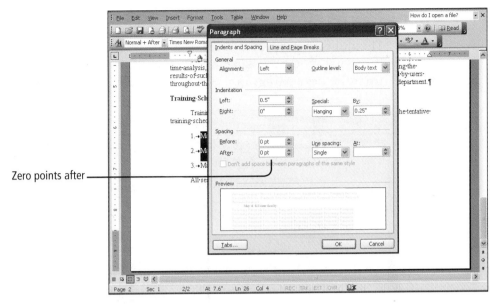

Zero points after

**Figure 2.43**

**6** Click **OK**.

The extra spaces between the items in the list are removed resulting in single spacing. The space after the third item remains, because it was not selected. See Figure 2.44.

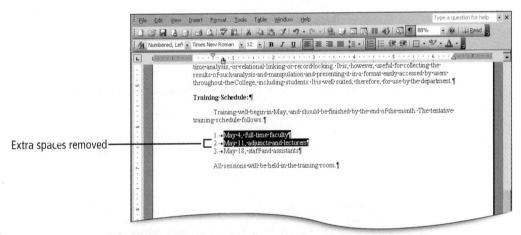

Extra spaces removed

**Figure 2.44**

**7** Scroll up to view the bulleted list on page 1, position the pointer in the margin until it displays as a white arrow, and then drag downward to select the five bulleted items.

**8** On the Formatting toolbar, click the **Decrease Indent** button .

All of the items in the list move to the left, and the ruler reflects the change.

**9** Select the first four bulleted items in the list. On the **Format** menu, click **Paragraph**.

The Paragraph dialog box displays.

**10** Under **Spacing**, in the **After** spin box, click the **down arrow** twice.

The value in the box changes from 12 pt. to 0 pt.

**11** Click **OK**.

The bulleted list is now formatted in the same manner as the numbered list. The extra spacing after the last item remains to set it off from the next paragraph. See Figure 2.45.

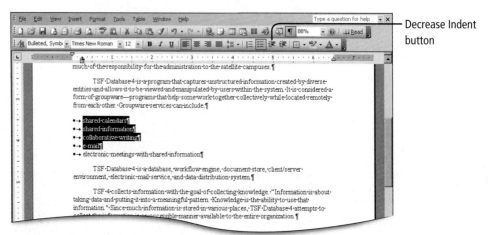

Decrease Indent button

**Figure 2.45**

### Activity 2.16 Customizing Bullets

You are not restricted to the bullet symbol that displays when you click the Bullets button. You can use any symbol from any font on your computer for your bullet character.

**1** From the margin area to the left of the five bulleted items, drag to select the five items in the list.

**2** On the **Format** menu, click **Bullets and Numbering**.

The Bullets and Numbering dialog box displays, showing you the most recently used bullets. Because the bullets displayed depend on previous usage at the computer at which you are seated, your screen may vary somewhat from Figure 2.46.

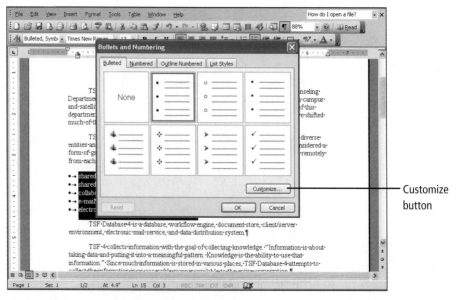

Customize button

**Figure 2.46**

**3** In the **Bullets and Numbering** dialog box, in the lower right corner click the **Customize** button.

The Customize Bulleted List dialog box displays, showing the options that are available for customizing a bullet character. See Figure 2.47.

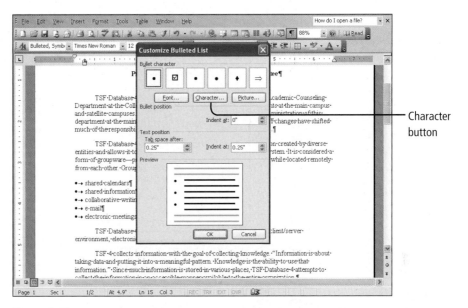

Character button

**Figure 2.47**

**4** Under **Bullet character**, click the **Character** command button.

A table of characters displays in the Symbol dialog box. The character that is currently used for your list is highlighted. The font name of the current bullet symbol also displays. See Figure 2.48.

Font name of the current bullet symbol

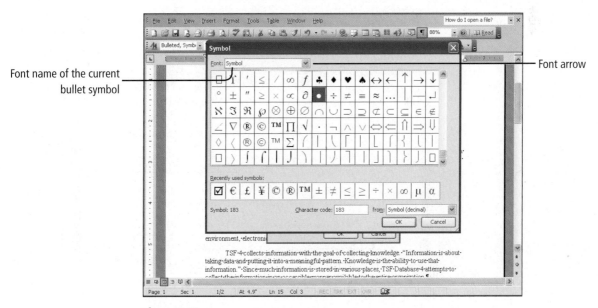

Font arrow

**Figure 2.48**

**5** At the top of the dialog box, click the **Font arrow** at the right of the font box, scroll as necessary, and then click **Wingdings**.

**6** Use the scroll bar on the right of the dialog box to scroll down the list of Wingding characters until you reach the end. Click the check mark in the last row as shown in Figure 2.49.

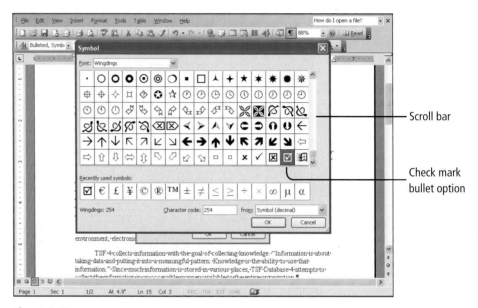

Scroll bar

Check mark
bullet option

**Figure 2.49**

**7** Click **OK** to close the **Symbol** dialog box. Click **OK** again to close the **Customize Bulleted List** dialog box.

**8** Click anywhere in the document to deselect the list.

The bullet character is changed to check marks in boxes, as shown in Figure 2.50.

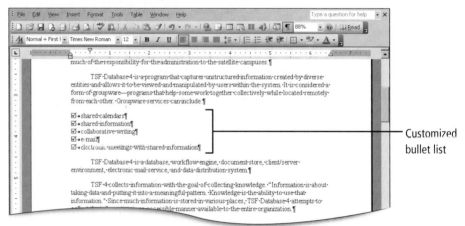

Customized
bullet list

**Figure 2.50**

**9** On the Standard toolbar, click the **Save** button 🖫.

## Objective 4
## Work with Headers and Footers

Text or graphics that you insert into a header or a footer display on every page of a document. On the first page of a document, it is common practice to suppress (hide) the header or footer, and Word provides an easy way to accomplish this. Within a header or footer, you can add automatic page numbers, dates, times, the file name, and pictures.

### Activity 2.17 Inserting and Formatting Page Numbers

**1** Position the insertion point at the top of the document. On the **View** menu, click **Header and Footer**.

The Header area displays.

**2** On the Formatting toolbar, click the **Align Right** button.

The insertion point moves to the right edge of the header box.

**3** On the Header and Footer toolbar, click the **Insert Page Number** button.

The page number, *1*, is inserted as shown in Figure 2.51.

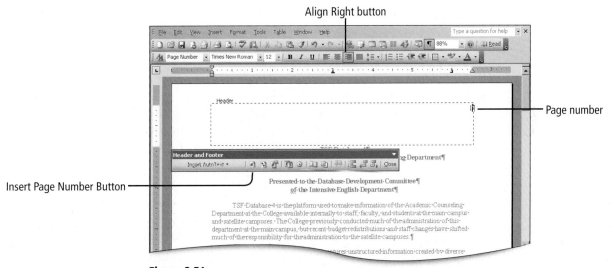

Align Right button

Page number

Insert Page Number Button

**Figure 2.51**

**4** On the Header and Footer toolbar, click the **Page Setup** button.

The Page Setup dialog box displays.

**5** On the **Page Setup** dialog box, click the **Layout tab**. Under **Headers and footers**, select (click to place a check mark in) the **Different first page** check box as shown in Figure 2.52.

The Different first page option enables you to remove the header or footer information from the first page.

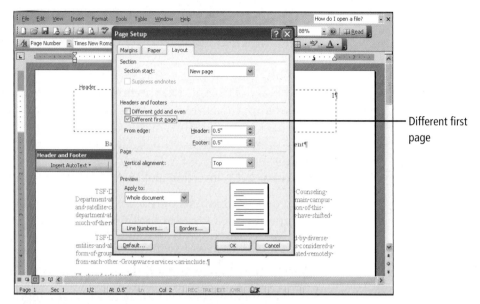

Different first page

**Figure 2.52**

**6** In the lower right corner of the dialog box, click **OK**.

The page number is removed from the header box and the name of the box changes to First Page Header.

**7** Use the vertical scroll bar to scroll down and bring the top of page 2 into view.

The page number is displayed on the second page, and will be displayed on every page thereafter. This is an easy way to suppress the header on page 1. Notice that the name of the footer box at the end of page 1 has been changed to First Page Footer. This reflects the change you made to create a header and footer on the first page of your document that is different from those on the remaining pages. See Figure 2.53.

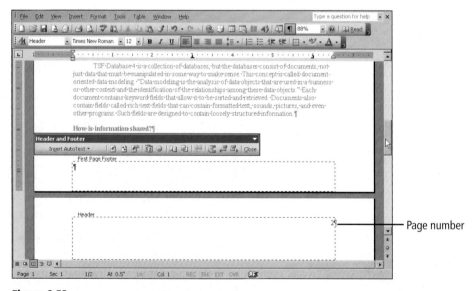

Page number

**Figure 2.53**

## Activity 2.18 Inserting AutoText

**1** On the Header and Footer toolbar, click the **Switch Between Header and Footer** button ⊞.

The insertion point is placed at the left edge of the First Page Footer box.

**2** On the Header and Footer toolbar, click the **Insert AutoText** button [Insert AutoText ▾]. Take a moment to look at the items that can be inserted in the header or footer. See Figure 2.54.

Inserts file name —

Switch Between Header and Footer button

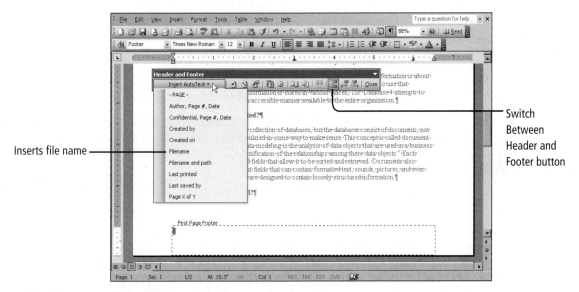

**Figure 2.54**

**3** Click **Filename**.

The file name displays in the First Page Footer. The file extension *.doc* may or may not display, depending on your Word settings. See Figure 2.55.

File name —

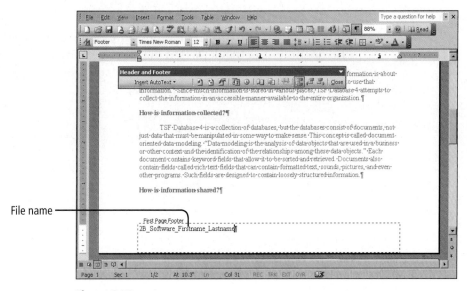

**Figure 2.55**

### Activity 2.19 Inserting the Current Date and Time

**1** Press Tab twice.

The insertion point moves to the right side of the footer box. Notice the location of the tab stop in the ruler bar.

**2** On the Header and Footer toolbar, click the **Insert Date** button, and then type a comma and press the Spacebar once.

The current date displays.

**3** On the Header and Footer toolbar, click the **Insert Time** button.

The current time displays. Your date and time will differ from the ones shown in Figure 2.56.

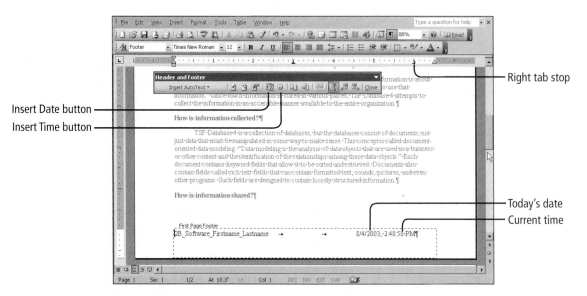

**Figure 2.56**

**4** On the Header and Footer toolbar, click the **Close** button.

**5** Scroll down as necessary to view the bottom of the first page and the top of the second page.

Notice that the text in the header and footer is gray, while the text in the document is black. When you are working in the header and footer, the header and footer text is black (active) and the document text is gray (inactive). See Figure 2.57.

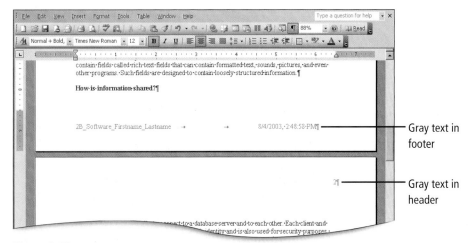

Figure 2.57

**Gray text in footer**

**Gray text in header**

6 On the Standard toolbar, click the **Save** button [img].

## Objective 5
## Insert Frequently Used Text

***AutoCorrect*** corrects common spelling errors as you type. When you type a word incorrectly, for example *teh*, Word automatically changes it to *the*.

If there are words that you frequently misspell, you can add them to the AutoCorrect list. Another feature, AutoText, lets you create shortcuts to quickly insert long phrases that are used regularly, such as a business name or your address, in a manner similar to AutoComplete.

Another type of frequently used text includes various symbols, such as the trademark symbol (™) or copyright symbol ©. These are accessed from the Insert Symbol dialog box.

### Activity 2.20 Recording AutoCorrect Entries

You probably have words that you frequently misspell. You can add these to the AutoCorrect list for automatic correction.

1 On the **Tools** menu, click **AutoCorrect Options**.

The AutoCorrect dialog box displays as shown in Figure 2.58. All of the check boxes on the left of the dialog box are selected by default. Yours may be different.

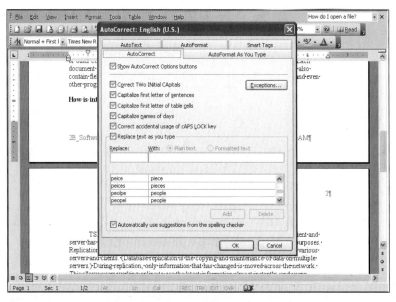

**Figure 2.58**

**2** Under **Replace**, type **peepel**

**3** Under **With**, type **people**

Your dialog box should be similar to Figure 2.59. If someone has already added this AutoCorrect entry, the Add button will change to a Replace button.

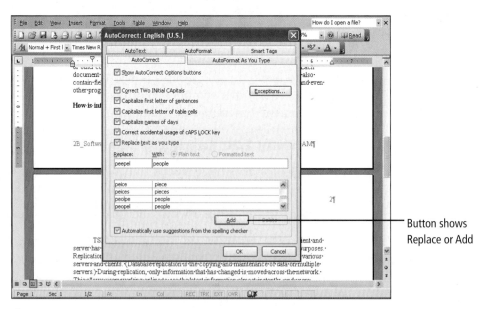

Button shows Replace or Add

**Figure 2.59**

**4** Click **Add**. If the entry already exists, click **Replace** instead, and then click **Yes**.

The new entry is added to the AutoCorrect list. See Figure 2.60.

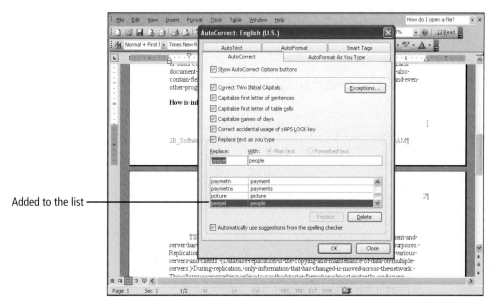

Added to the list ——

Figure 2.60

**5** Click **OK**.

The dialog box closes.

**6** Scroll to the top of page 1 and locate the paragraph that begins *TSF Database 4 is a program*, and then locate and double-click to select the word *some* in the third line.

**7** Watch the screen, type **peepel** and then press ⟨Spacebar⟩. If necessary, press ⟨←Bksp⟩ to get rid of the extra space between words.

Notice that the misspelled word is automatically corrected.

**8** Move the mouse pointer over the corrected word.

A blue line displays under the word. See Figure 2.61.

Corrected word ——

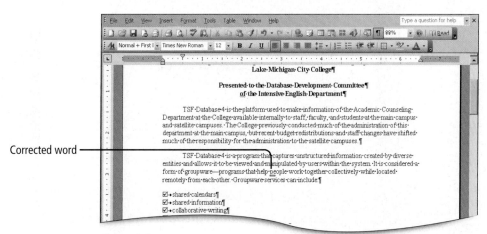

Figure 2.61

**9** Move the pointer over the blue line until the **AutoCorrect Options** smart tag button displays, and then click the button.

The AutoCorrect options menu displays. Notice that you have several commands available. The Control AutoCorrect Options selection will display the AutoCorrect dialog box.

**10** Click anywhere in the document to close the **AutoCorrect Options** menu without selecting a command.

> # More Knowledge — Other Uses of AutoCorrect
>
> AutoCorrect can also be used to
>
> • Correct two initial capital letters
>
> • Capitalize the first letter of sentences
>
> • Capitalize the first letter of table cells
>
> • Capitalize the names of days of the week
>
> • Turn off the Caps Lock key
>
> • Create exceptions to automatic corrections
>
> • Add your own AutoCorrect entries to the AutoCorrect list

### Activity 2.21 Using AutoCorrect Shortcuts

The AutoCorrect replacement is most commonly used to correct spelling errors, but it can also be used to insert symbols or to expand shortcut text into longer words or phrases.

**1** Scroll to the top of the document. In the fifth line of the title, select the words *Intensive English Department*.

Make sure you do not select the paragraph mark at the end of the title. See Figure 2.62.

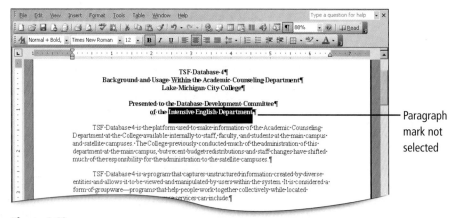

Paragraph mark not selected

**Figure 2.62**

**2** On the **Tools** menu, click **AutoCorrect Options**.

The AutoCorrect dialog box displays. Notice that the selected text displays in the With box. See Figure 2.63.

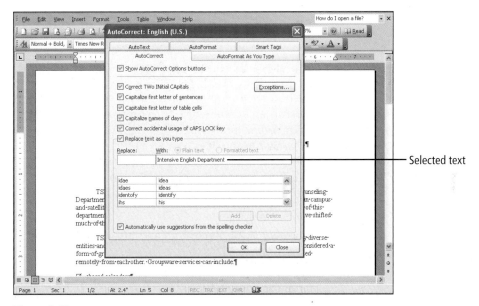

Selected text

**Figure 2.63**

**3** Under **Replace**, type **ied**, and then click **Add**. If this entry already exists, click the **Replace** button, and then click **Yes.**

The new shortcut is added to the list.

**4** Click **OK** to close the **AutoCorrect** dialog box, and then press [Ctrl] + [End] to move to the end of the document.

**5** Locate the *Training Schedule:* subheading and at the end of the sentence just above this subheading select the word *department* and the period at the end of the sentence.

**6** Type **ied.**

When you type the period, the AutoCorrect feature replaces the shortcut text with the text you defined. In order to activate the replace feature, you need to follow the shortcut with a space, a paragraph mark, or a punctuation mark. See Figure 2.64.

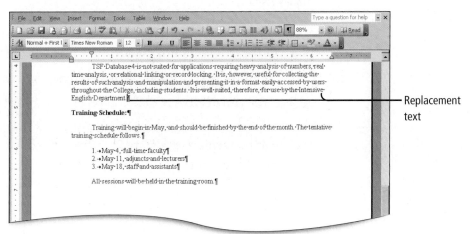

Replacement text

**Figure 2.64**

**7** On the Standard toolbar, click the **Save** button 🖫.

## More Knowledge — Creating AutoCorrect Shortcuts

When setting up an AutoCorrect shortcut, it is best not to use shortcut text that is an actual word or a commonly used abbreviation. Even though you can reverse an AutoCorrect replacement by using the AutoCorrect Options shortcut menu, it is best to avoid the problem by adding a letter to the shortcut text. For example, if you type both *LMCC* and *Lake Michigan City College* frequently, you might want to add *lmccx* (or just *lmx*) as an AutoCorrect shortcut for the text *Lake Michigan City College*.

### Activity 2.22 Recording and Inserting AutoText

AutoText stores, with a unique name, text and graphics that you use frequently. For example, at Lake Michigan City College, individuals in the counseling department frequently type *Academic Counseling Department*.

**1** Scroll to the top of the document. From the second title line, select *Academic Counseling Department*, but do not include the paragraph mark. See Figure 2.65.

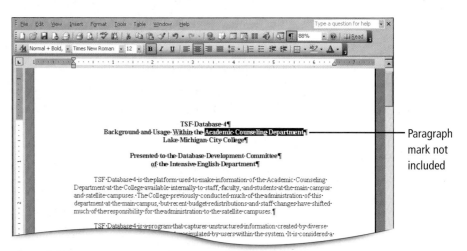

Paragraph mark not included

**Figure 2.65**

**2** On the **Tools** menu, click **AutoCorrect Options**.

The AutoCorrect dialog box displays.

**3** In the **AutoCorrect** dialog box, click the **AutoText tab**.

Notice that the selected text displays in the *Enter AutoText entries here* box. You can also type entries directly into this box. See Figure 2.66.

AutoText tab ——

Selected text ——

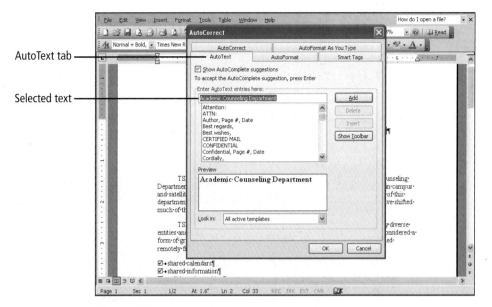

**Figure 2.66**

**4** Click **Add**.

The phrase is added to the AutoText entries, and the AutoCorrect dialog box closes. If the entry has already been created on this computer, click Yes to redefine the entry.

**5** Click outside the selected text to deselect it. On the **Edit** menu, click **Find**.

The Find and Replace dialog box displays. Using Find and Replace is not necessary to use AutoComplete—it just makes finding the text easier.

**6** In the **Find what** box, type **acd** and then click **Find Next**.

The next (and only) instance of ACD is found in the third subheading. See Figure 2.67.

Found text ——

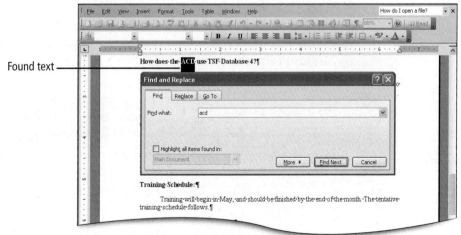

**Figure 2.67**

**7** Click **Cancel** to close the Find and Replace dialog box.

ACD remains selected.

**8** Type **acad** and look at the screen.

A ScreenTip displays the AutoCorrect entry that you just created. See Figure 2.68.

ScreenTip

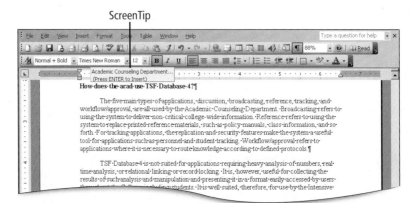

**Figure 2.68**

**9** Press `Enter`.

ACD is replaced with the AutoText entry Academic Counseling Department. Notice that the text is bold, as it was in the document title. The character formatting of an AutoText entry is the same as its source text.

**10** On the Standard toolbar, click the **Save** button ![save].

### Activity 2.23 Inserting Symbols

There are many symbols that are used occasionally, but not often enough to put on a standard keyboard. These symbols can be found and inserted from the Insert menu.

**1** Scroll to view the middle of the second page, and locate the paragraph following the subheading *How does the Academic Counseling Department use TSF Database 4?*

**2** After *The five main types of applications*, select the comma and space as shown in Figure 2.69.

Comma and space selected —

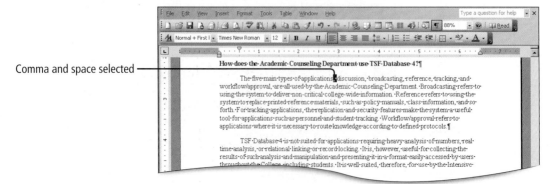

**Figure 2.69**

**3** On the **Insert** menu, click **Symbol**.

The Symbol dialog box displays. This is the same dialog box you used when you formatted bullets.

**4** Click the **Special Characters tab**.

A list of commonly used symbols displays. The keyboard shortcuts for inserting these commonly used symbols display to the right of the character name, as shown in Figure 2.70.

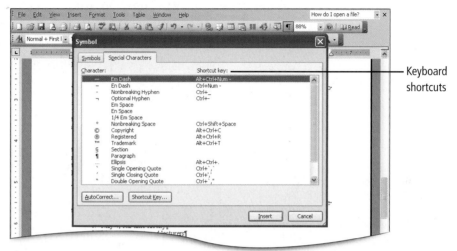

Keyboard shortcuts

**Figure 2.70**

**5** Be sure the *Em dash* is selected. In the lower right corner of the dialog box, click **Insert**, and then click **Close**.

An em dash replaces the selected text. An ***em dash*** is the word processing name for a long dash in a sentence. An em dash in a sentence marks a break in thought, similar to a comma but stronger.

**6** Select the em dash. On the Standard toolbar, click **Copy**.

**7** Near the end of the same sentence, in the second line, select the comma and space after *workflow/approval*. Click **Paste**.

A second em dash is inserted in the sentence. Because you used a paste operation to insert the em dash, the Paste Options smart tag also displays. See Figure 2.71.

Em dash

Copied em dash

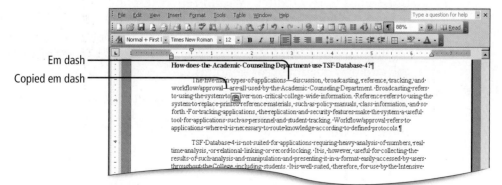

**Figure 2.71**

**8** Navigate to the top of the document by pressing Ctrl + Home. Position the insertion point at the end of the first title line. Type **(tm)**

Although this symbol, which indicates a trademark, is available from the Symbol dialog box, it is also included in Word's AutoCorrect list. The parentheses are necessary for AutoComplete to insert a trademark symbol.

**9** On the **Tools** menu, click **AutoCorrect Options** and then click the **AutoCorrect tab**.

Symbols that can be inserted automatically with AutoCorrect display at the top of the Replace With area. See Figure 2.72.

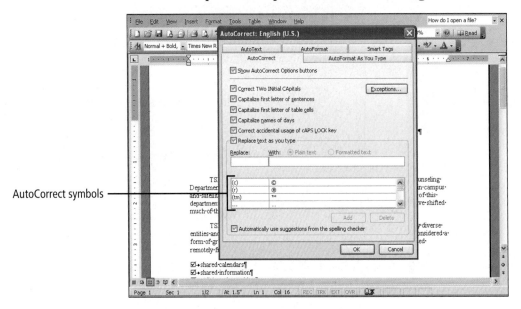

AutoCorrect symbols

**Figure 2.72**

**10** Scroll the list to view additional symbol shortcuts. When you are finished, click **OK** to close the dialog box. On the Standard toolbar, click the **Save** button ⊟.

## Objective 6
### Insert References

Reports frequently include information taken from other sources, and these need to be credited. Within report text, numbers mark the location of information that has been taken from another source, called ***references***. The numbers refer to ***footnotes*** (references placed at the bottom of the page containing the reference), or ***endnotes*** (references placed at the end of a document or chapter).

When footnotes or endnotes are included in a report, a page listing the references is also usually included. Such a list is usually titled *Bibliography, Works Cited, Sources* or *References*.

### Activity 2.24 Inserting Footnotes

Footnotes can be added when you type the document or after the document is complete. They do not need to be entered in order, and if one is removed, the rest are renumbered.

**1** In the lower half of page 1, in the paragraph that begins *TSF 4 collects information*, locate the quotation mark in the third line of text. Click to right of the quotation mark.

Direct quotes always need to be referenced.

**2** On the **Insert** menu, point to **Reference** and then click **Footnote**.

The Footnote and Endnote dialog box displays.

**3** Under **Location**, be sure the **Footnotes** option button is selected and that **Bottom of page** is selected. Under **Format**, be sure **Start at** is at **1**, and **Numbering** is **Continuous**.

**4** If necessary, under **Format** click the **Number format** arrow and, from the displayed list, click **1**, **2**, **3**.

The number format is selected.

Under Apply changes, *Apply changes to* the *Whole document* is selected by default. Compare your Footnote and Endnote dialog box to Figure 2.73.

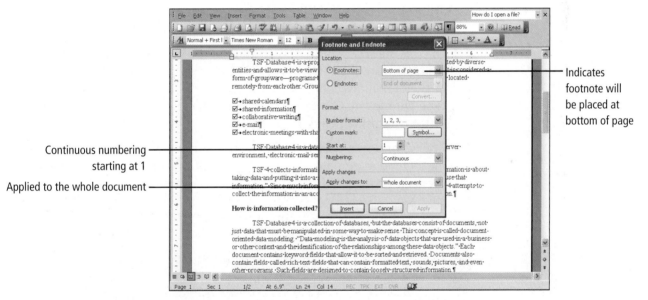

Continuous numbering
starting at 1

Applied to the whole document

Indicates
footnote will
be placed at
bottom of page

**Figure 2.73**

**5** Click **Insert**.

A footnote area is created at the bottom of the page, and a footnote number is added to the text at the insertion point location. Footnote 1 is placed at the top of the footnote area, and the insertion point is moved to the right of the number. You do not need to type a footnote number.

**6** Type **Blue, A. (1998). Davis drives home the importance of being knowledge based. Information Outlook, 2(5): 39.**

Footnote 1 is placed at the bottom of the page. See Figure 2.74.

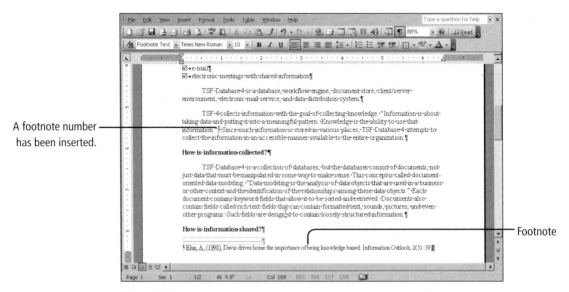

A footnote number has been inserted.

Footnote

**Figure 2.74**

**7** Scroll as necessary to position the top of page 2 in view. In the paragraph that begins *TSF Database 4 clients connect*, in the fifth line, locate servers.) and click to the right of the parenthesis.

**8** On the **Insert** menu, point to **Reference** and then click **Footnote**. Using the settings from your previous footnote, move to the bottom of the dialog box, click **Insert** and then in the inserted footnote box type **Thompson, Charles, "Database Replication," DBMS Magazine <http://dbmsmag.com/9705d15.html>**

The second footnote is placed at the bottom of the second page. The footnote feature places the footnote text on the same page as the referenced text and adjusts pages as necessary. The AutoCorrect feature may also replace straight quotes with curly quotes, depending on the settings on your computer. See Figure 2.75.

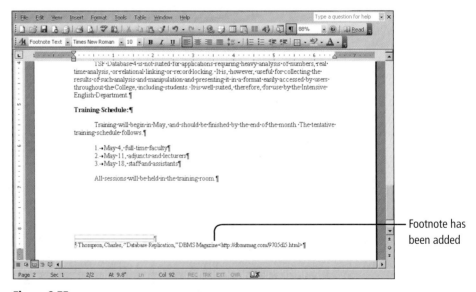

Footnote has been added

**Figure 2.75**

**Alert!**

### If the Web Address Changes to a Hyperlink

If you press the spacebar after you type the Web address in the footnote, the Web address text may be displayed in blue with an underline. This is the common format used to display a *hyperlink*—which is a link that can be used to open the Web page on the Internet that is related to this address. If this happens, click the Undo button once to reverse the formatting.

**9** In the lower half of page 1, in the paragraph that begins *TSF Database 4 is a collection of*, locate the closing quotation mark near the end of the fourth line and position the insertion point to the right of the quotation mark.

**10** On the **Insert** menu, point to **Reference**, and then click **Footnote**. Click **Insert**, and then type:
**Database.com search <http://searchdatabase.techtarget.com>**

This new footnote number is 2, and the footnote on page 2 becomes footnote 3. In this manner, Word makes it easy to insert footnotes in any order within your report, because it automatically renumbers and adjusts page endings. Compare your screen to Figure 2.76.

New footnote on page 1 —

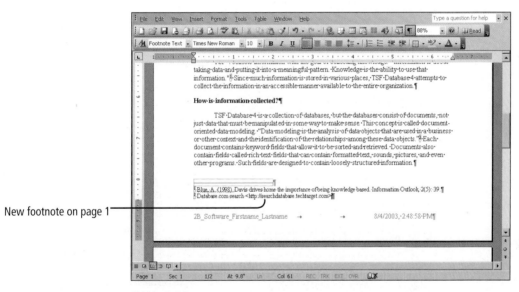

**Figure 2.76**

**11** Click to see if the *How is information shared?* subheading is at the bottom of the page. If so, position the insertion point to the left of the subheading, hold down Ctrl and press Enter.

A manual page break is inserted, the subheading is moved to the second page, but the footnotes remain on the proper page. See Figure 2.77.

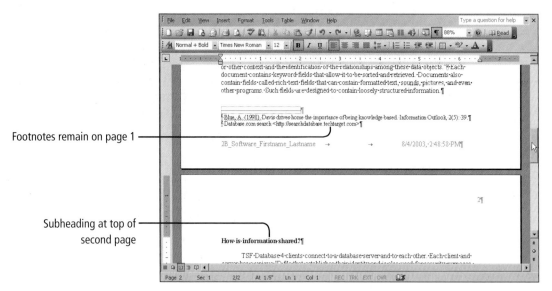

**Footnotes remain on page 1**

**Subheading at top of second page**

**Figure 2.77**

[12] On the Standard toolbar, click the **Save** button 🖫.

### Activity 2.25 Formatting Footnotes

Some parts of footnotes require special formatting. Magazine and book titles, for example, need to be italicized.

[1] At the end of the first page, in the first footnote, locate and select the magazine title, *Information Outlook*.

[2] Click the **Italic** button 🇮.

The magazine title is italicized as shown in Figure 2.78.

Italic button

**Figure 2.78**

[3] Scroll to the bottom of the document, locate and select the magazine title, *DBMS Magazine*.

[4] Click the **Italic** button 🇮.

The magazine title is italicized.

[5] On the Standard toolbar, click the **Save** button 🖫.

### Activity 2.26 Creating a Reference Page

In a long document, there will be many books, articles, and Web sites that have been referenced on the various pages. Some of them may be noted many times, others only once. It is common to include, at the end of a report, a single list of each source referenced. This list is commonly titled *References*, *Bibliography*, *Sources* or *Works Cited*.

**1** Press [Ctrl] + [End] to navigate to the end of the document.

**2** Hold down [Ctrl] and press [Enter].

A manual page break is inserted, and a new page is created.

**3** Press [CapsLock], type **BIBLIOGRAPHY** and press [Enter]. Turn off CapsLock. See Figure 2.79.

The paragraphs are double spaced and indented because the paragraph mark for the last paragraph of the document contains those instructions. Notice the indents in the ruler.

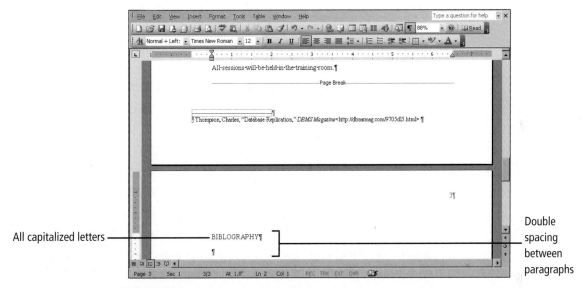

All capitalized letters ⎯ BIBLIOGRAPHY¶

Double spacing between paragraphs

**Figure 2.79**

**4** Type **Blue, A. (1998). Davis drives home the importance of being knowledge based. Information Outlook, 2(5): 39.** Press [Enter].

**5** Type **Thompson, Charles, "Database Replication," DBMS Magazine http://dbmsmag.com/9705d15.html** and then press [Enter].

When you type the Internet address, it may change to blue. This means that you have created a live Internet link. If this happens, move the pointer over the link, point to the small blue box under the first letter in the Internet address to display a white arrow, click the displayed AutoCorrect Options smart tag, and from the displayed menu, click Undo Hyperlink.

**6** Type **Database.com search <http://searchdatabase.techtarget.com>** and press [Enter]. If necessary, undo the hyperlink in the same manner as the previous step.

Compare your screen to Figure 2.80.

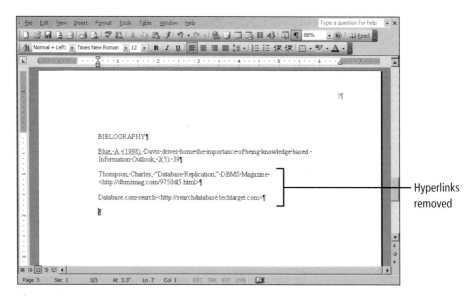

Hyperlinks removed

**Figure 2.80**

**7** On the Standard toolbar, click the **Save** button ![save icon].

### Activity 2.27 Formatting a Reference Page

Bibliographies have special formatting requirements. The title should be centered, the entries should be in alphabetical order, and the subsequent lines of an entry should be indented 0.5 inch to the right of the first line of the entry.

**1** Click anywhere in the title *BIBLIOGRAPHY*.

**2** On the Formatting toolbar, click the **Center** button ![center icon].

   The title is centered, but the centering is between the first line indent of 0.5" (instead of the left margin) and the right margin.

**3** On the **Format** menu, click **Paragraph**. On the **Indents and Spacing tab**, under **Indentation**, change the **Left** indent to 0. In the lower right corner of the dialog box, click **OK**.

**4** Select all three bibliographic entries. On the **Format** menu, click **Paragraph**.

**5** In the displayed **Paragraph** dialog box, under **Indentation**, change the **Left** indent to 0. Click the **Special arrow**, and from the displayed list, click **Hanging**. See Figure 2.81.

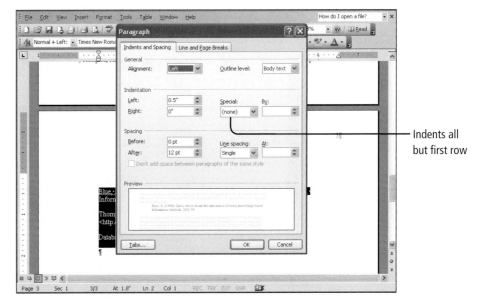

Indents all
but first row

**Figure 2.81**

6 Click **OK** to close the dialog box.

This paragraph style is called a ***hanging indent***, where the first line extends to the left of the rest of the lines in the same paragraph. Notice the indent markers on the toolbar. See Figure 2.82.

First Line Indent marker
Hanging Indent marker

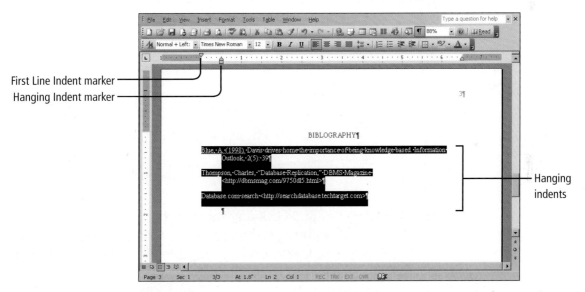

Hanging
indents

**Figure 2.82**

7 Be sure the three entries are still selected. From the **Table** menu, click **Sort**.

The Sort Text dialog box displays as shown in Figure 2.83.

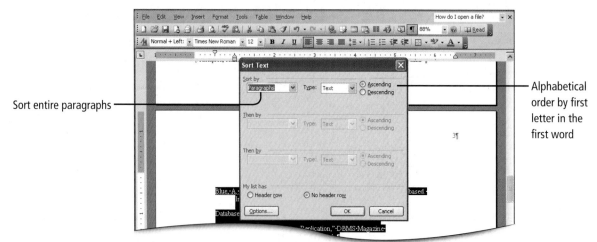

Sort entire paragraphs

Alphabetical order by first letter in the first word

**Figure 2.83**

**8** Accept the default sort options, which sort by paragraph in ascending (A-to-Z) order and click **OK**.

The paragraphs are sorted alphabetically.

**9** Click anywhere in the document to deselect the text.

Compare your Bibliography page with Figure 2.84.

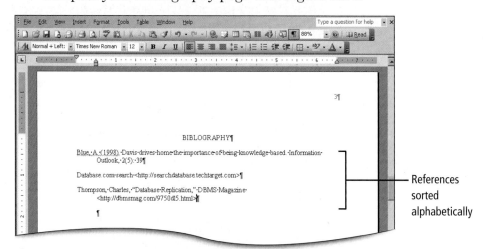

References sorted alphabetically

**Figure 2.84**

**10** Move to page 2 and click anywhere in the text. From the **View menu**, display the **Header** and Footer toolbar, switch to the footer and on the Header and Footer toolbar, click **Insert AutoText**, and then click **Filename**. Close the **Header** and Footer toolbar.

This is necessary because the Different First Page option was selected, and the footer you added earlier displays only on page 1. Adding the filename to the footer of page 2 displays the footer in the rest of the document.

**11** On the Standard toolbar, click the **Save** button 🔲 and then click the **Print Preview** button 🔍 to preview the document. Close the Print Preview window. Make any necessary changes, and then click the **Print** button 🖨. Close the document and save any changes.

**End** You have completed Project 2B

# Summary

In this chapter you practiced how to change the format of pages by setting the margins and how to change the format of paragraphs by changing indents, line spacing, and the spacing after paragraphs. You practiced applying the format from one paragraph to others using the Format Painter. Another paragraph formatting technique you used was creating bulleted and numbered lists and modifying the bullets from the Bullets and Numbering dialog box.

One of the most important features of word processing was presented in this chapter—moving and copying text. Both cut-and-paste and drag-and-drop techniques were demonstrated for moving text. You also practiced how to copy text and place it in a new location. You used the Find and Replace dialog box to locate text that you want to modify, and you practiced how to use the AutoCorrect, AutoText, AutoComplete, and Insert Symbols features.

In the header and footer areas, you accessed commands from the toolbar to add consecutive page numbers, the current date, the time, and the filename. Finally, you practiced how to add footnotes to a document, create a reference page with hanging indent paragraph format, and sort references in alphabetical order.

## In This Chapter You Practiced How To

• Change Document and Paragraph Layout

• Change and Reorganize Text

• Create and Modify Lists

• Work with Headers and Footers

• Insert Frequently Used Text

• Insert References

# Concepts Assessments

**Matching** Match each term in the second column with its correct definition in the first column by writing the letter of the term on the blank line in front of the correct definition.

_____ 1. Text that is aligned on both the left and right margins.

_____ 2. A temporary storage location that is used for text that is cut or copied.

_____ 3. The button that is used to reverse a previous action.

_____ 4. A small symbol that is used to begin each line of information in a list.

_____ 5. A reference that is placed at the bottom of a page.

_____ 6. The alignment of text in the middle of the document between the left and right margin.

_____ 7. The Word feature that is primarily responsible for correcting commonly misspelled words.

_____ 8. A paragraph style that positions the first line of text to the left of the rest of the paragraph.

_____ 9. In most documents, paragraphs are aligned on this side of the page.

_____ 10. The action that leaves text in its original location but also makes it available to place in a new location.

_____ 11. The name of a dialog box that you can use to locate specific text.

_____ 12. The command activated by the keyboard shortcut [Ctrl] + [X].

_____ 13. The command activated by the keyboard shortcut [Ctrl] + [V].

_____ 14. The area at the bottom of a page that shows the same information, or same type of information on every page of a document, with the possible exception of the first page.

_____ 15. The type of menu that displays by right-clicking on selected areas of a document.

**A** AutoCorrect

**B** Bullet

**C** Centered

**D** Copy

**E** Cut

**F** Find and Replace

**G** Footer

**H** Footnote

**I** Hanging indent

**J** Justified

**K** Left

**L** Office Clipboard

**M** Paste

**N** Shortcut menu

**O** Undo

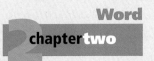

## Fill in the Blank  Write the correct answer in the space provided.

1. The width between the text and the edge of the paper is known as the _____.

2. The placement of text relative to the left and right side of a paragraph is known as _____.

3. When you drag-and-drop text, it is _____ from one place to another.

4. When you paste text, the text is taken from the _____ and placed where the insertion point is positioned.

5. The keyboard shortcut used to copy text is
Ctrl + _____.

6. If you need to create a list of items that is sequential, you should use a(n) _____ list.

7. When you click the Redo button, it reverses the action of the _____ _____.

8. If you want to create a shortcut that will automatically finish a frequently used phrase or name, use the _____ feature.

9. If you need to add a ™ ® or © to a document, display the _____ dialog box from the Insert menu.

10. A reference placed at the end of a document or a chapter is known as a(n) _____.

## Project 2C—Computer Lab

**Objectives:** *Change Document and Paragraph Layout, Change and Reorganize Text, Create and Modify Lists, Work with Headers and Footers, Insert Frequently Used Text, and Insert References.*

In the following Skill Assessment, you will format and modify a document regarding the Computer Lab policies at Lake Michigan City College. Your completed document will look similar to the one shown in Figure 2.85. You will save your document as *2C_Computer_Lab_Firstname_Lastname*.

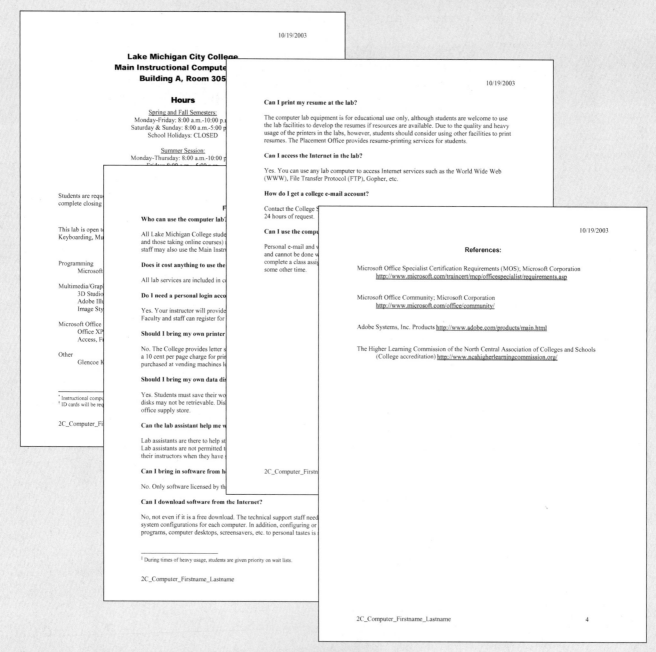

**Figure 2.85**

**(Project 2C–Computer Lab continues on the next page)**

**(Project 2C–Computer Lab continued)**

1. Start Word. On the Standard toolbar, click the **Open** button. Navigate to the location where the student files for this textbook are stored. Locate and open **w02C_Computer_Lab**. Be sure that non-printing characters are displayed. This is a three-page document; take a moment to scroll through the document to familiarize yourself with the overall content and layout.

2. Display the **File** menu and then click **Save As**. Navigate to the location where you are saving your projects for this chapter. In the **File name** box, type **2C_Computer_Lab_Firstname_Lastname** and then in the lower portion of the **Save As** dialog box, click the **Save** button.

3. Select the first four lines of text in the document, which comprise the document's title, two subtitles, and *Hours*. On the Formatting toolbar, click the **Center** button. With the four lines still selected, click the **Font button arrow**, click **Arial Black**, click the **Font Size button arrow**, and then click **14**. The title is centered and looks more distinctive.

4. Click anywhere to deselect. Select the title line and the first subtitle line—the first two lines of the document. Click the **Line Spacing button arrow** and, from the displayed list, click **1.0**. The line spacing for the first two lines of the document is changed, but the third line remains double-spaced so that it creates a space after effect.

5. Select the four lines of text that begin *Spring and Fall Semesters*. On the Formatting toolbar, click the **Center** button. Select the five lines of text that begin *Summer Session*, and click the **Center** button again. On the Standard toolbar, click **Save**.

6. Scroll to view the bottom of page 1, and click to position the insertion point at the beginning of the heading *Frequently Asked Questions*. Because it is not good document design to strand a subheading at the bottom of the page without any of its following information, press Ctrl + Enter to insert a hard page break if necessary and move this subheading to the next page.

7. Scroll to view the bottom of page 3, click to the left of the *References:* heading, and then press Ctrl + Enter to insert a page break and move the References portion to a separate page. This becomes page 4. Click the **Save** button.

**(Project 2C–Computer Lab continues on the next page)**

**(Project 2C–Computer Lab continued)**

8. Hold down Ctrl and press Home to move the insertion point to the top of the document. Click to place the insertion point at the end of *Main Instructional Computer Lab*. Display the **Insert** menu, point to **Reference**, and then click **Footnote**. In the **Footnote and Endnote** dialog box, under **Location**, be sure the **Footnotes** option button is selected and **Bottom of page** is displayed in the Footnotes box. Under **Format**, click the **Number format arrow**, and then click the sixth item in list, which is a group of symbols beginning with an *. These are appropriate to use when you are not making a specific reference to a document, but are noting additional information. In the lower left of the **Footnote and Endnote** dialog box, click **Insert**.

9. The insertion point is moved to the new footnote created at the bottom of page 1. Type the following note: **Instructional computer labs are also located at satellite campuses. See catalog or call campus for details.** Recall that you do not have to type the footnote symbol— Word places the symbol in the correct location for you.

10. Scroll to view the middle of page 1, and in the paragraph under the subheading *Courses Supported*, click to the right of the word *enrolled*. Display the **Insert** menu, point to **Reference**, and then click **Footnote**. In the displayed dialog box, in the lower left corner, click the **Insert** button to accept the settings. A new footnote is inserted, and the insertion point moves to the bottom of page 1. Type **ID cards will be required for entrance to lab.**

11. Navigate to the top of page 2. In the paragraph beginning *All Lake Michigan College students*, in the third line, click to place the insertion point to the right of the period following *Main Instructional Computer Lab*. Display the **Footnote and Endnote** dialog box, click the **Insert** button, and then type the following: **During times of heavy usage, students are given priority on wait lists.** This footnote, the third one you have added to the document, is placed at the bottom of page 2.

12. Navigate to page 4—the References page. Select the two lines beginning *Microsoft Office Specialist*. Hold down Ctrl and select the two lines beginning *Microsoft Office Community*. Continue to hold down Ctrl and select the text lines that form the remaining two references. All four references are selected, but the blank lines between them are not selected. From the **Format** menu, click **Paragraph**, and then click the **Indents and Spacing tab**. Under **Indentation**, click the **Special arrow** and then click **Hanging**. Under **Spacing**, in the **After** box, click the up arrow in the spin box to change the spacing after the paragraph to 12 pt. Click **OK**. The references are displayed with a hanging line indent and 12 points of space after each paragraph.

**(Project 2C–Computer Lab continues on the next page)**

**(Project 2C–Computer Lab continued)**

**13.** Click anywhere to deselect. On the **View** menu, click **Header and Footer**. With the header area displayed, on the Formatting toolbar, click the **Align Right** button. On the Header and Footer toolbar, click the **Insert Date** button. The current date is placed on the right side of the header.

**14.** On the Header and Footer toolbar, click the **Switch Between Header and Footer** button. In the footer area, on the **Header and Footer** toolbar, click **Insert AutoText**, and then click **Filename**. Press Tab twice to move the insertion point to the right side of the footer. On the Header and Footer toolbar, click the **Insert Page Number** button, and then click the **Close** button.

**15.** On the Standard toolbar, click the **Save** button to save the changes you have made to your document.

**16.** Press Ctrl + Home. On the Standard toolbar, click the **Print Preview** button to make a final check of your document before printing. Use the scroll bar to view each page in the document, and notice how Word formatted and placed your footnotes on pages 1 and 2. On the Print Preview toolbar, click the **Print** button, and then, on the same toolbar, click the **Close** button.

**17.** From the **File** menu, click **Close** to close the document, saving any changes if prompted to do so. Display the **File** menu again and then click **Exit** to close Word. Alternatively, you can close Word by clicking the Close button at the extreme right end of the blue title bar.

**End** You have completed Project 2C

## Project 2D — AFV Proposal

**Objectives:** *Change Document and Paragraph Layout, Create and Modify Lists, Work with Headers and Footers, and Insert Frequently Used Text.*

In the following Skill Assessment, you will format and edit a proposal for an Alternative Fuel Project that is being cosponsored by the college and several energy-related businesses. Your completed document will look similar to Figure 2.86. You will save your document as *2D_AFV_Proposal_Firstname_Lastname.*

**1.** On the Standard toolbar, click the **Open** button. Navigate to the location where the student files for this textbook are stored. Locate and open **w02D_AFV_Proposal**. Be sure that nonprinting characters are displayed. This is a two-page document. Take a moment to scroll through the document to familiarize yourself with the content and layout.

**(Project 2D–AFV Proposal continues on the next page)**

## (Project 2D–AFV Proposal continued)

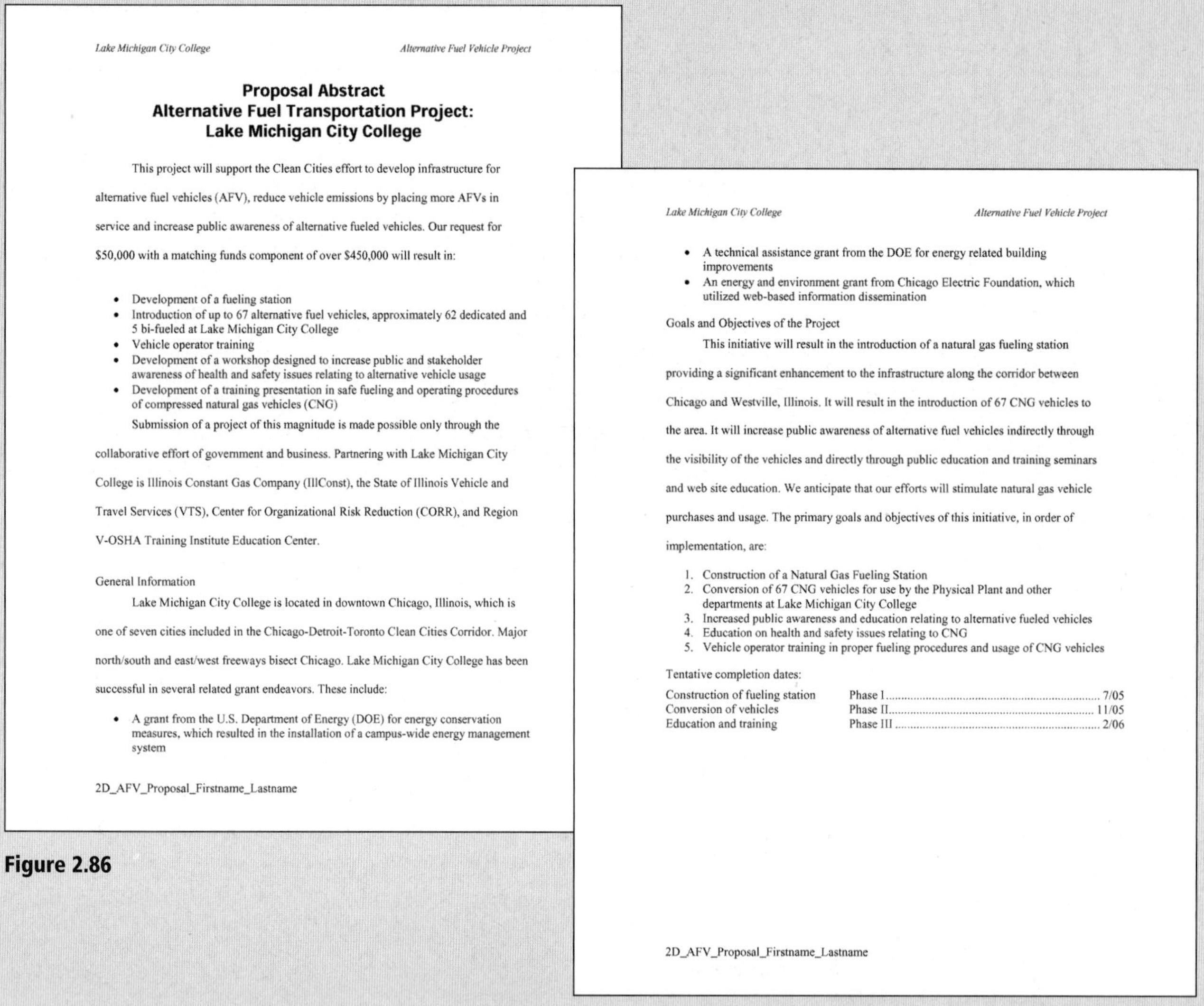

*Lake Michigan City College* *Alternative Fuel Vehicle Project*

**Proposal Abstract**
**Alternative Fuel Transportation Project:**
**Lake Michigan City College**

This project will support the Clean Cities effort to develop infrastructure for alternative fuel vehicles (AFV), reduce vehicle emissions by placing more AFVs in service and increase public awareness of alternative fueled vehicles. Our request for $50,000 with a matching funds component of over $450,000 will result in:

- Development of a fueling station
- Introduction of up to 67 alternative fuel vehicles, approximately 62 dedicated and 5 bi-fueled at Lake Michigan City College
- Vehicle operator training
- Development of a workshop designed to increase public and stakeholder awareness of health and safety issues relating to alternative vehicle usage
- Development of a training presentation in safe fueling and operating procedures of compressed natural gas vehicles (CNG)

Submission of a project of this magnitude is made possible only through the collaborative effort of government and business. Partnering with Lake Michigan City College is Illinois Constant Gas Company (IllConst), the State of Illinois Vehicle and Travel Services (VTS), Center for Organizational Risk Reduction (CORR), and Region V-OSHA Training Institute Education Center.

General Information
Lake Michigan City College is located in downtown Chicago, Illinois, which is one of seven cities included in the Chicago-Detroit-Toronto Clean Cities Corridor. Major north/south and east/west freeways bisect Chicago. Lake Michigan City College has been successful in several related grant endeavors. These include:

- A grant from the U.S. Department of Energy (DOE) for energy conservation measures, which resulted in the installation of a campus-wide energy management system

2D_AFV_Proposal_Firstname_Lastname

*Lake Michigan City College* *Alternative Fuel Vehicle Project*

- A technical assistance grant from the DOE for energy related building improvements
- An energy and environment grant from Chicago Electric Foundation, which utilized web-based information dissemination

Goals and Objectives of the Project
This initiative will result in the introduction of a natural gas fueling station providing a significant enhancement to the infrastructure along the corridor between Chicago and Westville, Illinois. It will result in the introduction of 67 CNG vehicles to the area. It will increase public awareness of alternative fuel vehicles indirectly through the visibility of the vehicles and directly through public education and training seminars and web site education. We anticipate that our efforts will stimulate natural gas vehicle purchases and usage. The primary goals and objectives of this initiative, in order of implementation, are:

1. Construction of a Natural Gas Fueling Station
2. Conversion of 67 CNG vehicles for use by the Physical Plant and other departments at Lake Michigan City College
3. Increased public awareness and education relating to alternative fueled vehicles
4. Education on health and safety issues relating to CNG
5. Vehicle operator training in proper fueling procedures and usage of CNG vehicles

Tentative completion dates:

| | | |
|---|---|---|
| Construction of fueling station | Phase I | 7/05 |
| Conversion of vehicles | Phase II | 11/05 |
| Education and training | Phase III | 2/06 |

2D_AFV_Proposal_Firstname_Lastname

**Figure 2.86**

2. From the **File** menu, click **Save As**. Navigate to the location where you are saving your projects for this chapter. In the **File name** box, type **2D_AFV_Proposal_Firstname_Lastname** and then in the lower portion of the **Save As** dialog box, click the **Save** button.

3. The name of the college needs to be added to the title and in several locations throughout the document. This will be easier if you first create an AutoText entry for Lake Michigan City College. From the **Tools** menu, click **AutoCorrect Options**. In the **AutoCorrect** dialog box, click the **AutoText tab**. In the **Enter AutoText entries here** box type **Lake Michigan City College** and click the **Add** button. (If the Add button is dimmed and *Lake Michigan City College* displays in the list, another student has already added this text to AutoText. Click Cancel and go on to the next step. You will be able to use the existing AutoText entry.) This AutoText is added to the list. In the lower portion of the **AutoText** dialog box, click **OK**.

**(Project 2D–AFV Proposal continues on the next page)**

**(Project 2D**–AFV Proposal continued)

4. On the second line of the document, click to place the insertion point following the colon after *Alternative Fuel Transportation Project:* and then press Enter. On the new line, start typing **Lake Michigan City College** When the AutoText ScreenTip displays, press Enter to finish the text.

5. Select the first three lines in the document and, on the Formatting toolbar, click the **Center** button. Click the **Font button arrow**, click **Tahoma**, click the **Font Size button arrow**, click **16**, and then click the **Bold** button. Click anywhere to deselect the title lines.

6. There are several places in the document where the phrase *the college* needs to be replaced with the phrase *Lake Michigan City College.* From the **Edit** menu, click **Replace**. In the **Find what** box type **the college** In the **Replace with** box type **Lake Michigan City College** In the **Find and Replace** dialog box, click the **Find Next** button. When the first occurrence of *the college* is highlighted, click **Replace**. When the second occurrence of *the college* is highlighted, click **Replace**. When the next occurrence is highlighted, click **Replace All**. When the message box displays that Word has finished searching the document, click **OK**, and then close the **Find and Replace** dialog box. Click the **Save** button.

7. Hold down Ctrl and press Home to move to the top of the document. In the paragraph beginning *This project will*, at the end of the fourth line, click at the end of the paragraph, to the right of *result in:* and then press Enter.

8. Beginning with *Development of a fueling*, select the next five short paragraphs—through *compressed natural gas vehicles (CNG)*. This is a list of results that are expected from the Alternative Fuel Project. With the list selected, on the Formatting toolbar, click the **Bullets** button.

9. The bullet symbol last used on your computer displays. With the list still selected, display the **Format** menu and then click **Bullets and Numbering**. In the first row, click the second box. If the second box is not solid black circles, in the lower left of the dialog box, click Reset and then click **Yes**. The selected box changes to its original setting—a solid black circle. Click **OK**.

10. Scroll as necessary to view the paragraphs below the bulleted list. Locate the subtitle *General Information*. Five lines below that, locate the paragraph that begins *A grant from*. Select the three paragraphs (five lines of text) beginning with *A grant from*. On the Formatting toolbar, click the **Bullets** button. The same bullet symbol that was used previously is applied to the list.

11. Scroll down to view the top portion of page 2. Select the six lines of text beginning with *Construction of a Natural*. On the Formatting toolbar, click the **Numbering** button. The result is five numbered items. Click the **Save** button.

**(Project 2D**–AFV Proposal continues on the next page)

**(Project 2D–AFV Proposal continued)**

**12.** Press Ctrl + Home to move to the top of the document, and then click to place the insertion point anywhere in the paragraph that begins *This project.* From the **Format** menu, click **Paragraph**. In the **Paragraph** dialog box, under **Indentation**, click the **Special arrow**, and then click **First line**. Under **Spacing**, click the **Line spacing arrow**, click **Double**, and then in the **Before** box, click the spin box up arrow once to display **6 pt**. Click **OK**.

**13.** The paragraph format that you just set will be applied to the other main paragraphs in the document. With the insertion point still in the formatted paragraph, on the Formatting toolbar, double-click the **Format Painter** button. Move the mouse pointer into a text portion of your document and verify that it takes on the shape of a paint brush. On this page, use the scroll bar to scroll down slightly below the first bulleted list, locate the paragraph that begins *Submission of a project* and then click in the paragraph. The paragraph format is applied, and the mouse pointer retains the paint brush. (If your mouse pointer no longer displays the paintbrush, double-click the Format Painter button again.)

**14.** Use the scroll arrow to move down slightly to view the paragraph beginning *Lake Michigan City College is located*—click in the paragraph to apply the formatting. Use the scroll bar to move to page 2, locate the paragraph that begins *This initiative will result*, and click in the paragraph. On the Formatting toolbar, click the **Format Painter** button once to turn it off.

**15.** Press Ctrl + Home to move to the top of the document. From the **View** menu, click **Header and Footer**. In the header area, type **Lake Michigan City College** (use AutoText to complete the entry if it displays), press Tab twice, and type **Alternative Fuel Vehicle Project** Select the text in the header and then, on the Formatting toolbar, click the **Italic** button.

**16.** On the Header and Footer toolbar, click the **Switch Between Header and Footer** button. On the Header and Footer toolbar, click the **Insert AutoText** button, point to **Header/Footer**, and then click **Filename** from the list that displays. Close the Header and Footer toolbar.

**17.** Click the **Save** button, then click the **Print Preview** button to see the document as it will print. Click the **Print** button, then close the file saving changes if prompted to do so.

**End** You have completed Project 2D

# Project 2E — Delivery Suggestions

**Objectives:** *Change Document and Paragraph Layout, Change and Reorganize Text, Create and Modify Lists, Work with Headers and Footers, and Insert Frequently Used Text.*

In the following Skill Assessment, you will format and edit a paper that discusses technology needed for delivering online courses at Lake Michigan City College. Your completed document will look similar to Figure 2.87. You will save your document as *2E_Delivery_Suggestions_Firstname_Lastname*.

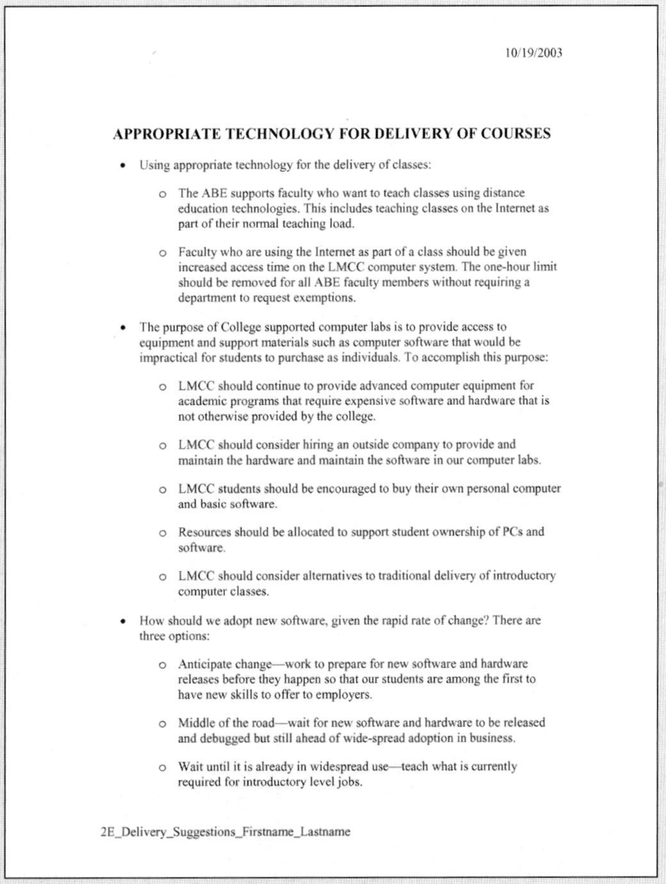

**Figure 2.87**

**(Project 2E–Delivery Suggestions continues on the next page)**

**(Project 2E–Delivery Suggestions continued)**

1. On the Standard toolbar, click the **Open** button. Navigate to the location where the student files for this textbook are stored. Locate and open **w02E_Delivery_Suggestions**. Be sure that nonprinting characters are displayed.

2. From the **File** menu, click **Save As**. Navigate to the location where you are saving your projects for this chapter. In the **File name** box, type **2E_Delivery_Suggestions_Firstname_Lastname** and then in the lower portion of the **Save As** dialog box, click the **Save** button.

3. Select the first line of the document and then, on the Formatting toolbar, click the **Center** button. From the **Format** menu, click **Change Case**. In the **Change Case** dialog box, click the **UPPERCASE** option button and then click **OK**. With the title still selected, on the Formatting toolbar, click the **Font Size button arrow**, click **14**, and then click the **Bold** button.

4. Click anywhere in the line beginning *1. Using*. Click the **Bullets** button. The last bullet symbol used on the computer at which you are seated is applied. Display the **Format** menu, and then click **Bullets and Numbering**. In the **Bullets and Numbering** dialog box, in the first row, click the second box. If the second box is not solid black circles, in the lower left of the dialog box, click Reset, and then click **Yes**. The selected box changes to its original setting—a solid black circle. Click **OK**.

5. On the Formatting toolbar, double-click the **Format Painter** button. When moved into the text area, the mouse pointer takes the shape of a paint brush. Use the scroll bar to scroll down until you see the next numbered paragraph beginning *1. The purpose of College supported* and then click in the numbered paragraph. A bullet replaces the number. Scroll down the document and click once in the next numbered paragraph, which begins *1. How should we*. On the Formatting toolbar, click the **Format Painter** button once to turn it off.

6. Scroll to position the second bulleted item and its following paragraphs into view on your screen. Select the paragraph that begins *Students should be*. On the Standard toolbar, click the **Cut** button. Click to place the insertion point at the beginning of the paragraph that begins *Resources should be allocated*. On the Standard toolbar, click the **Paste** button. The paragraph is moved.

7. Locate the paragraph under the second bulleted item that begins *We should consider hiring an outside company*. Select the word *software*, point to the selected word and drag it to the right of *hardware* and then release the mouse button. In the same sentence, select the second *and*, point to the selected word and drag it to the right of hardware, dropping it between *hardware* and *software*. Click to the left of *software*, and type **maintain the** The sentence should now read *...provide and maintain the hardware and maintain the software in our computer labs*.

**(Project 2E–Delivery Suggestions continues on the next page)**

**(Project 2E–Delivery Suggestions continued)**

8. Press [Ctrl] + [Home] to move to the top of the document. Under the first bulleted item, locate the paragraph that begins *Faculty who are using*. In the second line, select the text *LMCC* and click the **Copy** button.

9. In the second bulleted item, locate the paragraph that begins *The college should*. At the beginning of the paragraph, select the text *The college* and then click the **Paste** button. LMCC replaces the selected text.

10. In the first line of the next paragraph, select *We* and click the **Paste** button. In the next paragraph, select the S in *Students* click the **Paste** button, and then type **s** to provide the lower case letter at the beginning of the word *students*. Finally, select *We* at the beginning of the last paragraph under this bullet point and then click the **Paste** button.

11. Navigate to the top of the document and select the two paragraphs under the first bullet point. From the **Format** menu, click **Bullets and Numbering**. In the displayed dialog box, in the first row, click the third box, which should be a hollow circle. (If this bullet is not a hollow circle, in the lower left of the dialog box, click Reset. In the message box that displays, click Yes to reset the gallery position to the default setting. This resets the selected symbol to the default setting, which for the third box is a hollow circle.) Click **OK**. The selected text is formatted with a hollow circle bullet and is indented to the right under the first bullet.

12. Under the second bulleted item, select the five paragraphs that begin *LMCC should continue to provide*. On the Formatting toolbar, click the **Bullets** button and then click the **Increase Indent** button. When the bulleted text is indented, the bullets change to the hollow circle style.

13. Repeat this process to create the same style of bulleted list for the paragraphs that are listed under *How should we adopt*.

14. In the three bulleted items you just formatted, you will replace a colon (:) with an em dash. Position the bottom of the page into view on your screen. In the first bulleted item that begins *Anticipate*, select the colon and space following the text *Anticipate change*. From the **Insert** menu, click **Symbol**. In the **Symbol** dialog box, click the **Special Characters tab**. Make sure that **Em Dash** is highlighted, and then in the lower portion of the dialog box click **Insert**. The **Symbol** dialog box remains open on your screen.

**(Project 2E**–Delivery Suggestions continues on the next page)**

**(Project 2E–Delivery Suggestions continued)**

15. Point to the title bar of the **Symbol** dialog box, and then drag it to the right of your screen so that you can view the last two bulleted items on the page. Select the colon and space that follows *Middle of the road*, and then in the **Symbol** dialog box, click **Insert**. Moving the dialog box as necessary, repeat this process to replace the colon and space in the final bulleted item, found after *widespread use*. Close the **Symbol** dialog box. Click **Save** to save your changes.

16. From the **View** menu, click **Header and Footer**. In the header area, press  twice. On the Header and Footer toolbar, click the **Insert Date** button.

17. On the Header and Footer toolbar, click the **Switch Between Header and Footer** button. On the Header and Footer toolbar, click the **Insert AutoText** button, and then from the displayed list, click **Filename**. Close the Header and Footer toolbar.

18. From the **File** menu, click **Page Setup**. In the displayed **Page Setup** dialog box, click the **Margins tab**. Under **Margins**, click in the **Top** box and type **1.5** In the lower right corner of the dialog box, click **OK**.

19. On the Standard toolbar, click the **Save** button to save the changes to the document.

20. On the Standard toolbar, click the **Print Preview** button to view your document as it will print. On the Print Preview toolbar, click the **Print** button to print the document, and then on the same toolbar, click the **Close** button. Close the document and then close Word.

**End** You have completed Project 2E ————————————

# Project 2F — Computer Virus Policy

**Objectives:** *Change Document and Paragraph Layout, Change and Reorganize Text, Create and Modify Lists, Work with Headers and Footers, Insert Frequently Used Text, and Insert References.*

In the following Performance Assessment, you will format and edit a report regarding the Lake Michigan City College computer virus policy. Your completed document will look similar to Figure 2.88. You will save your document as *2F_Computer_Virus_Firstname_Lastname.*

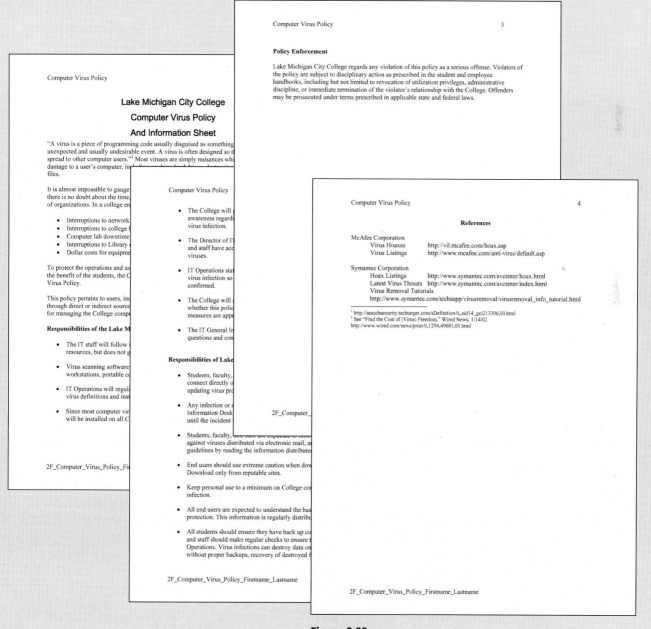

**Figure 2.88**

**(Project 2F–Computer Virus continues on the next page)**

**(Project 2F–Computer Virus Policy continued)**

1. Click the **Open** button. Navigate to the location where the student files for this textbook are stored. Locate and open **w02F_Computer_ Virus_Policy**. From the **File** menu click **Save As**. Navigate to the location where you are saving your projects for this chapter. In the **File name** box, and using your own name, type **2F_Computer_Virus_ Policy_Firstname_Lastname** and then click the **Save** button.

2. From the **File** menu, click **Page Setup**. In the **Page Setup** dialog box, change the left margin to **1"** and the right margin to **1"** and then click **OK**.

3. At the top of the document, select the first line, which will form the title and begins *Lake Michigan City College*. On the Formatting tool- bar, click the **Center** button. Click the **Font arrow**, scroll as needed and click **Arial Unicode MS**, click the **Font Size arrow**, and then click **16**. On the Formatting toolbar, click the **Bold** button. Place the insertion point at the end of the word *College* and press Enter. Place the insertion point at the end of the word *Policy* and press Enter again. The title is on three lines and is easier to read. If necessary, on the Standard toolbar, click the Show/Hide ¶ button to display nonprint- ing characters. Delete the spaces at the beginning of the second and third lines of the title.

4. The first two sentences in this document—beginning with *"A virus—* is a quote and needs to be referenced. In the third line of this para- graph, place the insertion point after the closing quote mark follow- ing *computer users."* From the **Insert** menu, point to **Reference**, and then click **Footnote**. In the **Footnote and Endnote** dialog box, under **Location**, click the **Endnotes** option button, and be sure **End of document** displays in the box to its right. Under **Format**, click the **Number format arrow**, and then click **1, 2, 3** from the list. Click **Insert**. In the endnote area type **http://searchsecurity.techtarget. com/sDefinition/0,,sid14_gci213306,00.html** but do not type a space or press Enter.

5. Because this is an Internet address, the Word program may auto- matically format it as a hyperlink—in blue and underlined—if you follow it with a space or Enter. If Word formats the address as a hyper- link, right-click on the address and click Remove Hyperlink.

6. Press Ctrl + Home. Locate the paragraph of text that begins *It is almost impossible* and place the insertion to the right of *viruses each year*—before the comma. Display the **Footnote and Endnote** dialog box again, click **Insert**, and then, without pressing Enter, but placing a space after the date, type **See "Find the Cost of (Virus) Freedom," Wired News, 1/14/02 http://www.wired.com/news/print/0,1294,49681,00.html**

   Your text may wrap at a different place than shown in Figure 2.88. Click the **Save** button.

**(Project 2F–Computer Virus continues on the next page)**

**(Project 2F–Computer Virus Policy continued)**

7. Near the top of the document, select the five one-line paragraphs starting with the paragraph that begins *Interruptions to network* and then click the **Bullets** button. (If the bullet that displays is not a solid round symbol, display the Format menu, click Bullets and Numbering, click the solid round bullet example, and then click OK.)

8. Position the lower portion of page 1 into view. In the paragraph beginning *The IT staff will follow,* click to left of the first word in the paragraph. Use the scroll arrow to view the top of the next page. Hold down Shift and, in the seventh line down, click after the period following the word *College.* This will select all the text paragraphs that follow this subheading. With these paragraphs selected, apply a solid round bullet. Display the **Format** menu, click **Paragraph**, and increase the spacing after to **12 pt**.

9. Using the technique in the previous step, select the paragraphs of text following the subheading *Responsibilities of Lake Michigan City College Students, Faculty, and Staff,* and use the same procedure to add solid round bullets and increase the space after to **12 pt**.

10. Navigate to the bottom of page 3, click to place the insertion point to the left of the word *References* and then press Ctrl + Enter to insert a page break and move this title to the next page. Select *References* and click the **Center** button.

11. On page 4, select *McAfee Corporation* and the two references listed under it. Click the **Cut** button. Place the insertion point to the left of *Symantec* and press the **Paste** button. The references are reordered. Insert an empty line between the Symantec and McAfee references.

12. Select the four lines listed under *Symantec Corporation*. Display the **Table** menu and then click **Sort**. In the **Sort Text** dialog box, under **Sort by**, be sure *Paragraphs* displays and then click **OK**. The references are resorted in alphabetical order. Right-click on any Web references that are formatted as hyperlinks (blue and underlined) and click **Remove Hyperlink**. Remove any empty paragraphs between the last reference and the beginning of the endnotes.

13. Display the **View** menu and then click **Header and Footer**. In the header area, type **Computer Virus Policy**, press Tab twice, and then click the **Insert Page Number** button. Switch to the footer area, click the **Insert AutoText** button, and insert the **Filename**. Close the Header and Footer toolbar.

14. Click the **Save** button, then click the **Print Preview** button. Compare the layout of your document to the figure. Click the **Print** button and then close the Print Preview window. Close the document, saving any changes and then close Word.

**End** You have completed Project 2F

# Project 2G—Interview Questions

**Objectives:** *Change Document and Paragraph Layout, Change and Reorganize Text, Create and Modify Lists, Work with Headers and Footers, Insert Frequently Used Text, and Insert References.*

In the following Performance Assessment, you will edit and format a list of questions from Lisa Huelsman, Associate Dean of Adult Basic Education, for use in an interview with candidates for a new Director of Distance Education at Lake Michigan City College. Your completed document will look similar to Figure 2.89. You will save your document as *2G_Interview_Questions_Firstname_Lastname.*

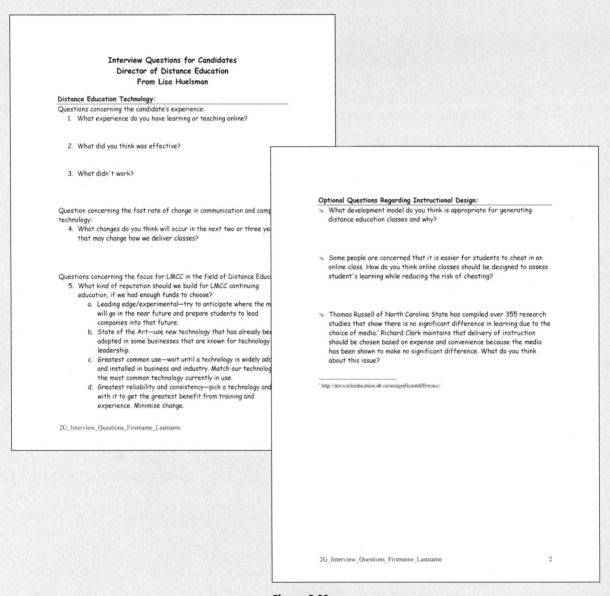

**Figure 2.89**

**(Project 2G–Interview Questions continues on the next page)**

**(Project 2G–Interview Questions continued)**

1. Click the **Open** button. Navigate to the location where the student files for this textbook are stored. Locate and open **w02G_Interview_ Questions**. From the **File** menu, click **Save As**. Navigate to the location where you are saving your projects for this chapter. In the **File name** box, using your own name, type **2G_Interview_Questions_Firstname_ Lastname** and then click the **Save** button. Make sure that nonprinting characters are displayed and take a moment to scroll through this two-page document to familiarize yourself with the layout and content.

2. In the first line of the document that begins *Interview Questions*, place your insertion point after *Candidates* and press [Enter]. Type **Director of Distance Education** and then press [Enter] again. There are now three title lines. Delete the space to the left of the third line.

3. Select the three title lines. On the Formatting toolbar, click the **Center** button and then click the **Bold** button. Change the **Font Size** to **14**.

4. Locate the first question beginning with *What experience*. Three questions are listed concerning the experience of the candidate. Select the three questions and, on the Formatting toolbar, click the **Line Spacing** arrow and then click **3.0**. This increases the spacing between the questions, which will provide space for the interviewer to make notes during the interview.

5. With the three questions still selected, on the Formatting toolbar, click the **Numbering** button.

6. Position the middle of page 1 into view. Select the paragraph that begins *What changes*. From the **Format** menu, click **Paragraph** and then click the **Indents and Spacing tab**. Under **Spacing**, change the **After** box to **36**. You can either type 36 or use the spin box arrow to increase the number displayed. Click **OK** to close the **Paragraph** dialog box. Notice that in this instance, the Line Spacing button was not used, because doing so would increase the space between the two wrapped lines of the paragraph. Because the goal is to add some space after the question for handwritten notes, the Spacing After paragraph feature is useful here.

7. With the question still selected, on the Formatting toolbar, click the **Numbering** button. The question is numbered 1, starting the numbering sequence over again, and the AutoCorrect Options button displays. Point to the **AutoCorrect Options** button, click its arrow to display the list of options available, and then, from the displayed list, click **Continue Numbering**. The number for this question is changed to 4.

8. Scroll down a few lines, select the question beginning *What kind of reputation,* and then click the **Numbering** button. The question is numbered 5, continuing the numbering sequence.

**(Project 2G–Interview Questions continues on the next page)**

**(Project 2G–Interview Questions continued)**

9. Select the four paragraphs following question 5, beginning with *Leading Edge*. Click the **Numbering** button. The numbering sequence continues—6 through 9. However, these paragraphs are a subset of question 5. With the four paragraphs still selected, on the Formatting toolbar, click the **Increase Indent** button. The paragraphs are indented and the numbers changed to letters a through d.

10. On the Standard toolbar, click the **Save** button. Each of the four paragraphs now labeled a. through d. has a colon followed by a space in the first line. In the paragraph beginning *a. Leading edge*, select the colon and its following space. From the **Insert** menu, click **Symbol**. In the **Symbol** dialog box, click the **Special Characters tab**; be sure that **Em Dash** is highlighted. Click **Insert**. The dialog box remains open on your screen. Select the colon and following space found in the first line of the paragraphs labeled, b., c., and d. and replace it by inserting an em dash from the **Symbol** dialog box. Move the dialog box on your screen as necessary and then close the dialog box.

11. Scroll as necessary to view page 2 on your screen. Select the paragraphs under *Instructional Design* including the two empty paragraphs between the questions. Display the **Paragraph** dialog box and increase the spacing after to **18**. Click **OK**. The space after formatting was applied to all of the paragraphs, including those without text.

12. With the paragraphs still selected, display the **Bullets and Numbering** dialog box and click the **Bulleted tab**. If necessary, click any bullet syles to activate the **Customize button**. In the lower right corner, click the **Customize button**. In the **Customize Bulleted List** dialog box, click the **Character button**. In the displayed **Symbol** dialog box, click the **Font** arrow, click **Wingdings**, scroll to the top of the list, and in the third row, click the first symbol-a hand with a pencil. Click **OK** twice. Then, click the **Decrease Indent** button as many times as necessary to align the bullets at the left margin.

    If the numbers continue sequentially with the number 6 from the previous list, instead of restarting at number 1, open the **Bullets and Numbering** dialog box and click again to select the **Restart Numbering** option button. Click **OK**.

13. From the **View** menu, click **Header and Footer**. Switch to the footer area and then, on the **Header and Footer** toolbar, click **Insert AutoText**. From the displayed list, click **Filename**. Press Tab and click the **Insert Page Number** button. Close the Header and Footer toolbar.

**(Project 2G–Interview Questions continues on the next page)**

**(Project 2G–Interview Questions continued)**

**14.** Press Ctrl + Home to move to the top of the document. In the first group of questions, the second and third questions need to be reversed. Select the question *What did you think was effective?* The number will not be highlighted. Point to the highlighted text. When the mouse pointer is in the shape of the white move arrow, drag the question and place the vertical line at the beginning of question 2— in front of the *W*—and then release the mouse button. The questions are reversed. On the Standard toolbar click the **Undo** button and then click the **Redo** button. Notice that the numbers stay in sequence.

**15.** Press Ctrl + End to move to the end of the document. In the paragraph beginning *Thomas Russell,* in the third line, click to place the insertion point following the period after the word *media.* From the **Insert** menu, point to **Reference** and then click **Footnote**. In the **Footnote and Endnote** dialog box, under **Location**, click the **Endnotes** option button and be sure **End of document** is displayed in its box. Under **Format**, click the **Number format arrow** and then click **i, ii, iii** from the list that displays. Click the **Insert** button. In the endnote area, type **http://nova.teleeducation.nb.ca/nosignificantdifference/**

**16.** Click the **Save** button and then click the **Print Preview** button to view the document. From the Print Preview toolbar, click the **Print** button and then, on the same toolbar, click the **Close** button. Close the document, saving changes if prompted to do so.

**End** You have completed Project 2G

# Performance Assessments (continued)

## Project 2H — Virtual Tour

**Objectives:** *Change Document and Paragraph Layout, Change and Reorganize Text, Work with Headers and Footers, and Insert Frequently Used Text.*

In the following Performance Assessment, you will edit and format a report written by students of the Advanced Web Design class, regarding a Web site they plan to create for members of the local community. Your completed document will look similar to Figure 2.90. You will save your document as *2H_Virtual_Tour_Firstname_Lastname.*

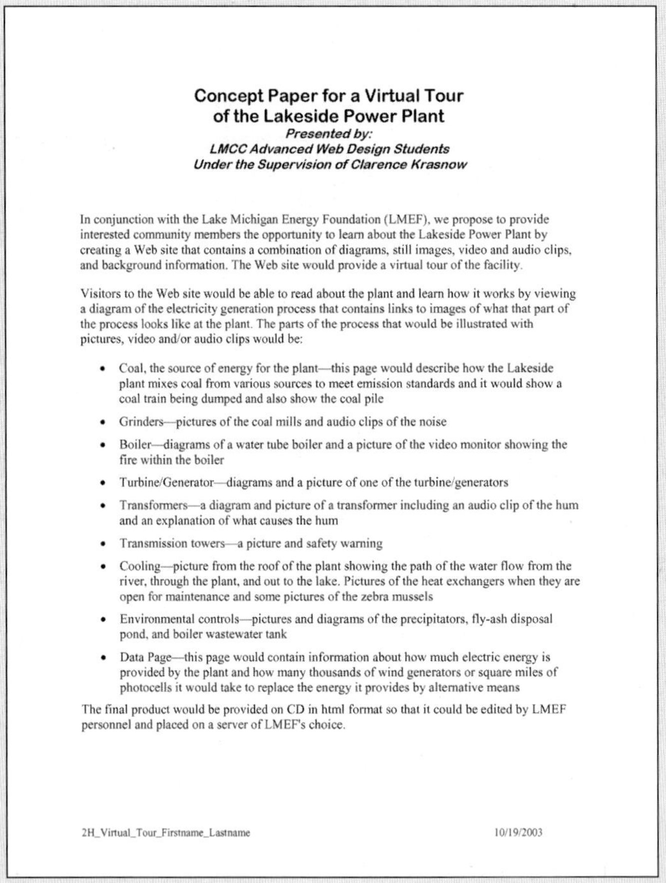

**Concept Paper for a Virtual Tour**
**of the Lakeside Power Plant**
***Presented by:***
***LMCC Advanced Web Design Students***
***Under the Supervision of Clarence Krasnow***

In conjunction with the Lake Michigan Energy Foundation (LMEF), we propose to provide interested community members the opportunity to learn about the Lakeside Power Plant by creating a Web site that contains a combination of diagrams, still images, video and audio clips, and background information. The Web site would provide a virtual tour of the facility.

Visitors to the Web site would be able to read about the plant and learn how it works by viewing a diagram of the electricity generation process that contains links to images of what that part of the process looks like at the plant. The parts of the process that would be illustrated with pictures, video and/or audio clips would be:

- Coal, the source of energy for the plant—this page would describe how the Lakeside plant mixes coal from various sources to meet emission standards and it would show a coal train being dumped and also show the coal pile
- Grinders—pictures of the coal mills and audio clips of the noise
- Boiler—diagrams of a water tube boiler and a picture of the video monitor showing the fire within the boiler
- Turbine/Generator—diagrams and a picture of one of the turbine/generators
- Transformers—a diagram and picture of a transformer including an audio clip of the hum and an explanation of what causes the hum
- Transmission towers—a picture and safety warning
- Cooling—picture from the roof of the plant showing the path of the water flow from the river, through the plant, and out to the lake. Pictures of the heat exchangers when they are open for maintenance and some pictures of the zebra mussels
- Environmental controls—pictures and diagrams of the precipitators, fly-ash disposal pond, and boiler wastewater tank
- Data Page—this page would contain information about how much electric energy is provided by the plant and how many thousands of wind generators or square miles of photocells it would take to replace the energy it provides by alternative means

The final product would be provided on CD in html format so that it could be edited by LMEF personnel and placed on a server of LMEF's choice.

2H_Virtual_Tour_Firstname_Lastname 10/19/2003

**Figure 2.90**

**(Project 2H–Virtual Tour continues on the next page)**

**(Project 2H**–Virtual Tour continued)

1. Click the **Open** button. Navigate to the location where the student files for this textbook are stored. Locate and open the file **w02H_Virtual_Tour**. From the **File** menu, click **Save As**. Navigate to the location where you are storing your projects for this chapter. In the **File name** box, using your own name, type **2H_Virtual_Tour_Firstname_Lastname**

2. From the **File** menu, click **Page Setup**. Change the left and right margin boxes to **1"**.

3. From the **Tools** menu, click **AutoCorrect Options** and then click the **AutoCorrect tab**. In the **Replace** box type: **xlmef** and in the **With** box type **Lake Michigan Energy Foundation**. Click the **Add** button and then click **OK**. If another student has already added this AutoCorrect entry, the Replace button will be indicated instead of the Add button. Click Replace, click Yes, and then click OK.

4. In the paragraph that begins with *In conjunction with*, in the first line, place the insertion point to the left of LMEF. Type **xlmef** and then press the spacebar. The name of the foundation replaces the shortcut you typed. Enclose *LMEF* in parentheses.

5. In the same paragraph, at the end of the third line, select *still images,*—be sure you include the comma and the space. Point to the selected text and drag it to the left of *video and audio clips* in the same sentence. Adjust the spacing if necessary.

6. Select the two paragraphs above the bulleted list, beginning with *In conjunction with*, point anywhere in the selected text and right-click, and then click **Paragraph** from the shortcut menu. Under **Spacing**, change the **After** box to **12**. Click **OK**.

7. In the bulleted list, rearrange the items into the following order: Coal, Grinders, Boiler, Turbine/Generator, Transformers, Transmission towers, Cooling, Environmental Controls, Data Page.

8. Press [Ctrl] + [Home] to move to the top of the document. Press [Ctrl] + [H] to open the **Find and Replace** dialog box. In the **Find what** box, type **web** In the **Replace with** box, type **Web** Click **Replace All**. Four replacements are made. Close the dialog box.

9. From the **View** menu, click **Header and Footer**. Switch to the footer area on the Header and Footer toolbar, click **Insert AutoText** and then click **Filename**. Press [Tab] two times to move to the right side of the footer area and then click the **Insert Date** button. Select the text in the footer and change the font size to **10 pt**. Close the Header and Footer toolbar.

10. Click the **Save** button and then click the **Print Preview** button. From the Print Preview toolbar, click the **Print** button and then, on the same toolbar, click the **Close** button. Close the document.

**End** You have completed Project 2H

# Mastery Assessments

## Project 2I — Organizations

**Objectives:** *Change Document and Paragraph Layout, Change and Reorganize Text, Create and Modify Lists, and Work with Headers and Footers.*

In the following Mastery Assessment, you will format and reorganize a list of the student organizations at LMCC. Your completed document will look similar to Figure 2.91. You will save your document as *2I_Organizations_Firstname_Lastname.*

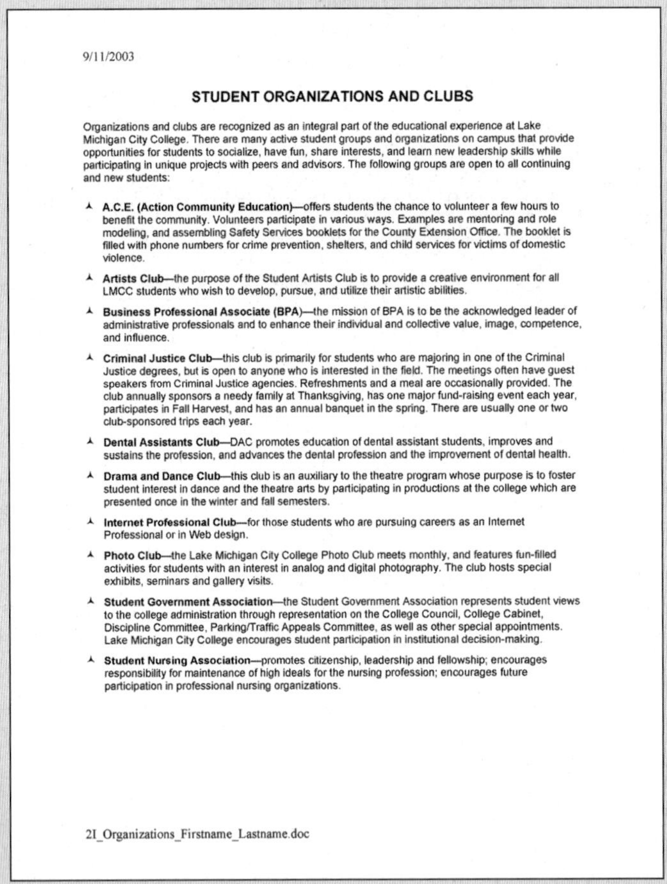
9/11/2003

**STUDENT ORGANIZATIONS AND CLUBS**

Organizations and clubs are recognized as an integral part of the educational experience at Lake Michigan City College. There are many active student groups and organizations on campus that provide opportunities for students to socialize, have fun, share interests, and learn new leadership skills while participating in unique projects with peers and advisors. The following groups are open to all continuing and new students:

- **A.C.E. (Action Community Education)**—offers students the chance to volunteer a few hours to benefit the community. Volunteers participate in various ways. Examples are mentoring and role modeling, and assembling Safety Services booklets for the County Extension Office. The booklet is filled with phone numbers for crime prevention, shelters, and child services for victims of domestic violence.
- **Artists Club**—the purpose of the Student Artists Club is to provide a creative environment for all LMCC students who wish to develop, pursue, and utilize their artistic abilities.
- **Business Professional Associate (BPA)**—the mission of BPA is to be the acknowledged leader of administrative professionals and to enhance their individual and collective value, image, competence, and influence.
- **Criminal Justice Club**—this club is primarily for students who are majoring in one of the Criminal Justice degrees, but is open to anyone who is interested in the field. The meetings often have guest speakers from Criminal Justice agencies. Refreshments and a meal are occasionally provided. The club annually sponsors a needy family at Thanksgiving, has one major fund-raising event each year, participates in Fall Harvest, and has an annual banquet in the spring. There are usually one or two club-sponsored trips each year.
- **Dental Assistants Club**—DAC promotes education of dental assistant students, improves and sustains the profession, and advances the dental profession and the improvement of dental health.
- **Drama and Dance Club**—this club is an auxiliary to the theatre program whose purpose is to foster student interest in dance and the theatre arts by participating in productions at the college which are presented once in the winter and fall semesters.
- **Internet Professional Club**—for those students who are pursuing careers as an Internet Professional or in Web design.
- **Photo Club**—the Lake Michigan City College Photo Club meets monthly, and features fun-filled activities for students with an interest in analog and digital photography. The club hosts special exhibits, seminars and gallery visits.
- **Student Government Association**—the Student Government Association represents student views to the college administration through representation on the College Council, College Cabinet, Discipline Committee, Parking/Traffic Appeals Committee, as well as other special appointments. Lake Michigan City College encourages student participation in institutional decision-making.
- **Student Nursing Association**—promotes citizenship, leadership and fellowship; encourages responsibility for maintenance of high ideals for the nursing profession; encourages future participation in professional nursing organizations.

2I_Organizations_Firstname_Lastname.doc

**Figure 2.91**

**(Project 2I–Organizations continues on the next page)**

**(Project 2I–Organizations continued)**

1. Display the **Open** dialog box. Navigate to the student files and then locate and open the file **w02I_Organizations**. In the **File name** box, type **2I_Organizations_Firstname_Lastname** Display nonprinting characters. Display the **File** menu and click **Save As**. Navigate to the location where you are storing your projects for this chapter.

2. From the **File** menu, display the **Page Setup** dialog box. Change the left and right margins to **1 inch**, and close the dialog box. Center the title of the document.

3. Select the list of student organizations, beginning with *Student Government* and continuing down through the end of the document. Recall that you can click at the beginning point in the text, scroll to the end, press [Shift], and then click at the end to select all of the text rather than dragging. Display the **Paragraph** dialog box, click the **Indents and Spacing tab**, and then, under **Spacing**, change the **After** box to **6**.

4. With the list of organizations still selected, display the **Bullets and Numbering** dialog box. Click the **Bulleted tab** and then click any of the bullet options. Click the **Customize** button and then click the **Character** button. In the **Symbol** dialog box, click the **Font arrow**, scroll, and then click **Wingdings**. Click a symbol of your choice that would serve as a bullet and then click **OK** twice to apply the bullet. Click the **Decrease Indent** button once to move the list to the left.

5. With the list of organizations still selected, from the **Table** menu, click **Sort**. Sort the list alphabetically by paragraph.

6. Display the footer area and then, using the **Insert AutoText** button, insert the **Filename**. Switch to the header area and insert the date at the left side of the header.

7. Save the changes. Preview and then print the document. Close the file.

 **End** **You have completed Project 2I** ————————————————

## Project 2J — Online Article

**Objectives:** *Change Document and Paragraph Layout, Change and Reorganize Text, Create and Modify Lists, Work with Headers and Footers, Insert Frequently Used Text, and Insert References.*

In the following Mastery Assessment, you will edit and format an article about one of the professors at LMCC who offers online classes. The completed article will look similar to Figure 2.92. You will save your document as *2J_Online_Article_Firstname_Lastname*.

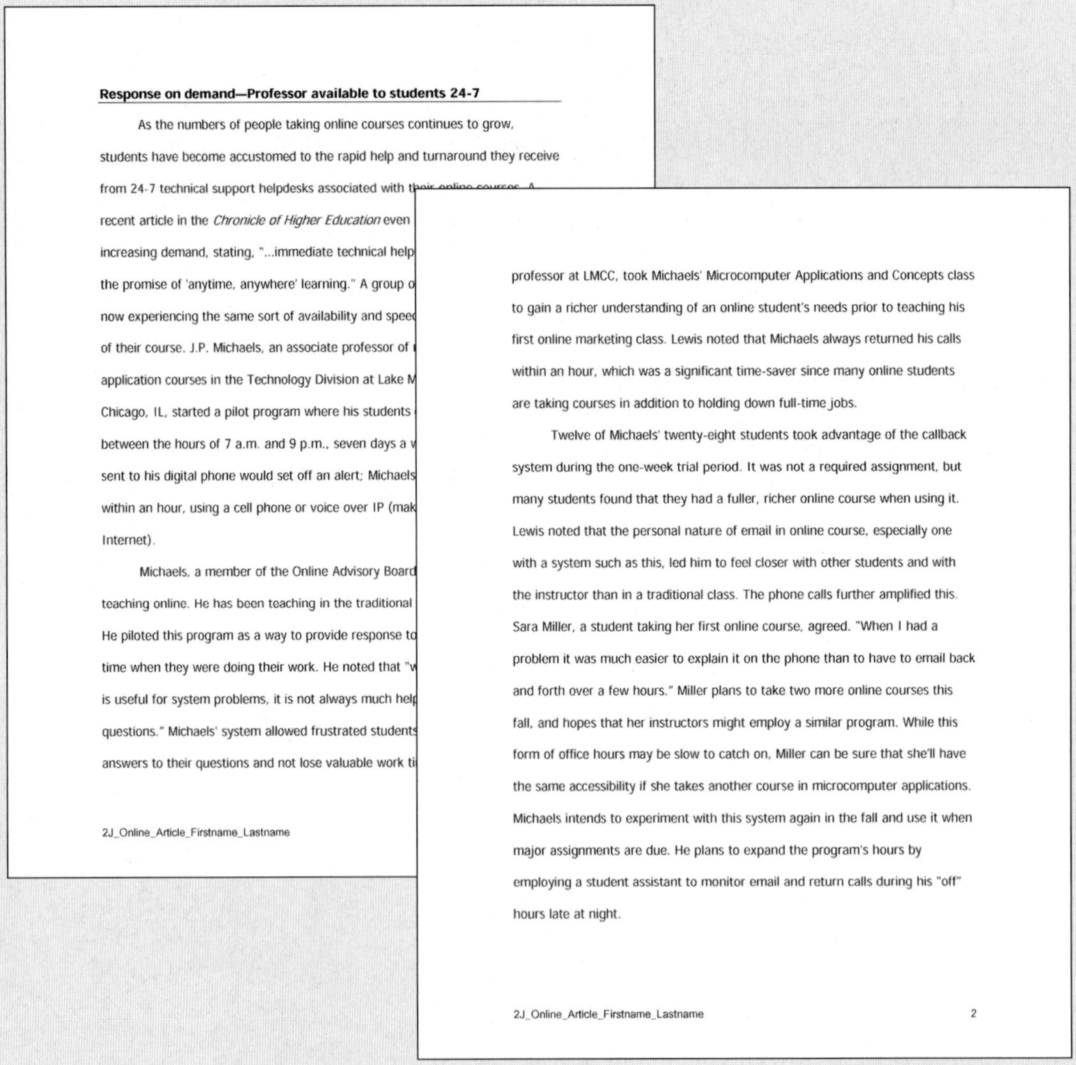

**Response on demand—Professor available to students 24-7**

As the numbers of people taking online courses continues to grow, students have become accustomed to the rapid help and turnaround they receive from 24-7 technical support helpdesks associated with their online courses. A recent article in the *Chronicle of Higher Education* even increasing demand, stating, "...immediate technical help the promise of 'anytime, anywhere' learning." A group o now experiencing the same sort of availability and speed of their course. J.P. Michaels, an associate professor of application courses in the Technology Division at Lake M Chicago, IL, started a pilot program where his students between the hours of 7 a.m. and 9 p.m., seven days a sent to his digital phone would set off an alert; Michaels within an hour, using a cell phone or voice over IP (mak Internet).

Michaels, a member of the Online Advisory Board teaching online. He has been teaching in the traditional He piloted this program as a way to provide response t time when they were doing their work. He noted that "w is useful for system problems, it is not always much help questions." Michaels' system allowed frustrated students answers to their questions and not lose valuable work ti

2J_Online_Article_Firstname_Lastname

professor at LMCC, took Michaels' Microcomputer Applications and Concepts class to gain a richer understanding of an online student's needs prior to teaching his first online marketing class. Lewis noted that Michaels always returned his calls within an hour, which was a significant time-saver since many online students are taking courses in addition to holding down full-time jobs.

Twelve of Michaels' twenty-eight students took advantage of the callback system during the one-week trial period. It was not a required assignment, but many students found that they had a fuller, richer online course when using it. Lewis noted that the personal nature of email in online course, especially one with a system such as this, led him to feel closer with other students and with the instructor than in a traditional class. The phone calls further amplified this. Sara Miller, a student taking her first online course, agreed. "When I had a problem it was much easier to explain it on the phone than to have to email back and forth over a few hours." Miller plans to take two more online courses this fall, and hopes that her instructors might employ a similar program. While this form of office hours may be slow to catch on, Miller can be sure that she'll have the same accessibility if she takes another course in microcomputer applications. Michaels intends to experiment with this system again in the fall and use it when major assignments are due. He plans to expand the program's hours by employing a student assistant to monitor email and return calls during his "off" hours late at night.

2J_Online_Article_Firstname_Lastname                    2

**Figure 2.92**

**(Project 2J–Online Article continues on the next page)**

**(Project 2J**–Online Article continued)

1. Display the **Open** dialog box. Navigate to the student files and then locate and open the file **w02J_Online_Article**. Display the **File** menu, click **Save As**, and navigate to the location where you are storing your projects for this chapter. In the **File name** box, type 2J_Online_Article_Firstname_Lastname

2. From the **File** menu, display the **Page Setup** dialog box. Change the left and right margins to **1.25"**.

3. Beginning with the paragraph *As the numbers*, select the entire body of the article, click the arrow on the **Line Spacing** button, and then click **2.0**.

4. With the text still selected, display the **Paragraph** dialog box, and then click the **Indents and Spacing tab**. Under **Indentation**, click the **Special arrow** and then click **First line**.

5. Position the insertion point at the top of the document and then display the **Find and Replace** dialog box. In the **Find what** box type **e-mail** and in the **Replace with** box type **email** Find and replace this word throughout the document.

6. Use the **Find and Replace** dialog box to locate **College of Technology** and replace it with **Technology Division** Make sure the insertion point is at the top of the document. Use the **Find and Replace** dialog box to locate the second occurrence of *Lake Michigan City College* and replace it with **LMCC** Finally, use the **Find and Replace** dialog box to find **Rosenthal** and replace each occurrence with **Miller**.

7. Move to the top of the document. In the paragraph beginning *As the numbers*, in the middle of the seventh line, locate the phrase *speed and availability*. Use drag-and-drop or cut-and-paste techniques to reword this to read *availability and speed*.

8. Press Ctrl + End to move to the end of the document. Select the last sentence in the document beginning with *Miller plans to take* (do not select the ending paragraph mark). In the same paragraph, locate the sentence that begins *While this form* and then use the drag-and-drop technique to move the selected sentence in front of the *While this form* sentence. Adjust the spacing if necessary. Be sure that you did not create a new paragraph.

9. View the footer area, click the **Insert AutoText** button, and then insert the **Filename**. Tab to the right side of the footer and insert the page number.

10. Save the changes. Preview and then print the document. Close the file.

**End** You have completed Project 2J

# Problem Solving

## Project 2K — Holidays

**Objectives:** *Change Document and Paragraph Layout, Change and Reorganize Text, Create and Modify Lists, Work with Headers and Footers.*

You will write a memo listing the holidays that will be taken during the calendar school year at Lake Michigan City College. You will save your document as *2K_Holidays_Firstname_Lastname*.

1. Open Word. Use the **Page Setup** dialog box to set the margins to **2 inches** at the top margin, and **1 inch** on the left and right sides.

2. Create a MEMO heading at the top of the document. Format the heading in a distinctive manner and align it on the right side of the page. Press Enter four times.

2. Type the heading of the memo as follows:

   **MEMO TO:**  **James Smith, Vice President of Student Affairs**
   **FROM:**  **Henry Sabaj, Vice President of Academic Affairs**
   **DATE:**  **August 1**
   **SUBJECT:**  **College Holidays**

3. Format the heading to be double-spaced and indent 1 inch from the left margin. Format the headings in uppercase bold.

4. Write one or two introductory sentences indicating that this is the list of holiday dates agreed to by the faculty and administration for the upcoming college year.

5. Use a calendar and create a bulleted list of official holiday names and dates for the September through May college year. Look at your own college calendar and include the dates for any winter or spring breaks that may be scheduled.

6. Format the list of holidays using a bullet symbol of your choice.

7. Save the memo in your storage location with the name **2K_Holidays_Firstname_Lastname**

8. View the footer area and insert the filename using AutoText.

9. Switch to the header area and type **Academic Affairs**

10. Preview and then print the memo. Close the file and close Word.

**End** **You have completed Project 2K** ——————————————

# Project 2L — Computer Information Memo

**Objectives:** *Change Document and Paragraph Layout, Change and Reorganize Text, Create and Modify Lists, Work with Headers and Footers.*

In this Problem Solving assessment, you will write a memo to the Vice President of Academic Affairs listing the Computer Information Systems courses at LMCC. You will save your memo as *2L_Computer_Information_Memo_Firstname_Lastname.*

1. Open Word. Use the **Page Setup** dialog box to set the margins to **2"** at the top margin, and **1"** on the left and right sides.

2. Create a MEMO heading at the top of the document. Format the heading in a distinctive manner and center it on the page. Press Enter four times.

3. Type the heading of the memo as follows:

   | | |
   |---|---|
   | MEMO TO: | Henry Sabaj, Vice President of Academic Affairs |
   | FROM: | Lisa Huelsman, Associate Dean of Adult Basic Education |
   | DATE: | September 30 |
   | SUBJECT: | Computer Information Systems Courses |

4. Format the heading area to be double-spaced and indent 1" from the left margin. Format the headings in uppercase bold.

5. Write one or two introductory sentences explaining that the list includes the current Computer Information Systems courses required for a certificate or degree at LMCC.

6. Using the course catalog and other information available via your college's Web site, create a bulleted list of the course numbers and names that are required as Computer Information Systems—or similar—classes at your college.

7. Add a closing to the memo requesting that Mr. Sabaj review the list for possible adjustments or modifications.

8. Save the memo in your storage location with the name **2L_Computer_Information_Memo_Firstname_Lastname**

9. View the footer area and insert the filename using AutoText.

10. Preview and then print the memo. Close the file and close Word.

**End** You have completed Project 2L ——————————————————

# On the Internet

## Finding More Bullet Styles To Use

The bullet symbols that display in the Symbols dialog box are used throughout Microsoft Office programs. You can also download and use symbols from other sites on the Internet.

1. Open your Web browser and go to a search engine such as www.google.com or www.yahoo.com. Type the key words **bullets** and **free** in the search box.

2. Look through the various sites for one you like that has a variety of interesting graphics that may be used for bullets. There are several that do not require that you sign up for advertising or provide your e-mail address.

3. Pick a bullet you like and right-click it. Click the **Save as Picture** option from the shortcut menu and save it to your disk.

4. Open a Word document and create a short bulleted list to demonstrate your new bullet.

5. Select the list and, on the Formatting toolbar, click the **Bullet** button.

6. From the **Format** menu, choose **Bullets and Numbering**. Click **Customize** and then **Picture**.

7. Click **Import**. In the **Add Clips to Organizer** dialog box, find the picture you saved to your disk, click it, and then click **Add**. Select your new picture, if necessary, click **OK**, and then click **OK** again to close the dialog boxes.

8. Close the file without saving the changes and then close Word.

# GO! with Help

## Restoring the Default Bullets and Numbering

If you have used a number of customized bullets in the Bullets and Numbering dialog box, you may want to restore the dialog box to its original configuration. The Word Help program gives you step-by-step instructions on how to restore a customized list format to its original setting.

1. Start Word. On the menu bar, in the *Type* a question for help box, type **How do I restore customized bullet list** and then press Enter.

2. Locate and then click the topic **Restore a customized list format to its original setting.**

3. Read the instructions that display and then follow the steps to restore the original settings to the Bullets and Numbering dialog box on your computer.

4. Close the Microsoft Word Help pane and then close the Search Results task pane.

# 3 chapterthree

# Using Graphics and Tables

**In this chapter, you will:** complete these projects **and** practice these skills.

| Project 3A **Creating a Flyer** | **Objectives** <br> • Insert Clip Art and Pictures <br> • Modify Clip Art and Pictures <br> • Work with the Drawing Toolbar |
|---|---|

| Project 3B **Formatting a Report** | **Objectives** <br> • Work with Tab Stops <br> • Create a Table <br> • Format Tables <br> • Create a Table from Existing Text |
|---|---|

# Sensation! Park

Sensation! Park is a "family fun center" theme park designed for today's busy families. The park offers traditional amusement park rides and arcade games along with new and popular water rides, surf pools, laser tag, video games, and a racetrack for all ages.

Situated on 100 acres, the park's mission is to provide a safe, clean, exciting environment where children and adults of all ages can find a game, ride, or event that suits their interests or discover something completely new!

© Getty Images, Inc.

# Adding Graphics and Tables to a Document

Adding graphics can greatly enhance the effectiveness of documents. Digital images, such as those obtained from a digital camera or a scanner, can be inserted into documents. A **clip** is a media file, including art, sound, animation, or movies. **Clip art** images—which are predefined graphic images included with Microsoft Office or downloaded from the Web—can be effective if used appropriately. You can also create your own graphic objects by using the tools on the Drawing toolbar.

Tabs can be used to horizontally align text and numbers. The Tab key is used to move to **tab stops**, which mark specific locations on a line of text. You can set your own tab stops and specify the alignment of each stop.

Tables are used to present data effectively and efficiently. The row and column format makes information easy to find and easy to read and helps the reader organize and categorize the data. The Word table feature has tools that enable you to format text, change column width and row height, change the background on portions or all of the table, and modify the table borders and lines.

# Project 3A Job Opportunities

In this chapter, you will create a document and add a picture from a file and a clip art image provided by Microsoft. You will format, resize, and move the images. You will add tab stops, and you will create and format two tables.

In Activities 3.1 through 3.9, you will edit a job announcement flyer for Sensation! Park. You will add a picture and a clip art image. You will also add objects from the Drawing toolbar. Your completed document will look similar to Figure 3.1. You will save your document as *3A_Job_Opportunities_Firstname_ Lastname.*

## Sensation! Park
### Summer Employment Opportunities

Are you looking for full- or part-time work in the most exciting surroundings in the greater Philadelphia area? Are you self-motivated, ambitious, friendly? Do you like working with people? If so, Sensation! Park has the job for you!

There are many advantages to working at Sensation! Park, including a strong benefits package, flexible hours, competitive wages, a friendly working environment, and the use of park facilities during off-peak hours.

We have jobs available in the following areas:
- Food service
- Ride management
- Security
- Transportation
- Clerical
- Maintenance

Some full- and part-time jobs are available immediately. Other jobs will begin in May. The park opens this year on May 20, the week before Memorial Day. Training sessions begin the week of May 13. There are also summer jobs available for college and high school students (minimum age 16).

The SuperSpeed Ferris Wheel, one of the new rides at Sensation!Park

### Call 215.555.1776

3A_Job_Opportunities_FirstName_Lastname

**Figure 3.1**
Project 3A—Job Opportunity Flyer

# Objective 1
## Insert Clip Art and Pictures

Graphic images can be inserted into a document from many sources. Clip art can be inserted from files provided with Microsoft Office or can be downloaded from the Microsoft Office Web site. Pictures can be scanned from photographs or slides, taken with a digital camera, or downloaded from the Web.

### Activity 3.1 Inserting Clip Art

**1** On the Standard toolbar, click the **Open** button. Navigate to the location where the student files for this textbook are stored. Locate **w03A_Job_Opportunities** and click once to select it. Then, in the lower right corner of the **Open** dialog box, click **Open**.

The w03A_Job_Opportunities file opens. See Figure 3.2.

**Figure 3.2**

**2** From the **File** menu, click **Save As**. In the **Save As** dialog box, click the **Save in** arrow and navigate to the location where you are storing your files for this chapter, creating a new Chapter 3 folder if you want to do so.

**3** In the **File name** box, type **3A_Job_Opportunities_Firstname_Lastname** and then click **Save**.

The document is saved with a new name. Make sure you substitute your name where indicated.

**4** If necessary, on the Standard toolbar, click the Show/Hide ¶ button to display the nonprinting characters.

**5** In the paragraph near the top of the document beginning *Are you looking*, click to place the insertion point to the left of the first word in the paragraph—*Are*.

6 From the **Insert** menu, point to **Picture**, and then click **Clip Art**.

The Clip Art task pane opens.

7 In the **Search in** box, verify that *All collections* displays and, if necessary, click the arrow, and then select the **Everywhere** check box. In the **Results should be** box, verify that *All media file types* displays and, if necessary, click the arrow, and then select the **All media types** check box.

8 In the **Search for** box, delete any existing text, type **roller coaster** and then click the **Go** button. Locate the roller coaster image from the task pane as shown in Figure 3.3. Use the scroll bar if necessary.

**Figure 3.3**

Clip art from all collections

Insertion point

Search for box

Search in box

Results should be box

Scroll bar

Desired image

---

**Alert!**

### Is the Image Missing from your Task Pane?

Many colleges perform minimum installations of software, including Microsoft Office. This means that little or no clip art is included with the program. When the program searches for an image, it looks on the hard drive and also tries to access the clip libraries on the Microsoft Office Web site. If you are not connected to the Web, your screen will not display the images shown in Figure 3.3.

If you do not see the appropriate image, click Organize clips at the bottom of the Clip Art task pane. From the File menu, point to Add Clips to Organizer, and then click Automatically. After a few minutes, all images on your computer are identified and organized. If the appropriate image is still not available, display the Insert menu, point to Picture, click From File, navigate to the location in which your student files are stored, click w03A_Roller_Coaster and then click the Insert button. Alternatively, use a similar image from the task pane.

**9** Click the roller coaster image if it is available. If you do not see the image, display the **Insert** menu, point to **Picture**, click **From File**, navigate to your student files and click **w03A_Roller_Coaster**, and then click the **Insert** button.

The clip art image is placed at the insertion point location. The image is inserted in the line of text in exactly the same manner as any other letter or number would be inserted—it becomes a part of the sentence. See Figure 3.4.

**Figure 3.4**

**10** On the Formatting toolbar, click the **Save** button.

### Activity 3.2 Inserting Pictures from Files

Pictures can also be added to a document, either by browsing for a picture on a disk drive or by using the Clip Art task pane.

**1** In the paragraph beginning *There are many advantages*, click to place the insertion point to the left of the first word in the paragraph—*There*.

**2** In the **Clip Art** task pane, in the **Search for** box, type **Ferris wheel**

**3** In the **Results should be** box, clear the check boxes of everything but **Photographs**.

Restricting the media type will limit the number of images found but will be helpful when you are searching for a topic with a large number of images. See Figure 3.5.

Search for photos    Type of photo

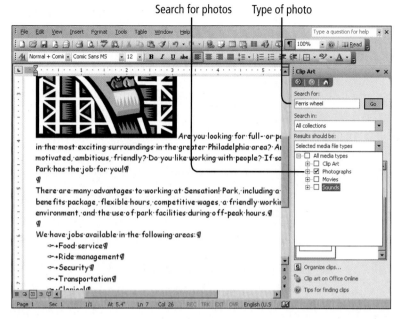

**Figure 3.5**

**4** Click **Go**.

One or more Ferris wheel photographs display.

**5** Click the Ferris wheel with the blue background. If the image is not available, select another similar image or display the **Insert** menu, point to **Picture**, click **From File**, navigate and click **w03A_Ferris_Wheel**, and click **Insert**. Scroll to the top of the second page.

The photograph is inserted at the insertion point location and the document expands to a second page. See Figure 3.6.

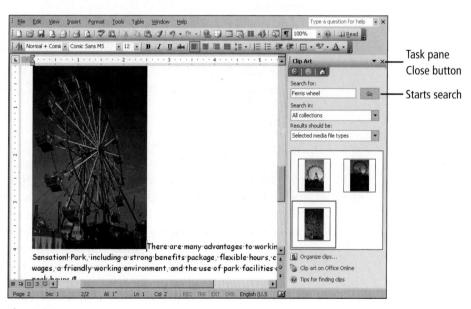

Task pane
Close button

Starts search

**Figure 3.6**

**6** On the **Clip Art** task pane title bar, click the **Close** button ☒.

**7** From the **View** menu, click **Header and Footer**.

The Header and Footer dialog box displays.

**8** On the Header and Footer toolbar, click the **Switch Between Header and Footer** button 🖽.

The insertion point is positioned in the footer box.

**9** On the Header and Footer toolbar, click the **Insert AutoText** button `Insert AutoText ▾`, and then click **Filename**.

The file name is inserted in the footer. The file extension .doc may or may not display, depending on your Word settings. See Figure 3.7.

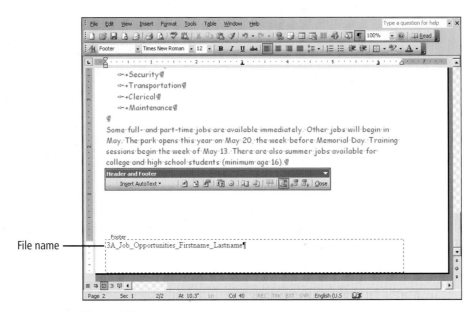

File name —— 3A_Job_Opportunities_Firstname_Lastname¶

**Figure 3.7**

**10** On the Header and Footer toolbar, click the **Close** button `Close`.

**11** On the Standard toolbar, click the **Save** button 🖫. Alternatively, press Ctrl + S to save your changes.

## Objective 2
## Modify Clip Art and Pictures

You can format clip art or pictures once you have placed them in a document. When images are placed in documents, they are placed inline. *Inline images* are just like characters in a sentence. You can change them to *floating images*—images that can be moved independently of the surrounding text—by changing the wrapping options. You can also change the size of an image to make it fit better in your document.

### Activity 3.3 Wrapping Text around Graphic Objects

Pictures and clip art images that are treated as characters in a sentence can cause awkward spacing in a document. To avoid this awkward spacing, you can format any graphic to move independently of the surrounding text.

**1** Locate and click the first image (the roller coaster) that you inserted.

*Sizing handles*, small black boxes, display around the image border. These handles are used to increase or decrease the size of the image. The sizing handles also indicate that the image is selected. The Picture toolbar may also open, either floating over the document, or added to the other toolbars. See Figure 3.8.

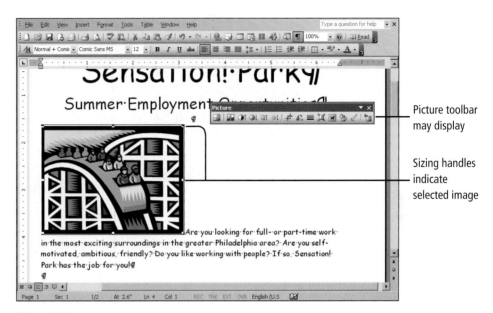

Picture toolbar may display

Sizing handles indicate selected image

**Figure 3.8**

**2** From the **Format** menu, click **Picture**. Alternatively, you can right-click the image and click Format Picture from the shortcut menu.

The Format Picture dialog box displays.

**3** In the **Format Picture** dialog box, click the **Layout tab**

The wrapping and alignment options display on the Layout tab. See Figure 3.9.

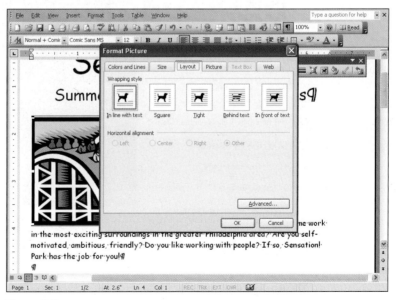

**Figure 3.9**

**4** Under **Wrapping style**, click **Tight**, and then click **OK**.

The text wraps tightly around the image, and the ferris wheel picture moves up from the second page. See Figure 3.10.

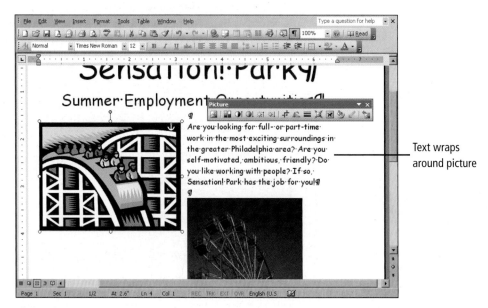

Text wraps around picture

**Figure 3.10**

**5** Scroll down and click the Ferris wheel picture.

**6** From the **Format** menu, click **Picture**, and then click the **Layout tab**.

**7** Under **Wrapping style**, click **Tight**, and then click **OK**.

The text wraps around the second image. See Figure 3.11. Because the spaces to the right of the pictures are used to display text, the document now occupies one page instead of two.

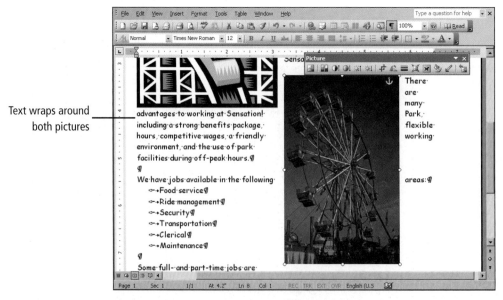

Text wraps around both pictures

**Figure 3.11**

**8** On the Standard toolbar, click the **Save** button.

### Activity 3.4 Resizing a Graphic Object

Usually you will want to adjust the size of the clip art and pictures that you place in documents. Use the sizing handles to resize images.

**1** Locate and click the first image you inserted (the roller coaster). Drag the image to the right side of the page so that its right edge aligns at approximately **6.5 inches on the horizontal ruler**.

Sizing handles, a *rotate handle*, and an *anchor* all display on or near the image. If your ruler is not displayed, from the View menu, click Ruler. You may need to use the horizontal scrollbar to move left to see the anchor. The table in Figure 3.12 describes the purpose of each of these formatting tools. Then refer to Figure 3.13 for placement of the image.

## Graphic Formatting Marks, Handles, and Anchors

| Mark | Purpose |
| --- | --- |
| Corner-sizing handles | Resizes images proportionally |
| Side-sizing handles | Stretches or shrinks the image in one direction |
| Rotate handle | Rotates the image clockwise or counterclockwise |
| Anchor | Indicates that the image is attached to the nearest paragraph |

**Figure 3.12**

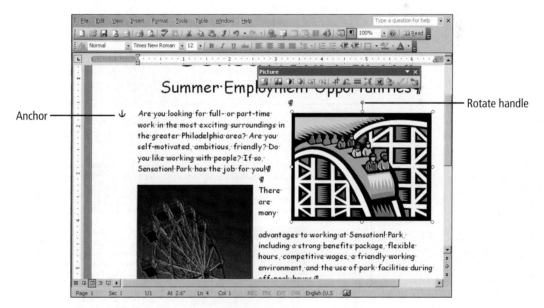

Anchor

Rotate handle

**Figure 3.13**

**2** Locate the sizing handle in the middle of the lower edge of the roller coaster image and drag it up until the image is about an inch high. Check the ruler height on the vertical ruler, although it need not be exact.

Notice that the image shape is distorted. See Figure 3.14.

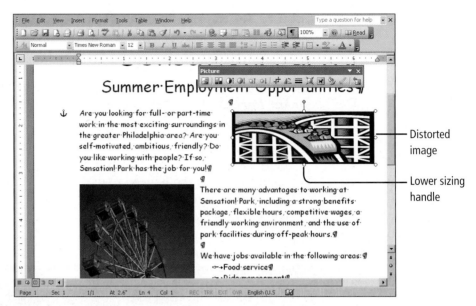

**Figure 3.14**

3 From the Standard toolbar, click the **Undo** button ⬚.

The image returns to its original size.

4 Locate the sizing handle on the lower right corner of the image and drag it up and to the left until the image is about an inch high.

Notice that the image is resized proportionally and not distorted. Do not be concerned if the words do not wrap exactly as shown in Figure 3.15.

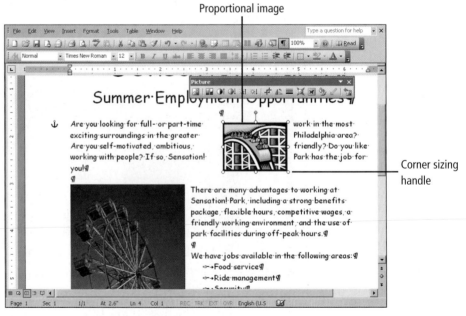

**Figure 3.15**

5 On the Standard toolbar, click the **Save** button ⬚.

## Activity 3.5 Moving a Graphic Object

Once you have chosen one of the image wrapping options, you can move the image anywhere on the page.

**1** Move the pointer to the middle of the roller coaster image but do not click.

The move pointer displays. See Figure 3.16.

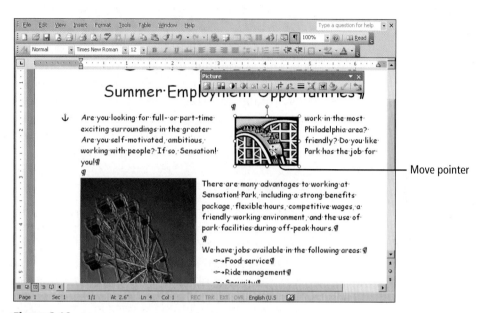

Move pointer

**Figure 3.16**

**2** Click in the middle of the image and, as shown in Figure 3.17, drag it to the right of the paragraph beginning *Are you looking for*.

A dashed border around the pointer indicates the potential position of the image. See Figure 3.17.

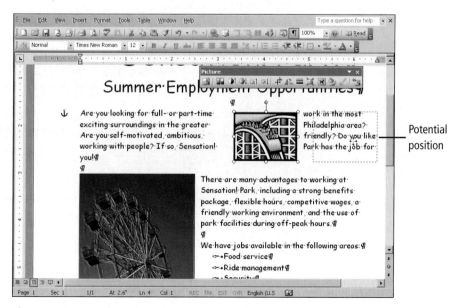

Potential position

**Figure 3.17**

**3** Release the mouse button.

The image moves to the pointer location, and the text wraps at the left border of the image.

**4** On the Standard toolbar, click the **Save** button 🔲.

## Objective 3
## Work with the Drawing Toolbar

The Drawing toolbar has tools to add text boxes, lines, arrows, boxes, circles, and predefined shapes to your document. Many of these drawing objects can be formatted; that is, you can increase line thickness and color, change font colors, and change the background colors and patterns. A drawing canvas is provided as a work area for complex drawings; however, when inserting and formatting simple drawing objects, it is more convenient to turn the drawing canvas off.

### Activity 3.6 Inserting a Text Box

A **text box** is a movable, resizable container for text or graphics. A text box is useful to give text a different orientation from other text in the document because it is can be placed anywhere in the document. A text box can be moved around the document just like a floating image. A text box is a drawing object and, as such, can be placed outside the document margin, resized, and moved. This is easier if you first turn off the drawing canvas. As you progress in your study of Word, you will learn more about using the drawing canvas.

**1** From the **Tools** menu, click **Options**, and then click the **General tab**.

**2** Under **General options**, locate the last check box, **Automatically create drawing canvas when inserting AutoShapes** and, if necessary, clear (click to remove the check mark). Click **OK** to close the **Options** dialog box.

The drawing canvas is turned off.

**3** Check to see the if your Drawing toolbar is displayed at the bottom of your screen. If it is not, right-click either toolbar to activate the Toolbars shortcut menu and then click Drawing.

The Drawing toolbar displays, usually at the bottom of the screen. You can also open the Drawing toolbar by clicking the Drawing button on the Standard toolbar.

**4** Position your document so the bulleted list is near the top of your screen. On the Drawing toolbar, click the **Text Box** button 🔲 and then move the pointer into the document window.

The pointer changes to a crosshair. See Figure 3.18.

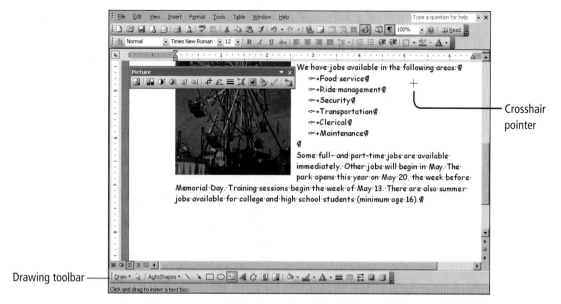

Drawing toolbar

Crosshair
pointer

**Figure 3.18**

**5** Position the crosshair pointer slightly to the right of *Food service* and then drag down and to the right to form an approximately 1½-inch square. Release the mouse button. Your measurement need not be exact.

A text box displays with the insertion point in the upper left corner, and the Text Box toolbar displays.

**6** Type **The SuperSpeed Ferris Wheel, one of the new rides at Sensation! Park**

The text wraps within the text box. See Figure 3.19.

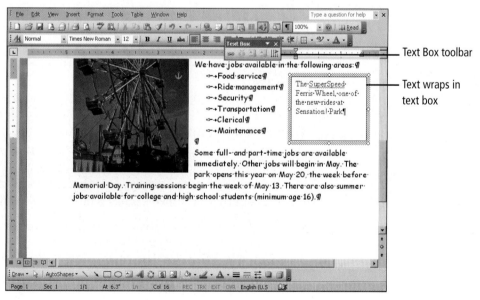

Text Box toolbar

Text wraps in
text box

**Figure 3.19**

**Activity 3.7** Moving and Resizing a Text Box

**1** On the Standard toolbar, click the **Zoom button arrow** `100%  ▾`, and then click **Page Width**.

**2** Move the pointer over a border of the text box until a four-headed arrow pointer displays.

The pointer changes to a move pointer, which looks like a four-way arrow.

**3** Drag the text box down to the empty area below the paragraph beginning *Some full- and part-time* as shown in Figure 3.20. A dashed border around the pointer indicates the potential position of the image.

**4** Release the mouse button.

The text box is moved to the new location. See Figure 3.20.

One-and-a-half inches wide

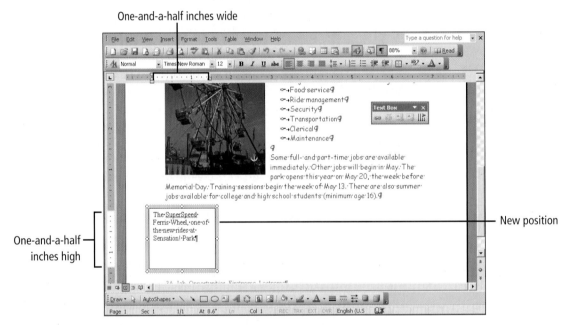

One-and-a-half inches high

New position

**Figure 3.20**

**5** Scroll down until you can see the whole text box. If necessary, position the pointer over the center right sizing handle to display a two-headed pointer and then drag to the right to adjust the text box size until all the text in the box displays on three lines. Drag the lower center handle up slightly to remove excess white space in the text box.

**6** On the Formatting toolbar, click the **Center** button �▤.

The text is horizontally centered within the text box. Compare your screen to Figure 3.21.

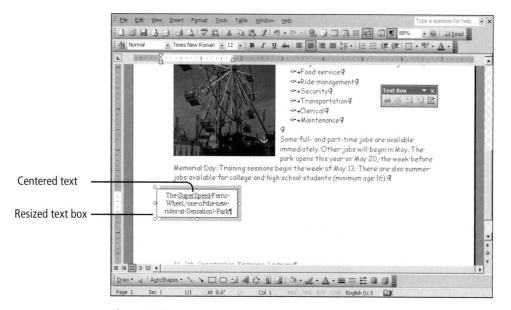

Centered text

Resized text box

**Figure 3.21**

**7** On the Standard toolbar, click the **Save** button.

### Activity 3.8 Inserting an Arrow

Buttons on the Drawing toolbar enable you to create shapes—circles, boxes, lines, and arrows. Arrows are very useful to point out features in graphic objects such as photographs and maps.

**1** On the Drawing toolbar, click the **Arrow** button and move your pointer into the document window.

The pointer changes to a crosshair.

---

**Alert!**

### Does a Large Drawing Box Display?

If you did not deactivate the drawing canvas earlier, clicking buttons on the Drawing toolbar results in the insertion of a large *drawing canvas*, which is a work area for creating drawings. This work area is very handy for combining several graphic objects but gets in the way when you try to add simple shapes to a document. To turn off the drawing canvas, click the Close button on the Drawing Canvas toolbar and click in the drawing canvas area.

The drawing canvas can be deactivated by choosing Tools, Options from the menu. Click the General tab. Clear the *Automatically create drawing canvas when inserting AutoShapes* check box.

**2** Position the crosshair pointer at the center of the left border of the text box.

**3** Drag up and to the right to draw a line to the Ferris wheel picture and then release the mouse button.

The arrowhead points in the direction you dragged the arrow. See Figure 3.22.

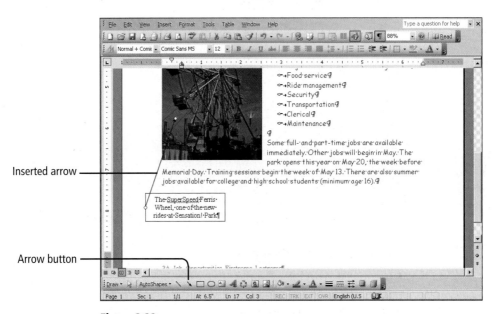

Inserted arrow ——

Arrow button ——

**Figure 3.22**

**4** With the arrow still selected, move your pointer over the white sizing handle on the lower end of the arrow to display a two-headed pointer and then drag up to shorten the arrow until its lower end is near the left edge of the top border of the text box as shown in Figure 3.23.

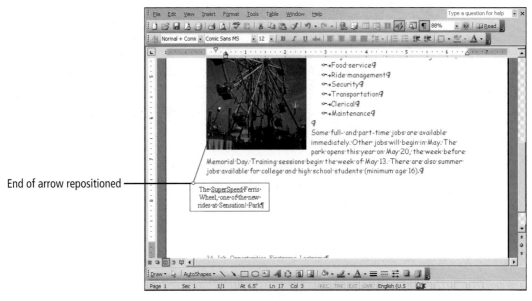

End of arrow repositioned ——

**Figure 3.23**

**5** Move the pointer over the selected arrow and right-click. From the shortcut menu, click **Format AutoShape** and, in the displayed **Format AutoShape** dialog box, click the **Colors and Lines tab**.

**6** Under **Line**, click the **Weight spin** box up arrow three times to select **1.5 pt**.

**7** Under **Arrows**, click the **End Size** arrow and, from the displayed menu, click the largest arrowhead—**Arrow R Size 9**.

Compare your dialog box to Figure 3.24.

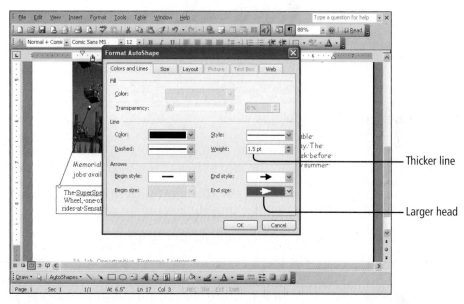

Thicker line

Larger head

**Figure 3.24**

**8** Click **OK**.

The arrow is thicker and has a larger arrowhead.

**9** On the Standard toolbar, click the **Save** button.

**Activity 3.9** Inserting an AutoShape

More than 150 predefined AutoShapes are available to use in documents. These include stars, banners, arrows, and callouts.

**1** On the Drawing toolbar, click the **AutoShapes** button AutoShapes.

Point to the **Stars and Banners** button.

Sixteen star and banner shapes display. See Figure 3.25.

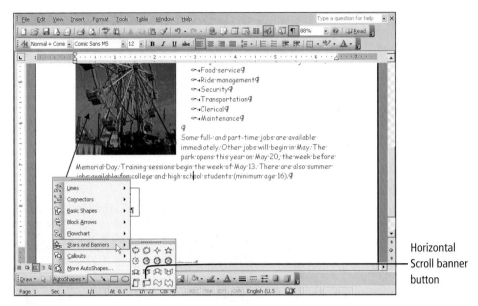

**Figure 3.25**

2️⃣ In the fourth row of the **Stars and Banners** menu, click the second shape, the **Horizontal Scroll** banner button 🔲, and move your pointer into the document window.

A crosshair pointer displays.

3️⃣ Position the crosshair to the right of the text box approximately **3 inches on the horizontal ruler**. As shown in Figure 3.25, drag down and to the right until the banner is about ¾ inch high and 3½ inches wide and release the mouse button. Use the horizontal and vertical rulers to help you determine the size of the banner. If you are not satisfied with your result, click Undo and begin again.

A banner is placed at the bottom of the flyer. See Figure 3.26.

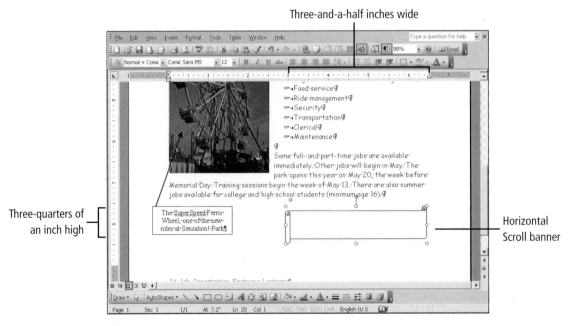

**Figure 3.26**

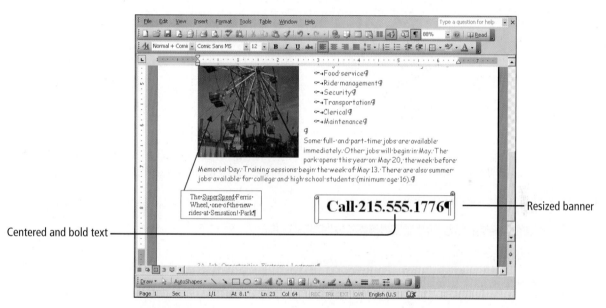

**4** Move the pointer over the banner and right-click. From the shortcut menu, click **Add Text**.

The insertion point is placed in the banner, and a slashed border surrounds the shape.

**5** Type **Call 215.555.1776**

**6** Select the text you just typed. From the Formatting toolbar, click the **Font Size arrow** and click **28**, as shown in Figure 3.27.

**7** Be sure the text is still selected and then on the Formatting toolbar, click the **Bold** button **B**. Adjust the height and width of the AutoShape as necessary.

**8** On the Formatting toolbar, click the **Center** button ▤. Use the sizing handles to adjust the banner until it looks similar to Figure 3.27. Click outside the banner to deselect it.

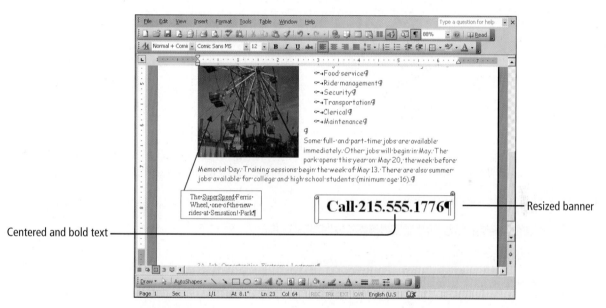

Centered and bold text ——

Resized banner

**Figure 3.27**

**8** On the Standard toolbar, click the **Save** button 🖫. Then, on the Standard toolbar, click the **Print Preview** button 🔍 to view your document.

**9** On the Print Preview toolbar, click the **Print** button 🖨. Close the document.

**End** You have completed Project 3A ————

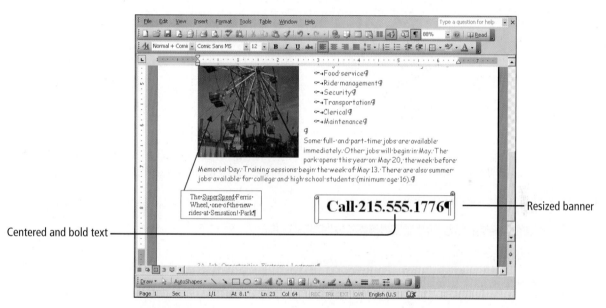

chapter three

# Project 3B **Park Changes**

In Project 3A you worked with clip art and the drawing features of Word. Now you will use tabs and tables to align and organize lists of information.

In Activities 3.10 through 3.24 you will edit a list of changes in age and height restrictions for the rides and other attractions for the coming Sensation! Park season. You will add a tabbed list and two tables. Your completed document will look similar to Figure 3.28. You will save your document as *3B_Park_Changes_Firstname_Lastname.*

**MEMO TO:** Dana Brothers, Vice President, Marketing

**FROM:** McNeal Blackmon

**DATE:** February 25

**SUBJECT:** Final Changes in Hours of Operation, Ticket Prices, and Restrictions

Here are the final changes in hours of operation, ticket prices, and restrictions for the new season. I know you are in a deadline crunch for the brochure, so please take a look at these changes and let me know if you see any problems. If you are comfortable with everything, go ahead and finish the brochure. Let's see if we can get it printed before the New Employee Orientation meetings.

The hours of operation are very similar to last year; the Sunday opening time is the only change:

| Monday-Thursday | 1 p.m. | 10 p.m. |
| Friday | 1 p.m. | 11 p.m. |
| Saturday and Holidays | 11 a.m. | 11 p.m. |
| Sunday | NOON | 11 p.m. |

Admission charges are significantly different, with the price of season passes reduced by $20 for Adults, and increased by $20 for Juniors. Let's hope the 15% increase in revenue is realistic!

| | Age | One Day | Season Pass |
|---|---|---|---|
| **Toddler** | 3 & under | Free | Free |
| **Junior** | 4 to 11 | $19 | $89 |
| **Adult** | 12 to 59 | $39 | $129 |
| **Senior** | 60+ | $29 | $99 |

Height and age restrictions are unchanged for most of the activities, with the following exceptions:

| Activity | Minimum height/age: | To be able to: |
|---|---|---|
| **Speedway Go-Karts** | 52" tall | Drive alone |
| | 16 years old | Drive with a passenger |
| | 40" tall | Ride as a passenger |
| **Bumper Boats** | 44" tall | Drive alone |
| | 14 years old | Drive with a passenger |
| | 32" tall | Ride as a passenger |
| **Miniature Golf** | 10 years old | Play without parent/guardian |
| | No age limit | Play with parent/guardian |
| | 5 years old | Play with 12+ year old companion |

3B_Park_Changes_Firstname_Lastname

**Figure 3.28**
Project 3B—Park Changes Memo

# Objective 4
## Work with Tab Stops

Tab stops are used to indent and align text. By default, tab stops are set every half inch, although the stops are not displayed on the horizontal ruler. Each time you press the tab key, the insertion point moves across the page a half inch. You can also customize tab stops by designating the location and characteristics of the tab stops. Custom tab stops override default tab stops that are to the left of the custom tab stop position. When you create a custom tab stop, its location and tab stop type is displayed on the ruler, as shown in Figure 3.29. The types of tab stops are shown in the table in Figure 3.29.

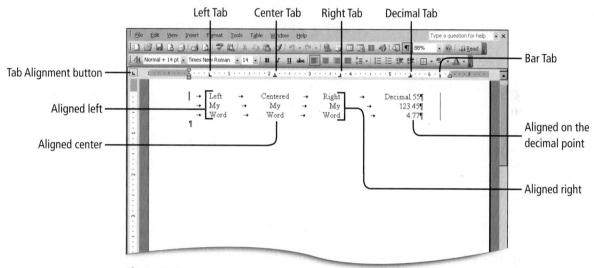

**Figure 3.29**

## Tab Alignment Options

| Type | Tab Alignment Button Displays This Marker | Description |
|------|-------------------------------------------|-------------|
| Left | ⌊ | Text is left aligned at the tab stop and extends to the right. |
| Center | ⊥ | Text is centered around the tab stop. |
| Right | ⌟ | Text is right aligned at the tab stop and extends to the left. |
| Decimal | ⊥ | The decimal point aligns at the tab stop. |
| Bar | ▯ | A vertical bar is inserted in the document at the tab stop. |
| First Line Indent | ▽ | Indents the first line of a paragraph. |
| Hanging Indent | ⊔ | Indents all lines but the first in a paragraph. |

**Figure 3.30**

## Activity 3.10 Setting Tab Stops

Tab stops enable you to position text on a line. Tab stops can be set before or after typing text, but it is easiest to set them before you type the text.

**1** On the Standard toolbar, click the **Open** button. Navigate to the location where the student files for this textbook are stored. Locate **w03B_Park_Changes** and click once to select it. Then, in the lower right corner of the **Open** dialog box, click **Open**.

The w03B_Park_Changes file opens. See Figure 3.31.

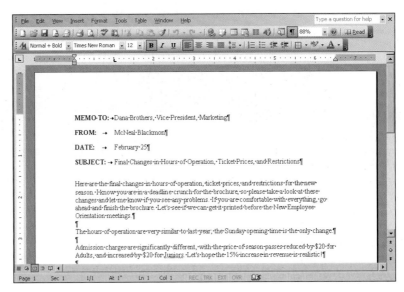

**Figure 3.31**

**2** From the **File** menu, click **Save As**. In the **Save As** dialog box, click the **Save in** arrow and navigate to the location in which you are storing your files for this chapter.

**3** In the **File name** box, type **3B_Park_Changes_Firstname_Lastname** and click **Save**.

The document is saved with a new name. Make sure you substitute your name where indicated.

**4** In the paragraph beginning *The hours of operation*, position the insertion point after the colon at the end of the paragraph. Press [Enter] two times.

**5** At the left end of the horizontal ruler, position the pointer over the **Tab Alignment** button.

A ScreenTip displays showing the type of tab currently selected, as shown in Figure 3.32.

Options for tab alignment ——

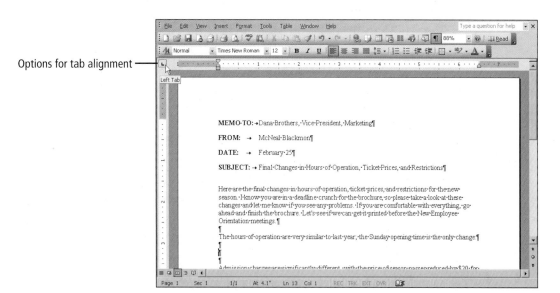

**Figure 3.32**

**6** Click the **Tab Alignment** button ⌊L⌋ once, move the mouse pointer away, and then point to the button again to display the next ScreenTip—*Center Tab*. Repeat this process to cycle through and view the ScreenTip for each of the types of tab stops, and then stop at the **Left Tab** button ⌊L⌋.

**7** Move the pointer over the horizontal ruler and click at the **1 inch mark**.

A left tab stop is inserted in the ruler. See Figure 3.33. Left tab stops are used when you want the information to align on the left.

Left alignment tab at the 1-inch mark

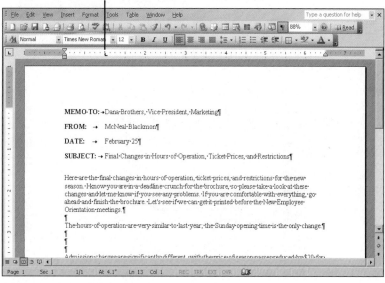

**Figure 3.33**

**8** Click the **Tab Alignment** button ⌊L⌋ two times to display the **Right Tab** button ⌊⌐⌋.

**9** At the **4 inch mark on the horizontal ruler**, click once.

A right tab stop is inserted in the ruler. See Figure 3.34. Right tab stops are used to align information on the right. As you type, the information will extend to the left of the tab stop.

Right alignment tab

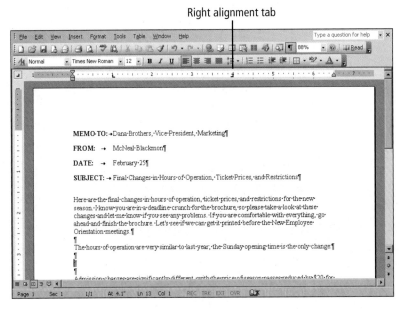

**Figure 3.34**

**10** Click the **Tab Alignment** button six times to display the **Center Tab** button.

**11** Click at the **5 inch mark on the horizontal ruler**, and then click again at the **6 inch mark**.

Two center tab stops are inserted in the ruler. See Figure 3.35. Center tab stops are used when you want the information to be centered over a particular point.

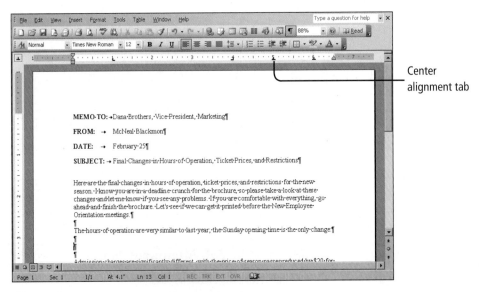

Center alignment tab

**Figure 3.35**

## Activity 3.11 Formatting and Removing Tab Stops

The Tabs dialog box enables you to add, remove, and format tab stops. You can also change the alignment of a tab stop.

**1** From the **Format** menu, click **Tabs**.

The Tabs dialog box displays. The tabs you just added to the ruler for the paragraph at the insertion point location are displayed under the *Tab stop position*, as shown in Figure 3.36.

Tabs you set on the ruler

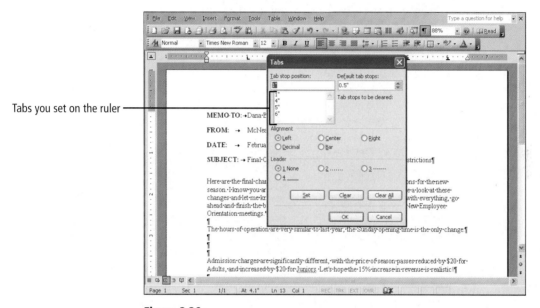

**Figure 3.36**

**2** Under **Tab stop position**, click **4"**.

The tab stop at the 4-inch mark is selected.

**3** At the bottom of the **Tabs** dialog box, click the **Clear** button.

The tab stop is ready to be removed, although it won't be removed until you close the dialog box. See Figure 3.37.

Tab stop removed

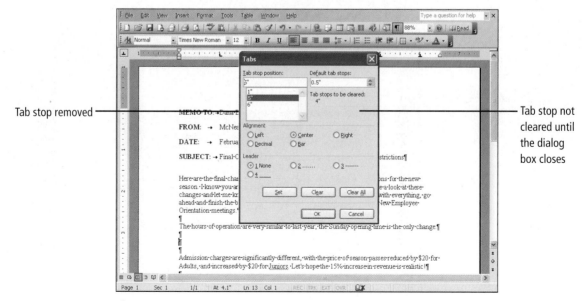

Tab stop not cleared until the dialog box closes

**Figure 3.37**

**4** Under **Tab stop position**, click **5"**.

**5** Under **Leader**, click the **2** option button. Near the bottom of the **Tabs** dialog box, click **Set**.

The Set button saves the change. The tab stop at the 5 inch mark now has a ***dot leader***. Dot leader tabs are used to help draw the reader's eye across the page from one item to the next. Later, when you tab to this spot, a row of dots will display. See Figure 3.38.

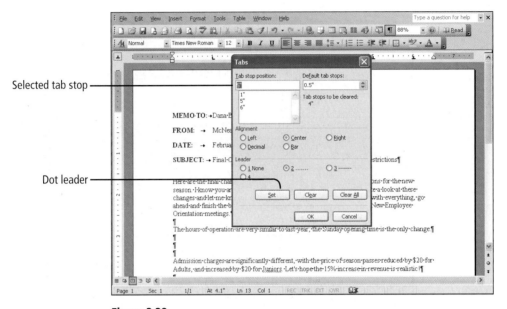

**Figure 3.38**

**6** Under **Tab stop position**, click **5"**.

**7** Under **Alignment**, click the **Right** option button. Near the bottom of the **Tabs** dialog box, click **Set**. Repeat this process to change the tab stop at the **6 inch mark** to a **Right** align tab stop as shown in Figure 3.39.

The tab stops at the 5- and 6-inch marks will be right aligned when the dialog box is closed.

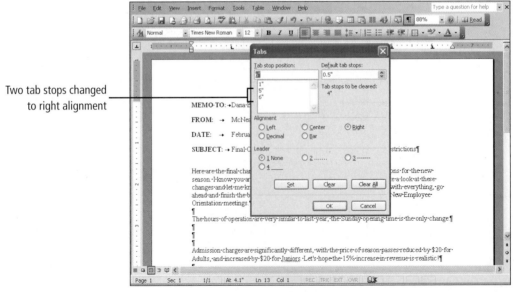

**Figure 3.39**

**8** At the bottom of the **Tabs** dialog box, click **OK**.

Notice that the changes are reflected in the ruler. See Figure 3.40.

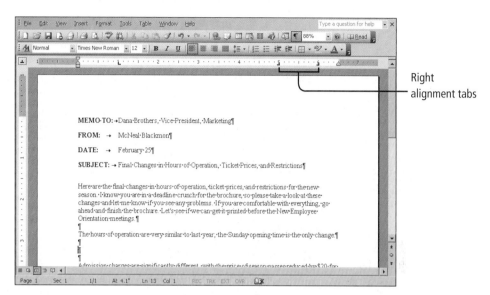

Right
alignment tabs

**Figure 3.40**

**9** From the **View** menu, click **Header and Footer**. On the Header and Footer toolbar, click the **Switch Between Header and Footer** button [icon].

**10** On the Header and Footer toolbar, click the **Insert AutoText** button `Insert AutoText ▾`, and then click **Filename**.

The filename is inserted in the footer. The file extension .doc may or may not display, depending on your Word settings.

**11** On the Header and Footer toolbar, click the **Close** button `Close`.

**12** On the Standard toolbar, click the **Save** button [icon].

### Activity 3.12 Using Tab Stops to Enter Text

**1** With the insertion point positioned at the beginning of the line with the new tab stops, press ⟨Tab⟩.

The insertion point moves to the first tab, which is at the 1 inch mark, and the nonprinting character for a tab (a small arrow) displays. See Figure 3.41.

Tab stop

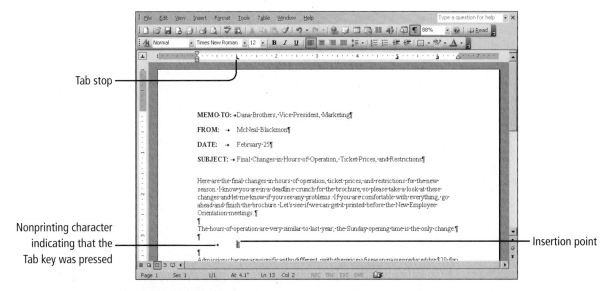

Nonprinting character
indicating that the
Tab key was pressed

Insertion point

**Figure 3.41**

**2** Type **Monday-Thursday**

Notice that the left edge of the text stays aligned with the tab stop.

**3** Press ⎣Tab⎦.

The insertion point moves to the tab stop at the 5 inch mark, and a dot leader is added, helping to draw your eye across the page to the next item. See Figure 3.42.

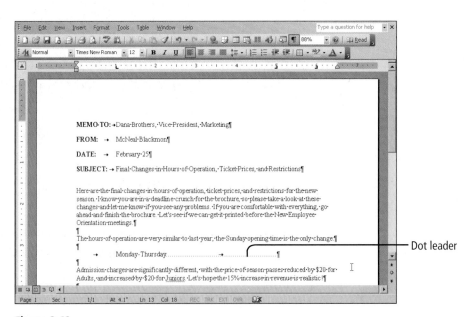

Dot leader

**Figure 3.42**

# More Knowledge — Using Dot Leaders

### A String of Periods Is Not the Same Thing

It is sometimes tempting to hold down the Period key on the keyboard to create a string of dots. This is not a good idea for several reasons. The periods, because of proportional spacing, may be spaced differently between rows, the periods will not line up, and, most importantly, the column on the right side of the string of periods may look lined up, but will be crooked when printed. If you need a string of dots, always use a tab with a dot leader.

**4** Type **1 p.m.**

With a right tab, the right edge of the text stays aligned with the tab mark, and the text moves to the left. See Figure 3.43.

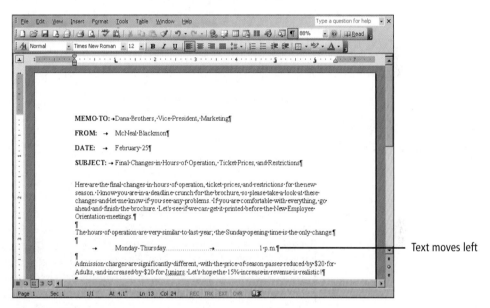

— Text moves left

**Figure 3.43**

**5** Press Tab. Type **10 p.m.**

The right edge of the text is aligned on the tab mark.

**6** Press Enter.

Recall that when you press Enter, the formatting of the previous paragraph, including tab stops, is copied to the new paragraph. Tab stops are a form of paragraph formatting, and thus, the information about them is stored in the paragraph mark to which they were applied.

**7** Type the following to complete the park schedule:

| | | |
|---|---|---|
| **Friday** | 1 p.m. | 11 p.m. |
| **Saturday and Holidays** | 11 a.m. | 11 p.m. |
| **Sunday** | NOON | 11 p.m. |

Compare your screen to Figure 3.44.

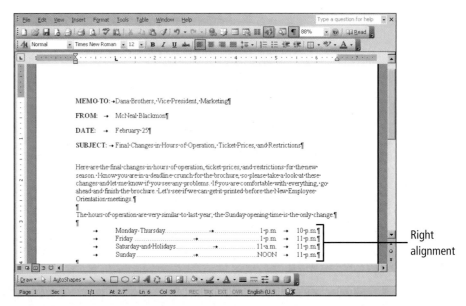

Right alignment

**Figure 3.44**

**8** On the Standard toolbar, click the **Save** button 🖫.

**Another Way** — **Indents versus Tabs**

### *Using an Indent to Start a Tabbed List*

If the items in the first column of a list are indented the same amount using a left-aligned tab, you can save keystrokes by indenting the paragraph instead. You can do this by using the Increase Indent button on the Formatting toolbar, or by using the Paragraph dialog box. You can also drag the Left Indent marker from the left side of the ruler and position it at the desired location. When you are finished typing the list, you can drag the marker back to the left margin position. When you use an indent at the beginning of the paragraph for a tabbed list, you do not have to press the Tab key before you type the first item in the list.

### **Activity 3.13** Moving Tab Stops

If you are not satisfied with the arrangement of your text after setting tab stops, it is easy to reposition the text by moving tab stops.

**1** In the four lines of tabbed text, disregard any wavy green lines or right-click them and click **Ignore Once** to remove them. Move the pointer into the left margin area, to the left of the first line of tabbed text. When the pointer changes to a white arrow, drag down to select the four lines of text as shown in Figure 3.45.

By selecting all of the lines, changes you make to the tabs will be made to the tabs in all four rows simultaneously.

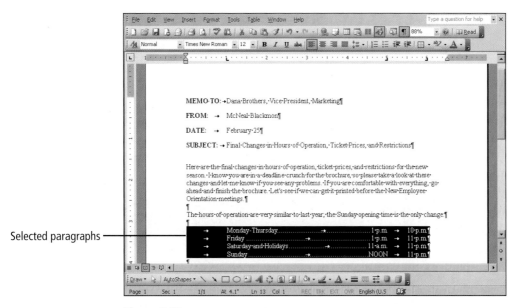

Selected paragraphs ——

**Figure 3.45**

**2** With the four lines of tabbed text selected, move the pointer into the horizontal ruler and position it so the tip of the pointer arrow is touching the 1 inch tab stop mark.

**3** When you see the ScreenTip *Left Tab*, drag the tab stop mark to the left to the **0.5 inch mark on the ruler** as shown in Figure 3.46 and then release the mouse button.

The first column of text is moved to the new location, as shown in Figure 3.46.

---

**Note** — Selecting Tab Stop Marks

Selecting and moving tab stop marks on the horizontal ruler requires fairly exact mouse movement. The tip of the pointer needs to touch the tab mark. If you miss it by even a little, you will probably insert another tab stop. One way to tell if you are in the right position to move a tab stop on the ruler is to look for a ScreenTip showing the tab type. To remove an accidental tab stop when you are trying to select an existing one, click the Undo button and try again. Alternatively, you can drag the unwanted tab stop marker below the ruler and release the mouse button.

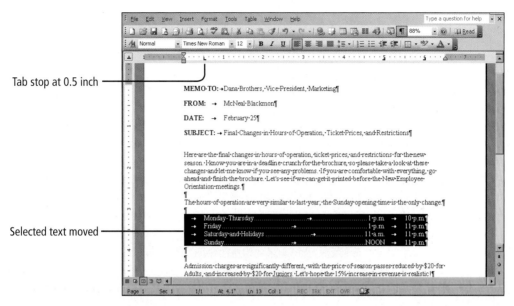

Tab stop at 0.5 inch

Selected text moved

**Figure 3.46**

**4** Move the pointer into the ruler, and position it so the tip of the pointer arrow is touching the 5 inch tab stop mark and you see the ScreenTip *Right Tab*. Drag the tab stop mark to the left to the **4.5 inch mark on the ruler**.

Compare your screen to Figure 3.47.

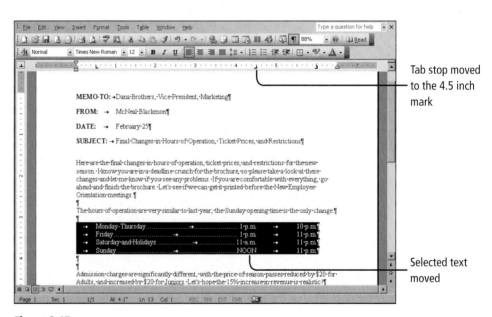

Tab stop moved to the 4.5 inch mark

Selected text moved

**Figure 3.47**

**5** Click anywhere to deselect and then, on the Standard toolbar, click the **Save** button 🔲.

# Objective 5
## Create a Table

The table feature in Word processing programs has largely replaced the use of tabs because of its flexibility and ease of use. **_Tables_** consist of rows and columns and are used to organize data. You can create an empty table and then fill in the boxes, which are also called **_cells_**. You can also convert existing text into a table if the text is properly formatted.

If a table needs to be adjusted, you can add rows or columns and change the height of rows and the width of columns. The text and numbers in the cells can be formatted, as can the cell backgrounds and borders.

### Activity 3.14 Creating a Table

**1** In the paragraph beginning _Admission charges_, position the insertion point after the exclamation point at the end of the second sentence. Press [Enter] two times.

**2** On the Standard toolbar, click the **Insert Table** button 🔲.

**3** Move the pointer down to the cell in the third row and third column of the **Insert Table** menu.

The cells are highlighted, and the table size is displayed at the bottom of the menu, as shown in Figure 3.48.

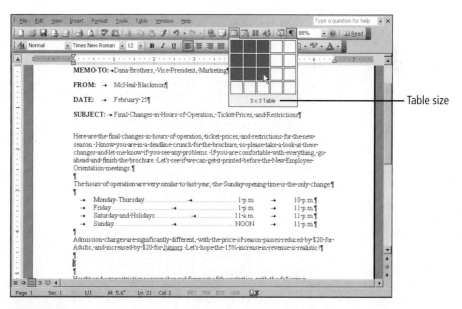

**Figure 3.48**

**4** Click the mouse button.

A table with three rows and three columns is created at the insertion point location and the insertion point is placed in the upper left cell. The table fills the width of the page, from the left margin to the right margin, as shown in Figure 3.49.

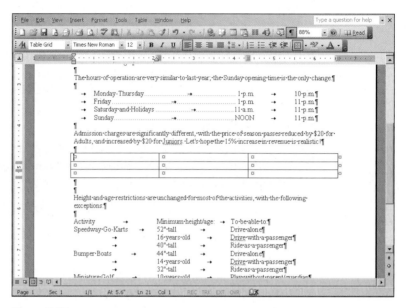

**Figure 3.49**

**5** Press ⎡Tab⎤ to the second cell in the first row of the table.

---

### **Note** — Moving Between Cells in a Table

**Using the Tab Key Rather than the Enter Key**

The natural tendency is to press Enter to move from one cell to the next. In a table, however, pressing Enter creates another line in the same cell, similar to the way you add a new line in a document. If you press Enter by mistake, you can remove the extra line by pressing the Backspace key.

---

**6** Type **Age** and press ⎡Tab⎤.

**7** Type **One Day** and press ⎡Tab⎤.

The text displays in the top row, and the insertion point moves to the first cell in the second row, as shown in Figure 3.50.

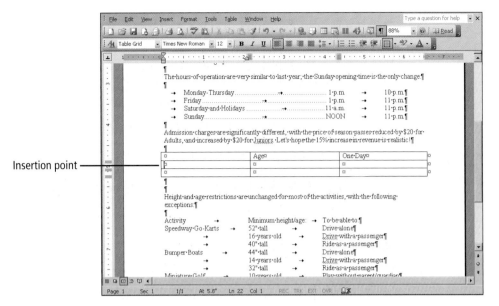

Insertion point

**Figure 3.50**

**8** Type the following to complete the table (do not press ⌨Enter or ⌨Tab after the last item):

| | | |
|---|---|---|
| **Toddler** | **3 & under** | **Free** |
| **Adult** | **12 to 59** | **$39** |

Compare your screen to Figure 3.51.

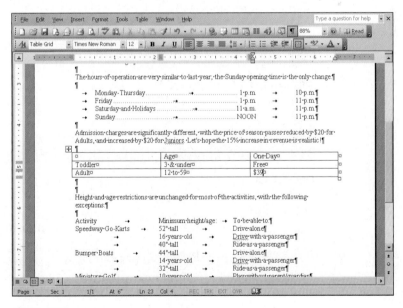

**Figure 3.51**

**9** On the Standard toolbar, click the **Save** button.

---

## More Knowledge — Navigating in a Table

### *Moving Between Cells in a Table*

You can move to a previous cell in a table by pressing Shift + Tab. This action selects the contents of the previous cell. The selection moves back one cell at a time each time you press Tab while holding down Shift. You can also use the up or down arrow keys to move up or down a column. The left and right arrow keys, however, move the insertion point one character at a time within a cell.

---

### Activity 3.15 Adding a Row to a Table

You can add rows to the beginning, middle, or end of a table.

**1** With the insertion point in the last cell in the table, press Tab.

A new row is added to the bottom of the table. See Figure 3.52.

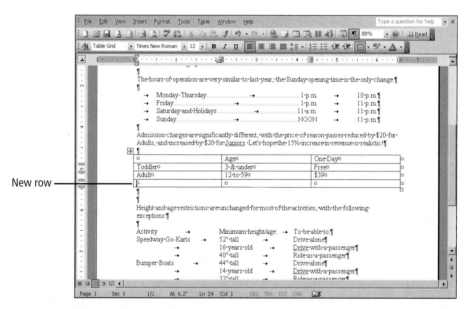

New row

**Figure 3.52**

**2** In the first cell of the new row, type **Senior** and then press Tab.

**3** Type **60+** and press Tab. Type **$29**

Compare your new row to Figure 3.53.

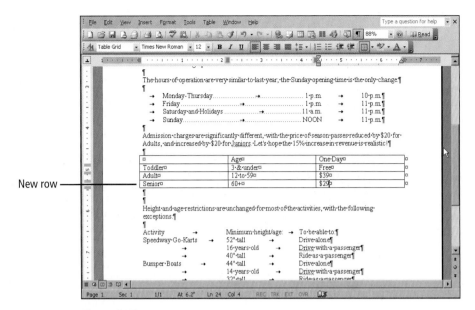

**Figure 3.53**

New row —

**4** In the table row beginning *Adult*, click anywhere to place the insertion point.

**5** From the **Table** menu, point to **Insert** and then click **Rows Above**.

A new row is added above the row containing the insertion point. See Figure 3.54.

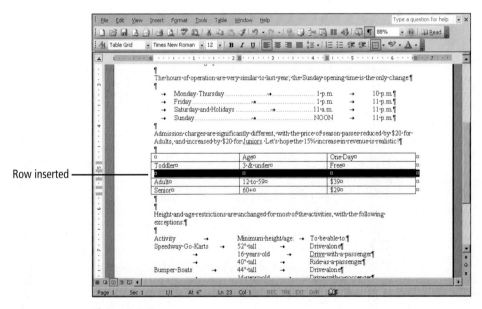

Row inserted —

**Figure 3.54**

**6** Type **Junior** and press Tab.

When the entire row is selected, text is automatically placed in the cell on the left.

**7** Type **4 to 11** and press Tab. Type **$19**

Compare your table to Figure 3.55.

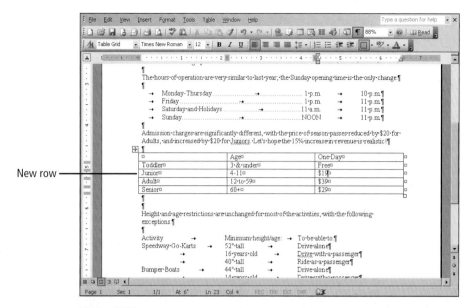

New row

**Figure 3.55**

**8** On the Standard toolbar, click the **Save** button.

### Activity 3.16 Changing the Width of a Table Column

In Word tables, you can change the column widths easily and quickly and adjust them as often as necessary to create a visually appealing table.

**1** Move the pointer over the right boundary of the first column until the pointer changes to a left- and right-pointing resize arrow, as shown in Figure 3.56.

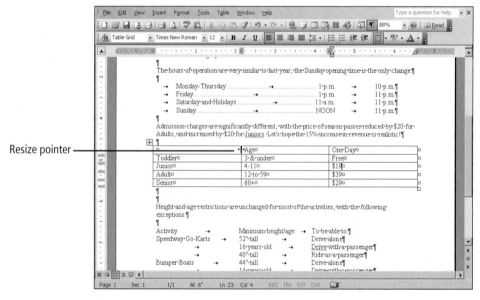

Resize pointer

**Figure 3.56**

**2** Drag the boundary to the left until the first column is about 1-inch wide, to approximately the **1 inch mark on the horizontal ruler**.

Use the horizontal ruler as a guide. If only one row resizes, click the Undo button and start again.

**3** Drag the right boundary of the second column to the left until the column is about 1-inch wide, to approximately the **2 inch mark on the horizontal ruler**.

**4** Drag the right boundary of the third column to the left until the column is about 1-inch wide, to approximately the **3 inch mark on the horizontal ruler**.

Compare your table to Figure 3.57.

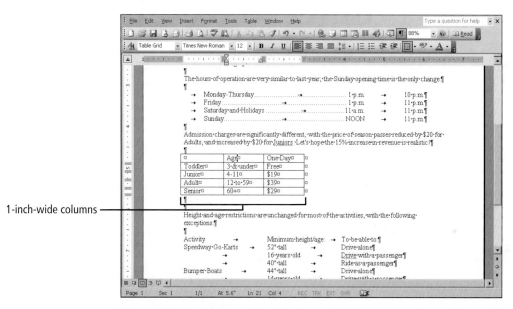

1-inch-wide columns

**Figure 3.57**

**5** On the Standard toolbar, click the **Save** button 🔲.

### Activity 3.17 Adding a Column to a Table

**1** In the last column of the table, click anywhere in the column to position the insertion point.

**2** From the **Table** menu, point to **Insert**, and then click **Columns to the Right**.

A new column is added to the right of the column containing the insertion point and is the same width as that column. See Figure 3.58.

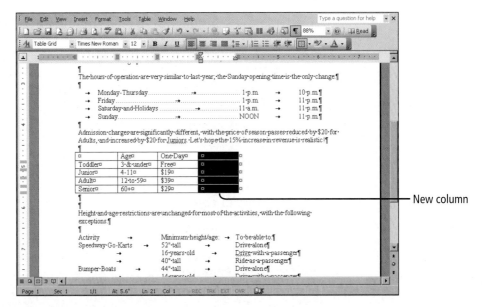

New column

**Figure 3.58**

**3** Type **Season Pass**

In a selected column, text is entered in the top cell when you type. If necessary, drag the column slightly to the right so that the text displays on one line.

**4** Complete the column with the following information. Compare your table with Figure 3.59.

Toddler **Free**
Junior **$89**
Adult **$129**
Senior **$99**

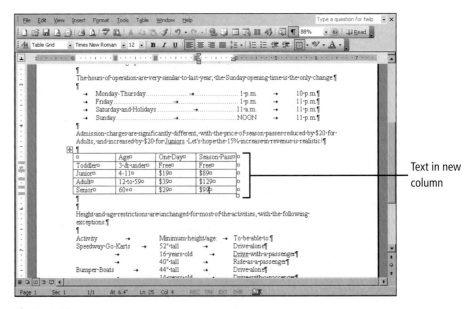

Text in new column

**Figure 3.59**

**5** On the Standard toolbar, click the **Save** button.

## More Knowledge — Using Tabs in Tables

You can also add tabs to a table column so you can indent items within a table cell. The easiest way to add a tab is to click on the ruler to set the location within a column. Then you can drag the tab stop indicator to change the location of the tab within the column or add the hanging indent marker so multiple lines in a list are evenly indented. To move to the tabbed location within the cell, press Ctrl + Tab.

## Objective 6
## Format Tables

Formatted tables are more attractive and easier to read. When you type numbers, for example, they line up on the left of a column instead of on the right until you format them. With Word's formatting tools, you can shade cells, format the table borders and grid, and center the table between the document margins. All of these features make a table more inviting to the reader.

### Activity 3.18 Formatting Text in Cells

In addition to aligning text in cells, you can also add emphasis to the text.

**1** Click anywhere in the cell containing the word *Age*, hold down the left mouse button, and then drag to the right until the second, third, and fourth cells in the top row are selected. See Figure 3.60.

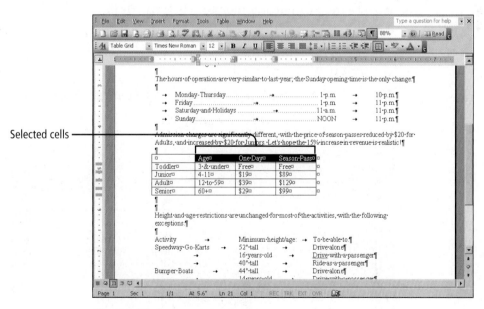

Selected cells ——

**Figure 3.60**

2 On the Formatting toolbar, click the **Bold** button [B], and then click the **Center** button [≣].

The text in the first row of cells is bold and centered, as shown in Figure 3.61.

Bold, centered text ———

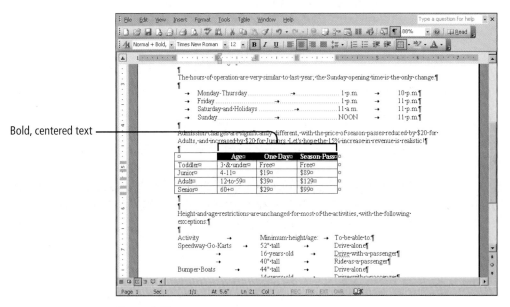

**Figure 3.61**

3 Click in the cell containing the word *Toddler* and then drag down to select the second, third, fourth, and fifth cells in the first column.

4 On the Formatting toolbar, click the **Bold** button [B].

5 In the third column, click in the cell containing *Free*, drag down and to the right until all of the cells in the last two columns, except the first row, are selected.

6 From the Formatting toolbar, click the **Align Right** button [≣].

Compare your table to Figure 3.62.

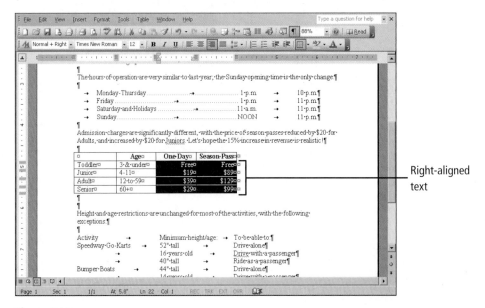

Right-aligned text

**Figure 3.62**

**7** Click anywhere to deselect, and then on the Standard toolbar, click the **Save** button 🖫.

### Activity 3.19  Shading Cells

Backgrounds can be added to cells to differentiate them from other cells.

**1** In the cell containing the word *Age*, drag to the right to select the second, third, and fourth cells in the top row.

**2** From the **Format** menu, click **Borders and Shading**.

The Borders and Shading dialog box displays.

**3** In the **Borders and Shading** dialog box click the **Shading tab**.

**4** Under **Fill**, in the second row, click the third button as shown in Figure 3.63.

The name of the shading option—*Gray-10%*—displays to the right of the shading option buttons, and the Preview area shows what the shading will look like in the table.

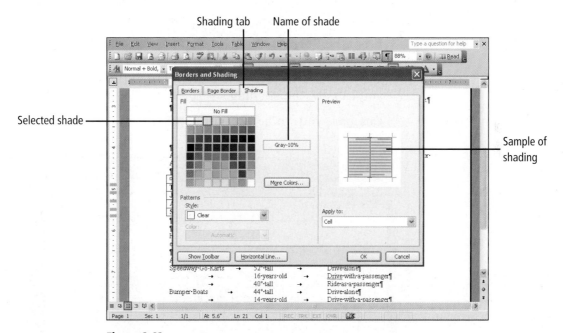

**Figure 3.63**

**5** Click **OK**. Click anywhere in the document to deselect the text.

A light gray background is applied to the three column headings. See Figure 3.64.

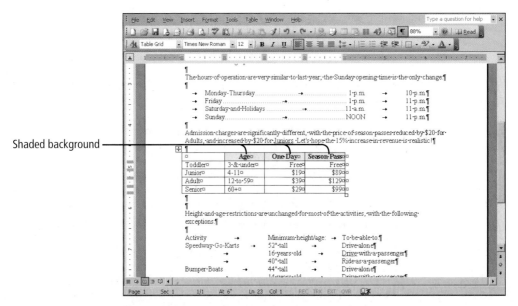

Shaded background

**Figure 3.64**

**6** Click in the cell containing the word *Toddler*, drag down until the second, third, fourth, and fifth cells in the first column are selected.

**7** From the **Format** menu, click **Borders and Shading**. Under **Fill**, click the same shading option you chose for the row headings— Gray-10%. Click **OK**. Click anywhere in the document to deselect so you can see the shading.

Compare your table to Figure 3.65.

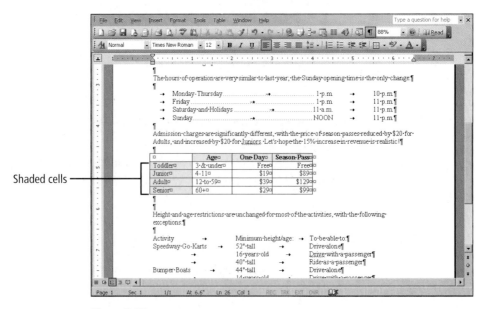

Shaded cells

**Figure 3.65**

**8** On the Standard toolbar, click the **Save** button.

### Activity 3.20 Changing the Table Border

You can modify or remove the border from the entire table, a selected cell, or individual boundaries of a cell.

**1** Click in any cell in the table. From the **Format** menu, click **Borders and Shading**.

The Borders and Shading dialog box displays.

**2** In the **Borders and Shading** dialog box, click the **Borders tab**.

**3** Under **Setting**, click **Grid**.

The Preview area in the right portion of the dialog box displays the current border settings, and the line width is displayed in the Width box, as shown in Figure 3.66.

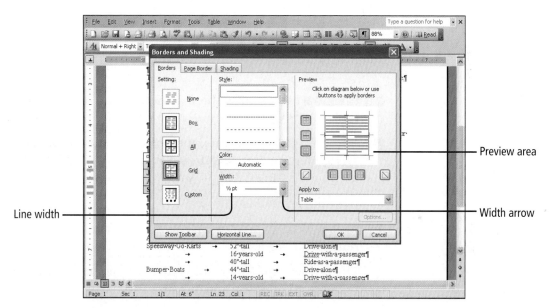

Line width ——

—— Preview area

—— Width arrow

**Figure 3.66**

**4** Click the **Width arrow**, and then from the displayed list, click **1½ pt**.

Notice, under Preview, the outside border is changed to a thicker 1½ point width, while the inner grid lines remain at ½ point width. See Figure 3.67.

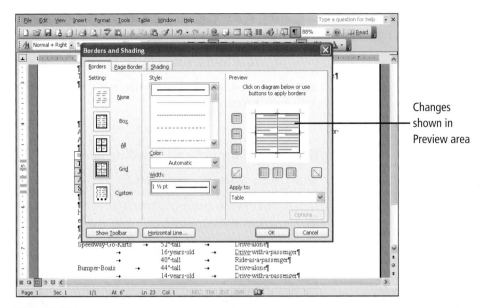

Changes shown in Preview area

**Figure 3.67**

[5] Click **OK**, and then click anywhere in the document to deselect the table.

[6] In the empty cell at the upper left of the table, click once. From the **Table** menu, point to **Select**, and then click **Cell**.

[7] From the **Format** menu, click **Borders and Shading**. Be sure that the **Borders tab** is selected.

[8] In the **Preview** area, point to and then click the top border twice to remove all borders.

The first click returns the border to ½ point, the second click removes the border. See Figure 3.68.

Top border line removed

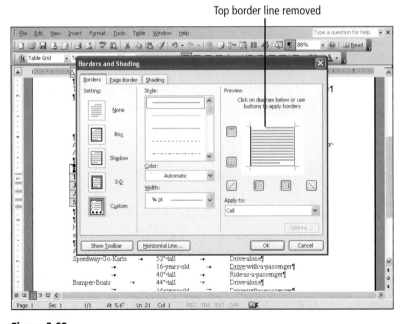

**Figure 3.68**

**9** In the **Preview** area, click the left border twice, until there is no border displayed.

The left border is removed.

**10** Click the **Width arrow**, and from the displayed list, click **1½ pt**.

**11** In the **Preview** area, click the bottom border once.

The bottom border is widened to 1½ point. ¶

**12** In the **Preview** area, click the right border once.

The right border is widened to 1½ point, as shown in Figure 3.69.

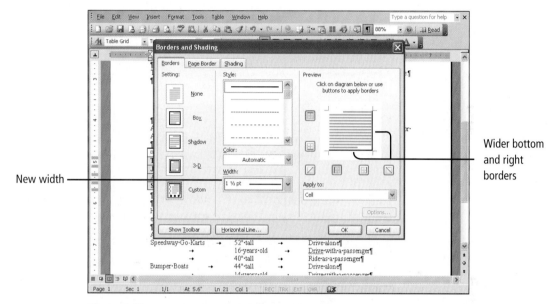

New width ——— ——— Wider bottom and right borders

**Figure 3.69**

**13** Click **OK**. Click anywhere in the document to deselect the table.

Compare your table to Figure 3.70.

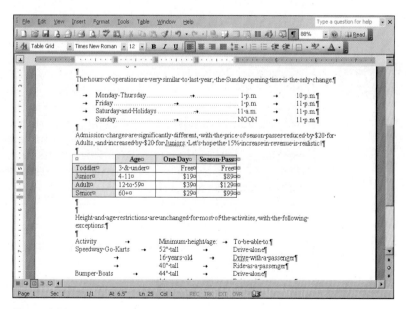

**Figure 3.70**

**14** On the Standard toolbar, click the **Save** button .

### Activity 3.21 Centering a Table

**1** Click anywhere in the table.

**2** From the **Table** menu, click **Table Properties**.

The Table Properties dialog box displays.

**3** In the **Table Properties** dialog box click the **Table tab**.

**4** Under **Alignment**, click **Center**. See Figure 3.71.

Table tab

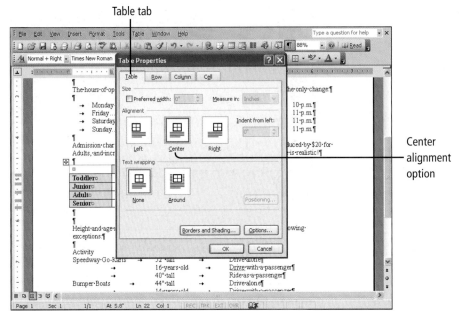

Center
alignment
option

**Figure 3.71**

**5** Click **OK**.

The table is centered horizontally between the left and right margins.

---

**Another Way** ── **Centering a Table**

You can center a table by clicking the Center button on the Formatting tool-bar. First you must select the entire table. To select a table, from the Table menu, point to Select and then click Table. Alternatively, in Print Layout view, rest the pointer on the upper left corner of the table until the table move handle appears, and then click the table move handle to select the table. After the table is selected, on the Formatting toolbar, click the Center button.

---

**6** Place the insertion point in the blank line just below the table and press Delete.

There should be only one empty paragraph before and one empty paragraph after the table.

**7** Click the **Show/Hide ¶** button 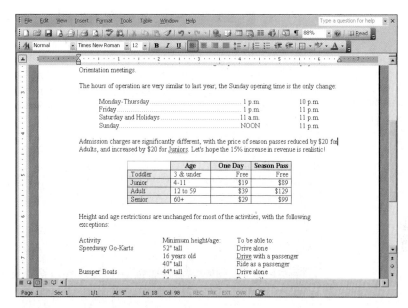.

The nonprinting characters are hidden. Your table should look like Figure 3.72.

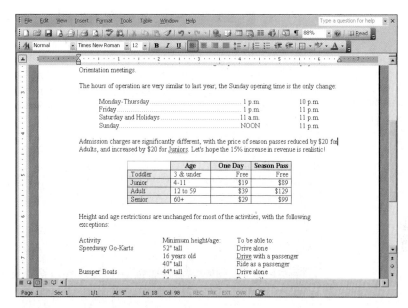

**Figure 3.72**

**8** Click the **Show/Hide ¶** button to redisplay the nonprinting characters.

**9** On the Standard toolbar, click the **Save** button.

## Objective 7
## Create a Table from Existing Text

The Insert Table feature is useful if you are beginning a new table, but Word also provides a tool that enables you to convert existing text into a table. The text needs to be marked using ***separator characters***—usually tabs or commas that separate the text in each line. When you convert text to a table, you can have Word optimize the column widths at the same time. You can also add blank rows or columns, if needed.

### Activity 3.22 Converting Text to Tables

If text is separated with a recognized separator character, and the text is selected, converting text to a table is an easy process.

**1** Scroll as necessary to view the lower portion of the document on your screen. In the block of text at the end of the document, beginning with *Activity* and continuing to the end of the document, notice the tab marks indicating where the [Tab] key was pressed.

The tab marks can act as separator characters for the purpose of converting text to a table. See Figure 3.73.

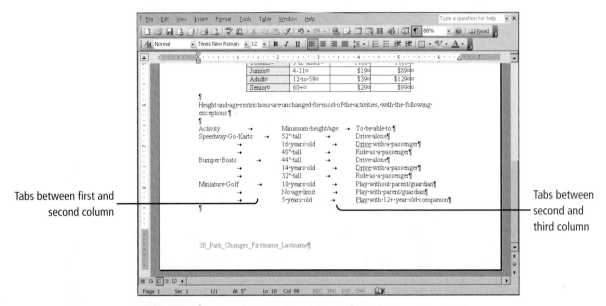

Tabs between first and second column

Tabs between second and third column

**Figure 3.73**

## More Knowledge — Formatting Text to Convert to a Table

If you have text you would like to convert into a table, you will need to separate the columns using a separator character. Tabs and commas are the most commonly used separators, but you can specify a number of different marks, including dashes, dollar signs, or colons. You must be consistent, however. Word will not recognize a mixture of tabs and commas as separators in the same block of text.

**2** Click to position the insertion point to the left of the word *Activity*, hold down ⬚Shift, and then click at the end of the last line, after the word *companion*.

**3** With the text selected, from the **Table** menu, point to **Convert**, and then click **Text to Table**.

The Convert Text to Table dialog box displays. Under Table size, the Number of columns should be 3.

**4** In the **Convert Text to Table** dialog box, under **AutoFit behavior**, click the **AutoFit to contents** option button.

**5** Under **Separate text at**, click the **Tabs** option button, if necessary.

Compare your dialog box to Figure 3.74.

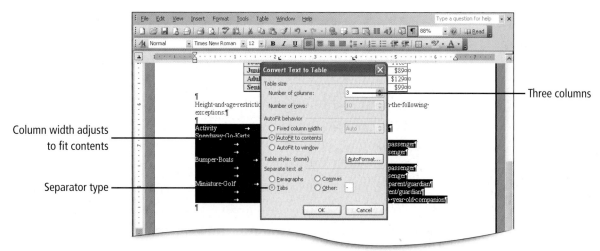

Column width adjusts to fit contents

Separator type

Three columns

**Figure 3.74**

## More Knowledge — Make Sure There Is Only One Separator Between Columns

Before you convert your text to a table, make sure there is only one separator between each column item. If you are using tabs, for example, each tab will move the subsequent item one more column to the right. An extra tab between items will mean that the item will eventually end up in the wrong column. There is an exception to this rule. If you have an empty cell, an extra tab will move the following item to the correct column. Always turn on the nonprinting characters in your document and visually scan the text for extra separators. Also, check the table once you have completed the conversion to make sure everything is in the right column.

**6** At the bottom of the **Convert Text to Table** dialog box, click **OK**. Click anywhere in the document to deselect the table.

Compare your table to Figure 3.75.

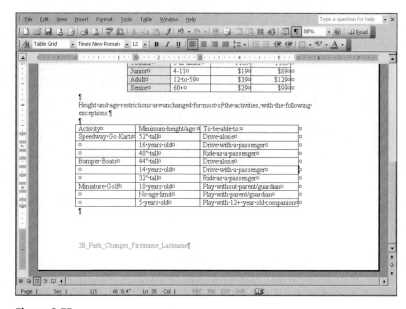

**Figure 3.75**

**7** On the Standard toolbar, click the **Save** button 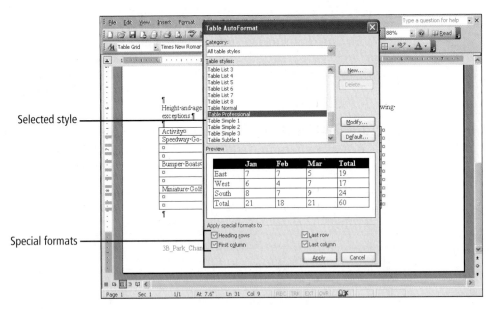.

### Activity 3.23 Applying a Predefined Format to a Table

You can format each of the table elements independently, but there is also a quick way to *AutoFormat* the whole table at one time, using predefined formats.

**1** In the table you just created, click anywhere to position the insertion point within the table.

You do not need to select the entire table to use the AutoFormat feature.

**2** From the **Table** menu, click **Table AutoFormat**.

**3** In the displayed **Table AutoFormat** dialog box, under **Table styles**, click any of the table styles and, under **Preview**, notice the style. Click several of the AutoFormat styles to see what types of formatting are available.

**4** Under **Table styles**, scroll toward the bottom of the list and click **Table Professional**. Under **Apply special formats to**, select the check boxes as necessary so that all four are selected, as shown in Figure 3.76.

Selected style —

Special formats —

**Figure 3.76**

**5** At the bottom of the **Table AutoFormat** dialog box, click **Apply**.

Compare your table to Figure 3.77.

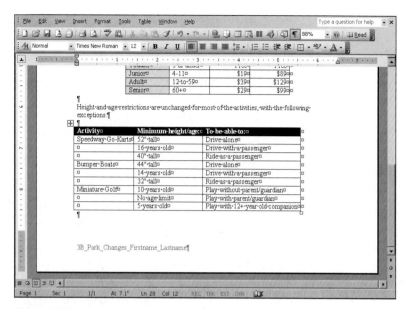

**Figure 3.77**

**6** On the Standard toolbar, click the **Save** button.

### Activity 3.24 Merging Cells and Aligning Text Vertically

Sometimes a title looks better if it spans two or more columns or rows. This can be accomplished by merging cells.

**1** In the table you just formatted, position your pointer over the second cell in the first column—the *Speedway Go-Karts* cell—and then drag down to select the cell and the two empty cells below.

Because of the formatting in the first row, it will appear that four cells are selected, but if you look closely, you will see that the selection area is indented slightly. See Figure 3.78.

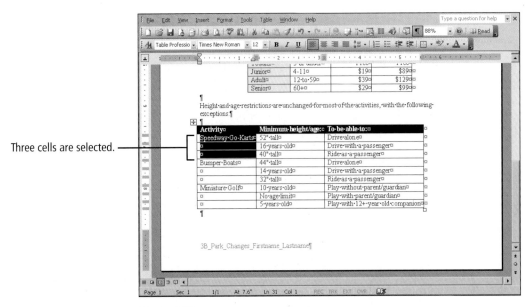

Three cells are selected. ——————————

**Figure 3.78**

**2** On the Formatting toolbar, click the **Bold** button **B**. From the **Table** menu, click **Merge Cells**.

The cells are merged, and the cell borders are removed. Notice that making the text bold also increased the width of the cell. The widths of all of the cells in the first column increased slightly.

**3** Repeat the procedure used in Steps 1 and 2 to bold and merge the three *Bumper Boats* cells and the three *Miniature Golf* cells.

Compare your table to Figure 3.79.

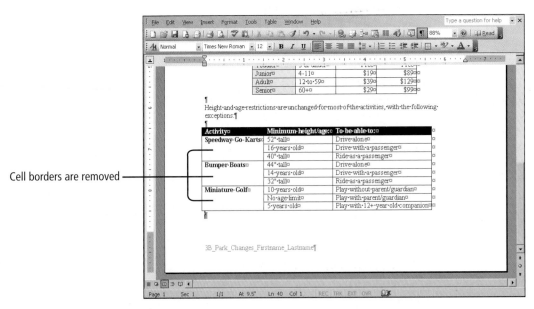

Cell borders are removed ——————————

**Figure 3.79**

**4** In the *Speedway Go-Karts* cell, click once to position the insertion point.

**5** From the **Table** menu, click **Table Properties**.

The Table Properties dialog box displays.

**6** In the **Table Properties** dialog box, click the **Cell tab**. Under **Vertical alignment**, click **Center**. See Figure 3.80.

Cell tab

Vertical center option ⎯

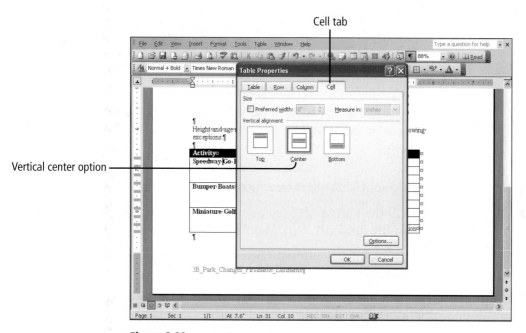

**Figure 3.80**

**7** At the bottom of the **Table Properties** dialog box, click **OK**.

The text is centered vertically.

**Another Way** ⎯ **Aligning Text in a Table**

**Use the Shortcut Menu**

You can use shortcut menus to align text in a table. Right-click the cell, point to Cell Alignment on the shortcut menu, and then click the alignment style you want from the Cell Alignment palette that displays. You can choose from both vertical and horizontal cell alignment options using the Cell Alignment palette.

**8** Drag to select the *Bumper Boats* and the *Miniature Golf* cells, display the **Table** menu, click **Table Properties**, and on the **Cell tab** under **Vertical alignment**, click **Center**. Click **OK**. Click anywhere in the document to deselect the selected cells.

Compare your table to Figure 3.81.

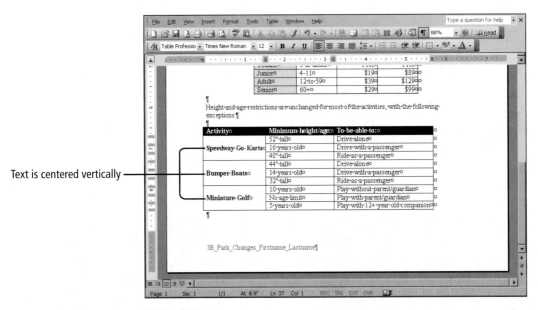

Text is centered vertically ————

**Figure 3.81**

**9** From the **Table** menu, point to **Select** and then click **Table**.

**10** On the Formatting toolbar, click the **Center** button [image]. Click anywhere in the document to deselect the table.

The table is centered horizontally on the page. Compare your finished table to Figure 3.82.

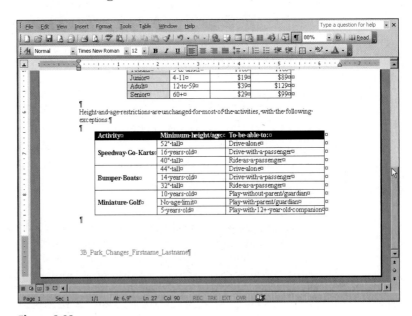

**Figure 3.82**

**11** Press [Ctrl] + [S] to save your changes. On the Standard toolbar, click the **Print Preview** button [image] to view your document.

**12** On the Print Preview toolbar, click the **Print** button [image]. Close Print Preview and close your document.

**End** **You have completed Project 3B** ——————————————————————————————

# Summary

Many graphical elements can be used with Word. In this chapter you practiced inserting, moving, and resizing clip art and pictures. You also worked with the Drawing toolbar and learned how to create basic shapes using the AutoShapes, line, and text box tools. You modified shapes by changing the size, shape, and background color.

An effective way to present information is with a tabbed list or a table. You have used tabs to display information in single rows with multiple columns. A variety of tabs can be used, such as dot-leader, decimal, centered, or right-aligned. You practiced setting, moving, and changing tabs, as well as entering text in a tabbed list.

Tables also have a row and column format, but have the advantage of displaying multiple lines of text in a cell and still maintaining a horizontal relationship with the other cells in the same row. Tables can be formatted to display the information in a manner that emphasizes certain parts of the table. You practiced how to format individual cells or an entire table, using both the Formatting toolbar and the AutoFormat with other commands found under the Table menu. Finally, you practiced how to convert text to a table.

## In This Chapter You Practiced How To

- Insert Clip Art and Pictures
- Modify Clip Art and Pictures
- Work with the Drawing Toolbar
- Work with Tabs
- Create a Table
- Format Tables
- Create a Table from Existing Text

# Concepts Assessments

**Matching**   Match each term in the second column with its correct definition in the first column by writing the letter of the term on the blank line in front of the correct definition.

_____ **1.** A tool that is used to resize an image proportionally.

_____ **2.** Images that can be moved independently of the surrounding text.

_____ **3.** A tool that is used to move an image in a clockwise or counterclockwise direction.

_____ **4.** The term used to identify commas or tabs when they are used to separate text in a line so it can be converted into a table.

_____ **5.** The general term used for any media file such as art, sound, animation, or movies.

_____ **6.** A button on the Drawing toolbar that can be used to insert and to draw a variety of forms.

_____ **7.** A mark on the ruler that indicates the location where the insertion point will be placed when you press Tab.

_____ **8.** The symbol that indicates that an image is attached to the nearest paragraph.

_____ **9.** A group of cells organized in rows and columns.

_____ **10.** Images that behave just like characters in a sentence.

_____ **11.** This button can be used to change the type of tab stop that will be set, before clicking on the ruler.

_____ **12.** The term used to refer to the boxes in a table where information is typed.

_____ **13.** Before you can move an image on your screen you first need to change this property.

_____ **14.** To change the color of the outside border on a table you would open this dialog box.

_____ **15.** To move vertically down a column in a table you can use this key.

**A** Anchor

**B** AutoShapes

**C** Borders and Shading

**D** Cells

**E** Clip

**F** Corner sizing handles

**G** Down arrow

**H** Floating images

**I** Inline images

**J** Rotate handle

**K** Separator characters

**L** Tab Alignment button

**M** Tab stop

**N** Table

**O** Wrapping

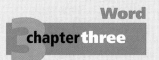
**Fill in the Blank** Write the correct answer in the space provided.

1. To create a table in Word, you can click on the _____ _____ button found on the Standard toolbar.

2. Predefined graphics such as those that come with the Word program or that can be downloaded from the Web are known as _____.

3. When a graphic image is selected, _____ _____ display around the edge of the image.

4. To align text to the contours of an irregularly shaped graphic, you would choose the _____ wrapping option.

5. A type of drawing object in which you can insert text, which can be placed outside of the document margin, is known as a _____ _____.

6. A series of dots following a tab that serve to guide the reader's eye is known as a dot _____.

7. A work area used for combining several graphic objects, known as the drawing _____, can also be turned off when adding simple shapes to a document.

8. To move from cell to cell across a table as you enter text, press _____.

9. To align a table on a page, you can use the _____ _____ dialog box.

10. A quick way to format a table is to use the _____ command found on the Table menu.

## Project 3C—Teacher Promotion

**Objectives:** *Create a Table, Format Tables, and Create a Table from Existing Text.*

In the following Skill Assessment, you will add a table to a planning meeting memo for the upcoming Teacher Appreciation Day at Sensation! Park. Your completed memo will look like the one shown in Figure 3.83. You will save your document as *3C_Teacher_Promotion_Firstname_Lastname.*

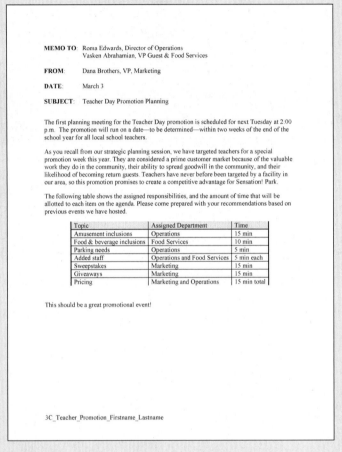

**Figure 3.83**

1. On the Standard toolbar, click the **Open** button. Navigate to the location where the student files for this textbook are stored. Locate and open **w03C_Teacher_Promotion**. On the Standard toolbar, click the **Show/Hide ¶** button if necessary to display the nonprinting characters.

2. From the **File** menu, click **Save As**. In the **Save As** dialog box, use the **Save in arrow** to navigate to the location where you are storing your files for this chapter. In the **File name** box, type **3C_Teacher_Promotion_Firstname_Lastname** using your own name. Click the **Save** button.

**(Project 3C**–Teacher Promotion continues on the next page)

**(Project 3C–Teacher Promotion continued)**

3. Scroll down to the middle of the document and locate the tabbed list. Click to place the insertion point to the left of *Amusement inclusions* in the list. Move the mouse pointer to the right of *Marketing and Operations*, the last item in the tabbed list, hold down Shift, and then click to select the entire list.

4. Display the **Table** menu, point to **Convert**, and then click **Text to Table**.

5. In the **Convert Text to Table** dialog box, under **Table size**, be sure **2** displays in the **Number of columns** box. Under **AutoFit behavior**, click the **AutoFit to contents** option button. Under **Separate text at** be sure **Tabs** is selected. Click **OK**. The tabbed list is converted to a table.

6. Click anywhere in the second column of the table. Display the **Table** menu, point to **Insert**, and then click **Columns to the Right**. In the newly inserted column (which may be quite narrow), position the mouse pointer over the right border until the left-right arrow pointer displays, and then drag the border to the right to approximately **5.25 inches on the horizontal ruler**.

7. Click in the first cell of the third column and type **15 min** Press ↓ to move to the second cell in the third column and type **10 min** Continue to use the ↓ to move down the column and enter the remaining time blocks that have been allotted for each topic as follows:

Parking needs     **5 min**

Added Staff       **5 min each**

Sweepstakes       **15 min**

Giveaways         **15 min**

Pricing           **15 min total**

8. Click anywhere in the first row of the table, display the **Table** menu, point to **Insert**, and then click **Rows Above**. In the first cell of the new row, type **Topic** and then press Tab, type **Assigned Department** and then press Tab and then type **Time**

9. With the insertion point anywhere in the table, display the **Table** menu and then click **Table AutoFormat**. In the **Table AutoFormat** dialog box, scroll down and click the **Table Grid 4** format. In the lower portion of the dialog box, under **Apply special formats to**, be sure there is no check mark in the Last row and Last column check boxes. Clear them, if necessary. Click **Apply**. The table is formatted.

10. With the insertion point still in the table, display the **Table** menu, point to **AutoFit**, and then click **AutoFit to Contents**.

**(Project 3C–**Teacher Promotion continues on the next page**)**

**(Project 3C–Teacher Promotion continued)**

11. Display the **Table** menu again and then click **Table Properties**. In the **Table Properties** dialog box, click the **Table tab** if necessary. Under **Alignment**, click the **Center** button and then click **OK**. The table is horizontally centered on the page.

12. Display the **View** menu and then click **Header and Footer**. On the Header and Footer toolbar, click the **Switch Between Header and Footer** button. With the insertion point positioned in the footer area, on the Header and Footer toolbar click the **Insert AutoText** button and then click **Filename**. Close the Header and Footer toolbar.

13. On the Standard toolbar, click the **Save** button and then click the **Print Preview** button to see the document as it will print. Click the **Print** button and then close Print Preview and close the file, saving changes if prompted to do so.

 **End** You have completed Project 3C

## Project 3D — Announcement Meeting

**Objectives:** *Insert Clip Art and Pictures, Modify Clip Art and Pictures, and Work with the Drawing Toolbar.*

In the following Skill Assessment, you will add graphics to an announcement for the upcoming Teacher Day promotion at Sensation! Park. Your completed announcement will look like the one shown in Figure 3.84. You will save your document as *3D_Announcement_Firstname_Lastname*.

1. On the Standard toolbar, click the **Open** button. Navigate to the location where the student files for this textbook are stored. Locate and open **w03D_Announcement**. The document opens at 75% zoom.

2. From the **File** menu, click **Save As**. In the Save As dialog box, use the **Save in arrow** to navigate to the location where you are storing your files for this chapter. In the **File name** box, type 3D_Announcement_Firstname_Lastname using your own name. Click the **Save** button.

3. From the **File** menu, display the **Page Setup** dialog box and click the **Margins tab**. Under **Orientation**, click **Landscape**. Under **Margins**, change the **Top** and **Bottom** boxes to **1.0** and then click **OK**.

4. From the **Tools** menu, click **Options**. Click the **General tab**. Under **General options**, locate the last check box—**Automatically create drawing canvas when inserting AutoShapes**—and be sure that it is unchecked. Clear the check box if necessary. Click **OK**. Recall that to use simple drawing tools, it is useful to turn off the drawing canvas.

**(Project 3D–Announcement Meeting continues on the next page)**

**(Project 3D–Announcement Meeting continued)**

**Figure 3.84**

5. Check to see if your Drawing toolbar is displayed at the bottom of your screen. If it is not, right-click on one of the toolbars and, from the displayed list, click Drawing. Click to place the insertion point to the left of the line that begins *It's been a LONG*. On the Drawing toolbar, click the **Line** button. Drawing a line is similar to drawing an arrow. Drag the crosshair pointer to draw a line under the text *Teacher Appreciation Day*. With the line still selected, on the Drawing toolbar, click the **Line Style** button and then click **2¼ pt**.

6. You can change the color of a line using the Line Color button, which is two buttons to the left of the Line Style button on the Drawing toolbar. With the line still selected, on the Drawing toolbar, locate the **Line Color** button and click its arrow to display a palette of colors. In the second row, click the **fourth color—green**.

7. Place the insertion point on the empty line under *And teachers deserve a break!* From the **Insert** menu, point to **Picture** and then click **Clip Art** from the submenu. In the **Clip Art** task pane, in the **Search for** box, type **teacher** In the **Search in** box, click the arrow and be sure **Everywhere** is selected. In the **Results should be box**, click the arrow and be sure **All media file types** are selected and then click the **Go** button. Locate the clip art image shown in Figure 3.84 and click the image to insert it. If you cannot locate that image, choose another image of a classroom teacher or insert the file **w03D_Teacher**. Close the Clip Art task pane.

**(Project 3D–Announcement Meeting continues on the next page)**

**(Project 3D–Announcement Meeting continued)**

8. Place the insertion point to the left of the line that begins *Come on June 22*. On the Drawing toolbar, click **AutoShapes**, point to **Stars and Banners** and then click the first shape—**Explosion 1**. Position the crosshair pointer at approximately **2.5 inches on the vertical ruler** and at the left margin in the horizontal ruler. Drag down so that one of the points is near the word *Come*, as shown in Figure 3.84. The size and placement need not be exact, but if you are not satisfied with your result, click Undo and begin again.

9. Right-click on the **Explosion 1 AutoShape** and, from the displayed shortcut menu, click **Add Text**. Type **Sweepstakes** and then select the text you typed. From the Formatting toolbar, change the font to **Comic Sans MS** and the font size to **16**. Point to a sizing handle and drag to expand the size of the shape until the text is displayed on one line.

10. With the Sweepstakes shape selected, locate the **Fill** button (paint can image) on the Drawing toolbar. Click the button's arrow and, on the displayed color palette, in the last row, click the **first color— Rose**. Click the arrow on the **Line Color** button and, from the displayed palette, click **Rose**. The line around the shape is the same color as the background color. Click the **Save** button.

11. Using the techniques you have just practiced, and using Figure 3.84 as a guide, create three more shapes as listed below. Use the Comic Sans MS 16-pt. font. Use the sizing handles to enlarge or to shrink your AutoShape, and recall that you can drag an AutoShape to a different position. Do not be concerned about exact placement.

| AutoShape | Placement | Text | Fill Color | Line Color |
|---|---|---|---|---|
| 24-point star | Lower left corner | **Door Prizes** | Light Yellow | Green |
| 24-point star | Lower right corner | **BBQ Lunch** | Light Yellow | Green |
| Explosion 1 | Right of date | **Discount Prices** | Bright Green | Bright Green |

12. Select *Sweepstakes* and, on the Formatting toolbar, click the **Center** button. Repeat this process to center the text in each of the other three AutoShapes.

13. Click the **Sweepstakes shape**. Drag the **Rotate** button to the right until the shape is pointing to the date as shown in Figure 3.84. Adjust the position and sizes of the other shapes so they resemble the arrangement shown in the figure.

**(Project 3D–Announcement Meeting continues on the next page)**

**(Project 3D–Announcement Meeting continued)**

**14.** Display the **View** menu, and then click **Header and Footer**. On the Header and Footer toolbar, click the **Switch Between Header and Footer** button. With the insertion point positioned in the footer area, on the Header and Footer toolbar, click the **Insert AutoText button** and then click **Filename**. Close the Header and Footer toolbar.

**15.** On the Standard toolbar, click the **Save** button and then click the **Print Preview** button to see the document as it will print. Make sure none of the shapes are outside of the margin area. Click the **Print** button, close Print Preview, and then close the file saving changes if prompted to do so.

**End** You have completed Project 3D ──────────────────

## Project 3E — Budget

**Objectives:** *Work with Tabs and Work with the Drawing Toolbar.*

In the following Skill Assessment, you will finish a memo by adding the results of the Teacher Promotion day at Sensation! Park. Your completed memo will look like the one shown in Figure 3.85. You will save your document as *3E_Budget_Firstname_Lastname.*

**1.** On the Standard toolbar, click the **Open** button. Navigate to the location where the student files for this textbook are stored. Locate and open **w03E_Budget**.

**2.** From the **File** menu, click **Save As**. In the **Save As** dialog box, use the **Save in arrow** to navigate to the location where you are storing your files for this chapter. In the **File name** box, using your own name, type **3E_Budget_Firstname_Lastname** Click the **Save** button.

**3.** If necessary, click the **Show/Hide ¶** button so you can see the non-printing characters as you complete this exercise. Place the insertion point at the end of the last paragraph—after the period following the word *below*—and press Enter. Spacing is added because spacing of 12 pt. after the paragraph has been set in this document.

**4.** On the Formatting toolbar, click the **Center** button and then click the **Underline** button. From the **Format** menu, click **Paragraph** and, under **Spacing**, use the spin box arrows to change **After** to **0 pt**. Click **OK**. Type **Attendance** and press Enter twice.

**5.** On the Formatting toolbar, click the **Align Left** button to change the alignment from Center, click the **Underline** button to turn off underline, and then click the **Increase Indent** button twice. This action indents the insertion point to the 1 inch mark—notice the indicator shown on the ruler.

**(Project 3E–Budget continues on the next page)**

**(Project 3E–Budget continued)**

MEMO TO:      McNeal Blackmon, President

FROM:         Dana Brothers, VP, Marketing

DATE:         July 1,

SUBJECT:      Teacher Day Promotion Results

The Teacher Day Promotion was a great success with our expected attendance exceeding our plan by 300 people.

Although attendance was higher than expected, actual promotion costs were still very close to our original budget number. The purchasing staff was able to negotiate lower prices on some food and promotional giveaways by making bulk purchases. The marketing team negotiated extremely favorable contracts with the entertainment providers; and, the human resources staff was able to adjust staff schedules for the week to keep overtime hours required to staff this event to a minimum. The budget vs. actual numbers is outlined below.

Attendance

| | |
|---|---|
| Teacher attendance: | 200 |
| Guests and families: | 700 |
| Total attendance for teacher promotion: | 900 |
| | |
| Total park attendance for day: | 3,000 |

Budget Figures

| Item | Budget | Actual |
|---|---|---|
| BBQ lunch | $7,200.00 | $9,000.00 |
| Refreshments/ice cream | 1,800.00 | 1,875.00 |
| Promotional giveaways | 5,000.00 | 3,320.64 |
| Additional parking shuttles | 2,250.00 | 2,032.99 |
| Additional park staff | 10,885.00 | 12,864.98 |
| Entertainment | 5,000.00 | 4,000.00 |
| Total | $32,135.00 | $33,093.61 |

3E_Budget_Firstname_Lastname

**Figure 3.85**

6.  At the left end of the horizontal ruler, click the **Tab Alignment** button until the **Decimal Tab** marker displays and then click the ruler at the **5 inch** mark. Type the following lines; press Tab after typing the text to move to the decimal tab stop and then press Enter at the end of each line. Refer to Figure 3.85.

    Teacher attendance:                            200

    Guests and families:                           700

    Total attendance for teacher promotion:   900

7.  Select 700 and, on the Formatting toolbar, click the **Underline** button. Position the insertion point to the right of 900, press Enter twice, and then type the following line pressing Tab before typing the number:

    Total park attendance for day:                3,000

8.  Press Enter twice. On the Formatting toolbar, click the **Decrease Indent** button twice to move the Left Indent indicator back to the left margin. On the Formatting toolbar, click the **Center** button and then click the **Underline** button. Type **Budget Figures** and press Enter twice.

**(Project 3E–Budget continues on the next page)**

**(Project 3E–Budget continued)**

9. On the Formatting toolbar, click the **Align Left** button to return to left alignment, click the **Underline** button to turn it off, and then click the **Increase Indent** button once.

10. From the **Format** menu, click **Tabs**. In the lower portion of the **Tabs** dialog box, click the **Clear All** button to remove any tabs from this line. In the **Tab stop position** box, type **3.5** Under **Alignment**, click **Center** and then click the **Set** button. This sets the first tab. In the **Tab stop position** box, type **5.5** and, under **Alignment**, click **Center** and then click **Set**. Two tabs have been set for this line of text. Click **OK** to close the dialog box, and notice the two Center tab stops indicated on the horizontal ruler.

11. Type the following, pressing Tab between each word:

    Item     Budget     Actual

12. Press Enter twice. From the **Format** menu, click **Tabs**. With **3.5** in the **Tab stop position** box, under **Alignment**, click **Decimal** and then click **Set**. Click the **5.5" tab** to select it, under **Alignment**, click **Decimal** and then click **Set**. The alignment of the two tabs is changed to Decimal. In a decimal tab stop, text aligns around the decimal point. Click **OK** to close the dialog box.

13. Type the following on separate lines, pressing Tab between the items listed in the columns:

    | Item | Budget | Actual |
    |---|---|---|
    | BBQ lunch | $7,200.00 | $9,000.00 |
    | Refreshments/ice cream | 1,800.00 | 1,875.00 |
    | Promotional giveaways | 5,000.00 | 3,320.64 |
    | Additional parking shuttles | 2,250.00 | 2,032.99 |
    | Additional park staff | 10,885.00 | 12,864.98 |
    | Entertainment | 5,000.00 | 4,000.00 |
    | Total | $32,135.00 | $33,093.61 |

14. On the Standard toolbar, click the **Save** button. On the line beginning with *Entertainment*, select **5,000.00**, click the **Underline** button, and then select **4,000.00** and click the **Underline** button.

15. The words *Budget* and *Actual* need to be better aligned over the columns of figures. Click anywhere on the line of headings above the budget figures. On the ruler, drag the first center tab stop one tick-mark (the tiny vertical lines between the numbers on the horizontal ruler) to the left between the 3 and 3.5 inch marks, so the word *Budget* is centered over the column of figures. Drag the second center tab stop one tick-mark to the left between the 5 and 5.5 inch marks to center the word *Actual* over the column of figures. When dragging tab stops, you can place the insertion point anywhere in the line.

**(Project 3E–Budget continues on the next page)**

**(Project 3E–Budget continued)**

16. From the **Tools** menu, click **Options** and then click the **General tab**. Under **General options**, in the last check box, if necessary, clear the *Automatically* create drawing canvas when inserting AutoShapes check box. Click **OK**. Recall that it is easier to create simple drawing objects with the drawing canvas turned off.

17. Check to see if your Drawing toolbar is displayed. If necessary, right-click on one of the toolbars and then click Drawing to display the Drawing toolbar. Place the insertion point on the empty line under *Total park attendance for day* and press [Enter] once. On the Drawing toolbar, click the **Line** button and then position the crosshair pointer at the left margin at approximately **5 inches on the vertical ruler**. Hold [Shift], and then drag to form a line from the left to the right margin. Holding down the [Shift] key ensures that your line will be straight, and not jagged. With the line selected, on the Drawing toolbar, click the **Line Style** button and click **1½ pt**.

18. With the line still selected, on the Standard toolbar, click the **Copy** button and then click the **Paste** button. A copy of the line is pasted under the first line. Drag the second line to a position under the budget as shown in Figure 3.85.

19. Display the **View** menu and then click **Header and Footer**. On the Header and Footer toolbar, click the **Switch Between Header and Footer** button. With the insertion point positioned in the footer area, on the Header and Footer toolbar, click the **Insert AutoText** button and then click **Filename**. Close the Header and Footer toolbar.

20. On the Standard toolbar, click the **Save** button and then click the **Print Preview** button to see the document as it will print. Click the **Print** button, close Print Preview, and then close the file saving changes if prompted to do so.

End **You have completed Project 3E** ——————————

# Project 3F—Refreshments

**Objectives:** *Insert Clip Art and Pictures, Modify Clip Art and Pictures, Work with the Drawing Toolbar, and Work with Tabs.*

In the following Performance Assessment, you will create a poster for one of the refreshment stands at Sensation! Park. Your completed document will look like the one shown in Figure 3.86. You will save your publication as *3F_Refreshments_Firstname_Lastname*.

**Figure 3.86**

1. Start Word and display a blank document. If necessary, close the Getting Started task pane. Be sure that nonprinting characters are displayed; if necessary, click the **Show/Hide ¶** button. Make sure the document is in the **Print Layout** view. From the **Tools** menu, click **Options** and then click the **General tab**. Under General Options, if necessary, clear the check box next to Automatically create drawing canvas when inserting AutoShapes and then click **OK**. Recall that if you want to use a simple drawing object, it is best to turn off the drawing canvas. If necessary, right-click on one of the toolbars and click **Drawing** to display the Drawing toolbar.

**(Project 3F–Refreshments continues on the next page)**

**(Project 3F–Refreshments continued)**

2. On the Drawing toolbar, click **AutoShapes** and point to **Stars and Banners**. In the displayed menu, in the fourth row, click the second shape—**Horizontal Scroll**. Position the crosshair pointer at the paragraph mark and then drag down and to the right to approximately **2 inches on the vertical ruler** and **6 inches on the horizontal ruler**, as shown in Figure 3.86.

3. Right-click in the **Horizontal Scroll** shape and, from the displayed menu, click **Add Text**. On the Formatting toolbar, change the font to **Comic Sans MS**, the font size to **48**, and the alignment to **Center**. Type **Refreshments** The text is added to the banner in a large font that is centered in the banner. If necessary, drag a sizing handle to adjust the size of the banner so the text is displayed on one line.

4. With the banner shape selected, on the Drawing toolbar, click the arrow on the **Line Color** button. From the displayed palette, click **Red**. Click the **Line Style** button and then click **1½ pt**. The outline of the banner is changed to a thicker red border.

5. Click the **Save** button. In the **Save As** dialog box, navigate to the location where you are saving your files. In the **File name** box, using your own name, type **3F_Refreshments_Firstname_Lastname** and then click the **Save** button.

6. Move the I-beam pointer just below the banner's left edge and double-click to insert one or two paragraph marks and to place the insertion point under the banner. With the insertion point positioned in front of the final paragraph mark, change the font to **Comic Sans MS** and the font size to **16 pt**. Notice that the paragraph mark reflects the changes.

7. From the **Format** menu, click **Tabs**. In the **Tabs** dialog box, in the **Tab stop position** box, type **1** and then, under **Alignment**, click **Left**. Click the **Set** button. The first tab is set. Set a second **Left** tab at **1.3 inches** and a third tab at **4.5 inches** that is a **Right** tab with **Leader option 2**. Click **Set** and then click **OK**.

8. Press Tab, type **Hot Dogs** press Tab, type **$2.25** and then press Enter. Repeat this pattern to add the next two items shown below. Press Enter once after the last line.

    Chili Dogs      2.75

    Knockwurst      3.25

**(Project 3F–Refreshments continues on the next page)**

**(Project 3F–Refreshments continued)**

Press [Tab] twice and type **Add Kraut** Press [Tab] again and type **.50** and then press [Enter]. This add-on is listed under Knockwurst. Press [Tab] twice and type **Add Chili** Press [Tab] again, type **.50** and then press [Enter] twice. Add the rest of the items listed below, pressing [Tab] once at the beginning of each line and again between the item and the price.

| | |
|---|---|
| Chips | 1.00 |
| Water/Pop | 1.50 |
| Child Size | 1.25 |
| Single Scoop | 2.00 |
| Double Scoop | 3.25 |

9. Click to the left of *Chips*, press [Enter] twice, and then press [Tab] once to restore the alignment of *Chips* in the listed items. Click to the left of *Child Size*, press [Enter] three times, and then press [Tab] once to restore the alignment. The prices for ice cream are moved down the page so you can add a subheading. Click the empty line above *Child Size*, change the font size to **22** and the alignment to **Center**, and then type **Ice Cream** Click the **Save** button.

10. Click to the left of *Hot Dogs*, to the left of the first tab mark. Display the **Insert** menu, point to **Picture**, and then click **Clip Art**. In the **Results should be** box, check that *All media file types* is displayed. In the **Search in box**, check that *All collections* is displayed. In the **Clip Art** task pane, in the **Search for** box, type **hot dog** and then click the **Go** button. Scroll down the list and locate the hot dog displayed in Figure 3.86. If you cannot find the hot dog shown in the figure, select another one of your choice or insert from your student files the file w03F_Hot_Dog. Click the image to insert it.

11. Click the inserted image to select it. Right-click to display the shortcut menu, and then click **Format Picture**. Click the **Layout tab**, click **Square**, and then click **OK**. In this case, you want the text to be aligned vertically in a list and not to wrap to the contour of the image. Drag the hot dog image as necessary to the left of the list of hot dog options as shown in Figure 3.86. Use the corner sizing handles to adjust the size of your image if needed. The size of the hot dog graphic used in Figure 3.86 was not changed.

12. Move your insertion point to the right of *1.25* on the *Child Size* row. In the **Clip Art** task pane, in the **Search for** box, replace *hot dog* with **ice cream cone** and then click the **Go** button. Scroll down the list and locate the ice cream cone displayed in Figure 3.86. If you cannot find the ice cream cone shown in the figure, select another one of your choice or, from your student files, insert w03F_Ice_Cream. Click the image to insert it.

**(Project 3F–Refreshments continues on the next page)**

**(Project 3F–Refreshments continued)**

13. Click the inserted image. Display the **Format Picture** dialog box, click **Layout**, click **Square**, and then click **OK**. Position the ice cream cone image to the right of the list of ice cream cone choices as shown in Figure 3.86. Be sure the top of the image is anchored to the Child Size line and not to the Ice Cream heading. Use the corner sizing handles to adjust the size of the image if needed. The image used in Figure 3.86 was not resized. Close the Clip Art task pane.

14. Display the **View** menu and then click **Header and Footer**. Switch to the footer area, click the **Insert AutoText** button, and click **Filename**. Close the Header and Footer toolbar.

15. Click the **Save** button and then click the **Print Preview** button to see the document as it will print. Click the **Print** button, close Print Preview, and then close the file, saving changes if prompted to do so.

**End** You have completed Project 3F

## Project 3G—Hours

**Objectives:** *Work with the Drawing Toolbar, Create a Table, and Format Tables.*

In the following Performance Assessment, you will create a poster listing the hours of operation at Sensation! Park. Your completed document will look like the one shown in Figure 3.87. You will save your document as *3G_Hours_Firstname_Lastname.*

1. On the Standard toolbar, click the **Open** button. Navigate to the location where the student files for this textbook are stored. Locate and open **w03G_Hours**.

2. From the File menu, open the **Save As** dialog box. Navigate to the location where you are storing your files for this chapter. In the **File name** box, type **3G_Hours_Firstname_Lastname** using your own name. Then click the **Save** button.

3. Click to the left of the first paragraph mark under *May Hours* to position your insertion point. On the Standard toolbar, click the **Insert Table** button, move the mouse pointer to select a table that is 3 columns wide by 4 rows high, and then click once to insert the table.

4. Enter the information in the table as shown below. Do not be concerned about the text alignment or formatting at this time.

| Monday-Thursday | 1 p.m. | 10 p.m. |
| Friday | 1 p.m. | 11 p.m. |
| Saturday and holidays | 11 a.m. | 11 p.m. |
| Sunday | NOON | 11 p.m. |

**(Project 3G–Hours continues on the next page)**

**(Project 3G–Hours continued)**

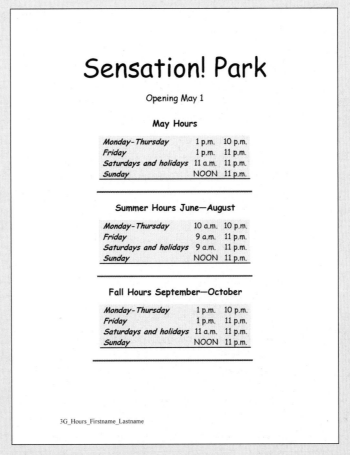

**Figure 3.87**

5. With your insertion point in the table, display the **Table** menu and then click **Table AutoFormat**. Under **Table styles**, scroll as necessary and then click **Table Colorful 2**. Under **Apply special formats to**, clear the **Heading rows** check box and, if necessary, clear the **Last column** check box. Click **Apply**.

6. Display the **Table** menu, point to **AutoFit**, and then click **AutoFit to Contents**.

7. Select the first column of the table. On the Formatting toolbar, click the **Align Left** button. From the **Table** menu, point to **Select** and then click **Table**. On the Formatting toolbar, click the **Center** button to center the table between the left and right margins.

8. With the table still selected, on the Standard toolbar, click the **Copy** button. Place the insertion point to the left of the first empty paragraph under *Summer Hours* and then click the **Paste** button. Click on the empty paragraph under *Fall Hours* and click the **Paste** button again. The table is copied to the two locations.

**(Project 3G–Hours continues on the next page)**

**(Project 3G–Hours continued)**

9. Change the hours in the table under *Summer Hours* as shown below:

| | | |
|---|---|---|
| Monday-Thursday | 10 a.m. | 10 p.m. |
| Friday | 9 a.m. | 11 p.m. |
| Saturday and holidays | 9 a.m. | 11 p.m. |
| Sunday | NOON | 11 p.m. |

10. On the Standard toolbar, click the **Save** button and then, if necessary, display the Drawing toolbar. If necessary, turn off the Drawing Canvas (Tools, Options, General tab). Click the **Line** button and drag a line under the first table between the two empty paragraph marks. Refer to Figure 3.87 to see where to position the line and how long to make it. With the line selected, click the **Line Color** arrow and click **Blue** (second row, sixth from the left) and then click the **Line Style** button and click **2¼**. With the line selected, click **Copy** and then click **Paste** two times. Drag the lines into position under the remaining two tables, similar to the position for the May table. Compare your document to Figure 3.87.

11. Display the **View** menu and click Header and Footer. Switch to the footer area, click the **Insert AutoText** button, and click **Filename**. Close the Header and Footer toolbar.

12. Click the **Save** button and then click the **Print Preview** button to see the document as it will print. Click the **Print** button, close Print Preview, and then close the file, saving changes if prompted to do so.

**End** You have completed Project 3G

## Project 3H — Prices

**Objectives:** *Create a Table from Existing Text and Format Tables.*

In the following Performance Assessment, you will create a poster with a list of prices for admission to Sensation! Park. Your completed document will look like the one shown in Figure 3.88. You will save your publication as *3H_Prices_Firstname_Lastname*.

1. On the Standard toolbar, click the **Open** button. Navigate to the location where the student files for this textbook are stored. Locate and open **w03H_Prices**.

2. From the **File** menu, open the **Save As** dialog box. Navigate to the location where you are storing your files for this Chapter. In the **File name** box, type **3H_Prices_Firstname_Lastname** using your own name. Then click the **Save** button.

**(Project 3H–Prices continues on the next page)**

**(Project 3H–Prices continued)**

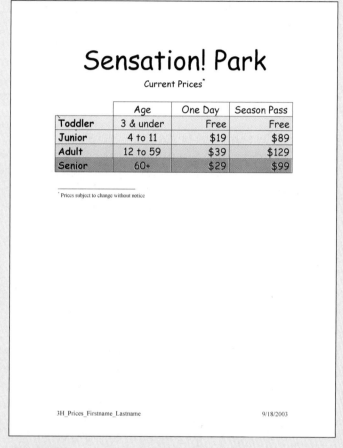

**Figure 3.88**

3. Click to the left of the first tab mark, left of *Age*, and select the five lines in the tabbed list. From the **Table** menu, point to **Convert** and then click **Text to Table**. In the **Convert Text to Table** dialog box, be sure **4** displays in the **Number of columns** box, and then click **OK**.

4. With the table still selected, using the Formatting toolbar, change the font to **Comic Sans MS** and the font size to **18**. Click anywhere to deselect the table.

5. Select the **first column** of the table and then click the **Bold** button. Select the **first row** of the table and then click the **Center** button. Select the four cells under *Age* and then click the **Center** button. In the last two columns, select the cells under the headings (do not select the headings) and click the **Align Right** button. Click the **Save** button.

**(Project 3H–Prices continues on the next page)**

**(Project 3H–Prices continued)**

6. Click in the first cell of the table—the one that is empty. From the Format menu, click **Borders and Shading**. In the Borders and Shading dialog box, on the right side, click the **Apply to arrow** and then, from the displayed list, click **Cell**. In the **Preview** area, click the **top** and **left** borders to deselect them and then click **OK**. Click the **Print Preview** button to verify that the top and left borders on the first cell will not print. Close the Print Preview window.

7. Select the row beginning with *Toddler*. From the **Format** menu, click **Borders and Shading** and then click the **Shading tab**. Under **Fill**, in the last row of the color palette, click **Light Turquoise**—the fifth color from the left. The name of the color displays to the right of the color palette after it is selected. Click **OK**.

8. Repeat Step 7 to apply colors to the three remaining rows of the table as follows:

    Junior     Light Yellow

    Adult      Light Green

    Senior     Lavender

9. Place the insertion point to the right of *Current Prices*. From the **Insert** menu, point to **Reference** and then click **Footnote**. In the **Footnote and Endnote** dialog box, under **Location**, click the **Endnotes** option button. Under **Format**, click the **Number format arrow** and, from the displayed list, click the last item—symbols that begin with *. At the lower left of the dialog box, click **Insert**. In the new endnote box, type **Prices subject to change without notice**

10. Display the **View** menu and then click **Header and Footer**. Switch to the footer area, click the **Insert AutoText** button, and then click **Filename**. Press Tab twice and then, on the Header and Footer toolbar, click the **Insert Date** button. Close the Header and Footer toolbar.

11. Click the **Save** button and then click the **Print Preview** button to see the document as it will print. Click the **Print** button, close Print Preview, and then close the file, saving changes if prompted to do so.

**End** You have completed Project 3H

## Project 3I—Water Rides

**Objectives:** *Insert Clip Art and Pictures, Modify Clip Art and Pictures, Create a Table, Format Tables, and Create a Table from Existing Text.*

In the following Mastery Assessment, you will create a table announcing new water rides at Sensation! Park. Your completed document will look like the one shown in Figure 3.89. You will save your publication as *3I_Water_Rides_ Firstname_Lastname.*

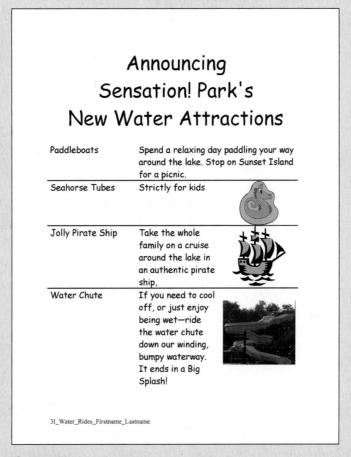

**Figure 3.89**

1. Start Word. From your student files, open **w03I_Water_Rides**. Save the file with the name **3I_Water_Rides_Firstname_Lastname** in the same location as your other files and using your own name. In the same manner as you have done in previous documents, display the footer and insert the AutoText filename.

2. Select the tabbed list, beginning with *Paddleboats* and ending with *Big Splash!* Convert this text to a two-column table.

3. Add a column to the right side of the table.

**(Project 3I–Water Rides continues on the next page)**

**(Project 3I**–Water Rides continued)

4. Drag to select the cell beginning with *Spend a relaxing day* and the empty cell to the right. Right-click the selected cells and click **Merge Cells** from the shortcut menu.

5. Click in the empty cell to the right of *Strictly for Kids*. Insert the file **w03I_Seahorse**. Use a corner sizing handle to resize the image to approximately 1 inch wide. With the image still selected, on the **Formatting** toolbar, click the **Center** button.

6. In the cell under the seahorse, insert file **03I_Pirate_Ship**. Resize the image so it is approximately 1 inch wide. With the image still selected, on the **Formatting** toolbar, click the **Center** button

7. Click in the empty cell in the last row. Press **Enter**, and then insert the **w03I_Waterride**.

8. Select the entire table and then display the **Borders and Shading** dialog box. Click the **Borders tab**. Under **Setting**, click **None** to remove all of the borders. In the lower middle of the dialog box, click the **Color arrow** and, from the displayed palette, in the second row, click the sixth color—**Blue**. Click the **Width arrow** and, from the displayed list, click **1½ pt**. In the Preview area, click the button that displays a **horizontal border line** between the rows. A horizontal border is added between the rows in the table preview graphic. Click **OK**.

9. Save the completed document. Preview the document and then print it.

**End**  **You have completed Project 3I** ————————————————————

## Project 3J—Events Memo

**Objectives:** *Create a Table, Format Tables, and Create a Table from Existing Text.*

In the following Mastery Assessment, you will add a table to a memo regarding the events that are planned for the upcoming season at Sensation! Park. In two columns in the memo, you will set tab stops and the hanging indent marker so you can create an indented list. Your completed document will look like the one shown in Figure 3.90. You will save your publication as *3J_Events_Memo_Firstname_Lastname.*

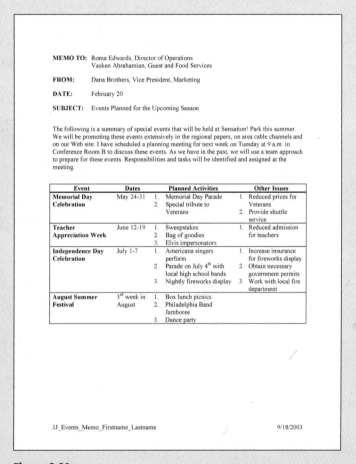

**Figure 3.90**

1. Start Word. From your student files, open **w03J_Events_Memo**. Save the file with the name **3J_Events_Memo_Firstname_Lastname** in the same location as your other files.

2. Click to position the insertion point to the left of the empty paragraph mark under the paragraph ending with *meeting* and insert a table that has four columns and four rows.

3. Be sure the ruler is displayed on your screen and the left tab indicator displays in the Tab Alignment button. Select the third

**(Project 3J–Events Memo continues on the next page)**

**(Project 3J–Events Memo continued)**

column of the table and then click on the ruler at the **3⅜** inch mark (third tick mark to the left of the 4 inch mark) to add a left tab. Point to the gray indent markers on the ruler until the *Hanging Indent* ScreenTip displays and then drag the hanging indent marker for that column to the **3⅜** inch position.

4. Select the fourth column of the table, click to place a left tab stop at **5.25** inches, and then drag the hanging indent marker to that tab stop.

5. Refer to Figure 3.90, and then in the first row of the table, type the information shown below. In the third cell, type **1.** and press Ctrl + Tab to move to the tab stop you created and then continue typing. Press Enter to move to the second line in this cell. Type **2.** press Ctrl + Tab and finish typing the information for the third cell.

Note that because numbers are used in this example, the AutoCorrect Options button may display to number the list for you. Click **Stop automatically creating numbered lists** from the displayed list. This will stop the AutoCorrect Options feature from creating a numbered list in each cell of the table.

| Memorial Day Celebration | May 24–31 | 1. Memorial Day Parade<br>2. Special tribute to Veterans | 1. Reduced prices for Veterans<br>2. Provide shuttle service |
|---|---|---|---|

Press Tab to move to the fourth cell and use same process to type the information so it aligns on the tab stop.

6. Enter the remaining information as shown in the table below. Use the same technique in the third and forth column—type the number and the period and then press Ctrl + Tab before continuing to type the rest of the data. Be sure to press Enter when multiple items are listed in a cell.

| Teacher Appreciation Week | June 12–19 | 1. Sweepstakes<br>2. Bag of goodies<br>3. Elvis impersonators | 1. Reduced admission for teachers |
|---|---|---|---|
| Independence Day Celebration | July 1–7 | 1. Americana singers perform<br>2. Parade on July 4th with local high school bands<br>3. Nightly fireworks display | 1. Increase insurance for fireworks display<br>2. Obtain necessary government permits<br>3. Work with local fire department |
| August Summer Festival | 3rd week in August | 1. Box lunch picnics<br>2. Philadelphia Band Jamboree<br>3. Dance party | |

**(Project 3J–Events Memo continues on the next page)**

**(Project 3J–Events Memo continued)**

7. Click in the first row of the table and insert a new row above. Type the following headings in this new first row:

   **Event    Dates    Planned Activities    Other Issues**

8. Select the table and use the **AutoFormat** dialog box to apply the **Table List 5** format to the table. Use **AutoFit** to fit the table to the contents and then center the column headings.

9. In the same manner as you have done in previous documents, display the footer and insert the **AutoText filename**. Press Tab to move to the right side of the footer. Notice that the right tab stop for the footer is not aligned with the right margin. On the ruler, drag the right tab stop to align with the right margin, and then click the **Insert Date** button.

10. Save the completed document. Preview the document and then print it.

**End** You have completed Project 3J

## Project 3K — Resume

**Objectives:** *Create a Table and Format Tables.*

The Table tool is convenient for creating resumes. In this Problem-Solving exercise, you will use a table to create your own resume. Your completed document will look similar to the one shown in Figure 3.91. You will save your resume as *3K_Resume_Firstname_Lastname.*

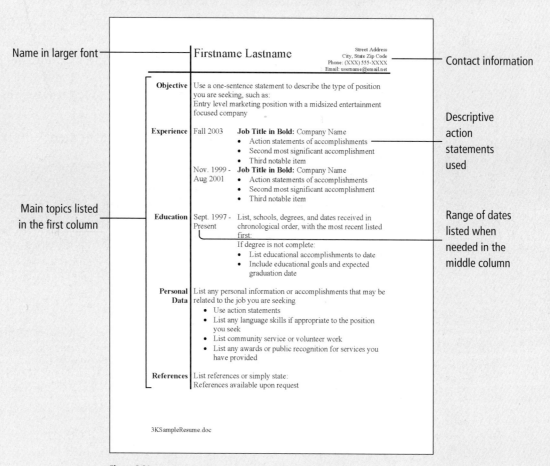

**Figure 3.91**

1. Examine Figure 3.91. This sample of a resume uses a three-column table with only a first column and first row border displayed. The middle column is used for dates when needed or merged with the third cell in the row to expand the text across a wider area.

2. Examine Figure 3.92, which displays the resume as it looks in Word. Notice the rows that have been added to increase space between major headings. The major topics in the left column have been aligned on the left and bold emphasis has been added.

**(Project 3K–Resume continues on the next page)**

**(Project 3K–Resume continued)**

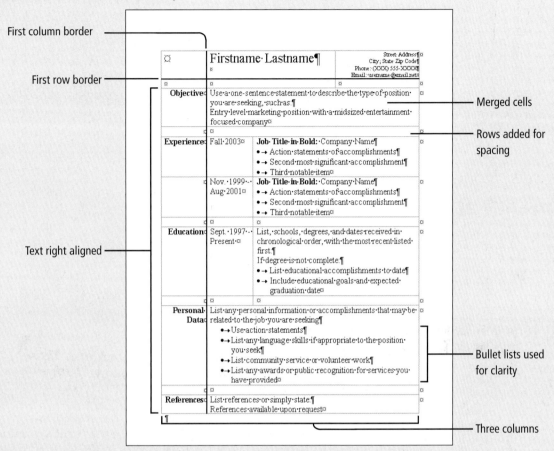

**Figure 3.92**

3. Create a three-column table with four rows to start—you can add more rows as needed. Remove all of the borders.

4. Select the top row and add a bottom border and then select the first column and add a right border. The bottom border of the first cell may be overwritten when you add the border to the right of the first column. Select the top left cell and re-apply the bottom border.

5. Fill in your name and personal information at the top of the table, formatting it appropriately.

6. The objective statement should be directed toward the job for which you are applying. You can write this as if applying for the job you already have, one you would like to have, or for a specific job posting.

7. Using the figures as a model, enter information for your own resume. The content of the figures provides tips on the type of information and format to use when writing a resume.

**(Project 3K–Resume continues on the next page)**

**(Project 3K–Resume continued)**

8. Proofread your resume and remove any spelling, grammar, or typographical errors. Save the document as **3K_Resume_Firstname_Lastname** In the footer area, using the AutoText button, insert the file name.

9. Print the document and then close the file, saving changes if prompted to do so.

**End** You have completed Project 3K ————————————————

# Project 3L — July 4th

**Objectives:** *Insert Clip Art and Pictures, Modify Clip Art and Pictures, Work with Tab Stops, Work with the Drawing Toolbar*

Sensation! Park has several events that it needs to promote for the upcoming season. In this Problem Solving exercise, you will create a promotional poster for the July 4th Celebration.

1. Type the name of the park at the top of the page and then use an AutoShape to create a banner for the event name. Add an event title in the shape you selected and format the font to a size and style that will make it stand out.

2. Using the skills you have practiced in this chapter and your imagination, create and format a table listing four to five planned activities and the scheduled day and times during the week of July 4.

3. Add clip art, such as fireworks, picnics, or pictures of parades to call attention to the events that are planned for the week.

4. Add a text box or a callout shape and draw a line to point out a special event or time.

5. Add a tabbed list of discounts that are offered for special groups or large parties.

6. Preview the document. Make sure the font style is consistent throughout and the various components are balanced on the page.

7. Save the document as **3L_July_4th_Firstname_Lastname** In the footer area, using the AutoText button, insert the file name.

8. Print the document and then close the file, saving changes if prompted to do so.

**End** You have completed Project 3L ————————————————

# On the Internet

## Clip Art on the Internet

You do not have to limit your choice of clip art or pictures to those images that come with Microsoft Word. You can download clip art images or select pictures to use from the Web. You can also insert pictures from your own files into any Word document. If you use images from a proprietary Web site, such as National Geographic, you must provide proper credit and reference to the location where the images were found. In some cases, a Web site will state specifically that all content is copyrighted and cannot be used without written permission. Web sites offering free clip art images do not have that requirement.

1. Open your Web browser and go to a search engine such as www.google.com or www.yahoo.com. Type the key words **clip art** and **free** in the search box.

2. Look through the various sites for one you like that has a variety of interesting graphics. There are several that do not require that you sign up for advertising or provide your e-mail address.

3. Find a site you like and practice inserting images in a Word document. When you right-click on an image, you can either copy it or use the Save as option from the shortcut menu to save it to your disk.

4. Open a Word document and insert some new images you found on the Web. Try more than one site to sample the variety of Web sites available.

5. If you like a site you found, you can add it to your Favorite Sites list or bookmark it.

6. Close your browser and close Word.

## Changing Text Orientation

You may want to change the orientation of text in a Word document so it is vertical instead of horizontal. You can do this in a table or by using a text box. There are several tutorials in the Word Help program that provide instructions on how to change the orientation of text.

1. Start Word. In the Type a Question for Help box, type **Text Orientation** Scroll through the list of topics that displays in the Search Results task pane. From this list of help topics, click **Change the orientation of text**.

2. In a blank document, create a text box and type your name. Follow the directions to practice changing the orientation in a text box.

3. Create a 3-by-2 (three columns by two rows) table and type random words in the table. Try changing the orientation of the first column of text in your table. Use Word Help if necessary to provide instructions. This process also works in drawing objects.

4. Close the Help task pane and exit Word.

# 4 chapterfour

# Creating Documents with Multiple Columns and Special Formats

**In this chapter, you will:** complete these projects **and** practice these skills.

| Project 4A **Creating a Newsletter** | **Objectives** |
|---|---|
| | • Create a Decorative Title |
| | • Create Multicolumn Documents |
| | • Add Special Paragraph Formatting |
| | • Use Special Character Formats |

| Project 4B **Creating a Web Page** | **Objectives** |
|---|---|
| | • Insert Hyperlinks |
| | • Preview and Save a Document as a Web Page |

| Project 4C **Creating a Memo** | **Objectives** |
|---|---|
| | • Locate Supporting Information |
| | • Find Objects with the Select Browse Object Button |

# The City of Desert Park

Desert Park, Arizona, is a thriving city with a population of just under 1 million in an ideal location serving major markets in the western United States and Mexico. Desert Park's temperate year-round climate attracts both visitors and businesses, and it is one of the most popular vacation destinations in the world. The city expects and has plenty of space for long-term growth, and most of the undeveloped land already has a modern infrastructure and assured water supply in place.

© Getty Images, Inc.

# Creating Documents with Multiple Columns and Special Formats

Creating a newsletter is usually a job reserved for **desktop publishing** programs, such as Microsoft Publisher. Word, however, has a number of tools that enable you to put together a simple, yet effective and attractive newsletter.

Newsletters consist of a number of elements, but nearly all have a title—called a **masthead**—story headlines, articles, and graphics. The text is often split into two or three columns, making it easier to read than one-column articles. Column widths can be changed, text is usually justified, and lines can be inserted to separate columns.

Newsletters are often printed, but they can also be designed as Web pages. Links to other Web sites can be included and can be accessed by clicking words or graphics. Microsoft Word provides research tools to find information included in the Office package or information on the Web. These materials can be collected and then pasted into different parts of the document.

# Project 4A **Garden Newsletter**

In this chapter, you will edit and format newsletters and add elements such as mastheads, borders, and shading. You will add links and save a document as a Web page. You will also use research tools to find information and place it in a document.

In Activities 4.1 through 4.10 you will edit a newsletter for the City of Desert Park Botanical Gardens. You will add a WordArt masthead and a decorative border line. You will also change the text of the articles from one column to two columns and then format the columns. Finally, you will use special text formatting features to change the font color and set off one of the paragraphs with a border and shading. Your completed document will look similar to Figure 4.1.

You will save your document as *4A_Garden_Newsletter_Firstname_Lastname.*

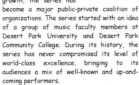

### GARDEN GETS NPS GRANT

The City of Desert Park received a $100,000 grant from the National Park Service (NPS) to be used in the Desert Park Botanical Garden. The grant comes from an NPS program entitled "Urban Park and Recreation Recovery" (UPARR).

UPARR grants can be used to renovate existing recreation areas and facilities. The grants highlight the importance of having safe and accessible neighborhood recreation facilities available for people of all ages.

To qualify for the grant, the Fine Arts and Parks Department followed the eligibility requirements and application procedures, which were posted in a Federal Register notice last January. Applications from around the nation were reviewed by NPS, and final selections were recently named by the NPS Director.

The UPARR program was established in 1978 to provide matching grants and technical assistance to urban communities. The law encourages systematic local planning and commitment to continuing operation and maintenance of recreation programs, sites, and facilities.

Additional information on the UPARR program can be found on the National Park Service's Web site at www.nps.gov/uparr.

### OUTDOOR MUSIC

Classical music is alive and well in Desert Park! Since 1986, the Desert Park Botanical Garden Outdoor Concert Series has presented over 600 high-quality events to audiences from Desert Park and from around the nation. With steady growth, the series has become a major public-private coalition of organizations. The series started with an idea of a group of music faculty members at Desert Park University and Desert Park Community College. During its history, the series has never compromised its level of world-class excellence, bringing to its audiences a mix of well-known and up-and-coming performers.

Please feel free to bring your picnic supper to enjoy in the Garden before the performance begins. Many of our attendees love to bring their bright table linens and vases of fresh flowers to accompany their picnics. (Due to fire danger, please no candles.)

4A_Garden_Newsletter_Firstname_Lastname

**Figure 4.1**
Project 4A—Garden Newsletter

## Objective 1
## Create a Decorative Title

The title at the top of a newsletter should be short and distinctive. Microsoft Word uses an Office program called **WordArt** to change text into a decorative graphic. WordArt can be formatted, even after the text has been changed to a graphic. Word also has attractive borders that can be used to separate the masthead from the articles.

### Activity 4.1 Inserting WordArt

**1** Start Word. On the Standard toolbar, click the **Open** button. Navigate to the location where the student files for this textbook are stored. Locate **w04A_Garden_Newsletter** and click once to select it. Then, in the lower right corner of the **Open** dialog box, click **Open**.

The w04A_Garden_Newsletter file opens.

**2** From the **File** menu, click **Save As**. In the **Save As** dialog box, click the **Save in arrow** and navigate to the location in which you are storing your files for this chapter, creating a new folder for chapter 4 if you want to do so.

**3** Type **4A_Garden_Newsletter_Firstname_Lastname** in the **File name** box, using your own name, and click **Save**. On the Standard toolbar, click the Zoom button arrow 100% , and then click Page Width.

**4** Be sure that you have the nonprinting characters displayed and notice the two blank lines at the top of the document. With the insertion point positioned to the left of the first blank paragraph mark, display the **Insert** menu, point to **Picture**, and then click **WordArt**.

The WordArt Gallery dialog box displays.

**5** Under **Select a WordArt style**, in the second row, click the fifth option as shown in Figure 4.2.

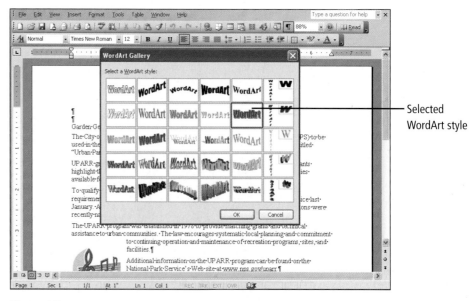

Selected WordArt style

**Figure 4.2**

**6** At the bottom of the **WordArt Gallery** dialog box, click **OK**.

The Edit WordArt Text dialog box displays with placeholder text *Your Text Here.* As soon as you begin to type, the placeholder text will be replaced.

**7** In the **Edit WordArt Text** dialog box, under **Text**, type **Botanical Notes**

The text you type displays. The default font size is 36 points, and the default font is Impact. Compare your Edit WordArt Text dialog box to Figure 4.3.

Default font — 
WordArt text — 

Default font size

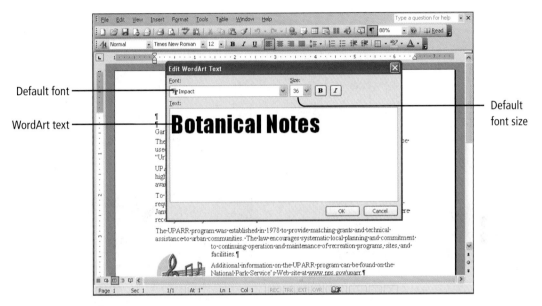

**Figure 4.3**

**8** At the bottom of the **Edit WordArt Text** dialog box, click **OK**.

The WordArt graphic is inserted at the insertion point location, as shown in Figure 4.4.

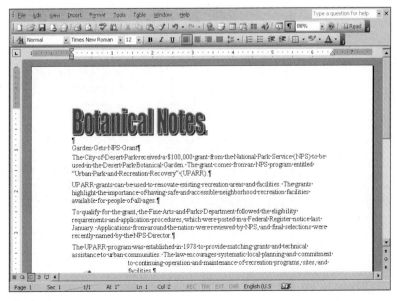

**Figure 4.4**

**9** On the Standard toolbar, click the **Save** button 💾.

### Activity 4.2 Formatting WordArt

When you create a WordArt image, a good technique is to create the graphic at the default (36-point) font size and then adjust it after you see how it fits in the allotted space.

**1** Click the **WordArt object** to select it, and notice that the WordArt toolbar displays, floating somewhere on your screen. Pause your mouse pointer over each button to display the ScreenTip and examine the description of each button in the table in Figure 4.5.

## Buttons on the WordArt Toolbar

| ScreenTip | Button | Description |
|---|---|---|
| Insert WordArt | | Inserts a new WordArt object. |
| Edit Text | Edit Text... | Opens the Edit WordArt dialog box so that the text for an existing WordArt object can be modified. |
| WordArt Gallery | | Opens the WordArt Gallery so that a new design can be applied to an existing WordArt object. |
| Format WordArt | | Opens the Format WordArt dialog box so that fill colors, size, position, and layout can be modified. |
| WordArt Shape | | Displays options for changing the shape of an existing WordArt object. |
| Text Wrapping | | Displays the text wrapping menu. |
| WordArt Same Letter Heights | Aa | Changes the height of lowercase letters so that they are the same height as uppercase letters. |
| WordArt Vertical Text | | Displays WordArt text vertically. |
| WordArt Alignment | | Applies alignment options to a WordArt object. |
| WordArt Character Spacing | AV | Adjusts the amount of spacing between WordArt characters. |

**Figure 4.5**

**2** On the WordArt toolbar, click the **Edit Text** button Edit Text.... Alternatively, move the pointer over the new WordArt graphic and double-click.

The Edit WordArt Text dialog box displays.

## **Note** — If the WordArt Toolbar Disappears

If the WordArt toolbar has been turned off, you may have to turn it on using the menu. Display the View menu, point to Toolbars, and click WordArt from the Toolbar menu. If you click outside of the WordArt graphic, the toolbar will close. To reactivate the toolbar, click the WordArt graphic again.

**3** In the **Edit WordArt Text** dialog box, click the **Size arrow** and then, from the displayed list, click **66**. Click **OK**.

The masthead of the newsletter you created using WordArt reaches nearly to the right margin.

**4** Look at the horizontal ruler and locate the boundary of the right margin—the area at 6.5 inches where the shading changes. On the right edge of the masthead, drag the middle sizing handle to align approximately with the right margin. See Figure 4.6.

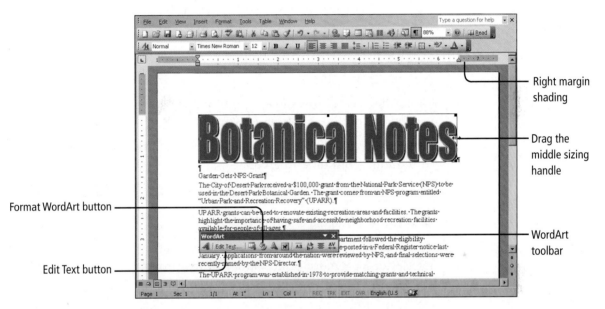

**Figure 4.6**

**5** On the **WordArt** toolbar, click the **Format WordArt** button 🎨. If necessary, click the Colors and Lines tab.

**6** Under **Fill**, click the **Color arrow**.

A color palette displays, as shown in Figure 4.7.

Colors and Lines tab —

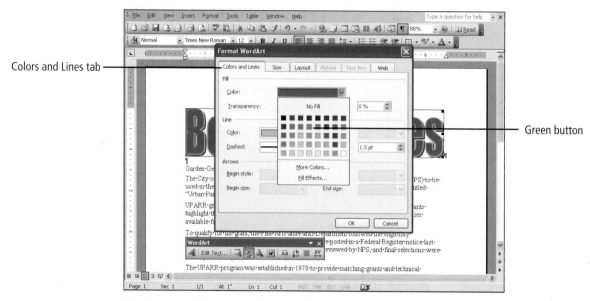

Green button

**Figure 4.7**

**7** In the second row of color options, click the fourth color—**Green**. At the bottom of the **Format WordArt** dialog box, click **OK**.

The WordArt letters that form the newsletter's masthead letters change from blue to green.

**8** On the Standard toolbar, click the **Save** button.

### Activity 4.3 Adding a Border Line

A line between the masthead and the rest of the material makes the newsletter look more professional. Word provides many decorative line types that you can add to your document.

**1** In the blank line below the masthead, click to position the insertion point.

**2** From the **Format** menu, click **Borders and Shading**.

The Borders and Shading dialog box displays.

**3** If necessary, click the Borders tab. Under **Setting**, click the **Custom** option.

**4** Under **Style**, scroll down about halfway and click the double line with the heavy top and lighter bottom lines.

**5** Under **Preview**, click the **Bottom Border** button.

Compare your dialog box to Figure 4.8.

Borders tab       Line style

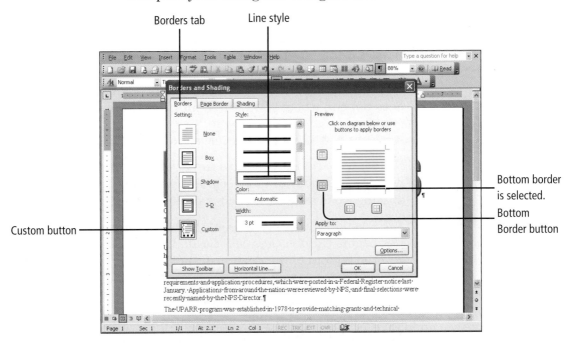

Custom button

Bottom border is selected.

Bottom Border button

**Figure 4.8**

**6** At the bottom of the **Borders and Shading** dialog box, click **OK**.

The double-line border is inserted at the bottom of the empty paragraph and stretches from the left margin to the right margin. See Figure 4.9.

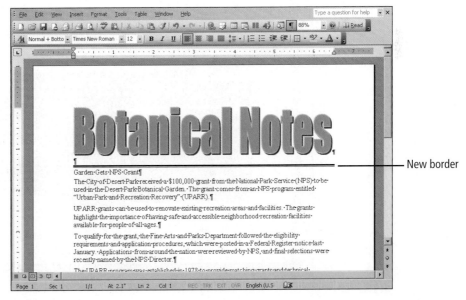

New border

**Figure 4.9**

**7** On the Standard toolbar, click the **Save** button 🖫.

## Objective 2
## Create Multicolumn Documents

All newspapers and most magazines and newsletters use multiple columns for articles because text in narrower columns is easier to read than text that stretches across a page. Word has a tool that enables you to change a single column of text into two or more columns. The columns can be formatted, and a line can be added between columns. If a column does not end where you want, a **_manual column break_** can be inserted.

### Activity 4.4 Changing One Column to Two Columns

Newsletters are nearly always two or three columns wide. It is probably not wise to create four or more columns because they are so narrow that word spacing looks awkward, often resulting in one long word by itself on a line.

**1** Position the insertion point to the left of the first line of text, which begins _Garden Gets NPS Grant._ Use the Scroll bar to scroll down to the bottom of the document, hold down Shift, and then click at the end of the last line.

All the text is selected. Do not be concerned about selecting the two pictures—they will be moved later, and they are not affected by changing the number of columns.

**2** On the Standard toolbar, click the **Columns** button ▦.

A Columns menu displays, showing up to four possible columns.

**3** Move the pointer over the second column.

Two columns are highlighted, and the bottom of the menu displays the number of columns, as shown in Figure 4.10.

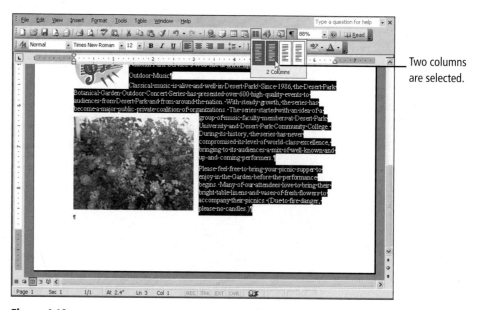

Two columns are selected.

**Figure 4.10**

**4** Click the mouse button and then scroll up as necessary to view the top of your document.

The text is divided into two columns, and a section break is inserted below the masthead, dividing the one-column section from the two-column section. Do not be concerned with the placement of the pictures—one may be displayed on top of the other, or one may display outside the document margin. See Figure 4.11.

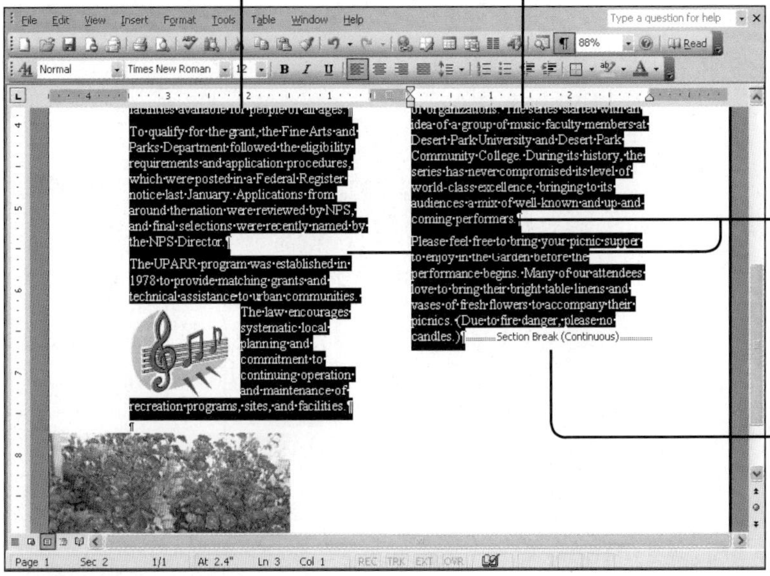

Two columns are created. ————

Uneven right margin

Section break

**Figure 4.11**

**5** On the Standard toolbar, click the **Save** button 🖫.

### Activity 4.5 Formatting Multiple Columns

The ragged right edge of a single page width column is readable. When you create narrow columns, justified text is preferable. The font you choose should also match the type of newsletter.

**1** With the text still selected, on the Formatting toolbar, click the **Font button arrow** Times New Roman ▾.

The Font menu displays.

**2** From the **Font** menu, scroll to and click **Comic Sans MS**. Alternatively, you can press C to move to the first font beginning with that letter, and then scroll down to the desired font.

Because the Comic Sans MS font is larger than Times New Roman, the text expands to a second page.

**3** On the Formatting toolbar, click the arrow **Font Size button arrow** 12 ▾ and then click **10**.

The document returns to a single page.

**4** On the Formatting toolbar, click the **Justify** button ![Justify icon]. Scroll to the top of the document and click anywhere in the document to deselect the text.

The font is changed to 10-point Comic Sans MS, an informal, easy-to-read font, and the text is justified. See Figure 4.12. The text at the top of the second column may differ from the figure because of the displaced pictures. This will be adjusted later.

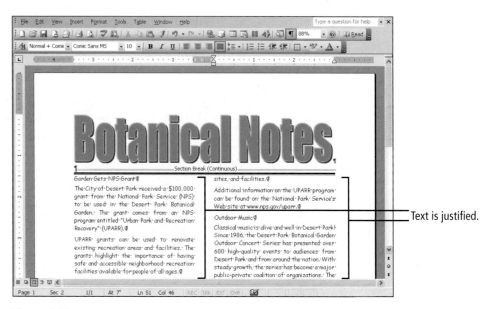

Text is justified.

**Figure 4.12**

**5** From the **View** menu, click **Header and Footer**.

The Header and Footer toolbar displays.

**6** On the Header and Footer toolbar, click the **Switch Between Header and Footer** button ![icon].

The insertion point is positioned in the footer box.

**7** On the Header and Footer toolbar, click the **Insert AutoText** button ![Insert AutoText], and then click **Filename**.

The file name is inserted in the footer. Do not be concerned if one of the pictures is covering your footer—this will be adjusted in a later activity.

**8** On the Header and Footer toolbar, click the **Close** button ![Close].

**9** On the Standard toolbar, click the **Save** button ![Save].

## Activity 4.6  Inserting a Column Break

Manual column breaks can be inserted to adjust columns that end or begin awkwardly or to make space for graphics or text boxes.

**1** On the Standard toolbar, click the **Print Preview** button.

If the newsletter was printed at this point, the ends of the columns would be uneven.

**2** On the Print Preview toolbar, click the **Close** button. Position the insertion point to the left of the paragraph at the bottom of the first column that begins *The UPARR program was established.*

**3** From the **Insert** menu, click **Break**.

The Break dialog box displays. See Figure 4.13. Here you can insert column breaks, page breaks, or text-wrapping breaks. You can also set four types of section breaks. The *Next page* break moves the text after the break to the next page of your document, whereas a *Continuous break* creates a section break on the same page. *Even page* and *Odd page* breaks are used when you need to have a different header or footer for odd and even pages in a manuscript, manual, or other long document that will be printed on two-sided paper.

Column break option

This text will be moved to the next column.

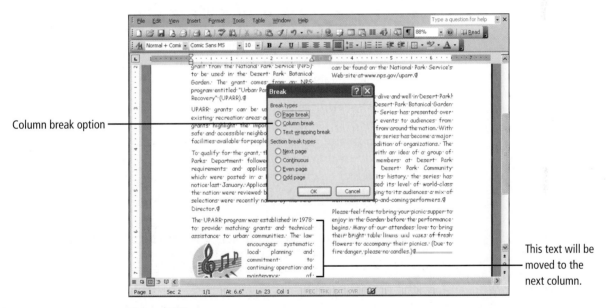

**Figure 4.13**

**4** Under **Break types**, click the **Column break** option button.

**5** At the bottom of the **Break** dialog box, click **OK**.

The column breaks at the insertion point, and the text following the insertion point moves to the top of the next column. See Figure 4.14.

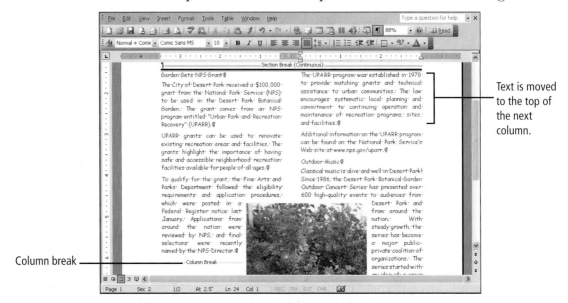

Text is moved to the top of the next column.

Column break

**Figure 4.14**

**6** Position the document so that you can view the lower portion on your screen. Point to the picture of the flowers, hold down the left mouse button, and then drag the picture of the flowers slightly below the column break you just inserted at the bottom of the first column. Align the top edge of the picture at approximately **6 inches on the vertical ruler**.

**7** In the second column, in the paragraph that begins *Classical music is alive and well*, drag the picture of the musical notes so the right border of the picture aligns with the right side of the column, then drag up or down as necessary to match Figure 4.15. Click anywhere to deselect the image.

Your newsletter should look similar to Figure 4.15.

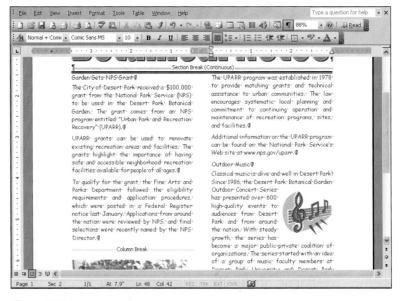

**Figure 4.15**

**8** On the Standard toolbar, click the **Save** button ⊞.

## More Knowledge — Balancing Column Breaks

You can also insert a column break to help balance columns so that they end evenly. This is important when the end of the columns is not the end of the document. If you want to balance the columns in a document, switch to Print Layout view, if necessary, and click at the end of the last column. On the Insert menu, click Break and then click the Continuous section break option. This will cause the end of the columns to be approximately even.

## Objective 3
## Add Special Paragraph Formatting

Sometimes you will want to call attention to specific paragraphs of text. One way to do this is to place a border around the paragraph. You can also shade a paragraph, although use caution not to make the shade too dark, because it will be hard to read the text.

### Activity 4.7 Adding a Border to a Paragraph

Paragraph borders provide strong visual cues to the reader.

**1** At the top of the second column, in the second paragraph that begins *Additional information on the UPARR program*, triple-click in the paragraph to select it.

The paragraph is selected.

**2** From the **Format** menu, click **Borders and Shading**.

The Borders and Shading dialog box displays.

## Note — Adding Borders to Text

*Add Simple Borders Using the Outside Border Button*

Simple borders, and border edges, can be added using the Outside Border button on the Formatting toolbar. This button offers very little control, however, because line thickness and color depends on the previous thickness and color chosen from the Borders and Shading dialog box.

**3** Under **Setting**, click **Box**.

**4** Under **Width**, click the arrow and then click **1½ pt**.

Compare your Borders and Shading dialog box to Figure 4.16. Notice that the Apply to box displays *Paragraph*. The Apply to box directs where the border will be applied—in this case, the border that has been set will be applied to the paragraph that is selected.

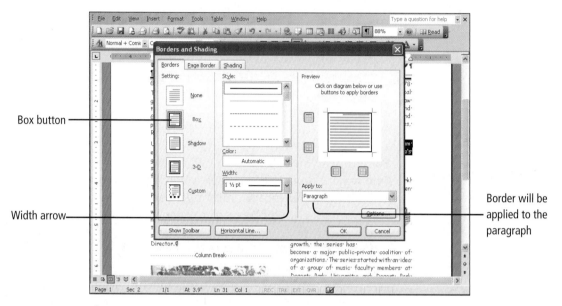

Box button ——

Width arrow——

Border will be applied to the paragraph

**Figure 4.16**

**5** At the bottom of the **Borders and Shading** dialog box, click **OK**.

A border has been placed around the paragraph, as shown in Figure 4.17.

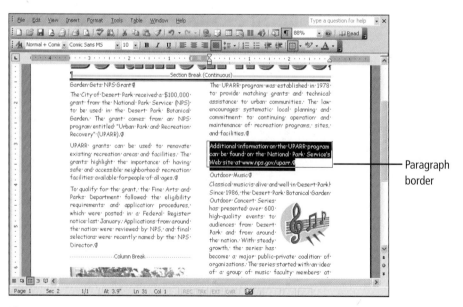

Paragraph border

**Figure 4.17**

**6** On the Standard toolbar, click the **Save** button .

## Activity 4.8 Shading a Paragraph

Shading can be used with or without borders. When used with a border, shading can be very effective.

**1** With the paragraph still selected, from the **Format** menu, click **Borders and Shading**.

The Borders and Shading dialog box displays.

**2** In the **Borders and Shading** dialog box, click the **Shading tab**.

**3** Under **Fill**, in the first row of the color palette, click the third button.

A box to the right of the palette indicates *Gray-10%*. See Figure 4.18.

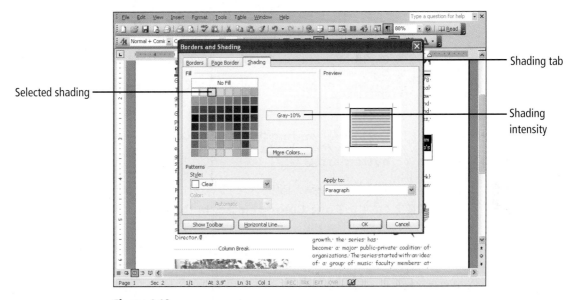

**Figure 4.18**

**4** At the bottom of the **Borders and Shading** dialog box, click **OK**. Click anywhere in the document to deselect the text.

The paragraph is shaded and has a border, as shown in Figure 4.19.

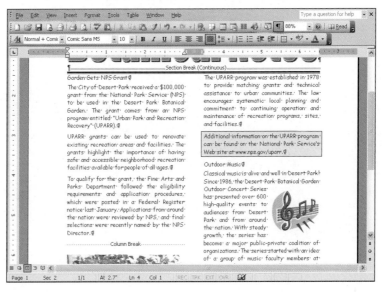

**Figure 4.19**

**5** On the Standard toolbar, click the **Save** button.

## Objective 4
## Use Special Character Formats

Headlines and titles should be set off from the rest of the text in a distinctive manner. This is usually done by emphasizing the text with the use of bold or italics, different fonts, or increased font size. If you are going to use a color printer or post the document on the Web, changing the color is very effective.

### Activity 4.9 Changing Font Color

**1** At the top of the first column, select the *Garden Gets NPS Grant* headline.

This is the headline for the first story in the newsletter.

**2** On the Formatting toolbar, click the **Bold** button 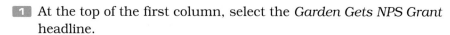.

**3** On the Formatting toolbar, click the **Font Size button arrow** , and then click **18**.

**4** On the Formatting toolbar, click the arrow click the **Font Color button arrow** .

The Font Color palette displays.

**5** On the **Font Color palette**, in the second row, click the fourth color—**Green**.

The first headline is bold, 18 point, and green. The Font Color button retains the color that was just applied, which means that if you click the button, it will apply Green to whatever text has been selected.

**6** Under the shaded paragraph, select the *Outdoor Music* headline. Repeat Steps 2 through 5 to apply the same format to the second headline. Alternatively, you could use the Format Painter to apply the format from the first headline to the second headline. Click anywhere in the document to deselect the text.

The second headline is formatted the same as the first, as shown in Figure 4.20.

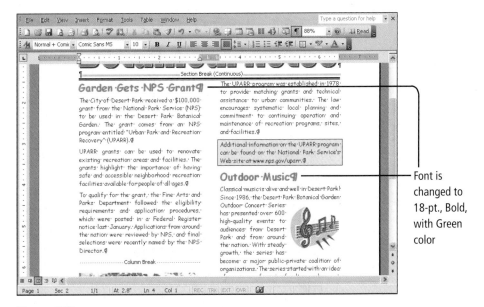

Font is changed to 18-pt., Bold, with Green color

**Figure 4.20**

**7** On the Standard toolbar, click the **Save** button.

### Activity 4.10 Using Small Caps

For headlines and titles, *small caps* is a useful font effect. Lower-case letters are changed to capital letters but remain the height of lower-case letters. Titles are often done in this style.

**1** Select the *Outdoor Music* title again. From the **Format** menu, click **Font**.

The Font dialog box displays. See Figure 4.21. There are several special effects that can be applied to fonts using the Font dialog box.

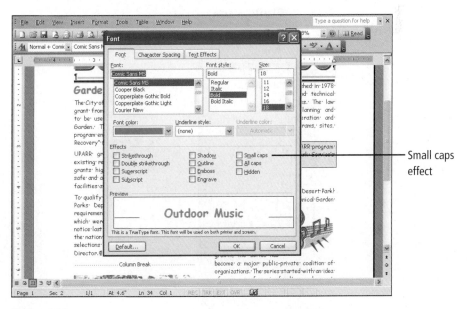

Small caps effect

**Figure 4.21**

**2** Under **Effects**, select the **Small caps** check box.

**3** At the bottom of the **Font** dialog box, click **OK**.

The second headline displays in small caps.

**4** In the first title, *Garden Gets NPS Grant*, repeat Steps 1 through 3. Alternatively, use the Format Painter to apply the small caps effect to the first title. Click anywhere in the document to deselect the text.

Both headlines display in small caps, as shown in Figure 4.22.

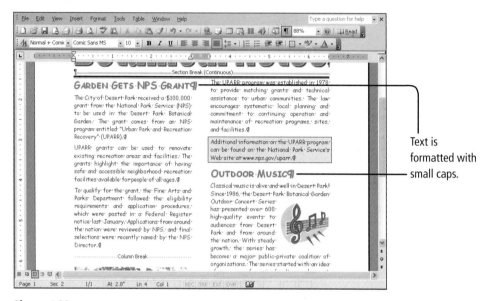

**Figure 4.22**

**5** On the Standard toolbar, click the **Show/Hide ¶** button ¶ to turn off the nonprinting characters.

**6** Click the **Zoom button arrow** 100% ▾, click the arrow and then click **Whole Page**.

The entire newsletter displays, as shown in Figure 4.23.

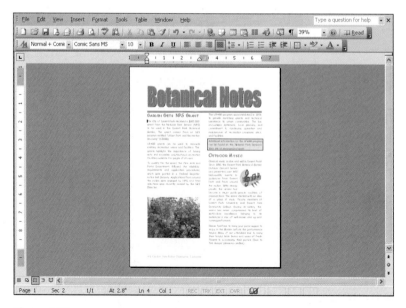

**Figure 4.23**

## More Knowledge — Removing Blank Pages

If you created empty paragraphs at the end of a document by pressing the Enter key too often, the result might be an extra blank page. To remove this page, click at the bottom of the document and press the Backspace key until the extra page is removed. It is best to use the Show/Hide ¶ button to show hidden characters so you can view the formatting marks that should be deleted.

**7** If your document looks different, make the necessary adjustments.

**8** On the Standard toolbar, click the **Show/Hide ¶** button 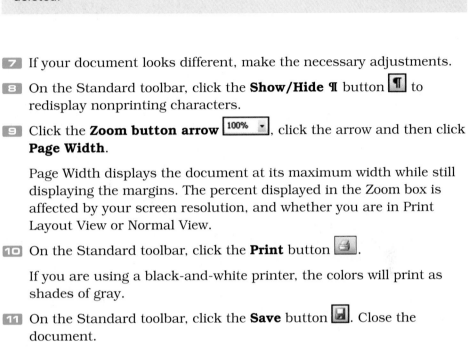 to redisplay nonprinting characters.

**9** Click the **Zoom button arrow**, click the arrow and then click **Page Width**.

Page Width displays the document at its maximum width while still displaying the margins. The percent displayed in the Zoom box is affected by your screen resolution, and whether you are in Print Layout View or Normal View.

**10** On the Standard toolbar, click the **Print** button.

If you are using a black-and-white printer, the colors will print as shades of gray.

**11** On the Standard toolbar, click the **Save** button. Close the document.

**End** You have completed Project 4A

# Project 4B **Water Matters**

In Project 4A you created titles and worked with paragraph and character formatting. In the following project, 4B, you will insert hyperlinks and practice saving documents as Web pages.

In Activities 4.11 through 4.15 you will edit a document that deals with water issues in the City of Desert Park. You will add links to text and graphics and then save the document as a Web page. Your completed document will look similar to Figure 4.24. You will save your document as *4B_Water_Matters_Firstname_Lastname.*

---

### City of Desert Park
# Water Matters

***Runoff Management***—Residents can visit the City's Web site to view the Urban Runoff Management Plan. The Plan details the City's action to protect and improve water quality of the lakes, rivers, and creeks in the region, and achieve compliance with the State Municipal Storm Water Permit.

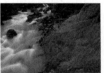 The Urban Runoff Management Plan has been posted to allow public access and understanding of the overall efforts of the City Manager's office to improve water quality in the City of Desert Park. Implementing the plan is one of the six objectives of the City's Storm Water Pollution Prevention Program to help improve water quality.

The City Council approved the plan last January, and is effective through February of 2006. At the City's Web site, click on "City Services," and choose "Storm Water Pollution Prevention." See the EPA Watershed site.

***Drinking Water***—Regulations from the State Public Health Services Drinking Water Program and the Environmental Protection Agency (EPA) require all community water systems to deliver an annual Consumer Confidence Report (water quality report) to customers. The City of Desert Park Water Bureau began sending this information to all postal customers in 1996, before these regulations went into effect in 1999.

 The most interesting information for most consumers is this: our drinking water supply continues to meet all state and federal regulations, without exception. This report includes other information of interest to many consumers: water quality test results; definitions; information on our sources of water supply; how to reduce exposure to lead in drinking water; and special notice for immuno-compromised persons. Copies of the report may also be ordered in Braille by calling the City Manager's office at 626-555-1234.

4B_Water_Matters_Firstname_Lastname

---

**Figure 4.24**
Project 4B—Water Matters

# Objective 5
## Insert Hyperlinks

Cities, businesses, and other organizations are publishing their important documents on the Web with increasing frequency. Web pages are easy to create using Microsoft Word features that enable the creation of Web pages directly from word processing documents. One of the strengths of using Web pages is that hyperlinks can be added to take the user to related sites quickly and easily. ***Hyperlinks*** are text or graphics that you click to move to a file, another page in a Web site, or a page in a different Web site.

You can create a Web page in Word, add text, graphics, and hyperlinks, and then preview the document in a Web browser to see how it looks. You can adjust the page to your satisfaction and then save the document as a Web page.

### Activity 4.11 Inserting Text Hyperlinks

The type of hyperlink used most frequently is one that is attached to text. Text hyperlinks usually appear underlined and in blue.

**1** On the Standard toolbar, click the **Open** button 📖. Navigate to the location where the student files for this textbook are stored. Locate **w04B_Water_Matters** and click once to select it. Then, in the lower right corner of the **Open** dialog box, click **Open**.

The w04B_Water_Matters file opens.

**2** From the **File** menu, click **Save As**. In the **Save As** dialog box, click the **Save in arrow** and navigate to the location in which you are storing your files for this chapter.

**3** Type **4B_Water_Matters_Firstname_Lastname** in the **File name** box, using your own name, and click **Save**.

The document is saved with a new name.

**4** On the Standard toolbar, click the **Show/Hide ¶** button ¶, if necessary, to display the nonprinting characters. On the Standard toolbar, click the Zoom button arrow 100%, and then click Page Width.

**5** Position the insertion point at the end of the paragraph beginning *The City Council approved*. Press [Spacebar] once and then type **See the EPA Watershed site.** In the sentence you just typed, select *EPA Watershed*.

**6** From the **Insert** menu, click **Hyperlink**. Alternatively, right-click on the selected text and click Hyperlink from the shortcut menu or click the Insert Hyperlink [button] button on the Standard toolbar.

The Insert Hyperlink dialog box displays, as shown in Figure 4.25.

Insert Hyperlink button

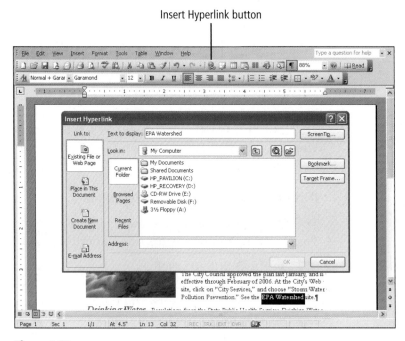

**Figure 4.25**

**7** Under **Link to**, click **Existing File or Web Page**. In the **Address** box, type **http://cfpub.epa.gov/surf/locate/map2.cfm** If another address displays while you are typing, ignore it and continue typing.

An address may display in the Address box as you type. This is AutoComplete at work. It displays the most recently used Web address for your computer.

**8** On the upper-right corner of the **Insert Hyperlink** dialog box, click **ScreenTip**.

The Set Hyperlink ScreenTip dialog box displays.

**9** In the **Set Hyperlink ScreenTip** dialog box, type **Watershed Map**

This is the ScreenTip that will display when the pointer is placed over the hyperlink. See Figure 4.26.

ScreenTip text —

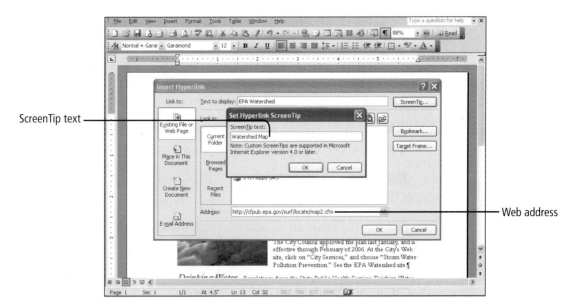

— Web address

**Figure 4.26**

**10** On the **Set Hyperlink ScreenTip** dialog box, click **OK**. At the bottom of the **Insert Hyperlink** dialog box, click **OK**.

The hyperlink is recorded, and the selected text changes to blue and is underlined.

**11** In the next paragraph, in the second line, select *Environmental Protection Agency (EPA)*. Repeat Steps 6 through 10 to create a hyperlink, but type **http://www.epa.gov** for the address and **EPA Home Page** for the ScreenTip.

The hyperlink is recorded, and the selected text changes to blue and is underlined, as shown in Figure 4.27.

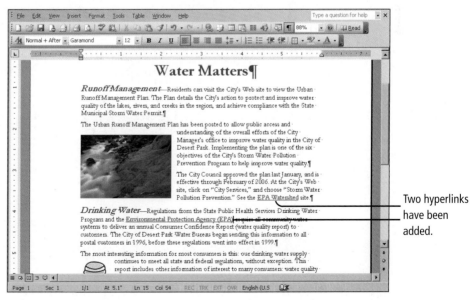

Two hyperlinks have been added.

**Figure 4.27**

**12** On the Standard toolbar, click the **Save** button ⊞.

## Activity 4.12 Adding a Hyperlink to a Graphic

When you move your pointer over a graphic on a Web page, and the pointer changes to a hand, it means a hyperlink has been added to the graphic. When you move your pointer over a hyperlink in a Word document, a ScreenTip displays with instructions for accessing the link.

**1** Scroll to the bottom of the document.

**2** Click the water cooler picture to select it.

**3** From the **Insert** menu, click **Hyperlink**.

The Insert Hyperlink dialog box displays.

**4** Under **Link to**, make sure **Existing File or Web Page** is selected. In the **Address** box, type **http://www.epa.gov**

**5** On the upper-right corner of the **Insert Hyperlink** dialog box, click **ScreenTip**.

The Set Hyperlink ScreenTip dialog box displays.

**6** In the **Set Hyperlink ScreenTip** dialog box, type **Drinking Water Standards**

Compare your dialog box with Figure 4.28.

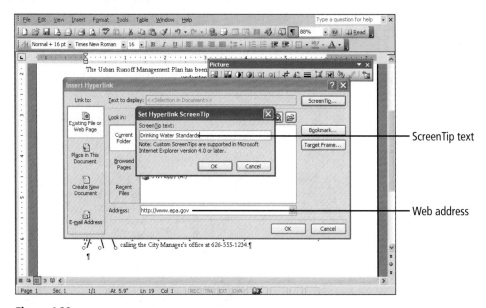

**Figure 4.28**

**7** On the **Set Hyperlink ScreenTip** dialog box, click **OK**. At the bottom of the **Insert Hyperlink** dialog box, click **OK**.

The hyperlink is recorded, but there is no visual indication that the link has been added.

**8** Move the pointer over the water cooler graphic.

The ScreenTip that you typed displays, as shown in Figure 4.29.

ScreenTip —

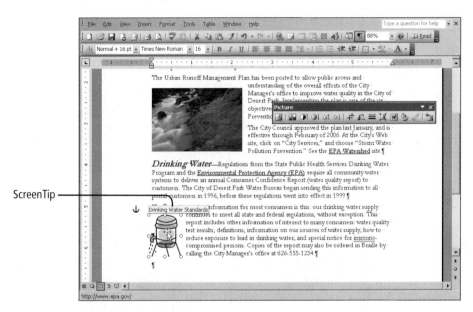

**Figure 4.29**

**9** On the Standard toolbar, click the **Save** button [icon].

### Activity 4.13 Modifying Hyperlinks

If you need to change a hyperlink, you will use a dialog box similar to the one you used to create it.

**1** Move the pointer over the water cooler and right-click.

A shortcut menu displays.

**2** From the shortcut menu, click **Edit Hyperlink**.

The Edit Hyperlink dialog box displays. Its components are similar to those of the Insert Hyperlink dialog box.

**3** At the bottom of the **Edit Hyperlink** dialog box, in the **Address** box, add **safewater** to the end of the Internet address.

Compare your dialog box to Figure 4.30.

## Note — If the Text Displays Automatically

When you begin typing the text in the text boxes of the Edit Hyperlink dialog box, the complete text may display after only a few letters. This results from someone else using the same computer to do this exercise before you. The text is completed only if the AutoComplete feature is turned on.

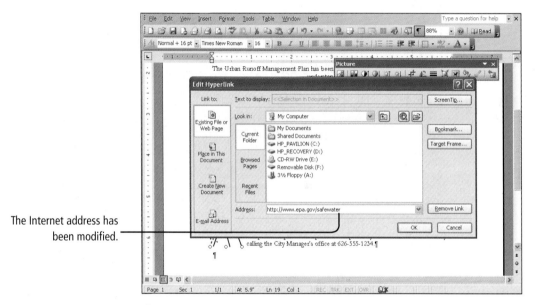

The Internet address has been modified.

**Figure 4.30**

**4** At the bottom of the **Edit Hyperlink** dialog box, click **OK**.

The hyperlink address is changed.

**5** From the **View** menu, click **Header and Footer**. On the Header and Footer toolbar, click the **Switch Between Header and Footer** button 🖻.

**6** On the Header and Footer toolbar, click the **Insert AutoText** button **Insert AutoText ▾** , and then click **Filename**.

The file name is inserted in the footer.

**7** On the Header and Footer toolbar, click the **Close** button 🔲ose .

**8** On the Standard toolbar, click the **Save** button 🔲 .

**9** On the Standard toolbar, click the **Print Preview** button 🔲 . Take a moment to check your work. On the **Print Preview** toolbar, click the **Close Preview** button 🔲ose .

**10** On the Standard toolbar, click the **Print** button 🔲 .

# Objective 6
## Preview and Save a Document as a Web Page

After you have created a document to be used as a Web page, you can see what the page will look like when displayed in a **Web browser** such as Internet Explorer or Netscape. A Web browser is software that enables you to use the Web and navigate from page to page and site to site. You can adjust the image and preview it until you get it exactly right. Once you are satisfied with the way the document looks when displayed in a Web browser, you can save the document as a Web page.

### Activity 4.14 Previewing a Document as a Web Page

**1** From the **File** menu, click **Web Page Preview**.

Your Web browser opens, and your document displays as a Web page. Your screen may look different, depending on your screen size, screen resolution, and the Web browser you use.

**2** Move your pointer over the *EPA Watershed* hyperlink.

The pointer changes to a hand, indicating that the text contains a link, as shown in Figure 4.31.

Document displayed in a Web browser ──

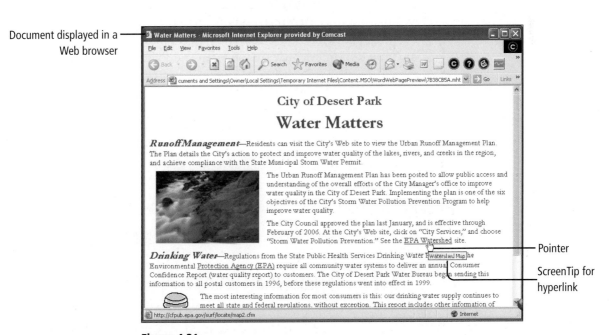

── Pointer

── ScreenTip for hyperlink

**Figure 4.31**

**3** On the vertical scroll bar, click the down arrow to scroll down the page, if necessary.

On some high-resolution screens, you will not need to scroll down. Notice that the file name you placed in the footer does not display on the Web page.

**4** Click the **water cooler image** to make sure your Web link works.

If you are connected to the Internet, you will see the *EPA Drinking Water* page.

**Alert!**

### If You Are Not Connected to the Internet

If you are not connected to the Internet, you will see a message box informing you that you are not connected, or the site could not be found. Click OK to acknowledge the message, and then resume with Step 6 of the instructions.

**5** On the Browser title bar, click the **Close** button ✕. Make any changes that you feel are necessary and preview your Web page again.

**6** On the Standard toolbar, click the **Save** button 🖫.

### Activity 4.15 Saving a Document as a Web Page

Once you are satisfied with your document, you can save it as a Web page.

**1** From the **File** menu, click **Save as Web Page**.

The Save As dialog box displays.

**2** In the **Save in** dialog box, navigate to the location in which you are saving your files.

Notice in the File name box that the file extension has changed from .doc to .mht. This is the extension of a single Web page. If file extensions have been turned off on your computer, you will not see the extension. The Save as type box displays *Single File Web Page*, and the document title displays as the Page title.

**3** Near the bottom of the **Save As** dialog box, click **Change Title**.

The Set Page Title dialog box displays. What you type here will become the Web page title; this is the title that displays in the browser title bar and shows up in the Web browser's history list.

**4** Type **City of Desert Park Water Issues** See Figure 4.32.

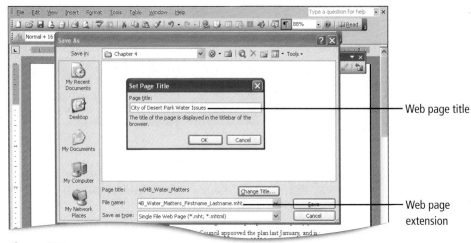

Figure 4.32

**5** Click **OK** to close the **Set Page Title** dialog box.

In the Save as dialog box, the new title for your Web page displays as the Page title. Accept the default File name for the Web page. When you save it, the Web page will have a different file extension and file type icon to distinguish it from the Word document by the same name.

**5** At the bottom of the **Save As** dialog box, click **Save**.

A dialog box displays stating that some of the elements in this page will not display properly on very early versions of Web browsers. See Figure 4.33.

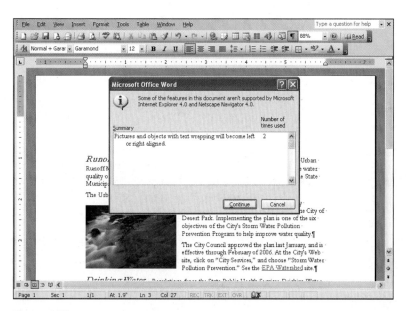

**Figure 4.33**

**6** At the bottom of the dialog box, click **Continue**.

The file is saved and the document displays on your screen in the Web page format, with text across the full width of the screen—no margins, and both pictures displayed on the left side.

**7** On the Standard toolbar, click the **Save** button. Close the document.

**End** You have completed Project 4B

# Project 4C **Recreation Ideas**

In Project 4B you practiced saving documents as Web pages. In Project 4C you will work with supporting information and objects.

In Activities 4.16 through 4.21, you will gather text and graphics that will be used in a Recreation Department newsletter. You will gather several documents and several pictures and then paste them from the Office Clipboard. You will use the *Thesaurus*—a language tool for finding alternative words with similar meanings—and then you will use special tools to browse a document. You will save your document as *4C_Recreation_Ideas_Firstname_Lastname.*

**MEMO TO:** Jane Romano

**FROM:** Ray Hamilton

**DATE:** March 5, 2005

**SUBJECT:** Ideas for the June Recreation Notes Newsletter

Here are some ideas for the June *Recreation Notes* newsletter, which should include the rough drafts of articles on Golf and Bicycling. I've also included some information on the history of each sport that you might be able to use for the *Did You Know?* boxes. Finally, I've added an image you might be able to use.

**GOLF**

*Draft of article:*
The Desert Park Fine Arts and Parks Department is hosting a golf clinic and nighttime golf benefit at the North Park Golf Course on Friday, August 21 to benefit the city's Youth Golf Program.
A PGA Tour Professional, recognized as one of the most accomplished golfers to play the game, will be at the North Park Golf Course to offer a free Golf Clinic. The clinic will run from 9 a.m. – 10:30 a.m. It's open to the public and there is no charge for admission. Come on out and learn some valuable tips from a pro!
Want to see how a pro applies those clinic techniques to an actual round of golf? As a follow-up to the clinic, our pro will join tournament guests in an exhibition round beginning at 12 noon. Plan to follow this foursome to see how they perform.
The nighttime event begins at 8 p.m. Pre-registration is required. The cost is $25 per person. Registration includes greens fees, glow balls, prizes, soft drinks, and pull carts. The tournament is a four-person scramble with a shotgun start at 8:15 p.m.
The tournament, which is played on the nine-hole course, is limited to the first 12 teams (48 players). The Youth Golf Program provides free golf lessons to youth at six of Desert Park's municipal golf courses. Funding makes it possible to provide year-round instruction, golf clubs, balls and other equipment for use during the classes. For more information, call 626-555-1131.
"The Golf Benefit is a fun and informal way to support hundreds of young people in Desert Park and the surrounding county," said Fred Stein, president of the Youth Golf Program Foundation. "The golf clinic is a great opportunity for children to learn about the game and be exposed to business leaders who can have an influence on their lives."
Last year the Youth Golf Program Foundation helped 145 young men and women learn to play the value of good sportspersonship. The organization is a non-profit organization that provides golf events through structured, school-based golf programs.

*Information for Did You Know? boxes:*
Some historians believe that golf originated in the Netherlands (the Dutch word *kolf* had a game played with a bent stick and a ball made of feathers that may have been th It has been fairly well established, however, that the game that is known today was ac the 14th or 15th century.
*Image:*

4C_Recreation_Ideas_Firstname_Lastname

**BICYCLING**

*Draft of article:*
The "Golden Age" of bicycling occurred during the development of Desert Park many years ago. Early photographs show street scenes with bicycles, horses, trolleys, and pedestrians. In fact, our first streets were arranged for these users. But Desert Park was ahead of its time, because this development pattern is actually an essential element of a livable community.
Desert Park is a city in which people can get around without cars, and the City hopes to make this a place where it is easier to ride a bicycle than to drive a car. Ideally, bicyclists should be able to circulate along city streets freely and safely. At the bicyclist's destination there should be safe, free, and accessible parking.
The City is working on a plan that identifies a network of bikeways that will connect bicycle riders to their destinations. The enhancements to the Agave Trail are an important part of this plan. The plan includes a list of other projects and programs, similar to the Agave Trail program, to be added to the Transportation Improvement Plan.

*Information for Did You Know? boxes:*
The bicycle was not invented by any one person. Rather, it is an outgrowth of ideas and inventions dating to the late 18th century. Some people claim the bicycle's history goes back even further, citing certain drawings by Leonardo da Vinci of a two-wheeled vehicle.
*Image:*

4C_Recreation_Ideas_Firstname_Lastname

**Figure 4.34**
Project 4C—Recreation Ideas

# Objective 7
## Locate Supporting Information

When you are writing, you may want to refer to information related to your topic. This **supporting information** could be located in other documents or on the Web. As you collect information for a new document, you can store all of the pieces (text and pictures) on the Office Clipboard. When you have all of the information pieces gathered, you can go to your document and paste the information one piece at a time. This feature is called **collect and paste**.

Word has a Thesaurus tool that enables you to find exactly the right word. Also, a special button can be used to quickly locate various elements in a document. For example, you can navigate through a document by moving from one section to the next or from one image to the next. It is recommended that you do these activities on a computer with an Internet connection. You will not be able to complete Activity 4.18 without a connection.

### Activity 4.16  Using Collect and Paste to Gather Images

Recall that the Office Clipboard is a temporary storage area maintained by your Windows operating system. When you perform the Copy command or the Cut command, the text that you select is placed on the Clipboard. From this Clipboard storage area, you can paste text into another location of your document, into another document, or into another Office program.

You can copy and then paste a single selection of text without displaying the Clipboard task pane. Displaying the Clipboard is essential, however, if you want to collect a group of selected text pieces or images and then paste them. The Clipboard can hold up to 24 items, and the Clipboard task pane displays a short representation of each item.

**1** On the Standard toolbar, click the **Open** button . Locate and open the **w04C_Recreation_Ideas** file.

**2** From the **File** menu, click **Save As**. Navigate to the location where you are storing your files for this chapter. In the **File name** box, type **4C_Recreation_Ideas_Firstname_Lastname** and click **Save**.

The document is saved with a new name. Be sure you substitute your name where indicated.

**3** From the **Edit** menu, click **Office Clipboard**.

The Clipboard task pane displays, as shown in Figure 4.35.

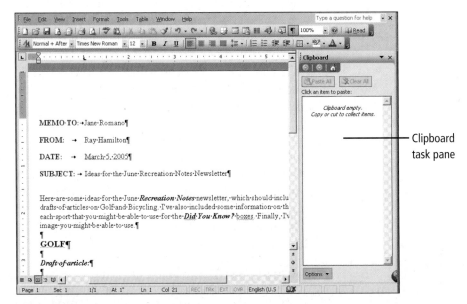

**Figure 4.35**

**Another Way**

### Other Ways to Display the Clipboard Task Pane

***There are two other ways to display the Clipboard task pane:***

- If a different task pane is displayed, click the Other Task Panes arrow and then click Clipboard.

- Select the first piece of text that you want to copy, hold down Ctrl, and then quickly press C two times.

**4** If the Office Clipboard displays any entries, from the top of the Clipboard task pane, click the **Clear All** button. From the **Insert** menu, point to **Picture** and then click **Clip Art**.

The Clip Art task pane replaces the Clipboard task pane.

**5** In the **Search for box**, type **golf** Click the **Search in arrow** and then select **Everywhere**. Click the **Results should be arrow**, be sure the **Clip Art** check box is selected, and then clear the other check boxes. Click **Go** twice.

**6** In the **Clip Art** task pane, move the pointer over the image of a woman golfer.

If the image shown in Figure 4.36 is not available, choose another golf picture.

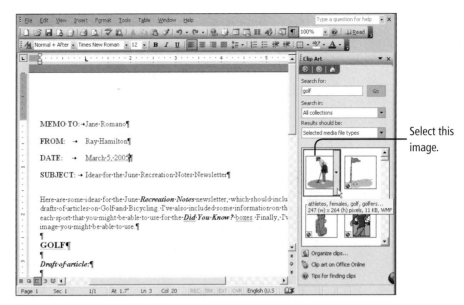

Select this image.

**Figure 4.36**

## Note — Inserting Clip Art Images from Your Student Files

If you do not have an Internet connection, and if you have a minimum Office installation, you may not have any images of golf available. Both images used for this activity have been included with the files for this chapter. To access those files, from the bottom of the Clip Art task pane, click *Organize clips*. In the Favorites-Microsoft Clip Organizer dialog box, display the File menu, point to Add Clips to Organizer, and then click On My Own. Use the Look in arrow to navigate to the location of your student files and find *w04C_Golf*. Select it and then, in the lower right corner of the dialog box, click Add. When the image displays in the dialog box, move the pointer over the arrow on the right side of the image and then click Copy. Close the dialog box. When prompted, click the Yes button to copy the image to the Office Clipboard. Continue with Activity 4.16.

**7** On the image of the woman golfer, click the arrow and then click **Copy**.

The image is copied to the Clipboard.

**8** In the title bar of the **Clip Art** task pane, click the **Other Task Panes arrow**. From the task pane menu, click **Clipboard**.

The image you selected displays in the Clipboard task pane. When copying clip art, you need to redisplay the Clipboard after you copy an image; otherwise, the next image you copy will replace the current image.

**9** In the title bar of the **Clipboard** task pane, click the **Other Task Panes arrow**. From the task pane menu, click **Clip Art**.

**10** In the **Search for** box, type **cycling** and then click **Go**.

**11** In the **Clip Art** task pane, move the pointer over the image of a cyclist on a trail.

If the image shown in Figure 4.37 is not available, choose another similar picture, or read the Note box for directions on how to find w04C_Cycling from your student files.

🔢 On the image of the cyclist, click the arrow and then click **Copy**.

The image is transferred to the Clipboard.

🔢 In the title bar of the **Clip Art** task pane, click the **Other Task Panes arrow**. From the task pane menu, click **Clipboard**.

Both images are displayed in the Clipboard task pane, with the most recently copied image on top. See Figure 4.37.

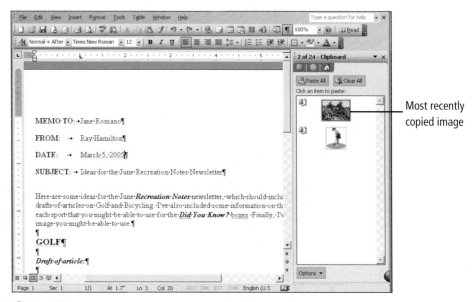

Most recently copied image

**Figure 4.37**

### Activity 4.17 Collecting Information from Other Documents

If you need information from another document, you can open the source document, copy the text you need onto the Clipboard, and then paste it into your document later.

1⃣ Be sure **4C_Recreation_Ideas** is still displayed on your screen, and the Clipboard task pane displays the two images you have copied.

On the Standard toolbar, click the **Open** button 📂. Locate and open the **w04C_Golf** file.

2⃣ In the **w04C_Golf** file, hold down Ctrl and press A.

All the text is selected.

3⃣ On the Standard toolbar, click the **Copy** button 📋.

The text is copied to the Clipboard, along with the two images.

4⃣ On the Standard toolbar, click the **Open** button 📂. Locate and open the **w04C_Bicycle** file.

5 In the **w04C_Bicycle** file, hold down Ctrl and press A to select the document.

6 On the Standard toolbar, click the **Copy** button.

The text is copied to the Clipboard along with the *Golf* text and the two images.

7 In the upper right corner of your screen, to the right of the *Type a question for help* box, click the **Close Window** button ✕ to close the **w04C_Bicycle** file.

8 Click the Close Window button ✕ to close the **w04C_Golf** file.

Compare your clipboard to Figure 4.38. Notice that as new items are copied to the Office Clipboard, the most recent item moves to the top of the list.

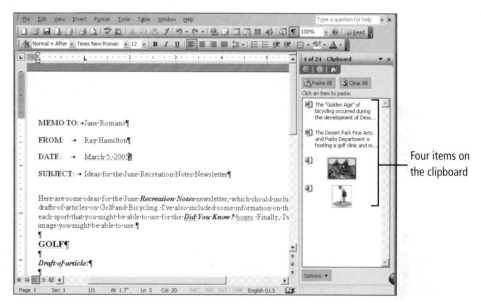

Four items on the clipboard

**Figure 4.38**

### Activity 4.18 Finding Supporting Information Using the Research Tool

Word includes a research tool that enables you to search for information on a variety of topics. You will need an Internet connection to complete this activity.

1 On the Standard toolbar, click the **Research** button.

The Research task pane displays.

2 In the **Search for** box, type **Golf**

3 Under the **Search for** box, in the second box, click the arrow, and then click **Encarta Encyclopedia**.

Your screen may indicate only *Encyclopedia* or it may display the language and version of the active encyclopedia. A list of golf topics displays. See Figure 4.39.

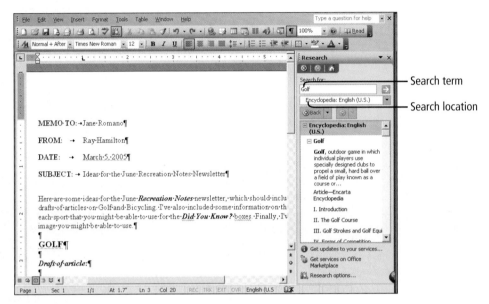

**Figure 4.39**

4 In the **Research** task pane list of topics, click **History**.

You may have to scroll down the list of topics. The program moves to the *MSN Learning & Research* site on the Web. The History section, which is in the middle of the document, displays at the top of the screen.

5 Move the pointer to the left of the top paragraph that begins *Some historians believe*. Drag to the end of the second sentence, which ends *the 14th or 15th century.*

Be sure you have only the two sentences selected. Your screen should look similar to Figure 4.40. Because the information on Web sites changes often, the information on your screen may look slightly different.

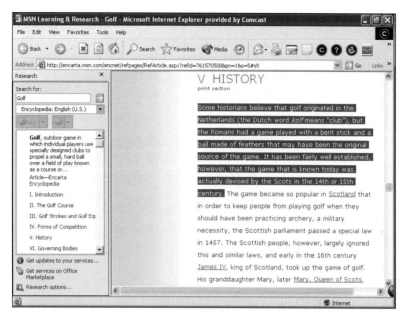

**Figure 4.40**

---

# More Knowledge — Being Careful of Copyright Issues

Nearly everything you find on the Web is protected by copyright law, which protects authors of original works, including text, art, photographs, and music. If you want to use text or graphics that you find online, you will need to get permission. One of the exceptions to this law is the use of small amounts of information for educational purposes, which falls under Fair Use guidelines.

Copyright laws in the United States are open to different interpretations, and copyright laws can be very different in other countries. As a general rule, if you want to use someone else's material, always get permission first.

---

**6** From the **Edit** menu, click **Copy**. Alternatively, right-click the selected text and from the shortcut menu click Copy.

The text is added to the Clipboard.

**7** Close the *MSN Learning & Research* window.

**8** In the title bar of the **Research** task pane, click the **Other Task Panes arrow**. From the task pane menu, click **Clipboard**.

The text you copied displays in the Clipboard task pane.

**9** Click the **Other Task Panes arrow** again and click **Research**. Use the same technique you used in Steps 2 through 7 for researching golf to research the **bicycle** You may have to scroll down the topics area to find **History of the Modern Bicycle**. Select and copy the first three sentences of the **History** area.

You should have six items in your Clipboard task pane, as shown in Figure 4.41.

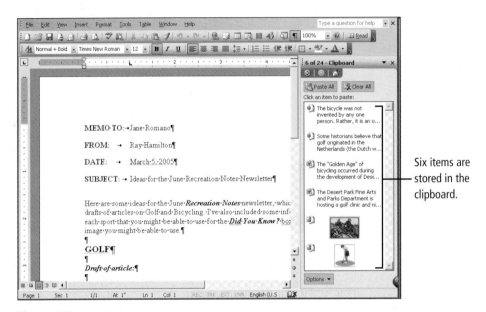

**Figure 4.41**

### Activity 4.19 Pasting Information from the Clipboard Task Pane

Once you have collected text and images from other documents or sources, such as the Internet, you can paste them into your document.

**1** With **4C_Recreation_Ideas_Firstname_Lastname** open, in the blank line under the **GOLF** *Draft of article*, click to position the insertion point.

**2** On the Clipboard task pane, under **Click an item to paste**, click the fourth item in the item list, the one that begins *The Desert Park Fine Arts*.

The text is pasted into the document at the insertion point location, as shown in Figure 4.42.

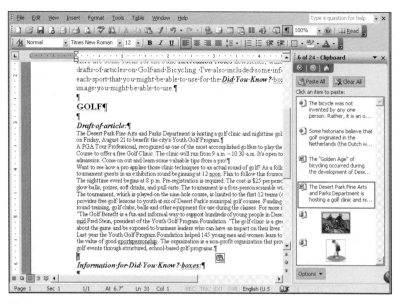

**Figure 4.42**

3 Position the insertion point in the blank line under the **GOLF** *Information for Did You Know? boxes*. From the **Click an item to paste** on the **Clipboard** task pane, click the second item in the item list, the one that begins *Some historians believe.*

The text is placed at the insertion point.

4 Position the insertion point in the blank line under the **GOLF** *Image*. From the **Click an item to paste** on the **Clipboard** task pane, click the sixth item in the item list, the graphic of the golfer.

The image is placed at the insertion point, as shown in Figure 4.43.

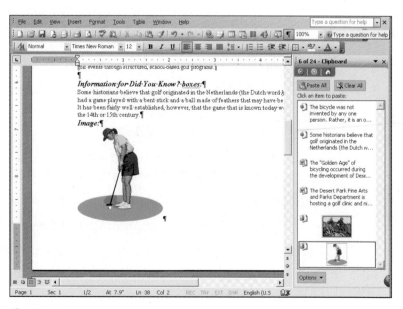

**Figure 4.43**

**5** In the blank line under the BICYCLING Draft of article, click to position the insertion point. On the Clipboard task pane, under Click an item to paste, click the third item in the item list, the one that begins The "Golden Age" of bicycling. The text is pasted into the document at the insertion point location.

**6** Position the insertion point in the blank line under the **BICYCLE** *Information for Did You Know? boxes*. From the **Click an item to paste** on the **Clipboard** task pane, click the text that begins *The bicycle was not invented.*

Compare your document to Figure 4.44.

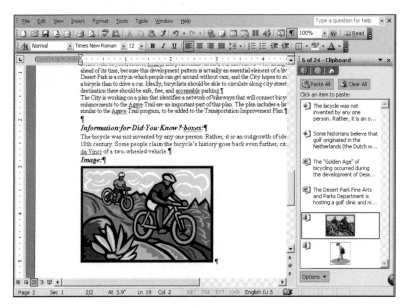

**Figure 4.44**

**7** Position the insertion point in the blank line under the **Bicycling** *Image*. From the **Click an item to paste** on the **Clipboard** task pane, click the fifth item in the item list, the graphic of the bicyclists.

**8** Under **Click an item to paste** on the **Clipboard** task pane, move the pointer over the first item in the list. Click the arrow.

**9** From the menu, click **Delete**.

The item is removed from the list. You can remove one item from the Clipboard without disturbing the rest of the items stored there.

**10** At the top of the **Clipboard** task pane, click **Clear All**.

All of the items are removed from the list.

**11** In the title bar of the **Clipboard** task pane, click the Close button ⊠.

The Clipboard task pane closes.

**12** On the Standard toolbar, click the **Save** button 🖫.

### Activity 4.20 Using the Thesaurus

The *thesaurus* is a language tool that assists in your writing by suggesting synonyms (words that have the same meaning) for words that you select.

**1** From the **Edit** menu, click **Find**.

The Find and Replace dialog box displays.

**2** In the **Find and Replace** dialog box, in the **Find what** box, type **training** and click **Find next**.

The word *training* in the Golf section is highlighted.

**3** In the **Find and Replace** dialog box, click **Cancel**.

**4** Right-click the selected word. From the shortcut menu, point to **Synonyms**.

A list of synonyms displays, as shown in Figure 4.45.

Selected word

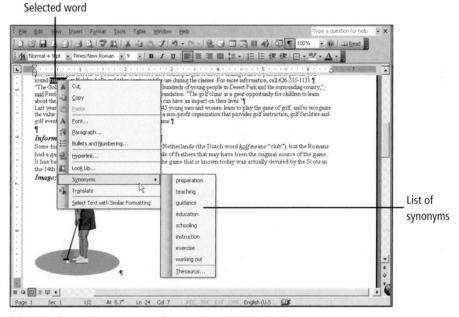

List of synonyms

**Figure 4.45**

**5** In the list of synonyms, click **instruction**.

*Instruction* replaces *training* in the document.

**6** From the **Edit** menu, click **Find**. In the **Find and Replace** dialog box, in the **Find what** box, type **impact** and click **Find next**.

The word *impact* in the Golf section is highlighted.

**7** In the **Find and Replace** dialog box, click **Cancel** to close the dialog box.

**8** Right-click the selected word. From the shortcut menu, point to **Synonyms**.

A list of synonyms displays. Sometimes the best word is not included in the list of synonyms.

**9** At the bottom of the synonym list, click **Thesaurus**.

The Research task pane displays and lists words from the English Thesaurus. Notice that there are more options available. See Figure 4.46.

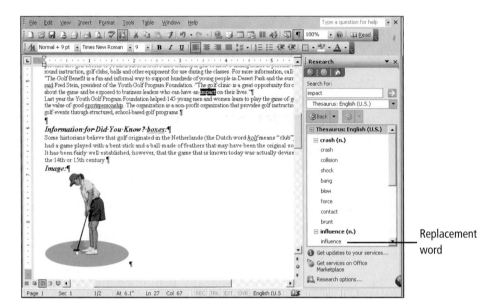

Replacement word

**Figure 4.46**

**10** In the **Research** task pane, point to *influence*, click the down arrow on the right side of the word, and then, from the displayed list, click **Insert**.

*Influence* replaces *impact* in the document.

**11** In the title bar of the **Research** task pane, click the **Close** button ☒.

On the Standard toolbar, click the **Save** button 🖫.

## Objective 8
## Find Objects with the Select Browse Object Button

The Select Browse Object button is located at the bottom of the vertical scroll bar and can be used to navigate through a document by type of object. For example, you can move from one footnote to the next or from one section to the next. This feature can be used on short documents but is most effective when you are navigating long documents. You can navigate using several different object elements, by graphic, table, section, footnote, or page.

**Activity 4.21** Using the Select Browse Object Menu to Find Document Elements

**1** With the **4C_Recreation_Ideas_Firstname_Lastname** open, at the bottom of the vertical scroll bar, click the **Select Browse Object** button.

The Select Browse Object palette displays, as shown in Figure 4.47. The order of the buttons in the Select Browse Object palette on your computer may be different from what is shown in the figure. Examine the Object buttons on the palette and compare them to the ones shown in the table in Figure 4.48 to identify each button and its purpose.

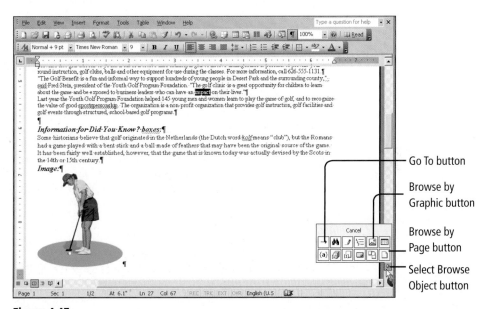

Go To button

Browse by Graphic button

Browse by Page button

Select Browse Object button

**Figure 4.47**

## Buttons on the Select Browse Object Palette

| ScreenTip | Button | Description |
|---|---|---|
| Browse by Field | {a} | Moves between objects in your document that have been defined as fields. |
| Browse by Endnote | | Moves from one endnote to the next. |
| Browse by Footnote | | Moves from one footnote to the next. |
| Browse by Comment | | Moves between comments that have been inserted in your document. |
| Browse by Section | | Moves from one section to the next. |
| Browse by Page | | Moves by page in your document. This is the most common way to browse a document and is the default setting for the Select Browse Object button. |
| Go To | → | Moves to the next occurrence of an object as defined in the Go To page of the Find and Replace dialog box. |
| Find | | Moves to the next word or phrase that has been entered in the Find and Replace dialog box. |
| Browse by Edits | | Moves between Edits that have been made to your document using the Track Changes command. |
| Browse by Heading | | Moves between Heading styles that have been applied to a document. |
| Browse by Graphic | | Moves between graphic objects that have been inserted in your document. |
| Browse by Table | | Moves between tables in your document. |

**Figure 4.48**

**2** On the **Select Browse Object** palette, click the **Browse by Page** button ▢.

The insertion point moves to the top of the second page.

**3** Click the **Select Browse Object** button ⊙ again. On the **Select Browse Object** palette, click the **Go To** button →.

The Find and Replace dialog box displays. Notice that the Go To tab at the top of the Find and Replace dialog box is selected. This page of the dialog box enables you to go to a specific page, or navigate by various objects.

**4** In the **Find and Replace** dialog box, under **Go to what**, scroll to the top of the list and click **Page**.

**5** Under **Enter page number**, type **1**

Compare your Find and Replace dialog box to Figure 4.49.

Go To tab

Page number

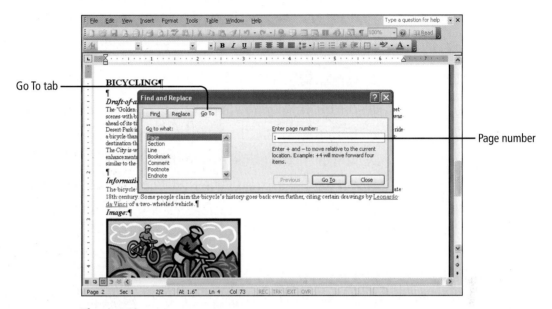

**Figure 4.49**

**6** In the **Find and Replace** dialog box, click **Go To**.

The insertion point moves to the top of the first page of the document.

**7** Close the **Find and Replace** dialog box. Click the **Select Browse Object** button. In the **Select Browse Object** palette, click the **Browse by Graphic** button.

The insertion point moves to the graphic of the golfer. The arrow buttons above and below the Select Browse Object button can be used to navigate to the next or previous object location. These buttons take on the name of the type of object that has been set with the Select Browse Object button.

**8** Click the **Next Graphic arrow** below the **Select Browse Object** button.

The insertion point moves to the graphic of the bicyclists.

**9** Click the **Select Browse Object** button ⬚. In the **Select Browse Object** palette, click the **Browse by Page** button ⬚.

This returns the Select Browse Object button to the Browse by Page function, which is the most common method for browsing a document. The Select Browse Object button retains the method of browsing that was last selected.

**10** From the **View** menu, click **Header and Footer**. On the Header and Footer toolbar, click the **Switch Between Header and Footer** button ⬚.

**11** On the Header and Footer toolbar, click the **Insert AutoText** button [ Insert AutoText ▾ ], and then click **Filename**.

The file name is inserted in the footer.

**12** On the Header and Footer toolbar, click the **Close** button [ Close ].

**13** From the Standard toolbar, click the **Save** button ⬚.

**14** On the Standard toolbar, click the **Print Preview** button ⬚. Take a moment to check your work. On the Print Preveiw toolbar, click the **Close Preview** button [ Close ].

**15** On the Standard toolbar, click the **Print** button ⬚. Close the document saving any changes.

**End** You have completed Project 4C ————————————————————

# Summary

Microsoft Word includes many features that can be used to create a newsletter or a Web page, similar to those created by desktop publishing or Web design programs. In this chapter, you created a masthead by changing text into a graphic element with the WordArt program, added borders and shading to paragraphs for special effect, and used special character formats to create more distinctive headings. You learned how to change from a single- to a multiple-column document and to control where a column ends. You practiced adding hyperlinks to a Word document and saving it as a Web page.

Finally, you practiced gathering information from several resources to create a new document. This collect-and-paste process can involve using the Office Clipboard, the Microsoft Research tools to find supporting information, and such common but helpful tools as a thesaurus. The Select Browse Object button was introduced as a tool to help navigate within a document.

## In This Chapter You Practiced How To

- Create a Decorative Title
- Create Multicolumn Documents
- Add Special Paragraph Formatting
- Use Special Character Formats
- Insert Hyperlinks
- Preview and Save a Document as a Web Page
- Locate Supporting Information
- Find Objects with the Select Browse Object Button

**Matching**    Match each term in the second column with its correct definition in the first column by writing the letter of the term on the blank line in front of the correct definition.

_____ 1. A Microsoft Office subprogram used to change text into a decorative graphic.

_____ 2. Text or graphic that you can click to move to a file, another page in a Web site, or a different Web site.

_____ 3. Laws that protect authors of original works, including text, art, photographs, and music.

_____ 4. The place where copied items are stored temporarily until they are pasted in another location.

_____ 5. The alignment used, especially in columns of text, to create a flush edge of text on both the left and right side of a column.

_____ 6. A button on the Standard toolbar that connects you to a group of resources for exploring information.

_____ 7. A special font effect where the lower-case letters are changed to capital letters but remain the height of lowercase letters.

_____ 8. The process of gathering various pieces of information together on the Office Clipboard for use in another document.

_____ 9. A dialog box used to add special formats to a paragraph so it stands out from the rest of the text.

_____ 10. A document that has been saved with a .mht extension so it can be viewed with a Web browser.

_____ 11. A dialog box used to change the appearance of a WordArt graphic.

_____ 12. The type of section break used when you want columns to end at approximately the same place on the page.

_____ 13. A dialog box used to create a Hyperlink.

_____ 14. An option used to expand a clip art search to include all possible locations.

_____ 15. A Word window that provides commonly used commands; useful for searching for clip art, researching information, or collecting items on the clipboard.

**A** Borders and Shading

**B** Collect and Paste

**C** Continuous

**D** Copyright

**E** Everywhere

**F** Format WordArt

**G** Hyperlink

**H** Insert Hyperlink

**I** Justified

**J** Office Clipboard

**K** Research

**L** Small caps

**M** Task pane

**N** Web page

**O** WordArt

**Fill in the Blank** Write the correct answer in the space provided.

1. Netscape and Internet Explorer are examples of _____

   _____.

2. To change the font size and style of a WordArt graphic, use the

   _____ _____ dialog box.

3. The title in a newsletter is known as a _____.

4. Microsoft Publisher is a _____ _____

   program.

5. The Office Clipboard can store up to _____ items.

6. To artificially end a column and move the rest of the text in

   that column to the top of the next column, you can insert a

   _____ _____.

7. When you change from a two-column format to a one-column

   format, Word inserts a _____ _____.

8. To change one column of text into two columns, use the

   _____ button on the Standard toolbar.

9. To move in a document from one section to the next, or from one

   graphic to the next, use the _____ button.

10. If you want to substitute one word for another and need to look up a

    synonym, use the Word language tool called a _____.

## Project 4D—Council News

**Objectives:** *Create a Decorative Title, Create Multicolumn Documents, Add Special Paragraph Formatting, Use Special Character Formats, and Find Objects with the Select Browse Object Button.*

In the following Skill Assessment, you will create a newsletter for the Desert Park City Council. Your completed document will look similar to Figure 4.50. You will save your publication as *4D_Council_News_Firstname_Lastname*.

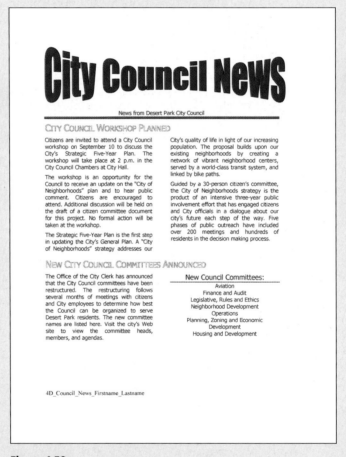

**Figure 4.50**

1. On the Standard toolbar, click the **Open** button and then navigate to the location where the student files for this textbook are stored. Locate **w04D_Council_News** and click once to select it. Then, in the lower right corner of the **Open** dialog box, click **Open**.

2. From the **File** menu, click **Save As**. In the **Save As** dialog box, click the **Save in arrow** and then navigate to the location in which you are storing your files for this chapter. In the **File name** box type **4D_Council_News_Firstname_Lastname** and click **Save**.

(**Project 4D–Council News continues on the next page**)

**(Project 4D–Council News continued)**

3. Be sure that the nonprinting formatting marks are displayed and then be sure the insertion point is at the top of the document, to the left of the empty paragraph mark. From the **Insert** menu, point to **Picture** and then click **WordArt**. In the **WordArt Gallery** dialog box, in the first row, click the fourth style and then click **OK**.

4. In the **Edit WordArt Text** dialog box type **City Council News** and then change the **Size** box to **66** Click **OK**.

5. Click the WordArt graphic to select it, if necessary. On the floating WordArt toolbar, click the **Format WordArt** button. In the **Format WordArt** dialog box, under **Fill**, click the **Color arrow**. On the displayed color palette, in the second row, click the first color—**Dark Red**. Under **Line**, click the **Color arrow**, click **Dark Red**, and then click **OK**. Alternatively, under Line, click the Color arrow, click No Line, and then click OK. The letters will appear slightly narrower. The color of the WordArt graphic is changed. On the Standard toolbar, click the **Save** button.

6. On the line below your inserted WordArt, click to the left of *City Council Workshop Planned* and press Enter. Notice that when the WordArt is deselected, the WordArt toolbar is closed. Move the insertion point to the left of the empty line you just created and type **News from Desert Park City Council** Select the text you just typed, on the Formatting toolbar click the **Center** button, and then click the arrow on the **Font Color** button. From the displayed palette, click **Dark Red**.

7. With the line you typed still selected, from the **Format** menu, click **Borders and Shading**. In the **Borders and Shading** dialog box, click the **Borders tab**. Under **Setting**, click **Custom**. Under **Style**, scroll down and click the option with a thick bottom line and a thin line above it (refer to Figure 4.50). Click the **Color arrow** and then click **Dark Red**. In the **Preview** area, click the **bottom line** in the preview graphic and then click **OK**. On the Standard toolbar, click **Save** to save the changes you have made.

8. Select the text *City Council Workshop Planned* and, from the **Format** menu, click **Font**. In the **Font** dialog box, change the number in the **Size** box to **18**. Click the **Font Color arrow** and click **Dark Red**. Under **Effects**, select the **Outline** and **Small caps** check boxes and then click **OK**. Scroll down to view the lower half of the document and then repeat this process to apply the same font format to the headline *New City Council Committees Announced*. Alternatively, apply the font format by using the Format Painter.

**(Project 4D–Council News continues on the next page)**

**(Project 4D–Council News continued)**

9. Scroll to view the upper portion of your document. Beginning with *Citizens are invited*, select the text between the two headlines. (Hint: Click to the left of *Citizens*, hold down Shift, and then click to the right of the period following *process*.) Do not include the paragraph mark at the end of the selected text. On the Standard toolbar, click the **Columns** button, drag to select **two columns**, and then release the left mouse button. The selected text is arranged into two columns, and section breaks are inserted before and after the selected text. Repeat this process to format the text under *New City Council*, beginning with *The Office of the City Clerk*, to a two-column format. On the Standard toolbar, click the **Save** button.

10. Place the insertion point to the left of *Aviation*. Type **New Council Committees:** and press Enter. Select the heading you just typed and the list of committees listed under it, including those in the second column, and then, on the Formatting toolbar, click the **Center** button.

11. Select *New Council Committees:* and, on the Formatting toolbar, click the **Font Color arrow** and then click **Dark Red**. Click the **Font Size arrow** and then click **14**. From the **Format** menu, display the **Borders and Shading** dialog box and click the **Borders tab**. Under **Style**, be sure the single line at the top of the style list is selected. Click the **Color arrow** and then click **Dark Red**. Click the **Width arrow** and then click **1 pt**. In the **Preview** area, click the **bottom line** and then click **OK**.

12. At the lower end of the vertical scroll bar, click the **Select Browse Object** button to display the menu. Point to the buttons until you locate the **Browse by Section** button and then click it. This sets the browse object so you can move from section to section and moves the insertion point to the next section. Point to the arrow below the Select Browse Object button; the ScreenTip displays *Next Section*. Point to the arrow above the Select Browse Object button; the ScreenTip displays Previous Section. Click the **Previous Section arrow**. The insertion point moves up the document to the previous section. Continue clicking the **Previous section arrow** until the insertion point is at the WordArt Graphic at the top of the document.

13. Click the **WordArt** graphic to select it and then, from the WordArt toolbar, click the **Format WordArt** button. In the **Format WordArt** dialog box, under **Line**, click the **Color arrow** and then click **black**—the first color in the first row. A graphic like WordArt has two parts—its surrounding line, and its interior fill. This action will change the surrounding line color to black. Click **OK**. Click in the body of the document to deselect the graphic.

**(Project 4D–Council News continues on the next page)**

**(Project 4D–Council News continued)**

14. From the **View** menu, display the Header and Footer toolbar, switch to the footer, and then, on the Header and Footer toolbar, click **Insert AutoText**. From the displayed list, click **Filename**. Close the Header and Footer toolbar.

15. On the Standard toolbar, click the **Save** button and then click the **Print Preview** button to preview the document. Click the **Print** button. Close the Print Preview window and close the document, saving changes if prompted to do so.

**End** You have completed Project 4D

# Project 4E — Public Safety

**Objectives:** *Insert Hyperlinks, Preview and Save a Document as a Web Page, and Locate Supporting Information.*

In the following Skill Assessment, you will create a Web page for the Desert Park Department of Public Safety. You will start with a file that contains the headings for the articles and then use the collect-and-paste technique to gather the necessary information for the article. You will add hyperlinks and save the document as a Web page. Your completed document will look similar to Figure 4.51. You will save your publication as *4E_Public_Safety_Firstname_Lastname*.

1. Be sure your computer is online and connected to the Internet. Start Word. On the Standard toolbar, click the **Open** button and navigate to the location where the student files for this textbook are stored. Locate **w04E_Public_Safety** and click once to select it. In the lower right corner of the **Open** dialog box, click **Open**.

2. From the **File** menu, click **Save As**. In the **Save As** dialog box, click the **Save in arrow** and navigate to the location in which you are storing your files for this chapter. In the **File name** box, type **4E_Public_Safety_Firstname_Lastname** and then click **Save**.

3. From the **Edit** menu, click **Office Clipboard**. If necessary, at the top of the Clipboard task pane, click the Clear All button to remove any items that display.

4. On the Standard toolbar, click the **Open** button. Locate and open the **w04E_Block_Clubs** file, and then press Ctrl + A to select all of the text. On the Standard toolbar, click the **Copy** button. The selected text is copied to the Office Clipboard. Close the w04E_Block_Clubs file.

5. Open and copy all of the text in the file **w04E_Fire**. Close the w04E_Fire file. The text is copied to the Clipboard.

**(Project 4E–Public Safety continues on the next page)**

**(Project 4E–Public Safety continued)**

## City of Desert Park
## Department of Public Safety

### Block Parties Scheduled

Friday, July 28 is designated as the Annual Party Night for all neighborhood Block Clubs in Desert Park. Block Clubs are groups of neighbors who get out and get acquainted, who watch out for each other, and keep an eye on the neighborhood. The Desert Park Block Clubs program is modeled after the National Neighborhood Watch program.

Any neighborhood club that would like to close a street in their neighborhood for the purpose of a neighborhood party can call the Desert Park Police Department for assistance. An officer will be assigned to your party and will assist with traffic flow, barricade setup, and perhaps even grilling a few hot dogs! The officer will also provide any necessary city permits—one call does it all.

Party planners can get assistance with party planning by calling the Block Clubs coordinator at the Department of Public Safety and requesting the Party Planning brochure.

### Seasonal Fire Danger

An unusually dry winter and spring, rising temperatures, and low humidity have combined to create extreme fire danger in Desert Park's mountain preserves and desert parks.

To reduce the risk of brush fires, a fire ban has been declared. This is the third straight year such a ban has been enacted.

The ban stipulates: no open or wood fires of any kind in any part of the preserves or parks; charcoal briquettes may be used only in established, department-installed grills in designated cooking areas; propane or gas grills may be used only in established picnic areas; motorists may not throw smoking materials from cars.

The fire restrictions are needed to protect against devastating wildfire during these times of extreme fire danger and severe drought. The complete text of the fire restrictions for the city limits is posted on the City's Web site.

Residents living on preserve boundaries can obtain a free informational brochure with tips on identifying vegetation they can legally remove from preserve boundary areas by calling 626-555-2222.

4E_Public_Safety_Firstname_Lastname

**Figure 4.51**

6. From the **Insert** menu, point to **Picture** and then click **Clip Art**. In the **Clip Art** task pane, in the **Search for** box, type **BBQ** If the **Search in** box does not display *All Collections*, click the **Search in arrow** and select **Everywhere**. Click the **Results should be arrow**, be sure only **Clip Art** is selected, and then click the **Go** button. Scroll the list of available images and locate the one shown in Figure 4.51. (If you cannot locate that image, choose one that is similar; alternatively, use the w04E_BBQ image that is with the student files for this book.) Copy the image to the Office Clipboard as described in Activity 4.16, step 11. On the image of the BBQ, click the arrow and then click Copy from the displayed menu.

7. In the title bar of the **Clip Art** task pane, click the **Other Task Panes arrow** and then click **Clipboard**. The image you copied is displayed at the top of the clipboard. Recall that as you copy items to the Clipboard, the most recent item moves to the top of the list.

**(Project 4E–Public Safety continues on the next page)**

**(Project 4E–Public Safety continued)**

8. Place the insertion point to the left of the empty paragraph mark under *Block Parties Scheduled*. On the **Clipboard** task pane, click the block of text beginning with *Friday, July 28 is*. The text is pasted to the Public Safety document at the location of your insertion point.

9. Place the insertion point to the left of the empty paragraph mark under *Seasonal Fire Danger*. On the **Clipboard** task pane, click the block of text beginning with *An unusually dry winter*. The text is pasted to the Public Safety document. On the Standard toolbar, click the **Save** button.

10. In the Block Parties article, click to the left of the paragraph that begins *Any neighborhood club*. In the **Clipboard** task pane, click the **BBQ image** to insert it in the article. Click the inserted image to select it and, on the floating Picture toolbar, click the **Text Wrapping** button. From the displayed list, click **Tight**. Drag the image to the right, as shown in Figure 4.51, aligning the right sizing handles with the right margin and the top sizing handles at approximately **2.5 inches on the vertical ruler**. Do not be concerned if your text does not wrap exactly as shown in the figure. In the **Clipboard** task pane, click the **Clear All** button and then close the Clipboard task pane.

11. In the *Seasonal Fire* article, click to the left of the paragraph that begins *To reduce the risk*. From the **Insert** menu, point to **Picture** and then click **From File**. In the **Insert Picture** dialog box, navigate to the location where the student files for this textbook are stored and locate **w04E_No_Fire**. If you do not see the file, click the Files of type box arrow and then click All files from the displayed list. Click the file to select it and then click Insert.

12. Click the inserted image to select it and, on the floating Picture toolbar, click the **Text Wrapping** button. From the displayed list click **Square**. Compare your document to Figure 4.51.

13. Under the *Block Parties Scheduled* heading, at the end of the paragraph that begins *Friday, July 28*, select *National Neighborhood Watch* in the last sentence. (Hint: Double-click *National* to select it, hold down Shift and hold down Ctrl, and then press → two times.) From the **Insert** menu click **Hyperlink**.

14. In the **Insert Hyperlink** dialog box, under **Link to**, click **Existing File or Web Page**. Under **Address**, type http://www.nnwi.org/

15. In the upper right corner of the **Insert Hyperlink** dialog box, click **ScreenTip**. In the **Set Hyperlink ScreenTip** dialog box, type **National Neighborhood Watch Institute** In the **Set Hyperlink ScreenTip** dialog box, click **OK**. At the bottom of the **Insert Hyperlink** dialog box, click **OK**. The hyperlink is recorded, and the selected text changes to blue and is underlined.

**(Project 4E–Public Safety continues on the next page)**

**(Project 4E–Public Safety continued)**

16. Right-click the **No Fire image** and then click **Hyperlink** from the shortcut menu. Repeat Steps 14 and 15, but type **http://www.smokey bear.com/** for the address and **Fire Safety Tips** for the ScreenTip.

17. From the **View** menu, display the Header and Footer toolbar, switch to the footer, and then, on the Header and Footer toolbar, click **Insert AutoText**. From the displayed list, click **Filename**. Close the Header and Footer toolbar. On the Standard toolbar, click the **Save** button.

18. From the **File** menu, click **Save as Web Page**. In the **Save As** dialog box, navigate to the location in which you are saving your files. In the lower portion of the **Save As** dialog box, click **Change Title**. The **Set Page Title** dialog box displays. Type **Public Safety** and then click **OK** to close the **Set Page Title** dialog box. In the lower right corner of the **Save As** dialog box, click **Save**. Click **Continue** to acknowledge the message box that displays. The Web page displays.

19. Point to the two hyperlinks you created to display the ScreenTips. Press Ctrl and click to go to the related Web site(s). Close the site(s) to return to your Web page.

20. On the Standard toolbar, click the **Print Preview** button. Take a moment to check your work. On the **Print Preview** toolbar, click the **Close Preview** button.

21. Click the **Print** button to print the Public Safety Web page and then close the document.

**End** You have completed Project 4E ————————————————

# Project 4F—IT Volunteers

**Objectives:** *Add Special Paragraph Formatting, Use Special Character Formats, Insert Hyperlinks, Locate Supporting Information, and Preview and Save a Document as a Web Page.*

In the following Skill Assessment, you will create a Web page notifying the citizens of Desert Park about an opportunity to volunteer their computer skills. Your completed document will look similar to Figure 4.52. You will save your publication as *4F_IT_Volunteer_Firstname_Lastname.*

1. On the Standard toolbar, click the **Open** button and navigate to the location where the student files for this textbook are stored. Locate **w04F_IT_Volunteer** and click once to select it. In the lower right corner of the **Open** dialog box, click **Open**.

2. From the **File** menu, click **Save As**. In the **Save As** dialog box, click the **Save in arrow** and navigate to the location in which you are storing your files for this chapter. In the **File name** box type **4F_IT_Volunteer_Firstname_Lastname** and click **Save**.

**(Project 4F–IT Volunteers continues on the next page)**

**(Project 4F–IT Volunteers continued)**

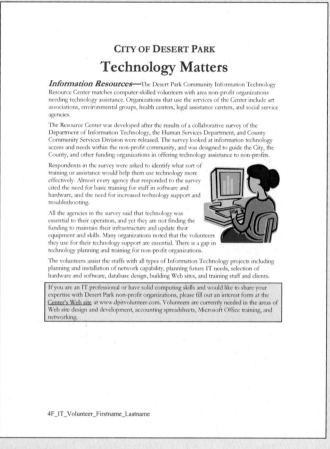

CITY OF DESERT PARK
# Technology Matters

***Information Resources***—The Desert Park Community Information Technology Resource Center matches computer-skilled volunteers with area non-profit organizations needing technology assistance. Organizations that use the services of the Center include art associations, environmental groups, health centers, legal assistance centers, and social service agencies.

The Resource Center was developed after the results of a collaborative survey of the Department of Information Technology, the Human Services Department, and County Community Services Division were released. The survey looked at information technology access and needs within the non-profit community, and was designed to guide the City, the County, and other funding organizations in offering technology assistance to non-profits.

Respondents in the survey were asked to identify what sort of training or assistance would help them use technology more effectively. Almost every agency that responded to the survey cited the need for basic training for staff in software and hardware, and the need for increased technology support and troubleshooting.

All the agencies in the survey said that technology was essential to their operation, and yet they are not finding the funding to maintain their infrastructure and update their equipment and skills. Many organizations noted that the volunteers they use for their technology support are essential. There is a gap in technology planning and training for non-profit organizations.

The volunteers assist the staffs with all types of Information Technology projects including planning and installation of network capability, planning future IT needs, selection of hardware and software, database design, building Web sites, and training staff and clients.

If you are an IT professional or have solid computing skills and would like to share your expertise with Desert Park non-profit organizations, please fill out an interest form at the Center's Web site at www.dpitvolunteer.com. Volunteers are currently needed in the areas of Web site design and development, accounting spreadsheets, Microsoft Office training, and networking.

4F_IT_Volunteer_Firstname_Lastname

**Figure 4.52**

3. Press `Ctrl` + `A` to select all of the text in the document. Change the font to **Garamond 12 pt**. From the **Format** menu, display the **Paragraph** dialog box. Under **Spacing**, change the number in the **After** box to **6 pt**. and click **OK**.

4. Hold down `Ctrl` and press `Home` to place the insertion point at the top of the document. Press `Enter` to create an empty line preceding the text. Click to the left of the empty line and on two separate lines type

**City of Desert Park**

**Technology Matters**

5. Select *City of Desert Park* and, from the **Format** menu, click **Font**. In the **Font** dialog box, under **Font style**, click **Bold**. Under **Size**, click **20**. Click the **Font color arrow** and, in the second row, click the sixth color—**Blue**. Under **Effects**, select the **Small caps** check box and then click **OK**.

**(Project 4F–IT Volunteers continues on the next page)**

**(Project 4F–IT Volunteers continued)**

6. Select *Technology Matters* and, on the Formatting toolbar, use the **Font Size** button to change the font size to **28 pt**. Click the **Bold** button and then click the **Font Color arrow**. From the displayed palette, click **Blue**. Select the two title lines you just formatted and then, on the Formatting toolbar, click the **Center** button.

7. Under the two heading lines, click to the left of *The Desert Park Community* and type **Information Resources** From the **Insert** menu, click **Symbol**. Click the **Special Characters** tab, be sure **Em Dash** is selected, and then click **Insert**. Close the **Symbol** dialog box. Select *Information Resources* and the following dash and then, using the Formatting toolbar, change the font size to **16 pt.**, change the font color to **Blue**, and add **Bold** and **Italic** for emphasis.

8. Place the insertion point at the start of the paragraph beginning *Respondents in the survey*. Display the **Insert** menu, point to **Picture**, and then click **Clip Art**. In the **Clip Art** task pane, in the **Search for** box, type **computer** Be sure the **Search in box** displays **All Collections**. Click the **Results should be arrow**, be sure only **Clip Art** is selected, and then click the **Go** button. Locate the image of a woman at a computer as shown in Figure 4.52. Click the figure to insert it in the document. Alternatively, insert the file w04F_Computer from your student files by displaying the insert menu, pointing to Picture, and then clicking From File.

9. Close the **Clip Art** task pane. Click the inserted image to select it and, on the floating Picture toolbar, click the **Text Wrapping** button. From the displayed list, click **Square**. Drag the image to the right of the paragraphs as shown in Figure 4.52, aligning its right edge with the right margin and the top edge at approximately **3 inches on the vertical ruler**. Do not be concerned if your text does not wrap exactly as shown in the Figure. On the Standard toolbar, click the **Save** button.

10. Scroll down the document until you can see the last paragraph, which begins *If you are*. Select the paragraph. From the **Format** menu, click **Borders and Shading**. In the **Borders and Shading** dialog box, click the **Shading tab**. Under **Fill**, in the last row, click the fifth color—**Light Turquoise**. Click the **Borders tab** and then, under **Settings**, click **Box**. Click the **Width** arrow and click **1 pt**. Click the **Color arrow** and click **Black**, if necessary, and then click **OK**. Click anywhere to deselect the paragraph and view your formatting. The special format is applied to the last paragraph.

11. In the same paragraph, select *Center's Web site* and then, from the **Insert** menu, click **Hyperlink**. In the **Insert Hyperlink** dialog box, under **Link to**, be sure **Existing File or Web Page** is selected. In the **Address** box, type **http://www.dpitvolunteer.com/**

**(Project 4F–IT Volunteers continues on the next page)**

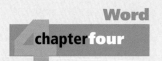
**(Project 4F–IT Volunteers continued)**

**12.** On the upper right corner of the **Insert Hyperlink** dialog box, click **ScreenTip**. In the **Set Hyperlink ScreenTip** dialog box, type **Click Here to Volunteer** and then click **OK**. At the bottom of the **Insert Hyperlink** dialog box, click **OK**. The hyperlink is recorded, and the selected text changes to blue and is underlined.

**13.** From the **Edit** menu, click **Find**. In the **Find and Replace** dialog box, in the **Find what** box, type **cooperative** and then click the **Find Next** button. If necessary, drag the dialog box away from the highlighted word. Leave the **Find and Replace** dialog box open and click the document to make it active. Right-click the highlighted word *cooperative* and point to **Synonyms** on the shortcut menu. To view additional synonyms for the word *cooperative*, click **Thesaurus**. The **Research** task pane displays. Under joint (adj.), point to *collaborative* and then click the arrow on *collaborative*. From the displayed list, click **Insert**; *cooperative* is replaced with *collaborative*.

**14.** Using the technique in step 13, from either the list of suggested synonymns or by opening the Thesaurus and finding additional synonymns, locate and replace *vital* with *essential* and *efficiently* with *effectively*. Close the **Find and Replace** dialog box and close the **Research** task pane.

**15.** From the **View** menu, display the Header and Footer toolbar, switch to the footer, and, on the Header and Footer toolbar, click **Insert AutoText**. From the displayed list, click **Filename**. Close the Header and Footer toolbar. On the Standard toolbar, click the **Save** button.

**16.** From the **File** menu, click **Save As Web Page**. In the **Save As** dialog box, navigate to the location in which you are saving your files. In the lower portion of the **Save As** dialog box, click **Change Title**. The **Set Page Title** dialog box displays. Type **IT Volunteer** and then click **OK** to close the **Set Page Title** dialog box. In the lower right corner of the **Save As** dialog box, click **Save**. Click **Continue** to acknowledge the message box that displays. The Web page is displayed in Word.

**17.** On the Standard toolbar, click the **Print Preview** button. Take a moment to check your work. On the **Print Preview** toolbar, click the **Close Preview** button.

**18.** Click the **Print** button and then close the document.

**End** You have completed Project 4F ───────────────

## Project 4G—Youth

**Objectives:** *Create a Decorative Title, Add Special Paragraph Formatting, Use Special Character Formats, Insert Hyperlinks, and Preview and Save a Document as a Web Page.*

In the following Performance Assessment, you will finish formatting a document for the Family Services Department of Desert Park. The document will then be saved as a Web page. Your completed document will look similar to Figure 4.53. You will save your document as *4G_Youth_Firstname_Lastname.*

**Figure 4.53**

1. Click the **Open** button and navigate to the location where the student files for this textbook are stored. Locate and open **w04G_Youth**. From the **File** menu, display the **Save As** dialog box. Navigate to the location in which you are storing your files for this chapter. In the **File name** box, type **4G_Youth_Firstname_Lastname** and click **Save**.

**(Project 4G–Youth continues on the next page)**

**(Project 4G–Youth continued)**

2. With the insertion point at the top of the document, click the **Insert** menu, point to **Picture**, and then click **WordArt**. In the third row, click the first style and then click **OK**. In the **Edit WordArt Text** dialog box, type **Desert Park Family Services** and click **OK**.

3. Click the **WordArt** graphic and, on the WordArt toolbar, click the **WordArt Shape** button. In the first row of the displayed palette, click the fifth style—the **Chevron Up** style. The WordArt graphic changes to the selected shape. Drag the right center sizing handle to the right margin—approximately **6.5 inches on the horizontal ruler**.

4. In the paragraph beginning with *The fair will focus*, select *dental care* at the end of the first line and then, from the **Insert** menu, display the **Insert Hyperlink** dialog box. Under **Link to**, be sure **Existing File or Web Page** is selected. In the **Address** box, type http://ada.org/public/topics/infants.html

5. In the upper right corner of the dialog box, click **ScreenTip**. Type **American Dental Association Tips** and then click **OK**. At the bottom of the **Insert Hyperlink** dialog box, click **OK**. The hyperlink is recorded, and the selected text changes to blue and is underlined.

6. In the same paragraph select *immunization*. Following the instructions in Steps 4 and 5, add a hyperlink to immunization, but for the address type **http://www.cdc.gov.nip/vfc/** and for the **ScreenTip** type **CDC Immunization Recommendations** and then click **OK** twice.

7. Scroll to the bottom of the page. In the paragraph beginning with *There's something*, click to place the insertion point to the left of *You* at the beginning of the second sentence. Press Enter. Select the paragraph you just created, beginning with *You can pick*, and, from the **Format** menu, display the **Borders and Shading** dialog box. Under **Setting**, click **Box**, change the **Width** of the border to **2¼ pt.**, and then change the **Color** to **Bright Green**—the fourth color in the fourth row. Click **OK**. Save your changes.

8. Select the text within the border and, from the **Format** menu, open the **Font** dialog box. Change the **Size** to **16**, the **Font style** to **Bold**, and the **Font color** to **Blue**. Under **Effects**, select the **Small caps** check box. Click **OK**. On the Formatting toolbar, click **Center** to center the text horizontally.

**(Project 4G–Youth continues on the next page)**

**(Project 4G–Youth continued)**

9. Scroll to view the upper portion of your document. In the Child Health Fair article, in the paragraph beginning with *The Fair is part*, click to place the insertion point to the right of Desert Park Month. From the **Insert** menu, point to **Picture** and then click **Clip Art**. In the **Clip Art** task pane, search for **toothbrush** in the Clip Art collection. Locate the toothbrush image displayed in Figure 4.53. (If you cannot locate that image, select another image of a toothbrush; alternatively, use the w04G_Toothbrush image that is included the student files for this book.) Click the image to insert it. With the image selected, on the Picture toolbar, click the **Text Wrapping** button and then click **Tight**. Use the Rotate handle to rotate the image so it is on an angle as displayed in Figure 4.53 and then position it in the approximate location shown in the figure. Do not be concerned if your text wraps differently than shown in the figure. Close the **Clip Art** task pane.

10. From the **View** menu, display the Header and Footer toolbar, switch to the footer, click **Insert AutoText**, and then click **Filename**. Close the Header and Footer toolbar. Save your changes.

11. From the **File** menu, click **Web Page Preview**. The document displays as it will when you save it as a Web page. Notice that the toothbrush that you placed in the middle of the paragraph displays on the left side of the text. In the **Web Page** title bar, click the **Close** button to close your browser and return to your 4G_Youth Word file.

12. From the **File** menu, click **Save As Web Page**. Navigate to the location where you are saving your files. In the **Save As** dialog box, click **Change Title**, type **Youth Programs** and then click **OK** to close the **Set Page Title** dialog box. Save the Web page and click **Continue** to acknowledge the message box that displays.

13. **Print** the Web page view of your document and then close it.

 You have completed Project 4G

## Project 4H — Cultural Affairs

**Objectives:** *Create a Decorative Title, Create Multicolumn Documents, Add Special Paragraph Formatting, and Locate Supporting Information.*

In the following Performance Assessment, you will gather information and create a newsletter concerning recent cultural activities in Desert Park. Your completed document will look similar to Figure 4.54. You will save your document as *4H_Cultural Affairs_Firstname_Lastname*.

**(Project 4H–Cultural Affairs continues on the next page)**

**(Project 4H–Cultural Affairs continued)**

Museum of Art Relocated

Thanks to a bond issue passed by the residents of Desert Park in 1998, the Desert Park Museum of Art has relocated to a new facility at 20th Street and Via Colinas. A gala dedication ceremony will be held on September 12, at 8:00 p.m. The ceremony is open to the public.

The new space was designed to allow a permanent exhibit area as well as changing exhibits area, museum store, collection storage, and children's museum. "I know that residents and visitors to the city will be impressed by the new museum," said Elizabeth Viejo, museum curator. "The space was specially designed with our collection in mind and it shows it off to the fullest."

This investment will ensure that the residents of Desert Park will have a beautiful museum to enjoy for many years to come. At the next meeting of the City Council, the various organizations that worked to get the bond measure passed will be recognized. They include the Heritage Commission, Friends of Fine Arts and Parks, Desert Park Citizens United, and many other individual citizens.

For exhibit information and museum hours, call 626-555-4ART or visit the Web site at www.desertparkmuseum.org.

**Did you know...**

An *exhibition*, or exhibit, is a display that incorporates objects and information to explain concepts, stimulate understanding, relate experiences, invite participation, prompt reflection, or inspire wonder.

Call for Artists

The Desert Park Fine Arts Commission is accepting applications from individual artists and artistic teams to design several public art projects for the City Hall Plaza mall. The goal of the public art projects is to provide an aesthetic link among intersections, bikeways, pedestrian bridges, and trails. Additionally, enhancements and artistic improvements to gateways to residential areas will be considered. The Commission hopes to add additional gardens, sculptures, walking paths, and pedestrian bridges to the area.

 A team can include artists, architects, and landscape architects. A selection committee will choose finalists to develop a preliminary proposal. Selected finalists must present their conceptual approach at a City Council meeting, and will receive a $1,000 honorarium for the proposals. Local artists and architects are encouraged to apply.

Students from the departments of Art and of Landscape Architecture at Desert Park University will assist the Fine Arts Commission in organizing submissions for judging. Dr. Betty Frank, the university's president, said, "We are proud to be a part of this artistic endeavor."

The deadline to apply is 5 p.m. Friday, September 1. Each team member should include a resume and a portfolio of relevant work. For more information or detailed submission requirements, call the Cultural Affairs office at 626-555-1234.

4H_Cultural_Affairs_Firstname_Lastname

**Figure 4.54**

1. Make sure you have an active Internet connection, which is required to complete this exercise. Click the **Open** button and navigate to the location where the student files for this textbook are stored. Locate and open **w04H_Cultural_Affairs**. From the **File** menu, display the **Save As** dialog box. Navigate to the location in which you are storing your files for this chapter. In the **File name** box, type **4H_Cultural_Affairs_Firstname_Lastname** and click **Save**.

2. With the insertion point at the top of the document, from the **Insert** menu, point to **Picture** and then click **WordArt**. In the fourth row, click the second style and then click **OK**. In the **Edit WordArt Text** dialog box, type **City of Desert Park** and press Enter. Type **Office of Cultural Affairs** and then click **OK**.

3. Click the **WordArt** graphic. Drag the right center sizing handle to approximately **6.5 inches on the horizontal ruler** to expand the shape and stretch it to the right margin. Click anywhere to deselect the **WordArt**.

**(Project 4H–Cultural Affairs continues on the next page)**

**(Project 4H–Cultural Affairs continued)**

4. From the **Edit** menu, click **Office Clipboard**. At the top of the **Clipboard** task pane, click the **Clear All** button to remove any items that may be displayed. From your student files, open **w04H_Museum**, select all of the text, click the **Copy** button, and then close the document. The copied text displays as the first item on the Office Clipboard. Open **w04H_Artists**, select all of the text, click the **Copy** button, and then close the document. The text of both articles displays in the Clipboard task pane.

5. On the Standard toolbar, click the **Research** button. In the **Research** task pane, in the **Search for** box, type **museum** and then click the arrow on the second box. From the displayed list, click **Encyclopedia (or Encarta or Encarta Encyclopedia)**. Your system searches and then displays a list. Click the topic *Exhibitions*. In the Encyclopedia window, in the first paragraph starting with *An Exhibition*, select the first sentence and then press [Ctrl] + [C] to copy this sentence to the clipboard. Close the encyclopedia.

6. Now you will collect clip art and place it on the Office Clipboard. Click the **Other Task Panes arrow** on the title bar of the **Research** task pane and then click **Clip Art**. In the **Search for** box, type **artist** Be sure the **Search in** box displays **All collections**. Click the arrow on the **Results should be** box and be sure just **Clip Art** is selected. Click the **Go** button. Locate the image shown in Figure 4.54. Click the arrow on the image and then click **Copy**. (If you cannot locate the image shown, select another image of an artist. Alternatively, use the w04H_Artist_Picture that is with the student files for this book.)

7. Click the **Other Task Panes** arrow on the title bar of the **Clip Art** task pane and then click **Clipboard**. Place the insertion point on the empty line under *Museum of Art Relocated* and then click the Clipboard item beginning with *Thanks to a bond issue*. The article is inserted.

8. Place the insertion point on the empty line under *Call for Artists* and insert the article beginning with *The Desert Park Fine Arts*. The artist article is inserted.

9. Select all of the text in the document except the WordArt graphic and the line below the graphic. Click the **Columns** button and drag to select **two columns**. With the text selected, on the Formatting toolbar, click the **Justify** button. Click the **Save** button.

10. With the text still selected, on the **Format** menu, click **Columns**. The **Columns** dialog box displays. The Columns dialog box allows you to control the width of columns and offers some other formatting options. On the right side of the dialog box, select the **Line between** check box. Notice at the bottom of the dialog box, the **Applies to** box displays *Selected Text*. Click **OK**.

**(Project 4H–Cultural Affairs continues on the next page)**

**(Project 4H–Cultural Affairs continued)**

11. Position the insertion point to the left of the heading *Call for Artists*. From the **Insert** menu, click **Break** and, in the **Break** dialog box, click **Column break**. Click **OK**. The artist article moves to the top of the second column. On the Standard toolbar, click the **Print Preview** button to see the result of your work so far. On the Print Preview toolbar, click the **Close** button.

12. In the artist article, position the insertion point at the start of the paragraph that begins *A team can include*. From the **Clipboard**, click the artist image to insert it. Use the lower right corner sizing handle to reduce the size of the image to about one quarter of its original size. With the image selected, on the floating Picture toolbar, click the **Text Wrapping** button and then click **Square**. Position the image as shown in Figure 4.54. Do not be concerned if your text does not align exactly as shown in the figure. Click the **Save** button.

13. In the first column of text, position the insertion point to the left of the empty paragraph mark at the end of the museum article. Type **Did you know...** and then press Enter. From the **Clipboard**, click the Encarta information to insert it. Close the **Clipboard** task pane.

14. Select the *Did you know* heading and the inserted reference and change the font size to **11 pt**. From the **Format** menu, display the **Borders and Shading** dialog box. Under **Settings**, click **Shadow**, change the **Color** to **Plum**—the seventh color in the fourth row—and the **Width** to **2¼**. Click the **Shading tab** and, in the first row under **No Fill**, click the second color—**5% gray** shading. Click **OK**.

15. Select the text *Did you know...* and add **Bold** emphasis. Then change the font size to **14** and the font color to **Plum** to match the other headings. Move to the top of the newsletter. Select the *Museum of Art Relocated* title and click **Center**. The selected text is centered over the column. Center the title *Call for Artists* over its column in the same manner.

16. Click the **Print Preview** button to see how the document will look when it is printed. Be sure you do not have a stray second page and that the columns are balanced—that is, their bottom edges align at approximately the same place. If you have an empty second page, remove any stray paragraph marks at the end of the document. Add the filename to the footer and save your changes. Print the newsletter and close the document.

**End** **You have completed Project 4H**

## Project 4I—Interns

**Objectives:** *Create a Decorative Title, Add Special Paragraph Formatting, Use Special Character Formats, and Preview and Save a Document as a Web Page.*

In the following Performance Assessment, you will create and format a document announcing the internship program for the city of Desert Park and then save the document as a Web page. Your completed document will look similar to Figure 4.55. You will save your document as *4I_Interns_Firstname_Lastname*.

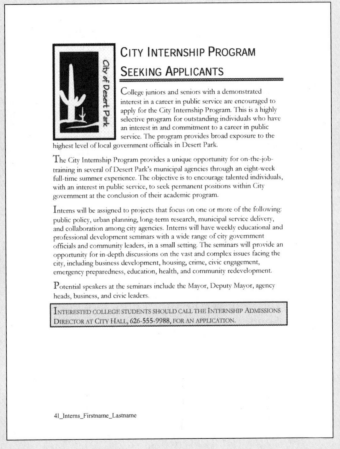

**Figure 4.55**

1. Click the **Open** button and navigate to the location where the student files for this textbook are stored. Locate and open **w04I_Interns**. From the **File** menu, display the **Save As** dialog box. Navigate to the location in which you are storing your files for this chapter. In the **File name** box type **4I_Interns_Firstname_Lastname** and click **Save**.

**(Project 4I–Interns continues on the next page)**

**(Project 4I–Interns continued)**

2. Select all of the text and change the font to **Garamond 14 pt**. From the **Format** menu, open the **Paragraph** dialog box and, under **Spacing**, increase the number in the **After** box to **6 pt**. Use the Spelling and Grammar Checker to correct the spelling errors in this document. Ignore grammar errors.

3. Select only the first letter in each paragraph and change the font size to **20** and the font color to **Dark Blue**—the sixth color in the first row. After you have formatted the first letter, use the **Format Painter** to copy the format to the first letter of each subsequent paragraph.

4. In the first paragraph, position the insertion point to the left of *College* and press Enter twice. Move the insertion point to the first empty line and type **City Internship Program** and press Enter. Type **Seeking Applicants**

5. Select the text you just typed and, from the **Format** menu, display the **Font** color dialog box. Change the **Font** to **Tahoma**, the **Size** to **24 pt.**, and the **Color** to **Dark Blue**. Under **Effects**, select the **Small caps** check box. Click **OK**.

6. With the title still selected, from the **Format** menu, display the **Borders and Shading** dialog box. Click the Borders tab if necessary. Under **Style**, scroll down and click the **double underline**, change the **Color** to **Dark Blue**, and then change the **Width** to **1½**. In the **Preview** area, be sure only the bottom line is displayed—click the left, right, and top lines to remove them from the preview if necessary. Check that **Paragraph** displays in the **Applies to** box and then click **OK**.

7. In the title, position the insertion point to the left of *City*. From the **Insert** menu, point to **Picture** and then click **From File**. Navigate to your student files and locate the **w04I_DPLogo** file. Click **Insert**. With the image selected, on the floating Picture toolbar, click the **Text Wrapping** button and then click **Square**. Remove the extra paragraph mark between the title and the first paragraph. The text moves up as shown in Figure 4.55. Save your changes.

8. Scroll to the bottom of the document and select the last paragraph. From the **Format** menu, display the **Borders and Shading** dialog box. Under **Setting**, click **Box**, change the **Color** to **Dark Blue** and the **Width** to **1½**. Be sure the preview area displays a dark blue border on all sides. Click the **Shading tab**. Under **Fill**, click **Light Yellow**—the third color in the last row. Click **OK**.

**(Project 4I–Interns continues on the next page)**

**(Project 4I–Interns continued)**

9.  With the text still selected, open the **Font** dialog box. Change the **Font color** to **Dark Blue**. Under **Effects**, select the **Small caps** check box and then click **OK**.

10. From the **View** menu, display the Header and Footer toolbar, switch to the footer, click **Insert AutoText**, and then click **Filename**. Close the Header and Footer toolbar. Save your changes.

11. From the **File** menu, click **Save As Web Page**. Navigate to the location where you are saving your files. In the **Save As** dialog box, click **Change Title**, type **Intern Program** and then click **OK** to close the **Set Page Title** dialog box.

12. **Save** the Web page and click **Continue** to acknowledge the message box that displays. Print thc Web page and then close it.

**End** You have completed Project 4I ────────────────────────

# Mastery Assessments

## Project 4J—Desert Oasis

**Objectives:** *Create a Decorative Title, Create Multicolumn Documents, Add Special Paragraph Formatting, Use Special Character Formats, and Locate Supporting Information.*

In the following Mastery Assessment, you will create a newsletter published by the Parks and Recreation Department in Desert Park. Your completed newsletter will look like Figure 4.56. You will save your document as *4J_Desert_Oasis_Firstname_Lastname.*

Desert Oasis

News from the Parks and Recreation Department of Desert Park

Finalists in Trail Design Competition

Residents of Desert Park are invited to preview what future enhancements to the Agave Trail may look like. Three architectural teams have been selected to design comprehensive improvement plans for the trail. Their prospective designs will be on display for public viewing and comment in the lobby of City Hall during the week of July 12.

The finalist teams' display will include artist renderings and maps showing proposed improvements such as interpretive signs, waterway enhancements, bicycle and pedestrian bridges, ramadas, lighting, transit shelters and other architectural and artistic features.

Final judging of the Trail Design Competition, which will be open to the public, will take place at noon on Saturday, July 17, at the Desert Park Botanical Garden located on the northwest corner of Agave Parkway and Ironwood Boulevard.

The winning team will be selected based on its ability to address the functional needs of the project, while providing complementary solutions to the area's unique environment and rich cultural traditions.

The Agave Trail is a 10-mile loop linking many of the area's significant historic, natural, cultural and recreational attractions. When complete, the Agave Trail will serve as an inviting destination for cyclists, pedestrians and hikers to enjoy the landscape of Desert Park.

City Beaches Are Open

Looking to cool off? The City's two beaches—at Blue Rock Lake and at Lake Roadrunner—are open now. And staying cool will be a bargain again this summer. Regular admission is just 50 cents for youths and seniors and $1 for adults. Coupon books and season passes are available by calling 626-555-SWIM.

The Desert Park Fine Arts and Parks Department will offer a variety of special summer programs and classes, which will include learn-to-swim and water safety instruction. Call the number above for more information and reservations.

Daily hours begin May 1, with the beaches open from 10 a.m. - 8 p.m. through the end of August. After August 31, beaches revert to weekend operations through October 15. Lifeguards are on duty during all open hours.

4J_Desert_Oasis_Firstname_Lastname

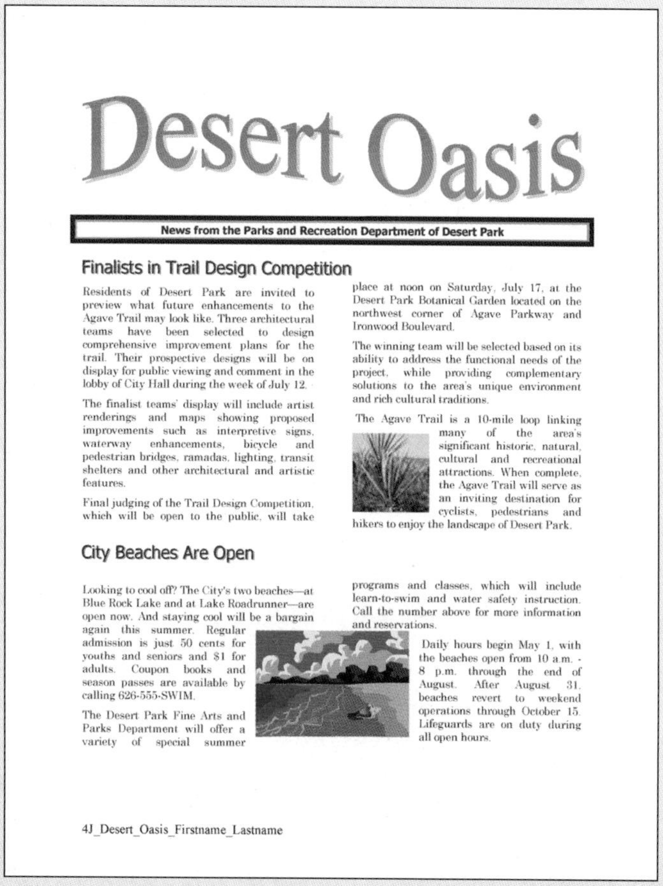

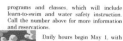

**Figure 4.56**

1. Start Word. In a blank document, open the **Page Setup** dialog box and change the left and right margins to 1 inch. Be sure you are in the **Print Layout View** and the nonprinting characters are displayed.
2. Display the **WordArt Gallery** dialog box and, in the third row, click the fifth style and click **OK**. In the **Edit WordArt Text** dialog box, type **Desert Oasis** Change the **Font Size** of the WordArt to **66** and then click **OK**.

**(Project 4J–Desert Oasis continues on the next page)**

**(Project 4J–Desert Oasis continued)**

3. With the WordArt graphic selected, drag the side sizing handle so it stretches between the left and right margins. Use the horizontal ruler to see the margins.

4. On the right side of the WordArt graphic, click in the margin to deselect and then press Enter twice to insert two paragraph marks at the left margin. Click the **Center** button and then type **News from the Parks and Recreation Department of Desert Park**

5. Select the text you just typed and change the font to **Tahoma**, **10 pt.**, **Bold**, and **Blue**. Open the **Borders and Shading** dialog box, click the **Box** setting, and then, in the **Style** list box, click the style that is third from the bottom. Change the color to **Teal** and click **OK**. Compare your banner to Figure 4.56.

6. Save your work as you have previously with the file name **4J_Desert_Oasis_Firstname_Lastname**

7. Position your I-beam pointer slightly below the banner at the left margin and double-click to place the insertion point just below the banner. Adjust as necessary so that two paragraph marks display and then position your insertion point to the left of the second paragraph mark and type **Finalists in Trail Design Competition**

   Select the text and change the font to **16-point Tahoma**. Change the font color to **Blue**. Open the **Font** dialog box and select the **Emboss** check box. Deselect the text.

8. Press Enter. Recall that paragraph marks retain the formatting of the preceding paragraph. To change the formatting, select the paragraph mark and open the **Font** dialog box. Change the font to **10-point Century Schoolbook** and change the font color to **Black**. Under **Effects**, clear the check box next to **Emboss**. Click **OK**. Now you will collect and paste the articles that will be used for this newsletter.

9. Display the **Office Clipboard** and click the **Clear All** button. From your student files, locate and open **w04J_Agave_Trail**. Select and copy all of the text and then close the file. Locate and open **w04J_Beaches**. Copy all of the text and then close the file.

10. Display the **Clip Art** task pane and search for *beaches*. Locate the beach image displayed in Figure 4.56, click the arrow on the image, and then click **Copy** to copy it to the Clipboard. (If you cannot locate the image that is shown in the figure, select another beach image; alternatively, use the w04J_Beach_Picture that is included with the student files for this book. Use the technique you practiced in Activity 4.16, step 11, to copy the picture from your student files to the Office Clipboard.) On the **Clip Art** task pane, click the **Other Task Panes arrow** and click **Clipboard** to see the image you copied and the two articles.

**(Project 4J–Desert Oasis continues on the next page)**

**(Project 4J–Desert Oasis continued)**

11. Display the **Research** task pane and type **Agave** and then select **Encyclopedia (or Encarta Encyclopedia)** as the research reference. In the list of choices displayed, under **Related items**, click *pictures of Agave plants*. In the MSN window that displays, locate the picture of a typical Agave type of plant. Right-click on the image and then click **Copy** to add the image to the Clipboard. Close the MSN window and then display the **Clipboard** task pane. Four items are displayed. Alternatively, insert the file w04J_Agave_Picture from your student files by displaying the Insert menu, pointing to Picture, and then clicking From File.

12. Position the insertion point in your document to the left of the last empty paragraph mark. From the **Clipboard** task pane, click the trail article that begins *Residents of Desert Park.* The article is inserted. Click the **Paste Options** button arrow that displays and click **Match Destination Formatting** to change the font to **Century Schoolbook, 10 pt**. Recall that the Paste Options button can be used to change the format of inserted text to match the formatting of the surrounding text.

13. Select the article text and change it to two columns, and then change the alignment to **Justify**. Display the **Paragraph** dialog box and add a **6-pt**. **Before** spacing to the article paragraphs. Save your changes.

14. To add the second article headline, click to the left of the empty paragraph mark on the left side of the screen, press Enter, and type **City Beaches Are Open**

Press Enter twice. Select the new headline and change the font so it matches the *Finalists in Trail Design Competition* headline.

15. Click to the left of the second paragraph mark under the *Beaches* headline and, from the Clipboard task pane, paste the beach article that begins *Looking to cool off?* Click the **Paste Options** button that displays and click **Match Destination Formatting**. Change the article to two columns and the alignment to **Justify**. Display the **Paragraph** dialog box and add a **6-pt**. **Before** spacing to the paragraphs.

16. In the *Finalists in Trail Design Competition* article, in the second column, place the insertion point to the left of the paragraph that begins *The Agave Trail.*

From the clipboard, paste the image of the Agave plant. Use a corner sizing handle to increase the size of the image until it is approximately 1 inch square. On the Picture toolbar, click the **Text Wrapping** button and click **Square**. Drag the image to position it in the article as shown in Figure 4.56. Do not be concerned if the text does not wrap around the image exactly as shown in the figure.

**(Project 4J–Desert Oasis continues on the next page)**

**(Project 4J–Desert Oasis continued)**

**17.** In the *City Beaches Are Open* article, place the insertion point at the beginning of the last paragraph that begins *Daily hours*. From the **Clipboard**, insert the beach picture. Set the **Text Wrapping** to **Square** and then position the image in the middle of the article as shown in Figure 4.56. If necessary, reposition the Agave plant image in the first article.

**18.** View the footer area and add the **AutoText file name** to the footer. Preview the document to be sure it is on one page. Make any necessary adjustments. Depending on your printer, the lines in the columns may be slightly different when compared to Figure 4.56. Print the newsletter, save your changes, and then close the document.

**End** You have completed Project 4J ————————————

## Project 4K — Recreation Notes

**Objectives:** *Create a Decorative Title, Create Multicolumn Documents, Add Special Paragraph Formatting, Use Special Character Formats, Insert Hyperlinks, and Locate Supporting Information.*

In the following Mastery Assessment, you will create a newsletter about upcoming sports events in Desert Park. Your completed newsletter will look similar to Figure 4.57. You will save your document as *4K_Recreation_Notes_Firstname_Lastname.*

**1.** Start Word. In a blank document open the **Page Setup** dialog box and set the left and right margins to 1 inch. Be sure you are in **Print Layout** view and that the nonprinting characters are displayed. If necessary, close the task pane.

**2.** Display the **WordArt Gallery** dialog box. In the fourth row, click the first style, click **OK**, and then type **Recreation Notes** Change the **Font Size** to **66** and then click **OK**. Select the **WordArt** graphic and open the **Format WordArt** dialog box. On the **Colors and Lines tab** of the dialog box, click the **Fill Color arrow** and then click **Fill Effects**. In the **Fill Effects** dialog box, click the **Texture tab** and then, in the first row, click the first texture—**Green marble**. Click **OK** twice.

**3.** On the right side of the **WordArt** graphic, click in the margin to deselect and then press [Enter] twice to insert two paragraph marks at the left margin. Click the **Center** button and then type **Sports News from the Parks and Recreation Department of Desert Park**

Select the text you just typed and change the font to **Comic Sans MS**, **10 pt.**, **Bold**. Change the font color to **Green**. Open the **Borders and Shading** dialog box, click the **3-D setting**, and then, in the **Style** list box, click the line style that displays a heavy top line and a narrow bottom line. Change the line color to **Green** and click **OK**. Compare your banner to Figure 4.57.

**(Project 4K–Recreation Notes continues on the next page)**

**(Project 4K–Recreation Notes continued)**

# Recreation Notes

Sports News from the Parks and Recreation Department of Desert Park

### GOLF FOR A CAUSE

The Desert Park Fine Arts and Parks Department is hosting a golf clinic and nighttime golf benefit at the North Park Golf Course on Friday, August 21 to benefit the city's Youth Golf Program.

A PGA Tour Professional, recognized as one of the most accomplished golfers to play the game, will be at the North Park Golf Course to offer a free Golf Clinic. The clinic will run from 9 a.m. – 10:30 a.m. It's open to the public and there is no charge for admission. Come on out and learn some valuable tips from a pro!

Want to see how a pro applies those clinic techniques to an actual round of golf? As a follow-up to the clinic, our pro will join tournament guests in an exhibition round beginning at 12 noon. Plan to follow this foursome to see how they perform.

The nighttime event begins at 8 p.m. Pre-registration is required. The cost is $25 per person. Registration includes greens fees, glow balls, prizes, soft drinks, and pull carts. The tournament is a four-person scramble with a shotgun start at 8:15 p.m.

The tournament, which is played on the nine-hole course, is limited to the first 12 teams (48 players). The Youth Golf Program provides free golf lessons to

youth at six of Desert Park's municipal golf courses. Funding makes it possible to provide year-round instruction, golf clubs, balls and other equipment for use during the classes. For more information, call 626-555-1131.

"The Golf Benefit is a fun and informal way to support hundreds of young people in Desert Park and the surrounding county," said Fred Stein, president of the Youth Golf Program Foundation. "The golf clinic is a great opportunity for children to learn about the game and be exposed to business leaders who can have an impact on their lives."

Last year the Youth Golf Program Foundation helped 145 young men and women learn to play the game of golf, and to recognize the value of good sportspersonship. The organization is a non-profit organization that provides golf instruction, golf facilities and golf events

4K_Recreation_Notes_Firstname_Lastname

through structured, school-based golf programs.

**Did You Know?**

Some historians believe that golf originated in the Netherlands (the Dutch word *kolf* means "club"), but the Romans had a game played with a bent stick and a ball made of feathers that may have been the original source of the game. It has been fairly well established, however, that the game that is known today was actually devised by the Scots in the 14th or 15th century.

### BICYCLING IN DESERT PARK

The "Golden Age" of bicycling occurred during the development of Desert Park many years ago. Early photographs show street scenes with bicycles, horses, trolleys, and pedestrians. In fact, our first streets were arranged for these users. But Desert Park was ahead of its time, because this development pattern is actually an essential element of a livable community.

Desert Park is a city in which people can get around without cars, and the City hopes to make this a place where it is easier to ride a bicycle than to drive a car. Ideally, bicyclists should be able to

circulate along city streets freely and safely. At the bicyclist's destination there should be safe, free, and accessible parking.

The City is working on a plan that identifies a network of bikeways that will connect bicycle riders to their destinations. The enhancements to the Agave Trail are an important part of this plan. The plan includes a list of other projects and programs, similar to the Agave Trail program, to be added to the Transportation Improvement Plan.

**Did You Know?**

The bicycle was not invented by any one person. Rather, it is an outgrowth of ideas and inventions dating to the late 18th century. Some people claim the bicycle's history goes back even further, citing certain drawings by Leonardo da Vinci of a two-wheeled vehicle.

4K_Recreation_Notes_Firstname_Lastname

**Figure 4.57**

4. Save your work as you have previously with the file name **4K_Recreation_Notes_Firstname_Lastname**

5. Position your I-beam pointer at the left margin and slightly under the banner you just created and then double-click to place the insertion point below the banner. Adjust as necessary so that two paragraph marks display, and then position your insertion point to the left of the second paragraph mark. Type **Golf for a Cause**

Select the text you just typed and change the font to **16 pt.**, **Bold**, and **Green**. Deselect the text.

**(Project 4K–Recreation Notes continues on the next page)**

**(Project 4K–Recreation Notes continued)**

6. Press Enter and drag to select the empty paragraph mark you just created. Change the font size to **11 pt.**, remove **Bold**, and change the font color to **Black**. Recall that paragraph marks retain the formatting of the preceding paragraph. You are ready to collect and paste the articles that will be used for this newsletter.

7. Display the **Office Clipboard** and, if necessary, click the **Clear All** button to clear the Clipboard. From the student files, locate and open **w04K_Recreation_Ideas**. This memo contains information that was gathered by the director of the Parks Department. You will copy each part separately so you can control the placement of the articles in the newsletter. Copy the golf article, starting with the paragraph that begins *The Desert Park*. Copy the first Did You Know paragraph, starting with *Some historians believe*. Copy the image of the woman golfer. Copy the bicycling article, starting at the paragraph that begins *The "Golden Age."* Copy the second Did You Know paragraph starting with *The bicycle was not*. Finally, copy the image of the bicyclers. Close the document.

8. Place the insertion point to the left of the last empty paragraph mark. From the **Clipboard** task pane, click the golf article that begins *The Desert Park*. The article is inserted. Point to the displayed **Paste Options** button and click the arrow. From the displayed list, click **Match Destination Formatting** to change the font to **Comic Sans, 11 pt.**

9. Press Enter and type **Did You Know?** Press Enter again and, from the Clipboard task pane, click the paragraph that begins *Some historians believe*. Click the **Paste Options button arrow** and then click **Match Destination Formatting**. Your newsletter expands to a second page.

10. On page 1, place the insertion point at the start of the paragraph that begins *"The Golf Benefit* and insert the woman golfer image. Select the image. From the displayed Picture toolbar, click the **Text Wrapping** button and then click **Top and Bottom**.

11. Hold down Ctrl and press End to move the insertion point to the end of the document. Press Enter and then type the headline for the next article: **Bicycling in Desert Park**

    Press Enter and then select the headline. Format the text the same as the *Golf for a Cause* headline—try using Format Painter to copy the format. Save your changes.

**(Project 4K–Recreation Notes continues on the next page)**

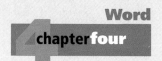
**(Project 4K**–Recreation Notes continued)

12. Click to the left of the paragraph mark under the new headline and then paste the bicycle article, which begins The *"Golden Age."* Use the **Paste Options** button to match the destination formatting. Press Enter to add a blank line after the article and then paste the image of the bicyclers. Click to the right of the image, press Enter, and then type **Did You Know?** Press Enter again, paste the text beginning with *The bicycle was not*, and then use the **Paste Options** button to match the destination formatting. A third page may be created in your newsletter. Close the Clipboard.

13. Move to the top of the first page. Place the insertion point to the left of the *Golf for a Cause* headline. Select all of the text in the newsletter except the banner and the Word Art Graphic. Open the **Paragraph** dialog box, set the spacing after to **6 pt.**, and then click **OK**.

14. With the text still selected, change the columns to **two** and change the alignment to **Justify**. Deselect the text. The newsletter is now on two pages. On page 1, drag as necessary to visually center the image of the woman golfer horizontally within the column, between the two paragraphs. Compare the placement of the image to Figure 4.57.

15. On page 2, in the first column, select the *Did You Know?* heading. Change the font to **Comic Sans MS**, **12-pt.**, **Bold**, and center it. In the second column, below the bicycle image, do the same to the second Did You Know? heading.

16. Select the first *Did You Know?* heading and the paragraph that follows it. Open the **Borders and Shading** dialog box and add a **Shadow** style, **2¼ pt.**, **Green** border around the paragraph to draw the reader's eye to it. Do the same for the second *Did You Know?* heading and paragraph.

17. Select the *Golf for a Cause* headline, open the **Borders and Shading** dialog box, click the **Shading tab**, and then apply a **light green** shading to the paragraph. Open the **Font** dialog box, apply the **Small caps** effect, and then center the headline. On page 2, apply the same formatting to the *Bicycling in Desert Park* headline.

18. View the footer area and add the **AutoText file name** to the footer. Preview the document, pressing PgUp and PgDn to move between the pages—your newsletter should occupy two pages. Compare your document to Figure 4.57 and the print it. Save your changes and close the document.

**End** **You have completed Project 4K**

## Project 4L—Tutoring Services

**Objectives:** *Create a Decorative Title, Add Special Paragraph Formatting, Use Special Character Formats, Insert Hyperlinks, and Preview and Save a Document as a Web Page.*

Use the skills you have learned in this and preceding chapters to create a one-page Word document to announce your services as a tutor for Microsoft Office applications. Save the document as a Web page with the file name *4L_Tutoring_Services_Firstname_Lastname.*

1. Start Word and create a headline to announce your services as a tutor. Use WordArt or any of the font characteristics you have practiced.

2. Write a paragraph or two to describe the skills you have acquired in Microsoft Word and other Microsoft programs. Include information about yourself that would make you qualified to be a tutor, such as patience or good listening skills. Think about the skills you would find helpful in a tutor. Format the text attractively so it is easy to read. When someone reads an announcement, they are usually seeking information about who, what, when, where, and why. Thus, be sure that your announcement describes who you are, what you do, when you are available to tutor, where tutoring can be held, and why you are qualified to be a tutor.

3. Add clip art or other pictures that are appropriate to the topic of tutoring using a computer.

4. Include a hyperlink to the Microsoft Web site— http://www.microsoft.com—or some other site appropriate to Microsoft Office programs.

5. Review your work and correct any errors. Be sure it is attractive and balanced on the page.

6. Save the document with the name **4L_Tutoring_Services_Firstname_ Lastname** Add the filename to the footer area. Then save the document as a Web Page. Print your results.

**End** **You have completed Project 4L** ──────────────────

## Project 4M — Personal Newsletter

**Objectives:** *Create a Decorative Title, Create a Multicolumn Document, Add Special Paragraph Formatting, Use Special Character Formats, and Locate Supporting Information.*

Create a one-page personal newsletter to send to your friends and family. Save your document as *4M_Personal_Newsletter_Firstname Lastname.*

1. From a blank document, create a WordArt heading for your personal newsletter. Add a decorative banner line under the newsletter heading.

2. Write a few paragraphs to describe the significant events in your life over the last few months to share with your family or friends. Write about two or more significant topics for which you could create a headline; for example, Enrolled In a Computer Course!

3. Create headlines for the topics you have chosen and then format them appropriately.

4. Change the text of the articles to two columns.

5. Add appropriate clip art or pictures. Select a significant paragraph and format it to stand out from the rest of the text.

6. If necessary, insert a continuous break at the end of the newsletter so the columns are even.

7. Save the file as **4M_Newsletter_Firstname_Lastname** Add the file name to the footer area and then print the document.

**End** You have completed Project 4M ⎯⎯⎯⎯⎯⎯⎯⎯⎯⎯⎯⎯

## On the Internet

### Locating Supporting Information on the Web

In this chapter, you were introduced to the Research feature of Microsoft Word. The Research button connects you to resources that you can use as you write. This includes the thesaurus and encyclopedia, which you used in the chapter, as well as many other tools. You can translate a word or a whole document into another language. Some of the resources that are displayed require that you pay a fee. Open Word and click the Research button. Explore the options available to you. Discover which ones are free, and which ones require you to sign up for the service and pay a fee. Try the translation feature, which will require that you have a document open. Think about how this compares to using your favorite Internet search engine to locate information. Also, think about how much you would be willing to pay for the resources available through the Research button.

## GO! with Help

### Special Column Formats

In the exercises in this chapter you created a simple one- or two-page newsletter. While desktop publishing software offers many more features for newsletter creation, Word can still be used—an advantage if you do not own desktop publishing software. Some additional features of Word can be applied to columns in a newsletter.

1. Start Word. On the menu bar, in the **Type a question for help** box, type **Columns** and then press Enter.

2. Expand and review the topics that display. This information is a good review of the content in this chapter related to columns and also introduces some new information.

3. Open **w04D_Council_News**. From the **Format** menu, click **Columns**. In the **Columns** dialog box, experiment with the different preset column formats displayed. Use the Help pane to assist you as you experiment with different column formats.

4. Close your document without saving changes. Close Help and then close Word.

# chapter**five**

# Using Charts, Special Effects, and Styles

**In this chapter, you will:** complete these projects **and** practice these skills.

**Project 5A**
**Creating a Chart**

**Objectives**
- Create a Chart with Microsoft Graph
- Format a Chart
- Add Special Text Effects

**Project 5B**
**Creating and Using Styles**

**Objectives**
- Use Existing Styles
- Create and Modify New Styles
- Modify the Document Window

**Project 5C**
**Creating an Outline**

**Objective**
- Create an Outline

**Project 5D**
**Creating a Program Outline**

**Objective**
- Create an Outline Using the Outline View and the Outlining Toolbar

# University Medical Center

The University Medical Center (UMC) is a premier patient-care and research institution serving Orange Beach, Florida. To maintain UMC's sterling reputation, the Office of Public Affairs (OPA) actively promotes UMC's services, achievements, and professional staff. The OPA staff interacts with the media, writes press releases and announcements, prepares marketing materials, develops public awareness campaigns, maintains a speakers bureau, and conducts media training for physicians and researchers. The UMC will soon be announcing successful results of a clinical trial of a new surgical technique, so this announcement will be a high priority for the OPA staff for the next several weeks.

©Photosphere Images Ltd.

# Making Professional Documents with Charts and Styles

Charts are visual representations of numeric data. Chart data is often easier to understand than textual data. Pie charts, which show the contributions of each piece to the whole, and column charts, which make comparisons among related numbers, are commonly used charts. Word features make it easy to design an effective chart.

Character, paragraph, and list styles provide a way to quickly apply formatting instructions to text. Character styles are applied to individual characters, paragraph styles are applied to entire paragraphs, and list styles are applied to bulleted or numbered lists. Word contains pre-defined styles, and you can also create your own styles.

Word also enables you to create and edit multiple-level outlines to organize an overview about a topic.

In this chapter, you will create and format charts. You will learn how to use existing styles and to create and modify new styles. Finally, you will create multilevel outlines.

# Project 5A Nutrition Flyer

Graphical representation of numbers helps a reader understand the implications and trends in a visual manner that is easier to interpret than lists of numbers. Using the Microsoft Graph program, you can add attractive charts to documents and reports.

In Activities 5.1 through 5.8, you will edit a nutrition flyer for the University Medical Center Nutrition Unit. You will add a chart to the flyer showing the results of a nutrition survey and format the chart to make it visually appealing. You will also use special formatting features to give your flyer a professional look. Your completed document will look similar to Figure 5.1. You will save your document as *5A_Nutrition_Flyer_Firstname_Lastname.*

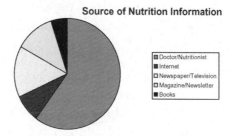

**Figure 5.1**
Project 5A—Nutrition Flyer

## Objective 1
## Create a Chart with Microsoft Graph

*Charts* are often used to make a set of numbers easier to understand. There are two ways to create a chart in Word using a built-in feature called *Microsoft Graph*. The easiest and most direct is to create a table with the data, and then create the chart directly from the table. You can also start Microsoft Graph and fill in the data in a table-like structure called a *datasheet*. There are 14 types of charts available in Word, each with a different purpose. The most commonly used are column, bar, pie, line, and area charts, as described in Figure 5.2.

| Chart Types Available in Word | |
|---|---|
| **Purpose of Chart** | **Chart Type** |
| Show comparison among data | Column, Bar |
| Show proportion of parts to a whole | Pie |
| Show trends over time | Line, Area |

**Figure 5.2**

### Activity 5.1 Creating a Chart from a Word Table

**1** On the Standard toolbar, click the **Open** button 🖼. Navigate to the location where the student files for this textbook are stored. Locate **w05A_Nutrition_Flyer** and click once to select it. Then, in the lower right corner of the **Open** dialog box, click **Open**.

The w05A_Nutrition_Flyer file opens.

**2** From the **File** menu, click **Save As**. In the **Save As** dialog box, navigate to the location where you are storing your files, creating a new folder for this chapter if you want to do so.

**3** In the **File name** box, type **5A_Nutrition_Flyer_Firstname_Lastname** and then click **Save**.

**4** Locate the table in the middle of the document, and then in the table, click anywhere to position the insertion point. From the **Table** menu, point to **Select**, and then click **Table**.

The table is selected, as shown in Figure 5.3. When creating a chart from a Word table, arrange the table so that the category labels form the first column and headings form the first row.

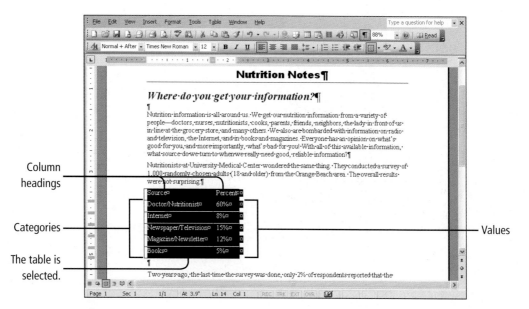

Column headings

Categories

The table is selected.

Values

**Figure 5.3**

---

**5** From the **Insert** menu, point to **Picture**, and then click **Chart**.

The Microsoft Graph program displays a three-dimensional column chart surrounded by a slashed border and a Datasheet table. New toolbars also display.

---

**Alert!**

**If the Datasheet Disappears**

If you click outside the chart, the datasheet will disappear, and the chart will no longer be in edit mode. To return to edit mode, double-click the chart. If the datasheet still does not display, from the View menu, click Datasheet.

---

**6** Look at Figure 5.4, and take a moment to become familiar with the parts of a chart with which you will be working.

The heading of the second column in the table—*Percent*—displays along the **category axis** (or x-axis). A **scale** of percentage values— from 0% to 60%—displays along the **value axis** (or y-axis). This scale is calculated by the Microsoft Graph program. The four categories from the first column are displayed in a **legend**, which relates the categories to the data in the chart. The chart graphic displays in the **plot area**; everything outside the plot area is the **chart area**. The table values have been copied to a datasheet, which is where future changes or additions to the data will be recorded. See Figure 5.4.

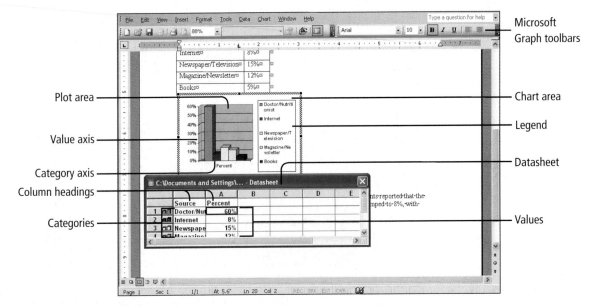

**Figure 5.4**

> ### Note — Chart Defaults
>
> If your chart does not look similar to the chart shown in Figure 5.4, it is because the default chart settings have been modified. Changing the chart default can be something as simple as changing the chart type for new charts, to custom changes of individual chart elements. Changes to the chart defaults should not interfere with completing the following activities, although your screens will look different from the ones in the book.

**7** On the Standard toolbar, click the **Save** button.

### Activity 5.2 Adding a Chart Title

Add a title to a chart to help the reader understand the topic of the chart's data.

**1** From the **Chart** menu, click **Chart Options**. If necessary, in the **Chart Options** dialog box, click the **Titles tab**. Alternatively, right-click on the chart area and click Chart Options from the shortcut menu.

**2** Click in the **Chart title** box and type **Source of Nutrition Information**

After a few seconds, the new title displays in the Preview area. See Figure 5.5.

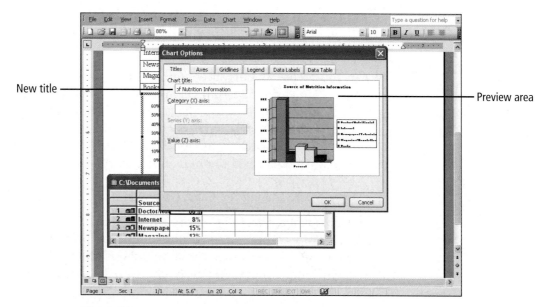

New title ——

Preview area ——

**Figure 5.5**

**3** At the bottom of the **Chart Options** dialog box, click **OK**. Click in the datasheet to remove the selection box from the title.

The title is added to the chart, and the size of the chart area is reduced, as shown in Figure 5.6.

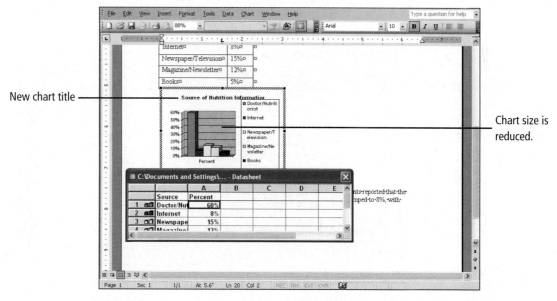

New chart title ——

Chart size is reduced.

**Figure 5.6**

**4** On the Standard toolbar, click the **Save** button.

## Objective 2
## Format a Chart

When you create a chart, it contains only the chart in default format and a legend. You can make changes to colors and backgrounds, change the size and page location of the chart, and add chart titles. Unless you have changed the default chart type, each new chart you create will be a **_column chart_**, which is used to compare data. Thus, if you need a pie chart or a line chart, you will need to change the chart type.

### Activity 5.3 Changing the Chart Type

The purpose of a chart is to graphically depict one of three types of relationships—a comparison among data, the proportion of parts to a whole, or trends over time. The data in your chart shows the parts of a whole, which is most effectively illustrated using a **_pie chart_**.

**1** Be sure that two toolbars display at the top of your screen. If only one toolbar row is displayed on your screen, at the right end of the Standard toolbar, click the **Toolbar Options** button █, and then click **Show Buttons on Two Rows**.

The Microsoft Graph Standard and Formatting toolbars are displayed in separate rows.

**2** On the Standard toolbar, click the **Chart Type button arrow** █.

A menu of chart type buttons displays. See Figure 5.7.

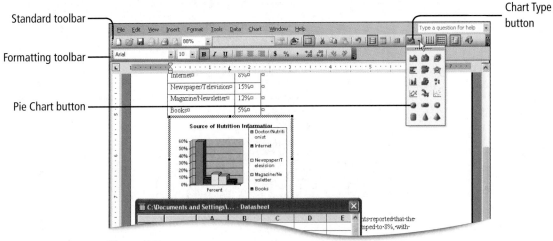

Standard toolbar

Formatting toolbar

Pie Chart button

Chart Type button

**Figure 5.7**

**3** Move the pointer over the chart buttons and take a moment to look at the buttons and ScreenTips.

Notice that the buttons depict the type of chart with which they are associated.

**4** From the **Chart Type** menu, click the **Pie Chart** button █.

The chart changes into a pie chart, but only the first row of information is charted, as indicated by the icon in the datasheet. See Figure 5.8.

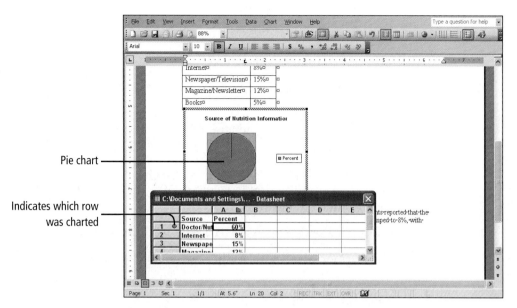

Pie chart

Indicates which row was charted

**Figure 5.8**

## More Knowledge — Two Ways of Displaying Chart Data

Charts can be displayed by row or by column. The difference can be very important. In a column chart, for example, changing the display from Rows to Columns switches the contents of the legend and the category (x) axis. In a pie chart this difference is particularly important. If you choose to display your data by rows, only the data in row 1 of the datasheet is displayed. If your data is in column format, you need to change the orientation of the chart to make the chart useful.

**5** On the Standard toolbar, click the **By Column** button.

The chart displays all the data, and icons in each row of the datasheet show that a pie slice has been added for each row. All of the slices together add up to 100 percent. See Figure 5.9.

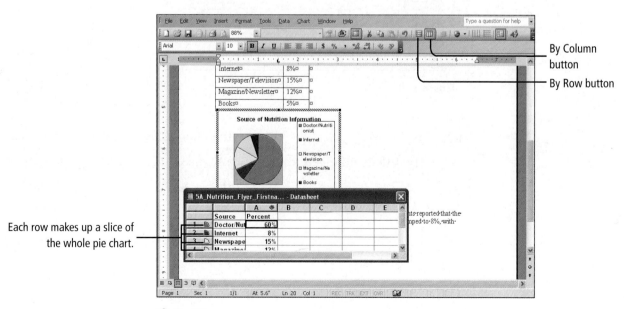

By Column button

By Row button

Each row makes up a slice of the whole pie chart.

**Figure 5.9**

**6** On the Standard toolbar, click the **Save** button 💾.

### Activity 5.4 Formatting Chart Text

You can format any text on a chart, including the title, axis titles, and text in legends.

**1** On the chart, click anywhere in the title *Source of Nutrition Information*.

A box with a gray border and sizing handles surrounds the title, indicating that the title is selected. You may have to click the title a second time to select it.

**2** From the **Format** menu, click **Selected Chart Title**.

The Format Chart Title dialog box displays.

**3** If necessary, on the **Format Chart Title** dialog box, click the **Font tab**.

Font options and a limited set of Effects are available in this dialog box.

**4** Click the **Color arrow** to display the color palette, as shown in Figure 5.10.

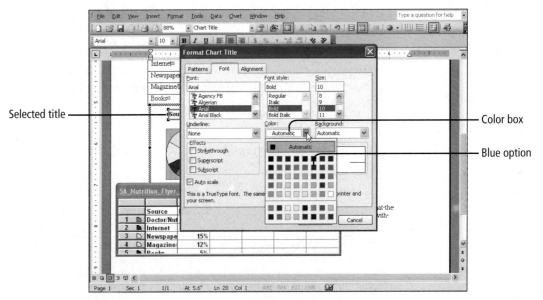

Selected title

Color box

Blue option

**Figure 5.10**

**5** In the second row, click the sixth color—**Blue**—and then click **OK**.

The title is changed to blue. See Figure 5.11.

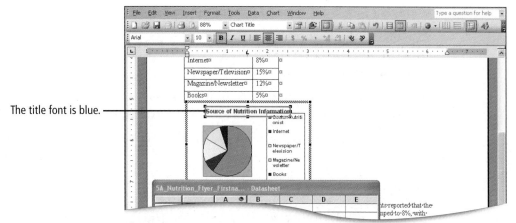

The title font is blue.

**Figure 5.11**

---

**6** Click to select the legend. From the **Format** menu, click **Selected Legend**.

The Format Legend dialog box displays.

**7** In the **Format Legend** dialog box, under **Font style**, click **Regular**, and then click **OK**.

The legend text changes from bold to regular, as shown in Figure 5.12.

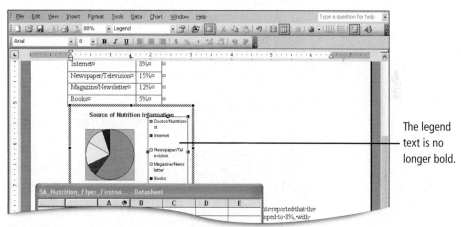

The legend text is no longer bold.

**Figure 5.12**

---

**8** On the datasheet, click in the title bar.

The Close button, which had been hidden while the datasheet was inactive, displays.

**9** On the datasheet title bar, click the **Close** button ☒.

The datasheet closes, but the chart remains active.

**10** On the Standard toolbar, click the **Save** button 🖫.

## Activity 5.5 Resizing and Centering a Chart

You can resize both the chart area and the individual chart elements. You can also position the chart on your page relative to the left and right margins.

**1** With the chart selected, drag the handle in the middle of the right border to approximately **5 inches on the horizontal ruler**.

Notice that the selection box stretches as you drag to the right. See Figure 5.13.

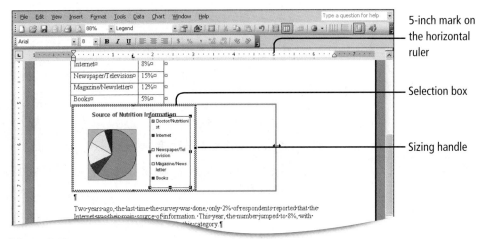

5-inch mark on the horizontal ruler

Selection box

Sizing handle

**Figure 5.13**

**2** Release the mouse button.

Notice that the text in the legend has expanded to display the widest entry, although the title may still be cut off.

**3** Move the pointer over the chart title and drag it to the right, near the edge of the chart box, as shown in Figure 5.14.

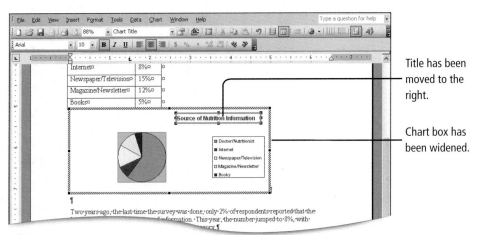

Title has been moved to the right.

Chart box has been widened.

**Figure 5.14**

**4** With the chart selected, drag the handle in the middle of the bottom border down to approximately **8 inches on the vertical ruler**.

The chart box is about 3 inches high. The legend and title size also increase, and the legend text may wrap.

**5** Move the pointer to one of the corners of the plot area, which is the area used for the pie.

A ScreenTip displays identifying the plot area.

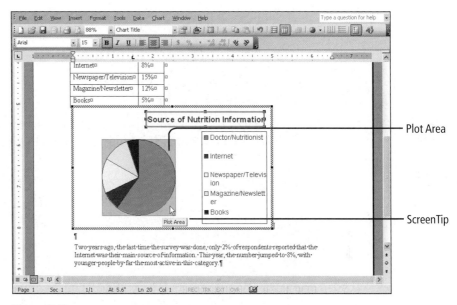

Plot Area

ScreenTip

**Figure 5.15**

**6** Click once to select the plot area. Using the sizing handle in the lower right corner of the plot area, drag down and to the right until the chart is near the lower border of the chart box.

**7** Using the sizing handle in the upper left corner of the plot area, drag up and to the left until the plot area is about 0.5 inch from the top border of the chart box.

Notice in Figure 5.16 that the legend text increases in size proportionally.

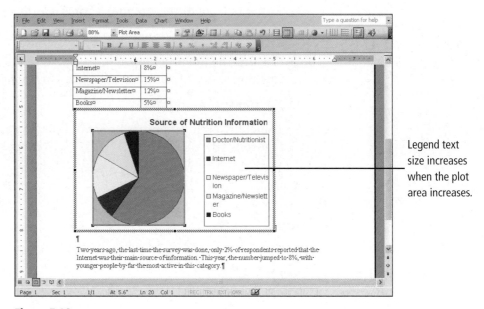

Legend text size increases when the plot area increases.

**Figure 5.16**

chapter**five**

**8** Click once on the legend. On the Formatting toolbar, click the **Font Size button arrow** 10, and then click **9**. If necessary, using the legend sizing handles, resize the legend box so that the text for each item displays on one line.

**9** Click once on the plot area outside the pie. From the **Format** menu, click **Selected Plot Area**.

The Format Plot Area dialog box displays.

**10** Under **Border**, click the **None** option button. Under **Area**, click the **None** option button.

This will remove the box and shading surrounding the pie. Compare your Format Plot Area dialog box with Figure 5.17.

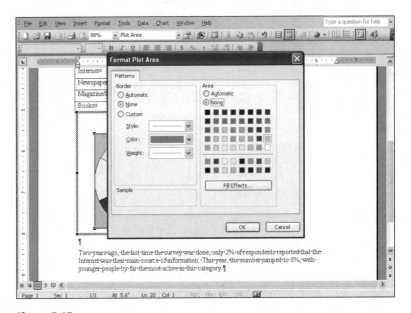

**Figure 5.17**

**11** At the bottom of the **Format Plot Area** dialog box, click **OK**.

The plot area border and shading are removed.

**12** Click in the document outside of the chart area to deselect the chart. Click once on the chart to select it. On the Formatting toolbar, click the **Center** button .

The chart area is centered horizontally on the page, as shown in Figure 5.18.

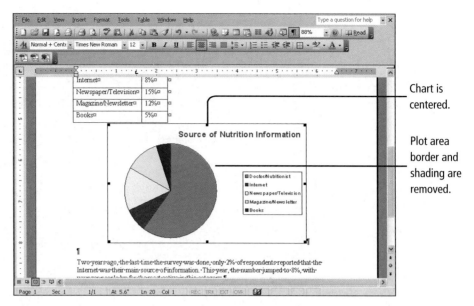

Chart is centered.

Plot area border and shading are removed.

**Figure 5.18**

**13** In the table, click anywhere to position the insertion point. From the **Table** menu, point to **Delete**, and then click **Table**.

The table is removed, but the chart retains its data because the data is stored in the datasheet associated with the chart.

**14** On the Standard toolbar, click the **Save** button ▣.

## Objective 3
## Add Special Text Effects

Word provides a number of methods to format text in a distinctive manner. For example, magazines and books sometimes use a large first letter to begin the first paragraph of an article or chapter. This is referred to as a ***drop cap***. The first letter can be three or four times taller than the rest of the text, which gives the text a finished look. Other distinctive text formatting is accomplished by adding a shadow effect, applying special underlining, or reducing the spacing between the letters.

### Activity 5.6 Creating a Drop Cap

A drop cap gives text a professional look, but use it only once in an article or chapter.

**1** Press Ctrl + Home to move to the top of the document. In the paragraph beginning *Nutrition information* select the letter *N* at the beginning of the paragraph.

**2** From the **Format** menu, click **Drop Cap**.

The Drop Cap dialog box displays. Under Position, notice that the default is *None*, and there are two other options. The ***Dropped*** position enlarges the letter and places it into the text, as illustrated by the small example. The ***In margin*** position places the enlarged letter in the left margin. See Figure 5.19.

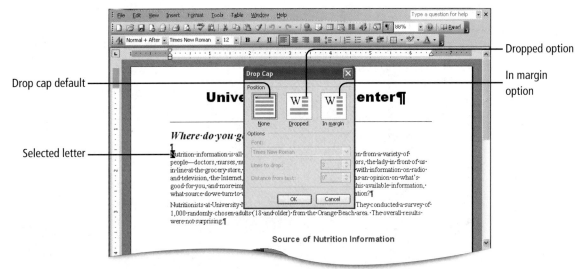

Drop cap default

Selected letter

Dropped option

In margin option

**Figure 5.19**

☒3 Under **Position**, click **Dropped**.

☒4 Under **Options**, click the **Lines to drop spin box up arrow** to change the line height of the drop cap to **4** lines.

Compare your Drop Cap dialog box with Figure 5.20.

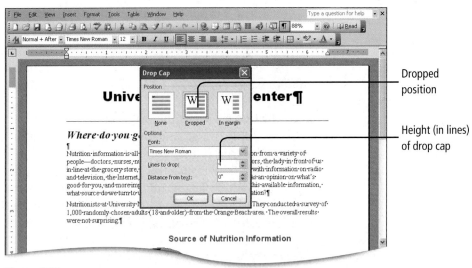

Dropped position

Height (in lines) of drop cap

**Figure 5.20**

☒5 In the **Drop Cap** dialog box, click **OK**.

The drop cap is inserted in the text, and resize handles display around its border indicating that it is selected.

☒6 On the Formatting toolbar, click the **Font Color button arrow** [A▾], and from the displayed palette in the second row, click the sixth color—**Blue**.

The drop cap color changes to blue.

☒7 Click anywhere in the document to deselect the drop cap.

Compare your screen with Figure 5.21.

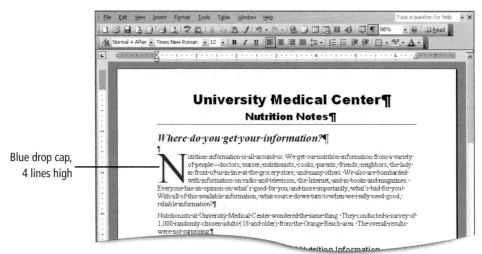

**Figure 5.21**

**8** On the Standard toolbar, click the **Save** button.

### Activity 5.7  Adding a Shadow to a Title

Special text effects, such as shadows, are effective when used sparingly. Use the Font dialog box to add text effects and also to change several font characteristics at the same time.

**1** Move to the top of the document. Move the pointer into the left margin to the left of the first line of text. When the pointer changes to a white arrow, click once to select the entire line.

**2** From the **Format** menu, click **Font**.

The Font dialog box displays.

**3** If necessary, at the top of the **Font** dialog box, click the **Font tab**.

In this dialog box, you can change many font characteristics, and a Preview window at the bottom of the dialog box will reflect the changes you make to the selected text. See Figure 5.22.

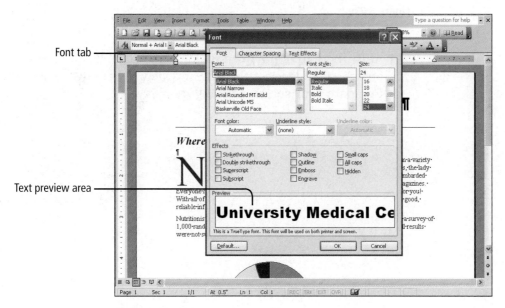

**Figure 5.22**

**4** In the **Font** dialog box, under **Font style**, click **Bold**.

Notice that the text in the preview box is shown in bold.

**5** In the **Size** box, select **24** and type **32**

The 32-point font size is not an option in the Size list. If you want a font size that does not appear in the list, you can type it in the Size box.

**6** Click the **Font color arrow**, and then in the second row, click **Blue**.

Blue is the sixth color in the second row. If you pause your mouse pointer over the colors, a ScreenTip displays the name of each color.

**7** Under **Effects**, select the **Small caps** check box.

**8** Under **Effects**, select the **Shadow** check box.

The changes to the text are reflected in the Preview box, as shown in Figure 5.23.

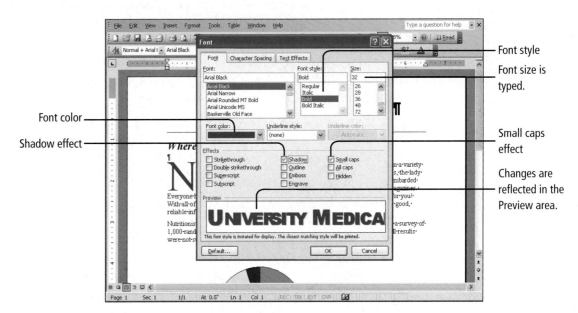

**Figure 5.23**

**9** At the bottom of the **Font** dialog box, click **OK**, and then click anywhere to deselect the title and view the changes you have made. Compare your screen with Figure 5.24.

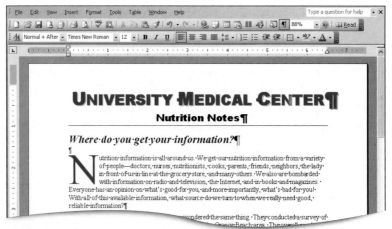

**Figure 5.24**

**10** Move the pointer into the left margin to the left of the subtitle line, *Nutrition Notes*. When the pointer changes to a white arrow, drag down to select the subtitle, the divider line, and the heading *Where do you get your information?*

The second and third lines of the document are selected.

**11** On the Formatting toolbar, click the **Font Color** button ![A] , which should have retained its previous usage of blue. If not, click the arrow on the right of the Font Color button ![A] and click the same color you used for the title and the drop cap. Click anywhere to deselect the text.

The top three lines of the document are blue, along with the drop cap and the title of the chart, as shown in Figure 5.25.

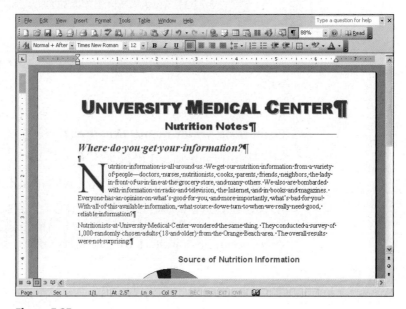

**Figure 5.25**

**12** On the Standard toolbar, click the **Save** button ![save] .

## Activity 5.8 Modifying Character Spacing

Increasing or decreasing font size changes the size of the letters and the spacing between the letters proportionally. You can make the text look denser by condensing (decreasing) the space between characters, which does not affect the font size. You can also expand (increase) the space between characters. This technique is useful to make text completely fill a page or to make text that is a little too long for a page or a text box fit precisely.

**1** Move the pointer into the margin to the left of the paragraph beginning *Nutrition information*. When the pointer changes to a white arrow, drag down to select that paragraph and the next one.

When you use this method to select a paragraph containing a drop cap, the paragraph marker above the drop cap is also selected, as shown in Figure 5.26. Notice the spacing of the letters in the selected paragraphs.

Paragraph above the
drop cap is selected.

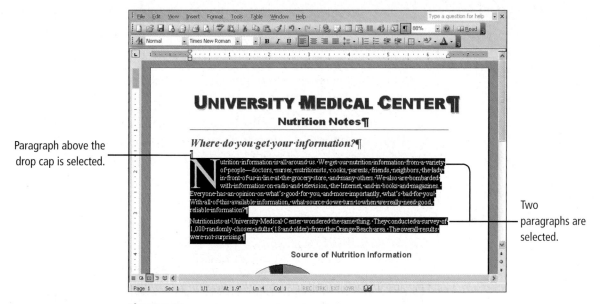

Two
paragraphs are
selected.

**Figure 5.26**

**2** From the **Format** menu, click **Font**.

The Font dialog box displays.

**3** At the top of the **Font** dialog box, click the **Character Spacing tab**.

In this dialog box you can adjust the scale, spacing, and position of characters, and a Preview window at the bottom of the dialog box will reflect changes made to the selected text.

**4** Look at the Preview box and notice the spacing. Click the **Spacing arrow**. From the displayed list, point to **Condensed**, and then watch the Preview area as you click.

The *By* box to the right of the *Spacing* box displays *1 pt.* This means that the characters are moved 1 point closer together.

**5** To the right of the **Spacing** box, click the **By spin box up arrow** to change the spacing to **0.3 pt**.

This will move the characters about a third of a point closer. Recall that a point is ½ of an inch. Compare your dialog box with Figure 5.27.

Character Spacing tab

Spacing type

Preview area

Spacing change

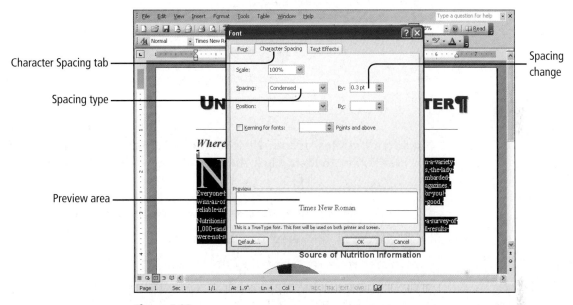

**Figure 5.27**

**6** At the bottom of the **Font** dialog box, click **OK**. Click anywhere to deselect the text.

Notice how much the text is condensed. The first paragraph, which was seven lines long, is now six lines long, but the font size remains unchanged. Compare the selected text in Figure 5.26 to the text in Figure 5.28.

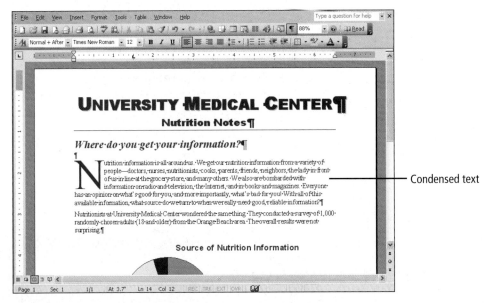

Condensed text

**Figure 5.28**

**7** From the **View** menu, click **Header and Footer**. On the Header and Footer toolbar, click the **Switch Between Header and Footer** button ⊞.

**8** On the **Header and Footer** toolbar, click the **Insert AutoText** button Insert AutoText ▾, and then click **Filename**.

The file name is inserted in the footer.

**9** On the **Header and Footer** toolbar, click the **Close** button Close.

**10** On the Standard toolbar, click the **Save** button ⊟.

**11** On the Standard toolbar, click the **Print Preview** button. Take a moment to check your work. On the Print Preview toolbar, click the **Close Preview** button Close.

**12** Make any necessary changes to your document. When you are satisfied, on the Standard toolbar, click the **Print** button. Close the document.

**End** You have completed Project 5A ————————————

# Project 5B **Medical Records**

Businesses often develop a uniform appearance for procedure and policy manuals that includes headings to help organize the material and make it easier for a user to find information. Microsoft Word includes a set of predefined styles with several heading levels, or you can create your own styles to use in your documents.

In Activities 5.9 through 5.17, you will edit a section of a medical center Policy and Procedure manual by applying new and existing styles. Your completed document will look similar to Figure 5.29. You will save your document as *5B_Medical_Records_Firstname_Lastname.*

---

**Medical Center Policy and Procedure Manual**

*Topic: Official Medical Records*

Policy and Procedure Manual Location: Section 1, Medical Center Administration

Section 1.4, Medical Records Policy and Procedure

Section 1.4.1, Integrated Central Medical Records System

*I. Purpose:*
The purpose of this policy is to provide guidance to **Medical Center** physicians, both faculty and staff, in the development and maintenance of an integrated, central medic[...] documentation will be develope[...] receives assessment or treatmen[...] unit. All documentation will be s[...] This makes it a more efficient an[...] patient, and also better serves the[...]

*II. Definitions:*
A. Integrated Medical Record – [...] the documentation and diagno[...] and those received from othe[...]
B. Centralized Medical Records[...] unique medical records of all[...] business functions.
C. Official Medical Record – A [...] current centralized system an[...] system includes those medica[...] Family Practice Center, Pedia[...] Women's Center, Plastic Surg[...]
D. Office/Shadow Records – Me[...] centralized medical records s[...] Official medical record.

*III. Policy:*
It is the policy of **Medical Cen**[...] medical records system and to [...] order to support patient care, [...] functions of the organization acc[...]
A. All original internal and exter[...] Medical Records to be assem[...] medical record.

5B_Medical_Records_Firstname_Lastna[...]

B. Appropriately document the encounter within the patient's Official medical record.
C. Discourage the creation or use of Office/Shadow medical records.

*IV. Procedure:*
Whenever possible, the patient's *Official medical record will be made available for each patient encounter with* **Medical Center** *physicians.*
A. All documentation should either occur directly within the Official medical record in accordance with applicable policies or should be forwarded to Medical Records after completed.
B. Any external patient information received should be appropriately reviewed by the responsible provider and forwarded to Medical Records.

5B_Medical_Records_Firstname_Lastname

**Figure 5.29**
Project 5B—Medical Records

## Objective 4
## Use Existing Styles

A **template** is a model for documents of the same type, and it stores information that determines the basic structure for a document in Word. The template information includes document settings such as page layout, fonts, special formatting, and styles. A **style** is a group of formatting commands that Word stores with a specific name, which you can retrieve by name and apply to text. Unless you select a specific template, all new Word documents are based on the **Normal template**—stored in your computer as *Normal.dot*.

The Normal template contains a small set of built-in styles that you can use to format text with one action instead of three or four. The default settings for the Normal template include such formatting as Times New Roman font, font size of 12 pt., single spacing, left alignment, 1" top and bottom margins, and 1.25" left and right margins. Styles are added to text using either the Style button in the Formatting toolbar, or the Styles and Formatting task pane. There are four types of styles, as shown in Figure 5.30.

## Word Style Types

| Style Type | Purpose |
|---|---|
| Paragraph style | Controls the formatting of a paragraph, including line spacing, indents, alignment, tab stops, font type, and size. |
| Character style | Affects the selected text within a paragraph, including font style, font size, bold, italic, and underline. |
| Table style | Formats border type and style, shading, cell alignment, and fonts in a table. |
| List style | Formats font style, font size, alignment, and bullet or number characteristics in lists. |

**Figure 5.30**

### Activity 5.9  Displaying Styles

You can display the styles available for paragraphs on the left side of a document and show all of the available styles in a task pane on the right side of the document.

**1** On the Standard toolbar, click the **Open** button. Navigate to the location where the student files for this textbook are stored. Locate and open **w05B_Medical_Records**. Save the file as **5B_Medical_Records_Firstname_Lastname**

**2** On the left edge of the horizontal scroll bar, click the **Normal View** button.

The document changes to Normal View. Recall that Normal view gives you more area in which to type, but does not display graphics or the edges of the page. It also enables you to see the styles used for each paragraph. Page breaks are indicated by a dotted line.

**3** From the **Tools** menu, click **Options**. Be sure the **View tab** is selected. See Figure 5.31.

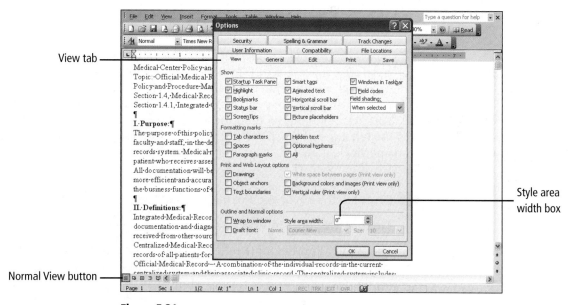

View tab

Style area
width box

Normal View button

**Figure 5.31**

> **Note — Is Your Style Area Already On?**
>
> If the last person to use the computer left the style area on, you may see it when you switch to Normal View. If this is the case, perform Steps 6 and 7 to verify that your style area is the right size.

**4** At the bottom of the **View tab**, under **Outline and Normal options**, click the **Style area width spin box up arrow** until the width is **0.6"**.

**5** In the lower right corner, click **OK**.

A style area opens at the left side of the document, and the style name for each paragraph displays. All of the paragraphs in this document use the default Normal style, except the section headings, which use a style named *Subheading*—a style created for this chapter. See Figure 5.32.

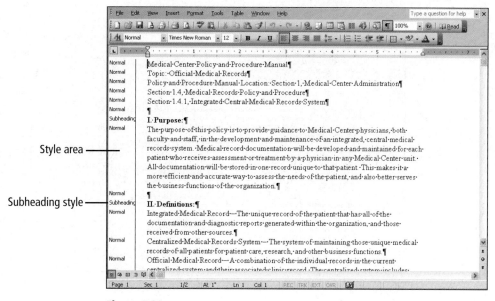

Style area

Subheading style

**Figure 5.32**

**Note** — Closing the Style Area

If you are working in a computer classroom or lab, you should close the style area before you close Word. To close the style area, from the Tools menu, click Options. Be sure the View tab is selected. Under Outline and Normal options, in the Style area width spin box, click the up arrow until the width is 0". Alternatively, you can drag the vertical line on the right of the style area to the left edge of the Word window. You can also use this method to resize an open style area.

**6** On the left side of the Formatting toolbar, click the **Styles and Formatting** button ![icon].

The Styles and Formatting task pane displays. The style of the paragraph that contains the insertion point is shown in the box at the top of this pane and is bordered in blue in the list of available styles.

**7** If the right edge of the text is hidden behind the task pane, on the Standard toolbar, click the **Zoom button arrow** ![100%], and then click **Page Width**.

**8** In your document, click to place the insertion point anywhere in the line that begins *II. Definitions*.

In the style area on the left, notice that this paragraph has the *Subheading* style applied. In the Styles and Formatting task pane, notice that the *Subheading* style is selected.

**9** In the **Styles and Formatting** task pane, under **Pick formatting to apply**, examine the list of style names. If necessary, at the bottom of the **Styles and Formatting** task pane, in the **Show** box, click the arrow, and then click **Available formatting**.

The built-in styles, plus the *Subheading* style that was created for this chapter, are listed. See Figure 5.33.

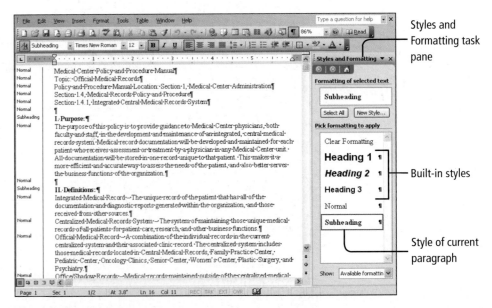

Styles and Formatting task pane

Built-in styles

Style of current paragraph

**Figure 5.33**

## Note — Style Names Do Not Print

Although the style area looks like it is part of the document, it is not. It does not print, and there is no method to print the style names as shown on the screen.

**10** On the Standard toolbar, click the **Save** button 🖫.

### Activity 5.10 Working with Default Styles

Four styles are included with every document created with the Normal template, which is the default template in Word. The four styles include three heading styles and the Normal style. The Subheading style was created for this chapter. Your version of Word may display other styles that have been added to the default template.

**1** At the top of the document, click to position the insertion point in the first line, which begins *Medical Center Policy.*

This is the document title. To apply a paragraph style, you need only position the insertion point somewhere in the paragraph—you do not need to select the entire paragraph.

**2** In the **Styles and Formatting** task pane, under **Pick formatting to apply**, click **Heading 1**.

The Heading 1 style is applied to the title. The Heading 1 style includes a font size of 16 and bold font style. Notice that the *Heading 1* name in the Styles and Formatting task pane has the same character formatting—the style name also acts as a style preview, as shown in Figure 5.34.

Style name in style area ——

Style has been applied to the title.

Selected style

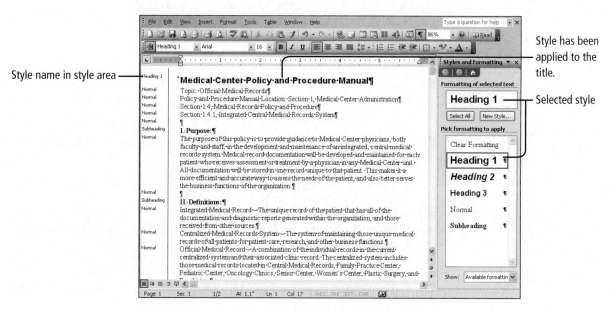

**Figure 5.34**

**3** Position the insertion point in the next line, beginning *Topic: Official*.

**4** In the **Styles and Formatting** task pane, under **Pick formatting to apply**, click **Heading 2**.

The Heading 2 style includes a font size of 14, smaller than Heading 1, and bold and italic font style.

**5** Position the insertion point in the next line, beginning *Policy and Procedure Manual*.

**6** In the **Styles and Formatting** task pane, under **Pick formatting to apply**, click **Heading 3**.

The Heading 3 style includes font size of 13 and bold font style, as shown in Figure 5.35.

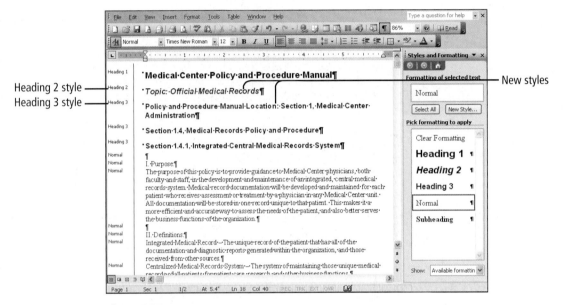

Heading 2 style

Heading 3 style

New styles

**Figure 5.35**

**7** Move the pointer to the left of the line beginning *Section 1.4, Medical*. When the pointer changes to a white arrow, drag down to select that paragraph and the next one, beginning *Section 1.4.1, Integrated*.

**8** In the **Styles and Formatting** task pane, under **Pick formatting to apply**, click **Heading 3**.

Notice that you can apply styles to more than one paragraph at a time.

**9** Click to position the insertion point in the next line, beginning *I. Purpose*. In the **Styles and Formatting** task pane, under **Pick formatting to apply**, click **Heading 3**.

**10** Click to position the insertion point in the line beginning *II. Definitions*. In the **Styles and Formatting** task pane, under **Pick formatting to apply**, click **Heading 3**.

**11** On the Standard toolbar, click the **Save** button.

**Activity 5.11** Clearing Styles

You can remove all formatting from a document or from selected text in a document, which removes any styles that were applied.

**1** If necessary, position the insertion point in the line beginning *II. Definitions*.

**2** In the **Styles and Formatting** task pane, under **Pick formatting to apply**, click **Clear Formatting**.

The Heading 3 style is removed, and the paragraph reverts to the Normal style. Notice that in task pane list, *Normal* is bordered.

**3** Click to position the insertion point in the line beginning *I. Purpose*.

**4** In the **Styles and Formatting** task pane, under **Pick formatting to apply**, click **Clear Formatting**.

The Heading 3 style is removed, and the paragraph reverts to the Normal style, as shown in Figure 5.36.

Paragraphs revert to Normal style.

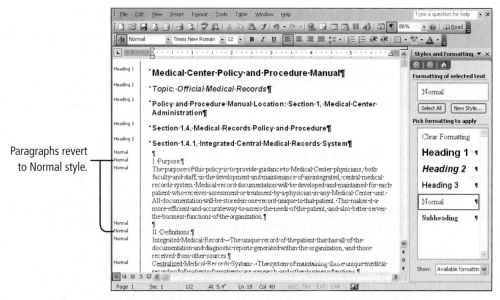

**Figure 5.36**

**5** Move the pointer into the left margin to the left of the paragraph beginning *I. Purpose*. When the pointer changes to a white arrow, click once.

**6** Move the pointer into the left margin to the left of the paragraph beginning *II. Definitions*. When the pointer changes to a white arrow, hold down Ctrl and click once.

Two nonadjacent paragraphs are selected, as shown in Figure 5.37.

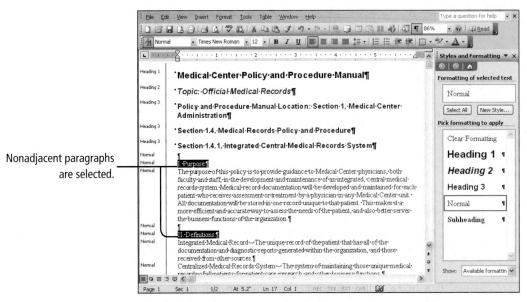

Nonadjacent paragraphs are selected.

**Figure 5.37**

**7** In the **Styles and Formatting** task pane, under **Pick formatting to apply**, click **Subheading**.

The Subheading style is restored to both paragraphs.

**8** On the Standard toolbar, click the **Save** button 🖫.

## Objective 5
## Create and Modify New Styles

By default, only a few styles are included with the Normal template, but you can create your own styles based on formats that you use often. For example, if you always type your name or company name in a distinctive manner (e.g., for example, bold, Verdana font, font size 14), you can create that as a style and apply it when needed. After you have created a style, you can modify it to suit your changing needs. One of the strengths of using styles is that it enables you to change all instances of a style throughout a document at the same time.

### Activity 5.12 Creating and Applying Paragraph Styles

When you need to match special formatting guidelines to complete a document, you can use paragraph styles that will enable you to perform several formatting steps with a single click.

**1** Move the pointer to the left of the line beginning *The purpose of this policy*. When the pointer changes to a white arrow, drag down to select the entire paragraph. Alternatively, you can double-click in the paragraph margin to select it.

**2** On the Formatting toolbar, click the **Italic** button $\boxed{I}$.

**3** From the **Format** menu, click **Paragraph**. If necessary, click the **Indents and Spacing tab**.

**4** Under **General**, click the **Alignment arrow**, and then click **Justified**.

**5** Under **Indentation**, click the **Left spin box up arrow** to set the left indent at **0.5"**.

**6** Under **Indentation**, click the **Right spin box up arrow** to set the right indent at **0.5"**.

Compare your Paragraph dialog box with Figure 5.38.

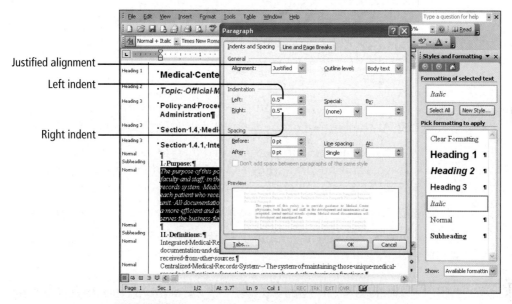

Justified alignment —
Left indent —
Right indent —

**Figure 5.38**

**7** At the bottom of the **Paragraph** dialog box, click **OK**.

The changes you made are reflected in the paragraph, and the paragraph remains selected.

**8** With the paragraph still selected, in the **Styles and Formatting** task pane, under **Formatting of selected text**, click **New Style**.

The New Style dialog box displays.

**9** In the **New Style** dialog box, under **Properties**, in the **Name** box, type **Intro**

A style formatting list displays under the preview window, as shown in Figure 5.39.

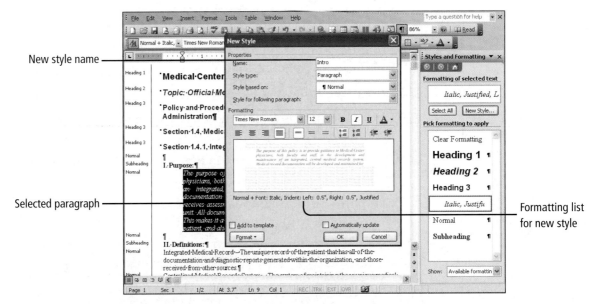

New style name

Selected paragraph

Formatting list for new style

**Figure 5.39**

**10** At the bottom of the **New Style** dialog box, click **OK**.

Even though you just created a style using the selected paragraph, you still need to apply the style. A temporary style displays the modifications you have made.

**11** In the **Styles and Formatting** task pane, click the **Intro** style.

The new style is applied to the selected paragraph.

---

## More Knowledge — Creating Styles Using the Style Box

There is a shortcut method to create styles using the Style box. Make the desired changes to a paragraph. In the Formatting toolbar, click once in the Style box. Type the name of the new style and press Enter. The new style is created and applied to the current paragraph. There are limitations to this method of creating styles. You can create only paragraph styles, and you have less control over the style than you have when creating a style in the New Style dialog box.

---

**12** Scroll down and, near the end of the first page, click to place the insertion point in the paragraph beginning *It is the policy*. In the **Styles and Formatting** task pane, click the **Intro** style.

The paragraph changes to the new style, with both margins indented, the text justified, with italic font style. See Figure 5.40.

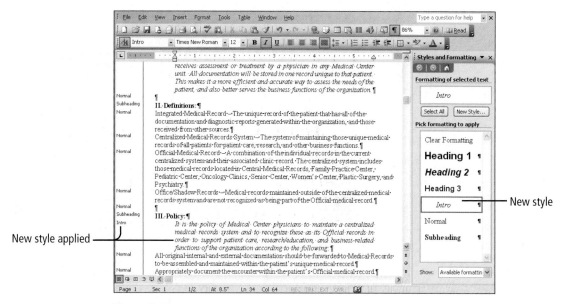

New style applied ———

New style ———

**Figure 5.40**

**13** Scroll down and click to place the insertion point in the paragraph beginning *Whenever possible* near the end of the document. In the **Styles and Formatting** task pane, click the **Intro** style.

The paragraph changes to the new style.

**14** On the Standard toolbar, click the **Save** button 🖫.

### Activity 5.13 Creating and Applying List Styles

Styles can be created for lists and then applied to any text, which will change the text to match the list characteristics of the style.

**1** Near the end of the document, move the pointer to the left of the line beginning *All documentation should*. When the pointer changes to a white arrow, drag down to select the last two paragraphs.

**2** On the Formatting toolbar, click the **Numbering** button 🗐.

The two paragraphs are numbered.

**3** From the **Format** menu, click **Bullets and Numbering**. In the displayed **Bullets and Numbering** dialog box, click the **Numbered tab**.

**4** From the **Bullets and Numbering** dialog box, click the option with capital letters, as shown in Figure 5.41. If that option is not displayed, at the bottom of the Bullets and Numbering dialog box, click the Reset button.

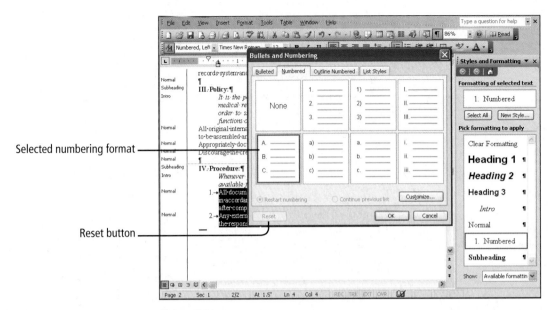

Selected numbering format

Reset button

**Figure 5.41**

**5** At the bottom of the **Bullets and Numbering** dialog box, click **OK**.

The numbers change to letters.

**6** From the Formatting toolbar, click the **Increase Indent** button .

The selected list items are indented to the right.

**7** In the **Styles and Formatting** task pane, under **Formatting of selected text**, click **New Style**.

The New Style dialog box displays.

**8** In the **New Style** dialog box, under **Properties**, in the **Name** box, type **Points**

**9** In the **New Style** dialog box, under **Properties**, click the **Style type arrow**, and then click **List**.

The list options display in the New Style dialog box, as shown in Figure 5.42.

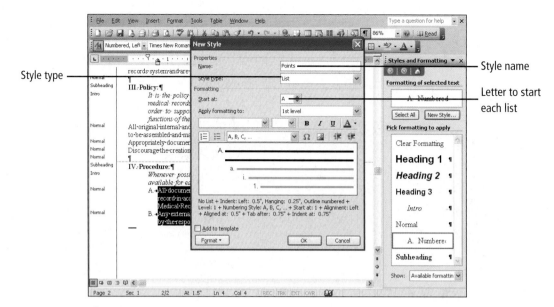

Style type

Style name

Letter to start each list

**Figure 5.42**

**10** At the bottom of the **New Style** dialog box, click **OK**.

The list changes to the new style, and the new style name is displayed in the list of styles in the Styles and Formatting task pane. Notice in Figure 5.43 that the new list style also displays a small icon indicating the style type.

**11** In the **Styles and Formatting** task pane, click the **Points** style.

Even though you just created a style using the selected paragraph, you still need to apply the style. When you apply a list style, the style displays in the Style box on the Formatting toolbar and in the Styles and Formatting task pane, but still displays Normal in the styles area. See Figure 5.43.

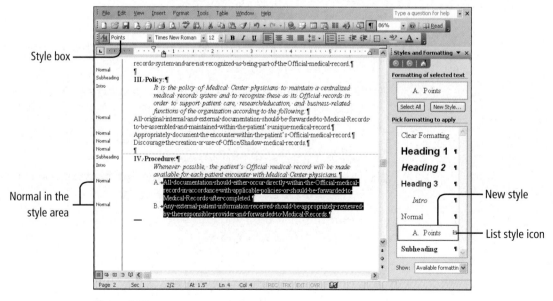

Style box

Normal in the style area

New style

List style icon

**Figure 5.43**

**12** Scroll up in the document. In each paragraph containing text that uses the Normal style, position the insertion point, and then in the **Styles and Formatting** task pane, click the **Points** style.

Your document should look similar to Figure 5.44.

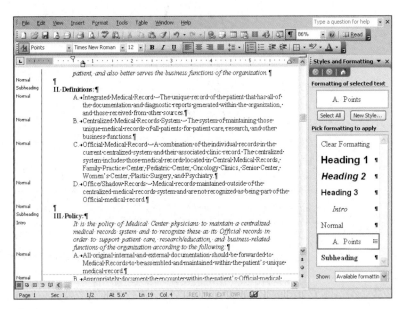

**Figure 5.44**

**13** On the Standard toolbar, click the **Save** button.

### Activity 5.14 Creating and Applying Character Styles

Character styles are applied to selected text within a paragraph; they do not affect the formatting of the entire paragraph.

**1** In the **Styles and Formatting** task pane, under **Formatting of selected text**, click **New Style**.

The New Style dialog box displays.

**2** In the **New Style** dialog box, under **Properties**, in the **Name** box, type **Med Center**

**3** Under **Properties**, click the **Style type arrow**, and then click **Character**.

Under Formatting, the character options display in the New Style dialog box.

**4** In the **New Style** dialog box, under **Formatting**, locate the two boxes with arrows.

From the first box, you can select a font, and from the second box you can select a font size.

**5** Click the **Font Size button arrow** and then click **14** points.

**6** In the **New Style** dialog box, under **Formatting**, click the **Bold** button **B**.

**7** In the **New Style** dialog box, under **Formatting**, click the **Font Color button arrow** **A▾**, and in the third row, click the first color—**Red**. Compare your dialog box with Figure 5.45.

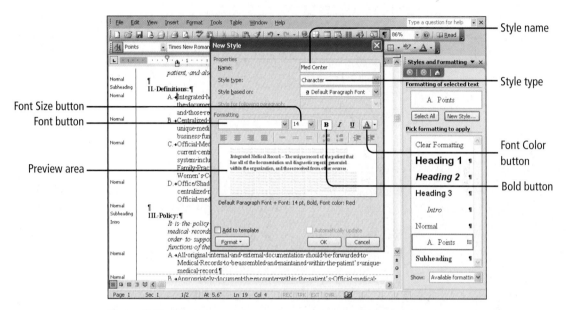

Style name

Style type

Font Size button

Font button

Preview area

Font Color button

Bold button

**Figure 5.45**

**8** At the bottom of the **New Style** dialog box, click **OK**. Scroll to the top of the document.

The style is added to the Styles and Formatting task pane list, but the style has not been used to modify any text. Notice that the symbol on the right of the new style is a small *a*, which indicates a character style.

**9** In the paragraph beginning *The purpose of this policy*, in the first sentence, select *Medical Center*.

**10** In the **Styles and Formatting** task pane, click the **Med Center** style. Click on the text you just formatted to deselect the text.

The three formatting changes you made in the New Style dialog box are applied. See Figure 5.46.

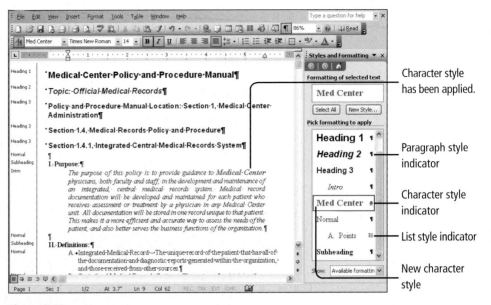

Character style
has been applied.

Paragraph style
indicator

Character style
indicator

List style indicator

New character
style

**Figure 5.46**

**11** In the same paragraph, in the fifth line, select **Medical Center**. In the **Styles and Formatting** task pane, click the **Med Center** style.

**12** Locate *Medical Center* in the Intro style paragraphs following *III. Policy* and *IV. Procedure*, and apply the **Med Center** style to both, as shown in Figure 5.47.

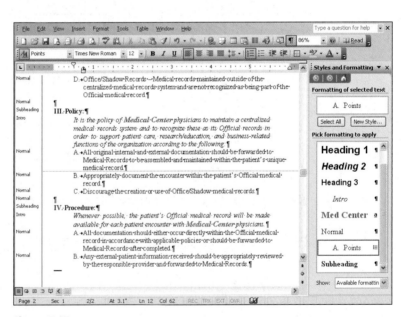

**Figure 5.47**

**13** On the Standard toolbar, click the **Save** button.

## Activity 5.15 Selecting and Modifying Styles

If you want to change a style, you can select all instances of the style, and then modify all of the paragraphs at once.

**1** In the **Styles and Formatting** task pane, pause the mouse pointer over the **Subheading** paragraph style. Click the arrow on the right of the **Subheading** style.

A short menu displays, as shown in Figure 5.48. Here you can select, delete, or modify this style.

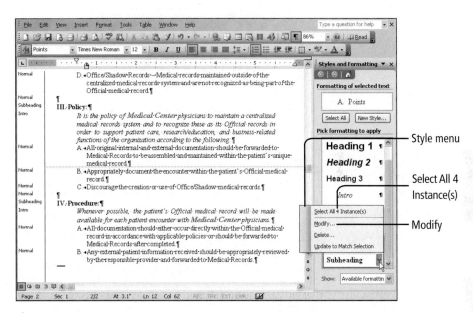

**Figure 5.48**

**2** From the displayed menu, click **Select All 4 Instance(s)**.

All four of the Subheading style paragraphs are selected. While not required to change all of the paragraphs at once, selecting all of the instances helps you see where the style is used in the document.

**3** Click the arrow on the right of the **Subheading** style again. From the displayed menu, click **Modify**.

The Modify Style dialog box displays.

**4** In the **Modify Style** dialog box, under **Formatting**, click the **Italic** button ⬚.

**5** Near the bottom of the **Modify Style** dialog box, select the **Automatically update** check box.

The Automatically update feature enables you to change all of the paragraphs using the same style, and the style itself, by selecting and modifying only one paragraph. Compare your dialog box with Figure 5.49.

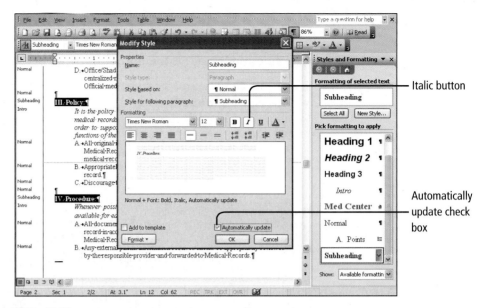

Italic button

Automatically update check box

**Figure 5.49**

**6** At the bottom of the **Modify Style** dialog box, click **OK**.

All of the paragraphs using the Subheading style are changed, as shown in Figure 5.50.

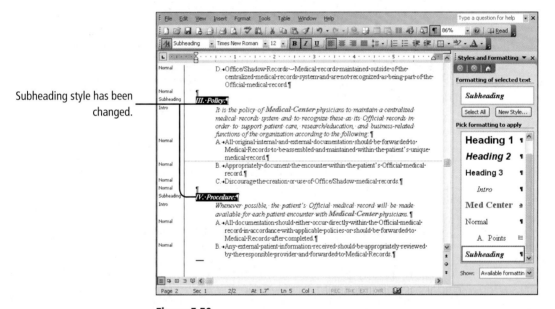

Subheading style has been changed.

**Figure 5.50**

**7** In the **Styles and Formatting** task pane, pause the mouse pointer over the **Med Center** character style. Click the arrow on the right of the **Med Center** style.

**8** From the displayed menu, click **Modify**.

The Modify Style dialog box displays.

**9** In the **Modify Style** dialog box, under **Formatting**, click the **Font Size button arrow**, and then click **12** points.

Compare your dialog box with Figure 5.51.

**Font size is changed.**

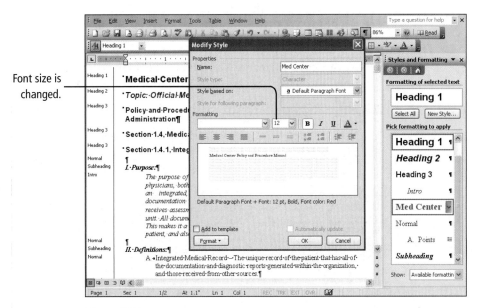

**Figure 5.51**

**10** At the bottom of the **Modify Style** dialog box, click **OK**.

All of the text using the Med Center style is changed.

**11** From the **Tools** menu, click **Options**. If necessary, click the **View tab**. Under **Outline and Normal options**, click the **Style area width spin box down arrow** until the style area width is **0"**. At the bottom of the **Options** dialog box, click **OK**. Alternatively, drag the vertical line on the right side of the style area to the left edge of the document window.

The style area on the left side of the screen closes.

**12** On the Standard toolbar, click the **Save** button 📖.

## Objective 6
## Modify the Document Window

When you are working in Print Layout View, the gap between pages can take up a large portion of the screen, particularly when you are working on a laptop computer. You can minimize the gap between the pages so you can see more of your document, yet still maintain the visual advantage of seeing the edges of the paper. You can also split the window so that you can view two parts of a document at the same time. This is especially useful in long documents when you need to see pages at the beginning of the document and pages at the end of the document at the same time.

### Activity 5.16 Hiding Spaces Between Pages

**1** In the **Styles and Formatting** task pane, in the title bar, click the **Close** button ✖.

**2** On the left edge of the horizontal scroll bar, click the **Print Layout View** button 🔲. If necessary, set the Zoom to 100%.

The document changes to Print Layout View.

**3** Scroll down until the break between the two pages is in view in the middle of your screen.

Notice how much of the screen is unused. You can see that a large portion of the screen contains blank white or gray space.

**4** Move the pointer into the gray area between the two pages.

The pointer changes to a Hide White Spaces pointer, as shown in Figure 5.52.

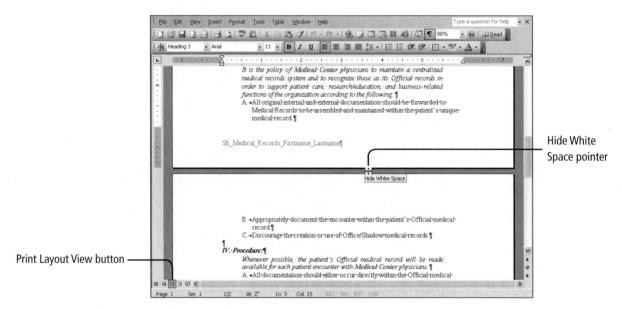

Hide White Space pointer

Print Layout View button

**Figure 5.52**

**5** With the pointer positioned between the pages, click once.

Notice that the gap is closed, and the text appears to be on one continuous page, with a line showing the page breaks, as shown in Figure 5.53. Notice also that the footer area is hidden. The headers and footer areas are removed from the display, although both will still print.

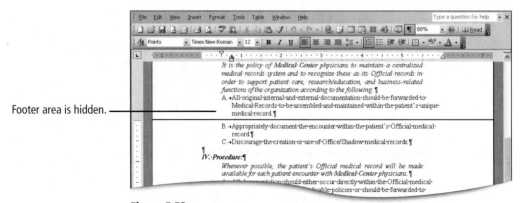

Footer area is hidden.

**Figure 5.53**

**6** Move the pointer over the black line between the two pages and click.

The gap between the pages displays again.

## Activity 5.17 Splitting the Window

**1** At the top of the vertical scroll bar, above the arrow, locate the small gray bar, called a ***split box***, and then move the pointer over the split box.

The pointer changes to a Resize Pointer, an up- and down-pointing arrow, as shown in Figure 5.54.

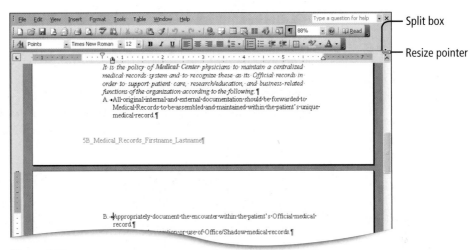

**Figure 5.54**

**2** With the Resize pointer displayed, drag about half way down the screen and release the mouse button.

The window splits in two, with a separate vertical and horizontal scroll bar for each portion of the window, as shown in Figure 5.55.

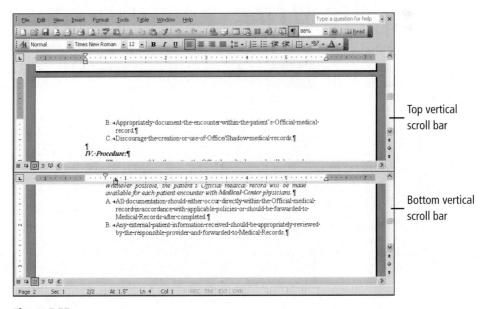

**Figure 5.55**

**3** Use the top vertical scroll bar to scroll to the top of the document.

**4** Use the bottom vertical scroll bar to scroll to the last section of the document, beginning with the *IV. Procedure* heading.

You can work on one part of the document while viewing another part, and you can cut or copy and paste between the two windows. If you are working in one window, you will need to click in the other window to make it active.

**5** In the upper window, move the pointer slightly below the horizontal scroll bar until the Resize pointer displays.

**6** Double-click or, alternatively, drag the bar to the top of the screen.

The second window is closed.

**7** From the **View** menu, click **Header and Footer**. On the Header and Footer toolbar, click the **Switch Between Header and Footer** button ⊡.

**8** On the **Header and Footer** toolbar, click the **Insert AutoText** button Insert AutoText ▾ , and then click **Filename**. On the **Header and Footer** toolbar, click the **Close** button Close .

**9** On the Standard toolbar, click the **Save** button 🖫.

**10** On the Standard toolbar, click the **Print Preview** button 🔍. Take a moment to check your work. On the Print Preview toolbar, click the **Close Preview** button Close .

**11** Make any necessary changes to your document, and then, on the Standard toolbar, click the **Print** button 🖨.

**12** On the far right edge of the menu bar, click the **Close Window** button ✕.

**End** You have completed Project 5B ─────────────────────────

# Project 5C **Policy Outline**

Outlines can help you organize the content of a document and provide a structure for writing. Microsoft Word has a built-in outline format that can be applied to documents.

In Activities 5.18 through 5.19, you will create a multilevel outline for a portion of a medical center policy manual. The manual will have eight sections, but the outline you will create will be for the Medical Center Facilities and Services section. Your completed document will look similar to Figure 5.56. You will save your document as *5C_Policy_Outline_Firstname_Lastname.*

**MEDICAL CENTER POLICY AND PROCEDURE MANUAL**

I. MEDICAL CENTER ADMINISTRATION
II. FACULTY POLICIES
III. STAFF POLICIES
IV. MEDICAL CENTER FACILITIES AND SERVICES
    **A. Equipment Center**
       1. Equipment Center Overview
       2. Checkout Procedures
       3. Equipment Purchases
       4. Equipment Repair
    **B. Medical Communications**
       1. Medical Communications Overview
       2. Medical Illustration Policies and Procedures
       3. Waiver Procedures
    **C. Medical Center Libraries**
       1. Graduate Library Policy and Procedures
       2. Medical Library Policy and Procedures
    **D. Space and Facilities**
       1. Medical Center Space Inventory
       2. Storage in Corridors
       3. Vacated Space
       4. Environmental Services
       5. Facilities Maintenance
       6. Cleanup Procedures
V. FINANCIAL MANAGEMENT
VI. HUMAN RESOURCES
VII. SAFETY AND SECURITY
VIII. FORMS

5C_Policy_Outline_Firstname_Lastname

**Figure 5.56**
Project 5C—Policy Outline

## Objective 7
## Create an Outline

An **outline** is a list of topics for an oral or written report that visually indicates the order in which the information will be discussed, and the relationship of the topics to each other and to the total report. Outlines are used in planning situations to organize and rearrange information. The most basic outline is a numbered list, which has only one outline level. Word provides up to nine levels in an outline.

### Activity 5.18  Creating a Multilevel Outline

The first step in creating an outline is to define the outline format.

**1** On the Standard toolbar, click the **Open** button. Navigate to the location where the student files for this textbook are stored. Locate and open **w05C_Policy_Outline**. Save the file as **5C_Policy_Outline_Firstname_Lastname**

**2** Click to position the insertion point to the left of the second line, which begins *Medical Center Administration*. Using the scroll bar, scroll down to the end of the document, hold down the Shift key, point to end of the last line, and then click again.

All of the text, with the exception of the title, is selected.

**3** On the **Format** menu, click **Bullets and Numbering**. In the displayed **Bullets and Numbering** dialog box, click the **Outline Numbered tab**. Click the second option in the first row.

The Bullets and Numbering dialog box should look like Figure 5.57. If the second option in the first row does not match the figure, see Step 4.

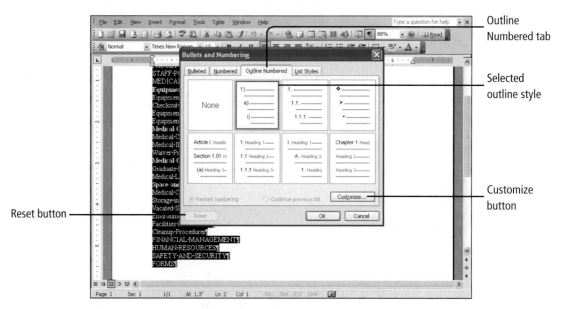

Figure 5.57

**4** Locate the **Reset** button at the bottom of the **Bullets and Numbering** dialog box. If the **Reset** button is active (dark), click it, and then click **Yes** when prompted to restore the default settings. If the **Reset** button is light gray, the button is inactive.

If someone has adjusted the outline settings on your computer, it is a good idea to restore the outline default settings.

**5** In the lower right corner of the **Bullets and Numbering** dialog box, click the **Customize** button.

The Customize Outline Numbered List dialog box displays. Under Number format, the Level starts at 1 by default. All formatting that you do will affect only the selected outline level.

**6** Under **Number format**, in the **Number style** box, click the arrow, and then click **I, II, III** from the list. In the **Number format** box, place the insertion point to the right of the parenthesis mark and press ⎗Bksp. Type a period.

Notice the format displayed in the Preview area.

**7** Under **Number format**, in the **Number position** box, click the arrow, and then click **Right** from the list. Under **Text position**, click the **Indent at spin box up arrow** to set the indent at **0.3"**.

In a formal outline, the Roman numerals should align on the decimal. These numbers need a little extra space to fit properly. Compare your Customize Outline Numbered List dialog box with Figure 5.58.

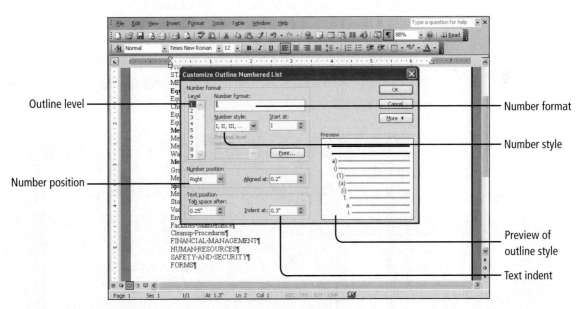

**Figure 5.58**

⬛ Under **Number format**, in the **Level** box, click **2**. In the **Number style** box, click the arrow, and then click **A, B, C** from the list. In the **Number format** box, place the insertion point to the right of the parenthesis mark and press Bksp. Type a period.

Compare your Customize Outline Numbered List dialog box with Figure 5.59.

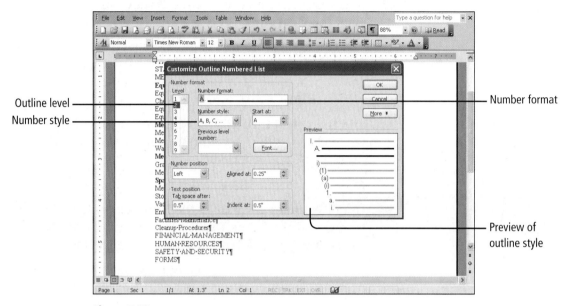

**Figure 5.59**

⬛ Under **Number format**, in the **Level** box, click **3**. In the **Number style** box, click the arrow, and then click **1, 2, 3** from the list. In the **Number format** box, place the insertion point to the right of the parenthesis mark and press Bksp. Type a period.

Compare your Customize Outline Numbered List dialog box with Figure 5.60.

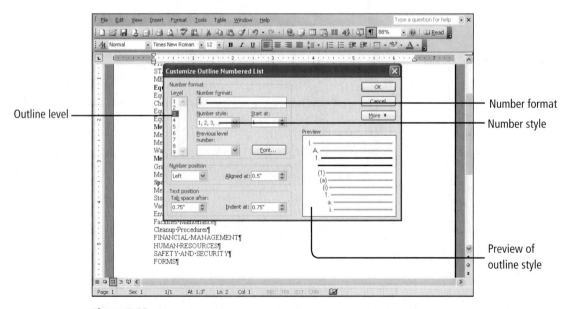

**Figure 5.60**

**10** In the upper right corner of the **Customize Outline Numbered List** dialog box, click **OK**. Hold down Ctrl and press Home.

The outline is created, but all items are at the top level—not visually indented to show different levels. See Figure 5.61.

Selected text is numbered. ——

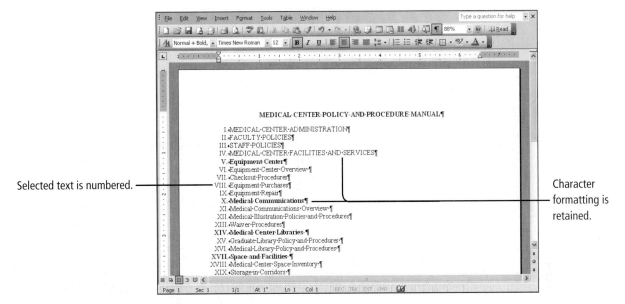

Character formatting is retained.

**Figure 5.61**

**11** On the Standard toolbar, click the **Save** button.

### Activity 5.19 Setting Outline Levels

After you set up a list as a multilevel outline, you can use the Increase Indent and Decrease Indent buttons on the Formatting toolbar to change outline levels. In this activity, you will set the lines shown in all caps at outline Level 1, the entries shown in bold at outline Level 2, and the entries shown in Normal text at outline Level 3.

**1** Click to position the insertion point anywhere in the paragraph beginning *V. Equipment Center*.

You do not need to select the entire paragraph to change the outline level.

**2** On the Formatting toolbar, click the **Increase Indent** button.

The line is indented 0.25 inch, and the number changes from *V* to *A*, a second-level outline entry. See Figure 5.62.

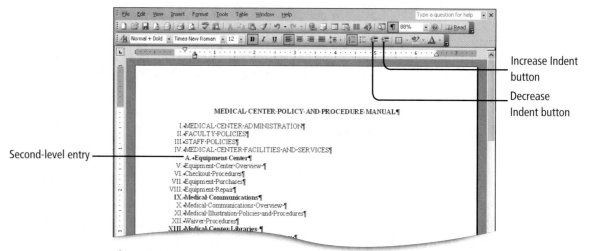

Second-level entry ————

Increase Indent button

Decrease Indent button

**Figure 5.62**

■3■ Move the pointer into the left margin to the left of the next line beginning *Equipment Center Overview*. When the pointer changes to a
white arrow, drag down to select that paragraph and the next three.

Four lines are selected.

■4■ On the Formatting toolbar, click the **Increase Indent** button ▣ twice.

All four lines become third-level outline entries, as shown in
Figure 5.63.

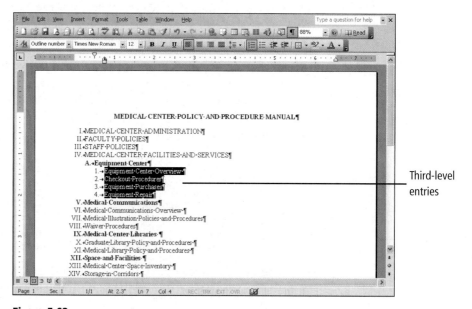

Third-level entries

**Figure 5.63**

■5■ Continue setting outline levels for the remainder of the document.
Recall that text in all caps retains its first-level setting, text in bold
should be set at the second level, and normal text should be set at

the third level. Use the **Increase Indent** button ▣ once on the bold
text and twice on the normal text.

On the Standard toolbar, click the **Show/Hide** button to hide the nonprinting characters.

Compare your outline with Figure 5.64. Notice that the first-level entries align on the decimal points, not the left margin. This is the proper format of a formal outline.

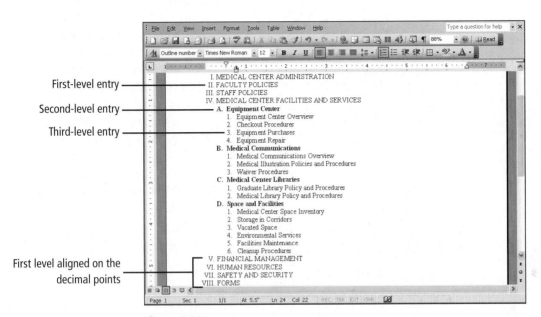

First-level entry

Second-level entry

Third-level entry

First level aligned on the decimal points

**Figure 5.64**

On the Standard toolbar, click the **Show/Hide** button to display the nonprinting characters again. From the **View** menu, click **Header and Footer**. On the Header and Footer toolbar, click the **Switch Between Header and Footer** button.

On the **Header and Footer** toolbar, click the **Insert AutoText** button `Insert AutoText ▾`, and then click **Filename**. On the **Header and Footer** toolbar, click the **Close** button `Close`.

On the Standard toolbar, click the **Save** button.

On the Standard toolbar, click the **Print Preview** button. Take a moment to check your work. On the Print Preview toolbar, click the **Close Preview** button `Close`.

Make any necessary changes to your document, and then, on the Standard toolbar, click the **Print** button.

On the far right edge of the menu bar, click the **Close Window** button `✕`.

**End** You have completed Project 5C

# Project 5D  Fitness

The Outline View enables you to use the Outlining toolbar to quickly create an outline based on heading styles. This outline can be rearranged, and heading levels can be changed with the click of a button.

In Activities 5.20 through 5.21 you will use the Outline View and the Outlining toolbar to create an outline for a summer fitness program at the University Medical Center. You will format existing text using the Outline toolbar, and you will modify and rearrange the outline. Your completed document will look similar to Figure 5.65. You will save your document as *5D_Fitness_Program_Firstname_Lastname.*

## Summer Sports and Fitness Program

The University Medical Center will off a full range of sports, fitness, and dance programs beginning after Memorial Day. The following programs are offered to all Medical Center staff and their families at no cost.

### Sports

Competitive sports will be offered in the mornings this summer. Slots fill up very quickly, especially for golf and tennis.

#### Golf

All rounds will be played on the University golf course on Monday and Wednesday mornings, except the week of the tournament. All participants will play in foursomes. Tee times will be at 6 a.m., 8 a.m., and 10 a.m.

#### Tennis

Matches will be played on the tennis courts at the IM building. If demand is great enough, the courts behind Married Housing will also be available. Court times will be assigned in one hour blocks on Monday or Thursday evenings. Players need to specify whether they are interested in singles, doubles, or mixed

#### Rowing

There were not a lot of people interested in two- and this summer only kayak racing will be offered. The ti determined.

### Fitness

#### Swimming

All swimming events will be held at the Natatorium pool will be used most of the summer by the high sch Summer Quest program. Free swimming will be avai Swimmersize classes will be held at noon on Monday The number of fitness programs has been increased b sessions last summer.

#### Aerobics

The aerobics program has not been finalized.

#### Martial Arts

The martial arts program has not been finalized.

5D_Fitness_Firstname_Lastname

#### Kickboxing

Kickboxing has become extremely popular with young adults and additional classes will be considered. The classes are currently scheduled on Wednesday evening and Saturday morning.

### Dance

#### Jazz and Tap

#### West Coast Swing

#### Ballroom Dance

5D_Fitness_Firstname_Lastname

**Figure 5.65**
Project 5D—Fitness

## Objective 8
## Create an Outline Using the Outline View and the Outlining Toolbar

When you display a document in Word's Outline View, Word treats each paragraph as a separate topic to which you can apply either Heading or Body Text styles. Word's built-in Heading 1 style represents the highest heading level, called Level 1, in an outline.

### Activity 5.20 Creating an Outline Using the Outlining Toolbar

An outline created using the Outline View and the Outlining toolbar enables you to look at sections of a document, and move all of the text under a heading by clicking that heading.

**1** On the Standard toolbar, click the **Open** button . Navigate to the location where the student files for this textbook are stored. Locate and open **w05D_Fitness**. Save the file as **5D_Fitness_Firstname_Lastname**

**2** To the left of the horizontal scroll bar, click the **Outline View** button . To the left of the Formatting toolbar, click the **Styles and Formatting** button .

The document displays in Outline View. The Outlining toolbar displays under the Formatting toolbar and the Styles and Formatting task pane displays on the right of the screen.

**3** Display the style area on the left of the screen by displaying the **Tools** menu, and then clicking **Options**. Click the **View tab**. Under **Outline and Normal options**, click the **Style area width spin box up arrow** until the style area width is **0.5"**. At the bottom of the **Options** dialog box, click **OK**.

In Outline View, each paragraph is considered a topic, and will be preceded by a symbol. If the paragraph does not have a Heading style, it is considered **body text**, and the symbol is a small box called a **topic marker**. Compare your screen with Figure 5.66.

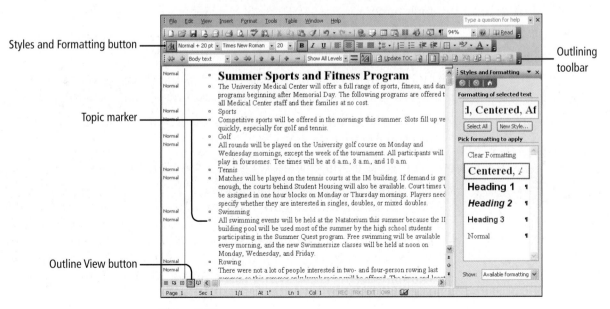

Styles and Formatting button

Topic marker

Outline View button

Outlining toolbar

**Figure 5.66**

**4** Click to position the insertion point in the fifth line of the document, which contains only the word *Sports*. In the Styles and Formatting task pane, under **Pick formatting to apply**, click **Heading 1**.

The paragraph changes to the Heading 1 style. The outline level, Level 1, displays in the Outline Level box. An open plus symbol, called an ***Expand button***, replaces the topic marker to the left of the paragraph, as shown in Figure 5.67. The expand button indicates that there is lower-level text associated with this heading, which in this instance is the remaining text in the document.

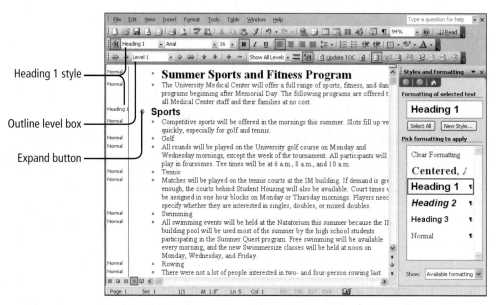

Heading 1 style

Outline level box

Expand button

**Figure 5.67**

**5** Scroll down and click to position the insertion point in the line that contains only the word *Fitness*. Press F4—the Repeat key. Repeat this process to change the *Kickboxing* line to a **Heading 1** style. Alternatively, click the Heading 1 style in the Styles and Formatting task pane.

The F4 button repeats the immediately-preceding command, in this instance the application of the Heading 1 style.

**6** Hold down Ctrl and press Home. Position the insertion point in the eighth line of the document, which contains only the word *Golf*.

Notice that this line currently uses the Normal style, and has a topic marker on the left.

**7** On the Outlining toolbar, click the **Demote** button ➡.

The paragraph changes to a Heading 2 style. The outline level is Level 2, as shown in Figure 5.68. All of the text following the word *Golf*, up to but not including the next heading, is also demoted and is treated as subordinate text to the *Golf* heading. The Demote and Promote buttons can be used to set the outline level of existing text, or you may find it faster to use the Styles and Formatting task pane along with the F4 key.

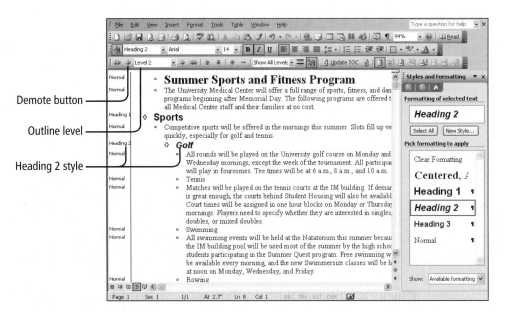

**Figure 5.68**

**8** Click to position the insertion point in the line that contains only the word *Tennis*. In the **Styles and Formatting** task pane, under **Pick formatting to apply**, click **Heading 2**.

**9** Scroll down and position the insertion point in the line that contains only the word *Swimming*. Press F4. Continue this process to the end of the document, changing *Rowing*, *Aerobics*, and *Martial Arts* to a **Heading 2** style. Hold down Ctrl and press Home.

Compare your document with Figure 5.69.

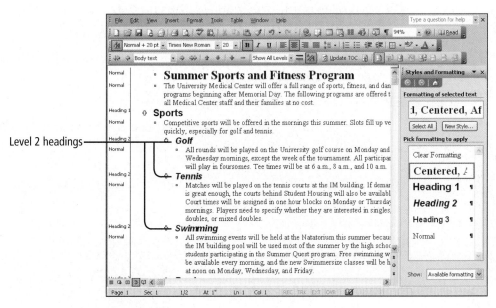

**Figure 5.69**

**10** On the Standard toolbar, click the **Save** button.

## Activity 5.21 Modifying an Outline in Outline View

In Outline View, you can change heading levels, rearrange headings in an existing outline, and show only the parts of the outline you want to see. You can also enter new text in the outline.

**1** To the left of the *Swimming* heading, click the **Expand** button.

The heading, along with all of its subordinate text (and headings if there were any) are selected, as shown in Figure 5.70.

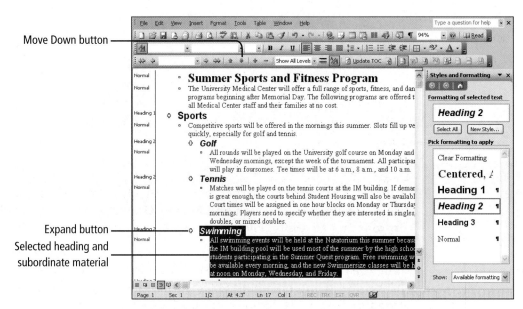

Figure 5.70

**2** Scroll down until you can see the end of the document. On the Outlining toolbar, click the **Move Down** button [⬇].

The Swimming heading and the subordinate paragraph move down one topic (paragraph).

**3** Click the **Move Down** button [⬇] twice more.

The *Swimming* heading and related text are moved to the *Fitness* section, as shown in Figure 5.71.

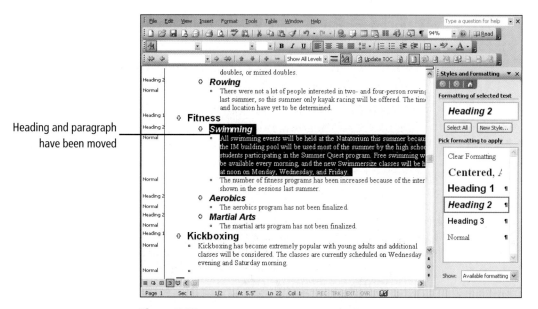

**Heading and paragraph have been moved**

**Figure 5.71**

4️⃣ Click to position the insertion point in the *Kickboxing* heading.

On the Outlining toolbar, click the **Demote** button 🔲.

The Kickboxing heading changes from a Heading 1 style to a Heading 2 style, and from Level 1 to Level 2. It is now subordinate to (a lower level than) the Fitness heading. See Figure 5.72.

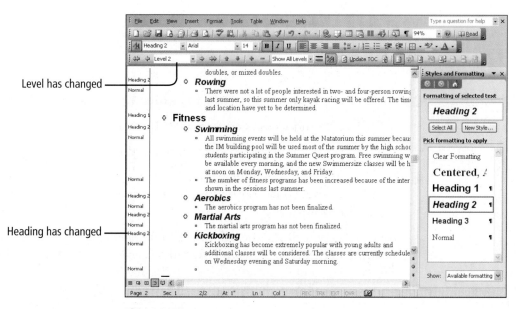

**Level has changed**

**Heading has changed**

**Figure 5.72**

**5** Hold down Ctrl and press Home. Hold down Ctrl and press A to select the entire document. On the Outlining toolbar, click the **Show Level button arrow** Show All Levels ▼ , and then click **Show Level 2**. Click anywhere to deselect the text.

Everything at Level 2 and higher is displayed, as shown in Figure 5.73. Headings underlined with wavy lines indicate that subordinate body text exists, but is currently hidden from view. In this manner, you can view the overall sections of your report (or presentation) without the clutter of the remaining text.

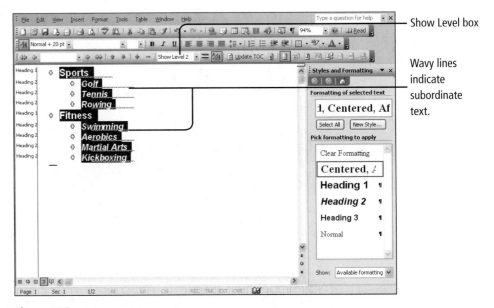

— Show Level box

Wavy lines indicate subordinate text.

**Figure 5.73**

**6** On the Outlining toolbar, click the **Show Level button arrow** Show Level 2 ▼ , and then click **Show All Levels**.

The headings and body text are all displayed.

**7** Near the top of the document, position the pointer over the **Expand** button to the left of the *Sports* heading. Double-click the **Expand** button.

All of the subordinate headings and text associated with the *Sports* heading are hidden—this is referred to as being **collapsed**. The Fitness heading is not affected. See Figure 5.74.

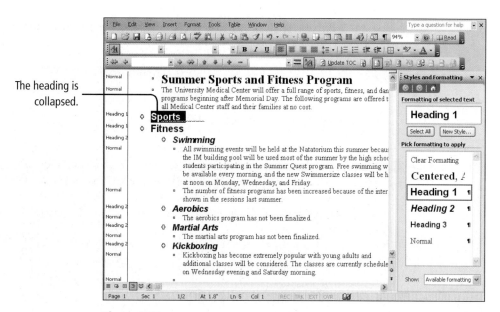

The heading is collapsed.

**Figure 5.74**

**8** Press Ctrl + End to position the insertion point at the end of the last line of the document, and then press Enter. Click the **Promote** button ⬅ twice. Type **Dance**

A new Level 1 heading is created.

**9** Press Enter. Click the **Demote** button ➡ and type **Jazz and Tap**

A new Level 2 heading is created.

**10** Press Enter and type **West Coast Swing** Press Enter again and type **Ballroom Dance**

The Dance heading now has three Level 2 headings under it. The Level 2 headings have no subordinate headings or text, indicated by a *Collapse button* to the left of each, as shown in Figure 5.75.

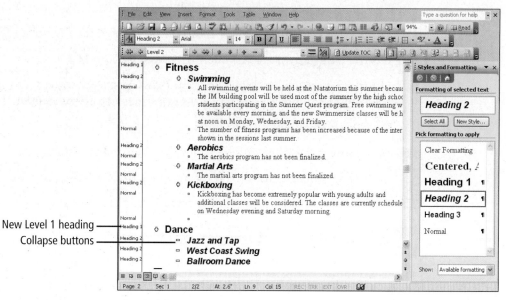

New Level 1 heading

Collapse buttons

**Figure 5.75**

**11** To the left of the Formatting toolbar, click the **Styles and Formatting** button 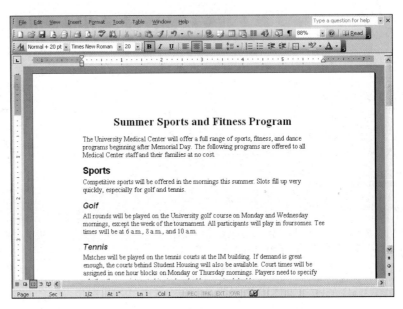 to close the Styles and Formatting task bar. To the left of the horizontal scroll bar, click the **Print Layout View** button. Hold down Ctrl and press Home.

Compare your document with Figure 5.76.

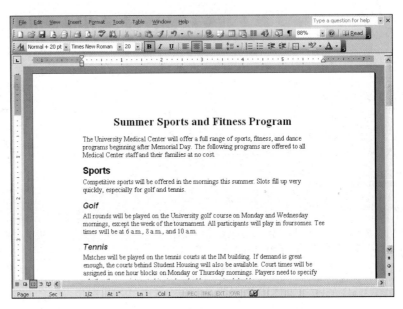

**Figure 5.76**

**12** From the **View** menu, click **Header and Footer**. On the Header and Footer toolbar, click the **Switch Between Header and Footer** button.

**13** On the **Header and Footer** toolbar, click the **Insert AutoText** button Insert AutoText ▾, and then click **Filename**.

The file name is inserted in the footer.

**14** On the **Header and Footer** toolbar, click the **Close** button Close.

**15** On the Standard toolbar, click the **Save** button.

**16** On the Standard toolbar, click the **Print Preview** button. Take a moment to check your work. On the Print Preview toolbar, click the **Close Preview** button Close.

**17** Make any necessary changes to your document. When you are satisfied, on the Standard toolbar, click the **Print** button.

**18** On the menu bar, click the **Close** button, saving any changes.

**End** **You have completed Project 5D** ————————————

# Summary

In this chapter, you used the Microsoft Graph program to create a chart from data displayed in a table. After the chart was created, you modified the elements of the chart by adding a title, changing the chart type, changing the font size and color and changing the size and placement of the chart in your document.

Some new character effects were demonstrated, including adding a drop cap to the first letter in the first paragraph of a document, adding a shadow effect to a title, and changing the character spacing in a paragraph.

Styles were introduced as a method to apply uniform formatting to long documents to achieve a consistent appearance. You practiced how to apply existing styles, set new styles, and modify styles for paragraph, character, and list style formats.

Techniques for modifying the Word window were demonstrated, including splitting a window so you can see the top and bottom of a document at the same time, and hiding the white space when you are in Print Layout view so that more text displays on the screen.

Finally, you practiced using a multilevel outline by modifying the outline format and applying it to text in a document. You also created an outline in the Outline View, and practiced changing ouline levels and moving blocks of text by move outline headings.

## In This Chapter You Practiced How To

- Create a Chart with Microsoft Graph
- Format a Chart
- Add Special Text Effects
- Use Existing Styles
- Create and Modify New Styles
- Modify the Document Window
- Create an Outline
- Create an Outline Using the Outline View and the Outlining Toolbar

**Matching**  Match each term in the second column with its correct definition in the first column by writing the letter of the term on the blank line in front of the correct definition.

_____ 1. A built-in feature of Word that is used to create charts.

_____ 2. A type of chart that shows comparison among data.

_____ 3. A type of chart that shows trends over time.

_____ 4. A type of chart that shows the proportion of parts to the whole.

_____ 5. A table-like structure that is part of the Microsoft Graph program in which you can enter the numbers used to create a chart.

_____ 6. The chart element that relates the data displayed to the categories.

_____ 7. The area on a chart where the graphic (pie or column) is placed, which can be resized by using sizing handles.

_____ 8. A text effect that adds a silhouette behind the letters.

_____ 9. A group of formatting commands that are stored with a specific name and can be retrieved and applied to text.

_____ 10. A type of style that controls the font, font size, and font style applied to individual characters.

_____ 11. The default Word template.

_____ 12. A list of topics that visually indicates the order in which information in an oral or written report will be presented and the relationship of the topics to each other.

_____ 13. The dialog box used to create an outline.

_____ 14. In the Styles and Formatting task pane, the term that describes the items listed under _Pick formatting to apply_.

_____ 15. An enlarged letter positioned at the beginning of text and displayed on several lines.

**A** Bullets and Numbering

**B** Character style

**C** Column

**D** Datasheet

**E** Drop cap

**F** Legend

**G** Line

**H** Microsoft Graph

**I** Normal

**J** Outline

**K** Pie

**L** Plot area

**M** Shadow

**N** Style

**O** Style names

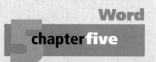

**Fill in the Blank** Write the correct answer in the space provided.

1. The data along the bottom of a chart displays in the
_____ axis.

2. The numbers along the left side of a chart display in the
_____ axis.

3. The numbers on the left side of a chart are called a(n)
_____ because they display a range of numbers.

4. A large first letter used to begin the first paragraph in a chapter or
article is known as a _____.

5. Increasing or decreasing the space between letters is accomplished
by changing the _____ spacing.

6. The information that determines the basic structure and format
of a document is known as a _____.

7. To change the line spacing, indents, alignment, and tab stops, you
could change the _____ style.

8. A quick way to create a new style is to set the style, and then type
a name in the _____ box.

9. An item in an outline can be moved to a lower level by clicking the
_____ button.

10. In the Styles and Formatting task pane, you can click the arrow
at the right end of a selected style and choose _____
to change the style.

## Project 5E — Service Area

**Objectives:** *Create a Chart with Microsoft Graph, Format a Chart, Add Special Text Effects, Use Existing Styles, Create and Modify New Styles, Modify the Document Window, and Create an Outline.*

In the following Skill Assessment, you will create and modify a pie chart that shows the geographic distribution of patients in the University Medical Center service area. Your completed document will look similar to the one shown in Figure 5.77. You will save your document as *5E_Service_Area_Firstname_Lastname.*

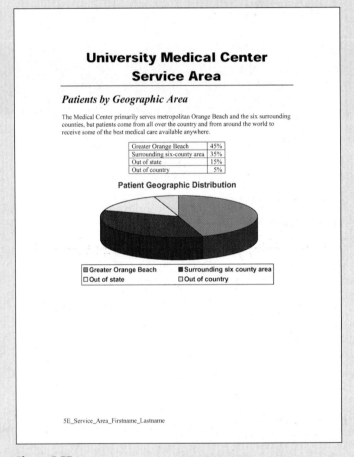

**Figure 5.77**

1. On the Standard toolbar, click the **Open** button. Navigate to the location where the student files for this textbook are stored. Locate and open **w05E_Service_Area**. Save the file as **5E_Service_Area_Firstname_Lastname**

2. In the table, click anywhere to position the insertion point in the table. From the **Table** menu, point to **Select**, and then click **Table**.

**(Project 5E–Service Area continues on the next page)**

**(Project 5E–Service Area continued)**

3. From the **Insert** menu, point to **Picture**, and then click **Chart**. The Microsoft Graph program displays and the data from the table displays in the datasheet.

4. Be sure that your Standard and Formatting toolbars are displayed on two rows. (If only one toolbar row is displayed on your screen, at the right end of the toolbar, click the Toolbar Options button, and then click Show Buttons on Two Rows.)

5. Click anywhere inside the **datasheet**, and then on the datasheet title bar, click the **Close** button. On the Chart toolbar, click the **By Column** button. Recall that the data must be displayed by column before you can change the default column chart into another type of chart.

6. On the Chart toolbar, click the **Chart Type arrow**, and then in the fifth row, click the second button—the **3-D Pie Chart**. Use the ScreenTip to help identify the chart type. The chart display changes to a pie chart. On the Standard toolbar, click the **Save** button.

7. From the **Chart** menu, click **Chart Options**. If necessary, in the Chart Options dialog box, click the Titles tab. Alternatively, right-click on the chart and click Chart Options from the shortcut menu. Click in the **Chart title** box, type **Patient Geographic Distribution** and then click **OK**.

8. Right-click the **Chart Title** and from the shortcut menu click **Format Chart Title**. In the **Format Chart Title** dialog box, click the **Font tab**. The font displayed is Arial, Bold, 10 pt. Click the **Color arrow**. From the displayed palette, in the second row, click the sixth color—**Blue**. Click **OK**.

9. Right-click the **Legend** and from the shortcut menu click **Format Legend**. In the **Format Legend** dialog box, click the **Placement tab**, and then click the **Bottom** option button. From this dialog box, you can move the legend to different areas on the chart. Click **OK**.

10. Drag the lower right sizing handle of the chart box down and to the right until the right edge of the chart area is at approximately **6 inches on the horizontal ruler** and the lower edge of the chart is at approximately **6 inches on the vertical ruler**.

11. Right-click in the **Plot Area**—the gray area behind the pie chart—and click **Format Plot Area** from the shortcut menu. Under **Border**, click **None**. Under **Area**, click **None**, and then click **OK**.

12. Click in the body of the document to close the Microsoft Graph program and return to the document window. Click on the chart once to select it, and then on the Formatting toolbar click the **Center** button to center the chart on the page. Compare your screen with Figure 5.77.

**(Project 5E–Service Area continues on the next page)**

**(Project 5E–Service Area continued)**

**13.** From the **View** menu, display the Header and Footer toolbar, switch to the footer, and then, on the Header and Footer toolbar, click **Insert AutoText**. From the displayed list, click **Filename**. Close the Header and Footer toolbar.

**14.** On the Standard toolbar, click the **Save** button, and then click the **Print Preview** button to see the document as it will print. Click the **Print** button, and then close the file, saving changes if prompted to do so.

**End** You have completed Project 5E

# Project 5F—Child Care

**Objectives:** *Add Special Text Effects, Create an Outline, and Modify the Document Window.*

In the following Skill Assessment, you will format a multilevel outline of the topics for a child care symposium that is being held by the University Medical Center. You will also add a drop cap to the title. Your completed document will look similar to the one shown in Figure 5.78. You will save your document as *5F_Child_Care_Firstname_Lastname.*

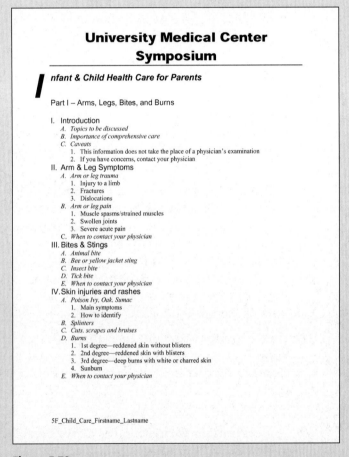

**Figure 5.78**

1. On the Standard toolbar, click the **Open** button. Navigate to the location where the student files for this textbook are stored. Locate and open **w05F_Child_Care**. Save the file as **5F_Child_Care_Firstname_Lastname**

2. Be sure the document is in **Print Layout View**. If necessary, change the Zoom setting to Page Width. Move the mouse pointer to the top edge of the document until you see the *Hide White Space* pointer, and then click. This will maximize your viewing area.

**(Project 5F–Child Care continues on the next page)**

**(Project 5F–Child Care continued)**

3. Notice that the lines in the body of the document are formatted in three ways—Arial 14 pt., Times New Roman italic 12 pt., and Times New Roman 12 pt. (no emphasis). Select the line *Infant & Child Health for Parents*. From the **Format** menu, click **Drop Cap**. In the **Drop Cap** dialog box, under **Position**, click **In margin**. Under **Options**, change the **Lines to drop** box to **2**, and then click **OK**.

4. Near the top of the document, click to position the insertion point to the left of *Introduction*. Use the scroll bar to view the end of the document, position the pointer to the right of the last word in the document, hold down Shift, and then click to select all the text from *Introduction* to the end.

5. With the text still selected, on the **Format** menu, click **Bullets and Numbering**. If necessary, in the Bullets and Numbering dialog box, click the Outline Numbered tab. In the first row, click the second **Outline Numbered** box. At the bottom of the **Bullets and Numbering** dialog box, check to see if the **Reset** button is active (not gray), and if it is, click it, and then click **Yes** when prompted to restore the default settings.

6. In the lower right, click the **Customize** button. Under **Number format**, in the **Number style** box, click the arrow, and then click **I, II, III** from the list. In the **Number format** box, place the insertion point to the right of the parenthesis mark and press Bksp. Type a period. Under **Number format**, in the **Number position** box, click the arrow, and then click **Right** from the list. Under **Text position**, click the **Indent at spin box up arrow** to set the indent at **0.3"**. The first level of the outline format is set.

7. Under **Number format**, in the **Level** box, click **2**. In the **Number style** box, click the arrow, and then click **A, B, C** from the list. In the **Number format** box, place the insertion point to the right of the parenthesis mark and press Bksp. Type a period. The second level of the outline format is set.

8. Under **Number format**, in the **Level** box, click **3**. In the **Number style** box, click the arrow, and then click **1, 2, 3** from the list. In the **Number format** box, place the insertion point to the right of the parenthesis mark and press Bksp. Type a period. In the upper right corner of the **Customize Outline Numbered List** dialog box, click **OK**.

9. Hold down Ctrl and press Home. On the Standard toolbar, click the **Save** button. Click to position the insertion point to the left of the paragraph beginning *II. Topics to be discussed* and drag down to select the next two lines, ending with *IV. Caveats.* (The Roman numerals will not be selected.) On the Formatting toolbar, click the **Increase Indent** button. These items become A.–C. Recall that the Increase Indent button is used to move items in an outline to a lower level.

**(Project 5F–Child Care continued)**

10. Move the pointer into the selection area to the left of the paragraph that begins *II. This information* and select that line and the following line. On the Formatting toolbar, click the **Increase Indent** button twice. These two lines are changed to the third level in the outline and become 1.–2.

11. Locate and select the remaining lines displayed in Times New Roman 12 pt. italic and set them to outline level two. (Hint: Hold down  and select each italic line.) Click Increase Indent once to get the result A. B. C. and so forth. Use the same technique to locate and select the remaining lines displayed in Times New Roman without emphasis, and then set them to outline level three (click Increase Indent twice to get the result 1. 2. 3. and so forth). Compare your document with Figure 5.78.

12. From the **View** menu, display the Header and Footer toolbar, switch to the footer and then, on the Header and Footer toolbar, click **Insert AutoText**. From the displayed list, click **Filename**. Close the Header and Footer toolbar.

13. On the Standard toolbar, click the **Save** button, and then click the **Print Preview** button to see the document as it will print. Click the **Print** button, and then close the file, saving changes if prompted to do so.

**End** You have completed Project 5F

## Project 5G—Art Program

**Objectives:** *Use Existing Styles and Create and Modify New Styles.*

In the following Skill Assessment, you will format an informational flyer about the University Medical Center arts program. You will use existing styles, create new styles, and modify a style. Your completed document will look similar to the one shown in Figure 5.79. You will save your document as *5G_Art_Program_Firstname_Lastname.*

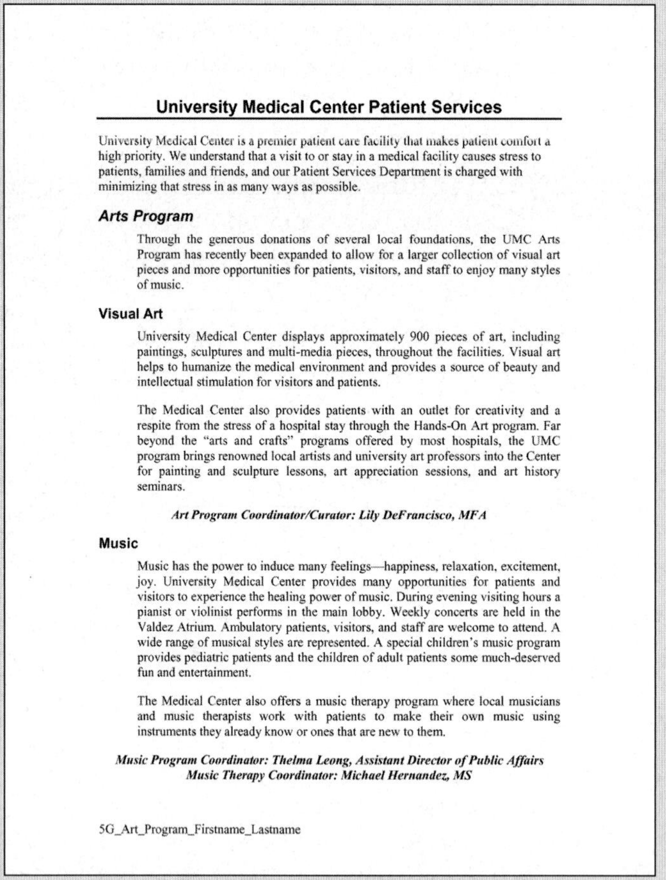

**University Medical Center Patient Services**

University Medical Center is a premier patient care facility that makes patient comfort a high priority. We understand that a visit to or stay in a medical facility causes stress to patients, families and friends, and our Patient Services Department is charged with minimizing that stress in as many ways as possible.

**Arts Program**

Through the generous donations of several local foundations, the UMC Arts Program has recently been expanded to allow for a larger collection of visual art pieces and more opportunities for patients, visitors, and staff to enjoy many styles of music.

**Visual Art**

University Medical Center displays approximately 900 pieces of art, including paintings, sculptures and multi-media pieces, throughout the facilities. Visual art helps to humanize the medical environment and provides a source of beauty and intellectual stimulation for visitors and patients.

The Medical Center also provides patients with an outlet for creativity and a respite from the stress of a hospital stay through the Hands-On Art program. Far beyond the "arts and crafts" programs offered by most hospitals, the UMC program brings renowned local artists and university art professors into the Center for painting and sculpture lessons, art appreciation sessions, and art history seminars.

*Art Program Coordinator/Curator: Lily DeFrancisco, MFA*

**Music**

Music has the power to induce many feelings—happiness, relaxation, excitement, joy. University Medical Center provides many opportunities for patients and visitors to experience the healing power of music. During evening visiting hours a pianist or violinist performs in the main lobby. Weekly concerts are held in the Valdez Atrium. Ambulatory patients, visitors, and staff are welcome to attend. A wide range of musical styles are represented. A special children's music program provides pediatric patients and the children of adult patients some much-deserved fun and entertainment.

The Medical Center also offers a music therapy program where local musicians and music therapists work with patients to make their own music using instruments they already know or ones that are new to them.

*Music Program Coordinator: Thelma Leong, Assistant Director of Public Affairs*
*Music Therapy Coordinator: Michael Hernandez, MS*

5G_Art_Program_Firstname_Lastname

**Figure 5.79**

1. On the Standard toolbar, click the **Open** button. Navigate to the location where the student files for this textbook are stored. Locate and open **w05G_Art_Program**. Save the file as **5G_Art_Program_Firstname_Lastname**

2. To the left of the horizontal scroll bar, click the **Normal View** button. From the **Tools** menu, click **Options**. Be sure the **View tab** is selected. At the bottom of the **View tab**, under **Outline and Normal options**, click the **Style area width spin box arrows** as necessary until the width is **0.6"**. Click **OK**.

**(Project 5G–Art Program continues on the next page)**

**(Project 5G–Art Program continued)**

3. On the left side of the Formatting toolbar, click the **Styles and Formatting** button. If the right edge of the text is hidden behind the task pane, on the Standard toolbar, click the Zoom button arrow, and then click Page Width.

4. Click anywhere in the first line, *University Medical Center Patient Services*. In the **Styles and Formatting** task pane, under **Pick formatting to apply**, click **Heading 1**. Click anywhere in the line *Arts Program*, and then click **Heading 2**. Click in the line *Visual Art*, and then click **Heading 3**. Scroll down the page, click in the line *Music*, and then click **Heading 3**. You have now completed applying existing heading styles to the major headings in this document.

5. Scroll to the top of the document, locate the paragraph beginning *Through the generous*, and then triple-click in the paragraph to select it. From the **Format** menu, click **Paragraph**. If necessary, click the **Indents and Spacing tab**. Under **General**, click the **Alignment arrow**, and then click **Justified**. Under **Indentation**, click the **Left spin box up arrow** to set the left indent at **0.5"**. Under **Spacing**, click the **Before spin box up arrow** to set the Before spacing to **6 pt**. Click the **After spin box up arrow** to set the After spacing to **12 pt**. Click **OK**.

6. With the paragraph still selected, in the **Styles and Formatting** task pane, under **Formatting of selected text**, click the **New Style** button. In the **New Style** dialog box, under **Properties**, in the **Name** box, type **Para** and then click **OK**. In the **Styles and Formatting** task pane, click the **Para** style. Recall that after you create a style, you must click it to apply the style to the selected paragraph.

7. Click in the first paragraph under *Visual Art* that begins *University Medical Center*, and then from the **Styles and Formatting** task pane, under **Pick formatting to apply**, click **Para**. Click in the next paragraph that begins *The Medical Center*, and then click **Para**. Scroll down until the paragraphs under the *Music* heading are displayed on your screen. Move the mouse pointer to the left margin until it changes to a white selection arrow, and then drag to select the first two paragraphs under *Music*, beginning with *Music has the power*. From the **Styles and Formatting** task pane, click **Para**.

8. Just above the *Music* heading, select the one-line paragraph that begins *Art Program Coordinator*. In the **Styles and Formatting** task pane, click the **New Style** button. In the displayed **New Style** dialog box, under **Properties**, in the **Name** box, type **Contact** In the **New Style** dialog box, under **Formatting**, click the **Bold** button, the **Italic** button, and the **Center** button. Click **OK**. In the **Styles and Formatting** task pane, click the **Contact** style to apply the style to the selected paragraph.

**(Project 5G–Art Program continues on the next page)**

## Skill Assessments (continued)

**(Project 5G–Art Program continued)**

9. Scroll down and select the last two paragraphs in the document, beginning with *Music Program Coordinator*. From the **Styles and Formatting** task pane, click **Contact** to apply the style to the selected paragraphs.

10. Hold down ⌨Ctrl and press ⌨Home. Click in the heading at the top of the document—*University Medical Center Patient Services*. On the Formatting toolbar, click the **Center** button. From the **Format** menu, display the **Borders and Shading** dialog box, and if necessary, click the **Borders tab**. Under **Style**, be sure the single line at the top of the Style area is selected. Click the **Width arrow**, and then click **1½ pt**. In the **Preview** area, click the **bottom** of the graphic to apply the line under the paragraph. Click **OK**.

11. From the **Format** menu, display the **Paragraph** dialog box. Under **Spacing**, change the **After** box to **12 pt.**, and then click **OK**.

12. In the **Styles and Formatting** task pane, click the **New Style** button. Under **Properties**, in the **Name** box, type **Title 1** and then click **OK**. In the **Styles and Formatting** task pane, click **Title 1** to apply the style to the title at the top of the document.

13. On the **Styles and Formatting** task pane's title bar, click the **Close** button. From the **Tools** menu, click **Options**. On the **View tab**, under **Outline and Normal options**, in the **Style area width** box, select the number, type **0** and then click **OK**.

14. To the right of the horizontal scroll bar, click the **Print Layout View** button. Compare your document with Figure 5.79. From the **View** menu, display the Header and Footer toolbar, switch to the footer, and then, on the Header and Footer toolbar, click **Insert AutoText**. From the displayed list, click **Filename**. Close the Header and Footer toolbar.

15. On the Standard toolbar, click the **Save** button, and then click the **Print Preview** button to see the document as it will print. Click the **Print** button, and then close the Print Preview. Close the file, saving changes if prompted to do so.

**End** You have completed Project 5G

## Project 5H — Daily Patients

**Objectives:** *Create a Chart with Microsoft Graph and Format a Chart.*

In the following Performance Assessment, you will create a column chart that shows the number of patients treated daily at University Medical Center by service provided. Your completed document will look similar to the one shown in Figure 5.80. You will save your document as *5H_Daily_Patients_Firstname_Lastname.*

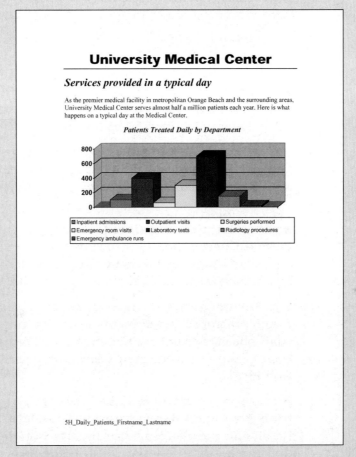

**Figure 5.80**

1. On the Standard toolbar, click the **Open** button. Navigate to the location where the student files for this textbook are stored. Locate and open **w05H_Daily_Patients**. Save the file as **5H_Daily_Patients_Firstname_Lastname**

2. Click anywhere in the table. Display the **Table** menu, point to **Select**, and then click **Table**. From the **Insert** menu, point to **Picture,** and then click **Chart**.

**(Project 5H–Daily Patients continues on the next page)**

**(Project 5H–Daily Patients continued)**

3. Be sure that two toolbar rows are displayed. If only one toolbar row is displayed on your screen, at the right end of the toolbar, click the Toolbar Options button, and then click Show Buttons on Two Rows.

4. Click in the **datasheet**, and then, on the datasheet title bar, click the **Close** button. Right-click in the white area of the chart, and then, from the shortcut menu, click **Chart Options**. Click the **Titles tab**. Click in the **Chart title** box, type **Patients Treated Daily by Department** and then click **OK**. On the Standard toolbar, click the **Save** button.

5. Scroll down so that you can see the 7-inch mark on the vertical ruler. Position the pointer over the right middle sizing handle on the outside border of the chart and drag to the right to approximately **6 inches on the horizontal ruler**. Point to the bottom middle sizing handle and drag down to approximately **6.5 inches on the vertical ruler**. Refer to Figure 5.80 as a guide.

6. Right-click the **Legend**, from the shortcut menu click **Format Legend**, and then click the **Font tab**. Change the **Size** box to **10** and the **Font style** box to **Regular**. Click the **Placement tab**, and then click **Bottom**. Click **OK**.

7. Right-click the **chart title**, and then, from the shortcut menu, click **Format Chart Title**. Click the **Font tab**. Under **Font**, scroll the list and click **Times New Roman**. Change the **Font style** box to **Bold Italic**, the **Size** box to **14**, and then click **OK**.

8. Click anywhere outside the selected chart to close the Microsoft Graph program and return to the document window. Click on the chart once to select it, and then, on the Formatting toolbar, click the **Center** button to center the chart on the page. Compare your screen with Figure 5.80.

9. Scroll as necessary to view the entire table, and then click in the table. From the **Table** menu, point to **Delete**, and then click **Table**. Recall that the data is now incorporated in the underlying datasheet that is represented by the chart—the table is no longer needed.

10. From the **View** menu, display the Header and Footer toolbar, switch to the footer, and then, on the Header and Footer toolbar, click **Insert AutoText**. From the displayed list, click **Filename**. Close the Header and Footer toolbar.

11. On the Standard toolbar, click the **Save** button, and then click the **Print Preview** button to see the document as it will print. Click the **Print** button, and then close the Print Preview. Close the file, saving changes if prompted to do so.

**End** You have completed Project 5H

# Performance Assessments (continued)

## Project 5I—Specialties

**Objectives:** *Add Special Text Effects, Create an Outline, and Modify the Document Window.*

In the following Performance Assessment, you will format the outline for an index of specialties available at University Medical Center. You will also apply a special text effect to the title. Your completed document will look similar to the one shown in Figure 5.81. You will save your document as *5I_Specialties_Firstname_Lastname*.

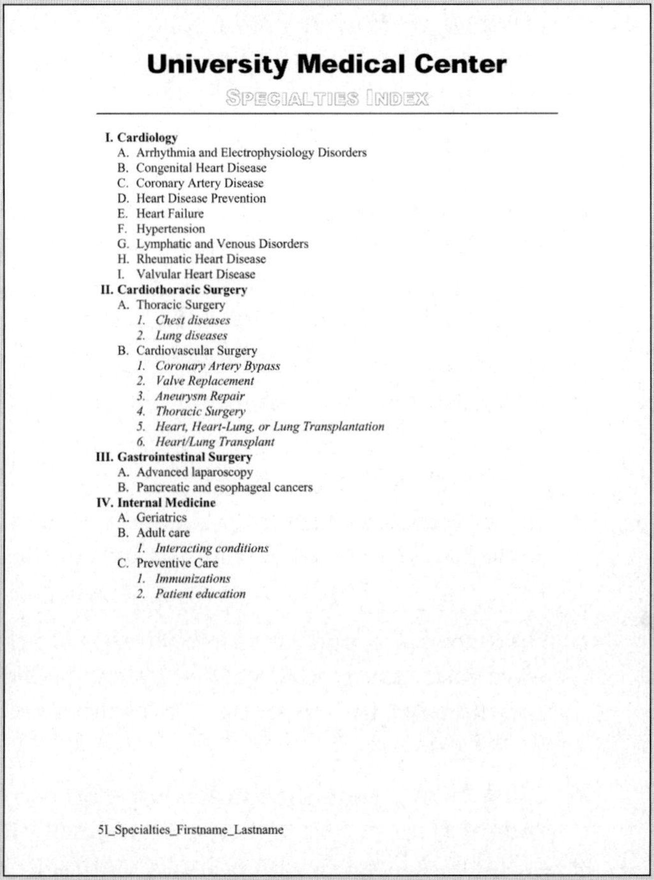

**University Medical Center**

SPECIALTIES INDEX

I. **Cardiology**
   A. Arrhythmia and Electrophysiology Disorders
   B. Congenital Heart Disease
   C. Coronary Artery Disease
   D. Heart Disease Prevention
   E. Heart Failure
   F. Hypertension
   G. Lymphatic and Venous Disorders
   H. Rheumatic Heart Disease
   I. Valvular Heart Disease
II. **Cardiothoracic Surgery**
   A. Thoracic Surgery
      *1. Chest diseases*
      *2. Lung diseases*
   B. Cardiovascular Surgery
      *1. Coronary Artery Bypass*
      *2. Valve Replacement*
      *3. Aneurysm Repair*
      *4. Thoracic Surgery*
      *5. Heart, Heart-Lung, or Lung Transplantation*
      *6. Heart/Lung Transplant*
III. **Gastrointestinal Surgery**
   A. Advanced laparoscopy
   B. Pancreatic and esophageal cancers
IV. **Internal Medicine**
   A. Geriatrics
   B. Adult care
      *1. Interacting conditions*
   C. Preventive Care
      *1. Immunizations*
      *2. Patient education*

5I_Specialties_Firstname_Lastname

**Figure 5.81**

1. On the Standard toolbar, click the **Open** button. Navigate to the location where the student files for this textbook are stored. Locate and open **w05I_Specialties**. Save the file as **5I_Specialties_Firstname_Lastname**

2. Open the header. Select the line *Specialties Index*. From the **Format** menu, display the **Font** dialog box. Under **Effects**, select the **Outline** check box and the **Small caps** check box. Click the **Character Spacing tab**. Click the **Spacing By up spin arrow** to display **0.5 pt**. Click **OK**. Close the header.

**(Project 5I–Specialties continues on the next page)**

**(Project 5I–Specialties continued)**

3. If necessary, click the Print Layout button, and then change the **Zoom** setting to **Page Width**. Move the mouse pointer to the top edge of the document until you see the **Hide White Space** pointer, and then click. This will maximize your viewing area.

4. Click to position the insertion point to the left of *Cardiology*. Use the scroll bar to move to the end of the document, and, at the end of the last word, hold down Shift and click to select all but the title lines in the document.

5. From the **Format** menu, display the **Bullets and Numbering** dialog box, and then click the **Outline Numbered tab**. In the first row, click the second option. Check to see if the **Reset** button is active or grayed. If it is active, click it, and then click **Yes** to reset the selected outline format.

6. Click the **Customize** button. In the **Customize Outline Numbered List** dialog box, in the **Number style** box, display the list and click **I, II, III**. In the **Number format** box, replace the parenthesis mark with a period. Change the **Number position** box to **Right**. Under **Text position**, change the **Indent at** box to **0.3"**.

7. Under **Number format**, in the **Level** box, click **2**. In the **Number style** box, click **A, B, C** from the list. In the **Number format** box, replace the parenthesis mark with a period.

8. Under **Number format**, in the **Level** box, click **3**. In the **Number style** box, click **1, 2, 3** from the list. In the **Number format** box, replace the parenthesis mark with a period. Click **OK**.

9. Hold down Ctrl and press Home to move to the top of the document. Save your changes. Select the items labeled *II.* through *X.* and click the **Increase Indent** button. These items display as specialties under *Cardiology*.

10. Click anywhere in the line *Thoracic Surgery* and click the **Increase Indent** button. Select the next two lines—*III. Chest diseases* and *IV. Lung diseases*—which are formatted in italic. Click the **Increase Indent** button twice.

11. Continue to format the outline. Items that are not bold or italic are Level 2 items. Items formatted in italic are Level 3 items. (Hint: Use Ctrl to select multiple lines, and then apply the indent formatting.) Compare your document with Figure 5.81.

12. Display the **View** menu and click **Header and Footer**. Switch to the footer area, click the **Insert AutoText** button, and then click **Filename**. Close the Header and Footer toolbar.

**(Project 5I–Specialties continues on the next page)**

**(Project 5I–Specialties continued)**

**13.** Click the **Save** button, and then click the **Print Preview** button to see the document as it will print. Click the **Print** button, and then close the Print Preview. Close the file, saving changes if prompted to do so.

**End** You have completed Project 5I

# Project 5J—Annual Report

**Objectives:** *Use Existing Styles, Create and Modify New Styles, Create an Outline Using the Outline View and the Outlining Toolbar.*

In the following Performance Assessment, you will format a draft outline of the annual report for the University Medical Center Foundation by using and creating styles and creating an outline. Your completed document will look similar to the one shown in Figure 5.82. You will save your document as *5J_Annual_Report_Firstname_Lastname*.

*ANNUAL REPORT, DRAFT OVERVIEW*

**University Medical Center Foundation**

**Introduction**

*University Medical Center in the Community*

This section will outline the programs and services UMC provides to the community. It will include a section of "quick facts" with statistics such as number of patients treated, number of procedures, etc.

**How UMC Foundation Impacts the Center**

This section will introduce the programs funded by the Foundation and how those programs serve the community.

**Section I**

*H. J. Worthington Hospice*

- Overview of the purpose of the hospice and the care provided to terminally ill patients
- Overview of operating expenses
- Narrative overview
- Pie chart showing department expenses as percentage of total

This section will include two quotes from patient family members on their experience with the hospice's programs and staff.

*University Medical Center Health Careers Scholarship Fund*

- Overview of why the scholarship was established
- Amount of the scholarship
- Overview of criteria for selection of recipient
- Short description of the qualifications of past two years' recipients
- Quotes from past two years' recipients

This section will include two quotes from recipients of University Medical Center scholarships.

*University Medical Center Cancer Center Fund*

- Overview of the Cancer Center
- Founding date
- Purpose
- Overview including types of state-of-the-art treatments, number of patients treated, support programs
- Overview operating expenses
- Percentage of expenses funded by the Foundation

This section will include a quote from one of the Center's physicians regarding the state-of-the-art treatments available at the center.

5J_Annual_Report_Firstname_Lastname

**Figure 5.82**

**(Project 5J–Annual Report continues on the next page)**

**(Project 5J–Annual Report continued)**

1. On the Standard toolbar, click the **Open** button. Navigate to the location where the student files for this textbook are stored. Locate and open **w05J_Annual_Report**. Save the file as **5J_Annual_Report_Firstname_Lastname**

2. To the left of the horizontal scroll bar, click the **Outline View** button. To the left of the Formatting toolbar, click the **Styles and Formatting** button. Set the Zoom to 100% if the text on the screen seems too large.

3. Display the style area on the left of the screen by displaying the **Tools** menu, and then clicking **Options**. Click the **View tab**. Under **Outline and Normal options**, click the **Style area width spin box up arrow** until the style area width is **0.5"**. At the bottom of the **Options** dialog box, click **OK**.

4. Click to position the insertion point in the second line of the document, which contains only the word *Introduction*. In the Styles and Formatting task pane, under **Pick formatting to apply**, click **Heading 1**.

5. Scroll down and click to position the insertion point in the line that contains only *Section I*. Press F4 —the Repeat key. Alternatively, click the Heading 1 style in the Styles and Formatting task pane.

6. Position the insertion point in the third line of the document, which begins *How UMC Foundation*. On the Outlining toolbar, click the **Demote** button.

7. Position the insertion point in the line that begins *University Medical Center in the Community*. In the **Styles and Formatting** task pane, under **Pick formatting to apply**, click **Heading 2**.

8. Use the same procedure to apply a **Heading 2** style to the other three lines that use an italic font style. Hold down Ctrl and press Home.

9. To the left of the third line, which begins *How UMC Foundation*, click the **Expand** button.

10. On the Outlining toolbar, click the **Move Down** button twice.

11. On the Outlining toolbar, click the **Show Level button arrow**, and then click **Show Level 2**. Click anywhere to deselect the text. Only Level 1 and Level 2 headings display; the remaining text is hidden from view so that you can see only the Level 1 and 2 headings.

12. Click to position the insertion point in the line that begins *H. J. Worthington*. On the Outlining toolbar, click the **Expand** button to expand only that section of the document.

13. Near the top of the document, position the pointer over the **Expand** button to the left of the line that begins *How UMC Foundation*. Double-click the **Expand** button to expand that section. This is another way to expand the text under a single section.

**(Project 5J–Annual Report continues on the next page)**

**(Project 5J–Annual Report continued)**

14. On the Outlining toolbar, click the **Show Level button arrow**, and then click **Show All Levels**.

15. To the left of the horizontal scroll bar, click the **Print Layout View** button. To the left of the Formatting toolbar, click the **Styles and Formatting** button to close the Styles and Formatting task pane. Compare your document with Figure 5.82.

16. Display the **View** menu and click **Header and Footer**. Switch to the footer area, click the **Insert AutoText** button, and then click **Filename**. Close the Header and Footer toolbar.

17. Click the **Save** button, and then click the **Print Preview** button to see the document as it will print. Close the Print Preview. Click the **Print** button, and then close the file, saving changes if prompted to do so.

**End** You have completed Project 5J

## Project 5K — Growth

**Objectives:** *Create a Chart with Microsoft Graph and Format a Chart.*

In the following Mastery Assessment, you will create a two-column chart for a University Medical Center report to show how staff levels have increased to keep up with the growing population of Orange Beach. Your completed document will look similar to the one shown in Figure 5.83. You will save your document as *5K_Growth_ Firstname_Lastname.*

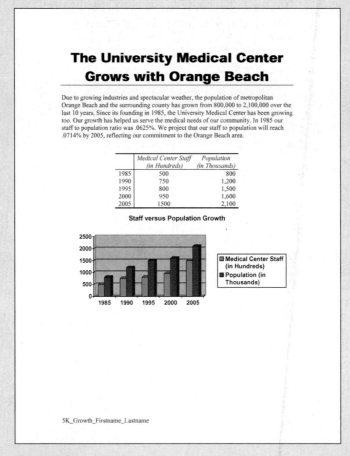

**Figure 5.83**

1. **Start** Word. From your student files, open **w05K_Growth**. Save the file with the name **5K_Growth_Firstname_Lastname** in the same location as your other files. In the same manner as you have done in previous documents, display the footer and insert the **AutoText** filename.

2. Select the entire table, display the **Insert** menu, point to **Picture**, and then click **Chart**. Close the datasheet. If necessary, click the Toolbar Options button, and then click Show Buttons on Two Rows to display both toolbars.

**(Project 5K–Growth continues on the next page)**

**(Project 5K–Growth continued)**

3. On the Chart toolbar, click the **By Column** button. To make a year-by-year comparison between staff and population, the data needs to be displayed by column.

4. Right-click in the white area of the chart, and then click **Chart Options**. In the **Chart title** box, type **Staff versus Population Growth** and then click **OK**.

5. Scroll so that you can view the 7-inch mark on the vertical ruler. Position the pointer over the right middle sizing handle of the chart and drag to approximately **6 inches on the horizontal ruler**. Point to the bottom middle sizing handle and drag down to approximately **7 inches on the vertical ruler**. Refer to Figure 5.83 as a guide.

6. Click in the body of the document to return to the document window. Click on the chart once to select it, and then, on the Formatting toolbar, click the **Center** button. Compare your screen with Figure 5.83.

7. Save the completed document. Preview the document, and then print it.

**End** You have completed Project 5K

# Project 5L — Speakers

**Objectives:** *Add Special Text Effects, Modify the Document Window, Create an Outline, and Apply and Modify Styles.*

In the following Mastery Assessment, you will format a speaker directory for the University Medical Center. You will apply an outline format that uses styles, modify one of the styles, add a special text effect to the opening paragraph, and modify the document window as you work. Your completed document will look similar to the one shown in Figure 5.84. You will save your document as *5L_Speakers_Firstname_Lastname*.

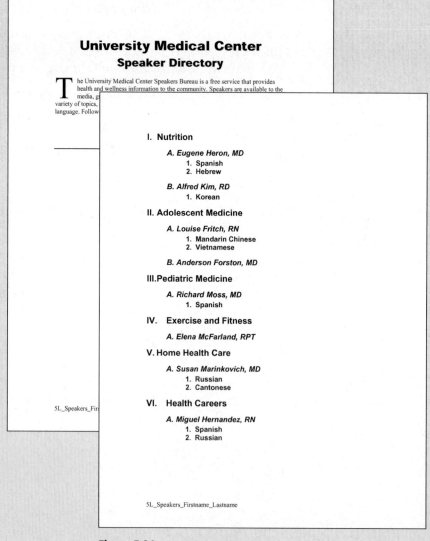

**Figure 5.84**

**(Project 5L–Speakers continues on the next page)**

**(Project 5L–Speakers continued)**

1. Start Word. From your student files, open **w05L_Speakers**. Save the file with the name **5L_Speakers_Firstname_Lastname** in the same location as your other files. In the same manner as you have done in previous documents, display the footer and insert the **AutoText** filename.

2. Position the insertion point in the paragraph beginning *The University Medical Center*. From the **Format** menu, open the **Drop Cap** dialog box, and then, under **Position**, click **Dropped**. Under **Options**, click the **Distance from text spin box up arrow** to add **0.1"** extra spacing between the drop cap and the text to its right. Click **OK**.

3. If necessary, change the Zoom setting to Page Width. Move the mouse pointer to the top edge of the document until you see the **Hide White Space** pointer, and then click.

4. Select the two paragraphs beginning *Ricardo*, which will include the phone number under his name. From the Formatting toolbar, change the selected lines to **14 pt.**, **Bold**, and **Italic**, and then **Center** the text.

5. Starting with *Nutrition,* select all of the remaining text through the end of the document. From the **Format** menu, display the **Bullets and Numbering** dialog box, and then click the **Outline Numbered tab**. In the second row, click the third option. Check to see if the **Reset** button is active or grayed. If active, click it to restore the original settings to this outline choice. This outline uses the I. A. 1. format you have practiced and combines it with the Heading 1, 2, 3, styles. Click **OK**.

6. Scroll up to view the result. A new page was created starting with *Nutrition.* Click in the paragraph that begins *II. Eugene Heron, MD* and click the **Increase Indent** button once. In this manner, the speakers need to be indented to Level 2. Listed under Dr. Heron are two languages—*II. Spanish* and *III. Hebrew.* Select these paragraphs and click the **Increase Indent** button twice. In this manner, the languages for each speaker need to be indented to Level 3. Continue down the page and indent the speaker names to Level 2 and the languages to Level 3. Compare your screen with Figure 5.84 to verify the outline levels.

7. On the Formatting toolbar, click the **Styles and Formatting** button. In the **Styles and Formatting** task pane, under **Pick formatting to apply**, scroll down the list, point to and then click the arrow to the right of **Heading 3**, and then click **Select All 10 Instance(s)**. Click the arrow again and click **Modify**. In the **Modify Style** dialog box, under **Formatting**, locate the second row of buttons. Point to the third button from the right to display the ScreenTip **Decrease Paragraph Spacing**. Click this button twice. Watch the preview window to see how the space before and after the example is decreased. Select the **Automatically Update** check box, and then click **OK**.

**(Project 5L–Speakers continues on the next page)**

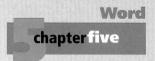
**(Project 5L–Speakers continued)**

8. Scroll the page to see the results. Close the **Styles and Formatting** task pane. Position the pointer at the top edge of the document and click the **Show White Space** pointer. Compare your screen with Figure 5.84.

9. Save the completed document. Preview the document, and then print it.

 **End** You have completed Project 5L

## Project 5M — Outline

**Objectives:** *Add Special Text Effects, Use Existing Styles, and Create an Outline.*

Outlines can help you organize information when you are writing research papers for your classes. In this Problem Solving exercise, you will create your own outline for a research paper on a topic of your choice. You will also use some of the styles you have practiced and apply some special text effects. You will save your outline as *5M_Outline_Firstname_Lastname.*

1. Select a topic for your paper. It can be a paper for another class, something you are interested in researching, or a topic related to the use of computers.

2. Enter the title of your research paper and apply the **Heading 1** style. **Center** the heading.

3. Under the title, type **Outline** Apply the **Heading 2** style and **center** this subheading. Select the *Outline* subheading and, from the **Font** dialog box, apply the **Outline** effect. Click the **Character Spacing tab** and expand the spacing to **1.0"**. Press Enter to move to any empty line.

4. Open the **Bullets and Numbering** dialog box. Click the **Outline Numbered tab** and, as practiced in the chapter, set the outline Level 1 format to I. II. III., set the Level 2 format to A. B. C., and set the Level 3 format to 1. 2. 3. Click **OK**.

5. Write your outline, using the **Increase Indent** button to position topics at the second or third level of the outline as appropriate. Include at least four Level 1 headings, at least two Level 2 headings under each major topic, and two instances of Level 3 headings somewhere in the outline.

6. Proofread your outline and remove any spelling, grammar, or typographical errors. In the footer area and using the **AutoText** button, insert the **Filename**. Save the document.

7. Print the document, and then close the file, saving changes if prompted to do so.

**End** **You have completed Project 5M** ————————————

## Project 5N—Personal Styles

**Objective:** *Create and Modify New Styles.*

The University Medical Center is issuing a press release about an upcoming health information series. In this Problem Solving exercise you will create new styles and apply them to the press release that has been written announcing this program. You will save the article as *5N_Press Release.*

1. Locate and open **w05N_Press Release**. Save it as **5N_Press_Release_Firstname_Lastname** with your other files. As you have with previous files, display the footer area and insert the **AutoText** filename.

2. Display the **Styles and Formatting** task pane. If necessary, change the view to **Normal**. Use the **Options** dialog box to display the **Styles area** on the left side of the window.

3. Using the skills you have practiced in this chapter, create a paragraph style named **PR** that is all **caps**, **Arial Black**, **18 pt.** and apply it to *Press Release.*

4. Create another paragraph style using font and paragraph styles of your own choice and apply it to the article headline that begins *The New Health.* Name the style **News Headline**.

5. Create a character style that is **Bold**, **Italic**, and **Red** and name it **UMC** Apply the **UMC** character style to all occurrences of *University Medical Center* in the body of the document—but not in the article headline.

6. Save the document, print it, and then close the file.

**End** You have completed Project 5N ——————————————————

## Downloading More Charting Tools

In this chapter you practiced using the Microsoft Graph program to create column charts, pie charts, and a line chart. There are other charting tools available as downloads from the Microsoft online support site.

1. Be sure that you are connected to the Internet. Open Word and, in the **Type a question for help** box, type **chart types** and press Enter.

2. In the Search Results task pane, click **Timeline**. A Template window opens on your screen with a Timeline chart displayed. Click the **Next arrow** at the bottom of the window to browse through the 10 templates that are available.

3. Click the **Previous** button until the screen returns to the Timeline template.

4. If you are working in a lab, check to be sure you can download files. If it is permitted, click the **Download** button. The template displays with instructions telling you how to use the template.

5. Follow the instructions and practice using the Timeline chart template you downloaded. Fill in the timeline with significant events in your life over the course of the time displayed. Follow the instructions to replace dates on the timeline as needed.

6. When you are done, close the file without saving changes, and then close Word.

### Styles in Word 2003 Help

Using styles can be very helpful if you need to format a large document. In this chapter you were introduced to the basics of how to create and apply styles. You can learn more about styles by reviewing some of the Word Help topics on the subject. One helpful technique when you are formatting a large document is to specify that one paragraph style follow another. For example, you may want a body text style to always follow a Heading 3 style.

1. Start Word. In the **Type a question for help** box, type **Styles**. Scroll through the list of topics that displays in the Search Results task pane.

2. From this list of help topics, click *Specify that one paragraph style follow another* and read the results. Print these instructions if you want.

3. In a blank document write two brief paragraphs. Format the first paragraph with a style of your choosing. Modify the style so it is followed by another specific paragraph style—not the Normal style. Using the Help instructions, update the style applied to the first paragraph to test the change. The style of the second paragraph should change if it was done correctly.

4. Review some of the other Help topics related to styles, printing any that interest you. Test some of the other instructions to learn more about applying styles.

5. Close the Help task pane, close your document without saving the changes, and then exit Word.

# chaptersix

# Working on a Group Project

**In this chapter, you will:** complete these projects **and** practice these skills.

| Project 6A **Creating a Document from a Template** | **Objective** <br>• Create a Document Using a Template |
| --- | --- |

| Project 6B **Preparing a Document for Distribution to Others** | **Objectives** <br>• Review and Modify Document Properties <br>• Use Comments in a Document <br>• Track Changes in a Document |
| --- | --- |

| Project 6C **Comparing Different Versions of a Document** | **Objectives** <br>• Circulate Documents for Review <br>• Compare and Merge Documents |
| --- | --- |

# The Management Association of Pine Valley

The Management Association of Pine Valley is an employers' group providing legal services, training, human resources consulting, and organizational development to member companies. Members are small and mid-size companies with 1 to 1,000 employees. Although most services come from the association's staff of experts, some services are outsourced. The association will also assist its members in procuring needed services from other organizations.

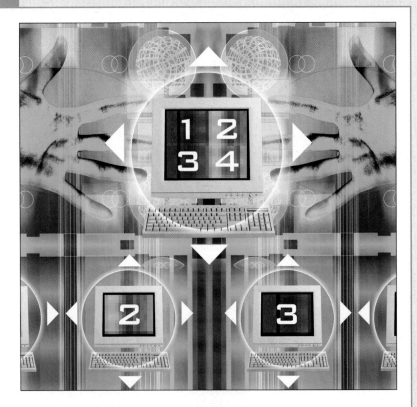

# Working on a Group Project

The process of creating documents is often a team effort. The people who need to review a document may be in the same office, in different cities, or even in different countries. After a document has been created, it is often necessary for several people to review it. Word includes several features that enable you to keep track of changes made to the original document and to add comments to the text. Changes made by others can be accepted or rejected by the document's author.

When no central network is available, documents can be distributed as attachments to email messages. If time is short and people are working on different copies of the same document, you can compare and merge them, using the Track Changes feature to accept or reject changes.

# Project 6A **Memo**

Templates contain predefined document formats that can be used to save time and to create a consistent look for similar documents. Templates exist for resumes, memos, letters, reports, brochures, faxes, and several other document types.

In Activities 6.1 through 6.2, you will use a template to create a memo for a team working on an upcoming conference for The Management Association of Pine Valley. You will replace existing text and replace placeholder text used to reserve areas of the document for specific kinds of information. Your completed document will look similar to Figure 6.1. You will save your document as *6A_Memo_Firstname_Lastname*.

**The Management Association of Pine Valley**

# Memo

**To:**      David Rosenberg, Siena Madison

**From:**   Deepa Patel, Director of Human Resource Counseling

**CC:**      Satarkta Kalam, Director of Labor Relations Services

**Date:**   August 19

**Re:**      Document Reviews

We will be working on two documents this week to present as part of a package to our members at next month's Human Resources Conference. Bill Newson finished the first drafts before he left on vacation. I would like you to read them carefully and give me your opinions. You can edit the documents I send you, but be sure you turn on the Track Changes feature in Word. I will need your edits by Friday.

6A_Memo_Firstname_Lastname

**Figure 6.1**
Project 6A—Memo

## Objective 1
## Create a Document Using a Template

A **template** is a model for documents of the same type; it is a predefined structure that contains the basic document settings, such as fonts, margins, and available styles. Unless otherwise specified, every Word document is based on the default Normal template. A document template can also store document elements such as headers, greetings, text blocks, and company logos. Word provides document templates for memos, resumes, and other common business documents. Other templates can be built using **wizards**, which ask you for information about the type of document you want to create. Document templates use a .dot file extension.

### Activity 6.1 Creating a Memo Using a Template

**1** Start Microsoft Word. From the **File** menu, click **New**.

The New Document task pane opens, as shown in Figure 6.2. If another Word document is open, it still displays in the document window.

On my computer option ───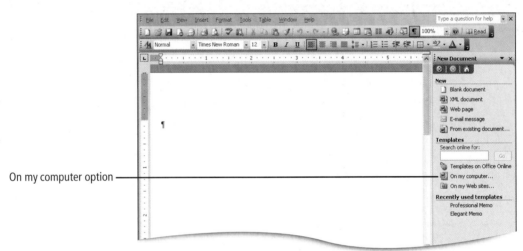

**Figure 6.2**

**2** In the **New Document** task pane, under **Templates**, click **On my computer**.

The Templates dialog box displays. Notice the template categories displayed in the tabs at the top of the dialog box.

**3** In the **Templates** dialog box, click the **Memos tab**, and then click the **Professional Memo** icon.

A preview of the memo displays in the Preview area. Under Create New, you have the option of creating a new document based on the Professional Memo template or of creating a new, customized template (document model) by modifying the existing template. See Figure 6.3.

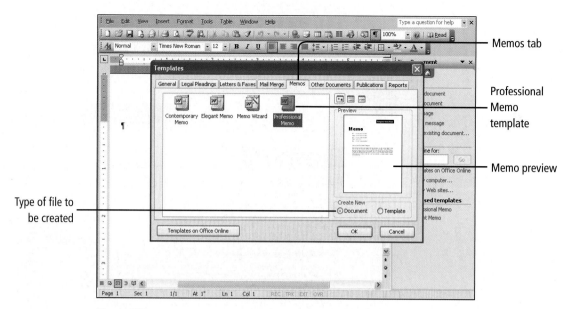

Type of file to be created

Memos tab

Professional Memo template

Memo preview

**Figure 6.3**

## More Knowledge — Templates on the Web

If you are connected to the Internet, you can click the *Templates on Office Online* button at the bottom of the Templates dialog box. This will give you access to hundreds of available templates for Word, Excel, Access, and PowerPoint. The Word templates will display the Word icon that appears on the left side of the Word title bar. Available Word templates on the Web include a performance review, a net worth calculator, many styles of calendars, and even a timeline diagram.

**4** At the bottom of the **Templates** dialog box, click **OK**. On the Standard toolbar, click the **Zoom button arrow** [100% ▾], and then click **Page Width**.

The Professional Memo template displays, and the new document is unnamed. See Figure 6.4. The small black squares in the left margin are part of the template and display when paragraphs are formatted with a style that keeps paragraphs together rather than splitting them across pages. You need not be concerned with styles in this project.

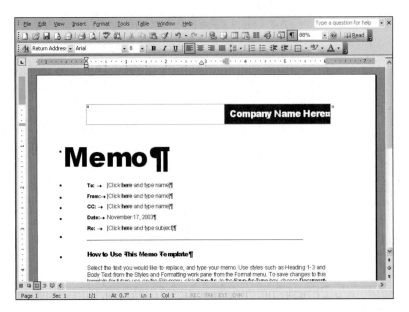

**Figure 6.4**

5 Be sure that you can see the nonprinting characters displayed on your screen. If necessary, on the Standard toolbar, click the Show/Hide ¶ button to display the formatting characters.

6 On the Standard toolbar, click the **Save** button . In the **Save As** dialog box, navigate to the location where you are storing your projects for this chapter, creating a new folder for Chapter 6 if you want to do so. In the **File name** box, type **6A_Memo_Firstname_Lastname** and then click **Save**.

Word saves the file as a document with a .doc extension, and the formatting is based on the template.

### Activity 6.2 Replacing Placeholder Text and Customizing the Memo

Sample text and **placeholder text** display in a document created from a template. Placeholder text reserves space for the text you will insert; it looks like text, but cannot be edited—it can only be replaced. You will edit all or some of this text and replace it with your personalized content.

1 At the top of the document, select the title **Company Name Here**. Type **The Management Association of** and then press Shift + Enter. Type **Pine Valley** to complete the company name. On the Formatting toolbar, click the **Center** button ![].

Because this placeholder title is formatted as a one-row table with two cells, the title is centered in the table's cell. Recall that pressing Enter while holding down Shift creates a manual line break, but keeps all of the text in the same paragraph with the same paragraph formatting. See Figure 6.5.

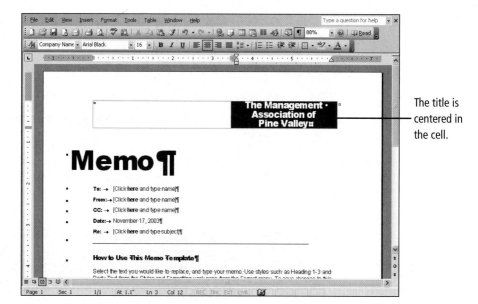

The title is centered in the cell.

**Figure 6.5**

**2** In the **To** line, click **[Click here and type name]**.

Notice that a single click selects the entire placeholder text. Placeholder text cannot be edited and behaves more like a graphic than text. See Figure 6.6.

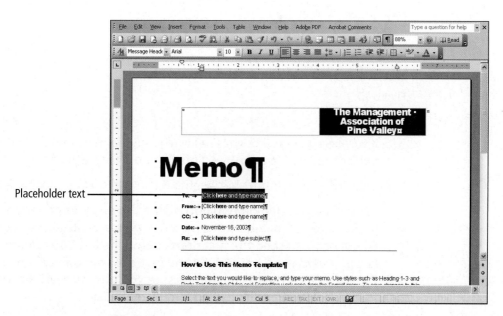

Placeholder text

**Figure 6.6**

**3** Type **David Rosenberg, Siena Madison**

The text you typed replaces the placeholder text.

**4** In the **From** line, click **[Click here and type name]**. Type **Deepa Patel, Director of Human Resource Consulting**

**5** In the **CC** line, click **[Click here and type name]**. Type **Satarkta Kalam, Director of Labor Relations Services**

**6** In the **Date** line, select the existing date and type **August 19**

This replaces the default date, which is the current date.

**7** In the **Re** line, click **[Click here and type subject]**. Type **Document Reviews**

Compare your document with Figure 6.7. You can see that using a predefined memo template saves you time in creating the basic parts of a memo.

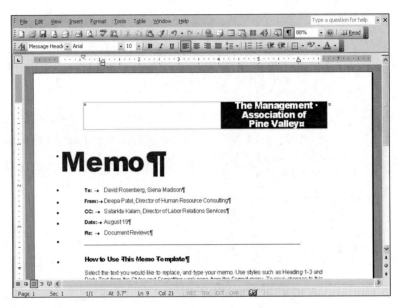

**Figure 6.7**

**8** If necessary, scroll down to view the middle portion of the document. Select the line **How to Use This Memo Template** and press Delete.

**9** Select the paragraph that begins *Select the text you would like.* Type

**We will be working on two documents this week to present as part of a package to our members at next month's Human Resources Conference. Bill Newson finished the first drafts before he left on vacation. I would like you to read them carefully and give me your opinions. You can edit the documents I send you, but be sure you turn on the Track Changes feature in Word. I will need your edits by Friday.**

Compare your memo with Figure 6.8.

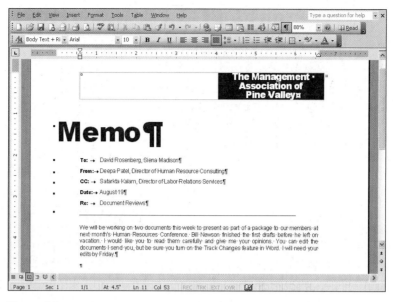

**Figure 6.8**

**10** From the **View** menu, click **Header and Footer**. On the Header and Footer toolbar, click the **Switch Between Header and Footer** button.

**11** Press [Delete] twice to remove the page number that was included as part of the template. On the **Header and Footer** toolbar, click the **Insert AutoText** button [Insert AutoText ▾]. Point to **Header/Footer** and click **Filename**.

The file name is inserted in the footer.

**12** On the Header and Footer toolbar, click the **Close** button [Close].

**13** On the Standard toolbar, click the **Save** button.

**14** On the Standard toolbar, click the **Print Preview** button. Take a moment to check your work. On the Print Preview toolbar, click the **Close Preview** button [Close].

**15** Make any necessary changes to your document. When you are satisfied, on the Standard toolbar, click the **Print** button. Close the document, saving changes if you are prompted to do so.

**End** You have completed Project 6A

# Project 6B **Exit Interview**

Microsoft Word records information about every document, such as document size, word count, date and time last edited, and author. This information is available to you from the Properties dialog box. When a document is edited by several people, changes and comments, along with the name of the person making each change or comment, can be displayed using the Track Changes feature.

In Activities 6.3 through 6.11, you will edit a draft document to be distributed to member businesses of The Management Association of Pine Valley, and you will look at the document summary. The draft document has been completed by one person; edits and comments have been added by another. You will make changes to the document and add more comments, and then you will accept or reject each of the changes. Your completed document will look similar to Figure 6.9. You will save your document as *6B_Exit_Interview_ Firstname_Lastname.*

**DRAFT: Exit Interviews – Voluntary Separation**

Exit interviews with employees who are voluntarily leaving the organization are useful to determine why an employee has decided to leave and to find opportunities for improving the organization's overall employee relations.

When conducting an exit interview, the interviewer should be relaxed and open to encourage honest feedback. The employee should be treated with respect and given time to discuss concerns and ask questions.

Sample questions for an exit interview include:

- What did you like most about your job?
- What did you like least about your job?
- What made you decide to leave this job?
- Do you feel adequate training was provided for you to do your job?
- Do you think your supervisor treated you and others fairly and reasonably? explain.
- Were you given access to information for promotional opportunities within organization?
- Do you believe you were given honest consideration for promotion?
- Do you feel your contributions were appreciated by your supervisor, co-w organization?
- Did you have the appropriate tools (equipment and resources) to do your j
- Do you believe your salary matched the job you were doing?
- Were you satisfied with the employee benefits? (Ask for details if necessa
- Was the physical environment comfortable and did it allow for productivit
- Was the job presented to you realistically at the time you were hired?

The organization should have strict confidentiality rules in place. These processes explained to the employee so they feel comfortable speaking freely, especially reg negative feedback.

For the exit interview information to be useful to the organization, the informatio interviews should be analyzed and summarized at least annually. Compare the inf turnover statistics for a period of time to identify trends. Appropriate feedback sh supervisors and managers while protecting the identity of employees who gave th

6B_Exit_Interview_Firstname_Lastname

| | |
|---|---|
| Filename: | 6B_Exit_Interview_Firstname_Lastname.doc |
| Directory: | C:\Student |
| Template: | C:\Documents and Settings\Bob\Application |
| | Data\Microsoft\Templates\Normal.dot |
| Title: | DRAFT: Exit Interviews |
| Subject: | Student Name |
| Author: | Bill Newsom |
| Keywords: | Exit Interviews, Fall Conference |
| Comments: | Draft copy of the Exit Interviews handout for the Fall conference. |
| Creation Date: | 9/5/2003 9:02:00 PM |
| Change Number: | 10 |
| Last Saved On: | 9/5/2003 11:40:00 PM |
| Last Saved By: | Siena Madison |
| Total Editing Time: | 133 Minutes |
| Last Printed On: | 9/6/2003 2:38:00 AM |
| As of Last Complete Printing | |
| Number of Pages: | 1 (approx.) |
| Number of Words: | 300 (approx.) |
| Number of Characters: | 1,713 (approx.) |

**Figure 6.9**
Project 6B—Exit Interview

# Objective 2
## Review and Modify Document Properties

*Document properties*—recorded statistics and other related information, such as the date the document was created, the date it was last modified, where the file is stored, and the author's name—are updated each time the document is modified.

Additionally, you can add document summary information to the properties area. You can give the document a title or a subject, and you can add the name of the company for which the document was created. Keywords can be added, which can help when searching for a document in Windows. The document properties also can be printed.

### Activity 6.3 Viewing the Summary

**1** On the Standard toolbar, click the **Open** button. Navigate to the location where the student files for this textbook are stored. Locate and open **w06B_Exit_Interview**. Save the file as **6B_Exit_Interview_Firstname_Lastname**

**2** On the Standard toolbar, click the **Zoom button arrow** 100%, and then click **Page Width**. If necessary, on the Standard toolbar, click the Show/Hide ¶ button to display formatting marks.

**Alert!**

### Check Your Screen

Changes were made to this document and comments have been added. Your screen may display the changes, or they may be hidden. The Reviewing toolbar may or may not be displayed. If the changes are displayed, they may be shown as multicolored text and balloons in the right margin of the document or just multicolored text in the document. Do not be concerned about the arrangement of your screen or the toolbar configuration at this point.

**3** From the **File** menu, click **Properties**. If necessary, click the General tab.

The document's Properties box displays, with the document name in the title bar. The General tab displays the type of document, file location, and file size. The creation date and date last modified also are displayed, as shown in Figure 6.10.

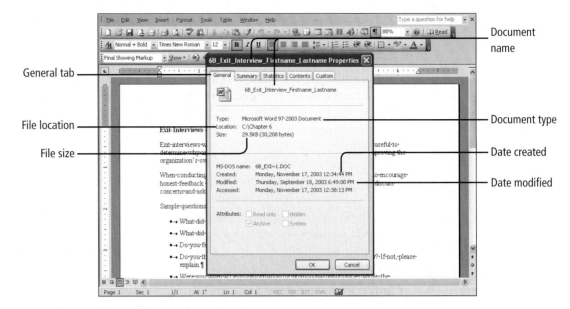

**Figure 6.10**

**4** In the **Properties** box, click the **Summary tab**.

The name in the Author box is the name of the person who originally registered the Office software, although the name can be changed at any time. The name in the Company box is the name of the last entry in that box; it will stay that way for each new document until it is modified. These two boxes are the only ones that are filled in automatically. See Figure 6.11.

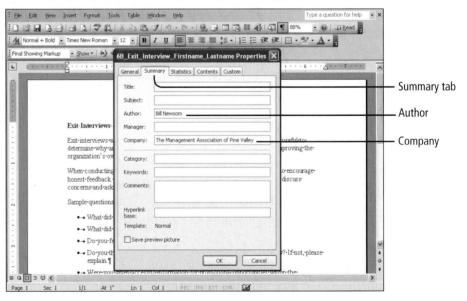

**Figure 6.11**

**5** In the **Properties** box, click the **Statistics tab**.

The Statistics tab expands on the information in the General tab, displaying the last time the document was printed, how many revisions have been made to the document, and how many minutes the document has been open—referred to as *editing time*. Editing time is not an exact measurement of actual time on task, because the document may have been left open overnight with no editing, and the time would still be added to the total. Document statistics are also displayed. See Figure 6.12.

Statistics tab ——

Number of revisions ——

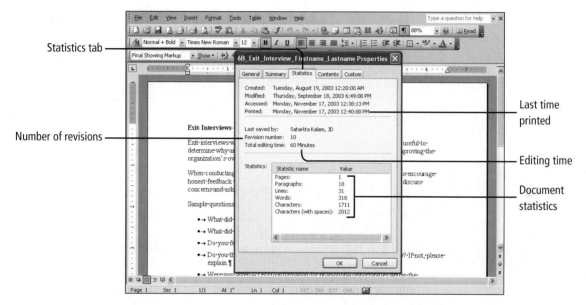

Last time printed

Editing time

Document statistics

**Figure 6.12**

## Activity 6.4 Editing the Summary and Printing the Document Properties

Editing summary information and adding more information can make the document easier to find using the Windows search feature. It also enables you to make notes about the document for future reference.

**1** In the **Properties** box, click the **Summary tab**.

**2** On the **Summary** sheet, in the **Title** box, delete the existing text, and then type **DRAFT: Exit Interviews**

**3** In the **Keywords** box, type **Exit Interviews, Fall Conference**

**4** In the **Comments** box, type **Draft copy of the Exit Interviews handout for the Fall conference.**

Compare your screen with Figure 6.13.

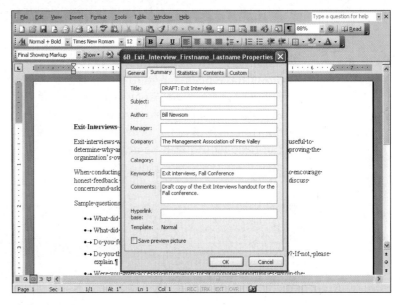

**Figure 6.13**

5 In the **Subject** box, type your name.

6 At the bottom of the **Properties** box, click **OK**.

7 On the Standard toolbar, click the **Save** button ⊞.

### Activity 6.5 Checking Word and Paragraph Counts

Some documents written for magazines or newsletters have word count or line count limits. Word enables you to open a toolbar that keeps track of the number of words, lines, and even characters in a document.

1 From the **Tools** menu, click **Word Count**.

The Word Count dialog box displays, as shown in Figure 6.14. These are the same statistics that were displayed in the Statistics sheet of the document's Properties box.

Show Toolbar button ——

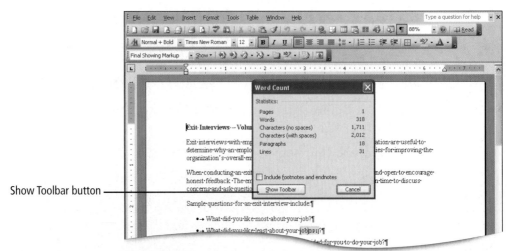

**Figure 6.14**

**2** At the bottom of the **Word Count** dialog box, click **Show Toolbar**.

The Word Count toolbar displays.

**3** At the bottom of the **Word Count** dialog box, click **Cancel**.

**4** In the Word Count toolbar, click the **Word Count Statistics** button <Click Recount to view> .

The list of statistics displays, as shown in Figure 6.15. Notice the number of words in the document.

Word Count toolbar ——

Word Count Statistics button ——

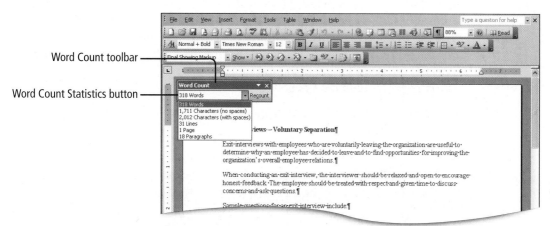

**Figure 6.15**

**5** Click to position the insertion point to the left of the first line of the document, beginning *Exit Interviews*, closing the displayed list. Type **DRAFT:** and then press Space.

Notice that the Word Count Statistics box displays *<Click Recount to view>*.

**6** In the Word Count toolbar, click the **Recount** button Recount .

The Word Count Statistics box displays the new number of words— 319—in the document.

**7** Leave the Word Count toolbar open for the following activities. On the Standard toolbar, click the **Save** button.

# Objective 3
## Use Comments in a Document

A ***comment*** is a note that an author or reviewer adds to a document. Word displays the comment in either a balloon-type graphic in the margin of the document or in a reviewing pane at the bottom of the document. Comments are a good way to communicate when more than one person is involved in the editing process.

Comments are like sticky notes attached to the document—they can be seen and read, but they do not print. When more than one person adds comments, each person's comments are displayed in a different color. The author's initials are also displayed in the comment box. Comments can be edited, and more than one author can edit the same comment.

### Activity 6.6 Adding a Comment

Comments can be added at a specific location in a document or to a selection of text.

**1** From the **Tools** menu, click **Options**, and then click the **Track Changes tab**.

The Options dialog box displays. See Figure 6.16.

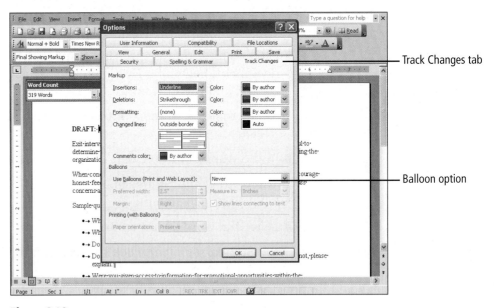

Figure 6.16

**2** Under **Balloons**, click the **Use Balloons (Print and Web Layout) arrow**, and then click **Always**.

When the Track Changes feature is active, this action will cause Word to always display comments and deletions in the right margin in a balloon when the document is displayed in Print Layout or Web Layout views.

## More Knowledge

In the Track Changes tab of the Options dialog box, you can change the width of the balloons. You can also set the balloons to display in the left margin.

**3** In the **Options** dialog box, click the **User Information tab**.

**4** Under **User information**, write down the current name and initials so that you can restore them when this project is completed. In the **Name** box type **Siena Madison** and in the **Initials** box type **SFM**

The name and initials will be used when comments are added and changes are made to the document. Compare your dialog box with Figure 6.17.

User Information tab
Name
Initials

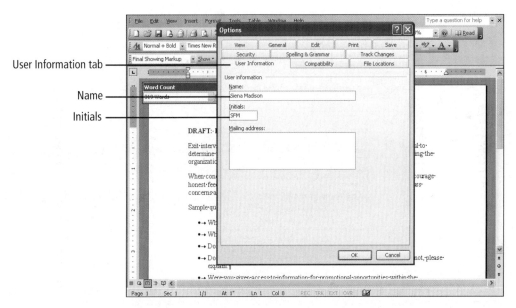

**Figure 6.17**

## Note — Restoring Word Settings

When you are using a computer that is used by more than one person, and you make a change to Word settings, it is always good practice and common courtesy to restore the setting when you are finished.

**5** Click **OK** to close the **Options** dialog box. From the **View** menu, point to **Toolbars**. Examine the list to see if the **Reviewing** toolbar is displayed (checked). If it is not checked, click it; if it is checked, click outside the menu to close it.

The Reviewing toolbar displays.

**6** On the Standard toolbar, click the **Zoom button arrow** 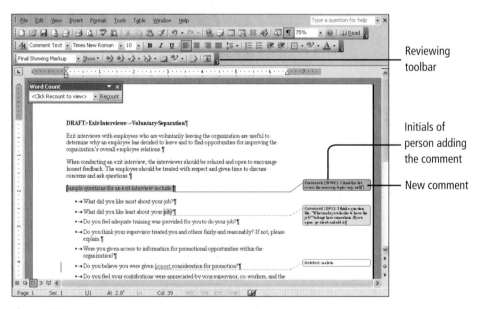, and then click **Page Width**. Be sure that you are in **Print Layout** view, and if necessary, from the View menu, click Print Layout.

The window adjusts to make more space for the balloons. On small screens, such as those on laptop computers, the text may be almost too small to read.

**7** Select the paragraph near the top of the document that begins *Sample questions*. If necessary, drag the Word Count toolbar away from the Reviewing toolbar. From the Reviewing toolbar, click the

**Insert Comment** button. Type **I think this list covers the necessary topics very well!**

The new comment displays in the right margin. The initials *SFM* appear at the beginning of the comment, followed by the number *1*, which means that this is the first comment in the document. See Figure 6.18.

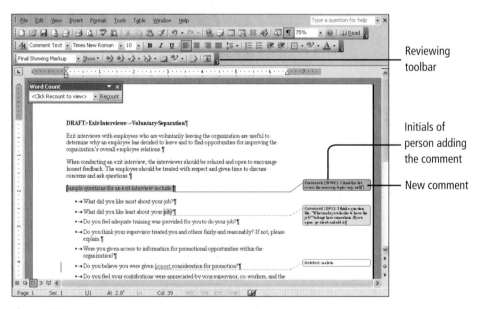

Reviewing toolbar

Initials of person adding the comment

New comment

**Figure 6.18**

**8** Click to position the insertion point at the end of the first (title) line of the document that begins *Draft Exit Interviews*. From the Reviewing toolbar, click the **Insert Comment** button ⬚. Type **Should there be a separate form for salaried vs. hourly employees?**

The last word of the line is highlighted, and the comment displays in the right margin. This comment is now *SFM1*, and the other comment you added changes to *SFM2*, as shown in Figure 6.19.

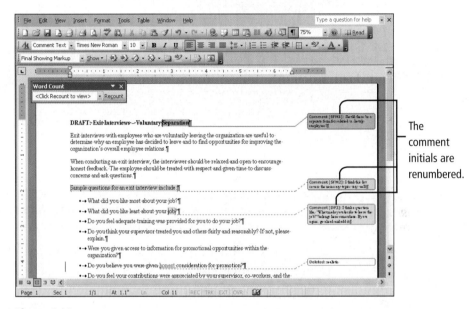

The comment initials are renumbered.

**Figure 6.19**

**9** On the Standard toolbar, click the **Save** button ⬚.

**Activity 6.7** Reading Comments Using the Reviewing Pane

You can view comments in a reviewing pane at the bottom of the screen as well as in balloons in the margin. The advantage to using the reviewing pane is that you can jump from comment to comment and read text that is sometimes too small to read in the margin.

**1** On the Word Count toolbar, click the **Recount** button `Recount`.

Notice that the document word count has not changed. Comments do not affect document statistics.

**2** On the Reviewing toolbar, click the **Reviewing Pane** button ⬚.

The reviewing pane displays at the bottom of the screen. The comment closest to the insertion point displays in the pane. The reviewing pane also includes the full name of the person who added the comment and the date and time of the comment, as shown in Figure 6.20.

Comments do not
affect word count.

Full name of the person
who added the comment

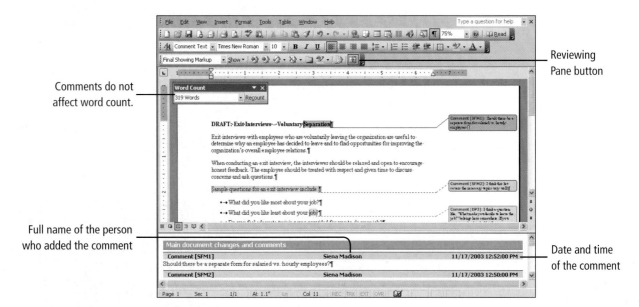

Reviewing
Pane button

Date and time
of the comment

**Figure 6.20**

3 In the upper window of your screen, use the vertical scroll bar to scroll down to the bottom of the document. Click to place the insertion point anywhere in the last paragraph, which has a comment attached.

The comment associated with this paragraph displays in the reviewing pane.

4 In the reviewing pane, use the small vertical scroll bar to scroll up. Click the comment labeled *SFM2*.

The upper window moves to display the selected comment so that the screen and reviewing pane comments match, as shown in Figure 6.21.

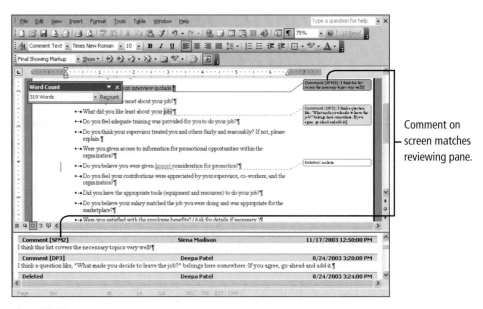

Comment on
screen matches
reviewing pane.

**Figure 6.21**

**5** From the **View** menu, point to **Toolbars**, and then click **Word Count** to close the Word Count toolbar.

**6** On the Standard toolbar, click the **Save** button 🖫.

### Activity 6.8 Editing a Comment

Comments can be edited in the balloons or in the reviewing pane. You can also add a response to someone else's comment.

**1** In the reviewing pane, in comment *DP3*, select the words *a question like*, press Delete, and then type **the following question:**

Be sure you remove the comma from the original text and add the colon to the end of the new text. Notice that the text is also changed in the balloon. Your reviewing pane should look like Figure 6.22.

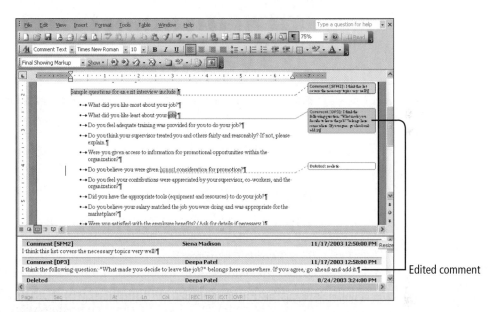

Edited comment

**Figure 6.22**

**2** In the reviewing pane, in comment *DP3*, place the insertion point at the end of the comment and press Enter.

A second line is added to the comment made by another person.

**3** In the reviewing pane, in the new line for comment *DP3*, type **I agree. Let's add this question. Siena**

Because the comment is being edited by someone other than the comment author, signing your name lets everyone know who responded to comment. See Figure 6.23.

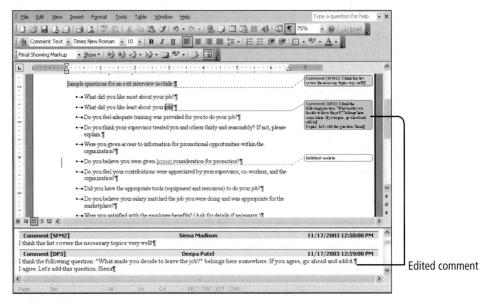

Edited comment

**Figure 6.23**

**4** On the Reviewing toolbar, click the **Reviewing Pane** button 📄.

The reviewing pane closes.

**5** On the Standard toolbar, click the **Save** button 💾.

## Objective 4
## Track Changes in a Document

The **Track Changes** feature in Word provides a visual indication of deletions, insertions, and formatting changes in a document. If the document is edited by more than one person, the changes are in different colors for each new reviewer. After the document has been reviewed by the appropriate individuals, the author can locate the changes and accept or reject the edits.

### Activity 6.9 Turning on Track Changes

While viewing a document with the Track Changes feature active, the document can be displayed in final form, showing what the document would look like if all suggested changes were accepted. Comments are also hidden.

**1** Hold down Ctrl and press Home.

The insertion point moves to the beginning of the document.

**2** On the Reviewing toolbar, click the **Display for Review button arrow** Final Showing Markup ▾ and click **Final**.

All comments and marked changes are hidden, and the document displays as it will print if all of the changes are accepted. See Figure 6.24.

Display for Review button ———

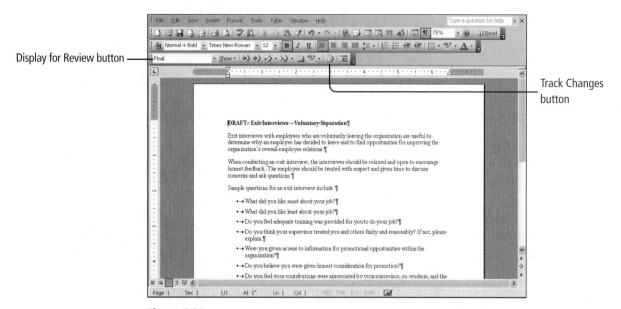

——— Track Changes button

**Figure 6.24**

**3** On the Reviewing toolbar, click the **Display for Review button arrow** [Final Showing Markup], and then click **Final Showing Markup**.

All changes to the document, such as deletions, insertions, and formatting modifications are displayed. Comments also are displayed.

**4** From the Reviewing toolbar, click the **Track Changes** button.

Track Changes is turned on, and any changes you make to the document will be visually indicated in the right margin and in the text. Notice that *TRK* is dark on the status bar.

**5** Position the insertion point at the end of the second bullet point, beginning *What did you like least.* Press Enter.

A bullet point is added to the list, and a line displays to the left of the new line, indicating that a change has been made to the document at this location.

**6** Type **What made you decide to leave this job?**

Notice that the inserted text is displayed with a different color and is underlined. The short vertical black line positioned in the left margin indicates the point at which a change has been made, but not what type of change. The type of change—formatting as a bullet point—is indicated in a balloon in the right margin.

**7** Point to the new bullet point.

A ScreenTip displays, showing who made the change and when. See Figure 6.25.

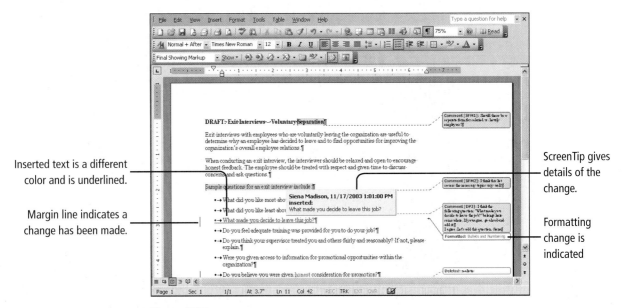

Inserted text is a different color and is underlined.

Margin line indicates a change has been made.

ScreenTip gives details of the change.

Formatting change is indicated

**Figure 6.25**

**8** Scroll down and locate the bullet point beginning *Do you believe your salary*. Select *and was appropriate for the marketplace*. Do not select the question mark. Press (Delete).

The selected text is deleted, and the deleted text is displayed in a balloon to the right of the line. A dotted line points to the location of the deleted text, as shown in Figure 6.26.

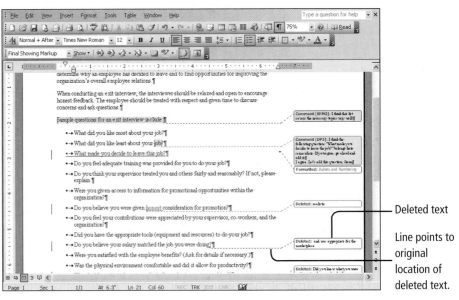

Deleted text

Line points to original location of deleted text.

**Figure 6.26**

**9** On the Standard toolbar, click the **Save** button [icon].

### Activity 6.10 Locating Changes in a Document

You can locate changes and comments in the order they appear in the document, or you can display only comments and changes by selected reviewers.

**1** Hold down [Ctrl] and press [Home] to move to the top of the document.

On the Reviewing toolbar, click the **Next** button 📄.

The insertion point moves to the first change or comment in the document. See Figure 6.27.

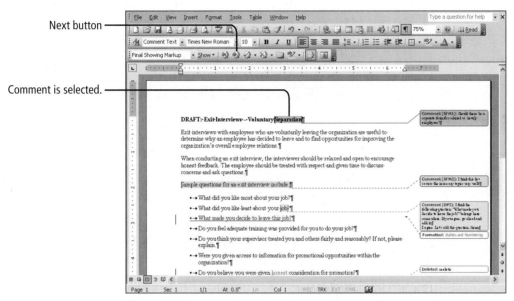

**Figure 6.27**

**2** On the Reviewing toolbar, point to the **Next** button 📄, and then watch your screen as you click the button five times.

The comments and changes are highlighted in the order they display in the document. The deletion of the word *realistic* is selected.

**3** On the Reviewing toolbar, click the **Next** button 📄 again.

The next comment or change is selected, in this case the insertion of the word *honest*. When the change was made, the word *realistic* was selected, and *honest* was typed to replace it. Deleting text and then inserting new text are treated as two separate changes to the document.

**4** On the Reviewing toolbar, click the **Show button arrow** Show ▾. Take a moment to study the available options.

You can display only comments, insertions and deletions, or formatting changes, or a combination of those changes. You can also display only the changes or comments by a specific reviewer.

**5** In the **Show** menu, point to **Reviewers**.

A list of all of the reviewers who have made changes to the document displays, as shown in Figure 6.28.

Show button ——

Check marks show which
reviewers' changes are
displayed.

List of
reviewers who
have made
changes

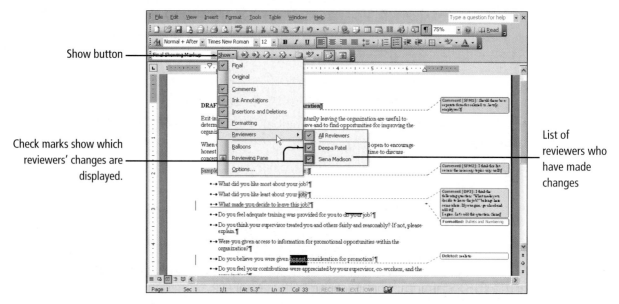

**Figure 6.28**

**6** From the **Reviewers** list, click **Deepa Patel**.

This action hides Deepa Patel's comments. Because only two reviewers
made changes to the document, only those of Siena Madison are now
displayed in the document.

**7** Click the **Show button arrow** Show ▼ again, and then point to
**Reviewers**.

Notice that the check box for Deepa Patel is cleared, as shown in
Figure 6.29.

Check box is cleared ——

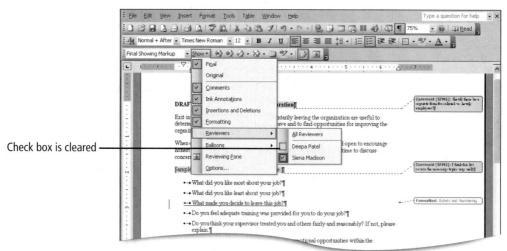

**Figure 6.29**

**8** From the **Reviewers** list, click **All Reviewers**.

All of the comments and changes are once again displayed.

**9** On the **Reviewing** toolbar, click the **Track Changes** button .

The Track Changes feature is turned off. Notice that *TRK* is gray on
the status bar. Changes made from this point on will not be marked,
but existing changes and comments still display in the document.

**10** On the Standard toolbar, click the **Save** button 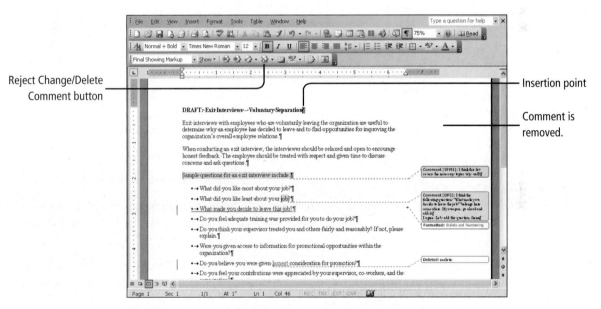.

### Activity 6.11 Accepting or Rejecting Changes in a Document

When all of the reviewers have made their suggestions and added their comments, the author must decide which changes to accept and which to reject, and which comments to act on. Unlike changes, comments are not accepted or rejected. The author reads the comments, decides whether any action is necessary, and then removes them.

**1** Hold down Ctrl and press Home to move to the top of the document. On the Reviewing toolbar, click the **Next** button.

The insertion point moves to the first comment in the document, which is a comment that will not be acted on.

**2** On the Reviewing toolbar, click the **Reject Change/Delete Comment** button.

The comment is deleted, and the insertion point remains at the comment location, as shown in Figure 6.30.

Reject Change/Delete Comment button

Insertion point

Comment is removed.

**Figure 6.30**

**3** On the Reviewing toolbar, click the **Next** button.

The next comment is selected. This comment requires no action and can be removed.

**4** On the Reviewing toolbar, click the **Reject Change/Delete Comment** button. On the Reviewing toolbar, click the **Next** button.

The next comment is selected. This comment has already been acted on when the third bullet point was added, so the comment can be removed.

**5** On the Reviewing toolbar, click the **Reject Change/Delete Comment** button. On the Reviewing toolbar, click the **Next** button.

The inserted bullet point is highlighted.

**6** On the Reviewing toolbar, click the **Accept Change** button.

The change is accepted, and the balloon is removed, as shown in Figure 6.31.

Accept Change button

Change is accepted.

**Figure 6.31**

**7** On the Reviewing toolbar, click the **Next** button.

The deleted word *realistic* in its balloon is selected.

**8** On the Reviewing toolbar, click the **Accept Change** button.

Recall that selecting and replacing text is actually two changes—a deletion and an insertion. Notice that the deletion has been accepted, but the insertion is still marked as a change.

**9** On the Reviewing toolbar, click the **Next** button to select the insertion. On the Reviewing toolbar, click the **Accept Change** button.

The insertion is accepted.

**10** On the Reviewing toolbar, click the **Accept Change button arrow**, and then click **Accept All Changes in Document**.

The remaining changes are accepted. The comment about the last paragraph is all that remains that requires action.

**11** On the Reviewing toolbar, click the **Next** button. On the Reviewing toolbar, click the **Reject Change/Delete Comment** button.

The last comment is removed. Because there are no other changes or comments, the extra space in the right margin closes, as shown in Figure 6.32.

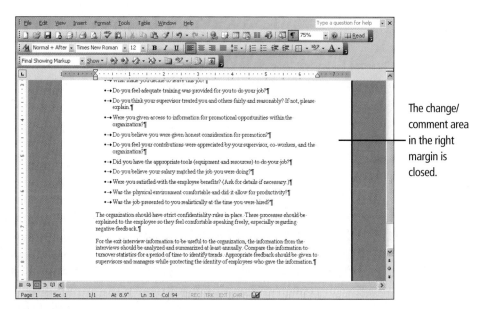

The change/comment area in the right margin is closed.

**Figure 6.32**

**12** From the **Tools** menu, click **Options**, and then click the **User Information tab**. Restore the name and initials that you changed earlier. Click **OK**.

**13** From the **View** menu, click **Header and Footer**. On the Header and Footer toolbar, click the **Switch Between Header and Footer** button 🖳.

**14** On the **Header and Footer** toolbar, click the **Insert AutoText** button Insert AutoText ▾, and then click **Filename**.

The file name is inserted in the footer.

**15** On the **Header and Footer** toolbar, click the **Close** button Close.

**16** On the Standard toolbar, click the **Save** button 🖫.

**17** From the **File** menu, click **Print**. Near the bottom of the **Print** dialog box, click the **Print what arrow**, and then click **Document properties**. Click **OK**.

All of the document properties are printed.

**18** On the Standard toolbar, click the **Print Preview** button 🔍. Take a moment to check your work. On the Print Preview toolbar, click the **Close Preview** button Close.

**19** Make any necessary changes to your document. When you are satisfied, on the Standard toolbar, click the **Print** button 🖨. Close the document, saving changes if you are prompted to do so.

**End** You have completed Project 6B ——————————————————

# Project 6C **Insurance**

Documents on which several people collaborate often need to be saved in a universal format that can be edited by reviewers using different word processing programs and that can be attached to emails for review. When reviewed documents are returned, Word has a feature that enables you to compare and merge edited documents.

In Activities 6.12 through 6.15, you will edit an article about health care benefits for the newsletter of The Management Association of Pine Valley. You will save the document in a universal document format and send it to another member of the reviewing team. Then you will compare and merge two versions of the same document. Your completed document will look similar to Figure 6.33. You will save your document as *6C_Insurance_Firstname_Lastname*.

---

Health Insurance: Preparing for Open Enrollment

In the fall, many companies will be offering open enrollment for health insurance. If you want to make your open enrollment season a success, it is a good idea to do a little groundwork well in advance. This is especially true if you are offering a new, more cost-effective plan with the same company or a more beneficial policy with another company. It is even more important that employees clearly understand the benefits of a new policy (or policy options) that they are not going to like.

Communication is the key to successful or at least non-acrimonious changes in employee benefits. Unfortunately, it is the weak link in most companies, at a time when the costs and complexities of health insurance plans make communication even more important.

The following steps need to be implemented well before the open enrollment period begins:

1. Map out changes in the plans, and carefully examine how these changes will affect the employees.
2. Check with the insurance provider to see if any sample guides are available that might help you present the information most effectively.
3. Craft a message to the employees, explaining the differences in the new plan, focusing on the positive provisions. Try to anticipate potential problem areas and defuse them, if possible.
4. Discuss the message with the union or other employee representatives.
5. Send the message to the employees. This is often best done in the summer during the vacation season.
6. Provide regular follow-ups for additional general information and to answer concerns that have been voiced.

The messages need to be well crafted, presenting the information in a positive light. Don't oversell one plan or the other a simple side-by-side comparison is far more effective, and can be designed to slightly favor a particular plan.

6C_Insurance_Firstname_Lastname

---

**Figure 6.33**
Project 6C—Insurance

# Objective 5
## Circulate Documents for Review

Documents created in Microsoft Word are saved in Microsoft's own format, which is indicated by the *.doc* extension on the document name. Some reviewers you work with may not be using Word, and their word processing program may not be able to read a Word document. You can save a Word document in **Rich Text Format (RTF)**, a universal document format that can be read by almost any word processing program. RTF files can be converted back to Word format when the editing process is complete. RTF documents use an *.rtf* extension.

Documents can be distributed as attachments to email messages. After the documents are returned from reviewers, they can be compared and merged.

### Activity 6.12 Saving a Document in a Different Format

When you save a Word document as an RTF file, all but the most complex formatting is translated into a format usable by nearly all word processing programs.

**1** On the Standard toolbar, click the **Open** button. Navigate to the location where the student files for this textbook are stored. Locate and open **w06C_Insurance**. Save the file as **6C_Insurance_Firstname_Lastname**

**2** On the Standard toolbar, click the **Zoom button arrow** 100%, and then click **Page Width**. Be sure that the nonprinting format marks are displayed, and if necessary, on the Standard toolbar, click the Show/Hide ¶ button to display formatting marks.

**3** From the **File** menu, click **Save As**.

The Save As dialog box displays.

**4** At the bottom of the **Save As** dialog box, click the **Save as type arrow** and scroll down until you can see **Rich Text Format (*.rtf)**. See Figure 6.34. (The *.rtf* may or may not display, depending on your system setup.)

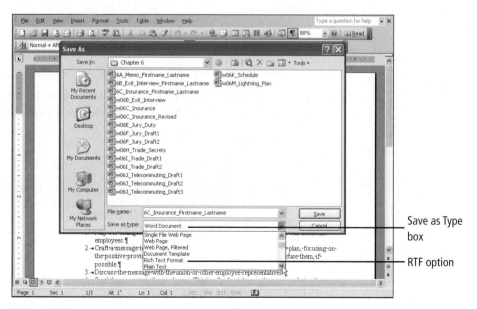

Figure 6.34

**5** From the **Save as type** list, click **Rich Text Format (*.rtf)**.

Notice that the file name in the File name box changes to 6C_Insurance_Firstname_Lastname.rtf. The extension may or may not display.

**6** At the bottom of the **Save As** dialog box, click **Save**.

The document is saved as an RTF document.

**7** From the **File** menu, click **Close**. From the **File** menu, click **Open**. Move to the location of your student files. If necessary, in the Open toolbar, click the **Views button arrow** 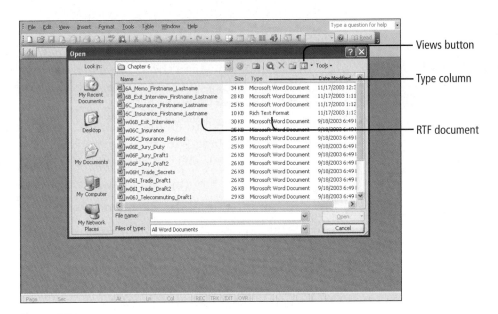, and then click **Details** to view the **Type** column.

The Open dialog box displays, showing a list of your documents, including the RTF file you just saved. The document type is shown in the *Type* column. See Figure 6.35.

Views button

Type column

RTF document

**Figure 6.35**

**8** In the **Open** dialog box, click **6C_Insurance_Firstname_Lastname.rtf**, and then click **Open**.

**9** From the **View** menu, click **Header and Footer**. On the Header and Footer toolbar, click the **Switch Between Header and Footer** button .

**10** On the **Header and Footer** toolbar, click the **Insert AutoText** button , and then click **Filename**.

The file name is inserted in the footer.

**11** On the **Header and Footer** toolbar, click the **Close** button Close.

**12** From the **File** menu, click **Save As**. At the bottom of the **Save As** dialog box, click the **Save as type arrow**, scroll, as necessary, and then click **Word Document (\*.doc)**.

The file name changes back to 6C_Insurance_Firstname_Lastname.doc, if extensions are displayed.

**13** At the bottom of the **Save As** dialog box, click **Save**.

A dialog box displays, indicating that a file of the same name already exists and asking what you want to do, as shown in Figure 6.36.

Replace existing file option —

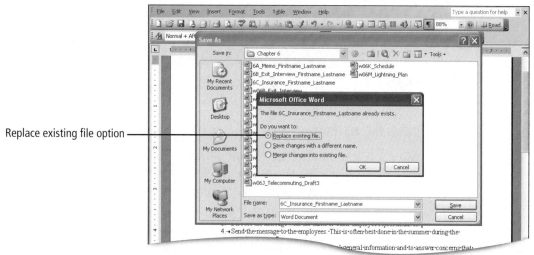

**Figure 6.36**

**14** From the dialog box, click **OK** to replace the existing file.

This Word file that you modified replaces the original RTF version of the same file. If you are not sure what to do when you see this dialog box, you should save the document under a different name.

### Activity 6.13 Attaching Documents to an Email Message

Documents can be attached to email messages and sent to others for them to review.

**1** From the **File** menu, point to **Send To**.

The *Send To* submenu displays. From this menu, you can send an email, attach the current document to an email, or send a fax. See Figure 6.37.

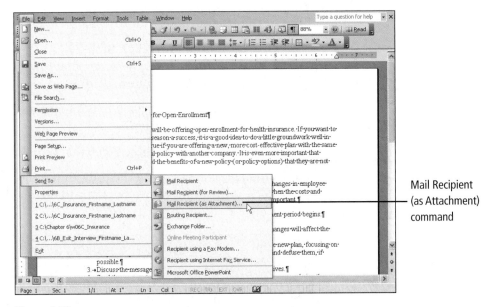

Mail Recipient
(as Attachment)
command

**Figure 6.37**

▣2 From the **Send To** menu, click **Mail Recipient (as Attachment)**.

After a few moments, an email window opens. The name of the document becomes the Subject text, and the name of the document also displays as the attachment name.

**Alert!** **Does Your Screen Differ?**

The appearance of your screen depends on various settings that your system administrator established when Office was installed and how the program has been used most recently. The email window may or may not be maximized, and the elements on the screen depend on the default email program on your computer. If you are using a non-Microsoft mail program, you may have to switch to the program yourself, or this feature may not work at all. Many organizations use Microsoft Outlook or Microsoft Outlook Express as their email program, but yours may differ. In this example, Outlook Express is the active email program.

▣3 Click within the white message area in the lower portion of the email window and type **David, Siena:** and press Enter.

▣4 Type **Please review this document and return it by Friday.**

▣5 In the top of the email window, in the **Subject** box, select the existing text and replace it with **Insurance document for your review**

▣6 In the **To** box, type **DRosenberg@mapv.org**

▣7 In the **Cc** box, type **SMadison@mapv.org**

This sends a copy of the email and attachment to Siena Madison. Compare your screen with Figure 6.38.

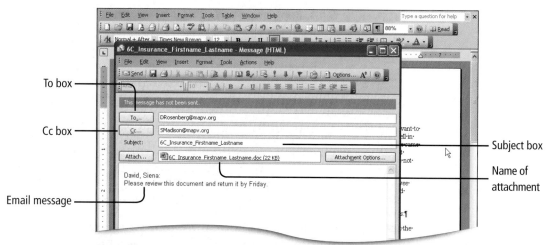

To box

Cc box

Email message

Subject box

Name of attachment

**Figure 6.38**

▣ Because you may or may not have an appropriate email connection at this time, rather than clicking the Send button, display the **File** menu, and then click **Close**. Do not save your changes when prompted.

No email is sent, and your document redisplays.

## Objective 6
### Compare and Merge Documents

It is not always possible for reviewers to make their comments and edits on a single copy of a document, as you practiced in Project B. When more than one person makes changes to different *copies* of the same document, identifying all the changes can be challenging. Word has a feature that combines the Track Changes feature with a document comparison operation. When you compare two or more documents, the changes are identified, and the Reviewing toolbar is used to decide which changes to accept and which ones to reject. The changes can be stored in the open document, or the combined documents can be saved as a new document.

There are three ways to merge documents, as shown in the table in Figure 6.39.

## Three Ways to Merge Reviewed Documents

| Type of Merge | Results |
|---|---|
| Merge | Differences in the documents are displayed as tracked changes in the unopened (baseline) document. |
| Merge into current document | Differences in the documents are displayed as tracked changes in the open document. |
| Merge into new document | Changes in both documents are merged into a new, third document, with differences shown as tracked changes. |

**Figure 6.39**

### Activity 6.14 Comparing and Merging Documents

To combine documents, you need one of the documents open and the other closed.

**1** With your **6C_Insurance_Firstname_Lastname** document open, from the **Tools** menu, click **Compare and Merge Documents**.

The Compare and Merge Documents dialog box displays.

**2** If necessary, at the bottom of the **Compare and Merge Documents** dialog box, clear the **Legal blackline** check box. Use the **Look in arrow** to navigate to the location where the student files for this textbook are stored. Locate and select **w06C_Insurance_Revised**.

**3** At the bottom of the **Compare and Merge Documents** dialog box, click the **Merge button arrow**.

The three merge commands are listed.

**4** From the **Merge** list, click **Merge into current document**.

The documents are compared and merged. The differences between the two documents are displayed as tracked changes in the open document, and the Reviewing toolbar opens. See Figure 6.40.

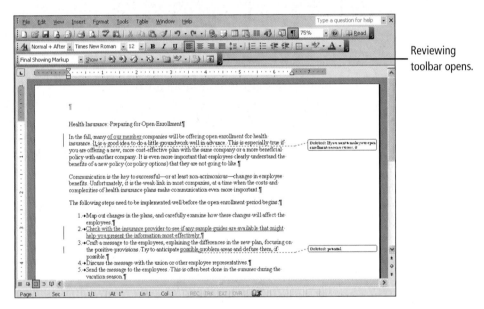

Reviewing toolbar opens.

**Figure 6.40**

**5** On the Standard toolbar, click the **Save** button.

### Activity 6.15 Accepting and Rejecting Merge Changes

Once you have identified the differences between two documents, you need to decide which changes to accept and which to reject.

**1** On the Reviewing toolbar, click the **Next** button.

The inserted text *of our member* is highlighted, as shown in Figure 6.41.

Reject Change/Delete
Comment button

Next button

Accept Change button

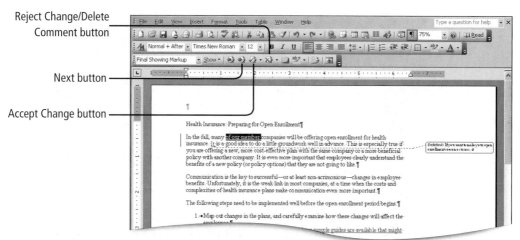

**Figure 6.41**

**2** On the Reviewing toolbar, click the **Reject Change/Delete Comment** button ![icon].

The change is removed from the document.

**3** On the Reviewing toolbar, click the **Next** button ![icon].

The phrase beginning *If you want to make* has been deleted, and the word *It* has been inserted.

**4** On the Reviewing toolbar, click the **Reject Change/Delete Comment** button ![icon].

The inserted text is removed, but the deleted text has not been addressed yet.

**5** On the Reviewing toolbar, click the **Next** button ![icon], and then click the **Reject Change/Delete Comment** button ![icon].

The deleted text is returned to the document.

**6** Click the **Next** button ![icon], and then click the **Accept Change** button ![icon].

The numbered item is added to the document.

**7** Click the **Next** button ![icon], and then click the **Reject Change/Delete Comment** button ![icon].

The inserted word *possible* is removed.

**8** Click the **Next** button ![icon], and then click the **Reject Change/Delete Comment** button ![icon].

The deleted word *potential* is returned to the document. That was the last tracked change in the document, so the expanded right margin is replaced by the standard document margin, as shown in Figure 6.42.

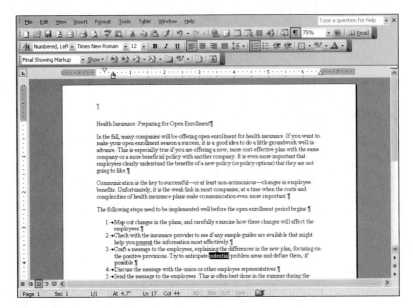

**Figure 6.42**

**9** Click the **Next** button ![Next button] once more.

A change was found in the footer—one document had the footer, the other did not.

**10** Click the **Accept Change** button ![Accept Change]. On the **Header and Footer** toolbar, click the **Close** button ![Close].

The footer is kept in the document.

**11** On the Standard toolbar, click the **Save** button ![Save].

**12** On the Standard toolbar, click the **Print Preview** button ![Print Preview]. Take a moment to check your work. On the Print Preview toolbar, click the **Close Preview** button ![Close].

**13** Make any necessary changes to your document. When you are satisfied, on the Standard toolbar, click the **Print** button ![Print]. Close the document, saving changes if you are prompted to do so, and close Word.

**End** You have completed Project 6C

# Summary

Businesses and organizations standardize document formats to give their printed materials a consistent look. Templates set up a document's structure, including page formatting, font, font size, margins, and indents. Templates are useful because they give all documents of a similar type the same look.

Business documents often are composed through a collaborative effort; that is, many individuals contribute text and ideas to the document. Word offers a number of collaboration tools. Document properties are statistics and document information that are stored with a document and can be used for document identification. These include the date the document was created and the date it was last modified. Summary information is also available and can include the document name, title, subject, and company. Information on the document category, keywords for document searches, and comments can also be added. Document statistics, such as word and line counts, enable you to keep within document guidelines.

When documents are exchanged between reviewers, comments can be added and edited, and changes can be tracked. Comments are identified by reviewer and can be added anywhere in the document, although they are not included in the final print version. The Track Changes option also enables the reader to see who made changes and exactly what changes were made. Once all of the comments have been added, and the changes by various reviewers are completed, the changes can be accepted or rejected, and the comments can be deleted.

While many companies provide a file server for quick access to group documents, it is often expedient to send document copies via email. Documents can be sent as attachments to email messages, and these documents can be compared and merged when the reviews are complete. Rich Text Format (RTF) is available if you need to send the document to someone using a word processor other than Microsoft Word.

## In This Chapter You Practiced How To

- Create a Document Using a Template
- Review and Modify Document Properties
- Use Comments in a Document
- Track Changes in a Document
- Circulate Documents for Review
- Compare and Merge Documents

**Matching** Match each term in the second column with its correct definition in the first column by writing the letter of the term on the blank line in front of the correct definition.

_____ **1.** Statistics and related information about a document, including file size and location, author, title, and subject.

_____ **2.** The template on which most documents are based; it contains the default Word document settings.

_____ **3.** The document property that shows the title, author, company, subject, and keywords for a document.

_____ **4.** A small, bordered shape in the right margin that displays a change or comment.

_____ **5.** A toolbar that keeps track of document statistics.

_____ **6.** A template set up with the elements necessary for a specific document type, such as a memo, resume, or letter.

_____ **7.** An area at the bottom of the screen that displays comments and tracked changes.

_____ **8.** A note attached to a document.

_____ **9.** The process by which documents are compared and differences are displayed as tracked changes in the unopened (baseline) document.

_____ **10.** The Word feature that enables you to see which reviewer made edits or added comments to a document.

_____ **11.** A universal document format that can be read by nearly all word processing programs.

_____ **12.** The command that compares two documents and creates a new document to display the differences.

_____ **13.** Text in a document created using a template; this text can be replaced but not edited.

_____ **14.** The toolbar button that highlights the first change or comment following the insertion point.

_____ **15.** A step-by-step program that asks you questions and then sets up a document based on your answers.

**A** Balloon

**B** Comment

**C** Document properties

**D** Document template

**E** Merge

**F** Merge into new document

**G** Next button

**H** Normal template

**I** Placeholder text

**J** Reviewing pane

**K** RTF

**L** Summary

**M** Track Changes

**N** Wizard

**O** Word Count

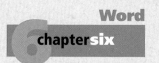
## Fill in the Blank  Write the correct answer in the space provided.

**1.** Document template files have a(n) _____ extension.

**2.** The _____ toolbar enables you to track, accept or reject changes, and delete comments.

**3.** _____ text is selected with a single click.

**4.** Microsoft Word files use a(n) _____ extension, which may or may not display depending on your system setup.

**5.** Adding Keywords to the _____ tab of the Properties dialog box is useful when you use the Windows Search command.

**6.** In the Properties dialog box, the _____ tab displays a document's word and line count.

**7.** On the Reviewing toolbar, click the Display for Review button arrow, and then click _____ to hide tracked changes and comments.

**8.** Rich Text Format documents use a(n) _____ extension.

**9.** To attach an open document to an email message using Word, click the _____ command from the File menu.

**10.** When using Track Changes, balloons are displayed in the _____ margin.

## Project 6D — Jury Duty Memo

**Objective:** *Create a Document Using a Template.*

In the following Skill Assessment, you will create a memo for The Management Association of Pine Valley. The memo will involve the review of a draft of a company policy regarding jury duty. Your completed document will look similar to the one shown in Figure 6.43. You will save your document as *6D_Jury_Duty_Memo_Firstname_Lastname.*

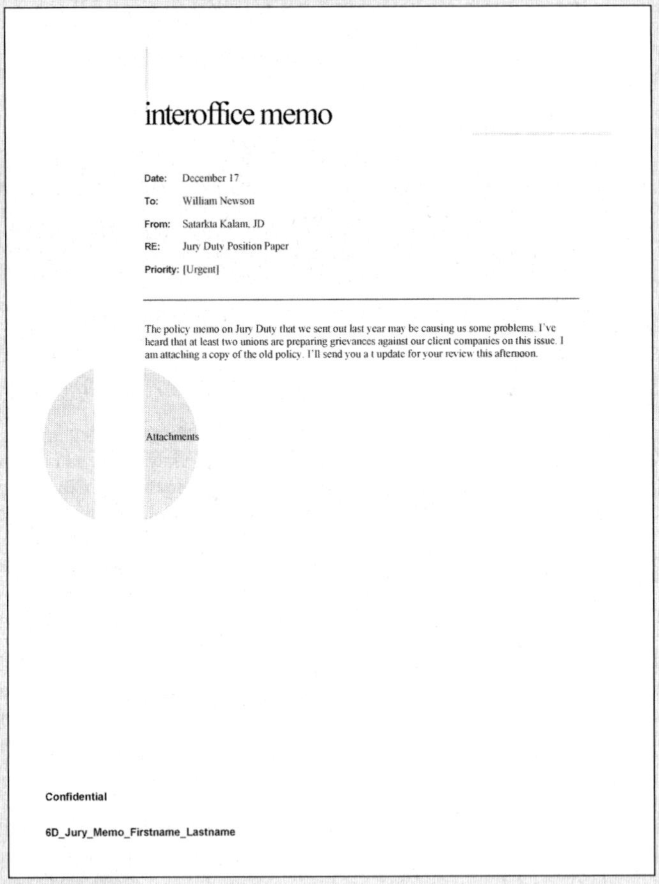

interoffice memo

Date:      December 17

To:        William Newson

From:      Satarkta Kalam, JD

RE:        Jury Duty Position Paper

Priority: [Urgent]

The policy memo on Jury Duty that we sent out last year may be causing us some problems. I've heard that at least two unions are preparing grievances against our client companies on this issue. I am attaching a copy of the old policy. I'll send you a t update for your review this afternoon.

Attachments

Confidential

6D_Jury_Memo_Firstname_Lastname

**Figure 6.43**

1. From the **File** menu, click **New**. In the **New Document** task pane, under **Templates**, click **On my computer**.

2. In the **Templates** dialog box, click the **Memos tab**, and then click the **Memo Wizard** icon. At the bottom of the **Templates** dialog box, click **OK**.

3. Examine the first **Memo Wizard** dialog box. Notice the sequence line on the left side, with the *Start* box highlighted in green. At the bottom of the dialog box, click **Next**.

**(Project 6D – Jury Duty Memo continues on the next page)**

**(Project 6D–Jury Duty Memo continued)**

4. In the *Style* **Memo Wizard** dialog box, click the **Contemporary** option button. Click **Next**.

5. In the *Title* **Memo Wizard** dialog box, accept *Interoffice Memo* as the title text by clicking **Next**.

6. In the *Heading Fields* **Memo Wizard** dialog box, if necessary, click to select (place a check mark in) the **Priority** check box. In the first three text boxes, substitute the following text, and then click **Next**. (Note that if another student has recently completed this exercise on the computer at which you are seated, the information may already be filled in.)

   Date:        **December 17**
   From:        **Satarkta Kalam, JD**
   Subject:     **Jury Duty Position Paper**

7. In the *Recipient* **Memo Wizard** dialog box, in the **To** text box, type **William Newson** and then click **Next**.

8. In the *Closing Fields* **Memo Wizard** dialog box, if necessary, select the **Attachments** check box, and then click **Next**.

9. In the *Header/Footer* **Memo Wizard** dialog box, under **Which items would you like in the footer for all pages?**, if necessary, clear the **Date** and **Page Number** check boxes, and then click **Next**.

10. In the *Finish* **Memo Wizard** dialog box, click **Finish** to display the customized memo. If the **Office Assistant** displays, click **Cancel** to close it.

11. On the Standard toolbar, click the **Save** button. Navigate to the location where the student files for this textbook are stored. Save the file as **6D_Jury_Duty_Memo_Firstname_Lastname**

12. Select the entire line **Cc: [Click here and type names]** and press Delete.

13. Click **[Click here and type your memo text]**. Type the following:

    **The policy memo on Jury Duty that we sent out last year may be causing us some problems. I've heard that at least two unions are preparing grievances against our client companies on this issue. I am attaching a copy of the old policy. I'll send you a draft of a possible update for your review this afternoon.**

14. From the **View** menu, click **Header and Footer**. On the Header and Footer toolbar, click the **Switch Between Header and Footer** button.

15. In the footer area, position the insertion point at the end of *Confidential*, and then press Enter. On the **Header and Footer** toolbar, click the **Insert AutoText** button, and then click **Filename**. Because of special formatting in the template, the file name overlaps the marked footer area; however, this will print properly.

**(Project 6D–Jury Duty Memo continues on the next page)**

**(Project 6D–Jury Duty Memo continued)**

16. On the **Header and Footer** toolbar, click the **Close** button.

17. On the Standard toolbar, click the **Save** button.

18. On the Standard toolbar, click the **Print Preview** button. Take a moment to check your work. On the Print Preview toolbar, click the **Close Preview** button.

19. Make any necessary changes to your document. When you are satisfied, on the Standard toolbar, click the **Print** button. Close the document, saving any changes.

**End** You have completed Project 6D ────────────────────

## Project 6E — Jury Duty

**Objectives:** *Use Comments in a Document, Track Changes in a Document, and Compare and Merge Documents.*

In the following Skill Assessment, you will edit an employee leave policy for jury duty. You will work with the document summary. You will add comments, track changes, and then accept or reject the changes and remove the comments. Your completed document will look similar to the one shown in Figure 6.44. You will save your document as *6E_Jury_Duty_Firstname_Lastname.*

1. Start Word. On the Standard toolbar, click the **Open** button. Navigate to the location where the student files for this textbook are stored. Locate and open **w06E_Jury_Duty**. Save the file as **6E_Jury_Duty_Firstname_Lastname**

2. On the Standard toolbar, click the **Zoom button arrow**, and then click **Page Width**. If necessary, on the Standard toolbar, click the Show/Hide ¶ button to display formatting marks.

3. From the **Tools** menu, click **Options**, and then click the **Track Changes tab**. Under **Balloons**, click the **Use Balloons (Print and Web Layout) arrow**, and then click **Always**.

4. In the **Options** dialog box, click the **User Information tab**. Note the name and initials and restore them when Project 6F is completed. Under **User information**, in the **Name** box, type **Satarkta Kalam, JD** and in the **Initials** box, type **SK** Click **OK**.

5. From the **View** menu, point to **Toolbars** and if necessary, click **Reviewing** to activate the Reviewing toolbar.

**(Project 6E–Jury Duty continues on the next page)**

**(Project 6E–Jury Duty continued)**

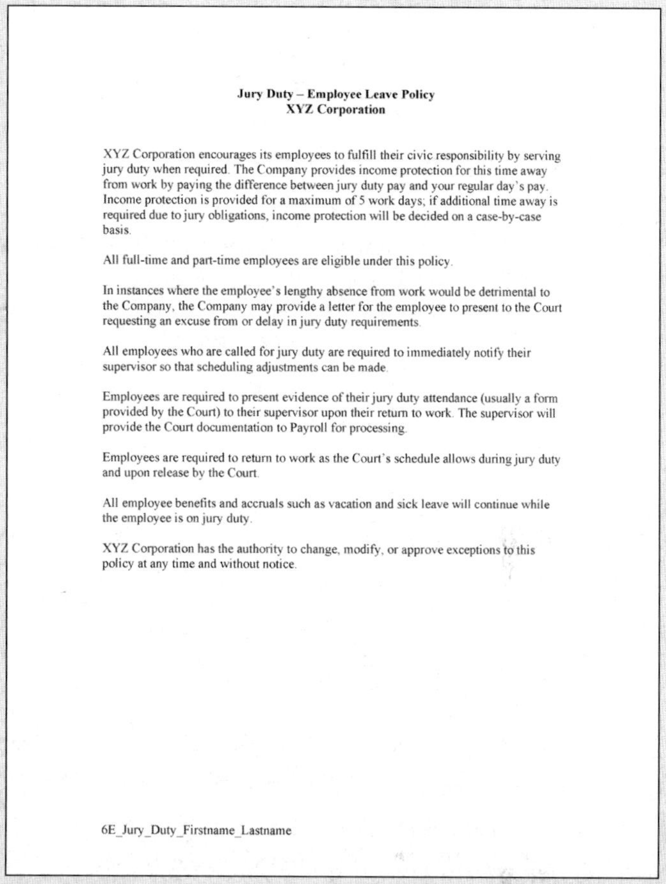

**Jury Duty – Employee Leave Policy**
**XYZ Corporation**

XYZ Corporation encourages its employees to fulfill their civic responsibility by serving
jury duty when required. The Company provides income protection for this time away
from work by paying the difference between jury duty pay and your regular day's pay.
Income protection is provided for a maximum of 5 work days; if additional time away is
required due to jury obligations, income protection will be decided on a case-by-case
basis.

All full-time and part-time employees are eligible under this policy.

In instances where the employee's lengthy absence from work would be detrimental to
the Company, the Company may provide a letter for the employee to present to the Court
requesting an excuse from or delay in jury duty requirements.

All employees who are called for jury duty are required to immediately notify their
supervisor so that scheduling adjustments can be made.

Employees are required to present evidence of their jury duty attendance (usually a form
provided by the Court) to their supervisor upon their return to work. The supervisor will
provide the Court documentation to Payroll for processing.

Employees are required to return to work as the Court's schedule allows during jury duty
and upon release by the Court.

All employee benefits and accruals such as vacation and sick leave will continue while
the employee is on jury duty.

XYZ Corporation has the authority to change, modify, or approve exceptions to this
policy at any time and without notice.

6E_Jury_Duty_Firstname_Lastname

**Figure 6.44**

6. Near the top of the document, locate the sentence that begins *The Company provides income protection*. Hold down [Ctrl] and click anywhere in the sentence to select it. From the Reviewing toolbar, click the **Insert Comment** button. Type **This phrase could cause trouble.**

7. In the lower portion of the page, select the sentence that begins *Employees are required to return to work*. From the Reviewing toolbar, click the **Insert Comment** button. Type **This is another controversial section.** On the Standard toolbar, click the **Save** button.

8. Hold down [Ctrl] and press [Home]. From the Reviewing toolbar, click the **Track Changes** button to turn the feature on. On the Reviewing toolbar, click the **Display for Review button arrow**, and then click **Final Showing Markup**. This will display the changes within the document.

**(Project 6E–Jury Duty continues on the next page)**

**(Project 6E–Jury Duty continued)**

9. In the paragraph that begins *In instances where the employee*, double-click *lengthy* and press Delete.

10. In the same paragraph, position the insertion point after *from* near the end of the paragraph. Press Space, and then type **or delay in**

11. In the paragraph that begins *All employees who are called*, select *who are* and press Delete.

12. On the **Reviewing** toolbar, click the **Track Changes** button to turn off Track Changes.

13. Hold down Ctrl and press Home to move to the top of the document. On the Reviewing toolbar, click the **Next** button.

14. On the Reviewing toolbar, click the **Reject Change/Delete Comment** button to delete the first comment.

15. On the Reviewing toolbar, click the **Next** button, and then click the **Accept Change** button to accept the insertion.

16. On the Reviewing toolbar, click the **Next** button, and then click the **Reject Change/Delete Comment** button to delete the second comment. Repeat this procedure to accept any changes and remove any other comments in the document.

17. From the **View** menu, click **Header and Footer**. On the Header and Footer toolbar, click the **Switch Between Header and Footer** button.

18. On the **Header and Footer** toolbar, click the **Insert AutoText** button, and then click **Filename**.

19. On the **Header and Footer** toolbar, click the **Close** button.

20. On the Standard toolbar, click the **Save** button.

21. On the Standard toolbar, click the **Print Preview** button. Take a moment to check your work. On the Print Preview toolbar, click the **Close Preview** button.

22. Make any necessary changes to your document. When you are satisfied, on the Standard toolbar, click the **Print** button.

23. From the **Tools** menu, click **Options**, and then click the **User Information tab**. Restore the name and initials that you changed earlier. Click **OK**. Close the file, saving any changes.

**End** You have completed Project 6E

## Project 6F — Jury Final

**Objectives:** *Review and Modify Document Properties, Circulate Documents for Review, and Compare and Merge Documents.*

In the following Skill Assessment, you will finalize edits on two different drafts of the employee leave policy for jury duty. You will work with the document summary and print the summary. You will also compare, merge, and respond to tracked changes in the two draft documents to produce a final document. Your completed document will look similar to the one shown in Figure 6.45. You will save your document as *6F_Jury_Final_Firstname_Lastname.*

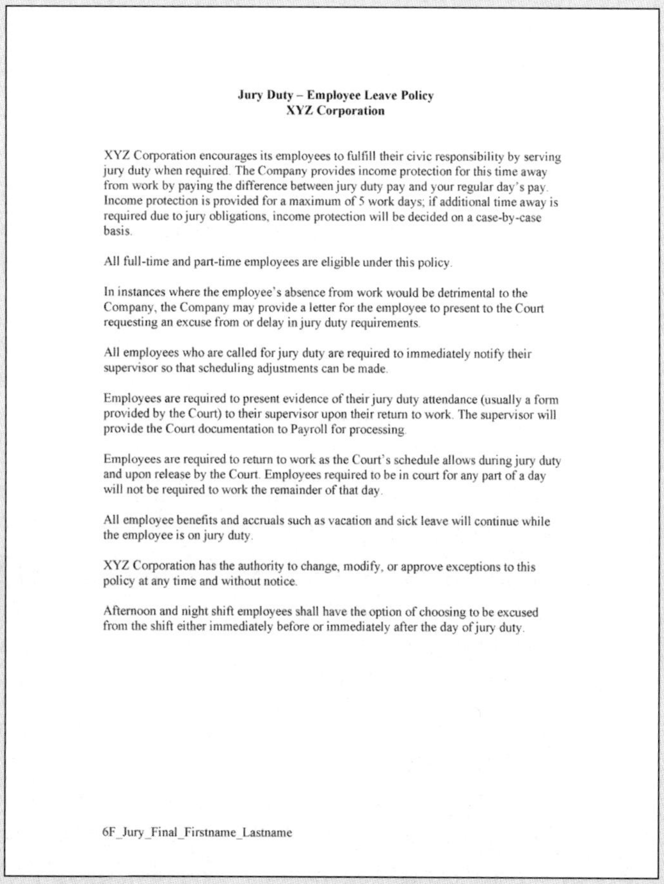

**Jury Duty – Employee Leave Policy**
**XYZ Corporation**

XYZ Corporation encourages its employees to fulfill their civic responsibility by serving jury duty when required. The Company provides income protection for this time away from work by paying the difference between jury duty pay and your regular day's pay. Income protection is provided for a maximum of 5 work days; if additional time away is required due to jury obligations, income protection will be decided on a case-by-case basis.

All full-time and part-time employees are eligible under this policy.

In instances where the employee's absence from work would be detrimental to the Company, the Company may provide a letter for the employee to present to the Court requesting an excuse from or delay in jury duty requirements.

All employees who are called for jury duty are required to immediately notify their supervisor so that scheduling adjustments can be made.

Employees are required to present evidence of their jury duty attendance (usually a form provided by the Court) to their supervisor upon their return to work. The supervisor will provide the Court documentation to Payroll for processing.

Employees are required to return to work as the Court's schedule allows during jury duty and upon release by the Court. Employees required to be in court for any part of a day will not be required to work the remainder of that day.

All employee benefits and accruals such as vacation and sick leave will continue while the employee is on jury duty.

XYZ Corporation has the authority to change, modify, or approve exceptions to this policy at any time and without notice.

Afternoon and night shift employees shall have the option of choosing to be excused from the shift either immediately before or immediately after the day of jury duty.

6F_Jury_Final_Firstname_Lastname

**Figure 6.45**

1. On the Standard toolbar, click the **Open** button. Navigate to the location where the student files for this textbook are stored. Locate and open **w06F_Jury_Draft1**. Save the file as **6F_Jury_Final_Firstname_Lastname**

2. On the Standard toolbar, click the **Zoom button arrow**, and then click **Page Width**. If necessary, to display formatting marks on the Standard toolbar, click the Show/Hide ¶ button.

**(Project 6F–Jury Final continues on the next page)**

**(Project 6F–Jury Final continued)**

3. From the **File** menu, click **Properties**. If necessary, click the **Summary tab**.

4. In the **Summary** sheet, in the **Author** box, type your name.

5. In the **Summary** sheet, type the following in the indicated boxes:

| | |
|---|---|
| Title | **Jury Duty Final** |
| Keywords | **Jury, Leave** |
| Comments | **Final Draft of the Jury Duty policy statement document** |
| Company | **The Management Association of Pine Valley** |

6. At the bottom of the **Properties** box, click **OK**. On the Standard toolbar, click the **Save** button.

7. From the **File** menu, click **Save As**. At the bottom of the **Save As** dialog box, click the **Save as type arrow**, scroll down, and then click **Rich Text Format**. At the bottom of the **Save As** dialog box, click **Save**.

8. From the **File** menu, click **Print**. Near the bottom of the **Print** dialog box, click the **Print what arrow**, and then click **Document properties**. Click **OK** to print the document properties. Notice that the document type is .rtf.

9. From the **File** menu, click **Close**. From the **File** menu, click **Open**. If necessary, move to the location of your student files. Check to see that the document type is visible, and if necessary, click the Views button arrow in the upper right corner of the dialog box, and then click Details. In the **Open** dialog box, click the *Word document* **6F_Jury_Final_Firstname_Lastname**, and then click **Open**.

10. From the **Tools** menu, click **Compare and Merge Documents**. In the displayed dialog box, navigate to the location where the student files for this textbook are stored. Locate and select **w06F_Jury_Draft2**.

11. At the bottom of the **Compare and Merge Documents** dialog box, click the **Merge button arrow**. If necessary, at the bottom of the **Compare and Merge Documents** dialog box, clear the **Legal blackline** check box. From the **Merge** list, click **Merge into current document**.

12. On the Standard toolbar, click the **Save** button.

13. On the Reviewing toolbar, click the **Next** button, and then click the **Accept Change** button to accept the deletion of *lengthy*.

14. On the Reviewing toolbar, click the **Next** button, and then click the **Accept Change** button to accept the insertion of the sentence beginning *Employees required to be in court.*

**(Project 6F–Jury Final continues on the next page)**

**(Project 6F–Jury Final continued)**

15. On the Reviewing toolbar, click the **Next** button, and then click the **Reject Change/Delete Comment** button to reject the deletion of *and without notice.*

16. On the Reviewing toolbar, click the **Next** button, and then click the **Accept Change** button to accept the addition of the paragraph beginning *Afternoon and night shift.*

17. On the Standard toolbar, click the **Save** button.

18. From the **View** menu, click **Header and Footer**. On the Header and Footer toolbar, click the **Switch Between Header and Footer** button. Click the **Insert AutoText** button, and then click **Filename**.

19. On the **Header and Footer** toolbar, click the **Close** button.

20. On the Standard toolbar, click the **Print Preview** button. Take a moment to check your work. On the Print Preview toolbar, click the **Close Preview** button. Make any necessary changes to your document. When you are satisfied, on the Standard toolbar, click the **Print** button.

21. If you are using your own computer and have it set up to use Word for email, from the **File** menu, point to **Send To**.

22. From the **Send To** menu, click **Mail Recipient (as Attachment)**. In the open area in the bottom part of the email window, type your name and press .

23. Type **Please review this document over the weekend and return it by Monday.**

24. In the top of the email window, in the **Subject** box, select the existing text and type **Jury Duty document**

25. In the **To** box, type your email address.

26. If you are sure you have an appropriate email configuration, click the **Send** button; otherwise, from the **File** menu, click **Close** and do not save your changes. If necessary, check your email to make sure the document arrived.

**End** You have completed Project 6F ―――――――――――――――――

## Project 6G — Trade Fax

**Objectives:** *Create a Document Using a Template and Circulate Documents for Review.*

In the following Performance Assessment, you will create a fax to a company about an enclosed trade secret and nondisclosure agreement. Your completed document will look similar to the one shown in Figure 6.46. You will save your document as *6G_Trade_Fax_Firstname_Lastname*.

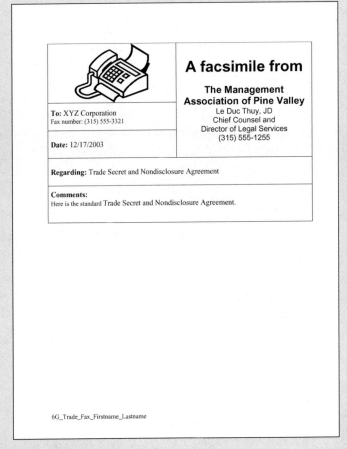

**Figure 6.46**

1. From the **File** menu, click **New**. In the **New Document** task pane, under **Templates**, click **On my computer**.

2. In the **Templates** dialog box, click the **Letters & Faxes tab**, and then click the **Business Fax** icon. At the bottom of the **Templates** dialog box, click **OK**. If you do not have the same business fax template as the one displayed in Figure 6.46, use a similar one and adjust your responses accordingly.

**(Project 6G–Trade Fax continues on the next page)**

**(Project 6G–Trade Fax continued)**

3. Save the document as **6G_Trade_Fax_Firstname_Lastname**

4. Replace the **To** placeholder with **XYZ Corporation**

5. Place the insertion point after *Fax number* and type **(315) 555-3321**

6. Replace the **Business name** placeholder with **The Management Association of Pine Valley**

7. Replace the **Contact information** placeholder with the following:

   **Le Duc Thuy, JD**
   **Chief Counsel and**
   **Director of Legal Services**
   **(315) 555-0155**

8. Replace the **Regarding** placeholder with **Trade Secret and Nondisclosure Agreement**

9. In the **Comments** box, on the line below *Comments*, type **Here is the standard Trade Secret and Nondisclosure Agreement.**

10. Use **Insert AutoText** to insert the file name in a footer, and then close the footer.

11. On the Standard toolbar, click the **Save** button. Preview the document, and then print it.

12. Save and close the document.

**End** You have completed Project 6G

## Project 6H — Trade Secrets

**Objectives:** *Use Comments in a Document and Track Changes in a Document.*

In the following Performance Assessment, you will add comments and make changes to a trade secrets and nondisclosure agreement policy statement, and then you will accept or reject changes. Your completed document will look similar to the one shown in Figure 6.47. You will save your document as *6H_Trade_Secrets_Firstname_Lastname.*

1. On the Standard toolbar, click the **Open** button. Navigate to the location where the student files for this textbook are stored. Locate and open **w06H_Trade_Secrets**. This file contains comments and changes that have been made with the Track Changes feature turned on. Save the file as **6H_Trade_Secrets_Firstname_Lastname**

2. On the Standard toolbar, click the **Zoom button arrow**, and then click **Page Width**. If necessary, on the Standard toolbar, click the Show/Hide ¶ button to display formatting marks.

**(Project 6H–Trade Secrets continues on the next page)**

**(Project 6H–Trade Secrets continued)**

**Trade Secret and Nondisclosure Agreement**

This Agreement is entered into on this ___ day of _____, 20__ by and between _____ ("Company") and _____ ("Employee").

Whereas, 1) Company has agreed to hire Employee; 2) as part of his/her employment, Employee will learn confidential information and trade secrets belonging to the Company; 3) the dissemination of such confidential information and trade secrets to persons inside or outside of the Company who are not entitled to receive such information is harmful to the company.

Therefore, Employee agrees not to disclose to any such person any confidential information or trade secret, directly or indirectly, whether for compensation or no compensation, without the written consent of the Company.

If Employee is not sure whether information he/she has obtained falls under said definition, Employee shall treat that information as confidential unless Employee is informed otherwise by the Company.

Employee acknowledges that a violation of this Agreement will cause damage and harm to the Company that can include loss of competitive advantage, loss of revenue, and other harm not specifically outlined in this Agreement. Employee agrees that upon written notice from Company of a breach of this agreement that Employee will immediately cease all activities which are or are claimed to constitute said breach. Employee agrees that Company may request relief for damages incurred by any such breach.

This agreement remains in effect until released in writing by the Company and is not cancelled by the end of Employee's employment with the company.

The parties have executed this Agreement on the date written above.

[Company Name]

_____
By: [Signer's name]

_____
By: [Employee's Name]

This Agreement is enforced under the laws of _____ [name of state].

6H_Trade_Secrets_Firstname_Lastname

**Figure 6.47**

3. From the **Tools** menu, click **Options**, and then click the **Track Changes tab**. Turn on balloons for all tracked changes.

4. In the **Options** dialog box, click the **User Information tab**. Note the name and initials and restore them when Project 6I is completed. Under **User information**, in the **Name** box, type **David Rosenberg** and in the **Initials** box, type **DR**

5. Right-click on any toolbar and if necessary, click Reviewing to display the toolbar. Turn on **Track Changes** (the button will display as orange when the feature is turned on and as blue when the feature is turned off).

6. Select the title (the first line of the document). Change the font to **Arial Black** and the font size to **14**.

7. In the paragraph that begins *Therefore, Employee agrees*, position the insertion point after the space following the word *confidential*. Type **or proprietary** and press Space.

**(Project 6H–Trade Secrets continues on the next page)**

**(Project 6H–Trade Secrets continued)**

8. In the paragraph that begins *Employee acknowledges that a violation*, near the end of the paragraph, position the insertion after the space following the word *request*. Type **equitable** and press ⎵.

9. Save the document. Hold down Ctrl and press Home to move to the beginning of the document. On the Reviewing toolbar, click the **Next** button, and then click the **Accept Change** button to accept the formatting change to the title. Press the **Next** button again, and then click the **Accept Change** button to accept the deletion of *4*.

10. Move to the next change, an insertion of *3*, and accept it. Move to the next change, the insertion of *or proprietary*, and accept it.

11. Move to the next change and click the **Reject Change/Delete Comment** button to reject the deletion of the paragraph beginning *If Employee is not sure*.

12. Move to the next change. Accept the insertion of *equitable*. Leave the comment at the end of the document for the next reviewer to read. Turn off **Track Changes**.

13. Use **Insert AutoText** to insert the file name in a footer, and then close the footer. In the **Reviewing** toolbar, click the **Display for Review arrow** and click **Final** to show the document without the comment in the margin.

14. If you are not going to do Project 6I, from the **Tools** menu, click **Options**, and then click the **User Information tab**. Restore the name and initials that you changed earlier. Click **OK**.

15. Save the document. Preview and print the document. Close all documents, saving any changes.

**End** You have completed Project 6H

## Project 6I — Trade Final

**Objectives:** *Review and Modify Document Properties and Compare and Merge Documents.*

In the following Performance Assessment, you will change the document properties for a trade secrets and nondisclosure agreement policy statement, and then you will compare and merge two drafts of the same documents. Your completed document will look similar to the one shown in Figure 6.48. You will save your document as *6I_Trade_Final_Firstname_Lastname*.

1. On the Standard toolbar, click the **Open** button. Navigate to the location where the student files for this textbook are stored. Locate and open **w06I_Trade_Draft1**.

**(Project 6I–Trade Final continues on the next page)**

**(Project 6I**–Trade Final continued)

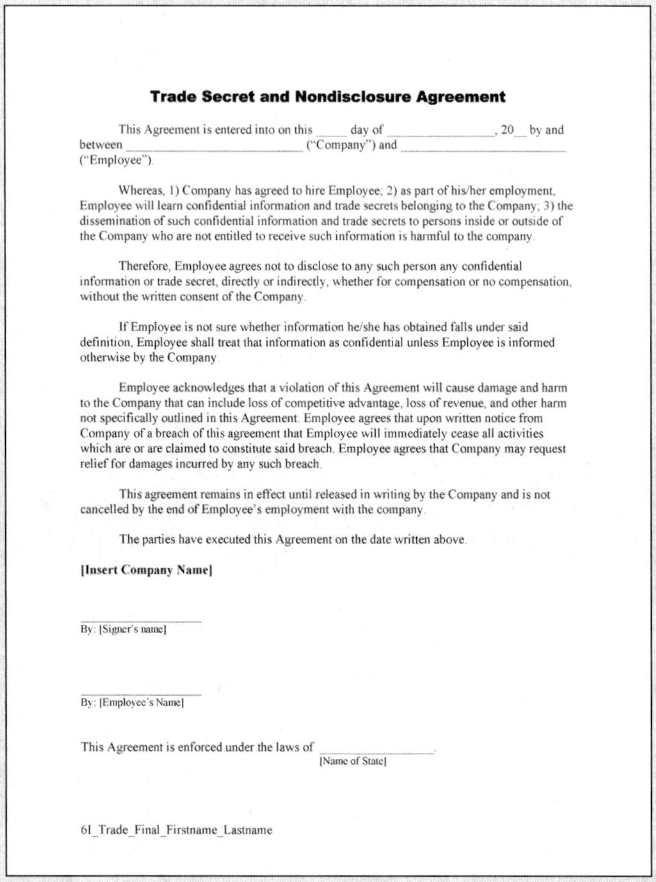

**Trade Secret and Nondisclosure Agreement**

This Agreement is entered into on this _____ day of _____, 20__ by and between _____ ("Company") and _____ ("Employee").

Whereas, 1) Company has agreed to hire Employee; 2) as part of his/her employment, Employee will learn confidential information and trade secrets belonging to the Company; 3) the dissemination of such confidential information and trade secrets to persons inside or outside of the Company who are not entitled to receive such information is harmful to the company.

Therefore, Employee agrees not to disclose to any such person any confidential information or trade secret, directly or indirectly, whether for compensation or no compensation, without the written consent of the Company.

If Employee is not sure whether information he/she has obtained falls under said definition, Employee shall treat that information as confidential unless Employee is informed otherwise by the Company.

Employee acknowledges that a violation of this Agreement will cause damage and harm to the Company that can include loss of competitive advantage, loss of revenue, and other harm not specifically outlined in this Agreement. Employee agrees that upon written notice from Company of a breach of this agreement that Employee will immediately cease all activities which are or are claimed to constitute said breach. Employee agrees that Company may request relief for damages incurred by any such breach.

This agreement remains in effect until released in writing by the Company and is not cancelled by the end of Employee's employment with the company.

The parties have executed this Agreement on the date written above.

**[Insert Company Name]**

_____
By: [Signer's name]


_____
By: [Employee's Name]


This Agreement is enforced under the laws of _____.
                                                [Name of State]


6I_Trade_Final_Firstname_Lastname

**Figure 6.48**

2. From the **Tools** menu, click **Options**, and then click the **Track Changes tab**. Under **Balloons**, be sure the **Use Balloons (Print and Web Layout)** box indicates **Always**. If necessary, change the **Zoom** to **Page Width** and turn on the formatting characters.

3. From the **Tools** menu, click **Compare and Merge Documents**. Navigate to the location where the student files for this textbook are stored. Locate and select **w06I_Trade_Draft2**.

4. At the bottom of the **Compare and Merge Documents** dialog box, click the **Merge button arrow**. From the **Merge** list, click **Merge into new document**. All differences between the two versions are displayed in an unnamed document, leaving the original documents unchanged.

5. Save the new document on your screen as **6I_Trade_Final_Firstname_Lastname**

**(Project 6I**–Trade Final continues on the next page)

**(Project 6I–Trade Final continued)**

6. On the Reviewing toolbar, click the **Next** button. All of the changes appear to be selected, but this is an indication that the document margins have changed, as shown in the first balloon. Click the **Accept Change** button to accept the new margins.

7. Move to the next change, which is inserted underlines to make the black lines longer, and accept the change. Repeat the procedure for the other three line changes.

8. Move to the next change, in which the word *Insert* was inserted, and accept the change.

9. On the Reviewing toolbar, click the **Next** button, and then click the **Accept Change button arrow**. Click **Accept All Changes in Document** to accept the remainder of the changes. If necessary, delete any remaining comments.

10. Create a footer, use **Insert AutoText** to insert the file name, and then close the footer. Save the document.

11. From the **File** menu, click **Properties** and move to the **Summary** sheet, if necessary.

12. In the **Summary** sheet, type the following in the indicated boxes:

| | |
|---|---|
| Author | **your name** |
| Title | **Trade Secrets Policy Statement** |
| Comments | **Final Draft of the Trade Secrets and Nondisclosure Agreement policy statement** |
| Company | **The Management Association of Pine Valley** |

13. Save your work. Preview the document and print it if you are satisfied with the way it looks.

14. From the **Tools** menu, click **Options**, and then click the **User Information tab**. Restore the name and initials that you changed earlier. Click **OK**. Close all documents, saving any changes.

**End** You have completed Project 6I

## Project 6J — Telecommuting

**Objectives:** *Compare and Merge Documents and Review and Modify Document Properties.*

In the following Mastery Assessment, you will compare and merge three drafts of a proposed Telecommuting Policy for The Management Association of Pine Valley. To merge three documents, you compare and merge two of them, and then compare the third document to the merged document. Your completed document will look similar to the one shown in Figure 6.49. You will save your document as *6J_Telecommuting_Firstname_Lastname*.

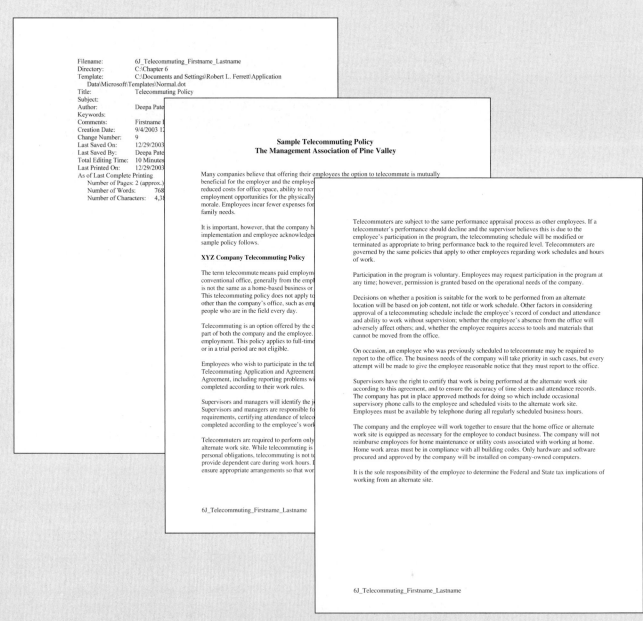

**Figure 6.49**

**(Project 6J–Telecommuting continues on the next page)**

**(Project 6J–Telecommuting continued)**

1. Start Word. From your student files, open **w06J_Telecommuting_Draft1**. Save the file with the name **6J_Telecommuting_Firstname_Lastname** in the same location as your other files from this textbook. In the same manner as you have done in previous documents, create a footer and insert the **AutoText** filename.

2. Compare and merge the document **w06J_Telecommuting_Draft2** into the current document. In the displayed box, be sure the first option— **Your document**—is selected, and then click **Continue with Merge**.

3. Accept changes until you reach the deletion of *means*. Reject the change from *means* to *is defined as*. Reject the deletion of the sentence that begins *It is the sole responsibility*. Accept all other changes and click Save.

4. Compare and merge the **w06J_Telecommuting_Draft3** document into the current document on your screen. Accept the default and click **Continue with Merge**. At the bottom of the document, reject the deletion of the sentence that begins *It is the sole responsibility*. Accept all other changes and save the document.

5. In the document summary, type **Telecommuting Policy** as the **Title**, **Deepa Patel** as the **Author**, and **The Management Association of Pine Valley** as the **Company**. Type your name in the **Comments** box.

6. Save the completed document. Preview and print the document, and then print the document properties. Save and close the document.

**End** You have completed Project 6J

## Project 6K — Schedule

**Objectives:** *Use Comments in a Document, Track Changes in a Document, Review and Modify Document Properties, and Circulate Documents for Review.*

In the following Mastery Assessment, you will edit a document regarding training sessions and seminars that has already been edited extensively by a colleague. You will make changes, and then print the document displaying all of the changes and comments. Your completed document will look similar to the one shown in Figure 6.50. You will save your document as *6K_Schedule_Firstname_Lastname*.

1. Start Word. From your student files, open **w06K_Schedule**. Save the file with the name **6K_Schedule_Firstname_Lastname** in the same location as your other files. In the same manner as you have done in previous documents, display the footer and insert the **AutoText** filename.

**(Project 6K–Schedule continues on the next page)**

**(Project 6K–Schedule continued)**

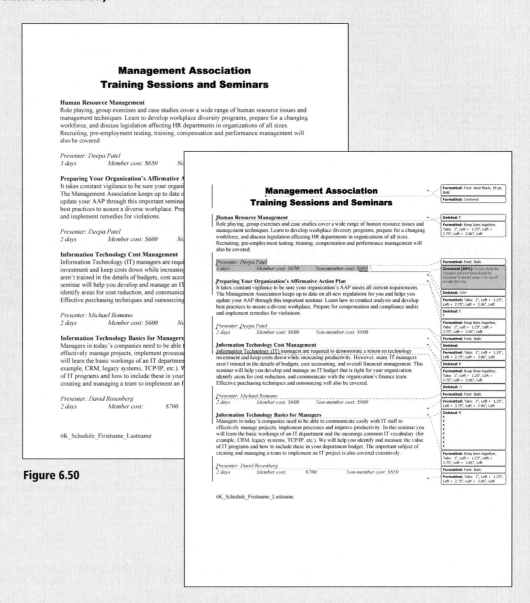

**Figure 6.50**

2. Turn on the Reviewing toolbar and, if necessary, turn on **Track Changes**. If necessary, turn on balloons for all tracked changes.

3. At the end of each Training Session description, the name of the Presenter is listed, followed in the next line by the date and cost. Go through the document and make all of these line pairs **Italic**. This will add additional tracked changes, but in a different color to identify you as a new reviewer.

**(Project 6K–Schedule continues on the next page)**

**(Project 6K–Schedule continued)**

4. In the middle of page 1, locate the first line following the *Information Technology Cost Management* heading, select *IT* (the first word in the sentence), and then replace it with **Information Technology (IT)**

5. Scroll down to examine the numerous changes to the document. To print these tracked changes, from the **Print** dialog box, click the **Print what** arrow, and then click **Document showing markup**. Under **Page range**, click the **Pages** option button, and then in the **Pages** box, type **1** so that only the first page prints. Click **OK**.

6. On the Reviewing toolbar, click the **Display for Review arrow**, and then click **Final** to see what the final document will look like. Print only the first page.

7. In the document summary, add your name and the current date to the **Comments** area. Change the **Title** to **Training Sessions and Seminars** and change the **Company** to **The Management Association of Pine Valley**

8. If your email system is set to do so, send the document as an email attachment to a friend or to yourself. Save your changes and close the document.

**End** You have completed Project 6K

## Project 6L — Resume

**Objectives:** *Create a Document Using a Template and Review and Modify Document Properties.*

Your resume is the first thing a prospective employer sees. Two things are important in an effective resume: the look of the document and the information about yourself. A professional-looking resume will give you a much better chance of having the potential employer take the time to read about your qualifications. In this project, you will create and save your resume as *6L_Resume_Firstname_Lastname*.

1. Create a new document using the **Professional Resume** template in the **Other Documents tab** of the **Templates** dialog box. Save the document as **6L_Resume_Firstname_Lastname**

2. At the top of the resume, enter your address and phone number as indicated by the placeholder text.

3. Write an objective for a job you are considering now or in the future after you have completed more education.

4. Replace the information in the various categories with your own information. If you have had only one job, delete the other job headings and their associated information.

5. Under *Education*, add any certificates or degrees you have. If you have not yet earned a certificate or degree, enter the expected date of certificate completion or graduation. Add any honors you have received, and/or your grade point average if it is above 3.0 on a 4.0 scale. Be sure you include your major, if you have one.

6. Add any interests where indicated, and then delete the *Tips* section, unless you have a category you would like to add (such as Public Service).

7. Go to the **Document Properties** dialog box and add your name in the **Author** box and the name of this document in the **Title** box. Type your college name for the **Company** name. In the **Comments** area, add the current date. Save your work and close the document. You might want to keep this file and update it whenever appropriate.

**End** You have completed Project 6L

## Project 6M — Lightning

**Objectives:** *Use Comments in a Document and Review and Modify Document Properties.*

In this project, you will add and edit comments in a draft copy of a lightning action plan document. You will save the document as *6M_Lightning_Firstname_Lastname*.

**1.** Locate and open **w06M_Lightning**. Save it as **6M_Lightning_Firstname_ Lastname** with your other files. As you have with previous files, display the footer area and insert the **AutoText** filename.

**2.** Turn on the **Reviewing** toolbar and open the **reviewing pane**.

**3.** Display the Properties sheet, write down the existing **User Information**, and then change the user information to your name and initials.

**4.** Look through the document and add two comments on any topic of your choice.

**5.** Respond to the comments of Satarkta Kalam as if you were a member of the team working on the document and knew the answers to his questions. Search the Web to find a site with information about lightning safety for outdoor workers and add a sentence about the site. Add a hyperlink to a word or phrase in the new sentence that will take the reader to the site you have found.

**6.** Restore the **User Information** to the original name and initials. Save the document, print it, and then close the file.

**End** You have completed Project 6M

## Downloading a Template from the Office Web Site

In this chapter you created a professional-looking memo using a template that was stored on your computer. Many templates are installed with Microsoft Office, but one that is exactly right for your purpose may not be included. Microsoft has an Internet site that makes many additional templates available.

1. Be sure that you are connected to the Internet. Open Word. In the **New Document** task pane, under **Templates**, click **Templates on Office Online**.

2. On the Templates page of Microsoft Office Online, scroll down to see the categories of templates that are available to you. Click on some of the categories to see what you can download.

3. Click the **Back** button until the screen returns to the Template page.

4. Under the **Health Care and Wellness** category, click **Diet and Exercise**. Click one of the templates that looks interesting to you. Make sure you select one that has the Word icon to the left of the template name. This list also includes Excel, PowerPoint, and Access templates. Notice the template is previewed on the screen.

5. If you are working in a lab, check to make sure you can download files. If it is permitted, click the **Download Now** button. The template displays with instructions explaining how to use the template.

6. Follow the instructions and practice using the template you downloaded.

7. When you are done, close the file without saving changes and then close Word. Remember that even though you have not saved your changes, the template is now available on the computer.

## Sending a Document for Review

In this chapter you practiced sending an email with a document attached. You can learn more about sending documents for review by examining some of the Word Help topics on the subject. Word includes a reviewing feature that makes the process much more interactive than attaching an email. When you send a document using the *Mail Recipient (for Review)* command instead of the *Mail Recipient (as Attachment)* command, the program keeps track of your messages, flags them, and turns on the Track Changes feature when the document is returned.

1. Start Word. In the **Type a Question for Help** box, type **mail for review** and press Enter.

2. Examine the list of topics that displays in the Search Results task pane. From this list of help topics, click **About sending a file for review** and read the results. At the top of the Help window, click the **Show All** button, and then print these instructions if you want.

3. In a blank document, write two brief paragraphs about how and when you might use email to work collaboratively on a document. In the Search Results pane, click **Send a document in e-mail**, and then click **Send a document for review**. Notice the restrictions on the email programs that will work for this procedure.

4. If you are using one of these email programs and have permission to do so, follow the instructions to create and send this document to a friend. In the email message, ask the friend to make several changes and send the message back.

5. When you get the message back, in the Search Results pane, click **End a review cycle**. Read the instructions. End the review cycle and respond to the tracked changes.

6. Close the Help window and the Help task pane, close your document without saving the changes, and exit Word.

# 7 chapterseven

# Working with Tables and Graphics

**In this chapter, you will:** complete these projects **and** practice these skills.

## Project 7A
### Creating a Custom Table

**Objectives**
- Create and Apply a Custom Table Style
- Format Cells in a Table

## Project 7B
### Applying Advanced Table Features

**Objectives**
- Modify Table Properties
- Use Advanced Table Features

## Project 7C
### Creating a Complex Table

**Objective**
- Draw a Complex Table

## Project 7D
### Inserting Objects in a Document

**Objectives**
- Insert Objects in a Document
- Modify an Image

# Oceana Palm Grill

Oceana Palm Grill is a chain of 25 upscale, casual, full-service restaurants based in Austin, Texas. The company opened its first restaurant in 1975 and now operates 25 outlets in the Austin and Dallas areas. Plans call for 15 additional restaurants to be opened in North Carolina and Florida by 2008. These ambitious plans will require the company to bring in new investors, develop new menus, and recruit new employees, all while adhering to the company's strict quality guidelines and maintaining its reputation for excellent service.

© Getty Images, Inc.

# Working with Tables and Graphics

To create consistent-looking tables, Word enables you to create custom table styles in the same way you create styles for characters, paragraphs, and lists. These styles control the structure of the table and the formatting of the text in the cells. Advanced table features enable you to use a vertical text orientation, to merge cells together to create more effective headings, and to align text in cells horizontally as well as vertically. You can also wrap text around a table. Text in cells can be sorted, and numbers can be added using formulas. Free-form tables can be created using an electronic pencil and eraser and other tools from the Tables and Borders toolbar.

Objects, such as tables from Excel and graphics from Web sites, can be imported into Word. With special formatting tools, you can rotate an object, resize it, and change the contrast and brightness.

# 7A

## Project 7A Grill Menu

Styles are used to perform several formatting procedures at once. In this project, you will create and use a table style. You also will apply special formatting tools to modify text formatting in table cells.

In Activities 7.1 through 7.5, you will create a table style and apply it to a draft of a new lunch menu for the Oceana Palm Grill. You will align text in a cell both horizontally and vertically, change text direction in a cell, and merge cells. Your completed document will look similar to Figure 7.1. You will save your document as *7A_Grill_Menu_Firstname_Lastname.*

Proposed lunch menu, Orlando, Florida: Restaurant scheduled to open on October 5

Note: Prices below are for formatting purposes only. Final pricing to be determined.

### Oceana Palm Grill
#### Lunch

| | |
|---|---|
| Blue Crab Chowder | $5.25 |
| Made with a broth of tomato, basil, and lobster | |
| Roasted Fresh Artichoke | $4.50 |
| Served with creamy dipping sauce | |
| Nicoise Salad | $12.95 |
| Seared tuna in olive oil with citrus-pomegranate vinaigrette | |
| Caesar Salad | $8.95 |
| With grated Reggiano Parmesan | |
| With grilled marinated chicken | $10.00 |
| With grilled shrimp | $11.50 |
| Herb Crusted Salmon | $12.95 |
| Served with fresh vegetables, potatoes Anna, and a light lemon sauce | |
| Sautéed Gulf Shrimp | $15.50 |
| Served over homemade linguini with roasted peppers and tomatoes and a bit of garlic | |
| Roasted Portabello Mushroom | $12.00 |
| Served with ratatouille over fresh fettuccine | |
| Charbroiled Prime Burger | $10.50 |
| Grilled to your specification with your choice of toppings and served with spiced fries and homemade mayonnaise | |

*Lunch menu is available from 11 a.m. until 2 p.m.*

**Appetizers**

**Main Courses**

*Executive Chef – Donna Rohan Kurian*

7A_Grill_Menu_Firstname_Lastname

**Figure 7.1**
Project 7A—Grill Menu

## Objective 1
## Create and Apply a Custom Table Style

Recall that a **style** is a combination of formatting steps, such as font, font size, and indentation, that you name and store as a set. You can create a table style to use over and over again, giving your tables a consistent format. For example, the Oceana Palm Grill uses a Word table to create all of its menus. By developing a table style, each new menu can be formatted with the same distinctive style.

### Activity 7.1 Creating a Table Style

When you create a table style, you can apply formats, such as borders, to the entire table, and you can add special formats to individual parts of the table, such as applying shading to specific rows and columns.

**1** On the Standard toolbar, click the **Open** button. Navigate to the location where the student files for this textbook are stored. Locate and open **w07A_Grill_Menu**. Save the file as **7A_Grill_Menu_Firstname_ Lastname** creating a new folder for Chapter 7 if you want to do so.

**2** On the Standard toolbar, click the **Zoom button arrow** 100%, and then click **Page Width**. If necessary, on the Standard toolbar, click the Show/Hide ¶ button to show formatting marks.

**3** From the **Format** menu, click **Styles and Formatting**.

The Styles and Formatting task pane opens.

**4** At the top of the **Styles and Formatting** task pane, click **New Style**.

The New Style dialog box displays. See Figure 7.2.

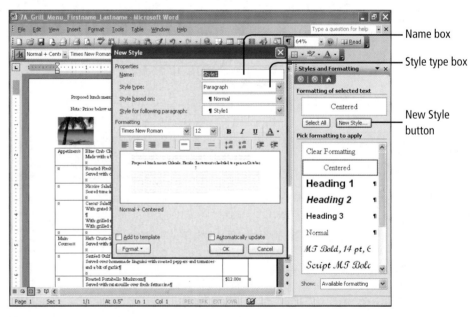

Name box
Style type box
New Style button

**Figure 7.2**

**5** In the **New Style** dialog box, under **Properties**, in the **Name** box type **Oceana Grill** Click the **Style type arrow** and from the displayed list, click **Table**.

A sample table displays in the preview area. Under Formatting, notice that the default setting is to apply the formatting to the *Whole table*, as shown in Figure 7.3.

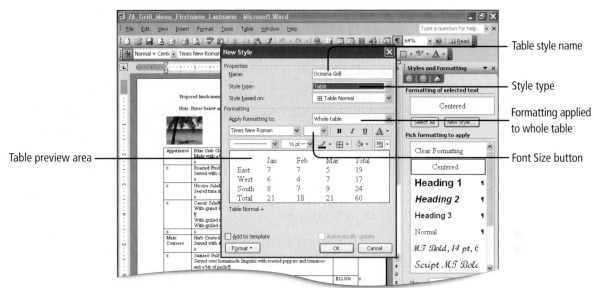

Table style name

Style type

Formatting applied to whole table

Font Size button

Table preview area

**Figure 7.3**

**6** Under **Formatting**, be sure that **Whole table** is displayed in the **Apply formatting to** box, and immediately below the box, locate the small two-row toolbar in the **New Style** dialog box. Click the **Font button arrow** [Times New Roman ▾], scroll up or down as necessary, and then click **Comic Sans MS**. Click the **Font Size button arrow** [12 ▾]—the button will be blank—and then click **12**.

**7** On the **New Style** dialog box toolbar, click the **Border button arrow** [⊞ ▾], and then click **No Border**.

The style is set to format an entire table with Comic Sans MS 12 point font and to remove all border lines. The new style settings display below the preview area. Compare your New Style dialog box with Figure 7.4.

Font button arrow ——

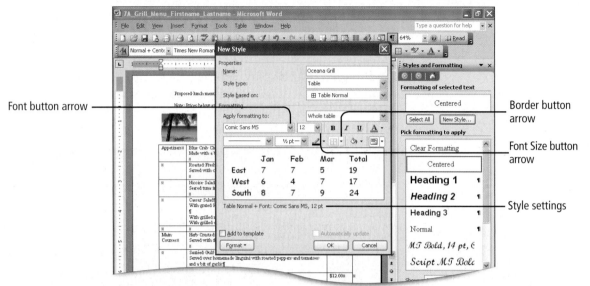

Border button arrow

Font Size button arrow

Style settings

**Figure 7.4**

**8** Under **Formatting**, click the **Apply formatting to arrow**, and then click **Left column**.

Any formatting changes you make at this point will affect only the left column of the table.

**9** On the **New Style** dialog box toolbar, click the **Bold** button **B**, and then click the **Italic** button **I**.

**10** On the **New Style** dialog box toolbar, click the **Shading Color button arrow**, and then in the first row, click the fourth color—**Gray-12.5%**.

When you use the new style, the left column of the table will be formatted with bold and italic text, and the column will be shaded in gray. A preview of the style displays in the preview area, as shown in Figure 7.5.

Preview area shows formatting. ——

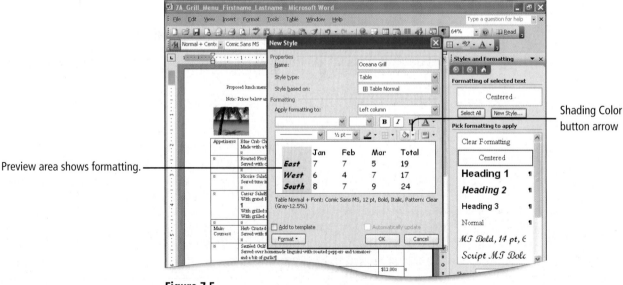

Shading Color button arrow

**Figure 7.5**

**11** Under **Formatting**, click the **Apply formatting to arrow**, and then click **Last row**.

Any formatting changes you make at this point will affect only the last row of the table.

**12** On the **New Style** dialog box toolbar, click the **Italic** button $I$.

**13** At the bottom of the **New Style** dialog box, click **OK**.

The style is saved with the document and displays in the Styles and Formatting task pane as a table style. A small boxed grid to the right of the style name *Oceana Grill* indicates that it is a table style, as shown in Figure 7.6.

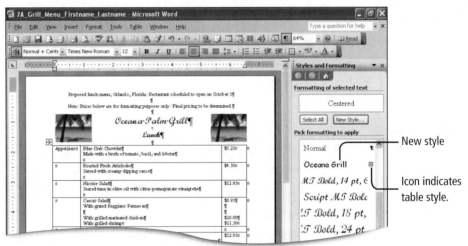

**Figure 7.6**

**14** On the Standard toolbar, click the **Save** button.

### Activity 7.2 Applying a Table Style

Applying a table style is a one-click process. After applying the style to your table, you can make further adjustments to the style.

**1** Click anywhere in the menu table in the **7A_Grill_Menu_Firstname_Lastname** document.

You do not need to select the whole table to apply a table style; it is sufficient to position the insertion point somewhere in the table.

**2** In the **Styles and Formatting** task pane, click the **Oceana Grill** style.

The formatting you created in the new table style is applied to the entire table, although the formatting to the last row will not be noticeable until text is entered. Light borders still display, but these are cell location indicators and will not print. See Figure 7.7.

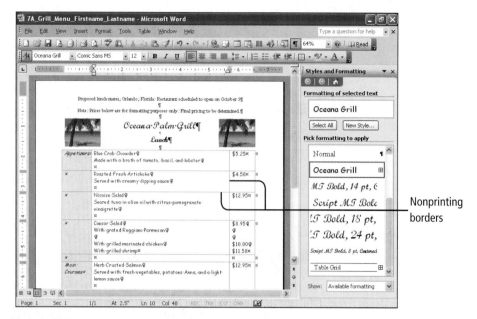

**Figure 7.7**

Nonprinting borders

**Alert!**

**Does Your Screen Differ?**

If you do not see the light borders, they probably have been deselected using the Table menu. From the Table menu, click Show Gridlines to reselect them.

**3** On the Standard toolbar, click the **Print Preview** button. Examine the table to verify that the light borders will not print. When you are through, on the Print Preview toolbar, click the **Close Preview** button.

**4** At the top of the table, move the pointer over the top edge of the middle column until it displays as a **black down arrow**, and then click once to select the column. Alternatively, click anywhere in the middle column and, from the Table menu, point to Select, and then click Column.

The middle column is selected.

**5** On the Formatting toolbar, click the **Center** button.

Within each row, the text in the middle column is centered.

**6** Use the technique you just practiced to select the right column of the table. On the Formatting toolbar, click the **Align Right** button.

Within each row, the text in the right column is aligned right. Because all of the menu prices use two decimal points, the numbers align appropriately.

**7** On the Standard toolbar, click the **Print Preview** button . Compare your screen with Figure 7.8.

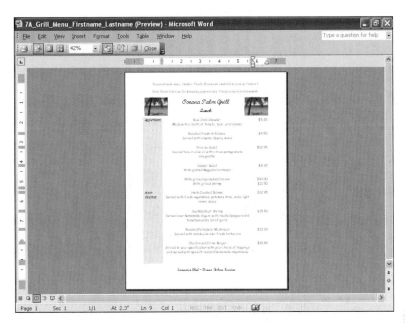

**Figure 7.8**

**8** On the Print Preview toolbar, click the **Close Preview** button . On the title bar of the **Styles and Formatting** task pane, click the **Close** button . On the Standard toolbar, click the **Save** button .

## Objective 2
### Format Cells in a Table

You have practiced formatting text in the cells of a table using the same formatting features that are available for use with paragraph text. These include text formatting such as bold and italic and text alignment such as centering. There are some special formatting features available in tables that are not available for use with paragraph text. These include vertical alignment in a cell and changing text direction from horizontal to vertical. When you want text to span multiple columns or rows, a table feature enables you to merge cells.

### Activity 7.3 Merging Cells

When you need a row or column heading to extend beyond one cell, merge adjacent cells. In this activity, you will use the Tables and Borders toolbar to merge cells. The Tables and Borders toolbar includes the buttons shown in Figure 7.9.

## Tables and Borders Toolbar Buttons

| Name | Button | Description |
| --- | --- | --- |
| Draw Table | | Creates a custom table. |
| Eraser | | Removes lines or portions of lines in a table. |
| Line Style | | Displays available line styles. |
| Line Weight | | Displays available line weights. |
| Border Color | | Displays border color choices. |
| Outside Border | | Displays border styles. |
| Shading Color | | Displays shading color choices. |
| Insert Table | | Displays the Insert Table dialog box. |
| Merge Cells | | Combines selected cells into one cell. |
| Split Cells | | Divides the selected cell into smaller cells. |
| Align | | Displays horizontal and vertical cell alignment choices. |
| Distribute Rows Evenly | | Makes selected row heights uniform. |
| Distribute Columns Evenly | | Makes selected column widths uniform. |
| Table AutoFormat | | Displays the Table AutoFormat dialog box. |
| Change Text Direction | | Changes horizontal text to vertical and vertical text to horizontal text. |
| Sort Ascending | | Sorts selected cells in ascending (a to z) order. |
| Sort Descending | | Sorts selected cells in descending (z to a) order. |
| AutoSum | | Sums the numbers in the row to the left of, or the column above, the selected cell. |

**Figure 7.9**

**1** From the **View** menu, point to **Toolbars**, and then click **Tables and Borders**.

The Tables and Borders toolbar displays. The toolbar may be docked with the other toolbars or floating above the text.

**2** Locate the upper left cell of the menu table, which contains *Appetizers*. Drag downward to select the first cell and the next three empty cells, as shown in Figure 7.10.

Selected cells

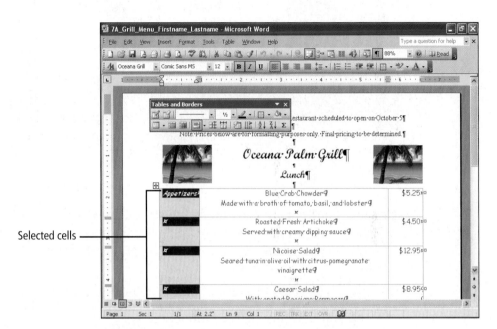

**Figure 7.10**

**3** On the Tables and Borders toolbar, click the **Merge Cells** button.

The four cells are merged into one, as shown in Figure 7.11.

Merge Cells button —

Four cells are merged. —

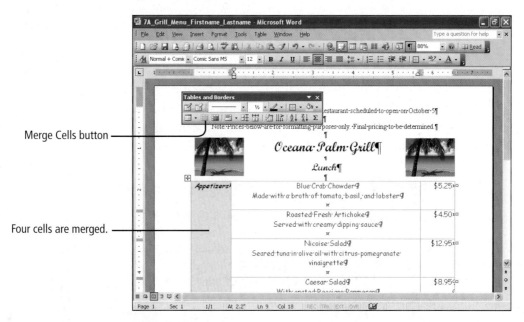

**Figure 7.11**

**4** Scroll down until you can see the last five rows of the table. Locate the *Main Courses* cell in the first column, and then drag downward to select that cell and the next three empty cells. Do not select the last cell in the column.

**5** On the Tables and Borders toolbar, click the **Merge Cells** button.

The four cells are merged into one.

**6** Move the pointer to the left of the last row of the table until it changes into a white arrow, and then click once to select the entire row. Alternatively, click in the first cell of the last row and drag to the right until all three cells are selected.

**7** On the Tables and Borders toolbar, click the **Merge Cells** button.

The three cells are merged into one.

**8** Click to position the insertion point in the last row of the table; the insertion point will blink at the right end. On the Formatting toolbar, click the **Center** button. Type **Lunch menu is available from 11 a.m. until 2 p.m.**

The text is centered across the bottom of the table. See Figure 7.12.

## Note — Formatting Changes

Notice that the text you typed in the merged cell is bold and italic, and the cell is shaded, although you did not specify bold when you created the Oceana Grill table style. When you merge cells horizontally, the new cell retains the formatting of the leftmost cell. When you merge cells vertically, the new cell retains the formatting of the topmost cell.

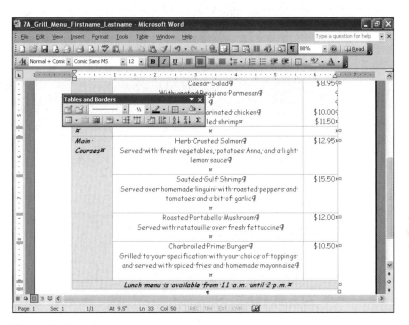

**Figure 7.12**

**9** Move the pointer to the left of the last row of the table until it changes into a white arrow, and then click once to select the row. On the Formatting toolbar, click the **Bold** button **B** to deselect bold. On the Formatting toolbar, click the **Font Size button arrow** 12 ▾, and then click **10**.

**10** On the Standard toolbar, click the **Save** button 🖫.

### Activity 7.4 Changing Text Direction

Word tables include a feature that enables you to change the text direction. This is effective for column titles that do not fit at the top of narrow columns or for row headings that cover multiple rows.

**1** Click to position the insertion point anywhere in the words *Main Courses*.

**2** In the Tables and Borders toolbar, click the **Change Text Direction** button ▥.

The text direction is changed to vertical, as shown in Figure 7.13.

Vertical text —

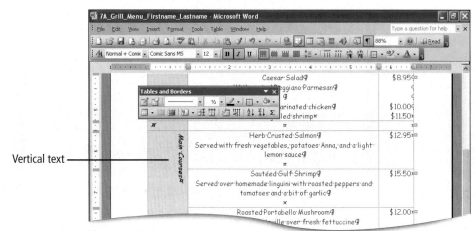

**Figure 7.13**

**3** In the Tables and Borders toolbar, click the **Change Text Direction** button ▥ again.

The text remains vertical, but faces the other direction and moves to the lower portion of the cell.

**4** In the Tables and Borders toolbar, click the **Change Text Direction** button ▥ again.

The text returns to horizontal. The Change Text Direction button is a three-way switch, moving among horizontal text and two vertical text orientations.

**5** In the Tables and Borders toolbar, click the **Change Text Direction** button [icon] twice. Move the insertion point over the beginning of the word *Main*.

Notice that the text select pointer [icon] is horizontal.

**6** Drag upward to select **Main Courses**. On the Formatting toolbar, click the **Font Size button arrow** [12 ▾], and then click **28**.

The font size increases, as shown in Figure 7.14.

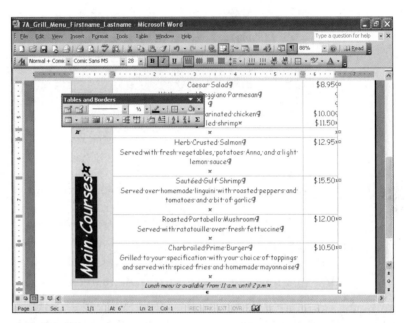

**Figure 7.14**

**7** Scroll up and position the insertion point in the *Appetizers* cell. In the Tables and Borders toolbar, click the **Change Text Direction** button [icon] twice.

**8** Move the pointer over the beginning of the word *Appetizers*. Drag up to select **Appetizers**. On the Formatting toolbar, click the **Font Size button arrow** [12 ▾], and then click **28**. Compare your screen with Figure 7.15.

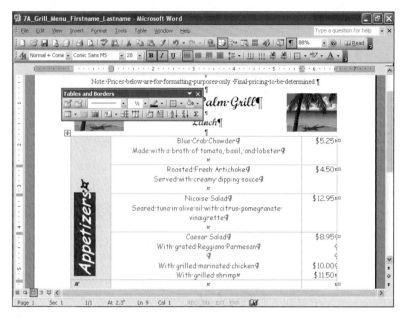

**Figure 7.15**

**9** On the Standard toolbar, click the **Save** button ⊞.

### Activity 7.5 Changing Text Position in a Cell

With paragraph text outside of a table, you are limited to horizontal alignment. In table cells, you can align text left, center, and right, as well as top, center, and bottom. You also can use all possible combinations of horizontal and vertical alignment, such as top left or bottom right.

**1** Click to position the insertion point anywhere in the *Appetizers* cell.

**2** On the Tables and Borders toolbar, click the **Align button arrow** ⊞.

The nine possible alignment combinations are displayed, as shown in Figure 7.16.

Align button arrow

Align Center button

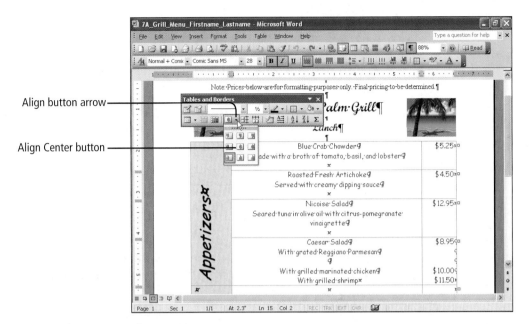

**Figure 7.16**

◻3 In the second row, click the second alignment—**Align Center**.

The text is centered left-to-right and top-to-bottom, as shown in Figure 7.17.

Text is aligned horizontally and vertically.

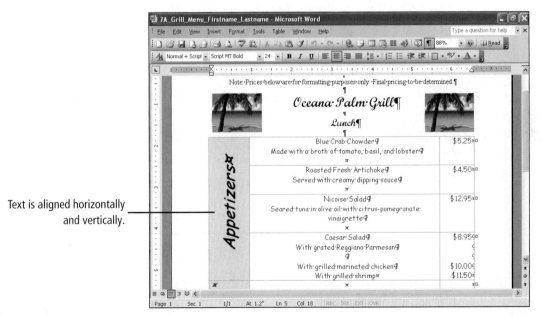

**Figure 7.17**

**4** Scroll down and click to position the insertion point anywhere in the *Main Courses* cell. On the Tables and Borders toolbar, click the **Align button arrow** [icon] and from the displayed menu, click **Align Center**.

**5** From the **View** menu, click **Header and Footer**. On the Header and Footer toolbar, click the **Switch Between Header and Footer** button [icon].

**6** On the Header and Footer toolbar, click the **Insert AutoText** button [Insert AutoText ▾], and then click **Filename**.

The file name is inserted in the footer.

**7** On the Header and Footer toolbar, click the **Close** button [Close]. Right-click any toolbar, and from the displayed list, click **Tables and Borders** to turn off the display of the toolbar.

**8** On the Standard toolbar, click the **Save** button [icon].

**9** On the Standard toolbar, click the **Print Preview** button [icon]. Take a moment to check your work. On the Print Preview toolbar, click the **Close Preview** button [Close].

**10** Make any necessary changes to your document. When you are satisfied, on the Standard toolbar, click the **Print** button [icon]. Close the document, saving any changes.

**End** You have completed Project 7A ——————————————————————————

# Project 7B Teen Safety

Word includes features to sort and summarize data in a table. Additionally, table properties can be adjusted to wrap text around a small table and to make text fit in a specified cell size.

In Activities 7.6 through 7.11, you will edit a memo about teen worker safety in Oceana Palm Grill restaurants. You will wrap text around a table and fit text in a cell. You will also sort information in a table, sum columns of numbers in a table, and add table captions. Your completed document will look similar to Figure 7.18. You will save your document as *7B_Teen_Safety_Firstname_Lastname.*

---

 *Oceana Palm Grill*

MEMO

To:      Devin Washington, Vice President, Quality and Customer Service

From:    Laura Mabry Hernandez, Vice President, Human Resources

Date:    July 7

Subject:   Teen Worker Safety in Our Restaurants

**Table 1. Oceana Teen Injuries**

| Year | Teen Injuries |
|------|---------------|
| 2000 | 47 |
| 2001 | 51 |
| 2002 | 39 |
| 2003 | 38 |

Approximately 15% of our current workforce is between 16 and 20 years old. As we expand into new geographic areas, that percentage is expected to increase. The Occupational Safety and Health Administration (OSHA) estimates that nationwide approximately 30% of food service employees are under 20 years old.

In the next few months, OSHA is expected to announce a new safety program for teen workers. In anticipation of this new program, I have put together some data about injuries. Table 1 shows injuries to our teenage employees from 2000-2003. Reported injuries to teenage restaurant workers in the eight-county area are shown in Table 2, although the data is by fiscal year (July through June) and does not directly match our company data.

**Table 2. Teen Worker Injuries in Restaurants**

|           | FY 99-00 | FY 00-01 | FY 01-02 | FY 02-03 |
|-----------|----------|----------|----------|----------|
| Burns     | 687      | 719      | 722      | 672      |
| Cuts      | 478      | 515      | 574      | 617      |
| Sprains   | 247      | 244      | 316      | 291      |
| Fractures | 29       | 31       | 19       | 40       |
| Total     | 1,441    | 1,509    | 1,631    | 1,620    |

7B_Teen_Safety_Firstname_Lastname

---

**Figure 7.18**

# Objective 3
## Modify Table Properties

Tables have properties that can be adjusted. For example, from the Table Properties dialog box you can wrap text around small tables, set row height and column width, set vertical alignment in cells, and force text to fit in a specified column width.

### Activity 7.6 Wrapping Text Around Tables

**1** On the Standard toolbar, click the **Open** button 📂. Navigate to the location where the student files for this textbook are stored. Locate and open **w07B_Teen_Safety**. Save the file as **7B_Teen_Safety_Firstname_Lastname** in the folder where you are storing your projects for this chapter.

**2** On the Standard toolbar, click the **Zoom button arrow** [100% ▾], and then click **Page Width**. If necessary, on the Standard toolbar, click the Show/Hide ¶ button to show formatting marks.

**3** Scroll down to display the small *Teen Injuries* table, and then click to position the insertion point anywhere in the table.

**4** From the **Table** menu, click **Table Properties**, and then in the displayed **Table Properties** dialog box, click the **Table tab**.

The Table tab of the Table Properties dialog box displays, as shown in Figure 7.19.

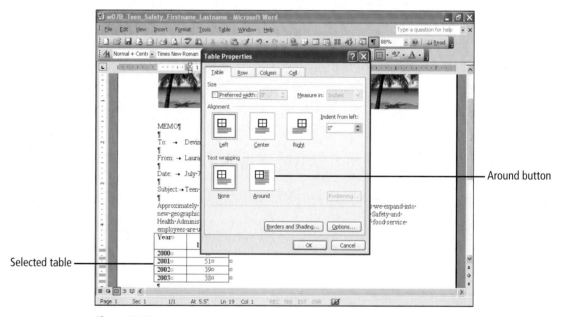

Figure 7.19

**5** Under **Text wrapping**, click **Around**, and then click **OK**.

Text wraps around the right side of the table.

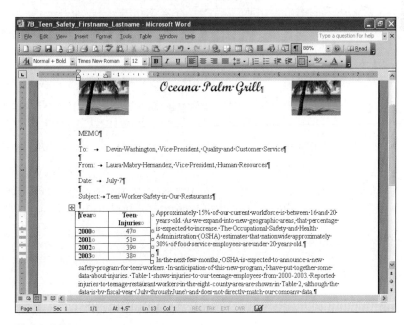

**6** Move the pointer over the table.

The ***table move handle*** displays above the upper left corner of the table, as shown in Figure 7.20. Using the table move handle, you can move the table without first selecting it.

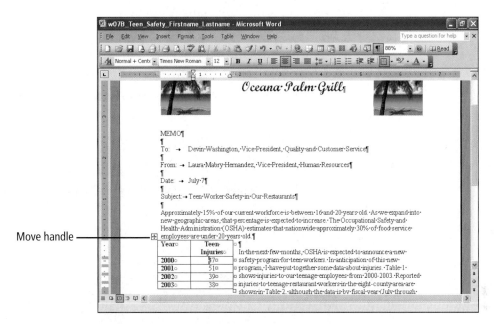

Move handle

**Figure 7.20**

**7** Point to the table move handle to display the move pointer, and then drag the table upward until the dotted box representing the table is even with the paragraph that begins *Approximately 15% of our current workforce.*

Compare your table with Figure 7.21.

**Figure 7.21**

**8** On the Standard toolbar, click the **Save** button.

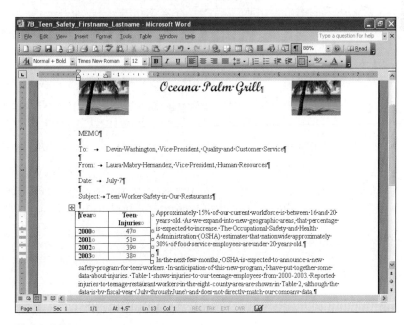

### Activity 7.7 Fitting Text in a Cell

If you want to squeeze a little more text into a cell or reduce two text lines to one, the text can be compressed to exactly the right size by using table properties.

**1** In the *Teen Injuries* table, click to position the insertion point in the *Teen Injuries* cell.

Notice that the text in this cell wraps to a second line, but could almost fit on one line.

**2** From the **Table** menu, click **Table Properties**, and then click the **Cell tab**.

The Cell tab of the Table Properties dialog box displays.

**3** In the lower right corner, click **Options**.

The Cell Options dialog box displays, as shown in Figure 7.22.

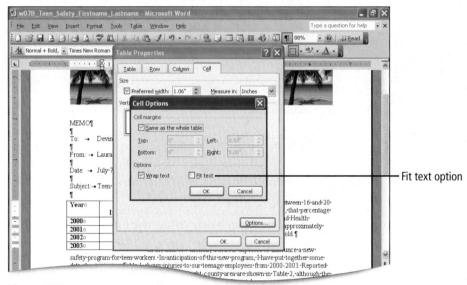

Figure 7.22

**4** In the **Cell Options** dialog box, under **Options**, clear the **Wrap text** check box, and then select the **Fit text** check box.

**5** In the **Cell Options** dialog box, click **OK**. In the **Table Properties** dialog box, click **OK**.

The text is compressed to fit on one line, as shown in Figure 7.23. A light blue line under the text indicates that the Fit text feature has been used in this cell.

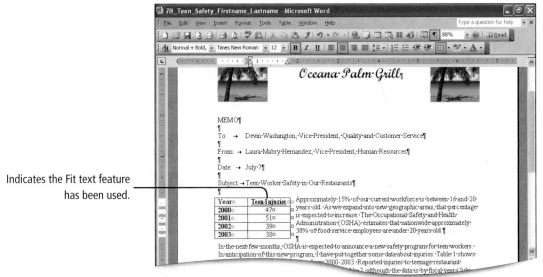

Indicates the Fit text feature has been used.

**Figure 7.23**

**6** On the Standard toolbar, click the **Save** button ⊞.

## Objective 4
## Use Advanced Table Features

Word tables have a few spreadsheet capabilities. For example, you can *sort*—organize in a particular order—the data in a table numerically or alphabetically in ascending or descending order on any of the columns. You also can use a limited group of formulas in a cell. These can be used to add a column or row or to calculate an average. Unlike a spreadsheet, however, if you change a number in a cell that is used in a formula, the formula must be recalculated manually.

*Captions* are titles that can be added to Word objects and are numbered sequentially as they are added. You can add a caption to each table in a document, which makes it easier to refer to the tables in the text.

### Activity 7.8 Sorting Tables by Category

Tables can be sorted by category (column) either alphabetically or numerically. No matter which column you sort on, the rows remain intact.

**1** In the second table, at the bottom of the document, click anywhere to position the insertion point.

The table does not need to be selected to perform a sort operation.

**2** From the **Table** menu, click **Sort**.

The table is selected, and the Sort dialog box opens, as shown in Figure 7.24.

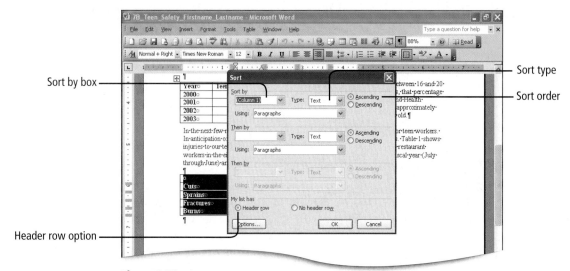

Sort by box

Header row option

Sort type

Sort order

**Figure 7.24**

**3** At the bottom of the dialog box, under **My list has**, be sure the **Header row** option button is selected. At the top of the dialog box, under **Sort by**, notice that the sort will be performed based on the data in **Column 1**. Accept all of the other defaults and click **OK**.

The text is sorted in alphabetical order by type of injury—the data in Column 1. Although the order of the rows has been changed to alphabetic order, the data attached to each type of injury remains with its appropriate row. If you do not indicate that the table has a header (column title) row, the first cell will be sorted along with the other cells in the column.

**4** From the **Table** menu, click **Sort** again. Click the **Sort by arrow**, and then click **FY 02-03**.

This will sort by the numbers in the last column.

**5** Under **Sort by**, click the **Descending** option button.

This will sort the numbers from highest to lowest.

**6** At the bottom of the **Sort** dialog box, click **OK**. Click anywhere in the document to deselect the table.

This process reordered the rows. They are no longer in alphabetic order by type of injury; rather, they are in numerical order based on the data for the fiscal year 2002–2003, from the highest number of injuries to the lowest. See Figure 7.25.

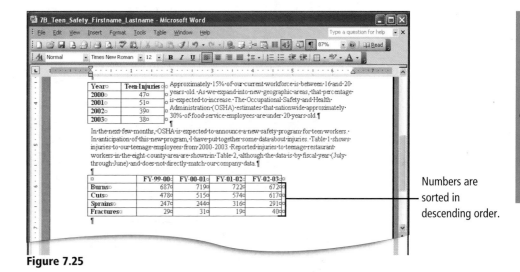

**Figure 7.25**

**Numbers are sorted in descending order.**

**7** On the Standard toolbar, click the **Save** button.

### Activity 7.9 Using Formulas in Tables

When you need to analyze numbers, it is best to use a spreadsheet program such as Microsoft Excel. However, when you need to do a simple calculation in Word, you can insert a formula in a table.

**1** In the table at the bottom of the page, click in the last row to position the insertion point. From the **Table** menu, point to **Insert**, and then click **Rows Below**.

A new row is added to the table.

**Another Way** — **To Add Rows to a Table**

You can add a row to the bottom of a table by pressing the Tab key when the insertion point is in the lower-right cell of the table. Also, when one or more rows are selected, the Insert Table button in the Standard toolbar changes to an Insert Rows button, which will insert the same number of blank rows as the number of existing rows that are selected.

**2** Click in the first cell of the new row, type **Total** and then press Tab to move to the second cell in the row.

**3** From the **Table** menu, click **Formula**.

The Formula dialog box displays. The default formula is =SUM(ABOVE). This formula calculates the sum of the numbers in all of the cells above the current cell—up to the first empty cell or cell that contains text—and places the result in the current cell. You can specify a special number format—for example, the number of decimal places—and you can use the Paste function box to specify a function other than the sum.

**4** Click the **Number format arrow** and from the displayed list, click **#,##0**.

This number format places a comma after every third digit and places a zero in empty cells. See Figure 7.26.

Default formula —

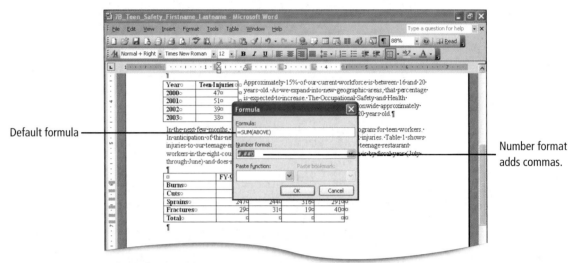

— Number format adds commas.

**Figure 7.26**

**5** In the **Formula** dialog box, click **OK**.

The column is summed, and the total displays in the active cell. Notice that a comma has been added to the total. See Figure 7.27.

A comma has been added to the sum. —

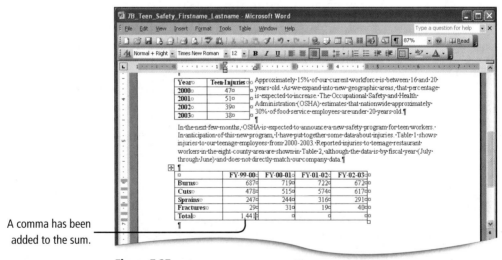

**Figure 7.27**

| Alert! | **Be Careful with Column Headings** |
| --- | --- |

If you are going to use formulas in a table, do not use numbers as column headings. In the column you just summed, a column heading such as *2000*, instead of a heading that began with text such as FY 99-00, would be included in the formula and the sum would have been in error by 2,000. Unlike an Excel spreadsheet, when using formulas, a Word table has no way to identify a numeric header as anything but a number.

**6** Repeat the procedure you used in Steps 3 through 5 to sum the other three columns of numbers. Compare your table with Figure 7.28.

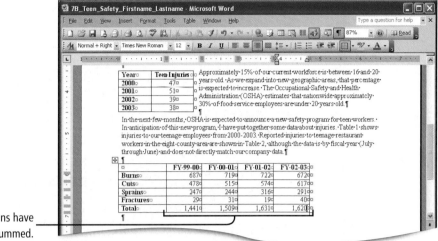

All columns have
been summed.

**Figure 7.28**

## Note — Summing Multiple Rows

When you place a formula in a table, the default formula is =SUM(ABOVE), assuming there is a number in the cell above the selected cell. If there is a number in the cell to the left of the selected cell and no number in the cell above, the default is =SUM(LEFT). If you need to sum several rows, place formulas in the lower rows first. This will keep the cell above the selected cell empty so that the default choice is =SUM(LEFT) instead of =SUM(ABOVE). Also, do not leave a cell empty within a range if you want to sum the entire range. If there is no value, then enter a 0.

**7** On the Standard toolbar, click the **Save** button ⊟.

### Activity 7.10 Adding Captions to Tables

Captions make it easy to refer to a table or figure in a document that contains multiple objects.

**1** Be sure the insertion point is still positioned somewhere in the lower table. From the **Insert** menu, point to **Reference**, and then click **Caption**.

The Caption dialog box displays. Because a table is selected, the default caption starts with *Table 1*. Word will assist you in numbering tables sequentially, as you will see as you progress through this activity.

**2** Refer to Figure 7.29, and then after *Table 1* type a period, press ⎵Spacebar⎵, and then type **Teen Worker Injuries in Restaurants**

Compare your Caption dialog box with Figure 7.29.

Table number ————

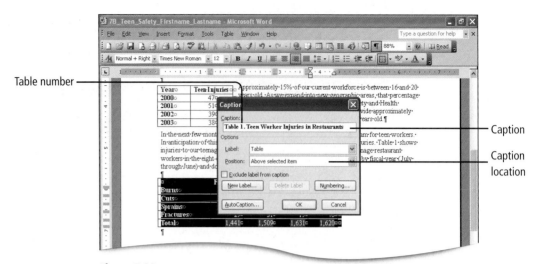

———— Caption

———— Caption location

**Figure 7.29**

**▣ 3** At the bottom of the **Caption** dialog box, click **OK**.

The caption is added to the top of the table, as shown in Figure 7.30. A green, wavy line may also display under the *Table 1* text.

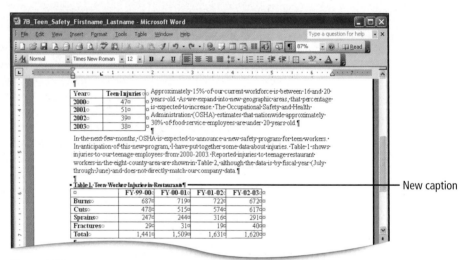

———— New caption

**Figure 7.30**

**▣ 4** Position the insertion point anywhere in the upper table. From the **Insert** menu, point to **Reference**, and then click **Caption**.

Notice that the caption box displays *Table 1* because the selected table comes before the one to which you just added a caption. The bottom table will be renumbered as *Table 2* when you add the caption to the current table.

**▣ 5** Under **Caption**, following *Table 1* type a period, press ⌷Spacebar⌷, type **Oceana Teen Injuries** and then click **OK**.

The caption is added to the first table, and the second table is renumbered. See Figure 7.31.

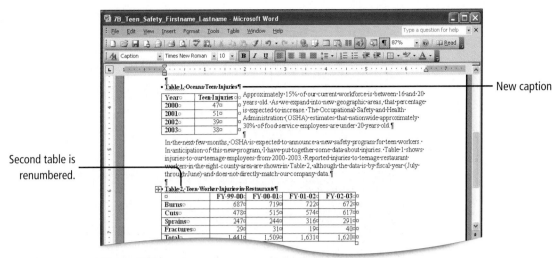

New caption

Second table is renumbered.

**Figure 7.31**

**6** On the Standard toolbar, click the **Save** button.

### Activity 7.11 Using the Toolbar to AutoFormat a Table

Recall that you can give your table a professional design by using any of the built-in table formats. This is quickly accomplished from the Table AutoFormat button on the Tables and Borders toolbar.

**1** Click to position the insertion point anywhere in the lower table. If necessary, right-click any toolbar and click Tables and Borders.

The Tables and Borders toolbar displays.

**2** On the Tables and Borders toolbar, click the **Table AutoFormat**

button. In the **Table AutoFormat** dialog box, under **Table styles**, scroll down and click **Table Simple 3**.

A preview of the table displays in the Preview area. Compare your dialog box with Figure 7.32.

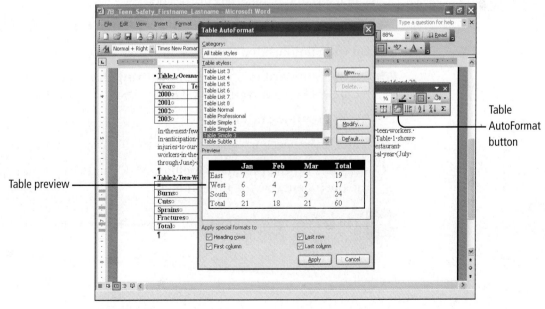

Table AutoFormat button

Table preview

**Figure 7.32**

**3** At the bottom of the **Table AutoFormat** dialog box, click **Apply**.

The AutoFormat is applied to the table.

**4** Use the procedure you practiced in Steps 2 and 3 to AutoFormat the other table using the **Table Simple 3** style. Close the Tables and Borders toolbar.

Compare your document with Figure 7.33.

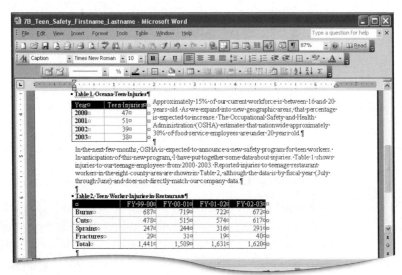

**Figure 7.33**

**5** From the **View** menu, click **Header and Footer**. On the Header and Footer toolbar, click the **Switch Between Header and Footer** button.

**6** On the Header and Footer toolbar, click the **Insert AutoText** button Insert AutoText ▾, and then click **Filename**.

The file name is inserted in the footer.

**7** On the Header and Footer toolbar, click the **Close** button Close.

**8** On the Standard toolbar, click the **Save** button.

**9** On the Standard toolbar, click the **Print Preview** button. Take a moment to check your work. On the Print Preview toolbar, click the **Close Preview** button Close.

**10** Make any necessary changes to your document. When you are satisfied, on the Standard toolbar, click the **Print** button. Close the document, saving any changes.

**End** You have completed Project 7B ─────────

# Project 7C **Purchase Order**

When you create a table using the Insert Table button or the Insert command from the Table menu, the result is a table structure comprised of rows and columns of uniform size. Sometimes, however, you need the structure of a table coupled with the flexibility to form rows and columns of varying size and format. For example, a form, such as a purchase order, not only needs the structure of a table, but also needs to have some flexibility in the sizing and shading of cells and rows and in the alignment of text.

In Activities 7.12 through 7.15, you will create a purchase order for the Oceana Palm Grill. You will draw a table, add and erase lines, change column widths and row heights, and format the table. Your completed document will look similar to Figure 7.34. You will save your document as *7C_Purchase_Order_Firstname_ Lastname.*

| Oceana Palm Grill | P.O. Number | Vendor | Date | |
|---|---|---|---|---|
| | Quantity | Description | Unit Price | Total |
| | | | | |
| | Authorization | | Department | |

7C_Purchase_Order_Firstname_Lastname

**Figure 7.34**

## Objective 5
## Draw a Complex Table

When you create a complex table using the Tables and Borders toolbar, you use an electronic pencil and eraser to sketch out the table shape you need. After the outline is created, you use the other buttons on the toolbar to refine the table format.

### Activity 7.12 Drawing a Complex Table

When you use the Draw Table command, first draw the outside, rectangular border of the table.

1. Start Word. From the Standard toolbar, click the **New Blank Document** button. Save the file as **7C_Purchase_Order_Firstname_Lastname** in the folder where you are storing your projects for this chapter.

2. On the Standard toolbar, click the **Zoom button arrow** [100% ▼], and then click **75%**. If necessary, on the Standard toolbar, click the Show/Hide ¶ button to show formatting marks.

3. If the Tables and Borders toolbar is not displayed, right-click on any toolbar, and then click Tables and Borders.

   The Tables and Borders toolbar displays, either floating on your screen or docked to the other toolbars.

4. On the Tables and Borders toolbar, click the **Draw Table** button, and then move the mouse pointer into the document area and notice the pencil shape of the pointer. On the Tables and Borders toolbar, click the **Line Style button arrow** [_____ ▼] to display the list of line styles. Drag the scroll box down and click the style with two thin outside lines and a thick inside line.

5. Move the pointer into the document window and locate the vertical and horizontal rulers.

   As you move the pointer within the document window, notice that faint dotted lines display in both the horizontal and vertical rulers. You will use these visual guides to determine the placement and dimensions of your table as you draw. Also notice that the Draw Table pointer looks like a pencil. See Figure 7.35.

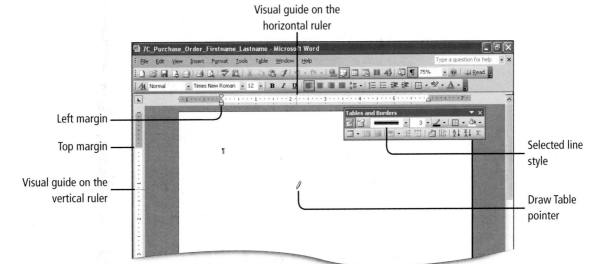

Visual guide on the
horizontal ruler

Left margin

Top margin

Visual guide on the
vertical ruler

Selected line
style

Draw Table
pointer

**Figure 7.35**

**6** Move your pointer so that, in the **horizontal ruler**, the guide is positioned **0.5 inches to the *left* of the left margin**—in the shaded area. Then, move the pointer so that, in the **vertical ruler**, the guide is positioned **even with the top margin**. Refer to Figure 7.35 to locate the top margin in the horizontal ruler.

**7** With your pointer positioned as described in Step 6, drag to the right to **6.5 inches on the horizontal ruler** (into the shaded area) and to **3.5 inches on the vertical ruler**. Release the mouse button. If you are not satisfied with your result, click the Undo button and begin again.

You have created outside boundaries with dimensions of 3.5 inches high and 7 inches wide, as shown in Figure 7.36.

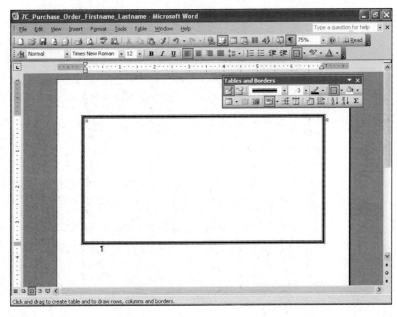

**Figure 7.36**

**8** On the Standard toolbar, click the **Save** button.

### Activity 7.13 Adding and Removing Table Lines

You can draw horizontal and vertical lines inside the table using the Draw Table pointer.

**1** If necessary, click the **Draw Table** button 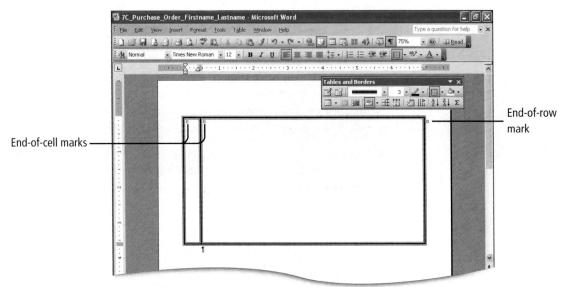 to activate the Draw Table pointer. Position the tip of the pencil pointer over the upper border of the table at **0.5 inch on the horizontal ruler**. Drag down, and when you see the dotted vertical line extending to the bottom table boundary, release the left mouse button.

A line in the same style as your border extends to the bottom table boundary. End-of-cell marks and the end-of-row mark indicate that you have created a Word table with a structure of two columns and one row. Compare your table with Figure 7.37.

End-of-cell marks

End-of-row mark

**Figure 7.37**

**2** With the **Draw Table** pointer still active, position the pointer on the right boundary of the first column at **1 inch on the vertical ruler**. Drag to the right, and when you see the dotted line extending to the right boundary, release the left mouse button.

A line in the same style as your border extends to the right table boundary.

**3** Repeat this process to draw two more horizontal lines—one beginning at **2 inches on the vertical ruler** and one beginning at **3 inches on the vertical ruler**. If you are not satisfied with your result, click the **Undo** button and begin again.

Compare your table with Figure 7.38.

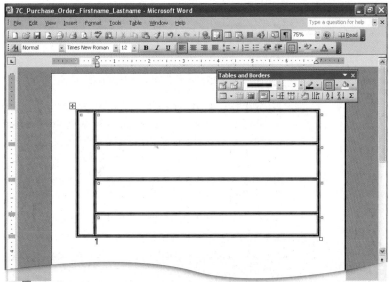

**Figure 7.38**

**4** On the Tables and Borders toolbar, click the **Eraser** button ▣.

The pointer becomes a small eraser.

**5** Position the **Eraser** pointer on the second horizontal line within the table (not including the top border line), and then click the left mouse button.

The line is erased.

**6** Position the pointer on the last horizontal line within the table (not including the bottom border line), and then click to erase it.

Compare your table with Figure 7.39.

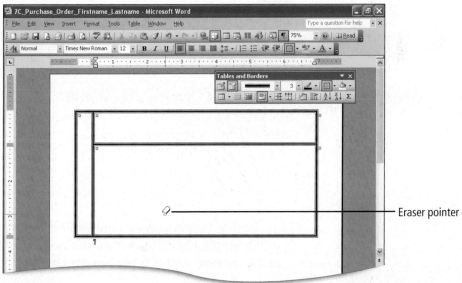

Eraser pointer

**Figure 7.39**

**7** On the Tables and Borders toolbar, click the **Line Style arrow** [image], scroll up to the top of the list, and then click the first border style—a single solid line.

The Draw Table pointer becomes active.

**8** In **Row 1**, **Column 2**, position your pencil pointer just below the top table border at approximately **2.5 inches on the horizontal ruler**. Drag down slightly, to the top border of the row below. In a similar manner, position your pencil pointer just below the top table border at approximately **4.5 inches on the horizontal ruler** and drag down slightly, to the top border of the row below.

Two vertical lines are added, as shown in Figure 7.40. You need not be positioned exactly at these measurements, because later you will use the Distribute Columns Evenly feature to set these measurements precisely.

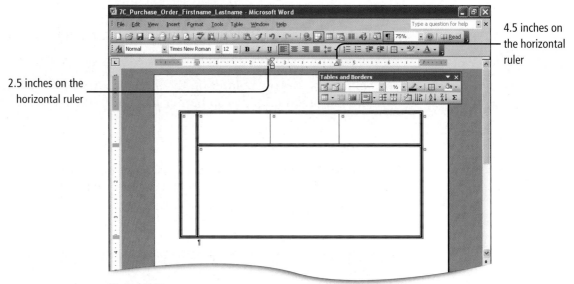

**Figure 7.40**

---

**Alert!**

### Accidentally Changing the Border

If you select a different line style and then click directly on the border when attempting to draw a line in a table, you might change the line formatting of the border to the current line style selection. Click the Undo button and begin again.

---

**9** In **Row 2**, position your pointer at the top edge of the row and draw three vertical lines to the bottom border at approximately **2 inches**, **3.75 inches**, and **5.5 inches on the horizontal ruler**.

**10** In **Column 2**, position your pointer on the left border, and draw two horizontal lines extending to the right table boundary at approximately **0.5 inches** and **1.5 inches** on **the vertical ruler**.

**11** On the Tables and Borders toolbar, click the **Line Style arrow** and click the first double-line border style. In **Column 2**, position your pointer on the left border at **3 inches on the vertical ruler** and draw a horizontal line extending to the right table boundary.

Click the **Draw Table** button to return to the I-beam pointer.

Compare your table with Figure 7.41.

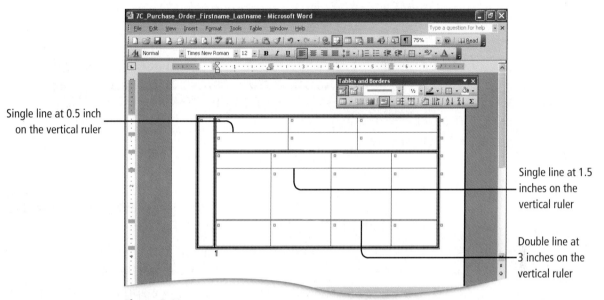

Single line at 0.5 inch on the vertical ruler

Single line at 1.5 inches on the vertical ruler

Double line at 3 inches on the vertical ruler

**Figure 7.41**

**12** On the Standard toolbar, click the **Save** button.

### Activity 7.14  Distributing Columns Evenly and Changing Text Direction

The **Distribute Columns Evenly** command formats columns so that their widths are equal within the boundaries that you select. A similar command—**Distribute Rows Evenly**—formats rows so that their heights are equal within the boundaries that you select.

**1** Select, by dragging, the six cells that comprise **Columns 2**, **3**, and **4** in **Rows 1** and **2**.

**2** On the Tables and Borders toolbar, click the **Distribute Columns Evenly** button.

The columns within the two rows are now equal in width and are evenly spaced, as shown in Figure 7.42.

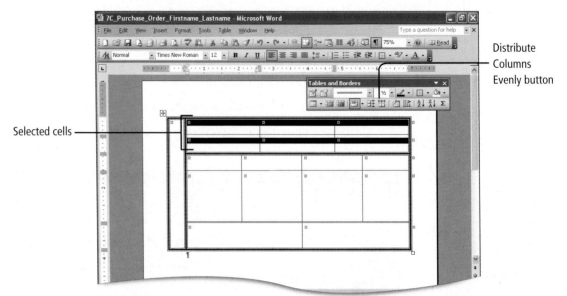

Distribute
Columns
Evenly button

Selected cells

**Figure 7.42**

3 On the Tables and Borders toolbar, click the **Eraser** button ![eraser]. In
Row 5, use the **Eraser** pointer to erase the first and third single-line
column borders.

4 On the Tables and Borders toolbar, click the **Eraser** button ![eraser] to
deselect the Eraser and redisplay the pointer as an I-beam.

5 Click anywhere in the first column to position the insertion point
to the left of its end-of-cell marker. On the Formatting toolbar, click
the **Center** button ![center]. On the Tables and Borders toolbar, click the
**Change Text Direction** button ![text direction] twice.

6 On the Formatting toolbar, click the **Bold** button ![B]. Click the **Font
Size arrow** and click **28**. Type **Oceana Palm Grill**

The text is displayed vertically, as shown in Figure 7.43.

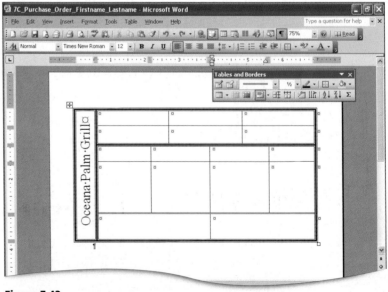

**Figure 7.43**

**7** On the Standard toolbar, click the **Save** button ![save].

### Activity 7.15 Formatting a Complex Table

Table cells can be formatted to enhance the appearance of a table.

**1** Move the pointer to the left of the first row of the table until it changes to a white arrow, and then click once.

The first row is selected—it includes the entire vertical column.

**2** On the Tables and Borders toolbar, click the **Shading Color button arrow** ![], and then in the first row, click the fourth color—**Gray-12.5%**.

The selected cells are shaded.

**3** In the third row, select the four cells. (Hint: Locate the end-of-row markers to help you locate the third row.) On the Tables and Borders toolbar, click the **Shading Color** button ![]. Click anywhere in the document to deselect the cells.

The selected cells are shaded Gray 12.5%. Compare your table with Figure 7.44.

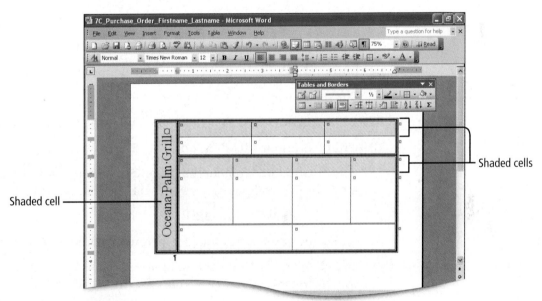

Shaded cell

Shaded cells

**Figure 7.44**

**4** In the first row, click to position the insertion point in the second column. Type **P. O. Number** and press Tab. Type **Vendor** and press Tab. Type **Date**

**5** In the third row, click to position the insertion point in the second column. Type **Quantity** and press Tab. Type **Description** and press Tab. Type **Unit Price** and press Tab. Type **Total**

**6** In the fifth row, click to position the insertion point in the second column. Type **Authorization** and press Tab. Type **Department**

Compare your table with Figure 7.45.

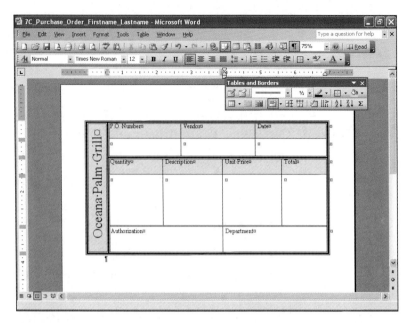

**Figure 7.45**

**7** Close the Tables and Borders toolbar. From the **View** menu, click **Header and Footer**. On the Header and Footer toolbar, click the **Switch Between Header and Footer** button.

**8** On the **Header and Footer** toolbar, click the **Insert AutoText** button Insert AutoText ▾, and then click **Filename**.

The file name is inserted in the footer.

**9** On the Header and Footer toolbar, click the **Close** button Close.

**10** On the Standard toolbar, click the **Save** button.

**11** On the Standard toolbar, click the **Print Preview** button. Take a moment to check your work. On the Print Preview toolbar, click the **Close Preview** button Close.

**12** Make any necessary changes to your document. When you are satisfied, on the Standard toolbar, click the **Print** button. Close the document, saving any changes, and close Word.

**End** You have completed Project 7C

# Project 7D **Special Event**

An **object** is any type of graphic—for example, a line, a shape, a WordArt, a text box, an AutoShape, a clip art image, a picture, or an Excel chart—that can be inserted in a document. Objects can be moved and resized, and some can be rotated. You can use special tools to modify graphic images in a variety of ways.

In Activities 7.16 through 7.20, you will complete a memo regarding a proposed cheese tasting night at the Oceana Palm Grill. You will insert and modify objects and wrap text around the objects. You will also lighten an image and place it behind text. Your completed document will look similar to Figure 7.46. You will save your document as *7D_Special_Event_Firstname_Lastname.*

 *Oceana Palm Grill*

MEMO TO:    Laura Mabry Hernandez, Seth Weddel, Duc Buy

FROM:         Donna Rohan Kurian, Executive Chef

DATE:          December 17

SUBJECT:     Cheese Specials on Tuesdays

I have been thinking about emphasizing cheese in our menus, but I'm not sure how to proceed. I have been considering a trial run in one of the restaurants, probably North Austin. I would like to try a weekly event, probably on Tuesday evenings, where the focus is on a good selection of cheese.

I can envision two possibilities—a selection of cheese plates, or a cheese bar (or possibly both). The cheeses would have to be matched with compatible fruit and bread or crackers. They could be used as appetizers, or for desserts, as is common in Europe.

The cheese plates should be varied and diverse, using a mixture of hard and soft, sharp and mild, unusual and familiar.

I am really excited about this possible new feature for our restaurants. I think that it will catch on in this area if it is done right. It will mean that our employees will need to become familiar with the various cheeses and their characteristics. I have included a link to a USDA document that gives lots of information. You will need Adobe Acrobat Reader to read it. Take a look and let me know what you think of the idea.

7D_Special_Event_Firstname_Lastname

**Figure 7.46**

# Objective 6
## Insert Objects in a Document

Clip art images, pictures, and other graphic objects are frequently inserted into Word documents. Another type of object that can be inserted is a **PDF document**. A PDF, as it is usually called, is a document formatted in the Portable Document Format developed by Adobe Systems. The format is recognized as one of the standard document formats. PDF files can be opened on most computers, using most operating systems. All that is required is the **Adobe Acrobat Reader**, which can be downloaded from the Adobe Systems Web site at no charge. Most computers in college computer labs have this program installed. If you are working on your own computer, you will need Adobe Acrobat Reader to complete these activities.

### Activity 7.16 Inserting Objects from Files

Some objects, when inserted into a Word document, do not display. Instead, an icon containing a link to the file displays. This is true when you insert a PDF.

**1** On the Standard toolbar, click the **Open** button. Navigate to the location where the student files for this textbook are stored. Locate and open **w07D_Special_Event**. Save the file as **7D_Special_Event_Firstname_Lastname**

**2** On the Standard toolbar, click the **Zoom button arrow** 100%, and then click **Page Width**. If necessary, on the Standard toolbar, click the Show/Hide ¶ button to show formatting marks.

**3** Click to position the insertion point at the beginning of the paragraph that begins *I have been thinking*. From the **Insert** menu, click **Object**. In the displayed **Object** dialog box, click the **Create New tab**.

The Object dialog box displays, as shown in Figure 7.47.

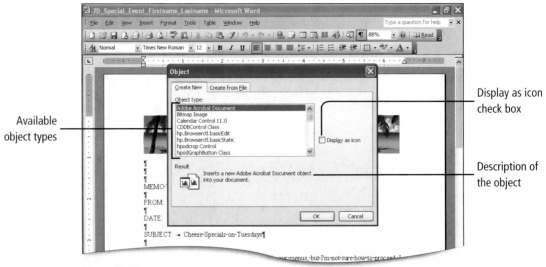

Figure 7.47

**4** Take a moment to scroll down and examine the types of objects that can be inserted into a Word document. When you are finished, under **Object type**, click **Adobe Acrobat Document**.

**Alert!**

### If the Adobe Acrobat Document Object Does Not Display

If the Adobe Acrobat Document option does not display in the Object type box, you will need to use the following procedure: In the Object dialog box, click the *Create from File* tab. Click the Browse button, locate the w07D_Cheese document in your student files, and then click Insert. Proceed to Step 5, ignoring references to PDF files.

**5** In the **Object** dialog box, select the **Display as icon** check box, and then click **Change Icon**.

The Change Icon dialog box displays.

**6** In the **Change Icon** dialog box, click the second icon, which displays *PDF* at the top. In the **Caption** box, select the text and type **USDA Cheese Information**

Compare your dialog box with Figure 7.48.

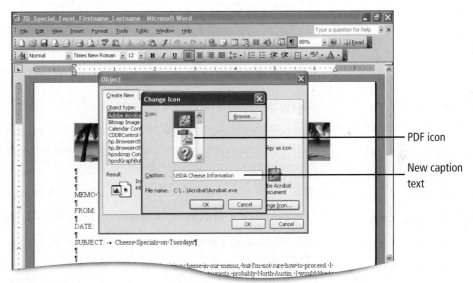

PDF icon

New caption text

**Figure 7.48**

**7** In the **Change Icon** dialog box, click **OK**. In the **Object** dialog box, click **OK**.

The Open dialog box displays, with *Acrobat(*.pdf)* selected in the *Files of type* box. Adobe Acrobat files use a *.pdf* file extension. There may be a delay before the dialog box displays.

**8** Navigate to the location where the student files for this textbook are stored. Locate and open **w07D_Cheese**.

The *How to Buy Cheese* PDF document opens in a separate window.

**9** In the title bar of the new window, click the **Close** button ☒.

The PDF file closes, and an icon is placed at the beginning of the paragraph. The icon is captioned *USDA Cheese Information.* See Figure 7.49. The PDF file is embedded in the Word document.

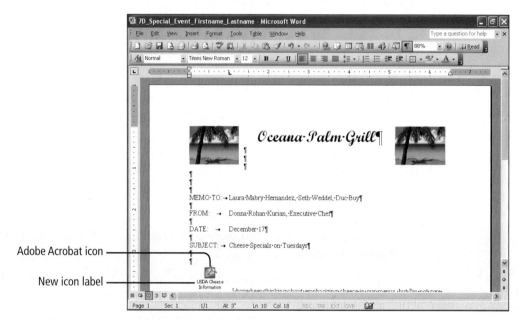

Adobe Acrobat icon ——

New icon label ——

**Figure 7.49**

**10** On the Standard toolbar, click the **Save** button 🖫.

### Activity 7.17 Modifying Objects

Each object type has a special set of features that can be modified. The PDF file icon can be resized, and you can wrap text around it. You can also change the icon border and color.

**1** Click once on the **Acrobat Document icon** to select it.

An object border with resizing handles displays.

**2** From the **Format** menu, click **Object**, and then click the **Layout tab**.

You can wrap text around a PDF icon in the same way that you wrap text around an image.

**3** Under **Wrapping style**, click **Square**. Under **Horizontal alignment**, click the **Right** option button, and then click **OK**.

The paragraph text wraps around the icon, and it is aligned at the right, as shown in Figure 7.50. An anchor symbol in the left margin indicates that the object is connected to the paragraph with the anchor.

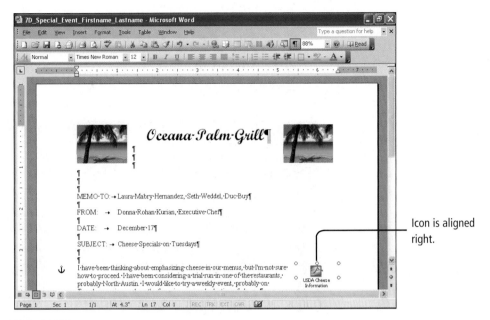

Icon is aligned right.

**Figure 7.50**

**4** Right-click the icon, and then from the displayed shortcut menu, click **Format Object**. In the **Format Object** dialog box, click the **Colors and Lines tab**.

**5** Under **Fill**, click the **Color arrow**. From the color palette, in the fourth row, click the third color—**Yellow**.

This will change the icon background to yellow.

**6** Under **Line**, click the **Color arrow**. From the color palette, in the third row, click the first color—**Red**.

**7** Under **Line**, click the **Weight up spin arrow** until the line weight is **1.5** pt.

Compare your Format Object dialog box with Figure 7.51.

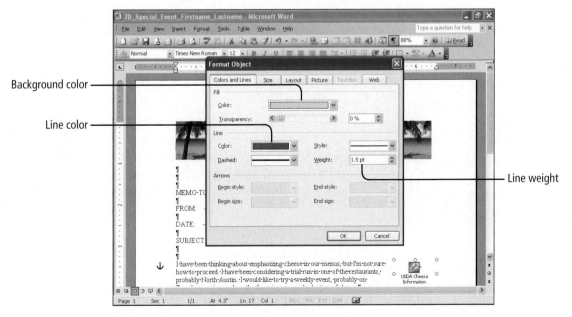

Background color

Line color

Line weight

**Figure 7.51**

**8** At the bottom of the **Format Object** dialog box, click **OK**. Scroll up so you can see the entire icon.

The icon box displays with a red border with yellow fill, as shown in Figure 7.52.

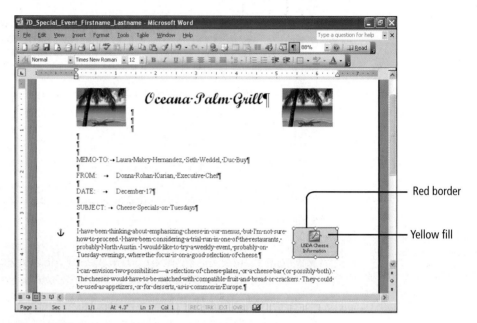

**Figure 7.52**

**9** Double-click the icon.

The Adobe Acrobat window opens, and the PDF document displays.

**10** If a task pane is open to the right of the document, click **Hide** to close it. Take a moment to scroll through the document. When you are finished, in the title bar of the **Adobe Acrobat** window, click the **Close** button ☒.

**11** On the Standard toolbar, click the **Save** button 🖫.

# Objective 7
## Modify an Image

You can use many tools in Word to modify a clip art image or a picture. You can **crop** an image, which hides part of the picture without resizing it. Pictures often are cropped to focus attention on a particular area or to remove unwanted parts of the picture. You can **scale** an image, which resizes the image, while keeping the same proportions. You can change the **contrast** and **brightness** of an image. Contrast is the differentiation between light and dark. When you increase contrast, the darks get darker and the lights get lighter. When you decrease the contrast, the dark areas brighten and the light areas darken. Changing the brightness brightens or darkens the bright areas and the dark areas at the same time.

### Activity 7.18 Cropping and Rotating Images

Unwanted or unnecessary parts of an image can be hidden by cropping, without affecting the rest of the image. The image can also be rotated to a more effective position.

**1** Click to position the insertion point at the beginning of the paragraph that begins *I have been thinking*. From the **Insert** menu, point to **Picture**, and then click **From File**. Navigate to the location where the student files for this textbook are stored. Locate and insert **w07D_Cheese_Wedge**.

The cheese wedge image is placed at the insertion point.

**2** Click to select the image and open the Picture toolbar. If the toolbar does not display, from the View menu, point to Toolbars, and then click Picture.

The Picture toolbar may be docked with other toolbars or may float, as shown in Figure 7.53.

**3** On the Picture toolbar, click the **Crop** button ⊡. Move the **Crop pointer** to the handle in the lower left corner of the image. Drag up and to the right until the image border is just to the left of and slightly below the cheese wedge, as shown in Figure 7.53.

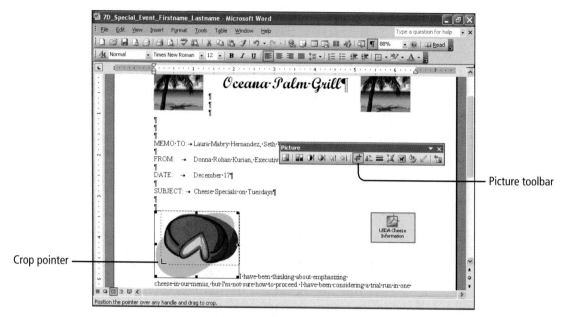

Crop pointer —————

Picture toolbar

**Figure 7.53**

**4** Release the mouse button.

The image is cropped, and the paragraph adjusts to the new image size. Recall that at this point the image is part of the text, and a change in the image size results in adjustments in the word wrap in the remainder of the paragraph.

## **Note** — Cropping Images

When you crop an image, part of the image is hidden, so the image size is reduced. The size of the remaining objects in the image, however, is not reduced. When you crop an image, you also can retrieve the cropped parts of the image by using the Crop pointer and dragging out to the former edges of the image.

**5** On the Picture toolbar, click the **Rotate Left 90°** button.

The image is rotated 90° to the left, and a rotate handle is added, as shown in Figure 7.54. You can drag the *rotate handle* to rotate an image to any angle.

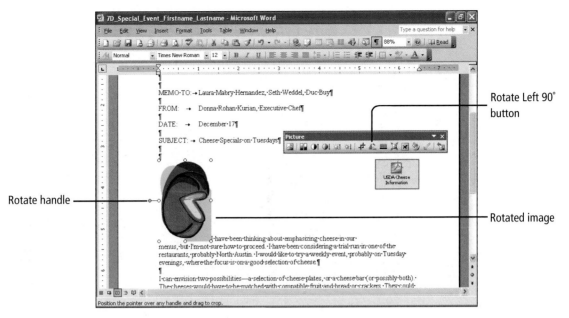

Rotate Left 90° button

Rotate handle

Rotated image

**Figure 7.54**

**Alert!**

### If the Rotate Handle Does Not Display

If you rotate the picture and the rotate handle does not display, right-click the image. From the shortcut menu, click Format Picture, and then click the Layout tab. Click Square, and then click OK. Your screens will look somewhat different than Figures 7.55 through 7.60.

**6** On the Picture toolbar, click the **Rotate Left 90°** button three more times.

The image returns to its original orientation.

**7** Move the pointer over the **rotate handle**. Using the ruler as a guide, drag the rotate handle to the left about 0.25 inches.

The image is rotated slightly. Compare your image with Figure 7.55.

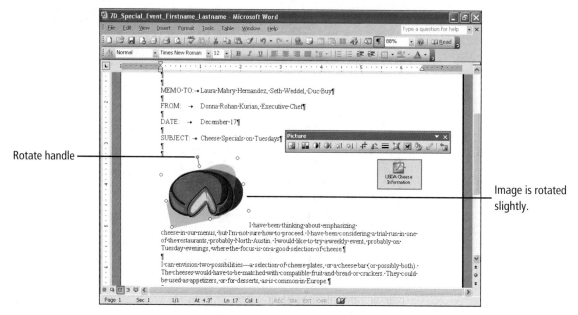

Rotate handle —

Image is rotated slightly.

**Figure 7.55**

**8** On the Standard toolbar, click the **Save** button 🖫.

### Activity 7.19 Scaling and Resizing Images

Images can be resized by dragging the resizing handles or by using the scaling feature in the Format Object dialog box.

**1** Move the pointer over the sizing handle in the middle of the right border of the image. Drag to the right about 2 inches.

The image is distorted, as shown in Figure 7.56.

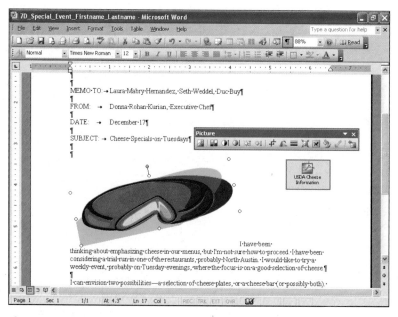

**Figure 7.56**

**2** On the Standard toolbar, click the **Undo** button.

The image returns to its original size.

**3** Right-click the image. From the shortcut menu, click **Format Picture**. From the **Format Picture** dialog box, click the **Size tab**.

**4** Under **Scale**, confirm that the **Lock aspect ratio** and the **Relative to original picture size** check boxes are selected.

The **aspect ratio** is the proportional relationship of the height and width of an image. When manually resizing a picture, always drag a corner sizing handle to retain the aspect ratio of an image.

**5** Under **Scale**, in the **Height** box, highlight **100%** and type **250**

The image will be 2.5 times as wide and high as it was originally. Compare your Format Picture dialog box with Figure 7.57. Your numbers may be slightly different.

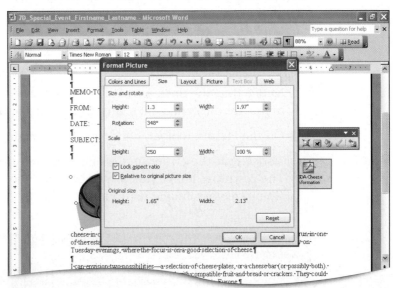

**Figure 7.57**

**6** At the bottom of the **Format Picture** dialog box, click **OK**.

**7** On the Standard toolbar, click the **Save** button.

### Activity 7.20 Controlling Image Contrast and Brightness

You can control the contrast and brightness of an image. Recall that when you increase contrast, the darks get darker and the lights get lighter, whereas changing the brightness brightens or darkens the bright areas and the dark areas at the same time.

**1** Scroll up so that you can see the entire image. On the Picture toolbar, click the **Color** button, and from the list, click **Grayscale**.

The image color is changed to grayscale. **Grayscale** displays colors as varying shades of gray, as shown in Figure 7.58.

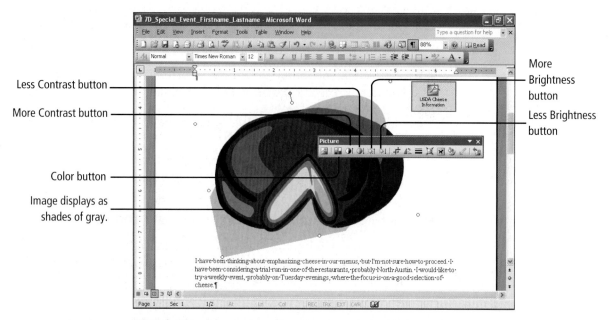

Less Contrast button

More Contrast button

Color button

Image displays as shades of gray.

More Brightness button

Less Brightness button

**Figure 7.58**

**2** On the Picture toolbar, click the **Less Contrast** button ▣ 12 times.

Notice that the dark parts of the image are lightened, and the light areas are darkened each time you click the button.

**3** On the Picture toolbar, click the **More Brightness** button ▣ 12 times.

Notice that the entire image lightens each time you click the button. The resulting image has a "washed out" look and is very light. Compare your image with Figure 7.59.

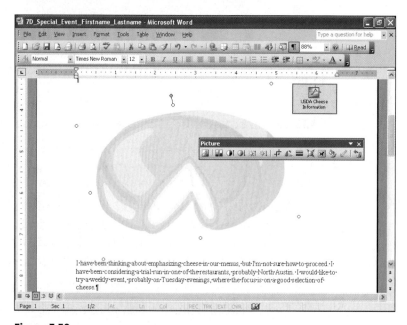

**Figure 7.59**

**Another Way**

### To Use the Format Picture Dialog Box to Adjust Contrast and Brightness

You also can adjust the contrast and brightness of an image using the menu. Right-click the image and click Format Picture (or Format Object) on the shortcut menu. In the Format Picture dialog box, click the Picture tab. Under Image control, type the desired percentages in the Brightness and Contrast boxes. Images by default use 50% Brightness and 50% Contrast. In the image you just adjusted, the Brightness should be 86% and the Contrast 14%.

**4** Right-click the image. From the shortcut menu, click **Format Picture**. In the **Format Picture** dialog box, click the **Layout tab**.

**5** Under **Wrapping style**, click **Behind text**, and then click **OK**.

The image is placed behind the text, but the image is still a little too dark.

**6** On the Picture toolbar, click the **More Brightness** button [▨] once.

The image is lightened slightly, and the text is easier to read.

**7** Hold down ⌈Ctrl⌉ and press ⌊↓⌋ eight times, watching the image as you press the key.

Notice that the image is *nudged*—moved in small increments—down slightly each time you press the arrow key. This technique enables you to position an image exactly where you want it.

**8** Hold down ⌈Ctrl⌉ and press ⌊→⌋ three times.

The image moves slightly to the right. See Figure 7.60. Use the nudge technique as necessary to move your image approximately as shown in Figure 7.60.

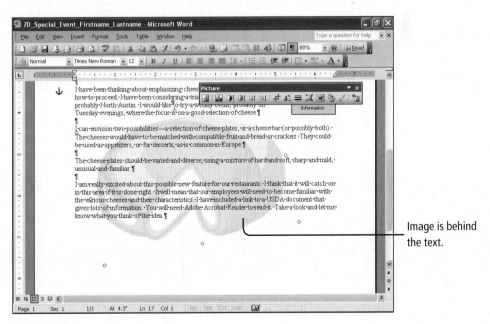

Image is behind the text.

**Figure 7.60**

**9** From the **View** menu, click **Header and Footer**. On the Header and Footer toolbar, click the **Switch Between Header and Footer** button ⊞.

**10** On the Header and Footer toolbar, click the **Insert AutoText** button Insert AutoText ▾ , and then click **Filename**.

The file name is inserted in the footer.

**11** On the Header and Footer toolbar, click the **Close** button Close .

**12** On the Standard toolbar, click the **Save** button 🖫 .

**13** On the Standard toolbar, click the **Print Preview** button 🔍 . Take a moment to check your work. On the Print Preview toolbar, click the **Close Preview** button Close .

**14** Make any necessary changes to your document. When you are satisfied, on the Standard toolbar, click the **Print** button 🖨 . Close the document, saving changes if necessary, and close Word.

**End** You have completed Project 7D ─────────────

# Summary

Tables are used for many purposes, and Word has advanced tools to enable you to present table data effectively and attractively. You can align text in cells horizontally (left, center, and right) and vertically (top, center, and bottom), giving you nine possible alignment combinations. When cell width is a concern, you can change the text direction from horizontal to vertical. Cells also can be merged horizontally or vertically to facilitate titles that extend beyond a cell's width or height.

If you create new tables often, you can standardize the look of your tables by creating a table style. Table styles enable you to format the whole table or just parts of a table, such as the left or right column or the top or bottom row. Once you have created a table style, a single click will result in the formatting changes saved in the style.

Sometimes you need the features of a table coupled with the flexibility to form rows and columns of varying size and format. The Draw Table command enables you to create a table with nonuniform rows and columns. When used with the other commands on the Tables and Borders toolbar, you can create a table with the exact specifications you need.

Clip art images and pictures can be modified using advanced formatting features. The contrast or brightness of an image can be modified to lighten or darken the whole image or to accentuate the difference between the light and dark areas. Color images can be changed to grayscale, which displays colors as shades of gray. You can crop an image to remove portions of the image without changing the size of the remaining image. An image can also be resized proportionally and rotated to any angle with precision.

# In This Chapter You Practiced How To

- Create and Apply a Custom Table Style
- Format Cells in a Table
- Modify Table Properties
- Use Advanced Table Features
- Draw a Complex Table
- Insert Objects in a Document
- Modify an Image

**Matching**  Match each term in the second column with its correct definition in the first column by writing the letter of the term on the blank line in front of the correct definition.

_____ 1. A small circle on a selected image that can be dragged to change the angle of an image.

_____ 2. The differentiation between light and dark parts of an image.

_____ 3. The light-to-dark ratio of an image.

_____ 4. A title that can be added to a table or figure.

_____ 5. A free program that is used to open Portable Document Format (PDF) files.

_____ 6. To resize an image, keeping the same image proportions.

_____ 7. Displays all colors as shades of gray.

_____ 8. Type of style that displays a small grid to the right of the style name in the Styles and Formatting task pane.

_____ 9. To trim part of a picture or clip art image without resizing the image.

_____ 10. Proportional relationship of the height and width of an image.

_____ 11. A combination of formatting steps, such as font, font size, and indentation, that you name and store as a set.

_____ 12. A small box that displays at the outside upper-left corner of a table that can be dragged to move the entire table to a different location in a document.

_____ 13. The process of organizing data in a particular order.

_____ 14. Any type of graphic—for example, a shape, a WordArt, an AutoShape, a clip art image, a picture, or an Excel chart— that can be inserted into a document.

_____ 15. A document formatted in the Portable Document Format developed by Adobe Systems.

**A**  Adobe Acrobat Reader

**B**  Aspect ratio

**C**  Brightness

**D**  Caption

**E**  Contrast

**F**  Crop

**G**  Grayscale

**H**  Object

**I**  PDF Document

**J**  Rotate handle

**K**  Scale

**L**  Sort

**M**  Style

**N**  Table

**O**  Table move handle

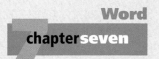

**Fill in the Blank**  Write the correct answer in the space provided.

1.  Text can be aligned in a cell both horizontally and

    _____.

2.  A(n) _____ enables you to sum numbers in a table

    row or column.

3.  If you increase the contrast of an image, the dark areas are made

    darker, and the light areas are made _____.

4.  Adobe Acrobat files use a(n) _____ extension.

5.  If you decrease the brightness of an image, the dark areas are made

    darker, and the light areas are made _____.

6.  You can create a table _____ to perform many

    formatting commands at one time.

7.  A(n) _____ is used as a numbered title for a table

    and can be placed above or below the table.

8.  PDF files can be read using Adobe Acrobat _____.

9.  You can _____ on a column in a table to arrange the

    contents of the column in alphabetical or numerical order.

10. An object can be rotated to any angle by dragging the

    _____.

## Project 7E — Staff Schedule

**Objectives:** *Create and Apply a Custom Table Style, Format Cells in a Table, and Use Advanced Table Features.*

In the following Skill Assessment, you will edit a table in a document for the Oceana Palm Grill, which describes an employee schedule for the lunch hour of the grand opening of a new restaurant in the chain. Your completed document will look similar to the one shown in Figure 7.61. You will save your document as *7E_Staff_Schedule_Firstname_Lastname*.

**Figure 7.61**

1. On the Standard toolbar, click the **Open** button. Navigate to the location where the student files for this textbook are stored. Locate and open **w07E_Staff_Schedule**. Save the file as **7E_Staff_Schedule_Firstname_Lastname**

2. On the Standard toolbar, click the **Zoom button arrow**, and then click **Page Width**. If necessary, on the Standard toolbar, click the Show/Hide ¶ button to show formatting marks. Right-click on any toolbar, and then click **Tables and Borders** from the shortcut menu. The Tables and Borders toolbar displays.

**(Project 7E–Staff Schedule continues on the next page)**

**(Project 7E–Staff Schedule continued)**

3. From the **Format** menu, click **Styles and Formatting**. At the top of the **Styles and Formatting** task pane, click **New Style**. In the displayed **New Style** dialog box, under **Properties**, in the **Name** box, type **Schedule**

4. Click the **Style type arrow** and from the displayed list, click **Table**.

5. Under **Formatting**, with **Whole table** displayed in the **Apply formatting to** box, on the **New Style** dialog box toolbar, click the **Font button arrow**, scroll as necessary, and then click **Arial**. Click the **Font Size button arrow**, and then click **12**. Click the **Border button arrow**, and then click **All Borders**.

6. Under **Formatting**, with **Whole table** still displayed in the **Apply formatting to** box, at the lower left side of the dialog box, click the **Format arrow**, and from the displayed list click **Table Properties**. If necessary, click the **Table tab**. Under **Alignment**, click **Center**, and then click **OK**.

7. Under **Formatting**, click the **Apply formatting to arrow**, and then click **Even row stripes**, which will shade every other row. On the **New Style** dialog box toolbar, click the **Shading Color button arrow**, and then in the first row, click the third color—**Gray-10%**.

8. Under **Formatting**, click the **Apply formatting to arrow**, and then click **Right column** to set formats for the right column of the table. On the **New Style** dialog box toolbar, click the **Align button arrow**, and then click **Align Center Right**. At the bottom of the **New Style** dialog box, click **OK**. Your new style is created, but has not yet been applied.

9. Click anywhere in the table in your **7E_Staff_Schedule_Firstname_ Lastname** document. In the **Styles and Formatting** task pane, click the **Schedule** style. Close the **Styles and Formatting** task pane.

10. In the first row of the table, select the right three cells, beginning with *Last Name* and ending with *Hourly Rate*. On the Tables and Borders toolbar, click the **Change Text Direction** button. On the Tables and Borders toolbar, click the **Align button arrow**, and then click the **Center** button.

11. Move the pointer into the left margin area of the first row of the table until it turns into a white arrow, and then click once to select the row. From the Formatting toolbar, click the **Bold** button. From the **Table** menu, point to **Insert**, and then click **Rows Above**.

12. With the first row still selected, on the Tables and Borders toolbar, click the **Merge Cells** button. Type **Tentative Schedule**

13. Select the text *Tentative Schedule* that you just typed. On the Formatting toolbar, if necessary, click the **Center** button. On the Formatting toolbar, click the **Font Size arrow**, and then click **24**.

**(Project 7E–Staff Schedule continues on the next page)**

**(Project 7E–Staff Schedule continued)**

14. Move the pointer to the left of the third row of the table, beginning *Host*, until it turns into a white arrow. Drag down to select the third row through the last row of the table. Be sure that you do *not* select the ending paragraph marker outside of the table.

15. From the **Format** menu, click **Paragraph**, and then click the **Indents and Spacing tab**. Under **Spacing**, in the **After** box, click the **up spin arrow** to add **6 pt.** spacing after each row.

16. With the rows still selected, from the **Table** menu, click **Sort**. Be sure that under **My list has**, the **No Header row** option is selected, and that the **Sort by** box displays **Column 1**. Be sure the **Ascending** option button is selected.

17. Click the first **Then by arrow** and click **Column 2**. This action directs Word to sort on the first column, and then, when two or more items in the first column are the same, to sort on the second column.

18. At the bottom of the **Sort** dialog box, click **OK** to sort the table by Position and, within position, by Last Name. Within groups, where the Position name is the same, Word further sorts the rows by Last Name (Column 2). Compare your document with Figure 7.61.

19. From the **View** menu, click **Header and Footer**. On the Header and Footer toolbar, click the **Switch Between Header and Footer** button. On the **Header and Footer** toolbar, click the **Insert AutoText** button, and then click **Filename**. On the **Header and Footer** toolbar, click the **Close** button.

20. On the Standard toolbar, click the **Save** button. On the Standard toolbar, click the **Print Preview** button. Take a moment to check your work. On the Print Preview toolbar, click the **Close Preview** button.

21. Make any necessary changes to your document. When you are satisfied, on the Standard toolbar, click the **Print** button. Close the document, saving it if you are prompted to do so.

**End** You have completed Project 7E ————————————

# Project 7F — Investment

**Objectives:** *Create and Apply a Custom Table Style, Modify Table Properties, and Use Advanced Table Features.*

In the following Skill Assessment, you will edit a letter to a potential investor in which you will wrap text around two tables, create and apply a custom table style, add table captions, and use a formula to calculate average sales. Your completed document will look similar to the one shown in Figure 7.62. You will save your document as *7F_Investment_Firstname_Lastname.*

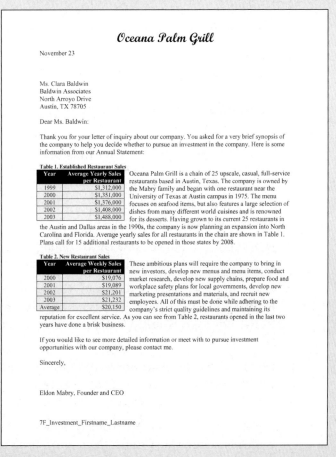

**Figure 7.62**

1. On the Standard toolbar, click the **Open** button. Navigate to the location where the student files for this textbook are stored. Locate and open **w07F_Investment**. Save the file as **7F_Investment_Firstname_Lastname**

**(Project 7F–Investment continues on the next page)**

**(Project 7F–Investment continued)**

2.  On the Standard toolbar, click the **Zoom button arrow**, and then click **Page Width**. If necessary, on the Standard toolbar, click the Show/Hide ¶ button to show formatting marks. Right-click on any toolbar, and then from the shortcut menu, click **Tables and Borders** to display the Tables and Borders toolbar. Drag the toolbar so that it is not blocking your view or dock it to the other toolbars on your screen.

3.  From the **Format** menu, click **Styles and Formatting**. At the top of the **Styles and Formatting** task pane, click **New Style**. In the displayed **New Style** dialog box, under **Properties**, in the **Name** box, type **Investment**

4.  Click the **Style type arrow** and from the displayed list, click **Table**.

5.  Under **Formatting**, be sure that **Whole table** displays in the **Apply formatting to** box. On the **New Style** dialog box toolbar, click the **Border button arrow**, and then click **All Borders**. Click the **Shading Color button arrow**, and then in the first row, click the second color—**Gray-5%**.

6.  Under **Formatting**, click the **Apply formatting to** arrow and from the displayed list, click **Header row**. On the **New Style** dialog box toolbar, click the **Shading Color button arrow**, and then in the fourth row, click the first color—**Black**. On the **New Style** dialog box toolbar, click the **Bold** button.

7.  At the bottom of the **New Style** dialog box, click **OK**. The new table style is created and listed in the Styles and Formatting task pane.

8.  Click anywhere in the **Average Yearly Sales** table. In the **Styles and Formatting** task pane, click the **Investment** style. Click anywhere in the **Average Weekly Sales** table. In the **Styles and Formatting** task pane, click the **Investment** style.

9.  Close the **Styles and Formatting** task pane. Right-click the **Average Yearly Sales** table, click **Table Properties**, and then click the **Table tab**. Under **Text wrapping**, click **Around**, and then click **OK**.

10. Right-click the **Average Weekly Sales** table, click **Table Properties**, and then click the **Table tab**. Under **Text wrapping**, click **Around**, and then click **OK**.

11. Position the insertion point anywhere in the **Average Weekly Sales** table. From the **Insert** menu, point to **Reference**, and then click **Caption**. Under **Caption**, at the insertion point type a period, press Spacebar, type **New Restaurant Sales** and then click **OK**.

12. Position the insertion point anywhere in the **Average Yearly Sales** table. From the **Insert** menu, point to **Reference**, and then click **Caption**. Under **Caption**, type a period, press Spacebar, type **Established Restaurant Sales** and then click **OK**.

**(Project 7F–Investment continues on the next page)**

**(Project 7F–Investment continued)**

**13.** Position the insertion point in the lower right cell of the **Average Weekly Sales** table and press `Tab`. In the left cell of the new row, type **Average** and then press `Tab`.

**14.** From the **Table** menu, click **Formula**. In the **Formula** dialog box, in the **Formula** box, select *SUM* and type **AVERAGE** The formula should indicate =*AVERAGE(ABOVE)*.

**15.** Click the **Number format arrow**, and then click **$#,##0.00;($#,##0.00)**. Delete everything from the first period on, so that the number format is *$#,##0* (without the period). This displays a number with a dollar sign and commas, but there is no preset formula for this format. Click **OK**. Compare your document with Figure 7.62.

**16.** From the **View** menu, click **Header and Footer**. On the Header and Footer toolbar, click the **Switch Between Header and Footer** button. On the Header and Footer toolbar, click the **Insert AutoText** button, and then click **Filename**. On the Header and Footer toolbar, click the **Close** button.

**17.** On the Standard toolbar, click the **Save** button.

**18.** On the Standard toolbar, click the **Print Preview** button. Take a moment to check your work. On the Print Preview toolbar, click the **Close Preview** button.

**19.** Make any necessary changes to your document. When you are satisfied, on the Standard toolbar, click the **Print** button. Close the document, saving it if you are prompted to do so.

**End** You have completed Project 7F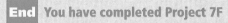

# Project 7G — Gift Card

**Objectives:** *Insert Objects in a Document and Modify an Image.*

In the following Skill Assessment, you will edit a poster announcing gift cards available at the Oceana Palm Grill. You will insert a picture from a file and rotate it, change the contrast and brightness of the picture, send an image behind text, and enlarge a picture proportionally. Your completed document will look similar to the one shown in Figure 7.63. You will save your document as *7G_Gift_Card_Firstname_Lastname*.

**1.** On the Standard toolbar, click the **Open** button. Navigate to the location where the student files for this textbook are stored. Locate and open **w07G_Gift_Card**. Save the file as **7G_Gift_Card_Firstname_Lastname**

**(Project 7G–Gift Card continues on the next page)**

**(Project 7G–Gift Card continued)**

**Figure 7.63**

2. On the Standard toolbar, click the **Zoom button arrow**, and then click **Page Width**. If necessary, on the Standard toolbar, click the Show/Hide ¶ button to display formatting marks.

3. Click to position the insertion point at the beginning of the line that begins *Give the gift*. From the **Insert** menu, point to **Picture**, and then click **From File**. Navigate to the location where the student files for this textbook are stored. Locate and select **w07G_Chef_Hat**, and then click **Insert**.

4. Click the **chef hat** image to select it. If necessary, display the Picture toolbar by right-clicking the image, and from the shortcut menu, clicking the Show Picture Toolbar. On the Picture toolbar, click the **Rotate Left 90°** button.

5. Drag the **Rotate** handle until the hat is tilted about 45° to the left. Refer to Figure 7.63.

6. On the Picture toolbar, click the **Less Contrast** button once, and then click the **More Brightness** button once.

**(Project 7G–Gift Card continues on the next page)**

**(Project 7G–Gift Card continued)**

7. Right-click the image. From the shortcut menu, click **Format Picture**. In the displayed **Format Picture** dialog box, click the **Layout tab**. Under **Wrapping style**, click **Behind text**, and then click **OK**.

8. Right-click the image. From the shortcut menu, click **Format Picture**. From the **Format Picture** dialog box, click the **Size tab**. Under **Scale**, confirm that the **Lock aspect ratio** and the **Relative to original picture size** check boxes are selected.

9. Under **Scale**, in the **Height** box, select **100%**, type **125** and then click **OK**.

10. Select the five lines that begin *Graduation* and end *Just because*. From the Formatting toolbar, click the **Font Size arrow**, and then click **36** to increase the font size.

11. From the Standard toolbar, click the **Zoom button arrow**, and then click **Whole Page**. Drag the image as necessary to visually center it on the poster. Hold down Ctrl and press the arrow keys to nudge the image into its final position, as shown in Figure 7.63. Return to **Page Width** zoom.

12. From the **View** menu, click **Header and Footer**. On the Header and Footer toolbar, click the **Switch Between Header and Footer** button. On the Header and Footer toolbar, click the **Insert AutoText** button, and then click **Filename**. On the Header and Footer toolbar, click the **Close** button.

13. On the Standard toolbar, click the **Save** button. Then, on the Standard toolbar, click the **Print Preview** button. Take a moment to check your work. On the Print Preview toolbar, click the **Close Preview** button.

14. Make any necessary changes to your document. When you are satisfied, on the Standard toolbar, click the **Print** button. Close the document.

**End** **You have completed Project 7G**

## Project 7H — Safety Training

**Objectives:** *Create and Apply a Custom Table Style, Format Cells in a Table, Use Advanced Table Features, and Insert Objects in a Document.*

In the following Performance Assessment, you will edit a memo about safety training for teenage workers at the Oceana Palm Grill. You will sort a table, merge cells, and change text direction. You also will insert and modify an image. Your completed document will look similar to the one shown in Figure 7.64. You will save your document as *7H_Safety_Training_Firstname_Lastname.*

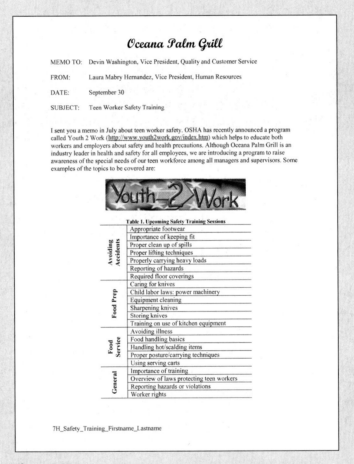

**Figure 7.64**

**1.** On the Standard toolbar, click the **Open** button. Navigate to the location where the student files for this textbook are stored. Locate and open **w07H_Safety_Training**. Save the file as **7H_Safety_Training_Firstname_Lastname**

**(Project 7H–Safety Training continues on the next page)**

**(Project 7H**–Safety Training continued)

2. Be sure that formatting marks are displayed and zoom to **Page Width**. Display the Tables and Borders toolbar. Scroll so that you can view the entire table in the middle of your screen. Click to position your insertion point somewhere in the table. From the **Table** menu, point to **Select**, and then click **Table**. On the Formatting toolbar, click the **Center** button.

3. From the **Table** menu, click **Sort**. Set the sort settings to sort first on **Column 1**, and **Then by Column 2**, both in **Ascending** order. Specify that the table has no header row, and then click **OK**.

4. In the first column, select all of the *Avoiding Accident* cells except the first one. Press [Del]. In the same manner, delete all but the first instance of *Food Prep*, *Food Service*, and *General*.

5. In the first column, select the *Avoiding Accident* cell and the blank cells under it (the top seven cells in the first column should be selected). On the Tables and Borders toolbar, click the **Merge Cells** button. In the same manner, merge *Food Prep*, *Food Service*, and *General* with the empty cells below them.

6. Move the pointer to the top of the first column until it turns to a black arrow, and then click to select the column. On the Tables and Borders toolbar, click the **Change Text Direction** button twice. On the Formatting toolbar, click the **Bold** button. On the Tables and Borders toolbar, click the **Align button arrow**, and then click the **Align Center** button.

7. From the **Table** menu, click **Table Properties**, and then click the **Column tab**. Under **Size**, change the **Preferred width** to .7

8. Click in the table to deselect all the rows. From the **Insert** menu, point to **Reference**, and then click **Caption**. Confirm that the Position is *Above selected item*. Under **Caption**, type a period and press [Spacebar]. Type **Upcoming Safety Training Sessions** and click **OK**. On the Formatting toolbar, click the **Center** button.

9. Click to position the insertion point in the blank line just above the caption. From the **Insert** menu, point to **Picture**, and then click **From File**. Navigate to the location where the student files for this textbook are stored. Locate and insert **w07H_Youth2Work**. From the Formatting toolbar, click the **Center** button. Press [Enter] to add a blank line after the graphic. Position the insertion point at the end of the paragraph before the graphic and press [Enter].

10. Click anywhere in the table. From the **Table** menu, point to **Select**, and then click **Table**. From the **Format** menu, click **Borders and Shading**, and then click the **Borders tab**. In the Preview area, click to deselect the left and right borders. Click **OK**.

**(Project 7H**–Safety Training continues on the next page)

**(Project 7H**–Safety Training continued)

11. From the **View** menu, click **Header and Footer**. On the Header and Footer toolbar, click the **Switch Between Header and Footer** button. Click the **Insert AutoText** button, and then click **Filename**. On the **Header and Footer** toolbar, click the **Close** button.

12. On the Standard toolbar, click the **Save** button. Preview the document, and then print it. Close the document.

**End** You have completed Project 7H

## Project 7I — Travel Form

**Objectives:** *Format Cells in a Table, Use Advanced Table Features, Draw a Complex Table, and Insert Objects in a Document.*

In the following Performance Assessment, you will edit a travel form for the Oceana Palm Grill. You will use the Draw Table feature, insert an object, and format the table. Your completed document will look similar to the one shown in Figure 7.65. You will save your document as *7I_Travel_Form_Firstname_Lastname*.

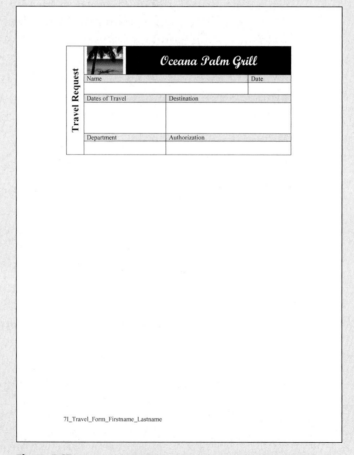

**Figure 7.65**
**(Project 7I**–Travel Form continues on the next page)

**(Project 7I–Travel Form continued)**

1. On the Standard toolbar, click the **Open** button. Navigate to the location where the student files for this textbook are stored. Locate and open **w07I_Travel_Form**. Save the file as 7I_Travel_Form_Firstname_Lastname

2. Right-click on the table, click **Table Properties**, and then click the **Table tab**. Under **Alignment**, click **Center**, and then click **OK**.

3. If necessary, display the Tables and Borders toolbar. On the Tables and Borders toolbar, click the **Eraser** button. Click the vertical line to the right of *Destination* to erase it. Erase the vertical line to the right of *Authorization*. Click the **Eraser** button to turn it off.

4. On the Tables and Borders toolbar, click the **Draw Table** button. Position the Draw Table pencil pointer on the upper left corner of the table. Drag to the left to **-0.5 inches on the horizontal ruler** (in the blue shaded area left of the table) and then down so the dotted line extends to the bottom of the table. This will add a narrow column to the left side of the table. Refer to Figure 7.65 for the size and location of the added table column. If you are not satisfied with your result, click the **Undo** button and begin again. Click the **Draw Table** button to turn it off.

5. On the Tables and Borders toolbar, click the **Change Text Direction** button twice. From the Formatting toolbar, click the **Bold** button. Click the **Font Size arrow** and click **16**. Click the **Font arrow**, and then click **Times New Roman**. Type **Travel Request**

6. On the Tables and Borders toolbar, click the **Draw Table** button. Move the Draw Table (pencil) pointer just under *Name*. Drag to the right until the dashed line touches the right table border. Repeat this procedure under *Dates of Travel* and *Department*. Refer to Figure 7.65. Click the **Draw Table** button to turn it off.

7. Click in the *Name* cell and drag to the right until the *Date* cell is also selected. On the Tables and Borders toolbar, click the **Shading Color button arrow**, and then in the first row, click the third button— **Gray-10%**. Repeat this procedure to shade the *Dates of Travel*, *Destination*, *Department*, and *Authorization* cells.

8. On the Tables and Borders toolbar, click the **Draw Table** button. Move the Draw Table (pencil) pointer to the top border of the table at **1.5 inches on the horizontal ruler**; drag down from the top border only to the bottom of the first row. This will create the cell in which you will insert the picture. Refer to Figure 7.65. Click the **Draw Table** button to turn it off.

**(Project 7I–Travel Form continues on the next page)**

**(Project 7I–Travel Form continued)**

9. Click to position the insertion point in the cell you just created (to the left of the *Oceana Palm Grill* cell). From the **Insert** menu, point to **Picture**, and then click **From File**. Locate and insert the **w07I_Grill_Logo** file. Click to select the image. Drag the lower right sizing handle up and to the left until the image is about 1 inch wide. Use the horizontal ruler as a guide.

10. Click to position the insertion point in the *Oceana Palm Grill* cell. On the Tables and Borders toolbar, click the **Shading Color button arrow**, and then in the fourth row, click the first button—**Black**. On the Tables and Borders toolbar, click the **Align button arrow**, and from the displayed palette, click the **Align Center** button. Click outside of the table to deselect. Compare your document with Figure 7.65.

11. From the **View** menu, click **Header and Footer**. On the Header and Footer toolbar, click the **Switch Between Header and Footer** button. Click the **Insert AutoText** button, and then click **Filename**. On the **Header and Footer** toolbar, click the **Close** button.

12. On the Standard toolbar, click the **Save** button. Preview the document, and then print it. Close the document.

**End** You have completed Project 7I

## Project 7J — Press Release

**Objectives:** *Create and Apply a Custom Table Style, Modify Table Properties, Use Advanced Table Features, Insert Objects in a Document, and Modify an Image.*

In the following Performance Assessment, you will edit a press release regarding the record growth of the Oceana Palm Grill. You will add a column of numbers in a table and insert and modify an image. Your completed document will look similar to the one shown in Figure 7.66. You will save your document as *7J_Press_Release_Firstname_Lastname*.

1. On the Standard toolbar, click the **Open** button 📂. Navigate to the location where the student files for this textbook are stored. Locate and open **w07J_Press_Release**. Save the new document as 7J_Press_Release_Firstname_Lastname

2. Display the **Styles and Formatting** task pane and create a **New Style**. At the top of the **New Style** dialog box, in the **Name** box, type **Growth**

**(Project 7J–Press Release continues on the next page)**

**(Project 7J**–Press Release continued)

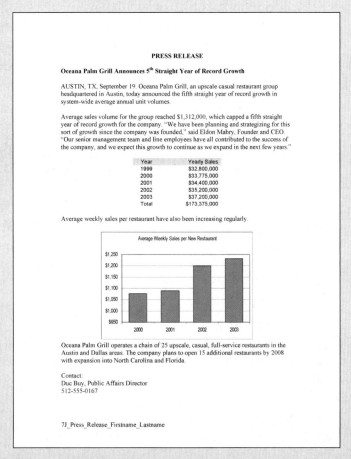

**Figure 7.66**

3. As the **Style type**, click **Table**. Under **Formatting**, click the **Apply formatting to arrow**, and then click **Header row**. On the **New Style** dialog box toolbar, click the **Bold** button. Click the **Border button arrow**, and then click **No Border**. Click the **Shading Color button arrow**, and then in the first row, click the third box—**Gray-10%**.

4. Under **Formatting**, click the **Apply formatting to arrow**, and then click **Left column**. On the **New Style** dialog box toolbar, click the **Align button arrow**, and then click **Align Center**. Click **OK**.

5. Position the insertion point in the table and click the **Growth** style. Close the task pane.

6. In the table, position the insertion point in the last row. From the **Table** menu, click **Insert**, and then click **Rows Below**. In the left cell of the new row, type **Total** and then press Tab.

7. From the **Table** menu, click **Formula**. In the **Number format** box, type **$#,##0** and then click **OK**.

**(Project 7J**–Press Release continues on the next page)

**(Project 7J–Press Release continued)**

8. Right-click on the table and click **Table Properties** from the shortcut menu. If necessary, click the **Table tab**. Under **Alignment**, click **Center**, and then click **OK**.

9. Click to position the insertion point in the blank line above the paragraph that begins *Oceana Palm Grill operates.*

10. From the **Insert** menu, point to **Picture**, and then click **From File**. From your student files, locate and insert **w07J_New_Locations**.

11. Click the chart to select it. Drag the middle sizing handle on the right border of the chart to the left approximately **1 inch**. Use the ruler as a guide. On the Formatting toolbar, click the **Center** button. Click to deselect the chart. Compare your document with Figure 7.66.

12. From the **View** menu, click **Header and Footer**. On the Header and Footer toolbar, click the **Switch Between Header and Footer** button. Click the **Insert AutoText** button, and then click **Filename**. On the **Header and Footer** toolbar, click the **Close** button.

13. On the Standard toolbar, click the **Save** button. Preview the document, and then print it. Close the document.

**End** You have completed Project 7J

# Project 7K — Locations

**Objectives:** *Format Cells in a Table, Modify Table Properties, and Use Advanced Table Features.*

In the following Mastery Assessment, you will edit a table of possible Oceana Palm Grill locations in North Carolina. You will sort the data, modify the table structure, and format the table data. Your completed document will look similar to the one shown in Figure 7.67. You will save your document as *7K_Locations_Firstname_Lastname*.

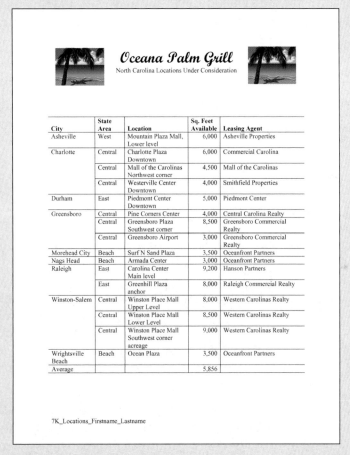

**Figure 7.67**

1. Locate and open **w07K_Locations**. Save the file as **7K_Locations_ Firstname_Lastname** in the same location as your other files for this chapter. In the same manner as you have done in previous documents, display the footer and insert the **AutoText** filename.

2. **Sort** the table on the **City** column in ascending order, specifying that you have a header row in this table.

**(Project 7K – Locations continues on the next page)**

**(Project 7K–Locations continued)**

3.  Display the Tables and Borders toolbar. In the first column of the table, delete the second and third instances of *Charlotte*. Select the *Charlotte* cell and the two empty cells below it. Merge the three cells.

4.  Use the same technique to delete duplicate city names and merge the city name cells with the empty cells below them.

5.  Select the top row of the table. Change the text to **Bold**. Align the first row text **Bottom Left**.

6.  Add a row to the bottom of the table. In the left cell, type **Average** In the fourth cell of the new row, add a formula to show the average square footage of the possible restaurant locations. (Hint: Delete *SUM* and insert *AVERAGE*.) Select **#,##0** as the number format, to match the numbers above.

7.  Select the table. Display the **Borders and Shading** dialog box and remove the left and right borders from the table.

8.  Save the completed document. Preview and print the document.

**End** You have completed Project 7K

## Project 7L — Regulations

**Objectives:** *Format Cells in a Table, Modify Table Properties, Use Advanced Table Features, Insert Objects in a Document, and Modify an Image.*

In the following Mastery Assessment, you will edit a memo regarding Oceana Palm Grill training sessions covering Texas Department of Health regulations. You will insert and modify graphics and create and modify a small table. Your completed document will look similar to the one shown in Figure 7.68. You will save your document as *7L_Regulations_Firstname_Lastname.*

1.  From your student files, open **w07L_Regulations**. Save the file with the name **7L_Regulations_Firstname_Lastname** in the same location as your other files from this chapter. Display the footer and insert the **AutoText** filename.

2.  Press Ctrl + End to move to the end of the document. At this location, create a 4-row by 2-column table. Add the following text:

| Date | Time |
|------|------|
| March 18 | 9 a.m. |
| March 18 | 3 p.m. |
| March 19 | 9 p.m. |

**(Project 7L–Regulations continues on the next page)**

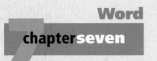
**(Project 7L–Regulations continued)**

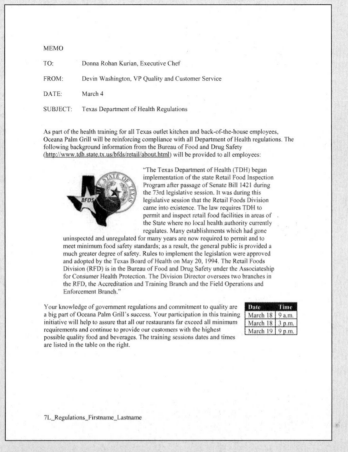

MEMO

TO:      Donna Rohan Kurian, Executive Chef

FROM:    Devin Washington, VP Quality and Customer Service

DATE:    March 4

SUBJECT: Texas Department of Health Regulations

As part of the health training for all Texas outlet kitchen and back-of-the-house employees, Oceana Palm Grill will be reinforcing compliance with all Department of Health regulations. The following background information from the Bureau of Food and Drug Safety (http://www.tdh.state.tx.us/bfds/retail/about.html) will be provided to all employees:

"The Texas Department of Health (TDH) began implementation of the state Retail Food Inspection Program after passage of Senate Bill 1421 during the 73rd legislative session. It was during this legislative session that the Retail Foods Division came into existence. The law requires TDH to permit and inspect retail food facilities in areas of the State where no local health authority currently regulates. Many establishments which had gone uninspected and unregulated for many years are now required to permit and to meet minimum food safety standards; as a result, the general public is provided a much greater degree of safety. Rules to implement the legislation were approved and adopted by the Texas Board of Health on May 20, 1994. The Retail Foods Division (RFD) is in the Bureau of Food and Drug Safety under the Associateship for Consumer Health Protection. The Division Director oversees two branches in the RFD, the Accreditation and Training Branch and the Field Operations and Enforcement Branch."

Your knowledge of government regulations and commitment to quality are a big part of Oceana Palm Grill's success. Your participation in this training initiative will help to assure that all our restaurants far exceed all minimum requirements and continue to provide our customers with the highest possible quality food and beverages. The training sessions dates and times are listed in the table on the right.

| Date | Time |
|------|------|
| March 18 | 9 a.m. |
| March 18 | 3 p.m. |
| March 19 | 9 p.m. |

7L_Regulations_Firstname_Lastname

**Figure 7.68**

**3.** Display the Tables and Borders toolbar. Select the table. Click the **Table AutoFormat** button. Under **Table styles**, click **Table Grid 8**. Be sure that special formatting is *not* applied to the last row or last column. From the **Table** menu, point to **AutoFit**, and then click **AutoFit to Contents**.

**4.** Change the table properties to wrap the text around the table. Use the table move handle to move the table to the right edge of the last paragraph, as shown in Figure 7.68.

**5.** Position the insertion point at the beginning of the paragraph that starts *The Texas Department*. From your student files, insert the **w07L_Texas** image.

**6.** Format the picture to wrap text **Tight** around the image. Change the **Scale** of the image to **125%** and be sure to retain the image proportions. Compare your document with Figure 7.68.

**7.** Save the completed document. Preview and print the document.

**End** You have completed Project 7L

## Project 7M — Employee

**Objectives:** *Insert Objects in a Document and Modify an Image.*

Good employees are critical to the success of a business. Employee of the Month awards help build team spirit and motivate individuals. In this project, you will complete an Employee of the Month announcement from Oceana Palm Grill. You will save your document as *7M_Employee_Firstname_Lastname.*

1. Locate and open **w07M_Employee**. Save the document as **7M_Employee_Firstname_Lastname** and add the file name to the footer.

2. Type your name as indicated as Employee of the Month.

3. Type two short paragraphs about why you think you won the award. For example, helping to train new employees, helping out when the restaurant was short of staff, and so forth. Give yourself any job title you like, other than CEO or President, and make sure the text fits the job.

4. Have someone take your picture with a digital camera. Insert your picture in the document as indicated. Scale your picture, making the width **4 inches**. Put a border around the picture, make the border line at least **2 pt.**, and change the color of the border to **blue**.

5. Save the completed document. Preview and print the document.

**End** You have completed Project 7M ————————————————————

## Project 7N — Personal Styles

**Objectives:** *Format Cells in a Table, Modify Table Properties, Use Advanced Table Features, Insert Objects in a Document, and Modify an Image.*

The United States Department of Agriculture has set nutrition guidelines, including a food pyramid. The food pyramid suggests the relative proportions of different foods that should be eaten to maintain a healthy diet. They include a list showing the optimum number of servings per day for different types of food.

1. You will use a PDF file to find the data needed for this project. Go to My Computer. Locate and open **w07N_Food_Pyramid**, which is a PDF file. If you cannot open the PDF file, it means that Adobe Acrobat Reader is not installed on your computer. To obtain Adobe Acrobat Reader, go to www.adobe.com and follow instructions for downloading and installing the program. You will need to register with Adobe, but there is no charge to download the program, or any obligation by registering.

**(Project 7N–Personal Styles continues on the next page)**

**(Project 7N–Personal Styles continued)**

2. Scroll down until you find the list of the recommended number of servings of different foods. Print just the pages containing that information.

3. Create a new document and save the document as *7N_Food_Pyramid_Firstname_Lastname*. Add a brief introductory paragraph, and then create a two-column table, with food types in the first column and number of servings in the second column.

4. Look through the information you printed, find the column that is appropriate for you, and create a table of recommended servings.

5. Find a clip art image of food and insert it into your document.

6. Change the color of the image to grayscale and change the contrast and brightness so it is light enough to place behind your table.

7. Scale the image to about 5 inches wide. Format the image so that it appears behind the table.

8. Save your work. Preview and print the document, and then close the document.

**End** You have completed Project 7N

### Downloading a Template from the Office Web Site

In this chapter, you formatted and modified several tables. Tables are also used for many of the templates that are available on the Microsoft Office Web site. Once these templates are downloaded to your computer, you can use the same techniques you practiced in this chapter to modify them.

1. Be sure that you are connected to the Internet. Open Word, and from the **File** menu, click **New**. In the **New Document** task pane, under **Templates**, click **Templates on Office Online** (you may have to select Templates Homepage to get to Office Online).

2. On the **Templates** page of Microsoft Office Online, scroll down to see the categories of templates that are available to you. Click on some of the categories to see what you can download.

3. Click the **Back** button until the screen returns to the **Template** page.

4. Under the **Healthcare and Wellness** category, click **Diet and Exercise**. Click the **Food Diary** template.

5. If you are working in a college computer lab, check to be sure you can download files. If it is permitted, click the **Download Now** button. You may be asked to install the Microsoft Office **Template and Media Control** program. You will need to install this program if you have not already done so. The template displays.

6. Save the template as a Word document using a name of your choice. Modify the information in the Food Group column. Find an appropriate clip art image or picture and insert it. Resize the image, lighten it, and place it behind the table.

7. When you are done, save and close the file. The original template is still available on your computer.

## Creating an Excel Chart in Word

In this chapter you practiced using the Insert menu to insert objects. In the Object dialog box, you had the choice of creating a new object or creating an object from a file. Among the new objects you can create in Word is an Excel chart.

1. Start Word. In the *Type a question for help* box, type **create Excel chart**

2. Examine the list of topics that displays in the **Search Results** task pane. From this list of help topics, click **Insert information by creating a linked object or embedded object**.

3. Locate and read the instructions for creating an embedded Excel chart in Word.

4. In a blank document, create a chart using the **Insert** menu command. You will need to switch between Excel worksheets in the Excel window in your document. You will add and edit your data in the **Sheet1** worksheet and format the chart in the **Chart1** worksheet. (Hint: To change the chart formatting, double-click on the chart element you want to change.)

5. Try using the various buttons on the Chart toolbar to see what you can do with an Excel chart.

6. Close the **Help** window and the **Help** task pane, close your document without saving the changes, and exit Word.

# 8 chaptereight

# Using Word with Other Office Programs and Creating Mass Mailings

**In this chapter, you will:** complete these projects **and** practice these skills.

| | |
|---|---|
| **Project 8A**<br>**Embedding and Linking Objects** | **Objectives**<br>• Embed Excel Charts and Data<br>• Link to Excel Charts and PowerPoint Presentations |

| | |
|---|---|
| **Project 8B**<br>**Using Mail Merge** | **Objectives**<br>• Create Labels Using the Mail Merge Wizard<br>• Create a Form Letter<br>• Merge Letters with Records from the Data Source |

# The Greater Atlanta Job Fair

The Greater Atlanta Job Fair is a nonprofit organization supported by the Atlanta Chamber of Commerce and Atlanta City Colleges. The organization holds several targeted job fairs in the Atlanta area each year. Candidate registration is free and open to area residents and students enrolled in certificate or degree programs at any of the City Colleges. Employers pay a nominal fee to participate in the fairs. When candidates register for a fair, their resumes are scanned into an interactive, searchable database that is provided to the employers.

© Getty Images, Inc.

# Working with Excel, Access, and PowerPoint

Microsoft Office 2003 is an integrated program, which means that individual Office programs are more useful by making use of the features of the other programs. Excel, the Office spreadsheet, is used frequently with Word. Excel data can be inserted as a Word table. Excel charts can be inserted as objects into Word documents, either as static (unchangeable) graphic objects or as dynamic objects that link back to the Excel program. In this arrangement, updates to the Excel data result in identical updates to the Word objects based on that data. PowerPoint presentations can be linked to a button in a Word document. Microsoft Access data can be inserted into Word tables, and Access reports can be exported into Word.

Creating form letters and labels is a common business task and one in which communication between programs is essential. For example, address information from Access databases, Excel lists, and Word tables can be inserted in Word to customize form letters and to create mailing labels.

## Project 8A Job Fair Overview

Information from other Office programs can be inserted into Microsoft Word documents. This information includes data from Excel spreadsheets, data from Access tables, Excel charts, or PowerPoint slides. The information can be embedded in the document or linked to the source document.

In Activities 8.1 through 8.6, you will add Excel data and charts to a Word document for Yolanda Strickland, the assistant to the employer coordinator. The document will be sent to potential organization participants in the Greater Atlanta Job Fair. You will also insert a link to a PowerPoint presentation. Your completed document will look similar to Figure 8.1. You will save your document as *8A_Job_Fair_Overview_ Firstname_Lastname*.

**MEMO TO**: Michael Augustino, Executive Director

**FROM**: Yolanda Strickland

**DATE**: February 26

**SUBJECT**: Charts and Data for Form Letter

I am working on the draft of the mass mailing form letter we are going to send to area businesses at the end of the month. I have chosen some data that I think is appropriate to help sell our services. The first chart I have chosen is a breakdown of the representation by industry at the 2004 job fairs. I am considering the following pie chart:

I think a table showing the attendance over a five year period wo[uld]
broken down by location and year. I do not have all of the inform[ation]
yet, but I should have those numbers by the end of the week. I ha[ve the]
spreadsheet that I took the data from, so when you open this next [week it will be]
updated.

**Job Fair Attendance**

| | 2000 | 2001 | 2002 |
|---|---|---|---|
| Atlanta | 7,873 | 8,145 | 9,683 |
| Decatur | 4,580 | 4,879 | 5,105 |
| East Point | 2,520 | 2,641 | 2,598 |
| Forest Park | 1,580 | 2,109 | 1,988 |
| Lawrenceville | 1,938 | 2,325 | 2,542 |
| Macon | 4,687 | 4,873 | 4,998 |
| North Atlanta | 3,647 | 3,879 | 3,764 |
| Total Attendance | 28,825 | 30,852 | 32,680 |

8A_Job_Fair_Overview_Firstname_Lastname

I would also like to include a chart showing total attendance at all of the job fairs over the last five years. This chart is also incomplete, but should be ready next week. The chart will update automatically.

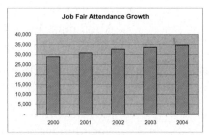

If you have any comments or questions, let me know. I would also appreciate your input on the charts and table I have selected. I have also created a PowerPoint presentation that we could put on our Web site and possibly use when talking to prospective businesses:

Greater Atlanta Job Fair

8A_Job_Fair_Overview_Firstname_Lastname

**Figure 8.1**
Project 8A—Job Fair Overview

# Objective 1
## Embed Excel Charts and Data

All Microsoft Office programs support **OLE**, which stands for **Object Linking and Embedding** and is pronounced *o-LAY*. OLE is a program-integration technology for sharing information between Office programs. Objects, for example, a table, chart, graphic, or other form of information created in one Office program—the **source file**—can be linked to or embedded in another Office program—the **destination file**.

To **embed** means to insert, using a format that you specify, information from a source file in one program into a destination file in another program. An embedded object maintains the characteristics of the original application, but is not tied to the original file. For example, the object's information in the destination file does not change if you modify the information in the source file.

### Activity 8.1 Embedding an Excel Chart

Excel has a more sophisticated charting program than Word. When a complex chart is required within a Word document, it makes sense to develop the chart in Excel, and then embed it in your Word document.

**1** Open Word. On the Standard toolbar, click the **Open** button. Navigate to the location where the student files for this textbook are stored. Locate and open **w08A_Job_Fair_Overview**. Save the file as **8A_Job_Fair_Overview_Firstname_Lastname** creating a new folder for this chapter if you want to do so.

**2** On the Standard toolbar, click the **Zoom button arrow** 100%, and then click **Page Width**. If necessary, on the Standard toolbar, click the Show/Hide ¶ button to show formatting marks.

**3** On the Windows taskbar, click the **Start** button start, navigate to the location of the Microsoft Office programs, and then open **Excel**.

On the Standard toolbar, click the **Open** button. Navigate to the location where the student files for this textbook are stored. Locate and open the **w08A_Job_Fair_Statistics** Excel file. Save the file as **8A_Job_Fair_Statistics_Firstname_Lastname** and save it in the same location as your **8A_Job_Fair_Overview** file.

**4** At the bottom of the Excel screen, click the **Representation by Industry sheet tab** to display the second worksheet in the workbook.

The worksheet contains data and a **_chart_**, which presents a graphical representation of the data. A **_worksheet_** is a grid pattern of rows and columns. The intersection of a row and a column is a **_cell_**, similar to the structure of a Word table. An Excel workbook consists of one or more worksheets.

**5** Click in a white area of the _Job Fair Representation by Industry_ Excel chart to select it.

Sizing handles display around the border of the chart, and colored borders surround the data that is represented in the chart, as shown in Figure 8.2.

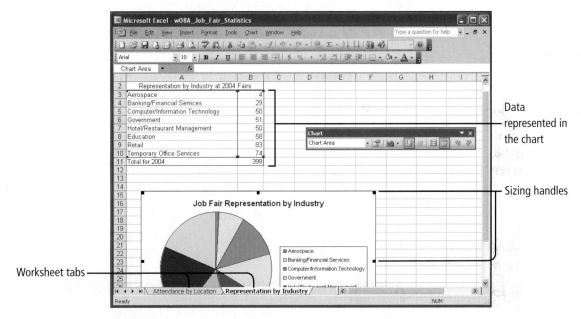

Figure 8.2

**6** From the Standard toolbar, click the **Copy** button 🖹.

The Excel chart is copied to the Office Clipboard.

**7** On the taskbar, click the Microsoft Word icon for your **8A_Job_Fair_ Overview** file.

**8** Locate the paragraph that begins *I am working* and click to position the insertion point in the second blank line below that paragraph. From the **Edit** menu, click **Paste Special**.

The Paste Special dialog box displays. The ***Paste Special*** command enables you to copy information from one location and paste it in another location using a different format, such as a Microsoft Excel Object, Picture, or Web format. Here you can paste the selected chart as an Excel Chart Object or as a Picture—as an embedded object. Or, if you click the Paste link option button, you can paste the selected chart as a linked object. See Figure 8.3.

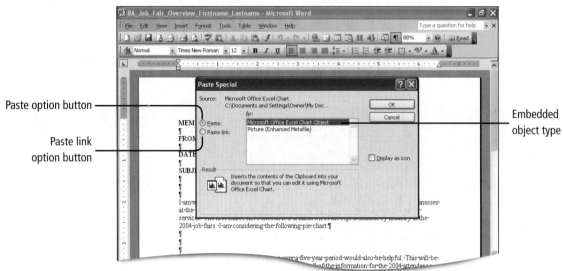

**Figure 8.3**

## More Knowledge — Pasting an Excel Chart into a Word Document

The Paste Special command enables you to embed an Excel chart in a Word document in two ways. If you embed the chart as a picture, you will be able to use picture formatting commands, but will not be able to edit the chart data. If you embed the chart as an Excel object, you will be able to edit the chart using Excel commands, but you will not have access to the original Excel data. Additionally, changes to the original data in the Excel file will not be reflected in the Word document. If you click the Paste link option button and link, rather than embed, the Excel chart, you can go back to the original source file and make changes that will be reflected in the linked chart within your Word document.

**9** In the **Paste Special** dialog box, click **OK** to accept the default option.

The chart is embedded at the insertion point location, as shown in Figure 8.4. As an embedded object, changes made to the original Excel file will not be reflected here in the Word document. The two charts are not tied to each other in any way.

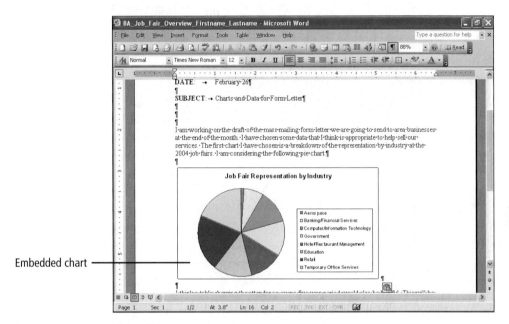

Embedded chart

**Figure 8.4**

**10** On the Standard toolbar, click the **Save** button.

### Activity 8.2 Embedding Excel Data

Excel data—the rows and columns of information—can be embedded using the same procedure you used to embed a chart.

**1** On the taskbar, click the Microsoft Excel icon for the **8A_Job_Fair_ Statistics** file. At the lower edge of the workbook, click the **Attendance by Location sheet tab**.

Excel data is stored in cells, which are labeled by column letter and row number. For example, the cell in the upper left corner of a worksheet is cell A1.

**2** Move the pointer to cell **A1** and drag down and to the right to cell **F10**.

The data table is selected, as shown in Figure 8.5.

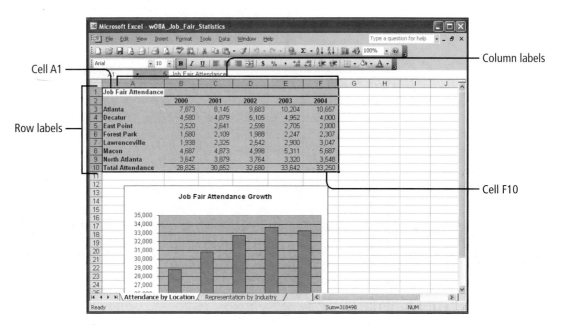

Cell A1

Row labels

Column labels

Cell F10

**Figure 8.5**

**3** On the Standard toolbar, click the **Copy** button.

The selected cells are placed on the Office Clipboard.

**4** On the taskbar, click the Microsoft Word icon for your **8A_Job_Fair_Overview** file. Locate the paragraph beginning *I think a table* and click to position the insertion point in the second blank line following that paragraph.

**5** From the **Edit** menu, click **Paste Special**.

The Paste Special dialog box displays. Selecting cells of data, rather than a chart as you did in Activity 8.1, offers more formats with which the information can be embedded.

**6** In the **Paste Special** dialog box, under **As**, click **Microsoft Office Excel Worksheet Object**, and then click **OK**.

The data table is embedded in the document, as shown in Figure 8.6.

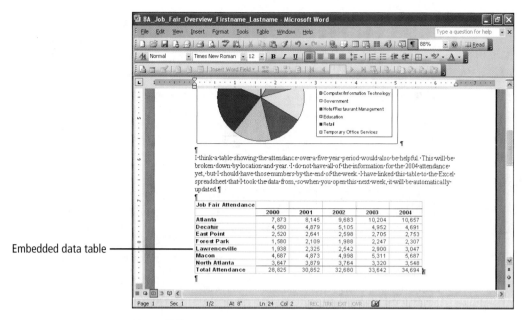

Embedded data table

**Figure 8.6**

**7** On the Standard toolbar, click the **Save** button 💾.

## Activity 8.3 Editing Embedded Excel Charts and Data

When you use the Paste Special command to embed a chart or data from an Excel worksheet as Excel objects into your Word document, you can activate the Excel commands to edit the objects without leaving the Word program.

**1** Scroll to position the colored pie chart, **Job Fair Representation by Industry**, in the center of your screen. Move your mouse pointer anywhere over the chart, right-click to display a shortcut menu, point to **Chart Object**, and then click **Edit**. Alternatively, double-click in the white area of the chart.

A slashed border surrounds the chart, and the worksheet tabs from the Excel file display at the bottom of the chart. Your chart number tab may display a different number. Excel buttons temporarily display in the toolbars, and Excel commands temporarily replace Word commands in the menus. The Chart toolbar may also display. See Figure 8.7.

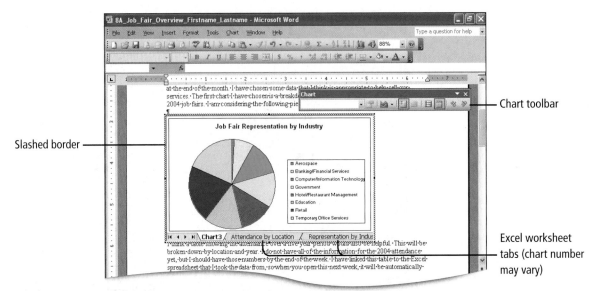

Slashed border ——————

Chart toolbar

Excel worksheet tabs (chart number may vary)

**Figure 8.7**

**2** Click anywhere in the **pie graphic**.

A sizing handle displays on each of the pie wedges.

**3** Click the **pale green pie wedge**.

Handles display around the pale green wedge only, indicating that it is selected. See Figure 8.8.

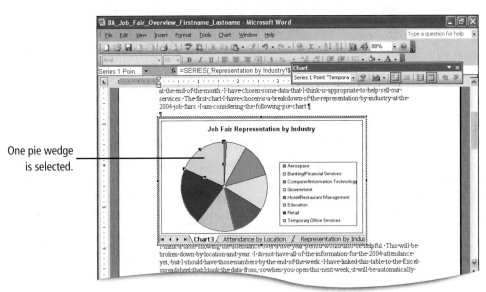

One pie wedge is selected.

**Figure 8.8**

**4** Right-click the selected pie wedge and from the shortcut menu, click **Format Data Point**.

The Format Data Point dialog box displays.

**5** Under **Area**, in the fourth row, click the fourth color—**Lime Green**.

Compare your Format Data Point dialog box with Figure 8.9.

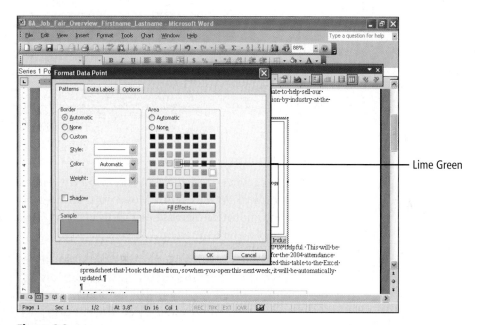

Figure 8.9

**6** At the bottom of the **Format Data Point** dialog box, click **OK**. Click anywhere in the document to deselect the chart.

Notice that the color of the pie wedge changes to lime green, as does the related box in the legend. See Figure 8.10. When you deselect, the Excel program is closed and the toolbars and menus return to the Word commands. Although you were able to activate Excel commands and edit the chart while in Word, this action did not make any changes to the original Excel file. The original Excel file remains unchanged.

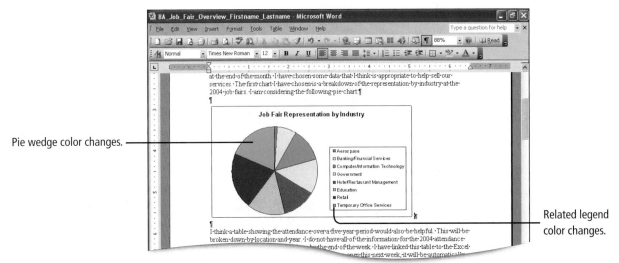

Pie wedge color changes.

Related legend color changes.

**Figure 8.10**

**7** Scroll down and display the *Job Fair Attendance* data table in the center of your screen. Move your mouse pointer over the table, right-click, point to **Worksheet Object**, and then click **Edit**. Alternatively, double-click on the table.

A slashed border surrounds the data table, and the worksheet tabs from the Excel file display at the bottom of the table. Excel buttons temporarily display in the toolbars, and Excel commands temporarily replace Word commands in the menus.

**8** At the intersection of **column F** and **row 4**, click cell **F4**, type **4691** and then press Enter.

The number changes, and the Total Attendance for 2004, in cell F10, is recalculated because cell F10 contains a formula that adds the numbers in the 2004 column. You do not need to type the comma—it is added by Excel.

**9** Click cell **F5**, type **2753** and then press Enter.

**10** Click anywhere in the document to deselect the data table.

Recall that these changes will not be reflected in the original Excel file. You can activate Excel commands to edit this table, but as an embedded Excel object, this table is no longer tied to the original Excel file. Compare your screen with Figure 8.11.

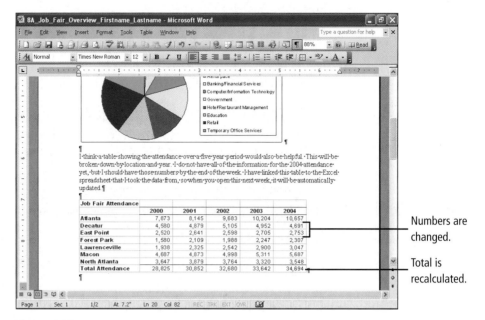

**Figure 8.11**

**11** On the Standard toolbar, click the **Save** button 🖫.

## Objective 2
## Link to Excel Charts and PowerPoint Presentations

In Activities 8.1 through 8.3, you embedded an Excel chart and Excel data into a Word document. Although you were able to activate Excel commands to edit the Excel objects, the objects themselves were not tied to the original Excel file. For example, the changes you made to the 2004 attendance numbers in the Word document were not made to the original Excel spreadsheet from which the data originated.

If you want to make changes to Excel data and have the changes also made to the corresponding Excel object in a Word document, then you should **link**, rather than embed, the Excel object. To link means to insert information from a source file in one program into a destination file in another program, while maintaining a connection between the two.

### Activity 8.4  Linking to an Excel Chart

A **linked object** is an object that maintains a direct connection to the source file. Linked data is stored in the source file (the Excel workbook); it is *not* stored in the destination file (the Word document). What you see in the Word document is only a representation of the Excel file. Unlike the embedded object, you cannot activate Excel commands while in Word, because the object is not a part of the actual Word document. Changes must be made by opening the source file (the original Excel workbook), after which the linked object in the destination file (the Word document) is also updated.

**1** On the taskbar, click the Microsoft Excel icon for the **8A_Job_Fair_ Statistics** file. Click the **Attendance by Location sheet tab** at the bottom of the worksheet.

**2** Click in the white area of the chart once to select it. From the Standard toolbar, click the **Copy** button.

**3** On the taskbar, click the Microsoft Word icon for your **8A_Job_ Fair_Overview** file. Scroll to the second page, locate the paragraph beginning *I would also like to include*, and then click to position the insertion point in the second blank line following that paragraph.

**4** From the **Edit** menu, click **Paste Special**.

The Paste Special dialog box displays.

**5** In the **Paste Special** dialog box, click the **Paste link** option button.

Under *As*, notice that *Microsoft Office Excel Chart Object* is the only choice, as shown in Figure 8.12.

Paste link option button

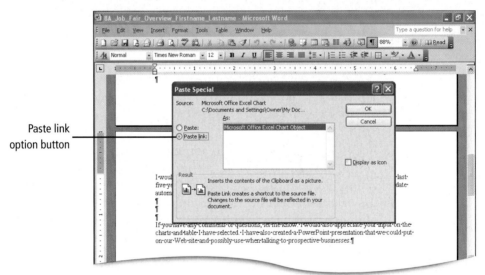

**Figure 8.12**

**6** In the upper right corner of the **Paste Special** dialog box, click **OK**.

The chart is placed at the insertion point location.

**7** On the Standard toolbar, click the **Save** button 🖫.

### Activity 8.5 Modifying Charts Linked to Excel Data

Recall that a linked object behaves differently from an embedded object. To edit the linked object, you must do so from the source file; thus you cannot activate the Excel commands within Word, as you did for an embedded object. Linking is especially useful when the Word document will be maintained as an online document. In that manner, any changes to the Excel data will be reflected automatically in the online Word document that contains the linked object.

**1** On the taskbar, click the Microsoft Excel icon for the **w08A_Job_Fair_Statistics** file.

**2** Click cell **F4** to select it, type **4691** and then press Enter.

The number changes, and the Total Attendance for 2004 in cell F10 is recalculated because cell F10 contains a formula that adds the 2004 column.

**3** Select cell **F5**, type **2753** and then press Enter.

The number changes, and the Total Attendance for 2004 is again recalculated. Because the chart in the worksheet is based on the data in the cells, it is also updated, as shown in Figure 8.13.

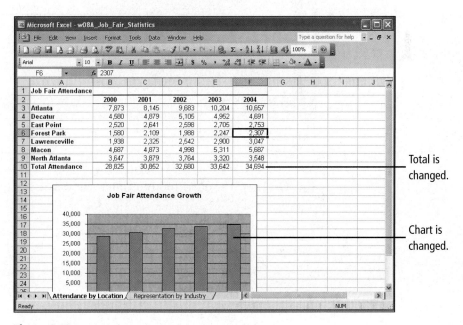

Total is changed.

Chart is changed.

**Figure 8.13**

**4** From the **File** menu, click **Save**. Close Excel. If necessary, on the taskbar click the Microsoft Word icon for your *8A_Job_Fair_Overview* file. Look at the last column in the chart.

Although this is a linked object, and you have changed information in the source file, the linked object is not updated automatically because the destination file is open. Only closed files are updated automatically, because before a document is opened, Word checks for any links and updates them.

**5** Right-click the **Job Fair Attendance Growth** chart and from the shortcut menu, click **Update Link**.

After a few seconds, the chart is updated to reflect the changes in the source file—the Excel worksheet. Compare your screen with Figure 8.14.

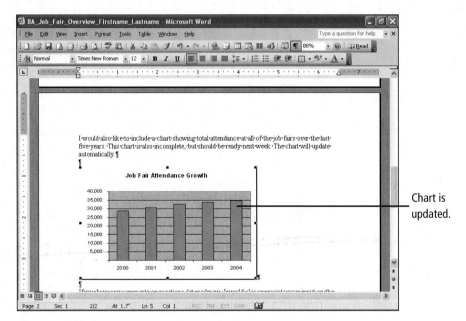

**Figure 8.14**

**6** On the Standard toolbar, click the **Save** button 🖫.

## Note — Updating Links

By default, Word updates any links in your document, provided the document is closed. Each time you open the document, Word checks whether any links have changed and updates them accordingly. This process can take a few minutes if your document has numerous links. If you make a change to the source file, and the destination file happens to be open, as you did in the previous activity, you will need to initiate the Update Link command manually.

### Activity 8.6 Linking to a PowerPoint Presentation

Within a Word document, you can insert a link to a PowerPoint presentation. Because this memo will be sent by e-mail, in this activity you will insert a link to a PowerPoint presentation that the e-mail recipient can view by clicking on the link.

**1** Hold down Ctrl and press End to move the insertion point to the end of the document.

**2** From the **Insert** menu, click **Object**. In the **Object** dialog box, click the **Create from File tab**.

**3** Click **Browse**, navigate to the location of your student files, and then click **w08A_Presentation**. Click **Insert**.

The file name displays in the *File name* box, as shown in Figure 8.15.

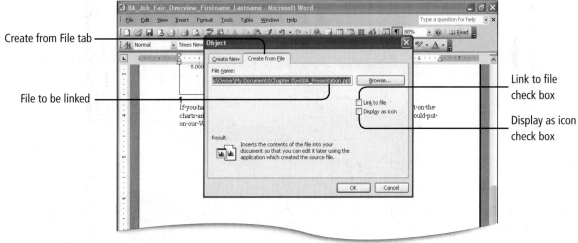

Create from File tab

File to be linked

Link to file check box

Display as icon check box

**Figure 8.15**

**4** At the right side of the **Object** dialog box, select the **Link to file** check box and select the **Display as icon** check box.

A preview PowerPoint icon displays near the bottom of the Object dialog box. The default caption for the icon is the document name and location. A Change Icon button displays under the preview icon. See Figure 8.16.

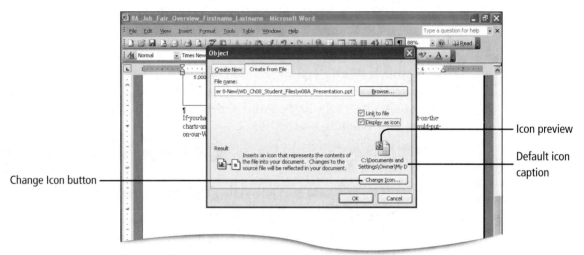

**Figure 8.16**

**5** Click **Change Icon**. In the **Caption** box, select and delete the text. Type **Greater Atlanta Job Fair** as shown in Figure 8.17.

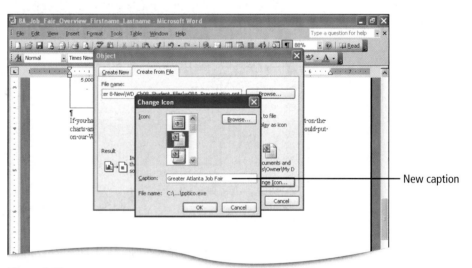

**Figure 8.17**

**6** At the bottom of the **Change Icon** dialog box, click **OK**. At the bottom of the **Object** dialog box, click **OK**.

The icon is placed in line with the text in the last paragraph.

**7** Right-click the new icon. From the shortcut menu, click **Format Object**. In the **Format Object** dialog box, click the **Layout tab**.

**8** Under **Wrapping style**, click **Square**. At the bottom of the **Format Object** dialog box, click **OK**.

**9** Drag the icon up and to the right until it is located at the right side of the last paragraph, as shown in Figure 8.18.

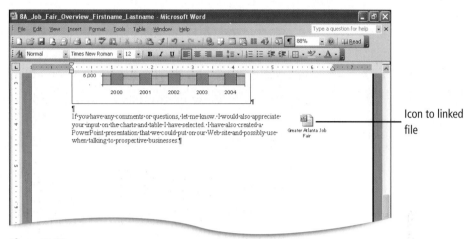

Icon to linked file

**Figure 8.18**

**10** Double-click the icon.

The PowerPoint presentation opens, as shown in Figure 8.19.

**Alert!**

### If the PowerPoint Presentation Does Not Run

If you do not have PowerPoint installed on your computer, you will get a message indicating that the associated program cannot be found. If this happens, click OK and move to Step 12.

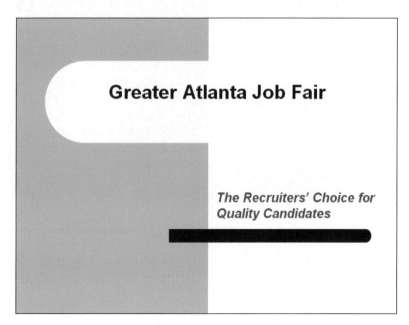

**Figure 8.19**

**11** Click the left mouse button to advance through the presentation one slide at a time. When you reach the black slide, which indicates the end of the slide show, click once.

The PowerPoint presentation closes, and your Word document redisplays.

**12** Press [Ctrl] + [Home] to move to the top of the document. Click the pie chart, and then on the Formatting toolbar, click the **Center** button ▤ to center the chart horizontally on the page. Select and then center horizontally the remaining two objects in the document.

**13** From the **View** menu, click **Header and Footer**. On the Header and Footer toolbar, click the **Switch Between Header and Footer** button ▣. Click the **Insert AutoText** button Insert AutoText ▾ , and then click **Filename**.

The file name is inserted in the footer.

**14** On the Header and Footer toolbar, click the **Close** button Close . On the Standard toolbar, click the **Save** button 🖫 .

**15** On the Standard toolbar, click the **Print Preview** button 🔍 . Use the PageDown and Page Up buttons to view both pages in Print Preview. Take a moment to check your work. On the Print Preview toolbar, click the **Close Preview** button Close .

**16** Make any necessary changes to your document. When you are satisfied, on the Standard toolbar, click the **Print** button 🖨 . Close the document, saving any changes.

**End** You have completed Project 8A ————————————————————

# Project 8B **Form Letter**

Form letters and mailing labels can be created quickly by merging names and addresses from a Word table, an Access database, or an Excel spreadsheet with a Word document. File folder labels, business cards, and index cards can be created in a similar manner.

In Activities 8.7 through 8.17, you will use a wizard to create and print a set of labels—from information in a Word table—suitable for printing on a sheet of blank mailing labels. You will save this document as *8B_Labels_ Firstname_Lastname*. You will also create a form letter that will be sent to individuals requesting information about the Greater Atlanta Job Fair. You will merge name and address data from an Access database with a letter in Word, and then preview and print one of the letters. Finally, you will customize another letter and print it. Your completed documents will look similar to Figure 8.20. You will save your letters as *8B_Form_Letter_ Firstname_Lastname* and *8B_Form_Letter2_ Firstname_Lastname*, and the label document as *8B_Labels_ Firstname_Lastname*.

February 14

Ms. Kelley Bondurant
179 Auburn Court
Cartersville, GA 30120

Subject: Greater Atlanta Job Fair Info

Dear Ms. Bondurant,

Thank you for your request for further
The Job Fair annually attracts more th
industries. This year's fair promises to
booklet of hints about effective intervi

Sincerely,

Yolanda Strickland
Publicity Manager

Enclosures

8B_Form_Letter_Firstname_Lastname

February 14

Ms. Kelley Bondurant
179 Auburn Court
Cartersville, GA 30120

Subject: Greater Atlanta Job Fair Informa

Dear Ms. Bondurant,

Thank you for your request for further in
The Job Fair annually attracts more than
industries. In answer to your question, the
year's fair promises to be the best yet. I h
about effective interview strategies.

Sincerely,

Yolanda Strickland
Publicity Manager

Enclosures

8B_Form_Letter2_Firstname_Lastname

Ms. Jacqui Epps
653 Constitution Ave.
Marietta, GA 30006

Mr. Byeong Chang
2221 Flowers Road South
Roswell, GA 30077

Ms. Kelley Bondurant
179 Auburn Court
Cartersville, GA 30120

Mr. David Feingold
1821 Alturas St.
#1442
Atlanta, GA 30301

Mr. Phillip Scroggs
1518 Orchard Place West
Kennesaw, GA 30327

Mr. Walter Perrie
2495 Sunset Drive
Conyers, GA 30012

Ms. Lenesha Barnett
2361 Bluebird Lane
#8
Smyrna, GA 30081

Ms. Jessica Pyun
1255 Miravista Street
Kennesaw, GA 30144

Mr. Daniel Echols
2000 St. Luke Place
Atlanta, GA 30313

Mr. Andrew Lau
975 Treetop Place
#G
Atlanta, GA 30327

Ms. Samira Ahmed
3418 Longview Drive
#320
Marietta, GA 30063

Mr. Bin Wu
676 North St. Clair St.
Smyrna, GA 30081

Ms. Samantha Quick
124 Whitworth Drive
#352
Atlanta, GA 30301

Mr. Mauro Calva
82 E. Ramona Blvd.
Atlanta, GA 30327

Mr. Taylor Dunnahoo
189 Ventura Street
Atlanta, GA 30330

8B_Labels_Firstname_Lastname

**Figure 8.20**

# Objective 3
## Create Labels Using the Mail Merge Wizard

Using Word's ***mail merge*** feature, labels are created by combining (merging) two documents—a ***main document*** and a ***data source***. The main document starts out blank, and is formatted for a specific label size. The data source contains the names and addresses of the individuals to whom the letters or postcards are being sent. Names and addresses in a data source can be contained in a Word table, an Excel spreadsheet, or an Access database.

The easiest way to perform a Mail Merge is to use the Mail Merge Wizard. Recall that a wizard asks you questions and, based on your answers, walks you step by step through a process. Labels are used to address envelopes or postcards or to label disks, name badges, file folders, and so on. Sheets of precut labels can be purchased from office supply stores.

### Activity 8.7 Adding an Address to a Word Address Table

Mail merge information can come from many sources, including Microsoft Word tables. These tables can be edited just like any other Word table.

**1** Open Word. On the Standard toolbar, click the **Open** button. Navigate to the location where the student files for this textbook are stored. Locate and open **w08B_Job_Fair_Addresses**. Save the file as **8B_Job_Fair_Addresses_Firstname_Lastname**

**2** On the Standard toolbar, click the **Zoom button arrow** 100%, and then click **Page Width**. If necessary, on the Standard toolbar, click the Show/Hide ¶ button to show formatting marks.

A table of addresses displays. The first row contains the column names. The remaining rows contain addresses. See Figure 8.21.

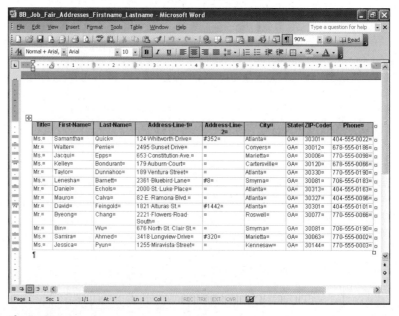

**Figure 8.21**

**3** Click to position the insertion point in the last cell of the last row. Press Tab.

A new row is added to the table.

**4** In the first cell of the new row, type **Mr.**

**5** In the second cell of the new row, type **Phillip**

**6** Type the following in the rest of the blank cells of the new row, leaving the Address Line 2 cell blank:

**Scroggs**

**1518 Orchard Place West**

[leave this cell blank]

**Kennesaw**

**GA**

**30152**

**770-555-0005**

Compare your table with Figure 8.22. The proper name *Scroggs* may display as a misspelled word on your system.

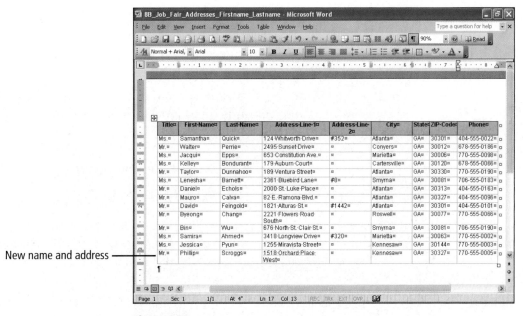

New name and address ——

**Figure 8.22**

**7** On the Standard toolbar, click the **Save** button 🔲. From the **File** menu, click **Close** to close the document.

**Activity 8.8** Starting the Mail Merge Wizard to Set Up Labels

The label feature in Word contains the product numbers of the standard Avery label products as well as several other brands. Each product number is associated with a layout in Word's table format consisting of the height and width of the label. Because the product numbers predefine the label layout, the creation of labels is a simple and automated process. The first two steps in creating labels using the Mail Merge Wizard are identifying the label type and identifying the data source.

**1** On the Standard toolbar, click the **New Blank Document** button. From the **Tools** menu, point to **Letters and Mailings**, and then click **Mail Merge**.

The Mail Merge task pane displays.

**2** In the **Mail Merge** task pane, under **Select document type**, click the **Labels** option button. At the bottom of the task pane, click **Next: Starting document**.

Step 2 of 6 of the Mail Merge Wizard displays—identified at the bottom of the task pane.

**3** In the middle of the task pane, under **Change document layout**, click **Label options**.

The Label Options dialog box displays.

**4** In the **Label Options** dialog box, under **Label information**, click the **Label products arrow**, and then click **Avery standard**. Under **Product number**, scroll as necessary and click **5160 - Address**. See Figure 8.23.

The Avery 5160 address label is a commonly used label. The precut sheets contain three columns of 10 labels each—for a total of 30 labels per sheet.

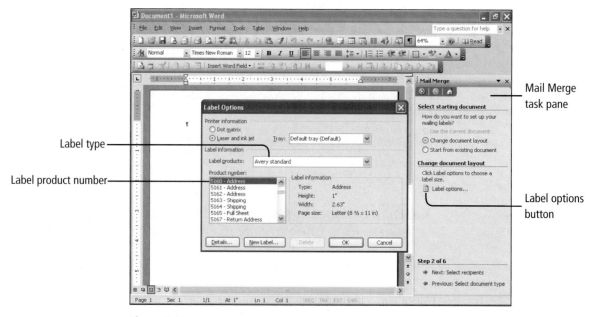

**Figure 8.23**

**5** At the bottom of the **Label Options** dialog box, click **OK**.

The label document displays, showing the label outlines. Recall that label layouts result in a predefined Word table.

**6** At the bottom of the **Mail Merge** task pane, click **Next: Select recipients**.

In Step 3 of the Mail Merge Wizard, you must identify the recipients—the data source. For your recipient data source, you can choose to use an existing list—for example, a list of names and addresses that you have in an Access database, an Excel spreadsheet, a Word table, or your Outlook contacts list. If you do not have an existing data source, you can type a new list at this point in the wizard.

---

## Note — Creating a New Address List

When you select the *Type a new list* option, the data that you enter will be stored in a Microsoft Access table but can be edited using Word.

---

**7** Be sure that the **Use an existing list** option button is selected, and then under **Use an existing list**, click **Browse**. Navigate to the folder where you are storing your projects for this chapter and click **8B_Job_Fair_Addresses_Firstname_Lastname**—the Word table you just edited—and then click **Open**.

The Mail Merge Recipients dialog box displays, as shown in Figure 8.24. In a database or Word address table, each row of information that contains data for one person is called a **record**. The column headings—for example, *Last Name* and *First Name*— are referred to as **fields**. A field describes the data in a record.

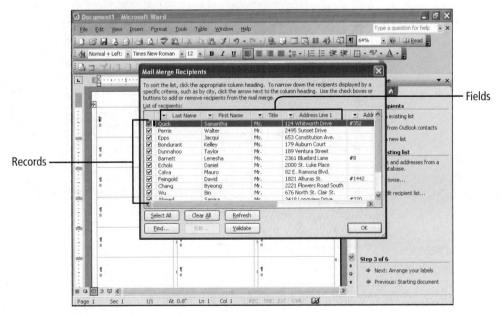

**Figure 8.24**

**8** Use the scroll bar in the lower portion of the dialog box to scroll to the right, and then click the **ZIP Code** field column heading.

The records are sorted in numerical order by ZIP code, and the dialog box data window shifts back to display the first column.

**9** At the bottom of the **Mail Merge Recipients** dialog box, click **OK**.

<<*Next Record*>> displays in each table cell.

**10** On the Standard toolbar, click the **Save** button 🖫. Navigate to the folder where you are storing your projects for this chapter, and in the **Save As** dialog box, type **8B_Labels_Firstname_Lastname** and then click **Save**.

### Activity 8.9 Completing the Mail Merge Wizard

You can add or edit names and addresses while completing the Mail Merge Wizard. You can also match your column names with preset names used in Mail Merge.

**1** In the **Mail Merge** task pane, under **Use an existing list**, click **Edit recipient list**.

The Mail Merge Recipients dialog box displays.

**2** At the bottom of the **Mail Merge Recipients** dialog box, click **Edit**.

The Data Form dialog box displays, as shown in Figure 8.25. You can edit or delete the selected record, or use the same dialog box to add a new recipient.

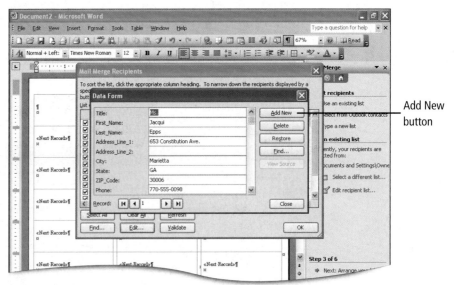

Add New button

**Figure 8.25**

**3** On the right side of the **Data Form** dialog box, click **Add New**.

The Data Form dialog box displays a new blank record.

**4** In the Data Form dialog box, type the following, using the Tab key to move from field to field.

| | |
|---|---|
| Title: | **Mr.** |
| First_Name: | **Andrew** |
| Last_Name: | **Lau** |
| Address_Line_1: | **975 Treetop Place** |
| Address_Line_2: | **#G** |
| City: | **Atlanta** |
| State: | **GA** |
| ZIP_Code: | **30327** |
| Phone: | **770-555-0008** |

Compare your Data Form dialog box with Figure 8.26.

New mail merge recipient —

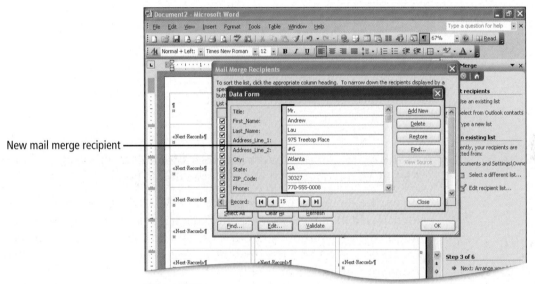

**Figure 8.26**

**5** At the bottom of the **Data Form** dialog box, click **Close**. At the bottom of the **Mail Merge Recipients** dialog box, click **OK**. At the bottom of the **Mail Merge** task pane, click **Next: Arrange your labels**.

In Step 4 of 6 of the Mail Merge Wizard, Word provides various ways to arrange and add features to your labels. For example, you can add a *Postal bar code*, which applies a bar code based on the ZIP code so that the address can be scanned and sorted electronically by the U.S. Postal Service.

**6** Under **Arrange your labels**, click **Address block**. In the **Insert Address Block** dialog box, under **Specify address elements**, examine the **Preview** area, and then clear the **Insert company name** check box.

This is a list of home addresses, so the organization name is not relevant. Notice that the label preview in the Preview box no longer displays a company. Compare your dialog box with Figure 8.27.

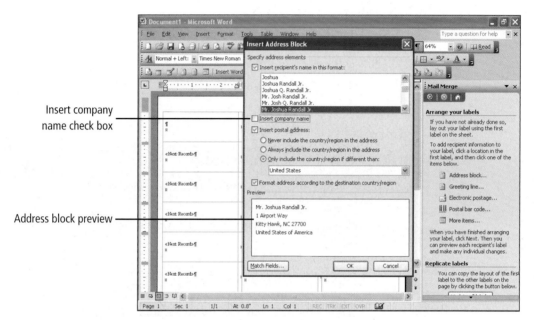

Insert company name check box

Address block preview

**Figure 8.27**

**7** At the bottom of the **Insert Address Block** dialog box, click **Match Fields**. Scroll down and examine the dialog box.

If your field names are descriptive, the Mail Merge program will identify them correctly, as is the case with the information in the Required Information section, as shown in Figure 8.28. If you need to match a field, use the drop-down list to choose the correct field from your database or table.

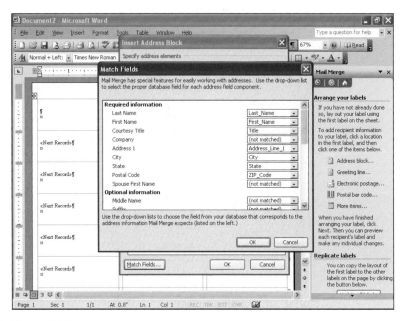

**Figure 8.28**

**8** At the bottom of the **Match Fields** dialog box, click **OK**. At the bottom of the **Insert Address Block** dialog box, click **OK**.

The Address block is inserted in the first label space and is surrounded by double angle brackets. Only the *Address Block* field name is displayed, but this represents the address block you saw in the Preview area of the Insert Address Block dialog box.

**9** In the task pane, under **Replicate labels**, click **Update all labels**.

An address block is inserted in each label space for each subsequent record.

**10** At the bottom of the task pane, click **Next: Preview your labels**.

Step 5 of the Mail Merge Wizard task pane displays, and the labels are filled in with the information from the data source. Notice that the labels are sorted numerically by the ZIP Code field. The order of the labels is from left to right and then down to the next row, as shown in Figure 8.29. Notice also that in some cases, where there is an apartment or unit number, there are addresses on two lines. This is done automatically when the *Address Block* is inserted.

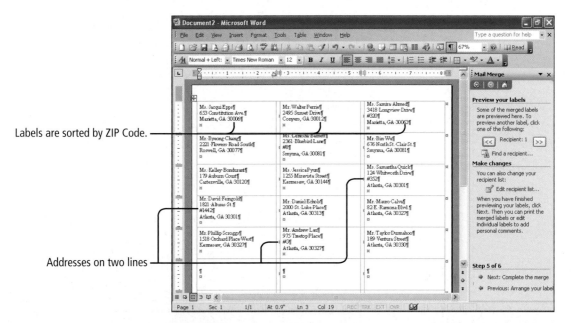

Labels are sorted by ZIP Code.

Addresses on two lines

**Figure 8.29**

## More Knowledge — Previewing Your Labels

When the labels are large, the *Preview your labels* button enables you to scroll through your labels to examine them. This is particularly useful when you are using the Mail Merge Wizard to create letters. You can also use *Find a recipient* to locate a particular record.

**11** At the bottom of the task pane, click **Next: Complete the merge**.

Step 6 of 6 of the Mail Merge task pane displays. At this point you can print or edit your labels.

**12** On the Standard toolbar, click the **Save** button.

### Activity 8.10 Editing Labels

Once the labels are created, you can edit individual labels when necessary.

**1** In the first row of labels, locate the label for Ms. Samira Ahmed. Click to place the insertion point to the left of the apartment number—**#320**.

The label text is shaded in gray, but the insertion point is still visible.

**2** Press Bksp twice.

The text is moved up to the end of the previous line.

**3** Press Spacebar to add a space before the apartment number.

**4** Repeat the procedure you used in Steps 1 through 3 to change the other four two-line addresses to one-line addresses.

Compare your labels to Figure 8.30.

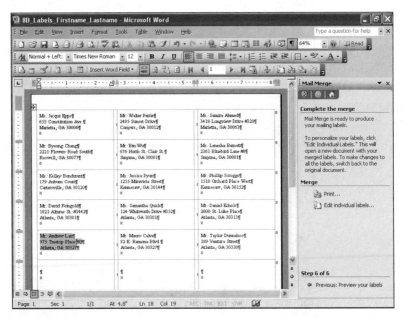

**Figure 8.30**

**5** On the Standard toolbar, click the **Save** button.

---

**More Knowledge** — Delivery Addresses for Envelopes and Labels

For more information from the United States Postal Service about addressing envelopes and labels, go to **www.usps.com/businessmail101/welcome.htm** and click Addressing.

---

### Activity 8.11 Previewing and Printing Labels

Before you print, it is always a good idea to preview your labels to be sure the information fits in the space reserved for each label.

**1** On the Standard toolbar, click the **Print Preview** button.

**2** Position the mouse pointer over the labels and click the **magnifying glass pointer**.

The labels are displayed at full size (100%), as shown in Figure 8.31.

**Figure 8.31**

**3** On the Print Preview toolbar, click the **Close** button Close.

**4** From the **View** menu, click **Header and Footer**. On the Header and Footer toolbar, click the **Switch Between Header and Footer** button. Click the **Insert AutoText** button Insert AutoText ▾, and then click **Filename**. On the Header and Footer toolbar, click the **Close** button Close.

The file name is inserted in the footer.

**5** On the Standard toolbar, click the **Save** button.

**6** In the **Mail Merge** task pane, under **Merge**, click **Print**. In the **Merge to Printer** dialog box, under **Print records**, click the **From** option button. In the **From** box, type **1** and in the **To** box, type **1**

This action will print only page 1. Adding a footer forced the last row of labels onto page 2, but because the labels on page 2 are empty, there is no need to print page 2.

**7** In the **Merge to Printer** dialog box, click **OK**.

The Print dialog box displays.

**8** At the bottom of the **Print** dialog box, click **OK** to print the labels. Close the document, saving any changes, and close Word.

The labels will print on whatever paper is in the printer. In this case, unless you have preformatted labels available, you will print your labels on a sheet of paper. This has the advantage of enabling you to proof the labels before you print them on more expensive label sheets.

## Objective 4
## Create a Form Letter

A **form letter** is a letter with standardized wording that can be sent to many different people. Each letter is customized to contain the name and address of the individual to whom the letter is being sent. The **salutation**, the part of the letter that begins *Dear*, and some information within the body of the letter also can be customized for each individual.

Using Word's mail merge feature, form letters are created by combining information from two documents—a main document and a data source. The main document contains the text and graphics that are the same for each version of the letter. This is called the **constant information**. The data source contains the information to be merged—for example, a list of names and addresses. This is called the **variable information** because it *varies* (differs) for each letter.

### Activity 8.12 Setting Up a Form Letter

First, create the main document—the letter containing the constant information. You can create or locate an existing data source later.

**1** In Word, display a new blank document, and if necessary, close the **Getting Started** task pane. On the Standard toolbar, click the **Zoom button arrow** 100% ▾, and then click **Page Width**. If necessary, on the Standard toolbar, click the Show/Hide ¶ button to show formatting marks.

**2** Right-click on any toolbar, and then click **Mail Merge**.

The Mail Merge toolbar displays, docked to the other toolbars at the top of your screen. Most of the buttons are gray because you have not yet begun the Mail Merge procedure.

**3** Take a moment to point to each button on the Mail Merge toolbar and study the information in the table shown in Figure 8.32.

## Mail Merge Toolbar Buttons

| Name | Button | Description |
| --- | --- | --- |
| Main document setup | | Displays the Main Document Type dialog box, where you specify the document type, such as labels, letters, or envelopes. |
| Open Data Source | | Displays the Select Data Source dialog box. |
| Mail Merge Recipients | | Displays the Mail Merge Recipients dialog box, where you select or deselect recipients or edit or add names and addresses. |
| Insert Address Block | | Displays the Insert Address Block dialog box, where you customize the data and format of the address block. |
| Insert Greeting Line | | Displays the Greeting Block dialog box, where you customize the data and format the greeting line. |
| Insert Merge Fields | | Displays the Insert Merge Field dialog box, showing the fields you can insert into the document. |
| Insert Word Field | Insert Word Field ▾ | Displays a menu of built-in fields. |
| View Merged Data | | Toggles between field names and values in the document. |
| Highlight Merge Fields | | Highlights merged fields in the active document. |
| Match Fields | | Displays the Match Fields dialog box, where you can match the fields in your database document with Mail Merge fields. |
| Propagate Labels | | Enables you to create a single label, and then use the same data and format to create labels for the remaining records in a data source. |
| First Record | | Displays the first merged record. |
| Previous Record | | Displays the previous merged record. |
| Go to Record | 1 | Moves to a specific merged record. |
| Next Record | | Displays the next merged record. |
| Last Record | | Displays the last merged record. |
| Find Entry | | Searches for a specific merged record. |
| Check for Errors | | Checks for errors before printing the file. |
| Merge to New Document | | Merges the source document and the data in a new document. |
| Merge to Printer | | Merges the source document and the data and sends the resulting documents to the printer. |
| Merge to E-mail | | Merges the source document and the data and sends the documents by e-mail. |
| Merge to Fax | | Merges the source document and the data and sends the documents by fax. |
| Toolbar Options | | Enables you to add or remove toolbar buttons. |

**Figure 8.32**

**4** On the Mail Merge toolbar, click the **Main document setup** button [icon].

The Main Document Type dialog box displays. See Figure 8.33.

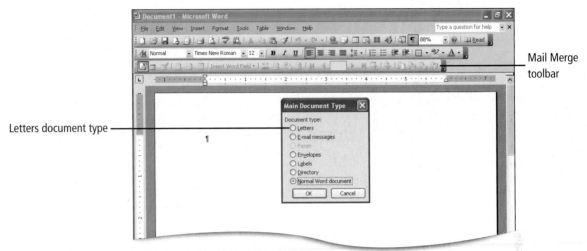

Letters document type

Mail Merge toolbar

**Figure 8.33**

**5** Under **Document type**, click the **Letters** option button, and then click **OK**.

Because you are creating this document from the Mail Merge toolbar, you can type the constant information and then use Mail Merge commands directly from the Mail Merge toolbar.

**6** Type **February 14** and then press Enter five times.

**7** Type the following text, pressing Enter twice after the Subject line:

**Subject: Greater Atlanta Job Fair Information**

**Thank you for your request for further information about the Greater Atlanta Job Fair. The Job Fair annually attracts more than 2,000 employers representing more than 70 industries. This year's fair promises to be the best yet. I have enclosed a brochure, and a booklet of hints about effective interview strategies.**

**8** Press Enter twice and type **Sincerely,**

**9** Press Enter four times and type **Yolanda Strickland**

**10** Press Enter and type **Publicity Manager**

**11** Press Enter twice and type **Enclosures**

**12** From the **File** menu, click **Page Setup**, and then click the **Layout tab**. Under **Page**, click the **Vertical alignment arrow**, and then click **Center**. Click **OK**.

Compare your screen with Figure 8.34.

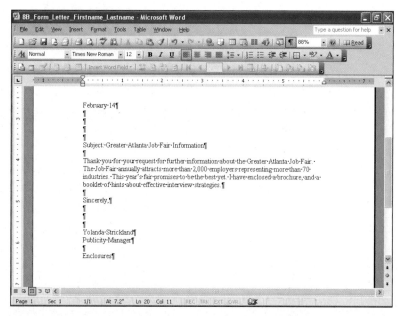

February 14

Subject: Greater Atlanta Job Fair Information

Thank you for your request for further information about the Greater Atlanta Job Fair. The Job Fair annually attracts more than 2,000 employers representing more than 70 industries. This year's fair promises to be the best yet. I have enclosed a brochure, and a booklet of hints about effective interview strategies.

Sincerely,

Yolanda Strickland
Publicity Manager

Enclosures

**Figure 8.34**

**13** On the Standard toolbar, click the **Save** button [image]. Navigate to the location in which you are storing your files for this chapter and save the file as **8B_Form_Letter_Firstname_Lastname**

### Activity 8.13 Opening, Editing, and Sorting a Data Source

Word provides two ways to merge the data source with the main document—you can use the Mail Merge Wizard, as you did in earlier activities with mailing labels, or you can use the Mail Merge toolbar. Using the toolbar gives you more flexibility in setting up your form letter.

**1** Near the left edge of the Mail Merge toolbar, click the **Open Data Source** button [image]. Navigate to the location where the student files for this textbook are stored. If necessary, in the Select Data Source dialog box, click the Views button arrow, and then click Details. Locate and select the **Access file** named **w08B_Job_Fair_Addresses**. Be sure that the file has an icon with a key in it, rather than the Word icon that displays a *W*. Click **Open**.

This file is a Microsoft Access database, and it contains a table of names and addresses. Most of the buttons on the Mail Merge toolbar become active.

**2** On the Mail Merge toolbar, click the **Mail Merge Recipients** button [image].

The Mail Merge Recipients dialog box displays a list of all of the names in the database table. Check marks to the left of each name indicate that the name currently is selected. See Figure 8.35.

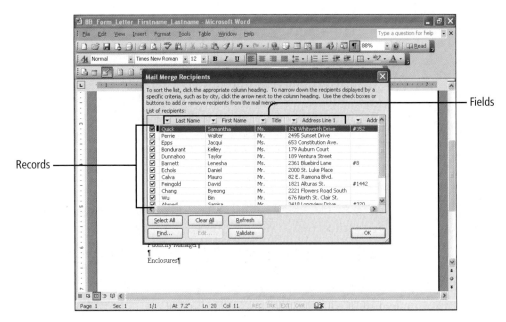

**Figure 8.35**

**3** Use the horizontal scroll bar to view all the fields included in the data table, and then scroll back to display the **Last Name** field.

You will not use all of these fields in the form letter.

**4** Click the **Last Name** column heading.

The records are reordered so that they are in alphabetical order by Last Name. Mailing lists are usually sorted by either the last name or the ZIP code. When sorted by ZIP codes, reduced rates, called **bulk mailing**, are available from the United States Postal Service.

**5** Locate the record for **Feingold** and click to clear the check mark next to Feingold's record.

By clearing the check box, Mail Merge will not generate a form letter for this individual. See Figure 8.36.

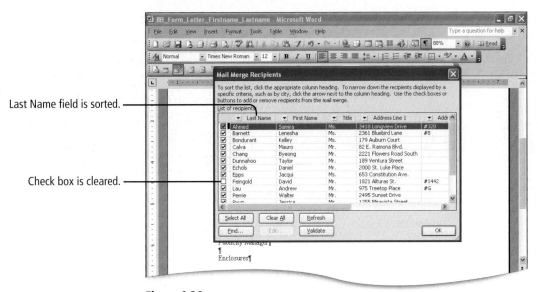

**Figure 8.36**

**Alert!**

**Editing and Adding Information to the Data Table**

An Edit button on the Mail Merge Recipients dialog box enables you to edit the selected record. You can also click Edit, and then click the New Entry button to add new records to the data table. Modifying the records in, or adding records to, the database in a Mail Merge operation also modifies and adds records in the original database file. Thus, use caution if you are using a database that is used by others and remember that you are making permanent changes to the data source.

**6** At the lower right corner of the **Mail Merge Recipients** dialog box, click **OK**.

**7** On the Standard toolbar, click the **Save** button 🖫

### Activity 8.14 Inserting Merge Fields

After you have created your main document—the letter—and identified your data source—the list of names and addresses—you are ready to insert **merge fields** into your main document. A merge field is a placeholder that you insert in the main document. For example, a specific merge field instructs Word to insert a city name that is stored in the City field of your data source. Merge fields are placed in the main document by displaying a field list, from which you can insert merge fields in any order.

**1** Click to position the insertion point in the blank line just above the *Subject* line.

**2** On the Mail Merge toolbar, click the **Insert Merge Fields** button 🔲.

A list of available fields displays, as shown in Figure 8.37. These are the same fields you saw in the Mail Merge Recipients dialog box. The *Title* field is selected by default.

Insert Merge Fields button ——

Title field ——

——— Available fields

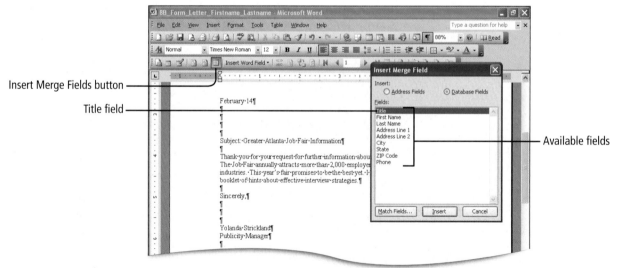

**Figure 8.37**

## More Knowledge — Inserting an Address Block

You also can add a complete address by clicking the Insert Address Block button on the Mail Merge toolbar. If all of your street addresses use a single address field, this procedure works well. When you have multiple address fields, as you do in the Job Fair Address database, using the Address Block would require you to adjust those addresses after the merge.

**3** With the **Title** field selected, at the bottom of the **Insert Merge Field** dialog box, click the **Insert** button.

The Title field is inserted into the document, surrounded by double angle brackets.

**4** Under **Fields**, click the **First Name** field, and then click the **Insert** button. Repeat this procedure to insert the **Last Name** field.

Notice that there are no spaces between the fields. These will be added later. See Figure 8.38.

Inserted fields

Double angle brackets indicate a merge field.

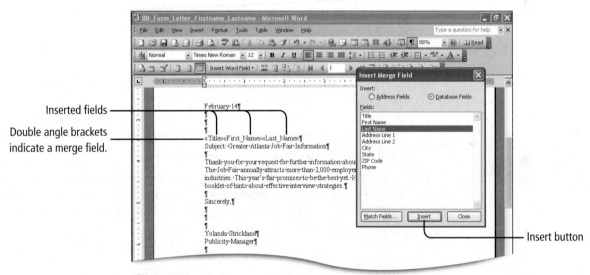

Insert button

**Figure 8.38**

**5** At the bottom of the **Insert Merge Field** dialog box, click the **Close** button. Press [Enter]. On the Mail Merge toolbar, click the **Insert Merge Fields** button ▣ again.

**6** Under **Fields**, click the **Address Line 1** field, and then click the **Insert** button. Repeat this procedure to insert the **Address Line 2** field.

**7** Close the **Insert Merge Field** dialog box and press [Enter]. On the Mail Merge toolbar, click the **Insert Merge Fields** button ▣ again.

**8** Use the same procedure you used in Step 6 to add the **City**, **State**, and **ZIP Code** fields. Click the **Close** button. Press [Enter].

Compare your document with Figure 8.39.

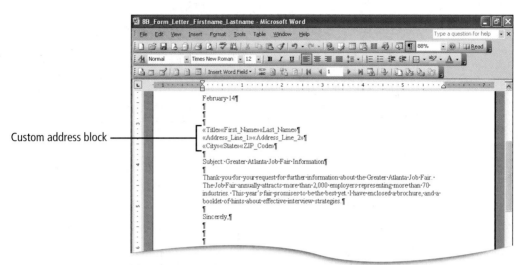

Custom address block

**Figure 8.39**

**9** Click to place the insertion point at the end of the *Subject* line, and then press ⟨Enter⟩ twice. Type **Dear** and then press ⟨Spacebar⟩.

**10** On the Mail Merge toolbar, click the **Insert Merge Fields** button 🔳. With **Title** selected, click **Insert** to insert the **Title** field. Click **Last Name**, and then click **Insert**. Click the **Close** button, and then type a comma.

**11** In the first row of fields, click to position the insertion point between the **Title** field and the **First Name** field (<<First_Name>> will appear to be shaded). Press ⟨Spacebar⟩. Repeat this procedure to insert a space between the **First Name** and **Last Name** fields and between the **Address Line 1** and **Address Line 2** fields.

**12** In the third row of fields, click to position the insertion point between the **City** field and the **State** field. Type a comma, and then press ⟨Spacebar⟩. Add a space between the **State** and **ZIP Code** fields. In the greeting line, add a space between the **Title** and **Last Name** fields.

The letter (main document) and the source data are now linked, although you still see only the field names, and not the names of the individuals in the source document. Compare your document with Figure 8.40.

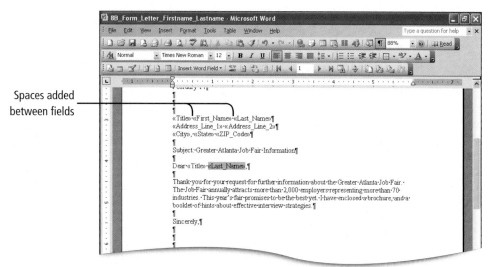

**Figure 8.40**

**13** On the Standard toolbar, click the **Save** button ⊞.

# Objective 5
## Merge Letters with Records from the Data Source

After the merge fields are added to the form letter—the main document—one letter for each person in the data source is created. You can preview the letters one at a time, print the letters directly from the Mail Merge document, or merge all of the letters into one Word document that you can edit. Merging the letters into one Word document is useful if you want to add customized information to individual letters.

### Activity 8.15 Previewing Merged Data

Before you print your form letters, it is a good idea to scan them to verify that you have the result you intended, and to make any necessary adjustments.

**1** On the Mail Merge toolbar, click the **Highlight Merge Fields** button 🗎.

Each of the merged fields is shaded in gray, enabling you to quickly examine each field that you have included, and the spacing and formatting within the fields. See Figure 8.41.

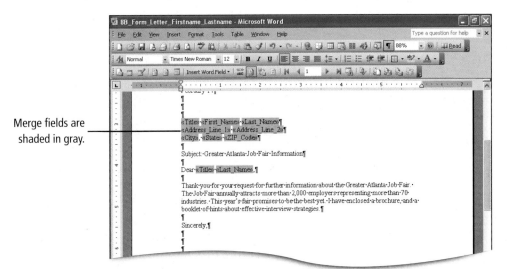

Merge fields are
shaded in gray.

**Figure 8.41**

**2** On the Mail Merge toolbar, click the **View Merged Data** button .

The first form letter displays. The highlighted fields indicate the data taken from the first record in the sorted data source. See Figure 8.42.

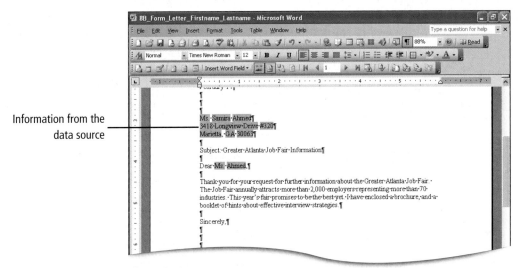

Information from the
data source

**Figure 8.42**

**3** On the Mail Merge toolbar, click the **Next Record** button  several times to examine the address block of the form letters.

Notice that the letters are addressed in alphabetical order by Last Name.

**4** On the Mail Merge toolbar, click the **Last Record** button , examine the last record, and then click the **First Record** button .

**5** On the Mail Merge toolbar, click the **Highlight Merge Fields** button to deselect the field highlights. If the insertion point is in a field, and the field is gray, then click anywhere in the body of the document to deselect the field. On the Formatting toolbar, click the **Show/Hide ¶** button.

**6** Using the **Next Record** button , scroll up or down through the letters with all of the formatting turned off to see what the final letters will look like. When you are through, on the Formatting toolbar, click the **Show/Hide ¶** button again to restore your view of the formatting marks.

**7** On the Standard toolbar, click the **Save** button .

### Activity 8.16 Printing Form Letters

You can print your form letters directly from your Mail Merge document.

**1** On the Mail Merge toolbar, click the **First Record** button .

**2** From the **View** menu, click **Header and Footer**. On the Header and Footer toolbar, click the **Switch Between Header and Footer** button . Click the **Insert AutoText** button Insert AutoText ▾ , and then click **Filename**.

The file name is inserted in the footer of each letter.

**3** On the Header and Footer toolbar, click the **Close** button Close .

**4** On the Mail Merge toolbar, click the **Merge to Printer** button .

The Merge to Printer dialog box displays, as shown in Figure 8.43.

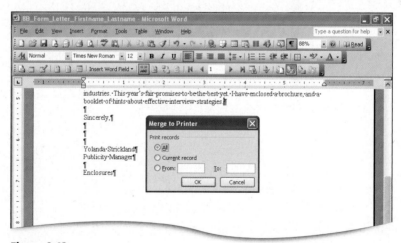

**Figure 8.43**

**5** Under **Print records**, click the **From** option button. In the **From** box, type **1** and in the **To** box, type **2**

**6** At the bottom of the **Merge to Printer** dialog box, click **OK**.

The Print dialog box displays.

**7** At the bottom of the **Print** dialog box, click **OK**. The first two form letters will print.

**8** On the Standard toolbar, click the **Save** button ![save icon].

### Activity 8.17 Merging Form Letters to a Word Document

If you need to customize the constant information—information in the main document—in the letters, you can merge all of the letters into one document and then edit only the letters you want to change. When you merge to a single document, a page break is inserted after each letter.

**1** On the Mail Merge toolbar, click the **Merge to New Document** button ![merge icon].

The Merge to New Document dialog box displays, as shown in Figure 8.44.

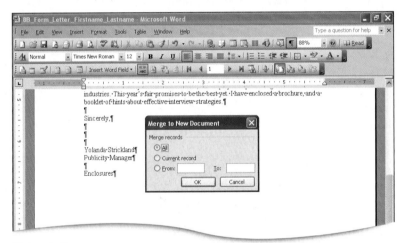

**Figure 8.44**

**2** Under **Merge records**, click the **All** option button, and then click **OK**.

All 14 letters are combined into one document, with page breaks between the letters. In the status bar, notice that *1/14* displays, indicating a Word document of 14 pages.

**3** At the bottom of the vertical scroll bar, click the **Select Browse Object** button ⊙, and then click the **Go To** button →.

The Find and Replace dialog box displays. The Go To tab is selected by default, as shown in Figure 8.45.

Go To tab

The first of 14 pages is displayed.

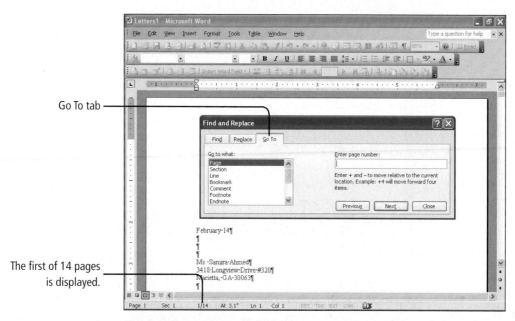

**Figure 8.45**

**4** In the **Find and Replace** dialog box, under **Enter page number**, type **3** and then, at the bottom of the dialog box, click the **Go To** button.

The insertion point moves to page 3.

**5** At the bottom of the **Find and Replace** dialog box, click **Close**.

**6** In the paragraph beginning *Thank you for your request*, click to position the insertion point in the third line, just after the period following *industries*. Press Spacebar and type **In answer to your question, there will be 17 medical firms represented.**

Compare your letter with Figure 8.46.

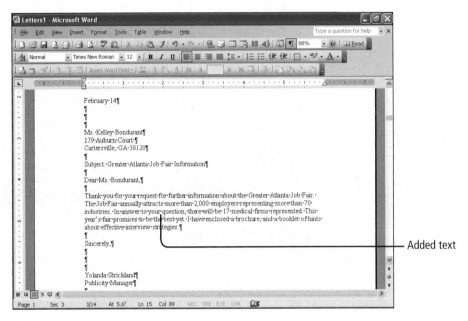

Figure 8.46

**7** On the **File** menu, click **Save As**. In the **Save As** dialog box, navigate to the folder where you are storing your projects for this chapter and type **8B_Form_Letter2_Firstname_Lastname** and then click **Save**.

**8** From the **File** menu, click **Print**. Under **Page range**, click in the **Pages** box, and then type **3** Click **OK** to print page 3, the third letter.

**9** Close both documents, saving any changes, and then close Word.

**End** You have completed Project 8B

# Summary

Microsoft Word documents can be integrated with other Office programs. It is common to combine a Word document with information in Excel and Access. Numbers and text from Access or Excel can be pasted into a Word document, where they become Word tables. You can use the Paste Special command to paste the data into the Word document, and then activate the source program's commands to edit the data while in Word. You also can paste the data and keep the link to the source program. When the data is edited in the source program, it can also be updated automatically in the Word document.

Charts from Excel can be pasted into Word documents and treated as images. As with data, the Paste Special command enables you to edit the Excel chart using the Excel program commands while viewing the document in Word. Excel charts can also be linked so that changes in the Excel spreadsheet are reflected in the Word document.

Links to other programs can be placed in Word documents in the form of icons. When you double-click on a linked icon, the program and program file open.

Word tables, Access databases, and Excel spreadsheets can be used to create customized form letters and labels, when the same basic letter must be sent to a number of different people. You can insert address information from Access databases and Excel lists in a Word document and customize each letter to contain the name and address of the individual to whom the letter is being sent. You can customize the text within the body of the letter. You can also customize the labels you create.

When creating a merge, the list of recipients is taken from a data source, which can be a Word table, an Excel spreadsheet, or an Access database. Within the data source, the columns of the table form the fields, and the rows of the table form the records. When the information in the data source document is merged with the text in the main document, one letter is generated for every record in the data source document.

## In This Chapter You Practiced How To

- Embed Excel Charts and Data
- Link to Excel Charts and PowerPoint Presentations
- Create Labels Using the Mail Merge Wizard
- Create a Form Letter
- Merge Letters with Records from the Data Source

**Matching**  Match each term in the second column with its correct definition in the first column by writing the letter of the term on the blank line in front of the correct definition.

_____ 1. To insert, using a format that you specify, information from a source file in one program, such as Excel, PowerPoint, or Access, into a destination file in another program, such as Word.

_____ 2. All of the fields containing information about one person and stored in a row in a data table.

_____ 3. In a mail merge for a form letter, the text and graphics that are the same from letter to letter.

_____ 4. A letter with standardized wording that can be sent to many different people when merged with an address list.

_____ 5. A Word feature that combines information from two documents—a main document and a data source—to create customized form letters or labels.

_____ 6. In a mail merge, the information, such as name and address, that varies from letter to letter.

_____ 7. In a mail merge, a placeholder inserted into the main document where information from the records in the data source will be placed.

_____ 8. The process of arranging the information in a data source in alphabetical or numerical order by a specific field.

_____ 9. An object that is created in a source file and inserted into a destination file, and which maintains a direct connection to the source file.

_____ 10. The column headings in a data source—for example, *Last Name* and *First Name*.

_____ 11. The acronym for Object Linking and Embedding, a term that refers to Microsoft's program-integration technology for sharing information between Office programs.

_____ 12. Mail sorted by ZIP code that qualifies for reduced postage rates from the United States Postal Service.

_____ 13. In a mail merge, the file that contains the information to be merged—for example, a list of names and addresses.

_____ 14. An arrangement of black bars based on a ZIP code and added to an envelope or label so that the address can be scanned and sorted electronically by the United States Postal Service.

_____ 15. In a mail merge, the document that contains the text and graphics that are the same for each version of the letter.

**A** Bulk mailing

**B** Constant information

**C** Data source

**D** Embed

**E** Fields

**F** Form letter

**G** Linked object

**H** Mail Merge

**I** Main document

**J** Merge field

**K** OLE

**L** Postal bar code

**M** Record

**N** Sort

**O** Variable information

**Fill in the Blank** Write the correct answer in the space provided.

1. To use mail merge, you need a main document and a(n)

   _____.

2. If you copy a range of cells from an Excel spreadsheet and then paste
   it into a Word document without using the Paste Special command,
   the result is a Word _____.

3. A linked object maintains a direct connection to the

   _____.

4. Microsoft Access is a(n) _____ program.

5. In a data table, click on the column heading to

   _____ the records by that field.

6. The _____ command allows you to copy information
   from one location and paste it in another location using a different
   format.

7. To create labels or form letters, use the Mail Merge toolbar or the

   Mail Merge _____, which walks you through the

   process step by step.

8. When you use the Paste Special command to _____
   an Excel chart into a Word document, you can use Excel commands
   to edit the chart.

9. A row of data in a data table is referred to as a(n)

   _____.

10. If you want to make changes to Excel data and have the changes
    also made to the corresponding Excel object in a Word document,
    then you should _____, rather than embed, the
    Excel object.

## Project 8C—Volunteers Letter

**Objectives:** *Embed Excel Charts and Data and Link to Excel Charts and PowerPoint Presentations.*

In the following Skill Assessment, you will embed an Excel chart into a letter to volunteers who will be working at the Greater Atlanta Job Fair. You also will insert a link to a PowerPoint presentation. Your completed document will look similar to the one shown in Figure 8.47. You will save your document as *8C_Volunteers_Letter_Firstname_Lastname*.

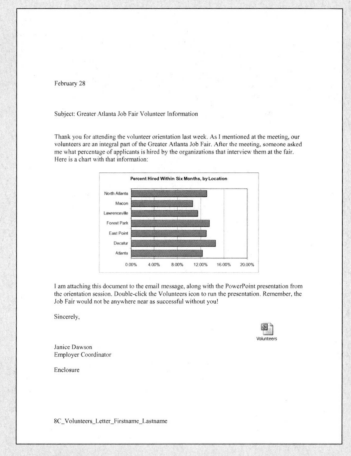

February 28

Subject: Greater Atlanta Job Fair Volunteer Information

Thank you for attending the volunteer orientation last week. As I mentioned at the meeting, our volunteers are an integral part of the Greater Atlanta Job Fair. After the meeting, someone asked me what percentage of applicants is hired by the organizations that interview them at the fair. Here is a chart with that information:

I am attaching this document to the email message, along with the PowerPoint presentation from the orientation session. Double-click the Volunteers icon to run the presentation. Remember, the Job Fair would not be anywhere near as successful without you!

Sincerely,

Janice Dawson
Employer Coordinator

Enclosure

8C_Volunteers_Letter_Firstname_Lastname

**Figure 8.47**

1. Start Word and on the Standard toolbar, click the **Open** button. Navigate to the location where the student files for this textbook are stored. Locate and open **w08C_Volunteers_Letter**. Save the file as **8C_Volunteers_Letter_Firstname_Lastname**

2. On the Standard toolbar, click the **Zoom button arrow**, and then click **Page Width**. If necessary, on the Standard toolbar, click the Show/Hide ¶ button to show formatting marks.

**(Project 8C–Volunteers Letter continues on the next page)**

**(Project 8C–Volunteers Letter continued)**

3. Click the **Start** button, locate the Excel program, and then start **Excel**. On the Standard toolbar, click the **Open** button. Navigate to the location where the student files for this textbook are stored. Locate and open the Excel file **w08C_Hiring_Results**.

4. Click in a white area of the bar chart entitled **Percent Hired Within Six Months, by Location** to select it. When the chart is selected, notice that in the cells above, the data represented in the chart is bordered. From the Standard toolbar, click the **Copy** button.

5. On the taskbar, click the Microsoft Word icon for your **8C_Volunteers_ Letter** file. Locate the paragraph that begins *I am attaching*, and then click to position the insertion point in the second blank line above that paragraph.

6. From the **Edit** menu, click **Paste Special**. In the displayed **Paste Special** dialog box, be sure the **Paste** option button is selected and that under **As**, **Microsoft Office Excel Chart Object** is selected. Click **OK**.

7. Click to select the chart. From the Formatting toolbar, click the **Center** button to center the chart horizontally.

8. Scroll down to view the lower half of the document on your screen. Click to position the insertion point at the end of the paragraph that begins *I am attaching*.

9. From the **Insert** menu, click **Object**. In the **Object** dialog box, click the **Create from File tab**.

10. Click **Browse**, navigate to the location of your student files, click to select the **w08C_Volunteers** PowerPoint presentation, and then click the **Insert** button. Select the **Link to file** check box and the **Display as icon** check box.

11. Click the **Change Icon** button. In the **Caption** box, select and delete the text. Type **Volunteers**

12. At the bottom of the **Change Icon** dialog box, click **OK**. At the bottom of the **Object** dialog box, click **OK**.

13. Right-click the new icon. From the shortcut menu, click **Format Object**. In the **Format Object** dialog box, click the **Layout tab**.

14. Under **Wrapping style**, click **Square**. At the bottom of the **Format Object** dialog box, click **OK**.

15. Drag the icon to an open area under the right side of the paragraph that begins *I am attaching*. The anchor should display to the left of the paragraph that begins *I am attaching*. Compare your document with Figure 8.47.

**(Project 8C–Volunteers Letter continues on the next page)**

**(Project 8C**–Volunteers Letter continued)

16. Double-click the new icon. Click the mouse button to advance through the presentation one slide at a time. When you reach a black slide, click once.

17. On the Standard toolbar, click the **Save** button. Use the taskbar to move to Excel and close the program. Do not save changes to the Excel file if prompted.

18. From the **View** menu, click **Header and Footer**. On the Header and Footer toolbar, click the **Switch Between Header and Footer** button. Click the **Insert AutoText** button, and then click **Filename**. On the Header and Footer toolbar, click the **Close** button. On the Standard toolbar, click the **Save** button.

19. On the Standard toolbar, click the **Print Preview** button. Take a moment to check your work. On the Print Preview toolbar, click the **Close Preview** button.

20. Make any necessary changes to your document. When you are satisfied, on the Standard toolbar, click the **Print** button. Close the document, saving your changes.

**End** You have completed Project 8C

## Project 8D—Volunteers Form Letter

**Objectives:** *Create a Form Letter and Merge Letters with Data from a Data Source.*

In the following Skill Assessment, you will use the Mail Merge Wizard to address letters to volunteers who will be working at the Greater Atlanta Job Fair. You will also use the Mail Merge toolbar to insert the name of the organization that the volunteer has been asked to assist, and then you will print the form letters. Your completed document will look similar to the one shown in Figure 8.48. You will save your document as *8D_Volunteers_Form_Letter_Firstname_Lastname*.

1. On the Standard toolbar, click the **Open** button. Navigate to the location where the student files for this textbook are stored. Locate and open **w08D_Volunteers_Form_Letter**. Save the file as **8D_Volunteers_Form_Letter_Firstname_Lastname**

2. On the Standard toolbar, click the **Zoom button arrow**, and then click **Page Width**. If necessary, on the Standard toolbar, click the Show/Hide ¶ button to show formatting marks.

**(Project 8D**–Volunteers Form Letter continues on the next page)

**(Project 8D–Volunteers Form Letter continued)**

February 28

Mary Martinez
3293 Nyland Ave.
Atlanta, GA 30327

Subject: Greater Atlanta Job Fair Volunteer Information
Your Assigned Organization: Atlanta Insurance Brokers

Thank you for attending the volunteer orientation last week. As I mentioned at the meeting, our
volunteers are an integral part of the Greater Atlanta Job Fair. After the meeting, someone asked
me what percentage of applicants is hired by the organizations that interview them at the fair.
Here is a chart with that information:

The organization you have been assigned to work with is mentioned at the top of this letter. We
have tried to find the best match between organization and volunteer whenever possible. As I
mentioned after the meeting, the Job Fair would not be anywhere near as successful without you!

Sincerely,

Janice Dawson
Employer Coordinator

Enclosure

8D_Volunteers_Form_Letter_Firstname_Lastname

**Figure 8.48**

3. On the Windows taskbar, click the **Start** button, navigate to the location of the Microsoft Office programs, and then open **Excel**. On the Standard toolbar, click the **Open** button. Navigate to the location where the student files for this textbook are stored. Locate and open the Excel file **w08D_Volunteer_Help**. Examine the table, which will be used as the data source for a mail merge. Close Excel. Do not save changes if prompted.

4. Click to position the insertion point at the end of the first line—the line containing the date. Press Enter three times. From the **Tools** menu, point to **Letters and Mailings**, and then click **Mail Merge**. In the **Mail Merge** task pane, be sure the **Letters** option button is selected, and then at the bottom of the task pane, click **Next: Starting document**.

5. Under **Select starting document**, be sure the **Use the current document** option button is selected. At the bottom of the task pane, click **Next: Select recipients**.

**(Project 8D–Volunteers Form Letter continues on the next page)**

**(Project 8D**–Volunteers Form Letter continued)

6. Under **Use an existing list**, click **Browse**. Navigate to the location where the student files for this textbook are stored. Locate and click the **w08D_Volunteer Help** Excel file, and then click **Open**.

7. In the **Select Table** dialog box, **Volunteer_Help** is the only data table identified. Be sure the **First row of data contains column headers** check box is selected, and then click **OK**.

8. In the **Mail Merge Recipients** dialog box, click the **Last Name** column header to sort the recipient list by the last names of the volunteers.

9. Use the horizontal scroll bar in the **Mail Merge Recipients** dialog box to scroll to the right. Notice that there is a field for *Assigned Organization*. Recall that each volunteer will be assigned one organization to assist during the job fair. At the bottom of the **Mail Merge Recipients** dialog box, click **OK**. At the bottom of the task pane, click **Next: Write your letter**.

10. At the top of the task pane, under **Write your letter**, click **Address block**. In the **Insert Address Block** dialog box, under **Specify address elements**, clear the **Insert company name** check box because there is no company field associated with this data source. Click **OK**.

11. At the bottom of the **Mail Merge** task pane, click **Next: Preview your letters**. In the upper portion of the task pane, under **Preview your letters**, click the **Next Record** (>>) and **Previous Record** (<<) buttons as necessary to scroll through the letters and examine the address blocks. There are a total of 15 letters.

12. At the bottom of the task pane, click **Next: Complete the merge**. Close the **Mail Merge** task pane.

13. If necessary, display the Mail Merge toolbar.

14. Locate the line *Your Assigned Organization:* and click to position the insertion point following the space at the end of that line. On the Mail Merge toolbar, click the **Insert Merge Fields** button. (Display ScreenTips if you are not sure which button to click.)

15. In the **Insert Merge Field** dialog box, click **Assigned Organization**, and then click **Insert**. Notice that the field names are the column headings from the Excel table you examined. Click **Close** to close the dialog box. Notice that for the displayed letter, an Organization name is inserted. On the Standard toolbar, click the **Save** button. Compare your document with Figure 8.48.

16. On the Mail Merge toolbar, click the **Highlight Merge Fields** button so that you can view the areas that contain merged information. On the Mail Merge toolbar, click the **Next Record** button or **Previous Record** button to scroll through the letters. Examine the *Assigned Organization* field.

**(Project 8D**–Volunteers Form Letter continues on the next page)

**(Project 8D**–Volunteers Form Letter continued)

17. On the Mail Merge toolbar, click the **Highlight Merge Fields** button to deselect the field highlights. On the Formatting toolbar, click the **Show/Hide ¶** button.

18. Scroll through the letters with all of the formatting turned off to see what the final letters will look like. When you are through, on the Formatting toolbar, click the **Show/Hide ¶** button again to restore formatting marks.

19. From the **View** menu, click **Header and Footer**. On the Header and Footer toolbar, click the **Switch Between Header and Footer** button. Click the **Insert AutoText** button, and then click **Filename**. Click the **Close** button.

20. On the Mail Merge toolbar, click the **Merge to Printer** button. Under **Print records**, click the **From** option button. In the **From** box, type **1** and in the **To** box, type **2**

21. At the bottom of the **Merge to Printer** dialog box, click **OK**. At the bottom of the **Print** dialog box, click **OK**. The first two letters of the 15 will print. Close the document, and save your changes.

**End** You have completed Project 8D

## Project 8E — Volunteers Mailing Labels

**Objective:** *Create Labels Using the Mail Merge Wizard.*

In the following Skill Assessment, you will use the Mail Merge Wizard to create mailing labels for letters sent to volunteers who will be working at the Greater Atlanta Job Fair. Your completed document will look similar to the one shown in Figure 8.49. You will save your document as *8E_Volunteers_Mailing_Labels_Firstname_Lastname*.

1. Start Word and be sure a new blank document is displayed. From the **Tools** menu, point to **Letters and Mailings**, and then click **Mail Merge**.

2. In the **Mail Merge** task pane, under **Select document type**, click the **Labels** option button, and then at the bottom of the task pane, click **Next: Starting document**.

3. Under **Change document layout**, click **Label options**.

4. In the **Label Options** dialog box, under **Label information**, click the **Label products arrow** and then click **Avery standard**. Under **Product number**, scroll down the list and click **5160 - Address**.

5. At the bottom of the **Label Options** dialog box, click **OK**. The blank labels, formatted as a Word table, display. At the bottom of the task pane, click **Next: Select recipients**.

**(Project 8E**–Volunteers Mailing Labels continues on the next page)

**(Project 8E–Volunteers Mailing Labels continued)**

| | | |
|---|---|---|
| Kimberly Anderson<br>221 Julian Ct.<br>Atlanta, GA 30330 | Jewell Barick<br>226 S. Hillcrest St.<br>Marietta, GA 30063 | Monique Bernier<br>218 ½ W. Harvard Blvd.<br>Atlanta, GA 30330 |
| Steven Bradley<br>811 E. Santa Paula Pl. #335<br>Smyrna, GA 30081 | Janna Carras<br>1810 Muirfield Dr.<br>Atlanta, GA 30301 | Nicole Clark<br>309 Wolff Street<br>Marietta, GA 30063 |
| Tina Cunningham<br>1278 Ramona Blvd. #1<br>Marietta, GA 30063 | Rashad Dinola<br>3953 Bolero Ct.<br>Kennesaw, GA 30152 | Ronnie Littlejohn<br>201 Claressa Ave.<br>Atlanta, GA 30327 |
| Mary Martinez<br>3293 Nyland Ave.<br>Atlanta, GA 30327 | Lois Maxwell<br>3953 Cecilia Drive<br>Atlanta, GA 30327 | Katherine Stork<br>1950 Ginger St.<br>Kennesaw, GA 30144 |
| Tabitha Suhr<br>795 N. Olive Pl.<br>Smyrna, GA 30081 | Tyree Swayne<br>2203 Los Encinos<br>Smyrna, GA 30081 | Tamika Tetrault<br>1643 Urbana Lane<br>Atlanta, GA 30327 |

8E_Volunteers_Mailing_Labels_Firstname_Lastname

**Figure 8.49**

6. Under **Use an existing list**, click **Browse**. Navigate to the location where the student files for this textbook are stored. Locate and click the Access file **w08E_Job_Fair_Addresses**, and then click **Open**. The **Select Table** dialog box displays, showing two data tables in the database. Click **Volunteer Help**, and then click **OK**.

7. Click the **Last Name** field column heading to sort the records alphabetically by last name, and then click **OK**. At the bottom of the task pane, click **Next: Arrange your labels**.

8. Under **Arrange your labels**, click **Address block**. In the **Insert Address Block** dialog box, under **Specify address elements**, clear the **Insert company name** check box. Click **OK**.

9. If necessary, scroll down in the task pane. Under **Replicate labels**, click **Update all labels**. At the bottom of the task pane, click **Next: Preview your labels**. Examine your labels. Compare your document with Figure 8.49.

**(Project 8E–Volunteers Mailing Labels continues on the next page)**

**(Project 8E–Volunteers Mailing Labels continued)**

10. Now that you have viewed the preview of the labels, at the bottom of the task pane, click **Next: Complete the merge**. Close the **Mail Merge** task pane.

11. On the **File** menu, click **Save As**. In the **Save As** dialog box, type 8E_Volunteers_Mailing_Labels_Firstname_Lastname and then click **Save**.

12. On the Standard toolbar, click the **Print Preview** button. Click the magnifying glass pointer in the middle of the labels. On the Print Preview toolbar, click the **Close** button.

13. From the **View** menu, click **Header and Footer**. On the Header and Footer toolbar, click the **Switch Between Header and Footer** button. Click the **Insert AutoText** button, and then click **Filename**. On the Header and Footer toolbar, click the **Close** button.

14. On the Standard toolbar, click the **Save** button.

15. In the Mail Merge toolbar, click the **Merge to Printer** button. Under **Print records**, click the **From** option button. In the **From** box, type **1** and in the **To** box, type **1** (Because page 2 contains no labels, it is not necessary to print it.)

16. At the bottom of the **Merge to Printer** dialog box, click **OK**. At the bottom of the **Print** dialog box, click **OK** to print the labels. Close the document, saving any changes.

**End** You have completed Project 8E

## Project 8F—Financial Information

**Objectives:** *Embed Excel Charts and Data and Link to Excel Charts and PowerPoint Presentations.*

In the following Performance Assessment, you will edit a memo about financial results from the Greater Atlanta Job Fair, one of the regional job fairs in the Greater Atlanta area. You will embed a table and link a chart. Your completed document will look similar to the one shown in Figure 8.50. You will save your document as *8F_Financial_Information_Firstname_Lastname*.

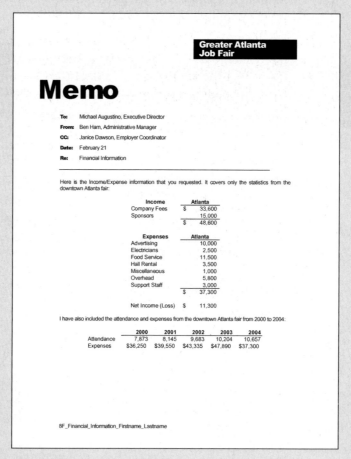

**Figure 8.50**

1. On the Standard toolbar, click the **Open** button. Navigate to the location where the student files for this textbook are stored. Locate and open **w08F_Financial_Information**. Save the file in your storage location as **8F_Financial_Information_Firstname_Lastname**

2. Start Excel, and then locate and open the **w08F_Atlanta_Information** Excel file. If necessary, click the **2004 Income sheet tab** at the bottom of the worksheet. Save the file in your storage location as **8F_Atlanta_Information_ Firstname_Lastname**

3. Click in cell **A3** and drag to the right one column and then down to cell **B18**. On the Standard toolbar, click the **Copy** button.

**(Project 8F–Financial Information continues on the next page)**

**(Project 8F–Financial Information continued)**

4. On the taskbar, click the Microsoft Word icon for your **8F_Financial_ Information** file. Locate the paragraph that begins *I have also included* and then click to position the insertion point in the second blank line above the paragraph.

5. From the **Edit** menu, click **Paste Special**. In the **Paste Special** dialog box, click the **Paste link** option button, and then click **Microsoft Office Excel Worksheet Object**. Click **OK** to paste the selected cells from the Excel worksheet into the Word document and to create a link to the source document.

6. Examine the *Expenses* and the *Net Income (Loss)* for Atlanta in the new table. Double-click the new table to return to the linked work-sheet. Click cell **B13**. Type **1000** and press Enter.

7. From the taskbar, switch back to your Word **8F_Financial_ Information** file. Right-click anywhere on the table and click **Update Link** from the shortcut menu. Notice that the *Miscellaneous* expense, the *Expenses* total, and the *Net Income (Loss)* are updated.

8. From the taskbar, navigate to the Excel spreadsheet and click on the **Atlanta Expenses sheet tab**. Click in cell **A3** and drag to the right through column F and then down to cell **F5**. On the Standard toolbar, click the **Copy** button.

9. Navigate back to your Word document. Click to position the insertion point in the last blank line of the document. From the **Edit** menu, click **Paste Special**. Be sure the **Paste** option button is selected and under **As**, click **Microsoft Office Excel Worksheet Object**. Click **OK**.

10. To edit the new table, double-click anywhere in the table to activate Excel. Click in the lower right cell—$36,800—press Delete, and type **37300**

11. Click outside the table. Click the table to select it, and, on the Formatting toolbar, click the **Center** button. Center the other table in the same manner. Compare your document with Figure 8.50.

12. From the **View** menu, click **Header and Footer**. On the Header and Footer toolbar, click the **Switch Between Header and Footer** button. Click the **Insert AutoText** button, point to **Header/Footer**, and then click **Filename**. On the Header and Footer toolbar, click the **Close** button. On the Standard toolbar, click the **Save** button.

13. On the Standard toolbar, click the **Print Preview** button. Take a moment to check your work. On the Print Preview toolbar, click the **Close Preview** button.

14. Make any necessary changes to your document. When you are satisfied, on the Standard toolbar, click the **Print** button. Close the document, saving your changes.

**End** You have completed Project 8F

## Project 8G — Confirmation Letter

**Objectives:** *Create a Form Letter and Merge Letters with Data from a Data Source.*

In the following Performance Assessment, you will use the Mail Merge Wizard to add an address block to a letter to the organizations that are participating in the Greater Atlanta Job Fair. Then you will use the Mail Merge toolbar to insert the number of booths ordered and the booth charges for each organization. You will also add a greeting line. Your completed document will look similar to the one shown in Figure 8.51. You will save your document as *8G_Confirmation_Letter_Firstname_Lastname*.

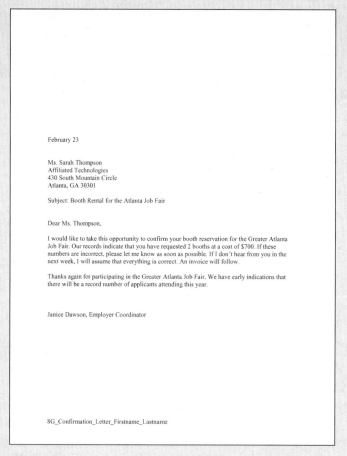

**Figure 8.51**

1. On the Standard toolbar, click the **Open** button. Navigate to the location where the student files for this textbook are stored. Locate and open **w08G_Confirmation_Letter**. In your storage location, save the file as **8G_Confirmation_ Letter_Firstname_Lastname**

2. Click to position the insertion point at the end of the first line—the line containing the date. Press Enter three times.

**(Project 8G–Confirmation Letter continues on the next page)**

**(Project 8G**–Confirmation Letter continued)

3. From the **Tools** menu, point to **Letters and Mailings**, and then click **Mail Merge**. In the **Mail Merge** task pane, be sure the **Letters** option button is selected, and then at the bottom of the task pane, click **Next: Starting document**.

4. Be sure you are using the current document for the mail merge, and then click **Next: Select recipients**.

5. Under **Use an existing list**, click **Browse**. Navigate to the location where the student files for this textbook are stored. Locate and click the Access file **w08G_Job_Fair_Addresses**, and then click **Open**.

6. In the **Select Table** dialog box, click **Organization_Addresses**, and then click **OK**. Scroll to view the fields at the right of list, and notice that fields are included for both the number of Booths the organization has requested, and the Amount Due for booth rental. At the bottom of the **Mail Merge Recipients** dialog box, click **OK**. At the bottom of the task pane, click **Next: Write your letter**.

7. Under **Write your letter**, click **Address block**. Because there is a Company Name field, do not deselect the Insert Company Name check box. Click **OK**. At the bottom of the task pane, click **Next: Preview your letters**. In the task pane, click the **Next Record** and **Previous Record** buttons as necessary to scroll through the letters and examine the address blocks.

8. At the bottom of the task pane, click **Next: Complete the merge**. Close the **Mail Merge** task pane. If necessary, right-click any toolbar, and click Mail Merge to open the Mail Merge toolbar. Click the **View Merged Data** button to display the field names, rather than the recipient names.

9. Position the insertion point at the end of the *Subject* line and press Enter three times. Type **Dear** and then press Spacebar. On the Mail Merge toolbar, click the **Insert Merge Fields** button. In the **Insert Merge Fields** dialog box, click **Title**, and then click **Insert**. Use the same procedure to insert the **Lastname** field, and then click **Close**. Add a space between the title and last name and add a comma after the last name.

10. In the paragraph that begins *I would like*, click to position the insertion point just after the word *requested* and add a space. On the Mail Merge toolbar, click the **Insert Merge Fields** button, click the **Booths** field, and then click **Insert**. Close the **Insert Merge Field** dialog box.

11. At the end of the same sentence, position the insertion point before the period. Press Spacebar and type **$** On the Mail Merge toolbar, click the **Insert Merge Fields** button, click the **Amount Due** field, and then click **Insert**. Close the **Insert Merge Field** dialog box.

**(Project 8G**–Confirmation Letter continues on the next page)

**(Project 8G**–Confirmation Letter continued)

12. On the Mail Merge toolbar, click the **Highlight Merge Fields** button. Click the **View Merged Data** button. Scroll through the form letters using the **Next Record** button and examine the inserted fields. Compare your document with Figure 8.51.

13. From the **File** menu, click **Page Setup**, and then click the **Layout tab**. Under **Page**, click the **Vertical alignment arrow**, and then click **Center**. Create a footer and insert the file name.

14. On the Mail Merge toolbar, click the **Merge to Printer** button. In the **From** box, type **1** and in the **To** box, type **2**

15. At the bottom of the **Merge to Printer** dialog box, click **OK**. At the bottom of the **Print** dialog box, click **OK**. The first two letters will print. Close the document and save any changes.

**End** **You have completed Project 8G**

## Project 8H — Confirmation Labels

**Objective:** *Create Labels Using the Mail Merge Wizard.*

In the following Performance Assessment, you will use the Mail Merge Wizard to create a set of mailing labels for the organizations participating in the Greater Atlanta Job Fair. Because the addresses are long, and the name and title of the contact person and the organization will be included, you will need to use a large label. Your completed document will look similar to the one shown in Figure 8.52. You will save your document as *8H_Confirmation_Labels_Firstname_Lastname.*

1. Open Word and display a new blank document. From the **Tools** menu, point to **Letters and Mailings**, and then click **Mail Merge**. In the **Mail Merge** task pane, click the **Labels** option button, and then at the bottom of the task pane, click **Next: Starting document**.

2. Under **Change document layout**, click **Label options**. In the **Label Options** dialog box, under **Label information**, click the **Label products arrow**, and then click **Avery standard**. Under **Product number**, scroll down the list and click **5162 - Address**. Click **OK**, and then click **Next: Select recipients**.

3. Under **Use an existing list**, click **Browse**. Navigate to the location where the student files for this textbook are stored. Locate and click the Access file **w08H_Job_Fair_Addresses**, and then click **Open**. In the **Select Table** dialog box, click **Organization_Addresses**, and then click **OK**.

**(Project 8H**–Confirmation Labels continues on the next page)

**(Project 8H**–Confirmation Labels continued)

Mr. Carson Fallacker
Director of Human Resources
A&G Consulting
107 Marguerite Drive South, Suite 15
Roswell, GA 30077

Ms. Sarah Thompson
Director of Recruiting
Affiliated Technologies
430 South Mountain Circle
Atlanta, GA 30301

Ms. Christa Jakabowski
Vice President, Administration
Atlanta Insurance Brokers
352 Piedmont Circle
Roswell, GA 30077

Mr. Sun Cho
Director, Professional Recruiting
Atlanta Veterans Medical Center
8553 Hunters Glen Blvd.
Atlanta, GA 30301

Mr. Lamar Caldwell
Director of Operations
Derrikson Brothers Construction
2215 Lake Park Drive
Marietta, GA 30063

Ms. Gail Bradley
Vice President Human Resources
DYCarlson Corp.
511 King Street
Smyrna, GA 30081

Mr. Shawn McFarland
Recruiting Representative
Georgia US Bank
980 Peachtree St., Suite 3200
Atlanta, GA 30313

Ms. Cianna Williams
Recruiting Representative
GR Data Storage
415 Technology Drive
Atlanta, GA 30330

Ms. Julie Lewis
HR Director
Olivare Corporation
2000 Delowe St., Suite 5
Atlanta, GA 30327

Mr. Brian Garcia
VP Administration
Southeast and Coastal Recycling Systems
698 Rosedale Circle SE, Suite 550
Kennesaw, GA 30144

Mr. Jared Simmons
HR Representative
Thinkanswer Technologies
898 Lakeview Drive
Conyers, GA 30012

Mr. Bilal Hadad
Medical Technology Recruiter
Underwood Medical Systems
1558 McVie Plaza Drive
Marietta, GA 30006

Mr. Nicholas Russo
Director of Human Resources
Verasound Energy
1 Verasound Way
Smyrna, GA 30080

Ms. Maya Brock
Office Manager
Wisener Heating & Air Conditioning
862 Ingleside Way, #315
Cartersville, GA 30120

8H_Confirmation_Labels_Firstname_Lastname

**Figure 8.52**

4. Scroll to the right, click the **Organization Name** field column heading to sort the records alphabetically by Organization Name, and then click **OK**. At the bottom of the task pane, click **Next: Arrange your labels**.

5. Under **Arrange your labels**, click **More items**. In the **Insert Merge Field** dialog box, under **Fields**, click **Title**, and then click **Insert**. Use the same procedure to add the **Firstname** and **Lastname** fields. Click **Close**. In the first label, add a space between each of the new fields. Click at the end of the new line and press [Enter] to create another label line.

6. Click **More items**. In the **Insert Merge Field** dialog box, under **Fields**, click **Job Title**. Click **Insert**, and then click **Close**. Press [Enter] to create another label line.

7. Click **Address block**. Under **Specify address elements**, clear the **Insert recipient's name in this format** check box, because you have already added a customized recipient's name.

**(Project 8H**–Confirmation Labels continues on the next page)

**(Project 8H—Confirmation Labels continued)**

8. Click the **Match Fields** button. Under **Required information**, click the **Company box arrow**, click **Organization Name**, and then click **OK**. Click **OK** to close the **Insert Address Block** dialog box.

9. Under **Replicate labels**, click **Update all labels**. At the bottom of the task pane, click **Next: Preview your labels**. Examine your labels.

10. At the bottom of the task pane, click **Next: Complete the merge**. Close the **Mail Merge** task pane. Compare your document with Figure 8.52.

11. On the **File** menu, click **Save As**. In the **Save As** dialog box, type **8H_Confirmation_Labels_Firstname_Lastname** and then click **Save**.

12. On the Standard toolbar, click the **Print Preview** button. Click the magnifying glass pointer in the middle of the labels. On the Print Preview toolbar, click the **Close** button.

13. Create a footer and add the file name. On the Standard toolbar, click the **Save** button.

14. In the Mail Merge toolbar, click the **Merge to Printer** button. In the **From** box, type **1** and in the **To** box, type **1**

15. At the bottom of the **Merge to Printer** dialog box, click **OK**. At the bottom of the **Print** dialog box, click **OK** to print the labels. Close the document.

**End** You have completed Project 8H

# Project 8I — Cover Sheet

**Objectives:** *Create a Form Letter, Merge Letters with Records from the Data Source, and Create Labels Using the Mail Merge Wizard.*

In the following Mastery Assessment, you will use the Mail Merge Wizard to create file folder labels for the organizations participating in the Greater Atlanta Job Fair. You will also create a paper cover sheet for a file folder. Your completed document will look similar to the one shown in Figure 8.53. You will save your documents as *8I_Cover_Sheet_Firstname_Lastname* and *8I_Folder_Labels_Firstname_Lastname*.

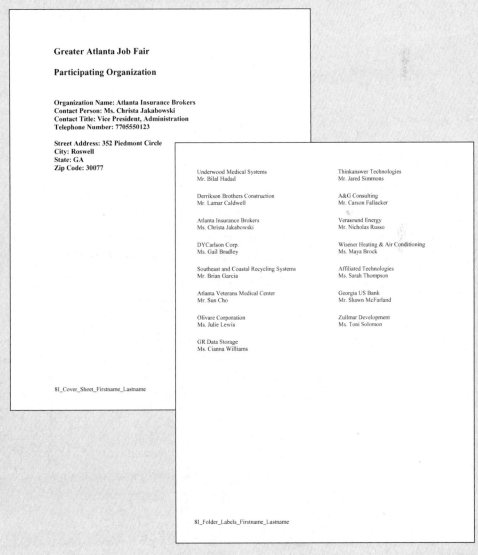

**Figure 8.53**

(**Project 8I**–Cover Sheet continues on the next page)

**(Project 8I**–Cover Sheet continued)

1. Start Word. From your student files, locate and open **w08I_Cover_Sheet**. Save the file as **8I_Cover_Sheet_Firstname_Lastname** in the same location as your other files from this chapter. Create a footer and insert the **AutoText** filename.

2. Display the Mail Merge toolbar, if necessary. Click the **Open Data Source** button and open the Access file **w08I_Job_Fair_Addresses**. Select the **Organization_Addresses** table.

3. Click at the end of the line *Organization Name* and press [Spacebar] once following the colon. Click the **Insert Merge Fields** button, click **Organization Name**, click **Insert**, and then click **Close**. Using this technique, insert the Merge Fields for the remaining lines, using the **Title**, **Firstname**, and **Lastname** fields for the Contact Person. Be sure you add a space after the colons and a space between fields in the *Contact Person* line.

4. Beginning with the line *Organization Name*, select all of the text through the end of the page. Change the **Font Size** to **14 pt.** and apply **Bold**.

5. Click the **View Merged Data** button and scroll through the 15 records. Save your changes.

6. Preview and print the first two cover sheets, and then close the document.

7. In a new document, open the **Mail Merge Wizard**. Choose **Labels**, and then select the **5766 - File Folder** Avery label option.

8. Select recipients from the Access file **w08I_Job_Fair_Addresses** and select the **Organization_Addresses** table.

9. Under **Arrange your labels**, click **More items** and insert the **Organization Name**. Close the dialog box and move down one line. Click **More items** and add the three contact person fields—**Title**, **Firstname**, and **Lastname**. Add a space between the contact person fields. Click **Update all labels**.

10. Preview your labels, and then complete the merge. Compare your document with Figure 8.53. Save the document as **8I_Folder_Labels_Firstname_ Lastname**.

11. Print page 1 of 1 of the file folder labels. Close the document, saving any changes, and then close Word.

**End** You have completed Project 8I

## Project 8J — Successful Applicants

**Objectives:** *Embed Excel Charts and Data and Link to Excel Charts and PowerPoint Presentations.*

In the following Mastery Assessment, you will edit a memo about the number of applicants hired per job fair location. You will embed a chart and link to a data table. Your completed document will look similar to the one shown in Figure 8.54. You will save your document as *8J_Successful_Applicants_Firstname_Lastname.*

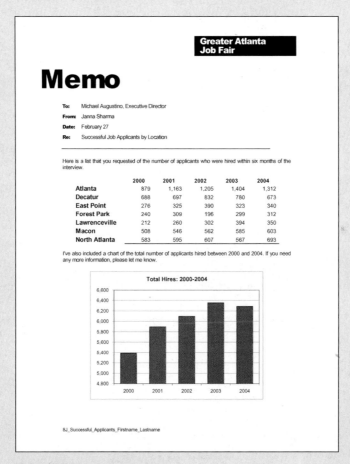

**Figure 8.54**

**(Project 8J–Successful Applicants continues on the next page)**

**(Project 8J–Successful Applicants continued)**

1. Start Word. From your student files, open **w08J_Successful_Applicants**. Save the file with the name 8J_Successful_Applicants_Firstname_Lastname in the same location as your other files from this chapter. Display the footer and insert the **AutoText** filename.

2. Start Excel and open the **w08J_Job_Fair_Hires** Excel file. Save the file as 8J_Job_Fair_Hires_Firstname_Lastname

3. Select and then copy cells **A3** through **F10**. Be sure you do not include the *Total Hires* row.

4. Switch to Word and click in the blank line above the paragraph that begins *I've also included*. Then, use the **Paste Special** command to embed the Excel data as a **Microsoft Office Excel Worksheet Object**. Add a blank line after the new table.

5. Position the insertion point at the end of the last paragraph and press Enter twice.

6. Switch to Excel, select and copy the chart, and then return to Word. Use the **Paste Special** command to link the chart to the spreadsheet.

7. Switch to Excel. Examine the chart for the year 2004. Change cell **F10** from *593* to **693** and press Enter. Notice that the chart changes. Save your work and switch to Word. Right-click the chart and click **Update Link** from the shortcut menu. Notice the change in the chart.

8. In the table, locate and double-click the lower right cell—the one that you changed in the Excel worksheet. Change *593* to **693** in the selected cell. Notice that the changes are made in Excel, even though the table is in Word. Click outside the table.

9. Center both the table and the chart. Save your work. Preview and print the document. Compare your document with Figure 8.54. Close Word and Excel.

**End** You have completed Project 8J

# Project 8K — Index Cards

**Objectives:** *Create a Form Letter and Merge Letters with Data from the Data Source.*

For quick reference, many organizations use index cards. The organizers of the Greater Atlanta Job Fair use index cards for businesses and job seekers. You will create a set of index cards for the volunteers who work at the various fairs. These index cards are available in letter-size sheets with four cards to a sheet. You will save your document as *8K_Index_Cards_Firstname_Lastname*.

1. Start Word. Start the Mail Merge Wizard. Use **w08K_Job_Fair_Addresses** as the mail merge source.

2. Create labels based on the Avery **5315 - Note Card** label.

3. Set up the cards to show the last name, followed by a comma and space, and then the first name. Add the full address in a format of your choice. Be sure you include the phone number and the company with which the volunteer has been assigned to work.

4. Format the volunteer's name in a slightly larger font than the rest of the card and emphasize the name in a distinctive manner.

5. Save the completed document as **8K_Index_Cards_Firstname_Lastname**

6. Preview and print the first page of labels.

**End** You have completed Project 8K

# Project 8L — Press Release

**Objective:** *Embed Excel Charts and Data.*

In this chapter, you practiced embedding Excel charts and data, and linking to PowerPoint presentations. There are other objects you can create and embed.

1. Create a new document and save the document as **8L_Press_Release_Firstname_Lastname** Add a brief introductory paragraph announcing the text of the new radio advertisement regarding the upcoming job fairs.

**(Project 8L**–Press Release continues on the next page)

**(Project 8L**–Press Release continued)

2. If you have access to a microphone, plug it in to the computer as instructed. From the **Insert** menu, click **Object**. In the **Object** dialog box, click the **Create New tab**, and under **Object type**, click **Wave Sound**. Select the **Display as icon** check box. (If you cannot record your voice, in the Object dialog box, click the Create from File tab, and browse to and select the **w08L_Press_Release** file that is included with your student files. Insert the object from a file the same way you embed an Excel chart from a file.) Display the sound as an icon.

3. In your textbook, turn to the second page of this chapter—the one that contains a picture depicting the Greater Atlanta Job Fair. Locate the paragraph to the left of the picture that begins *The Greater Atlanta Job Fair is a non-profit*. On the **Sound Object** dialog box, click the **Record** button (the button with the circle on it). Read the paragraph about the Greater Atlanta Job Fair into the microphone. When you are finished, click the **Stop** button (the button with the black rectangle on it).

4. Click the **Play** button (the button with the triangle pointing to the right) to listen to your announcement. If you are not satisfied, from the Sound Object File menu, click New and try again. When you are satisfied with your result, from the **Sound Object** dialog box **File** menu, click **Exit & Return**. Double-click your sound icon to listen to your recording.

5. Save your document and close Word.

**End** You have completed Project 8L —————————————————

## Downloading a Data Table from a Web Site

In this chapter you used data from Access and Excel in a Word document. Often, a table on the Web can also be inserted into a Word document as a Word table, after which it can be edited—unless the table on the Web site is a graphic.

1. Be sure that you are connected to the Internet. Open Word.

2. Go to a Web site that has data in a table format. The following sites might be useful, although you can use any site you like:

| | |
|---|---|
| **www.yahoo.com** | Click the **Finance** icon at the top of the Yahoo window. Under **Market Summary**, click **Dow**. In the task pane, at the left side of the screen, click **Historical Prices**. In the **Prices** table, highlight the column headings and four or five rows of data. |
| **www.spc.noaa.gov/ archive/tornadoes** | Scroll down and click **Tables: (HTML format)**. Choose one of the tables and highlight the column headings and a few rows of data. |

3. After you have selected the data, copy and then paste it into a Word document. Try changing information in the table cells. If the data is in table format, it can be edited. If it is text lined up to look like a table, it can be changed, but probably will need to be edited. If the table is an image, you will not be able to make any changes to the data.

4. When you are done, close the file without saving your changes.

## Updating Links

In this chapter you practiced linking data in a Word document to data in a source document created in Excel or Access. The links can be updated regularly, as long as the source file remains in the same folder in which it was stored when the link was created. If the file is moved, however, you will not be able to use Word to reopen the link without taking steps to reconnect the link.

1. Start Word. In the *Type a question for help* box, type **update a link**

2. In the **Search Results** task bar, click **Reconnect a linked object**.

3. Read the instructions for reconnecting a link, and print these instructions.

4. Open your **8A_Job_Fair_Statistics** file. Scroll down and right-click the second chart. Click **Update Link** to be sure the link is still active.

5. In **My Computer**, move the **w08A_Job_Fair_Statistics** file to a different folder. Try to update the link to the chart again.

6. Use the Help information to reconnect the link. Open the Excel document and change one of the numbers in the 2004 column to change the total attendance for that year. Go back to the Word document and update the link again to confirm that the link has been reestablished.

7. Close the **Help** window and the **Help** task pane, close your document without saving the changes, and then exit Word. Move the **w08A_Job_Fair_Statistics** file back to its original folder. Because you did not save your changes to the Word document, the link to the original source document folder remains.

# 9 chapternine

# Working with Long Documents

**In this chapter, you will:** complete these projects and practice these skills.

| Project 9A **Creating a Master Document** | **Objectives** |
|---|---|
| | • Create a Master Document and Subdocuments |
| | • Manage a Master Document and Subdocuments |

| Project 9B **Preparing an Index and Table of Contents** | **Objectives** |
|---|---|
| | • Add an Index |
| | • Create a Table of Contents |

| Project 9C **Using Pagination, Navigation, and Summary Tools** | **Objectives** |
|---|---|
| | • Control the Flow and Formatting of Pages and Text |
| | • Navigate Within Long Documents |
| | • Use AutoSummarize and Determine Readability Statistics |

# City of Desert Park

The City of Desert Park, Arizona, is a thriving city with a population of just under 1 million in an ideal location serving major markets in the western United States and Mexico. Desert Park's temperate year-round climate attracts both visitors and businesses, and it is one of the most popular vacation destinations in the world. The city expects and has plenty of space for long-term growth, and most of the undeveloped land already has a modern infrastructure and assured water supply in place.

© Getty Images, Inc.

# Working with Long Documents

When two or more people work on a document at the same time, it is a challenge to keep track of versions and styles. In this chapter, you will work with a master document and several subdocuments, which are stored in a shared folder so that different parts of the same document can be edited by different people at the same time, and then reassembled into a finished document.

A table of contents, an index, and page numbers assist the reader in finding information in a long document. In this chapter you will insert a table of contents that identifies main document sections and an index that points to specific information in the document. You will insert page numbers that can be updated as the document is changed. You will help the reader navigate the document quickly on the computer or on the Web by electronically marking important text.

Page formatting is important in long documents. You will practice techniques to specify text and titles that should not be separated by page breaks, and you will check the flow of text from one page to the next using advanced print preview features.

# Project 9A **Employment**

Long documents can be divided so that two or more people can work on different portions of the document independently. When the document is complete, all of the document portions can be tied together as a single document, using common features such as indexes and tables of contents.

In Activities 9.1 through 9.5, you will create a master document with three subdocuments. The finished document will be a set of job descriptions for administrative support positions in the City of Desert Park. Your completed document will look similar to Figure 9.1. You will save your document as *9A_Employment_Firstname_Lastname*.

### City of Desert Park

#### Administrative Support Positions

The City of Desert Park accepts applications for administrative support positions by mail, via the Internet, and in person. To request an application by mail, call the automated employment hotline at 626-555-0133 or send an email including your name and address to the City employment office. Applications are available online at the City's Web site and can also be picked up at the City Hall employment office.

#### Application Tips:

- Carefully review the requirements of the position for which you are applying to be sure you have the necessary skills and experience.
- If there is an application deadline for a particular job, be sure your application is received in time.
- Be sure to complete the entire application. Incomplete applications may not be processed.
- You may submit a resume with your application, but the application must still be thoroughly completed.

---

### Accounting Specialist

#### Highlights

- Excellent position for those who like to calculate and work with numbers
- Wages range from minimum wage to $13.75 per hour
- Uses spreadsheet and other computer software
- Training is available at a community college

#### Job Description and Work Conditions

Accounting Specialists help the City keep track of money coming in and going out, and they do much of the clerical work related to accounting and bookkeeping. They open mail to look for checks or bills, prepare bank deposits, write bills, receipts or invoices, file and make copies. They record debits and credits and enter data on computers using spreadsheets or specialized accounting software. They perform a wide range of calculations using 10-key calculators. Other tasks include balancing accounts, preparing purchase orders, sales tickets, charge slips and bank deposits, computing interest charges on loans or purchases and checking loans and accounts to be sure payments are up to date. Specialists may follow up with suppliers to check on orders or payments.

---

Benefits for full-time jobs include paid holidays, vacations and sick leave, health and life insurance and retirement plans.

#### Qualifications, Skills and Training

Entry-level Accounting Specialist positions require a high school diploma or GED. High school classes in business math, computers and data entry are useful. Entry-level positions may require six months experience in clerical, cash handling (such as bank teller), or customer service positions. Specialized positions generally require one to two years experience as an Accounting Specialist. Some positions require college courses or an associate degree in business or accounting.

Accounting Specialists must have good math skills and be detail oriented. As with all City employees, Accounting Specialists must be able and willing to comply with City policies and procedures and government regulations. The City also looks for honesty and trustworthiness because Accounting Specialists often handle cash and checks, and may have access to confidential records.

Ability to use a 10-key calculator and accurate data entry skills are essential. Knowledge of spreadsheet and word processing programs are required for these jobs and most positions also require knowledge of computer databases.

1

---

### Data Entry Specialist

#### Highlights

- Excellent position for those with computer skills who want to get started in a business career
- Wages range from minimum wage to $12.00 per hour
- Some limited opportunities for telecommuting
- Often advance to higher-paying jobs with more responsibility

#### Job Description and Work Conditions

Data entry is often used as a stepping stone to other careers that offer higher wages and more responsibilities, such as administrative assistant or accounting specialist. Data Entry Specialists are responsible for entering lists of data into computers using word processing, databases, and spreadsheets. They may also be responsible for editing data already existing in the database. Much of the data that is entered deals with numbers (for example, cancelled checks, financial reports, utility bills, time cards, etc.). The job requires organizational skills and the ability to focus and type with speed and accuracy. Commonly, a typing speed of 45-50 words per minute is desired.

Other duties may include sorting mail, photocopying documents, or compiling information. The ability to communicate effectively through both speaking and writing is very important, therefore

---

often hired and trained for the position. The ability to type with accuracy and speed is important. The ability to focus and handle repetition is also important.

The skills required for data entry (i.e. keyboarding, knowledge of word processing, databases, and spreadsheets) may be gained from a variety of different sources. Vocational programs, high schools, community colleges, business schools, temporary help agencies, books, tapes, or the Internet are all useful sources for becoming efficient in the skills necessary for data entry.

#### Career Advancement and Related Jobs

The City encourages promotion from within based on education, experience, performance, and computer knowledge. Those who continue to get additional education and/or training, and advance their knowledge in the appropriate computer software will be at the highest advantage. With sufficient education and/or training, Data Entry Specialists may advance to a variety of different positions including administrative assistant, supervisor, accounting specialist, dispatcher, etc.

3

---

### Records Specialist

#### Highlights

- Positions available in all City departments
- Wages range from minimum wage to $13.00 per hour
- Good entry-level job because little training is required

#### Job Description and Work Conditions

Working as a Records Specialist can be a very good way to get started in a career in business. Although the position involves responsibility, it requires a minimum of technical skills. Records Specialists are needed in all City departments and are relied upon by a variety of employees.

Records Specialists store and maintain material in several forms including on paper, electronically, on microfilm and microfiche. Files can be stored in traditional file cabinets, mechanized filing systems, on film, or in computerized systems on a network hard drive, floppy disk or CD ROM. They may sort, code and file items alphabetically, numerically, or by subject. They may also scan information to optical disks using imaging systems. Creating new folders or files and assigning ID numbers may be a part of this job.

Records Specialists are responsible for keeping records up-to-date, discarding old records, and checking files to make sure the data is complete and in correct order. Records Specialists may be asked to locate missing materials and resolve discrepancies. Additional tasks for Records Specialists could include word processing, data entry, operating copy, fax, scanners and other business machines, sorting mail and performing other general receptionist or office duties.

Records Specialists sometimes work in a specialized file or records room, and the job requires a combination of independent work and contact with co-workers and/or the public. Records Specialists must be able to work well independently but also have good people skills. Records Specialists may have to bend, stoop, and stand and lift or push from 25 to 50 lbs.

The usual work week is 40 hours, Monday through Friday. Overtime is sometimes required.

#### Qualifications, Skills and Training

The City requires Records Specialists to have a high school diploma or GED. Some entry-level Records Specialists are hired with no experience; more often, the City hires people who have 6 months to a year of experience. A filing test and general clerical skills exam is required to interview for positions. Other key requirements are a good attitude, ability to follow directions, and a willingness to learn.

Accurate typing skills are required, and if an employee has no experience with personal computers or word processing, they may be required to attend training classes. Good

---

handwriting, English, spelling skills, and the ability to quickly read and accurately interpret information are often important. Honesty and trustworthiness are important because Records Specialists need to be able to appropriately handle sensitive and confidential data.

#### Career Advancement and Related Jobs

Records Specialists may advance into other administrative support roles such as data entry specialists, bookkeepers, office machine operators, receptionists and administrative assistants. If remaining in the records department, they may become filing supervisors or trainers.

5

---

**Figure 9.1**
Project 9A—Employment

# Objective 1
## Create a Master Document and Subdocuments

Long documents contain numerous pages and must be organized in a manner so that the reader can easily locate material. Use Word's *master document* feature to manage the numerous pages and parts of a long document. A master document is a Word document that functions as a container for a set of separate files called *subdocuments*.

There are four reasons to organize a long document as a master document and subdocuments. First, it is easier to organize and maintain a long document by dividing it into smaller, more manageable subdocuments. Second, a master document helps you maintain consistent formats and styles across all the subdocuments—especially if different people are working on different subdocuments. Third, a master document lets you assign the writing of various subdocuments to different people with the assurance that Word will be able to bring all the parts back into one large integrated document. Finally, a master document uses Word's outline view so that you can see the overall organization of the document's parts in an easy-to-read outline format.

### Activity 9.1 Creating a Master Document from an Existing Document

In Activity 9.1, you will create a master document by starting with an existing document, and then changing it into a master document by creating subdocuments within it. All the files for master and subdocuments are stored in the same folder. If several individuals are contributing to the development of the document, the folder is commonly stored in a shared location on a network where everyone can access the files in the folder.

**1** **Start** Word. On the Standard toolbar, click the **Open** button.

Navigate to the location where the student files for this textbook are stored. Locate and open **w09A_Employment**. In your storage location, save the file as **9A_Employment_Firstname_Lastname** creating a new folder for this chapter if you want to do so.

**2** On the Standard toolbar, click the **Zoom button arrow** `100%`, and then click **Page Width**. If necessary, on the Standard toolbar, click the **Show/Hide ¶** button to show formatting marks.

**3** To the left of the horizontal scroll bar, click the **Outline View** button.

The document displays in Outline view, and the Outlining toolbar displays. The eight buttons on the right side of the Outlining toolbar are Master Document buttons.

**4** Take a moment to point to each Master Document button on the Outlining toolbar and study the information in the table shown in Figure 9.2.

## Master Document Buttons on the Outlining Toolbar

| Name | Button | Description |
|---|---|---|
| Master Document View | 🖹 | Switches the display to the master document view, from which you can see the subdocument icons. |
| Collapse Subdocuments | 🖹 | Reduces the display of subdocuments to their heading levels. |
| Expand Subdocuments | 🖹 | Displays all of the subheadings and subordinate text for all of the subdocuments. |
| Create Subdocument | 🖹 | Creates a subdocument from the selected text. |
| Remove Subdocument | 🖹 | Removes subdocument status and adds the subdocument text back into the master document. |
| Insert Subdocument | 🖹 | Creates a subdocument in a master document from an existing file. |
| Merge Subdocument | 🖹 | Combines two or more subdocuments into a single subdocument. |
| Split Subdocument | 🖹 | Divides a subdocument into two separate subdocuments. |
| Lock Document | 🖹 | Prevents further editing to a subdocument. |

**Figure 9.2**

**5** Scroll to view the middle of the first page. To the left of the *Accounting Specialist* heading, point to the **Expand** icon 🖸 to display the pointer 🖸, and then click.

The *Accounting Specialist* heading and its subordinate headings and text are selected, as shown in Figure 9.3.

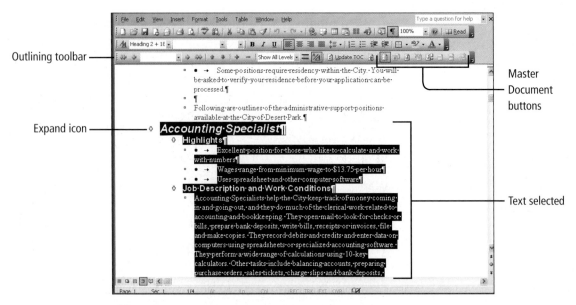

**Figure 9.3**

---

**6** From the Outlining toolbar, click the **Create Subdocument** button .

A Continuous Section Break is added above the *Accounting Specialist* heading and at the end of the selected text. A **section break** is a mark that stores the section formatting information, such as the margins, page orientation, headers and footers, and sequence of page numbers.

A section break mark stores information about the formatting in a section in the same manner that a paragraph mark stores information about the formatting in a paragraph. A **continuous section break** indicates that the section will begin on the same—not on a new—page. Additionally, a light gray box is placed around the subdocument, and a subdocument icon is placed to the left of the first line of the new subdocument. The light gray box is formed with solid lines at the top and bottom of the section and broken lines on the left and right of the section. All of the text that was *not* selected remains as text within the master document. See Figure 9.4.

Master document

Subdocument icon

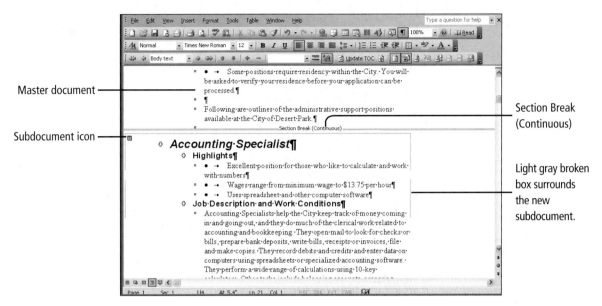

Section Break (Continuous)

Light gray broken box surrounds the new subdocument.

**Figure 9.4**

## Note — Saving and Naming the Subdocument

The file name for the new subdocument is created automatically using the heading text of the subdocument. Thus, in this example, the file name for the new subdocument will be *Accounting Specialist*. Subdocuments cannot be renamed. The new file will also be stored automatically in the same folder as the master document. Recall that all files for master and subdocuments must be stored in one folder.

**7** Scroll down until you can see the *Records Specialist* heading. To the left of *Records Specialist*, click the **Expand** icon.

All of the subordinate headings and text following *Records Specialist* are selected.

**8** From the Outlining toolbar, click the **Create Subdocument** button.

Continuous Section Breaks are added before and after the selected text, and the text is surrounded by a light gray box. Recall that a Continuous Section Break will begin the section on the same—not on a new—page. The subordinate text and headings under *Records Specialist* are designated as a subdocument, which will be created and named *Records Specialist* when the next Save operation is performed on the displayed master document. See Figure 9.5.

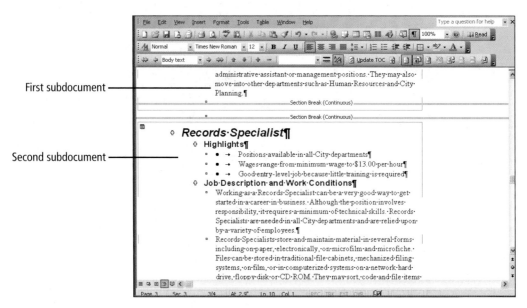

First subdocument

Second subdocument

**Figure 9.5**

**9** On the Standard toolbar, click the **Save** button .

The changes to the master document are saved, and the two new subdocuments are also created and saved. You will be able to open and edit the subdocuments independently of the master document. Any changes made to subdocuments will also be reflected in the master document.

**10** To view the file names of the new subdocuments, from the **File** menu, click **Save As**.

Two new files have been created—**Accounting Specialist** and **Records Specialist**. See Figure 9.6. Recall that the file names are automatically created using the text of the heading in the selected text.

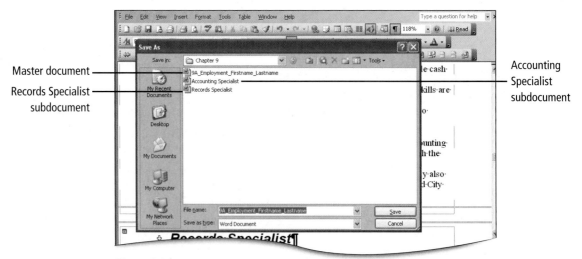

Master document

Records Specialist subdocument

Accounting Specialist subdocument

**Figure 9.6**

**11** In the **Save As** dialog box, click **Cancel**.

**Another Way** ── **To Create a Master Document**

If you are at the very early stages of planning a long document and have no existing document to start with, begin by creating a new Word document in Outline view. Create the outline headings, and then begin writing and inserting the subdocuments as they are written by you, or by others to whom they are assigned. When you create a subdocument, it remains unnamed until you save the master document. After the master document is saved, each subdocument that was created is saved in a separate, related file, using the heading text as the file name.

**Activity 9.2** Expanding and Collapsing Subdocuments

Recall that one advantage of using a master document with subdocuments is to be able to see the overall arrangement of the master document—without the distraction of seeing all the text of each subdocument. The ease with which you can expand (view) or collapse (hide) subdocuments is the reason that you will want to create all of your long and complex documents using this feature. Expand and collapse subdocument headings using the same procedure you used to expand and collapse outline headings.

**1** Press Ctrl + Home to move to the beginning of the master document.

**2** Scroll down until you can see the *Accounting Specialist* subdocument. To the left of *Accounting Specialist*, double-click the **Expand** icon ⬚.

The subdocument is collapsed and displays only its Level 2 heading—*Accounting Specialist*. The subordinate headings and text within the subdocument are hidden from view. Double-clicking the Expand icon on the left of a heading hides all subordinate text and subheadings.

**3** Locate the next subdocument title—*Records Specialist*—and click to position the insertion point anywhere within the title. On the Outlining toolbar, click the **Collapse** button ⬚.

The *Records Specialist* subdocument displays only its Level 2 (title) and Level 3 headings; all the nonheading text is hidden, as indicated by the faint jagged gray lines.

**4** Click to position the insertion point in the subheading that begins *Job Description*. On the Outlining toolbar, click the **Expand** button ⬚.

The nonheading text is displayed for the *Job Description* subheading only. Compare your screen with Figure 9.7.

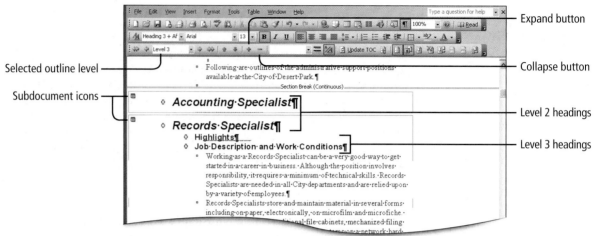

Expand button

Collapse button

Selected outline level

Subdocument icons

Level 2 headings

Level 3 headings

**Figure 9.7**

**5** Click to position the insertion point in the *Records Specialist* subdocument title. On the Outlining toolbar, click the **Collapse** button twice.

Both subdocuments—*Accounting Specialist* and *Records Specialist*— are collapsed to their top-level heading. Without the distraction of all the details of each subdocument, it is easier to get an overall view of the arrangement of this long document. Jagged gray lines below each heading provide a visual indication that some of the text is collapsed (hidden from view).

**6** To the left of the *Accounting Specialist* heading, double-click the **Subdocument icon** .

The *Accounting Specialist* subdocument opens in Print Layout view, as shown in Figure 9.8. Use this procedure to open and view subdocuments or to edit subdocuments while the master document is still open in Outline view.

New name for subdocument visible in title bar

Subdocument is open.

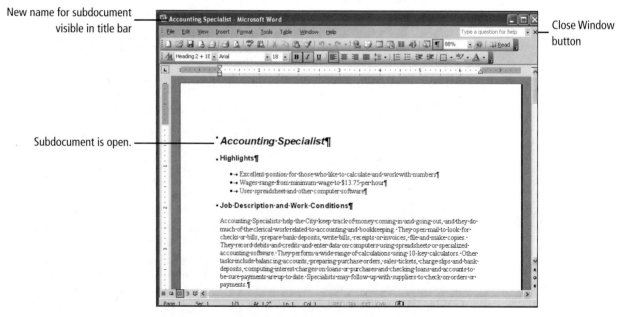

Close Window button

**Figure 9.8**

**7** At the far right of the menu bar, click the small **Close Window** button ⊠.

The *Accounting Specialist* subdocument closes, and the master document redisplays.

**8** On the Standard toolbar, click the **Save** button 🔲.

### Activity 9.3 Inserting an Existing File as a Subdocument

Existing files can be inserted into a master document to become new subdocuments. For example, information about the job title *Data Entry Specialist* has already been created by the City in another Word document. In Activity 9.3, you will insert this Word document as a new subdocument.

**1** Scroll down until you can see the *Accounting Specialist* subdocument.

To the left of *Accounting Specialist*, double-click the **Expand** icon ⬚.

The Accounting Specialist subdocument is fully expanded and selected.

**2** Scroll down to view the bottom of the *Accounting Specialist* subdocument. In the right half of the screen where there is no text, point to the **second Section Break (Continuous) line** between the two subdocuments, and then click to place the insertion point on the line and deselect the text.

The insertion point should be between the light gray boxes surrounding the subdocuments, as shown in Figure 9.9.

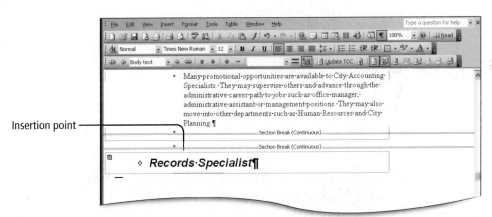

Insertion point

**Figure 9.9**

---

**Alert!**

### Two Special Conditions for Inserting Subdocuments

There are two things to know when inserting new subdocuments. First, you cannot insert a new subdocument between two fully collapsed subdocuments—the subdocument *above* the insertion point must be fully expanded. Second, the insertion point must be directly on the section break line. Otherwise, the new subdocument will be placed *inside* either the upper or lower subdocument. You will know you have successfully inserted a new subdocument if you see its subdocument icon and light gray boundary box. If you are not satisfied with your result, click Undo and begin again.

**3** On the Outlining toolbar, click the **Insert Subdocument** button.

The Insert Subdocument dialog box displays.

**4** Navigate to the location where the student files for this textbook are stored. Locate and select **w09A_Data_Entry**.

**5** At the bottom of the **Insert Subdocument** dialog box, click **Open**. Then, scroll up to view the *Data Entry Specialist* heading and the inserted **Section Break (Next Page)** section break above it as shown in Figure 9.10.

The w09A_Data_Entry file is inserted in the master document at the insertion point, as shown in Figure 9.10. When an existing Word document is inserted into a master document, a Next Page Section Break is inserted before the subdocument, which will begin the inserted section on a new page rather than on the same page.

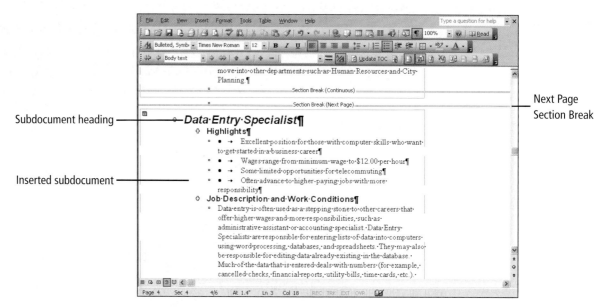

Figure 9.10

---

**Note** — **The Inserted Document May Not Be Fully Expanded**

Sometimes the inserted document is not fully expanded—only the subdocument heading and the last paragraph of the subdocument display. If this happens, place the insertion point anywhere in the new section and, from the Outlining toolbar, click the Expand Subdocuments button.

---

**6** On the Standard toolbar, click the **Save** button.

**7** On the right side of the menu bar, click the **Close Window** button.

**8** **Open** 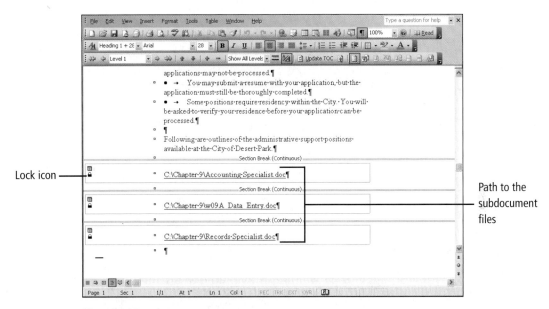 your **9A_Employment_Firstname_Lastname** master document. Scroll down to see the subdocuments.

Instead of displaying the documents, the locations of the subdocument files are displayed as blue hyperlinks, as shown in Figure 9.11. When subdocuments are collapsed in the master document, each subdocument appears as a hyperlink. Additionally, the subdocuments all display a **Lock icon** under the Subdocument icon, which is inserted when you save a master document.

Lock icon ⟶

Path to the
subdocument
files

**Figure 9.11**

---

## More Knowledge — What Is a Locked Subdocument?

When you open a master document, the Lock icon displays next to the link for each subdocument. While a subdocument is locked, no one else can make changes to it. When you expand a subdocument, the subdocument can be edited by those who have permission to do so. The person who creates a master document can specify who can edit different parts of the document and can also lock out others.

---

**9** On the Outlining toolbar, click the **Expand Subdocuments** button.

The subdocuments are fully displayed, and the Locked Document icon is removed. Those who have permission to do so can once again edit the subdocuments.

**10** On the Standard toolbar, click the **Save** button.

There are two ways to edit a subdocument. Regardless of the way you choose to edit, the changes will display in both the master document file and the subdocument file. The first way to edit a subdocument is to do so directly in the master document. Expand the subdocument to view all the headings and text and to make the changes you want. Although you can do this in Outline View, you will find it easier to switch to Print Layout View when editing directly in the master document.

The second way to edit a subdocument is to open it independently of the master document and then make your desired changes.

### Activity 9.4  Editing a Subdocument

If you choose to edit your subdocument directly within the master document, it is easier if you first switch to Print Layout View.

**1** To the left of the horizontal scroll bar, click the **Print Layout View** button 🔲.

**2** Scroll down and locate the first bulleted list in the *Accounting Specialist* section. Click to place the insertion point at the end of the third bulleted point that begins *Uses spreadsheet*. Press (Enter) to insert another bullet.

**3** Type **Training is available at a community college**

Compare your screen with Figure 9.12.

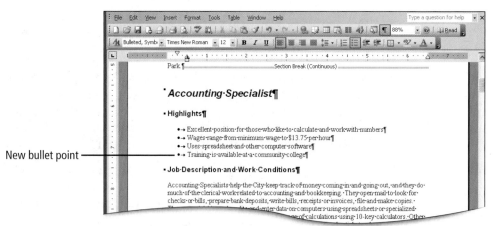

New bullet point ——

**Figure 9.12**

**4** On the Standard toolbar, click the **Save** button 🔲. On the right side of the menu bar, click the **Close Window** button ❌ to close the master document.

**5** On the Standard toolbar, click the **Open** button 📂. Navigate to your chapter folder and open the **Accounting Specialist** subdocument.

**6** Examine the bulleted list near the top of the screen.

Notice that the bullet point you added in the master document has also been added in the subdocument.

**7** Scroll down and locate the paragraph that begins *Two specialty areas*. Double-click to select the word *Two* and type **Three**

Compare your screen with Figure 9.13.

Edited word —

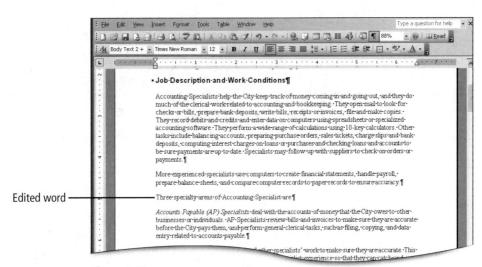

**Figure 9.13**

**8** On the Standard toolbar, click the **Save** button. On the right side of the menu bar, click the **Close Window** button to close the subdocument.

**9** **Open** your **9A_Employment_Firstname_Lastname** master document.

**10** Scroll to the bottom and notice that the three subdocuments are not expanded—only the path to their location is indicated. Switch to **Outline View**, and then on the Outlining toolbar, click the **Expand Subdocuments** button.

**11** Scroll down to the *Accounting Specialist* subdocument. Confirm that the two changes you made in the subdocument are reflected in the master document. Recall that the first change was made directly in the master document, and that the second change was made by opening the subdocument independently of the master document. Editing either way updates both the master and subdocument.

**Activity 9.5** Adding Footers to and Printing a Master Document

One advantage of a master document is that styles and headers and footers that you create in the master document are automatically applied to all of the subdocuments. This helps you maintain consistency of style and format across all the parts of your long document. Another advantage of a master document is that you can print all the subdocuments without opening them individually. You can also print the master document at a specific level; for example, you can print only the headings and subheadings.

**1** Be sure that all subdocuments are fully expanded. Then, scroll as necessary and click in the title *Accounting Specialist*.

**2** From the **File** menu, click **Page Setup**, and then click the **Layout tab**. Under **Section**, click the **Section start arrow**, and from the displayed list, click **New page**. Click **OK**.

Recall that when an existing document is inserted into a master document as a new subdocument, a New Page Section Break is inserted. Changing this section to *New page* will begin it on a new page, in a manner similar to the inserted subdocument *Data Entry*.

**3** Scroll as necessary, and click in the title *Records Specialist*. From the **File** menu, click **Page Setup**, click the **Layout tab**, and then under **Section**, change the **Section start** to **New page**. Click **OK**.

Each job description heading will now begin on a new page.

**4** Press [Ctrl] + [Home], and then to the left of the horizontal scroll bar, switch to **Print Layout View** ⊡. From the **View** menu, click **Header and Footer**. On the Header and Footer toolbar, click the **Switch Between Header and Footer** button ⬚. Click the **Insert AutoText** button [Insert AutoText ▾], click **Filename**, and then click the **Close** button.

**5** From the **Insert** menu, click **Page Numbers**. Be sure that **Position** indicates **Bottom of page (Footer)** and **Alignment** indicates **Right**. Leave the checkbox selected. Click **OK**.

**6** On the Standard toolbar, click the **Save** button ⬛. From the **File** menu, click **Print**, and then under **Page range**, be sure that the **All** option button is selected as shown in Figure 9.14.

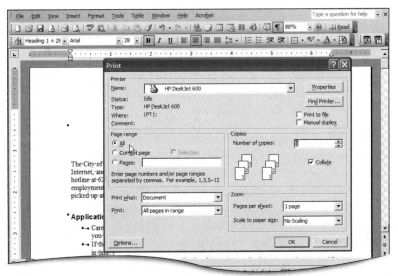

**Figure 9.14**

**7** At the bottom of the **Print** dialog box, click **OK**. Close all documents.

---

## More Knowledge — Converting Subdocuments into Part of the Master Document

You can convert a subdocument back into the text of the master document. Expand and unlock the subdocument that you want to convert, click its subdocument icon, and then on the Outlining toolbar, click Remove Subdocument. Additionally, you can convert *all* of the subdocuments and the accompanying master document text back into one single Word document. You may want to do this if the document is going to be circulated to people who are not connected to the shared folder location, or if the file is going to be uploaded to the Web. Hold down the Shift key while clicking the subdocument icons to select a group of subdocuments, and then on the Outlining toolbar, click Remove Subdocument.

---

**End** You have completed Project 9A

# Project 9B **Job Descriptions**

Word includes features that help the reader find information in a long document. An index points to important words and phrases in the document, and a table of contents (TOC) directs the reader to major document sections.

In Activities 9.6 through 9.11 you will start with a document containing a set of job descriptions for administrative support positions in the City of Desert Park. The file contains a modified version of the information contained in the previous project. Several index entries have been marked. You will create an index at the end of the document, mark additional words and phrases, and then update the index. You will also create and modify a table of contents for the document. Your completed document will look similar to Figure 9.15. You will save your document as *9B_Job_Descriptions_Firstname_Lastname*.

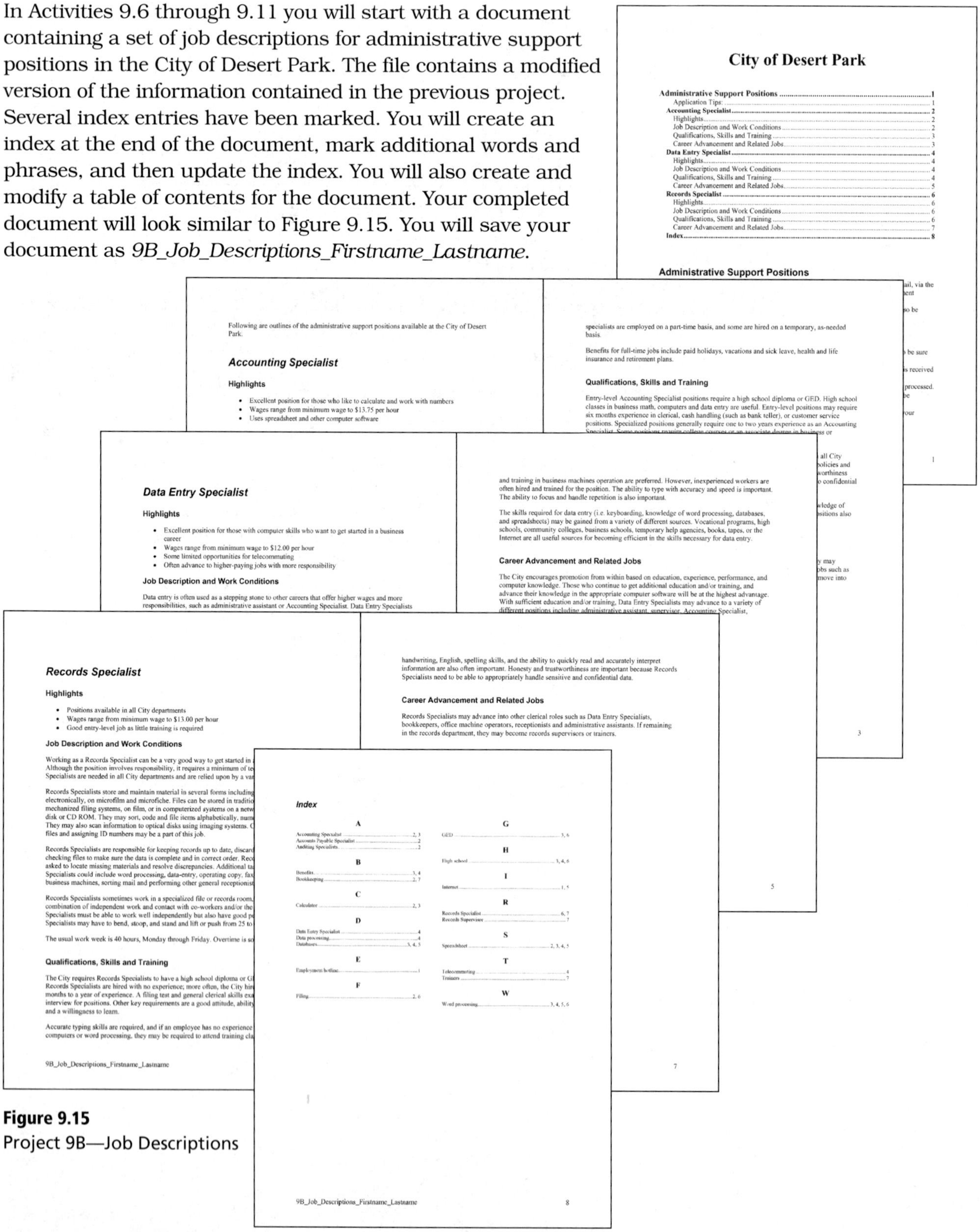

**Figure 9.15**
Project 9B—Job Descriptions

# Objective 3
## Add an Index

An **index** is placed at the end of a document and consists of topics, names, and terms within a document accompanied by the page number on which they can be found. To create an index, you mark the words you want to include in the index as an **index entry**. An index entry marks specific text for inclusion in an index. As you mark new index entries and the document is edited, the index is updated to keep the page numbers shown in the index current.

### Activity 9.6  Creating an Index

After you mark text as an index entry, Word inserts the code **XE (Index Entry)** formatted as hidden text. Then you choose an index design and build the finished index. Word collects the index entries, sorts them alphabetically, references their page numbers, finds and removes duplicate entries from the same page, and displays the index in the document.

**1** **Start** Word. On the Standard toolbar, click the **Open** button. Navigate to the location where the student files for this textbook are stored. Locate and open **w09B_Job_Descriptions**. Save the file as **9B_Job_Descriptions_Firstname_Lastname**

This document does not use the master/subdocument feature. However, the index and table of contents features work the same, whether you are using one long document or a master/subdocument arrangement.

**2** On the Standard toolbar, click the **Zoom button arrow** 100%, and then click **Page Width**.

**3** Be sure that the formatting marks are displayed. If necessary, on the Standard toolbar, click the Show/Hide ¶ button to show formatting marks.

Notice that, in addition to spaces, tabs, and paragraph marks, the index entries are displayed. The format of an index entry is { XE "Internet" }, as shown in Figure 9.16. The brackets and everything inside the brackets define the text and page number for the index entry and are called a **field code**. Inside the brackets, *XE* indicates an **indeX Entry field code**, and the word or phrase inside the quotation marks will appear in the index.

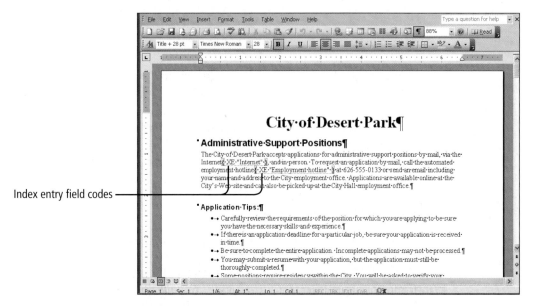

Index entry field codes

**Figure 9.16**

**4** Scroll through the document and examine the other marked index entries.

Notice that a number of words and phrases are marked as index entries. It is easy to choose which words or phrases you want to include in the index.

**5** On the Standard toolbar, click the **Show/Hide ¶** button ![¶] to hide formatting marks to ensure correct page numbers for the index entries.

**Alert!**

## Hide Formatting Marks to Ensure the Correct Page Numbers in an Index

When formatting marks are displayed, the index entries take up about a quarter of a line each. In long documents with a lot of marked index entries, the document with the formatting marks displayed can be several pages longer than the same document with the formatting marks hidden. Thus, when creating or updating the index, hide the formatting marks. Otherwise, page references in the index will be incorrect.

Sometimes, when you click the Show/Hide ¶ button, some or all of the hidden characters are still displayed. If this happens, from the Tools menu, click Options, and then click the View tab. Under *Formatting marks*, deselect the formatting marks that are displayed, and then click OK.

**6** Press ⌈Ctrl⌉ + ⌈End⌉ to place the insertion point at the end of the document. Press ⌈Ctrl⌉ + ⌈Enter⌉ to create a new page.

**7** Type **Index** and press ⌈Enter⌉.

**8** From the **Insert** menu, point to **Reference**, and then click **Index and Tables**. Click the **Index tab**.

The Index and Tables dialog box displays, as shown in Figure 9.17. A preview of the default index style displays under *Print Preview*.

Index tab —

Preview of default index style —

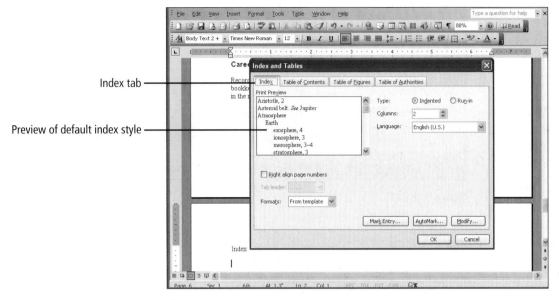

**Figure 9.17**

**9** At the bottom left of the dialog box, click the **Formats arrow**, and then click **Classic**.

The Classic index style is previewed in the Print Preview area.

> ## Note — The Order of Selection Is Important
>
> The layout of the Index and Tables dialog box suggests that you choose alignment options before selecting a format. However, the format type must be selected before you change the number alignment and add tab leaders.

**10** Select the **Right align page numbers** check box.

The Tab leader box becomes active. Recall that a *leader* is a series of dots or other characters that connects related items that are spaced some distance apart, which serves to guide the reader's eye.

**11** Click the **Tab leader arrow**, and then click the series of dots near the top of the list. In the upper right section of the dialog box, be sure that the number of **Columns** is **2**.

Compare your Index and Tables dialog box with Figure 9.18.

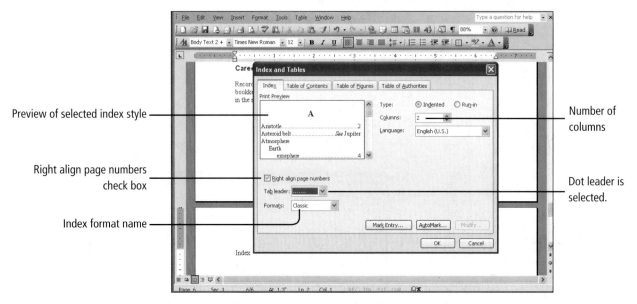

**Figure 9.18**

**12** Click **OK**.

The index is built based on the index entry field codes. The index is actually one large *field*—a set of codes that instructs Word to insert material automatically. This is a two-column index, with the page numbers tabbed to the right side of each column. Dot leaders have been added between the entry and the page number to guide the reader's eye to the page number. Some entries are found on multiple pages. See Figure 9.19.

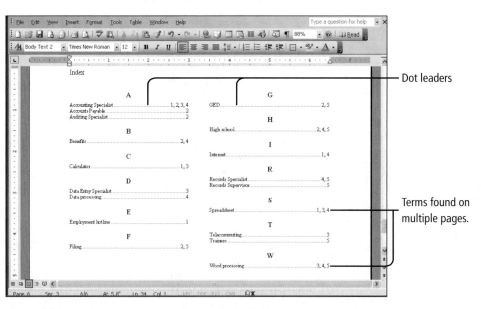

**Figure 9.19**

**13** On the Standard toolbar, click the **Save** button .

### Activity 9.7 Marking Index Entries

Index entries can be marked while you are entering the text or after the document is complete. The index entry inside the brackets can also be changed.

**1** Click the **Show/Hide ¶** button ¶ to show formatting marks, and then press Ctrl + Home to move to the top of the document.

**2** From the **Edit** menu, click **Find**. Alternatively, press Ctrl + F.

The Find and Replace dialog box displays.

**3** In the **Find and Replace** dialog box, click **More**. Be sure that all check boxes are cleared. Click **Less**. Click in the **Find what** box, type **Database** and then click **Find Next**.

The first instance of *database* is highlighted. By typing just the beginning of the word, Word will find all words beginning with those letters, including *database* and *databases*.

**4** Leave the **Find and Replace** dialog box open. Move the pointer over the selected word and double-click.

The entire word *databases* is selected. You do not need to close the Find and Replace dialog box to work in the document.

**5** From the **Insert** menu, point to **Reference**, and then click **Index and Tables**.

The Index and Tables dialog box displays, as shown in Figure 9.20.

Highlighted word ——

Mark Entry button

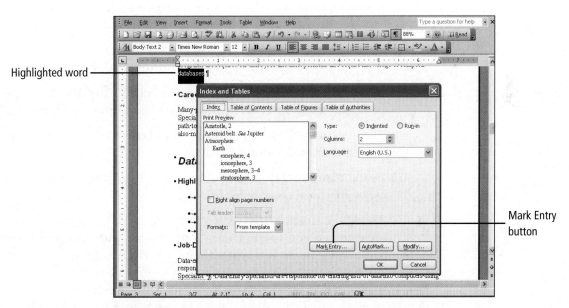

**Figure 9.20**

### Another Way — Using a Concordance File to Build an Index

You can also build an index by using a *concordance* file, which is a list of words to include in an index. Create a two-column table, with the words from the document in the left column and the index entries in the right column. Then, in the Index and Tables dialog box, click the AutoMark button and enter the name of the concordance file.

**6** At the bottom of the **Index and Tables** dialog box, click **Mark Entry**.

The Mark Index Entry dialog box displays. The selected word displays in the Main entry box, as shown in Figure 9.21.

Selected word

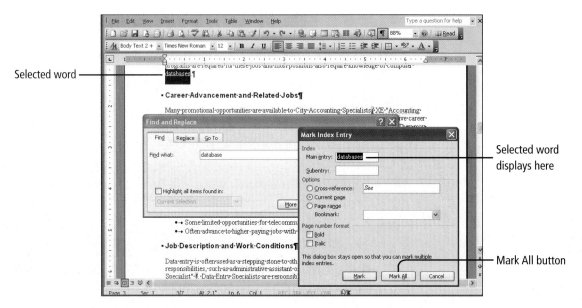

Selected word displays here

Mark All button

**Figure 9.21**

**7** In the **Mark Index Entry** dialog box, in the **Main entry** box, edit to place an initial capital letter to form *Databases*. At the bottom of the **Mark Index Entry** dialog box, click **Mark All**, and then click **Close**.

Each instance of *databases* is marked as an index entry. However, other forms of the word, such as *database*, have not been marked.

**8** In the **Find and Replace** dialog box, click **Find Next** several times until the singular form of the word—*database*—is selected.

The singular form of the word—*database* without the *s*—does not yet have an index entry.

**9** In the **Find and Replace** dialog box, click **Cancel**. Hold down Alt + Shift, and then press X.

The Mark Index Entry dialog box displays. This shortcut is a time-saver when you are marking a document with many index entries. It not only saves you from having to use the menu, which is the purpose of most keyboard shortcuts, but also skips the Index and Tables dialog box. Because this shortcut opens a dialog box, be sure to close any other open dialog boxes before performing the shortcut.

**10** In the **Mark Index Entry** dialog box, in the **Main entry** box, edit to place an initial capital letter and an **s** on the end to form *Databases*. At the bottom of the **Mark Index Entry** dialog box, click **Mark All**, and then click **Close**.

Each instance of *database* is marked as a *Databases* index entry.

**11** Press ⌃Ctrl + ⌃Home to move to the top of the document. From the **Edit** menu, click **Find**. Alternatively, press ⌃Ctrl + ⌃F.

The Find and Replace dialog box displays.

**12** In the **Find what** box, type **bookkeep** and then click **Find Next**.

The first instance of *bookkeeping* is highlighted. By typing just the first few letters, Word will find all words beginning with those letters, including *bookkeeper* and *bookkeepers*, which you will index using the *bookkeeping* entry, in the same way you grouped *database* and *databases* together under one index entry.

**13** In the **Find and Replace** dialog box, click **Cancel**. Double-click *bookkeeping* to select the entire word. Hold down ⌃Alt + ⌃Shift, and then press ⌃X.

The Mark Index Entry dialog box displays.

**14** Under **Index**, in the **Main entry** box, edit to place an initial capital letter to form *Bookkeeping*.

Compare your dialog box with Figure 9.22.

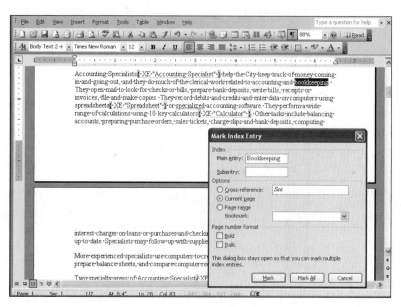

**Figure 9.22**

**15** At the bottom of the **Mark Index Entry** dialog box, click **Mark All**, and then click **Close**.

**16** Using the technique you just practiced, find *bookkeepers* and mark an index entry as *Bookkeeping*.

The index entry does not have to be the same as the selected text. This enables you to index *bookkeeping* and *bookkeepers* using only one index entry.

**17** On the Standard toolbar, click the **Save** button 🖫.

**Activity 9.8** Updating an Index

You must manually update the index when you add new index entries to an existing index.

**1** Click the **Show/Hide ¶** button ¶ to hide the formatting marks and index entries.

Recall that formatting marks and hidden text should not be displayed when you create or update an index, because the space taken up by the index entries can cause incorrect page numbers.

**2** Press Ctrl + End. Scroll up slightly to view the entire index. Click anywhere in the index to select it.

Notice that the index displays in gray, and that *Databases* and *Bookkeeping* are not yet displayed in the index. See Figure 9.23. If your selected index does not display in gray, from the Tools menu, click Options, and then click the View tab. Under Show, click the Field shading arrow, and then click When selected. This displays a gray field background when any field is selected.

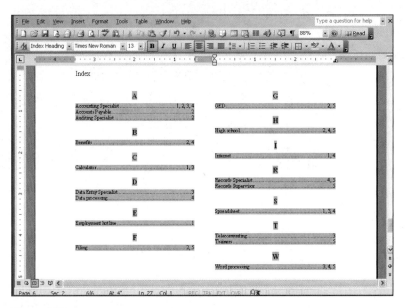

**Figure 9.23**

**3** Right-click anywhere on the index. From the shortcut menu, click **Update Field**. Alternatively, you can select the index and press F9.

Notice that the index displays the *Databases* and *Bookkeeping* entries, as shown in Figure 9.24.

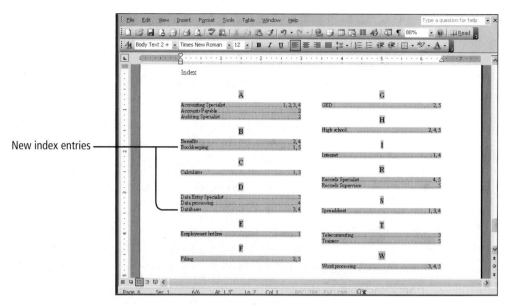

New index entries

**Figure 9.24**

**Alert!**

### Editing Index Entries

When you need to edit an index entry, do so in the bracketed field code in the document—*not* in the index at the end of the document. Although you can edit the text in the index, because it is generated from index field codes, the editing will be lost the next time the index is updated.

**4** Leave the formatting marks hidden. On the Standard toolbar, click the **Save** button .

## Objective 4
## Create a Table of Contents

A *table of contents*, often abbreviated and referred to as a *TOC*, is placed near the beginning of a long document and indicates, in order of appearance, the headings and subheadings of the document and the associated page numbers. A table of contents benefits the reader by providing an overall view of the important topics covered in the document.

### Activity 9.9 Creating a Table of Contents

If you use the default Word heading styles for the main topics and subtopics, creating a table of contents is a simple and automated process.

**1** Move the insertion point to the top of the document. To the left of the horizontal scroll bar, click the **Normal View** button . From the **Tools** menu, click **Options**, and then click the **View tab**.

**2** Under **Outline and Normal options**, click the **Style area width up spin arrow** until the width is set at **0.6"**. Click **OK**.

The paragraph styles display on the left side of the document.

**3** Scroll down and observe the heading styles.

The default table of contents will use the first three heading levels. Notice also that the document title uses the default *Title* style rather than a Heading 1 style. The document title is usually omitted from a TOC.

**4** Press [Ctrl] + [Home], and then press [End] to position the insertion point at the right end of the document title. Press [Enter] twice.

**5** From the **Insert** menu, point to **Reference**, and then click **Index and Tables**. Click the **Table of Contents tab**.

The Index and Tables dialog box displays, with the default table of contents shown under *Print Preview*. See Figure 9.25.

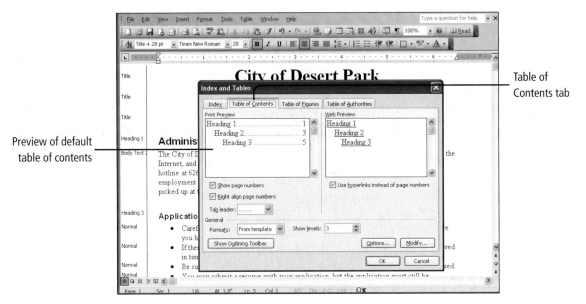

**Figure 9.25**

**6** At the bottom of the **Index and Tables** dialog box, click **OK**.

The default table of contents is built as a single field. Paragraphs formatted with the Heading 1, Heading 2, or Heading 3 style display, along with their corresponding page numbers. *TOC* (table of contents) styles have replaced the corresponding Heading styles.

**7** Move the pointer over the *Records Specialist* entry in the table of contents.

A ScreenTip displays, indicating that the TOC entries are also hyperlinks to the topics in the document. See Figure 9.26. If saved as a Web page, the TOC entries will be hyperlinks formatted in blue and underlined.

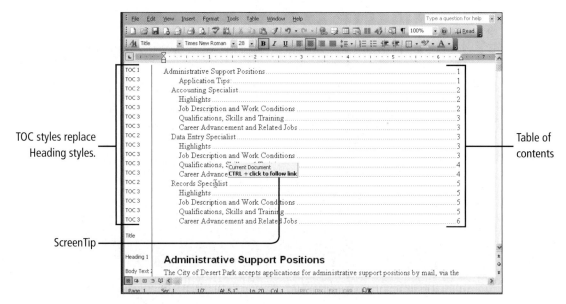

TOC styles replace
Heading styles.

Table of
contents

ScreenTip

**Figure 9.26**

[8] Hold down Ctrl and click the **Records Specialist** entry.

The insertion point moves to page 5, where the related text begins, and is positioned to the left of the *Records Specialist* heading.

[9] Move the insertion point to the top of the document, and then on the Standard toolbar, click the **Save** button.

**Activity 9.10** Customizing a Table of Contents

You can customize different table of contents levels to make the entries stand out. The formatting changes that you make to the TOC do not affect the text in the document.

[1] Scroll so that you can see the entire table of contents. Right-click anywhere on the table of contents, and then from the shortcut menu, click **Edit Field**.

The Field dialog box displays. Here you can edit any field type available in a Word document, including index fields, mail merge fields, and TOC fields.

[2] Click the **Categories arrow**, and then click **Index and Tables**. Under **Field names**, click **TOC**.

A Table of Contents button displays under Field properties. See Figure 9.27.

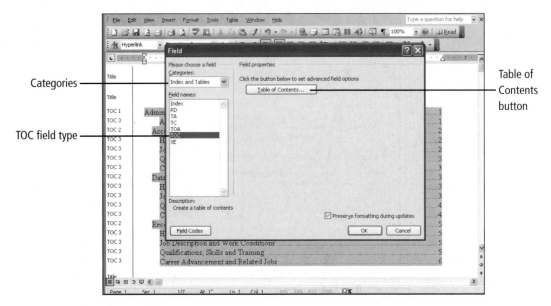

**Figure 9.27**

**3** Under **Field properties**, click the **Table of Contents** button.

The Table of Contents dialog box displays.

**4** At the bottom of the **Table of Contents** dialog box, click **Modify**.

The Style dialog box displays, with nine TOC levels shown. Recall that the TOC levels are linked to the Heading styles—Heading 1 is the same as TOC 1. See Figure 9.28.

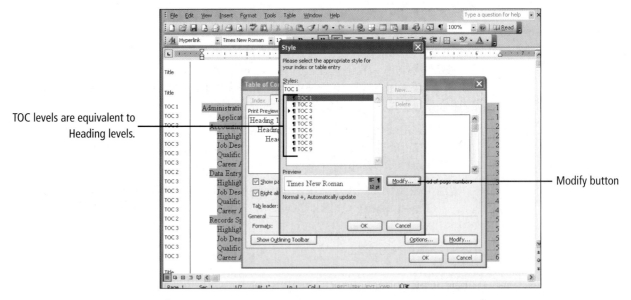

**Figure 9.28**

**5** To the right of the **Preview** box, click **Modify**.

The Modify Style dialog box displays. Notice that under Properties, the Name is *TOC 1*. Any formatting you do will affect only the TOC 1 heading level. See Figure 9.29.

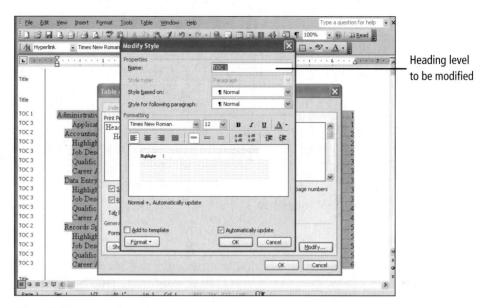

Heading level to be modified

**Figure 9.29**

**6** On the dialog box Formatting toolbar, click the **Bold** button **B**. Click the **Font Size button arrow** 12 ▾, and then click **14**. Click **OK**.

The changes to TOC 1 are recorded, and the Style dialog box displays.

**7** Under **Styles**, click **TOC 2**, and then click **Modify**.

**8** On the dialog box Formatting toolbar, click the **Bold** button **B**. Click **OK** to close the **Modify Style** dialog box. Click **OK** to close the **Style** dialog box.

Examine the Print Preview area of the Table of Contents dialog box. Notice that the formatting for the first two levels has changed, as shown in Figure 9.30.

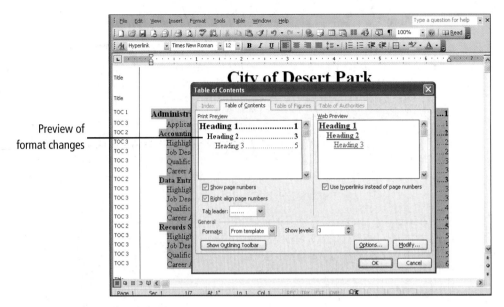

Preview of format changes

**Figure 9.30**

**9** Click **OK** to close the **Table of Contents** dialog box.

A dialog box displays asking whether you want to replace the selected table of contents. This has the same effect as updating the TOC.

**10** Click **OK** to replace the table of contents.

Notice that the formatting has changed for the first two TOC levels—they are formatted in bold. See Figure 9.31.

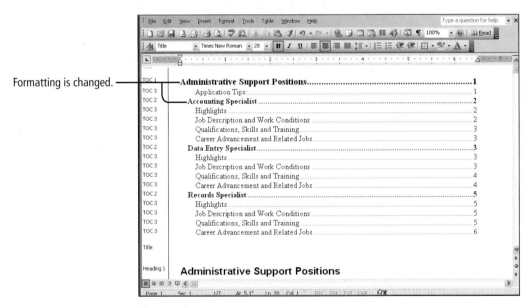

Formatting is changed.

**Figure 9.31**

**11** On the Standard toolbar, click the **Show/Hide ¶** button ¶ to display the formatting marks and field codes.

Notice that tabs with dot leaders are used to display the page numbers on the right side of the page.

**12** On the Standard toolbar, click the **Save** button ⊟.

### Activity 9.11 Updating a Table of Contents

When you edit a document containing a table of contents or an index, as a last step prior to closing the document, be sure to turn off the formatting marks and hidden text and update the TOC field.

**1** On the Standard toolbar, click the **Show/Hide ¶** button ![¶] to hide the formatting marks and field codes.

**2** Move the pointer over the *Data Entry Specialist* entry in the TOC.

A ScreenTip displays, indicating that this is a hyperlink. Also notice that the page number for the Data Entry Specialist entry is *3*.

**3** Hold down Ctrl, and then click **Data Entry Specialist**.

The insertion point moves to page 3, positioned at the beginning of the *Data Entry Specialist* heading.

**4** Press Ctrl + Enter to begin a new page.

The Data Entry Specialist heading is moved to the top of page 4.

**5** Press Ctrl + Home to move to the top of the document, and notice in the TOC that the page number for the *Data Entry Specialist* is still *3*.

**6** Move the pointer over the *Records Specialist* entry in the table of contents. Hold down Ctrl, and then click **Records Specialist**.

**7** Press Ctrl + Enter to move the *Records Specialist* section of the document to a new page.

**8** Scroll down to view the **Index page**. Click on the word *Index*. On the Formatting toolbar, click the **Style box arrow**, and then click **Heading 2**.

The formatting of the Index heading now matches the other Level 2 headings, as shown in Figure 9.32. Notice that in Normal View, the index is displayed in one column; it will, however, print in two columns.

Heading 2 style —

Style applied —

Index displays in one column —

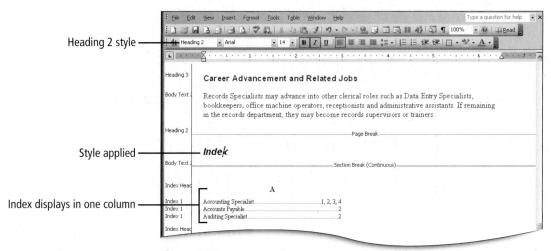

**Figure 9.32**

**9** Move the insertion point to the top of the document, and then scroll down slightly so that you can see the entire TOC.

**10** Right-click anywhere on the TOC. From the shortcut menu, click **Update Field**.

The Update Table of Contents dialog box displays. Here you have the option of updating only the page numbers or updating the entire TOC. In this case, because you added a new heading, you will need to update the entire TOC.

**11** Click the **Update entire table** option button, and then click **OK**.

The page numbers are updated, and the new *Index* Heading 2 entry has been added, as shown in Figure 9.33.

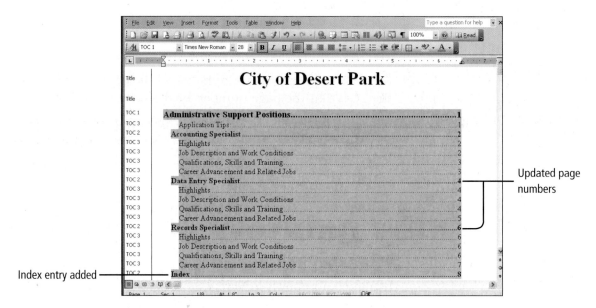

Updated page numbers

Index entry added

**Figure 9.33**

**12** In the Table of Contents, move the pointer over the **Index** entry. Hold down Ctrl, and then click **Index**.

You have made significant changes to the document since the last time the index was updated.

**13** Right-click anywhere on the index. From the shortcut menu, click **Update Field**.

The index page numbers are updated.

## More Knowledge — Updating All Reference Tables and the Index at the Same Time

You can create a *table of figures*, which references figure captions, or a *table of authorities*, which lists legal references. When you have more than one reference table and index in a document, be sure to update each one after the document has been edited. To update all fields at once, press Ctrl + A to select the entire document (alternatively, from the Edit menu, click Select All), and then press F9. You can also right-click anywhere in the document and, from the shortcut menu, click Update Fields. Any dialog boxes—such as the one used for updating the TOC—will be displayed one at a time, until all options are chosen. All of the fields are then updated at once.

**14** From the **Tools** menu, click **Options**, and then click the **View tab**. Under **Outline and Normal options**, click the **Style area width down spin arrow** until the width is set at **0"**. Click **OK**. To the left of the horizontal scroll bar, click the **Print Layout View** button 🔲.

Notice that the index again displays in two columns.

**15** Press Ctrl + Home. From the **View** menu, click **Header and Footer**. On the Header and Footer toolbar, click the **Switch Between Header and Footer** button 🔲. Click the **Insert AutoText** button Insert AutoText ▾, and then click **Filename**.

**16** Press Tab twice. If necessary, from the View menu, click Ruler to display the ruler. On the ruler at the top of the page, locate the right tab mark at **6 inches** and drag it to **6.5 inches**—on top of the gray triangle at the right margin of the document.

**17** On the Header and Footer toolbar, click the **Insert Page Number** button 🔲. On the Header and Footer toolbar, click the **Close** button.

**18** **Save** 🔲 your file, and then from the **File** menu, click **Print**. **Close** the document, and then close Word.

**End** You have completed Project 9B ——

# Project 9C City Jobs

When you are working on long, complex documents, Word provides various formatting techniques to improve the document's appearance and to help the reader navigate the document more easily. You can apply formatting to specific sections of a document. You can adjust paragraphs so that single lines do not appear at the top or bottom of pages, and so that paragraph text remains together on one page—or stays with a topic heading.

In Activities 9.12 through 9.21, you will begin with a set of job descriptions for administrative support positions in the City of Desert Park—a single document that is similar to the document you used earlier in the chapter. You will create section breaks in the text, control the text flow from page to page, and then examine several pages at the same time using Print Preview. You will add tools to improve onscreen document navigation. Finally, you will summarize the document and produce readability statistics. Your completed document will look similar to Figure 9.34. You will save your document as *9C_City_Jobs_Firstname_Lastname*.

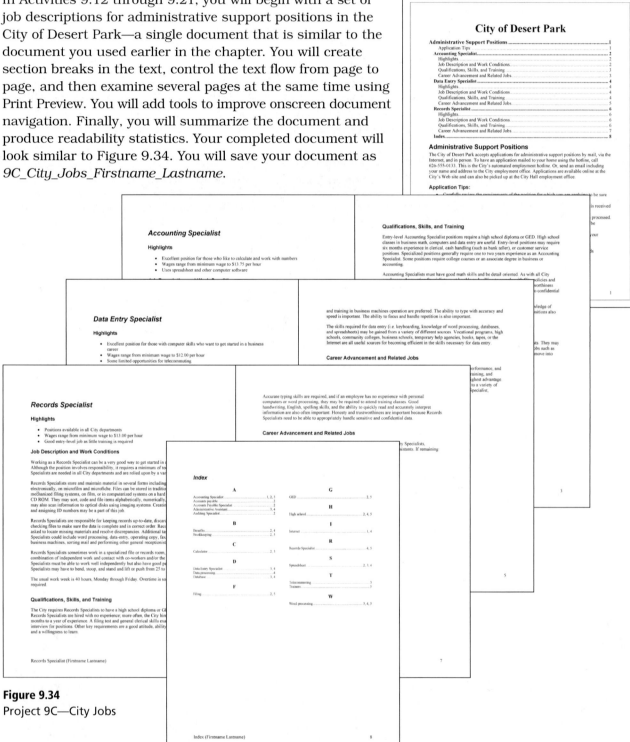

**Figure 9.34**
Project 9C—City Jobs

## Objective 5
## Control the Flow and Formatting of Pages and Text

**Pagination** is the process of dividing a document into pages for printing. As you type in a document, text fills the page from the top margin to the bottom margin. When your insertion point reaches the bottom margin, Word inserts a page break, adds a new page, and moves the insertion point to the top of the new page. This is called an **automatic page break**, also referred to as a **soft page break**. To end a page *before* reaching the bottom margin, insert a **manual page break**, also referred to as a **hard page break**, by holding down the Ctrl key and pressing the Enter key.

Different formatting can be applied to different parts of a document by inserting a **section break**. A **section** is a part of a document that has different formatting from the rest of the document. For example, a section can have different margin settings from those set for the document. The section break mark stores the formatting information for the section.

### Activity 9.12 Inserting Section Breaks

Insert section breaks when you want to apply a different format to a portion of a document. In the following activity, you will create new sections so that you can use different formatting in one section and different footers in each section.

**1** **Start** Word. On the Standard toolbar, click the **Open** button 📁. Navigate to the location where the student files for this textbook are stored. Locate and open **w09C_City_Jobs**. Save the file as **9C_City_Jobs_Firstname_Lastname**

**2** On the Standard toolbar, click the **Zoom button arrow** 100% ▾, and then click **Page Width**. Hide the formatting marks, if necessary, by clicking the **Show/Hide ¶** button ¶ to turn off their display.

**3** Scroll down so that you can see the bottom of page 1 and the top of page 2. Click to position the insertion point at the beginning of the *Accounting Specialist* title.

The information regarding *Accounting Specialist* will be placed in a separate section so that it can have a distinct footer and a different first page format.

**4** From the **Insert** menu, click **Break**.

The Break dialog box displays. Figure 9.35 describes the four section break types.

## Types of Section Breaks

| Type of Section Break | Results |
| --- | --- |
| Next page | Inserts a section break and starts a new section at the top of a new page. |
| Continuous | Inserts a section break and starts a new section on the same page. |
| Odd page | Inserts a section break and starts a new section on the next odd-numbered page. |
| Even page | Inserts a section break and starts a new section on the next even-numbered page. |

**Figure 9.35**

**5** Under **Section break types**, click the **Next page** option button, and then click **OK**. On the Standard toolbar, click the **Show/Hide ¶** button ▣ to show formatting marks.

Notice that *Section Break (Next Page)* displays at the end of the last sentence on page 1, and a new page begins at the insertion point location. Sections are numbered consecutively from the beginning of the document; thus the section you just added is Section 2. The new section number is displayed in the status bar, as shown in Figure 9.36.

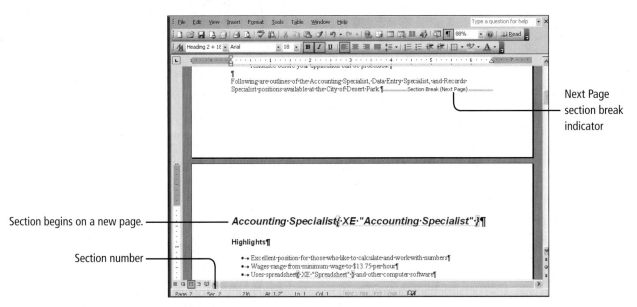

Next Page section break indicator

Section begins on a new page.

Section number

**Figure 9.36**

**6** Scroll down to view the lower half of page 3. Click to position the insertion point at the beginning of the *Data Entry Specialist* title.

On the Standard toolbar, click the **Show/Hide ¶** button ▣ to hide formatting marks.

**7** From the **Insert** menu, click **Break**. Under **Section break types**, click the **Next page** option button, and then click **OK**.

A new section for the Data Entry Specialist information is created, and the section begins on a new page. This becomes Section 3.

8. Scroll down to the middle of page 5. Click to position the insertion point at the beginning of the *Records Specialist* title. Insert a **Next page** section break.

A new section for the Records Specialist information is created, and the section begins on a new page. As indicated in the status bar, this becomes Section 4.

9. Press Ctrl + End to move to the end of the document. Click anywhere in the index. Examine the section area of the status bar.

In the status bar, notice that the index is labeled *Sec 5*, indicating that a new section was created when the index was created.

10. Scroll up slightly to the *Index* title and click to the left of the word *Index*. Examine the section area of the status bar.

When you began adding section breaks, all of the text in the document except the index was in Section 1. Notice that the Index title is labeled *Sec 4*, indicating that the title is part of the original document section, not part of the *Index* section.

11. From the **Insert** menu, click **Break**. Under **Break types**, click the **Next page** option button, and then click **OK**.

A new section is created for the index information, and the section begins on a new page. Additionally, the *Index* title is now in Section 5, as shown in Figure 9.37.

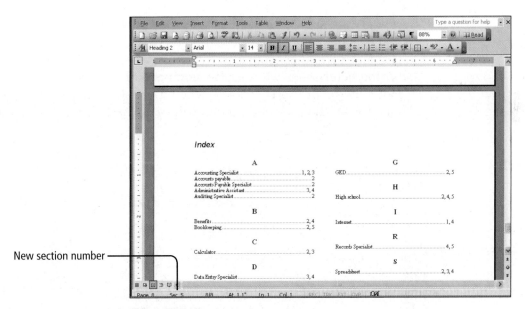

New section number

**Figure 9.37**

12. Click anywhere in the index. Examine the section area of the status bar.

Notice that the index entries are in Section 6.

13. On the Standard toolbar, click the **Save** button.

## Note

A section break controls the section formatting of the text that comes *before* it. For example, if you delete a section break, the preceding text becomes part of the following section and assumes its section formatting. The last paragraph mark in the document controls the section formatting of the last section in the document—or of the entire document if it does not contain sections.

### Activity 9.13 Applying Different Formats for Document Sections

Recall that the purpose of creating a section is to apply different formats, such as headers and footers or page formatting, to each section.

**1** Press Ctrl + Home to move to the top of the document. From the **View** menu, click **Header and Footer**. On the Header and Footer toolbar, click the **Switch Between Header and Footer** button. Click the **Insert AutoText** button Insert AutoText ▾, and then click **Filename**. On the Header and Footer toolbar, click the **Close** button Close.

The file name is placed in the footer.

**2** Scroll down and click anywhere in page 2, which is the beginning of **Section 2**. From the **View** menu, click **Header and Footer**. On the Header and Footer toolbar, click the **Switch Between Header and Footer** button.

Notice that the Footer section is labeled *Footer -Section 2-* and *Same as Previous* displays on the right side of the footer area. Also, in the Header and Footer toolbar, the *Link to Previous* button is active. This button determines whether the new section will display the same footer as the previous section. When it is active, as it is here, the footer from the previous section will be carried over to this section. See Figure 9.38.

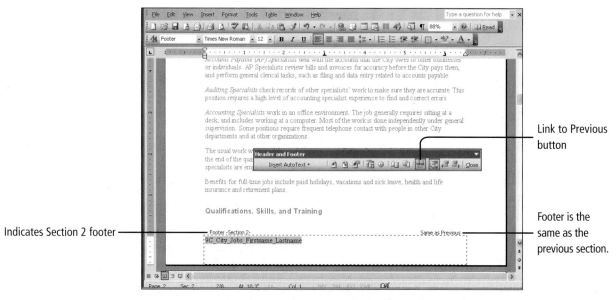

Indicates Section 2 footer

Link to Previous button

Footer is the same as the previous section.

**Figure 9.38**

**3** On the Header and Footer toolbar, click the **Link to Previous** button 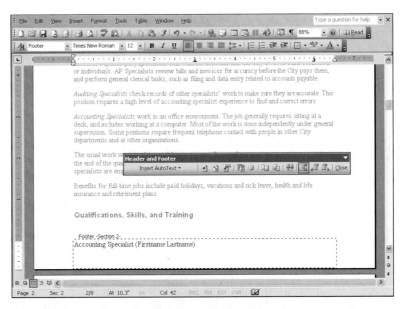 to turn it off.

The *Same as Previous* indicator is removed from the footer area. Now that the link between the footer in Section 1 and the footer in Section 2 is removed, you can type new text into the footer that will display only in this section.

**4** Select the footer text and press ⌜Delete⌝. Using your own name, type **Accounting Specialist (Firstname Lastname)**

Compare your footer with Figure 9.39.

**Figure 9.39**

**5** On the Header and Footer toolbar, click the **Show Previous** button and confirm that the Section 1 footer—the filename—on the first page has not changed. Scroll down to view the footer area on the bottom of page 3 and confirm that the footer displays the new Section 2 footer text—*Accounting Specialist*.

**6** Scroll to the footer at the bottom of page 4 and click to position the insertion point anywhere in the footer area.

Notice that the footer for Section 3 displays the same text— *Accounting Specialist*—as the footer for Section 2.

**7** On the Header and Footer toolbar, click the **Link to Previous** button to turn it off. Select *Accounting Specialist*—but not your name— and then press ⌜Delete⌝. Type **Data Entry Specialist** and leave your name in parentheses following the text.

**8** Scroll to view the Section 4 footer at the bottom of page 6. Click in the footer, remove the link, delete the job title text, and then type **Records Specialist**

Compare your Section 4 footer with Figure 9.40.

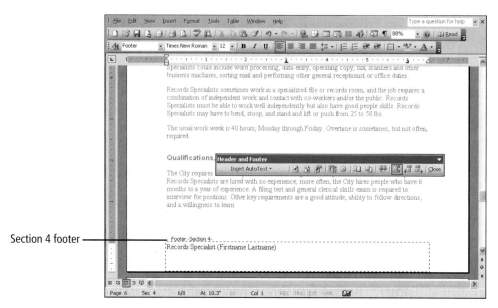

**Figure 9.40**

Section 4 footer

9. Scroll to view the footer at the bottom of page 8. Click in the footer, check to be sure the link is turned off (turn it off if necessary), delete the job title text, leaving your name, and then type **Index**

   New formatting—individualized footers—has been added to each of the sections you created. Recall that the purpose of creating sections is to apply formatting to the section that differs from the formatting of the rest of the document.

10. On the Header and Footer toolbar, click the **Show Previous** button to scroll back through the document. Examine the footers to be sure each section has a different footer. When you are satisfied, on the Header and Footer toolbar, click the **Close** button.

**Alert!** — **Are Some of the Footers Incorrect?**

If the wrong footers display in one or more sections, it is likely that the Link to Previous button on the Header and Footer toolbar was not turned off (deselected). Go back to the first instance of an incorrect footer, click to position the insertion point anywhere in the footer, and then click the Link to Previous button to deselect it (so it does not display in orange). Type the correct footer text and recheck the remainder of the document.

11. Press Ctrl + Home to move to the top of the document. From the **Format** menu, click **Borders and Shading**. In the **Borders and Shading** dialog box, click the **Page Border tab**. Under **Setting**, click the **Box** setting. In the lower right corner, click the **Apply to arrow**, and then click **This section**.

   This will add a border to the first page (Section 1) but will not affect any of the other sections of the document. Compare your Borders and Shading dialog box with Figure 9.41.

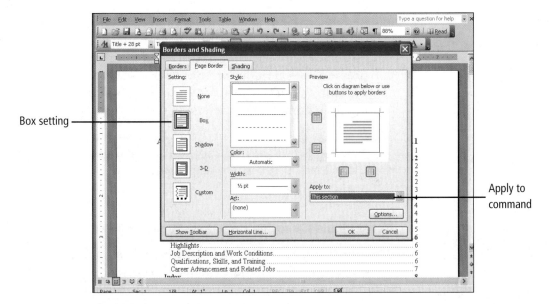

Box setting

Apply to command

**Figure 9.41**

**12** Click **OK**. Scroll to display the bottom of page 1 and the top of page 2. Confirm that the page border displays only in Section 1—the first page.

Compare your document with Figure 9.42.

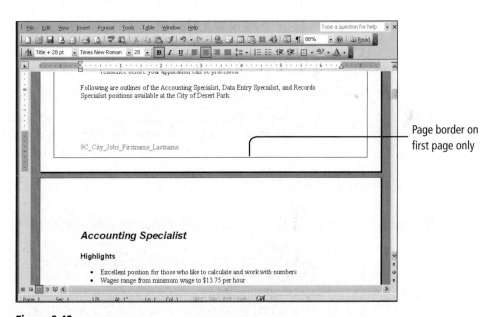

Page border on first page only

**Figure 9.42**

**13** Press Ctrl + Home. From the **Insert** menu, click **Page Numbers**. Be sure the **Position** is **Bottom of page (Footer)** and that **Alignment** is **Right**. Leave the **Show number on first page** check box selected. Click **OK**.

**14** Scroll down and click anywhere in **Section 2**. From the **Insert** menu, display the **Page Numbers** dialog box. Click the **Format** button, and notice that under **Page numbering**, the **Continue from previous section** option button is selected. Click **OK** twice. Click in **Section 3** and repeat to add the page number. Add the page number to all sections *except* the single section for the title *Index*.

**15** Press [Ctrl] + [Home]. Display **Print Preview**, and use the [PageDown] key to view each page and be sure that the pages are numbered correctly. **Close** Print Preview. On the Standard toolbar, click the **Save** button 🖫.

### Activity 9.14 Keeping Paragraphs Together on a Page

Sometimes it is desirable to keep two or more paragraphs together on the same page. For example, to make your document easy for the reader to follow, avoid stranding a heading at the bottom of a page and then beginning its first paragraph on the next page. Setting the **_Keep with next_** feature keeps a selected paragraph, such as a heading, together with its following paragraph.

**1** If necessary, on the Standard toolbar, click the **Show/Hide ¶** button ¶ to hide formatting marks. Press [Ctrl] + [G].

The Find and Replace dialog box displays, with the *Go To* tab active and *Page* selected under *Go to what*.

**2** In the **Enter page number** box, type **3** and then click **Go To**. Click **Close** to close the dialog box.

The insertion point moves to the top of page 3.

**3** Scroll up so you can see the bottom of page 2 and the top of page 3.

Notice that the title *Qualifications, Skills, and Training* is the last line on page 2. With the heading placed on the same page as its first paragraph, the document is easer for the reader to follow and looks more professional.

---

**Alert!**    **Avoid Pressing the Enter Key to Adjust Pagination**

It may be tempting to place the insertion point to the left of text that you want to move to the next page and press [Enter]—inserting blank lines and forcing the text to move down. If the document is complete, this may be OK. However, if the document is going to be edited further, using blank lines to push text down the page can leave large gaps in the document when text is added or deleted earlier in the document.

---

**4** Click to position the insertion point anywhere in the title at the bottom of page 2 that begins *Qualifications*. From the **Format** menu, click **Paragraph**, and then click the **Line and Page Breaks tab**.

The pagination controls display.

**5** Under **Pagination**, click to select the **Keep with next** check box. Click **OK**.

The title moves to the top of the next page and will remain connected to the paragraph that follows, regardless of other additions or deletions of blocks of text. See Figure 9.43. The connection is to the paragraph immediately following the title, so if a new paragraph is inserted just below the title, the title will be connected to the new paragraph.

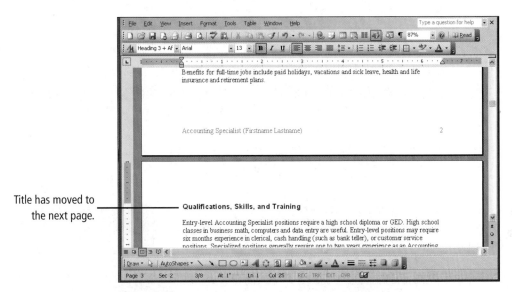

Title has moved to the next page.

**Figure 9.43**

## More Knowledge — Controlling *Widows* and *Orphans*

Widows and orphans are controlled by default in Word. A **widow** occurs when the last line of a paragraph flows onto the top of a new page. An **orphan** occurs when the first line of a paragraph is stranded at the bottom of a page and the remainder of the paragraph flows to the top of a new page. Sometimes, when you import documents created using other programs or open a document created using a previous version of Word, your document will contain widows, orphans, or both. To control for this situation, from the Format menu, click Paragraph, and then click the Line and Page Breaks tab. Under Pagination, select the *Widow/Orphan control* check box.

**6** On the Standard toolbar, click the **Show/Hide ¶** button ¶ to show formatting marks.

Notice that a small square displays to the left of the *Qualifications* title. This indicates that the title will be kept with the following text. The *keep with next* feature can also be used to keep two text paragraphs together—it is not restricted to title text.

**7** On the Standard toolbar, click the **Show/Hide ¶** button ¶ to hide formatting marks. On the Standard toolbar, click the **Save** button.

**Activity 9.15** Viewing Text Flow Using Print Preview

Print Preview is often the most efficient tool to examine the text flow from page to page.

**1** Press [Ctrl] + [Home] to move to the beginning of the document. On the Standard toolbar, click the **Print Preview** button [icon].

A single page displays. If a single page does not display, on the Print Preview toolbar, click the One Page button [icon].

**2** On the Print Preview toolbar, click the **Multiple Pages** button [icon]. From the **Multiple Pages** menu, move the pointer over the third icon in the second row.

Notice that all six icons are selected, and the number of pages is displayed at the bottom of the menu, as shown in Figure 9.44.

Multiple Pages button ——

Number of pages to display ——

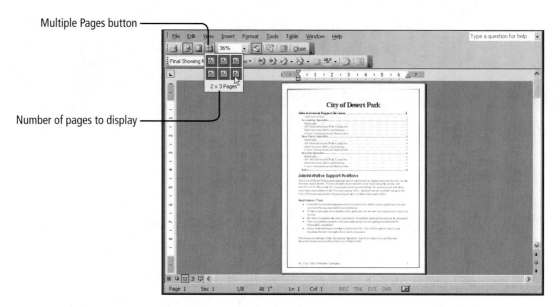

**Figure 9.44**

**3** Click the third button in the second row.

Six small pages are displayed. The text is too small to read, but you can see the titles and amount of space at the bottom of the pages, along with the placement of the footers. Compare your screen with Figure 9.45.

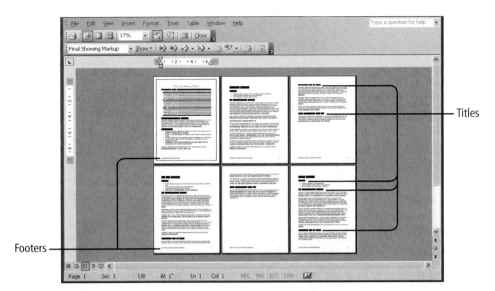

Titles

Footers

**Figure 9.45**

**4** On the Print Preview toolbar, click the **Multiple Pages** button again. From the **Multiple Pages** menu, click the third icon in the first row.

Only three pages display, and you can see much more detail, as shown in Figure 9.46. The fewer pages you show, the more detail you can see.

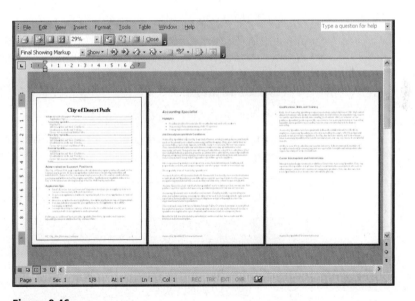

**Figure 9.46**

**5** On the Print Preview toolbar, click the **One Page** button to return to a single page preview. Then, press PageDown and Page Up as necessary to view each page.

**6** On the Print Preview toolbar, click the **Close Preview** button .

## Objective 6
## Navigate Within Long Documents

Long documents designed to be read on a computer screen, such as a Web-based document, can benefit from Word's long document navigation features. This set of features includes **bookmarks**, which identify a location or selection of text that you name and identify for future reference. One way that bookmarks can be accessed is through text links—called **cross-references**—in the document. Cross-references can link to headings, footnotes, endnotes, or captions.

You also can move quickly from one section of the document to another by activating the **document map**, a pane on the side of the screen that displays a linked outline of the document. **Thumbnails** are displayed in the same location as the document map, but rather than text, small icons display. Click on the thumbnail icon to move directly to the page it represents.

### Activity 9.16 Creating Bookmarks

Bookmarks identify the exact location of text, tables, charts, images, or any other objects in a document. You can create as many bookmarks as you want. You can use them to locate a particular part of the document quickly or as the target location of a hyperlink.

**1** Press Ctrl + G, in the **Enter page number** box, type **2** and then click **Go To**. Click **Close**.

The insertion point is positioned at the beginning of the first line—*Accounting Specialist*—of page 2.

**2** On the Standard toolbar, click the **Show/Hide ¶** button ¶ to display formatting marks. Select the title text—*Accounting Specialist*. Do not select the index entry or paragraph mark. From the **Insert** menu, click **Bookmark**.

The Bookmark dialog box displays.

**3** In the **Bookmark** dialog box, in the **Bookmark name** box, type **Accounting_Specialist**

Because spaces are not allowed in bookmarks, be sure you add the underscore between the two words. See Figure 9.47.

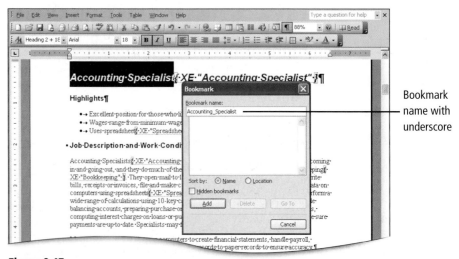

Bookmark name with underscore

**Figure 9.47**

## More Knowledge — Naming Bookmarks

Bookmark names cannot contain a space. If your bookmark title is more than one word, use an underscore to separate the words. If you leave a space in a bookmark name, the Add button at the bottom of the Bookmark dialog box will remain inactive (gray) until you change the name. Colons, dashes, pound signs, and most other special characters are also not allowed.

**4** At the bottom of the **Bookmark** dialog box, click **Add**.

The bookmark is added to a bookmark list, and the Bookmark dialog box closes.

**5** Press Ctrl + PageDown twice to move to the top of page 4. Select the title text—*Data Entry Specialist*.

**6** From the **Insert** menu, click **Bookmark**. In the **Bookmark name** box, type **Data_Entry_Specialist** over the existing text.

Be sure to use underscores between each word.

**7** At the bottom of the **Bookmark** dialog box, click **Add**.

**8** Using the technique you just practiced, go to page 6 and add a bookmark for the title *Records Specialist*.

**9** Press Ctrl + G. Under **Go to what**, click **Bookmark**.

**10** Click the **Enter bookmark name arrow**.

Notice that all three bookmarks display in the bookmark list. Compare your dialog box with Figure 9.48.

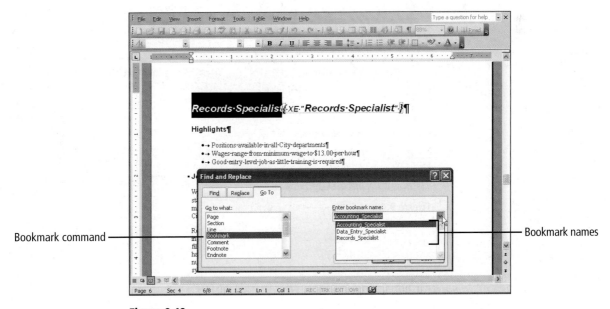

Figure 9.48

**11** Under **Enter bookmark name**, click **Data_Entry_Specialist**. Click **Go To**, and then click **Close**.

The page that begins with the bookmark displays. In a long document, this is a convenient way to quickly move to the page with the information you need.

**12** On the Standard toolbar, click the **Save** button 🖫.

### Activity 9.17 Creating Cross-References

A cross-reference refers to an item that appears in another location in the document, such as a heading, a caption of a figure, a footnote, or a bookmark. A cross-reference functions as an internal hyperlink that enables you to move quickly to specific locations in a document.

**1** Press Ctrl + Home to move to the top of the document. On the Standard toolbar, click the **Show/Hide ¶** button ¶ to hide formatting marks. Scroll down to view the bottom of the first page.

**2** In the sentence that begins *Following are outlines*, select **Accounting Specialist**. From the **Insert** menu, point to **Reference**, and then click **Cross-reference**. In the **Cross-reference** dialog box, click the **Reference type arrow**, and then click **Bookmark**.

The Cross-reference dialog box displays, as shown in Figure 9.49.

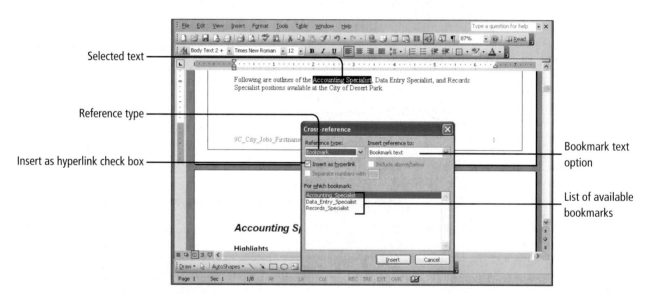

**Figure 9.49**

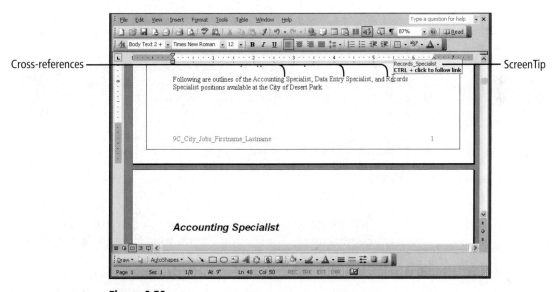

**3** Be sure the **Insert reference to** is **Bookmark text**, and the **Insert as hyperlink** check box is selected. Under **For which bookmark**, click **Accounting_Specialist**, and then click **Insert**. Click **Close**.

The text that you selected when you created the bookmark replaces the existing text. The bookmark text retains some of its formatting, including the font. The font size, however, changes, and italic and bold emphasis is also removed.

**4** Select the **Accounting Specialist** cross-reference text that you just inserted. From the Formatting toolbar, click the **Font Size button arrow** [12 ▾], and then click **12**. From the Formatting toolbar, click the **Font Color button arrow** [A ▾], and then click **Blue**—the sixth color in the second row.

The font of the cross-reference is the same size as the surrounding text, but the color is blue, indicating a hyperlink. Blue was chosen because most hyperlinks are displayed in this color. The color of the cross-reference, however, does not create the hyperlink; creating the cross-reference does.

**5** In this same sentence, and using the technique you just practiced, add **Data Entry Specialist** and **Records Specialist** cross-references. Move your pointer over the **Records Specialist** cross-reference.

A ScreenTip displays with instructions on how to activate the hyperlink. See Figure 9.50.

Cross-references —

ScreenTip

**Figure 9.50**

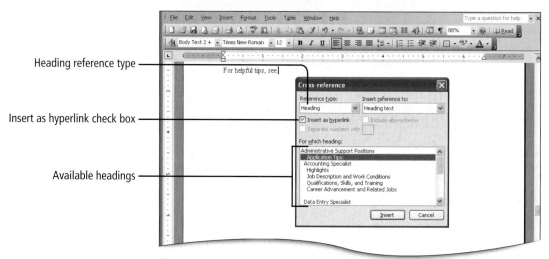

6 Hold down Ctrl, which displays the **Link Select pointer** 🖑, and then click **Records Specialist**.

The Records Specialist page (page 6) displays at the bookmark location.

7 Scroll to the end of the *Records Specialist* section text on page 7. Click to position the insertion point to the right of the period at the end of the paragraph that begins *Records Specialists may advance*. Press Enter.

8 Type **For helpful tips, see** and then press Spacebar.

9 From the **Insert** menu, point to **Reference**, and then click **Cross-reference**.

10 Click the **Reference type arrow** and examine the other reference types that are available. Click **Heading**.

A list of headings used in the document displays.

11 Click **Application Tips**. Be sure the **Insert as hyperlink** check box is selected.

Your Cross-reference dialog box should be similar to Figure 9.51, although a blank line may follow *Application Tips*.

Heading reference type

Insert as hyperlink check box

Available headings

**Figure 9.51**

12 Click **Insert**, and then click **Close** to close the dialog box. Select the inserted text—*Application Tips:*—and from the Formatting toolbar, click the **Font Color** button 🅰▾.

The inserted cross-reference displays as a hyperlink. Recall that changing the font color does not create the hyperlink. It is intended to give a visual cue to the reader.

13 Hold down Ctrl and click the new **Application Tips** cross-reference.

The page containing the Application Tips heading displays.

14 Use the technique you just practiced to add the same message at the end of the *Accounting Specialist* and *Data Entry Specialist* sections.

On the Standard toolbar, click the **Save** button 🔲.

**Activity 9.18** Using the Document Map

The **Document Map** is a separate pane that displays a list of headings in your document. It is useful for quickly navigating through the document and for keeping track of your location in it. When displayed, the document map remains on the screen, regardless of the section of document on which you are working. This is an advantage over using the TOC to move around the document, because the TOC is visible only on one page.

**1** Move the insertion point to the top of the document.

**2** On the Standard toolbar, click the **Document Map** button 📄.

The Document Map pane displays on the left side of the screen. All document headings, based on heading styles, display. Some of the longer headings are too long to view in the pane and appear to be cut off. Small Collapse buttons display to the left of any headings for which there are subheadings, as shown in Figure 9.52.

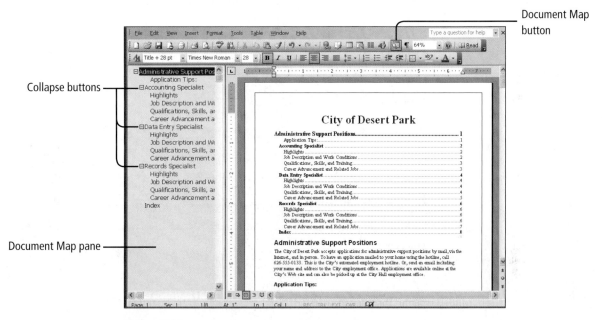

Document Map button

Collapse buttons

Document Map pane

**Figure 9.52**

**3** In the **Document Map** pane, click **Data Entry Specialist**.

The beginning of the *Data Entry Specialist* section displays.

**4** In the **Document Map** pane, under **Data Entry Specialist**, click **Qualifications, Skills, and Training**.

The *Qualifications, Skills, and Training* heading of the *Data Entry Specialist* section displays at the top of the screen.

**5** In the **Document Map** pane, click **Index**.

The page containing the *Index* heading displays.

**6** In the **Document Map** pane, click **Administrative Support Positions**.

The *Administrative Support Positions* heading displays at the top of the screen. Notice that this is not the top of the document, and there is no heading to take you to the top of the document. This is because the title at the top of the document does not use a built-in heading style.

**7** On the Standard toolbar, click the **Save** button 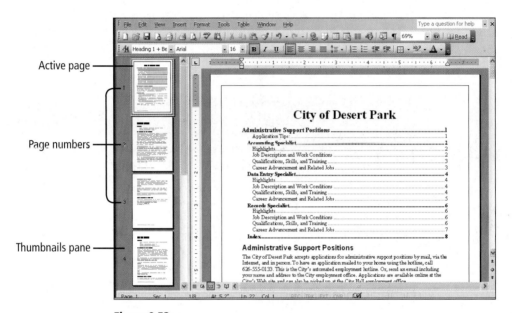.

### Activity 9.19 Using Thumbnails

Thumbnails function in much the same way as the Document Map, but they take you to specific pages instead of headings.

**1** From the **View** menu, click **Thumbnails**.

Page icons replace the Document Map in the pane. The Thumbnails pane is usually narrower than the Document Map pane. The active page is highlighted with a wide outline. Notice that the page numbers display to the left of the page icons, as shown in Figure 9.53.

Active page

Page numbers

Thumbnails pane

**Figure 9.53**

**2** In the **Thumbnails** pane, click the icon for page 3.

The top of page 3 displays.

**3** In the **Thumbnails** pane, use the vertical scroll bar to scroll down to the icon for the last page—page 8—and click it.

The *Index* section displays.

**4** Move the pointer over the thin gray vertical bar between the pane scroll bar and the vertical ruler in the document window.

The pointer changes to a two-sided arrow Resize pointer.

**5** Use the Resize pointer to drag the separator line to the right until two columns of page icons display. If necessary, scroll to the top of the pane.

Page numbers display for the left pages only. The pages are displayed from left to right and from top to bottom, as shown in Figure 9.54. The Thumbnails task pane is very effective for navigating within a long document, especially on larger monitors, where the page icons can be displayed without having to reduce the size of the document display.

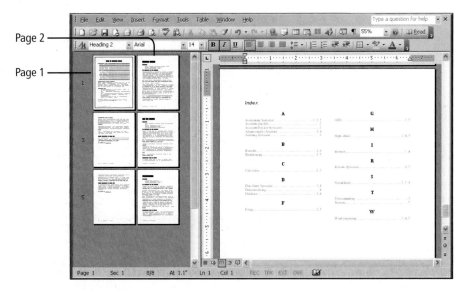

Page 2
Page 1

**Figure 9.54**

**6** From the **View** menu, click **Thumbnails** to close the Thumbnails task pane.

**7** On the Standard toolbar, click the **Save** button 🔲.

## Objective 7
## Use AutoSummarize and Determine Readability Statistics

**AutoSummarize** determines the key points in a document by looking for frequently used words. **Readability statistics** determine how easy it is for someone to read the document based on the average number of syllables per word and words per sentence.

### Activity 9.20 Using AutoSummarize

The AutoSummarize feature is useful not only to highlight important parts of your own document but also to skim quickly through a document you have received from someone else. This tool works best on well-structured documents, such as reports, articles, and scientific papers.

**1** Move the insertion point to the top of the document. From the **Tools** menu, click **AutoSummarize**.

**2** In the displayed **AutoSummarize** dialog box, under **Type of summary**, be sure **Highlight key points** is selected. Under **Length of summary**, click the **Percent of original arrow**, and then click **25%**.

The statistics under *Length of summary* show how many words and sentences are in the document and how many words and sentences will be included in the summary at the chosen *Percent of original*. Compare your dialog box with Figure 9.55.

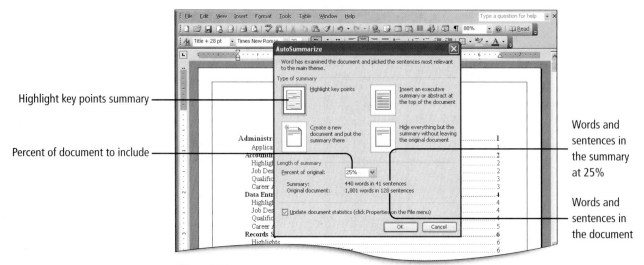

Highlight key points summary

Percent of document to include

Words and sentences in the summary at 25%

Words and sentences in the document

**Figure 9.55**

**3** At the bottom of the **AutoSummarize** dialog box, click **OK**.

The parts of the document that the AutoSummarize tool has determined are most important are highlighted in yellow, and the AutoSummarize toolbar displays.

**4** Scroll through the document and examine the key points that Word identified based on a system of assigning scores to sentences containing frequently used words.

Notice that the TOC and index are not highlighted.

**5** Scroll to display the bottom half of the first page.

Notice that only one sentence in the *Application Tips* bulleted points has been highlighted. See Figure 9.56.

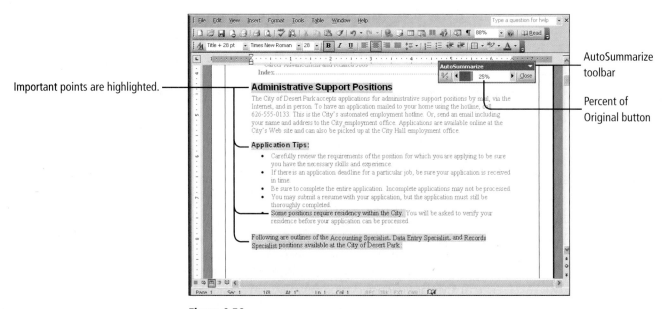

Important points are highlighted.

AutoSummarize toolbar

Percent of Original button

**Figure 9.56**

**6** On the displayed AutoSummarize toolbar, click the **Percent of Original button right arrow** (see Figure 9.56) twice.

The Percent of Original button displays 35%, and a second point in the Application Tips bulleted list is highlighted.

**7** Read through the Application Tips.

Word looks for key words and phrases and other characteristics to determine which points are important. All major headings are highlighted. Also, sentences containing certain key words or phrases are highlighted. Notice that the two highlighted sentences in the bulleted points contain *may not be* and *require*, both of which are strong words or phrases.

**8** From the **File** menu, click **Print**. Under **Page range**, in the **Pages** box, type **1** and click **OK**.

The first page prints. If you are using a black-and-white printer, the background of the highlighted text will print as a shade of gray. If you are using a color printer, the background of the highlighted text is yellow.

**9** On the AutoSummarize toolbar, click the **Close AutoSummarize** button Close .

The AutoSummarize toolbar closes, and the highlighting is removed.

**10** On the Standard toolbar, click the **Save** button.

### Activity 9.21 Reviewing Readability Statistics

Readability statistics are displayed only at the end of a spelling and grammar check.

**1** Move the insertion point to the top of the document. From the **Tools** menu, click **Options**, and then click the **Spelling & Grammar tab**.

**2** Under **Grammar**, select the **Show readability statistics** check box, and then click **OK**.

**3** On the Standard toolbar, click the **Spelling and Grammar** button . Click **Ignore Once**, and keep clicking it until you get a dialog box telling you the spelling and grammar check is complete.

You must perform the spelling and grammar check before the program will display the readability statistics.

**4** Click **OK** to close the dialog box.

The Readability Statistics dialog box displays. This dialog box shows the word, sentence, and paragraph counts and also gives the average number of sentences in each paragraph, the average number of words in each sentence, and the average word length (Characters per Word). Readability indicators are displayed at the bottom of the dialog box. This document is written at a twelfth-grade reading level. See Figure 9.57.

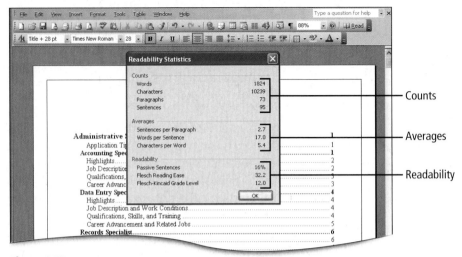

Counts

Averages

Readability

**Figure 9.57**

## More Knowledge — What the Readability Statistics Mean

The two qualitative statistics displayed in the Readability Statistics dialog box are based on the averages displayed in the Averages section. The Flesch Reading Ease score is rated on a scale of 1–100, with a higher score indicating easier reading. The Flesch-Kincaid Grade Level score rates the document based on U.S. grade levels. A 9.0 score means that the document is written at about a ninth-grade reading level. Microsoft suggests that for a standard document, you should aim for a 60–70 on the Flesch Reading Ease score and a Flesch-Kincaid Grade Level score of 7.0–8.0. For more information, look up readability in Help, and click on the *Readability scores* topic.

5 Click **OK** to close the dialog box. From the **Tools** menu, click **Options**, and then click the **Spelling & Grammar tab**.

6 Under **Grammar**, deselect the **Show readability statistics** check box, and then click **OK**.

7 From the **File** menu, click **Print**, and then print the entire document. On the Standard toolbar, click the **Save** button . Close the file.

**End** You have completed Project 9C ——————————————————

# Summary

A special set of Word tools are useful for long documents. These features enable several writers to write collaboratively, help the reader navigate the document, and enable you to summarize and evaluate the text.

A master document coordinates and keeps track of related documents and subdocuments from a single Word file. Subdocuments can be opened and edited independently of the master document, and changes are reflected in the master document. A master document and several subdocuments can be stored in a shared folder; thus, different people simultaneously can edit different parts of the same document and can use common features such as indexes and tables of contents (TOCs). When finished, the document and subdocuments can be assembled into a finished document.

A TOC gives the reader a quick view of the important topics covered in a long document and also provides page numbers for each topic. An index enables the reader to look for key words or phrases in the document and provides the page number where they can be found. You can create an index and format it in one of several styles. As new index entries are marked, the index can be updated to keep the page numbers current.

In this chapter you practiced how to keep text together that should not be separated by page breaks, and you examined page formatting using advanced print preview features. You also created a new page by inserting a section break. You created a new section, which is part of a larger document but can be formatted independently of the rest of the document.

Word offers long document navigation features that include bookmarks, cross-references, a document map, and thumbnails. Bookmarks enable you to move quickly to specific locations in the document. You can also move quickly from one part of a document to another using the document map, a pane on the side of the screen that displays a linked outline of the document. You can click any heading in the document map to move to a section. Thumbnails are displayed in the same location as the document map, but display page icons rather than a text outline. Thumbnails enable you to click a page icon to move quickly to the page.

The AutoSummarize tool analyzes a document, looks for key words and phrases, and then highlights what it determines to be the most important text. Readability statistics are part of the spelling and grammar checker. The program analyzes a document and computes the reading level of the text.

## In This Chapter You Practiced How To

- Create a Master Document and Subdocuments
- Manage a Master Document and Subdocuments
- Add an Index
- Create a Table of Contents
- Control the Flow and Formatting of Pages and Text
- Navigate Within Long Documents
- Use AutoSummarize and Determine Readability Statistics

**Matching**   Match each term in the second column with its correct definition in the first column by writing the letter of the term on the blank line in front of the correct definition.

_____ 1. An alphabetical list of words and phrases in a document, along with the page numbers on which they are found.

_____ 2. A Word document that functions as a container for a set of separate files called subdocuments.

_____ 3. A list placed near the beginning of a long document that indicates, in order of appearance, the headings and subheadings in a document and the page numbers on which they can be found.

_____ 4. Hidden text, displayed in brackets and beginning with *XE*, that indicates an index entry and how it will be displayed.

_____ 5. A portion of a document that can be formatted independently of the rest of the document.

_____ 6. The process of dividing a document into pages for printing.

_____ 7. Formatting marks that divide a document into areas that can use different page formatting and different headers and footers.

_____ 8. A button on the Master Document toolbar that creates, from an existing file, a subdocument in a master document.

_____ 9. The term that describes the result when the last line of a paragraph flows onto the top of a new page.

_____ 10. The term that describes the result when the first line of a paragraph is stranded at the bottom of a page and the remainder of the paragraph flows to the top of a new page.

_____ 11. A Word feature that determines the key points in a document by looking for frequently used words.

_____ 12. A Word feature that determines how easy it is for someone to read the document based on the average number of syllables per word and words per sentence.

_____ 13. A separate Word file linked to a master document.

_____ 14. An internal link in a document to specific locations, such as bookmarks, footnotes, endnotes, captions, or objects.

_____ 15. A separate pane that displays a list of headings in a document and is used to quickly navigate within a document.

**A** AutoSummarize

**B** Cross-reference

**C** Document map

**D** Index

**E** Index entry field code

**F** Insert Subdocument

**G** Master document

**H** Orphan

**I** Pagination

**J** Readability Statistics

**K** Section

**L** Section breaks

**M** Subdocument

**N** Table of contents

**O** Widow

## Fill in the Blank  Write the correct answer in the space provided.

1. A master document helps you maintain consistent _____ and _____ across all the subdocuments.

2. A master document uses Word's _____ view so that you can see the overall organization of the document's parts in an outline format.

3. All files for master and subdocuments must be stored in one _____.

4. An existing file can be inserted into a master document to become a new _____.

5. When you open a master document, the _____ icon displays next to the link for each subdocument.

6. When you edit a subdocument, the changes will display in both the _____ document file and the subdocument file.

7. A table that references figure captions is called a table of _____.

8. A table that lists legal references is called a table of _____.

9. To end a page before reaching the bottom margin, insert a _____ page break.

10. A section break controls the section formatting of the text that comes _____ it.

# Skill Assessments

## Project 9D — Job Seeking

**Objectives:** *Create a Master Document and Subdocuments and Manage a Master Document and Subdocuments.*

In the following Skill Assessment, you will create a master document with subdocuments using information about job opportunities for the City of Desert Park and the surrounding metropolitan area. You also will insert another document as a subdocument. Your completed document will look similar to Figure 9.58. You will save your document as *9D_Job_Seeking_Firstname_Lastname*.

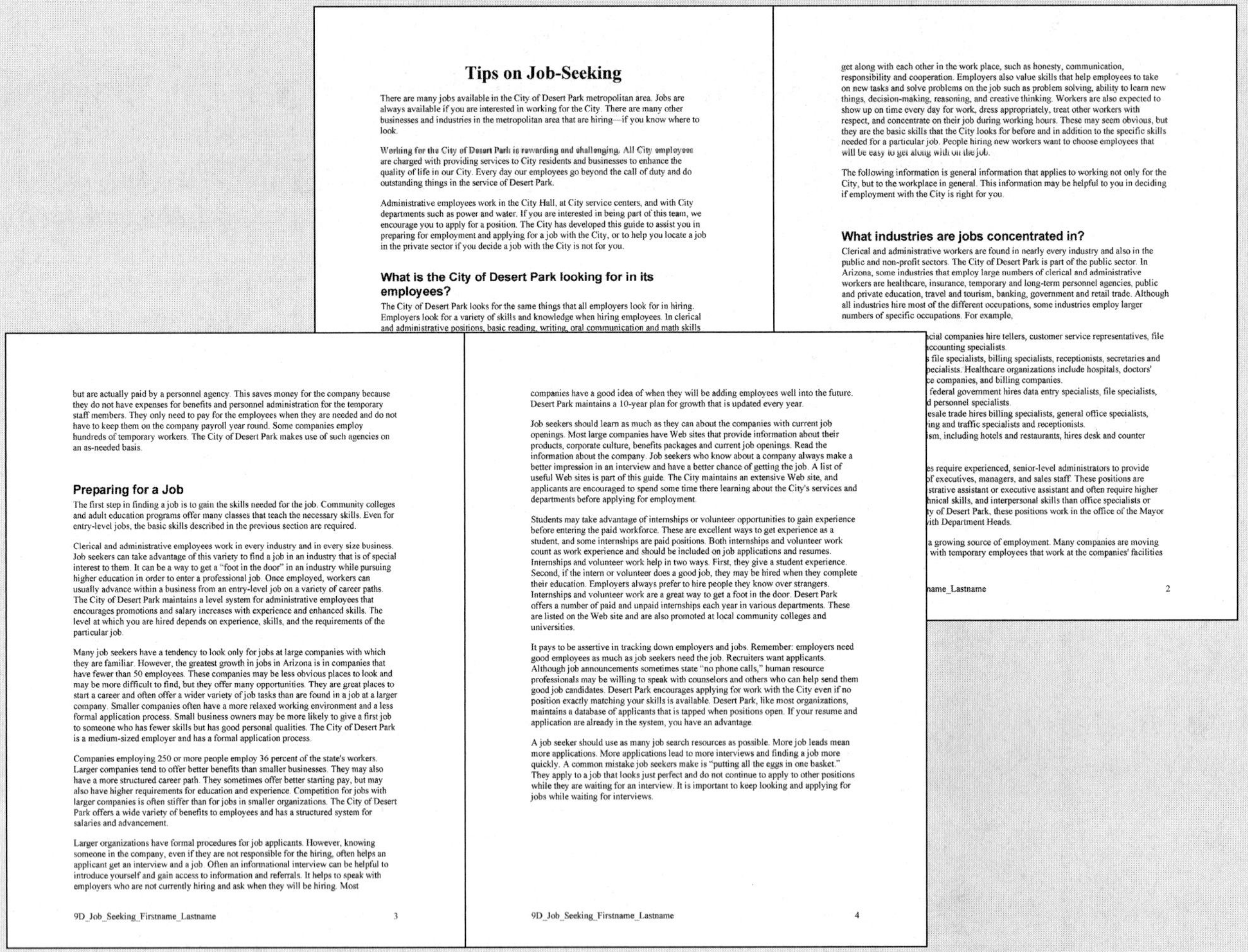

Tips on Job-Seeking

There are many jobs available in the City of Desert Park metropolitan area. Jobs are always available if you are interested in working for the City. There are many other businesses and industries in the metropolitan area that are hiring—if you know where to look.

Working for the City of Desert Park is rewarding and challenging. All City employees are charged with providing services to City residents and businesses to enhance the quality of life in our City. Every day our employees go beyond the call of duty and do outstanding things in the service of Desert Park.

Administrative employees work in the City Hall, at City service centers, and with City departments such as power and water. If you are interested in being part of this team, we encourage you to apply for a position. The City has developed this guide to assist you in preparing for employment and applying for a job with the City, or to help you locate a job in the private sector if you decide a job with the City is not for you.

What is the City of Desert Park looking for in its employees?

The City of Desert Park looks for the same things that all employers look for in hiring. Employers look for a variety of skills and knowledge when hiring employees. In clerical and administrative positions, basic reading, writing, oral communication and math skills

get along with each other in the work place, such as honesty, communication, responsibility and cooperation. Employers also value skills that help employees to take on new tasks and solve problems on the job such as problem solving, ability to learn new things, decision-making, reasoning, and creative thinking. Workers are also expected to show up on time every day for work, dress appropriately, treat other workers with respect, and concentrate on their job during working hours. These may seem obvious, but they are the basic skills that the City looks for before and in addition to the specific skills needed for a particular job. People hiring new workers want to choose employees that will be easy to get along with on the job.

The following information is general information that applies to working not only for the City, but to the workplace in general. This information may be helpful to you in deciding if employment with the City is right for you.

What industries are jobs concentrated in?

Clerical and administrative workers are found in nearly every industry and also in the public and non-profit sectors. The City of Desert Park is part of the public sector. In Arizona, some industries that employ large numbers of clerical and administrative workers are healthcare, insurance, temporary and long-term personnel agencies, public and private education, travel and tourism, banking, government and retail trade. Although all industries hire most of the different occupations, some industries employ larger numbers of specific occupations. For example,

...cial companies hire tellers, customer service representatives, file
...ccounting specialists.
...s file specialists, billing specialists, receptionists, secretaries and
...pecialists. Healthcare organizations include hospitals, doctors'
...ce companies, and billing companies.
... federal government hires data entry specialists, file specialists,
...d personnel specialists.
...esale trade hires billing specialists, general office specialists,
...ing and traffic specialists and receptionists.
...ism, including hotels and restaurants, hires desk and counter

...es require experienced, senior-level administrators to provide
...of executives, managers, and sales staff. These positions are
...strative assistant or executive assistant and often require higher
...hnical skills, and interpersonal skills than office specialists or
...ty of Desert Park, these positions work in the office of the Mayor
...ith Department Heads.

...a growing source of employment. Many companies are moving
... with temporary employees that work at the companies' facilities

...name_Lastname 2

but are actually paid by a personnel agency. This saves money for the company because they do not have expenses for benefits and personnel administration for the temporary staff members. They only need to pay for the employees when they are needed and do not have to keep them on the company payroll year round. Some companies employ hundreds of temporary workers. The City of Desert Park makes use of such agencies on an as-needed basis.

Preparing for a Job

The first step in finding a job is to gain the skills needed for the job. Community colleges and adult education programs offer many classes that teach the necessary skills. Even for entry-level jobs, the basic skills described in the previous section are required.

Clerical and administrative employees work in every industry and in every size business. Job seekers can take advantage of this variety to find a job in an industry that is of special interest to them. It can be a way to get a "foot in the door" in an industry while pursuing higher education in order to enter a professional job. Once employed, workers can usually advance within a business from an entry-level job on a variety of career paths. The City of Desert Park maintains a level system for administrative employees that encourages promotions and salary increases with experience and enhanced skills. The level at which you are hired depends on experience, skills, and the requirements of the particular job.

Many job seekers have a tendency to look only for jobs at large companies with which they are familiar. However, the greatest growth in jobs in Arizona is in companies that have fewer than 50 employees. These companies may be less obvious places to look and may be more difficult to find, but they offer many opportunities. They are great places to start a career and often offer a wider variety of job tasks than are found in a job at a larger company. Smaller companies often have a more relaxed working environment and a less formal application process. Small business owners may be more likely to give a first job to someone who has fewer skills but has good personal qualities. The City of Desert Park is a medium-sized employer and has a formal application process.

Companies employing 250 or more people employ 36 percent of the state's workers. Larger companies tend to offer better benefits than smaller businesses. They may also have a more structured career path. They sometimes offer better starting pay, but may also have higher requirements for education and experience. Competition for jobs with larger companies is often stiffer than for jobs in smaller organizations. The City of Desert Park offers a wide variety of benefits to employees and has a structured system for salaries and advancement.

Larger organizations have formal procedures for job applicants. However, knowing someone in the company, even if they are not responsible for the hiring, often helps an applicant get an interview and a job. Often an informational interview can be helpful to introduce yourself and gain access to information and referrals. It helps to speak with employers who are not currently hiring and ask when they will be hiring. Most

9D_Job_Seeking_Firstname_Lastname 3

companies have a good idea of when they will be adding employees well into the future. Desert Park maintains a 10-year plan for growth that is updated every year.

Job seekers should learn as much as they can about the companies with current job openings. Most large companies have Web sites that provide information about their products, corporate culture, benefits packages and current job openings. Read the information about the company. Job seekers who know about a company always make a better impression in an interview and have a better chance of getting the job. A list of useful Web sites is part of this guide. The City maintains an extensive Web site, and applicants are encouraged to spend some time there learning about the City's services and departments before applying for employment.

Students may take advantage of internships or volunteer opportunities to gain experience before entering the paid workforce. These are excellent ways to get experience as a student, and some internships are paid positions. Both internships and volunteer work count as work experience and should be included on job applications and resumes. Internships and volunteer work help in two ways. First, they give a student experience. Second, if the intern or volunteer does a good job, they may be hired when they complete their education. Employers always prefer to hire people they know over strangers. Internships and volunteer work are a great way to get a foot in the door. Desert Park offers a number of paid and unpaid internships each year in various departments. These are listed on the Web site and are also promoted at local community colleges and universities.

It pays to be assertive in tracking down employers and jobs. Remember: employers need good employees as much as job seekers need the job. Recruiters want applicants. Although job announcements sometimes state "no phone calls," human resource professionals may be willing to speak with counselors and others who can help send them good job candidates. Desert Park encourages applying for work with the City even if no position exactly matching your skills is available. Desert Park, like most organizations, maintains a database of applicants that is tapped when positions open. If your resume and application are already in the system, you have an advantage.

A job seeker should use as many job search resources as possible. More job leads mean more applications. More applications lead to more interviews and finding a job more quickly. A common mistake job seekers make is "putting all the eggs in one basket." They apply to a job that looks just perfect and do not continue to apply to other positions while they are waiting for an interview. It is important to keep looking and applying for jobs while waiting for interviews.

9D_Job_Seeking_Firstname_Lastname 4

**Figure 9.58**

1. **Start** Word. On the Standard toolbar, click the **Open** button. Navigate to the location where the student files for this textbook are stored and open **w09D_Job_Seeking**. Save the file as **9D_Job_Seeking_Firstname_Lastname** in your chapter folder.

**(Project 9D–Job Seeking continues on the next page)**

**(Project 9D**–Job Seeking continued)

2. On the Standard toolbar, click the **Zoom button arrow**, and then click **Page Width**. If necessary, on the Standard toolbar, click the **Show/Hide ¶** button to show formatting marks.

3. To the left of the horizontal scroll bar, click the **Outline View** button. To the left of the heading that begins *What is the City*, click the **Expand** icon once to select the heading and all subordinate text. From the Outlining toolbar, click the **Create Subdocument** button.

4. Scroll down until you can see the *Preparing for a Job* heading. To the left of *Preparing for a Job*, click the **Expand** icon. From the Outlining toolbar, click the **Create Subdocument** button.

5. Press Ctrl + Home to move to the beginning of the document. Scroll down until you can see the subdocument that begins *What is the City*. To the left of the heading, double-click the **Expand** icon to collapse the subdocument.

6. On the next subheading title—*Preparing for a Job*—click to position the insertion point anywhere in the title. On the Outlining toolbar, click the **Collapse** button—another way to collapse the subordinate material under a heading. Notice the subdocument icons to the left of both subheading titles. Recall that by creating a master document with subdocuments, and then collapsing the subdocuments, you can easily view the overall content of your document.

7. Click to position the insertion point in the subheading that begins *What is the City*. On the Outlining toolbar, click the **Expand** button. Scroll down to the second subheading—*Preparing for a Job*. To the left of the *Preparing for a Job* heading, double-click the **Expand** icon. Both subdocuments are fully expanded. On the Standard toolbar, click the **Save** button.

8. Scroll down until you can see the section breaks between the two subdocuments. Click to position the insertion point on the second **Section Break line**. On the Outlining toolbar, click the **Insert Subdocument** button.

9. Navigate to the location where the student files for this textbook are stored. Locate and select **w09D_Job_Concentrations**. At the bottom of the **Insert Subdocument** dialog box, click **Open**. Scroll through the document to examine the subdocuments. Recall that when an existing document is inserted as a subdocument, Word automatically creates a Next Page Section Break.

**(Project 9D**–Job Seeking continues on the next page)

**(Project 9D–Job Seeking continued)**

10. Be sure that all the subdocuments are fully expanded. Then, scroll as necessary and click in the title beginning *What industries*. Display the **Page Setup** dialog box and click the **Layout tab**. Under **Section**, click the **Section start arrow**, and click **Continuous**. Click **OK**. On the Standard toolbar, click the **Save** button. On the right side of the menu bar, click the **Close Window** button.

11. On the Standard toolbar, click the **Open** button. Navigate to your files for this chapter and open your **9D_Job_Seeking_Firstname_Lastname** document.

12. Notice that the subdocuments are referred to by their file names and location. On the Outlining toolbar, click the **Expand Subdocuments** button. To the left of the horizontal scroll bar, click the **Print Layout View** button.

13. Click the **Open** button and navigate to your files. Locate and open **What is the City of Desert Park looking for in its employees**, which is the name of the first subdocument that you created in your master document. In the paragraph beginning *Computer skills*, at the end of the third line, select *every community college* and type **all area community colleges**

14. On the Standard toolbar, click the **Save** button. On the right side of the menu bar, click the **Close Window** button to close the subdocument. In the displayed master document, examine the paragraph you just edited in the subdocument, and confirm that the changes have been made.

15. From the **Insert** menu, click **Page Numbers**. Be sure that **Position** indicates **Bottom of page (Footer)** and **Alignment** indicates **Right**. Leave the check box selected and click **OK**. Press Ctrl + Home. From the **View** menu, click **Header and Footer**. On the Header and Footer toolbar, click the **Switch Between Header and Footer** button. Click the **Insert AutoText** button, and then click **Filename**. On the **Header and Footer** toolbar, click the **Close** button.

16. On the Standard toolbar, click the **Save** button. From the **File** menu, click **Print**. At the bottom of the **Print** dialog box, click **OK**. Close the document, saving any changes.

**End** You have completed Project 9D ─────────────────

## Project 9E—Finding Jobs

**Objectives:** *Control the Flow and Formatting of Pages and Text and Navigate Within Long Documents.*

In the following Skill Assessment, you will use a longer version of the job handout document that you used in Project 9D. You will create section breaks and work with document pagination. You will create bookmarks and then use them as cross-references. Finally, you will preview the document using the multipage print preview feature, and you will use the document map and thumbnails to navigate the document. Your completed document will look similar to Figure 9.59. You will save your document as *9E_Finding_Jobs_Firstname_Lastname*.

1. **Start** Word. On the Standard toolbar, click the **Open** button. Navigate to the student files for this textbook and open **w09E_Finding Jobs**. Save the file as **9E_Finding_Jobs_Firstname_Lastname** in your chapter folder.

2. On the Standard toolbar, click the **Zoom button arrow**, and then click **Page Width**. If necessary, on the Standard toolbar, click the **Show/Hide ¶** button to display formatting marks.

3. Locate the first subheading, which begins *What is the City*, and click to position the insertion point to the left of *What*. From the **Insert** menu, click **Break**. Under **Section break types**, click the **Next page** option button, and then click **OK**.

4. Scroll to the bottom of page 2. Click to position the insertion point at the beginning of the *What industries* subheading. Press F4 to repeat the section break procedure that you used in Step 3.

5. Scroll to the bottom of page 3 and add a section break to move the *Preparing for a job* subheading to the next page. Finally, begin a new section for the *Where to look for a job* subheading. Recall that the purpose of creating sections is to apply formatting to the section that is different from the format of the document.

6. On the Standard toolbar, click the **Save** button. Press Ctrl + Home. From the **View** menu, click **Header and Footer**. On the Header and Footer toolbar, click the **Switch Between Header and Footer** button. Click the **Insert AutoText** button, and then click **Filename**.

7. On the Header and Footer toolbar, click the **Show Next** button to move to the Section 2 footer. Click to place the insertion point anywhere in the footer. On the Header and Footer toolbar, click the **Link to Previous** button to turn off the link. By breaking the link in this manner, the footnote from the previous section will *not* be carried over to this section. Select the footer text and press Delete. Type **What is the City Looking For? (Firstname Lastname)**

**(Project 9E–Finding Jobs continues on the next page)**

**(Project 9E–Finding Jobs continued)**

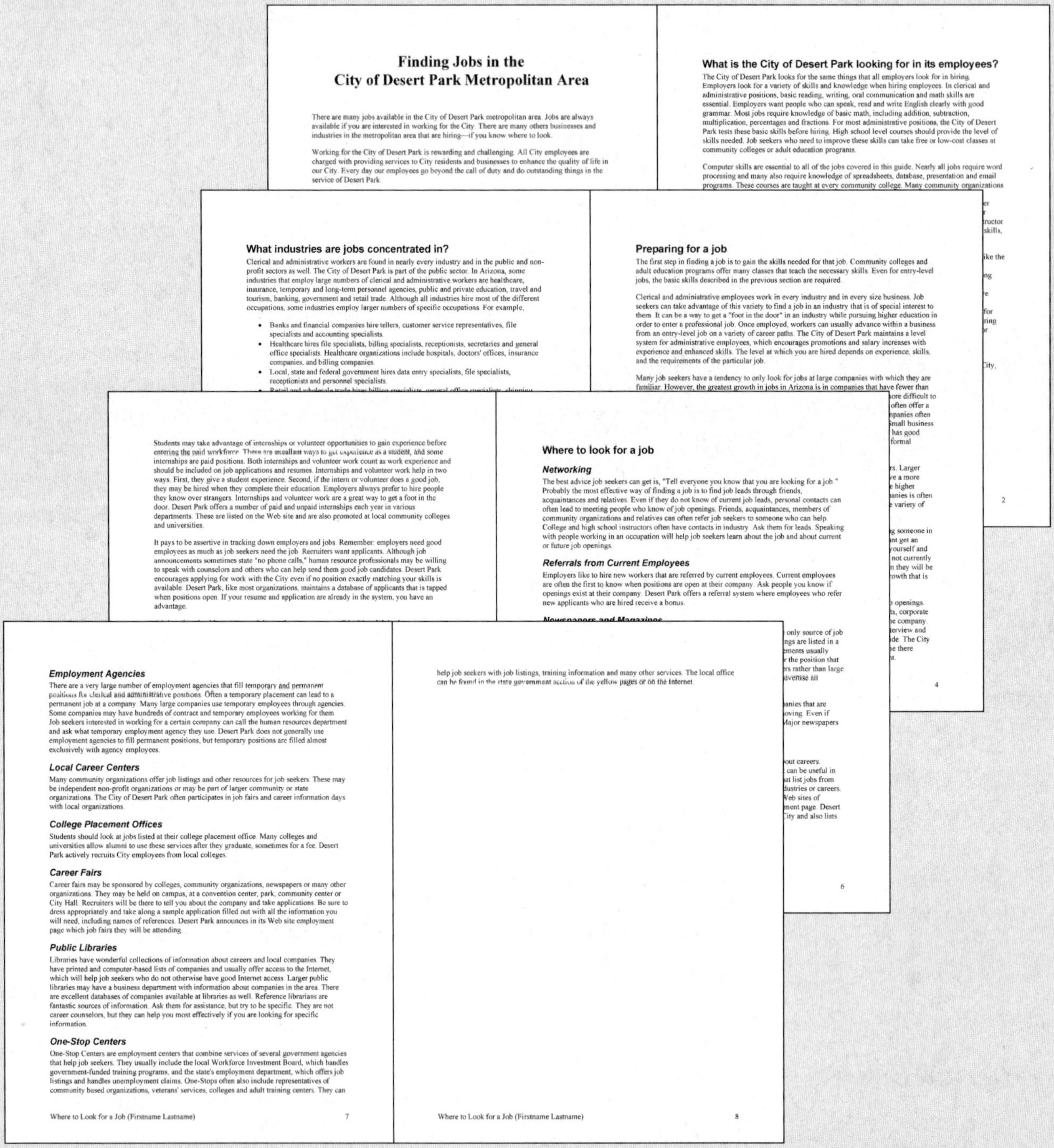

**Figure 9.59**

8. On the Header and Footer toolbar, click the **Show Next** button to move to the Section 3 footer. On the Header and Footer toolbar, click the **Link to Previous** button to turn off the link. This will prevent the previous section's footer from carrying over to this section. Select the text on the left side of the footer (not including your name) and press Delete. Type **What Industries are Jobs Concentrated In?**

**(Project 9E–Finding Jobs continues on the next page)**

**(Project 9E–Finding Jobs continued)**

9. Click **Show Next** to move to the Section 4 footer. Turn off the **Link to Previous** button, delete the footer text (but not your name), and then type **Preparing for a Job** Click **Show Next** to move to the Section 5 footer, break the link, delete the text, and type **Where to Look for a Job**

10. On the Header and Footer toolbar, click the **Close** button. On the Standard toolbar, click the **Save** button. Drag the scroll box on the vertical scroll bar until you can see the bottom of page 6 and the top of page 7. Notice that the subheading *Employment Agencies* is at the bottom of page 6, separated from its accompanying text.

11. Click in the **Employment Agencies** subheading at the bottom of page 6. From the **Format** menu, click **Paragraph**. Click the **Line and Page Breaks tab**. Under **Pagination**, select the **Keep with next** check box, and then click **OK** to keep the subheading and the following paragraph together. Recall that the small black square formatting mark indicates that the *Keep with next* feature has been applied.

12. On the Standard toolbar, click the **Save** button. Move to the top of page 2. Select the subheading text—beginning *What is the City*. Be sure you do not select the paragraph mark at the end of the subheading. From the **Insert** menu, click **Bookmark**. In the **Bookmark name** box, type **Employee_Attributes** At the bottom of the **Bookmark** dialog box, click **Add**.

13. Repeat the technique you just practiced to add bookmarks to the other three sections of the document. Name Section 3 **Jobs_by_Industry** and name Section 4 **Job_Preparation** and name Section 5 **Where_to_Look**

14. On the Standard toolbar, click the **Save** button. Press Ctrl + Home to move to the top of the document.

15. In the bulleted list at the end of page 1, select **What the city is looking for**. Do not select the paragraph mark at the end of the line. From the **Insert** menu, point to **Reference**, and then click **Cross-reference**.

16. Click the **Reference type arrow**, and then click **Bookmark**. Be sure the **Insert reference to** is **Bookmark text**, and the **Insert as hyperlink** check box is selected. Under **For which bookmark**, click **Employee_Attributes**, and then click **Insert**. Click **Close** to close the **Cross-reference** dialog box. The bookmarked heading replaces the text in the bulleted list.

17. Select the cross-reference text that you just inserted. From the Formatting toolbar, click the **Font Color button arrow**, and then click **Blue**—the sixth color in the second row. This will give readers a visual cue that the text is also a link.

18. Use the technique you just practiced to replace the remaining bullet point with a cross-reference, using the bookmarks *Jobs_by_Industry*, *Job_Preparation*, and *Where_to_Look*, respectively.

**(Project 9E–Finding Jobs continues on the next page)**

**(Project 9E–Finding Jobs continued)**

**19.** Hold down Ctrl and in the bulleted list, click **Preparing for a Job** to test the cross-reference. On the Standard toolbar, click the **Save** button. Press Ctrl + Home to move to the beginning of the document. From the **Insert** menu, click **Page Numbers**, be sure the **Position** is **Bottom of page (Footer)** and the **Alignment** is **Right**. Click **OK**.

**20.** Scroll down and click anywhere in Section 2. From the **Insert** menu, display the **Page Numbers** dialog box. Click the **Format** button, and notice that under **Page numbering**, the **Continue from previous section** option button is selected. Click **OK** twice. Click in Section 3 and repeat, and then repeat for all the remaining sections.

**21.** Press Ctrl + Home to move to the beginning of the document. On the Standard toolbar, click the **Print Preview** button. On the Print Preview toolbar, click the **Multiple Pages** button. From the **Multiple Pages** menu, move the pointer over the second icon in the second row to display the first four pages of the document. Examine the flow of text and the footers. On the Print Preview toolbar, click the **Close Preview** button.

**22.** On the Standard toolbar, click the **Document Map** button. In the **Document Map** task pane, click **Preparing for a job**. In the **Document Map** task pane, under *Where to look for a job*, click **Internet**. Try moving to other headings. When you are through, press Ctrl + Home to move to the beginning of the document.

**23.** From the **View** menu, click **Thumbnails**. In the **Thumbnails** task pane, click the icon for page 2. In the **Thumbnails** task pane, use the vertical scroll bar to scroll down to the icon for page 7, and click it. Move the pointer over the vertical bar that separates the Thumbnails task pane from the document window. Use the Resize pointer to drag the separator line to the right until two rows of page icons display.

**24.** From the **View** menu, click **Thumbnails** to close the Thumbnails task pane. On the Standard toolbar, click the **Save** button. From the **File** menu, click **Print**. At the bottom of the **Print** dialog box, click **OK**. Close the document.

**End** You have completed Project 9E

# Project 9F — Job Search

**Objectives:** *Add an Index, Create a Table of Contents, and Use AutoSummarize and Determine Readability Statistics.*

In the following Skill Assessment, you will make the job handout document for the City of Desert Park more user friendly by adding a table of contents and an index. You also will summarize the document and determine its readability level. Your completed document will look similar to Figure 9.60. You will save your document as *9F_Job_Search_Firstname_Lastname*.

1. **Start** Word. On the Standard toolbar, click the **Open** button. Navigate to the student files for this textbook and open **w09F_Job_Search**. Save the file as **9F_Job_Search_Firstname_Lastname** in your chapter folder.

2. On the Standard toolbar, click the **Zoom button arrow**, and then click **Page Width**. On the Standard toolbar, click the **Show/Hide ¶** button to show formatting marks.

3. Scroll through the document, examine the marked index entries, and then on the Standard toolbar, click the **Show/Hide ¶** button to hide formatting marks.

4. Press Ctrl + End to move to the end of the document. Press Ctrl + Enter to create a new page.

5. Type **Index** and press Enter. From the **Insert** menu, point to **Reference**, click **Index and Tables**, and then click the **Index tab**.

6. Click the **Formats arrow**, and then click **Modern**. Select the **Right align page numbers** check box. Click the **Tab leader arrow**, and then click the series of dots at the top of the list. Be sure that the number of columns is **2**. Click **OK**. The marked index entries are placed in the index using the format you selected.

7. On the Standard toolbar, click the **Save** button. Click the **Show/Hide ¶** button to show formatting marks. Press Ctrl + Home to move to the top of the document.

8. From the **Edit** menu, click **Find**. In the **Find what** box, type **Healthcare** and then click **Find Next**. Close the **Find and Replace** dialog box.

9. With the first instance of *healthcare* selected, from the **Insert** menu, point to **Reference**, and then click **Index and Tables**. At the bottom of the **Index and Tables** dialog box, click **Mark Entry**. In the **Mark Index Entry** dialog box, in the **Main entry** box, edit to capitalize *Healthcare*. At the bottom of the **Mark Index Entry** dialog box, click **Mark All**, and then click **Close**.

**(Project 9F–Job Search continues on the next page)**

**(Project 9F–Job Search continued)**

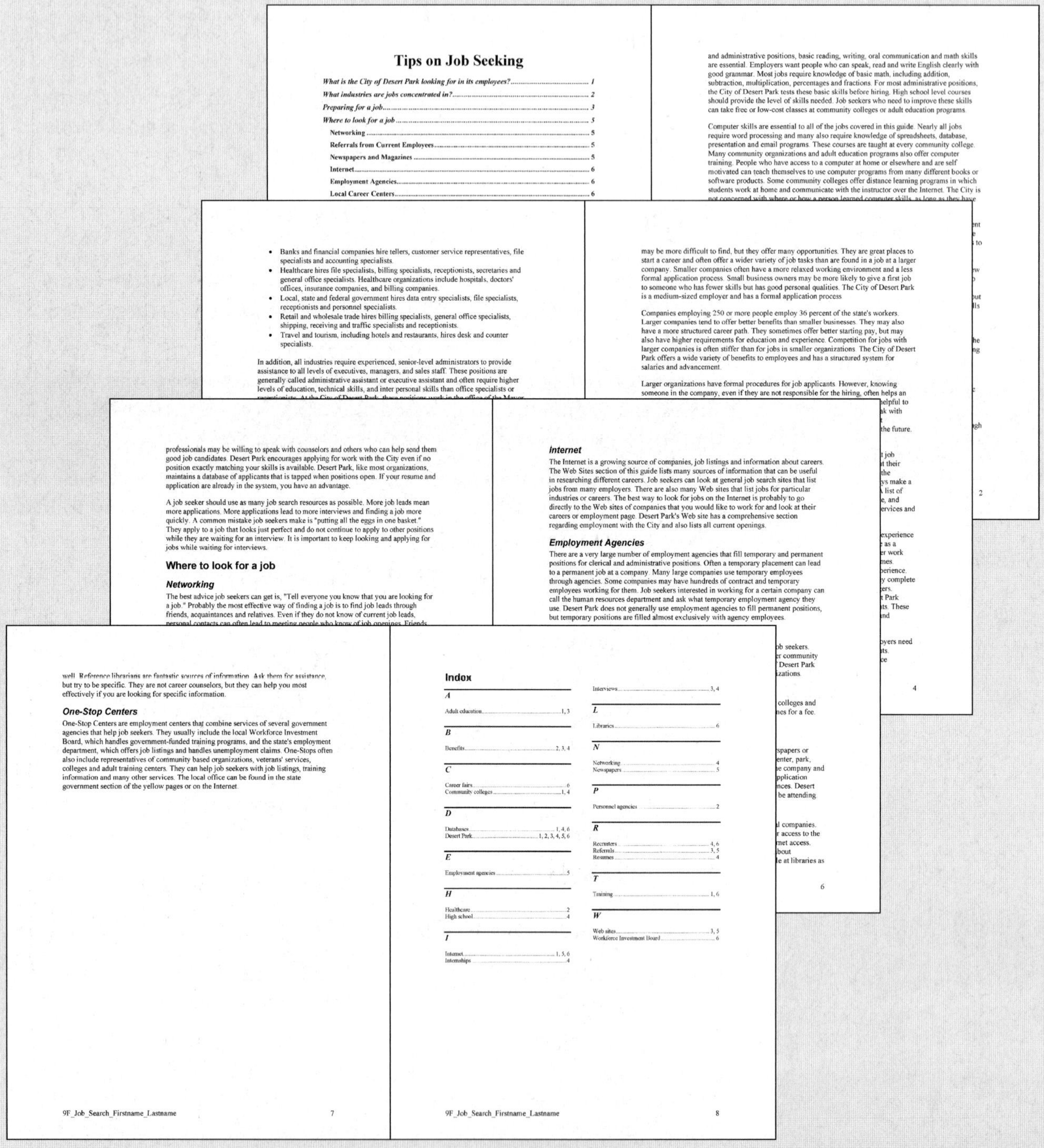

**Figure 9.60**

**10.** From the **Edit** menu, click **Find**. In the **Find what** box, type **high school** and then click **Find Next**. Close the **Find and Replace** dialog box. Hold down [Alt] + [Shift], and then press [X]—an alternative method to display the Mark Entry dialog box.

**(Project 9F–Job Search continues on the next page)**

**(Project 9F–**Job Search continued)

**11.** In the **Mark Index Entry** dialog box, in the **Main entry** box, edit to capitalize *High school*. At the bottom of the **Mark Index Entry** dialog box, click **Mark All**, and then click **Close**. Click the **Show/Hide ¶** button to hide the formatting marks and index entries.

**12.** Press Ctrl + End. Scroll up to display the entire index. Notice your new entries are not yet displayed. Right-click anywhere on the index. From the shortcut menu, click **Update Field**. Check to confirm that *Healthcare* and *High school* have been added to the index.

**13.** Leave the formatting marks hidden. On the Standard toolbar, click the **Save** button. Press Ctrl + Home. Press End to position the insertion point at the right edge of the document title. Press Enter.

**14.** From the **Insert** menu, point to **Reference**, and then click **Index and Tables**. Click the **Table of Contents** tab. Under **General**, click the **Formats arrow**, and then click **Distinctive**. Click the **Tab leader arrow**, and then click the series of dots at the top of the list.

**15.** At the bottom of the dialog box, click **OK**. Move the pointer over the *Employment Agencies* entry in the TOC. Notice the ScreenTip. Hold down Ctrl, and then click the **Employment Agencies** entry to move to that section of the document.

**16.** On the Standard toolbar, click the **Save** button. Press Ctrl + End, and then scroll to view the top of the index page.

**17.** Click to position the insertion point in the *Index* heading. On the left side of the Formatting toolbar, click the **Style button arrow**, and then click **Heading 1** to make the *Index* heading consistent with the other document headings.

**18.** Press Ctrl + Home. Right-click anywhere on the TOC. From the shortcut menu, click **Update Field**. Click the **Update entire table** option button, and then click **OK**. Confirm that *Index* has been added to the table of contents.

**19.** Move the pointer over the *Index* entry in the TOC. Hold down Ctrl, and then click **Index** to confirm that the new TOC entry works properly. Press Ctrl + Home to move to the top of the document.

**20.** From the **View** menu, click **Header and Footer**. On the Header and Footer toolbar, click the **Switch Between Header and Footer** button. Click the **Insert AutoText** button, and then click **Filename**. Press Tab twice. On the **Header and Footer** toolbar, click the **Insert Page Number** button. On the **Header and Footer** toolbar, click the **Close** button.

**21.** On the Standard toolbar, click the **Save** button. From the **File** menu, click **Print**, and then click **OK**.

**(Project 9F–**Job Search continues on the next page)

**(Project 9F**–Job Search continued)

22. From the **Tools** menu, click **AutoSummarize**. Under **Type of summary**, be sure **Highlight key points** is selected. Under **Length of summary**, click the **Percent of original arrow**, and then click **25%**. Click **OK**.

23. Scroll through the document and examine the yellow-highlighted text that Word has identified as important. On the AutoSummarize toolbar, click the **Close** button.

24. From the **Tools** menu, click **Options**, and then click the **Spelling & Grammar tab**. Under **Grammar**, select the **Show readability statistics** check box, and then click **OK**.

25. On the Standard toolbar, click the **Spelling and Grammar** button. Click **Ignore Once**, and keep clicking it until a dialog box displays indicating that the spelling and grammar check is complete. Click **OK** to close the dialog box, leaving the Readability Statistics window displayed.

26. Examine the averages, reading level, and other readability statistics. When you are through, at the bottom of the **Readability Statistics** dialog box, click **OK**. From the **Tools** menu, click **Options**, and then click the **Spelling & Grammar tab**. Under **Grammar**, clear the **Show readability statistics** check box, and then click **OK**. On the Standard toolbar, click the **Save** button. Close the document.

**End** You have completed Project 9F

## Project 9G — Internship Positions

**Objectives:** *Create a Master Document and Subdocuments and Manage a Master Document and Subdocuments.*

In the following Performance Assessment, you will create a master document using Outline view and then insert other documents as subdocuments. The document describes the college internship program for the City of Desert Park. Your completed document will look similar to the one shown in Figure 9.61. You will save your document as *9G_Internship_Positions_Firstname_Lastname.*

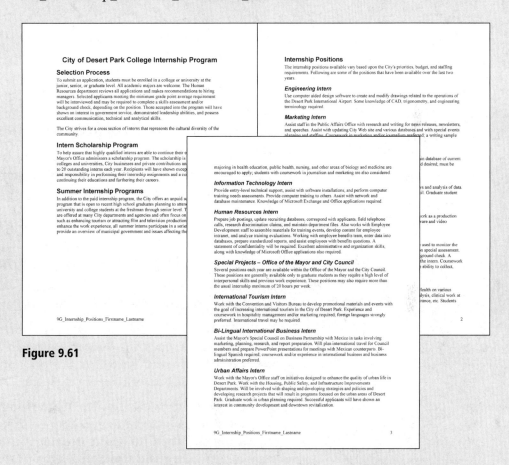

**Figure 9.61**

1. **Start** Word. On the Standard toolbar, click the **New Blank Document** button. Be sure the formatting marks are displayed, and then zoom to **Page Width**. Click the **Outline View** button. Type **City of Desert Park College Internship Program** and press Enter. Save the file as **9G_Internship_Positions_Firstname_Lastname** in your chapter folder.

2. From the Outlining toolbar, click the **Insert Subdocument** button. Locate and open **w09G_Internship_Information**. The file is inserted as a subdocument. A Next Page section break is added at the top of the subdocument, and a Continuous section break is added at the bottom.

**(Project 9G–Internship Positions continues on the next page)**

**(Project 9G–Internship Positions continued)**

3. With the insertion point positioned after the Continuous section break, insert **w09G_List_of_Positions** as a subdocument. Scroll through the list of positions. Click in any of the headings. On the Formatting toolbar, notice that in the Style box, these headings are formatted in the Heading 2 style.

4. Move to the top of the document. In the upper left corner of the first subdocument, click the **Subdocument icon** to select the entire subdocument. On the Outlining toolbar, click the **Remove Subdocument** button to incorporate this text as part of the master document.

5. Following the title of the document, click on the **Next Page section break line** and press Delete. Close the master document, saving your changes.

6. Open the **w09G_List_of_Postions** file. Scroll to locate the information for the *International Tourism Intern*. As the last sentence of this information, type **International travel may be required.** Close the document and save the changes.

7. Open your **9G_Internship_Positions_Firstname_Lastname** master document. Scroll to the end of the document, and notice that the subdocument is reduced to its path name. On the Outlining toolbar, click the **Expand Subdocuments** button. Verify that in the information for the *International Tourism Intern*, the sentence you added to the subdocument has been added to the master document.

8. Press Ctrl + Home and switch to **Print Layout View**. Select the document title, change the **Font Size** to **18**, and **Center** the title.

9. From the **View** menu, click **Header and Footer**. On the Header and Footer toolbar, click the **Switch Between Header and Footer** button. Click the **Insert AutoText** button, and then click **Filename**. On the Header and Footer toolbar, click the **Close** button.

10. From the **Insert** menu, display the **Page Numbers** dialog box, and insert page numbers in the footer, aligned at the right. On the Standard toolbar, click the **Print Preview** button. On the Print Preview toolbar, click the **Multiple Pages** button. From the **Multiple Pages** menu, move the pointer over the third icon in the first row to display the entire document.

11. On the Print Preview toolbar, click the **Close** button. On the Standard toolbar, click the **Show/Hide ¶** button to hide the formatting marks. From the **File** menu, click **Print**. At the bottom of the **Print** dialog box, click **OK**. Close the document, saving any changes.

**End** You have completed Project 9G

# Performance Assessments (continued)

## Project 9H—Internship Program

**Objectives:** *Add an Index, Create a Table of Contents, Navigate Within Long Documents, and Use AutoSummarize and Determine Readability Statistics.*

In the following Performance Assessment, you will work with a modified version of the internship document you used in the previous project. You will add a table of contents and an index to an expanded version of the document. You will also use the document map to navigate the document. Your completed document will look similar to Figure 9.62. You will save your document as *9H_Internship_Program_Firstname_Lastname*.

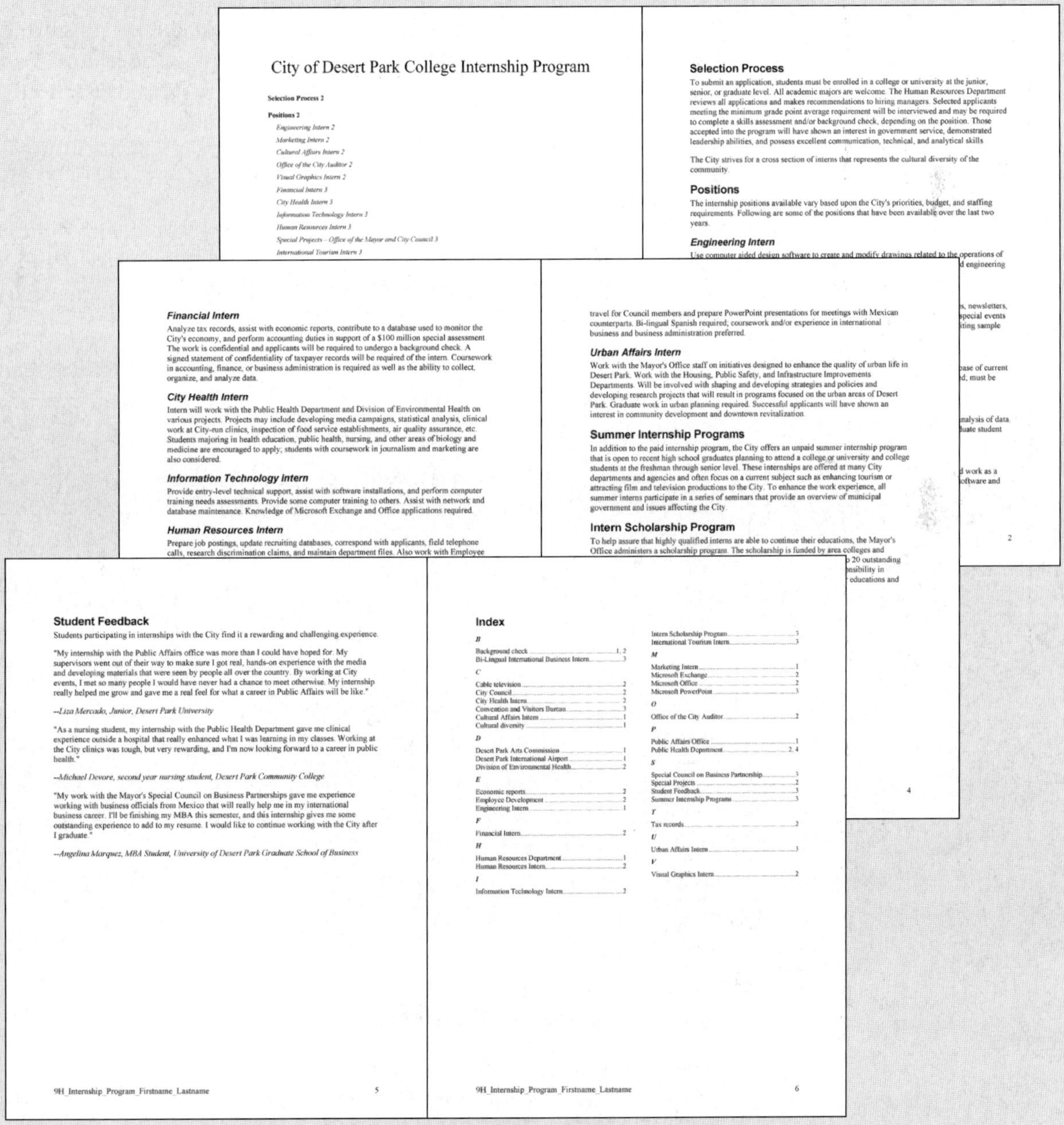

**Figure 9.62**

**(Project 9H–Internship Program continues on the next page)**

**(Project 9H**–Internship Program continued)

1.  **Start** Word, navigate to the location where the student files for this textbook are stored, and then open **w09H_Internship Program**. Save the file as **9H_Internship_Program_Firstname_Lastname** in your chapter folder.

2.  Be sure the formatting marks are displayed, and zoom to **Page Width**. Scroll through the document and examine the marked index entries. When you are through, hide the formatting marks.

3.  Press Ctrl + End to place the insertion point at the end of the document. Press Ctrl + Enter to create a new page.

4.  Type **Index** and then press Enter. From the **Insert** menu, point to **Reference**, and then display the **Index tab** of the **Index and Tables** dialog box. Set the index **Format** to **Formal** and **Right align page numbers**. Set the **Tab leader** to the series of dots at the top of the list. **Save** your work. **Close** the dialog box. The index is created as the last page of the document.

5.  Display the formatting marks and move to the top of the document. From the **Edit** menu, display the **Find** dialog box. In the **Find what** box, type **Background** and then click **Find Next**. Close the dialog box, and then select the text *background check*.

6.  Hold down Alt + Shift, and then press X. In the **Mark Index Entry** dialog box, in the **Main entry** box, edit to capitalize *Background check*. Click **Mark All**, and then **Close** the dialog box.

7.  Move to the top of the document. Display the **Find** dialog box and find **Microsoft Exchange** In this sentence, select the word *Office*, and add it as an index entry. Edit the **Main entry** to read **Microsoft Office** and use the **Mark** command—not the Mark All command. Otherwise, every occurrence of the word *office* mentioned in the document will be indexed as *Microsoft Office*. Close the dialog box.

8.  Find and select *Arts Commission*. Display the **Mark Index Entry** dialog box, change the **Main entry** to **Desert Park Arts Commission** and then click **Mark All**. **Close** the dialog box.

9.  Hide the formatting marks and move to the end of the document. Right-click anywhere on the index, and then from the shortcut menu, click **Update Field**. Check to confirm that your new index entries are now included in the index. **Save** your changes.

10. Press Ctrl + Home. Press End to position the insertion point at the right edge of the document title. Press Enter. Display the **Index and Tables** dialog box and click the **Table of Contents tab**. Set the **Formats** for the TOC to **Simple**. **Close** the dialog box.

11. Move to the *Index* heading on the last page. Click anywhere in the word *Index* and apply the **Heading 1** style to make the *Index* heading consistent with the other document headings.

**(Project 9H**–Internship Program continues on the next page)

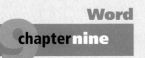
**(Project 9H–Internship Program continued)**

12. Move back to the table of contents, right-click anywhere on the TOC, and **Update Field**. Click the **Update entire table** option button. Notice that *Index* is added to the TOC.

13. Move the pointer over the *Index* entry in the TOC. Hold down Ctrl, and then click **Index** to confirm that the new TOC entry works properly. Press Ctrl + Home to move back to the top of the document.

14. From the **View** menu, click **Header and Footer**. On the Header and Footer toolbar, click the **Switch Between Header and Footer** button. Click the **Insert AutoText** button, and then click **Filename**. Press Tab. On the ruler, move the last tab marker to the **6.5 inch mark**. On the **Header and Footer** toolbar, click the **Insert Page Number** button. On the **Header and Footer** toolbar, click the **Close** button.

15. Navigate to the bottom of page 1, click to the left of *Selection Process*, and then insert a **Next page** section break. Navigate to page 4 and click to the left of *Student Feedback*. Insert a **Next page** section break. Navigate to the bottom of page 2. Click to the left of *Financial Intern*. Display the **Paragraph** dialog box, click the **Line and Page Breaks tab**, and then select the **Keep with next** check box.

16. On the Standard toolbar, click the **Document Map** button. In the **Document Map** task pane, click **Index**. In the **Document Map** task pane, under **Positions**, click **Financial Intern**. Try moving to other headings. When you are through, press Ctrl + Home to move to the beginning of the document. Turn off the document map.

17. On the Standard toolbar, click the **Save** button. From the **File** menu, click **Print**, and then click **OK**.

18. From the **Tools** menu, click **AutoSummarize**. Under **Type of summary**, be sure **Highlight key points** is selected. Under **Length of summary**, click the **Percent of original arrow**, and then click **25%**. Click **OK**.

19. Scroll through the document and examine the text that Word identified as important. On the AutoSummarize toolbar, click the **Close** button.

20. From the **Tools** menu, click **Options**, and then click the **Spelling & Grammar tab**. Under **Grammar**, select the **Show readability statistics** check box, and then click **OK**.

21. On the Standard toolbar, click the **Spelling and Grammar** button. Click **Ignore Once**, and keep clicking it until a dialog box notifies you that the spelling and grammar check is complete. Notice that this document has a fairly high readability level. Click **OK** to close the dialog box. On the Standard toolbar, click the **Save** button. Close the document.

**End** You have completed Project 9H

## Project 9I — Internship Application

**Objectives:** *Control the Flow and Formatting of Pages and Text and Navigate Within Long Documents.*

In the following Performance Assessment, you will use a version of the internship document that includes instructions for applying for a position. You will create section breaks and control document flow. You also will create a bookmark, and then use it as a cross-reference. Finally, you will preview the document using thumbnails. Your completed document will look similar to the one shown in Figure 9.63. You will save your document as *9I_Internship_Application_Firstname_Lastname.*

1. **Start** Word, navigate to the location where the student files for this textbook are stored, and then open **w09I_Internship_Application**. Save the file as **9I_Internship_Application_Firstname_Lastname** in your chapter folder.

2. If necessary, turn off formatting marks. In the TOC, hold down Ctrl, point to and then click **Selection Process** to move the insertion point to that position in the document. With the insertion point to the left of *Selection*, from the **Insert** menu, display the **Break** dialog box, and then insert a **Next page** section break.

3. Using the technique you practiced in the previous step, from the TOC, move to the *Positions* subheading. With the insertion point to the left of *Positions*, insert a **Continuous** section break. Notice that the text remains on the same page, but a new section is created. Recall that a section can have formatting different from that applied to the rest of the document.

4. From the TOC, move to the *Summer Internship Programs* heading and insert a **Next page** section break. Move to the *Student Feedback* heading and insert a **Next page** section break.

5. On page 2, click to the left of the *Positions* heading. Use the scroll bar to navigate to page 4, hold down Shift, and then click to the right of the period at the end of the sentence ending in *revitalization.* All of the text in the *Positions* section is selected. From the **File** menu, click **Page Setup**, and change the **Left Margin** and the **Right Margin** to **1.25**.

6. Move to the top of the document and click **Print Preview**. Click the One Page button. Press PageDown once. Using Print Preview, you can easily see the new margins applied to the *Positions* section. Press PageDown again to view page 3, and notice that at the bottom of page 3, the heading *Bilingual International Business Intern* is separated from its following text. **Close** Print Preview, locate and click anywhere in the heading. From the **Format** menu, display the **Paragraph** dialog box, click the **Line and Page Breaks tab**, and then click to select the **Keep with next** check box.

**(Project 9I–Internship Application continues on the next page)**

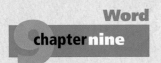
**(Project 9I–Internship Application continued)**

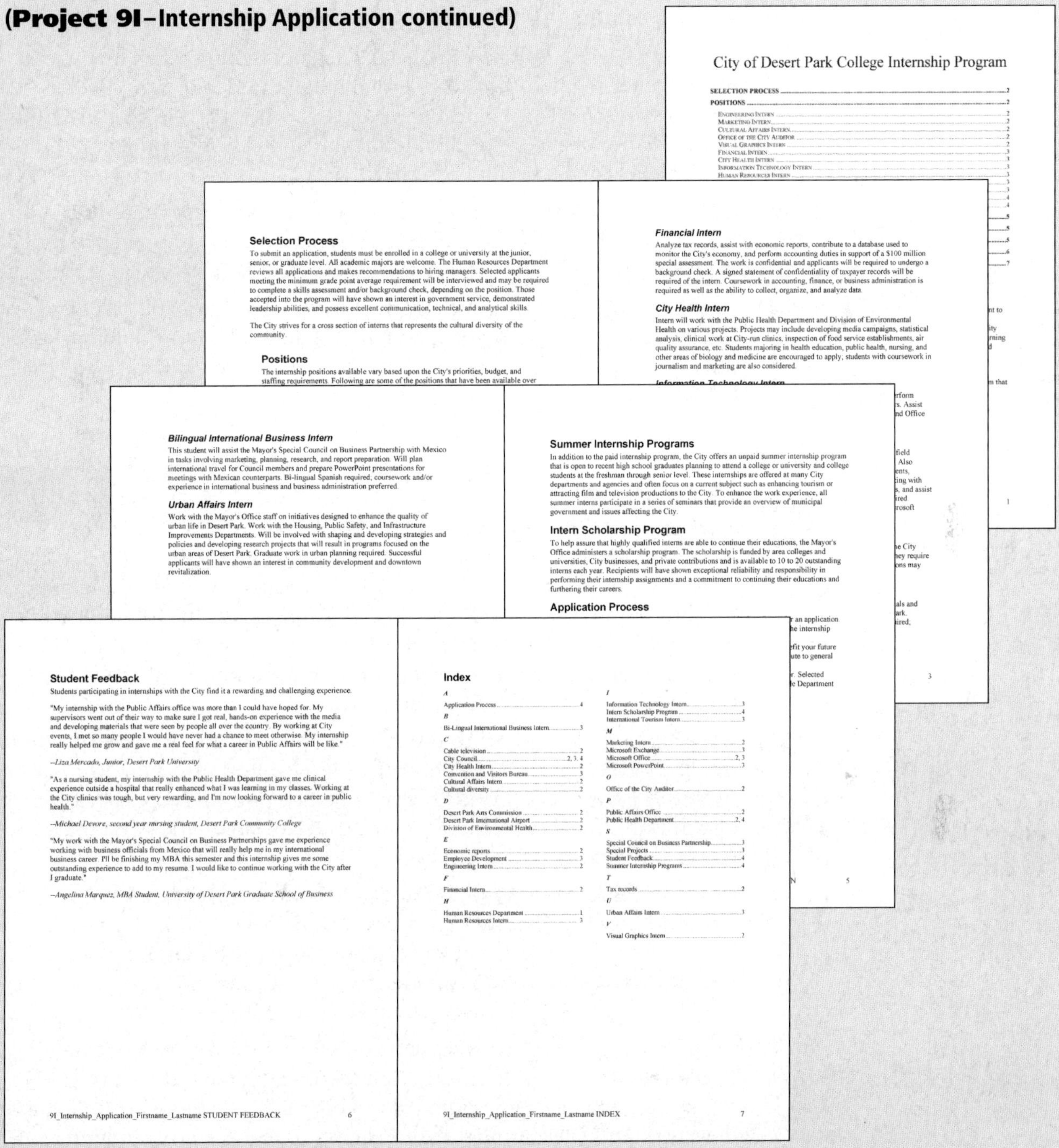

**Figure 9.63**

7. **Save** your changes, and then move to the beginning of the document. From the **View** menu, click **Header and Footer**. On the Header and Footer toolbar, click the **Switch Between Header and Footer** button. Click the **Insert AutoText** button, and then click **Filename**. **Close** the Header and Footer toolbar.

8. From the **Insert** menu, insert **Page Numbers** in the footer, aligned at the right.

**(Project 9I–Internship Application continues on the next page)**

**(Project 9I**–Internship Applications continued)

9. Scroll to view the bottom of page 2, and then double-click anywhere in the footer to open the footer and display the Header and Footer toolbar. On the Header and Footer toolbar, click the **Link to Previous** button to break the link. Click immediately following your name, press Spacebar once, and type **POSITIONS**

10. Scroll to the footer at the bottom of page 5. Click anywhere in the footer, and then click the **Link to Previous** button to break the link. Delete *POSITIONS* and type **PROGRAM INFORMATION**

11. In the footer on page 6, click in the footer, break the link, replace *PROGRAM INFORMATION* with **STUDENT FEEDBACK** In the footer on page 7, repeat the process, and replace *STUDENT FEEDBACK* with **INDEX**

12. **Close** the Header and Footer toolbar and click **Save**. Use **Print Preview** to view all the pages and be sure that appropriate footers display on each page.

13. Navigate to page 5 and display the formatting marks. Locate and select the **Application Process** subheading. Be sure you do not select the index entry or the paragraph mark at the end of the sub-heading. From the **Insert** menu, click **Bookmark**. In the **Bookmark** dialog box, in the **Bookmark name** box, type **Application_Process** Remember to use the underscore between the words. At the bottom of the **Bookmark** dialog box, click **Add**.

14. Press Ctrl + Home to move to the top of the document. Click to position the insertion point at the end of the paragraph that begins *The City of Desert Park offers*. Press Spacebar, type **See** and then press Spacebar again. From the **Insert** menu, point to **Reference**, and then click **Cross-reference**.

15. Click the **Reference type arrow**, and then click **Bookmark**. Be sure the **Insert reference to** is **Bookmark text**, and the **Insert as hyperlink** check box is selected. Under **For which bookmark**, accept **Application_Process**, and then click **Insert**. **Close** the dialog box. Press Spacebar, and then type **for more information.**

16. In the sentence you just inserted, select the cross-reference text *Application Process*. Change the **Font Color** to **Blue**—the sixth color in the second row. On the Standard toolbar, click the **Save** button. Hold down Ctrl and click **Application Process** to test the cross-reference. Press Ctrl + Home to move to the beginning of the document.

17. From the **View** menu, click **Thumbnails**. In the **Thumbnails** task pane, click the icon for page 3. Practice moving among pages using the Thumbnails pane.

18. From the **View** menu, click **Thumbnails** to close the Thumbnails pane. On the Standard toolbar, click the **Save** button. From the **File** menu, click **Print**. Close the document, saving any changes.

**End** You have completed Project 9I

# Project 9J—Tech Plan

**Objectives:** *Create a Master Document and Subdocuments, Manage a Master Document and Subdocuments, Create a Table of Contents, Control the Flow and Formatting of Pages and Text, Navigate Within Long Documents, and Use AutoSummarize and Determine Readability Statistics.*

In the following Mastery Assessment, you will work with an overview of the functions of a strategic planning team for information technology in the City of Desert Park. You will create and manage a master document, creating subdocuments and adding a table from another document. You will create and modify a table of contents, and use the Document Map and Print Preview to navigate and view text flow. Finally, you will AutoSummarize the document, and change the summary settings. Your completed document will look similar to the one shown in Figure 9.64. You will save your document as *9J_Tech_Plan_Firstname_Lastname*.

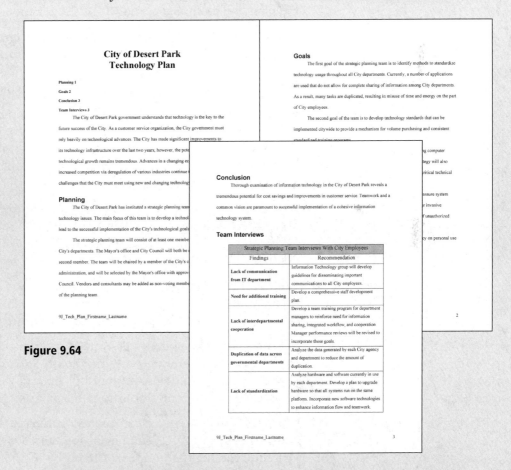

**Figure 9.64**

1. **Start** Word. From the student files that accompany this textbook, open **w09J_Tech_Plan**. Save the file as **9J_Tech_Plan_Firstname_Lastname** in your chapter folder.

2. In the title, remove the space between *Park* and *Technology*. Press Shift + Enter to create a manual line break that places *Technology Plan* on the second line of the title.

**(Project 9J–Tech Plan continues on the next page)**

**(Project 9J**–Tech Plan continued)

3. Switch to **Outline View**, and if necessary, display the formatting marks. Click the **Expand** icon to select the **Planning** subheading and all of the subordinate text. On the Outlining toolbar, click the **Create Subdocument** button.

4. Create another subdocument with the **Goals** subheading.

5. Press Ctrl + End to move to the end of the document and press Enter. Click the **Insert Subdocument** button, and then insert the **w09J_Interview_Table** document. **Save** and **Close** your master document.

6. Open the **Planning** subdocument, and if necessary, display formatting marks. At the end of the last paragraph, add the following sentence, being sure to type in front of the section break mark: **Vendors and consultants may be added as non-voting members at the invitation of the planning team. Save** and **Close** the document.

7. Open your **9J_Tech_Plan_Firstname_Lastname** document. On the Outlining toolbar, click the **Expand Subdocuments** button. Notice that the text you typed into the *Planning* subdocument displays in this master document. Hide the formatting marks.

8. Switch to **Print Layout View**. Move to the top of the document. Click to position the insertion point to the left of the paragraph that begins *The City of Desert Park Government*. Insert a table of contents using the **Simple** format. Be sure that the TOC displays page numbers, but that they are not right aligned.

9. Above the table on page 4, add the subheading **Team Interviews** and apply the **Heading 1** style. Add a blank line between the *Team Interviews* subheading and the table. Move to the top of the document, and then update the entire table of contents.

10. Display the formatting marks. Go to page 3 and delete the section break at the end of the text. The *Team Interviews* subheading and table move to page 3. Update the table of contents.

11. On the Standard toolbar, click the **Document Map** button. In the Document Map pane, move to the **Team Interviews** subheading, and then move up the document by clicking each heading. When you are finished, close the **Document Map** pane.

12. From the **Tools** menu, click **AutoSummarize** and accept the default settings. Use the AutoSummarize toolbar to view **35%** of the original. Examine the highlighted text. **Close** the AutoSummarize toolbar.

13. Create a footer and insert the **Filename**. **Close** the Header and Footer toolbar, and then add page numbers to the footer, aligned at the right. Use **Print Preview** and display three pages at the same time. Examine the flow of the text from page to page. **Save** your changes. **Print** the document. **Close** the document and close Word.

 **End** You have completed Project 9J

# Project 9K — City Guide

**Objectives:** *Add an Index, Control the Flow and Formatting of Pages and Text, Navigate Within Long Documents, and Use AutoSummarize and Determine Readability Statistics.*

In the following Mastery Assessment, you will edit a guide for new residents in the City of Desert Park. You will keep titles with subsequent text, add an index, mark index entries, and update the index. You will use thumbnails to navigate the document. Finally, you will check the readability statistics of the document. Your completed document will look similar to the one shown in Figure 9.65. You will save your document as *9K_City_Guide_Firstname_Lastname.*

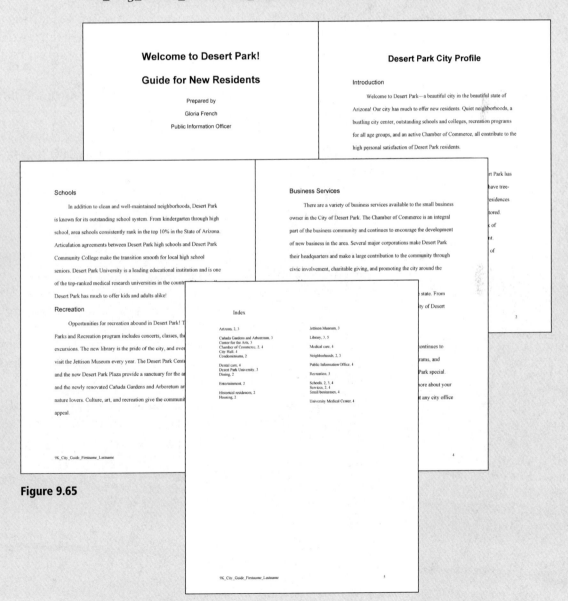

**Figure 9.65**

**(Project 9K–City Guide continues on the next page)**

**(Project 9K** – City Guide continued)

1. **Start** Word. From the student files, open **w09K_City_Guide**. Save the file as **9K_City_Guide_Firstname_Lastname** in your chapter folder. Add a footer, and from the **Insert AutoText** list, insert the **Filename**. Close the Header and Footer toolbar, and insert page numbers to the footer, aligned at the right.

2. If necessary, turn off formatting marks. At the bottom of page 2, click in the *Schools* subheading. Apply the Keep with next formatting to keep this subheading with the paragraph that follows it. Scroll through the document, repeating this procedure wherever you find a heading that is separated from its following text.

3. Move to the top of the document and display formatting marks. Scroll through the document to examine the index entries. Move to the end of the document and press Ctrl + Enter to create a new page. Type **Index** and then press Enter.

4. Insert an index using the **Simple** format. Clear the *Right align page numbers* check box if necessary.

5. Move to the top of the document, find the word **neighborhoods** and mark all instances of the word, edited to **Neighborhoods** as an index entry. Repeat the procedure with *Dining* and *Entertainment*. Hide the formatting marks. Move to the index, and update the index field.

6. From the **View** menu, click **Thumbnails**. Usc the page icons to move to the first page, and then move to the last page. Close the **Thumbnails** pane.

7. From the **Tools** menu, click **Options**, and then move to the **Spelling & Grammar tab**. If necessary, select the **Show readability statistics** check box, and then close the dialog box. Run a spelling and grammar check, ignoring any flagged items until the readability statistics display. Examine the statistics, from the **Tools** menu, display the **Options** dialog box, and then on the **Spelling & Grammar tab**, clear the **Show readability statistics** check box.

8. Use **Print Preview** to examine the text flow of all five pages at the same time. **Save** your changes. **Print** the document. **Close** the document and close Word.

**End** You have completed Project 9K

# Problem Solving

## Project 9L — Research Project

**Objectives:** *Create a Master Document and Subdocuments, Manage a Master Document and Subdocuments, Create a Table of Contents, and Add an Index.*

In this project, you will create a research document about professional jobs in city government. It will include a master document and subdocuments, an index, a table of contents, and footnotes. You will assemble the document, maintaining consistent formatting throughout. You will create a title page as well as separate footers for different sections of the document. You will save your document as *9L_Research_Project_ Firstname_Lastname*.

1. **Start** Word. Open a blank document and save it as **9L_Research_Project_ Firstname_Lastname** in your chapter folder.

2. Create a title page with a document title, followed by your name and then the date, all on separate lines. If you are not certain what a title page should look like, go to www.google.com and search for **research paper title page** Find the title page instructions using an acceptable style such as APA, MLA, or the Chicago Manual of Style. Or, consult an office reference manual or Business Communications textbook. Add a next page section break at the bottom of the first page text. Center the text vertically on the page.

3. Five subdocuments will be inserted into the document:

   w09L_City_Government

   w09L_Chief_Executive

   w09L_Architect

   w09L_Urban_Planner

   w09L_Civil_Engineer

   Open each of the documents, and give the document titles a style that can be used with master/subdocuments. Close the files.

4. Insert each of the subdocuments into the master document. The *City Government* document is the introduction, and thus should come first. Use your judgment to place the other documents in a logical order. Examine the footnotes to be sure they are numbered consecutively. In the *Chief Executive* section, the last bulleted list has a source. Use that information to add a footnote to the last item in the bulleted list, and then delete the source information.

5. Add the filename to the footer, and also add the title of each section to separate footers in a manner similar to that used in this chapter. Add page numbers to the header at the right margin.

**(Project 9L–Research Project continues on the next page)**

**(Project 9L–Research Project continued)**

6. If desired, format all the text as double spaced, common in a research paper, and then delete extra lines as necessary. After you have set the spacing you like, scroll through to see if there are instances where you should use the *Keep with next* feature. Then, create a TOC at the top of the first subdocument.

7. Mark at least ten index entries in the document. Create a new page at the end of the document, and then create an index with a title at the same heading level as the headings in the rest of the document.

8. Add a References page. If you are not sure what should go on the page, perform a Google search for **research paper reference page**, or consult an appropriate reference manual.

9. Save, print, and then close your document.

**End** You have completed Project 9L

# Project 9M—Outdoor Activities

**Objectives:** *Create a Master Document and Subdocuments, Manage a Master Document and Subdocuments, Create a Table of Contents, Control the Flow and Formatting of Pages and Text, Navigate Within Long Documents, and Use AutoSummarize and Determine Readability Statistics.*

In this project, you will work on a document created by the City of Desert Park Department of Parks and Recreation. You will use the master/subdocument procedure to incorporate three documents into your master document. You will create a table of contents, and then add bookmarks to the subtitles. You will create different footers for different sections. Finally, you will use the AutoSummarize feature, and then print with the summary highlighting turned on. You will save your document as *9M_Outdoor_Activities_Firstname_Lastname.*

1. **Start** Word. From the student files, open **w09M_Outdoor_Activities** and save it as **9M_Outdoor_Activities_Firstname_Lastname** in your chapter folder.

2. Create a subdocument from the *Golf for a Cause* section. At the end of the document, insert the **w09M_Bicycling**, **w09M_Desert_Oasis**, and **w09M_Garden** documents as subdocuments.

3. If necessary, change the subheadings of the three subdocuments to **Heading 1** style. In the *Botanical Notes* area, use the **Heading 2** style for **Garden Gets NPS Grant** and **Outdoor Music**. Make the subheading color consistent with the green titles at the top of the document. Create a TOC following the paragraph near the top of the first page that begins *The following is a brief description.* Use a style of your choice. Make the color of the TOC consistent with the rest of the titles.

4. Locate the title below the box at the top of the first page that begins *The City of Desert Park.* Create a line break to move **Outdoor Activities** to another line.

5. Create bookmarks for each of the document subheadings. Practice going to the bookmarks using the **Go To** command.

6. Create a footer with your name, and then create different footers for each section of the document, using text of your choice.

7. **Save** your work. Use **AutoSummarize** to summarize **30%** of the document. With **AutoSummarize** still active, print the document. Close the document.

**End** You have completed Project 9M

## On the Internet

### Learning More About the Table of Contents Feature

In this chapter you worked with a table of contents. You can do much more with a table of contents, and Microsoft provides an online tutorial on the topic.

1. Be sure that you are connected to the Internet. **Start** Word.

2. In the **Type a question for help box**, type **table of contents**

3. Locate **Explore tables of contents in Word** in the **Search Results** task pane, and then click it. Notice the methods other than using built-in heading styles to add entries to a table of contents.

4. Scroll to the bottom of the tutorial, and then read the section on keyboard shortcuts.

5. When you are done, close the file without saving your changes.

## GO! with Help

### Creating a Table of Figures

In this chapter, you practiced creating a table of contents. Word also helps you create a table of authorities and a table of figures. The table of authorities is a list of the references in a legal document, such as references to cases, statues, and rules, along with the number of the pages on which the references appear. A table of figures lists the captions for pictures, charts, graphs, slides, or other illustrations in a document, along with the numbers of the pages on which the captions appear. The table of figures can be used in any document that contains clip art, pictures, tables, or other objects to which captions can be attached.

1. **Start** Word. In the *Type a Question for Help* box, type **table of figures** and then press Enter.

2. In the **Search Results** task bar, click **Create a table of figures**.

3. Click the link to **table of figures** at the top of the task pane to see a definition of the term.

4. Expand and read the **Use captions created with the Caption command** topic. When you come to a link in the text, click it, and then read the information, particularly the section on adding captions automatically.

5. If you want to do so, open the **9M_Outdoor_Activities** file that you created in Project 9M. If you did not complete that project, substitute a file you have worked on that contains graphics and/or tables. Add captions to the figures, and then follow the instructions to create a table of figures. (Note: Try this with the figures inline with the text, and then with the figures floating unattached to the text, updating your table of figures each time.)

6. When you are finished, close the document without saving your changes.

# 10 chapterten

# Creating Standardized Forms and Documents

**In this chapter, you will:** complete these projects **and** practice these skills.

| Project 10A **Creating and Modifying Forms** | **Objectives**<br>• Create a Customized Form<br>• Modify a Form<br>• Save a Form as a Template and Use the Template to Create a New Form |
|---|---|

| Project 10B **Automating a Form with Macros and Visual Basic for Applications (VBA)** | **Objectives**<br>• Automate a Form with Macros<br>• Control a Form with Visual Basic for Applications (VBA)<br>• Add an ActiveX Control to a Form |
|---|---|

# Jefferson Inn

About two and a half hours outside of Washington, DC, the Jefferson Inn is located in Charlottesville, Virginia. The Inn's proximity to Washington, DC, and Richmond, VA, makes it a popular weekend getaway for locals and a convenient base for out-of-town vacationers. The Inn offers 12 rooms, all individually decorated. A fresh country breakfast and afternoon tea are included each day. Meeting rooms offering the latest high-tech amenities, such as high-speed Internet connections, have made the Inn an increasingly popular location for day-long corporate meetings and events.

© Getty Images, Inc.

# Creating Standardized Forms and Documents

A form is a structured document with spaces reserved for entering information. After you design the form, others can fill it in on paper or on a computer screen by viewing it in Microsoft Word. For creating everyday forms, Word 2003 has many features, such as check boxes, drop-down lists, bookmarks, automatic dates, and text fields. Forms can be protected to prevent unauthorized changes and they can be automated for convenient use.

Using forms that people complete in Word has some advantages: Word can verify the input, such as a date, or update other fields based on the input in an associated field, such as a city associated with a specific postal code.

Standardized forms are useful in the operation of any business, such as the Jefferson Inn, which handles large numbers of reservations. If you need to use the same form repeatedly, or if you will be creating additional forms based on the form you create, you can save the form as a template and reuse it.

# Project 10A **Reservation Form**

Microsoft's *InfoPath 2003* is a specialized tool for creating data-gathering forms that are tied to a database. For forms that are not tied to a specific database, you can use Word to create forms that must be printed, viewed in Word, or placed on a Web page to collect information online. You can create a form using Word that does not require knowledge of programming, databases, or server software. You can use any of the Word features in a form, including the drawing tools, graphics, and tables.

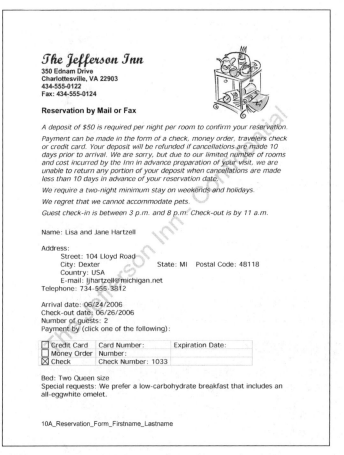

In Activities 10.1 through 10.13 you will create a form from an existing document and then save the form as a template, which can be used again. The finished template will be a reservation form for the Jefferson Inn that may be filled in by guests who want to reserve a room by mail or fax. Your completed document will look similar to Figure 10.1. You will save your document as *10A_Reservation_Form_Firstname_Lastname*.

**Figure 10.1**

## Objective 1
## Create a Customized Form

A **form** is a document that contains fill-in areas, or **form fields**, in which you can enter information. A form field is a location in a form where a particular type of information, such as a name or address, is stored. For example, you can create an online reservation form in Word that uses drop-down lists from which users can select entries. Paragraphs of standard text can also be included.

A form is usually stored as a template so that it can be used repeatedly without changing the original form. Recall that a **template** is a model for documents of the same type; it stores basic information such as formatting, styles, and—in a form—standard text. Automated features such as check boxes and lists are added to forms to ensure uniform responses to specific questions.

### Activity 10.1 Creating a Customized Form

For guests who want to make room reservations by mail, fax, or e-mail, the Jefferson Inn wants a form that the guest can download, fill in, and submit. In this activity, you will open an existing document, save it with a new name, copy standard paragraphs from another document, and then add some text to complete the standardized portion of the form.

**1** **Start** Word. From the student files that accompany this textbook, locate and open **w10A_Reservation_Form**. If you want to do so, create a new folder for this chapter, and then save the file as **10A_Reservation_Form_Firstname_Lastname**

**2** On the Standard toolbar, click the **Zoom button arrow** `100% ▾`, and then click **Page Width**. If necessary, on the Standard toolbar, click the **Show/Hide ¶** button `¶` to show formatting marks.

**3** From the student files that accompany this textbook, locate and open **w10A_Standard_Text**. Press `Ctrl` + `A` to select all the text. Click the **Copy** button `📋`, and then close the document; if prompted, do not save changes.

**4** In your **10A_Reservation_Form_Firstname_Lastname** file, click to position the insertion point in the empty line above *Name:* and then click the **Paste** button `📋`.

The text that you copied is inserted.

**5** In the heading, click to the right of the telephone number and press `Enter`. Type **Fax: 434-555-0124** as shown in Figure 10.2.

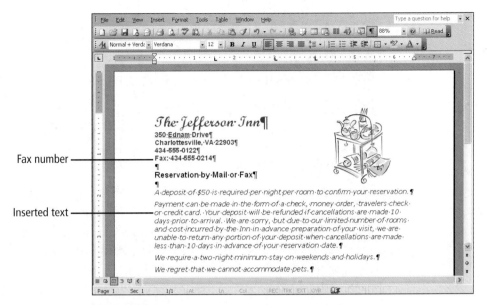

Fax number ——

Inserted text ——

**Figure 10.2**

**6** From the **View** menu, display the Header and Footer toolbar, and then click the **Switch Between Header and Footer** button ⊡. Click the **Insert AutoText** button ⌊Insert AutoText ▾⌋, and then click **Filename**. On the **Header and Footer** toolbar, click the **Close** button ⌊Close⌋.

**7** On the Standard toolbar, click the **Save** button ⊟.

### Activity 10.2 Adding Text Fields

Use a text form field when you want to control the type of text that the person filling in the form types. In this activity, you will add text form fields to the form.

**1** From the **View** menu, point to **Toolbars**, and then click **Forms**.

**2** Take a moment to point to each button on the Forms toolbar, which may be floating on your screen or docked to other toolbars, and view the ScreenTips. Examine the information in the table shown in Figure 10.3.

## Buttons on the Forms Toolbar

| Button | Name | Description |
|---|---|---|
| abl | Text Form Field | Inserts a text field. |
| ☑ | Check Box Form Field | Inserts a check box field. |
| | Drop-Down Form Field | Inserts a drop-down field for selecting from a list. |
| | Form Field Options | Sets options such as font. |
| | Draw Table | Opens the Tables and Borders toolbar from which you can draw a table. |
| | Insert Table | Opens a grid of cells from which you can select the number of rows and columns in the table. |
| | Insert Frame | Activates the cross-shaped mouse pointer with which you can drag to insert a frame, which is a container for text that can be positioned anywhere on a page. |
| | Form Field Shading | Toggles shading on and off. |
| | Reset Form Fields | Restores the default values to fields. |
| | Protect Form | Prevents users from making changes to the form. |

**Figure 10.3**

**3** Click to position the insertion point to the right of *Name:* and press Spacebar. If necessary, click the **Show/Hide ¶** button ¶ to display the formatting marks. On the **Forms** toolbar, click the **Text Form Field** button.

A series of small circles in a gray box indicates the location of the text form field.

**4** Repeat this process to place a space and a text form field to the right of **Street**, **City**, **State**, **Postal Code**, **Country**, **E-mail**, **Telephone**, **Arrival date**, **Check-out date**, **Number of guests** and **Special requests**. Do not place a field next to *Payment by* or *Bed*.

Compare your screen with Figure 10.4.

Text Form Field button ——

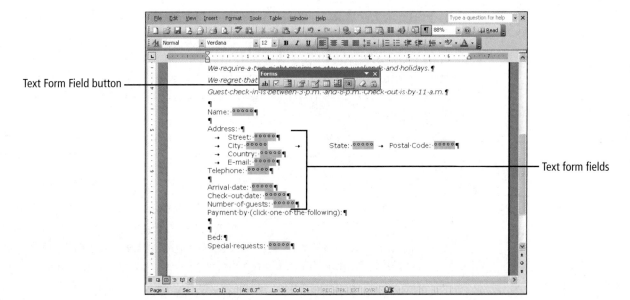

—— Text form fields

**Figure 10.4**

**5** On the Standard toolbar, click the **Save** button.

## Activity 10.3 Inserting a Table

In a form, you can insert a table to display information or to organize a group of related check boxes and text form fields. In this activity, you will insert a table to indicate the method of payment and related information.

**1** In the second empty line below *Payment*, click to position the insertion point.

**2** On the Forms toolbar, click the **Insert Table** button. In the displayed palette, move the pointer to the cell in the third column and the third row to select a **3 x 3 Table**, and then click.

A table with three rows and three columns is inserted, as shown in Figure 10.5.

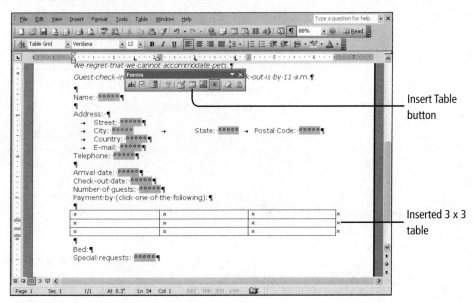

—— Insert Table button

—— Inserted 3 x 3 table

**Figure 10.5**

**3** On the Standard toolbar, click the **Save** button.

**Activity 10.4** Adding Check Boxes and Text Form Fields to a Table

By adding a check box to a form, the person filling out the form can select—or *not* select—specific options. The Check Box field is empty until the person filling out the form clicks on it, which places an X in the check box. In this activity, you will insert a table to offer various choices for payment.

**1** If necessary, click to position the insertion point in the first cell in the first row of the table. On the Forms toolbar, click the **Check Box Form Field** button [✓]. Press [Spacebar], and then type **Credit Card**

A check box is inserted in the first cell of the table along with text to explain the purpose of the check box.

**2** Press [Tab] to move the insertion point to the second cell in the first row of the table. Type **Card Number:** Press [Spacebar], and then on the Forms toolbar, click the **Text Form Field** button [abl].

A field for recording the credit card number is placed in the cell.

**3** Press [Tab] to move to the third cell in the first row of the table. Type **Expiration Date:** Press [Spacebar], and then on the Forms toolbar, click the **Text Form Field** button [abl].

A field for recording the credit card expiration date is placed in the cell.

**4** Press [Tab] to position the insertion point in the first cell in the second row of the table. On the Forms toolbar, click the **Check Box Form Field** button [✓]. Press [Spacebar], and then type **Money Order**

**5** Press [Tab] and type **Number:** Press [Spacebar], and then on the Forms toolbar, click the **Text Form Field** button [abl].

A field for recording the number of the money order is placed in the cell.

**6** Move to the first cell in the third row of the table. Click the **Check Box Form Field** button [✓], press [Spacebar], and then type **Check**

**7** Press [Tab], and in the second cell in the third row of the table, type **Check Number:** Press [Spacebar], and then on the Forms toolbar, click the **Text Form Field** button [abl].

The three payment options display check boxes and text form fields for additional information as shown in Figure 10.6.

Text Form Field button ——

Check box form fields ——

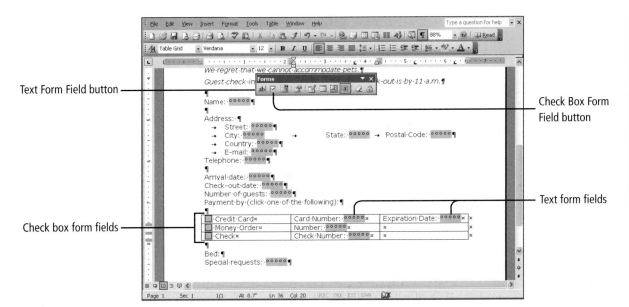

Check Box Form
Field button

Text form fields

**Figure 10.6**

■8 On the Standard toolbar, click the **Save** button 🔲.

### Activity 10.5 Adding a Drop-Down List to a Form

Use a drop-down form field when the field has many options and it is not important to see the options that were *not* selected. By inserting a drop-down list, you ensure acceptable responses because the person filling out the form is limited to the responses on the list. In this activity, you will insert a drop-down list so that guests can request the type of bed arrangement in their room.

■1 Near the bottom of the document, click to position the insertion point to the right of *Bed:*.

■2 Press Spacebar once. Click the **Drop-Down Form Field** button 🔲.

A space and a small gray rectangle are inserted to the right of *Bed:* as shown in Figure 10.7. The field is ready to accept entries for the list.

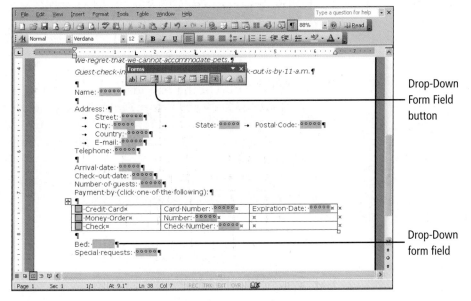

Drop-Down
Form Field
button

Drop-Down
form field

**Figure 10.7**

■3 On the Standard toolbar, click the **Save** button 🔲.

**Activity 10.6** Setting Options on the Form Fields

With a form, you can manage the information that the person filling in the form provides. Six text form field types—Regular text, Number, Date, Current date, Current time, and Calculation—can be applied to control the characteristics or behavior of a text form field. Setting a text form field to a specific type ensures that the person filling in the form enters a valid date, enters a number and not text, or does not exceed a specified amount of text. In this activity, you will set form field options.

**1** To the right of **Name:**, click to select the gray text form field. On the Forms toolbar, click the **Form Field Options** button 🔲.

**2** In the displayed **Text Form Field Options** dialog box, under **Text form field**, in the **Maximum length** box, select the text *Unlimited*, and then type **60**

This action will limit the number of characters that can be typed in the field to 60. See Figure 10.8. Notice that a bookmark has been created for the form field. Recall that a bookmark identifies a location in the document—in this case it also identifies the field so that the contents of the field can be referenced later, if necessary.

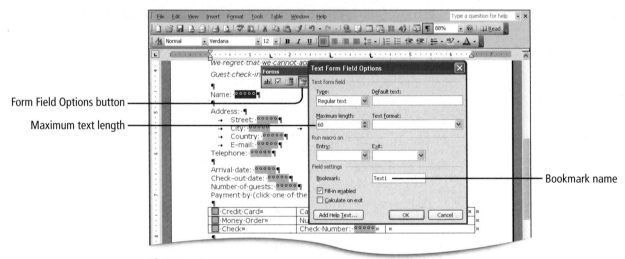

Form Field Options button

Maximum text length

Bookmark name

**Figure 10.8**

**3** Click **OK**. On the text form field to the right of **Street:**, double-click to open the **Text Form Field Options** dialog box. Set the **Maximum length** to **60** and click **OK**. Using this technique, assign maximum text lengths to the text form fields to the right of the following labels:

City—**25**

State—**2**

Postal Code—**11**

Country—**60**

E-mail—**60**

Telephone—**12**

Card Number—**19**

Expiration date—**5**

**4** On the text form field to the right of **Arrival date:**, double-click to open the **Text Form Field Options** dialog box. Under **Text form field**, click the **Type arrow**, and then click **Date**. Click **OK**. Repeat this procedure for the text box to the right of **Check-out date:**.

This action limits the type of information entered in these fields to dates.

**5** On the text form field to the right of **Number of guests:**, double-click to open the **Text Form Field Options** dialog box. Under **Text form field**, click the **Type arrow**, and then click **Number**. Click the **Number format arrow**, and then click **0**. Click **OK**. Repeat this process for the fields to the right of **Number** and **Check Number**.

Defining the type as *Number* ensures that entries in these text form fields will display as a number. Defining the Number format as *0* ensures that the number will be an ***integer***—a whole number rather than a decimal or a fraction.

**6** On the drop-down form field to the right of **Bed:**, double-click to open the **Drop-Down Form Field Options** dialog box. In the **Drop-down item** box, type **One King size** and then click the **Add** button.

The option you typed displays in the *Items in drop-down list* box.

**7** In the **Drop-down item** box, type **Two Queen size** and click the **Add** button. In the **Drop-down item** box, type **One Queen size and two bunk beds** and then click the **Add** button.

Compare your dialog box with Figure 10.9.

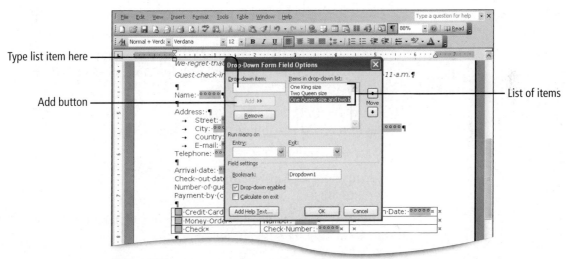

Type list item here

Add button

List of items

**Figure 10.9**

**8** Click **OK**. Click anywhere in the table. From the **Table** menu, point to **AutoFit**, and then click **AutoFit to Contents**.

When the form is filled in, the column widths will adjust automatically to accommodate the maximum field size, which in this case is 19—the character field for the credit card number.

**9** On the Standard toolbar, click the **Save** button ⊞.

**Activity 10.7** Protecting and Testing the Form

Before you distribute a form that people will view and fill in, you must protect it so that people can enter information only in the form fields. Protecting a form as you are designing it is also helpful to test how the final version of the form will work. While you are testing the form, you should try out examples of each of the different types of fields to be sure they behave as you intended.

**1** On the Standard toolbar, click the **Show/Hide ¶** button ¶ to hide formatting marks. On the Forms toolbar, click the **Protect Form** button 🔒.

Use the Protect Form button to toggle back and forth between the final form and form editing. When the form is protected, no changes can be made to the form text—you can only enter information into form fields. When you click the Protect Form button to turn protection off, you can change anything on the form but cannot enter data into the form fields. Notice that the small circles in the form field boxes no longer display, and the first item in the *Bed* form field displays by default.

**2** Press the Tab key repeatedly to observe how the insertion point moves from one form field to the next. Stop when the insertion point arrives at the **State** field.

Earlier, you limited the State field to two characters.

**3** Type **ILL**

Notice that the field accepts only the first two characters that you type.

**4** Press the Tab key five times to move the insertion point to the **Arrival date:** field. Type **9/31/06** and then press Tab.

Because September has only 30 days, a warning box displays to indicate that this is an invalid date. Word checks date fields for valid dates.

**5** In the warning box, click **OK**. Type the current date in the **Arrival date:** box. To the left of **Credit Card**, click to select the check box.

An X fills the box.

**6** To the right of **Expiration Date:**, click the text form field, and then type **07/08**

This text form field will accept any five characters because its type was not specifically defined as a date field.

**7** To the right of **Bed:**, click in the drop-down form field to display the list. From the list, click **Two Queen size**.

Your choice from the list fills the field.

**8** To the right of **Special requests:**, click the text form field and type the following paragraph: **My husband is very allergic to cats. It is very important to us that no one has had a cat in the room.**

Notice that the text wraps within the margins of the page and that this text form field allows an unlimited amount of text. Your test form should be partially filled in as shown in Figure 10.10.

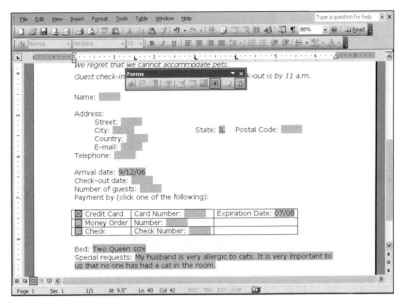

**Figure 10.10**

**9** On the Standard toolbar, click the **Save** button 🖫.

## Objective 2
## Modify a Form

When you test a form, you may discover that it does not work the way you want, or you may decide to add additional information. You can modify forms by changing the text or the fields. You can add form fields or change the options of existing form fields. Protection must be turned off to modify the form.

### Activity 10.8 Modifying Form Fields

Several form field options can be modified, such as the field type, the maximum length of the field, the default value of the text, and the format of the text. Additionally, you can add a Help message to a form field. In this activity, you will change a text form field from text type to a date type.

**1** On the Forms toolbar, click the **Protect Form** button 🔒 to turn off protection. On the Standard toolbar, click the **Show/Hide ¶** button ¶ to display formatting marks. On the Forms toolbar, click the **Reset Form Fields** button 🖉.

Protection is turned off and the sample data you entered is removed.

**2** On the text form field to the right of **Expiration Date:**, double-click to display the **Text Form Field Options** dialog box. Under **Text form field**, click the **Type arrow**, and then click **Date**. Leave the **Maximum length** at 5.

Expiration dates on credit cards typically show the month and two-digit year separated by a slash, which takes only five characters. Because this is an unusual date format, adding a Help message would be helpful for the person filling in the form.

**3** At the bottom of the **Text Form Fields Option** dialog box, click the **Add Help Text** button.

**4** In the **Form Field Help Text** dialog box, be sure the **Status Bar tab** is selected. Click the **Type your own** option button, and then type **Provide the expiration date exactly as printed on your credit card in mm/yy format.**

Compare your dialog box with Figure 10.11. When people are filling out the form, this Help message will display on the status bar at the bottom of the window when the insertion point is placed in the Expiration date field.

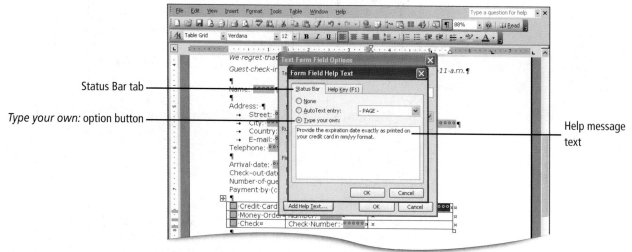

**Figure 10.11**

**5** Click **OK** twice to close both dialog boxes. On the Forms toolbar, click the **Protect Form** button [icon]. Press Tab repeatedly until the field to the right of **Expiration Date:** is selected.

The form is protected and the Help message you typed displays on the status bar at the bottom of the window as shown in Figure 10.12.

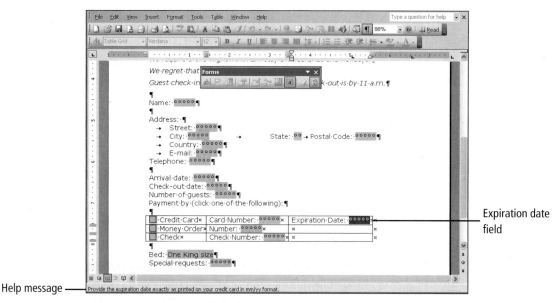

Help message ——

**Figure 10.12**

6 On the Forms toolbar, click the **Protect Form** button 🔒 to turn off protection. Click the **Save** button 💾.

**Activity 10.9** Applying a Theme

A *theme* is a set of unified design elements that provides a uniform look for your document by using coordinated colors, fonts, and graphics. In this activity, you will apply a nonprinting theme to improve the appearance of the form when it is displayed on a computer screen.

1 From the **Format** menu, click **Theme**. Under **Choose a Theme**, click a few of the available themes and examine them in the Sample area. When you are through, click **Echo**.

Notice in the *Sample of theme Echo* preview area, the background changes to a light blue-green or gray texture, as shown in Figure 10.13.

Echo theme ——

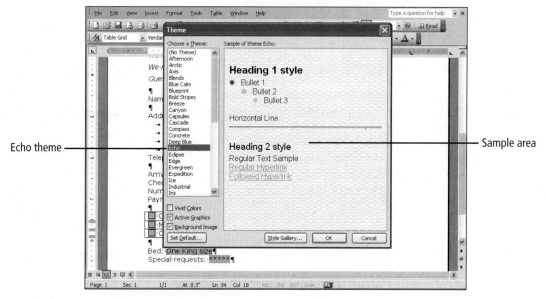

—— Sample area

**Figure 10.13**

**2** Click **OK** to apply the background theme color to your form.

**3** On the Standard toolbar, click the **Print Preview** button and notice that the background color is *not* applied to the printed version of the form.

**4** On the Print Preview toolbar, click the **Close** button <u>Close</u>, and then click the **Save** button.

### Activity 10.10 Creating a Background

A theme includes a nonprinting background that is designed to complement the other colors of the theme. However, you may choose your own background color and add special effects, such as gradients, textures, patterns, or pictures.

**1** From the **Format** menu, point to **Background**, and then click **Fill Effects**. Click the **Texture tab**. Under **Texture**, in the first row, click the third texture—**Parchment**—as shown in Figure 10.14.

Texture tab —

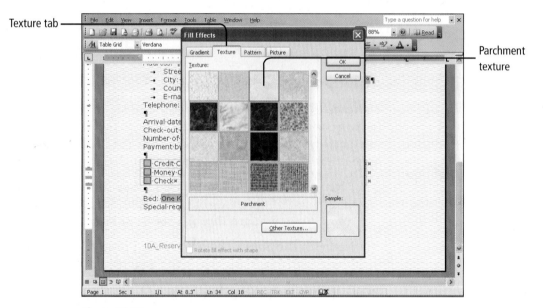

Parchment texture

**Figure 10.14**

**2** Click **OK** to apply the Parchment background to the form.

**3** On the Standard toolbar, click the **Print Preview** button, and notice that the background texture is not applied to the printout.

**4** **Close** <u>Close</u> Print Preview and click the **Save** button.

**Activity 10.11** Creating a Watermark

*Watermarks* are text or pictures that display behind document text. A watermark adds interest or identifies the document status, for example, marking a document as a *Draft*. Watermarks are intended for printed documents. In this activity, you will add a watermark to indicate that the document is for confidential use only.

**1** From the **Format** menu, point to **Background**, and then click **Printed Watermark**.

The Printed Watermark dialog box displays with options for pictures or text as watermarks. If you select text as the watermark, you can also set the size, font, color, and layout of the printed watermark.

**2** Click the **Text watermark** option button. Click the **Text arrow** and examine some of the common choices for watermark text. Then, select the existing text and type **The Jefferson Inn - Confidential**

Compare your dialog box with Figure 10.15.

Text watermark option button ——

Text for the watermark

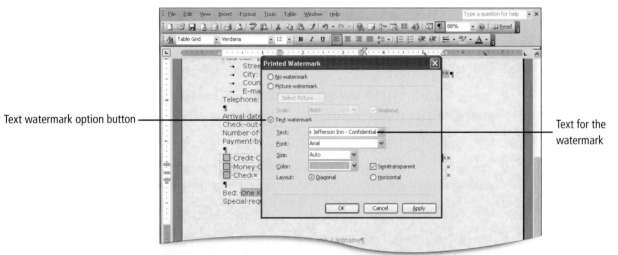

**Figure 10.15**

**3** At the bottom of the **Printed Watermark** dialog box, click **Apply**, and then click **Close**.

The watermark text is semitransparent and angled in the background.

**4** On the Standard toolbar, click the **Print Preview** button.

Notice that the watermark text will print in the background, but the colored texture will not print. See Figure 10.16.

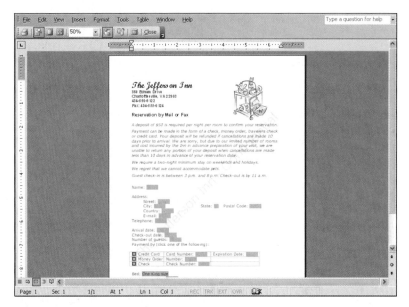

**Figure 10.16**

**5** On the Print Preview toolbar, click **Close** [Close], and then click **Save** [💾].

## Objective 3
### Save a Form as a Template and Use the Template to Create a New Form

A form is usually stored as a template so that it can be used repeatedly without changing the original form. The form you have created can be sent to a guest as an e-mail attachment and used to create a printed form that can be returned by e-mail, regular mail, or fax. Employees at the Inn can also use the form to take reservation information by phone. Recall that templates are stored in a dedicated folder that is accessible whenever you create a new document.

### Activity 10.12 Protecting the Form and Saving It as a Template

Before you save it as a template, the form must be protected.

**1** On the Standard toolbar, click the **Show/Hide ¶** button [¶] to hide the formatting marks. On the Forms toolbar, click the **Reset Form Fields** button [⟳]. On the Forms toolbar, click the **Protect Form** button [🔒] to turn on protection.

**2** From the **File** menu, click **Save As**. At the bottom of the **Save As** dialog box, click the **Save as type arrow**, and then click **Document Template**. In the **File name** box, type **10A_Reservation_Form_Firstname_Lastname**

The form will be saved as a template in the default Templates folder as shown in Figure 10.17.

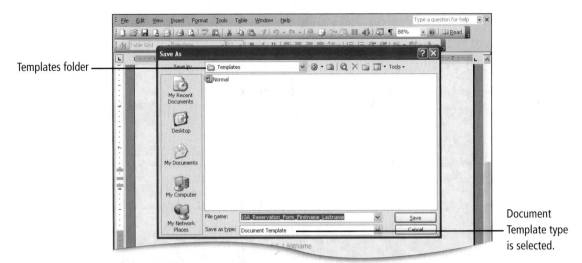

Templates folder

Document Template type is selected.

**Figure 10.17**

**Alert!**

### Is the Templates Folder Blocked?

If you are working in a college computer lab, your college may have placed restrictions on saving files to the Templates folder. Saving to the Templates folder makes the template available to anyone at this computer when they display the File menu, click New, and then click the General Templates tab. If you cannot store to the Templates folder, you can still save and use the template. The difference is that it will be available only to you. If you are unable to save your template in the Templates folder, navigate to the location where you are storing your files for this chapter, and save it there.

**3** Near the bottom of the **Save As** dialog box, click the **Save** button. At the right end of the menu bar, click the small **Close Window** button ☒. **Close** the Forms toolbar.

### Activity 10.13 Filling in the Form and Saving the Document

In this activity, you will create a new document using the template, fill in the form, and save the document.

**1** From the **File** menu, click **New**. If you saved the template in your student folder, click the Start button, click My Documents, navigate to your folder, double-click the template, and then move directly to Step 4.

**2** In the **New Document** task pane, under **Templates**, click **On my computer**.

The Templates dialog box displays.

**3** Be sure the **General tab** is selected. Click your **10_Reservation_ Firstname_Lastname** template, and then click **OK**.

A new document opens as Document1 (or other Document number depending on how many new documents you have started in this session). It displays the watermark but not the textured background, which is not saved in a template. The field to the right of *Name:* is selected.

chapter ten

**4** Type **Lisa and Juan Hartzell** and then press ⟨Tab⟩.

The first field is filled, and the insertion point moves to the field to the right of *Street:* as shown in Figure 10.18.

Document is unnamed. ——

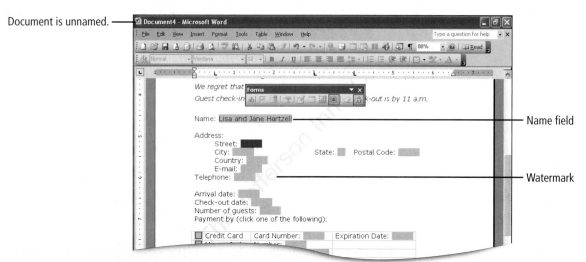

Name field

Watermark

**Figure 10.18**

**5** In the **Street:** field box, type **104 Lloyd Road** and then press ⟨Tab⟩. Use this process to fill in the following fields with the data shown below:

City: **Dexter**

State: **MI**

Postal Code: **48118**

Country: **USA**

E-mail: **ljhartzell@michigan.net**

Telephone: **734-555-3812**

Arrival date: **06/24/2006**

Check-out date: **06/26/2006**

Number of guests: **2**

**6** Click in the box to the left of **Check:** and then press ⟨Tab⟩. Type **1033**

**7** Click the field to the right of **Bed:**, and then click **Two Queen size**. Alternatively, you can press ⟨Alt⟩ + ⟨↓⟩ to display a drop-down list. Press ⟨Tab⟩. Type **We prefer a low-carbohydrate breakfast that includes an all-eggwhite omelet.** Compare your screen with Figure 10.19.

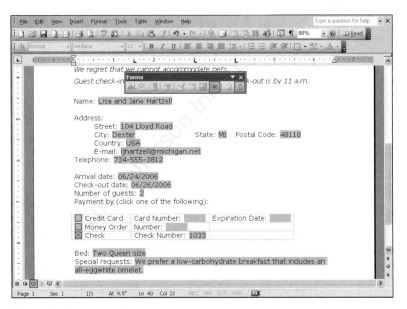

**Figure 10.19**

8  From the **File** menu, click **Save As**. In the **Save As** dialog box, navigate to the location where you are storing your files for this chapter. In the **File name** box, and using your own name, type **10A_Reservation_Form_Firstname_Lastname** and then click the **Save** button.

Because a file with the same name already exists, a dialog box displays.

9  Click **OK** to replace the existing file. On the Standard toolbar, click the **Print Preview** button ⊡ to see the document as it will print. Click the **Print** button ⊟.

10  If necessary, close the Forms toolbar, and then close the file, saving changes if prompted to do so.

11  If you are working in a lab and saved the template to the Templates folder, remove the template from the system. From **My Computer**, navigate to the **Templates** folder (C:/Documents and Settings/Owner Name/Application Data/Microsoft/Templates). Right-click your **10A_Reservation_Form_Firstname_Lastname** file, click **Delete**, and then click **Yes** if prompted to send the document to the Recycle bin. Close **My Computer**.

**End** You have completed Project 10A ─────────────

# Project 10B **Meetings**

A Word document or form can include programming that is activated by keystrokes, by mouse clicks, or automatically when a document opens.

In Activities 10.14 through 10.26, you will assist Elena Brondello, the Manager of Corporate Meetings, in automating tasks by adding computer programming code to a meeting reservation form. The form is used to take meeting reservations over the phone and then send out confirmations by fax. You will create a macro to print a fax cover sheet for every reservation. You also will add a message that displays when the *Computer* checkbox is checked. Your completed reservation document and fax cover sheet will look similar to Figure 10.20. You will save your documents as *10B_Fax_Firstname_Lastname* and *10B_Meetings_Firstname_Lastname*.

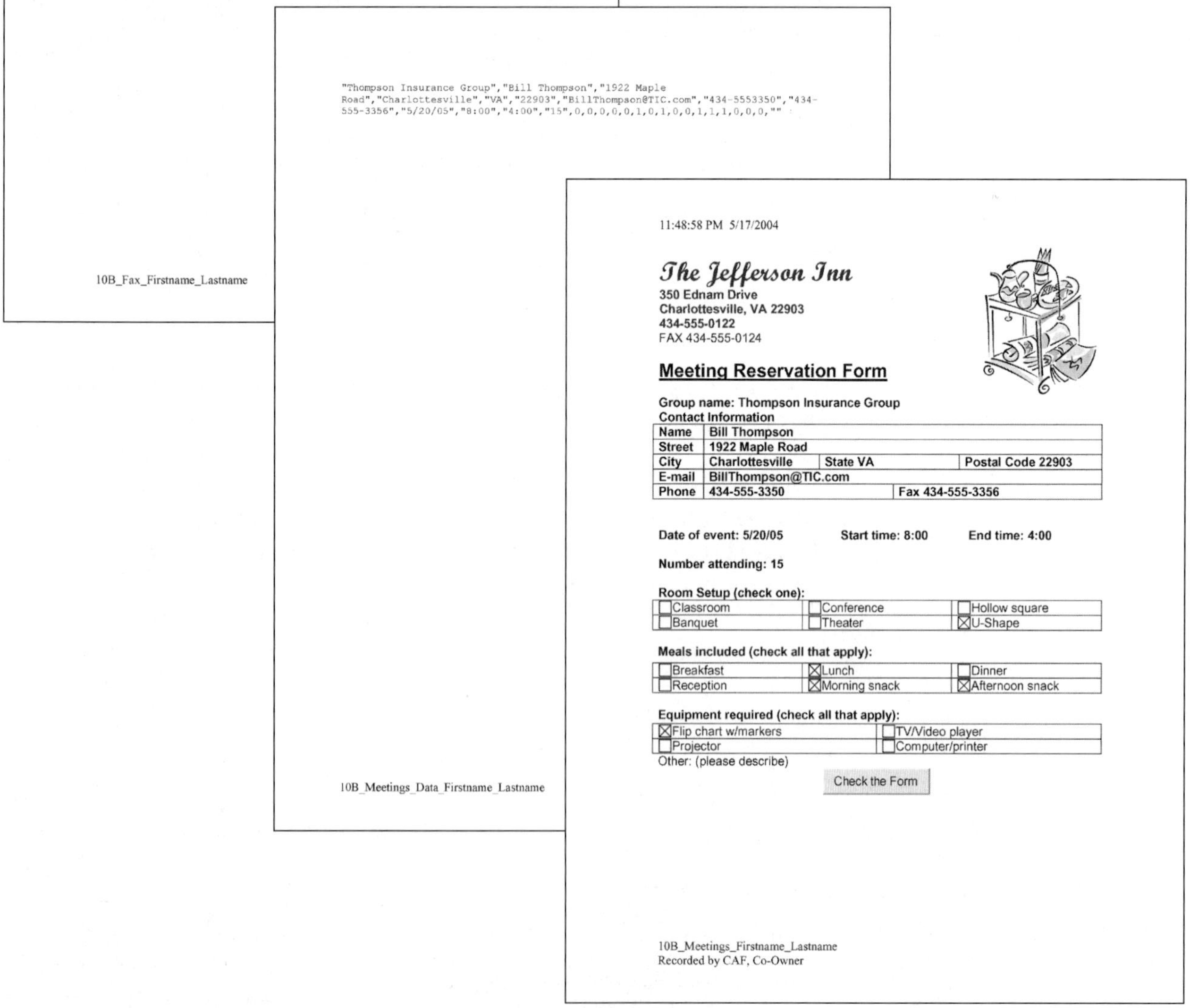

A fax from

*The Jefferson Inn*

To: **Bill Thompson**
Fax number: 434-555-3356

350 Ednam Drive
Charlottesville, VA 22903
434-555-0122
FAX: 434-555-0124

**Today's Date: 5/17/2004**

**Regarding: Meeting reservation for Thompson Insurance Group**

10B_Fax_Firstname_Lastname

"Thompson Insurance Group","Bill Thompson","1922 Maple Road","Charlottesville","VA","22903","BillThompson@TIC.com","434-5553350","434-555-3356","5/20/05","8:00","4:00","15",0,0,0,0,0,1,0,1,0,0,1,1,1,0,0,0,""

10B_Meetings_Data_Firstname_Lastname

11:48:58 PM  5/17/2004

*The Jefferson Inn*
350 Ednam Drive
Charlottesville, VA 22903
434-555-0122
FAX 434-555-0124

### Meeting Reservation Form

**Group name: Thompson Insurance Group**
**Contact Information**

| Name | Bill Thompson | | |
|---|---|---|---|
| Street | 1922 Maple Road | | |
| City | Charlottesville | State VA | Postal Code 22903 |
| E-mail | BillThompson@TIC.com | | |
| Phone | 434-555-3350 | Fax 434-555-3356 | |

**Date of event: 5/20/05**     **Start time: 8:00**     **End time: 4:00**

**Number attending: 15**

**Room Setup (check one):**

| ☐ Classroom | ☐ Conference | ☐ Hollow square |
|---|---|---|
| ☐ Banquet | ☐ Theater | ☒ U-Shape |

**Meals included (check all that apply):**

| ☐ Breakfast | ☒ Lunch | ☐ Dinner |
|---|---|---|
| ☐ Reception | ☒ Morning snack | ☒ Afternoon snack |

**Equipment required (check all that apply):**

| ☒ Flip chart w/markers | ☐ TV/Video player |
|---|---|
| ☐ Projector | ☐ Computer/printer |

Other: (please describe)

Check the Form

10B_Meetings_Firstname_Lastname
Recorded by CAF, Co-Owner

**Figure 10.20**

# Objective 4
## Automate a Form with Macros

A *macro* is a series of commands and instructions that are grouped together as a single command. Create a macro to perform a set of actions automatically—with a single mouse-click, with a keyboard shortcut, or when a document opens or closes. For example, a macro could open a new document, create a 3x3 table, format the table with specific colors and fonts, and then type your name in the first cell of the table.

Using the macro command, you record a series of actions, which are stored by Word as a single command. When you run the macro, the series of commands is performed automatically.

### Activity 10.14  Renaming Form Field Bookmarks

Recall that when you add a form field, a bookmark is created for that field. Each field is given a unique bookmark name. To use the data from one form in another form, the bookmark names need to match. In this activity, you will rename three bookmarks in each of two different files.

---

**Note — Completing This Project**

It is recommended that you allow enough time to complete this entire project in one working session.

---

**1** **Start** Word. From the student files that accompany this textbook, locate and open **w10B_Meetings**. Save the file in your chapter folder as **10B_Meetings_Firstname_Lastname**

**2** Set the **Zoom** 100% to **Page Width**. If necessary, click **Show/Hide ¶** button ¶ to show formatting marks. Display the Forms toolbar.

This form is used to reserve meeting rooms at the Jefferson Inn.

**3** Display the Header and Footer toolbar, switch to the footer area, click the **Insert AutoText** button Insert AutoText ▾, and then click **Filename**. Close the Header and Footer toolbar.

**4** From the student files that accompany this textbook, locate and open **w10B_Fax** and save the file in your chapter folder as **10B_Fax_Firstname_Lastname**

This is the fax form that will be used to confirm meeting reservations.

**5** Set the **Zoom** 100% to **Page Width**. If necessary, click **Show/Hide ¶** button ¶ to show formatting marks.

**6** Display the Header and Footer toolbar, switch to the footer area, click the **Insert AutoText** button Insert AutoText ▾, and then click **Filename**. Close the Header and Footer toolbar.

**7** On the taskbar, click the **10B_Meetings_Firstname_Lastname** document button.

The contents of three of the form fields—*Group name*, *Name*, and *Fax*—will be used in the fax form.

**8** To the right of **Group name:** right-click on the form field and click **Properties**.

This is another way to display the Text Form Field Options dialog box. Under *Field settings*, notice that *Text1* displays in the Bookmark box. Recall that a bookmark is created and named for each form field added to a document. The default bookmark name for a form text field is *Text*, followed by a number.

**Alert!**

## Is the Properties Command Available?

If you right-click the text form field and the Properties command is unavailable, unprotect the form. Recall that editing a form requires that the form be unprotected. In the Forms toolbar, click the Protect Form button. The Properties command will be available in the shortcut menu.

**9** Under **Field settings**, in the **Bookmark** box, select the existing text, and then type **Groupname**

Compare your dialog box with Figure 10.21.

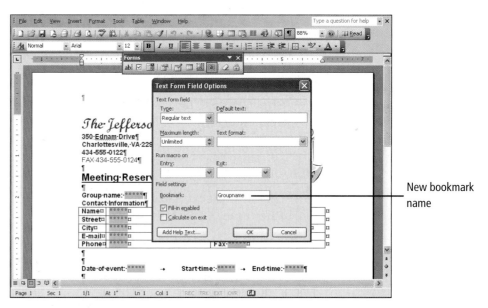

New bookmark name

**Figure 10.21**

**10** Click **OK**. Right-click the form field to the right of **Name**. From the shortcut menu, click **Properties**. In the **Text Form Field Options** dialog box, change the bookmark name to **Contactname** and click **OK**. Repeat this technique to change the bookmark name of the text field to the right of **Fax** to **Contactfax**

The date field automatically inserts the current date, and the bookmark name does not need to be changed.

**11** From the taskbar, switch to the **10B_Fax_Firstname_Lastname** document.

**12** Right-click the **To:** form field and click **Properties** from the shortcut menu. Change the bookmark text to **Contactname**

**13** Right-click the **Fax number** form field, click **Properties**, and then change the bookmark text to **Contactfax** Right-click the **Regarding: Meeting reservation for** form field, and then change the bookmark text to **Groupname**

The three fields on the fax form now have the same bookmark names as the associated form fields in the *10B_Meetings_Firstname_Lastname* document. This will enable you to fill in these forms automatically using a macro. The date field automatically inserts the current date and will not need to have its bookmark name changed.

**14** If necessary, display the Forms toolbar, and then click the **Protect Form** button to protect the form. Click the **Show/Hide ¶** button to hide the formatting marks, and then click the **Save** button. Close the **10B_Fax_Firstname_Lastname** document.

**Activity 10.15** Setting the Security Level and Filling in the Form

Opening a Word document that has a macro attached may cause a security warning to display indicating that macros may contain viruses. Because a macro is a computer program, programming code that erases or damages files can be inserted. This unauthorized code is called a *macro virus*. To protect systems from this type of virus, organizations commonly set their security programs to disable macros automatically or block any e-mail attachment that contains a macro. The Jefferson Inn uses macros to automate some of the repetitive tasks encountered when making meeting reservations over the phone. In this activity, you will adjust the security level in Word to allow macros to run.

**1** With your **10B_Meetings_Firstname_Lastname** form displayed, from the **Tools** menu, point to **Macro**, and then click **Security**. In the displayed **Security** dialog box, be sure the **Security Level tab** is selected. Click the **Medium** option button.

The medium level of security for dealing with macros is selected, as shown in Figure 10.22. This is the default security setting and enables you to choose whether to open a document that contains macros.

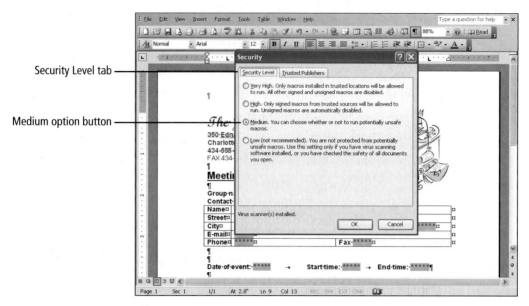

Security Level tab

Medium option button

**Figure 10.22**

▣ Click **OK**. If necessary, display the Forms toolbar, and then click the **Protect Form** button 🔒. Click the **Group name** form field to select it. Fill in the following Meeting Reservation information. Use the Tab key to move from field to field.

Group name: **Thompson Insurance Group**

Name: **Bill Thompson**

Street: **1922 Maple Road**

City: **Charlottesville**

State: **VA**

Postal Code: **22903**

E-mail: **BillThompson@TIC.com**

Phone: **434-555-3350**

Fax: **434-555-3356**

Date of event: **5/20/05**

Start time: **8:00**

End time: **4:00**

Number attending: **15**

Under **Room Setup**, click to select the **U-Shape** check box.

Under **Meals included**, click to select the **Lunch**, **Morning snack**, and **Afternoon snack** check boxes.

Under **Equipment required**, click the **Flip chart w/markers** check box.

To deselect a check box selected by mistake, click it again. Compare your form with Figure 10.23.

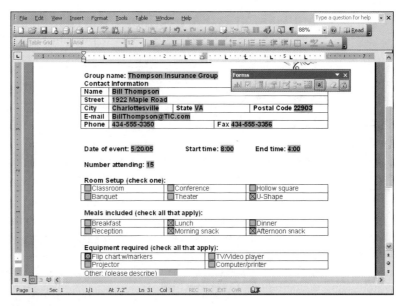

**Figure 10.23**

**3** On the Standard toolbar, click the **Save** button 🖫.

### Activity 10.16 Recording a Keyboard-Activated Macro

After Elena takes a meeting reservation by phone using the form, she confirms the reservation by sending a fax to the contact person. The cover sheet for the fax uses the same information that she has typed into the reservation form. In this activity, you will create a macro to automate the task of filling in the fax cover sheet form by using the information that is already in the reservation form. The macro will open the fax cover sheet form, copy information from the reservation form, and place it on the Office Clipboard. From the Office Clipboard, Elena can paste the appropriate information into the fax cover sheet without retyping it.

**1** On the Forms toolbar, click the **Protect Form** button 🔒 to turn *off* the protection—the button is *not* surrounded by an orange frame after the mouse pointer is moved away from the button.

The protection must be off to record a macro.

**2** On the **Tools** menu, point to **Macro**, and then click **Record New Macro**.

**3** In the displayed **Record Macro** dialog box, in the **Macro name** box, type **Fax** Click the **Store macro in arrow**, and then click your **10B_Meetings_Firstname_Lastname** document.

The macro named *Fax* will be stored in your form, rather than being added to the macros available to all documents. You can assign a macro to a key combination, or you can add a button to a toolbar and use the mouse to activate the macro.

**4** Under **Assign macro to**, click the **Keyboard** button.

**5** In the displayed **Customize Keyboard** dialog box, with the insertion point positioned in the **Press new shortcut key** box, hold down Alt and press F.

*Alt+F* displays in the *Press new shortcut key* box. This enables you to activate the macro you are about to create by holding down Alt and pressing F. (Note: If the shortcut key is already in use, try another letter.)

**6** Under **Specify keyboard sequence**, click the **Save changes in arrow**, and then click your **10B_Meetings_Firstname_Lastname** document.

The Customize Keyboard dialog box displays your keyboard shortcut and location where the macro will be saved, as shown in Figure 10.24.

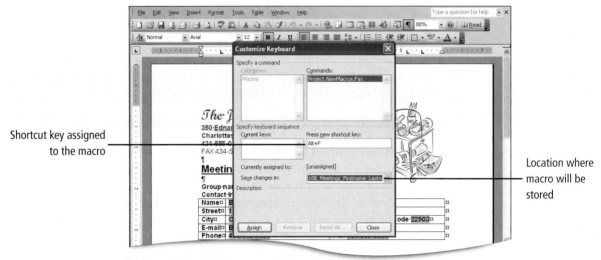

Shortcut key assigned to the macro

Location where macro will be stored

**Figure 10.24**

**7** At the bottom of the dialog box, click the **Assign** button, and then click **Close**.

The Record Macro toolbar displays on the screen, and the pointer displays a tape cassette icon, as shown in Figure 10.25. From this point forward, the macro recorder will record all your actions. The amount of time you take between actions is not recorded, so do not feel rushed. If you make an error, continue with the next step; later you will practice editing and deleting a macro.

Macro Recorder pointer ———

Record Macro toolbar ———

**Figure 10.25**

---

**8** Take your time; the macro recorder is recording all of your actions. From the **Edit** menu, click **Office Clipboard**. In the **Clipboard** task pane, click the **Clear All** button to clear any preexisting items.

**9** From the **Edit** menu, click **Go To**. In the **Find and Replace** dialog box, in the **Go to what** list, click **Bookmark**.

Recall that each field in the form has a default bookmark name— *Text1*, *Text2*, and so on—and that you renamed three of the fields with specific names.

**10** Click the **Enter bookmark name arrow**. Scroll down the list and click **Groupname**. Near the bottom of the dialog box, click the **Go To** button, and then to the right of the Go To button, click the **Close** button.

The field to the right of *Group name* is selected.

**11** On the Standard toolbar, click the **Copy** button 📋.

The name of the group is stored in the Office Clipboard as shown in Figure 10.26.

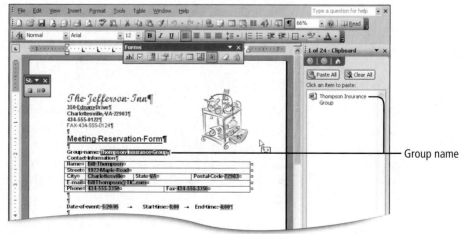

——— Group name

**Figure 10.26**

**12** From the **Edit** menu, click **Go To**. Click the **Enter bookmark name arrow**. Scroll down the list and click **Contactfax**. Click the **Go To** button and then click the **Close** button.

The field to the right of *Fax* is selected.

**13** On the Standard toolbar, click the **Copy** button.

The fax number of the group is added to the top of the list on the Office Clipboard.

**14** From the **Edit** menu, click **Go To**. Click the **Enter bookmark name arrow**. Scroll down the list and click **Contactname**. Click the **Go To** button and then the **Close** button.

The field to the right of *Name* is selected.

**15** On the Standard toolbar, click the **Copy** button.

The name of the contact person is stored in the Office Clipboard as shown in Figure 10.27.

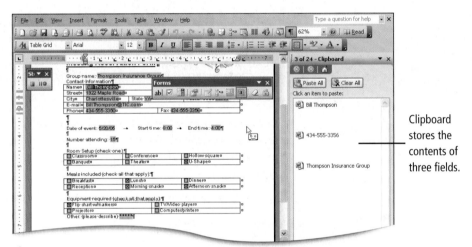

Clipboard stores the contents of three fields.

**Figure 10.27**

**16** From the **File** menu, click **Open**. Locate your **10B_Fax_Firstname_Lastname** file, click to select the file name, and then in the lower right corner of the dialog box, click **Open** to display the fax cover sheet form. From the **Edit** menu, click **Office Clipboard** to display the **Clipboard** task pane. On the Record Macro toolbar, click the **Stop Recording** button.

All of your mouse clicks and keystrokes were recorded. Now the fax cover sheet form can be filled out by pasting the appropriate information from the Office Clipboard into the form. Each time a Meeting Reservation form is filled out, this macro will gather the information for the fax cover sheet and place it on the Office Clipboard.

The macro recording feature has some limitations. It does not work within wizards, and you cannot select things using the click and drag method. This is why you used bookmarks to locate and select the fields in the Meetings Reservation form. You have created a macro to perform part of the work but have left the final steps to the person completing the form.

**17** In the **Clipboard** task pane, click **Bill Thompson**.

The name is pasted into the field to the right of *To:* in the form, which is the form's first field.

**18** Press Tab. In the **Clipboard** task pane, click **434-555-3356**.

**19** Press Tab. In the **Clipboard** task pane, click **Thompson Insurance Group**.

The cover sheet is filled in with information from the reservation form, as shown in Figure 10.28.

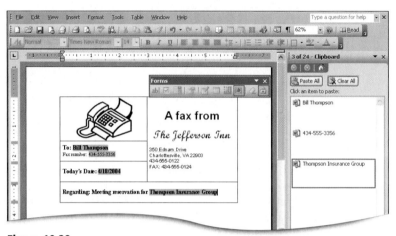

**Figure 10.28**

**20** On the Standard toolbar, click the **Print** button [icon] to print the form. **Close** [X] the Clipboard task pane, and then close the form and do *not* save the changes.

The fax cover sheet form is closed, and your 10B_Meetings_ Firstname_Lastname form remains open.

**21** In the **Clipboard** task pane, click the **Clear All** button. **Close** [X] the task pane.

**22** On the Standard toolbar, click the **Save** button [icon].

### Activity 10.17 Running and Testing Macros

You may need several attempts to create a successful macro. A simple method for correcting errors is to test the macro, delete it if it does not work correctly, and then record a new one.

**1** With your **10B_Meetings_Firstname_Lastname** form displayed, be sure that the form is still unprotected—the Protect Form button is *not* surrounded by an orange frame.

With the form unprotected, macros can be recorded or tested.

**2** From the **Tools** menu, point to **Macro**, and then click **Macros**.

The Macros dialog box displays.

**3** Click the **Macros in arrow** and click your **10B_Meetings_Firstname_Lastname** document.

The list of macros recorded in this document displays. The list has only one entry—Fax—as shown in Figure 10.29.

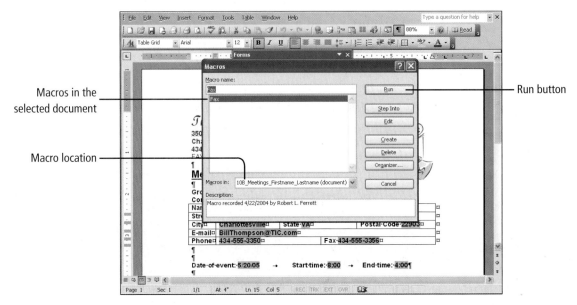

Macros in the selected document

Macro location

Run button

**Figure 10.29**

**4** In the **Macro name** list, click **Fax**, and then click the **Run** button.

If you recorded the macro correctly, the fax cover sheet file opens, and the three fields display in the Clipboard task pane, as shown in Figure 10.30. If your macro did not run correctly, move directly to Activity 10.18.

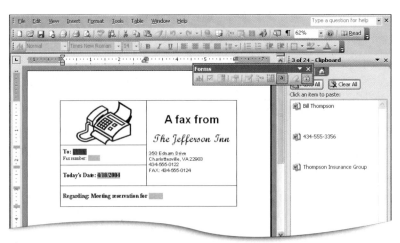

**Figure 10.30**

**5** In the **Clipboard** task pane, click the **Clear All** button. Close your **10B_Fax_Firstname_Lastname** file; if prompted, do not save any changes.

**6** Press [Alt] + [F].

The Fax macro will run again, assuming it was correctly assigned to the [Alt] + [F] keys.

**7** Clear the Office Clipboard and close your **10B_Fax_Firstname_Lastname** file; if prompted, do not save any changes.

---

**More Knowledge** — Running Macros in **Protected Documents**

If you record a macro and then protect the document, the macro will perform only the tasks that are available in a protected document. For example, if you create a macro to place a date in a form header, and then protect the form, the macro will display an error message because the header and footer areas are not accessible in a protected form. If you receive an error message of this type, click OK, and the macro will move to the next step, ignoring the date in the header.

---

**Activity 10.18** Deleting a Macro

If your macro does not work properly, or if you desire to make an improvement, you can delete the macro and record it again.

**1** If your macro did *not* work properly, follow the steps below to delete it and repeat Activity 10.16. If your macro *did* work properly, perform the following steps up to the point of actually deleting the macro.

**2** **Close** the **Clipboard** task pane. Confirm that the form is unprotected—the Protect Form button on the toolbar is not selected.

The form must be unprotected to add or delete macros.

**3** From the **Tools** menu, point to **Macro**, and then click **Macros**. In the **Macros** dialog box, click the **Macros in arrow**, and then click your **10B_Meetings_Firstname_Lastname** document.

The macros attached to this file are displayed, as shown in Figure 10.31.

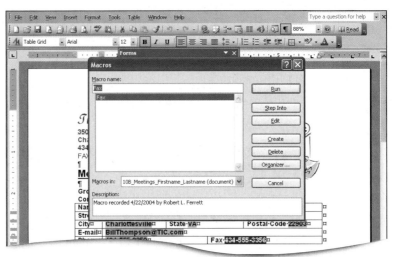

**Figure 10.31**

**4** Under the **Macro name** box, click **Fax**. If you want to delete this macro and record it again, click the **Delete** button. Otherwise, proceed to the next step.

**5** Click **Cancel** to close the **Macros** dialog box.

### Activity 10.19 Creating a Toolbar-Activated Macro

In Activities 10.16 through 10.18, you set your macro to activate by using the keyboard shortcut Alt + F. You can also set your macro to activate from a button on a toolbar. In the following activity, you will record a macro that will place the initials of the person who took the meeting reservation in the footer area.

**1** Confirm that your **10B_Meetings_Firstname_Lastname** file is open and the form is unprotected. If you are reopening the document, enable macros when prompted.

The form must be unprotected to add or delete macros.

**2** From the **Tools** menu, point to **Macro**, and then click **Record New Macro**.

The Record Macro dialog box opens.

**3** In the **Record Macro** dialog box, in the **Macro name** box, type Initials Click the **Store macro in arrow**, and then click your **10B_Meetings_Firstname_Lastname** document.

The *Initials* macro will be stored in your form, rather than as a macro available to all documents.

**4** Under **Assign macro to**, click the **Toolbars** button, and then in the displayed **Customize** dialog box, click the **Commands tab**.

The Customize dialog box displays the macros assigned to the toolbar, as shown in Figure 10.32.

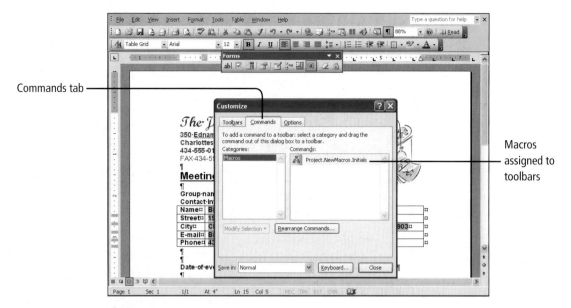

**Figure 10.32**

Commands tab ——

Macros assigned to toolbars

**5** In the **Commands** box, move the mouse pointer over **Project.NewMacros.Initials**. Drag this command onto the Formatting toolbar to the left of the **Bold** button **B**. Release the mouse button.

A button is added to the Formatting toolbar with the name of the macro on it. Your Formatting toolbar may wrap to a second row, depending on your screen resolution and the number of buttons on the toolbar.

**6** Click the **Modify Selection** button. In the displayed menu, click **Name** to select the default macro name. Type **Initials** and then press Enter.

The word *Initials* replaces the text on the button, as shown in Figure 10.33.

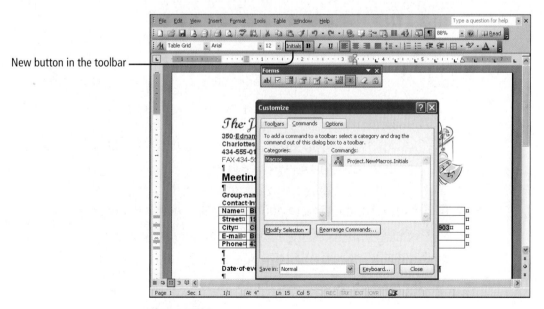

**Figure 10.33**

New button in the toolbar ——

chapter**ten**

**7** At the bottom of the dialog box, click the **Close** button.

The text on the button changes to *Initials* and the Record Macro toolbar displays.

**8** Take your time; your actions are now being recorded for your macro. From the **View** menu, click **Header and Footer**. On the Header and Footer toolbar, click the **Switch Between Header and Footer** button 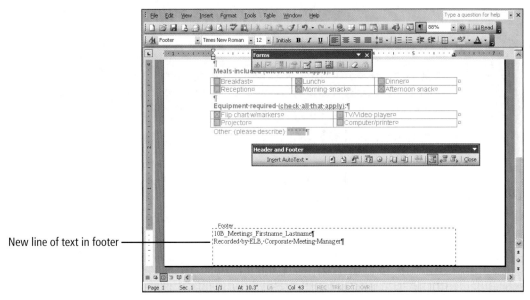.

**9** Press the End key, and then press Enter to move the insertion point to the beginning of a new line in the footer. Type **Recorded by ELB, Corporate Meeting Manager**

The phrase with the Elena's initials, *ELB*, is added to a new line in the footer as shown in Figure 10.34.

New line of text in footer ———

**Figure 10.34**

**10** On the Header and Footer toolbar, click the **Close** button.

**11** On the Record Macro toolbar, click the **Stop Recording** button.

A macro to add the phrase is recorded and attached to a button on the toolbar.

**12** On the Standard toolbar, click the **Undo** button to remove the new line from the footer. Scroll to the bottom of the document to confirm that the text with the initials has been removed.

**13** On the Formatting toolbar, click your new **Initials** button.

The macro runs and places the text in the footer.

**14** Confirm that the new line has been added to the footer. On the Standard toolbar, click the **Save** button.

### Activity 10.20 Creating a Macro That Runs Automatically When the Document Closes

You can create a macro that runs automatically based on the occurrence of a specific event. For example, when you close Word, Word searches the Normal template for a macro named **AutoClose**, which it runs before it closes Word. In this activity, you will create a macro to add the date and time to the header when the document is closed.

**1** Be sure that your **10B_Meetings_Firstname_Lastname** file is open and then, if necessary, click to unprotect the form.

The form must be unprotected to add or delete macros.

**2** From the **Tools** menu, point to **Macro**, and then click **Record New Macro**.

The Record Macro dialog box displays.

**3** In the **Record Macro** dialog box, in the **Macro name** box, type **AutoClose** Under **Assign macro to**, click the **Store macro in arrow**, and then click your **10B_Meetings_Firstname_Lastname** document.

Do not use spaces between the words in the macro name. The macro named *AutoClose* will be stored in your form as shown in Figure 10.35.

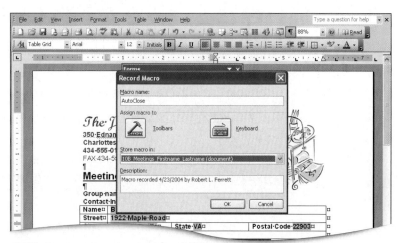

**Figure 10.35**

---

**Alert!**

### Do Not Save the Macro in the Normal Template

Be careful that you save this macro in your document rather than in the Normal.dot template. If you save the macro in the Normal.dot template on your computer, the macro will run every time a document is closed.

---

**4** Click **OK**. Take your time; the recorder is now recording all of your actions. From the **View** menu, click **Header and Footer**.

**5** From the **Edit** menu, click **Select All**. From the **Edit** menu, point to **Clear**, and then click **Contents**.

Any previous header is deleted.

**6** On the Header and Footer toolbar, click the **Insert Time** button ▣. Press ⌈Spacebar⌋ twice.

The time and two spaces are inserted.

**7** On the Header and Footer toolbar, click the **Insert Date** button ▣.

Word checks your computer's internal clock and calendar and inserts the current time and date as shown in Figure 10.36.

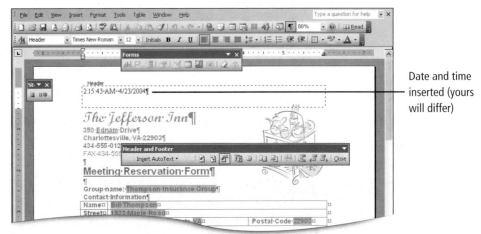

Date and time inserted (yours will differ)

**Figure 10.36**

**8** On the Header and Footer toolbar, click the **Close** button ⌈Close⌋. On the Record Macro toolbar, click the **Stop Recording** button ▣.

The AutoClose macro will add the time and date when the document is closed.

**9** On the Standard toolbar, click the **Undo** button ▣ three times to remove the date, spaces, and time from the header, as shown in Figure 10.37.

Date and time are removed.

**Figure 10.37**

**10** Close the document and save the changes.

The macro should run and place the date and time in the header, and then close the document.

**11** Open your **10B_Meetings_Firstname_Lastname** document. If prompted, click **Enable Macros**.

Notice that the time and date have been placed in the header. The current time and date will be added automatically each time the document is closed.

---

### More Knowledge — AutoRunning Macros

If you create a new document from a template, Word checks the template for a macro named *AutoNew* that runs when a new document is created from the template. Individual documents may contain macros named *AutoOpen* and *AutoClose* that run automatically when the document is opened or closed, respectively.

---

## Objective 5
## Control a Form with Visual Basic for Applications (VBA)

The macro command records your actions in the Visual Basic for Applications (VBA) programming language and builds the program code for you. To take advantage of all the options available in the VBA programming language, you must work directly with the code. Microsoft provides a *Visual Basic Editor (VBE)*, with which you can modify existing macro code or write new code.

### Activity 10.21 Editing a Macro Using the Visual Basic Editor

In this activity, you will edit the *Initials* macro and change the initials that are placed automatically in the footer by the macro. This approach is faster than recording a new macro.

**1** Be sure your **10B_Meetings_Firstname_Lastname** file is displayed and that the protection is turned off.

**2** From the **Tools** menu, point to **Macro**, and then click **Macros**.

**3** In the **Macros** dialog box, under **Macro name**, click **Initials**, and then click the **Edit** button. If necessary, **Maximize** the Visual Basic Editor window and the editing window that displays the programming code.

The Microsoft Visual Basic Editor window displays the code for the *Initials* macro in the editing window. See Figure 10.38.

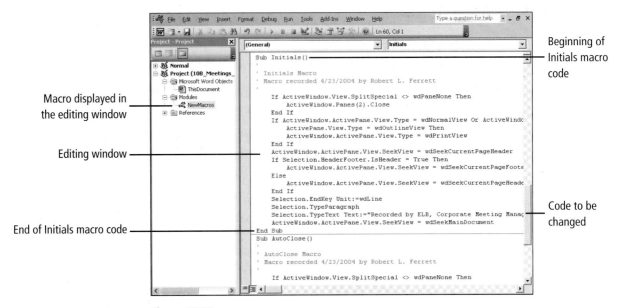

**Figure 10.38**

> **Note** — **If Your Screen Differs**
>
> When you open the Visual Basic Editor, you may see the programming code for all of the macros attached to the document. This occurs if the last person to use the VBE chose to view *(Declarations)* instead of an individual macro. If more than one macro displays at the top of the edit window, click the arrow in the right box—the one that displays *(Declarations)*—and then click Initials.

**4** At the top of the editing window that displays the programming code, if the box on the right displays *(Declarations)*, click the arrow to the right of *(Declarations)*, and then click **Initials** to display only the code for the *Initials* macro.

**5** Near the end of the *Initials* macro code, locate the initials **ELB**. Select the text *ELB, Corporate Meeting Manager*—but not the quotation mark—and type **CAF, Co-Owner** for Carmen Fredericks, co-owner of the Inn.

The macro attached to the toolbar button will now use the new initials.

**6** From the **File** menu, click **Close and Return to Microsoft Word**.

The revised macro is ready to use.

**7** From the **View** menu, click **Header and Footer**. On the Header and Footer toolbar, click the **Switch Between Header and Footer** button. Select and delete *Recorded by ELB, Corporate Meeting Manager*, including the paragraph mark at the end of the line. On the Header and Footer toolbar, click the **Close** button.

**8** On the Standard toolbar, click the **Initials** button that you created earlier.

The macro places the new initials in the footer, as shown in Figure 10.39.

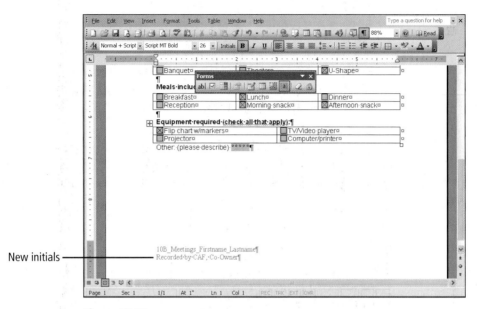

New initials

**Figure 10.39**

**9** From the **View** menu, point to **Toolbars**, and then at the bottom of the list click **Customize**. With the **Customize** dialog box displayed, point to the **Initials button** that you created and drag it off of the toolbar into an empty place below the toolbar area in the document window. Release the mouse button.

The button is removed from the toolbar.

**10** In the **Customize** dialog box, click **Close**.

The Initials macro still exists, but the button has been removed from the Standard toolbar to return it to its original condition.

**11** On the Standard toolbar, click the **Save** button 🔲.

### Activity 10.22 Writing a Procedure in VBA to Save Data

You can use the Visual Basic Editor to write code in the Visual Basic for Applications language. To write effective VBA procedures, plan to enroll in a formal course in VBA programming. However, you can gain some familiarity with VBA by entering a prewritten program. In this activity, you will write a program to save the contents of the form fields without the rest of the form's text. By doing this, the data can be used in this format by other Office programs to store reservations and produce reports.

**1** From the **Tools** menu, point to **Macro**, and then click **Visual Basic Editor**.

The code for the *Initials* macro displays, because this was the last macro edited in the editing window.

**2** Scroll to the bottom of the code window and click in the empty line at the bottom. Type the following lines. Substitute today's date and your name as indicated, in place of the example text:

**Sub SaveAsData()**
**'**

**' SaveAsData Macro**
**' Macro recorded Today's Date by Firstname Lastname**
**'**

The first line declares the following section to be a section of code named *SaveAsData*. The name of the code is followed by two parentheses with no space between them. An End Sub statement is added automatically.

The other lines begin with a single quotation mark, which means these are comments that the program will ignore. This is space for **documentation**, which is information added by programmers to identify who wrote the code and when it was written. Use the current date and your name as shown in Figure 10.40.

Start of new macro —————

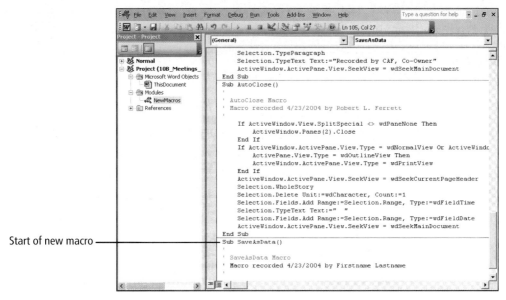

**Figure 10.40**

**3** Press Enter. On the next three lines type the following, leaving the insertion point at the end of the last line. Be sure to start the middle line with a period. The *With* and *End With* statements enclose a statement that turns on the feature that saves only the data. Use the space bar to indent the second line to make it easier to identify as a statement that goes between the other two lines. The number of spaces you use for indents is up to you. You can also use Tab to indent lines. As you type the second line, an AutoComplete feature displays options for completing the command. Ignore them for now.

**With ActiveDocument**
**    .SaveFormsData = True**
**End With**

**4** From the taskbar, return to your **10B_Meetings_Firstname_ Lastname** document.

The Visual Basic Editor window remains open.

**5** On the Standard toolbar, click the **Open** button . Navigate to the location where the student files for this textbook are stored. Locate and open **w10B_VBA_Text**. Press Ctrl + A to select all of the text. On the Standard toolbar, click the **Copy** button . Close the **w10B_VBA_Text** file.

**6** From the taskbar, return to the Visual Basic Editor. Press Enter, and then from the toolbar in the VBE window, click the **Paste** button . Compare your screen with Figure 10.41.

New VBA code —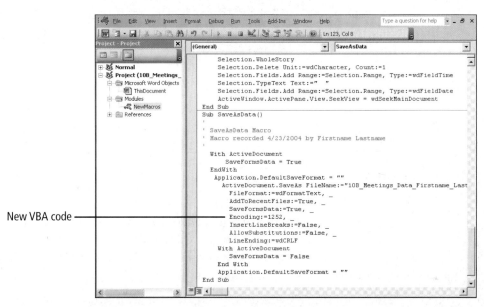

**Figure 10.41**

**7** From the **File** menu, click **Close and Return to Microsoft Word**.

You have completed a program in VBA named *SaveAsData*.

**8** From the **Tools** menu, point to **Macro**, and then click **Macros**. In the **Macro name** box, click **SaveAsData**, and then click the **Run** button.

Nothing appears to happen, but if your macro worked correctly, a text file with the data from the form was written to the folder where you keep your other files for this chapter.

**Alert!**

## If You Receive a Compile Error Message

Any typing error in the program code will cause a compile error. When this occurs, the Visual Basic Editor will open, and the line with the error will be highlighted. The usual cause of error is an extra space or an omitted space. For example, if you type *End With* as *EndWith*, the program will not work. Also, if you type *End Sub* at the end of a macro, and the program also adds this command, the program will display a compile error. You can correct the mistake in the editor, save your changes, and then close the editor.

**9** From the **File** menu, click **Open**. If necessary, navigate to your chapter folder. Confirm that the **Files of type** box displays **All Files**.

Click the **Views button arrow** ▦▾ and click **Details**. Locate the text document that has the same name as the Word document form. Click the text document **10B_Meetings_Firstname_Lastname** and then click **Open**.

Notice that the text file icon and the Word document icon are different and that the description in the Type column is also different. The contents of the form fields have been saved as data. Empty check boxes are represented by zeros, and checked boxes are represented by ones, as shown in Figure 10.42.

Form data ——————

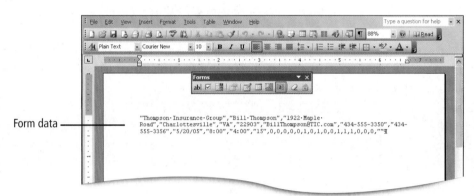

**Figure 10.42**

**10** From the **File** menu, click **Save As**. At the bottom of the **Save As** dialog box, click the **Save as type arrow**, and then click **Word Document**. Save the document as **10B_Meetings_Data_Firstname_Lastname**

**11** From the **View** menu, click **Header and Footer**. On the Header and Footer toolbar, click the **Switch Between Header and Footer** button 🖹. Click the **Insert AutoText** button Insert AutoText ▾, and then click **Filename**. On the **Header and Footer** toolbar, click the **Close** button Close.

**12** On the Standard toolbar, click the **Print** button 🖨. Close the document, saving any changes.

The *10B_Meetings_Firstname_Lastname* document displays again.

**13** On the Forms toolbar, click the **Reset Form Fields** button ⬚. Leave the form unprotected. On the Standard toolbar, click the **Save** button 🖫.

# Objective 6
## Add an ActiveX Control to a Form

An **ActiveX control** is a small program attached to an object, such as a check box or button, that offers options to users or that runs macros or scripts that automate a task. Use an ActiveX control on a form to add more powerful functionality to a form in Word. For example, you can add an ActiveX control to a button that will add text to a form if the button is clicked.

In the following activities, you will add a button to check the form after the form has been completed. It will determine whether the *Computer/printer* check box has been selected to indicate that computer equipment is needed for a meeting. If the *Computer/printer* check box has been selected, a message is generated describing the computers that are available in the meeting rooms. The process of adding a control has four steps: inserting, formatting, writing code, and testing.

### Activity 10.23 Inserting an ActiveX Control

An ActiveX control provides a user interface, such as a command button, a check box, or a spin box with up and down arrows, for the person filling out the form. In the following activity, you will add a command button—a type of ActiveX Control—that will be used when a computer is requested for a meeting.

**1** On the **View** menu, point to **Toolbars**, and then click **Control Toolbox**.

The Control Toolbox toolbar displays. The most commonly used controls are displayed on the Control Toolbox toolbar. The More Controls button at the bottom of the toolbar links to more than a hundred additional controls. The buttons on the toolbar are described in the table shown in Figure 10.43.

## Buttons on the Control Toolbox Toolbar

| Button | Name | Description |
|---|---|---|
| | Design Mode | Toggles between Design Mode and Run Mode. |
| | Properties | Displays the Properties dialog box. |
| | View Code | Displays the related code in the VBA editor. |
| | Check Box | Inserts a check box. |
| | Text Box | Inserts a text box. |
| | Command Button | Inserts a command button to which code can be attached. |
| | Option Button | Indicates an on/off choice. |
| | List Box | Displays a list of choices. |
| | Combo Box | Displays a list of choices from another source. |
| | Toggle Button | Indicates two option choices. |
| | Spin Button | Displays a range of numbers from which to choose. |
| | Scroll Bar | Adds a scroll bar to a box. |
| | Label | Adds a text label. |
| | Image | Inserts a picture. |
| | More Controls | Displays a list of additional controls. |

**Figure 10.43**

**2** If the Control Toolbox toolbar displays in a column two buttons wide, move the pointer over the right edge of the toolbar and drag the right edge to the right until the toolbar consists of three rows of buttons. Confirm that the form is unprotected. Press Ctrl + End to position the insertion point at the end of the document, and then press Enter. On the Control Toolbox, click the **Command Button** button ▣.

The Command Button control is placed at the insertion point, and a one-button Design toolbar opens, as shown in Figure 10.44. Notice that all except the three buttons in the top row of the control toolbox are inactive (dim).

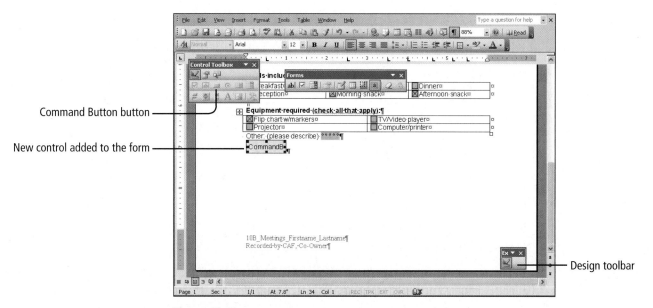

Command Button button

New control added to the form

Design toolbar

**Figure 10.44**

■ On the Standard toolbar, click the **Save** button 🖫.

### Activity 10.24 Formatting an ActiveX Control

When a control is inserted into a document, the control toolbox switches to **design mode**, in which you can change the properties and the code of the control.

■ Be sure the command button is still selected. On the **Control Toolbox** toolbar, click the **Properties** button 🖳.

■ In the displayed **Properties** dialog box, if necessary, click the **Alphabetic tab**. In the **Name** column, double-click **Caption**.

The *Caption* property is selected along with the default text in the box to the right.

■ Type **Check the Form**

The button caption is changed in the dialog box and on the button. Notice the text does not fit within the default button size. See Figure 10.45.

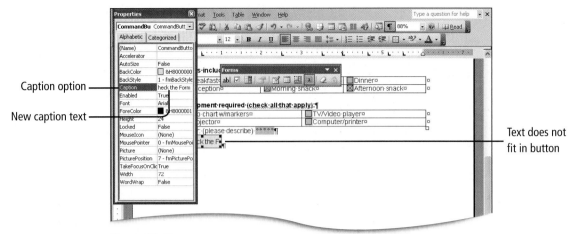

Caption option ———

New caption text ———

Text does not fit in button

**Figure 10.45**

**4** On the Properties list, to the right of the **AutoSize** property, click **False**. Click the arrow to the right of **False** and click **True**.

The AutoSize property adjusts the width of the button to accommodate the text, as shown in Figure 10.46.

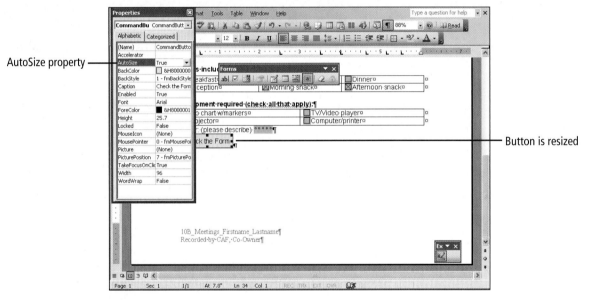

AutoSize property ———

Button is resized

**Figure 10.46**

**5** On the **Properties** dialog box title bar, click the **Close** button ☒.

On the Formatting toolbar, click the **Center** button ▤.

The button is centered horizontally.

**6** On the Standard toolbar, click the **Save** button ▤.

## Activity 10.25 Writing Code for an ActiveX Control

A thorough knowledge of programming is required to take full advantage of ActiveX controls, but you can gain an understanding of their power by editing existing code or by entering code written by someone else. In this activity, you will enter a program that checks the condition of the check box next to the *Computer/printer* option. If the *Computer/printer* check box is selected, a message will display describing the equipment available in the meeting rooms.

The program you will insert uses a common programming technique called *If-Then-Else-End If*. The first line starts with *If* and is followed by a condition to be checked and then the terms *Then* and *Else*. Each of these terms is followed by an action—such as displaying an appropriate message. If the condition is true, the first message displays; if the condition is not true, the second message displays. The End If statement marks the end of this group of code lines.

**1** In your displayed **10B_Meetings_Firstname_Lastname** form, locate the check box to the left of **Computer/printer**, and then right-click on the check box. From the displayed shortcut menu, click **Properties**.

The Check Box Form Field Options dialog box displays. Under Field settings, notice that the bookmark for this check box is *Computer*. The bookmark name is used in the program to identify this checkbox.

**2** In the **Check Box Form Field Options** dialog box, click **Cancel**. Click the **Check the Form** command button to select it. On the Control Toolbox toolbar, click the **View Code** button [icon].

The Microsoft Visual Basic window opens. The opening and closing statements of the code group and the default name of the command button are added automatically, as shown in Figure 10.47.

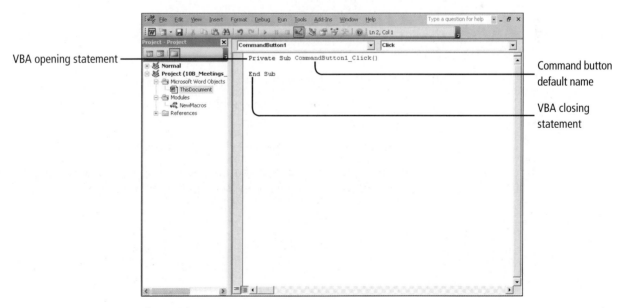

VBA opening statement

Command button default name

VBA closing statement

**Figure 10.47**

**3** Press Spacebar three times to indent the first line of the program. Type **'Program to check for the type of computer requested** and then press Enter.

Recall that lines that begin with a single quote mark contain comments. The line also displays in green. The program ignores them; they are used to explain what the program does. Spaces or tabs are used to indent the lines of text to make subsections of code distinctive. In this example, the *Private Sub* and *End Sub* commands contain the remaining lines of this program; therefore, they are not indented.

**4** Type **If ActiveDocument.FormF**

An AutoComplete box opens to help with writing the code. As you type more letters, the list changes until it chooses the one you want. In this case, you want FormFields.

**5** Press Tab to accept the suggested text.

The selected term is added by the AutoComplete feature, as shown in Figure 10.48.

VBA command

VBA comment

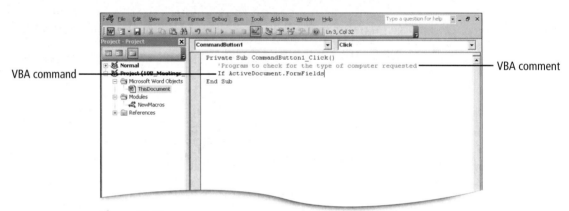

**Figure 10.48**

**6** Continuing on the same line, type **("Computer")**

Recall that *Computer* is the bookmark name of the check box next to the Computer/printer text.

**7** Continuing on the same line, type **.Checkbox.Value = True**

Be sure you type the period to the left of *Checkbox*. This completes the condition that examines the check box to see if it is checked.

**8** Continuing on the same line, press [Spacebar], type **Then** and then press [Enter].

This line contains the condition and the two commands, *If* and *Then*. If the condition is met, the next line of code will be executed.

**Alert!** | **Syntax Mistakes Produce Error Boxes**

If you make an error while typing one of the lines of code, the Visual Basic Editor will display an error message describing the type of error. Depending on the type of error, the editor may highlight the line of code and place the insertion point at the point of the error. Check what you typed against the instructions in the step to determine the location of the error. Edit the code as necessary.

**9** Press [Spacebar] three times to indent the next line. Type **'Display message if computer is requested** and press [Enter].

This line is a comment that describes what this section of the program does. Notice that the editor helps with indenting the text by returning to the same horizontal position on the next line.

**10** Type **TitleBarText = "Computer Requested"** and press [Enter]. Type **MessageText = "The computer provided will be a PC running Office 2003. If you need a different type of computer, please describe it in the 'Other' option and we will do our best to accommodate you."** and press [Enter].

These two lines determine the title and text of a message box. Notice that single quotation marks may be used inside of the double quotes if quotation marks are needed.

**11** Type **MsgBox MessageText, , TitleBarText** and then press [Enter].

This line displays the message box with the title and text from the two lines above.

**12** Press [←] to reduce the indent by one space. Type **Else** and press [Enter].

The lines following this statement will be executed if the *If* condition is false—the check box is not checked. If the condition is true, the lines of code in this section will be skipped. Execution will pass to the next line of code following the *End If* statement.

**13** Press Spacebar once to indent the following lines of text. Type **'Display message if no computer is requested** and press Enter. Type **TitleBarText = "Form Checked"** and press Enter. Type **MessageText = "We look forward to making your meeting a success."** and press Enter. Type **MsgBox MessageText, , TitleBarText** and press Enter.

These lines set the title and message in a second text box that displays if the Computer/printer box is not checked.

**14** Press ← to reduce the indent by one space and then type **End If**

Compare what you have typed with Figure 10.49. Some of the text may be off the screen. If necessary, use the scroll bar to view it.

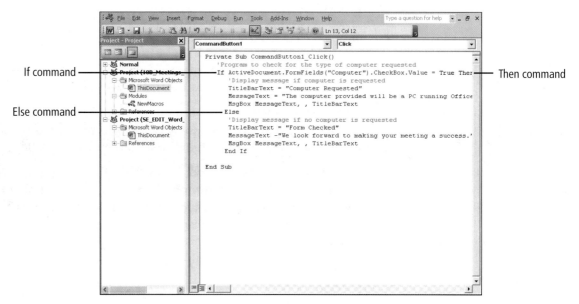

If command

Else command

Then command

**Figure 10.49**

**15** From the **File** menu, click **Close and Return to Microsoft Word**.

On the Standard toolbar, click the **Save** button ⊞.

**Activity 10.26** Running and Testing an ActiveX Control

In this example, two actions can be taken, depending on the condition of one of the check boxes. Both options should be tested to see how the control behaves. In this activity, you will test the ActiveX control that you have created.

**1** On the Control Toolbox toolbar, click the **Exit Design Mode** button ⊠.

**2** If necessary, click an empty part of the form to deselect the command button. On the Forms toolbar, click the **Protect Form** button 🔒.

The form is ready to test.

**3** To the left of the **Computer/printer** text, click the check box. Click the **Check the Form** command button.

The code associated with the command button runs and finds the check box selected. The *If* condition is true, so the code displays the first message box. See Figure 10.50.

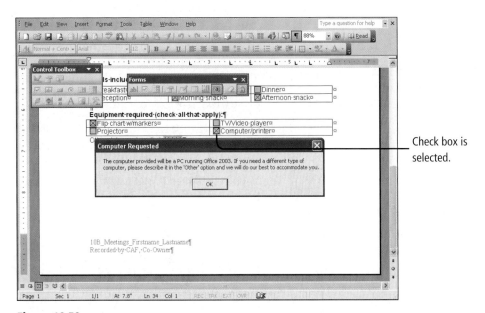

Check box is selected.

**Figure 10.50**

**4** In the message box, click **OK**. To the left of the *Computer/printer* text, click the check box to deselect it, and then click the **Check the Form** button.

The code associated with the command button runs and finds the check box not selected. The *If* condition is false so the code following the Else statement displays the second message box. See Figure 10.51.

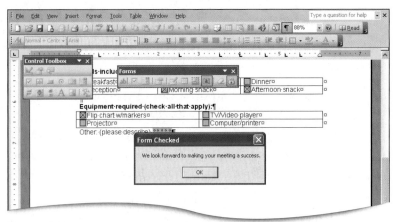

**Figure 10.51**

**5** Click **OK**. Close the Control Toolbox toolbar.

**6** On the Standard toolbar, click the **Save** button 🖫. On the Standard toolbar, click the **Print** button 🖨. Close the Forms toolbar. On the **File** menu, click **Close**, saving any changes.

**End** You have completed Project 10B

# Summary

A form is a document with spaces—form fields—reserved for entering information. When a form is created, others can use Microsoft Word to fill in the form on a computer screen. Microsoft Office has a special form-creation program called InfoPath 2003 for complex forms that are tied to a database. For creating everyday forms, Word 2003 has many features, such as check boxes, drop-down lists, and text fields. Forms can be protected to prevent unauthorized changes and forms can be automated for convenient use.

Forms created in Word can be printed, viewed, or placed on a Web page to collect information online. Creating a form with Word does not require knowledge of programming, databases, or server software. You can use any of the Word features in a form, including the drawing tools, graphics, and tables. A form is often stored as a template that can be used repeatedly without changing the original form.

Forms can contain any Word features, for example, you can include custom backgrounds and watermarks, which are text or pictures that display behind document text.

A macro is useful to automate multiple steps in a procedure. A macro is a series of commands and instructions that are grouped together as a single command. Macros can be activated with a single mouse click or a keyboard shortcut. You can also create a macro that runs automatically based on the occurrence of a specific event, such as opening or closing a document.

A macro can be created automatically by letting Word record your actions. The macro is written in the Visual Basic for Applications (VBA) programming language. You can also open the Visual Basic Editor (VBE) and use it to modify existing macro code or write new code.

An ActiveX control is a control, such as a check box or button, that offers options to users or that runs macros that automate a task. For example, you can add an ActiveX control to a button that will add text to a form if the button is clicked. A thorough knowledge of programming is required to take full advantage of ActiveX controls.

## In This Chapter You Practiced How To

- Create a Customized Form
- Modify a Form
- Save a Form as a Template and Use the Template to Create a New Form
- Automate a Form with Macros
- Control a Form with Visual Basic for Applications (VBA)
- Add an ActiveX Control to a Form

**Matching**   Match each term in the second column with its correct definition in the first column by writing the letter of the term on the blank line in front of the correct definition.

_____ **1.** A button on the Forms toolbar that restores the default values to a field.

_____ **2.** A type of ActiveX control in which the person filling out the form can select, or not select, specific options.

_____ **3.** A series of commands and instructions that are grouped together as a single command.

_____ **4.** The default document template in Word, in which, if you store a macro, the macro will run every time a document is closed.

_____ **5.** A document that contains fill-in areas—form fields—in which an individual can enter data.

_____ **6.** The default macro security level setting in Word.

_____ **7.** A macro that can be stored in a document and that runs automatically when the document is opened.

_____ **8.** A location in a form where a particular type of data, such as a name or address, is stored.

_____ **9.** A picture or text displayed behind the document text.

_____ **10.** A tool for modifying existing macro code, or writing new code, directly within the VBA programming language.

_____ **11.** The dialog box that displays as a result of clicking the Form Field Options button on the Forms toolbar with a text form field selected, and in which you can set the type, length, and format of a form field.

_____ **12.** Information provided in VBA code that is added by programmers to identify the author and the purpose of the code.

_____ **13.** Unauthorized programming code inserted into a macro that erases or damages files.

_____ **14.** A message that displays if an error is detected when writing VBA code.

_____ **15.** A control, such as a check box or button, that offers options to users or runs macros or scripts that automate a task and that adds functionality to a form.

**A** ActiveX control

**B** AutoOpen

**C** Check box

**D** Compile error

**E** Documentation

**F** Form

**G** Form field

**H** Macro

**I** Macro virus

**J** Medium

**K** Normal.dot

**L** Reset Form Field button

**M** Text Form Field Options

**N** Visual Basic Editor

**O** Watermark

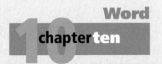

**Fill in the Blank** Write the correct answer in the space provided.

1. A form is usually stored as a(n) _____ so it can be used over and over again.

2. You can type information in a(n) _____ field.

3. The _____ button turns shading on and off.

4. A(n) _____ is a set of unified design elements that provides a uniform look for a document.

5. A unique _____ is created for every form field added to a form.

6. Macros can be run using keyboard commands or _____ on a toolbar.

7. A(n) _____ macro runs automatically every time a document is closed.

8. Click the _____ button to change the formatting of a form field.

9. Use a(n) _____ form field to present information in a list.

10. You must _____ a form before entering information into the form fields.

# Project 10C—Web Contact Form

**Objectives:** *Create a Customized Form and Modify a Form.*

In the following Skill Assessment, you will create a contact form for the Jefferson Inn. The form will contain text form fields, check boxes, and a drop-down form field. Because the form will be used on a Web site, you will not save it as a template. Your completed document will look similar to Figure 10.52. You will save your document as *10C_Web_Contact_Form_Firstname_Lastname.*

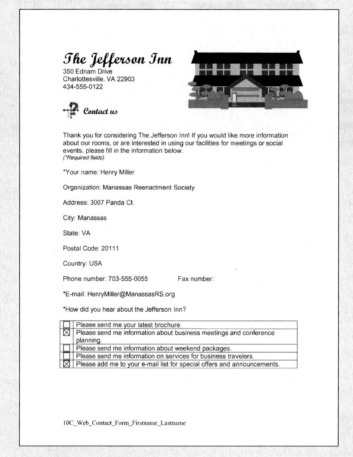

**Figure 10.52**

1. **Start** Word. From the student files that accompany this textbook, locate and open **w10C_Web_Contact_Form**. Save the file as **10C_Web_Contact_Form_Firstname_Lastname** in your chapter folder.

2. Set the **Zoom** to **Page Width**. If necessary, click the **Show/Hide ¶** button to show formatting marks.

3. Display the Header and Footer toolbar, switch to the footer area, click the **Insert AutoText** button, and then click **Filename**. **Close** the Header and Footer toolbar.

**(Project 10C–Web Contact Form continues on the next page)**

**(Project 10C–Web Contact Form continued)**

4. From the **View** menu, point to **Toolbars**, and then click **Forms**. Click to position the insertion point to the right of *Your Name: and press Spacebar. On the **Forms** toolbar, click the **Text Form Field** button.

5. Repeat this process to place a space and a text form field to the right of **Organization**, **Address**, **City**, **State**, **Postal Code**, **Country**, **Phone number**, **Fax number**, and *E-mail. Do not place a field next to *How did you hear about the Jefferson Inn? On the Standard toolbar, click the **Save** button.

6. Press Ctrl + End, and then press Enter. From the **Table** menu, point to **Insert**, and then click **Table**. In the **Insert Table** dialog box, under **Table size**, set the **Number of columns** to **2**. Set the **Number of rows** to **5**. Under **AutoFit behavior**, click the **AutoFit to contents** option button. Click **OK**.

7. With the insertion point in the first cell in the first row of the table, from the Forms toolbar, click the **Check Box Form Field** button. Repeat this procedure to place check boxes in the first cell of each of the five rows.

8. Click to position the insertion point in the second cell of the first row. Type **Please send me your latest brochure.**

9. In the remaining four cells in the second column, type:

   **Please send me information about business meetings and conference planning.**

   **Please send me information about weekend packages.**

   **Please send me information on services for business travelers.**

   **Please add me to your e-mail list for special offers and announcements.**

10. Position the insertion point to the right of the line that begins *How did you hear. Press Spacebar. From the Forms toolbar, click the **Drop-Down Form Field** button.

11. Double-click on the drop-down form field that you just created to display the **Drop-Down Form Field Options** dialog box. In the **Drop-down item** box, press Spacebar five times, and then click the **Add** button. (Because a drop-down list displays whatever item is first in its list, this action will ensure that the box is empty, rather than filled with the first item on the drop-down list.) In the **Drop-down item** box type **Friend** and then click the **Add** button. Repeat this procedure to add:

   **Magazine ad**

   **Newspaper/magazine article**

   **Travel professional**

   **Other**

**(Project 10C–Web Contact Form continues on the next page)**

**(Project 10C–Web Contact Form continued)**

12. Click **OK** to close the **Drop-Down Form Field Options** dialog box. On the Forms toolbar, click the **Protect Form** button to turn on protection. Press [Tab] several times to test how the form will work. When you get to *Your Name*, type your name. Move through the form and fill out the remaining two required form fields—*e-mail* and *How did you hear...*—to test the form.

13. On the Forms toolbar, click the **Protect Form** button to turn off protection. On the Forms toolbar, click the **Reset Form Fields** button.

14. Double-click the text form field to the right of *E-mail*. In the **Text Form Field Options** dialog box, click the **Add Help Text** button. If necessary, click the Status Bar tab. Click the **Type your own** option button. In the box, type **This should be in the format myname@myemail.com** Click **OK** twice to close the dialog box.

15. On the Forms toolbar, click the **Protect Form** button to turn on protection. Press [Tab] until you reach the *E-mail* field. Confirm that the Help message displays in the status bar at the bottom of the screen. Press [Tab] once. In the line that begins *\*How did you hear*, click the arrow and confirm that the five choices are available in the drop-down list. Click **Newspaper/magazine article**.

16. Click in the **Your name** text form field. Type **Henry Miller** and then type the following information in the remaining text form fields:

    Organization: **Manassas Reenactment Society**

    Address: **3007 Panda Ct.**

    City: **Manassas**

    State: **VA**

    Postal Code: **20111**

    Country: **USA**

    Phone number: **703-555-0055**

    Fax number: (leave blank)

    E-mail: **HenryMiller@ManassasRS.org**

17. In the table at the bottom of the page, in the first column, click the second and fifth check boxes.

18. On the Standard toolbar, click the **Save** button. From the **File** menu, click **Print**. At the bottom of the **Print** dialog box, click **OK**. Close the document, saving any changes.

**End** You have completed Project 10C

# Project 10D — Call-In Contact Form

**Objectives:** *Save a Form as a Template and Use the Template to Create a New Form and Automate a Form with Macros.*

In the following Skill Assessment, you will edit a form similar in content to the form that you used in the previous project; however, this form is used at the Jefferson Inn offices to record requests for information received by telephone. You will add a watermark to the form, save the form as a template, and open a new form using the template. You will create a macro to add the current date and time to the form header and then print the form. Your completed document will look similar to Figure 10.53. You will save your document as *10D_Call-In_Contact_Form_Firstname_Lastname*. Then you will fill out a form and save it as *10D_Freeman_Firstname_Lastname*.

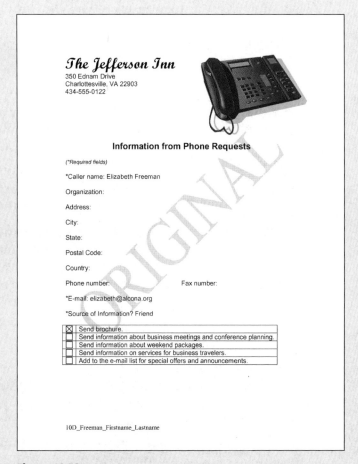

**Figure 10.53**

1. **Start** Word. From the student files that accompany this textbook, locate and open **w10D_Call-In_Contact_Form**. In your chapter folder, save the file as **10D_Call-In_Contact_Form_Firstname_Lastname**

(**Project 10D**–Call-In Contact Form continues on the next page)

**(Project 10D – Call-In Contact Form continued)**

2.  Set the **Zoom** to **Page Width**. From the **View** menu, point to **Toolbars**, and then click **Forms** to display the Forms toolbar. If necessary, on the Standard toolbar, click the **Show/Hide ¶** button to display formatting marks.

3.  Display the Header and Footer toolbar, switch to the footer area, click the **Insert AutoText** button, and then click **Filename**. **Close** the Header and Footer toolbar.

4.  From the **Format** menu, point to **Background**, and then click **Printed Watermark**. Click the **Text watermark** option button. Click the **Text arrow**, and then click **ORIGINAL**. Be sure the **Size** box displays **Auto**, which positions and resizes the text on the page. Click **OK**. (Note: If part of the page becomes unreadable when you click OK, click the Print Preview button, and then close Print Preview.)

5.  On the Standard toolbar, click the **Print Preview** button. Examine the watermark. On the Print Preview toolbar, click **Close**, and then click **Save**.

6.  Be sure protection is turned off. On the **Tools** menu, point to **Macro**, and then click **Record New Macro**.

7.  In the **Record Macro** dialog box, in the **Macro name** box, type **SaveAndPrint** Click the **Store macro in arrow**, and then click your **10D_Call-In_Contact_Form_Firstname_Lastname** document.

8.  Under **Assign macro to**, click the **Toolbars** button. In the displayed **Customize** dialog box, be sure the **Commands tab** is selected and the project name is displayed in the box on the right.

9.  Under **Commands**, drag **Project.NewMacros.SaveAndPrint** to the left of the **Numbered List** button on the Formatting toolbar. Near the bottom of the **Customize** dialog box, click the **Modify Selection** button. Click **Name** to select the default macro name, and then type **SaveAndPrint**

10. Press ⎆Enter to record the name change. At the bottom of the **Customize** dialog box, click **Close**.

11. Take your time; your actions are now being recorded in the macro. From the **File** menu, click **Save**. From the **File** menu, click **Print**. At the bottom of the **Print** dialog box, click **OK**. On the Recording toolbar, click the **Stop Recording** button.

12. On the Standard toolbar, click the **Show/Hide ¶** button to hide the formatting marks. On the Forms toolbar, click the **Protect Form** button to turn on protection.

**(Project 10D – Call-In Contact Form continues on the next page)**

### (Project 10D – Call-In Contact Form continued)

**13.** From the **File** menu, click **Save As**. At the bottom of the **Save As** dialog box, click the **Save as type arrow**, and then click **Document Template**. At the top of the dialog box, click the **Save in arrow**, navigate to your chapter folder, and then click **Save** to accept *10D_Call-In_Contact_Form_Firstname_Lastname* as the file name for the template.

**14.** **Close** the Forms toolbar. At the right end of the menu bar, click the small **Close Window** button.

**15.** Click the **Start** button, click **My Computer**, navigate to your folder, and then double-click the template you just created. Click **Enable Macros** when prompted.

**16.** Type **Elizabeth Freeman** and then press  until the **E-mail** field is selected. Type **elizabeth@alcona.org** and press Tab. Click the drop-down form field arrow and click **Friend**. Click the **Send brochure** check box.

**17.** On the Formatting toolbar, click the **SaveAndPrint** button that you created. Because the document has not yet been saved, the **Save As** dialog box displays. In the **File name** box, type **10D_Freeman_Firstname_Lastname** and click **Save**. Because you are running a macro, the macro continues and prints the document.

**18.** If necessary, display the Forms toolbar, and then click the **Protect Form** button to remove protection. From the **Tools** menu, click **Customize**. Drag your new **SaveAndPrint** button off the toolbar into a blank area of the document, and then release the mouse button. **Close** the dialog box and then close the document, saving any changes. If necessary, close the Forms toolbar.

**End** You have completed Project 10D —————————————————

# Project 10E — Phone Contact Form

**Objectives:** *Automate a Form with Macros and Control a Form with Visual Basic for Applications (VBA).*

In the following Skill Assessment, you will edit a form that the Jefferson Inn uses when receiving a call requesting information about the Inn's facilities and services. Employees view and complete the form on a computer screen. You will create a keyboard-activated macro to place your name and other text in the footer. Then you will edit the macro to add a command to save the document when the macro runs. You also will add a toolbar button to write the form data to a text file for use in a contact list database. Your completed document will look similar to Figure 10.54. You will save your document as *10E_Phone_Contact_Form_Firstname_Lastname*.

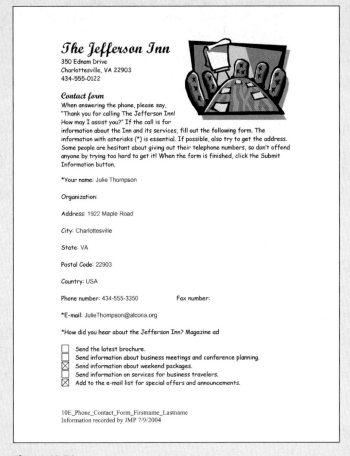

**Figure 10.54**

1. **Start** Word. From the student files that accompany this textbook, locate and open **w10E_Phone_Contact_Form**. Save the file in your chapter folder as **10E_Phone_Contact_Form_Firstname_Lastname**

**(Project 10E–Phone Contact Form continues on the next page)**

**(Project 10E–Phone Contact Form continued)**

2. Set the **Zoom** to **Page Width**. On the Standard toolbar, click the **Show/Hide ¶** button to show formatting marks. From the **View** menu, point to **Toolbars**, and then click **Forms**. On the Forms toolbar, click to turn protection *off*.

3. From the **Tools** menu, point to **Macro**, and then click **Record New Macro**. In the **Record Macro** dialog box, in the **Macro name** box, type **AddFooter** Click the **Store macro in arrow**, and then click your **10E_Phone_Contact_Form_Firstname_Lastname** document. Under **Assign macro to**, click the **Keyboard** button.

4. Press [Alt] + [F]. If that key combination is already assigned, use another combination, but make a note of the combination you use. Under **Specify keyboard sequence**, click the **Save changes in arrow**, and then click your **10E_Phone_Contact_Form_ Firstname_Lastname** document.

5. At the bottom of the dialog box, click the **Assign** button, and then click **Close**. Take your time; your actions are now being recorded. From the **View** menu, click **Header and Footer**. On the Header and Footer toolbar, click the **Switch Between Header and Footer** button. From the **Edit** menu, click **Select All**. From the **Edit** menu, point to **Clear**, and then click **Contents** to remove any text in the footer. On the Header and Footer toolbar, click the **Insert AutoText** button, and then click **Filename**.

6. Press [Enter]. Type **Information recorded by SFF** and then press [Spacebar]. On the Header and Footer toolbar, click the **Insert Date** button. On the Header and Footer toolbar, click the **Close** button.

7. On the Stop Recording toolbar, click the **Stop Recording** button to complete the macro. On the Standard toolbar, click the **Undo** button three times to remove the text from the footer so you can test your macro. Press [Alt] + [F] (or whatever key combination you used) and confirm that the macro has created the two-line footer.

8. **Save** your form. From the **Tools** menu, point to **Macro**, and then click **Macros**. In the **Macros** dialog box, click the **Macros in arrow**, and then click your **10E_Phone_Contact_Form_Firstname_Lastname** document. Be sure your **AddFooter** macro is selected, and then click the **Edit** button.

9. Near the bottom of the program code, locate and select the initials **SFF**. Replace the selected text with **JMP** and then position the insertion point at the end of the line just above the last line of the macro—*End Sub*.

10. Press [Enter] to create a new line before *End Sub*. Type **ActiveDocument.Save** to have the macro add the footer and save the document at the same time. From the **File** menu, click **Close and Return to Microsoft Word**.

**(Project 10E–Phone Contact Form continues on the next page)**

**(Project 10E–Phone Contact Form continued)**

**11.** Press [Alt] + [F] (or whatever key combination you used) to activate the macro. Confirm that the initials have changed and that the new footer text has replaced the old footer text and did not add two more lines to the footer. **Close** the document, reopen the document and enable macros, and then confirm that your addition to the macro saved the document with the new initials—*JMP*.

**12.** From the **Tools** menu, point to **Macro**, and then click **Visual Basic Editor**. Scroll to the bottom of the code window and click below the last line of code—the End Sub command. Type the following five lines—the single quotes count as lines—and press [Enter] after the last line. Substitute today's date and your name as indicated in place of the example:

**Sub SaveAsData()**
**'**
**' SaveAsData Macro**
**' Macro recorded Today's Date by Firstname Lastname**
**'**

**13.** On the taskbar, click the **10E_Phone_Contact_Form_Firstname_ Lastname** button to minimize the VBE window and return to your document. On the Standard toolbar, click the **Open** button. Navigate to the location where the student files for this textbook are stored. Locate and open **w10E_VBA_Text**. Press [Ctrl] + [A] to select all of the text. Click the **Copy** button. **Close** the **w10E_VBA_Text** document.

**14.** On the taskbar, click the button to return to the VBE window. Be sure you are positioned on a blank line below the text you typed in Step 12. From the VBE window toolbar, click the **Paste** button. Scroll to the bottom of the code and examine the last lines. If two lines display *End Sub*, delete one of them. From the **File** menu, click **Close and Return to Microsoft Word**.

**15.** From the **Tools** menu, point to **Macro**, and then click **Visual Basic Editor**. Scroll to the bottom of the code window and verify that only one End Sub command is at the bottom of the macro code. Remove the duplicate code if the editor has added it. Close the VBE window and return to the form.

**16.** On the **Forms** toolbar, click the **Protect Form** button to turn on protection. Fill in the following contact information, leaving the *Organization* and *Fax number* form fields blank. Use the [Tab] key to move from field to field.

Your name: **Julie Thompson**

Organization:

Address: **1922 Maple Road**

**(Project 10E–Phone Contact Form continues on the next page)**

**(Project 10E–Phone Contact Form continued)**

City: **Charlottesville**

State: **VA**

Postal Code: **22903**

Country: **USA**

Phone number: **434-555-3350**

Fax number:

E-mail: **JulieThompson@alcona.org**

How did you hear about the Jefferson Inn: **Magazine ad**

Check the **Send information about weekend packages** check box.

Check the **Add to the e-mail list** check box.

17. On the Standard toolbar, click the **Save** button. On the **Forms** toolbar, click the **Protect Form** button to turn off protection. To add a button to the toolbar to run the *SaveAsData* macro, from the **Tools** menu, click **Customize**. Be sure the **Commands tab** is selected. Under **Categories**, scroll down and click **Macros**. Click the **Save in arrow** and select your **10E_Phone_Contact_Form_Firstname_Lastname** document.

18. Under **Commands**, drag the **Project.NewMacros.SaveAsData** macro to the toolbar and place it to the right of the **Underline** button. Near the bottom of the **Customize** dialog box, click the **Modify Selection** button. In the **Name** box, select the existing macro name. Type **SaveAsData** and press Enter. Click the **Close** button.

19. On the Standard toolbar, click the **Save** button. On the **Formatting** toolbar, click the **SaveAsData** button. If a compile error message displays, it is likely that the program added another *End Sub* command to the macro. To correct this, click **OK** to close the message box. Scroll to the bottom of the window, select, and then delete the second *End Sub* command. From the **File** menu, click **Close and Return to Microsoft Word**. Run the macro again by clicking your toolbar button.

20. Click the **Start** button and click **My Computer**. Locate the **10E_Phone_Data_Firstname_Lastname** text file—not the Word file. Open the text file and verify that the data you typed has been saved in this document. **Close** the file and **Close My Computer**. Your form redisplays.

21. From the **File** menu, click **Print**. At the bottom of the **Print** dialog box, click **OK**. From the **Tools** menu, click **Customize**. Drag your **SaveAsData** button off the toolbar and release the mouse button. Close the document, saving any changes.

**End** You have completed Project 10E

## Project 10F — Breakfast Menu

**Objectives:** *Create a Customized Form, Modify a Form, Save a Form as a Template and Use the Template to Create a New Form.*

In the following Performance Assessment, you will edit a form that is used for two purposes—as a paper form filled in by the guests at the Jefferson Inn and as an electronic form filled in by Inn employees. The form is a breakfast room service menu, as shown in Figure 10.55. You will save your document as *10F_Breakfast_Menu_Firstname_Lastname*. You will also save a template of the form as *10F_Breakfast_Menu_Template_Firstname_Lastname*, and a completed form as *10F_Room_14_Firstname_Lastname*.

**Figure 10.55**

1. **Start** Word. From the student files that accompany this textbook, locate and open **w10F_Breakfast_Menu**. Save the file in your chapter folder as **10F_Breakfast_Menu_Firstname_Lastname**

2. Be sure the formatting marks are displayed, and then zoom to **Page Width**. If necessary, open the Forms toolbar. Be sure the form protection is turned *off*.

**(Project 10F–Breakfast Menu continues on the next page)**

**(Project 10F–Breakfast Menu continued)**

3. Place the insertion point after **Name:** and press `Spacebar`. On the Forms toolbar, click the **Text Form Field** button. Repeat this procedure to add a text form field after **Room:**.

4. In the line that begins *Please deliver*, place the insertion point to the right of *at* and add a space. Add a text form field between *at* and *a.m.*

5. Place the insertion point in the upper left cell in the table—the cell to the left of *Fresh-brewed coffee*. On the Forms toolbar, click the **Check Box Form Field** button. Repeat this procedure to add a check box form field in each cell in the narrow columns that precede each beverage name. When complete, you should have nine check box text fields.

6. With the insertion point still in the table, from the **Table** menu, point to **Select**, and then click **Table**. From the **Format** menu, click **Borders and Shading**. Be sure the **Borders tab** is selected. Under **Setting**, click **None** to remove the table borders. Click **OK**. To preview the table, on the Standard toolbar, click the **Print Preview** button. **Close** Print Preview.

7. In the *Entrée* section, position the insertion point to the left of *Basket*. Insert a **Check Box Form Field** button, and then add a space. Repeat this procedure to add check boxes to all of the lines in the *Entrée* section that are not indented. **Save** your document.

8. Under *Selection of cold cereals*, add a check box form field to the left of the three milk options. Be sure to add a space after the check boxes. (Note: A drop-down form field could also be useful here for a computerized form, but because the Inn will use this as both an online and a paper form, check boxes are appropriate.)

9. Under *American Breakfast*, add a check box form field to the left of *hash browns* in the second line. Be sure to add a space after the check box. Add check boxes to the left of *ham* and to the left of *bacon* in the first line and to the left of *wheat toast* and to the left of *white toast* in the third line. Double-click the long line in the fourth line to select it. Replace the line with a text form field.

10. From the **Format** menu, point to **Background**, and then click **Printed Watermark**. Click the **Text watermark** option button. In the **Text** box, select the existing text, replace it with **Jefferson Inn** and then click **Apply**. **Close** the dialog box. (Note: If your form appears to be partially blacked out, click the Print Preview button, and then Close Print Preview.)

11. Display the Header and Footer toolbar, switch to the footer area, click the **Insert AutoText** button, and then click **Filename**. **Close** the Header and Footer toolbar. **Print** the form with the form field shading still displayed. **Save** the form.

**(Project 10F**–Breakfast Menu continues on the next page)

**(Project 10F**–Breakfast Menu continued)

**12.** On the Forms toolbar, click the **Form Field Shading** button to turn off the shading. Click the **Show/Hide ¶** button to hide the formatting marks. On the Forms toolbar, click the **Protect Form** button to turn on protection. Close the Forms toolbar.

**13.** Because the form will also be used as an electronic form by the Inn's staff, you will need to save the form as a template so it can be used repeatedly. From the **File** menu, click **Save As**. At the bottom of the **Save As** dialog box, click the **Save as type arrow**, and then click **Document Template**. In the **Save in** box, navigate to your chapter folder. In the **File name** box type **10F_Breakfast_Menu_Template_ Firstname_Lastname**

**14.** Near the bottom of the **Save As** dialog box, click the **Save** button. **Close** the template.

**15.** Click the **Start** button, click **My Computer**, navigate to your folder, and double-click the template you just created. For the first three fields, type the following:

Name: **Elizabeth Freeman**

Room: **14**

Please deliver at **8:30** a.m.

**16.** In the *Your beverages* area, click the check boxes for **Fresh-brewed coffee** and **Orange juice**. In the *Entrée* area, click the check boxes for **Selection of cold cereals**, **soy milk**, and **Homemade cinnamon roll**.

**17.** Save the form in your chapter folder as **10F_Room_14_Firstname_ Lastname** and then **Print** the form. **Close** Print Preview. **Close** the document.

**End** You have completed Project 10F

# Project 10G — Breakfast Data

**Objectives:** *Modify a Form, Automate a Form with Macros, and Control a Form with Visual Basic for Applications (VBA).*

In the following Performance Assessment, you will work with a modified version of the Jefferson Inn breakfast menu form you used in Project 10F. You will change the watermark from text to a picture. You also will add macros to the document and create a new macro using the Visual Basic Editor. Your completed document will look similar to Figure 10.56. You will save your document as *10G_Breakfast_Data_Firstname_Lastname*.

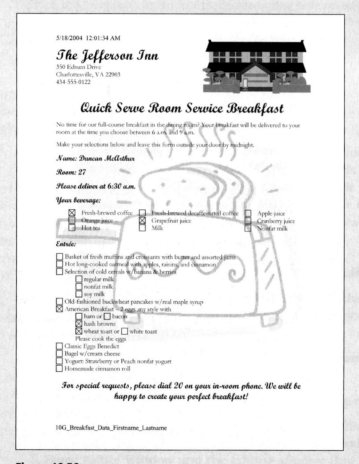

**Figure 10.56**

1. **Start** Word. From the student files that accompany this textbook, locate and open **w10G_Breakfast_Data**. Save the file in your chapter folder as **10G_Breakfast_Data_Firstname_Lastname**

2. Be sure the formatting marks are displayed, and then zoom to **Page Width**. Display the Forms toolbar and be sure the form protection is turned off.

**(Project 10G–Breakfast Data continues on the next page)**

**(Project 10G–Breakfast Data continued)**

3. Take a moment to examine the form. Display the **Printed Watermark** dialog box, and then click **Picture watermark**. Click the **Select Picture** button and navigate to the location where the student files for this textbook are stored. Locate and insert **w10G_Toaster**. Be sure **Auto** displays in the **Scale** box and the **Washout** check box is selected. Click **Apply**, and then close the dialog box. (Note: If part of the screen is blacked out, click the Print Preview button, and then close Print Preview to refresh the screen.)

4. Display the **Record Macro** dialog box. Name the macro **AddHeaderAndFooter** Store the macro in your **10G_Breakfast_ Data_ Firstname_Lastname** document.

5. Assign the macro to **Toolbars**. In the displayed **Customize** dialog box, be sure the **Commands** tab is selected, and the project name is displayed in the box on the right.

6. Drag **Project.NewMacros.AddHeaderAndFooter** to the left of the **Numbered List** button on the Formatting toolbar. Near the bottom of the **Customize** dialog box, click the **Modify Selection** button. To the right of the *Name* command, select the text, and then type **Header/Footer** Press Enter, and then **Close** the dialog box.

7. Take your time; your actions are now being recorded. From the **View** menu, click **Header and Footer**. On the Header and Footer toolbar, click the **Insert Date** button, press Spacebar twice, and then click the **Insert Time** button. Click the **Switch Between Header and Footer** button. Click the **Insert AutoText** button, and then click **Filename**. Click **Close**. On the Recording toolbar, click the **Stop Recording** button.

8. Start a new macro and name it **SaveAndPrint** Store the macro in your **10G_Breakfast_Data_Firstname_Lastname** document. Assign the macro to **Toolbars**.

9. Under **Commands**, drag **Project.NewMacros.SaveAndPrint** to the right of the **Header/Footer** button you just added to the Formatting toolbar. Near the bottom of the **Customize** dialog box, click the **Modify Selection** button. As the button name, type **Save/Print** and press Enter. **Close** the **Customize** dialog box.

10. From the **File** menu, click **Save**. From the **File** menu, click **Print**. In the **Print** dialog box, click **OK**. On the Recording toolbar, click the **Stop Recording** button. You should have two macro buttons next to each other on the Formatting toolbar.

11. Click **Save**. Close and reopen the document. Enable macros if prompted. Open the header and footer area and delete the header and footer text. Close the header and footer. Test your macros to confirm that they both work.

**(Project 10G–Breakfast Data continues on the next page)**

**(Project 10G–Breakfast Data continued)**

**12.** From the **Tools** menu, point to **Macro**, and then click **Visual Basic Editor**. If the edit window does not display, double-click the Modules folder in the Project pane on the left side of the screen. (Note: If the Project pane is closed, from the View menu, click Project Explorer.) If the code for your new macros does not display, under Modules, double-click NewMacros.

**13.** Scroll to the bottom of the code window and click in the empty line at the bottom. From the taskbar, return to the **10G_Breakfast_Data_Firstname_Lastname** document. On the Standard toolbar, click the **Open** button. Locate and open **w10G_VBA_Text**. Press Ctrl + A to select all of the text. On the Standard toolbar, click the **Copy** button. Close the **w10G_VBA_Text** file.

**14.** From the taskbar, return to the Visual Basic Editor. Press Enter and from the Visual Basic Editor window toolbar, click the **Paste** button. From the **File** menu, click **Close and Return to Microsoft Word**. **Save** your document. On the Forms toolbar, click the **Protect Form** button to turn protection *on*. Enter the following information in the first three text form fields:

Name: **Duncan McArthur**

Room: **27**

Please deliver at **6:30** a.m.

**15.** In the *Your beverage* area, click the check boxes for **Fresh-brewed decaffeinated coffee** and **Grapefruit juice**. In the *Entrée* area, click the check boxes for **American Breakfast**, **hash browns**, and **wheat toast**. In the *Please cook the eggs* text form field, type **Over easy** and then from the Formatting toolbar, click the **Save/Print macro button** that you created earlier.

**16.** Save the form as **10G_Room_14_Firstname_Lastname** Reopen your **10G_Breakfast_Data_Firstname_Lastname** document.

**17.** On the Forms toolbar, click the **Protect Form** button to turn off protection. From the **Tools** menu, click **Customize**. Be sure the **Commands tab** is selected. Under **Categories**, scroll down and click **Macros**. Near the bottom of the **Customize** dialog box, click the **Save in arrow**, and then click **10G_Breakfast_Data_Firstname_Lastname**.

**18.** Drag the **SaveAsData** macro to the right of the **Save/Print** button on the Formatting toolbar. Near the bottom of the **Customize** dialog box, click the **Modify Selection** button. To the right of the *Name* command, select the text. Type **SaveAsData** and press Enter. Click **Close**.

**(Project 10G–Breakfast Data continues on the next page)**

**(Project 10G–Breakfast Data continued)**

 **19.** On the Formatting toolbar, click the **SaveAsData** button. Click the **Start** button and then open **My Computer**. Locate and open your **10G_Breakfast_Data_Firstname_Lastname** text file and confirm that the data has been stored. Close the file and return to your form.

**20.** From the **Tools** menu, display the **Customize** dialog box, and click the **Commands tab** if necessary. On the Formatting toolbar, drag each of the three buttons you created off the toolbar and into the white space in the document. Close the **Customize** dialog box.

**21.** Close the document, saving your changes when prompted.

**End** You have completed Project 10G ——————————————

## Project 10H—Breakfast Form Check

**Objectives:** *Modify a Form and Add an ActiveX Control to a Form.*

In the following Performance Assessment, you will edit a version of the breakfast menu for the Jefferson Inn. You will change the background of the form and then add an ActiveX control that will do three things. First, it will check to see if a field was selected and, if so, display a message. Then, it will prompt you to save the document under another name by displaying the Save As dialog box. Finally, it will print the document. Your completed document will look similar to the one shown in Figure 10.57. You will save your document as *10H_Breakfast_Form_Check_Firstname_Lastname* and the completed document as *10H_Room_28_Firstname_Lastname*.

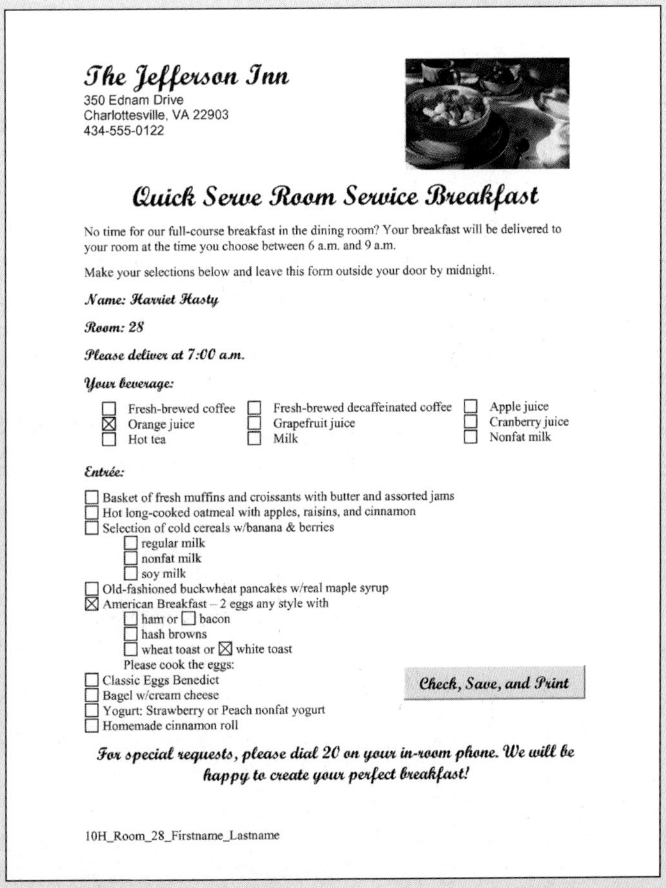

*The Jefferson Inn*
350 Ednam Drive
Charlottesville, VA 22903
434-555-0122

*Quick Serve Room Service Breakfast*

No time for our full-course breakfast in the dining room? Your breakfast will be delivered to your room at the time you choose between 6 a.m. and 9 a.m.

Make your selections below and leave this form outside your door by midnight.

*Name: Harriet Hasty*

*Room: 28*

*Please deliver at 7:00 a.m.*

*Your beverage:*

☐ Fresh-brewed coffee ☐ Fresh-brewed decaffeinated coffee ☐ Apple juice
☒ Orange juice ☐ Grapefruit juice ☐ Cranberry juice
☐ Hot tea ☐ Milk ☐ Nonfat milk

*Entrée:*

☐ Basket of fresh muffins and croissants with butter and assorted jams
☐ Hot long-cooked oatmeal with apples, raisins, and cinnamon
☐ Selection of cold cereals w/banana & berries
  ☐ regular milk
  ☐ nonfat milk
  ☐ soy milk
☐ Old-fashioned buckwheat pancakes w/real maple syrup
☒ American Breakfast – 2 eggs any style with
  ☐ ham or ☐ bacon
  ☐ hash browns
  ☐ wheat toast or ☒ white toast
  Please cook the eggs:
☐ Classic Eggs Benedict
☐ Bagel w/cream cheese
☐ Yogurt: Strawberry or Peach nonfat yogurt
☐ Homemade cinnamon roll

*Check, Save, and Print*

*For special requests, please dial 20 on your in-room phone. We will be happy to create your perfect breakfast!*

10H_Room_28_Firstname_Lastname

**Figure 10.57**

1. **Start** Word. From the student files that accompany this textbook, locate and open **w10H_Breakfast_Form_Check**. Save the file in your chapter folder as **10H_Breakfast_Form_Check_Firstname_Lastname** Display the Forms toolbar; be sure the form is *not* protected.

**(Project 10H–Breakfast Form Check continues on the next page)**

**(Project 10H**–Breakfast Form Check continued)

2. Create a footer, click the **Insert AutoText** button, and then click **Filename**. **Close** the Header and Footer toolbar.

3. To change the form background, display the **Fill Effects** dialog box, click the **Texture tab**, and then click the first button—**Newsprint**. Click **OK**.

4. Scroll down and double-click the form check box to the left of *American Breakfast*. In the **Check Box Form Field Options** dialog box, change the *Bookmark* text for this field to **American** and then click **OK**.

5. Display the **Control Toolbox** toolbar. Press Ctrl + End to position the insertion point at the end of the document, and then press Enter. On the Control Toolbox toolbar, click the **Command Button** button.

6. Right-click on the command button. From the shortcut menu, click **Format Control**. On the **Layout tab**, change the **Wrapping style** to **Square**. Click **OK**. Recall that a command button can be treated like any other graphic object in Word. Drag the command button to an open area to the right of *Classic Eggs Benedict*. Place the button far enough to the right so that it does not overlap any of the text, but do not be concerned with the precise placement.

7. Right-click the command button, and click **Properties**. Point to and click the word *Caption*, and then type **Check, Save, and Print**

8. Click the **AutoSize arrow**, and then click **True** to resize the command button. **Close** the **Properties** dialog box. On the command button, drag the sizing handle on the right edge to the right about an eighth of an inch.

9. Double-click the command button to open the VBA code window for the ActiveX control button. Use the taskbar to move back to the Word document. On the Standard toolbar, click the **Open** button. Locate and open the **w10H_ActiveX_Text** document. Select all of the text, copy it, and then close the document. On the taskbar, click to return to the Visual Basic Editor.

10. In the VBA code window, on the toolbar, click the **Paste** button. Take a moment to examine the code. The code includes an If/Then statement (without the Else section that you used earlier). After the If/Then statement is complete, the two other commands are run. Notice that the **MessageText** is blank.

**(Project 10H**–Breakfast Form Check continues on the next page)

**(Project 10H–Breakfast Form Check continued)**

**11.** In the *MessageText* line, place the insertion point between the two quotation marks. Type: **The Virginia Board of Health does not allow us to serve eggs cooked Over Easy. If the guest has requested this option, please call and offer alternatives.** Press Home to move back to the left edge of the VBA code. The VBA code will check to see if eggs have been ordered and display a message box if they have. Then the code will save and print the form.

**12.** From the **File** menu, click **Close and Return to Microsoft Word**. **Save** your document. On the Control Toolbox toolbar, click the **Exit Design Mode** button. **Close** the Control Toolbox toolbar. On the Forms toolbar, click the **Protect Form** button to turn on protection. Hide the formatting marks.

**13.** Enter the following information in the first three text form fields:

Name: **Harriet Hasty**

Room: **28**

Please deliver at **7:00** a.m.

**14.** In the *Your beverage* area, click the **Orange juice** check box. In the *Entrée* area, click the **American Breakfast** check box and the **white toast** check box. Click the **Check, Save, and Print** command button that you just added. Read the message box, and then click **OK**.

**15.** In the **Save As** dialog box, change the name of the file to **10H_Room_28_Firstname_Lastname** and click **Save**. In the **Print** dialog box, click **OK** to print the document. **Close** the document.

**End** **You have completed Project 10H** ————————

# Mastery Assessments

## Project 10I—Local Attractions

**Objectives:** *Create a Customized Form, Modify a Form, Save a Form as a Template and Use the Template to Create a New Form.*

The Charlottesville area has numerous attractions for visitors to the Jefferson Inn. Many hotels, motels, inns, and bed and breakfast establishments are participating in a Chamber of Commerce survey to analyze information about what people do when they visit the city. In the following Mastery Assessment, you will add form fields to the survey document and create tables for some of the information. You will save the form as a template and then save the data in a text file. Your completed document will look similar to the one shown in Figure 10.58. You will save your document as *10I_Local_Attractions_Firstname_Lastname* and the completed document as *10I_Stanley_Firstname_Lastname*. You also will save a template and text file using the same document name, but with different filename extensions.

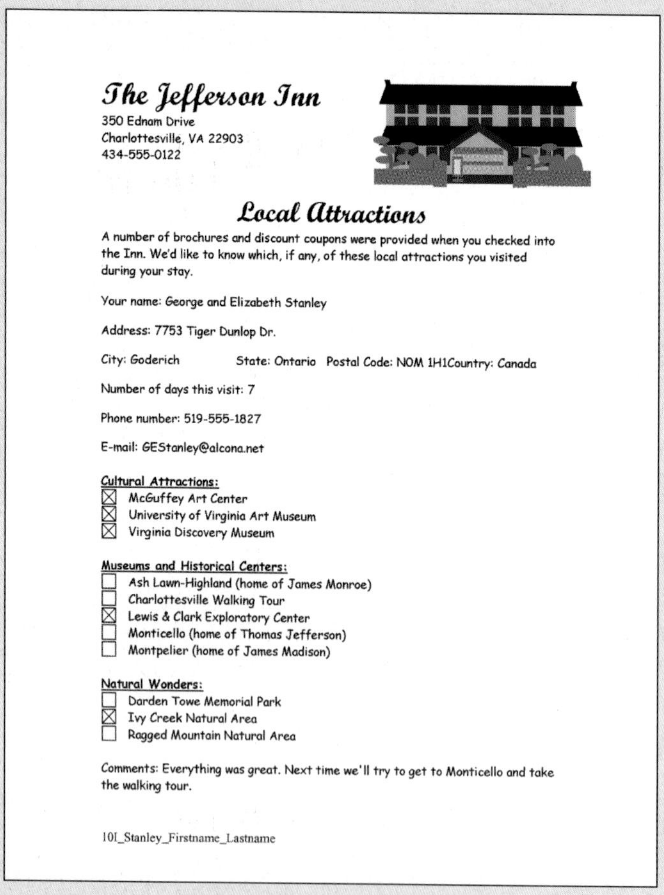
The Jefferson Inn
350 Ednam Drive
Charlottesville, VA 22903
434-555-0122

Local Attractions

A number of brochures and discount coupons were provided when you checked into the Inn. We'd like to know which, if any, of these local attractions you visited during your stay.

Your name: George and Elizabeth Stanley

Address: 7753 Tiger Dunlop Dr.

City: Goderich State: Ontario Postal Code: NOM 1H1Country: Canada

Number of days this visit: 7

Phone number: 519-555-1827

E-mail: GEStanley@alcona.net

Cultural Attractions:
- [x] McGuffey Art Center
- [x] University of Virginia Art Museum
- [x] Virginia Discovery Museum

Museums and Historical Centers:
- [ ] Ash Lawn-Highland (home of James Monroe)
- [ ] Charlottesville Walking Tour
- [x] Lewis & Clark Exploratory Center
- [ ] Monticello (home of Thomas Jefferson)
- [ ] Montpelier (home of James Madison)

Natural Wonders:
- [ ] Darden Towe Memorial Park
- [x] Ivy Creek Natural Area
- [ ] Ragged Mountain Natural Area

Comments: Everything was great. Next time we'll try to get to Monticello and take the walking tour.

10I_Stanley_Firstname_Lastname

**Figure 10.58**

**(Project 10I–Local Attractions continues on the next page)**

**(Project 10I–Local Attractions continued)**

1. **Start** Word. From the student files that accompany this textbook, locate and open **w10I_Local_Attractions**. Save the file as **10I_Local_Attractions_Firstname_Lastname** in your chapter folder.

2. Display the Forms toolbar and be sure protection is turned off. Display the formatting marks. Add text form fields to the first nine items, including **E-mail**.

3. Change the form field type for the **Number of days** item to **Number**. Recall that you can double-click a form field to open the **Text Form Field Options** dialog box.

4. Select the three lines under **Cultural Attractions**. Be sure you do not select the title—*Cultural Attractions*. From the **Table** menu, point to **Convert**, and then click **Text to Table**. Click **OK** to accept the defaults and create a one-column table. From the **Table** menu, point to **Insert**, and then click **Columns to the Left**.

5. Add a check box form field to each of the empty cells in the first column. From the **Table** menu, point to **AutoFit**, and then click **AutoFit to Contents**. Select the table and remove the borders.

6. Repeat Steps 4 and 5 to create borderless tables for the *Museums and Historical Centers* and *Natural Wonders* lists. Add a text form field after *Comments*. Save your work.

7. From the **Tools** menu, point to **Macro**, and then click **Visual Basic Editor**. If necessary, in the Project pane, double-click **ThisDocument** under the document name to open the editing window. **Minimize** the VBE window, and then copy and paste the code in **w10I_VBA_Text** to create a macro that will save the form data in a text document. Replace *Firstname Lastname* with your name. Close and return to Word.

8. Place the document filename in the footer. Protect the form, hide the formatting marks, and save your work.

9. Save the form as a template and be sure you save it in your chapter folder using the default filename. Close the template. Open the template, and enable macros when prompted.

**(Project 10I–Local Attractions continues on the next page)**

**(Project 10I–Local Attractions continued)**

**10.** Fill out the form as follows:

Your name: **George and Elizabeth Stanley**

Address: **7753 Tiger Dunlop Dr.**

City: **Goderich**

State: **Ontario**

Postal Code: **N0M 1H1**

Country: **Canada**

Number of days this visit: **7**

Phone number: **519-555-1827**

E-mail: **GEStanley@alcona.net**

**11.** Click the check boxes next to the three items under **Cultural Attractions**. Also click the check box next to the **Lewis & Clark Exploratory Center** and the **Ivy Creek Natural Area**. Under comments, type **Everything was great. Next time we'll try to get to Monticello and take the walking tour.** Display the **Save As** dialog box, change the files of type to **Word document**, and type **10I_Stanley_Firstname_Lastname** as the file name. On the Forms toolbar, click to unprotect, and leave the document displayed on your screen.

**12.** From the **Tools** menu, point to **Macro**, and then click **Macros**. Click the **Macros in arrow** and click **10I_Stanley_Firstname_Lastname**. Be sure **SaveAsData** is selected, and then click **Run**. Open **My Computer** and locate the *10I_Local_Attractions_Firstname_Lastname* text file. Open the text file to confirm that the data has been saved. Close the file and return to your form.

**13.** Close the document, saving any changes.

**End** You have completed Project 10I ————————————

# Project 10J — Business Evaluation

**Objectives:** *Create a Customized Form, Modify a Form, and Automate a Form with Macros.*

A few days after a business meeting, the Jefferson Inn e-mails a brief evaluation form to the meeting organizer. In the following Mastery Assessment, you will edit the Meeting Evaluation form. You will convert text to a table and then add drop-down and text form fields. You also will add an AutoExit macro to add the date and time to the header when the meeting organizer closes the form. Your completed document will look similar to the one shown in Figure 10.59. You will save your document as *10J_Business_Evaluation_Firstname_Lastname*. The Contact Information has already been filled in.

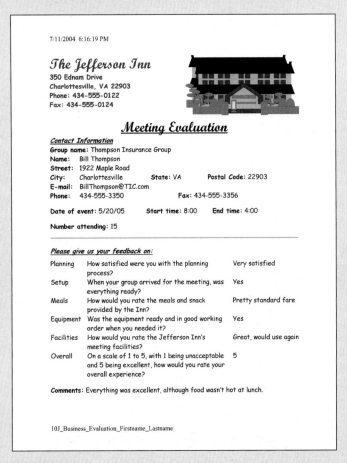

**Figure 10.59**

(**Project 10J**–Business Evaluation continues on the next page)

**(Project 10J–Business Evaluation continued)**

1. **Start** Word. From the student files that accompany this textbook, locate and open **w10J_Business_Evaluation** and enable macros. Save the file in your chapter folder as **10J_Business_Evaluation_Firstname_ Lastname** Display the footer and insert the **AutoText** filename.

2. Display the formatting marks and display the Forms toolbar. Be sure the form is unprotected.

3. Select the text between (but not including) *Please give us your feedback on* and *Comments*. From the **Table** menu, point to **Convert**, and then click **Text to Table**. Select **3** columns, and then click **OK**. From the **Table** menu, point to **AutoFit**, and then click **AutoFit to Contents**.

4. In the empty cell at the end of the first row, insert a drop-down form field. Double-click on the new form field and add the following items to the list:

   **Please select from list**

   **Very satisfied**

   **Mostly satisfied**

   **Needs improvement (see comments)**

5. Repeat the procedure you used in Step 4 and add a drop-down form field to the empty cells in the **Setup** and **Equipment** rows. Add the following items to the lists:

   **Please select from list**

   **Yes**

   **No**

   **See comments**

6. Add a drop-down form field in the empty cell in the **Meals** row, using the following list items:

   **Please select from list**

   **Food was excellent**

   **Pretty standard fare**

   **Needs improvement (see comments)**

7. Add a drop-down form field in the empty cell in the **Facilities** row, using the following list items:

   **Please select from list**

   **Great, would use again**

   **Adequate for our needs**

   **Needs improvement (see comments)**

**(Project 10J–Business Evaluation continues on the next page)**

**(Project 10J–Business Evaluation continued)**

8. In the empty cell in the **Overall** row, add a drop-down form field. Add **Please select from list** as the first item and the numbers **1** through **5** as the next five items. Add a text form field after *Comments*.

9. From the **Tools** menu, point to **Macro**, and then click **Record New Macro**. Type **AutoExit** as the macro name. Store the macro in your **10J_Business_Evaluation_Firstname_Lastname** document. Assign the macro to the keyboard, and assign the macro to [Alt] + [C].

10. Take your time; your macro is now recording. Open the header/footer, clear any text in the header, and then add the **Date** and **Time**. Close the Header and Footer toolbar. Stop recording the macro.

11. Hide the formatting marks and protect the form. Fill in the bottom half of the form with the following information:

    Planning: **Very satisfied**

    Setup: **Yes**

    Meals: **Pretty standard fare**

    Equipment: **Yes**

    Facilities: **Great, would use again**

    Overall: **5**

    Comments: **Everything was excellent, although the food wasn't hot at lunch.**

12. **Save** your changes. **Print** the document. In the Forms toolbar, click the **Protect Form** button to remove protection. Close the Forms toolbar. **Close** the document, saving any changes, and close Word. If a Compile Error dialog box displays, click End to ignore the message.

**End** You have completed Project 10J ────────────────────────

## Project 10K — Guest Satisfaction

**Objectives:** *Create a Customized Form, Modify a Form, and Automate a Form with Macros.*

In the following Mastery Assessment, you will work on a Customer Satisfaction form. You will determine the questions that need to be asked and the type of form fields to use. You will also add a picture watermark to the form. You can create the form for use on the computer or as a paper form. The Contact Information has already been filled in. You will save your document as *10K_Guest_Satisfaction_Firstname_Lastname.*

1. **Start** Word. Open **w10K_Guest_Satisfaction**. Save the file with the name **10K_Guest_Satisfaction_Firstname_Lastname** in your chapter folder. Display the footer and insert the **AutoText** filename.

2. Add a picture watermark to the background of the form. The watermark should be appropriate for a country inn. You might want to search the clip art images on the Microsoft Web site. Be sure to use the **Washout** option so the text in front of the watermark is readable.

3. Create at least four questions that can be used on a form. If you are creating an electronic form, use at least two drop-down form fields. If you are creating a form for paper, create a check box form field for each option. You might want to create questions about the food, room cleanliness, staff friendliness, or surrounding attractions.

4. Add a toolbar macro to save and print the document. Test your macro.

5. Protect the form and fill out the survey. Save, print, and close your document.

**End** You have completed Project 10K

# Project 10L — Guest Registration

**Objectives:** *Create a Customized Form, Modify a Form, Save a Form as a Template and Use the Template to Create a New Form.*

When guests check into the Jefferson Inn, they fill out a registration form. It includes questions designed to help the owners of the Inn determine the demographics of their guests and thus help determine their marketing strategies for the future. A paper version of this form will be given to the guests. This is the form that the Inn staff members will fill in using the computer. Therefore, drop-down list form fields are acceptable where appropriate. In this project, you will determine which form fields are appropriate, and create the form. You also will write a macro to save the data to a text file so it can be analyzed in a database. You will save your document as *10L_Guest_Registration_Firstname_Lastname*. You will also save a template and text file using the same document name, but with different filename extensions.

1. **Start** Word. Open **w10L_Guest_Registration** and save it as **10L_Guest_Registration_Firstname_Lastname**

2. Possible form items have been included. Examine the data that is provided, and add at least two more items that you think should be on the form. Decide which fields should be filled in by the guests, and which fields should be filled in by Inn personnel. Move the items to be filled in by the employees below the line.

3. Lay out the form by moving fields. You might want to use one or more tables and turn off table borders. Add text form fields and check box form fields where appropriate. Add a drop-down form field for the bed type, as you did earlier in this chapter.

4. Change the field options where appropriate. Recall that you can double-click a form field to open the Form Field Options dialog box. For example, add a text form field for *Arrival date*, and then use a date type for the form field. Use a number type for the number form fields. (Note: Do not use a number type for the Postal Code text form field—many countries, such as Canada and England, use letters in their postal codes.)

5. Create a macro to save the data in a text file. Use the default name for the file. (Hint: You might want to use the text from the **w10L_VBA_Text** to complete this macro.)

**(Project 10L–Guest Registration continues on the next page)**

**(Project 10L**–Guest Registration continued)

6. When you complete the form, save it as a document template, using the default document name. Close the template, open it again, and then enter your name and information as if you were staying at the Inn. Run the macro to save the data.

7. Insert the filename in the footer. Save, print, and then close the document.

 **End** You have completed Project 10L ────────────────

## Creating Sophisticated Forms Using InfoPath 2003

InfoPath 2003 is a specialized tool for creating data-gathering forms. It enables you to gather information flexibly and efficiently and more effectively share, reuse, and repurpose information throughout a team or organization. InfoPath 2003 enables you to efficiently collect the information needed to make better informed decisions, to enable teams and organizations to reuse any information they collect, and then share that information across business processes and organizations.

In this exercise, you will navigate to the Microsoft Office InfoPath 2003 Web site to get an overview of what the software can do. If you are working on a computer that enables you to install software, Microsoft provides a 60-day evaluation copy of the InfoPath 2003 software.

1. Be sure that you are connected to the Internet. Open your browser and go to **www.microsoft.com**

2. Under **Product Families**, click **Office**. Under **Microsoft Office**, click **InfoPath**.

3. Under **Discover InfoPath 2003**, click **Product Information**, and then use this page to navigate to the various sections that describe the uses and benefits of InfoPath.

4. Under **Overview**, click **See a Demo**. Go through the demo to familiarize yourself with InfoPath 2003. This is an excellent demo that enables you to determine whether you might have a future use for this product.

5. Return to the InfoPath 2003 Product Information page. If you think InfoPath 2003 might be useful to you, order and install a trial version.

6. When you are done, close the browser.

## Use Visual Basic Help

In this chapter you used VBA. When you recorded macros, Word wrote the code for you. When you opened the Visual Basic Editor, you changed the code and created a macro. The code you wrote for the ActiveX control button was also VBA. The Help feature that is available when you are editing a document only gives brief information. Word offers more in-depth Visual Basic help.

1. **Start** Word. In the *Type a Question for Help* box, type **Visual Basic** and press [Enter]. Notice the limited help available.

2. From the **Tools** menu, point to **Macro**, and then click **Visual Basic Editor**. On the Standard toolbar, click the **Help** button to open the *Visual Basic Help* pane.

3. Under **Table of Contents**, click **Microsoft Word Visual Basic Reference**. Click **Microsoft Word Object Model**, and then maximize the screen. Examine the objects that can be used with VBA. Click on a few of them to see the type of help that is available.

4. Close the Object Model window. Under **Table of Contents**, type **if then** in the **Search** box. Scroll down the **Search Results** pane about two-thirds of the way. Click **Using If...Then...Else Statements**, which you used earlier in this chapter. Examine the examples provided.

5. Spend some time looking through the other sections of VBA Help. When you are through, close the VBE, and then close the document without saving your changes.

# 11 chaptereleven

# Creating a Web Page and Managing Documents

In this chapter, you will: complete these projects and practice these skills.

| Project 11A Creating a Web Page Using Frames | **Objectives** |
|---|---|
| | • Create a Web Page with Frames |
| | • Edit Web Pages Using Word |

| Project 11B Protecting Documents and Using Versions | **Objectives** |
|---|---|
| | • Protect Documents |
| | • Attach Digital Signatures to Documents |
| | • Use Document Versions |

# Southland Gardens

With gardening booming as a hobby, Southland Media, a TV production company headquartered in Irvine, California, saw a need for practical and entertaining information on the subject. *Southland Gardens* was developed especially for year-round gardeners in Southern California. The show features experts on vegetable and flower gardening, landscape design, projects for kids, and tours of historical and notable gardens. The company also offers a companion Web site where viewers can get more information about show segments, purchase supplies, and e-mail guests of the show.

# Creating a Web Page and Managing Documents

Earlier, you practiced saving a Word document as a Web page. For a more complex Web page—such as dividing the screen into multiple areas to show several documents or objects at the same time—Word enables you to create and resize separate rectangular screen areas that can contain text or objects. You can also use Word to edit an existing Web page.

Microsoft Word includes tools for sharing documents with others and enabling two or more people to edit the same document at the same time. Restrictions can be added to documents that identify who can open a document and what types of edits each person can make. A password can be used to restrict individuals from changing document formatting or from editing all or part of the document. Documents can also be electronically signed to verify that the document has not been altered.

Sometimes you will need to keep different versions of a document as the editing process continues. Word enables you to save various versions of the document in one file, eliminating the need for saving and keeping track of separate files.

# Project 11A **Television Schedule**

Web pages can contain independent rectangular areas of the screen in which you can place different kinds of content. Using independent areas of the screen enables, for example, a title to stay in place while the document below it is scrolled up or down. Each of the areas in a Web page can use scroll bars if the item is larger than the area in which it is placed.

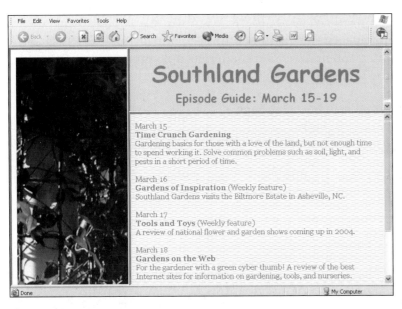

**Figure 11.1**

In Activities 11.1 through 11.10, you will create a Web page that is divided into three areas. One area will contain a picture, a second area will contain a title, and the third and largest area will contain the weekly television schedule for the Southland Gardens TV show. You will also edit the Web page in Word. The finished document will be a Web page that will look similar to Figure 11.1. You will save your document as *11A_Television_Schedule_Firstname_Lastname.*

## Objective 1
## Create a Web Page with Frames

You have practiced saving a Word document as a Web page. For a Web page that is more sophisticated than just a single Word document, use Word's **frames page** feature. A frames page is a Web page that divides a Web browser window into different scrollable areas—called **frames**—that can independently display several Web pages. The frame, when named, is referred to as a **subwindow**. Frames can be resized and often use vertical or horizontal scrollbars to display their contents.

A common Web page arrangement is a three-frame layout—a title frame, a frame containing the main content, such as a document, and a third frame containing an image or a table of contents.

### Activity 11.1 Creating a New Web Page

If you know your document will be used as a Web page, create it using the Web page template.

**1** **Start** Word. From the **File** menu, click **Close** to close the blank Document1. From the **File** menu, click **New**.

The New Document task pane displays. One of the new document types is a Web page, as shown in Figure 11.2.

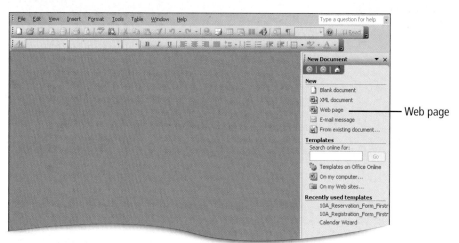

**Figure 11.2**

**2** In the **New Document** task pane, under **New**, click **Web page**.

The document opens in Web Layout view, and the New Document button changes to a New Web Page button. The work area covers the entire width of the Word window, as shown in Figure 11.3.

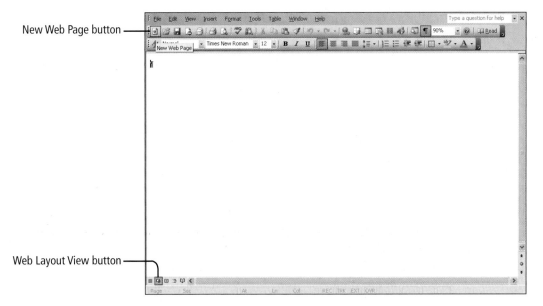

New Web Page button

Web Layout View button

**Figure 11.3**

**Another Way** — **To Create a Web Page Using the View Buttons**

You can open a new document in any view, and then click the Web Layout View button, located to the left of the horizontal scroll bar. You can also prepare an existing document for the Web by switching to Web Layout view.

**3** On the Standard toolbar, click the **Show/Hide ¶** button, if necessary, to show formatting marks.

**4** On the Standard toolbar, click the **Save** button. In the **Save as type** box, be sure **Single File Web Page** displays.

**5** In the **Save As** dialog box, navigate to your storage location, creating a new folder for this chapter if you want to do so. In the **File name** box, type **11A_Television_Schedule** but do *not* add your name. Click **Save**.

At the time you create and save the frames on your Web page, you must rename the document; thus, at that point you will add your name to the file.

**Activity 11.2** Inserting and Naming Frames in a Web Page

From the Frames toolbar, you can add frames to a Web page. Because your frames page will contain links to each frame page, you will also need to name and save the individual frames.

**1** From the **View** menu, point to **Toolbars**, and then click **Frames**.

The Frames toolbar displays, floating on your screen.

**2** On the Frames toolbar, point to unlabeled buttons to display the ScreenTips. Take a moment to examine the description of each button in the table in Figure 11.4.

## Buttons on the Frames Toolbar

| Name | Button | Description |
|---|---|---|
| Table of Contents in Frame | | Places the table of contents field in a frame to the left of the frame containing the insertion point |
| New Frame Left | New Frame Left | Creates a vertical frame to the left of the frame containing the insertion point |
| New Frame Right | New Frame Right | Creates a vertical frame to the right of the frame containing the insertion point |
| New Frame Above | New Frame Above | Creates a vertical frame above the frame containing the insertion point |
| New Frame Below | New Frame Below | Creates a vertical frame below the frame containing the insertion point |
| Delete Frame | | Removes the frame containing the insertion point |
| Frame Properties | | Displays the Frame Properties dialog box for the frame containing the insertion point |

**Figure 11.4**

**3** On the Frames toolbar, click the **New Frame Left** button New Frame Left.

A frame is added to the left side of the screen, dividing the screen into two frames of equal size. A *frame border* divides the frames, and the insertion point displays in the new frame, as shown in Figure 11.5.

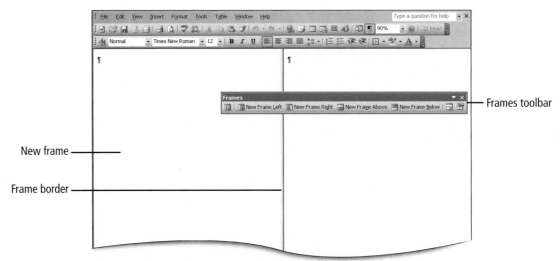

New frame

Frame border

Frames toolbar

**Figure 11.5**

**4** Click to position the insertion point in the frame on the right—if necessary, move the toolbar so that you can see the insertion point. On the Frames toolbar, click the **New Frame Above** button New Fra<u>m</u>e Above.

The frame on the right side of the screen is split into two frames of equal size, and the insertion point moves to the new upper frame. Your Web page consists of three frames.

**5** Right-click anywhere in the upper right frame. From the shortcut menu, click **Save Current Frame As**. At the bottom of the dialog box, in the **Save as type** box, be sure **Single File Web Page** is selected. In the **File name** box, type **Southland_Title** and then click **Save**.

The frame is saved in the same folder as the frames page—*11A_Television_Schedule*. Notice that the name of the frame does not display in the title bar.

**6** Click in the lower right frame, and then right-click in the frame. From the shortcut menu, click **Save Current Frame As**. Be sure the type is **Single File Web Page** and then name and save the document as **Southland_Schedule**

**7** Click in the left frame, and then right-click in the frame. Save the frame as a **Single File Web Page** with the name **Southland_Picture**

### Activity 11.3 Adding Text to a Frame

Type text in a frame in the same manner as you would type text into a Word document; use the same tools to format the text.

**1** Click to position the insertion point in the upper right frame. Type **Southland Gardens** and then press Enter. Type **Episode Guide: March 15-19**

**2** Select the two lines of text you just typed. Change the **Font** Times New Roman to **Comic Sans MS**.

**3** Click the **Font Color button arrow** A, and then in the second row, click the fourth color—**Green**. Click the **Bold** button B.

**4** Select the first line of text—*Southland Gardens*—and change the **Font Size** 12 to **48**.

Depending on your screen settings, the text may wrap to two lines.

**5** Select the second line of text—*Episode Guide: March 15-19*—and change the **Font Size** 12 to **24**. Click anywhere in the frame to deselect the text.

Compare your screen with Figure 11.6; your text may wrap differently.

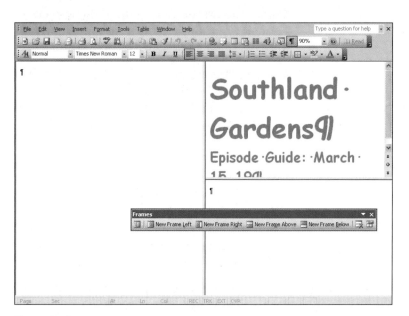

**Figure 11.6**

**6** On the Standard toolbar, click the **Save** button ▣.

Although you have already saved, the Save As dialog box displays. When you add frames, you must give the document a new name, at which time you can also add a Web page title. Notice that the temporary file name and the three frame names display in the folder.

**7** Near the bottom of the **Save As** dialog box, click **Change Title**.

The Set Page Title dialog box displays, as shown in Figure 11.7. The title that you enter here will display in the browser title bar when the Web page is displayed in a Web browser such as Internet Explorer.

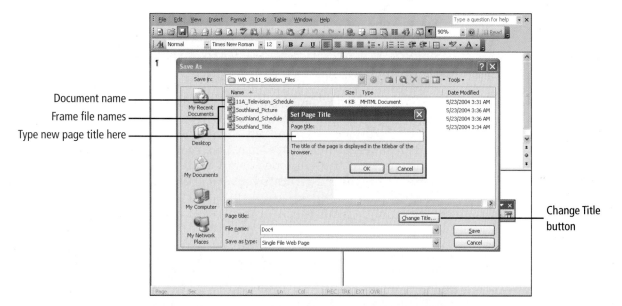

Figure 11.7

**8** In the **Set Page Title** dialog box, in the **Page title** box, type **11A_Television_Schedule_Firstname_Lastname** and then click **OK**.

Notice that the new page title displays to the left of the Change Title button.

**9** In the **File name** box, type **11A_Television_Schedule_Firstname_ Lastname**

**10** Near the bottom of the **Save As** dialog box, click **Save**.

### Activity 11.4 Inserting Graphics in a Frame

Pictures and clip art can be inserted or pasted into Web frames.

**1** Click to position the insertion point in the frame on the left side of the screen.

**2** From the **Insert** menu, point to **Picture**, and then click **From File**.

**3** Navigate to the location where the student files for this textbook are stored. Locate and select **w11A_Garden_Picture**. At the bottom of the **Insert Picture** dialog box, click **Insert**.

The picture is inserted into the frame. Because the picture is taller than the screen, a vertical scroll bar is added to the frame, as shown in Figure 11.8.

---

## More Knowledge — Horizontal Scroll Bars

Although the picture in the left frame is wider than the frame, no horizontal scrollbar has been added. When a horizontal scroll bar is necessary, it is displayed only when the Web page is viewed using a Web browser. By default, text frames automatically adjust text using word wrap when the frames are resized or displayed in a screen with a different resolution. Horizontal scroll bars are added only if the text has been set with a fixed width. The need for a vertical scrollbar will depend on your screen resolution.

---

Vertical scroll bar

**Figure 11.8**

**4** **Save** your work.

**Activity 11.5** Inserting a Word File in a Frame

If the text you want on your Web page already exists in a Word document, you can insert the Word document directly into a frame.

**1** Click to position the insertion point in the empty frame in the lower right corner of the screen.

**2** From the **Insert** menu, click **File**.

**3** In the displayed **Insert File** dialog box, navigate to the student files that accompany this textbook. Locate and select **w11A_Episode_ Guide**. At the bottom of the **Insert File** dialog box, click **Insert**.

The *w11A_Episode_Guide* document is inserted in the frame.

**4** If necessary, on the right side of the frame that contains the Word document, use the vertical scroll bar to scroll to the top of the document and drag the Frames toolbar so that it is not blocking your view of the frame.

Compare your screen with Figure 11.9.

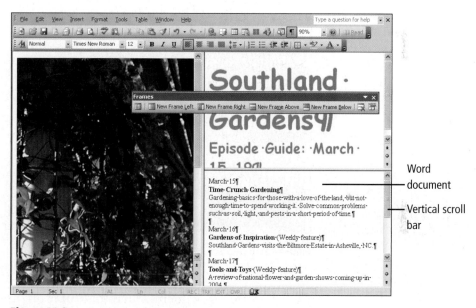

Figure 11.9

**5** Click **Save** .

## Activity 11.6  Resizing Frames in a Web Page

Each time you create a frame, the frame in which the insertion point is positioned is divided in half to create the new frame. After you have placed the text and graphics in the frames, you can resize them to get the effect you want.

**1** If necessary, from the View menu, click Ruler to turn on the rulers.

Notice that only horizontal rulers display.

**2** In the center of the screen, move the pointer over the vertical frame border to display the **Resize** pointer ⟷.

**3** Drag the vertical frame border to the left to **2.75 inches on the horizontal ruler** and release the mouse button.

All three frames are resized, and in the two frames on the right, word wrap fits the text to the new frame width. See Figure 11.10.

2.75 inch mark —

Text wraps to fit frame width.

**Figure 11.10**

**4** From the **View** menu, turn the **Ruler** off, and then close the Frames toolbar.

**5** Move the pointer over the horizontal frame border and drag up until the border is just below the second line of text that begins *Episode Guide*. If necessary, drag the vertical frame border to the left until the *Southland Gardens* title fits on one line.

Compare your screen with Figure 11.11.

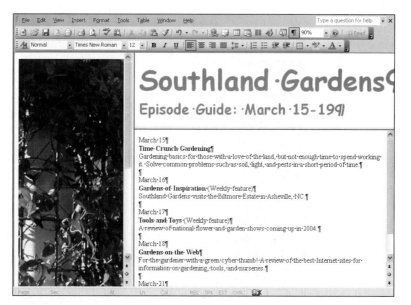

**Figure 11.11**

6 **Save**  your work.

### Activity 11.7 Adding Themes and Backgrounds to a Web Page

You can use themes and backgrounds in your Web page frames.

1 Click to position the insertion point in the upper right frame, which begins *Southland Gardens*.

2 From the **Format** menu, point to **Background**, and then in the fifth row, click the fourth color—**Light Green**.

The dark green text contrasts nicely with the light green background.

3 Click to position the insertion point in the lower right frame, which begins *March 15*. From the **Format** menu, click **Theme**. In the **Theme** dialog box, under **Choose a Theme**, click **Edge**.

The theme is previewed under *Sample of theme Edge*, as shown in Figure 11.12. The Edge theme uses a patterned background and the Georgia font.

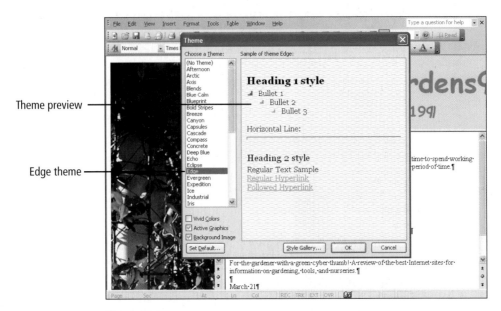

**Figure 11.12**

4 Click **OK**, and then click **Save** ![save icon].

Notice that the theme is applied only to the active frame—the
frame that contained the insertion point. Compare your screen
with Figure 11.13.

**Figure 11.13**

**Activity 11.8** Previewing a Web Page Containing Frames

**1** Be sure the insertion point is positioned in the lower right frame. From the **File** menu, click **Web Page Preview**. If necessary, **Maximize** 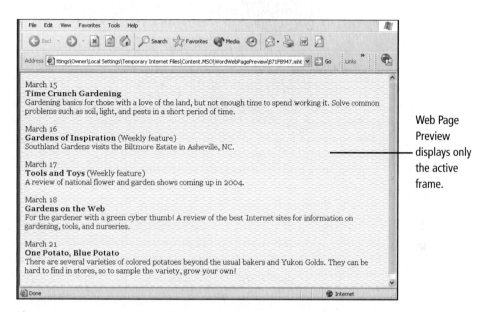 the Internet Explorer window that displays.

The Internet Explorer browser window opens but displays only the contents of the active frame, as shown in Figure 11.14.

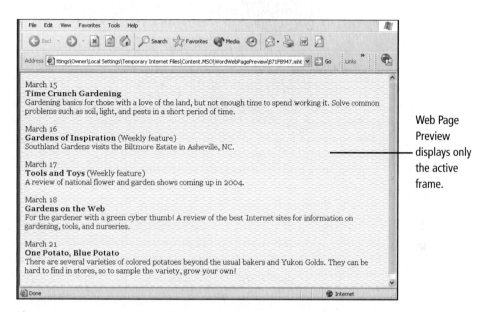

> March 15
> **Time Crunch Gardening**
> Gardening basics for those with a love of the land, but not enough time to spend working it. Solve common problems such as soil, light, and pests in a short period of time.
>
> March 16
> **Gardens of Inspiration** (Weekly feature)
> Southland Gardens visits the Biltmore Estate in Asheville, NC.
>
> March 17
> **Tools and Toys** (Weekly feature)
> A review of national flower and garden shows coming up in 2004.
>
> March 18
> **Gardens on the Web**
> For the gardener with a green cyber thumb! A review of the best Internet sites for information on gardening, tools, and nurseries.
>
> March 21
> **One Potato, Blue Potato**
> There are several varieties of colored potatoes beyond the usual bakers and Yukon Golds. They can be hard to find in stores, so to sample the variety, grow your own!

Web Page Preview displays only the active frame.

**Figure 11.14**

**2** On the browser title bar, click the **Close** button ⊠ to close the preview. On the **Word** menu bar, click the **Close Window** button ⊠, saving your changes if prompted to do so.

**3** On the taskbar, click the **Start** button, and then click **My Computer**. Navigate to your chapter folder. Locate and double-click your **11A_Television_Schedule_Firstname_Lastname** file. If necessary, **Maximize** the window.

Notice that the Web page opens in your browser software, but the text in the title frame may need to be adjusted, depending on the resolution of your screen. See Figure 11.15 (your screen may vary).

**Figure 11.15**

**4** Test the vertical scroll bars to confirm that the text or picture in the frame moves up and down. Move the pointer over the frame borders and drag the horizontal frame border up and down, and the vertical border left and right. Move the borders to *approximately* the same positions as those shown in Figure 11.15—this need not be precise.

**5** **Close** the browser. From the taskbar, click Microsoft Word to return to the Word window.

## Objective 2
## Edit Web Pages Using Word

Most Web pages can be edited in Word, regardless of whether they were created in Word. Everything in a Web page can be edited, from simple text to frame properties, such as borders and size.

### Activity 11.9 Editing a Web Page in Word

Web pages can be opened in your browser software or in Word. If the Web page is opened in Word, you can use Word's editing features to modify the page.

**1** Display the **Open** dialog box, click the **Files of type arrow**, and then click **All Web Pages**. Navigate to your chapter folder.

Only the Web pages (and any subfolders in the folder) display.

**2** Click to select your **11A_Television_Schedule_Firstname_ Lastname** file, and then click **Open**.

**3** In the upper right frame, select the text *Southland Gardens*. Change the **Font Size** [12 ▾] to **36**, and then click the **Center** button [▤].

**4** Select the text *Episode Guide: March 15-19*. Change the **Font Size** [12 ▾] to **18**, and **Center** [▤] the text.

**5** Click anywhere in the upper right frame to deselect the text. Move the pointer over the horizontal frame border and drag upward to position it slightly below the *Episode Guide* line as shown in Figure 11.16.

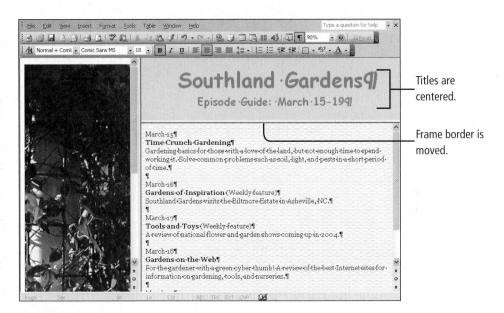

Titles are centered.

Frame border is moved.

**Figure 11.16**

**6** If necessary, in the lower right frame, scroll down until you can see the last item. Change *March 21* to March **19**

**7** From the **Edit** menu, click **Select All**. Alternatively, press Ctrl + A.

**8** Change the **Font Color** [A ▾] of the selected text to **Green**. Click anywhere in the frame to deselect the text. **Save** [▤] your work.

All of the text in the frame is changed to green to match the title text in the upper frame, as shown in Figure 11.17.

Selected text is changed to green.

**Figure 11.17**

### Activity 11.10 Changing Frame Properties

Similar to other Word objects, frames have properties that can be changed. These properties include border width, border color, and scrollbars.

**1** Right-click in either of the frames on the right portion of the screen.

**2** From the shortcut menu, click **Frame Properties**. Click the **Borders tab**.

**3** Under **Frames page**, click the **Border color arrow**, and then in the second row, click the fourth color—**Green**.

Changes made in the *Frames page* area of this dialog box affect all frames in the document, as shown in the preview area. See Figure 11.18.

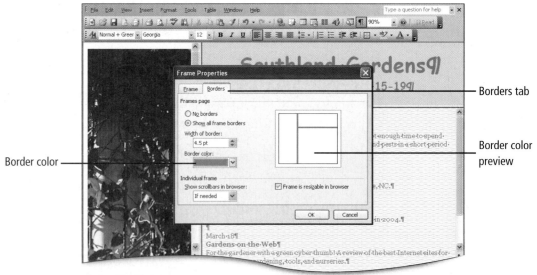

Borders tab

Border color preview

Border color

**Figure 11.18**

**4** Click **OK**.

Both frame borders match the text color, as shown in Figure 11.19.

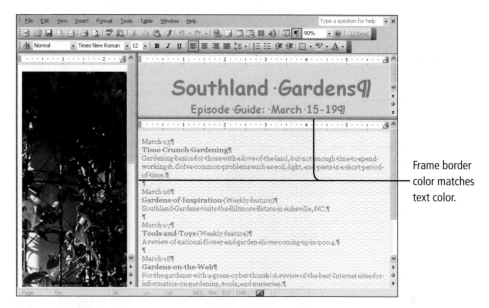

Frame border
color matches
text color.

**Figure 11.19**

**5** Click the left frame on the screen, and then right-click in the frame.

Notice that you cannot access Frame Properties for this frame by clicking the picture area.

**6** Move the pointer over the vertical frame border to display the horizontal resize pointer, and then drag to the right until you can see white space to the right of the picture. If you did not drag far enough, you may have to do this a second time to see the white area. Refer to Figure 11.20 for the position of the vertical frame border. Position the pointer over the white space and right-click.

Notice that the shortcut menu displays the Frame Properties command when you right-click in the white space.

**7** From the shortcut menu, click **Frame Properties**. Be sure the **Borders tab** displays.

**8** Under **Individual frame**, click the **Show scrollbars in browser arrow**, and then click **Never**.

Because the picture is purely decorative, it is unnecessary—and possibly distracting—to have another set of scroll bars on the screen. Changes made in the *Individual frame* area of this dialog box affect only the active frame. See Figure 11.20.

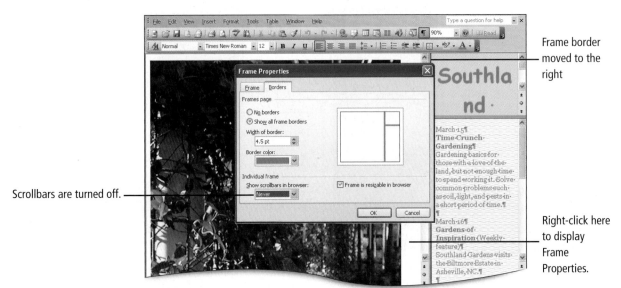

**Figure 11.20**

**9** Click **OK**. From the **View** menu, click **Ruler** to display the rulers. Drag the vertical frame border to the left to **2.75 inches on the horizontal ruler**. Turn off the ruler. Click in the upper right frame, and then from the Standard toolbar, click the **Show/Hide ¶** button 【¶】 to hide the formatting marks. Repeat this procedure in the lower right frame. Compare your screen with Figure 11.21.

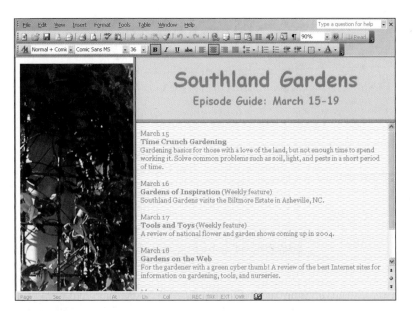

**Figure 11.21**

**10** **Save** your work and then click the **Open** button. In the **Files of type** box, select **All Word Documents**, and then click **Cancel**.

This will restore the document type that is displayed the next time you use the Open dialog box.

**11** **Close** the document. Click the **Start** button, and then click **My Computer**. Navigate to your chapter folder. Locate and double-click your **11A_Television_Schedule_Firstname_Lastname** file.

The browser opens to display the Web page.

**12** From the **File** menu, click **Print Preview**. Because Web pages are designed to be viewed on a screen rather than printed, the formatting of the printed document will differ from the formatting on the Web page. Confirm that the file name containing your name displays at the top of document—to the left of *Page 1 of 1*. **Close** the Print Preview window.

**Alert!**

**Does Only One Frame Display?**

If only one frame displays in the Print Preview window, check the box to the right of the Zoom box in the Print Preview toolbar. If *All frames individually* displays, click the button and select *As laid out on screen*.

**13** From the **File** menu, click **Print**, and then click **OK**. **Close** ☒ the Web browser, and then close any open windows from My Computer. **Close** ☒ Word.

**Note — Moving the Web Page**

When you create a Web page using frames, the Web page and the frame pages must be kept in the folder in which they were created. If you need to submit a copy of the Web page electronically, you have two choices. First, you can capture the Web page and paste it into a Word document. With the Web page displayed using your browser, press [Shift] + [PrtScr] to place a copy of the screen in your Office Clipboard. Open a blank document, change the Orientation to Landscape, and then click the Paste button. Save the document as 11A_Television_Schedule_Firstname_Lastname and submit it.

The second way to move (or submit) the Web page is to save it as a complete Web page in its own folder, and then move the folder to a new location. Open Word in your browser. From the File menu, click Save As. From the Save Web Page dialog box, click the Create New Folder button and create and open a new folder. Under Save as type, click Web Page, and then complete. The entire folder can then be moved and opened in another location.

**End** You have completed Project 11A ——————————————

# Project 11B Human Resources

Word includes several features that help you work with others on the same document. These include password protection and document validation. You can also save different versions of the same document in a single file.

To:         Danny Golden, President

From:       Yumiko Sato, Southland Gardens Producer

Date:       March 8

Subject:    Next Fiscal Headcount and Outsourcing

In accordance with this year's budget and production schedule, Southland Gardens' headcount requirements will remain even with last year. We anticipate a turnover of approximately 15%, based on past years. With no planned changes in number of episodes or major increases in production requirements, Southland Gardens should be well prepared to maintain its quality programming with no increases in personnel.

Several job descriptions have been changed and current employees will be invited to apply for those new positions. We believe that current employees will be able to fill all the new positions, and we do not anticipate any layoffs based on these changes. We have the resources available to provide new or additional training where necessary and our staff has always been willing to take on new responsibilities and learn new things when called on.

We have been working with the Southland Media marketing group to determine which pieces of our marketing program can be outsourced. Some of the larger, more complex multi-media development will be outsourced, and preference will be given to California companies employing local personnel. We will also continue to use locally-based film crews for location shooting to avoid travel and equipment transport costs. Post-production will continue to be done in house, which may require hiring temporary or contract personnel. This is covered in our budget.

In accordance with the recently revised Southland Media policies and our own internal guidelines, we will continue to strive for an employee base that is diverse, both behind the camera and on camera. Southland Gardens actively recruits minorities, veterans, and people with physical challenges.

11B_Human_Resources_Firstname_Lastname

**Figure 11.22**

In Activities 11.11 through 11.18 you will work with a Human Resources memo from the Southland Gardens television producer. You will restrict access to the document and specify the types of changes that can be made. You will also save and delete versions of the document. Your completed document will look similar to Figure 11.22. You will save your document as *11B_Human_Resources_Firstname_Lastname*.

# Objective 3
## Protect Documents

Document security is important when different members of a group have access to the folder in which shared documents are stored. You can use passwords to keep people from opening confidential documents. You can also use a password to restrict the types of formatting that can be applied to a document. Finally, a password can prevent someone viewing the document from making changes to the document.

### Activity 11.11 Protecting a Document with a Password

***Password protection*** is the use of passwords as a means of allowing only authorized individuals access to a computer system or to specific computer files. Password protection is commonly used for documents that contain confidential or proprietary information. Word offers two ways to add a password to a document. As the author of a document, you can create a password that must be typed to open the document. Thus, only individuals who know the password can open the document. You can also create a password that must be typed to modify the document—anyone can open and view the document, but only those who know the password can modify the document.

**1** **Start** Word. From the student files that accompany this textbook, locate and open **w11B_Human_Resources**. Save the file in your chapter folder as **11B_Human_Resources_Firstname_Lastname**

**2** Set the **Zoom** `100%` to **Page Width**, and if necessary, click **Show/Hide ¶** button `¶` to show formatting marks.

**3** From the **Tools** menu, click **Options**, and then click the **Security tab**.

The Options dialog box displays several security settings, as shown in Figure 11.23. Use ***file encryption*** to scramble the contents of the file mathematically. Only individuals who know the password can open and edit the document. A file encryption password can be combined with other security tools to restrict the editing capabilities of other users. The ***Password to modify*** option enables users who know the password to edit the document—usually a document stored in a shared file on an organization's network.

Password to open a document ————

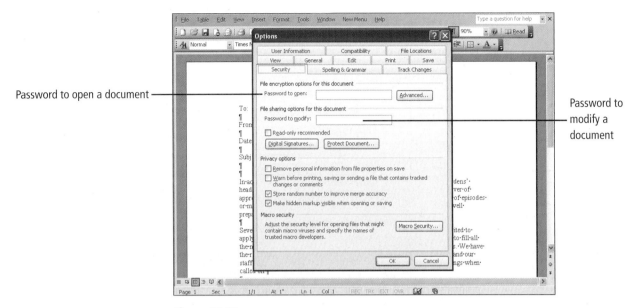

———— Password to
modify a
document

**Figure 11.23**

**Alert!**

**Remember Your Password**

You must remember the password you choose for a document. If you forget the password, you will be unable to open the document.

**4** Under **File encryption options for this document**, in the **Password to open** box, type **Practice**

Notice that as you type the password, only black dots (or asterisks) display, which prevents someone from reading your password as you type it.

**5** Click **OK**.

The Confirm Password dialog box displays, asking you to reenter your password. This prevents you from making a typographical error in your intended password. If the two passwords do not match, you can enter them again. See Figure 11.24.

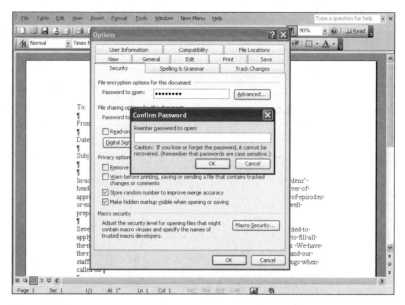

**Figure 11.24**

## Note — Using Uppercase and Lowercase Letters

When you type a password to open a document, you must type it exactly as it was created in this dialog box. Passwords are *case sensitive*, which means that if you use a capital letter, for example, as the first character of a password at the time you create the password, you will be unable to open the document unless you use a capital letter in the same position every time you type the password.

**6** Type **Practice** again and click **OK**. If the passwords do not match, you will be asked to try again.

**7** On the right side of the document window, click the **Close Window** button ☒, and then save your changes when prompted.

**8** On the Standard toolbar, click the **Open** button 📂. Select your **11B_Human_Resources_Firstname_Lastname** file, and then click **Open**.

**9** In the **Password** dialog box, type **Practice** and then click **OK**. If the document does not open, type the password again. Be sure you use a capital letter at the beginning of the password.

**10** **Save** 🖫 your document.

## Activity 11.12 Setting Formatting Restrictions

When several people will be working on the same document, you can prevent others from applying styles that you do not explicitly make available. You can also prevent users from applying formatting directly to the text—for example, bulleted or numbered lists. When you restrict formatting in this manner, the commands and keyboard shortcuts for applying formatting directly are unavailable.

**1** From the **Tools** menu, click **Protect Document**.

The Protect Document task pane displays on the right side of your screen, as shown in Figure 11.25.

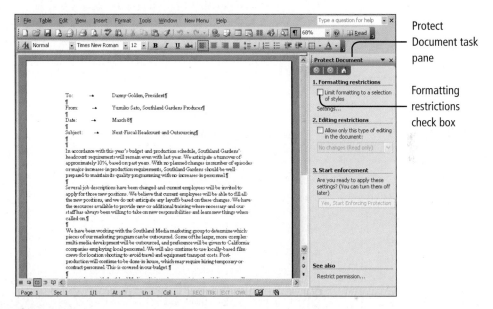

**Figure 11.25**

**2** In the **Protect Document** task pane, under **Formatting restrictions**, click the **Limit formatting to a selection of styles** check box. Under **Formatting restrictions**, click **Settings**.

The Formatting Restrictions dialog box displays, showing a list of styles used on your computer. See Figure 11.26.

Limit formatting check box ———

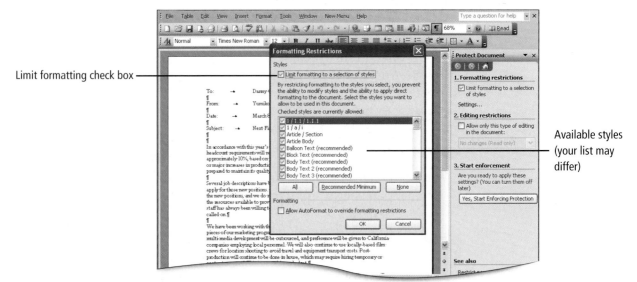

**Figure 11.26**

▣ In the **Formatting Restrictions** dialog box, be sure the **Limit formatting to a selection of styles** check box is selected. In the lower portion of the dialog box, click the **Recommended Minimum** button.

Any styles that have been created and saved with other documents are deselected, and the built-in Word styles remain selected. See Figure 11.27.

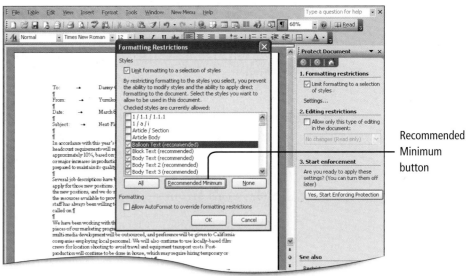

Available styles (your list may differ)

Recommended Minimum button

**Figure 11.27**

**4** Scroll through the list of styles to see which are still selected and which have been deselected.

Notice, for example, that many table styles, which are not used in this document, are deselected, although the default (recommended) table styles remain selected.

## Note — If Your Dialog Box Differs

Computers in a college computer lab sometimes use minimum installations that do not use many of the available styles. If you are working in a lab where the computers are reconfigured every night, and additional user-created styles are removed, your dialog box may show no deselected styles.

**5** At the bottom of the **Formatting Restrictions** dialog box, click **OK**.

A message box indicates that styles may exist in the document that are not allowed and asks if you want to remove them.

**6** Click **No** to retain all existing styles in the document. In the **Protect Document** task pane, under **Start enforcement**, click **Yes, Start Enforcing Protection**.

The Start Enforcing Protection dialog box displays, asking you to enter a password for this document. Those who know the password will be able to turn off the protection and format text and paragraphs. Those who do not know the password will be unable to make formatting changes. See Figure 11.28.

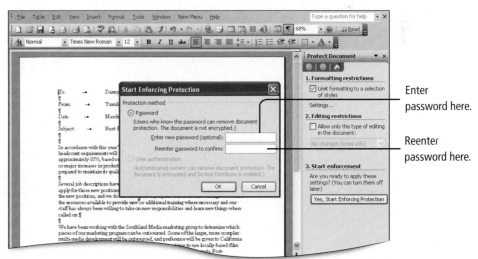

**Figure 11.28**

**7** Under **Protection method**, in the **Enter new password (optional)** box, type **format** and then press [Tab]. Retype the password and click **OK**.

**8** Click to position the insertion point in the paragraph that begins *In accordance.*

Examine the Formatting toolbar. Most of the buttons on the Formatting toolbar are inactive as a result of restricting formatting.

**9** Select the text *In accordance.* On the Formatting toolbar, click the **Italic** button [*I*].

A message box indicates that the command is unavailable because formatting is currently restricted in the document. See Figure 11.29.

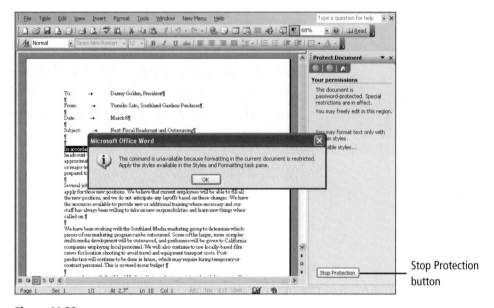

Stop Protection button

**Figure 11.29**

---

**Note** — The Effects of Using Document Protection

Passwords are applied only to the current document—no other documents are affected. When the document is unprotected, Word does not remember the password. If you want to protect the document again, you will have to repeat the procedure to create a password.

**10** Click **OK** to close the message box.

The Styles and Formatting task pane replaces the Protect Document task pane.

**11** At the top of the task pane, click the **Other Task Panes arrow**, and then click **Protect Document**. At the bottom of the displayed **Protect Document** task pane, click the **Stop Protection** button.

The Unprotect Document dialog box displays. If you know the password, you can turn off protection by typing the password in this dialog box.

**12** In the **Password** box, type **format** and then click **OK**.

Formatting restrictions are removed, and the buttons on the Formatting toolbar are active again. See Figure 11.30.

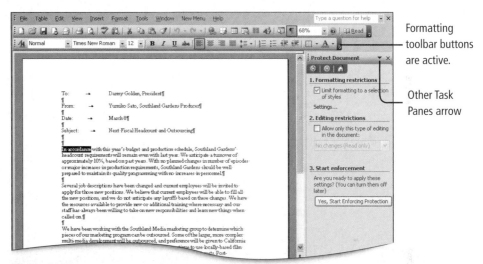

Formatting toolbar buttons are active.

Other Task Panes arrow

**Figure 11.30**

**13** Click the **Save** button 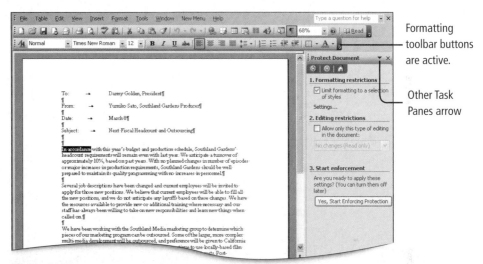.

**Activity 11.13** Setting Editing Restrictions

In addition to setting formatting restrictions, you can restrict which parts of the document can be edited, what type of editing can be done, and who has permission to make changes.

**1** In the **Protect Document** task pane, under **Formatting restrictions**, click to clear the **Limit Formatting to a selection of styles** check box.

**2** Under **Editing restrictions**, click to select the **Allow only this type of editing in the document** check box.

The *Editing restrictions* box activates, and the *Exceptions (optional)* section displays in the task pane.

**3** Click the **Editing restrictions arrow** and examine the available restriction types as shown in Figure 11.31.

The four restriction types are described in the table in Figure 11.32.

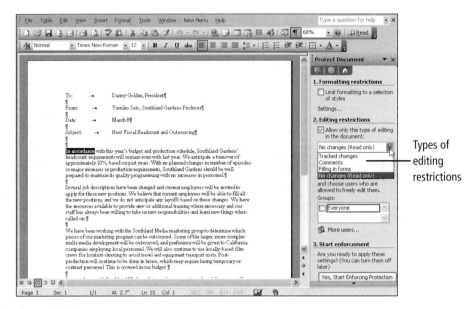

Figure 11.31

## Editing Restriction Types

| Restriction Type | Description |
| --- | --- |
| Tracked changes | All changes made are tracked using the Track Changes tool. |
| Comments | Comments can be added to the document using the Word Comments tool, but no changes can be made. |
| Filling in forms | Only form fields—check boxes, drop-down lists, and text fields—created using Word form tools can be filled in. |
| No changes (Read only) | The document can be viewed but not edited. This is the default restriction type. |

Figure 11.32

**4** On the displayed list, click **Comments**.

## More Knowledge — Making Exceptions to Editing Restrictions

Exceptions can be made to editing restrictions using the *Exceptions (optional)* section of the Protect Document task pane. To make exceptions, select a portion of the document, and then click either one of the groups in the Groups box or click *More users* and type in the e-mail addresses (or Microsoft Windows user account names) of the people who are allowed to work on the selected part of the document. You can identify different people who can work on different parts of the document. These exceptions work only for editing restrictions, not for formatting restrictions.

**5** In the **Protect Document** task pane, under **Start enforcement**, click **Yes, Start Enforcing Protection**.

The Start Enforcing Protection dialog box displays. Those who know the password will be able to turn off the protection. Those who do not know the password can add comments only; they can make no changes. See Figure 11.33.

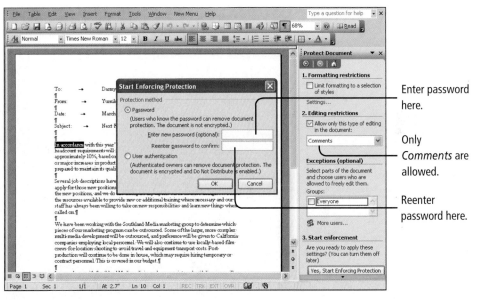

Enter password here.

Only *Comments* are allowed.

Reenter password here.

**Figure 11.33**

**6** In the **Enter new password (optional)** box, type **restricted** and then reenter the password in the confirmation box. Click **OK**.

Notice that a Stop Protection button is available at the bottom of the Protect Document task pane.

**7** In the paragraph that begins *In accordance*, locate and select **10%**. Watch the status bar, and attempt to type **20%**

You are unable to make changes. A message in the status bar momentarily displays indicating that the modification is not allowed.

**8** From the **View** menu, point to **Toolbars**, and then click **Reviewing**.

The Reviewing toolbar displays.

**9** Be sure *10%* is still selected. From the Reviewing toolbar, click the **Insert Comment** button. Type **This number will probably be closer to 15%**. If the comment is not displayed in the right margin, from the Tools menu, click Options, and then click the Track Changes tab. Under Balloons, click the Use Balloons arrow and click Always. Click anywhere in the document to deselect the text.

Compare your screen with Figure 11.34.

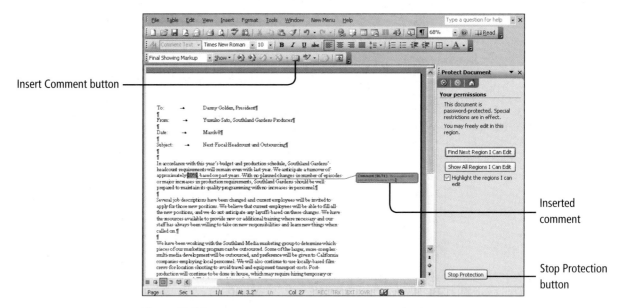

Insert Comment button

Inserted comment

Stop Protection button

**Figure 11.34**

**10** Near the bottom of the **Protect Document** task pane, click **Stop Protection**.

The Unprotect Document dialog box displays.

**11** In the **Password** box, type **restricted** and then click **OK**. Close the task pane.

**12** On the Reviewing toolbar, click the **Display for Review button arrow** `Final Showing Markup ▾`, and then click **Final** to hide the comment.

**13** From the **View** menu, point to **Toolbars**, and then click **Reviewing** to close the Reviewing toolbar. Click the **Save** button 🖫.

## Objective 4
## Attach Digital Signatures to Documents

Because sending documents electronically is common, receivers must be able to confirm the source of the document. With paper documents, a signature and notarization are legal tools to identify the source of the document and the validity of the signature. A *digital signature* is an electronic, encryption-based, secure stamp of authentication on a document, which confirms that the document originated from the signer and has not been altered. This requires a *digital certificate*—an attachment that vouches for authenticity, provides secure encryption, or supplies a verifiable signature. The digital certificate verifies the source and also verifies that the document has not been changed since the signature was added. The digital certificate contains personal information about the person who signed the document.

You can obtain a digital certificate in one of three ways. The most secure and most widely accepted way is a certificate purchased from a commercial verification company, such as VeriSign or E-Lock. You may also be able to obtain a certificate that will be accepted within your organization from your organization's network administrator. Finally, you can create a local certificate using *SelfCert*, a program that is included with Microsoft Office 2003.

### Activity 11.14 Creating a Personal Digital Signature with SelfCert

You can use the *SelfCert* program to create your own digital signature, which vouches for the authenticity of the document to which it is attached.

**1** On the taskbar, click the **Start** button `🏁 start` and point to **All Programs** (point to **Programs** if you are using Windows 2000). Point to **Microsoft Office**, point to **Microsoft Office Tools**, and then click **Digital Certificate for VBA Projects**.

The Create Digital Certificate dialog box displays, as shown in Figure 11.35.

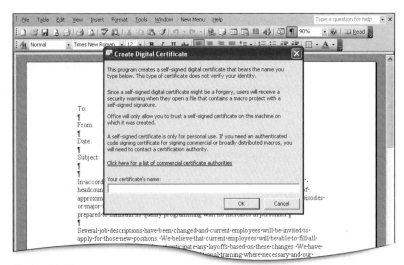

**Figure 11.35**

**Alert!**

### If You Don't See the Digital Certificate Command

You may not see the Digital Certificate for VBA Projects command using the procedure outlined in Step 1, for several reasons. The Microsoft Office Tools folder may be in a different location than the one described. If you find the Microsoft Office Tools folder, but do not see the Digital Certificate for VBA Projects command, SelfCert may not be installed on your computer. Finally, you may not be able to access the Microsoft Office folder because of security set by your local system administrator.

**2** Take a moment to read the description of the digital certificate created using the SelfCert program. Then, in the **Create Digital Certificate** dialog box, in the **Your certificate's name** box, type **Southland Gardens** and then click **OK**.

The SelfCert Success message box displays, indicating that the new certificate has been created. See Figure 11.36.

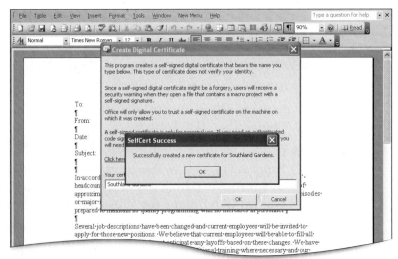

**Figure 11.36**

**3** In the **SelfCert Success** message box, click **OK**.

### Activity 11.15 Using a Digital Signature to Authenticate a Document

When you attach a digital signature and send the document as an e-mail attachment, or when you make the document available in a shared folder, the signature indicates that the document came from you and that it has not been altered. Because of the low level of security provided by certificates created by SelfCert, they are often useful only within a company.

**1** On the **Tools** menu, click **Options**, and then click the **Security tab**.

**2** Under **File sharing options for this document**, click the **Digital Signatures** button.

The Digital Signature dialog box displays, as shown in Figure 11.37.

Digital Signatures button —

Add button —

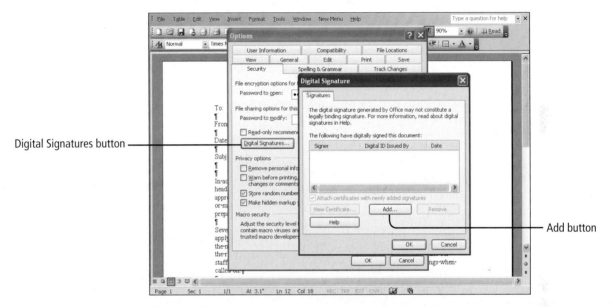

**Figure 11.37**

---

**Alert!** — **If the Digital Signature Does Not Work Properly**

Digital signatures are related to the security system built into Microsoft Office. Your system configuration and your Office settings can affect the way digital signatures work. If you have difficulty attaching a digital signature, consult with your instructor or move to Activity 11.16.

**3** Near the bottom of the **Digital Signature** dialog box, click the **Add** button.

A message box may display, indicating that one or more fonts are not installed, and that some content may not display.

## Note — If Your Dialog Box Differs

The message that displays here depends on the configuration of Microsoft Office on your computer. If your message box asks if you want to proceed without reviewing the document, click Yes. If another dialog box displays, close the dialog box and continue to Step 4.

**4** If the font warning message box displays, click **OK** to close it.

The Select Certificate dialog box displays, showing a list of digital signatures available to you. See Figure 11.38. Your dialog box may display more certificates, including several with the same name if you are using a lab computer.

List of available certificates ——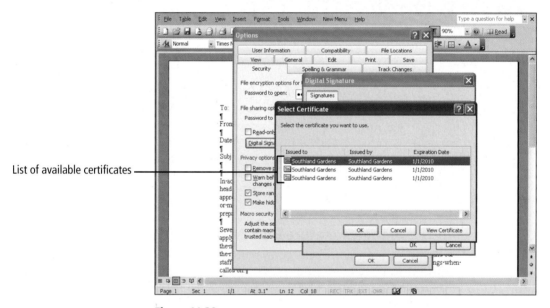

**Figure 11.38**

**5** Click to select the **Southland Gardens** certificate (the top one in the list if two or more have the same name), and then click **OK**.

The Southland Gardens certificate is added to the signature list for this document, as shown in Figure 11.39.

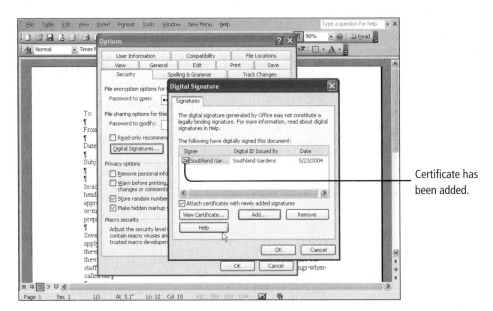

Certificate has been added.

**Figure 11.39**

**6** Click to select the digital signature, and then click the **View Certificate** button. Read the certificate information, and then click **OK** to close the **Certificate** dialog box. Click to select the digital signature again. At the bottom of the **Digital Signature** dialog box, click **OK**. At the bottom of the **Options** dialog box, click **OK**.

Notice that the signature is indicated in the title bar. If you were using an organization-wide or purchased certificate, the word *unverified* would not display. In the status bar, an icon indicates that a certificate is attached to the document.

---

### **Note** — If the Signature Does Not Display in the Title Bar

The process of adding a digital signature may not work if there are other Word documents open. If the digital signature icon does not display on the status bar, and is not included in the file name, close any other Word documents and try again.

You also may have to close and reopen the document to display the digital signature. Recall that your password for this document is Practice. You will need to open the Reviewing toolbar and change the Display for Review box to Final to hide the comment.

**7** In the status bar, double-click the digital signature icon, as shown in Figure 11.40.

The Digital Signature dialog box displays.

Title bar indicates a certificate is attached.

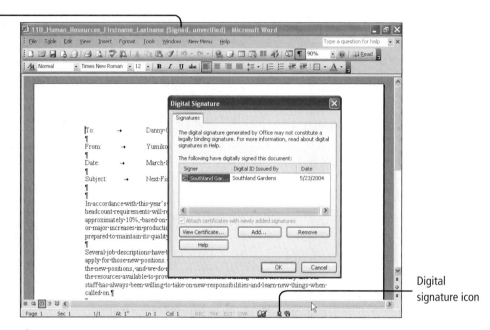

Digital signature icon

**Figure 11.40**

**8** Click **Cancel** to close the **Digital Signature** dialog box.

**9** On the Standard toolbar, click the **Save** button.

# Objective 5
## Use Document Versions

As you create, save, edit, and resave a document numerous times, you may want to return to an earlier revision to retrieve something that has been changed. You can review earlier revisions in two ways. The first is to save each revision, using the Save As command, with a new file name that indicates, with a version number or date and time you assign, the chronological order of the documents. The other way to keep track of revisions is to use Word's Versions feature. A **version** is a revision that is saved with the current document. If you save versions, you can open any previous revision along with the current version and cut and paste between the two documents. You can also abandon the current version and revert to an earlier version.

### Activity 11.16  Saving a Version

If you are going to use the versions feature, it is a good idea to save a new version each time significant changes are made to the document.

**1** In the paragraph that begins *In accordance*, select **10%** and change it to **15%**

**2** From the **View** menu, point to **Toolbars**, and then click **Reviewing** to display the Reviewing toolbar.

**3** On the Reviewing toolbar, click the **Display for Review arrow** `Final Showing Markup ▾`, and then click **Final Showing Markup**.

The comment that you added earlier displays.

**4** On the Reviewing toolbar, click the **Next** button ⇥. On the Reviewing toolbar, click the **Reject Change/Delete Comment** button ⊗▾. Close the Reviewing toolbar.

**5** Scroll to the last paragraph in the document. In the first sentence, click to position the insertion point immediately to the right of *In accordance with* and press ⎵Spacebar. Type **the recently revised**

**6** From the **File** menu, click **Versions**.

The Versions dialog box displays showing previously saved versions of the document, as shown in Figure 11.41. The versions display from newest to oldest.

Save Now button ———

Previous versions of the document ———

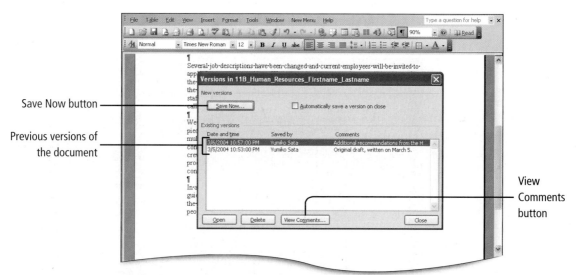

View Comments button

**Figure 11.41**

**7** Near the bottom of the **Versions** dialog box, click the **View Comments** button.

The View Comments dialog box displays. The comments written when the selected version was saved are displayed in the message box, as shown in Figure 11.42.

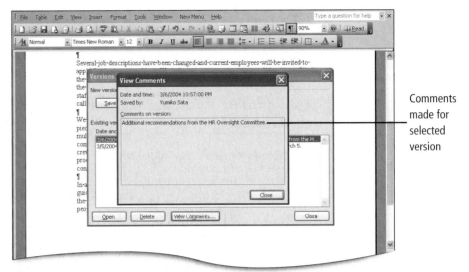

**Figure 11.42**

Comments made for selected version

**8** In the lower right corner of the **View Comments** dialog box, click the **Close** button. Under **New versions**, click the **Save Now** button.

**9** In the displayed **Save Versions** dialog box, under **Comments on version**, type **Final Draft**

Compare your dialog box with Figure 11.43.

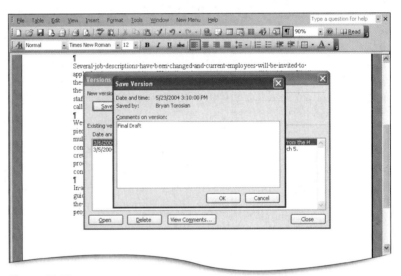

**Figure 11.43**

**10** At the bottom of the **Save Version** dialog box, click **OK**.

A message box displays, indicating that saving the document will remove all digital signatures. Recall that one of the purposes of using digital signatures is to indicate that the file has not been altered since the certificate was attached.

**11** Click **Yes** to save the new version and remove the digital signature.

Notice that the extra text in the file name in the title bar and the digital signature icon in the status bar are also removed.

---

## More Knowledge — File Size Issues When Using Versions

If you save a number of versions of the document, you would expect the document size to get very large. Word solves this potential problem by saving only the changes from one version to the next. Text and graphics that are unchanged are not saved again.

---

### Activity 11.17 Viewing Versions

**1** From the **File** menu, click **Versions**.

The Versions dialog box displays, showing previously saved versions of the document, as shown in Figure 11.44. The versions display from newest (at the top of the list) to oldest.

Previous versions —

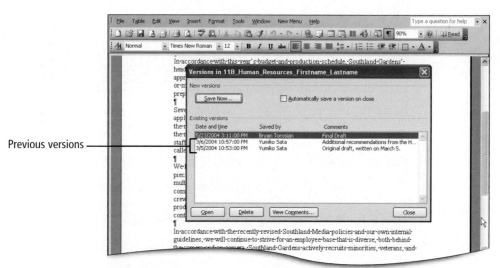

**Figure 11.44**

**2** Under **Existing versions**, click the oldest version, which will be at the bottom of the list.

**3** At the bottom of the **Versions** dialog box, click **Open**.

The first version opens in a separate window at the bottom of the screen. The current version displays in a window at the top of the screen.

**4** In the lower window, scroll up or down until you can see the first paragraph that begins *In accordance*. Click in the upper window and scroll up or down until you can see the same paragraph.

Notice that a long sentence has been added to the paragraph since the first version was saved. The date of the earlier version displays in the window title bar at the bottom of the screen. See Figure 11.45.

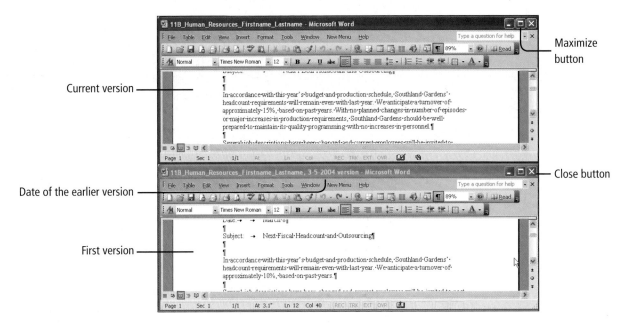

**Figure 11.45**

**5** In the title bar of the bottom window, click the **Close** button ![X]. In the title bar of the top window, click the **Maximize** button ![□].

### Activity 11.18 Deleting Unwanted Versions

If you are certain you will no longer need them, you can remove old versions of the document.

**1** From the **File** menu, click **Versions**. Under **Existing versions**, click the oldest version, which will be at the bottom of the list.

**2** At the bottom of the **Versions** dialog box, click **Delete**.

The Confirm Version Delete message box displays, asking you to confirm that you want to delete the selected version, and noting that you cannot undo this action once you have clicked *Yes*. See Figure 11.46.

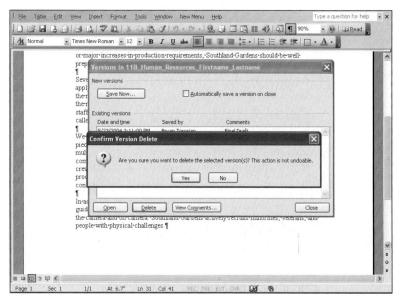

**Figure 11.46**

**3** In the **Confirm Version Delete** message box, click **Yes**. At the bottom of the **Versions** dialog box, click **Close**.

**4** From the **View** menu, click **Header and Footer**. On the Header and Footer toolbar, click the **Switch Between Header and Footer** button . Click the **Insert AutoText** button Insert AutoText ▾, and then click **Filename**. On the **Header and Footer** toolbar, click the **Close** button Close.

**5** On the Standard toolbar, click the **Save** button 🔲, and then click the **Print** button 🖨. Close the document and close Word.

**End** You have completed Project 11B ————————————————————

# Summary

Organizations commonly post important documents on the Web. Word documents can be saved as Web pages, but to take full advantage of the features available on the Web, Word also includes tools to divide the screen into different sections, called frames. Using frames, several different pages can be displayed on one Web screen. The frames can expand and contract, depending on the size of the user's browser window. Scrollbars can also be used to make long documents or other objects available in a single window.

After you have created a Web page using Word's frame features, you can still use Word to edit the Web document. You can also use Word to edit Web pages created using other programs.

When a document is stored in a shared folder that can be accessed by many people, Word offers several tools to restrict access to the document. A password can be added to prohibit those who do not have the password from opening the document. After the document is opened, passwords can be used to restrict the editing capabilities of each person who has access to the document. Individuals viewing the document can be prohibited from making formatting changes or restricted to adding only comments.

Digital signatures can be added to a document to confirm the identity of the author and assure the reader that no changes have been made to the document. Adding a digital signature attaches a digital certificate to the document. This certificate gives the reader information about who created the document and when it was created. When edits are made to the document, the certificate is removed.

When you want to see the progress of a document or need to be able to look at older editions of the file, you can use the Versions feature. This enables you to save older versions of a document in the same file as the current version. Version information, including comments, is stored along with the version. Documents saved with older versions do not take up excessive disk space, because only the changes from the current document are saved.

## In This Chapter You Practiced How To

- Create a Web Page with Frames
- Edit Web Pages Using Word
- Protect Documents
- Attach Digital Signatures to Documents
- Use Document Versions

# Concepts Assessments

**Matching** Match each term in the second column with its correct definition in the first column by writing the letter of the term on the blank line in front of the correct definition.

_____ 1. A Web page that divides a Web browser screen into different scrollable areas.

_____ 2. A method to restrict access to a document or to restrict what a user can do to a document—commonly applied to documents that contain confidential or proprietary information.

_____ 3. The name of the dialog box in which the characteristics of frame borders are controlled in a Web page document.

_____ 4. A scrollable and resizable area on a Web page that can independently display pages and may contain text, tables, graphics, or other objects.

_____ 5. A type of restriction that you can apply to a document allowing the reader to view the document but not edit or make comments.

_____ 6. When applying password protection to a document, an option that enables individuals who know the password to edit the document.

_____ 7. The Word document view that enables you to see what your document will look like when displayed on the Web.

_____ 8. The command that enables you to type the text that will display in the title bar of the browser software when people view your Web page on the Internet.

_____ 9. A technique that scrambles the contents of a file mathematically so that only individuals who know the password can open and edit the document.

_____ 10. The term that refers to discrimination between uppercase (capital) letters and lowercase letters, especially when typing a password.

_____ 11. A type of restriction that you can apply to a document that enables the reader to view the document and to type in comments, but not to make any changes to the document.

_____ 12. An electronic, encryption-based, secure stamp of authentication on a document, which confirms that the document originated from the signer and has not been altered.

_____ 13. In a frames page, the command that creates a new subwindow directly above the active frame.

_____ 14. An attachment that vouches for authenticity, provides secure encryption, or supplies a verifiable signature.

_____ 15. One of several commercial certification authorities, to which you can submit an application for a commercial digital certificate.

**A** Case sensitive

**B** Comments

**C** Digital certificate

**D** Digital signature

**E** File encryption

**F** Frame

**G** Frame Properties

**H** Frames page

**I** New Frame Above

**J** No changes (Read only)

**K** Password protection

**L** Password to modify

**M** Set Page Title

**N** VeriSign

**O** Web Layout View

**Fill in the Blank** Write the correct answer in the space provided.

1. The Web Page Preview command from the File menu does not display all elements of a Web page document that contains

   _____.

2. Frames are stored on a single Web page called a(n)

   _____ page.

3. When you type a password for a Word document, only

   _____ appear in the password box.

4. Word passwords are _____; that is, uppercase and lowercase letters that you type must match the password exactly or the password will not work.

5. Web design tools are found on the _____ toolbar.

6. A(n) _____ scroll bar does not display at the bottom of a frame while you are editing the Web page in Word.

7. _____ is the Office program that enables you to create your own digital signature.

8. When you use a digital signature, a(n) _____ is attached to the document.

9. A(n) _____ is one or more revisions of a document saved with the current document.

10. A subwindow is another name for a(n) _____.

# Project 11C — Special Show

**Objective:** *Create a Web Page with Frames.*

In the following Skill Assessment, you will create a Web page that describes the First Annual California Japanese Garden Symposium, which is sponsored by Southland Gardens. You will create a Web page that contains four frames, and insert two images and two text files. Your completed Web page will look similar to Figure 11.47. You will save your document as *11C_Special_Show_Firstname_Lastname*.

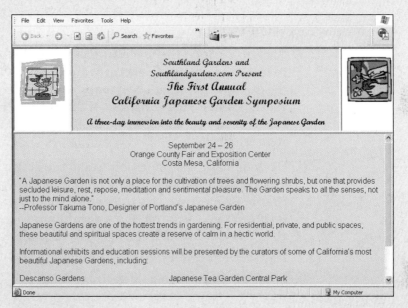

**Figure 11.47**

1. **Start** Word. From the **File** menu, click **New**. In the **New Document** task pane, under **New**, click **Web page**.

2. If necessary, on the Standard toolbar, click the **Show/Hide ¶** button to show formatting marks. From the **View** menu, point to **Toolbars**, and then click **Frames**.

3. On the Frames toolbar, click the **New Frame Above** button.

4. With the insertion point in the upper frame, click the **New Frame Right** button. With the insertion point in the upper right frame, click the **New Frame Right** button again. Your screen should display three frames in the upper half of the page and a single frame in the lower half of the page.

**(Project 11C–Special Show continues on the next page)**

**(Project 11C–Special Show continued)**

5. Right-click anywhere in the upper right frame. From the shortcut menu, click **Save Current Frame As**. Navigate to your chapter folder, and in the **Save as type** box, be sure **Single File Web Page** is selected. Type **Southland_Picture2** as the file name, and then click **Save**.

6. Click to position the insertion point in the upper middle frame, and then right-click in the upper middle frame. From the shortcut menu, click **Save Current Frame As**. In the **Save as type** box, be sure **Single File Web Page** is selected. Type **Southland_Heading** as the file name, and then click **Save**. Use the same technique to save the upper left frame as **Southland_Picture1** and the bottom frame as **Southland_Text**

7. Click to position the insertion point in the upper left frame. From the **Insert** menu, point to **Picture**, and then click **From File**. Navigate to the student files that accompany this textbook. Locate and select **w11C_Plant1**. At the bottom of the **Insert Picture** dialog box, click **Insert**. Use the same technique to insert **w11C_Plant2** in the upper right frame.

8. Click to make the upper left frame the active frame. Then, right-click in an open area of the frame and from the shortcut menu, click **Frame Properties**. In the **Frame Properties** dialog box, click the **Borders tab**. Click the **Show scrollbars in browser arrow**, and then click **Never**. Click **OK**. Repeat this technique to turn off the display of scroll bars in the other two frames at the top of the screen.

9. From the **View** menu, click **Ruler** to display the rulers. Click the upper left frame to make it active, and then select the image. Drag the lower right sizing handle up and to the left until the right edge of the image is at **1 inch on the horizontal ruler**. Select the image in the upper right frame. Drag the lower-right sizing handle down and to the right until the right edge of the image is at **1 inch on the horizontal ruler**. From the Formatting toolbar, click the **Align Right** button.

10. Click the upper middle frame to make it active. From the **Insert** menu, click **File**. Locate, and then insert **w11C_Garden_Title**. Use the same technique to insert **w11C_Garden_Text** in the lower frame.

11. Click **Save** to display the **Save As** dialog box. In the **Save as type** box, be sure **Single File Web Page** is selected. Near the bottom of the **Save As** dialog box, click the **Change Title** button. Type **11C_Special_Show_Firstname_Lastname** and click **OK**. Recall that this procedure will place the file name and your name in the browser title bar. In the **File name** box, select the existing text, type **11C_Special_Show_Firstname_Lastname** and then click **Save**.

**(Project 11C–Special Show continues on the next page)**

**(Project 11C**–Special Show continued)

**12.** In the upper left frame, drag the right vertical frame border to the left to **1.25 inches on the horizontal ruler**. In the upper middle frame, drag the right vertical frame border to the right to **6.5 inches on the horizontal ruler**. (Hint: Drag a little further so that you can see the markings, and then position the border more precisely.)

**13.** From the **View** menu, click **Ruler** to turn off the rulers. Drag the horizontal frame border upward until it is just under the last line of title text. **Close** the Frames toolbar.

**14.** Select all of the text lines in the title, and then click the **Center** button. Select the two title lines that begin *The First Annual* and *California*. Click the **Bold** button, and then change the **Font Size** to **18**.

**15.** Click to make the lower frame active and scroll to the top of the frame. From the **Format** menu, point to **Background**, and then in the fifth row, click the fourth color—**Light Green**. Repeat this technique to apply a **Light Green** background to the upper middle frame.

**16.** At the right end of the **Word** menu bar, click the **Close Window** button and save your changes.

**17.** Click the **Start** button, and then click **My Computer**. Navigate to your chapter folder, and then double-click your **11C_Special_Show_Firstname_Lastname** file to open it in your browser. Drag the horizontal border down, if necessary, to display the entire title in the upper middle frame.

**18.** From the **File** menu, click **Print Preview**. Notice that the formatting of the printed document will be different from the formatting on the Web page. Confirm that the file name is in the upper left corner. If only one frame displays, in the Print Preview toolbar, change *All frames individually* to *As laid out on screen*. **Close** the **Print Preview** window. From the **File** menu, click **Print**. Close the Web browser, and close **My Computer**.

**End** You have completed Project 11C ─────────────────

# Project 11D—Japanese Gardens

**Objective:** *Edit Web Pages Using Word.*

In the following Skill Assessment, you will work on a different version
of the Japanese Gardens Web page. This page was created without
frames. You will edit the text in the document, and convert two
columns of text to a table. You will add and resize a picture. Finally,
you will save and view the Web page. Your finished document should
be similar to Figure 11.48. You will save your document as
*11D_Japanese_Gardens_Firstname_Lastname.*

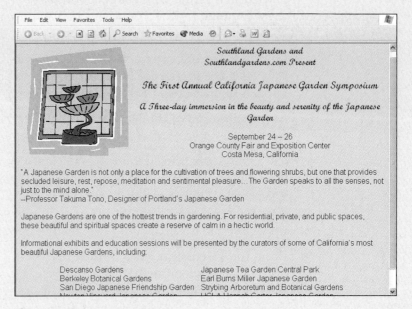

**Figure 11.48**

1. From **My Computer**, navigate to the student files that accompany
   this textbook. Locate and open the **w11D_Japanese_Gardens** file
   and examine the Web page in your browser. Close the browser when
   you are finished.

2. **Start** Word. On the Standard toolbar, click the **Open** button. Click
   the **Files of type arrow**, and click **All Web Pages**. Navigate to the
   student files that accompany this textbook, and open the file
   **w11D_Japanese_Gardens**. The document opens in Web Layout
   View.

**(Project 11D–Japanese Gardens continues on the next page)**

**(Project 11D–Japanese Gardens continued)**

3. From the **File** menu, click **Save As**. Near the bottom of the **Save As** dialog box, click the **Change Title** button. Type **11D_Japanese_ Gardens_Firstname_Lastname** as the title that will display in the browser title bar. Click **OK**.

4. Under **Save as type**, be sure **Single File Web Page** is selected. In the **File name** box, type **11D_Japanese_Gardens_Firstname_Lastname** and then click **Save**.

5. If necessary, on the Standard toolbar, click the Show/Hide ¶ button to show formatting marks. Select the four lines of text at the bottom of the page, beginning with *Descanso Gardens*. Be sure to include all four paragraph marks at the end of the four lines, but not the paragraph marks in the blank lines before or after the text.

6. From the **Table** menu, point to **Convert**, and then click **Text to Table**. In the **Convert Text to Table** dialog box, be sure the *Number of columns* is **2**, and then click **OK**.

7. With the table still selected, from the **Table** menu, point to **AutoFit**, and then click **AutoFit to Contents**. From the Formatting toolbar, click the **Center** button. From the **Format** menu, click **Borders and Shading**, and then click the **Borders tab**. Under **Setting**, click **None**, and then click **OK**.

8. From the **File** menu, click **Web Page Preview** to examine the change to the table. If necessary, **Maximize** the browser window. When you are finished, close the browser.

9. Press Ctrl + Home to move to the top of the document. Press Enter, and then position the insertion point in the new blank line at the top of the document.

10. From the **Insert** menu, click **File**. Locate and select **w11D_Garden_Title**, and then click **Insert**. Select the inserted title text. From the Formatting toolbar, click the **Center** button.

11. Press Ctrl + Home to move to the top of the document. From the **Insert** menu, point to **Picture**, and then click **From File**. Locate and select **w11D_Plant**, and then click **Insert**.

12. Right-click the image. From the shortcut menu, click **Format Picture**. In the **Format Picture** dialog box, click the **Layout tab**. Under **Wrapping style**, click **Square**. Under **Horizontal alignment**, click the **Left** option button, and then click **OK**.

**(Project 11D–Japanese Gardens continues on the next page)**

**(Project 11D**–Japanese Gardens continued)

13. From the **File** menu, click **Web Page Preview** to examine the position of the image and the text wrapping. Compare your Web page with Figure 11.48. Close the browser.

14. Use the resizing handles on the picture to resize the image as necessary. Preview the Web page to be sure the text is aligned properly. If necessary, resize the image again, and preview until your Web page looks like Figure 11.48. When you are satisfied, close the browser to return to Word.

15. Click to position the insertion point anywhere in the text. From the **Format** menu, point to **Background**, and then click **Light Green**— the fourth button in the fifth row.

16. On the **Word** menu bar, click the **Close Window** button, and save your changes. Click the **Start** button, and then click **My Computer**. From your chapter folder, locate and open your **11D_Japanese_ Gardens_Firstname_Lastname** file; the file opens in your browser.

17. From the **File** menu, click **Print Preview**. Confirm that the file name is in the title bar. Notice that when printed, the Web page does not match exactly the layout of the Web page on the screen. **Close** the **Print Preview** window. From the **File** menu, click **Print**. Close your browser, close My Computer, and close Word.

**End** You have completed Project 11D ⎯⎯⎯⎯⎯⎯⎯⎯⎯⎯⎯⎯⎯⎯

# Project 11E — Privacy Policy

**Objectives:** *Use Document Versions and Protect Documents.*

In the following Skill Assessment, you will work on a new version of the Southland Gardens privacy policy. You will make changes in the document, save a new version, and delete an old version. You also will add password protection to the document and restrict document formatting. Your document will look similar to Figure 11.49. You will save your document as *11E_Privacy_Policy_Firstname_Lastname.*

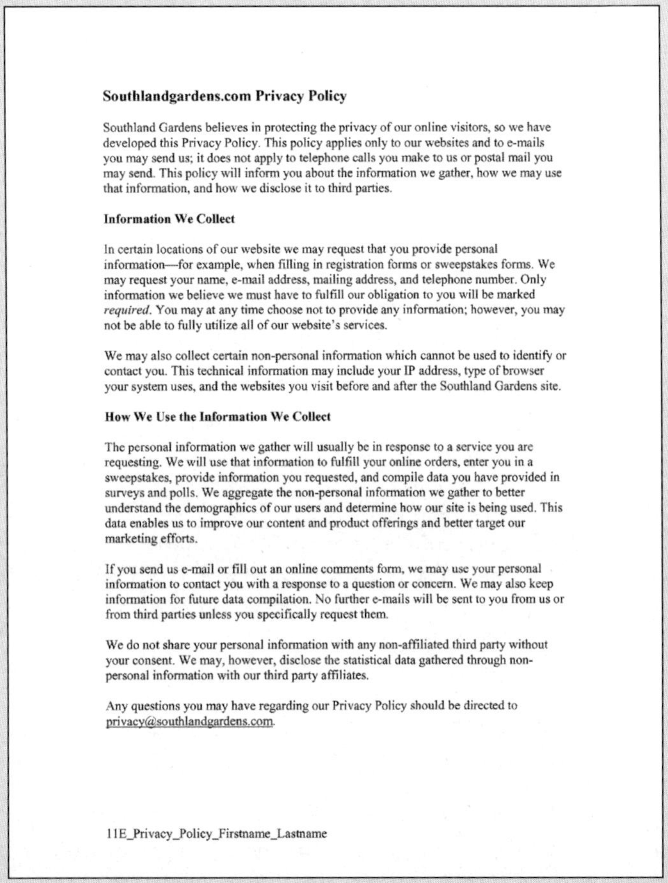

**Southlandgardens.com Privacy Policy**

Southland Gardens believes in protecting the privacy of our online visitors, so we have developed this Privacy Policy. This policy applies only to our websites and to e-mails you may send us; it does not apply to telephone calls you make to us or postal mail you may send. This policy will inform you about the information we gather, how we may use that information, and how we disclose it to third parties.

**Information We Collect**

In certain locations of our website we may request that you provide personal information—for example, when filling in registration forms or sweepstakes forms. We may request your name, e-mail address, mailing address, and telephone number. Only information we believe we must have to fulfill our obligation to you will be marked *required*. You may at any time choose not to provide any information; however, you may not be able to fully utilize all of our website's services.

We may also collect certain non-personal information which cannot be used to identify or contact you. This technical information may include your IP address, type of browser your system uses, and the websites you visit before and after the Southland Gardens site.

**How We Use the Information We Collect**

The personal information we gather will usually be in response to a service you are requesting. We will use that information to fulfill your online orders, enter you in a sweepstakes, provide information you requested, and compile data you have provided in surveys and polls. We aggregate the non-personal information we gather to better understand the demographics of our users and determine how our site is being used. This data enables us to improve our content and product offerings and better target our marketing efforts.

If you send us e-mail or fill out an online comments form, we may use your personal information to contact you with a response to a question or concern. We may also keep information for future data compilation. No further e-mails will be sent to you from us or from third parties unless you specifically request them.

We do not share your personal information with any non-affiliated third party without your consent. We may, however, disclose the statistical data gathered through non-personal information with our third party affiliates.

Any questions you may have regarding our Privacy Policy should be directed to privacy@southlandgardens.com.

11E_Privacy_Policy_Firstname_Lastname

**Figure 11.49**

1. **Start** Word. Display the **Open** dialog box, navigate to the location where the student files for this textbook are stored, and then be sure **All Files** is selected in the **Files of type** box. Locate and open **w11E_Privacy_Policy**. Save the file in your chapter folder as 11E_Privacy_Policy_Firstname_Lastname

2. Set the **Zoom** to **Page Width**, and if necessary, click the Show/Hide ¶ button to show formatting marks.

**(Project 11E–Privacy Policy continues on the next page)**

**(Project 11E–Privacy Policy continued)**

3. From the **File** menu, click **Versions**. Under **Existing versions**, click the oldest version, which displays at the bottom of the list. Near the bottom of the **Versions** dialog box, click the **View Comments** button. Read the comments, and then click the **Close** button.

4. In the lower left corner of the **Versions** dialog box, click **Open**. The older version—in the lower window—displays the creation date and time in its title bar. In the older version in the lower window, scroll until you can see the heading *Information We Collect* and its following paragraph. In the upper window—the current version—click, and then scroll up or down until you can see the same heading and paragraph. Notice the changes: In the first line under the heading, an em dash replaces the hyphen, and an additional sentence has been added to the end of the paragraph.

5. In the title bar of the lower window—the older version—click the **Close** button. **Maximize** the top window.

6. From the **Tools** menu, click **Options**, and then click the **User Information tab**. Write down the existing *Name* and *Initials*. Under **User information**, change the **Name** to **Miguel Harris** and then change the **Initials** to **MH** Click **OK**.

7. Scroll down to the paragraph that begins *The personal information*. In the sixth line of the paragraph, locate and select *allows*, and then type **enables**

8. Scroll to view the paragraph that begins *In certain locations*. In the fifth line of the paragraph, locate and select the word *required*. From the Formatting toolbar, click the **Italic** button. Delete the quotation marks before and after the word.

9. Near the end of the document, position the insertion point at the end of the paragraph that begins *If you send us e-mail*, and then press Spacebar. Type **No further e-mails will be sent to you from us or from third parties unless you specifically request them.**

10. From the **File** menu, click **Versions**. Under **New versions**, click the **Save Now** button. Under **Comments on version**, type **These are the final changes.** and then click **OK**.

11. From the **File** menu, click **Versions**. Under **Existing versions**, confirm that your new version—with the name *Miguel Harris*—displays. Click the oldest version, which will be at the bottom of the list, and then click the **Delete** button. In the **Confirm Version Delete** dialog box, click **Yes** to delete the version. Click the **Close** button.

12. From the **Tools** menu, click **Options**, and then click the **User Information tab**. Restore the original *Name* and *Initials*, and then click **OK**.

**(Project 11E–Privacy Policy continues on the next page)**

**(Project 11E–Privacy Policy continued)**

**13.** From the **View** menu, click **Header and Footer**. On the Header and Footer toolbar, click the **Switch Between Header and Footer** button. Click the **Insert AutoText** button, and then click **Filename**. On the Header and Footer toolbar, click the **Close** button.

**14.** On the Standard toolbar, click **Save**, and then click **Print**. From the **Tools** menu, click **Options**, and then click the **Security tab**.

**15.** In the **Options** dialog box, under **File encryption options for this document**, in the **Password to open** box, type **Privacy** and then click **OK**. Be sure you type a capital letter at the beginning of the password. Reenter your password and click **OK**.

**16.** Click the **Close Window** button and save your changes when prompted. On the Standard toolbar, click the **Open** button. Select and open your **11E_Privacy_Policy_Firstname_Lastname** file.

**17.** In the **Password** message box, type **Privacy** and then click **OK**. If the document does not open, try the password again. Be sure you type a capital letter at the beginning of the password.

**18.** From the **Tools** menu, click **Protect Document**. In the **Protect Document** task pane, under **Formatting restrictions**, select the **Limit formatting to a selection of styles** check box. Under **Formatting restrictions**, click **Settings**.

**19.** In the **Formatting Restrictions** dialog box, be sure the **Limit formatting to a selection of styles** check box is selected. Near the lower portion of the dialog box, click the **Recommended Minimum** button.

**20.** At the bottom of the **Formatting Restrictions** dialog box, click **OK**. Click **No** to leave all existing styles in the document. In the **Protect Document** task pane, under **Start enforcement**, click **Yes, Start Enforcing Protection**.

**21.** In the **Start Enforcing Protection** dialog box, under **Protection method**, in the **Enter new password (optional)** box, type **Format** Press Tab, and then reenter the password in the next box. Click **OK**.

**22.** Select the document title, which begins *Southlandgardens.com.* On the Formatting toolbar, click the **Bold** button. Because you have restricted formatting, a message displays. Read the message box, and then click **OK**.

**23.** On the Standard toolbar, click the **Save** button. Close the **Protect Document** task pane, and then close the document.

**End** You have completed Project 11E

# Project 11F — Biltmore Itinerary

**Objectives:** *Create a Web Page with Frames and Edit Web Pages Using Word.*

Because many employees need to refer to them, Southland Gardens posts draft copies of production schedules and itineraries on its internal network. In the following Performance Assessment, you will create a Web page for the itinerary for Miguel Harris, who is working on a special series on the gardens of the Biltmore estate. Your completed document will look similar to Figure 11.50. You will save your document as *11F_Biltmore_Itinerary_Firstname_Lastname.*

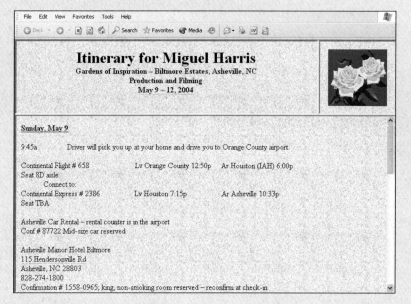

**Figure 11.50**

1. **Start** Word. From the **New Document** task pane, click **Web page**, and then display the Frames toolbar.

2. Add a **New Frame Below**. Click to make the upper frame active, and then create a **New Frame Right**.

3. In the upper right frame, from your student files, insert the **w11F_Flower** picture file. In the lower frame, insert the **w11F_Biltmore_Itinerary** document file.

4. Scroll to the top of the Itinerary text. Select and **Cut** the four title lines beginning with *Itinerary for Miguel Harris*. Delete the empty line at the top of the lower frame. **Paste** the title text in the upper left frame.

**(Project 11F–Biltmore Itinerary continues on the next page)**

**(Project 11F–Biltmore Itinerary continued)**

5.  Right-click anywhere in the upper left frame. From the shortcut menu, click **Save Current Frame As**. Navigate to your chapter folder, and then be sure **Single File Web Page** is displayed in the **Save as type** box. In the **File name** box, type **Itinerary_Title** Use the same procedure to name the upper right frame **Itinerary_Picture** and the bottom frame **Itinerary_Text**

6.  Right-click in an open area of the upper left frame, and then click **Frame Properties** from the shortcut menu. Click the **Borders tab**, click the **Individual frame arrow**, and then click **Never**. Click **OK**. Repeat this procedure to turn off the scroll bars in the upper right frame.

7.  Right-click the picture, click **Format Picture** from the shortcut menu, and then click the **Size tab**. Under **Size and rotate**, click the **Height down spin arrow** until the height is **1.2"** (or type as necessary in the box). Click **OK**. **Center** the picture. Resize both the left and lower borders of the upper right frame so that it is only slightly larger than the picture of the flower.

8.  Select the first line of text—*Itinerary for Miguel Harris*. Increase the **Font Size** to **24**.

9.  Click the **Save** button. In the **Save as type** box, be sure **Single File Web Page** is selected. Change the title to **11F_Biltmore_Itinerary_ Firstname_Lastname** In the **File name** box, type **11F_Biltmore_Itinerary_ Firstname_Lastname** and then click **Save**.

10. Click to position the insertion point in the lower frame. From the **Format** menu, point to **Background**, and then click **Fill Effects**. Click the **Texture tab**, and then in the first row, click the first texture—**Newsprint**. Click **OK**. Repeat this procedure to change the background texture of the other two frames. (Hint: When you click in the upper right frame, use caution to select the frame and not the picture.)

11. **Close** the document and save your changes. **Close** the Frames toolbar. Click the **Start** button, and then click **My Computer**. Locate and open your **11F_Biltmore_Itinerary_Firstname_Lastname** file.

12. Note any changes that might be necessary, especially in the upper right frame, where the borders might be too close to the picture— refer to Figure 11.50. If you notice any changes that need to be made, **Close** the browser. **Start** Word, and then open the same file in Word; make and save any necessary adjustments. Close the document, and close Word.

13. If necessary, reopen your **11F_Biltmore_Itinerary_Firstname_ Lastname** file in your browser. Open Print Preview and if necessary select *As laid out on screen*. **Print**, and then **Close** the document.

**End** You have completed Project 11F

## Project 11G — Program Hosts

**Objectives:** *Create a Web Page with Frames and Edit Web Pages Using Word.*

Southland Gardens is developing a Web page that profiles the program hosts. The draft copy has been saved as a Web page but does not contain frames. To add pictures to both the right and left sides of the page, frames need to be added. In the following Performance Assessment, you will create five frames, add two pictures, and divide the existing text among three frames. Your Web page will look similar to Figure 11.51. You will save your document as *11G_Program_Hosts_Firstname_Lastname*.

**Figure 11.51**

1. **Start** Word. On the Standard toolbar, click the **Open** button. Under **Files of type**, select **All Web Pages**. From the student files that accompany this textbook, locate, select, and then open **w11G_Program_Hosts**.

2. Be sure the formatting marks are displayed, and display the **Frames** toolbar. Add a **New Frame Above**. With the insertion point in the upper frame, click the **New Frame Right** button twice to create three frames in the upper half of the page.

3. Position the insertion point at the beginning of the text in the lower frame. Add a **New Frame Left**. All of the text should display in the lower right frame. **Close** the Frames toolbar.

**(Project 11G–Program Hosts continues on the next page)**

**(Project 11G–Program Hosts continued)**

4. In the lower right frame, select and **Cut** the two title lines. **Paste** the title lines in the upper middle frame.

5. In the lower right frame, remove the blank line above the first line of text—*Victor Ortiz*. Position the insertion point to the left of *Victor Ortiz*. Scroll down, if necessary, and locate the end of the Ortiz biography—the one that ends just above *Elizabeth Robinson*. Press Shift, and click at the end of the paragraph to select the two paragraphs about Victor Ortiz. **Cut** the selected text. **Paste** the text in the lower left frame. Remove the blank line above *Elizabeth Robinson* in the lower right frame.

6. Make the upper left frame active, and then right-click in the frame. From the shortcut menu, click **Save Current Frame As**. Navigate to your chapter folder. Be sure that **Save as type** is **Single File Web Page**. Save the frame as **Hosts_Ortiz_Picture** Use the same technique to name the other frames as indicated below. Be sure to select **Single File Web Page** each time.

   Upper middle: **Hosts_Title**

   Upper right: **Hosts_Robinson_Picture**

   Lower left: **Hosts_Ortiz_Text**

   Lower right: **Hosts_Robinson_Text**

7. In the lower left frame, select *Victor Ortiz*. Change the **Font Size** to **16** and apply **Bold**. In the lower right frame, if necessary, delete any blank lines at the top of the text. Select *Elizabeth Robinson*, change the **Font Size** to **16**, and then apply **Bold**.

8. In the upper middle frame, edit *Southland Gardens* to **Font Size 20** and apply **Bold**. Edit *Meet the Hosts* to **Font Size 28** and apply **Bold**. **Center** both title lines.

9. Click to make the upper left frame active. Insert the **w11G_Victor_Ortiz** picture file. In the upper right frame, insert the **w11G_Elizabeth_Robinson** picture file.

10. Click the **Save** button. Be sure **Save as type** is **Single File Web Page**. Change the title to **11G_Program_Hosts_Firstname_Lastname** In the **File name** box, type **11G_Program_Hosts_Firstname_Lastname** and then click **Save**.

**(Project 11G–Program Hosts continues on the next page)**

**(Project 11G–Program Hosts continued)**

11. Make the upper left frame active, and then right-click in an open area to the right of Victor's picture. From the shortcut menu, click **Frame Properties**. If necessary, click the Borders tab. Under **Frames page**, click the **Border color arrow**, and then in the second row, click the fourth color—**Green**. Under **Individual frame**, click the **Show scrollbars in browser arrow**, and then click **Never**. Repeat this last step to remove scrollbars from the upper middle and upper right frames. Recall that you need to change the border color only once.

12. Place the insertion point in the upper left frame. Change the **Background** color to **Light Green**. Repeat this procedure to change the background color of all of the frames.

13. Right-click the picture in the upper left frame, click **Format Picture** from the shortcut menu, and then click the **Size tab**. Under **Size and rotate**, select the number in the **Height** box, type **2** and then click **OK**. Repeat this procedure for the picture in the upper right frame, and then click the **Align Right** button. Adjust the borders around the pictures so that they are similar to Figure 11.51.

14. Click to position the insertion point in the top line of the title—*Southland Gardens*. Display the **Paragraph** dialog box, and under **Spacing**, change the number in the **Before** box to **36** and then click **OK**. This will move the title down in the frame.

15. **Close** the Word window, saving your changes. From **My Computer**, locate and open your **11G_Program_Hosts_Firstname_Lastname** file.

16. Examine your Web page. Close the browser, close My Computer, and then open your **11G_Program_Hosts_Firstname_Lastname** file in Word. Resize the pictures and frames, if necessary. Close the Word window, saving your changes, and open the Web page in your browser again.

17. If you are satisfied with the look of the Web page, **Print** the page, and close the browser.

**End** You have completed Project 11G ————————————————

# Project 11H — Employment Projections

**Objectives:** *Use Document Versions and Protect Documents.*

In the following Performance Assessment, you will edit a document from the Southland Gardens producer, Yumiko Sato. This document has been saved using two versions. You will make changes, and then save a third version. You also will apply password protection to the document, and, for those who have the document password, restrict editing to comments only. Your completed document will look similar to Figure 11.52. You will save your document as *11H_Employment_Projections_Firstname_Lastname*.

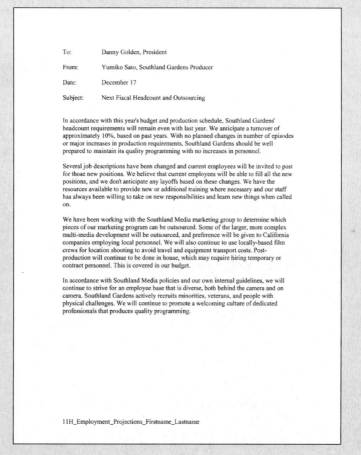

**Figure 11.52**

**(Project 11H–Employment Projections continues on the next page)**

**(Project 11H—Employment Projections continued)**

1. **Start** Word. From the student files that accompany this textbook, locate and open **w11H_Employment_Projections**. If necessary, change **Files of type** to **All Files**. In your chapter folder, save the file as **11H_Employment_Projections_Firstname_Lastname**

2. Display the **Versions in** dialog box for this document. Under **Existing versions**, click the oldest version—the bottom one in the list. View and read the comments for this version, and then close the **View Comments** dialog box.

3. In the lower left corner of the **Versions in** dialog box, click **Open**. Scroll and compare the first two paragraphs of the document—starting with the paragraph that begins *In accordance with this year's budget*. Notice that in the newer (upper) version, the paragraphs have been greatly expanded.

4. **Close** the older version, and **Maximize** the current Word window.

5. Display the **Options** dialog box, and click the **User Information tab**. Write down the existing *Name* and *Initials*. Change the **Name** to **Yumiko Sata** and change the **Initials** to **YS** Click **OK**.

6. Scroll to the paragraph that begins *In accordance with this year's budget*. Locate and select *15%*. Edit to change the number to **10%**

7. Scroll to the paragraph that begins *We have been working*. Locate the sentence that begins *Some of the larger*. Place the insertion point to the left of the period at the end of the sentence. Add a comma and a space, and then type **and preference will be given to California companies employing local personnel**

8. At the end of the same paragraph, add the following sentence: **This is covered in our budget.** Display the **Versions in** dialog box for this document and then under **New versions**, click the **Save Now** button. In the **Comments on version** box, type **These are the final changes.** and click **OK**.

9. Display the **Versions in** dialog box again, and under **Existing versions**, confirm that your new version displays. Click the **Close** button.

10. Display the Header and Footer toolbar and create a footer containing the file name. **Save** and **Print** your document.

11. Display the **Options** dialog box and click the **Security tab**. As the **Password to open**, type **Security** and then click **OK**. Be sure you type a capital letter at the beginning of the password. Reenter your password, and click **OK**.

12. Close your document, saving the changes. Open the document again. Type the password you just created.

**(Project 11H—Employment Projections continues on the next page)**

**(Project 11H–Employment Projections continued)**

13. Display the **Protect Document** task pane, and then select the **Limit formatting to a selection of styles** check box. Under **Editing restrictions**, select the **Allow only this type of editing in the document** check box. Click the **Editing restrictions arrow**, and then click **Comments** to restrict changes to comments only.

14. Under **Start enforcement**, click **Yes, Start Enforcing Protection**. In the **Start Enforcing Protection** dialog box, click **OK** *without* entering a password.

15. Near the top of the document, in the line that begins *From*, click to position the insertion point to the left of *Producer*. Attempt to type **Executive** Because you have restricted the formatting in this document, you will not be able to make any changes.

16. Select the word *Producer*. Display the Reviewing toolbar, and then click the **Insert Comment** button. Type **Should this be Executive Producer?**

17. Display the **Options** dialog box and click the **User Information tab**. Restore the original *Name* and *Initial*, and then click **OK**. Save your changes.

18. Close the **Protect Document** task pane, close the Reviewing toolbar, and then close Word, saving any changes.

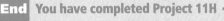 **End** You have completed Project 11H

## Project 11I — Gardens of Inspiration

**Objectives:** *Create a Web Page with Frames and Edit Web Pages Using Word.*

In the following Mastery Assessment, you will create a Web page listing the upcoming series on Gardens of Inspiration for the Southland Gardens television show. You will create frames and insert a Word document. You will also insert a picture into one of the text frames, and edit the picture. Your completed document will look similar to the one shown in Figure 11.53. You will save your document as *11I_Gardens_of_Inspiration_Firstname_Lastname.*

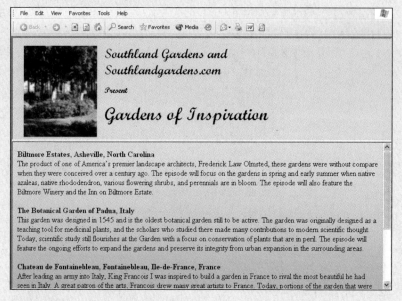

**Figure 11.53**

1. **Start** Word. Display the **New Document** task pane and click **Web page**. Show formatting marks, and display the **Frames** toolbar.

2. Add a **New Frame Above**. In the upper frame, insert the text file **w11I_Inspiration_Title**. In the lower frame, insert the **w11I_Inspiration_Text** text file. **Close** the Frames toolbar.

3. Save the upper frame as a **Single File Web Page** with the name **Inspiration_Title** and use the same procedure to save the lower frame as **Inspiration_Text**

4. On the Standard toolbar, click the **Save** button. Under **Save as type**, be sure **Single File Web Page** is selected. Change the title to **11I_Gardens_of_Inspiration_Firstname_Lastname** In the **File name** box, type **11I_Gardens_of_Inspiration_Firstname_Lastname** and then click **Save**.

**(Project 11I–Gardens of Inspiration continues on the next page)**

**(Project 11I**–Gardens of Inspiration continued)

5. Remove the blank line at the end of the text in the upper frame. Change the emphasis of the text in the upper frame to **Bold**. Increase the **Font Size** of the last line—*Gardens of Inspiration*— to **28**. Increase the **Font Size** of the first two title lines in the upper frame to **20**.

6. Change the **Background** of the top frame to **Light Green**. Move the frame border to just below the last line of the title in the upper frame.

7. Move the insertion point to the beginning of the text in the upper frame. Insert the picture **w11I_Garden_Picture** from your student files. Select the picture. If necessary, open the Picture toolbar. On the Picture toolbar, click the **Text Wrapping** button, and then click **Square**. Adjust the frame border to make space for the entire picture in the upper frame. Display the **Frame Properties** dialog box, and turn off the scroll bar in the upper frame.

8. Click to position the insertion point in the lower frame. Display the **Fill Effects** dialog box and click the **Gradient tab**. If necessary, under **Colors**, click the **One color option** button, click the **Color 1 arrow**, and then click **Light Green**. Under **Shading styles**, be sure the **Horizontal** option button is selected. Click **OK**.

9. Scroll through the lower frame. If the background shading is too dark near the bottom, return to the **Fill Effects** dialog box and, under **Colors**, adjust the color by moving the **Dark Light** slider toward **Light**.

10. **Close** the document and save your changes. From **My Computer**, locate and open your **11I_Gardens_of_Inspiration_Firstname_ Lastname** file.

11. Note any changes that might be necessary. Close the browser. Open the file in Word, and then make and save any necessary adjustments.

12. If necessary, open **11I_Gardens_of_Inspiration_Firstname_ Lastname** in your browser. From the **File** menu, click **Print**. Close the browser, close **My Computer**, and close **Word**.

**End** **You have completed Project 11I**

## Project 11J — Inspiration Memo

**Objectives:** *Use Document Versions, Protect Documents, and Attach Digital Signatures to Documents.*

In the following Mastery Assessment, you will edit a memo written to the Southland Gardens hosts about the upcoming Gardens of Inspiration series. You will save a new version of the document. You also will apply password protection to the document and add a digital signature. Your completed document will look similar to the one shown in Figure 11.54. You will save your document as *11J_Inspiration_Memo_Firstname_Lastname*.

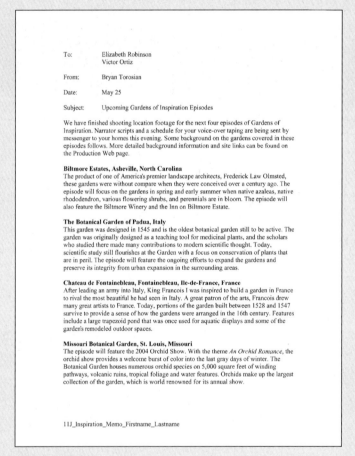

**Figure 11.54**

1. From the student files that accompany this textbook, locate and open the file **w11J_Inspiration_Memo**. Save the file in your chapter folder as **11J_Inspiration_Memo_Firstname_Lastname**

2. Display the **Versions in** dialog box for this document. Examine the previous versions of the document and the comments associated with the versions, and then close the dialog box.

**(Project 11J–Inspiration Memo continues on the next page)**

**(Project 11J–Inspiration Memo continued)**

3. At the end of the paragraph that begins *We have finished shooting location footage*, add the following sentence: **More detailed background information and site links can be found on the Production Web page**. Delete the paragraph that begins *If you would like* and the blank line following the paragraph.

4. Display the **Options** dialog box, and then click the **User Information tab**. Write down the existing *Name* and *Initials*. Change the **Name** to **Bryan Torosian** and change the **Initials** to **BLT** Click **OK**.

5. From the **Versions in** dialog box, save a new version of the document. As the comment, type **Final version**. **Delete** the oldest saved version.

6. Display the Header and Footer toolbar, and add the file name to the document footer. Save and print your document.

7. Display the **Options** dialog box, and click the **Security tab**. As the password to open the document, type **security** and then click **OK**. Be sure not to type a capital letter at the beginning of the password. Reenter your password, and click **OK**.

8. **Close** the document and save your changes. Open the document again. In the **Password** message box, type **security** and then click **OK**. If the document does not open, try the password again.

9. Click the **Start** button and point to **All Programs**. Point to **Microsoft Office**, point to **Microsoft Office Tools**, and then click **Digital Certificate for VBA Projects**. Name the certificate **Southland Gardens Firstname Lastname** and then click **OK**.

10. Display the **Options** dialog box. On the **Security tab**, under **File sharing options for this document**, click the **Digital Signatures** button. Near the bottom of the **Digital Signature** dialog box, click the **Add** button. Click to select the **Southland Gardens Firstname Lastname** certificate, and then close the dialog boxes.

11. In the status bar, double-click the digital signature icon. Click **View Certificate** to read about the digital signature. Close the dialog boxes.

12. Display the **Options** dialog box, and on the **User Information tab**, restore the original *Name* and *Initial*. Click **OK**. Save your changes.

13. Close the document, and close Word.

**End** You have completed Project 11J ——————————

## Project 11K — Personal Web Page

**Objectives:** *Create a Web Page with Frames and Edit Web Pages Using Word.*

In this project, you will create a personal Web page using frames. You will create at least three frames. One of the frames will be used for a title, one for a picture of yourself, and one for some text with personal information. You will use your own text in the two text frames. You will save your document as *11K_Personal_Web_Page_Firstname_Lastname.*

1. **Start** Word. Open a new document, and click the **Web Layout View** button.

2. Display the Frames toolbar. Create a **New Frame Above**. In the lower half of the page, create a **New Frame Left**. Save each frame with a descriptive name of your choice.

3. In the upper right frame, add a title to your Web page. It should be at least two lines long and centered in the frame.

4. Obtain a digital picture of yourself, either by using a digital camera or by scanning an existing photograph. If you cannot obtain a digital image of yourself, use a ClipArt image. Insert the image in the upper left frame.

5. In the lower frame, add some text about yourself. You could include your background, hobbies, or other interests. You can insert an existing file if you have one that is appropriate. For example, a resume would be appropriate text.

6. Resize the frames to fit the content. Save the document as **11K_Personal_Web_Page_Firstname_Lastname**

7. View your Web page in your Web browser. Print and close your document.

**End** You have completed Project 11K ─────────────────────

## Project 11L — Ornamental Grasses

**Objectives:** *Create a Web Page with Frames and Edit Web Pages Using Word.*

In this project, you will work on a Web page for the Southland Gardens intranet. The page will provide links to Web sites specializing in ornamental grasses and will be used by the interns preparing the background material for the upcoming Ornamental Grasses Series. The page will consist of a title and a picture of ornamental grasses. You will save your document as *11L_Ornamental_Grasses_Firstname_Lastname*.

1. **Start** Word. Open a new document in **Web Layout View**.

2. Display the Frames toolbar. Create two frames in the upper half of the page and a single frame in the lower half. Reserve the upper left frame for the title and the upper right frame for a picture. The bottom frame will contain a list of hyperlinks. Save each frame with a descriptive name of your choice.

3. In the upper right frame, insert the **w11L_Title** file. In the last line of the title, change the **Font Size** to **20**, and apply **Bold**.

4. Open your browser, and open your favorite search engine—such as *www.google.com*. Search for **ornamental grasses** and browse a few sites, making note of the ones you want to include in your Web page.

5. Find a picture that you like. If you have time, click the e-mail link on the page and ask permission to use the picture for a class project. Most businesses will allow you to use an image that will not be published on the Web. If you do not have time, check with your instructor to find out if Fair Use guidelines cover the use of a downloaded picture in this instance.

6. When you have determined that it is appropriate to use the picture, right-click the image, and use the appropriate command from the shortcut menu to transfer the picture to your hard disk. Insert the picture into the upper right frame.

7. In the lower frame, type a short description of what the links will do. Switch between your browser and your Word document, copying the Web addresses of several sites that you think are particularly good and pasting them into your Web page. Add some descriptive text below each URL describing the site.

8. If a link is not created automatically when you paste the URL into your document, select and right-click the URL text. From the shortcut menu, click **Hyperlink**, and then click **OK**.

9. Adjust the frame sizes to fit the content. Save and print your work. Test your Web page, and test the hyperlinks. Make any necessary adjustments.

10. Close the document, saving any changes.

**End** You have completed Project 11L

## Learning More About Digital Certificates

In this chapter you used a digital signature by creating a local certificate using the SelfCert program that is included with Microsoft Office 2003. If you need to use a trusted digital signature on documents that you send to others, consider using the services of a commercial security firm, such as VeriSign, E-Lock, or InfoMosaic.

1. Be sure that you are connected to the Internet.

2. Type one of the following URLs in the Address box on your browser:

   **www.verisign.com**

   **www.elock.com**

   **www.infomosaic.net**

3. Read the options available, and find the price of using the service.

4. Check the other two services to compare features and price.

5. If you are interested in obtaining a commercial digital signature, continue with the process of signing up with one of the companies.

6. When you are done, close the browser.

# GO! with Help

## Protecting Different Parts of the Document

In this chapter you practiced protecting your document by adding password protection to the entire document and by requiring a password to make formatting or editing changes. You also have the option of restricting editing access to different parts of the document to different people.

1. **Start** Word and display a new document. In the *Type a Question for Help* box, type **edit protected document** and press [Enter].

2. In the **Search Results** task pane, click **Allow editing in a protected document**.

3. Read through the description.

4. Expand and read the **Allow particular individuals to edit the part you selected** topic.

5. Scroll to the bottom of the **Search Results** pane. Click the **Tip** link and read about different ways to add user names.

6. When you are finished, close the document without saving your changes.

# chaptertwelve

# Managing Documents as Data with XML

**In this chapter, you will:** complete this project **and** practice these skills.

| Project 12A Use XML Tags and a Schema | Objectives |
|---|---|
| | • Create a Well-Formed XML Document and Use a Schema |
| | • Standardize and Validate an XML Document with a Schema |
| | • Import XML Data into Excel |
| | • Transform a Document |

# Lake Michigan City College

Lake Michigan City College is located along the lakefront of Chicago—one of the country's most exciting cities. The college serves its large and diverse student body and makes positive contributions to the community through relevant curricula, partnerships with businesses and nonprofit organizations, and learning experiences that allow students to be full participants in the global community. The college offers three associate degrees in 20 academic areas, adult education programs, and continuing education offerings on campus, at satellite locations, and online.

© Getty Images, Inc.

# Managing Documents as Data with XML

Word documents often contain valuable information that can be sorted, analyzed, and shared with other computer applications. The key to using the data that is stored within Word documents is to mark sections of text with identifying tags.

In this chapter you will use a markup standard called XML with which you can define tags and use them to identify the enclosed text as data. Both XML and HTML tags can be used to produce Web pages. Web browsers use HTML tags to control the appearance of the document on the screen and use the XML tags to manage the data.

Another use of XML is to provide convenient ways for different computer systems to talk to each other. XML tags that are attached to data from one computer can be understood by another computer. This feature is useful for an organization that is trying to coordinate its computer system with that of a newly acquired business, a customer, or a supplier.

# Project 12A Business Advising

In this project, you will work with advising documents used at Lake Michigan City College. You will use tags to capture data from Word documents and then gather that data into Excel where it can be analyzed.

In Activities 12.1 through 12.4, you will use Notepad to create an XML file and you will save your document as *12A_Advising_Firstname_Lastname.xml*. In Activity 12.5, you will add data between the start and end tags. Your printout will look similar to Figure 12.1a. In Activities 12.6 through 12.8, you will add comments to a schema to explain some of the important features. Your printout will look similar to Figure 12.1b. In Activities 12.9 through 12.13, you will modify a schema and attach it to an advising document. The finished document will be an advising form and will look similar to Figure 12.1c. You will save your document as *12A_Business_Advising_1_Firstname_Lastname.xml*. In Activity 12.13, you will save only the data from the advising form as *12A_Business_Advising_Data_1_Firstname_ Lastname.xml*. You will open the data in Word, add a footer, and then print it. Your document will look similar to Figure 12.1d. You will not save the document again with the footer because the footer is not data. In Activities 12.14 through 12.16, you will import data from three forms into Excel; your result will look similar to Figure 12.1e. In Activity 12.17, you will add comments to a transform in Notepad to explain important features. Your transform will look similar to Figure 12.1f.

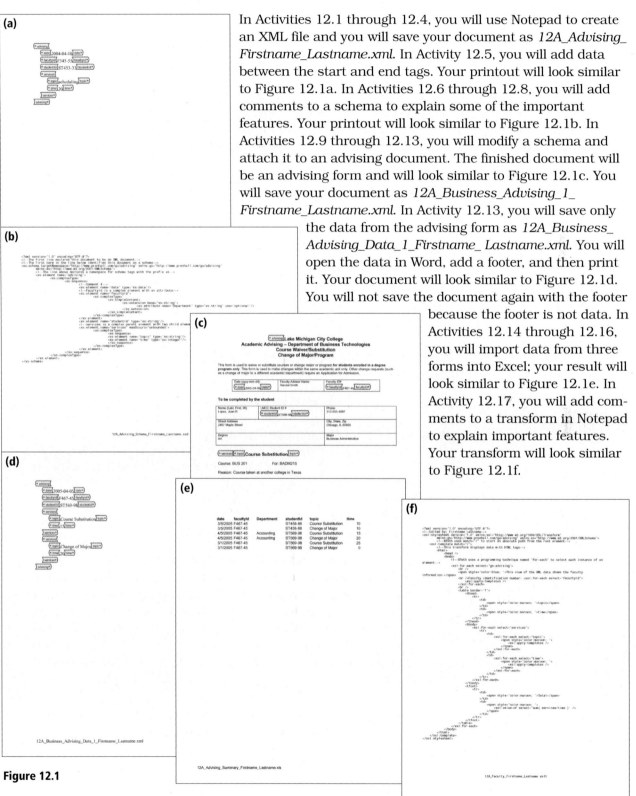

**Figure 12.1**

# Objective 1
## Create a Well-Formed XML Document and Use a Schema

You probably think of **data**—information that can be sorted and analyzed—as being stored in a database or in an Excel spreadsheet. A Word document can also contain data that can be sorted and analyzed. **eXtensible Markup Language**, also called **XML**, lets you apply **tags** to text in a Word document. The tags identify text as data, and then the data can be extracted from Word documents for use by other programs like Microsoft Excel.

For example, faculty members at Lake Michigan City College advise students about courses and majors, and the faculty member completes a Word form about each advising session with a student. The data on the forms can be sorted and analyzed by marking text with XML tags.

You may be familiar with **Hypertext Markup Language**, also called **HTML**, which is the standard markup language used to display documents on the Web. HTML uses a similar system of applying tags, but with XML you can create and define your own sets of tags. The XML standard is provided by the **World Wide Web Consortium**, also known as the **W3C**, which is a group of representatives from leading Internet companies that oversees research and sets standards and guidelines for many areas of the Internet.

---

### More Knowledge — Web Browsers Use a Markup Language

HTML uses tags to indicate how Web browsers should display page elements. For example, the tags <b> and </b> mark the start and end of the text to be displayed as bold. Web browsers such as Internet Explorer, Netscape, and Mozilla recognize a standard set of HTML tags that tell the browser software how to format text on the screen. Newer browsers can use XML as well as HTML. The combination is called **XHTML**.

---

### Activity 12.1 Writing XML Tags with a Text Editor

XML files are text files that contain text enclosed by tags. They are usually identified with the three-letter extension **.xml**. If you open a file with this extension in Microsoft Word, it displays the tags in a user-friendly manner, but it also hides the underlying simple text that creates the tags. To create and edit the basic underlying XML text, you need to use a simpler program than Word. Additionally, to manage these files, you must be able to see the file extensions when you display lists of files in a dialog box.

In this activity, you will display the file extensions for all file types and then create pairs of XML tags to identify text as data.

**1** **Start My Computer**. On the menu bar, click **Tools**, and then click **Folder Options**. In the **Folder Options** dialog box, click the **View tab**. If necessary, clear the check mark from the **Hide extensions for known file types** check box.

By clearing this check box, as shown in Figure 12.2, every time you display a list of files, the extensions will be displayed for all types of files. For example, an Excel file has the extension *.xls* and a Word file has the extension *.doc*. File extensions must be visible so that you can open and save files in Notepad with the appropriate file extensions.

Check box cleared so that file extensions will be visible in file lists

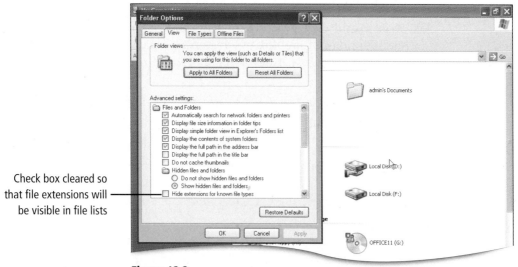

**Figure 12.2**

**2** Click **OK**. On the title bar of the **My Computer** window, click the **Close** button ☒.

## Another Way ──┌ To Change the Folder Options

You can also use Windows Explorer to change the Folder Options. Right-click the Start button and then click Explore. In the Start Menu window, from the Tools menu, click Folder Options. Click the View tab, and then clear the *Hide extensions for known file types* check box.

**3** Click **Start**. Point to **All Programs**. On the displayed list, point to **Accessories**, and then click **Notepad**. On the title bar, click the **Maximize** button ☐.

The Notepad window opens. *Notepad* is a simple word processor, also called a *text editor*; it has only a few menus of commands and no toolbars. *Notepad* is the name of the text editor included with the Windows operating system.

**4** Type **<date></date>** and then press Enter. Check to be sure the capitalization and spelling of *date* is exactly the same in both tags.

*<date>* is a **start tag**, which is text preceded with a left angle bracket (<) and followed by a right angle bracket (>). It contains the name of the **element**, which in this instance is *date*. An element is the combination of the set of tags, any content between the tags, and any properties the tag may have. *</date>* is the **end tag**, which is like its corresponding start tag except that it includes a slash (/) followed by the element name. Start and end tags are used to enclose and identify the actual data. In this manner, a pair of tags indicates an element.

**5** Type **<facultyId></facultyId>** and then press Enter. Type **<studentId></studentId>** and then be sure that you have no extra spaces or differences in capitalization in your three lines.

You have created tags for three elements—*date, facultyId,* and *studentId.* Compare what you have typed with Figure 12.3. The start and end tags must be exactly the same except for the slash mark.

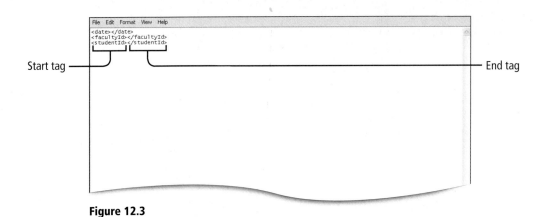

**Figure 12.3**

**6** Check your XML text against the following rules and conventions in the table shown in Figure 12.4.

## Rules and Conventions for Writing Simple XML Tags

| Rule | Example | Correct? | Common Practice |
|------|---------|----------|-----------------|
| Every start tag must have an end tag. | <date> </date> | This example is correct because the two tags are the same, except there is a slash in the end tag. | |
| Tag names are case sensitive. | <FacultyId> </facultyId> | This example is incorrect because these two tags do not match due to the difference in capitalization. | The first letter is usually lowercase and capital letters are used to break up the name into identifiable segments such as <facultyId>. |
| Special characters are not allowed, except hyphens, underscores, and periods. | <student-name> </student-name> | This example is correct. | Special characters can be used to make identifiable segments. |
| Tag names can be any length. | <theMostImportant IdeaInTheDocument> </theMostImportant IdeaInTheDocument> | This example is correct but not preferred. | Shorter tag names are preferred. |
| Tag names must start with a letter or underscore. | <1stDate> </1stDate> | This example is incorrect because the first character is a number, not a letter. | |
| Tag names cannot include spaces. | <faculty Id> </faculty Id> | This example is incorrect because there is a space within the angle brackets. | |
| Text between the tags cannot contain the symbols & or <. | <text>Use <p> to mark the end of a paragraph in HTML.</text> | The use of <p> as part of the enclosed text is incorrect because angle brackets are used exclusively to enclose the tag name. | The character < is not allowed because it is used to identify the XML start tag. Special substitution codes are available. |

**Figure 12.4**

### Activity 12.2 Creating Parent–Child Elements

Some elements contain other elements. This relationship is called **parent–child**. The start and end tags of the child elements must be placed—**nested**—between the start and end tags of the parent element. The child of one element can be the parent of another. In this activity, you will create a parent element named *<advising></advising>* that will contain all the other elements. You also will create a parent element named *<services></services>* that will contain the child elements *<topic></topic>* and *<time></time>*.

**1** At the beginning of the first line, to the left of *<date>*, click to place the insertion point. Type **<advising>** and then press Enter.

**2** Press Tab.

The second line is indented. Although you cannot type spaces or tabs *within* a tag name, you can use spaces and tabs outside of tag names to visually arrange the code in a way that is easy to read. Here, a tab visually places the child element *date* within the parent tag *advising*.

**3** At the beginning of the third line, to the left of *<facultyId>*, click to place the insertion point, and then press Tab.

*facultyId* visually becomes the second child element to the parent element *advising*.

**4** At the beginning of the fourth line, to the left of *<studentId>*, click to place the insertion point, and then press Tab.

**5** At the end of the fourth line, to the right of *</studentId>*, click to place the insertion point, and then press Enter. Press Tab and then type **<services>** Press Enter.

**6** Press Tab twice and then type **<topic></topic>**

**7** Press Enter and then press Tab two times. Type **<time></time>** and then press Enter.

The *topic* and *time* elements are visually placed as child elements of *services*.

**8** Press Tab once and then type **</services>**

The end tag of the *services* element encloses the tags for the *topic* element and the *time* element—they are nested within the *services* element.

**9** Press Enter and then type **</advising>**

The tags for the *advising* element enclose all the other elements. The *advising* element is the parent of *date*, *facultyId*, *studentId*, and *services*. *services* is the parent of *topic* and *time*. Compare your screen with Figure 12.5.

The *services* element is a parent to the elements *topic* and *time*.

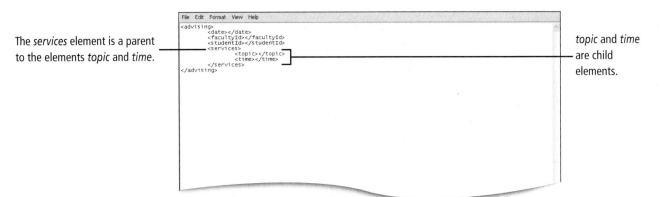

topic and time are child elements.

**Figure 12.5**

### Activity 12.3 Adding Declarations and Comments

A text file is not an XML document until you declare it to be so in the first line of text. Other declarations can be added to identify how the files work with each other. You can add comments to the document to identify the author or provide information about the structure of the XML document for the next person who reads it. A document that is correctly declared with properly marked elements is said to be ***well formed***. In this activity, you will add declarations and comments to your XML document.

**1** At the beginning of the first line to the left of *<advising>*, click to place the insertion point. Type **<?xml version ="1.0"?>** and then press Enter.

This line is the ***XML declaration***, which identifies the document as an XML document and specifies the XML version number. Currently, only one version of XML is available, but newer versions will be developed; thus, this specification will be important in the future. A declaration must begin with <? and end with ?> and must be the first line of the document.

**2** Use your own name and type **<!--written by: Firstname Lastname-->** and then press Enter.

Because programs that work with XML documents ignore anything typed between <!-- and -->, use this code to bracket comments and other helpful information. These can be placed on any line.

**3** Carefully examine your text to confirm that it matches Figure 12.6. Be sure each end tag has a slash and the element names have no spaces. If you discover an error, correct it before moving to the next activity.

Declaration ——

Elements ——

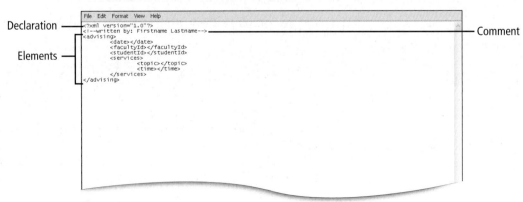

—— Comment

**Figure 12.6**

**Activity 12.4** Saving an XML Document with Selected Encoding

When you save an XML file, you choose the **encoding** method and the file extension. Encoding is the process of converting your typed words, letters, and characters into zeros and ones so that a computer can work with them. Older encoding standards were based on the English language. Newer encoding standards make it possible to write XML in a variety of human languages.

**1** From the **File** menu, click **Save As**. With the **Save in arrow**, navigate to the location where you are storing your projects for this chapter, creating a new folder for Chapter 12 if you want to do so.

**2** Near the bottom of the displayed **Save As** dialog box, click the **Save as type arrow**, and then click **All Files**.

**3** Click the **Encoding arrow**, and then click **UTF-8**.

As one of the new standards, **UTF-8** not only recognizes older encoding formats but is also compatible with newer international standards. UTF-8 incorporates the commonly used **ASCII** (American Standard Code for Information Interchange) standard.

**4** In the **File name** box, type **12A_Advising_Firstname_Lastname.xml**

The file extension *.xml* must be used, and it must be at the end of the file name. If you do not type the file extension, the program will attach *.txt* instead.

**5** Click **Save**. From the **File** menu, click **Print**. In the displayed dialog box, click the **Print** button.

**6** On the Notepad title bar, click the **Close** button ⊠.

**Activity 12.5** Editing and Printing XML Files in Word

Microsoft Word 2003 has a user-friendly interface for working with XML files. It automatically displays the tags and facilitates entering and saving data. You can use XML tags in Word to save parts of a document as data, or you can save the entire document and all of its formatting with XML tags. In this activity, you will view tagged data elements in Word and print tagged data with the tags displayed.

**1** Start **Word**. On the Standard toolbar, click the **Open** button 🖼. Navigate to your chapter folder. Click the **Files of type arrow** and then click **All Files (*.*)**. Locate and then open your **12A_Advising_Firstname_Lastname.xml** file.

The tags are displayed and the XML Document task pane opens.

**Alert!**

**Errors in the XML document**

If the XML document is not well formed, it will not open, and a dialog box will display a warning. Click the Details button to see an explanation of the problem. Start Notepad, set the Files of type to *All files*, and then open the document. Refer to the error message and to the table in Figure 12.4, and then find and correct the error. Follow the steps in Activity 12.4 to save the file. Replace the existing file with the revised file.

**2** Move the pointer to the location between the two **date tags** and click. Type **2004-04-10**

A sample date is placed between the two *date* tags. *Year-month-day* is the default date format for XML documents.

**3** Move the pointer to the location between the two **facultyId tags** and click. Type **F345-55**

A sample faculty identification number is placed between the two *facultyId* tags.

**4** Move the pointer to the location between the two **studentId tags** and click. Type **ST453-33**

A sample student identification number is placed between the two *studentId* tags.

**5** Move the pointer to the location between the two **topic tags** and click. Type **scheduling**

The topic of *scheduling* is placed between the two topic tags.

**6** Move the pointer to the location between the two **time tags** and click. Type **20**

The number of minutes spent in the advising session is placed between the two *time* tags. Compare your screen with Figure 12.7.

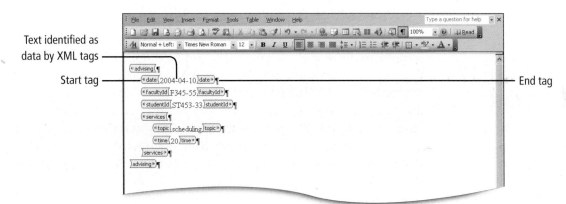

Text identified as data by XML tags

Start tag

End tag

**Figure 12.7**

**7** From the **View** menu, click **Header and Footer**. On the Header and Footer toolbar, click the **Switch Between Header and Footer** button. Click the **Insert AutoText** button, and then click **Filename**. On the Header and Footer toolbar, click the **Close** button.

The tags, text, and footer complete the document.

**8** From the **File** menu, click **Print**. In the lower left corner of the displayed **Print** dialog box, click the **Options** button. Under **Include with document**, if necessary, select the **XML tags** check box, which will print the tags. Compare your dialog box with Figure 12.8.

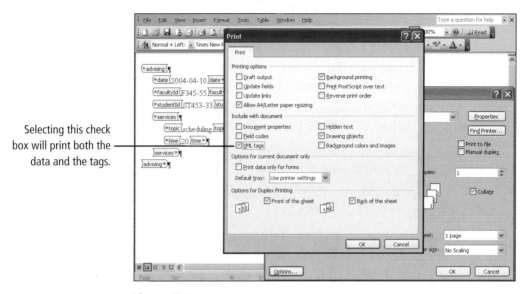

Selecting this check box will print both the data and the tags.

**Figure 12.8**

**9** Click **OK** twice to close the dialog boxes. On the title bar, click the **Close** button ![X]. Click **No**—do *not* save the changes.

The document with the sample data you inserted is *not* saved at this time.

### Activity 12.6 Declaring a Schema

XML is most valuable when it is used to share information. This presents a problem if everyone is allowed to define different tag names for the same type of data. To overcome this problem, a separate XML document called a **schema** is provided to define the tag names and the relationships among the tagged elements. The schema specifies which elements are required and in what order, and additional information about each element. Schemas themselves are XML documents that are written using standardized XML tags so that all other applications can read the schema.

A schema can be written using a text editor like Notepad, but is usually created with a special program that has a convenient graphic interface. In this activity, you will open an existing schema that defines the relationships among the elements of the college's advising form, and you will add comments that describe important parts of the document.

**1** Click **Start**. Point to **All Programs**. On the displayed list, point to **Accessories**, and then click **Notepad**. **Maximize** ![icon] the Notepad window.

**2** From the **File** menu, click **Open**. In the **Open** dialog box, click the **Files of type arrow**, and then click **All Files**. Navigate to the folder where the student files that accompany this textbook are stored, and then click the **w12A_Advising_Schema.xsd** file.

Schema files use *.xsd* as the file extension.

**3** Click the **Open** button. Examine your screen. As shown in Figure 12.9, identify the XML declaration and the schema declaration.

Declaration that this document is a schema

XML declaration

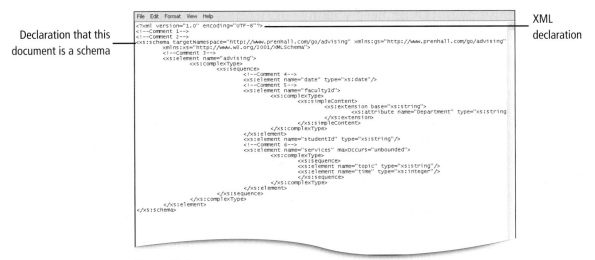

**Figure 12.9**

**4** In line 1, select the text *Comment 1* and type **The first line declares this document to be an XML document**

**5** In line 3, select the text *Comment 2*, type **The first term in the line below identifies this document as a schema** and then compare your screen with Figure 12.10.

The schema declaration begins with the prefix *<xs:schema*

Comment

Schema declaration

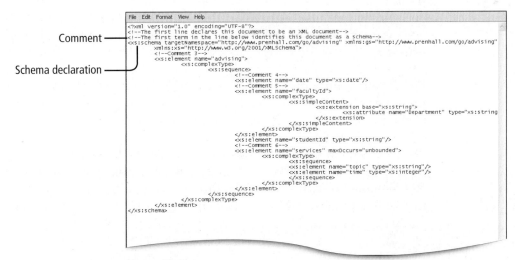

**Figure 12.10**

**6** From the **File** menu, click **Save As**. Click the **Save as type arrow**, and then click **All Files**. Click the **Encoding arrow**, and then click **UTF-8**.

**7** In the **File name** box, type **12A_Advising_Schema_Firstname_Lastname.xsd**

The file extension *.xsd* must be typed, and it must be at the end of the file name. By adding the *.xsd* extension, you ensure that the file will be recognized as a schema by other programs.

**8** With the **Save in arrow**, navigate to your chapter folder, and then click **Save**.

The document is saved as a schema in your folder and remains displayed on your screen.

### Activity 12.7 Defining Elements with a Namespace

Recall that you can define your own element names in your XML documents and then set the rules for how they are used by writing a schema. Other people can do the same thing, but their elements refer to different data. So, what happens if you want to mix documents together in the same place? How do you communicate with others if everyone gets to define their own tag names?

The first step is to agree on a common set of tags that are used to write schemas. Schemas are themselves XML documents that use tags. The standardization is provided by the World Wide Web Consortium (W3C). The W3C publishes a list of tags you can use to write schemas. A set of tags created for a specific purpose is called a **namespace**, which has a unique name that looks like the address of a Web page. For convenience, you can declare a short prefix called an **alias**, which can be used with each element name to identify the namespace to which the element belongs.

For example, if we declare that the W3C namespace will use the *xs:* prefix, when you see an element name like *xs:sequence* you know this element name is from the W3C namespace.

The next step is to declare a unique namespace for *your* set of tags, declare that other XML documents with this namespace should use this schema, and choose an alias to use as a prefix. If an element name in your set of tags is the same as an element in the W3C namespace, confusion is avoided because they have different prefixes. In this activity, you will identify namespaces and their aliases in the schema.

**1** In the displayed schema, read line 4 and line 5.

These two lines comprise the start tag of the schema element. The tag is continued on a second line to make it easier to read. The end tag is on the last line of the document. Start tags can contain additional information following the name of the tag.

**2** Near the end of line 5, find the text that resembles a Web address with *w3.org* in the term.

This is the namespace for schema tags created by the World Wide Web Consortium. The term *xmlns* indicates an *XML namespace* and *xs:* is the prefix that identifies element names from this namespace in this schema.

**3** In line 6, select the text *Comment 3* and type **The line above declares a namespace for schema tags with the prefix xs**

## More Knowledge — Using the URI to Identify Namespaces

The designers of XML recognized that a worldwide method for creating unique names already exists—the *Uniform Resource Identifier* (*URI*). A common use of URIs is to provide a unique name for a Web page for the purpose of locating the computer that hosts the Web page. In that case, a URI is called a *Uniform Resource Locator* (*URL*). If you own the rights to a domain name such as *prenhall.com*, you can create your own URI for a namespace; no one else in the world will have a duplicate name. The URI in an XML document is not necessarily used to display a Web page. It is used as a unique name. Programs that use schemas, like Microsoft Word, recognize *http://www.w3.org/2001/XMLSchema* as the name of a set of standard schema terms that are already stored in the program. You do not have to have Internet access to use a schema. The URI is simply used as a name that is unique worldwide.

**4** In line 4, find the term **targetNamespace**.

If you declare a namespace as the *targetNamespace* in the schema, other XML documents that use the designated namespace will be associated with this schema automatically.

## More Knowledge — Namespaces Used by Organizations

Namespaces with sets of tags that are commonly used by a specific industry, for example, electronic parts manufacturing, can be created by a professional organization to make it easy to exchange XML documents among members of the group.

### Activity 12.8 Using Simple and Complex Elements with Constraints and Attributes

A schema can be used to define the relationships among elements, restrict their contents and their sequence, and provide options for appending additional information. An element that is a parent, or that has additional information attached to it, is called a **complex element**. **Attributes** specify additional information for an element. Restrictions applied to the elements and attributes are called **constraints**.

In this activity, you will identify a complex element that has child elements, a complex element that has an attribute, a constraint on the type of data entered in an element, and a constraint on the order of child elements. These features of a schema will affect the way XML data is imported or exported from Excel worksheets. In the following activity, you will identify a complex element that contains the elements used to record the type of advising and the amount of time spent on that activity.

**1** Locate the line below *Comment 6* that begins *<xs:element name= "services"*

services is the parent of *topic* and *time*. Therefore, it is a complex element.

**2** Notice that in the next line, a *complexType* element is declared, as shown in Figure 12.11. Select the text *Comment 6* and type **services is a complex parent element with two child elements**

Complex element with child elements

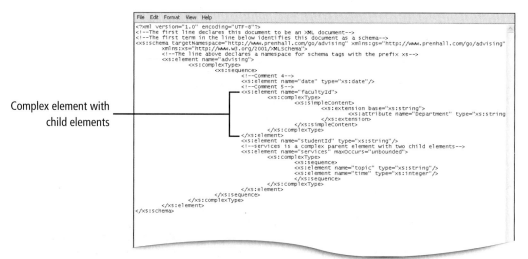

**Figure 12.11**

**3** Locate the line below *Comment 5* that begins with *<xs:element name="facultyId">*.

This element is complex because it has an attribute named *Department*.

**4** Select the text *Comment 5* and type **facultyId is a complex element with an attribute** as shown in Figure 12.12.

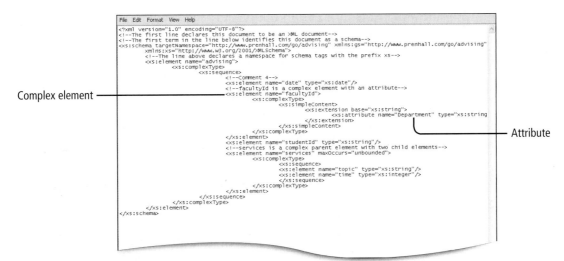

Complex element ──────────── [pointing to XML code]

Attribute ──────────── [pointing to XML code]

**Figure 12.12**

> **5** Refer to Figure 12.13, where two types of constraints are identified. The child elements must be in the specified sequence, and date, time, and topic must be particular types of data.

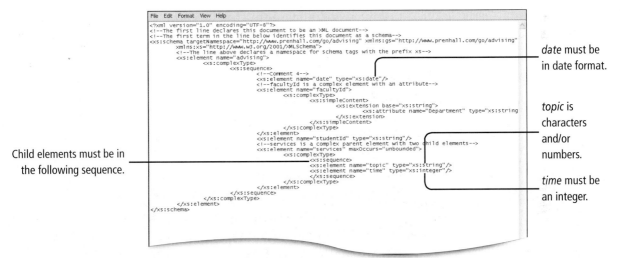

Child elements must be in the following sequence. ──────────── [pointing to XML code]

*date* must be in date format.

*topic* is characters and/or numbers.

*time* must be an integer.

**Figure 12.13**

> **6** From the **File** menu, click **Page Setup**. Under **Orientation**, click **Landscape**. In the **Header** box, delete the existing code if necessary. In the **Footer** box, delete the existing code, if necessary, and type **&f**
>
> The code &f will place the file name, centered, in the footer.

> **7** Click **OK**. From the **File** menu, click **Print**. In the **Print** dialog box, click the **Print** button. From the **File** menu, click **Save**, and then **Close** ☒ Notepad.

## Objective 2
### Standardize and Validate an XML Document with a Schema

A schema provides a defined structure that is added to a Word document for the purpose of extracting text as data. Once extracted, the data can be shared or analyzed. Word 2003 makes it easy to work with schemas. The process of using a schema with a Word 2003 document has five steps: (1) add the schema to the schema library, (2) attach the schema to a document, (3) mark the document with XML tags, (4) validate the document, and (5) save the document as an XML file.

In Activities 12.9 through 12.14, you will attach the advising schema to two different Word forms that are used for advising in different departments on campus. Then you will create Word templates for each department so that faculty members can continue to use their favorite forms yet still capture important data about the advising session.

**Activity 12.9** Adding a Schema to the Schema Library and Attaching a Schema to a Document

A schema, once developed and tested, can be used repeatedly with a variety of documents. To reuse a schema, the schema is added to the *schema library*, which is a list of schemas that are available in Word 2003. In this activity, you will add the advising schema to the schema library.

**1** **Start** Word. On the Standard toolbar, click the **Open** button. Navigate to the student files that accompany this textbook and open **w12A_Business_Advising_1.doc**. Save the file in your chapter folder as **12A_Business_Advising_1_Firstname_Lastname.doc**

The file extension *.doc* is visible because the settings on your computer were changed to display file extensions.

**2** If the task pane is not displayed, from the **View** menu, click **Task Pane**. Click the **Other Task Panes arrow**, and then click **XML Structure**. In the **XML Structure** task pane, click **Templates and Add-Ins**.

**3** In the displayed **Templates and Add-ins** dialog box, click the **XML Schema tab**.

If a list of schemas used in other documents or by other users displays, you will delete them in the next step. Refer to Figure 12.14.

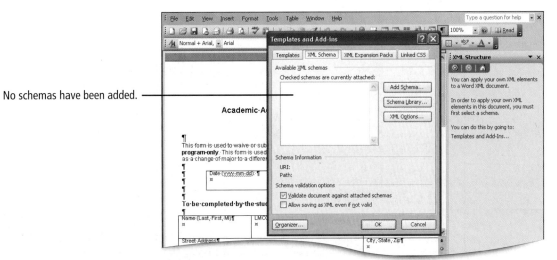

No schemas have been added.

**Figure 12.14**

4 Click the **Schema Library** button. If the Schema Library is not empty, click the first schema on the list, click the Delete Schema button, and then click **Yes**. Repeat this process until the schema library is empty.

Deleting schemas from the library does not actually delete the schema files; rather, the reference to the files in the library is deleted.

5 In the **Schema Library** dialog box, click the **Add Schema** button. In the displayed **Add Schema** dialog box, navigate to your chapter folder and click your file **12A_Advising_Schema_Firstname_Lastname.xsd**. Click the **Open** button.

6 In the **Schema Settings** dialog box, in the **Alias** box, type **advising** and then confirm that the **Changes affect current user only** check box is selected.

In the library's list of schemas, this alias will be used as the short name for this schema.

7 Click **OK**.

If the file has a schema declaration and is a well-formed XML document, it will be added to the library as shown in Figure 12.15.

New schema added
to the library

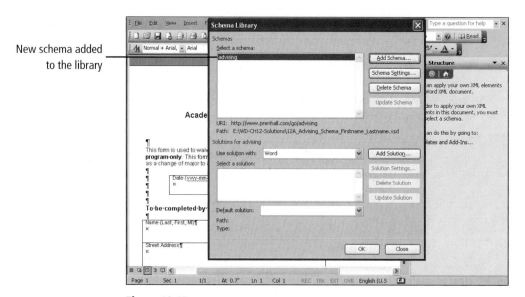

**Figure 12.15**

**Alert!**

### Errors in the Schema

If the program does not add the schema to the library because it is not a valid schema, it is likely that you altered one or more of the lines of code outside of a comment. Reopen the schema within Notepad and make the necessary corrections. Look for missing characters that start or end the comments you edited. Alternatively, from the student files that accompany this textbook, add the original schema, *w12A_Advising*.

**8** Click **OK**.

The advising schema is added to the schema library. The Templates and Add-ins dialog box displays with the advising schema listed, as shown in Figure 12.16.

Available schema

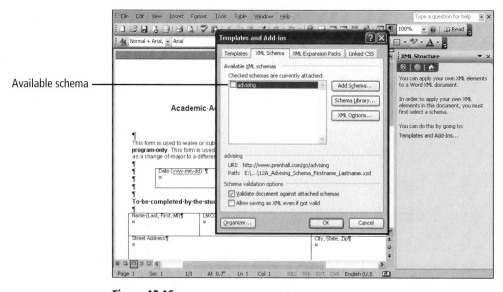

**Figure 12.16**

> **9** In the **Checked schemas are currently attached** list, select the **advising** check box.

> **10** In the **Templates and Add-ins** dialog box, confirm that the **Validate document against attached schemas** check box is selected and that the **Allow saving as XML even if not valid** is *not* selected.

The document will not be saved as XML if it does not use the structure or meet the constraints of the advising schema. Refer to Figure 12.17.

Checks document against the schema

Will not allow an invalid document to be saved

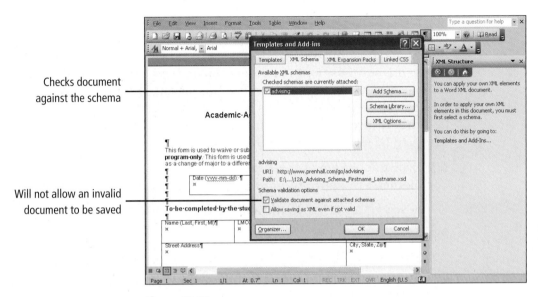

**Figure 12.17**

> **11** Click **OK**.

The XML Structure task pane displays the parent element, *advising*, in a box at the bottom of the pane, as shown in Figure 12.18.

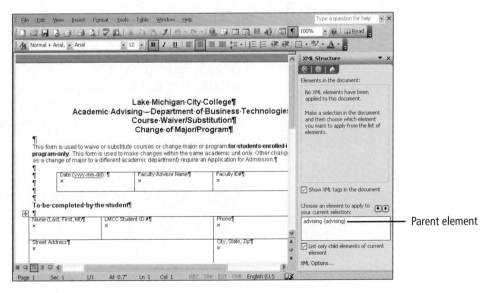

Parent element

**Figure 12.18**

**12** At the bottom of the **XML Structure** task pane, click **XML Options**. In the **XML Options** dialog box, under **Schema validation options**, select the **Ignore mixed content** check box.

Some of the text in this document will *not* be marked with tags from the advising schema. This situation is known as ***mixed content***—some, but not all, of the text is tagged.

**13** Click **OK**.

### Activity 12.10 Marking Up a Document and Validating Against a Schema

The task pane is used to display the schema structure. By clicking the element name in the task pane, parts of a document can be selected and then marked with a tag. In this activity, you will tag the *date*, *facultyId*, *studentId*, *services*, *topic*, and *time* elements in this document. The schema allows for an unlimited number of topic and time elements; two of each will be marked. Once tagged—or ***marked***—the marked text can be extracted from the document and saved as structured data. The data can then be evaluated in another program such as Excel.

**1** Near the bottom of the **XML structure** task pane, in the **Choose an element to apply to your current selection** list, point to **advising**.

A ScreenTip displays the alias and URI for this schema.

**2** Click **advising**.

After you click *advising*, the Apply to entire document? dialog box displays. The advising element is the parent of all the other elements in this schema.

**3** Click **Apply to Entire Document**.

Because you chose to ignore mixed content, the text you do not select does not need to be tagged; thus, it is safe to select the entire document.

**4** Click anywhere in the document to cancel the selection.

The advising start tag is placed at the beginning of the document, and its closing tag is placed at the end. A wavy pink line displays along the left side of the document to indicate an error. In the XML Structure task pane, the *advising* element is listed with a diamond and *x* symbol to the left that indicates an error. The schema has several required elements that have not yet been added, which is the cause for the error indicators. See Figure 12.19.

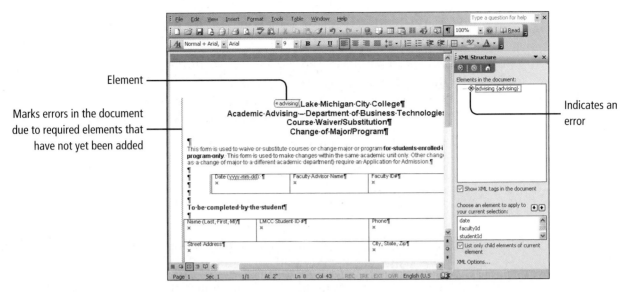

Element

Marks errors in the document due to required elements that have not yet been added

Indicates an error

**Figure 12.19**

**5** Under the introductory text, Word tables have been used to create cells where data can be entered in the form. In the first table, click below *Date*, and then in the list at the bottom of the **XML Structure** task pane, click **date**.

At the top of the task pane, the *date* element is added as a child of *advising* with an *x* to indicate a problem. A question mark is added next to the *advising* element to indicate that required content is missing. See Figure 12.20.

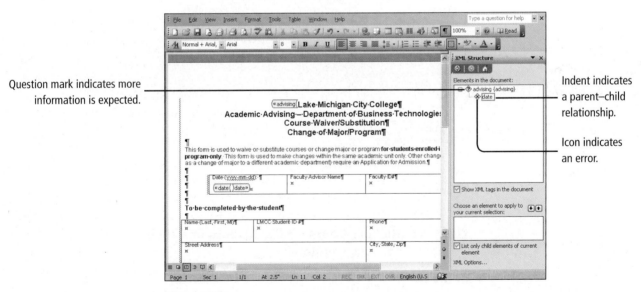

Question mark indicates more information is expected.

Indent indicates a parent–child relationship.

Icon indicates an error.

**Figure 12.20**

**6** In the **XML Structure** task pane, under **Elements in the document**, right-click **date**.

A message indicates that a date is required in a specific format that starts with a four-digit year followed by a two-digit month and a two-digit day. This is an example of how specific a schema can be, which is beneficial because it forces consistency in the data.

**7** In the first table, click in the cell under *Faculty ID#*, and then from the list at the bottom of the task pane, click **facultyId**. Click outside the tags.

This element does not require content at this time, so no error symbol displays next to it in the task pane.

**8** In the second table, click below **LMCC Student ID#**, and then in the task pane, click **studentId**.

The first three elements, which are child elements of *advising*, are now tagged. The next element, *services*, is a complex element with its own child elements—*topic* and *time*.

**9** Scroll down to position the center portion of the document on your screen. Beginning with the line *Course Substitution*, select all the lines, including the blank lines, above *Change of Major*. Then, at the bottom of the task pane, click **services**. Click outside the selected area.

The first type of service is selected and tagged as shown in Figure 12.21.

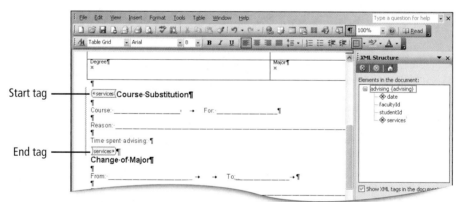

**Figure 12.21**

**10** Select the text **Course Substitution**, and then at the bottom of the task pane, click **topic**.

The *topic* element is a child of *services*.

**11** Click to the right of *Time spent advising:* and then at the bottom of the task pane, click **time**.

The end tag for time does not show the element name, and it is underlined with a wavy line. This indicates that a number is required.

**12** Select the lines from the beginning of *Change of Major* through the blank line below *Time spent advising*, and then in the task pane, click **services**. Click outside the selected area.

**13** Select the text *Change of Major*, and then from the bottom of the task pane, click **topic**.

The schema allows for more than one *services* element along with its child elements.

**14** Click to the right of *Time spent advising:* and then from the bottom of the task pane, click **time**.

The error symbols in the task pane indicate missing data that is required or other errors that make the document invalid according to the schema. You cannot save this document until the errors are resolved. See Figure 12.22.

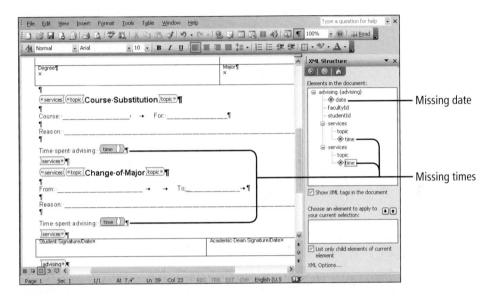

**Figure 12.22**

## Activity 12.11 Adding Attributes and Content

Recall that an attribute is an additional piece of information that is attached to an element. An attribute can be used by another program to filter or sort the data elements. Attributes can be added to XML tags provided the attribute is defined in the schema. In this activity, you will add an attribute to the *facultyId* tag and then fill in the form.

**1** Scroll to view the upper portion of the document. Right-click the **facultyId start tag**, and then on the shortcut menu, click **Attributes**.

The Attributes for facultyId dialog box displays. The schema defined an attribute for the *facultyId* element named *Department*. This attribute could be used to filter or sort the data during the analysis of the advising data.

**2** In the **Value** box, type **Accounting** and then click the **Add** button.

The *Department* attribute is assigned the value *Accounting* for this faculty member, as shown in Figure 12.23.

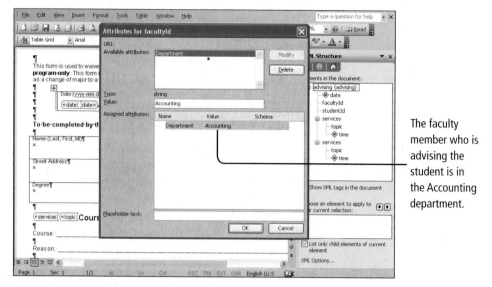

The faculty member who is advising the student is in the Accounting department.

**Figure 12.23**

**3** Click **OK**. Click between the **date start tag** and the **date end tag** and type **2005-04-05** Complete the top portion of the form using the information below: Be sure the tagged data is placed between the start and end tags. This is an example of mixed content. Only the text between tags will be identified as data that can be extracted and analyzed.

| | |
|---|---|
| Faculty Advisor Name | **Randal Smith** |
| Faculty ID# | **F467-45** |
| Name | **Lopez, Juan R.** |
| LMCC Student ID# | **ST569-98** |
| Phone | **312-555-4587** |
| Street Address | **2467 Maple Street** |
| City, State, Zip | **Chicago, IL 60605** |
| Degree | **A.A.** |
| Major | **Business Administration** |

**4** To the right of *Course:* select the underscore characters, and then type **BUS201**

---

## More Knowledge — Using Placeholder Text Instead of XML Tags

The XML tags can take up more space in the form than the data they will enclose. An alternative to showing XML tags is to use placeholder text. To use placeholder text, right-click on one of the XML tags, and then choose Attributes. At the bottom of the Attributes window in the Placeholder text box, you can type text that serves as a prompt or placeholder. Remove the check mark from Show XML tags in the document in the Attributes window. The placeholder text displays instead of the tags. When you select the placeholder text, you can enter the text for that element.

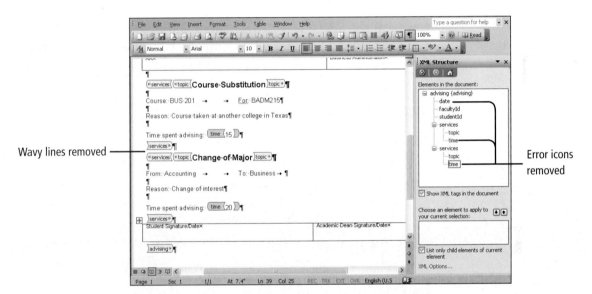

Using the technique you just practiced, fill out the rest of the form with the information below. Refer to Figure 12.24 for placement of nontagged data.

| | |
|---|---|
| For | **BADM215** |
| Reason | **Course taken at another college in Texas** |
| Time spent advising | **15** |

Under Change of Major

| | |
|---|---|
| From | **Accounting** |
| To | **Business** |
| Reason | **Change of interest** |
| Time spent advising | **20** |

Because all the required elements, according to the schema, are now complete, the error indicators are removed from the document and the task pane, as shown in Figure 12.24.

Wavy lines removed ———

Error icons removed

**Figure 12.24**

Examine the document for vertical wavy lines that may indicate an XML error. Examine the task pane for any warning symbols next to the element name.

Your document should have no XML wavy lines or error symbols as shown in Figure 12.24. This document is valid according to the schema and can be saved as an XML document. If you see wavy lines or error symbols, review the preceding steps and figures to locate the error and make the necessary revisions.

**Activity 12.12** Saving an XML Document with WordML

A normal Word document stores formatting information as hidden codes. If you try to open a Word document in Notepad, Notepad does not recognize the codes used by Word and it displays them as an array of symbols next to the words of normal text that it can recognize. Most advanced word processing programs use codes like this; however, they do not use the *same* codes. This practice limits the exchange of formatted documents between programs.

Word 2003 can convert all of its formatting into XML tags. Over 400 tags make up a language for describing Word documents called *WordML*. These tags are written in plain text, like all XML tags, which enables programmers at other organizations to write programs that will display the document using their own codes for the same type of formatting. If a schema is attached to the document, and it is saved as XML, the resulting file shows WordML tags in addition to tags from the schema. The advantage of saving the document with WordML and tagged data is that you retain all of the *untagged* data.

In this activity, you will save the form as an XML document with the tags from the advising schema. The resulting document will be used as a template for advising; the template will capture some of the text as tagged data while retaining all the formatting of a normal Word document. This option preserves the document and tagged data for use with document management programs provided to the college by other organizations.

**1** From the **File** menu, click **Save As**. Click the **Save as type arrow**, and then click **XML Document**. Navigate to your chapter folder, and then click the **Save** button.

The document is saved as an XML file named 12A_Business_Advising_1_Firstname_Lastname.xml.

**2** At the right end of the menu bar, click the **Close Window** button ⊠ to close the document, and then **Close** ⊠ Word.

**3** Click **Start**. Point to **All Programs**. On the displayed list, point to **Accessories**, and then click **Notepad**. **Maximize** ▣ the window if necessary.

**4** From the **File** menu, click **Open**. Click the **Files of type arrow** and then click **All Files**. Navigate to your chapter folder and then click **12A_Business_Advising_1_Firstname_Lastname.doc**. Click the **Open** button.

Figure 12.25 shows what the normal Word document looks like if you try to view the codes you have used to format the advising form.

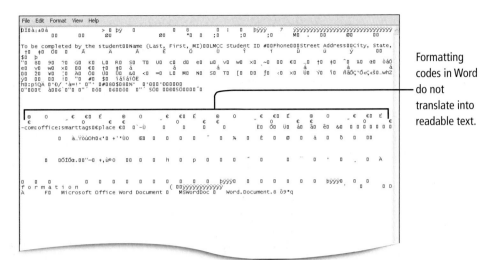

Figure 12.25

> Formatting codes in Word do not translate into readable text.

**5** From the **File** menu, click **Open**. Click the **Files of type arrow** and then click **All Files**. Navigate to your chapter folder, and then click **12A_Business_Advising_1_Firstname_Lastname.xml**. Click the **Open** button.

Figure 12.26 shows the same file saved with WordML tags and the tags from the advising schema. Because WordML has approximately 400 tags, the document is still complex; however, programmers from other software companies can write programs to use this file should the need arise.

Figure 12.26

**6** On the Notepad title bar, click the **Close** button ☒.

**Activity 12.13** Saving Tagged Data

Recall that by tagging parts of a Word document, you can extract the tagged parts and treat them as data that can be sorted and analyzed. For example, by collecting the data from a number of the completed forms, the college might discover that many students are changing their major from Accounting to Business Administration.

To make it easy to extract only the relevant data from the completed forms, Word provides another option for saving the file. This option saves only the text that has been tagged as elements of an attached schema.

**1** Start **Word**, click **Open** 📂, and then navigate to your chapter folder. Click the **Files of type arrow** and then click **All Files (*.*)**. Locate and then open your file **12A_Business_Advising_1_Firstname_ Lastname.xml**.

The Word form with tags is displayed.

**2** From the **View** menu, click **Header and Footer**. Switch to the footer, insert the **Filename**, and then **Close** [Close] the Header and Footer toolbar.

**3** Click the **Print Preview** button 🔍 to preview your Word form. Then, on the Print Preview toolbar, click the **Print** button 🖨. **Close** [Close] and then **Save** 💾 your document.

**4** From the **File** menu, click **Save As**. Click the **Save as type arrow**, and then click **XML Document**. Navigate to your chapter folder. In the **File name** box, delete the existing text, and then type **12A_Business_Advising_Data_1_Firstname_Lastname.xml**

**5** To the right of the **File name** box, select the **Save data only** check box.

Only the tagged data will be saved; the remaining text on the form will not be saved. Compare your Save As dialog box with Figure 12.27.

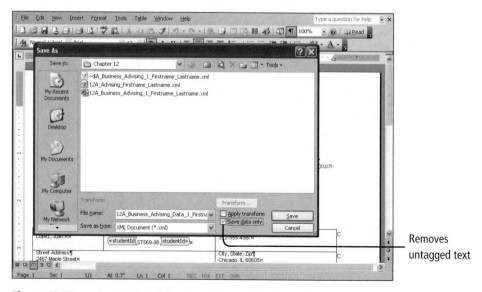

Removes untagged text

**Figure 12.27**

6. In the **Save As** dialog box, click the **Save** button.

A warning displays, indicating that most of the document will be lost. This is not a problem; recall that you are saving only the tagged data.

7. In the **Microsoft Office Word** dialog box, click the **Continue** button. From the **File** menu, click **Close**.

8. Click the **Open** button , click the **Files of type arrow**, and then click **All Files**. In your folder click **12A_Business_Advising_Data_1_Firstname_Lastname.xml**, and then click **Open**.

The tagged data is displayed as shown in Figure 12.28.

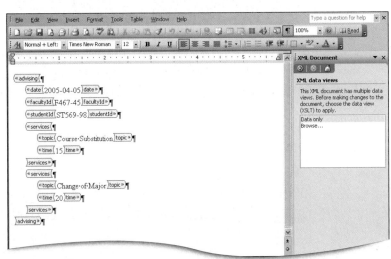

**Figure 12.28**

9. From the **View** menu, click **Header and Footer**. Switch to the footer, insert the **Filename**, and then **Close** [Close] the Header and Footer toolbar.

10. Click the **Print Preview** button , and notice that the data will print, along with the tags. On the Print Preview toolbar, click the **Print** button , and then click the **Close** button [Close].

11. On the right end of the menu bar, click the **Close Window** button [X]. Do *not* save your changes.

Although the footer printed when you printed the document, the footer is not data and therefore cannot be saved with the document. Thus, it is unnecessary to save the changes.

### Activity 12.14 Marking Up Existing Documents

You can attach a schema to existing documents and then save the tagged data. This feature allows you to extract data from older documents or documents that were created without a schema. For example, many advising documents may have been created in an earlier version of Word before tagging data was an option.

**1** Click the **Open** button [icon] and navigate to the student files that accompany this textbook. Click the **Files of type arrow** and then click **Word Documents (*.doc)**. Locate and then open **w12A_Business_Advising_2.doc**.

A business advising form, which was completed by faculty advisor *Randal Smith*, displays. Although this Word form was created before the XML version of the advising form was developed, you can still extract the data by attaching a schema to the old form and then using the *Save as data* option.

**2** Display the **XML Structure** task pane, and then click **Templates and Add-Ins**. Click the **XML Schema tab** if necessary, and then select the **advising** check box.

The advising schema will be attached to the document, as shown in Figure 12.29.

Attached schema —

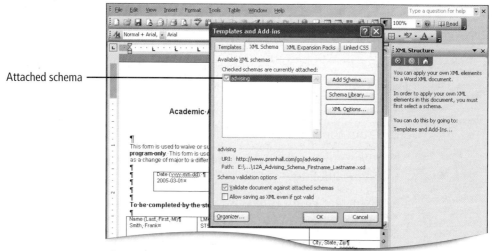

**Figure 12.29**

**3** Click **OK**. In the **XML Structure** task pane, confirm that both the **Show XML tags in the document** and the **List only child elements of current element** check boxes are selected.

The *advising* element is displayed in the *Choose an element to apply* list as an element that may be applied.

**4** At the bottom of the **XML Structure** task pane, click **XML Options**.

**5** In the **XML Options** dialog box, under **Schema validation options**, select the **Ignore mixed content** check box.

By selecting this check box, the parts of the form that are not tagged will be ignored when you save the data. Compare your screen with Figure 12.30.

Untagged text will not be saved or considered for validation.

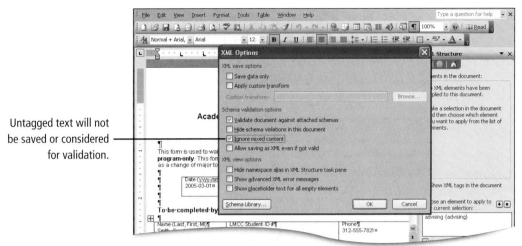

**Figure 12.30**

**6** Click **OK**. At the bottom of the **XML Structure** task pane, click **advising**, click **Apply to Entire Document**, and then click anywhere in the document to cancel the selection.

A wavy line displays at the left to indicate that some required elements have not yet been tagged, and the advising tag is added to the *Elements in the document* list as shown in Figure 12.31.

Document is not yet valid.

Indicates an incomplete document

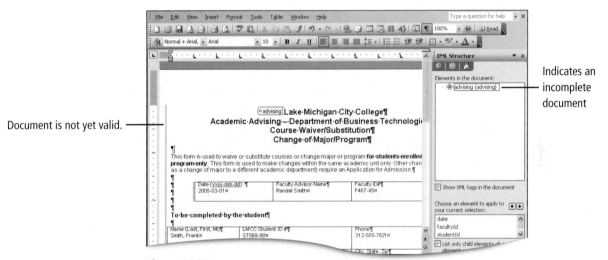

**Figure 12.31**

**7** On the form, in the **Date** box, select the date, and then in the lower portion of the **XML Structure** task pane, click **date**.

The date of the advising session is tagged as the *date* element.

**8** In the **Faculty ID# box**, select the faculty ID number, and then in the **XML Structure** task pane, click **facultyId**.

The faculty identification number is tagged as the *facultyId* element.

**9** In the **LMCC Student ID# box**, select the student ID number, and then in the **XML Structure** pane, click **studentId**.

The student identification number is tagged as the *studentId* element as shown in Figure 12.32.

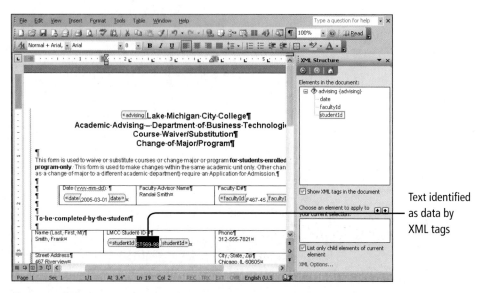

Text identified as data by XML tags

**Figure 12.32**

**10** Select the eight text and blank lines beginning with *Course Substitution*, and then in the **XML Structure** task pane, click **services**.

This section is one of the services provided by the advisor, and *services* is a child of *advising*. The element is marked with start and end tags, and the diagram in the task pane displays an icon indicating that it is not yet complete. See Figure 12.33.

Indicates a problem area

Indicates an incomplete element

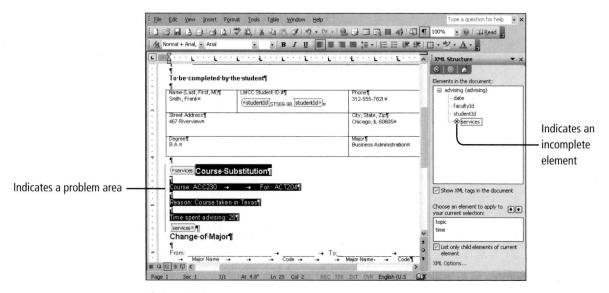

**Figure 12.33**

**11** Select the text *Course Substitution*, and then in the **XML Structure** task pane, click **topic**. In the *Course Substitution* section, to the right of *Time spent advising*, double-click **25** to select it, and then in the **XML Structure** task pane, click **time**.

The *topic* and *time* spent elements are tagged within the *services* element as shown in Figure 12.34.

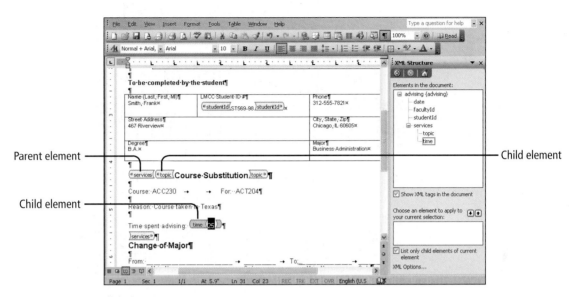

Parent element — Child element — Child element

**Figure 12.34**

**12** Select the nine text and blank lines beginning with *Change of Major*. In the **XML Structure** task pane, click **services**.

This section is one of the services provided by the advisor, and *services* is a child of *advising*. The element is marked with start and end tags, and the diagram in the task pane displays an icon indicating that it is not yet complete.

**13** Select the text *Change of Major*, and then in the **XML Structure** task pane, click **topic**. In the *Change of Major* section, to the right of *Time spent advising*, double-click **0** to select it, and then in the **XML Structure** task pane, click **time**.

The *topic* and *time* elements are tagged within the services element. There are no wavy lines at the left of the screen or warning icons in the task pane that indicate problems. Compare your screen with Figure 12.35.

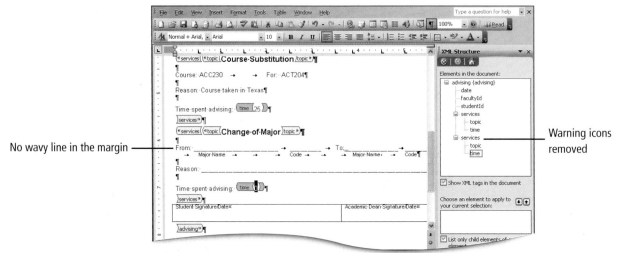

No wavy line in the margin

Warning icons removed

**Figure 12.35**

14 From the **File** menu, click **Save As**. Click the **Save as type arrow**, and then click **XML Document**.

15 Select the **Save data only** check box. Navigate to your chapter folder. In the **File name** box, delete the file name, and then type **12A_Business_Advising_Data_2_Firstname_Lastname.xml**

16 Click **Save**. In the warning box, click **Continue**.

The tagged data is saved as an XML file.

17 At the right end of the menu bar, click the **Close Window** button ☒.

18 Using the technique you have just practiced, open **w12A_Business_ Advising_3.doc**, repeat Steps 2–13 to attach the **advising** schema, ignore mixed content, apply the **advising element** to the whole document, and then apply the XML tags to the data as shown in Figure 12.36.

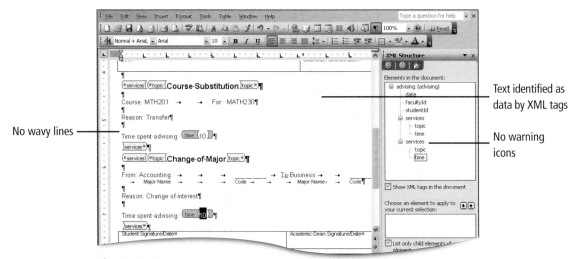

No wavy lines

Text identified as data by XML tags

No warning icons

**Figure 12.36**

**19** From the **File** menu, click **Save As**. Click the **Save as type arrow**, and then click **XML Document**. Select the **Save data only** check box. Navigate to your chapter folder, and in the **File name** box type **12A_Business_Advising_Data_3_Firstname_Lastname.xml** Click **Save** and **Continue**.

**20** **Close** ⊠ the file and then **Close** ⊠ Word.

## Objective 3
## Import XML Data into Excel

If multiple documents are created using the same schema that is used to save the data, Excel can import the data into a worksheet. For example, from the hundreds of individual advising forms filled out by faculty members who spend time advising students, the tagged data can be imported into an Excel worksheet. After the data is in an Excel worksheet, it can be sorted, totaled, and charted to show how much time faculty members are spending advising students.

Excel 2003 allows you to select a group of XML documents and then import the data from all the documents in the group at the same time. The process of importing data is controlled by the schema. In Activities 12.15 and 12.16, you will assist the Dean of the college in selecting a few documents submitted by one faculty member to test this process.

### Activity 12.15  Adding a Schema as an XML Map

Recall that Excel works with data arranged in columns and rows. If you assign an XML element to a column, the element name becomes the column heading and the individual values are filled into the rows beneath. Assigning elements from a schema to columns is accomplished by defining a *Map*.

In this activity, you will define a map to place the elements in the advising schema into columns in an Excel worksheet.

**1** **Start** Excel; be sure that you have a new empty workbook displayed. From the **Data** menu, point to **XML**, and then click **XML Source**.

The XML Source task pane opens, and the List toolbar may display floating on your screen.

**2** At the bottom of the **XML Source** task pane, click **XML Maps**.

---

### More Knowledge — Importing XML Files
### Without a Map

If you do not specify a schema to use as a map, a dialog box will display and provide the option of creating a map. If you approve, Excel creates a simple map that places each element in its own column.

---

**3** In the **XML Maps** dialog box, click **Add**. Navigate to the folder where the student files that accompany this textbook are stored, click **w12A_Advising_Schema.xsd**, and then click **Open**.

The advising schema named *advising_Map* is added to the list of XML maps as shown in Figure 12.37.

Schema used as a map ——

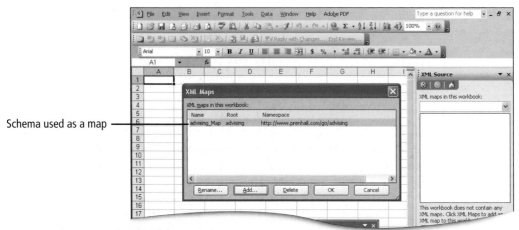

**Figure 12.37**

**4** Click **OK**.

The elements of the advising schema are displayed in the task pane, as shown in Figure 12.38.

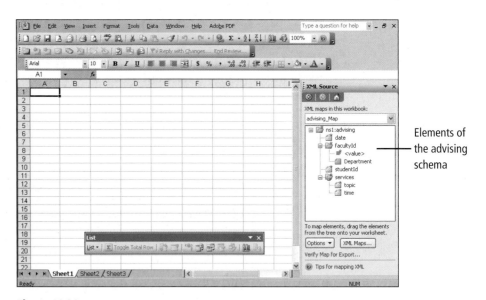

Elements of the advising schema

**Figure 12.38**

**5** From the **XML Source** task pane, drag the **ns1:advising** element to cell **B3**.

Excel assigns its own namespace prefixes to element names, regardless of the prefix used in the schema. The prefix *ns1:* indicates *namespace1*. Each of the child elements of *advising*, and the *Department* attribute, is mapped to a column heading. Each column heading displays a filter button, as shown in Figure 12.39.

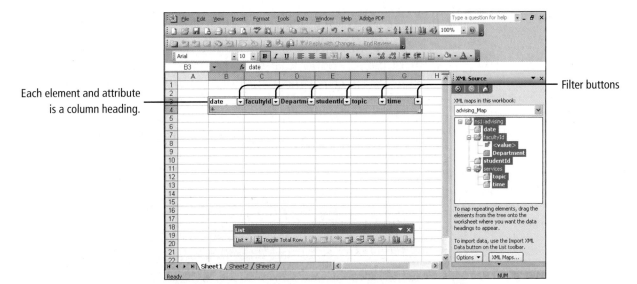

Each element and attribute is a column heading.

Filter buttons

**Figure 12.39**

### Activity 12.16 Importing Multiple XML Documents

When you import XML data into Excel, parent–child relationships can be converted into repeating rows in the table, where each parent element is listed in its own column.

If documents in a group all share the same schema, data from the documents can be imported into Excel at the same time. After the data is in Excel, you can use Excel's advanced analysis features to calculate, sort, filter, or chart the data. In this activity, you will import the data from three advising forms from one faculty member to test how Excel can import from multiple files with one operation.

**1** From the **Data** menu, point to **XML**, and then click **Import**.

## More Knowledge — Preserving Parent–Child Relationships with Excel

You can preserve one level of a parent–child relationship in Excel by dragging the parent element to its own cell and the child elements to a different cell, where they will form a list. This type of worksheet can be exported as XML with the parent–child relationship intact. More complex XML files with multiple levels of parent–child relationships—for example, where a child element is the parent of its own child elements—are not supported by Excel 2003.

**2** In the Import XML dialog box, navigate to your chapter folder. Hold down Ctrl and click the following documents, which are the three advising forms that you saved as data:

**12A_Business_Advising_Data_1_Firstname_Lastname.xml**

**12A_Business_Advising_Data_2_Firstname_Lastname.xml**

**12A_Business_Advising_Data_3_Firstname_Lastname.xml**

**3** In the **Import XML** dialog box, click **Import**.

The data from all three documents is added to the rows beneath the element names. Notice that the *Department* attribute is also displayed. A value for the *Department* attribute was present in one of the forms but not the other two, which results in blanks for those cells. The sequence of the rows of data may differ on your screen depending on the order in which you selected the files for import. Compare your screen with Figure 12.40.

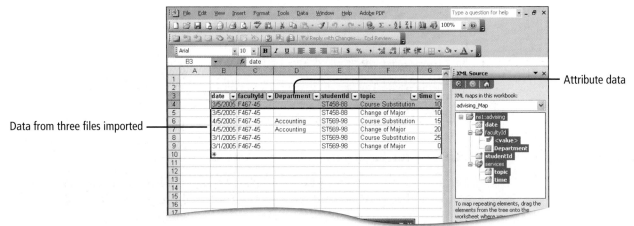

Data from three files imported

Attribute data

**Figure 12.40**

**4** From the **View** menu, click **Header and Footer**. In the **Page Setup** dialog box, on the **Header/Footer tab**, click **Custom Footer**. With the insertion point in the **Left section**, click the **Filename** button 🔲.

The filename is added to the Left section of the custom footer as shown in Figure 12.41.

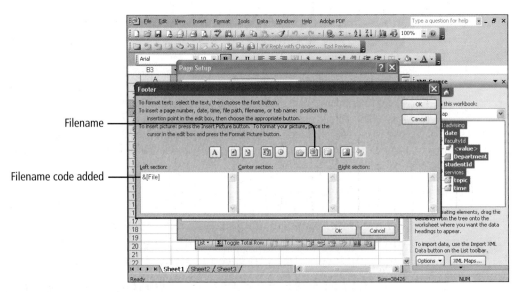

Filename

Filename code added

**Figure 12.41**

**5** Click **OK** twice to close the two dialog boxes. From the **File** menu, click **Save As**. Navigate to your chapter folder. In the **File name** box, type **12A_Advising_Summary_Firstname_Lastname.xls** and then click **Save**.

**6** On the Standard toolbar, click the **Print Preview** button , and check to confirm that the file name displays in the footer. Click **Print** and then click **OK**. **Close** Excel.

## Objective 4
## Transform a Document

You have practiced applying a schema to a Word document and saving the tagged portions as data using tags with names of your choice. This data can be exchanged with other computers or displayed in a variety of ways by applying a **transform**. A transform changes the tag names from those used in one computer database to a different set used in another computer database. This feature allows two computers to exchange data without requiring either one to revise its database naming conventions. Transforms are also used to create files that can be displayed by specific programs such as an Adobe PDF file or an HTML file for display in a Web browser. This type of transform is applied when the file is saved and converts it into the desired format. The data is matched with certain conditions to control the way the file is transformed.

### Activity 12.17 Using Transforms and Modifying Stylesheets

Transforms can control how data is displayed in Word. Word uses a method called **stylesheets** to allow you to change display styles, and these stylesheets can be used as XML transforms. This type of transform is a well-formed XML file that uses an **.xslt** file extension. XML transforms use the **XML Path Language (XPath)** to write transforms. **XPath** is a language that describes a way to locate and process elements in an XML document based on the parent–child relationships, attributes, and constraints. In this activity, you will open a transform in Notepad and add comments that identify lines of the document where XPath applies formatting to the elements. This transform uses HTML tags to display the advising data, including a table of the time faculty members spent advising students.

**1** Click **Start**. Point to **All Programs**. On the displayed list, point to **Accessories**, and then click **Notepad**. **Maximize** the window if necessary.

**2** From the **File** menu, click **Open**. In the **Open** dialog box, click the **Files of type arrow**, and then click **All Files**. Navigate to the student files that accompany this textbook and click **w12A_Faculty.xslt**.

Stylesheet transforms use *.xslt* as the file extension.

**3** Click the **Open** button. On line 2, select the text *Comment 1*, and then using your name type **Edited by: Firstname Lastname** Compare your screen with Figure 12.42.

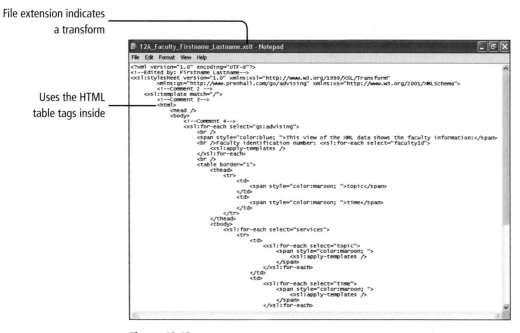

**Figure 12.42**

**4** From the **File** menu click **Save As**. Click the **Save as type arrow**, and then click **All Files**.

**5** Click the **Encoding arrow**, and then click **UTF-8**. In the **File name** box, type **12A_Faculty_Firstname_Lastname.xslt**

The file extension *.xslt* must be typed, and it must be at the end of the file name.

**6** Navigate to your chapter folder and click **Save**.

The document is saved as a schema in your folder and it is still open, as shown in Figure 12.43.

File extension indicates
a transform

Uses the HTML
table tags inside

**Figure 12.43**

**7** On line 5, select the text *Comment 2*, and then type **XPath uses match="/" to start an absolute path from the root element**

An ***absolute path*** refers to a particular element and its parents, such as *advising/services/topic*. A ***relative path*** refers to any child of *services*.

**8** On line 7, select the text *Comment 3*, and then type **This transform displays data with HTML tags**

XPath matches all the advising elements and makes them part of the html section.

**9** Select the text *Comment 4*, and then type **XPath uses a programming technique named "for-each" to select each instance of an element**

This transform displays some introductory text and then shows the services provided by the faculty member in a table. It uses HTML tags to display the data as a table. See Figure 12.44.

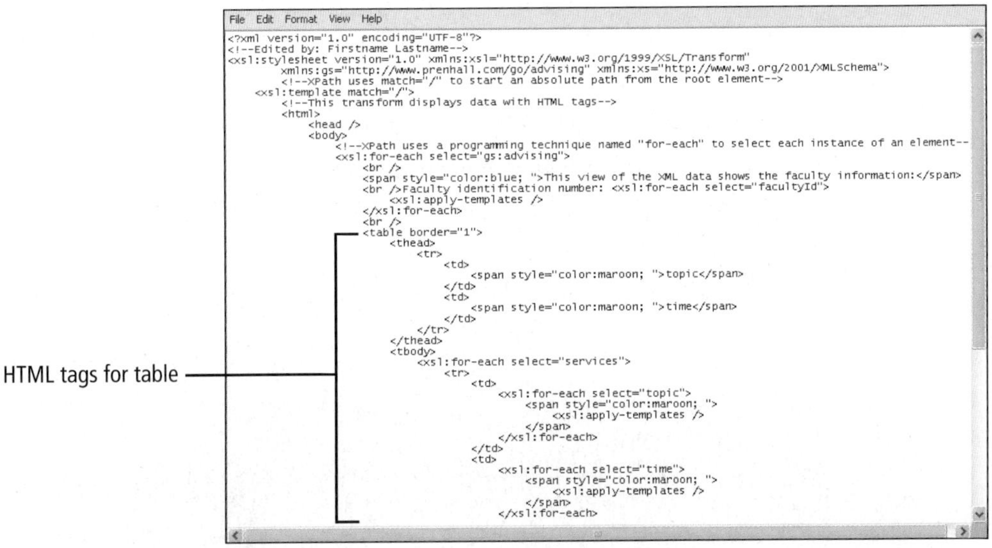

HTML tags for table ———

```
File  Edit  Format  View  Help
<?xml version="1.0" encoding="UTF-8"?>
<!--Edited by: Firstname Lastname-->
<xsl:stylesheet version="1.0" xmlns:xsl="http://www.w3.org/1999/XSL/Transform"
    xmlns:gs="http://www.prenhall.com/go/advising" xmlns:xs="http://www.w3.org/2001/XMLSchema">
    <!--XPath uses match="/" to start an absolute path from the root element-->
    <xsl:template match="/">
        <!--This transform displays data with HTML tags-->
        <html>
            <head />
            <body>
                <!--XPath uses a programming technique named "for-each" to select each instance of an element--
                <xsl:for-each select="gs:advising">
                    <br />
                    <span style="color:blue; ">This view of the XML data shows the faculty information:</span>
                    <br />Faculty identification number: <xsl:for-each select="facultyId">
                        <xsl:apply-templates />
                    </xsl:for-each>
                </xsl:for-each>
                <br />
                <table border="1">
                    <thead>
                        <tr>
                            <td>
                                <span style="color:maroon; ">topic</span>
                            </td>
                            <td>
                                <span style="color:maroon; ">time</span>
                            </td>
                        </tr>
                    </thead>
                    <tbody>
                        <xsl:for-each select="services">
                            <tr>
                                <td>
                                    <xsl:for-each select="topic">
                                        <span style="color:maroon; ">
                                            <xsl:apply-templates />
                                        </span>
                                    </xsl:for-each>
                                </td>
                                <td>
                                    <xsl:for-each select="time">
                                        <span style="color:maroon; ">
                                            <xsl:apply-templates />
                                        </span>
                                    </xsl:for-each>
```

**Figure 12.44**

**10** From the **File** menu, click **Page Setup**. Under **Orientation**, be sure **Portrait** is selected. If necessary, in the Footer box, delete the existing code and type **&f**

A few of the longer lines of code may wrap to the next line.

**11** Click **OK**. From the **File** menu, click **Print**. In the **Print** dialog box, click the **Print** button.

The transform prints with the file name in the footer.

**12** From the **File** menu, click **Save**. From the **File** menu, click **Open**. In the **Open** dialog box, click the **Files of type arrow**, and then click **All Files**. Navigate to the student files that accompany this textbook and click **w12A_Student.xslt**. Click the **Open** button.

The stylesheet is displayed. This stylesheet is similar to the Faculty stylesheet, but it displays the student identification number instead of the faculty number.

**13** From the **File** menu, click **Save As**. Click the **Save as type arrow** and then click **All Files**. Click the **Encoding box arrow** and then click **UTF-8**. Navigate to your chapter folder, and then in the **File name** box, type **12A_Student_Firstname_Lastname.xslt** Click **Save**.

The document is saved as a schema in your folder.

**14** On the title bar, click the **Close** button ☒ to close Notepad.

### Activity 12.18 Using Stylesheets as XML Data Views

Stylesheets can be temporarily attached to a document so that you can view the data. In this activity, you will use the two stylesheets to view faculty and student information.

**1** **Start** Word. From the **File** menu, click **Open**. Navigate to your chapter folder and change **Files of type** to **All Files**. Click your **12A_Business_Advising_Data_1_Firstname_Lastname.xml** file, and then click **Open**.

The file opens displaying the tagged data. The XML Document task pane is also open. In the task pane, notice that this document may have more than one view of the data.

**2** In the **XML Document** task pane, click **Browse**.

**3** In the **XSL Transformation** dialog box, navigate to your chapter folder, click **12A_Student_Firstname_Lastname.xslt**, and then click **Open**.

The data is displayed using the stylesheet for student information as shown in Figure 12.45.

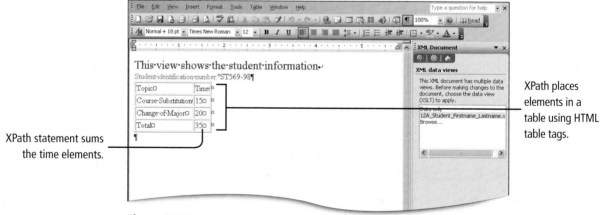

XPath statement sums the time elements.

XPath places elements in a table using HTML table tags.

**Figure 12.45**

**4** In the **XML Document** task pane, click **Browse**.

**5** In the **XSL Transformation** dialog box, navigate to your chapter folder, click **12A_Faculty_Firstname_Lastname.xslt**, and then click **Open**.

The data is displayed using the stylesheet for faculty information, as shown in Figure 12.46.

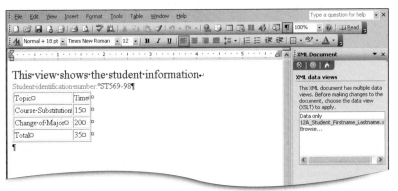

**Figure 12.46**

**6** At the right end of the menu bar, click the **Close Window** button ☒.

**7** From the **File** menu, click **Open**. Navigate to your chapter folder. Click **12A_Business_Advising_Data_1_Firstname_Lastname.xml**, and then click **Open**.

In the task pane, notice the faculty and student views are not in the XML data views. These styles were not saved with the worksheet.

### Activity 12.19 Adding Solutions to the Schema Library

Adding a transform to the XML Document task pane makes it available temporarily until you close the file. To make the transform available every time the file is opened, attach the transform to the schema. When the XML file opens, the schema and the transforms that are attached to it open.

**1** From the **Tools** menu, click **Templates and Add-ins**. Click the **XML Schema tab**.

A list of available schemas is displayed indicating those that are attached.

**2** In the **Templates and Add-ins** dialog box, click **Schema Library**.

The Schema Library dialog box opens.

**3** In the **Select a schema** list, click **advising**, and then click the **Add Solution** button.

**4** In the **Add Solution** dialog box, navigate to your chapter folder, and then click **12A_Faculty_Firstname_Lastname.xslt**. In the **Add Solution** dialog box, click the **Open** button.

**5** In the displayed **Solution Settings** dialog box, in the **Alias** box, type **faculty advising information** and then click **OK** to add the transform as a solution. Compare your screen with Figure 12.47.

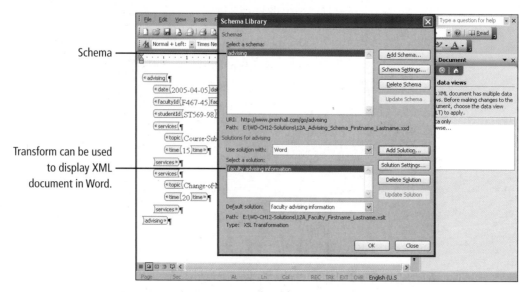

**Schema** ———

**Transform can be used to display XML document in Word.** ———

**Figure 12.47**

6. In the **Schema Library** dialog box, click the **Add Solution** button.

7. Navigate to your chapter folder and click **12A_Student_Firstname_Lastname.xslt**. In the **Add Solution dialog box**, click the **Open** button.

8. In the **Alias** box, type **student advising information** and then click **OK**. Click **OK** again.

   The transform is added as a solution, and the Schema Library dialog box closes.

9. In the **Templates and Add-ins** dialog box, click **OK**.

   Both transforms are added as solutions in the XML data view task pane. In the task pane, you now have three views and a Browse option from which to choose, as shown in Figure 12.48.

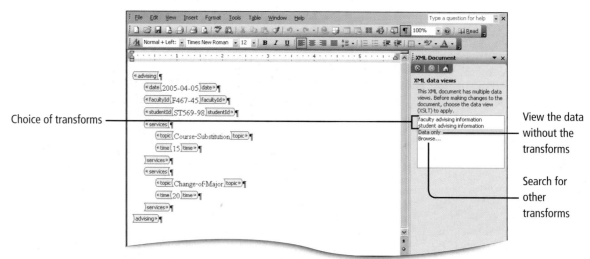

**Choice of transforms** ———

**View the data without the transforms**

**Search for other transforms**

**Figure 12.48**

**10** Click the **Close Window** button ✕. From the **File** menu, click **Open**. In your chapter folder, click **12A_Business_Advising_ Data_1_Firstname_Lastname.xml**, and then click **Open**.

Notice that the two transforms—*faculty advising information* and *student advising information*—display in the XML list of the task pane because they are attached to the schema.

**11** In the **XML Document** task pane, click **student advising information**, and then click **faculty advising information**.

The data displays in two different views.

**12** At the right end of the menu bar, click the **Close Window** button ✕ to close the document, and then on the title bar, **Close** ✕ Word.

**Activity 12.20** Returning Word and Windows Settings to Previous Values

If you share a computer with others, you must return the settings to the default values or the values used by the owner.

**1** **Start My Computer**. From the **Tools** menu, click **Folder Options**. In the **Folder Options** dialog box, click the **View tab**. Select the **Hide extensions for known file types** check box as shown in Figure 12.49.

Hide extensions for known file types check box selected ——

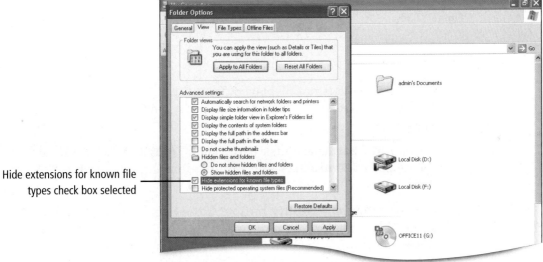

**Figure 12.49**

**2** Click **OK**. **Close** 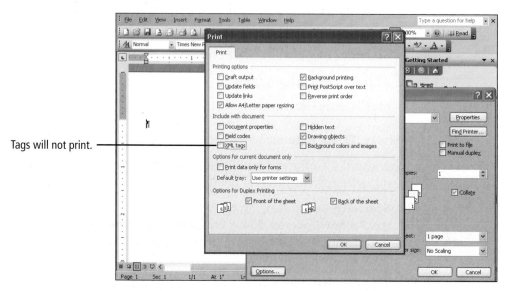 **My Computer**.

**3** **Start** Word. Confirm that a blank document is open. From the **File** menu, click **Print**. In the **Print** dialog box, click the **Options** button.

**4** Under **Include with document**, click to clear the **XML tags** check box as shown in Figure 12.50.

Tags will not print. ⎯⎯⎯⎯

**Figure 12.50**

**5** Click **OK** and then click **Close**.

**6** If the task pane is not displayed, from the **View** menu, click **Task Pane**. Click the **Other Task Panes arrow**, and then click **XML Structure**.

**7** In the **XML Structure** task pane, click **Templates and Add-Ins**. In the displayed **Templates and Add-ins** dialog box, click the **XML Schema tab**.

**8** Click the **Schema Library** button. If the Schema Library is not empty, click the first schema on the list, and then click the **Delete Schema** button. Click the **Yes** button to confirm that you want to delete the schema. Repeat this process until the schema library is empty.

**9** Click **OK** twice. **Close**  Word.

**End** You have completed Project 12A ⎯⎯⎯⎯⎯⎯⎯⎯⎯⎯⎯⎯⎯⎯⎯⎯

# Summary

EXtensible Markup Language (XML) provides a method for identifying data in a document by marking portions of text with start and end tags. You can define the tag names, which is why the language is eXtensible— it can be extended. Elements are tagged data that can be nested in parent–child relationships. The start and end tags of a child element must be within the start and end tags of the parent element. An element can have additional information attached to it as attributes. The first line of an XML document is always a declaration that identifies the document as an XML document. Documents that meet these rules are said to be well formed.

Additional rules and requirements can be written in a separate XML document called a schema. Schemas specify what elements must be present, the type of data in each element, and the sequence. A Uniform Resource Identifier (URI) that looks like a Web address is used to provide a unique name. The XML document and the schema can both use the URI to indicate that they are associated with each other. If an XML document meets all the rules and requirements of a schema, the document is valid.

Microsoft Word 2003 has a complete set of XML tags to identify all of the formatting and functions in Word. If you save a Word document as XML, the resulting text file does not contain any proprietary codes and can be used by any program that uses XML. If you save a Word document as data only, only the elements that have been defined by an attached schema are saved.

If multiple files are saved as *data only* using the same schema, they can be imported into Excel. Excel can use the schema to map the elements to columns in a worksheet and then fill in the contents of the elements from multiple files into the rows of the worksheet. Once in the worksheet, you can analyze the data that was formerly inaccessible.

Transforms can be used to transfer data between different computer systems by converting the names of the element tags. Transforms can also be used to control which elements are displayed on the screen and their appearance. This type of transform is called a stylesheet. Several stylesheets can be attached to a document or a schema to provide choices on how the data is displayed.

## In This Chapter You Practiced How To

- Create a Well-Formed XML Document and Use a Schema
- Standardize and Validate an XML Document with a Schema
- Import XML Data into Excel
- Transform a Document

**Matching**   Match each term in the second column with its correct definition in the first column by writing the letter of the term on the blank line in front of the correct definition.

_____ 1. The abbreviation for eXtensible Markup Language, a method for creating structured data that follows standard guidelines and that can be read by a variety of applications.

_____ 2. A general term that refers to the use of start and end tags to enclose parts of a document to identify it.

_____ 3. A markup language that combines the markup method of HTML with XML, and which can be read by new versions of Web browsers.

_____ 4. Text defined in an XML document that is enclosed with a start tag and an end tag, and which is the basic building block of XML.

_____ 5. A simple word processing program—a text editor—that is included with the Windows operating system and that is useful for editing XML files.

_____ 6. The standard set of tags used to format documents that will be viewed on the Web using browser software such as Microsoft's Internet Explorer.

_____ 7. The term given to a document that meets the basic requirements of XML.

_____ 8. A standard for encoding text that not only recognizes older encoding formats, but is also compatible with newer international standards.

_____ 9. A document attached to an XML document that defines the elements, entities, and content allowed; uniquely identifies the tag names; and defines the order, relationship, and data types used with each tag.

_____ 10. A unique name used to find a Web page on the Internet.

_____ 11. A group of representatives from leading Internet companies that oversees research and sets standards and guidelines for many areas of the Internet.

_____ 12. A grouping of one or more names in a shared computing environment, such as a network, in which each name is unique, and which is used by an organization to create its own unique set of XML tags.

_____ 13. A worldwide system for creating unique names.

_____ 14. The relationship that exists when XML elements are contained within other XML elements.

_____ 15. An XML element that is a parent or that has additional information attached to it.

**A** Complex

**B** Element

**C** HTML

**D** Markup language

**E** Namespace

**F** Notepad

**G** Parent–child

**H** Schema

**I** URI

**J** URL

**K** UTF-8

**L** W3C

**M** Well formed

**N** XHTML

**O** XML

**Fill in the Blank** Write the correct answer in the space provided.

1. In Excel, the relationship between the elements in a schema and locations on a worksheet is called a(n) _____.

2. In Word, a transform that is attached to a schema that can be used to control how the data appears on the screen is called a(n) _____.

3. An XML file that can change the names of tags to facilitate the transfer of data between computer systems or control the appearance of data on the screen or in print form is called a(n) _____.

4. The markup language that allows you to make up your own tag names is the _____ markup language.

5. Text that is enclosed by an XML start tag and end tag is called a(n) _____.

6. If a parent–child relationship exists, the start and end tags of the child must be between the start and end tags of the parent if the XML document is _____ _____ (two words).

7. Changing the text of a document into numbers that are easy for a computer to understand is called _____, an example of which is the UTF-8 standard.

8. A transform that controls the display in Word may also be called a(n) _____.

9. The requirement, by a schema, for specific types of data and the order of the data is called _____.

10. The letters at the beginning of an element name that identify a namespace is called a(n) _____.

## Project 12B — New Course Schema

**Objective:** *Standardize and Validate an XML Document with a Schema.*

Lake Michigan City College limits to three the number of prerequisites for any class. In the following Skill Assessment, you will add comments to a schema and edit one of the constraints to limit the number of prerequisites to three. Forms that use this schema will not be valid XML documents and cannot be saved as XML documents if they have more than three prerequisite courses as child elements of the *NewCourse* element. By changing the schema, the new policy will be enforced. Because schemas are also well-formed XML documents, you will check to see that the document has the necessary characteristics of a well-formed XML document. Your completed document will look similar to Figure 12.51. You will save your document as *12B_New_Course_Schema_Firstname_Lastname.xsd.*

```
<?xml version="1.0" encoding="UTF-8"?>
<!--First line declares the document to be an XML document-->
<!--The start and end tags of each child element are between the start and end tags of parent elements-->
<xs:schema targetNamespace="http://www.prenhall.com/go/newcourse" xmlns:xs="http://www.w3.org/2001/XMLSchema"
xmlns:gs="http://www.prenhall.com/go/newcourse">
    <xs:element name="NewCourse">
        <xs:complexType>
            <xs:sequence>
                <xs:element name="code" type="xs:string"/>
                <xs:element name="title" type="xs:string"/>
                <xs:element name="creditHours" type="xs:integer"/>
                <xs:element name="description" type="xs:string"/>
                <!--Maximum number of prerequisite courses set to 3-->
                <xs:element name="prerequisites" maxOccurs="3">
                    <xs:complexType>
                        <xs:sequence>
                            <xs:element name="pcode" type="xs:string"/>
                            <xs:element name="ptitle" type="xs:string"/>
                            <xs:element name="pcreditHours" type="xs:integer"/>
                        </xs:sequence>
                    </xs:complexType>
                </xs:element>
            </xs:sequence>
        </xs:complexType>
    </xs:element>
</xs:schema>
```

12B_New_Course_Schema_Firstname_Lastname.xsd

**Figure 12.51**

1. **Start My Computer**. From the **Tools** menu, click **Folder Options**, and then click the **View tab**. If necessary, clear the **Hide extensions for known file types** check box; recall that you need to be able to view the file extensions when working in Notepad. Click **OK**. Close the **My Computer** window. You will be able to view the file extensions and locate schema files by their extensions.

**(Project 12B–New Course Schema continues on the next page)**

**(Project 12B–New Course Schema continued)**

2. Click **Start**. Point to **All Programs**. On the displayed list, point to **Accessories**, click **Notepad**, and then **Maximize** the window if necessary.

3. From the **File** menu, click **Open**. In the **Open** dialog box, click the **Files of type arrow**, and then click **All Files**. Navigate to the student files that accompany this textbook, select **w12B_New_Course_ Schema.xsd**, and then click the **Open** button. This schema controls the form used to request new courses. A well formed XML schema displays in Notepad.

4. In line 2, select *Comment 1* and type **First line declares the document to be an XML document**

5. In line 3, select *Comment 2* and type **The start and end tags of each child element are between the start and end tags of parent elements**

6. In line 12, select *Comment 3* and type **Maximum number of prerequisite courses set to 3**

7. In line 13, select *unbounded* and type **3** This changes the limit on the number of prerequisite classes to three.

8. From the **File** menu, click **Save As**. Click the **Save as type arrow** and then click **All Files**. Click the **Encoding arrow** and then click **UTF-8**. This saves the schema in an internationally recognized standard text format.

9. Navigate to your chapter folder. In the **File name** box, type **12B_New_Course_Schema_Firstname_Lastname.xsd** Click **Save**.

10. From the **Format** menu, click **Font**. Under **Size**, click **8**, and then click **OK**. The smaller font will allow the printout to fit on one page.

11. From the **File** menu, click **Page Setup**. Under **Orientation**, click **Landscape**. In the **Header** box, delete any existing text. In the **Footer** box, delete any existing text, type **&f** and then click **OK**. Notepad uses this code for the file name.

12. From the **File** menu, click **Print**. In the **Print** dialog box, click the **Print** button. From the **File** menu, click **Save**. On the title bar, click the **Close** button.

13. If you are completing your working session at this computer, reset the computer to hide file extensions by repeating Step 1 and then selecting the check box.

**End** You have completed Project 12B

## Project 12C — New Course

**Objective:** *Standardize and Validate an XML Document with a Schema.*

In the following Skill Assessment, you will add a schema to the schema library and then tag portions of the document. The schema will allow you to tag and save the data from a form that is used at the college to request a new course. You will save the tagged portions as data and then open the file in Word. Your completed document will look similar to Figure 12.52. You will save your document as *12C_New_Course_Firstname_Lastname.xml.*

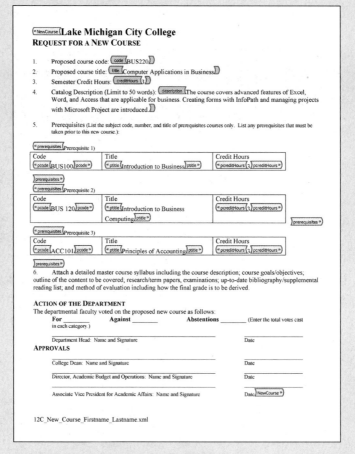

**Figure 12.52**

1. **Start My Computer**. From the **Tools** menu, click **Folder Options**, and then click the **View tab**. If necessary, clear the **Hide extensions for known file types** check box. Click **OK**. Close the **My Computer** window. You will be able to view the file extensions and locate schema files by their extensions.

**(Project 12C–New Course continues on the next page)**

**(Project 12C–New Course continued)**

2. **Start** Word. Click the **Open** button, navigate to the student files that accompany this textbook, and then open **w12C_New_Course.doc**. This is a form used to request the creation of a new course at the college.

3. Display the **XML Structure** task pane, and then in the task pane, click **Templates and Add-Ins**. Click the **XML Schema tab**.

4. Click the **Schema Library** button. If any schemas display on the list, select and delete each one. Then, click the **Add Schema** button. Navigate to the student files and click **w12C_New_Course_Schema.xsd**. Click the **Open** button.

5. In the **Alias** box, type **newCourse** Confirm that the **Changes affect current user only** check box is selected. Click **OK** in both dialog boxes.

6. In the **Templates and Add-ins** dialog box, under **Checked schemas are currently attached**, select **newCourse**. Confirm that the **Validate document against attached schemas** check box is selected and that the **Allow saving as XML even if not valid** check box is *not* selected. Click **OK**. If you apply tags from the schema to the new document, the program will check to be sure the rules of the schema are met. If the form is filled out in a way that violates the rules of the schema, the individual filling out the form will not be able to save the form as an XML document.

7. At the bottom of the **XML Structure** task pane, click **XML Options**. In the **XML Options** dialog box, under **Schema validation options**, select the **Ignore mixed content** check box. Click **OK**. The parts of the form that are not tagged will not be considered when the document is checked against the schema.

8. In the **XML structure** task pane, in the **Choose an element to apply to your current selection** list, click **NewCourse**. Click **Apply to Entire Document**. Click anywhere in the document to cancel the selection.

9. Click to the right of *Proposed course code:* to position the insertion point, and then from the element list at the bottom of the **XML Structure** task pane, click **code**. Between the start and end tags for the **code** element type **BUS220** This is the code for the proposed course.

10. Click to the right of *Proposed course title:* to position the insertion point, and then from the element list at the bottom of the task pane, click **title**. Between the start and end tags for the **title** element, type **Computer Applications in Business** This is the proposed title.

**(Project 12C–New Course continues on the next page)**

**(Project 12C–New Course continued)**

11. Click to the right of *Semester Credit Hours:* to position the insertion point, and then from the element list at the bottom of the task pane, click **creditHours**. Between the start and end tags for the **creditHours** element, type **3**

12. Click to the right of *Catalog Description (Limit to 50 words):* to position the insertion point and click the **description** element. Between the start and end tags for the **description** element type **The course covers advanced features of Excel, Word, and Access that are applicable for business. Creating forms with InfoPath and managing projects with Microsoft Project are introduced.**

13. Beginning with the line *Prerequisite 1)*, select the lines up to and including the blank line above *Prerequisite 2)* and then in the task pane click the **prerequisites** element. Click outside the selected area. This is the parent element for *prerequisite* child elements.

14. In the table below *Prerequisite 1)*, click below **Code** and then in the task pane, click the **pcode** element. Between the start and end tags for **pcode**, type **BUS100** This is the code for the first prerequisite class.

15. In the table below *Prerequisite 1)*, click below **Title** and then in the task pane, click the **ptitle** element. Between the start and end tags for **ptitle**, type **Introduction to Business**

16. In the table below *Prerequisite 1)*, click below **Credit Hours**, and then in the task pane, click the **pcreditHours** element. Between the start and end tags for **pcreditHours**, type **3**

17. Beginning with the line *Prerequisite 2)*, select the lines up to and including the blank line above *Prerequisite 3)*, and then in the task pane, click **prerequisites**. In the table below *Prerequisite 2)*, click below *Code*, and then in the task pane click **pcode**. Between the start and end tags for **pcode**, type **BUS120** This is the second prerequisite class.

18. In the table below *Prerequisite 2)*, click below *Title*, and then in the task pane, click **ptitle**. Between the start and end tags for **ptitle**, type **Introduction to Business Computing**

19. In the table below *Prerequisite 2)*, click below *Credit Hours*, and then in the task pane, click **pcreditHours**. Between the start and end tags for **pcreditHours**, type **3**

20. Beginning with the line *Prerequisite 3)*, select the lines up to and including the blank line below *Prerequisite 3)*, and then in the task pane, click **prerequisites**. In the table below *Prerequisite 3)*, click below *Code*, and then in the task pane, click **pcode**. Between the start and end tags for **pcode**, type **ACC101** This is the third prerequisite class.

**(Project 12C–New Course continues on the next page)**

**(Project 12C–New Course continued)**

**21.** In the table below *Prerequisite 3)*, click below *Title*, and then in the task pane, click **ptitle**. Between the start and end tags for **ptitle**, type **Principles of Accounting**

**22.** In the table below *Prerequisite 3)*, click below *Credit Hours*, and then in the task pane, click **pcreditHours**. Between the start and end tags for **pcreditHours**, type **3** Confirm that there are no error indicators at the left side of the text, under any of the tags, or in the task pane.

**23.** From the **File** menu, click **Save As**. Click the **Save as type arrow**, and then click **XML Document**. Navigate to your chapter folder. In the **File name** box, type **12C_New_Course_Firstname_Lastname.xml** and then click the **Save** button. This version of the document displays the tags.

**24.** From the **View** menu, click **Header and Footer**. On the Header and Footer toolbar, click the **Switch Between Header and Footer** button. Click the **Insert AutoText** button, and then click **Filename**. On the Header and Footer toolbar, click the **Close** button.

**25.** From the **File** menu, click **Print**. In the **Print** dialog box, click the **Options** button. Under **Include with document**, select the **XML tags** check box to show the tags. In the **Print** dialog box, click **OK**. Click **OK** again to print with the tags displayed.

**26.** From the **File** menu, click **Save As**. Select the **Save data only** check box. Navigate to your chapter folder, in the **File name** box delete the file name, and then type **12C_New_Course_Data_Firstname_Lastname.xml** This version saves only the tagged data that can be collected and used for other purposes.

**27.** Click the **Save** button, and then click the **Continue** button. At the right end of the menu bar, click the **Close Window** button to close the document.

**28.** If you are completing your working session at this computer, reset the computer to hide file extensions by repeating Step 1 and then selecting the check box.

**End** You have completed Project 12C

# Project 12D — New Course Summary

**Objectives:** *Transform a Document and Import XML Data into Excel.*

After data is available in XML form, you can view it using transforms or import it into another application such as Excel for analysis. To check individual requests for new courses, the data from a new course application form can be viewed using a transform that shows the prerequisite courses in a table that sums the credit hours. This type of transform makes it easier to see how many total credit hours of prerequisites are required. Another option is to import the data from several course requests into Excel where its analysis tools can be used. In the following Skill Assessment, you will view XML data in a Word document using a transform attached to a schema as a solution. Your completed document will look similar to Figure 12.53a. The transforms allow you to view the data in several different ways. You will name the view *12D_New_Course_View_Firstname_Lastname* and print the transform. This transform is temporarily used with the document and is not saved as an individual file. You will use a schema as a map to import XML data into an Excel worksheet and save the workbook as *12D_New_Course_Summary_Firstname_Lastname.xls.*

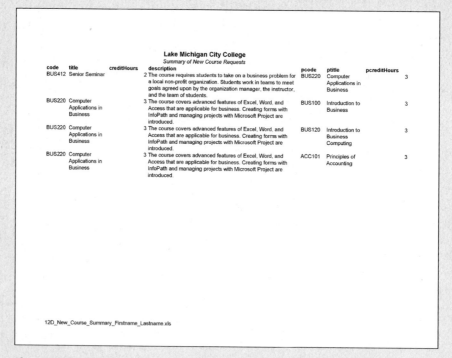

**Lake Michigan City College**
*Summary of New Course Requests*

| code | title | creditHours | description | pcode | ptitle | pcreditHours |
|------|-------|-------------|-------------|-------|--------|--------------|
| BUS412 | Senior Seminar | 2 | The course requires students to take on a business problem for a local non-profit organization. Students work in teams to meet goals agreed upon by the organization manager, the instructor, and the team of students. | BUS220 | Computer Applications in Business | 3 |
| BUS220 | Computer Applications in Business | 3 | The course covers advanced features of Excel, Word, and Access that are applicable for business. Creating forms with InfoPath and managing projects with Microsoft Project are introduced. | BUS100 | Introduction to Business | 3 |
| BUS220 | Computer Applications in Business | 3 | The course covers advanced features of Excel, Word, and Access that are applicable for business. Creating forms with InfoPath and managing projects with Microsoft Project are introduced. | BUS120 | Introduction to Business Computing | 3 |
| BUS220 | Computer Applications in Business | 3 | The course covers advanced features of Excel, Word, and Access that are applicable for business. Creating forms with InfoPath and managing projects with Microsoft Project are introduced. | ACC101 | Principles of Accounting | 3 |

12D_New_Course_Summary_Firstname_Lastname.xls

**Figure 12.53**

**(Project 12D–New Course Summary continues on the next page)**

**(Project 12D–New Course Summary continued)**

1. **Start My Computer**. From the **Tools** menu, click **Folder Options**, and then click the **View tab**. If necessary, clear the **Hide extensions for known file types** check box. Click **OK**. Close the **My Computer** window. You will be able to view the file extensions and locate files by their extensions. **Start** Word. Display the **Open** dialog box, navigate to the student files that accompany this textbook, click the **Files of type** arrow, and then click **XML Files**. Locate and open **w12D_New_Course_Data_1.xml**.

2. Display the **XML Document** task pane, and under **XML data views**, click **Browse**. Navigate to the student files for this textbook and then locate and open **w12D_New_Course_View.xslt**.

3. From the **View** menu, click **Header and Footer**. On the Header and Footer toolbar, click the **Switch Between Header and Footer** button. In the footer, type **12D_New_Course_View_Firstname_Lastname** On the Header and Footer toolbar, click the **Close** button. This footer name is different than the file name.

4. From the **File** menu, click **Print**. In the **Print** dialog box, click **OK**. On the **Word** menu bar, click the **Close Window** button, and then click **No**. You need not save the file, because the view is temporary.

5. Click the **New Blank Document** button to open a blank document. A document must be open to reset the XML tags option. From the **File** menu, click **Print**. In the **Print** dialog box, click the **Options** button. Under **Include with document**, if necessary, clear the **XML tags** check box to reset the dialog box. Click **OK**, and then click **Close** to accept the new setting but not print. **Close** Word.

6. **Start** Excel. From the **File** menu, click **Open**. Navigate to the student files for this textbook and click **w12D_New_Course_Summary.xls**. Click **Open**.

7. From the **Data** menu, point to **XML**, and then click **XML Source**. At the bottom of the **XML Source** task pane, click **XML Maps**.

8. In the **XML Maps** dialog box, click **Add**. Navigate to the student files, click **w12D_New_Course_Schema.xsd**, click **Open**, and then click **OK**.

9. From the **XML Source** task pane, drag the **ns1:NewCourse** element to cell **A3**. From the **Format** menu, click **Cells**, and then click the **Alignment tab**. Under **Text alignment**, click the **Vertical arrow**, and then click **Top**. Under **Text control**, select the **Wrap text** check box, and then click **OK**.

**(Project 12D–New Course Summary continues on the next page)**

**(Project 12D**–New Course Summary continued)

10. From the **Data** menu, point to **XML**, and then click **Import**. Navigate to the student files, press and hold Ctrl, click **w12D_New_Course_Data_1.xml** and **w12D_New_Course_Data_2.xml** to select both files, and then click **Import**. The data for two new courses is imported into Excel. This technique can be used to import the data for dozens of new courses. After the data is in Excel, you can use Excel's filter and subtotal features to total the credit hours of prerequisite courses for each new course.

11. From the **File** menu, click **Save As**. Navigate to your chapter folder, and in the **File name** box, type **12D_New_Course_Summary_Firstname_Lastname** and then click **Save**.

12. From the **View** menu, click **Header and Footer**. In the **Page Setup** dialog box, on the **Header/Footer tab**, click **Custom Footer**. With the insertion point in the **Left section**, type &[File] and then click **OK**. In the **Page Setup** dialog box, click **OK**.

13. From the **File** menu, click **Page Setup**. On the **Page tab**, click **Landscape**, and then click the **Fit to** option button. Confirm that the Fit to options are **1 page wide by 1 page tall**. Click **OK**.

14. From the **File** menu, click **Print Preview**. Confirm that all the text fits on one page and that the file name is in the footer. Click the **Print** button. In the Print dialog box, click **OK**. On the title bar, click the **Close** button, and then click **Yes** to save the changes.

15. If you are completing your working session at this computer, reset the computer to hide file extensions by repeating Step 1 and then selecting the check box.

**End** You have completed Project 12D

# Performance Assessments

## Project 12E—Financial Aid Schema

**Objective:** *Standardize and Validate an XML Document with a Schema.*

The Student Services office wants to use XML with its applications for financial aid to ensure that all the required fields are filled in and that they contain data in the correct format. In the following Performance Assessment, you will modify a schema using Notepad to add comments that identify sections of the schema that control the required elements for student information, other schools the student has attended, and references. Because schemas must be well-formed XML documents, you will check to see that the schema has the necessary characteristics of a well-formed XML document. Your completed document will look similar to Figure 12.54. You will save your document as *12E_Financial_Aid_Schema_Firstname_Lastname.xsd.*

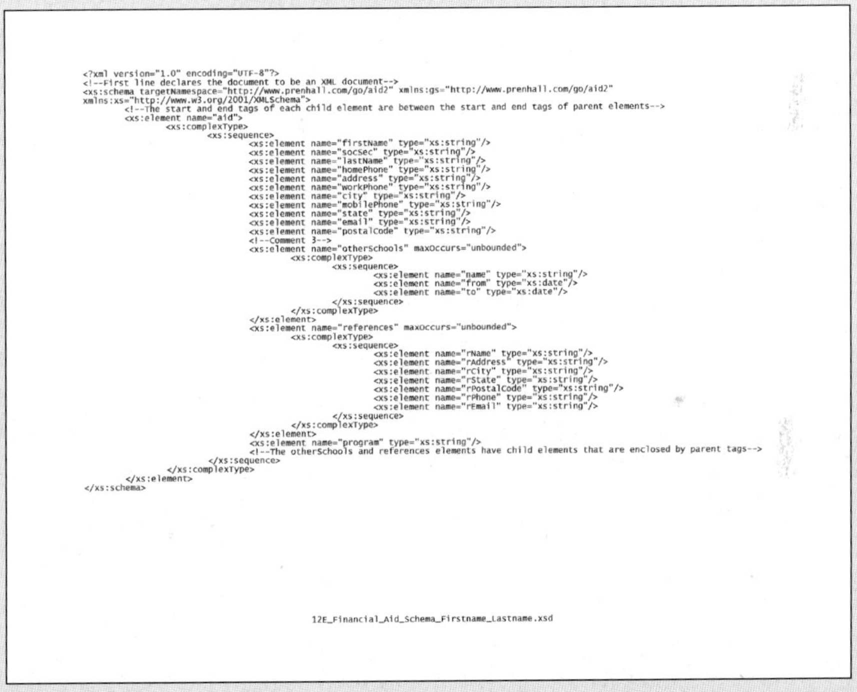

```
<?xml version="1.0" encoding="UTF-8"?>
<!--First line declares the document to be an XML document-->
<xs:schema targetNamespace="http://www.prenhall.com/go/aid2" xmlns:gs="http://www.prenhall.com/go/aid2"
xmlns:xs="http://www.w3.org/2001/XMLSchema">
	<!--The start and end tags of each child element are between the start and end tags of parent elements-->
	<xs:element name="aid">
		<xs:complexType>
			<xs:sequence>
				<xs:element name="firstName" type="xs:string"/>
				<xs:element name="socSec" type="xs:string"/>
				<xs:element name="lastName" type="xs:string"/>
				<xs:element name="homePhone" type="xs:string"/>
				<xs:element name="address" type="xs:string"/>
				<xs:element name="workPhone" type="xs:string"/>
				<xs:element name="city" type="xs:string"/>
				<xs:element name="mobilePhone" type="xs:string"/>
				<xs:element name="state" type="xs:string"/>
				<xs:element name="email" type="xs:string"/>
				<xs:element name="postalCode" type="xs:string"/>
				<!--Comment 3-->
				<xs:element name="otherSchools" maxOccurs="unbounded">
					<xs:complexType>
						<xs:sequence>
							<xs:element name="name" type="xs:string"/>
							<xs:element name="from" type="xs:date"/>
							<xs:element name="to" type="xs:date"/>
						</xs:sequence>
					</xs:complexType>
				</xs:element>
				<xs:element name="references" maxOccurs="unbounded">
					<xs:complexType>
						<xs:sequence>
							<xs:element name="rName" type="xs:string"/>
							<xs:element name="rAddress" type="xs:string"/>
							<xs:element name="rCity" type="xs:string"/>
							<xs:element name="rState" type="xs:string"/>
							<xs:element name="rPostalCode" type="xs:string"/>
							<xs:element name="rPhone" type="xs:string"/>
							<xs:element name="rEmail" type="xs:string"/>
						</xs:sequence>
					</xs:complexType>
				</xs:element>
				<xs:element name="program" type="xs:string"/>
				<!--The otherSchools and references elements have child elements that are enclosed by parent tags-->
			</xs:sequence>
		</xs:complexType>
	</xs:element>
</xs:schema>
```

12E_Financial_Aid_Schema_Firstname_Lastname.xsd

**Figure 12.54**

1. **Start My Computer**. From the **Tools** menu, click **Folder Options**, and on the **View tab**, if necessary, clear the **Hide extensions for known file types** check box. Click **OK** and **Close My Computer**.
2. **Start** Notepad and **Maximize** the window. From the **File** menu, click **Open**, change the **Files of type** to **All Files**, and then navigate to the student files for this textbook. Open the file **w12E_Financial_Aid_Schema.xsd**.

(**Project 12E**–**Financial Aid Schema continues on the next page)**

**(Project 12E**–Financial Aid Schema continued)

3. In line 2, select *Comment 1* and type **First line declares the document to be an XML document**

4. In line 4, select *Comment 2* and type **The start and end tags of each child element are between the start and end tags of parent elements**

5. In line 22, select *Comment 3* and type **The otherSchools and references elements have child elements that are enclosed by parent tags** Read the comments to review how they relate to the schema.

6. From the **File** menu, click **Save As**, change **Save as type** to **All Files**, and then encode the file using **UTF-8**. Save the file in your chapter folder as **12E_Financial_Aid_Schema_Firstname_Lastname.xsd**

7. From the **Format** menu, click **Font**. Under **Size**, click **8**, if necessary, and then click **OK**.

8. From the **File** menu, display the **Page Setup** dialog box. Change the **Orientation** to **Landscape**. In the **Header** box, delete any existing text. In the **Footer** box, delete any existing text, type **&f** and then click **OK**. Print the file, and save it. **Close** Notepad.

9. If you are completing your working session at this computer, reset the computer to hide file extensions by repeating Step 1 and then selecting the check box.

**End** You have completed Project 12E

# Project 12F — Financial Aid

**Objective:** *Standardize and Validate an XML Document with a Schema.*

The Student Services office wants to apply a schema to existing financial aid applications to see if they have all the required information and to extract the data for analysis in other programs. In the following Performance Assessment, you will add a schema to the schema library and then tag portions of the document. You will fill out the form with data and your completed document will look similar to Figure 12.55a and b. You will save your document as *12F_Financial_Aid_Firstname_Lastname.xml.* You will save only the tagged data from the form as *12F_Financial_Aid_data.xml* and then open it in word. The document that consists of only the tagged data will look similar to Figure 12.55c and d.

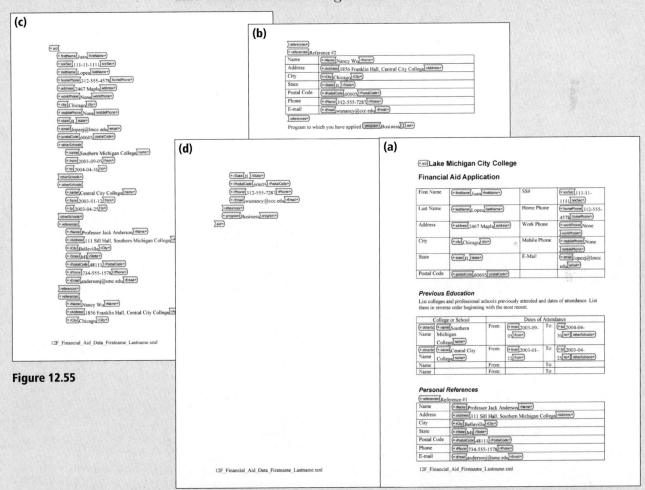

**Figure 12.55**

1. **Start My Computer**. From the **Tools** menu, click **Folder Options**, and on the **View tab**, if necessary, clear the **Hide extensions for known file types** check box. Click **OK** and **Close My Computer**. **Start** Word. Display the **Open** dialog box, navigate to the student files for this textbook, change the **Files of type** to **All Files**, and then open **w12F_Financial_Aid.doc**.

**(Project 12F–Financial Aid continues on the next page)**

**(Project 12F–Financial Aid continued)**

2. Display the **XML Structure** task pane and click **Templates and Add-Ins**. Click the **XML Schema tab**.

3. Click the **Schema Library** button. Delete any existing schemas. Click the **Add Schema** button. Navigate to the student files for this textbook and open **w12F_Financial_Aid_Schema.xsd**. In the **Alias** box, type **aid** Confirm that the **Changes affect current user only** check box is selected. Click **OK** twice.

4. In the **Templates and Add-ins** dialog box, under **Checked schemas are currently attached**, select **aid**. Confirm that the **Validate document against attached schemas** check box is selected and the **Allow saving as XML even if not valid** is *not* selected. Click **OK**.

5. At the bottom of the **XML Structure** task pane, click **XML Options**. Under **Schema validation options**, select **Ignore mixed content**. Click **OK**.

6. In the **XML Structure** task pane, from the element list at the bottom, click **aid**. Click **Apply to Entire Document**. Click anywhere in the document to cancel the selection.

7. In the empty table cell to the right of *First Name*, click to position the insertion point. From the element list at the bottom of the task pane, click **firstName**. Between the start and end tags for the *firstName* element, type **Juan**

8. Repeat this technique to place tags in the empty cells of the first table. Place the following data between the appropriate tags:

| Last Name | Lopez |
|---|---|
| Address | 2467 Maple |
| City | Chicago |
| State | IL |
| Postal Code | 60605 |
| SS# | 111-11-1111 |
| Home Phone | 312-555-4587 |
| Work Phone | None |
| Mobile Phone | None |
| E-mail | lopezj@lmcc.edu |

9. Move the mouse pointer to the left of the second table in line with the second row of the table and click. The entire row below the headings is selected. This row is used for information about the most recent school previously attended. In the **XML Structure** task pane, click **otherSchools**. The start tag is placed at the beginning of the row, and the end tag is placed in the last cell.

**(Project 12F–Financial Aid continues on the next page)**

**(Project 12F–Financial Aid continued)**

10. In the second table, in the second row, click in the empty cell to the right of *Name*. In the task pane, click **name**. Type **Southern Michigan College**

11. In the empty cell to the right of **From:**, click to place the insertion point. From the task pane, click **from**, and then type **2003-09-05**

12. In the empty cell to the right of **To:**, click to place the insertion point to the left of the *otherSchools* end tag. From the task pane, click **to**, and then type **2004-04-30** Confirm that the start and end tags for *name*, *from*, and *to* are enclosed by the start and end tags of *otherSchools*.

13. Use the technique you just practiced to enter the information for another school: **Central City College** from **2003-01-12** to **2003-04-25**

14. Below **Personal References**, click to the left of *Reference #1*, and then drag to select the lines up to and including the empty line below the table. In the task pane, click **references**.

15. In the second column of the table, click in the empty cell in the first row. In the task pane, click **rName**, and then type **Professor Jack Anderson**

16. Fill in the remainder of the first reference with the XML tags from the task pane and the following data:

| Field | XML tag | Data |
|---|---|---|
| Address | **rAddress** | **111 Sill Hall, Southern Michigan College** |
| City | **rCity** | **Belleville** |
| State | **rState** | **MI** |
| Postal Code | **rPostalCode** | **48111** |
| Phone | **rPhone** | **734-555-1578** |
| E-mail | **rEmail** | **andersonj@smc.edu** |

17. Use the same technique to enter tags and data for the second reference. Use the following data:

| Name | **Nancy Wu** |
|---|---|
| Address | **1856 Franklin Hall, Central City College** |
| City | **Chicago** |
| State | **IL** |
| Postal Code | **60605** |
| Phone | **312-555-7287** |
| E-mail | **wunancy@ccc.edu** |

**(Project 12F–Financial Aid continues on the next page)**

**(Project 12F–Financial Aid continued)**

18. To the right of the last line that ends with *you have applied:*, click, and then in the task pane, click **program**. Type **Business** Confirm that there are no error indicators at the left side of the text, under any of the tags, or in the task pane.

19. From the **File** menu, click **Save As**. Click the **Save as type arrow**, and then click **XML Document**. Navigate to your chapter folder. In the **File name** box, type **12F_Financial_Aid_Firstname_Lastname.xml** Click the **Save** button.

20. From the **View** menu, click **Header and Footer**. On the Header and Footer toolbar, click the **Switch Between Header and Footer** button. Click the **Insert AutoText** button, and then click **Filename**. On the Header and Footer toolbar, click the **Close** button.

21. From the **File** menu, click **Print**. In the **Print** dialog box, click the **Options** button. Under **Include with document**, select the **XML tags** check box to show the tags. Click **OK** to close the dialog box. Click **OK** to print the file. Some printers will not print this document without warning you that the print area is outside the margins. You may ignore that warning for this document.

22. From the **File** menu, click **Save As**. Click the **Save data only** check box. Navigate to the folder where you are saving your files for this chapter. In the **File name** box, delete the file name, and then type **12F_Financial_Aid_Data_Firstname_Lastname.xml** Click the **Save** button, and then click **Continue**, if necessary.

23. On the menu bar, click the **Close Window** button. Open your **12F_Financial_Aid_Data.xml** file.

24. From the **View** menu, click **Header and Footer**. On the Header and Footer toolbar, click the **Switch Between Header and Footer** button. In the **footer**, type **12F_Financial_Aid_Data_Firstname_Lastname.xml** Close the Header and Footer toolbar.

25. Print the file. Display the **Print** dialog box, and then click the **Options** button. Under **Include with document**, clear the **XML tags** check box. Click **OK** and **Close** to close the dialog boxes.

26. On the menu bar, click the **Close Window** button. Click **No**. Do not save the changes. **Close** Word.

27. If you are completing your working session at this computer, reset the computer to hide file extensions by repeating Step 1 and then selecting the check box.

**End** You have completed Project 12F

# Project 12G — Financial Aid View

**Objectives:** *Transform a Document and Import XML Data into Excel.*

After the data is available in an XML form, you can view it using transforms or import it into another application such as Excel for analysis. To check individual requests for financial aid, the data from a financial aid form can be viewed using a transform that shows the schools attended and references in tabular form, which makes them easier to read. Another option is to import the data from several aid requests into Excel, where you can use Excel's analysis tools. In the following Performance Assessment, you will view XML data in a Word document using a transform attached to a schema as a solution. Your completed document will look similar to Figure 12.56a. The transforms allow you to view the data in several different ways. You will name the view *12G_Financial_Aid_View_Firstname_Lastname* and print it but not save it as a separate file. You will use a schema as a map to import XML data into an Excel worksheet and save the workbook as *12G_Financial_Aid_Firstname_Lastname.xls.* Your completed document will look similar to Figure 12.56b.

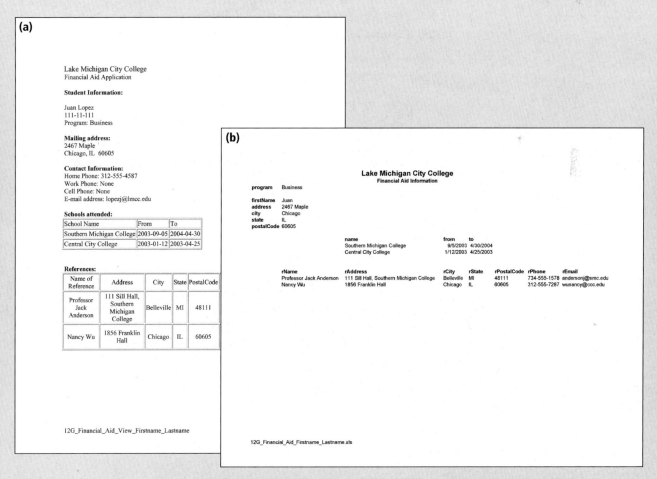

**Figure 12.56**

(**Project 12G**–Financial Aid View continues on the next page)

**(Project 12G–Financial Aid View continued)**

1. **Start My Computer**. From the **Tools** menu, click **Folder Options**, and on the **View tab**, if necessary, clear the **Hide extensions for known file types** check box. Click **OK** and **Close My Computer**. **Start** Word. Navigate to the folder where the student files for this textbook are located and open **w12G_Financial_Aid_Data.xml**.

2. From the **View** menu, click **Task Pane**, if necessary, to open the task pane. In the **XML Document** task pane, in the **XML data views** list, click **Browse**.

3. Navigate to the student files for this textbook and open **w12G_Financial_Aid_View.xslt**.

4. From the **View** menu, click **Header and Footer**. On the Header and Footer toolbar, click the **Switch Between Header and Footer** button.

5. Type **12G_Financial_Aid_View_Firstname_Lastname** Close the Header and Footer toolbar.

6. Print the file. Close the file but do not save the changes. Close **Word**.

7. **Start** Excel. From the **File** menu, click **Open**. Navigate to the folder where the student files for this chapter are stored and click **w12G_Financial_Aid_Information.xls**. Click **Open**.

8. From the **Data** menu, point to **XML**, and then click **XML Source**. At the bottom of the **XML Source** task pane, click **XML Maps**.

9. In the **XML Maps** dialog box, click **Add**. Navigate to the student files, click **w12G_Financial_Aid_Schema.xsd**, click **Open**, and then click **OK**.

10. From the **XML Source** task pane, drag the **firstName** element to cell **B4**. Click the **Smart tag** that appears next to the cell and click **Place XML heading to the left**.

11. In the **XML Source** task pane, drag the **lastName** element to cell **B5**. Click the **Smart tag** that displays next to the cell and click **Place XML Heading to the Left**.

12. Repeat the same technique to place **address**, **city**, **state**, and **postalCode** in cells **B6** through **B9** with the headings on the left.

13. In the **XML Source** task pane, drag the **otherSchools** element to cell **C11**. In the **XML Source** task pane, drag the **references** element to cell **B16**.

**(Project 12G–Financial Aid View continues on the next page)**

**(Project 12G**–Financial Aid View continued)

14. In the **XML Source** task pane, drag the **program** element to cell **B3**. Click the **Smart tag** that displays next to the cell, and then click **Place XML Heading to the Left**.

15. From the **Data** menu, point to **XML**, and then click **Import**. From the student files, click **w12G_Financial_Aid_Data.xml**, and then click **Import**. A notice may display indicating that rows have been inserted into the list. If so, click **OK**.

16. From the **File** menu, click **Save As**. Navigate to the folder where you are saving your files for this chapter. In the **File name** box, type **12G_Financial_Aid_Firstname_Lastname** and then click **Save**.

17. From the **File** menu, click **Page Setup**. Click the **Header/Footer tab** and then click **Custom Footer**. With the insertion point in the **Left section**, type &[File] and then click **OK**. Click the **Page tab**, click **Landscape**, and then click **Fit to**. Confirm that the Fit to options are **1 page wide by 1 page tall**. Click **OK**.

18. From the **File** menu, click **Print Preview**. Confirm that all the text fits on one page and the file name is in the footer. Click the **Print** button. In the **Print** dialog box, click **OK**.

19. **Close** the file and save the changes. **Close** Excel. If you are completing your working session at this computer, reset the computer to hide file extensions by repeating Step 1 and then selecting the check box.

**End** You have completed Project 12G ——————————————

# Project 12H — Faculty Activity

**Objectives:** *Standardize and Validate an XML Document with a Schema.*

In the following Mastery Assessment, you will open a form that each faculty member must fill out annually to summarize their activity for the past 12 months. A schema is provided to capture data from these documents. You will attach the schema to the document and tag the fields. Then you will fill out a form and save the data. You will print the form with the XML tags. You will save your document as *12H_Faculty_Activity_Firstname_Lastname.xml*. You will open the data-only version of the document, create the footer *12H_Faculty_Activity_Data_Firstname_Lastname*, and then print the data-only version. Your completed documents will look similar to the ones shown in Figure 12.57.

1. **Start My Computer**. From the **Tools** menu, click **Folder Options**, and on the **View tab**, if necessary, clear the **Hide extensions for known file types** check box. Click **OK** and **Close My Computer**. **Start** Word. Locate and open **w12H_Faculty_Activity.doc**. In your chapter folder, save the file as an XML document named **12H_Faculty_Activity_Firstname_Lastname.xml**

2. Open the **Schema Library**. Delete any existing schemas. From the student files for this chapter, add **w12H_Faculty_Activity.xsd** to the schema library, and then attach it to the document. Use **activity** as the alias for this file.

3. Set the XML options to ignore mixed content. Apply the **Activity** element to the whole document.

4. Apply the biographical data elements to individual cells. Use the following data:

| Location in Table | Element Name | Data to Enter |
| --- | --- | --- |
| Name | facultyName | **Frank Howard** |
| Date | date | **2005-10-15** |
| Faculty ID# | facultyID | **F12-456** |
| Years at LMCC | years | **7** |
| Department | department | **Business** |
| Rank | Rank | **Lecturer** |

**(Project 12H–Faculty Activity continues on the next page)**

## (Project 12H–Faculty Activity continued)

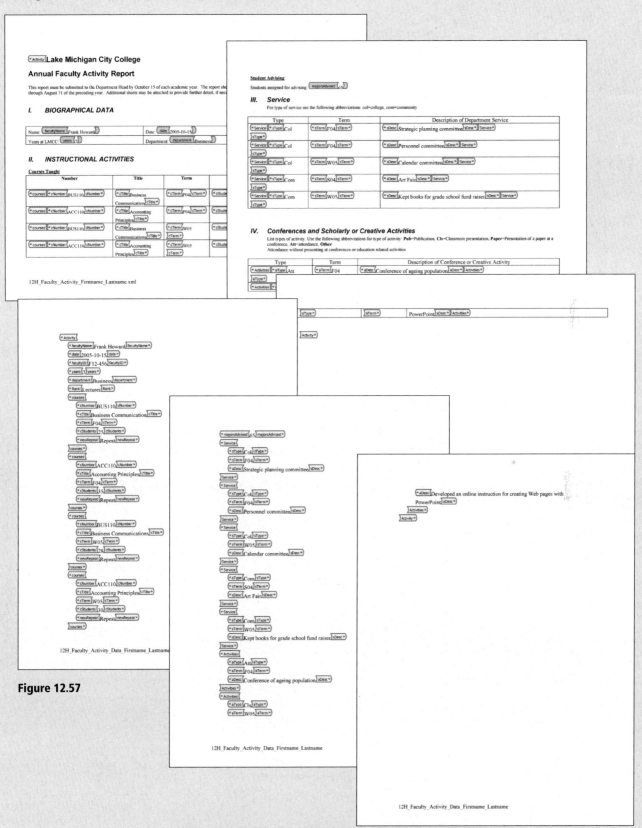

**Figure 12.57**

**(Project 12H–Faculty Activity continued)**

5. Apply the **courses** element to the first non-heading row of the **Instructional Activities** table, and then apply the child elements to each of the cells in the row. Fill in the first row with the following data:

| Number | Title | Term | Students | New/Repeat |
|---|---|---|---|---|
| BUS110 | Business Communications | F04 | 25 | Repeat |

6. Apply the **Courses** element and the child elements to the next three rows. Fill in the following data:

| Number | Title | Term | Students | New/Repeat |
|---|---|---|---|---|
| ACC110 | Accounting Principles | F04 | 35 | Repeat |
| BUS110 | Business Communications | W05 | 28 | Repeat |
| ACC110 | Accounting Principles | W05 | 30 | Repeat |

7. Apply the **majorsAdvised** element to the right of *Students assigned for advising:* and enter **65**

8. Apply the **Service** element to the first non-heading row of the **Service** table, and then apply the child elements to each of the cells in the row. Fill in the first row with the following data:

| Type | Term | Description |
|---|---|---|
| Col | F04 | Strategic planning committee |

9. Apply the **Service** element and the child elements to the next two rows. Fill in the following data.

| Type | Term | Description |
|---|---|---|
| Col | F04 | Personnel committee |
| Col | W05 | Calendar committee |

**(Project 12H–Faculty Activity continues on the next page)**

**(Project 12H–Faculty Activity continued)**

10. Press Tab. A new row is added to the table with all the tags in place. Use the Tab key to move between sets of tags to enter the data for the next two rows.

| Type | Term | Description |
|------|------|-------------|
| Com | S04 | Art Fair |
| Com | W05 | Kept books for grade school fund-raiser |

11. Apply the **Activities** element to the first non-heading row of the **Conferences and Scholarly or Creative Activities** table, and then apply the child elements to each of the cells in the row. Fill in the first row with the following data:

| Type | Term | Description |
|------|------|-------------|
| Att | F04 | Conference on ageing populations |

12. Apply the **Activities** element and the child elements to the next row. Fill in the following data:

| Type | Term | Description |
|------|------|-------------|
| Cls | W05 | Developed an online instruction for creating Web pages with PowerPoint |

13. Confirm that there are no error indicators at the left side of the text, under any of the tags, or in the task pane. Turn on the ability to print the XML tags, add the file name to the footer, and then print the document. Save your changes.

14. Save the document as XML data only using the file name **12H_Faculty_Activity_Data_Firstname_Lastname** Close the document.

15. Open **12H_Faculty_Activity_Data_Firstname_Lastname.xml**. In the footer, type the following file name using your name: **12H_Faculty_Activity_Data_Firstname_Lastname** Print the document. Close the document but do not save changes.

16. **Close** Word. If you are completing your working session at this computer, reset the computer to hide file extensions by repeating Step 1 and then selecting the check box.

**End** You have completed Project 12H

## Project 12I — Teaching Solution

**Objective:** *Transform a Document.*

The annual activity report includes information on faculty activity in several areas. Using transforms, the user can conveniently switch views of the data to show the faculty member's activity in different areas. In the following Mastery Assessment, you will attach transforms to a schema that allows you to view the data three different ways. Your completed document views will look similar to the ones shown in Figure 12.58. You will print your documents with the following names in the footer of each: *12I_Teaching_Solution_Firstname_Lastname*, *12I_Activities_Solution_Firstname_Lastname*, and *12I_Service_Solution_Firstname_Lastname*. You will not create files with these names.

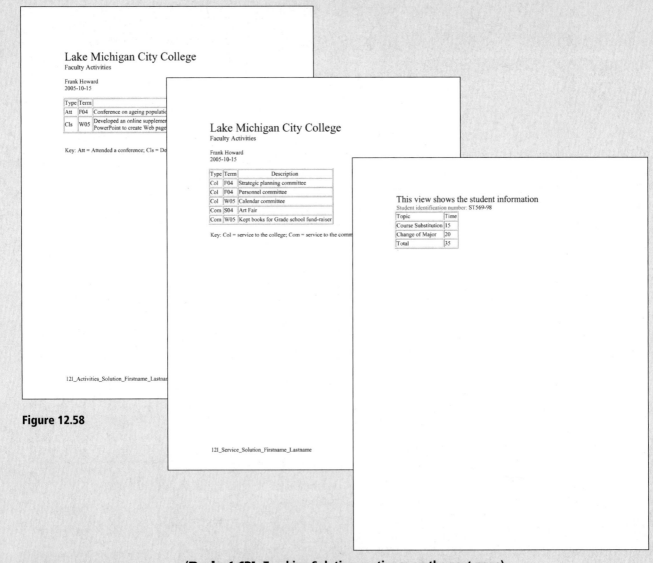

**Figure 12.58**

**(Project 12I–Teaching Solution continues on the next page)**

**(Project 12I–Teaching Solution continued)**

1. **Start My Computer**. From the **Tools** menu, click **Folder Options**, and on the **View tab**, if necessary, clear the **Hide extensions for known file types** check box. Click **OK** and **Close My Computer**. **Start** Word. From your student files, open the XML document **w12I_Faculty_Activity_Data.xml**. Display the **XML Structure** task pane, click **XML Options**, and then click the **Schema Library** button.

2. Select the **activity** schema. If the schema is not in the library, add **w12I_Faculty_Activity.xsd** to the library, and then use **activity** for its alias.

3. In the **Schema Library** dialog box, click the **Add Solution** button. Add **w12I_Activities.xslt** and give it the alias **activities** Add **w12I_Service.xslt** and **w12I_Teaching.xslt** and give them aliases of **service** and **teaching** respectively.

4. Close the document and reopen it. From the **XML Document** task pane, in the **XML data views** box, click **teaching**.

5. In the **footer**, type 12I_Teaching_Solution_Firstname_Lastname and then print this view.

6. Choose the **activities** view. In the **footer**, type 12I_Activities_Solution_Firstname_Lastname and then print this view.

7. Choose the **service** view. In the **footer**, type 12I_Service_Solution_Firstname_Lastname and then print this view. Close the document. Do not save changes.

8. **Close** Word. If you are completing your working session at this computer, reset the computer to hide file extensions by repeating Step 1 and then selecting the check box.

**End** **You have completed Project 12I**

## Project 12J — Schema Design

**Objective:** *Standardize and Validate an XML Document with a Schema.*

In this exercise, you will design a schema for an existing form used at your college. You will identify the elements that an administrator would like to extract from the document and the parent–child relationships between those elements. The schema will be created by the college's computing professionals but will capture the elements you choose. You will save your document as *12J_Schema_Design_Firstname_Lastname.doc.*

1. Pick a document that is used at your college that contains information that an administrator might want to extract for record keeping or analysis.

2. Start Word. Open a blank document and save it as **12J_Schema_Design_Firstname_Lastname.doc** Place the file name in the footer.

3. Choose at least 10 elements from the document where a group of three or more are child elements of one of the other elements.

4. At the top of the document, type **Schema design for** and then type the title of the document you are using.

5. On the next line, type **suggested namespace URI:** and then type a URI that begins with your college's home page URL and ends with the name of the document. For example, if the URL for the home Web page of Lake Michigan City College is http://www.lmcc.edu, and you are designing a schema for the form used to apply for parking permits, the suggested namespace URI would be *http://www.lmcc.edu/parking*

**(Project 12J–Schema Design continues on the next page)**

**(Project 12J – Schema Design continued)**

6. List the elements vertically in your document and indent the child elements below the parent element to indicate the parent–child relationship. An example of a completed assignment would be the following:

Schema Design for Parking Permit Request Form

Suggested namespace: http://www.lmcc.edu/parking

List of elements

      firstname

      lastname

      address

      city

      state

      postalCode

      phone

      cars

      license

      make

7. Save, print, and close your document. Provide a copy of the form with your printout.

8. **Close** the file and save the changes. **Close** Word. If you are completing your working session at this computer, reset the computer to hide file extensions.

**End** You have completed Project 12J

## Project 12K — Apply Schema

**Objective:** *Standardize and Validate an XML Document with a Schema.*

In this exercise, you will work with a schema provided by the college to create a computer inventory form. The schema uses tags with the same names as the data fields in a property management database on the college's main computer, so this will facilitate transfer of the data. You will attach the schema to a blank document, create a form, and then attach the tags to the form. You will save your document as *12K_Apply_Schema_Firstname_Lastname.xml*.

1. Start Word. Open a blank document. From the student files, attach the schema file **w12K_Computer_Schema.xsd**.

2. Type a suitable title and subheading that identify the purpose of the form. Apply the root element, **computers**, to the whole document, and then set the program to ignore mixed content.

3. Apply the elements to the document and fill in example data. If you do not know what typical values are for the hardware on your computer, click Start, point to All Programs, Accessories, System Tools, and then click System Information. The processor speed is measured in Mhz, and the RAM memory is called *Physical Memory*. You can find the capacity of the hard drive by using Windows Explorer or My Computer. Right-click on the drive letter and click **Properties** from the menu.

4. Save the file as an XML file named **12K_Computer_Inventory_ Firstname_Lastname**

5. Add the name of the file to the footer. Save the file again, and then print it with the XML tags displayed. Close the document.

6. **Close** the file and save the changes. **Close** Word. If you are completing your working session at this computer, reset the computer to hide file extensions by repeating Step 1 and then selecting the check box.

**End** You have completed Project 12K ────────────────────

## Download and Install a Schema and Transform Generator

In this chapter the schemas and transforms were provided. These files were created with a special-purpose software. If you know all the rules of writing a schema or a transform, you can use a simple text editor like Notepad. However, it is much faster to use a special-purpose software that provides a graphic user interface that is similar to the Microsoft Office software with which you are already familiar. Some of these programs are simple assistants that speed the process of writing and checking code, although you still have to know the details of the language. Others are more sophisticated graphic design tools that require little programming knowledge. In this exercise, you will download an evaluation copy of XMLSpy enterprise edition that includes a schema design program and a transform design program. If you are using a computer that is not your own, obtain permission to download and install software on the computer. This activity may be blocked or not allowed in some computer laboratories.

1. Be sure that you are connected to the Internet and open your Web browser. Go to a search engine site such as www.google.com or www.yahoo.com and search for keywords **XML schema** and **"Free trial"** to find a variety of XML editors. Alternatively, search directly for **XMLSpy**.

2. Download an evaluation copy of an XML editor such as XMLSpy, and install it. From the menu bar, click **Help**, click **Table of Contents**, and then click **Tutorial**.

3. Use the editor to create a schema that has at least five elements with a parent element and at least two child elements. Save the schema.

4. Open a Word document, and attach the schema. Enter some appropriate data, and tag it with the schema. Save the file as **12L_New_Schema_Firstname_Lastname.xml**

5. Add the file name to the footer, and print it with the XML tags showing. Close the file.

### Learn About InfoPath

Microsoft incorporated XML into Word 2003, Excel 2003, and Access 2003. These programs are designed to work together to provide solutions. You can tag data in existing Word documents and gather the data from several XML data documents into a single worksheet. You can import and export XML data with Access. In previous versions of Office, Word was used to create forms, but that role has been taken over by a new program named *InfoPath*. InfoPath is designed to create forms that use XML to capture data and save it as XML for use by other programs. No treatment of XML in Office 2003 is complete without an introduction to InfoPath. In this exercise, you will read more about InfoPath in Help, and then learn more from the online help at Microsoft's Web site.

1. **Start** Word. In the *Type a Question for Help* box, type **InfoPath** and then press Enter.

2. In the **Search Results** taskbar, click **What's new in Microsoft Office 2003** and then click **Microsoft InfoPath.**

3. Read the page on InfoPath 2003 to get an overview of InfoPath's role.

4. Return to the **Search Results** task pane. Be sure you are connected to the Internet. Under **Other places to look**, click **Knowledge Base Search**.

   The Office Online Web page opens.

5. In the **Search for** pane, click the **All of Microsoft.com** option, and then click the green and white arrow. From the list of articles, click the **Microsoft Office InfoPath 2003 Virtual Press Kit**. Read the press releases about InfoPath.

6. In your browser's **Address** box, type **http://www.microsoft.com/ infopath** Locate the virtual tour of InfoPath, and take the tour to see some of the forms and their features. If you want to learn more, download and install the free demonstration copy of InfoPath.

7. When you are through, close the document without saving your changes.

# appendixA

# Customizing Word

**In this appendix, you will:** practice these skills.

## Objectives

- Modify Word Default Settings
- Customize Toolbars and Menus

# Customizing Word

Microsoft applications can be customized to match your needs and preferences. You can change the default font settings, add or remove buttons from toolbars, create or customize menus, and change the default location where files are saved.

In this appendix you will explore the default settings and practice changing them. You will then return the original settings to the computer you are using.

# Objective 1
## Modify Word Default Settings

When you install Microsoft Office, default settings are created for many features, including font type and size, page margins, and file locations. When you save a file, for example, the default location that displays in the Save As dialog box is the Documents folder for the owner of the computer. In a lab setting, this default location may have been changed to another folder. You can create your own folder and change the default location where files (or templates) are saved to your folder. This saves time navigating to your folder when you save files. You can also change the default font and font size and the default document margins.

In this appendix, you will practice customizing Word by changing some of the default settings for the font, font size, and default file location. When you are done, you will return the original settings to the computer you are using.

### Activity A.1 Changing Default Font Settings

If you prefer a different font or font size, you can change the default settings so all of your documents use a font and font size of your choice.

1. **Start** Word. Close the **Getting Started** task pane. Click the **Save** button. In the **Save As** dialog box, navigate to the location where you save your files, and then click the **Create New Folder** button. The New Folder dialog box displays.

2. In the displayed dialog box, using your name, type **Firstname Lastname** and then click **OK**.

   A new folder is created, and the folder name is displayed in the Save in box.

3. Click the **Save in arrow** to display the path where your folder is located. Write down the file path so you can use it later. See Figure Ap1.

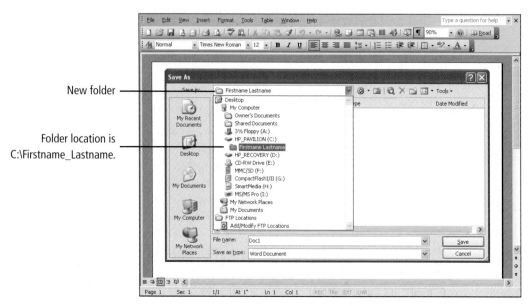

New folder

Folder location is
C:\Firstname_Lastname.

**Figure Ap1**

**4** In the **File name** box, type **Appendix_Firstname_Lastname** and then click **Save**.

The document is saved in the new folder.

**5** From the **Format** menu, click **Font**, and then click the **Font tab**.

Here you can change the font, font style, and font size. The current default font settings are displayed. When Word is installed, the default font is Times New Roman, and the default font size is 12 point.

**6** Examine and jot down the font and size settings so you can reset them at the end of this exercise. Under **Font**, click **Arial**. Under **Size**, click **11**. Near the bottom of the dialog box, click the **Default** button.

A message box displays asking if you want to change the default font. See Figure Ap2. Notice that the message box indicates that the changes will be made to the Normal template.

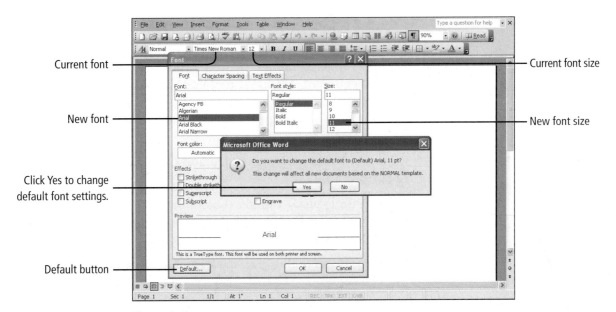

Current font

New font

Click Yes to change
default font settings.

Default button

Current font size

New font size

**Figure Ap2**

**Alert!**

### Changing Defaults in a Lab Setting

You can change the default settings on your personal computer, but it is always a good idea to check with your lab manager before changing the default settings on computers in a lab. In fact, most labs have security settings that limit or prevent changes to any of the default settings in Office.

**7** Click **Yes** to accept the changes to the default font settings. Close the document.

**8** On the Standard toolbar, click the **Open** button . Open the **Appendix_Firstname_Lastname** document and type your name. On the Formatting toolbar, examine the **Font** button and the **Font Size** button .

Notice that the font is Arial, and the font size is 11 point.

**9** From the **Format** menu, click **Font**. Restore the font and size to their original settings. Click the **Default** button. In the message box, click **Yes**.

The original font settings are restored. When you work in a lab or on a computer in a public location, it is proper computer etiquette to return the computer to its original settings.

### Activity A.2 Changing the Default File Location

When you install Office, a folder is set by default to receive all Office documents. You can change the folder using the Save in box each time you save a document, or you can change the default file location. By familiarizing yourself with this procedure, you can change the default file locations on your computer each time you start working on a new project that requires its own folder.

**1** From the **Tools** menu, click **Options**, and then click the **File Locations tab**.

**2** Under **File types**, examine the default **Documents** file **Location** box. Write down the file location so you can change it back to the original setting at the end of this exercise.

**3** In the **Options** dialog box, click the **Modify** button. Locate and select the **Firstname Lastname** folder you created, and then click **OK**.

The Firstname Lastname folder displays as the default document folder, as shown in Figure Ap3.

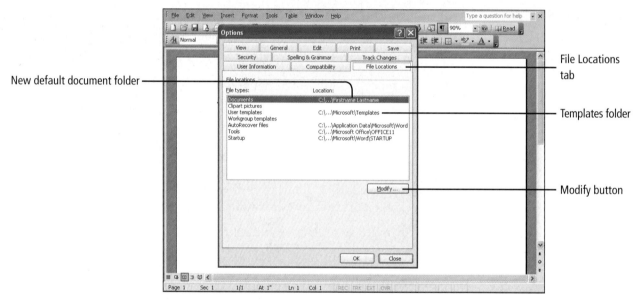

**Figure Ap3**

4 Click **OK**. **Close** the document. From the Standard toolbar, click the **New Blank Document** button ⬚, and then click the **Save** button ⬚.

The Save As dialog box displays. In the Save in box, notice that the default directory is the folder that you designated in Step 3.

## More Knowledge — Changing the Default Template Location

By default, templates are stored in a Templates folder located in the Documents and Settings folder, several levels below the root directory. You can change the template storage location the same way you changed the Documents default location.

5 Click **Cancel**. From the **Tools** menu, click **Options**. Restore the default file location.

### Activity A.3 Working with the Default Dictionary

Microsoft Office comes with an extensive built-in dictionary. When you add words to the dictionary, they are added to a default user dictionary called ***custom.dic***. You can create other custom dictionaries for special topics or special projects or add commercial dictionaries that include specialized words related to a particular topic, such as physics, law, or medicine. You also can direct Word to make changes to a different default dictionary.

**1** From the **Tools** menu, click **Options**, and then click the **Spelling & Grammar tab**. Under **Spelling**, click **Custom Dictionaries**.

The Custom Dictionaries dialog box displays. You can click the Modify button to view a list of words that have been added, and then add, edit, or delete words. You can also Add a new dictionary or Remove an old one.

**2** Click the **New** button to open the **Create Custom Dictionary** dialog box. Under **File name**, type **Special** and then click **Save**.

The new dictionary has been added to the dictionary list, as shown in Figure Ap4.

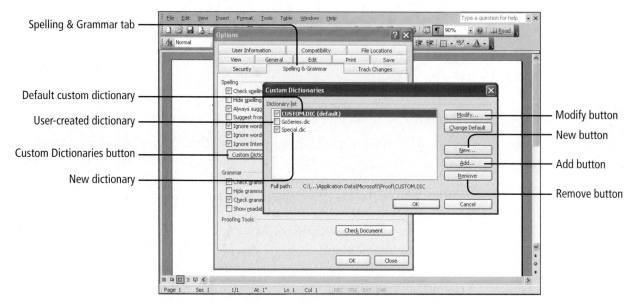

Spelling & Grammar tab

Default custom dictionary

User-created dictionary

Custom Dictionaries button

New dictionary

Modify button

New button

Add button

Remove button

**Figure Ap4**

**3** Under **Dictionary list**, click the **Special.dic** dictionary, and then click the **Modify** button.

The Special.dic dialog box displays.

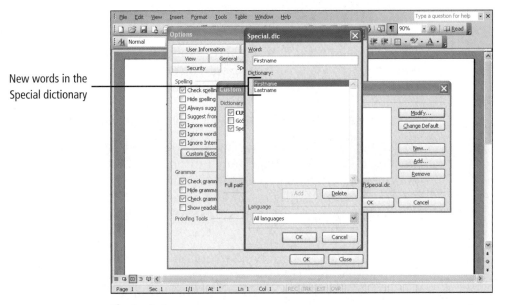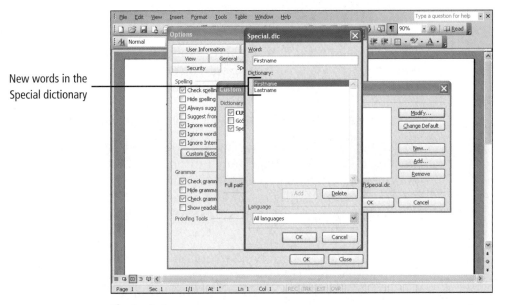

**4** In the Word box, type **Lastname** (substituting your last name), and then click **Add**. Select the text in the **Word** box, type **Firstname** (substituting your first name), and then click **Add**.

Compare your screen with Figure Ap5.

New words in the Special dictionary

**Figure Ap5**

**5** Click **OK**.

The changes to your Special dictionary are saved.

---

## **Note** — Changing the Default Dictionary

If you decide you want to save your new words to a different dictionary, click the dictionary name in the Dictionary list, and then click the Change Default button.

---

**6** Under **Dictionary list**, click the **Special.dic** dictionary. Click the **Remove** button to remove the new dictionary. Click **Cancel** to close the **Custom Dictionaries** dialog box, and then **Close** the **Options** dialog box. **Exit** Word.

## Objective 2
### Customize Toolbars and Menus

Toolbars and menus appear to be permanent parts of the Word screen. You can, however, add and remove buttons from toolbars. You can also add and remove menu commands and menu options, and you can create your own menus.

In this appendix, you will add and remove buttons from a toolbar, and then reset the toolbar to its original settings. You also will create a new menu command, and then remove the menu command.

### Activity A.4 Adding and Removing Toolbar Buttons and Resetting a Toolbar

When you worked with macros, you practiced creating new buttons and adding them to a toolbar. Many buttons built into Word are not displayed on the toolbars. You can add these buttons to any toolbar, and you can remove existing buttons that you do not use regularly. If you find a computer with buttons missing, you also can reset the toolbar to its default button list.

**1** **Start** Word. From the **View** menu, point to **Toolbars**, and then confirm that only the **Standard** and **Formatting** toolbars are displayed. **Close** any other toolbars that are open.

**2** On the right side of the Standard toolbar, click the **Toolbar Options** button ▪, point to **Add or Remove Buttons**, and then click **Customize**.

The Customize dialog box displays.

**3** Click the **Commands tab**. Under **Categories**, click **Format** to display the complete list of formatting commands.

**4** Under **Commands**, scroll down and examine the list of available buttons. Locate the **Strikethrough** command.

**5** Drag the **Strikethrough** command to the Formatting toolbar. Place the I-beam pointer just to the right of the **Underline** button and release the mouse button.

The Strikethrough button is added to the Formatting toolbar, as shown in Figure Ap6.

Strikethrough button ——

Format category ——

Strikethrough command

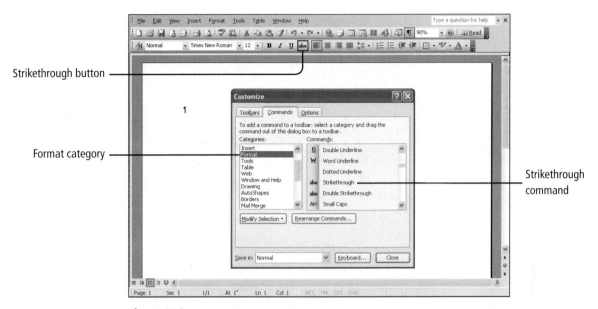

**Figure Ap6**

**6** On the Formatting toolbar, locate the **Highlight** button , drag it below the toolbar, and then release the mouse button.

The button is removed from the toolbar. This method of removing buttons only works when the Customize dialog box is open. You can add or remove as many buttons as you wish from any toolbar using this method.

**Another Way** ——

### Removing a Button from a Toolbar

If the Customize dialog box is not open, you can remove a button from a toolbar by holding down Alt and dragging the button off the toolbar.

**7** In the **Customize** dialog box, click the **Toolbars tab**. Under **Toolbars**, click to select the **Formatting** toolbar. Click the **Reset** button.

The Reset Toolbar message box displays, asking if you want to restore the toolbar to its default settings using the Normal template. See Figure Ap7.

Formatting toolbar is selected. ———

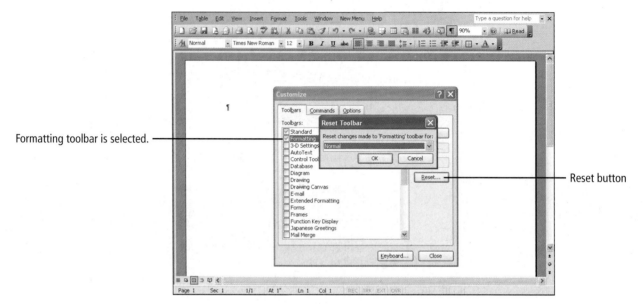

Reset button

**Figure Ap7**

**8** Click **OK**, and then examine the Formatting toolbar.

Notice that the Strikethrough button is removed, and the Highlight button is restored to the toolbar. If you are using a lab computer, it is always good practice to leave the computer settings the way you found them.

**9** **Close** the dialog box.

### Activity A.5 Modifying Menus

You can add or remove menu options, or you can rearrange menu commands on the menu bar. You also can create your own menu for options that you would like to make easily available.

**1** From the **Tools** menu, click **Customize**. In the menu bar, drag the **Table** command to the left until the I-bar pointer is between *File* and *Edit*, and then release the mouse button.

The Table menu command is moved to a new location.

**2** In the **Customize** dialog box, click the **Commands tab**. Scroll to the bottom of the **Categories** list, and click **New Menu**. Under **Commands**, drag **New Menu** to the menu bar, and drop it between *Window* and *Help*.

A new menu command is added to the menu bar, as shown in Figure Ap8.

Table menu command is in a new location.

New menu command has been added.

New Menu command

New Menu category

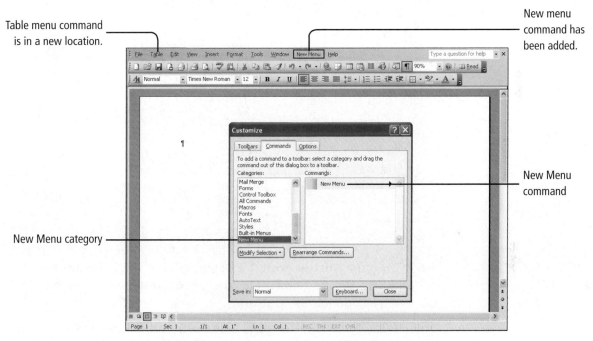

**Figure Ap8**

**3** In the Customize dialog box, click the **Modify Selection** button, click **Name**, type **Favorites** and then press ⏎.

The name of the new menu command is changed to *Favorites*. No menu options are associated with this new command.

**4** Under **Categories**, click **Format**. Under **Commands**, drag the **Grow Font 1 Pt** command to the *Favorites* menu. Position the I-bar pointer in the box below the *Favorites* command, as shown in Figure Ap9.

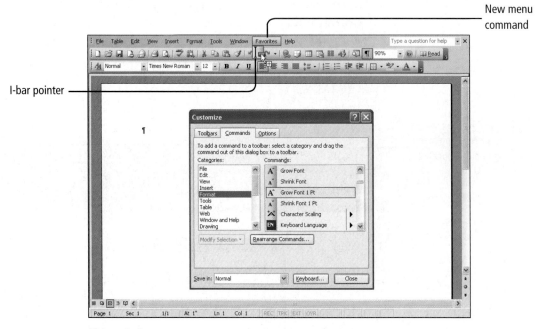

New menu command

I-bar pointer

**Figure Ap9**

**5** Drag the **Shrink Font 1 Pt** command to the *Favorites* menu, position the horizontal I-bar under the **Grow Font 1 Pt** command, and then release the mouse button.

**6** Drag the **Strikethrough** command to the *Favorites* menu, position the horizontal I-bar under the **Shrink Font 1 Pt** command, and then release the mouse button.

Your new menu now contains three commands, as shown in Figure Ap10. (Note: You can mix commands from different categories if you wish.)

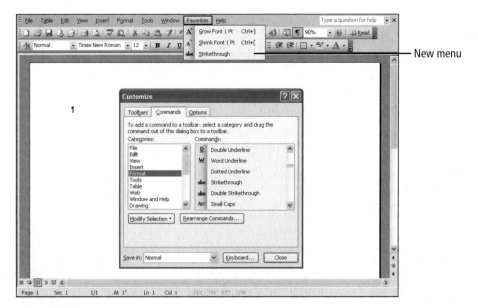

New menu

**Figure Ap10**

**7** In the **Customize** dialog box, click the **Close** button. Type your first name and last name, and then select your last name. From the **Favorites** menu, click **Grow Font 1 Pt**. Select your first name. From the **Favorites** menu, click **Strikethrough**.

Notice that the menu commands in the new menu work the same as the default menu commands.

**8** From the **Tools** menu, click to **Customize**, and then click the **Toolbars tab**. Under **Toolbars**, click once to select menu bar, and then click the **Reset** button.

The Reset Toolbar message box displays.

**9** Click **OK** to reset the menu bar.

Notice that the **Table** command returns to its original location, and the custom toolbar that you created is removed.

**10** **Close** Word but do not save your changes.

# Word 2003 Task Guide

Each book in the *GO! Series* is designed to be kept beside your computer as a handy reference, even after you have completed all the activities. Any time you need to recall a sequence of steps or a shortcut needed to achieve a result, look up the general category in the alphabetized listing that follows and then find your task. To review how to perform a task, turn to the page number listed in the second column to locate the step-by-step exercise or other detailed description. Additional entries without page numbers describe tasks that are closely related to those presented in the chapters.

| Word Task | Page | Mouse | Menu Bar | Shortcut Menu | Shortcut Keys |
|---|---|---|---|---|---|
| ActiveX control, format | 775 | In design mode, select control; on Control Toolbox toolbar | | In design mode, right-click control; Properties | |
| ActiveX control, insert | 773 | From Control Toolbox, click control | View \| Toolbars \| Control Toolbox; click control; click or drag in document | Right-click a toolbar; Control Toolbox; click control; click or drag in document | |
| ActiveX control, run and test | 780 | on Control Toolbox toolbar (to exit design mode); on Forms toolbar; click controls to test | | | |
| ActiveX control, toggle design mode | 773 | on Control Toolbox toolbar | | | |
| ActiveX control, write code for | 777 | In design mode, select control; on Control Toolbox toolbar; type code<br><br>Double-click control; type code | | In design mode, right-click control; View Code; type code | |
| Align, center | 86 | on Formatting toolbar | Format \| Paragraph \| Indents and Spacing tab, Alignment | Right-click, Paragraph \| Indents and Spacing tab, Alignment | Ctrl + E |
| Align, justify | 86 | on Formatting toolbar | Format \| Paragraph \| Indents and Spacing tab, Alignment | Right-click, Paragraph \| Indents and Spacing tab, Alignment | Ctrl + J |
| Align, left | 86 | on Formatting toolbar | Format \| Paragraph \| Indents and Spacing tab, Alignment | Right-click, Paragraph \| Indents and Spacing tab, Alignment | Ctrl + L |
| Align, right | 86 | on Formatting toolbar | Format \| Paragraph \| Indents and Spacing tab, Alignment | Right-click, Paragraph \| Indents and Spacing tab, Alignment | Ctrl + R |

| Word Task | Page | Mouse | Menu Bar | Shortcut Menu | Shortcut Keys |
|-----------|------|-------|----------|---------------|---------------|
| **Arrow, insert and format** | 185 | ↖ on Drawing toolbar | Format \| Auto-Shape \| Colors and Lines tab | Right-click arrow, Format \| AutoShape | |
| **AutoComplete, use** | 34 | | | | Begin typing the first few letters of a month (or other AutoComplete text); when a ScreenTip displays, press [Enter] |
| **AutoCorrect, record entries** | 121 | | Tools \| AutoCorrect Options \| AutoCorrect tab | | |
| **AutoCorrect, use shortcuts** | 124 | | | | Type shortcut text and press [Enter], [Spacebar], or [Tab], or add punctuation mark |
| **AutoFormat, table** | 222 | ▦ on Tables and Borders toolbar | Table \| Table AutoFormat | Select table, right-click, Table AutoFormat | |
| **AutoShape, insert** | 187 | AutoShapes ▾ on Drawing toolbar | Insert \| Picture \| AutoShapes | | |
| **AutoSummarize, use** | 695 | | Tools \| AutoSummarize | | |
| **AutoText, insert** | 126 | | Insert \| AutoText | | Begin typing the first few letters of AutoText text; when a ScreenTip displays, press [Enter] |
| **AutoText, insert in header or footer** | 119 | Insert AutoText ▾ on Header and Footer toolbar | Insert \| AutoText | | |
| **AutoText, record entries** | 126 | | Tools \| AutoCorrect Options \| AutoText tab | | Select, [Alt] + [F3] |
| **Background, create** | 744 | | Format \| Background | | |
| **Bookmark, go to** | 688, 755 | ◉ on vertical scroll bar; → ; click Bookmark; select bookmark name; click Go To | Insert \| Bookmark; select bookmark name; click Go To. Edit \| Go To; Bookmark; select bookmark name; click Go To | | [Ctrl] + [G]; Bookmark; select bookmark name; |
| **Bookmark, insert** | 690 | | Insert \| Bookmark | | [Ctrl] + [Shift] + [F5] |
| **Border, add to paragraph** | 271 | ▦ ▾ on Formatting toolbar | Format \| Borders and Shading \| Borders tab, Box | | |
| **Border, insert custom** | 264 | | Format \| Borders and Shading \| Borders tab, Custom | | |

| Word Task | Page | Mouse | Menu Bar | Shortcut Menu | Shortcut Keys |
|---|---|---|---|---|---|
| Browse, select browse object | 301 | [icon] on vertical scroll bar, select object on palette, use [icon] for next object | | | |
| Browse, by comment | 301 | [icon] on vertical scroll bar, [icon] | Edit \| Go To, Comment | | Ctrl + G |
| Browse, by edits | 301 | [icon] on vertical scroll bar, [icon] | | | |
| Browse, by endnote | 301 | [icon] on vertical scroll bar, [icon] | Edit \| Go To, Endnote | | Ctrl + G |
| Browse, by field | 301 | [icon] on vertical scroll bar, [icon] | Edit \| Go To, Field | | Ctrl + G |
| Browse, by footnote | 301 | [icon] on vertical scroll bar, [icon] | Edit \| Go To, Footnote | | Ctrl + G |
| Browse, by graphic | 301 | [icon] on vertical scroll bar, [icon] | Edit \| Go To, Graphic | | Ctrl + G |
| Browse, by heading | 301 | [icon] on vertical scroll bar, [icon] | Edit \| Go To, Heading | | Ctrl + G |
| Browse, by page | 301 | [icon] on vertical scroll bar, [icon] | Edit \| Go To, Page | | Ctrl + G |
| Browse, by section | 301 | [icon] on vertical scroll bar, [icon] | Edit \| Go To, Section | | Ctrl + G |
| Browse, by table | 301 | [icon] on vertical scroll bar, [icon] | Edit \| Go To, Table | | Ctrl + G |
| Browse, find | 301 | [icon] on vertical scroll bar, [icon] | Edit \| Find | | Ctrl + F |
| Browse, go to | 301 | [icon] on vertical scroll bar, [icon] | Edit \| Go To | | Ctrl + G |
| Bulleted list, create | 109 | [icon] on Formatting toolbar | Format \| Bullets and Numbering | Select text, right-click, Bullets and Numbering | |
| Bulleted list, customize | 114 | | Select list, Format \| Bullets and Numbering \| Bulleted tab; select style and then click Customize | Select list, right-click, Bullets and Numbering \| Bulleted tab; select style and then click Customize | |
| Character style, create for selected character(s) | 372 | Apply formatting and then click New Style; in Style type box, click Character | | | |
| Chart, add title | 342 | | Activate chart, Chart \| Chart Options \| Titles tab | Activate chart; right-click chart area, Chart Options \| Titles tab | |
| Chart, center | 348 | [icon] on Formatting toolbar | Format \| Paragraph \| Indents and Spacing tab, Alignment | | Ctrl + E |
| Chart, change type | 344 | [icon] on Graph Standard toolbar | Activate chart, Chart \| Chart Type | Activate chart; right-click chart area, Chart Type | |

| Word Task | Page | Mouse | Menu Bar | Shortcut Menu | Shortcut Keys |
|---|---|---|---|---|---|
| Chart, close datasheet | 347 | [X icon] on datasheet title bar<br><br>[grid icon] on Standard toolbar when the datasheet is open | View \| Datasheet | Activate chart; right-click, Datasheet | |
| Chart, create from table | 340 | | Activate table, Insert \| Picture \| Chart | | |
| Chart, display datasheet | 341 | | Activate chart, View \| Datasheet | | |
| Chart, edit | 341 | Double-click chart | Activate chart, Edit \| Chart Object \| Edit | Double-click chart; right-click chart, Chart Object \| Edit | |
| Chart, format text | 346 | [icon] on Graph Standard toolbar | Activate chart, Format \| Selected <object> | Activate chart; right-click text, Format <object> | |
| Chart, graph by column | 345 | [icon] on Graph Standard toolbar | Activate chart, Data \| Series in Columns | | |
| Chart, graph by row | 345 | [icon] on Graph Standard toolbar | Activate chart, Data \| Series in Rows | | |
| Chart, resize | 348 | Drag a selection handle | Activate chart, Format \| Object \| Size tab | Double-click chart; right-click chart, Format Object | |
| Chart, select | 341 | Click chart | | | |
| Clip art, insert | 172 | [icon] on Drawing toolbar<br><br>[arrow icon] in task pane and then click Clip Art | Insert \| Picture \| Clip Art | | |
| Clip art, resize | 179 | Drag sizing handle<br><br>[icon] on Picture toolbar | Select picture, Format \| Picture \| Size tab | Right-click image, Format Picture \| Size tab | |
| Clip art, wrap text around | 176 | [icon] on Picture toolbar<br><br>Draw ▾ on Drawing toolbar, Text Wrapping | Select picture, Format \| Picture \| Layout tab | Right click image, Format Picture \| Layout tab | |
| Clipboard, clear | 289 | [icon] Clear All in Clipboard task pane | | | |
| Clipboard, clear individual items | 296 | Click arrow next to item in Clipboard, click Delete | | Right-click item in Clipboard, Delete | |
| Clipboard, collect and paste | 289, 296 | Display Clipboard task pane, [icon] or [icon] multiple objects; in new location(s), click objects on Clipboard to paste<br><br>or [icon] Paste All | Collect objects on Clipboard using Edit \| Copy; Edit \| Cut; then paste in new location | Display Clipboard; right-click objects in document, Copy or Cut; right-click objects in Clipboard and Paste | Ctrl + C (copy) or Ctrl + X (cut) |

| Word Task | Page | Mouse | Menu Bar | Shortcut Menu | Shortcut Keys |
|---|---|---|---|---|---|
| Clipboard, collect from other documents | 292 | Display Clipboard, [icon] document selections to Clipboard | Collect objects on Clipboard using Edit \| Copy; Edit \| Cut | Display Clipboard; right-click objects in documents, Copy or Cut | Ctrl + C (copy) or Ctrl + X (cut) |
| Clipboard, display task pane | 289 | [icon] in any task pane and then click Clipboard | Edit \| Office Clipboard | | Ctrl + F1, and click Clipboard<br>Ctrl + C twice |
| Close, document | 292 | [X] on menu bar | File \| Close | | Ctrl + F4 or Ctrl + W |
| Close, file | 48 | [X] on menu bar | File \| Close | | Ctrl + F4 or Ctrl + W |
| Close, header or footer | 26 | Close on Header and Footer toolbar<br>Double-click in text area of document | | | |
| Close, print preview | 34 | Close or [X] | | | |
| Collect and paste, multiple selections | 289, 296 | Display Clipboard task pane, [icon] or [icon] multiple objects; in new location(s), click objects on Clipboard to paste or [icon] Paste All | Collect objects on Clipboard using Edit \| Copy; Edit \| Cut; then paste in new location | Display Clipboard; right-click objects in document, Copy or Cut; right-click objects in Clipboard, Paste | Ctrl + C (copy) or Ctrl + X (cut) |
| Columns, balancing breaks | 269 | | Insert \| Break, Continuous | | |
| Columns, change number | 266 | [icon] on Standard toolbar | Format \| Columns | | |
| Columns, insert break | 269 | | Insert \| Break, Column break | | |
| Command, repeat | 390 | | | | F4 |
| Command button, insert | 773 | [icon] on Control Toolbox toolbar | | | |
| Comment, delete | 451 | [icon] on Reviewing toolbar | | Right-click comment balloon or comment in reviewing pane, and then click Delete Comment | |
| Comment, insert | 442 | [icon] on Reviewing toolbar | Insert \| Comment | | Alt + Ctrl + M |
| Comment, modify | 445 | Click in comment balloon or in reviewing pane, edit text | | | |

| Word Task | Page | Mouse | Menu Bar | Shortcut Menu | Shortcut Keys |
|---|---|---|---|---|---|
| Comment, read in reviewing pane | 443 | on Reviewing toolbar; click in text that has a comment, and then read in reviewing pane | | | |
| Copy | 102 | on Standard toolbar | Edit \| Copy | Right-click selected text, Copy | Ctrl + C |
| Create, new document | 33 | Start Word (opens blank document) on Standard toolbar<br><br>Click *Create a new document* in Getting Started task pane<br><br>Click *Blank document* in New Document task pane | File \| New | | Ctrl + N |
| Create, new folder | 28 | in Open or Save As dialog box | | | |
| Create, new table | 203 | on Standard toolbar | Table \| Insert \| Table | | |
| Crop image | 535 | on Picture toolbar | | | |
| Cross-reference, insert | 690 | | Insert \| Reference \| Cross-reference | | |
| Cut | 99, 104 | on Standard toolbar | Edit \| Cut | Right-click selected text or object, Cut | Ctrl + X |
| Date and time, insert in header or footer | 120 | on Header and Footer toolbar | Insert \| Date and Time | | Alt + Shift + D and Alt + Shift + T |
| Delete, text | 39, 97 | | Edit \| Clear \| Contents | | Bksp or Delete |
| Digital signature, attach | 853 | | Tools \| Options \| Security tab; Digital Signatures | | |
| Digital signature, create | 851 | start on Windows taskbar; All Programs \| Microsoft Office \| Microsoft Office Tools \| Digital Certificate for VBA Projects | | | |
| Display, ScreenTip | 13 | Point to a screen element | | | |
| Display, toolbar | 4 | | View \| Toolbars | Right-click any toolbar, click toolbar name | |
| Display/hide, task pane | 9 | | View \| Task Pane | | Ctrl + F1 |
| Document, accept merge changes | 461 | on Reviewing toolbar | | | |

| Word Task | Page | Mouse | Menu Bar | Shortcut Menu | Shortcut Keys |
|---|---|---|---|---|---|
| Document, attach to email message | 457 | | File \| Send To \| Mail Recipient (as Attachment) | | |
| Document, create new | 33 | Start Word (opens blank document) <br><br> ☐ on Standard toolbar <br><br> Click Create a new document in Getting Started task pane <br><br> Click Blank document in New Document task pane | File \| New | | Ctrl + N |
| Document, protect | 843, 847 | | Tools \| Protect Document; perform steps in Protect Document task pane | | |
| Document, reject merge changes | 461 | ✍ ▾ on Reviewing toolbar | | | |
| Document, save | 34 | ☐ | File \| Save | | Ctrl + S |
| Document, save in another format | 455 | | File \| Save As; change *Save as type* to another format | | |
| Document map | 693 | ☐ on Standard toolbar | View \| Document Map | | |
| Documents, compare and merge | 459 | | Tools \| Compare and Merge Documents | | |
| Drag-and-drop, turn off/on | 104 | | Tools \| Options \| Edit tab | | |
| Drawing canvas, hide | 182 | | Tools \| Options \| General tab | | |
| Drop cap, create | 351 | | Format \| Drop Cap | | |
| Editing restrictions, set | 847 | | Tools \| Protect Document; perform Steps 2 and 3 in Protect Document task pane | | |
| Em dash, insert | 128 | | Insert \| Symbols \| Special Characters tab | | Alt + Ctrl + − |
| Email, document as attachment | 457 | | File \| Send To \| Mail Recipient (as Attachment) | | |
| Endnote insert | 130 | | Insert \| Reference \| Endnote | | Alt + Ctrl + F |
| Excel chart, edit embedded chart | 577 | | Double-click embedded chart; make changes | Right-click embedded chart; Chart Object; Edit | |
| Excel chart, embed | 572 | ☐ on Excel Standard toolbar; ☐ on Word Standard toolbar | Edit \| Copy (in Excel); Edit \| Paste (or Paste Special) in Word | Right-click chart in Excel; Copy \| right-click in Word; Paste | Ctrl + C in Excel; Ctrl + V in Word |

| Word Task | Page | Mouse | Menu Bar | Shortcut Menu | Shortcut Keys |
|---|---|---|---|---|---|
| Excel chart, link to | 581 | | Edit \| Copy (in Excel); Edit \| Paste Special (in Word); Paste link | | |
| Excel chart, modify linked chart | 583 | | Change the data (in Excel); Edit \| Update Link (in Word) | Change the data (in Excel); right-click the chart (in Word); Update Link (if necessary) | F9 |
| Excel data, embed | 575 | | Edit \| Copy (in Excel); Edit \| Paste Special (in Word) \| click Microsoft Office Excel Worksheet Object | | |
| Excel worksheet, edit embedded worksheet object | 577 | | Double-click embedded worksheet object; make changes | Right-click embedded worksheet; Worksheet Object; Edit | |
| Exit Word | 31 | X | File \| Exit | | Alt + F4 |
| File, close | 48 | X on menu bar | File \| Close | | |
| File, view properties | 435 | | File \| Properties | | |
| File extensions, show/hide | 892, 935 | | In My Computer or Windows Explorer: Tools \| Folder Options \| View tab; *Hide extensions for known file types* | Right-click Windows Start button; Explore; Tools \| Folder Options \| View tab; *Hide extensions for known file types* | |
| Find and replace text | 95 | on Select  Browse Object palette and then click Replace tab | Edit \| Replace | | Ctrl + H |
| Folder, create new | 28 | in Open or Save As dialog box | | | |
| Font, apply bold or italic style | 47 | B  I | Format \| Font, Font style | Right-click and then click Font | Ctrl + B or Ctrl + I |
| Font, apply underline | 47 | U | Format \| Font, Underline | Right-click and then click Font | Ctrl + U |
| Font, change | 44 | Times New Roman ▾ on Formatting toolbar | Format \| Font | Right-click and then click Font | |
| Font, change size | 44 | 12 ▾ on Formatting toolbar | Format \| Font, Size | Right-click and then click Font | |
| Font, color | 274 | A ▾ on Formatting toolbar | Format \| Font, Font color | Right-click and then click Font | |
| Font, effects | 275 | | Format \| Font, Effects, select effect | Right-click and then click Font | |
| Footnote, insert | 130 | | Insert \| Reference \| Footnote | | Alt + Ctrl + F |

| Word Task | Page | Mouse | Menu Bar | Shortcut Menu | Shortcut Keys |
|-----------|------|-------|----------|---------------|---------------|
| **Format Painter** | 94 | on Standard toolbar (double-click to apply repeatedly) | | | Ctrl + Shift + C and Ctrl + Shift + V |
| **Format, paragraph** | 366 | | Format \| Paragraph | Paragraph | |
| **Formatting marks, display/hide** | 17 | ¶ on Standard toolbar | Tools \| Options \| View tab, Formatting marks | | |
| **Form field, rename bookmark** | 751 | on Forms toolbar; Bookmark  Double-click form field; Bookmark | | Right-click form field; Properties; Bookmark | |
| **Form fields, add help text** | 741 | on Forms toolbar; click Add Help Text  Double-click form field; click Add Help Text | | Right-click form field; Properties; click Add Help Text | |
| **Form fields, modify** | 741 | on Forms toolbar  Double-click form field | | Right-click form field; Properties | |
| **Form fields, reset** | 741 | on Forms toolbar | | | |
| **Form fields, set options** | 738 | on Forms toolbar  Double-click form field | | Right-click form field; Properties | |
| **Form letters, set up mail merge** | 601 | on Mail Merge toolbar; Letters | Tools \| Letters and Mailings \| Mail Merge; Letters in task pane | | |
| **Form letters, merge to Word document** | 612 | on Mail Merge toolbar | | | |
| **Form letters, print** | 611 | on Mail Merge toolbar  on Standard toolbar | File \| Print in merged document | | Ctrl + P |
| **Form, add check box field** | 736 | on Forms toolbar | | | |
| **Form, add drop-down form field** | 737 | on Forms toolbar | | | |
| **Form, add text field** | 733, 736 | abl on Forms toolbar | | | |
| **Form, apply theme** | 743 | | Format \| Theme | | |

| Word Task | Page | Mouse | Menu Bar | Shortcut Menu | Shortcut Keys |
|---|---|---|---|---|---|
| Form, create custom | 732 | Open form document; insert text and use Forms toolbar to insert form fields | | | |
| Form, fill in | 747, 753 | Open form document; enter or select data in form field; press Tab to move to next field | | | |
| Form, insert table | 735 | ▦ on Forms or Standard toolbar | | | |
| Form, protect | 740, 746 | 🔒 on Forms toolbar | | | |
| Form, save as template | 746 | | File \| Save As; click Save as type arrow; Document Template | | |
| Form, set security level | 753 | | Tools \| Macro \| Security \| Security Level tab | | |
| Form, test | 740 | Fill in sample data | | | |
| Formatting marks, display/hide | 17 | ¶ on Standard toolbar | Tools \| Options \| View tab; Fomatting marks | | |
| Formatting restrictions, set | 843 | | Tools \| Protect Document; perform Steps 1 and 3 in Protect Document task pane | | |
| Forms toolbar, display | 733 | | View \| Toolbars \| Forms<br><br>Tools \| Customize; Toolbars tab; click check box next to Forms | Right-click toolbar; Forms | |
| Frame, add text | 824 | Click in frame; type | | | |
| Frame, change border properties | 834 | 🖼 on Frames toolbar; Borders tab | | Right-click in frame; Frame Properties; Borders tab | |
| Frame, change properties | 834 | 🖼 on Frames toolbar; Frame tab | | Right-click in frame; Frame Properties; Frame tab | |
| Frame, insert above | 822 | New Frame Above on Frames toolbar | | | |
| Frame, insert graphics | 826 | 🖼 on Drawing toolbar | Insert \| Picture \| From File<br><br>Insert \| Picture \| Clip Art | | |
| Frame, insert to left | 822 | New Frame Left on Frames toolbar | | | |

| Word Task | Page | Mouse | Menu Bar | Shortcut Menu | Shortcut Keys |
|---|---|---|---|---|---|
| Frame, insert Word file | 827 | | Insert \| File | | |
| Frame, resize | 828 | Drag frame border | | | |
| Frame, save current | 822 | [icon] on Standard toolbar | | Right-click in frame; Save Current Frame As | |
| Frames toolbar, display/hide | 822, 828 | | View \| Toolbars \| Frames<br><br>Tools \| Customize; Toolbars tab; click check box next to Frames | Right-click a toolbar; Frames | |
| Graphic image, move | 181 | Drag image; [icon] and [icon] on Standard toolbar | Edit \| Cut<br>Edit \| Paste | Right-click image, Cut, and then right-click at new location and choose Paste | Ctrl + X and Ctrl + V<br><br>Select image, ← → ↑ ↓ |
| Header or footer, add to document | 26 | Double-click in a header or footer area on a page (only if header or footer is not empty) | View \| Header and Footer; position insertion point in header or footer area and then enter text | | |
| Header or footer, close and return to document | 26 | Close on Header and Footer toolbar<br><br>Double-click in text area of document | | | |
| Header or footer, insert date and time | 120 | [icon] [icon] on Header and Footer toolbar | Insert \| Date and Time | | Alt + Shift + D and Alt + Shift + T |
| Header or footer, insert page numbers | 117 | [icon] on Header and Footer toolbar | Insert \| Page Numbers | | Alt + Shift + P |
| Header or footer, switch between | 26 | [icon] on Header and Footer toolbar | | | |
| Help, display in Word | 51 | [icon] on Standard toolbar<br><br>Click the *Type a question for help* box; type text and press Enter | Help \| Microsoft Office Word Help | | F1 |
| Help, hide Office Assistant | 8 | | Help \| Hide the Office Assistant | Right-click Office Assistant and then click Hide | |
| Help, show Office Assistant | 51 | | Help \| Show the Office Assistant | | |
| Hide/Show, space between pages (Print Layout View) | 377 | Point between pages to display Hide/Show White Space pointer, and then click | Tools \| Options \| View tab, White space between pages | | |

| Word Task | Page | Mouse | Menu Bar | Shortcut Menu | Shortcut Keys |
|---|---|---|---|---|---|
| Hyperlink, graphic | 282 | on Standard toolbar | Insert \| Hyperlink | Right-click and then click Hyperlink | Ctrl + K |
| Hyperlink, modify | 283 | on Standard toolbar | Insert \| Hyperlink | Right-click and then click Edit Hyperlink | Ctrl + K |
| Hyperlink, text | 279 | on Standard toolbar | Insert \| Hyperlink | Right-click and then click Hyperlink | Ctrl + K |
| Image, brightness | 539 | and on Picture toolbar | Format \| Picture \| Picture tab; Brightness | Right-click on picture; Format Picture \| Picture tab; Brightness | |
| Image, contrast | 539 | and on Picture toolbar | Format \| Picture \| Picture tab; Contrast | Right-click on picture; Format Picture \| Picture tab; Contrast | |
| Image, crop | 535 | on Picture toolbar | | | |
| Image, resize | 538 | Drag a sizing handle | Format \| Picture \| Size tab; set Height and Width | Right-click on picture; Format Picture \| Size tab; set Height and Width | |
| Image, rotate | 535 | on Picture toolbar<br><br>Drag rotate handle | Format \| Picture \| Size tab; Rotation | Right-click on picture; Format Picture \| Size tab; Rotation | |
| Image, scale | 538 | | Format \| Picture \| Size tab; set Scale options | Right-click on picture; Format Picture \| Size tab; set Scale options | |
| Image, wrapping style | 539 | on Picture toolbar | Format \| Picture \| Layout tab | Right-click on picture; Format Picture \| Layout tab | |
| Indent, decrease left indent | 197 | on Formatting toolbar | Format \| Paragraph \| Indents and Spacing tab, Left | Right-click, Paragraph \| Indents and Spacing tab \| Left | Ctrl + Shift + M |
| Indent, first line | 93 | on ruler | Format \| Paragraph \| Indents and Spacing tab, Special | Right-click, Paragraph \| Indents and Spacing tab, Special | |
| Indent, hanging | 136 | on ruler | Format \| Paragraph \| Indents and Spacing tab, Special | Right-click, Paragraph \| Indents and Spacing tab, Special | Ctrl + T |
| Indent, increase left indent | 197 | on Formatting toolbar<br><br>Drag Left Indent marker on ruler | Format \| Paragraph \| Indents and Spacing tab, Left | Right-click, Paragraph \| Indents and Spacing tab \| Left | Ctrl + M |
| Indent, left | 93 | on ruler | Format \| Paragraph \| Indents and Spacing tab, Left | Right-click, Paragraph \| Indents and Spacing tab, Left | |
| Index and reference tables, update all | 673 | | Edit \| Select All; F9 | Right-click in document; Update Fields | Ctrl + A ; F9 |

| Word Task | Page | Mouse | Menu Bar | Shortcut Menu | Shortcut Keys |
|---|---|---|---|---|---|
| Index, create | 659 | | Insert \| Reference \| Index and Tables \| Index tab | | |
| Index, edit entry | 666 | Edit in bracketed field code, not in the index | | | |
| Index, mark entry | 663 | | Insert \| Reference \| Index and Tables \| Index tab; click Mark Entry | | Alt + Shift + X |
| Index, update | 666 | | | Right-click in index; Update Field | F9 |
| Insert mode, toggle between overtype/ insert | 40 | Double-click OVR in status bar | | | Insert |
| Insert, clip art | 172 | ▣ on Drawing toolbar<br><br>▼ in task pane, then click Clip Art | Insert \| Picture \| Clip Art | | Ctrl + F1, then choose Clip Art |
| Insert, text box | 182 | ▣ on Drawing toolbar | Insert \| Text Box | | |
| Keyboard shortcut | 9 | | | | Press and hold down the first key, such as Ctrl, and then press the second key (if any), such as F1 |
| Labels, create with mail merge | 592, 594 | | Tools \| Letters and Mailings \| Mail Merge; Labels in task pane | | |
| Labels, edit after mail merge | 598 | Click in label; edit text | | | |
| Labels, preview after merge | 599 | ▣ on the Standard toolbar | | | |
| Labels, print after merge | 599 | In the Mail Merge task pane, click Print | | | |
| Line break, insert | 677 | | Insert \| Break; Text wrapping break | | Shift + Enter |
| Line spacing | 88 | ▣▼ on Formatting toolbar | Format \| Paragraph \| Indents and Spacing tab, Line spacing | Right-click, Paragraph \| Indents and Spacing tab, Line spacing | Ctrl + 1 (single)<br>Ctrl + 2 (double)<br>Ctrl + 5 (space and one half) |
| List style, create for selected list | 369 | Apply formatting, and then click New Style button in Styles and Formatting task pane; in Style type box, click List | | | |

| Word Task | Page | Mouse | Menu Bar | Shortcut Menu | Shortcut Keys |
|-----------|------|-------|----------|---------------|---------------|
| Macro, create to run when document closes | 765 | Double-click REC on status bar; name the macro AutoClose; click Store macro in arrow; select current document<br><br>[icon] on Visual Basic toolbar; name the macro AutoClose; click Store macro in arrow; select current document | Tools \| Macro \| Record New Macro; name the macro AutoClose; click Store macro in arrow; select current document | | |
| Macro, delete | 761 | | Tools \| Macro \| Macros; select macro name; Delete | | Alt + F8; select macro name; Delete |
| Macro, edit using VBA editor | 767 | | Tools \| Macro \| Macros; select macro name; Edit | | Alt + F8; select macro name; Edit |
| Macro, record (keyboard-activated) | 755 | Double-click REC on status bar; click Keyboard<br><br>[icon] on Visual Basic toolbar; click Keyboard | Tools \| Macro \| Record New Macro; click Keyboard | | |
| Macro, record (toolbar-activated) | 762 | Double-click REC on status bar; click Toolbars; click Commands tab; drag command to a toolbar<br><br>[icon] on Visual Basic toolbar; click Toolbars; click Commands tab; drag command to a toolbar | Tools \| Macro \| Record New Macro; click Toolbars; click Commands tab; drag command to a toolbar | | |
| Macro, run | 759 | [icon] on Visual Basic toolbar | Tools \| Macro \| Macros; select macro name; Run | | Alt + F8; select macro name; Run |
| Macro, stop recording | 755 | Double-click REC on status bar<br><br>[icon] on Stop Recording toolbar | | | |
| Mail merge, add recipients | 604 | [icon] on Mail Merge toolbar; click Edit; click New Entry | | | |
| Mail merge, display toolbar | 601 | | View \| Toolbars \| Mail Merge<br><br>Tools \| Customize; Toolbars tab; click check box next to Mail Merge | Right-click toolbar; Mail Merge | |
| Mail merge, edit merged labels | 598 | Click in label; edit text | | | |
| Mail merge, edit recipients | 604 | [icon] on Mail Merge toolbar; clear check box to remove recipient; click Edit to change data | | | |

| Word Task | Page | Mouse | Menu Bar | Shortcut Menu | Shortcut Keys |
|---|---|---|---|---|---|
| Mail merge, form letters to Word document | 612 | on Mail Merge toolbar | | | |
| Mail merge, highlight merged fields | 609 | on Mail Merge toolbar | | | |
| Mail merge, insert merge fields | 606 | on Mail Merge toolbar | | | |
| Mail merge, open data source | 604 | on Mail Merge toolbar | | | |
| Mail merge, preview merged data | 609 | on Mail Merge toolbar; navigate using | | | |
| Mail merge, set up form letter | 601 | on Mail Merge toolbar; Letters | Tools \| Letters and Mailings \| Mail Merge; Letters in task pane | | |
| Mail merge, set up labels | 592, 594 | on Mail Merge toolbar; Labels | Tools \| Letters and Mailings \| Mail Merge; Labels in task pane | | |
| Mail merge, sort recipients | 604 | on Mail Merge toolbar; click a column heading | | | |
| Margins, set | 84 | Double-click at right of ruler and then click | File \| Page Setup \| Margins tab | | |
| Markup, show/hide | 446 | Final Showing Markup on Reviewing toolbar | View \| Markup | | |
| Master document, add footer | 656 | Double-click in footer area on a page (only if footer is not empty) | View \| Header and Footer; position insertion point in footer area and then enter text | | |
| Master document, create from blank document | 644 | on Standard toolbar; on View toolbar; create outline headings and then write and insert subdocuments | File \| New \| Blank Document; View \| Outline; create outline headings and then write and insert subdocuments | | |
| Master document, create from existing document | 644 | on View buttons; assign heading styles; select heading of subdocument content; on Outlining toolbar | View \| Outline; assign heading styles; select heading of subdocument content; on Outlining toolbar | | |
| Master document, print with subdocuments | 656 | on Standard toolbar | File \| Print | | Ctrl + P |

| Word Task | Page | Mouse | Menu Bar | Shortcut Menu | Shortcut Keys |
|---|---|---|---|---|---|
| Memo, create from template | 428 | Click *On my computer* on New Document task pane, and then click Memos tab | File \| New, *On my computer,* click Memos tab | | |
| Memo, replace placeholder text | 430 | Click in a placeholder and then type | | | |
| Menu bar, use | 9 | Click menu name and then click a command | | | Alt + under-lined letter on menu and then underlined letter of command |
| Menu, display full | 9 | Double-click menu name in menu bar<br><br>Wait a few seconds after displaying menu<br><br>Click expand arrows at bottom of menu | Tools \| Customize \| Options tab, Always show full menus | | |
| Menu, display full always | 9 | | Tools \| Customize \| Options tab, Always show full menus | Right-click any toolbar and then click Customize; on Options tab, select Always show full menus | |
| Menu, use keyboard shortcut shown on menu | 9 | | | | Press and hold down the first key, such as Ctrl, and then press the second key (if any), such as F1 |
| Merge, accept changes | 461 | on Reviewing toolbar | | | |
| Merge, documents | 460 | | Tools \| Compare and Merge Documents | | |
| Merge, reject changes | 461 | on Reviewing toolbar | | | |
| Move, graphic image | 181 | Drag image; and on Standard toolbar | Edit \| Cut and Edit \| Paste | Right-click image, Cut, and then right-click at new location and choose Paste | Ctrl + X and Ctrl + V<br><br>Select image ← → ↑ ↓ |
| Move, text | 99, 104 | and on Standard toolbar<br><br>Drag selected text to new location | Edit \| Cut Edit \| Paste | Right-click selected text, Cut, and then right-click at new location and choose Paste | Ctrl + X and Ctrl + V |
| Multiple pages, preview | 686 | on Standard toolbar; on Print Preview toolbar | View \| Zoom \| Many pages | | |

| Word Task | Page | Mouse | Menu Bar | Shortcut Menu | Shortcut Keys |
|---|---|---|---|---|---|
| Navigate, down, a line at a time | 13 | ⌄ at the bottom of vertical scroll bar | | | ↓ |
| Navigate, up/down, screen at a time | 13 | Click in gray area above/below scroll box on vertical scroll bar | | | Page Up PageDown |
| Navigate, to beginning of current line | 16 | Click at beginning of line | | | Home |
| Navigate, to beginning of document | 16 | Drag vertical scroll bar to top, click before first line | | | Ctrl + Home |
| Navigate, to beginning of next word | 16 | Click at beginning of next word | | | Ctrl + → |
| Navigate, to beginning of previous word | 16 | Click at beginning of previous word | | | Ctrl + ← |
| Navigate, to end of current line | 16 | Click at end of line | | | End |
| Navigate, to end of document | 16 | Drag vertical scroll bar to lower end, click after last line | | | Ctrl + End |
| Navigate, up a line at a time | 13 | ⌃ at the top of the vertical scroll bar | | | ↑ |
| Normal view, display | 18 | ☰ in lower left corner of Word window | View \| Normal | | Alt + Ctrl + N |
| Numbered list, create | 110 | ▤ on Formatting toolbar | Format \| Bullets and Numbering | Select text, right-click Bullets and Numbering | |
| Object, insert | 530 | | Insert \| Object \| Create New tab | | |
| Object, modify | 532 | | Format \| Object | Right-click object; Format Object | |
| Open, existing document | 8 | ⌹ on Standard toolbar

More or document name in Getting Started task pane | File \| Open

File \| document name at bottom of File menu | | Ctrl + O |
| Outline entry, collapse | 395 | ▬ on Outlining toolbar

Double-click Collapse indicator | | | |
| Outline entry, demote | 390 | ⇨ on Outlining toolbar | | Increase Indent | Tab or Alt + Shift + → |

| Word Task | Page | Mouse | Menu Bar | Shortcut Menu | Shortcut Keys |
|---|---|---|---|---|---|
| Outline entry, expand | 392 | [icon] on Outlining toolbar<br><br>Double-click Expand indicator | | | |
| Outline entry, move up | 392 | [icon] on Outlining toolbar | | | In Outline View, drag Expand/ Collapse button up |
| Outline entry, move down | 392 | [icon] on Outlining toolbar | | | In Outline View, drag Expand/ Collapse button down |
| Outline entry, promote | 395 | [icon] on Outlining toolbar | | Decrease Indent | Shift + Tab or Alt + Shift + ← |
| Outline view, display | 18 | [icon] in lower left corner of Word window | View \| Outline | | Alt + Ctrl + O |
| Outline, set numbering | 382 | | Format \| Bullets and Numbering \| Outline Numbered tab | Bullets and Numbering \| Outline Numbered tab | |
| Page break, insert manual | 130 | | Insert \| Break, Page break | | Ctrl + Enter |
| Page numbers, different on first page | 117 | [icon] on Header and Footer toolbar | File \| Page Setup \| Layout tab | | |
| Page numbers, format in header or footer | 117 | [icon] on Header and Footer toolbar | | | |
| Page numbers, in header or footer | 117 | [icon] on Header and Footer toolbar | Insert \| Page Numbers | | Alt + Shift + P |
| Page setup | 34 | Double-click left or right of ruler | File \| Page Setup | | |
| Paragraph style, create for selected paragraph | 366 | Apply formatting, and then click New Style button in Styles and Formatting task pane<br><br>Normal [box] on Formatting toolbar; type a new name and then press Enter | | | |
| Paragraph, border | 271 | [icon] on Formatting toolbar | Format \| Borders and Shading \| Borders tab, Box | | |
| Paragraph, decrease left indent | 112 | [icon] on Formatting toolbar | Format \| Paragraph \| Indents and Spacing tab, Left | Right-click, Paragraph \| Indents and Spacing tab, Left | Ctrl + Shift + M |
| Paragraph, increase left indent | 112 | [icon] on Formatting toolbar | Format \| Paragraph \| Indents and Spacing tab, Left | Right-click, Paragraph \| Indents and Spacing tab, Left | Ctrl + Shift + M |

| Word Task | Page | Mouse | Menu Bar | Shortcut Menu | Shortcut Keys |
|-----------|------|-------|----------|---------------|---------------|
| Paragraph, format | 366 | | Format \| Paragraph | Paragraph | |
| Paragraph, hanging indent | 136 | on ruler | Format \| Paragraph \| Indents and Spacing tab, Special | Right-click, Paragraph \| Indents and Spacing tab, Special | Ctrl + T |
| Paragraph, indent first line | 93 | on ruler | Format \| Paragraph \| Indents and Spacing tab, Special | Right-click, Paragraph \| Indents and Spacing tab, Special | |
| Paragraph, Indent left margin | 88 | on ruler | Format \| Paragraph \| Indents and Spacing tab, left | Right-click, Paragraph \| Indents and Spacing tab, Left | |
| Paragraph, line spacing | 88 | on Formatting toolbar | Format \| Paragraph \| Indents and Spacing tab, Line spacing | Right-click, Paragraph \| Indents and Spacing tab, Line spacing | Ctrl + 1 (single) Ctrl + 2 (double) Ctrl + 5 (space and one half) |
| Paragraph, shading | 273 | | Format \| Borders and Shading \| Shading tab | | |
| Paragraph, spacing | 90, 112 | | Format \| Paragraph \| Indents and Spacing tab, Before/After | Right-click, Paragraph \| Indents and Spacing tab, Before/After | |
| Paragraphs, keep together | 684 | | Format \| Paragraph \| Line and Page Breaks tab; Keep with next | Right-click first paragraph; Paragraph \| Line and Page Breaks tab; Keep with next | |
| Password, set to modify document | 840 | | Tools \| Options; Security tab; type in *Password to modify* text box; OK; retype same password | | |
| Password, set to open document | 840 | | Tools \| Options; Security tab; type in *Password to open* text box; OK; retype same password | | |
| Paste | 99 | on Standard toolbar Click item in Office Clipboard | Edit \| Paste | Right-click, then choose Paste | Ctrl + V |
| Paste options | 99 | after Paste | | | |
| Picture, insert | 124 | on Drawing toolbar then choose | Insert \| Picture \| From File | | Ctrl + F1 and then choose Clip Art |
| Picture, resize | 179 | Drag sizing handle on Picture toolbar | Format \| Picture \| Size tab | Right-click image, Format Picture \| Size tab | |
| Picture, wrap text around | 176 | on Picture toolbar Draw ▾ on Drawing toolbar, Text Wrapping | Format \| Picture \| Layout tab | Right-click image, Format Picture \| Layout tab | |
| PowerPoint presentation, link to | 585 | | Insert \| Object \| Create from File tab; Browse for file; select Link to file | | |

| Word Task | Page | Mouse | Menu Bar | Shortcut Menu | Shortcut Keys |
|---|---|---|---|---|---|
| Preview, as Web page | 285 | | File \| Web Page Preview | | |
| Print Layout view, display | 18 | [icon] in lower left corner of Word window | View \| Print Layout | | Alt + Ctrl + P |
| Print, document | 31, 48 | [icon] on Standard toolbar | File \| Print | | Ctrl + P |
| Print, document properties | 437 | | File \| Print; click Print what, and then click Document properties | | |
| Print, form letters | 611 | [icon] on Mail Merge toolbar [icon] on Standard toolbar | File \| Print in merged document | | Ctrl + P |
| Print, from preview | 187 | [icon] on Print Preview toolbar | | | |
| Print, preview | 34 | [icon] on Standard toolbar | File \| Print Preview | | Ctrl + F2 |
| Readability statistics, review | 697 | | Tools \| Options \| Spelling & Grammar tab; Show readability statistics check box; run spell check | | |
| Reading Layout view, close | 18 | [icon] Close on Reading Layout toolbar | | | |
| Reading Layout view, display | 18 | [icon] in lower left corner of Word window [icon] Read on Standard toolbar | View \| Reading Layout | | |
| Redo an action (after Undo) | 106 | [icon] on Standard toolbar | Edit \| Redo | | Ctrl + Y |
| Research | 293 | [icon] on Standard toolbar, type a search topic and select a source | Tools \| Research | | Alt + click word(s) |
| Resize image | 538 | Drag resizing handle | Format \| Picture \| Size tab; set Height and Width | Right-click image; Format Picture \| Size tab; set Height and Width | |
| Reviewing pane, show/hide | 443 | [icon] on Reviewing toolbar | | | Alt + Shift + C (hide only) |
| Rotate image | 535 | [icon] on Picture toolbar Drag rotate handle | Format \| Picture \| Size tab; Rotation | Right-click image; Format Picture \| Size tab; Rotation | |
| Ruler, display/hide | 84, 828 | | View \| Ruler | | |
| Save, document | 34 | [icon] | File \| Save | | Ctrl + S |

| Word Task | Page | Mouse | Menu Bar | Shortcut Menu | Shortcut Keys |
|---|---|---|---|---|---|
| Save, document (new name, location, or type) | 28 | | File \| Save As | | F12 |
| Save, document as Web page | 286 | | File \| Save as Web Page | | |
| Save, document in another format | 455 | | File \| Save As; change *Save as type* to another format | | |
| Scale image | 538 | | Format \| Picture \| Size tab; set Scale options | Right-click image; Format Picture \| Size tab; set Scale options | |
| ScreenTip, display | 13 | Point to a screen element | | | |
| Section break, insert | 677 | | Insert \| Break; click a Section break type | | |
| Sections, apply different headers/footers | 680 | [icon] on Header and Footer toolbar | Click in section; View \| Header and Footer; click to deselect Link to Previous button | | |
| Sections, apply page formatting | 680 | | Click in section; Format \| Borders and Shading; choose settings; in *Apply to* list, click *This section* | Right-click in section; Borders and Shading; choose settings; in *Apply to* list, click *This section* | |
| Security, set password to modify document | 840 | | Tools \| Options; Security tab; type in *Password to modify* text box; OK; retype same password | | |
| Security, set password to open document | 840 | | Tools \| Options; Security tab; type in *Password to open* text box; OK; retype same password | | |
| Sort, paragraphs | 136 | [icon] or [icon] on Tables and Borders toolbar | Table \| Sort | | |
| Spelling and Grammar, check entire document | 23 | [icon] on Standard toolbar | Tools \| Spelling and Grammar, then choose an action for each suggestion | | F7 |
| Spelling and Grammar, check individual errors | 21 | | | Right-click word or phrase with red or green wavy underline and then choose a suggested correction or other action | |
| Spelling and Grammar, turn on/off features | 21 | | Tools \| Options \| Spelling & Grammar tab, then choose Check spelling as you type and/or Check grammar as you type | | |
| Start Word | 4 | [start] on Windows task-bar and then locate and click Microsoft Office Word 2003 | Start \| All Programs \| Microsoft Office \| Microsoft Office Word 2003 | | |

| Word Task | Page | Mouse | Menu Bar | Shortcut Menu | Shortcut Keys |
|---|---|---|---|---|---|
| **Statistics, view properties** | 435 | | File \| Properties \| Statistics tab | | |
| **Style area, display (Normal View)** | 360 | | Tools \| Options \| View tab, Style area width (increase) | | |
| **Style area, hide (Normal View)** | 362 | Drag style areas vertical border to left edge of window | Tools \| Options \| View tab, Style area width (set to 0) | | |
| **Style, apply** | 363, 365, 371 | Normal [ ] on Formatting toolbar<br><br>Click Style in Styles and Formatting task pane | | | |
| **Style, clear** | 365 | Normal [ ] on Formatting toolbar, and then click *Clear Formatting*<br><br>Click *Clear Formatting* in Styles and Formatting task pane | | | |
| **Style, modify** | 376 | In Styles and Formatting task pane, point to style, click arrow, and then click Modify | | Right-click style in Styles and Formatting task pane, and then click Modify | |
| **Styles and Formatting task pane, display/hide** | 360 | on Formatting toolbar | Format \| Styles and Formatting | | Ctrl + F1, then choose Styles and Formatting |
| **Stylesheet, modify** | 929 | In Notepad, edit the .xslt file | | | |
| **Stylesheet, save** | 929 | | In Notepad: File \| Save As; click *Save as type* arrow; All Files; click *Encoding* arrow; UTF-8; in File name box, type file name with .xslt extension; Save | | |
| **Stylesheet, use as XML data view** | 932 | Open .xml file; in XML Document task pane, click Browse; open a stylesheet (.xlst file) | | | |
| **Subdocument, collapse/expand** | 649 | or double-click the Expand icon or click a heading and to collapse or to expand | | | |
| **Subdocument, create** | 644 | on View buttons; select heading; on Outlining toolbar | View \| Outline; select heading; on Outlining toolbar | | |
| **Subdocument, create from existing file** | 651 | Place insertion point on section break line after an expanded subdocument; | | | |

| Word Task | Page | Mouse | Menu Bar | Shortcut Menu | Shortcut Keys |
|---|---|---|---|---|---|
| Subdocument, edit within master document | 654 | ▣ on View buttons; edit | | | |
| Subdocument, lock/unlock | 651 | ; click in subdocument; | | | |
| Subdocument, open in Print Layout view | 649 | To the left of a master document heading, double-click ▣ | | | |
| Subdocument, remove (convert into part of master document) | 656 | ▣ | | | |
| Summary, view or edit properties | 435, 437 | | File \| Properties \| Summary tab | | |
| Symbols, insert | 128 | | Insert \| Symbols \| Special Characters tab | | |
| Tab stops, clear | 195 | Drag tab stop off ruler | Format \| Tabs, Clear or Clear All | | |
| Tab stops, dot leaders | 197 | | Format \| Tabs, Leader | | |
| Tab stops, format | 195 | | Format \| Tabs, Set | | |
| Tab stops, move | 200 | Drag markers on ruler | Format \| Tabs, Set | | |
| Tab stops, set | 192 | ▣ on ruler; click to cycle tab types, then click ruler | Format \| Tabs, Set | | |
| Tab stops, use | 197 | | | | Tab while typing |
| Table of contents, create | 667 | | Insert \| Reference \| Index and Tables \| Table of Contents tab | | |
| Table of contents, customize | 669 | | Insert \| Reference \| Index and Tables \| Table of Contents tab | Right-click in table of contents; Edit Field | |
| Table of contents, update | 673 | | | Right-click in table of contents; Update Field | F9 |
| Table, add caption | 515 | | Insert \| Reference \| Caption | | |
| Table, add lines | 522 | ▣ on Tables and Borders toolbar | Table \| Draw Table | | |
| Table, add row at bottom | 513, 590 | Position insertion point in last row; ▣ ▾ arrow on Tables and Borders toolbar, Insert Rows Below | Table \| Insert \| Rows Below | | Tab in last cell |

| Word Task | Page | Mouse | Menu Bar | Shortcut Menu | Shortcut Keys |
|---|---|---|---|---|---|
| Table, align | 218 | Select table, [icon] or [icon] or [icon] on Formatting toolbar | Table \| Table Properties \| Table tab | Right-click, Table Properties, Table tab | |
| Table, align cells | 223 | [icon] on Tables and Borders toolbar | Table \| Table Properties \| Cell tab | Right-click in cell, Cell Alignment | |
| Table, AutoFormat | 222, 517 | [icon] on Tables and Borders toolbar | Table \| Table AutoFormat | Select table, right-click, Table AutoFormat | |
| Table, change border | 215 | [icon] on Tables and Borders toolbar | Format \| Borders and Shading \| Borders tab | Right-click, Borders and Shading \| Borders tab | |
| Table, column width | 208 | Drag column boundary | Table \| Table Properties \| Column tab, Preferred width | Right-click in column, Table Properties \| Column tab, Preferred width | |
| Table, convert from text | 219 | | Table \| Convert \| Text to Table | | |
| Table, create new | 203 | [icon] on Standard toolbar | Table \| Insert \| Table | | |
| Table, delete | 351 | | Click in table, Table \| Delete \| Table | | |
| Table, distribute columns evenly | 525 | [icon] on Tables and Borders toolbar | | | |
| Table, draw | 520 | [icon] on Tables and Borders toolbar | Table \| Draw Table | | |
| Table, fit text in cell | 510 | | Table \| Table Properties \| Cell tab; select Options, then select Fit text | Right-click in cell; Table Properties; click Cell tab, click Options, then click Fit text | |
| Table, fit to contents | 738 | | Table \| AutoFit \| AutoFit to Contents | Right-click in table; AutoFit \| AutoFit to Contents | |
| Table, format cell text | 211 | Formatting toolbar | | | |
| Table, insert column | 209 | [icon] arrow on Tables and Borders toolbar, Insert Columns to the Left or Insert Columns to the Right | Table \| Insert \| Columns to the Left or Columns to the Right | Right-click in selected column, Insert Columns | |
| Table, insert formula | 513 | | Table \| Formula | | |
| Table, insert row | 206 | [icon] arrow on Tables and Borders toolbar, Insert Rows Above or Insert Rows Below | Table \| Insert \| Rows Above or Rows Below | Right-click to left of row, Insert Rows | |

| Word Task | Page | Mouse | Menu Bar | Shortcut Menu | Shortcut Keys |
|---|---|---|---|---|---|
| Table, line style | 520 | [___] on Tables and Borders toolbar | Table \| Table Properties \| Table tab; Borders and Shading, Borders tab; Style | Right-click in cell; Borders and Shading, Borders tab; Style | |
| Table, merge selected cells | 223, 497 | on Tables and Borders toolbar | Table \| Merge Cells | Right-click in selected cells, Merge Cells | |
| Table, move between cells | 203 | Click in cell | | | Tab, Shift + Tab, → ← ↑ ↓ |
| Table, remove lines | 522 | on Tables and Borders toolbar | | | |
| Table, select | 218 | Click table move handle in Print Layout view | Table \| Select \| Table | | Alt + 5 |
| Table, shading cells | 213 | on Tables and Borders toolbar | Format \| Borders and Shading \| Shading tab | Right-click in selected cells, Borders and Shading \| Shading tab | |
| Table, shading color | 527 | on Tables and Borders toolbar | Table \| Table Properties \| Table tab; Borders and Shading, Shading tab | Right-click in cell; Borders and Shading, Shading tab | |
| Table, sort | 511 | (ascending) or (descending) on Tables and Borders toolbar | Table \| Sort | | |
| Table, text alignment | 504 | on Tables and Borders toolbar | Table \| Table Properties \| Cell tab | Right-click in cell, Cell Alignment | |
| Table, text direction | 502, 525 | on Tables and Borders toolbar | | Right-click in cell, Text Direction | |
| Table, wrap text around | 508 | | Table \| Table Properties \| Table tab; select Around | Right-click in cell; Table Properties; click Table tab, then click Around | |
| Tables and Borders toolbar, display | | on Standard toolbar | View \| Toolbars \| Tables and Borders | Right-click in any toolbar, click Tables and Borders | |
| Table style, apply | 495 | Normal on Formatting toolbar; on Formatting toolbar; click style name in task pane | Format \| Styles and Formatting; select style name | | Ctrl + Shift + S, ↑ or ↓ to display style, then Enter |
| Table style, create | 492 | on Formatting toolbar; New Style, then click Style type arrow and select Table | Format \| Styles and Formatting; New Style, then in Style type list, select Table | | |
| Task pane, display/hide | 9 | | View \| Task Pane | | Ctrl + F1 |

| Word Task | Page | Mouse | Menu Bar | Shortcut Menu | Shortcut Keys |
|---|---|---|---|---|---|
| Template, find on Web | 429 | Click *Templates on Office Online* on New Document task pane | File \| New, *Templates on Office Online* | | |
| Template, use to create document | 428, 747 | Click *On my computer* on New Document task pane | File \| New, *On my computer* | | |
| Text box, insert | 182 | [icon] on Drawing toolbar | Insert \| Text Box | | |
| Text box, move | 184 | Drag border; [icons] and on Standard toolbar | Edit \| Cut and Edit \| Paste | Right-click border, Cut, then right-click at new location and choose Paste | `Ctrl` + `X` and `Ctrl` + `V` `←` `→` `↑` `↓` |
| Text box, resize | 184 | Drag sizing handle | Format \| Text Box \| Size tab | Right-click border, Format Text Box \| Size tab | |
| Text, align | 86 | [alignment icons] | Format \| Paragraph \| Indents and Spacing tab, Alignment | Right-click, Paragraph \| Indents and Spacing tab, Alignment | `Ctrl` + `L` (left) `Ctrl` + `E` (center) `Ctrl` + `R` (right) `Ctrl` + `J` (justify) |
| Text, cancel selection | 42 | Click anywhere in document | | | |
| Text, change font | 44 | Times New Roman [box] on Formatting toolbar | Format \| Font | Right-click and then click Font | |
| Text, change font size | 44 | 12 [box] on Formatting toolbar | Format \| Font | Right-click and then click Font | |
| Text, character spacing | 356 | | Format \| Font \| Character Spacing tab | Font \| Character Spacing tab | |
| Text, copy | 102 | [icon] on Standard toolbar | Edit \| Copy | Right-click selected text, Copy | `Ctrl` + `C` |
| Text, delete | 39, 97 | | Edit \| Clear \| Contents | | `Bksp` or `Delete` |
| Text, drop cap | 351 | | Format \| Drop Cap | | |
| Text, enter | 34 | Click to place insertion point and then type text | | | |
| Text, find and replace | 95 | [icon] on Select Browse Object palette and then click Replace tab | Edit \| Replace | | `Ctrl` + `H` |
| Text, move (cut) | 99, 104 | [icons] and on Standard toolbar Drag selected text to new location | Edit \| Cut Edit \| Paste | Right-click selected text, Cut, click at new location, and choose Paste | `Ctrl` + `X` `Ctrl` + `V` |
| Text, new paragraph or blank line | 34 | | | | `Enter` once or twice |
| Text, overtype/ insert | 40 | Double-click OVR in status bar, then type | | | `Insert` and then type |

| Word Task | Page | Mouse | Menu Bar | Shortcut Menu | Shortcut Keys |
|---|---|---|---|---|---|
| Text, paste | 99 | on Standard toolbar | Edit \| Paste | Right-click and then choose Paste | Ctrl + V |
| Text, paste options | 99 | after pasting | | | |
| Text, select | 42 | Drag over text | | | Click at beginning, Shift + click at end of selection |
| Text, select consecutive lines | 42 | | | | Shift + ↑ or ↓ |
| Text, select consecutive paragraphs | 42 | | | | Shift + Ctrl ↑ or ↓ |
| Text, select entire document (including objects) | 42 | Triple-click in selection bar | Edit \| Select All | | Ctrl + A |
| Text, select line | 42 | Click next to line in selection bar | | | |
| Text, select one character at a time | 42 | | | | Shift + → or ← |
| Text, select one word at a time | 42, 97 | | | | Shift + Ctrl + → or ← |
| Text, select paragraph | 42 | Triple-click in paragraph  Double-click in selection bar next to paragraph | | | |
| Text, select sentence | 42 | | | | Ctrl + click sentence |
| Text, select word | 42 | Double-click word | | | |
| Text, shadow effect | 353 | | Format \| Font \| Font tab, Shadow | Font \| Font tab, Shadow | |
| Text, small caps effect | 354 | | Format \| Font \| Font tab, Small Caps | Font \| Font tab, Small Caps | Ctrl + Shift + K |
| Theme, apply to form | 743 | | Format \| Theme | | |
| Thesaurus | 299 | on Standard toolbar, select Thesaurus in Research task pane | Tools \| Language \| Thesaurus | Right-click a word, Synonyms \| Thesaurus | Shift + F7 |
| Thumbnails, view | 694 | | View \| Thumbnails | | |
| Toolbar, display | 4 | | View \| Toolbars | Right-click any toolbar, click toolbar name | |

| Word Task | Page | Mouse | Menu Bar | Shortcut Menu | Shortcut Keys |
|---|---|---|---|---|---|
| Toolbars, show on one or two rows | 4 | ▪ on Standard or Formatting toolbar, Show Buttons on One Row / Two Rows | Tools \| Customize \| Options tab, Show Standard and Formatting toolbars on two rows<br><br>View \| Toolbars \| Customize \| Options tab, Show Standard and Formatting toolbars on two rows | Right-click any toolbar and then click Customize; on Options tab, select or clear Show Standard and Formatting toolbars on two rows | |
| Track changes, accept change | 452 | ▨ ▾ on Reviewing toolbar | | | |
| Track changes, locate next change | 449 | ▧ on Reviewing toolbar | | | |
| Track changes, reject change | 451 | ▨ ▾ on Reviewing toolbar | | | |
| Track changes, reviewers | 449 | Show ▾ on Reviewing toolbar; click Reviewers and then click All Reviewers or a reviewer's name | | | |
| Track changes, show settings | 449 | Show ▾ on Reviewing toolbar | | | |
| Track changes, show/hide markup | 446 | Final Showing Markup ▾ on Reviewing toolbar | View \| Markup | | |
| Track changes, turn on/off | 446 | Show ▾ on Reviewing toolbar | Tools \| Track Changes | Right-click a tracked change, and then click Track Changes | Ctrl + Shift + E |
| Transforms, save | 929 | | In Notepad: File \| Save As; click *Save as type* arrow; All Files; click *Encoding* arrow; UTF-8; in File name box, type file name with .xslt extension; Save | | |
| Transforms, use | 929 | | In Notepad: File \| Open; click *Files of type* arrow; All Files; locate and open file with .xslt extension | | |
| Undo an action | 106 | � ▾ on Standard toolbar | Edit \| Undo | | Ctrl + Z |
| VBA editor, close | 767 | ✕ in Microsoft Visual Basic title bar | File \| Close and Return to Microsoft Word | | Alt + Q |
| VBA editor, use | 767 | | Tools \| Macro \| Macros; select macro name; Edit<br><br>Tools \| Macro \| Visual Basic Editor | | Alt + F8; select macro name; Edit<br><br>Alt + F11 |

| Word Task | Page | Mouse | Menu Bar | Shortcut Menu | Shortcut Keys |
|---|---|---|---|---|---|
| VBA, write procedure | 769 | | Tools \| Macro \| Visual Basic Editor; type code | | Alt + F11 ; type code |
| Versions, create | 856 | | File \| Versions; Save Now | | |
| Versions, delete | 860 | Double-click Versions icon on status bar; Select version; Delete | File \| Versions; Select version; Delete | | |
| Versions, view | 859 | | File \| Versions; click a version; Open | | |
| View, Normal | 18 | ▤ in lower left corner of Word window | View \| Normal | | Alt + Ctrl + N |
| View, Outline | 18 | ▤ in lower left corner of Word window | View \| Outline | | Alt + Ctrl + O |
| View, Print Layout | 18 | ▤ in lower left corner of Word window | View \| Print Layout | | Alt + Ctrl + P |
| View, Reading Layout | 18 | ▤ in lower left corner of Word window; 📖 Read on Standard toolbar | View \| Reading Layout | | |
| View, Web Layout | 18 | ▤ in lower left corner of corner of Word window | View \| Web Layout | | |
| Watermark, create | 745 | | Format \| Background \| Printed Watermark | | |
| Web Layout view, display | 18 | ▤ in lower left corner of Word window | View \| Web Layout | | |
| Web page, add background | 829 | | Format \| Background | | |
| Web page, add theme | 829 | | Format \| Theme | | |
| Web page, capture as image | 834 | In browser: Shift + PrtScr ; in Word: 🖻 on Standard toolbar | In browser: Shift + PrtScr ; in Word: Edit \| Paste | In browser: Shift + PrtScr ; in Word: right-click; Paste | In browser: Shift + PrtScr ; in Word: Ctrl + V |
| Web page, create | 820 | ▤ in view buttons | File \| New; *Web page* in New Document task pane; View \| Web Layout | | |
| Web page, edit in Word | 832 | Open in Word; use Word's editing features | | | |
| Web page, insert frame above | 822 | New Frame Above on Frames toolbar | | | |

| Word Task | Page | Mouse | Menu Bar | Shortcut Menu | Shortcut Keys |
|---|---|---|---|---|---|
| Web page, insert frame to left | 822 | New Frame Left on Frames toolbar | | | |
| Web page, move by saving in its own folder | 834 | | Open page in browser: File \| Save As; open or create new folder; click *Save as type* arrow; Web Page, complete | | |
| Web page, open in browser | 831 | Double-click Web page file name in *My Computer* to display in browser | | Right-click file name in *My Computer*; Open with; Microsoft Word | |
| Web page, open in Word | 832 | on Standard toolbar; click *Files of type* arrow; All Web Pages | | Right-click file name in *My Computer*; Open with; Microsoft Word | |
| Web page, preview active frame | 831 | | File \| Web Page Preview | | |
| Web page, preview page (all frames) | 831 | Double-click Web page file name in *My Computer* to display in browser | | | |
| Web page, print | 834 | on MS Internet Explorer's Standard Buttons bar | Open page in browser; File \| Print | Right-click page in browser; Print | |
| Web page, print preview | 834 | | Open page in browser; File \| Print Preview | | |
| Web page, save document | 286 | | File \| Save as Web Page | | |
| Web page, save as single file | 820 | | File \| Save As; click *Save as type* arrow; Single File Web Page  File \| Save as Web Page | | Ctrl + S; click *Save as type* arrow; Single File Web Page |
| Window, remove split | 379 | Double-click split bar between panes  Drag split bar up | Window \| Remove Split | | |
| Window, split | 379 | Drag split box (above vertical scroll bar) | Window \| Split | | |
| WordArt, alignment | 262 | on WordArt toolbar | | | |
| WordArt, change shape | 262 | on WordArt toolbar | | | |
| WordArt, character spacing | 262 | on WordArt toolbar | | | |
| WordArt, display toolbar | 262 | Click the WordArt image | View \| Toolbars \| WordArt | | |

| Word Task | Page | Mouse | Menu Bar | Shortcut Menu | Shortcut Keys |
|---|---|---|---|---|---|
| WordArt, edit text | 262 | Edit Text... on WordArt toolbar | | Right-click WordArt, Edit Text | |
| WordArt, format | 262 | on WordArt toolbar | Format \| WordArt | Right-click WordArt, Format WordArt | |
| WordArt, gallery | 262 | on WordArt toolbar | | | |
| WordArt, insert | 260 | on Drawing toolbar | Insert \| Picture \| WordArt | | |
| WordArt, same letter heights | 262 | Aa on WordArt toolbar | | | |
| WordArt, text wrapping | 262 | on WordArt toolbar | Format WordArt \| Layout tab | Right-click WordArt, Format WordArt \| Layout tab | |
| WordArt, vertical text | 262 | Ab b on WordArt toolbar | | | |
| Word count, check | 438 | <Click Recount to view> on Word Count toolbar | Tools \| Word Count<br><br>View \| Toolbars \| Word Count | | Ctrl + Shift + G, and then Enter |
| Word count, recheck | 439 | Recount on Word Count toolbar | Tools \| Word Count<br><br>View \| Toolbars \| Word Count | | Ctrl + Shift + G, and then Enter |
| XML document, add attributes | 913 | | | Right-click a start tag; Attributes | |
| XML document, add comment | 897 | Type text between <!-- and --> | | | |
| XML document, add content | 913 | Type text between tags and elsewhere in document | | | |
| XML document, declare | 897 | Type <?xml version="1.0"?> as the first line of the XML document | | | |
| XML document, edit in Word | 898 | Type or edit text between existing tags | | | |
| XML document, import multiple | 927 | | In Excel: Data \| XML \| Import; press Ctrl and select multiple .xml files; Import | In Excel: Right-click XML map; XML \| Import; press Ctrl and select multiple .xml files; Import | |
| XML document, mark up | 910 | In XML Structure task pane, click element tag and then select the text in the document to be tagged | | | |
| XML document, open in Word | 898 | on Standard toolbar; click *Files of type* arrow; XML Files; open | File \| Open; click *Files of type* arrow; XML Files; open | | Ctrl + O |

| Word Task | Page | Mouse | Menu Bar | Shortcut Menu | Shortcut Keys |
|---|---|---|---|---|---|
| XML document, print in Word | 898 | | File | Print; Options; select XML tags check box | | |
| XML document, save tagged data | 918 | | File | Save As; click *Save as type* arrow; XML Document (.xml); select *Save data only* | | |
| XML document, save with encoding | 898 | | In Notepad: File | Save As; click *Save as type* arrow; All Files; click *Encoding* arrow; UTF-8; in File name box, type file name with .xml extension; Save | | |
| XML document, save with WordML | 916 | | File | Save As; click *Save as type* arrow; XML Document (.xml) | | |
| XML schema, add as XML map | 925 | | In Excel: Data | XML | XML Source; click XML Maps in task pane; Add; open the .xsd file; click OK; drag element from task pane to worksheet cell | | |
| XML schema, add solutions to Schema Library | 933 | In XML Structure task pane, click Templates and Add-Ins; on XML Schema page, click Schema Library; select a schema; Add Solution | Tools | Templates and Add-Ins | XML Schema tab; Schema Library; select a schema; Add Solution | | |
| XML schema, add to Schema Library | 906 | In XML Structure task pane, click Templates and Add-Ins; on XML Schema page, click Schema Library; Add Schema | Tools | Templates and Add-Ins | XML Schema tab; Schema Library; Add Schema | | |
| XML schema, attach to document | 906 | In XML Structure task pane, click Templates and Add-Ins; on XML Schema page, select a schema check box | Tools | Templates and Add-Ins | XML Schema tab; select a schema check box | | |
| XML schema, declare | 900 | In Notepad: type a statement beginning with **<xs:schema** after the XML document declaration. xs: is an optional namespace prefix | | | |
| XML schema, define elements with a namespace | 902 | In Notepad: Use XML rules to declare the schema and namespace used for standard tag names | | | |
| XML schema, mark up existing document | 920 | In XML Structure task pane, click Templates and Add-Ins; on XML Schema page, select schema check box(es); see "XML document, mark up" | Tools | Templates and Add-Ins | XML Schema tab; select schema check box(es); see "XML document, mark up" | | |
| XML schema, open in Notepad | 900 | | In Notepad: File | Open; click *Files of type* arrow; All Files; open file with .xsd extension | | |

| Word Task | Page | Mouse | Menu Bar | Shortcut Menu | Shortcut Keys |
|---|---|---|---|---|---|
| XML schema, save | 900 | | In Notepad: File \| Save As; click *Save as type* arrow; All Files; click *Encoding* arrow; UTF-8; in File name box, type file name with .xsd extension; Save | | |
| XML schema, use simple and complex elements | 904 | In Notepad: Type schema elements using XML rules | | | |
| XML, create parent–child element | 896 | Type XML element (child) between start and end tags of another element (parent) and declare the constraints according to XML rules | | | |
| XML, set options | 906 | In XML Structure task pane, click Templates and Add-Ins; on XML Schema page, click XML Options | Tools \| Templates and Add-Ins; XML Schema tab; XML Options | | |
| XML, type element | 892 | In Notepad: Type elements using XML tag rules | | | |
| Zoom, magnify or shrink the view of a document | 19 | `100% ▾` arrow on Standard toolbar and then choose a display percentage  Click in Zoom box `100% ▾` and then type a percentage | View \| Zoom | | |
| Zoom, maximum page width | 19 | `100% ▾` arrow on Standard toolbar and then choose Page Width | View \| Zoom, Page Width | | |

# Glossary

**Absolute path** An XPath term used to locate a specific element.

**ActiveX control** A control, such as a check box or button, that enables users to run macros in a Web document.

**Adobe Acrobat Reader** A free program that is used to open Portable Document Format (PDF) files.

**Alias** A short name that is substituted for a longer name.

**Aligned left** The most common text alignment, with the left edge of the text straight, and the right edge uneven.

**Aligned right** The right edge of the text is straight, and the left edge is uneven.

**Alignment** The placement of paragraph text relative to the left and right margins.

**Anchor** Indicates that an object is attached to the nearest paragraph.

**ASCII** American Standard Code for Information Interchange, a commonly used code format.

**Aspect ratio** Proportional relationship of the height and width of an image.

**Attributes** In XML, additional information attached to an element that further defines the element.

**AutoClose** A macro that runs automatically when a document is closed.

**AutoComplete** A Word feature that assists in your typing by suggesting words or phrases.

**AutoCorrect** A feature that corrects common typing and spelling errors, and can also be used as a shortcut for typing commonly used text.

**AutoExec** A macro that runs automatically when Word is started.

**AutoFormat, Table** Uses predefined formats to create a professional-looking table.

**Automatic page break** A page break inserted by Word when the insertion point reaches the bottom margin of a page. Also referred to as a soft page break.

**AutoNew** A macro that runs automatically when a Word document is created using a template.

**AutoOpen** A macro that runs automatically when a document is opened.

**AutoSummarize** Analyzes a document, and then identifies and highlights the document's key points.

**AutoText** A feature that stores commonly used text and graphics for easy retrieval.

**Background** Colors, patterns, or pictures applied behind the text in a document. Backgrounds are displayed on the screen, but not printed.

**Body text** Text in the Outline View that does not use a heading style.

**Bookmark** Named location in a document. Bookmarks can be accessed using the Go To menu or with cross-references.

**Brightness** The light-to-dark ratio of an image. Increasing the brightness brightens both the dark areas and the light areas in an image. Decreasing the brightness darkens both the dark areas and the light areas in an image.

**Bullet** A symbol used at the beginning of each item in a bulleted list.

**Bulleted list** A group of items formatted in a similar manner, and preceded by a symbol, called a bullet.

**Caption** A title that can be added to a table or figure.

**Case-sensitive** When typing a password, uppercase and lowercase letters must be used exactly as typed when the password was created.

**Category axis (x-axis)** The horizontal axis along the bottom of a chart that displays labels.

**Cell** The intersection of a row and column in a table.

**Center alignment** Text is spaced equally between the left and right margins.

**Character style** Style that contains a set of instructions for changing a group of formatting characteristics, such as font and font size, for text only. All changes are applied together.

**Chart** A graphic representation of numbers used to display comparisons, change over time, contributions to the whole, or some other relationship that is easier to understand with a picture.

**Chart area** The part of the chart that displays the chart graphic.

**Clip** A media file, such as sound, art, animation, or movies.

**Clip art** Graphic images included with the Microsoft Office program or obtained from other sources.

**Clipboard** Shortcut term for the Office Clipboard.

**Collapse button** An open minus symbol to the left of a heading in an outline indicating that no text or lower-level headings are associated with the heading.

**Collapsed** Subordinate headings and text associated with a heading are hidden.

**Collect and paste** Microsoft Office feature that enables you to place up to 24 objects in the Office Clipboard, and then paste them as needed, and in any order.

**Column chart** A graph with vertical columns that is used to make comparisons among related numbers.

**Comment** A note attached to a document. By default, comments do not print.

**Complex element** In XML, an element that is a parent or that has additional information attached to it.

**Constant information** The information that does not change from letter to letter in a form letter created using Mail Merge.

**Constraints** In XML, the requirement that child elements must be used in a certain order or combination.

**Contrast** The differentiation between light and dark. When you increase contrast, the darks get darker and the lights get lighter. Decreasing the contrast brightens the dark areas and darkens the light areas.

**Control Toolbox** A toolbar, similar to the Forms toolbar, that offers over 100 control options.

**Copy** Send a graphic or block of text to the Office Clipboard, while also leaving it in its original location.

**Copyright** Laws that protect the rights of authors of original works, including text, art, photographs, and music.

**Crop** To trim part of a picture or clip art image without resizing the image.

**Cross-reference** An internal link in a document to specific locations such as bookmarks, footnotes, endnotes, captions, or objects.

**Custom.dic** A default user dictionary that comes with Microsoft Office.

**Cut** Send a graphic or block of text to the Office Clipboard and remove it from its original location.

**Data** Information that can be sorted and analyzed.

**Datasheet** A special table that holds chart data. Each chart has its own datasheet.

**Data source** A list of variable information that is merged with a main document to create customized form letters or labels.

**Desktop publisher** A program, such as Microsoft Publisher, that is used to create newsletters, posters, greeting cards, and even Web pages.

**Design mode** Enables you to work on an ActiveX control that has been inserted into a document.

**Destination file** A file in which an object from another Office file is linked or embedded.

**Digital certificate** An attachment that vouches for authenticity, provides secure encryption, or supplies a verifiable digital signature.

**Digital signature** An electronic, encryption-based secure stamp of authentication on a document, which confirms that the document originated from the signer and has not been altered.

**Distribute columns evenly** Formats columns so that their widths are equal within the boundaries that you select.

**Distribute rows evenly** Formats rows so that their heights are equal within the boundaries that you select.

**Documentation** Comments added to Visual Basic code to help explain the purpose for each section of code, who wrote the code, and when the code was written.

**Document map** A pane on the left side of the document that contains a linked outline to document headings.

**Document properties** Statistics and related information about a document, including file size and location, author, title, and subject.

**Dot leader** A series of dots preceding a tab; often used between a text entry and a page number in a table of contents.

**Double-click** The action of clicking the left mouse button twice in rapid succession.

**Drag** Hold the left mouse button down over selected text or a graphic element and move it by moving the mouse; also, to hold down the left mouse button and move over text to select it.

**Drag-and-drop** A method of moving text and graphics from one location to another by selecting it and then clicking and holding the mouse button and moving the text.

**Drawing canvas** A work area for creating and editing complex figures created using the drawing tools.

**Drop cap** The first letter (or letters) of a paragraph, enlarged and either embedded in the text or placed in the left margin.

**Dropped** Drop cap position embedded in the text, rather than in the margin.

**Edit** Make changes to the text or format of a document.

**Editing time** In document Properties, the total number of minutes the document has been open. Editing time is not an exact measurement of actual time on task.

**Element** In XML, the tagged portion of text or numbers.

**Embed** To insert an object from another program. The object maintains the characteristics of the original application, but is not tied to the original file.

**Embedded object** An object contained in a source file and inserted into a destination file. Once embedded, the object becomes part of the destination file. Changes you make to the embedded object are reflected in the destination file, but not the source file.

**Em dash** A long dash that separates distinct phrases in a sentence. It is about four times as long as a hyphen.

**Encoding** The process of converting letters and characters to zeros and ones so a computer can work with them.

**Endnote** A reference placed at the end of a section or the end of the document.

**End tag** The second of a pair of XML tags that enclose data.

**Expand button** An open plus symbol to the left of a heading in an outline indicating that there is text associated with the heading. If double-clicked, it acts as an on/off button to display subordinate text.

**eXtensible Markup Language (XML)** A markup language that enables the user to define the tags and use them to identify the enclosed text as data.

**Field** A category of information stored in columns in a data table.

**File encryption** Scrambling the contents of a file for document security using a mathematical algorithm.

**Floating image** A graphic that moves independently of the surrounding text.

**Font** A set of characters with the same design and shape.

**Font styles** Bold, italic, and underline used to enhance text.

**Footer** Area reserved at the bottom of each page for text and graphics that appear at the bottom of each page in a document or section of a document.

**Footnote** A reference placed at the bottom of a page.

**Form** A document with places reserved for filling in individualized information.

**Format text** The process of establishing the overall appearance of text in a document.

**Formatting marks** Characters that display on the screen, but do not print, indicating where the Enter key, the Spacebar, and the Tab key were pressed. Also called nonprinting characters.

**Formatting toolbar** Contains buttons for some of the most common formatting tasks in Word. It may occupy an entire row or share a row with the Standard toolbar.

**Form field** A location in a form where a particular type of information, such as a name or address, is stored.

**Form letter** A letter containing constant information (a fixed message) that can be merged with an address list to create customized letters.

**Frame** A rectangular window on the screen that displays a Web page, also referred to as a subwindow.

**Frame border** The line that separates two frames on a Web page.

**Frames page** A Web page that divides a Web browser window into different scrollable areas—called frames—that can independently display several Web pages.

**Grayscale** Displays all colors as shades of gray.

**Hanging indent** A paragraph where the first line extends to the left of the rest of the lines in the same paragraph. Hanging indents are often used for bibliographic entries.

**Hard page break** A page break inserted before the reaching the bottom margin of a page. Also referred to as a manual page break.

**Header** Area reserved for text and graphics that appear at the top of each page in a document or section of a document.

**Horizontal scroll bar** Enables you to move left and right in a document that is wider than the screen.

**Hyperlink** Text that you click to go to another location in a document, another document, or a Web site. Hyperlinks are often a different color (usually blue) than the surrounding text, and are often underlined.

**Hypertext Markup Language (HTML)** The standard markup language used to display documents on the Web.

**If-Then-Else-End If** A programming technique that determines what is done next if a condition is true or false.

**Index** An alphabetical list of words and phrases in a document, along with the page numbers on which they are found.

**Index entry** Hidden text that marks a word or phrase for inclusion in the index.

**InfoPath 2003** A specialized Microsoft program used to create online forms that gather information.

**In margin** Drop cap position with the letter in the margin, rather than embedded in the text.

**Inline image** A graphic that acts like a character in a sentence.

**Insert mode** The mode in which text moves to the right to make space for new characters or graphic elements.

**Insertion point** A blinking vertical line that indicates where text or graphics will be inserted.

**Justified alignment** Both the left and right margins are straight (aligned). Text in books and magazines is nearly always justified.

**Keep with text** Pagination feature that keeps consecutive paragraphs—sometimes a title and paragraph—on the same page.

**Keyboard shortcut** A combination of keys on the keyboard, usually using the Ctrl key or the Alt key, that provides a quick way to activate a command.

**Legend** A key in a chart that identifies the data series by color, shade of gray, or pattern.

**Line spacing** The distance between lines of text in a paragraph.

**Link** To insert an object from another program that maintains a connection to the file that contains the original information.

**Linked object** An object that is created in a source file and inserted into a destination file, while maintaining a connection between the two files. The linked object in the destination file can be updated when the source file is updated.

**List style** Formats font style, font size, alignment, and bullet or number characteristics in lists.

**Macro** A series of actions that are recorded or written in VBA so that all of the steps can be run with one keyboard or mouse action.

**Macro virus** Programming code inserted into a macro that can cause damage to or even erase files.

**Mail Merge** A feature that joins a main document and a data source to create customized form letters or labels.

**Main document** The text that contains the constant information (the information that remains the same) in a form letter.

**Manual column break** An artificial end to a column used to balance columns or to provide space for the insertion of other objects.

**Manual page break** A page break inserted before reaching the bottom margin of a page. Also referred to as a hard page break.

**Map** In XML, assigning elements from a schema to columns in Excel.

**Margin** The white space at the top, bottom, left, and right sides of a page.

**Markup language** A method of using tags to format or add information to text.

**Master document** A file that coordinates and keeps track of related subdocuments.

**Masthead** The large title at the top of a newsletter.

**Menu** A list of commands within a category.

**Menu bar** The bar beneath the blue title bar that lists the names of menu categories.

**Microsoft Graph** A subprogram built into Microsoft Office that is used to create charts.

**Mixed content** In XML, a document in which some of the text is not tagged.

**Namespace** A group of tags that are created to make it easier to exchange XML documents between members of a group.

**Navigate** To move within a document.

**Nested** A procedure embedded in another procedure.

**Nonprinting characters** Characters that display on the screen, but do not print, indicating where the Enter key, the Spacebar, and the Tab key were pressed. Also called formatting marks.

**Normal template** The template on which most documents are based, which contains the default Word document settings.

**Normal View** A simplified view of a document that does not show graphics, margins, headers, or footers.

**Notepad** A simple text-editing program provided with the Windows operating system.

**Nudge** To move an object in small increments using the arrow keys.

**Numbered list** A group of items formatted in a similar manner, with each item preceded by a number. Numbered lists are used for items that have some relationship (chronological or sequential).

**Object** A portion of a document, such as a range of data from Excel, an Excel chart, or a PowerPoint slide or presentation. Objects can be copied and moved to another document or another application.

**Object Linking and Embedding (OLE)** A program-integration technology for sharing information between Office programs.

**Office Clipboard** A memory area that can hold up to 24 graphics or blocks of text. Items are placed in the Office Clipboard when the Cut or Copy commands are used.

**Orphan** The first line of a paragraph printed by itself at the bottom of a page.

**Outline** A list of topics for an oral or written report that visually indicates the order in which the information will be discussed, as well as the relationship of the topics to each other and to the total report.

**Outline view** A document view that shows headings and subheadings, which can be expanded or collapsed.

**Overtype mode** A mode for entering text in which existing text is replaced as you type.

**Pagination** The placement of text and other objects on the pages of a document and the location of page breaks.

**Paragraph style** Style that contains a set of instructions for changing a group of formatting characteristics in a paragraph, such as font, font size, line spacing, and indentation. All changes are applied together.

**Parent–child** In XML, identifies the relationship between elements in tagged data where the child element is subordinate to and contained within the parent element.

**Password to modify** Security option that enables users who know a document password to turn off editing restrictions.

**Password protection** Enables the author of a document to restrict access to a file.

**Paste** Insert an object from the Office Clipboard into a document.

**Paste Special** Enables you to copy information from one location and paste it in another location using a different format.

**Pie chart** A graph in the shape of a pie that is used to show the contribution of each part to the whole.

**Placeholder text** Text or graphic used as an indicator that the users should enter their own text. Placeholder text can be replaced but not edited.

**Plot area** The portion of a chart occupied by the chart graphic—a pie or columns. It does not include the title or legend areas.

**Point** A measurement of the size of a font. There are 72 points in an inch, with 10–12 points being the most commonly used font size.

**Portable Document Format (PDF)** A standard document format that enables the document to be opened on different computers using different operating systems. PDF files can be opened with Adobe Acrobat Reader, a free program.

**Print Layout View** A view of a document that looks like a sheet of paper. It displays margins, headers, footers, and graphics.

**Pt.** Abbreviation for point in terms of font size.

**Readability Statistics** A Spelling and Grammar tool that analyzes a document and determines the reading level of the text.

**Reading Layout View** Displays easy-to-read pages that fit on the screen.

**Recognizer** A purple dotted underscore beneath a date or address indicating that the information could be placed into another Microsoft Office application program such as Outlook.

**Record** All of the fields containing information about one topic (a person or organization) and stored in a row in a data table.

**Reference** The source of information, taken verbatim or paraphrased, from another location, usually indicated by a mark or a number. References can be placed at the bottom of each page (footnote) or the end of the section or document (endnote).

**Relative path** Reference to any child of an XML element.

**Reviewing pane** An area at the bottom of the screen that displays comments and tracked changes.

**Rich Text Format (RTF)** A universal document format that can be read by nearly all word processing programs.

**Right-click** The action of clicking the right mouse button, usually to display a shortcut menu.

**Rotate handle** A handle on a selected image that can be dragged to rotate the image to any angle.

**Ruler** Displays the exact location of paragraph margins, indents, and tab stops.

**Sans serif font** A font with no lines or extensions on the bottoms of characters; usually used for titles or headlines.

**Scale** (1) The range of numbers in the data series that controls the minimum, maximum, and incremental values on the value axis of a chart. (2) To resize an image, keeping the same image proportions.

**Schema** An XML document that specifies which elements are required, their sequence, and other attributes about each element.

**Schema library** A list of schemas that are available in Office 2003.

**ScreenTip** A small box, activated by holding the pointer over a button or other screen object, that displays the name of a screen element.

**Scroll box** Box in a scroll bar that provides a visual indication of your location in a document. It can also be used with the mouse to drag a document up and down or left and right.

**Section** A portion of a document that can be formatted independently of the rest of the document.

**Section break** Divides a document into areas that can use different page formatting and different headers and footers.

**Selecting text** Highlighting text so that it can be formatted, deleted, copied, or moved.

**SelfCert** A program, included with Microsoft Office, that enables you to create a local digital certificate.

**Separator character** A character used to identify column placement in text; usually a tab or a comma.

**Sequence** In XML, the requirement that child elements must be used in a certain order.

**Serif font** A font that contains extensions or lines on the ends of the characters; usually the easiest type of font to read for large blocks of text.

**Shortcut menu** A context-sensitive menu that displays commands relevant to the selected object.

**Sizing handle** A small square or circle in the corners and the middle of the sides of a graphic that can be used to increase or decrease the size of the graphic.

**Small caps** Text format, usually used in titles, that changes lowercase text into capital letters using a reduced font size.

**Soft page break** A page break inserted by Word when the insertion point reaches the bottom margin of a page. Also referred to as an automatic page break.

**Sort** A command used to organize table data numerically or alphabetically.

**Source file** The file in which an Office object is created.

**Spin box arrow** The up and down arrows in an option box that enable you to increase or decrease a value incrementally.

**Split box** The short gray bar at the top of the vertical scroll bar that can be dragged to split the screen and as a result display two different parts of the document.

**Standard toolbar** Contains buttons for some of the most common commands in Word. It may occupy an entire row or share a row with the Formatting toolbar.

**Start tag** The first of a pair of XML tags that enclose data.

**Status bar** A horizontal bar at the bottom of the document window in Microsoft Word that provides information about the current state of what you are viewing in the window, including the page number, and whether overtype or track changes are on or off.

**Style** A set of formatting characteristics that is stored in one shortcut command. All formatting characteristics, such as font, font size, and indentation, are applied together.

**Stylesheet** Library of styles that can be used with XML transforms.

**Subdocument** A document linked to a master document. Changes made in the subdocument are reflected in the master document.

**Subwindow** A named Web page frame.

**Tab stop** A mark on the ruler bar to which the insertion point will jump when the Tab key is pressed.

**Table** Rows and columns of text or numbers, used to organize data and present it effectively.

**Table of authorities** A list of the references in a legal document.

**Table of contents (TOC)** A list of topics and subtopics in a document and the page numbers on which they can be found.

**Table of figures** A list of the captions for pictures, charts, graphs, slides, or other illustrations in a document.

**Table move handle** A four-way arrow that displays near the upper left corner of a table and enables you to move the table by dragging the handle.

**Table style** Formats border type and style, shading, cell alignment, and fonts in a table.

**Tag** (1) In HTML, a symbol that identifies a page element's type, format, and appearance. (2) In XML, a symbol that identifies text as data.

**Task pane** Displays commonly used commands or utilities available for use with the current task.

**Taskbar** Displays the Start button and any open documents. The taskbar may also display shortcut buttons for other programs.

**Template** Predefined document structures defining the basic document settings, such as font, margins, and available styles.

**Text editor** A simple text-editing program that is less powerful than a word processor; one text editor is Notepad.

**Theme** A document format that coordinates fonts, colors, and background images.

**Thesaurus** A language tool that helps add variety to your writing by suggesting synonyms (words that have the same meaning) for words that you select.

**Thumbnail** Page icons in a pane on the left side of the screen that contain links to document pages.

**Title bar** Displays the program icon, the name of the document, and the name of the program. The Minimize, Maximize/Restore Down, and Close buttons are grouped on the right side of the title bar.

**TOC** Abbreviation for a table of contents.

**Toggle switch** A button, such as the Numbering or Bold button, that turns on with a click, and then off with another click.

**Toolbar** A row of buttons that activate commands, such as Undo or Bold, with a single click of the left mouse button.

**Toolbar Options** Button that enables you to see all of the buttons associated with a toolbar. It also enables you to place the Standard and Formatting toolbars on separate rows or on the same row.

**Topic marker** A small open square symbol to the left of body text in an outline.

**Track Changes** A feature in Word that provides a visual indication of deletions, insertions, and formatting changes in a document.

**Transform** In XML, changes the tag names from those used in one computer database to a different set used in another computer, allowing two computers to exchange data without requiring either to revise database naming conventions.

**Uniform Resource Identifier (URI)** A worldwide method of creating unique names for use on the Internet.

**Uniform Resource Locator (URL)** A unique name for a Web page that is used to locate the computer that hosts the Web page.

**URI** A worldwide method of creating unique names for use on the Internet.

**URL** A unique name for a Web page that is used to locate the computer that hosts the Web page.

**UTF-8** A new standard for encoding that recognizes older encoding formats and newer international standards.

**Value axis (y-axis)** The vertical line on the left side of the chart that displays the numeric scale for numbers in the selected data.

**Variable information** The information, such as name and address, which varies from letter to letter in a form letter created using Mail Merge.

**VBA** The acronym for Visual Basic for Applications.

**VBE** The acronym for Visual Basic Editor.

**Version** A revision of a document saved with other revisions in the same document.

**Vertical scroll bar** Enables you to move up and down in a document.

**Visual Basic Editor (VBE)** A programming area that enables you to modify or create VBA code.

**Visual Basic for Applications (VBA)** A programming language that can be used to write code to attach to an Office file. VBA can be used to write macros

**W3C** World Wide Web Consortium: A group of representatives from leading Internet companies that oversees research and sets standards and guidelines for many areas of the Internet.

**Watermark** Semitransparent text displayed behind the text and objects in a document. Unlike backgrounds, watermarks appear when the document is printed.

**Web browser** Software that enables you to use the Web and navigate from page to page and site to site.

**Web Layout View** A document view that shows how the document would look if viewed with a Web browser.

**Well formed** The term applied to an XML document that meets all of the rules for creating XML and is declared with properly marked elements.

**Widow** The last line of a paragraph printed by itself at the top of a page.

**Wizard template** A step-by-step program that asks you questions and then sets up a document based on your answers.

**WordML** A language created using XML, with over 400 tags that identify nearly all of Word's features.

**WordPad** A text editing program provided with the Windows operating system; often used to create and edit XML text.

**Word wrap** Automatically moves text from the right edge of a paragraph to the beginning of the next line as necessary to fit within the margins.

**WordArt** A Microsoft Office drawing tool that enables you to turn text into graphics.

**Worksheet** In Excel, a set of cells that are identified by row and column headings. An Excel spreadsheet can contain more than one worksheet.

**World Wide Web Consortium (W3C)** A group of representatives from leading Internet companies that oversees research and sets standards and guidelines for many areas of the Internet.

**XE (Index Entry)** Formatted hidden text designating a word or phrase as an index entry.

**XHTML** A document containing both HTML formatting tags and XML data tags.

**XML** eXtensible Markup Language: A markup language that enables the user to define the tags and use them to identify the enclosed text as data.

**XML declaration** Line of code identifying the document as an XML document and specifying the version number: for instance, <?xml version ="1.0"?>.

**xml extension** The extension used for an XML file.

**xmlns** An XML namespace.

**XML Path Language (XPath)** In XML, the language used to write transforms.

**xsd extension** The extension used for XML schema files.

**xslt extension** The extension used for an XML transform.

**Zoom** To get a closer view of a document, or to see more of the document on the screen.

# Index

## Symbols

✔ (check mark), Word menus, 12
... (ellipsis), Word menus, 12
< (left angle bracket), 894
<!—comments—!>, 897
<? declaration ?>, 897
<xs:element name, 904
<xs:schema, 901, 903
? (question mark), missing content, 911
> (right angle bracket), 894
► (right arrow), Word menus, 12

## A

absolute path, XPath, 931
Accept Change button arrow (Reviewing toolbar), 452, 461–462
accepting changes, 451–453, 460–462
Access, 604
   editing caution, 606
accessing
   headers and footers, 26–27
   menu commands, 9–13
Acrobat Document icon, 532
activating the spelling/ grammar checkers, 21
active documents, 7
ActiveX controls, 773
   adding to forms, 773
   comments, 779
   formatting, 775–776
   running and testing, 780–782
   writing code, 777–780
Add New button (Mail Merge Recipients dialog box), 594–595
Add Schema dialog box, 907
Add Solution dialog box, 933
Add Text shortcut menu, 189
Add to Dictionary button, 24
adding
   ActiveX control to forms, 773
   addresses to tables, 590–591
   border lines, 264–265, 271–272
   check boxes and text form fields to tables, 736
   comments, 849–850, 857
   drop-down lists to forms, 737
   emphasis to text, 47
   graphics, 170
   hyperlinks to graphics, 282–283
   rows to tables, 591

shading to paragraphs, 273
special paragraph formatting, 271
text form fields, 733–734
text to Web page frames, 824–825
themes and backgrounds to Web pages, 829–830
Address Block, inserting, 596–597, 607
addresses
   adding to tables, 590–591
   creating new list, 593
   U.S. Postal Service guidelines, 599
Adobe Acrobat Document object type, 531
Adobe Acrobat Reader, 530, 534
After spin box, 112
aliases, XML namespaces, 902
Align button (Tables and Borders toolbar), 498, 504–506
Align Right button (Formatting toolbar), 496
aligning
   page numbers in index, 661
   paragraphs, 360
   text, 86–88
     *headers, 117*
     *tables, 212, 223–226, 496, 502–506*
     *using tab stops, 191*
alphabetical sorting, 511–512
anchors, 179
Apply formatting to box (New Style dialog box), 493–495
Apply to Entire Document dialog box, 910
applying styles
   character styles, 372–374
   font styles, 47–48
   list styles, 369–372
   table styles, 495–497
area charts, 340, 360
arrows
   black down, 496
   down, 13
   Encoding, 902
   inserting, 185–187
   up, 14
   white, 500–501, 527
aspect ratio of image, 539
assistance, getting, 51–53
attachments, email, 455–459
attributes
   adding to elements, 913–915
   using simple and complex elements, 904–905

Attributes for <tag> dialog box, 913
AutoClose macro, 765–767
AutoComplete, 34, 284, 770, 778
AutoCorrect
   recording entries, 121–124
   shortcuts, 124–126
   Spelling and Grammar dialog box, 24
AutoCorrect dialog box, 121–123, 126
AutoCorrect Options smart tag, 123, 135
AutoFit command (Table menu), 739
AutoFit to contents option button, 220
AutoFormat, tables, 517–518
automatic page break, 677
Automatically update check box (Modify Style dialog box), 375
AutoNew macro, 767
AutoOpen macro, 767
AutoShapes, inserting, 187–189
AutoSize property, 776
AutoSum button (Tables and Borders toolbar), 498
AutoSummarize documents, 695–697
AutoSummarize toolbar, 696–697
   Close AutoSummarize button, 697
   Percent of Original button right arrow, 696–697
AutoText, inserting, 120–121, 126–128
Avery labels, 592

## B

background
   creating, 744
   forms color, 743–744
   Web pages, 829–830
Background command (Format menu), 744–745, 829
Backspace key, 30, 39–40, 204
   versus using Delete key or Cut command, 99
balancing column breaks, 271
bar charts, 340
bar code on labels, 595
bar tab stops. *See* tabs

**Internet**
accessing templates, 429
connection to, 286. *See also under* Web
**Internet Explorer, 831, 892**
**Italic button (Formatting toolbar), 47–48, 134, 367, 494–495**

## J-K

**justified text, 86–87, 278–268**

**Keep with next, 684–685**
**keyboard-activated macros, 755–759**
**keyboard shortcuts, 10, 16**
cutting/copying/pasting text, 95
navigating documents, 16
text formatting, 47
**keystrokes, 17.** *See also* **nonprinting characters**

## L

**Label button (Control Toolbox toolbar), 774**
**label feature, 592**
**Label Options dialog box, 592–593**
**Label products arrow, 592**
**labels**
Avery, 592
bar codes, 595
editing, 598–599
previewing, 598
*printing, 599–601*
using Mail Merge Wizard, 592–594
**Last Record button (Mail Merge toolbar), 602, 610**
**laws, copyright, 295**
**layouts, changing document and paragraph, 84–95**
**leader, 661**
**left alignment of text, 86**
**left angle bracket (<), 894**
**Left Tab button, 193**
**left tab stops.** *See* **tabs**
**legal references, 675**
**legends, 341**
**Less Brightness button (Picture toolbar), 540**
**Less Contrast button (Picture toolbar), 540**
**letters.** *See* **form letters**
**Letters and Mailings command (Tools menu), 592**
**Letters option button (Main Document Type dialog box), 603**
**Level 2 and 3 headings, 649–650**

**levels, setting outline, 385–387**
**lightening images, 539**
**Limit formatting check box (Protect Document task pane), 843–844, 847**
**line charts, 340, 360**
**Line Spacing button, 88–90**
**Line Style button (Tables and Borders toolbar), 498, 520, 524**
**Line Weight button (Tables and Borders toolbar), 498**
**lines**
changing space between, 88–90, 360
dotted in tables, 522
faint dotted, 520
green wavy, 516
jagged gray, 649–650
line weight, 533
selecting, 44
table usage, 522–525
**Link Select pointer, 692**
**Link to file check box (Object dialog box), 585–586**
**Link to Previous button (Header and Footer toolbar), 680–682**
**linking, 581**
Excel charts, 581–583
main document and data source, 608
objects, 574
PowerPoint presentations, 585–588
**List Box button (Control Toolbox toolbar), 774**
**List toolbar, 925**
**lists**
creating/modifying, 109–116
*styles, 338, 360, 369–372*
formatting, 112–113
**locating**
changes, 449–451
supporting information, 289–300
**Lock aspect ratio check box (Format Picture dialog box, Size tab), 539**
**Lock Subdocument button (Outlining toolbar), 645**
**locked subdocuments, 653**
**losing work, 29–30**

## M

**Macro command (Tools menu)**
Macros, 759, 761, 767, 771
Record New Macro, 755, 762, 765
Security, 753
Visual Basic Editor, 769

**macro virus, 753**
**macros, 751**
AutoClose, 765–766
automate forms, 751
automatic running, 767
deleting, 761–762
editing with Visual Basic Editor, 767–769
recording
*event-driven, 765–767*
*keyboard-activated, 755–759*
*toolbar-activated, 762–764*
running
*protected documents, 761*
*testing, 759–761*
security level, 753–754
**Macros dialog box, 759–761, 767**
**magnifying glass pointer, 599**
**Mail Merge Recipients button (Mail Merge toolbar), 602, 604**
**Mail Merge Recipients dialog box, 593–595, 604–606**
**Mail Merge task pane, 592–595, 600**
**Mail Merge toolbar, 602**
First Record button, 610
Highlight Merge Fields button, 609, 611
Insert Address Block button, 607
Insert Merge Fields button, 606–608
Last Record button, 610
Mail Merge Recipients button, 604
Merge to New Document button, 612
Merge to Printer button, 611
Next Record button, 610
Open Data Source button, 604
View Merged Data button, 610
**Mail Merge Wizard**
completing, 594
setting up labels, 592–594
**mail programs, 458**
**mailing labels, 589**
**Main document setup button (Mail Merge toolbar), 602–603**
**main documents, 590, 606.** *See also* **documents**
linking with data source, 608
merging
*data source, 604*
*records, 609*
*Word documents, 612–613*
**manual breaks**
column breaks, 266
page breaks, 677

# X-Z

x-axis, 341
XE (Index Entry), 659. *See also* index
XHTML, 892
XML (eXtensible Markup Language), 892
  data
    *applying tags, 921–924*
    *importing to Excel, 925*
    *saving tagged data as XML document, 918–919*
  documents
    *adding declarations and comments, 897*
    *applying elements to entire document, 921*
    *attaching schema to old document, 920*
    *attaching transform to schema, 933–934*
    *defining elements with namespace, 902–903*
    *editing and printing in Word, 898–899*
    *importing to Excel, 927–929*
    *marking, 910–912*
    *saving tagged data, 918–919*
    *saving with encoding, 898*
    *saving with WordML, 916–917*
    *using elements with constraints and attributes, 904–905*
    *using stylesheets as data views, 932*
    *well-formed documents, 897–898*
  elements
    *adding attributes, 913–915*
    *applying to entire document, 921*
    *creating parent–child, 896*
    *defining with namespace, 902–903*
    *marking in documents, 910*
    *nesting elements, 896*
    *using with constraints and attributes, 904–905*
  namespace, 902
  schemas
    *adding as XML Map, 925–926*
    *attaching to documents, 906–909, 920*
    *declaring, 900–902*
    *validating, 910–912*
  tags, 892
    *applying to data, 921–924*
    *attaching attributes, 913–915*
    *creating parent–child elements, 896*
    *editing XML document, 899*
    *end tags, 895*
    *rules and conventions, 895*
    *start tags, 895*
    *using placeholder text, 914*
    *writing with text editor, 892–894*
XML command (Data menu)
  Import, 927
  XML Source, 925
XML data view task pane, 934
XML Document task pane, 898, 932
XML Maps, 925–926
XML Options dialog box, 910, 920
XML Path Language (XPath), 929, 931–932
XML Source task pane, 925–926
XML Structure task pane
  Apply to Entire Document, 921
  Choose an element to apply, 910
  confirming check box use, 920
  date element, 911
  Elements in the document, 912, 922–923
  error symbols, 910
  parent element displayed, 909
  Templates and Add-Ins, 906, 920, 936
  time element, 912, 923
  XML Options, 910
XPath (XML Path Language), 929, 931–932
XSL Transformation dialog box, 932
xs:schema, 901–903

y-axis, 341

zero value in cells, 515
ZIP codes, 595, 597–598, 605
Zoom button arrow (Standard toolbar), 19, 277
  75%, 520
  Page Width, 492, 508
  Whole Page, 276
  zoom options, 19